Kister's Best Encyclopedias
A Comparative Guide to General and Specialized Encyclopedias
Second Edition

❀ ❀

Kenneth F. Kister

ORYX PRESS
1994

have inspired the myth of the unicorn. This desert n the early 1960s. At that time several groups of ed to have 9 animals sent to the Phoenix Zoo to be d. Today the Oryx population is nearly 800, and over 400 have been returned to reserves in the Middle East.

Copyright © 1994 by Kenneth F. Kister
Published by The Oryx Press
4041 North Central at Indian School Road
Phoenix, AZ 85012-3397

Published simultaneously in Canada

Printed and Bound in the United States of America

∞ The paper used in this publication meets the minimum requirements of American National Standard for Information Science—Permanence of Paper for Printed Library Materials, ANSI Z39.48, 1984.

Library of Congress Cataloging-in-Publication Data

Kister, Kenneth F., 1935–
   Kister's best encyclopedias: a comparative guide to general and specialized encyclopedias / by Kenneth F. Kister.—2nd ed.
      p. cm.
   Includes bibliographical references and index.
   ISBN 0-89774-744-5
   1. Encyclopedias and dictionaries—Book reviews. 2. Encyclopedias and dictionaries—Miscellanea. 3. Encyclopedias and dictionaries—Bibliography. 4. Encyclopedias and dictionaries—History and criticism. 5. Bibliography—Best books—Encyclopedias and dictionaries. I. Title. II. Ttile: Best encyclopedias.
AE1.K57   1994
031—dc20   94-11282
                                           CIP

Contents

❦ ❦ ❦ ❦ ❦ ❦ ❦ ❦ ❦

Preface vii

Acknowledgments xiii

About Encyclopedias 1
  Questions and Answers about
  Encyclopedias 3
    What Is an Encyclopedia? 3
    How Did Encyclopedias Come
    About? 5
    What Types of Encyclopedias Are
      Available? 8
    Are Teachers Biased against
      Encyclopedias? 9
    Who Makes and Publishes
      Encyclopedias? 10
    How Are Encyclopedias Bought and
      Sold? 12
    What About a Secondhand
      Encyclopedia? 14
    What Should You Look for When
      Choosing an Encyclopedia? 15

General Encyclopedias 21
  Large Encyclopedias for Adults and Older
  Students 23
    Overview 23
    Collier's Encyclopedia 24
    Encyclopedia Americana 31
    New Encyclopaedia Britannica 37
    Comparison Chart 50

  Medium-Sized Encyclopedias for Adults
  and Older Students 51
    Overview 51
    Academic American Encyclopedia 53
    Barnes & Noble New American
      Encyclopedia 59

Compton's Encyclopedia 60
Funk & Wagnalls New Encyclopedia 69
Global International Encyclopedia 74
Grolier Academic Encyclopedia 75
Grolier Encyclopedia of Knowledge 76
Grolier International Encyclopedia 80
Lexicon Universal Encyclopedia 81
Macmillan Family Encyclopedia 81
New Standard Encyclopedia 82
Oxford Illustrated Encyclopedia 88
Webster's Family Encyclopedia 93
World Book Encyclopedia 97
Comparison Chart 105

**Small Encyclopedias for Adults and Older
Students** 108
  Overview 108
  American Spectrum Encyclopedia 109
  Barnes & Noble Encyclopedia 114
  Barron's New Student's Concise
    Encyclopedia 115
  Cambridge Encyclopedia 118
  Cambridge Paperback Encyclopedia 124
  Columbia Encyclopedia 126
  Concise Columbia Encyclopedia 131
  Dictionary of Cultural Literacy 136
  Knowledge Encyclopedia 140
  New American Desk Encyclopedia 143
  Random House Encyclopedia 146
  Running Press Cyclopedia 153
  Volume Library 156
  Webster's New World Encyclopedia 161
  Webster's New World Encyclopedia:
    College Edition 166
  Webster's New World Encyclopedia: Pocket
    Edition 168
  Comparison Chart 170

Large and Medium-Sized Encyclopedias for
Children and Younger Students 173
Overview 173
Charlie Brown's 'Cyclopedia 174
Childcraft 177
Children's Britannica 182
Compton's Encyclopedia 186
Compton's Precyclopedia 190
Golden Book Encyclopedia 191
Grolier Children's Encyclopedia 195
New Book of Knowledge 195
New Grolier Student Encyclopedia 201
Oxford Children's Encyclopedia 202
World Book Encyclopedia 206
Young Children's Encyclopedia 210
Young Students Learning Library 213
Comparison Chart 218

Small Encyclopedias for Children and
Younger Students 220
Overview 220
Barron's Junior Fact Finder 221
Facts Plus 223
First Dictionary of Cultural Literacy 225
Kingfisher Children's Encyclopedia 228
My First Encyclopedia
    (Dorling Kindersley) 231
My First Encyclopedia (Troll) 233
Random House Children's
    Encyclopedia 235
Random House Library of Knowledge: First
    Encyclopedia 238
Troll Student Encyclopedia 241
Usborne Children's Encyclopedia 243
Webster's Beginning Book of Facts 245
World Almanac Infopedia 248
Comparison Chart 251

Electronic Encyclopedias 253
Overview 253
Academic American Encyclopedia
    (Online) 256
Brittanica Instant Research System
    (CD-ROM) 259
Brittanica Online (Online) 261
Columbia Electronic Encyclopedia
    (Hand-held) 264
Compton's Concise Encyclopedia
    (CD-ROM) 266
Compton's Encyclopedia (Online) 268

Compton's Family Encyclopedia
    (CD-ROM) 269
Compton's Interactive Encyclopedia
    (CD-ROM) 271
Compton's Multimedia Encyclopedia
    (CD-ROM) 272
Concise Columbia Encyclopedia
    (CD-ROM) 275
Everyman's Encyclopaedia (Online) 277
First Connections (CD-ROM) 279
Information Finder (CD-ROM) 281
Kussmaul Encyclopedia (Online) 283
Microsoft Encarta Multimedia
    Encyclopedia (CD-ROM) 285
New Grolier Multimedia Encyclopedia
    (CD-ROM) 287
Random House Electronic Encyclopedia
    (Hand-held) 291
Random House Encyclopedia
    (Floppy Disks) 293
Software Toolworks Illustrated Encyclopedia
    (CD-ROM) 296
Comparison Chart 297

Out-of-Print Encyclopedias 299
Overview 299

Subject and Foreign Encyclopedias 321

Subject Encyclopedias 323
Overview 323
Art (General), Architecture, and
    Photography 324
Astronomy and Space Science 327
Biology and Animal Life 329
Botany and Horticulture 334
Business, Economics, and Statistics 337
Chemistry and Chemical
    Engineering 340
Computer and Electronic Sciences 342
Decorative Arts and Antiques 344
Earth, Energy, and Environmental
    Sciences 346
Education and Libraries 349
Engineering and Building
    Construction 352
Film, Radio, Television, and Mass
    Communications 355
Food, Nutrition, and Agriculture 359
Geography and Area Studies 361
Health, Medicine, and Drugs 368

History and Archaeology 375
Law and the Judicial System 382
Literature, Language, and Publishing .. 385
Military Science and History 392
Music 396
Physics and Mathematics 401
Political Science and Government 403
Psychology, Psychiatry, and
   Parapsychology 407
Religion, Philosophy, and Mythology . 412
Science and Technology (General) 420
Sexuality, Human Reproduction, and
   Child Care 424
Social Science, Sociology, and
   Anthropology 427
Sports and Games 433
Theater and Dance 436
Transportation 440

Foreign-Language Encyclopedias 443
   Overview 443
   Chinese 444
   Dutch 445
   French 445
   German 447
   Italian 447
   Japanese 448
   Korean 448
   Russian 449
   Spanish 449

Appendixes 453

A. Encyclopedia Resources 455
B. Directory of Encyclopedia Publishers
   and Distributors 460

Index 477

Preface

* * * * * * * * *

Practically everyone has used an encyclopedia at one time or another and knows from experience how valuable a good one can be for quickly locating basic factual information or an understandable overview of an unfamiliar or complicated subject. But finding the best encyclopedia—the one that most effectively meets *your* particular needs—is not so easy. The average consumer more often than not finds the process of choosing an encyclopedia a trying and even intimidating experience, due in large part to the many titles on the market and also to the lack of easy opportunity to size them up comparatively.

Few people know offhand how one encyclopedia differs from another. How, for instance, does *Collier's Encyclopedia* compare with *Encyclopedia Americana? Compton's Encyclopedia? Funk & Wagnalls New Encyclopedia? The New Standard Encyclopedia?* What are the strengths of these encyclopedias? Their limitations? Are the two best-known encyclopedias in North America, namely the *New Encyclopaedia Britannica* and the *World Book Encyclopedia*, works of exceptional quality or are their reputations inflated by high-powered advertising and slick promotion? How do relative newcomers like the *Academic American Encyclopedia*, the *Cambridge Encyclopedia*, and the *Oxford Children's Encyclopedia* stack up against older, more established titles in their respective classes? What advantages, if any, do the new electronic encyclopedias on CD-ROM (or compact disk), such as *Compton's Multimedia Encyclopedia, Informa-*tion *Finder, Microsoft Encarta,* the *New Grolier Multimedia Encyclopedia,* and others, have over traditional print encyclopedias? Is now the time to buy an electronic encyclopedia or are these products merely a fad? When might a substantial subject encyclopedia such as the *Encyclopedia of Human Biology* or the *International Encyclopedia of Linguistics* be preferable to any general encyclopedia, print or electronic?

Kister's Best Encyclopedias—subtitled *A Comparative Guide to General and Specialized Encyclopedias*—provides authoritative answers to such questions. Now in its second edition, the guide introduces and evaluates the full range of English-language encyclopedias available to North American consumers. Major foreign-language encyclopedias are also covered, albeit briefly. In all, *Kister's Best Encyclopedias* furnishes descriptive and critical information about more than 1,000 encyclopedias and encyclopedic works.

The main purpose of *Kister's Best Encyclopedias* is to help any interested consumer in the United States or Canada distinguish good encyclopedias from bad and mediocre ones, and, further, to determine which encyclopedia among the many available will best serve that consumer's specific informational needs. Bear in mind that no one encyclopedia is best for everyone; if that were the case, there would be no need for encyclopedia reviews or a guide like this one. The encyclopedia most appropriate for, say, a newspaper editor or university professor will almost certainly not be the first choice for parents with school-age children or a retired postal worker.

Kister's Best Encyclopedias also offers extensive consumer information about encyclopedias as a type of reference source. In "Questions and Answers about Encyclopedias" at the front of the book, interested readers will find notes concerning all important aspects of encyclopedias, including their purpose, history, types, uses, publication, merchandising, and evaluation. "What Should You Look for When Choosing an Encyclopedia?" will be especially helpful to those seeking criteria, or guidelines, for determining the merits of any encyclopedia.

GENERAL ENCYCLOPEDIAS

General English-language encyclopedias receive the most attention in this guide, simply because this type of encyclopedia is, by its very nature, of greatest interest to the largest number of consumers in the U.S. and Canada. Specifically, this edition of *Kister's Best Encyclopedias* reviews 77 general encyclopedias currently on the North American market. They range from very large multivolume sets for adults, such as the *New Encyclopaedia Britannica* and *Encyclopedia Americana*, to small single-volume works for young people, such as the *Kingfisher Children's Encyclopedia* and the *Random House Library of Knowledge: First Encyclopedia*. General encyclopedias in electronic form—most on CD-ROM—are also covered.

Reviews of in-print encyclopedias are grouped in six logical categories: (1) "Large Encyclopedias for Adults and Older Students"; (2) "Medium-sized Encyclopedias for Adults and Older Students"; (3) "Small Encyclopedias for Adults and Older Students"; (4) "Large and Medium-sized Encyclopedias for Children and Younger Students"; (5) "Small Encyclopedias for Children and Younger Students"; and (6) "Electronic Encyclopedias." This arrangement facilitates comparison of encyclopedias of similar size, format, price, and intended usership.

A headnote, or "Overview," introduces each of these sections. These notes furnish a broad perspective on comparable encyclopedias and identify the best titles in each group.

For instance, by scanning the "Overview" that introduces "Medium-Sized Encyclopedias for Adults and Older Students," the reader quickly receives a sense of how the titles in that category compare and learns which ones—the *Academic American Encyclopedia*, *Compton's Encyclopedia*, and the *World Book Encyclopedia*—stand out as works of exceptional quality and represent the best buys.

At the end of each section is a "Comparison Chart." These charts group factual information about similar encyclopedias in handy tabular form. In addition to providing core data about each title, the charts represent yet another way of looking at encyclopedias comparatively. Note that the charts include a rating for each encyclopedia in the form of a letter grade, with A representing the best and F the worst.

The Reviews

The reviews of general encyclopedias in *Kister's Best Encyclopedias* describe and evaluate all significant aspects of each title, beginning with the basic facts—the encyclopedia's editor, publisher, number of volumes, words, pages, articles, illustrations and maps, cross-references, index entries, physical size, and price and sales information. This descriptive information is followed by critical commentary on the work's history and authority, scope and coverage, accuracy, recency, objectivity, clarity and readability, organization and accessibility, pictures and graphics, bibliographies, special features, etc. The reviews also include a performance report, called "Report Card," which grades selected articles in each encyclopedia on the quality of their coverage, accuracy, recency, and clarity—all key evaluative criteria. Each review concludes with a wrap-up statement, the summary.

During the review process, the author systematically checked selected topics in each encyclopedia. The topics, which represent all major areas of knowledge, were chosen by the author before examining any encyclopedia—a procedure designed to avoid prejudgment and ensure fair and honest comparison.

In all, 51 topics were checked in each encyclopedia for adults and older students:

abortion	Gilman, Charlotte Perkins	Rhodes scholars and scholarships
adoption	Glass, Philip	Roman Catholic church
apartheid	Gordimer, Nadine	rose (flower)
carpal tunnel syndrome	Hare Krishnas	Rutherford, Ernest
chelation therapy	heart disease	Scientology
Christian Science church	hypnosis	Seventh-Day Adventist church
circumcision	Intelligence Quotient (IQ)	sexual harassment
Dead Sea Scrolls	Islam	sexually transmitted diseases
depression (economic)	Medjugorje	Shroud of Turin
depression (psychological)	melaleuca trees	sinkholes
dinosaurs	Motherwell, Robert	stingrays
Drew, Dr. Charles	Mozart, Wolfgang Amadeus	Tchaikovsky, Peter Ilich
drunk driving	Nicaragua	Uranus
euthanasia	nuclear energy	Uzbekistan
fluoridation	Olympic Games	Vietnam War
Galileo	panda bears	Veterans Memorial
genetics and gene-splicing	poetry (contemporary American and British)	
Germany		

General encyclopedias for children and younger students are naturally less detailed and sophisticated than those intended for adults and older students. Accordingly, the topics (25 in all) checked in children's encyclopedias are geared to the interests and concerns of young people and school curricula:

alcoholic beverages	measles	rose (flower)
baseball	Mozart, Wolfgang Amadeus	Russia
comets	Nicaragua	Scouts (Girl and Boy)
computers	nuclear energy	sex education
dinosaurs	panda bears	snakes
Halloween	poetry	space program
heredity	puppets and puppetry	Uranus
Islam	rock music	vaccination
Johnson, Earvin (Magic)		

Users of *Kister's Best Encyclopedias* who lack the time or inclination to read the reviews in their entirety can obtain a concise appraisal of any general encyclopedia covered in the book by turning to the "Summary" in the encyclopedia review, or the "Overview" or "Comparison Chart" in each section, or all three.

Electronic Encyclopedias

Today, more and more encyclopedias are published in both print and electronic (or automated) form. Electronic encyclopedias may appear in any one or all of these three distinct formats:

1. An online database transmitted from a remote source via telephone lines to a personal computer (PC) in the home, business, school, or library; the database is marketed through information vendors such as, for example, Dialog (for institutions), and CompuServe, GEnie, or Prodigy (for homes).

2. A compact disc called a CD-ROM (Compact Disk Read-Only-Memory) that employs laser optical technology to read and retrieve data; operated on a PC equipped with a CD-ROM drive, it can and usually does include multimedia features, such as video, animation, and sound.

3. A portable hand-held, battery-operated electronic device that stores and retrieves information by means of ROM computer chip technology; the device, which can be as small as a pocket calculator, has a small typewriter-like keyboard accompanied by a display screen.

Reviews of electronic encyclopedias in *Kister's Best Encyclopedias* generally follow the same style and organization as those for print encyclopedias, although the automated format requires comment on such additional concerns as user interface with the machine, search options unique to electronic products (e.g., Boolean searching), software and hardware requirements, and multimedia capabilities.

Out-of-Print Encyclopedias

Following the reviews of in-print general encyclopedias on the North American market is a section devoted to general English-language encyclopedias that have come and gone during the past 30 or so years. These encyclopedias have been reported out of print by their publishers or distributors and consequently are no longer available through normal retail channels. In almost all instances they are quite dated, sometimes severely so.

Still, out-of-print encyclopedias command attention because consumers frequently encounter them in secondhand bookstores, in discount stores as remainder items, or for sale at flea markets, estate and garage sales, and the like. The possibility also exists that a discontinued encyclopedia—an example is the excellent *Merit Students Encyclopedia*, which has only recently ceased publication—might be revived and returned to in-print status at any time. Likewise, an out-of-print encyclopedia is sometimes reissued with little or no revision and offered for sale as a new work, often under a different title. Old editions of the now defunct *Encyclopedia International*, for instance, have appeared in recent years under a variety of titles, including *Webster's New Family Encyclopedia* and *Webster's New Age Encyclopedia*.

Finally, out-of-print encyclopedias will sometimes be found in library reference collections. They might be reputable works of considerable substance (albeit no longer current), such as the *Lincoln Library of Essential Information*, *Chambers's Encyclopaedia*, the *Britannica Junior Encyclopaedia*, the *New Caxton Encyclopedia*, or the aforementioned *Merit Students Encyclopedia*. Or they might be practically valueless as sources of information. Because recently discontinued encyclopedias have a way of popping up in various places and guises, the most prominent or visible of them—73 in all—are briefly reviewed in *Kister's Best Encyclopedias*.

SUBJECT ENCYCLOPEDIAS

Most people who set out to buy an encyclopedia have in mind a general work covering all areas of knowledge from A to Z. Some prospective purchasers, however, may find that a good subject encyclopedia—one that covers a particular area of knowledge or topic in some depth—is a wiser or more practical choice. After carefully considering all the options, others might decide that both a general and subject encyclopedia are needed and begin looking for some logical combination based on their specific circumstances. Consumer A, for instance, might settle on an expensive multivolume subject encyclopedia and augment it with a reasonably priced single-volume general work. Consumer B might take the opposite approach, investing in a substantial general encyclopedia and supplementing it with an affordable one-volume work devoted to a particular subject. Ultimately, such decisions come down to each consumer's informational needs, intellectual interests, and financial resources.

Fortunately for those interested in subject encyclopedias, many quality works are currently available, with new titles appearing at a record pace. Some of these encyclopedias deal with very broad areas of knowledge or whole disciplines, such as the *McGraw-Hill Encyclopedia of Science and Technology* and the *Encyclopedia of Sociology*, whereas others focus on quite specialized or narrow topics, as in the case of the *Encyclopedia of Fluid Mechanics* and the *Heritage Encyclopedia of Band Music*.

Kister's Best Encyclopedias provides extensive coverage of the universe of subject encyclopedias, describing or listing more than 800 of the best or most useful titles published in recent years. Limited to works in English, the encyclopedias are grouped under 30 broad subjects, beginning with "Art (General), Architecture, and Photography" and ending with "Transportation."

FOREIGN-LANGUAGE ENCYCLOPEDIAS

The last type of encyclopedia covered in *Kister's Best Encyclopedias* is the foreign-language encyclopedia. This book lists and briefly discusses selected general foreign-language encyclopedias of potential interest to North Americans in nine languages: Chinese, Dutch, French, German, Italian, Japanese, Korean, Russian, and Spanish. Each encyclopedia is described in a short annotation.

The introduction to this section of the guide identifies several prominent North American booksellers specializing in foreign-language reference materials, including encyclopedias, and offers cogent acquisitions advice by Emanuel Molho, a leading foreign book dealer located in New York City.

APPENDIXES

Kister's Best Encyclopedias has two appendixes. Appendix A provides an annotated bibliography of other sources of encyclopedia reviews as well as books and articles about

using encyclopedias and their history. Appendix B is a directory of all encyclopedia publishers and distributors whose products are covered in the guide.

FINDING INFORMATION IN THIS BOOK

To find a specific encyclopedia or title in *Kister's Best Encyclopedias*, always turn first to the index at the back of the book. The index offers complete and easy alphabetical access to all encyclopedias reviewed or otherwise mentioned in the guide. In addition, the index includes former and variant titles. For example, the review of the *New American Desk Encyclopedia* notes that this work has also been published as the *University Desk Encyclopedia* and the *Concord Desk Encyclopedia*; the index includes entries for all three of these titles.

The index also provides cross-references, such as "*Britannica*. See "NEW ENCYCLOPAEDIA BRITANNICA*"; "*Americana*. See ENCYCLOPEDIA AMERICANA." Likewise, subject entries in the index help access the many specialized encyclopedias covered in the guide. The index entry "India," for instance, brings together the *Cambridge Encyclopedia of India, Pakistan, Bangladesh, Sri Lanka, Nepal, Bhutan, and the Maldives* (reviewed under "Geography and Area Studies") and the *Encyclopaedia of Indian Archaeology* (reviewed under "History and Archaeology').

Following customary practice, the words *encyclopaedia* and *encyclopaedic* are alphabetized throughout as if they were spelled *encyclopedia* and *encyclopedic*.

In the encyclopedia reviews, cross-references, printed in SMALL CAPITAL LETTERS, frequently appear, directing the user to competing or related titles. For example, a reference to COMPTON'S MULTIMEDIA ENCYCLOPEDIA in the *Compton's Encyclopedia* review indicates that *Compton's Multimedia Encyclopedia* is reviewed elsewhere in this book.

ABOUT THIS EDITION

This is the second edition of *Kister's Best Encyclopedias*. The first edition appeared in 1986 under the title *Best Encyclopedias* and was also published by the Oryx Press. The new edition is current as of March 1, 1994, the closing date for adding new titles, review citations, price changes, and the like. Encyclopedias reviewed are 1992-93 editions or printings, or the latest edition published; for example, the 1989 (second) edition of the *Concise Columbia Encyclopedia* is reviewed because it is the most recent edition of that encyclopedia.

Users of this guide should be aware of the distinction between a new printing and a new edition of an encyclopedia. Briefly, a new printing implies routine revision on a continual basis, whereas a new edition connotes substantial change on a scale well beyond the ordinary bounds of continual revision.

In most instances, encyclopedia statistics reported in *Kister's Best Encyclopedias*—number of pages, articles, words, illustrations, cross-references, and the like—are actual counts or estimates furnished by the publisher or distributor and verified via sampling by the author of this guide. Responsibility for all descriptive matter and unattributed opinion in the book rests with the author, a nationally known authority on reference materials.

Acknowledgments

* * * * * * * *

A few personal remarks about the many people who have contributed in one way or another to the making of *Kister's Best Encyclopedias*:

I am grateful to Cindy Luiaconi, Media Specialist at Northwest Elementary School in Tampa, Florida, for allowing me to use various electronic encyclopedias in her library, for talking candidly with me about her experience with these exciting new encyclopedias, and for arranging for me to interview students at her school about their use of and attitudes toward encyclopedias; to Jessica Deforno, Megan Gales, Samantha Garis, Tracee Goodman, Andrew Schrader, and Troy Turriate, all students (in 1992) at Northwest Elementary in Tampa, for so openly sharing their thoughts about print and electronic encyclopedias with me.

I am likewise indebted to Norman Horrocks of Scarecrow Press for including me in his informal clipping service of English-language publications from abroad, which has brought many useful encyclopedia articles and reviews to my attention I otherwise would not have seen; to Emanuel Molho, president of French & European Publications, Inc., for his invaluable assistance in preparing the section on foreign-language encyclopedias; and to the many reviewers in such publications as *American Reference Books Annual, Basic Information* Sources (6th ed., McGraw-Hill, 1992) by William A. Katz, *Choice, Library Journal, Reference Books Bulletin* (in *Booklist*), and *Wilson Library Bulletin*, whose criticisms are cited or incorporated in the book.

I am also grateful to those publishers and distributors who generously provided examination copies or sets of their encyclopedias, shared reports and documents with me, patiently answered my many questions, and, in some instances, made special arrangements at great inconvenience to themselves to introduce me to a new product.

My thanks particularly to David Arganbright (Grolier Electronic Publishing); Lauren Bahr (P.F. Collier), Leon Bram (Funk & Wagnalls); Craig Bartholomew (Miscrosoft Corporation); Jim Burnette (Encyclopaedia Britannica Educational Corporation); Phil Cox (Encyclopaedia Britannica Educational Corporation); Doug Downey (Standard Educational Corporation); Debbie Farber (Arrow Trading Company); Dale Good (Compton's); Sonja Gustafson (Microsoft Corporation); Robert Janus (World Book Publishing); Bernard Johnston (P.F. Collier); Madelyn Lesnick (Encyclopaedia Britannica Educational Corporation); Lawrence Lorimer (Grolier, Inc.); Linda Maxwell (Hartley Courseware); Robert McHenry (Encyclopaedia Britannica, Inc.); Bill Nault (World Book Publishing); Janet Peterson (World Book Publishing); James Raimes (Columbia University Press); Steve Riggio (Barnes & Noble); and Jonathan Weiss (Oxford University Press).

My gratitude to Anne Thompson, managing editor at the Oryx Press, is immense. This is the fifth book I have written with Anne as editor and my admiration for her editorial skills, knowledge, patience, and good common sense has deepened with each project. I am also grateful to the rest of the Oryx Press staff who worked on this book, especially Susan Slesinger, vice president of editorial and production, and Linda Vespa, typesetter, for their commitment to quality publishing.

To Clarice Ruder—spouse, colleague, and best friend—I am constantly and forever appreciative.

Finally, I welcome comments about *Kister's Best Encyclopedias* as well as questions, experiences, observations, and so forth from encyclopedia consumers everywhere.

Kenneth F. Kister
3118 San Juan Street
Tampa, Florida 33629
March 1994

About Encyclopedias

* * * * * * * * *

Questions and Answers about Encyclopedias

* * * * * * * * *

WHAT IS AN ENCYCLOPEDIA?

When most people think of an encyclopedia they envision a handsomely bound set of alphabetically arranged volumes brimming with information on every conceivable subject from the aardvark to zucchini. This popular conception, while not wrong, hardly tells the whole story of what an encyclopedia is or can be.

Today, an encyclopedia is a reference source published in either print or electronic form that summarizes basic knowledge and information on all important subjects or, in the case of a specialized encyclopedia, a particular subject. The encyclopedist's goal is to make this material accessible, both physically and intellectually, to students and other users in as fair, accurate, and precise a manner as possible. The historian François Guizot once characterized the famous eighteenth-century French *Encyclopédie* as a "vast intellectual bazaar where the results of all the works of the human spirit are offered to whosoever stops to satisfy his curiosity," an apt description of any large encyclopedia, no matter when or where it was made.

Encyclopedias, in short, aim to encompass and codify that knowledge and information educated people deem essential or universally worth knowing—the word *encyclopedia* coming to us from the Greek *enkyklios* (circle) and *paideia* (of learning). Perhaps Henry David Thoreau put it best in his classic *Walden* when he called an encyclopedia "an abstract of human knowledge."

Typically, encyclopedias contain articles describing important people, places, things, events, concepts, and activities. The written text is normally accompanied by such enhancements as photographs, diagrams, charts, chronologies, fact boxes, maps, bibliographies, and glossaries—complements designed to assist the reader's comprehension. The new electronic encyclopedias on compact disc (or CD-ROM)—appropriately called multimedia encyclopedias—also convey information via sound and video clips, thus expanding the sensory reach of the traditional encyclopedia. For instance, *Microsoft Encarta*, the newest of the multimedia encyclopedias, includes not only standard information about T.S. Eliot and his poetry but the added dimension of the poet readings from his works.

Because their reason for being involves making knowledge and information as readily accessible as possible, encyclopedias are always organized in some systematic manner, usually alphabetically but not always. Sometimes, as in the case of the *Random House Encyclopedia*, the arrangement is by subject, customarily referred to as a thematic, or topical, arrangement. Retrieval of an encyclopedia's contents, no matter whether the arrangement is alphabetical or topical, is normally facilitated by an index at the end of the work and a network of cross-references throughout the text. Physical size and intended readership dictate an encyclopedia's range and depth. A multivolume set intended for adult use, for instance, will naturally provide broader and deeper coverage than a single-volume work for children.

In addition to being a prime source for quick reference information, a good encyclopedia will furnish reliable summaries or digests of potentially unfamiliar or complicated subjects, rendering them comprehensible to the ordinary person. For example, any reputable general encyclopedia for adults and older students can be expected to explain clearly and succinctly such complexities as the underlying causes of economic depression and recession, the major types of psychological depression and their etiology and treatments, how genetic (or DNA) fingerprinting works, the pros and cons of nuclear power, the political and economic tenets of Marxism, and the distinguishing characteristics of abstract expressionism, a contemporary school of art. The best encyclopedias make such difficult subjects intelligible to the average reader without sacrificing accuracy to oversimplification.

Users of encyclopedias should understand, however, that these most basic of all reference sources are not, nor do they pretend to be, substitutes for in-depth study or mastery of a subject. No encyclopedia, no matter how voluminous or erudite it might be, can begin to include everything worth knowing about any topic. The article on Abraham Lincoln in any decent encyclopedia, for instance, will almost certainly record the highlights of Lincoln's life, including his political achievements and defeats, the presidential years and his handling of the Civil War, and his tragic assassination. On the other hand, an encyclopedic account of Lincoln cannot be expected to include relatively minor facts. Did you know, for instance, that a march called *Honor to Our Soldiers* composed by William Withers, Jr. was scheduled as the finale at Ford's Theatre the night John Wilkes Booth shot Lincoln but never got

played because of the attack on the president? This sort of interesting historical tidbit might well be included in a biography of Lincoln but not an encyclopedia article; it is too trivial, too insignificant, too anecdotal to warrant encyclopedic attention. Encyclopedias deal only in the bare bones of knowledge and information.

In this same vein, encyclopedia editors and writers do not conduct original research, nor do they normally base their articles on primary sources. Rather, practically all encyclopedias are tertiary—or third-stage—compilations, meaning that they base their text on secondary sources (such as trade books, popular journals, and newspapers), which in turn derive from primary sources (scholarly studies, laboratory tests, interviews, speeches, and the like). To repeat: A good encyclopedia summarizes basic factual and conceptual information on important subjects; the goal is not comprehensive treatment but provision of a frame of reference for initial understanding or a starting point that might serve as a springboard to further investigation. George Sarton, the science historian, has put the encyclopedia and its purpose into good perspective: "It is wise to refer to encyclopedias for first guidance; it is priggish to disregard them. But it is foolish to depend too much on them."

One final note about what an encyclopedia is—and is not. Consumers should know that encyclopedias are sometimes called "dictionaries," "handbooks," etc. By way of example, the eight-volume *Dictionary of American History* is actually a subject encyclopedia, containing well over 6,000 substantial articles written by some 800 authorities; the use of "dictionary" in this instance refers simply to the work's alphabetical (or dictionary) arrangement. Nor is every reference work with "encyclopedia" in its title really an encyclopedia. The well-known *Encyclopedia of Associations*, for instance, is a directory.

HOW DID ENCYCLOPEDIAS COME ABOUT?

Encyclopedias date back to antiquity, well before the advent of the printing press, although the word *encyclopedia* itself was not used until the middle of the sixteenth century.

The first encyclopedias represented attempts by individual scholars to classify and organize what was then a relatively small but growing body of knowledge in some systematic fashion. Such compendiums served the educated elite as codifications of what was known—or thought to be known—at the time. Pliny the Elder's *Historia Naturalis* (A.D. 77) exemplified the early encyclopedic impulse. Considered the most influential of the Roman encyclopedias and sometimes cited as the first bona fide encyclopedia produced in the west, *Historia Naturalis* divided ancient scientific scholarship into 37 books comprising some 2,500 chapters under such rubrics as geography, physiology, zoology, botany, and medicine.

As Pliny's compilation suggests, early encyclopedias differed markedly from those published today. Most twentieth-centry encyclopedists agree, for instance, that the best way to arrange encyclopedic material is alphabetically, with access to specific facts expedited by a detailed index, not topically as Pliny did. Most also agree that encyclopedias should be as up-to-date as humanly possible and that, conversely, out-of-date information is tantamount to misinformation, a problem of minimal concern to Pliny and his contemporaries. Likewise, practically all editors today consider pictures, graphics, and maps to be an integral part of any successful encyclopedia, whereas in Pliny's day encyclopedias had little if any pictorial matter.

Prior to the beginning of the eighteenth century, when the modern encyclopedia began to take shape, quite different editorial attitudes and realities prevailed. For good technical reasons, pictorial illustrations did not begin to appear with any frequency in encyclopedias until a few hundred years ago and only recently have they come to be regarded as essential to the encyclopedic mix. Alphabetical arrangement—admittedly easier to understand and access than any thematic or classified scheme—and cumulative indexes have become firm fixtures only since the eighteenth century, due chiefly to the increased use of general encyclopedias by schoolchildren as a result of the introduction of universal education in Europe and North America. Similarly, the importance of keeping encyclopedias as current as possible has paralleled the growth of modern communications and the resulting speed-up in information creation and exchange.

Another striking difference between present-day encyclopedias and those of earlier times concerns the changing role or mission of encyclopedias. Today, editors and publishers universally agree that encyclopedias are obliged not only to codify existing knowledge and information but to accomplish that task as impartially and objectively as possible. The notion of an encyclopedia promoting a particular religious doctrine or political philosophy or excluding certain ideas as heretical or subversive is contrary to the intellectual instincts of practically all contemporary encyclopedia-makers. Yet the encyclopedic tomes of yesterday were often conspicuously and deliberately biased in their presentation, serving as vehicles for the compiler's or publisher's or sponsor's vision of what was right or true; similarly, any ideas, theories, or beliefs deemed wrong or false were ignored or condemned. The rationale was betterment of the human lot through dissemination of correct knowledge, not deceit or censorship.

Indeed, the historical record is full of encyclopedias intended as purveyors of immutable truth and moral ballast, especially during the early Christian and medieval periods, when church scholars and monks saw encyclopedias as a means of interpreting and promulgating knowledge according to established ecclesiastical dogma. Secular thinkers also viewed encyclopedias as a way to improve people and society. The thirteenth-century French savant Vincent of Beauvais, author of *Speculum Majus* (translated as *The Greater Mirror*), for example, suggested that his work (completed in 1244) not only depicted the world as it was but reflected how it might be made better in the future. In similar fashion, the Spanish humanist Juan Luis Vives presented his *De Disciplinis* (*On the Disciplines*), published in 1531, as more a guide to the search for truth than a precis of established knowledge.

Later, English intellectuals like Sir Francis Bacon, concerned with developing the ideal person, and Samuel Taylor Coleridge, the Romantic poet, formulated encyclopedias based on the principle of knowledge as a progressive, edifying, and unifying force. In Coleridge's introductory essay in the initial volume of *Encyclopaedia Metropolitana* (1822–45), a splendid failure that he planned but did not edit, the poet describes the encyclopedia's purpose as rendering "the pure and unsophisticated knowledge of the past . . . to aid the progress of the future." In modern parlance, encyclopedists like Vincent of Beauvais, Vives, Bacon, and Coleridge had their own agendas.

While the basic function of the encyclopedia as an all-encompassing source of universal or specialized knowledge has remained relatively constant through the ages, its style, format, contents, and intended readership have changed, in some cases dramatically, over the years in response to new social, political, educational, and technological conditions.

The term *encyclopedia* first appeared in the title of a book in 1559, namely a work in Latin by Paul Scalich called *Encyclopaedia; seu, Orbis Disciplinarium, tam Sacrarum quam Prophanum Epistemon*, which translates as *Encyclopedia; or Knowledge of the World of Disciplines, Not only Sacred but Profane*. Like the works of Scalich and Pliny before him, most early encyclopedias were the creations of a single individual, always a person of wide learning and, during the Middle Ages when the Roman Catholic church so completely dominated western scholarship, most likely a cleric. Interestingly, the church's theocentric monopoly on knowledge during the medieval period relied as much on control of the supply of parchment (which was scarce) and the ready availability of monks as reliable and cheap copyists as it did content of the message. That the church's influence began to wane just as the movable-type printing press and its handmaiden, paper, arrived on the scene is no historical accident.

The coming of the modern printing press and papermaking industry—both fifteenth-century developments—stimulated an enormous increase in book production, which in turn fueled the growth of literacy, education, and, broadly speaking, the intellectual awakening historians call the Renaissance. The ferment of the Renaissance affected the entire world of learning, including encyclopedias and how they were compiled and used. Specifically, as they became more widely available, encyclopedias broadened their readership to include not only educational elites but ordinary people now able to read for the first time. At the same time, encyclopedias expanded their scope to accommodate the avalanche of new ideas, new theories, new attitudes, new inventions, new discoveries, and new vocations spawned by the Renaissance and the incipient Industrial Revolution.

The sheer quantity of new knowledge and information meant that for the first time in history no one person, no matter how brilliant and industrious, could hope to know all that was worth knowing. It also meant that the day when one person working alone à la Pliny or Scalich could create an authoritative encyclopedia was gone. Increasingly, encyclopedia-making became a cooperative endeavor, involving a staff of editors, artists, contributors, consultants, and production personnel. The solitary genius capable of synthesizing all knowledge in all areas of intellectual discourse soon became as obsolete as the parchment scroll.

Most authorities agree that the first true English-language encyclopedia (despite its Latinate title) was John Harris's *Lexicon Technicum, or, An Universal English Dictionary of the Arts and Sciences*. A single-volume work published in London in 1704, *Lexicon Technicum* was alphabetically arranged (a first in English) and emphasized articles of interest to British readers on practical and scientific subjects. Not long thereafter, Ephraim Chambers published his popular and prestigious *Cyclopaedia* (London, 1728), a two-volume set that measurably improved on Harris's encyclopedia by incorporating several innovative features, including an elaborate system of cross-references. More important, Chambers's *Cyclopaedia* inspired the greatest encyclopedia project of the eighteenth century, the French *Encyclopédie*, a massive work begun in 1751 that eventually comprised 70 volumes when completed in 1772.

Edited by the philosopher Denis Diderot and mathematician Jean Le Rond d'Alembert, the *Encyclopédie*, though condemned by Pope Clement VIII and censored at various times by the French government, had a profound effect on the radical thought of the day, ultimately helping to pave the way for the French Revolution. Its contributors—Voltaire, Rousseau, Turgot, Montesquieu, Quesnay, Condorcet, et al.—included some of the most distinguished intellectuals of eighteenth-century France. Hans Koning has described the *Encyclopédie*'s impact in an article in the *New Yorker* (March 2, 1981, p. 67): "The Encyclopédie raised a storm that blew away the smells of powdered wigs, love potions, and alchemists' retorts; shook the

salons of the court and the chambers of bishops and parliamentarians still meeting in the shadow of stake and rack; and astounded the still humble new middle class." For a fascinating scholarly account of the publishing history of the *Encyclopédie*, see Robert Darnton's *The Business of Enlightenment* (Harvard University Press, 1979); complementing Darnton's history is *The Encyclopédie and the Age of Revolution* (G.K. Hall, 1992), a collection of essays edited by Clorinda Donato and Robert Maniquis on encyclopedia production in the latter part of the eighteenth century.

Among its many accomplishments, the *Encyclopédie* stimulated the compilation of similar multivolume works in other countries. In Britain, for instance, what has come to be the best known of all English-language encyclopedias, the *Encyclopaedia Britannica*, first appeared in three volumes during 1768–71; in Germany, *Konversations-Lexikon*, later and better known as the *Brockhaus Enzyklopadie* (or simply *Brockhaus*), was initially published between 1796 and 1811. *Brockhaus*, named for its influential founding editor Friedrich Arnold Brockhaus, treated knowledge in short, fact-filled, popularly written articles noted for their accuracy, objectivity, and timeliness. The encyclopedia's success was immediate and contagious. *Brockhaus* in turn served as the model for numerous other national encyclopedias begun in the nineteenth century, most prominently the *Encyclopedia Americana*, a large English-language work originally published in the United States between 1829 and 1833 and still a major multivolume set on the North American market.

Unlike the French *Encyclopédie*, however, these new national encyclopedias did not attempt to fan the flames of revolution or alter the course of human society. Rather, they tended to be works of solid, unbiased scholarship tailored to satisfy the most basic informational and educational needs of the now dominant (and no longer humble) middle classes, particularly the growing student population at all levels. It comes as no surprise, then, that modern encyclopedias customarily have shorter entries and are more popularly written and heavily illustrated than those of the past. Like their antecedents, today's encyclopedias mirror the intellectual conditions and interests of the people and times that create them.

WHAT TYPES OF ENCYCLOPEDIAS ARE AVAILABLE?

Encyclopedias come in every shape and size imaginable, from the massive *New Encyclopaedia Britannica*, which comprises 44 million words in 32 stately volumes, to the *Running Press Cyclopedia*, a fat little one-volume paperback that stands only 5 inches high and contains just 100,000 words. In addition, more and more encyclopedias are published today in electronic (or automated) form, either online or on disks for use with personal computers. A few hand-held electronic encyclopedias not much larger than pocket calculators have also appeared in recent times.

Encyclopedias are written in numerous languages representing all major and many minor countries, nationalities, and cultures. Some (called general encyclopedias) treat all areas of knowledge and information, while others (subject encyclopedias) concentrate on a particular topic or field of study, such as art, chemistry, the environment, film, geography, law, music, sports, and so on. Some are intended specifically for adult readers, others for children; some for generalists, others for specialists. In sum, the versatile encyclopedia assumes as many guises as there are ways to record and communicate basic knowledge and information.

Encyclopedias of principal interest to North American consumers fall into four broad types or categories:

- General English-language encyclopedias published in print (or hardcover) form.
- General English-language encyclopedias published in electronic (or automated) form.
- Subject (or specialized) encyclopedias, usually published in print but increasingly in electronic form.

- Foreign-language encyclopedias—that is, encyclopedias published in languages other than English, the dominant language of North America.

General English-Language Print Encyclopedias. General English-language encyclopedias in print form receive more attention in *Kister's Best Encyclopedias* than any other type because, by their very nature, these encyclopedias are of the greatest interest to the largest number of consumers in the U.S. and Canada. These encyclopedias cover universal knowledge in the language most people speak and in a traditional format almost everyone understands and can use with a minimum of difficulty.

For comparative purposes, it is useful (and fair) to classify general English-language print encyclopedias by size and intended usership. The categories used in *Kister's Best Encyclopedias* are: Large Encyclopedias for Adults and Older Students; Medium-Sized Encyclopedias for Adults and Older Students; Small Encyclopedias for Adults and Older Students; Large and Medium-Sized Encyclopedias for Children and Younger Students; and Small Encyclopedias for Children and Younger Students.

General English-Language Electronic Encyclopedias. General English-language encyclopedias in electronic form are relatively new, part of the communications and information revolution currently sweeping the world. Thus far, all electronic encyclopedias derive from a print counterpart. For example, *Compton's Concise Encyclopedia, Compton's Family Encyclopedia, Compton's Interactive Encyclopedia,* and *Compton's Multimedia Encyclopedia*—all CD-ROM products—are based on *Compton's Encyclopedia*, the 26-volume print set. Electronic encyclopedias are normally classified by how they deliver their information: Dial-up online; CD-ROM (which may include moving pictures and sound); Floppy disk; and Hand-held (which works off a ROM chip). For additional information about electronic encyclopedias, see "Electronic Encyclopedias" beginning on page 253.

Subject Encyclopedias. Hundreds of new subject (or specialized) encyclopedias appear in North America every year. The proliferation and popularity of these encyclopedias reflect the irresistible human urge toward specialization. General encyclopedias effectively serve a large number of people, particularly school and college students. But in the case of scholars, researchers, teachers, advanced students, and professional people, an encyclopedia dedicated entirely to their field or area of intellectual interest is usually preferable due to its deeper treatment and greater authority.

Subject encyclopedias are logically classified by specialty. *Kister's Best Encyclopedias* groups them under 30 broad headings: Art (General), Architecture, and Photography; Astronomy and Space Science; Biology and Animal Life; Botany and Horticulture; Business, Economics, and Statistics; Chemistry and Chemical Engineering; Computer and Electronic Sciences; Decorative Arts and Antiques; Earth, Energy, and Environmental Sciences; Education and Libraries; Engineer-

ing and Building Construction; Film, Radio, Television, and Mass Communications; Food, Nutrition, and Agriculture; Geography and Area Studies; Health, Medicine, and Drugs; History and Archaeology; Law and the Judicial System; Literature, Language, and Publishing; Military Science and History; Music; Physics and Mathematics; Political Science and Government; Psychology, Psychiatry, and Parapsychology; Religion, Philosophy, and Mythology; Science and Technology (General); Sexuality, Human Reproduction, and Child Care; Social Science, Sociology, and Anthropology; Sports and Games; Theater and Dance; and Transportation.

Foreign-Language Encyclopedias. Although English remains very much the preferred language in the U.S. and Canada (with the obvious exception of the province of Quebec), encyclopedias in languages other than English can be invaluable reference sources for North Americans, particularly students who are studying another language or culture. Such encyclopedias often provide biographical, geographical, and historical information not ordinarily found in English-language reference works. *Kister's Best Encyclopedias* briefly covers selected titles in nine major foreign languages: Chinese, Dutch, French, German, Italian, Japanese, Korean, Russian, and Spanish. A good source for concise information about encyclopedias in other languages is the *Guide to Reference Books* (American Library Assn., 1986; supplement, 1992).

ARE TEACHERS BIASED AGAINST ENCYCLOPEDIAS?

Yes, some–but certainly not all–teachers discourage or prohibit outright the use of encyclopedias in elementary and secondary school. They sincerely believe that students will rely too heavily or exclusively on "the encyclopedia" for homework assignments, while neglecting other pertinent library resources such as indexes, almanacs, magazines, and books.

"The danger of an encyclopedia," a prominent educator once said, "is that a child may see it as the easy way out of some assignment. It can have a detrimental effect on the development of a child's ability to search and learn to use the full library. Instead, he learns to take shortcuts." Some teachers also complain that students copy, or plagiarize, articles from encyclopedias, which accomplishes little except to promote cheating among the young.

Not everyone agrees with this reasoning, including the author of this book. Mindlessly insisting that students not use encyclopedias in the course of their school work is, frankly, a strange approach to education. It suggests a weak and rigid teacher who lacks understanding of the spirit of learning. Nearly 30 years ago the historian Richard B. Morris, a longtime teacher himself, forcefully addressed this issue in an article entitled "Adventures in the Reference Room" (*Wilson Library Bulletin*, January 1967, p. 498):

> I know there are some teachers who try to keep their students out of the reference room....I don't feel this way at all. I think a student should be taught how to use the tools of the trade without hurting himself or injuring others. I see my responsibility as a teacher to encourage curiosity and suggest where it can be satisfied. I don't think a teacher should act as a policeman, and I do not feel that reference books should be restricted.

Ann Scarpellino has looked at the problem from the librarian's perspective in her article "School-Public Library Cooperation: Some Practical Approaches," which appeared in 1979 in the *U*N*A*B*A*S*H*E*D Librarian* (No. 32, p. 29); her comments are as pertinent today as they were 15 years ago:

Too many young people come into the library needing to find out, but knowing nothing about Henry VIII, say, the Sumerians, or the mastodon. The encyclopedia is the only tool that can be used initially by a student working alone, to place the topic in time, country of origin, or within broad subjects which he can then use to find broad-based books which will include information on his topic. The encyclopedia, in short, is the preferred tool, the necessary first step, for the young person with no background of knowledge in the subject. And the young, who are most likely to lack that knowledge, are the very ones who are not allowed to use it....An encyclopedia is, in itself, a small research library. Many librarians feel that asking anyone learning to do research to forego use of it is on a level with teaching someone to play tennis with the use of only the left hand.

The real issue here goes well beyond encyclopedias. What will determine whether a child fully uses the library and its various resources is not use or nonuse of "the encyclopedia," but rather the quality of instruction the student receives, the type of assignments involved, and the student's own intellectual motivation and maturity. Still, despite the feeble logic behind, the fact is that some educators are hostile to encyclopedias. It therefore behooves consumers thinking seriously of buying an encyclopedia for their school-age children to check with local teachers and principals before making a final purchase decision.

WHO MAKES AND PUBLISHES ENCYCLOPEDIAS?

Three well-known, highly regarded publishers dominate the general encyclopedia market in North America today: Encyclopaedia Britannica, Inc.; Grolier, Inc.; and World Book, Inc. Together, they account for about 75 percent of all general print (or hardcover) encyclopedia sales in North America. Total industry sales typically average 800,000 sets each year with gross revenues in the neighborhood of $600-700 million. (These figures represent informed estimates; both

Encyclopaedia Britannica and World Book are privately held and accordingly do not disclose their unit sales or dollar volume.)

Encyclopaedia Britannica, Inc. The cornerstone of EB's publishing empire, of course, is the 32-volume *New Encyclopaedia Britannica*, the oldest, largest, and most prestigious general encyclopedia in the English language. The *Britannica* is also now published in electronic form on disk as the *Britannica Instant Research System* and online as *Britannica Online*; the latter will shortly become available via Internet. EB also publishes and distributes two multivolume sets for young people, the *Children's Britannica* (which replaces the now defunct *Britannica Junior Encyclopaedia*) and the *Young Children's Encyclopedia*. For many years, the company also published *Compton's Encyclopedia*, but that property, including the electronic versions (*Compton's Multimedia Encyclopedia, Compton's Interactive Encyclopedia*, etc.), was sold in 1993 to the Tribune Company of Chicago.

In addition, EB publishes or distributes a number of fine foreign-language sets, such as *Encyclopaedia Universalis, Enciclopedia Hispánica*, and the *Chinese-Language Concise Encyclopaedia Britannica*. Encyclopaedia Britannica Educational Corporation (EBEC) distributes Britannica products to schools and libraries, along with many reference titles published by other companies.

Grolier, Inc. Grolier, along with its school and library arm, Grolier Educational Corporation (GEC), offers a strong product line. At the top of the company's encyclopedia hierarchy is the 30-volume *Encyclopedia Americana*, a major work for adults and older students; it was the first encyclopedia of any consequence to be produced in North America (1829–).

Next in line is the *Academic American Encyclopedia*, the newest (1980–) general English-language multivolume set on the market—and the first encyclopedia to be created in machine-readable form from the start, which helps account for its prominent position among electronic encyclopedias; for instance, the *Academic American* dominates the major commercial online information services (CompuServe, GEnie, Prodigy, etc.), and it is published on CD-ROM as the *New Grolier Multimedia Encyclopedia* (a product of Grolier Electronic Publishing). The *Academic American* is also published in print form under numerous other titles, such as the *Global International Encyclopedia*, the *Grolier Aca-*

demic Encyclopedia, the *Grolier International Encyclopedia, Lexicon Universal Encyclopedia*, and the *Macmillan Family Encyclopedia*. There is also an abridged version, the *Grolier Encyclopedia of Knowledge*.

The last major encyclopedia in the Grolier family is the 21-volume *New Book of Knowledge*, a longtime favorite with young readers. In addition, GEC distributes many non-Grolier products (e.g., the *Grolier Children's Encyclopedia*; the *New Grolier Student Encyclopedia*) to schools and libraries.

World Book, Inc. Unlike its chief publishing rivals, World Book has a relatively small product line, headed by the 22-volume *World Book Encyclopedia*, unquestionably the bestselling encyclopedia in North America. The encyclopedia is now available on CD-ROM under the title *Information Finder. Information Finder* lacks sound and moving pictures, but the 1994 edition has added illustrations. The company also publishes *Childcraft: The How and Why Library*, a quality set in 15 volumes for very young children. In addition, World Book offers a few subject encyclopedias, including the *World Book Encyclopedia of People and Places* and the *World Book/Rush-Presbyterian-St. Luke's Medical Center Medical Encyclopedia*.

Other Major Publishers. Other general multivolume print encyclopedias include those published by P.F. Collier, Inc. (*Collier's Encyclopedia*), Compton's Learning Company (*Compton's Encyclopedia*), Funk & Wagnalls (*Funk & Wagnalls New Encyclopedia*), and Standard Educational Corporation (*New Standard Encyclopedia*). Publishers of one- and two-volume general encyclopedias also claim a small share of the market. The leading small-volume publishers are Columbia University Press (the *Columbia Encyclopedia*; *Concise Columbia Encyclopedia*), Random House, Inc. (the *Random House Encyclopedia*), Cambridge University Press (the *Cambridge Encyclopedia*), Prentice Hall (*Webster New World Encyclopedia*), and the Southwestern Company (the *Volume Library*).

Electronic products are the new kids on the encyclopedia block. One of the main players is Compton's NewMedia, a sister company to Compton's Learning Company (together they form Compton's Multimedia Publishing Group, Inc.); Compton's NewMedia publishes *Compton's Multimedia Encyclopedia* and its various spin-offs. Grolier Electronic Publishing (a subsidiary of Grolier, Inc.) is also a key player, responsible for the online version of the aforementioned *Academic American Encyclopedia* and the CD-ROM *New Grolier Multimedia Encyclopedia*. Brand new to the encyclopedia business is Microsoft Corporation, which has staked out a strong claim with its *Microsoft Encarta Multimedia Encyclopedia*, based on *Funk & Wagnalls New Encyclopedia*. Other publishers in the electronic arena are Franklin Electronic Publishers, Inc. (the *Columbia Electronic Encyclopedia*), Hartley Courseware (*First Connections*), and Microlytics (a floppy disk version of the *Random House Encyclopedia*).

Subject (or specialized) encyclopedias, which can be viewed as either complements or alternatives to general encyclopedias, are produced and sold by a great variety of publishers and distributors in the U.S. and Canada. Among the most prominent and prolific of these are the Academic Press, Cambridge University Press, Facts on File, Gale Research, Garland Publishing, Greenwood Publishing Group, Grove's Dictionaries of Music, HarperCollins, Macmillan, Marshall Cavendish, McGraw-Hill, Oxford University Press, Pergamon Press, Prentice Hall, St. Martin's Press, Charles Scribner's Sons, Van Nostrand Reinhold Company, and John Wiley & Sons.

For further information about all of the publishers mentioned here, see the directory at the back of this book (Appendix B). The directory provides the address and telephone numbers of North American encyclopedia publishers, along with lists of their products.

HOW ARE ENCYCLOPEDIAS BOUGHT AND SOLD?

The adage that "encyclopedias are sold not bought" contains more than a grain of truth. Most people perceive encyclopedias, unlike automobiles and toothpaste, to be a discretionary, or luxury, item. Hence, potential customers usually must be convinced that an encyclopedia, which can cost as much as $1,500.00 or more, is a necessary purchase. It should come as no surprise, then, that most encyclopedias—that is, most print (or hardcover) encyclopedias—are sold in the home, where sales representatives are able to demonstrate the product at length with minimum interruption, pointing out its excellent qualities and occasionally sneaking in disparaging comments about the competition.

This system has advantages for the seller, who loves (and needs) a captive audience. But from the consumer's point of view it leaves much to be desired. For openers, in-

home selling hampers comparison shopping. When consumers shop for, say, a new car or television set, they can go to various dealerships or stores and look over the merchandise, kick the tires, push the buttons, and so on. They are able to get a comparative sense of the models and brands on the market. Not so with encyclopedias, which traditionally have not been sold in bookstores or similar retail outlets.

Another consumer problem inherent in in-home selling is the overly aggressive sales representative who bends or breaks the rules of fair business conduct. For years, encyclopedia salespeople have been portrayed in cartoons and movies as the worst sort of hucksters. This image—though unfair to the large majority of sales reps today, who are honest, hardworking people—is unfortunately grounded in historical fact. Because encyclopedias rarely sell themselves, and because encyclopedia salespeople work on commission, and because the encyclopedia business is extremely competitive, hard-sell tactics are not uncommon. According to one former encyclopedia salesman, "We were trained to play on guilt by telling parents their children might grow up to be dummies if they didn't have an encyclopedia." (Quoted from Tyler Mathisen's article "All About Encyclopedias" in *Money*, October 1983, p. 209.)

And sometimes encyclopedia sales reps cross the line from high-pressure to fraudulent and deceptive practices, such as misrepresenting the purpose of their call or using false and misleading advertising. In an old but still valid article entitled "Buying an Encyclopedia" in *Consumers' Research Magazine* (Febrruary 1975, p. 12), W.T. Johnston and Joy B. Trulock discuss the time-honored techniques employed by unscrupulous sales reps:

> [D]on't be caught in the trap of the claim that he has only one bargain or "demo," or sample set left. The prices on most standard and good encyclopedias are fairly rigid. Watch, too, that he hasn't quoted you an inflated price and makes the offer to throw in a dictionary and an atlas free of charge when in reality these volumes were included in the price he gave you to begin with. And last, don't accept a "free" set and then sign a contract agreeing to pay $400 for an annual updating service for the next 10 years.

Happily, the most blatant encyclopedia sales abuses have declined in recent years. Much of the credit for this improvement belongs to the Federal Trade Commission (FTC), a regulatory agency of the U.S. government, which instituted several consumer protection measures during the 1970s designed to curb the overzealous salesperson. The most effective of these measures has been the so-called "cooling-off" regulation, which allows consumers to cancel a contract for any in-home purchase of $25.00 or more within three business days after signing the contract. Moreover, in the 1970s and 1980s, the FTC investigated the whole encyclopedia industry for questionable sales practices, resulting in regulatory action against most of the major companies, including Collier, Encyclopaedia Britannica, and Grolier. All of this public attention has helped persuade encyclopedia publishers and distributors to get rid of the rotten apples on their sales force and otherwise clean up their act.

Furthermore, those who sell print encyclopedias have begun to explore new, more inventive ways to merchandise their products. Selling door-to-door is no longer practical or profitable in many areas of the U.S. and Canada; fewer people are at home during the day and those who are often refuse to open the door for fear of crime—even the venerable Fuller Brush Man, part of the American scene since 1906, is an endangered species. One observer of the encyclopedia industry noted recently, "It's always been a competitive market. But now, there's been a shift to new, more sophisticated ways of marketing." (Quoted from Warren Berger's "What New in Encyclopedias," *New York Times*, May 28, 1989, p. 15-F.) Direct mail and telemarketing are on the increase in the encyclopedia business. Likewise, publishers and distributors are looking anew at selling through bookstores, especially the big chains and superstores. Mall kiosks are also being tried. And some encyclopedias (particularly Grolier titles) are now being sold alongside cartons of dog food in the large discount warehouse stores, such as PACE, Sam's Club, Price Club, and Costco.

The advent of electronic encyclopedias, particularly those on CD-ROM with multimedia capabilities, is also affecting the print encyclopedia sales environment today. CD-ROM encyclopedias, which are merchandised through computer software stores and catalogs and therefore require no formidable company sales force, have been enormously successful in marketplace during the 1990s. Compton's, Grolier, and Microsoft all report impressive sales figures for their multimedia encyclopedias. Naturally, this success has cut into the print side of the business, prompting layoffs and early retirements of salespeople in the largest companies.

To meet the electronic challenge, some former encyclopedia sales reps are setting up as independent distributors and selling selected titles at discount prices to the home market, foregoing the large markups and commissions typical in the industry. An example of this trend is Educational Home Systems (EHS) located outside Atlanta (4290 Bells Ferry Road, Suite 106-636, Kennesaw, GA 30144; 800-435-2349). EHS currently offers such titles as *Encyclopedia Americana*, the *New Standard Encyclopedia*, and the *Academic American Encyclopedia* at roughly half their suggested retail price. Such efforts can only benefit consumers.

Finally, encouraging trends notwithstanding, encyclopedia consumers would be wise to remain alert for sharp sales practices. Here are seven cautions that should be kept in mind when dealing with any encyclopedia representative:

- Do **not** be pressured into making a purchase decision until you are ready. As consumer advocate Herb Denenberg has advised (in *Caveat Emptor*, August-September 1979, p. 19), "The surest earmark of a phony salesman with a lousy deal is the one who insists you have to buy right now

or you'll miss a monumental bargain. What you'll probably miss if you don't buy in a hurry is a monumental rip-off."

- Do **not** sign a blank or incomplete contract.
- Do **not** talk with a salesperson when you are tired or not feeling well.
- Do **not** fall for come-ons like "free" gifts or prizes. Inevitably they are not free, not gifts, and not prizes.
- Do **not** buy an encyclopedia—any encyclopedia—unless it will be used sufficiently to justify the expense.
- Do **not** automatically sign up for the encyclopedia's yearbooks, traditionally part of the print encyclopedia package. Although some are excellent, yearbooks (or annual supplements) are usually expensive, only indirectly related to the encyclopedia, and often never used.
- Do **not** be suckered into buying an adult encyclopedia for a child. Specifically, the 24-volume *Collier's Encyclopedia*, the 30-volume *Encyclopedia Americana*, and the 32-volume *New Encyclopaedia Britannica* are much too advanced for most young people. Some sales reps will try to convince you that a child—your child, such a bright child—will "grow into" an adult encyclopedia. Don't believe it. By the time your youngster is ready for such an encyclopedia, it will be ancient history.

WHAT ABOUT A SECONDHAND ENCYCLOPEDIA?

New encyclopedias can be expensive, ranging from $600.00 to $1,500.00 or more for a quality multivolume adult set. *Collier's Encyclopedia*, for instance, now costs around $1,000.00 to individual consumers and just slightly less to schools and libraries, which usually receive a discount; the *Academic American Encyclopedia* currently goes for more than $1,100.00 to individuals and $700.00 to schools and libraries; and the *New*

Encyclopaedia Britannica starts at nearly $1,200 for individuals and about the same in a library binding for educational institutions. Subject (or specialized) encyclopedias of comparable size and quality are equally or more expensive. For example, the multivolume *Encyclopedia of Religion* (Macmillan, 1986) currently sells for $1,400.00; the most recent edition (seventh) of the 15-volume *McGraw-Hill*

Encyclopedia of Science and Technology (McGraw-Hill, 1992) today costs the consumer $1,900.00.

One way around the high cost of encyclopedias is to buy a secondhand, or used, set. Substantial savings can be realized by investing in an older encyclopedia. Saul Shine, who runs the Reference Book Center in New York City with his wife Margery, estimates such savings "at 25 to 30 percent or more, depending on the date, condition, and binding of the encyclopedia." For example, Shine currently has older editions of the *Britannica* in stock priced between $400.00 and $1,000.00.

Like most products, encyclopedias begin to lose value the minute they are purchased. The general rule of thumb is that an encyclopedia depreciates between 15 and 20 percent the first year and 5 to 10 percent each year thereafter.

Naturally, a secondhand encyclopedia will not be as current as a new set. How important a consideration should up-to-dateness be when buying an encyclopedia? If the informational needs of those who will be using the set are mainly in the area the humanities—history, literature, music, philosophy, religion, etc.—where knowledge is not as volatile and readily discarded as in the sciences, then a used encyclopedia several years old can be a good buy—if it was a quality set to begin with. If, on the other hand, the encyclopedia will be consulted chiefly for information in the physical, technical, bio-logical, or behavioral sciences, where knowledge changes very rapidly and currency is often essential, a secondhand encyclopedia makes little sense, no matter how inexpensive it might be. Generally speaking, any encyclopedia over 10 years old should be avoided, unless it has some special historical significance, such as the ninth and eleventh editions of *Encyclopaedia Britannica*.

Who sells secondhand encyclopedias? Sometimes they can be found through classified advertisements in the local newspaper or at estate and garage sales or flea markets. But the best place to locate a used or older encyclopedia is through a bookstore that specializes in such materials. Most large cities have at least one bookstore that trades in secondhand and remainder books, including large reference sets. Two of the most active dealers in North America are Saul and Margery Shine, who operate the aforementioned Reference Book Center. The Shines have been in the business for years and are thoroughly knowledgeable about titles, editions, etc. Contact them at the Reference Book Center, Inc. 175 Fifth Avenue, Room 701, New York, NY 10010; 212-677-2160. Interested consumers should also contact the Strand Book Store at 828 Broadway, New York, NY 10003; 212-473-1452; the Strand usually has a modest selection of secondhand encyclopedias, all in good or excellent condition. Both the Reference Book Center and the Strand Book Store will send you a catalog of their reference books on request.

WHAT SHOULD YOU LOOK FOR WHEN CHOOSING AN ENCYCLOPEDIA?

Obviously, not all encyclopedias are of equal merit or value. Like all products, a few encyclopedias stand out as works of exceptional quality while others are out-and-out clunkers—with the vast majority somewhere in between. Given the large number and variety of titles available in both print and electronic form, how does the ordinary person with no special training in the evaluation of reference products go about deciding which encyclopedia to buy or use? How can you find the best encyclopedia for your needs without spending an inordinate amount of time or becoming bogged down in confusing and conflicting claims?

A simple and time-honored solution is to seek the advice of a knowledgeable friend, colleague, teacher, or librarian. Certainly this approach represents a good starting point. Reference librarians can be especially helpful. Specialists in finding information, they use numerous reference sources, including encyclopedias, day in and day out during the course of their work; they know the pluses and minuses of individual titles as well as anyone.

Also, this book—*Kister's Best Encyclopedias*, a comprehensive consumer guide to all types of encyclopedias currently on the North American market—can help prospective purchasers determine which titles seem most suitable based on such key considerations as size, format, content, intended readership, quality, and price. For example, if you are interested in a multivolume print (or hardcover) encyclopedia for general family use, a perusal of the sections of the book devoted to large and medium-sized general encyclopedias for adults and older students will provide an honest sense of the strengths and weaknesses of each title in those categories, as well a comparative overview of the lot. Or, if you decide that a computerized encyclopedia is the way to go, the section on electronic encyclopedias will help you focus on those titles that deserve serious consideration and ultimately on which one to buy. Likewise, if you are interested in a particular area of knowledge, such as music or engineering, the subject encyclopedias section of *Kister's Best Encyclopedias* will guide you through the thicket of available titles.

Talking to experts and consulting an authoritative guide will normally satisfy casual encyclopedia consumers who lack the time and/or inclination to formulate their own opinions about specific titles. But serious consumers—teachers, journalists, writers, editors, researchers, librarians, advanced students, etc.—will want to inspect *firsthand* any encyclopedia being considered for purchase or extensive use in fact-checking or preparation of a term paper, thesis, article, book, or similarly important project. *Nothing beats personal examination when it comes to evaluating and selecting reference materials.* This is particularly true in the case of encyclopedias, where the expense involved can be quite high.

How, then, does the serious consumer go about personally evaluating an encyclopedia? The author of *Kister's Best Encyclopedias* recommends this general procedure:

After locating an examination set or copy at a library or bookstore or from the publisher (on a trial basis), ask the encyclopedia some questions it might reasonably be expected to answer—and demand clear, accurate, impartial, up-to-date, easily retrievable information in return. Interrogate the encyclopedia as if you were an investigative reporter on the trail of a hot story. Think of yourself as Mike Wallace (of TV's *60 Minutes*) grilling a particularly cunning malefactor. Ask the encyclopedia for information on topics you know something about, as well as those you would like to know more about. By way of example, you might ask the encyclopedia about sodium pentothal, popularly known as "truth serum." How effective is sodium pentothal at eliciting the truth? How does it work biochemically? Are there different kinds of truth serum? Are confessions obtained using truth serum admissible as evidence in a court of law? Does the encyclopedia indicate who first used or developed truth serum? Still in search of the truth (appropriately enough), you might also ask the encyclopedia similar questions about the polygraph, or lie detector, test.

The object, of course, is to discover the encyclopedia's strengths and weaknesses through actual use. When possible, the encyclopedia's chief competitors should be asked the same questions for the purpose of head-to-head comparison. The results can be revealing. Also, if children will be using the encyclopedia, include them in the examination and selection process. Make certain, for instance, that the encyclopedia's written text is comprehensible to everyone who will be using it.

To repeat: Ask the encyclopedia questions, the more the better. Cross-examine it, checking topics based on your knowledge and interests and those of your family. Very quickly you will begin to learn whether or not the encyclopedia under scrutiny is clearly written, intelligently organized, reasonably current, sufficiently detailed, and so on.

To achieve a full and fair sense of the overall quality of the encyclopedia, consider these 15 points during the evaluation process:

1. Does the encyclopedia provide the material you and others who will be using it are likely to need? How extensive is the encyclopedia's coverage? How deep? Are there any noticeable or glaring gaps in the coverage? Are all basic areas of knowledge adequately covered, or does the encyclopedia emphasize one area to the detriment of another? In some general encyclopedias, scientific and technical subjects tend to predominate while the humanities or social sciences (or both) are given short shrift. If you or the encyclopedia's principal users are mainly interested in a particular subject or field of knowledge (art, astronomy, biology, botany, business, chemistry, computer science, etc.), ought not a subject encyclopedia be considered?

2. Is the encyclopedia comprehensible to you and others who will be using it? For whom is the encyclopedia intended? Adults? High school and college students? Children? Specialists? The introduction or preface to the work should make this plain, but unfortunately some encyclopedia makers have a habit of exaggerating reader suitability claims. Is the writing style clear and interesting? Are potentially difficult or unfamiliar terms defined and explained, either in context or in glossaries? Is the vocabulary controlled? That is, are the words used in the encyclopedia

checked for recognition and comprehension against scientifically conducted age- and grade-level vocabulary studies? Are jargon and buzzwords avoided? Is the writing style relatively consistent throughout, or does it vary from article to article or section to section? To evaluate the encyclopedia's clarity and reader suitability, read several articles on subjects about which you have little or no knowledge. Then ask yourself, do I understand what is being said? Do the same with others who will be using the encyclopedia heavily—especially children.

3. Is the encyclopedia produced by reputable people? Who made the encyclopedia? What are the credentials of the contributors, consultants, and top editorial staff? Such information should be provided in the front matter, or introductory material. Has the encyclopedia achieved recognition over the years as a work of quality? If it is a comparatively new or little-known work, has it received favorable notices in such major review publications as *American Reference Books Annual, Reference Books Bulletin* (in *Booklist*), and *Kister's Best Encyclopedias*? What is the reputation of the publisher or distributor? For an informed opinion on this last question, read "Who Makes and Publishes Encyclopedias?" beginning on page 10 of this book; you might also check with your local public or school librarian.

4. Is the encyclopedia reliable? Are the facts right 99.9 percent of the time? Are the encyclopedia's interpretations of historical events in accord with responsible contemporary scholarship? No encyclopedia is entirely without error or dubious interpretation, but users have a right to expect a very high level of accuracy from any encyclopedia. If several or more errors are found after casual examination, the consumer is right to question the encyclopedia's overall reliability, just as the clock that strikes 13 once too often is suspect. Check a number of topics on which you are well versed to test the encyclopedia's dependability. You might also ask a friend or neighbor who has some particular expertise to read an article or two.

5. Is the encyclopedia free from bias and stereotyping? Are such polemical or sensitive subjects as abortion, circumcision, electroshock therapy, euthanasia, fluoridation, homosexuality, hypnosis, nuclear power, sexual harassment, and the Vietnam War treated as fairly and impartially as possible? Are differing points of view on such issues presented in an evenhanded manner, or does the encyclopedia simply avoid controversial topics—a form of bias by omission? Do the contributors bring an objective perspective to the encyclopedia, or are they open to charges of partisanship, as in the case of, say, a nuclear power industry executive writing about the accidents at Three Mile Island in 1979 and Chernobyl in 1986? Bias, favoritism, prejudice, propaganda, and stereotyping of any kind—racial, sexual, political, religious, etc.—have no place in a quality encyclopedia.

6. Is the encyclopedia reasonably current? Encyclopedias, even those in electronic form, cannot be expected to be as current as the daily newspaper or television news report. On the other hand, an encyclopedia boasting a recent copyright should cover important recent developments in the world. (The latest date on the reverse side of the title page indicates the most recent copyrighted edition or printing.) An encyclopedia with a 1994 copyright, for example, should include information on such 1990s concerns and events as the end of apartheid in South Africa, the invention of cellular telephones, the spread of such horrific diseases as AIDS and Alzheimer's, the growing debate over euthanasia and doctor-assisted suicide, the unification of East and West Germany, the end of the Cold War and demise of the Soviet Union, and the changing attitudes toward adoption and the rights of adoptees. As a rule, at least 10 percent of the contents of a continuously published encyclopedia ought to

be revised each year. With regard to so-called encyclopedia updating supplements or yearbooks, consumers should understand that these annual publications, though often handsomely produced and useful as sources of new information, do not really keep an encyclopedia up-to-date, despite vigorous claims to the contrary by some encyclopedia sales representatives.

7. Is the encyclopedia easy to use and are its contents readily accessible? How is the encyclopedia arranged? If arranged alphabetically, is the filing letter-by-letter (in which case "Newspaper" precedes "New York") or is it word-by-word ("New York" precedes "Newspaper")? Are cross-references used throughout? If so, are they helpful? Is there a detailed general index? Is the index analytical? That is, are broad entries like "Islam" broken down under specific subentries, such as "Islam—Afghanistan," "Islam—Allah," "Islam—Egypt," "Islam—Koran," "Islam—Shites," and "Islam—Sunnites"? In the case of electronic encyclopedias, additional search options are normally available, including keyword and full-text searching. The latter enables the user to access the entire database for all references containing a particular word (e.g., "Islam") or combination of words ("Islam" AND "Koran"). The prospective purchaser needs to determine what search capabilities the electronic encyclopedia offers and how effective they are. Here hands-on demonstration is a must.

8. Does the encyclopedia include well-selected bibliographies? An encyclopedia is frequently the first—but not the last—place one looks for knowledge and information. Hence, most quality encyclopedias include bibliographies, or lists of recommended materials the reader might consult for additional information on a subject. Are the bibliographies, which customarily appear at the end of an encyclopedia's articles, reasonably current? Do they include the most important or best-known works on the subject? Are both print and nonprint materials listed?

9. Is the encyclopedia adequately illustrated? Does the encyclopedia's pictorial content—photographs, drawings, diagrams, cutaways, reproductions of paintings and other works of art, transparencies, maps, and the like—enhance the written text, or are the illustrations merely pretty page fillers? Are the illustrations large enough? Are they clearly and sharply reproduced? Are they of recent vintage? Or are the illustrations too often small, out-of-register visual images that bespeak another era? Browse through the encyclopedia with an eye to ascertaining how well the words and pictures interface with one another. In the case of electronic encyclopedias on CD-ROM with multimedia capability, the user will encounter moving as well as still pictures, plus sound. How substantial is the encyclopedia's "multimedia" content, which normally includes video clips, animations, and a variety of audio (speeches, music, voice-over narrations, sound effects)? Do the multimedia features add significantly to the informational value of the encyclopedia, or are they bells and whistles intended chiefly to entertain television-bred youngsters?

10. Is the encyclopedia in book version physically well-made and aesthetically pleasing? Is the page layout varied, uncluttered, and attractive to the eye? Is the type large and legible enough for those who will be using the encyclopedia, including children and older adults? Does the binding seem sturdy enough to hold up under heavy use? Do the volumes lie flat when open (for easy consultation on a desk or stand), or are they so tightly bound that they spring shut? Spend some time examining the physical construction of the encyclopedia.

11. Does the encyclopedia offer any special or unique features? If so, do they add to the basic value of the encyclopedia, or are they simply promotional gimmicks? Some encyclopedias, for instance, include dictionaries, atlases, study guides, parents' manuals, and the like as supplements to the basic work. Others offer research services to customers. Still others boast a unique arrangement (as in the case of the tripartite *New Encyclopaedia Britannica*) or include sound and moving pictures (e.g., *Compton's Interactive Encyclopedia, Compton's Multimedia Encyclopedia, First Connections, Microsoft Encarta Multimedia Encyclopedia*, the *New Grolier Multimedia Encyclopedia*). Any special features claimed by the encyclopedia will almost certainly be ballyhooed in its introductory material.

12. Is the encyclopedia available in both print and electronic form and, if so, which version do you want? A growing number of print (or hardcover) encyclopedias have recently become available in electronic (or automated) form, including the *Academic American Encyclopedia, Compton's Encyclopedia*, the *Concise Columbia Encyclopedia, Funk & Wagnalls New Encyclopedia*, the *Golden Book Encyclopedia*, the *New Encyclopaedia Britannica*, the *Random House Encyclopedia*, and the *World Book Encyclopedia*. Not only are electronic encyclopedias now available via the various commerical online information services (such as America Online, CompuServe, Dialog, GEnie, and Prodigy) and the Internet, they have exploded onto the market in the the 1990s in the form of compact discs (CD-ROM) used in conjunction with a personal computer. As noted, encyclopedias on CD-ROM now usually include sound and moving pictures, a tremendous advance in the presentation of encyclopedic information. Still, the traditional print encyclopedia retains great appeal. Using it requires no special or costly equipment, nor does the user need to worry about a tangle of cords, surge protectors, compatibility problems, and, for some, intimidating computer commands. Print or electronic? It's a key question for today's encyclopedia consumers. Consider it carefully.

13. Is the encyclopedia fairly priced? What is the encyclopedia's lowest retail price? Do educational institutions (schools, libraries, etc.) receive a discount? If so, how much? Is the price competitive for an encyclopedia of this type, size, and quality? (*Kister's Best Encyclopedias* includes price information at the beginning of each review and in the comparison charts that conclude each section of general encyclopedia reviews.) Consumers should be aware that the price of print encyclopedias can vary greatly depending on the type of binding, even though the encyclopedia's contents are exactly the same. For the overwhelming majority of consumers, the least expensive binding will suffice just as well as a higher-priced one. Prices may also be affected by "package deals," wherein the consumer agrees to buy not only the encyclopedia but a number of additional products, such as anthologies of children's stories, yearbooks, dictionaries, atlases, globes, bookcases, and research services. If you only want the encyclopedia, do not be cajoled or dunned into buying unwanted extras. In the case of CD-ROM encyclopedias, the price continues to come down, down, down—good news for consumers.

14. What do published reviews say about the encyclopedia? Has the encyclopedia received favorable notices from responsible critics? Are the reviews mostly in agreement? Mixed? How do they square with your own findings? The principal encyclopedia review publications in North America are *American Reference Books Annual* (ARBA), published each year since 1970 by Libraries Unlimited in Littleton, Colorado; *Reference Books Bulletin*, a twice-monthly review journal published as part of *Booklist* by the American Library Association; and the book you are now reading, *Kister's Best Encyclopedias* by Kenneth F. Kister, published by Oryx Press in 1994 (second edition). These sources can be found in most sizable public and academic libraries. For further information about these and other publications that review encyclopedias, see Appendix A ("Encyclopedia Resources") at the back of this book.

15. How does the encyclopedia compare with its major competitors? Which encyclopedias compete directly with the one under review? How do these works match up in terms of coverage? Readability? Authority? Reliability? Objectivity? Recency? Bibliographies? Illustrations? Format? Special features? Price? Reviewer opinion? Comparative analysis of competing encyclopedias, print or electronic, can be a time-consuming as well as frustrating business, but the serious consumer will find it well worth the effort. Only through this process can one begin to appreciate fully an encyclopedia's strengths and weaknesses and, if you will, its personality.

General
Encyclopedias

* * * * * * * * * *

Large Encyclopedias for Adults and Older Students

❖ ❖ ❖ ❖ ❖ ❖ ❖ ❖ ❖

OVERVIEW

The three titles reviewed in this sec
tion—COLLIER'S ENCYCLOPEDIA, ENCY
CLOPEDIA AMERICANA, and the NEW EN-
CYCLOPEDIA BRITANNICA—represent the largest general encyclopedias currently published
in North America. They range in size from
24 to 32 volumes, 21 to 44 million words,
and 20,000 to 32,000 densely packed pages—
huge, scholarly compendiums of basic knowledge and information intended chiefly for
college educated adults and professional
people (teachers, editors, writers, doctors,
lawyers, librarians, the clergy, business ex-
ecutives, administrators, architects, engineers, researchers, et al.) as well as serious
students at the high school level and beyond.

Sometimes called the ABC's of encyclopedias, the AMERICANA, BRITANNICA, and
COLLIER'S are also found in the reference collections of most public, academic, and school
libraries.

As might be expected, these three
heavyweight encyclopedias are not inexpensive. They require an enormous financial
outlay to produce and maintain, a reality
reflected in their prices, which currently start
at $1,000.00 (COLLIER'S) and go up to
$1,400.00 (AMERICANA). Purchase of year-
books and other extras can jack the final
price tag up to $2,000.00 or more. Obvi-
ously, not everyone needs an encyclopedia
as large and costly as these three sets. Indeed, most people in North America who
buy a multivolume encyclopedia chose one
in the medium-sized adult and older student

class (see page 51). Ordinarily comprising
only about nine or 10 million words, mid-
sized encyclopedias tend to be less intimidating and more reasonably priced than the
AMERICANA, BRITANNICA, and COLLIER'S. Also,
they are designed to meet the needs of a
broader readership, including students in junior high school or even the upper elementary grades.

But for those consumers who truly want
or need a very large and scholarly general
encyclopedia, the choice is limited to the
AMERICANA, the BRITANNICA, and COLLIER'S—
happily, all works of considerable merit. But
which one of the three sets is best? COLLIER'S
is the smallest, youngest, and least well-
known of the three, but it is also the best
maintained, best indexed, best illustrated,
and least expensive. On the other hand, the
BRITANNICA is the oldest, largest, most learned,
and most prestigious of the three, but it is
also the least user-friendly because of its un-
conventional arrangement. Finally, the
AMERICANA, the first major encyclopedia to
be published on this side of the Atlantic
(1829–), offers the strongest coverage of
North American people, places, and events
of the three sets, but it has the poorest revision record and it costs the most.

Which is best? Each of these large encyclopedias is, on balance, a fine reference
work that can be recommended without hesitation to those in search of a major adult
encyclopedia. Each has its particular
strengths and weaknesses; each will appeal
to some readers and not others. This re-

viewer personally prefers COLLIER'S, but has used all three sets at one time or another profitably. Because of the importance of the choice and the expense involved, consum-

ers are urged to examine all three encyclopedias closely and comparatively prior to making a final purchase decision.

COLLIER'S ENCYCLOPEDIA

FACTS

Full Title: *Collier's Encyclopedia with Bibliography and Index.* **Editorial Director:** Lauren S. Bahr. Editor in Chief: Bernard Johnston. **Editorial Director:** P.F. Collier, Inc. **Date Published:** First published in 1950–51; new printing with revisions published annually.
Volumes: 24. **Words:** 21 million. **Pages:** 19,844. **Articles:** 25,000. **Bibliographies:** 11,500. **Illustrations and Maps:** 19,000. **Cross-references:** 13,000. **Index entries:** 450,000. **Editorial Staff, Advisers, and Contributors:** 5,000. Trim Size: 8¼ × 10½ in.

Price and Sales Information: $999.00 retail; $995.00 to schools and libraries. *Collier's Encyclopedia* is sold to individual consumers and educational institutions (schools, libraries, etc.) through authorized sales representatives of the publisher. The set is not sold in bookstores or similar retail outlets. For additional information about the encyclopedia or to order it, consumers should call toll-free 1-800-257-2755 or write P.F. Collier, Inc., 866 Third Avenue, 17th Floor, New York, NY 10022-6299.

EVALUATION

Collier's, which first appeared in 1950–51 in 20 volumes, is a relatively new encyclopedia when compared with its principal competitors, the NEW ENCYCLOPAEDIA BRITANNICA and ENCYCLOPEDIA AMERICANA, which date back to the eighteenth and nineteenth centuries respectively. In 1962, a major revision expanded *Collier's* to its present size of 24 volumes. During its more than four decades of existence, the set has achieved a reputation as one of the five or six truly first-rate general multivolume encyclopedias published in North America.

The encyclopedia's publisher, P.F. Collier, was a longtime subsidiary of Macmillan, Inc. until last year, when the company was acquired by Istituto Geografico de Agostini (an Italian publisher noted for its fine cartographic work) and Planeta Internacional S.A. (a major Spanish refer-

ence book publisher) in a 50–50 joint venture. The sale of P.F. Collier became inevitable when Macmillan's parent company, Maxwell Communication, went bankrupt after the untimely death in 1991 of Robert Maxwell, the British publishing magnate who headed Maxwell Communication. Maxwell's companies, it developed, were billions of dollars in debt and his unexpected exit forced the dissolution of his worldwide empire, which included newspapers, publishing houses, and Berlitz, the language school. Exactly what P.F. Collier's new ownership augers for it and its principal publication, *Collier's Encyclopedia*, remains to be seen. Apparently both De Agostini and Planeta believe *Collier's* will do well in their respective international markets, which have little overlap.

From the beginning, *Collier's* has been blessed with strong editorial leadership, a tradition that continues today. The creative force behind the planning of the set was the late Louis Shores, dean of the library school at Florida State University for many years and a noted authority on reference books. Shores served as the encyclopedia's editorial coordinator from 1946 until its publication in 1950–51. Later, in 1960, he became editor in chief, holding that position into the 1970s. Currently, Lauren Bahr is editorial director, the only woman so far to achieve such a high position among the principal U.S. encyclopedia publishers, and Bernard Johnston is editor in chief. Both Bahr and Johnston bring years of experience and a strong commitment to quality publishing to their work.

These two top editors are supported by a sizable in-house staff, plus approximately 120 advisers who are academic specialists and more than 4,500 contributors, all of whom are listed at the front of Volume 1. The contributors—mostly university professors and writers from the U.S. and Great Britain—are usually well qualified in their specific areas of knowledge. Indeed, the list of contributors is studded with some very prominent names from the world of academe and publishing, such as Daniel Aaron, Richard Aldington, Paul M. Angle, Isaac Asimov, Carlos Baker, Albert C. Baugh, John Malcolm Brinnin, Henry Steele Commager, Norman Dorsen, Philip S. Foner, Anne Fremantle, John Gassner, Henry F. Graff, Chandler Grannis, Louis J. Halle, Oscar Handlin, Cyril M. Harris, Gerald W. Johnson, Walter Kaufmann, Russell Kirk, David Lodge, Margaret Mead, Roy A. Medvedev, Richard B. Morris, Reinhold Niebuhr, J.H. Plumb, Anthony Powell, Sir Herbert Read, Arnold M. Rose, A.L. Rowse, Gerard Salton, Mark Schorer, B.F. Skinner, Barbara Tuchman, Clement Vose, and Norbert Wiener.

As this sampling shows, quite a few of the contributors are now retired or deceased, but the editors continue to add new writers to the list each year. In 1993, for example, 87 new contributors were recruited, including Pierre Broué, a French scholar and authority on Leon Trotsky, and Roy Medvedev, a prominent Russian historian who furnishes a fresh biography of Joseph Stalin.

An infrequent but nevertheless troubling problem concerning some of the contributors involves natural bias on the part of the writer. *Example:* Articles on certain religious groups have been prepared by officers of the church, as in the case of "Christian Science," whose author, William Duncan Kilpatrick, is described in Volume 1 as "Late Manager, Committees on Publication, First Church of Christ Scientist, Boston, Mass." Not surprisingly, the article reads like an official history or press release, sans any hint of criticism or debate about the church's teachings on health and medicine or recent internal problems. In any event, Kilpatrick was surely not the right person to choose to write on Christian Science. In the case of Scientology, another religion that has had its share of public controversy, *Collier's* ignores the subject altogether.

Unlike most multivolume encyclopedias, *Collier's* is a broad-entry (as opposed to specific-entry) encyclopedia—meaning that small related topics tend to be treated within a long, essay-length omnibus article rather than separately. An example is the *Collier's* article "Occupational Disease," which includes information on such maladies as carpal tunnel syndrome, leucoderma, and pneumoconiosis (black lung disease). In a specific-entry encyclopedia, these topics (if covered) would most likely have their own entries. Another example is the subject of fluoridation, which is discussed in *Collier's* in "Water Resources," "Water Treatment," and "Teeth," but has no entry of its own; in a specific-entry encyclopedia (such as rival ENCYCLOPEDIA AMERICANA) fluoridation would almost certainly be treated separately.

The broad-entry approach has the virtue of placing discrete, or specific, topics within the framework of a larger context, thus providing the reader with an expanded view and better overall understanding of the subject. On the other hand, a broad-entry encyclopedia is usually not as effective for quick and easy retrieval of specific topics or facts in the text. Moreover, the broad-entry work forces users to rely heavily on the index to find information—and studies of reference book use indicate many people resist using indexes or simply do not remember to consult them.

The encyclopedia's coverage tends to be well balanced, with prominent people, places, events, and concepts in all major knowledge areas receiving adequate attention. The editors estimate that about 20 percent of the coverage is devoted to the arts and humanities, 25 percent to science and technology, 35 percent to geography and area studies, and the remaining 20 percent to the social and behavioral sciences—a fair division reflecting contemporary educational interests and trends.

Biographical articles in *Collier's* are particularly commendable. Ordinarily, they furnish not only the pertinent facts about the biographee but attempt to summarize the person's ideas and achievements, placing them in historical or intellectual perspective. Articles on the countries of the world, the U.S. states, and Canadian provinces are also impressive, both in terms of quantity and quality. The article on China, for example, comprises more than 60 pages and is admirably current and authoritative. Uzbekistan, one of the smaller former Soviet republics, is accorded more than five pages of coverage and, again, the article is up-to-date and reliable.

In fact, one of *Collier's* special strengths is its extensive coverage of what is now the former Communist world in Eastern Europe, including all of the republics of the old Soviet Union, the Communist political system (before and after the collapse of the U.S.S.R.), and its leaders, such as Lenin, Trotsky, Stalin, Khrushchev, Gorbachev, and Yeltsin. Doubtless this emphasis stems from the encyclopedia's effort to provide strong international coverage, but it also reflects Macmillan's longtime involvement with the GREAT SOVIET ENCYCLOPEDIA, an English-language translation of the massive Russian BOL'SHAIA SOVETSKAIA ENTSIKLOPEDIIA that required more than a decade (1973–83) and much treasure to complete.

The encyclopedia also includes a considerable amount of information on practical subjects. The article "Insurance," for instance, provides a down-to-earth discussion of the various types of insurance (automobile, home, health, etc.) and what to look for when considering their purchase. Similarly, "Child Psychology and Development" includes a section called "Practical Problems of Childhood," which gives much useful information on such matters as day care, divorce, child abuse, sibling rivalry, fears and nightmares, bed-wetting, and the potentially harmful effects of too much television on children. "Drug Abuse" offers realistic counsel on treatment. "Sewing" discusses basic equipment, fabric selection, and the various steps in making a garment.

Occasionally, *Collier's* fails to provide adequate information on a topic users might reasonably expect to find in a large, up-to-date general encyclopedia. *Examples:* Carpal tunnel syndrome is mentioned in a brief paragraph on chronic repetitive trauma in "Occupational Disease," but there is no detailed description of the condition or its symptoms or possible treatments. Chelation therapy, a controversial "miracle cure" that has been in the news off and on for a decade or more, receives no coverage. Likewise,

Maya Angelou, the writer, and Glenn Gould, the pianist, are missing from the pages of *Collier's*, as is Scientology and sexual harassment. Philip Glass, an important contemporary American composer, is mentioned only in passing in "Music, History of." But on balance, considering the natural limitations of any encyclopedia, *Collier's* usually lives up to its claim to be "a scholarly, systematic, continuously revised summary of the knowledge that is most significant to mankind" (preface).

Collier's can be trusted to have its facts right almost all of the time. Editor Johnston and his staff are careful to check and double-check all articles for errors prior to publication. Still, like us all, even the most meticulous encyclopedia editors slip up every now and then. For instance, *Collier's* erroneously reports that the giant panda is a "member of the raccoon family," when in fact genetic tests conducted at the National Zoo in Washington, D.C. in the 1980s have clearly established the exotic animal as a member of the bear family. In another instance, the encyclopedia's index gives an incorrect page number under the entry "Fluoridation" (the entry should read 23–352d, not 23–325d).

Information in the encyclopedia is never intentionally biased, and often articles on controversial or sensitive subjects present both the pros and cons of the issue, as in "Abortion" and "Intelligence." The latter, for instance, devotes a lengthy paragraph to the "Intelligence Controversy," which discusses Arthur Jensen's hotly debated findings some years ago concerning race and intelligence based on differences in IQ test scores. Sometimes, however, such subjects are ignored or glossed over, as in "Circumcision," which notes that the procedure is "practiced as a religious rite by Jews, Muslims, and many primitive peoples" and that it is "also extensively practiced in modern medicine as a sanitary measure," but fails to mention any of the contemporary arguments against circumcision or even to acknowl-

edge the controversy. Interestingly, this article was written not by someone with medical training but a rabbi and professor of rabbinical literature.

Collier's has one of the most aggressive and successful revision programs among the major multivolume encyclopedias currently on the North American market. It consistently outpaces its major competitors, ENCYCLOPEDIA AMERICANA and the NEW ENCYCLOPAEDIA BRITANNICA, in this area. The publisher invests on average more than $2 million each year in maintaining the set. In 1993, the editors added 61 new articles, completely reworked 88, and revised nearly 1,400 others in some manner or other. In addition, almost 800 new illustrations and maps were added, most in color. In all, the 1993 revision entailed resetting 3,638 of the set's nearly 20,000 pages. As a result, the encyclopedia is ordinarily as current as can be expected in a large reference work that is published just once a year.

This does not mean, though, that every article in the encyclopedia is completely up-to-date or that there is no room for improvement. Some articles—"Adoption," "Christian Science," "Circumcision," "Dead Sea Scrolls," "Galileo," and "Rose" to name a few—fail to include important recent developments. Bill Katz, in an incisive and quite positive review of *Collier's* in his *Basic Information Sources* (6th ed., McGraw-Hill, 1992, p. 243) finds that, "While most of the material is under continuous revision, and the 'news' items are current, there is evidence that some basic articles are not."

Prospective purchasers of *Collier's* should be aware that sales representatives will almost certainly promote the *Collier's Year Book* (1960–) as a convenient way of keeping the encyclopedia up-to-date on an annual basis. The yearbook, which is lavishly and colorfully illustrated, includes a detailed review of the previous year's events, plus many articles on people in the news, the countries of the world, the U.S. states, Canadian provinces, and new developments in all areas of knowledge. Unlike most encyclopedia yearbooks, the *Collier's Year Book* can a good investment—if it is used. Efforts are made to relate its contents to those of the encyclopedia by means of gummed cross-reference tabs found at the front of the yearbook. The publisher also offers an informative medical yearbook entitled *Health and Medical Horizons*. Again, it is intended as a supplement to the encyclopedia and should be purchased only if the consumer has a real need for it.

The encyclopedia's writing style is typically clear and to the point. In most instances, the text will be comprehensible to adults and college and high school students who possess good-to-average reading skills. Because the editors do not employ a controlled vocabulary or attempt to write to grade level, the set is normally well beyond the reading capabilities of elementary school students as well as most students at the junior high level. True, many articles begin simply by defining the topic, but even this device does not automatically ensure easy comprehension. The first sentence of the article "Adoption," for instance, reads "Adoption is the establishment of the relationship of parent and child, in contemplation of law, between persons not so related by nature."

The first two paragraphs of the article "Heart" offer a more extensive example of the *Collier's* style:

> HEART, a powerful muscular organ, which pumps blood through a system of chambers and valves into a distributing network known as the cardiovascular, or circulatory, system. In man the heart is located near the center of the chest. It is made primarily of a tough resilient tissue, called cardiac muscle, which contracts rhythmically throughout the lifetime of the individual, sending blood pulsing through the arteries and capillaries of the tissues of the body. With each contraction the heart pumps about 2 to 2½ ounces (60–75 milliliters) of blood or, at an average rate of 70 beats per minute, 4 to 5 quarts (4–5

liters) per minute. In 70 years the heart beats more than 2.5 billion times and pumps about 165 million quarts (156 million liters) of blood.

> This seemingly tireless pump is about the size of a clenched fist and weighs slightly more than half a pound. Lying nearly on its side beneath the breastbone, it rests upon the dome-shaped diaphragm below, and between the right and left lungs, which fold partially around its front side. It has a truncated conical shape, somewhat bulging at one end like a pear, and its tip lies to the left of the breastbone, directed toward the front of the chest. The large vessels, which carry blood to and from the heart, emerge from the portion away from the tip.

As these paragraphs plainly indicate, *Collier's* does not write down to its readers. It does sometimes define or explain potentially difficult or unfamiliar terms in context, as in the case of *cardiovascular system* and *cardiac muscle* in the excerpt above, but this again does not ensure comprehension on the part of young readers. Ultimately, the encyclopedia is for literate adults and older students— and not for young people, despite what some overzealous publicists and sales representatives might say.

Along these lines, for many years Macmillan published the MERIT STUDENTS ENCYCLOPEDIA, a very serviceable 20-volume set that *was* intended for students in the upper elementary grades on through college. But the encyclopedia was discontinued in 1992, most likely a victim of the sudden collapse of the Maxwell empire. Whether P.F. Collier and its new owners will revive the worthy MERIT STUDENTS ENCYCLOPEDIA is not known at this time.

As previously explained, *Collier's* is a broad-entry encyclopedia, which means that use of the index is often essential for finding specific topics and facts in the set. Fortunately, COLLIER'S possesses an excellent index. The index, which makes up the bulk of Volume 24, contains more than 400,000 entries—or one entry for approximately every 50 words in the 21-million-word encyclopedia. This ratio of index entries to text words (1:50) easily beats the competition in the large adult class (both ENCYCLOPEDIA AMERICANA and the NEW ENCYCLOPAEDIA BRITANNICA have approximate ratios of 1:90) and is second only to the ACADEMIC AMERICAN ENCYCLOPEDIA (1:45) among all general encyclopedias. The set also includes some 13,000 cross-references in the text, which help steer the reader to related articles.

Unlike most encyclopedias, *Collier's* publishes a separate bibliography rather than appending bibliographies—lists of recommended sources for additional information—to articles throughout the set. The bibliography section, found at the beginning of Volume 24 preceding the index, contains roughly 11,500 titles grouped by broad subjects and then subdivided into more specific topics, e.g., a book on Galileo is found under "General Science—History of Science and Biographies of Scientists." The titles listed usually represent good selections for students and are briefly annotated. The Galileo entry, for instance, is for Stillman Drake's *Galileo* (Oxford Univ. Press, 1980), described as a "Short biography of the founder of modern physics." Also, very important, the bibliographies can be located via the index, designated by the subentry "—BIB."

Unfortunately, the bibliographies in Volume 24 are not always as up-to-date as they could or should be. *Examples:* Of the 16 titles listed under "Economics and Business—History of Economic Thought—General Studies," the most recent was published in 1983 and half were published in the 1960s, or 30 years ago. Of the 15 titles under "Economics and Business—Circulation of Wealth—Investments," none is more recent than 1984; two were published in the 1960s. Apparently in order to help rectify this problem, the editors have recently begun to include selected bibliographies with the articles themselves; "Abortion" and "Black Americans" are examples of this new policy.

Illustrations in *Collier's* have improved dramatically over the past several years. Many dreary black-and-white photographs have been replaced by striking four-color illustrations. For example, well over 2,000 color photos alone have been added to the set thus far in the 1990s. The color reproduction is excellent, due in large measure to the use of new paper especially designed to enhance color quality. Many examples could be cited, but perhaps the article "Painting" is most representative of the encyclopedia's new visual appeal. The set's major maps, by Rand McNally, are quite satisfactory.

Some years ago, the encyclopedia critic Harvey Einbinder wrote (in *Wilson Library Bulletin*, December 1980, p. 261) that "readers who peruse the pages of *Collier's* today are carried back three decades in a time machine—viewing a 1950 black-and-white kinescope instead of a bright, multi-colored video image." This was true in 1980, but no longer. The editors of *Collier's* are succeeding in their sustained effort to bring the encyclopedia up to speed visually. More work remains—the articles "Motion Pictures" and "Circus," for instance, still include the type of graphics Einbinder was complaining about—but great strides have been made and, unless the set's new owners turn out to be cheapskates, *Collier's* will soon be among the best illustrated encyclopedias on the market.

The set's physical format is well constructed and aesthetically appealing. The binding—black Fabrikoid with red panels and gold lettering—is both sturdy and attractive. The paper is of very good quality and particularly suitable for color reproduction. The two-column page layout lacks flair but is clean and functional. The many new color illustrations add much to improve the set's overall appearance. In sum, *Collier's* is not a flashy encyclopedia, but it is a well-built, smartly put together set of reference books.

REPORT CARD: COLLIER'S ENCYCLOPEDIA

Topic	Coverage	Accuracy	Recency	Clarity
Circumcision	D	A	D	C
Drew, Charles	B	A	B	A
Galileo	B	A	C	A
Glass, Philip	D	A	A	A
Heart Disease	A	A	B	A
IQ	A	A	B	A
Panda Bear	A	D	B	A
Sexual Harassment	F*	NA	NA	NA
Shroud of Turin	A	A	A	A
Uzbekistan	A	A	A	A

A = Excellent; B = Above Average; C = Average; D = Below Average; F = Poor; NA = Not Applicable
*No Article

SUMMARY

The newest of the so-called ABCs (AMERICANA, BRITANNICA, and *Collier's*), *Collier's Encyclopedia* first appeared in the early 1950s and, over the years, has gained a reputation as one of the best large sets on the North American market. Intended chiefly for adults and older students with good reading skills, *Collier's* is usually accurate, authoritative, impartial, clearly written, and up-to-date. Its coverage is well-balanced and its illustrations—long a weak point—have improved dramatically in the 1990s. A broad-entry encyclopedia, *Collier's* includes a detailed analytical index that facilitates quick and easy retrieval of specific topics and facts. On the negative side, *Collier's* sometimes avoids controversial or sensitive issues and its bibliographies tend to be dated. The bottom line: Kister's choice as the best of the big sets.

OTHER OPINIONS

American Reference Books Annual, 1992, pp. 16–17 (review by Anna Grace Patterson); *Basic Information Sources* by William A. Katz (vol. 1 of *Introduction to Reference Work*, 6th ed., New York: McGraw-Hill, 1992), 242–43; *Reference Books Bulletin* (in *Booklist*), September 15, 1993, pp. 174–76 (unsigned review); *Reference Sources for Small and Medium-Sized Libraries* (5th ed., Chicago: American Library Assn., 1992), pp. 30–31 (review by Jovian P. Lang).

ENCYCLOPEDIA AMERICANA

FACTS

Full Title: *The Encyclopedia Americana: International Edition.* **Editorial Director:** Lawrence T. Lorimer. Editor in Chief: Mark Cummings. **Publisher:** Grolier Inc. Former Title: *The Americana* (1907–12). **Date Published:** First published between 1829 and 1833; International Edition first published 1918–20; new printing with revisions published annually.

Volumes: 30. **Words:** 30.8 million. **Pages:** 26,740. **Articles:** 52,000. **Illustrations and Maps:** 24,170. **Cross-references:** 40,000. **Index Entries:** 353,000. **Editorial Staff, Advisors, and Contributors:** 6,650. **Trim Size:** 7¼ × 10 in.

Price and Sales Information: $1,400.00 publisher's suggested retail price; $999.00 plus $35.00 shipping and handling to schools and libraries. *Encyclopedia Americana* is sold to individual consumers by independent distributors who purchase quantities of the encyclopedia from the publisher, Grolier Inc., which functions as a wholesaler. Distributors set their own prices. In most instances, distributors attempt to sell the prospective purchaser a package deal consisting of the encyclopedia and various other reference materials at $1,400.00 or more. For further information about the encyclopedia or to obtain the name of a local distributor, consumers should call 1–203-796-2602 (not a toll-free number) or write Grolier Inc., Sherman Turnpike, Danbury, CT 06816.

Encyclopedia Americana is sold to educational institutions (schools, libraries, etc.) by authorized sales representatives of Grolier Educational Corporation. For additional information or to place an order, call toll-free 1-800-243-7256 or write Grolier Educational Corporation, Sherman Turnpike, Danbury, CT 06816.

EVALUATION

The first general encyclopedia of any magnitude to be published in North America, *Encyclopedia Americana* originally appeared in Philadelphia between 1829 and 1833 in a 13-volume set edited by Francis Lieber, an influential nineteenth-century German-American scholar. At first, Lieber planned only an English-language translation of the seventh edition of the popular German encyclopedia *Konversations-Lexikon*, familiarly known as *Brockhaus* after its publisher Friedrich Arnold Brockhaus (see BROCKHAUS ENZYKLOPADIE on page 447 for more information about this encyclopedia). But as work on the new encyclopedia progressed, Lieber sought and added original articles by leading U.S. writers and intellectuals of the day. United States Supreme Court Justice Joseph Story, for instance, contributed more than 120 pages of legal material to the first edition. Hence, when the *Americana* began appearing some 165 years ago, it represented a hybrid of two cultures, German and American.

Around the turn of the century the *Americana* grew to 16 volumes under the editorship of Frederick Converse Beach. Beach, who also edited the magazine *Scientific American*, expanded the encyclopedia's coverage, especially (no surprise here) in the area of the physical and life sciences. The set reached its present size of 30 volumes during the period 1918–20 with publication of the International Edition, the last entirely new edition of the encyclopedia. Since that time the set has been maintained by continuous annual revisions and several volume-by-volume rebuilding programs.

The people who produce the *Americana* today bring good credentials to their work. Grolier, which has published the set since 1945, is a major force in encyclopedia publishing in North America and throughout the world; the *Americana* is its largest set, followed by the mid–sized ACADEMIC AMERICAN ENCYCLOPEDIA and the NEW BOOK OF KNOWLEDGE, which is for children. The *Americana's* editorial director, Lawrence T. Lorimer, has worked on a number of encyclopedia projects over the years (at Grolier and elsewhere) and is thoroughly knowledgeable about what constitutes a quality encyclopedia and how to achieve it. The editor in chief, Mark Cummings, has held that position since 1991. Prior to joining Grolier, Cummings worked at Oxford University Press, where he developed both academic and trade reference books; he holds advanced degrees in Asian studies and religion, with special interest in the religions of China.

Assisting Lorimer and Cummings is an editorial staff of about 60, plus 50 advisory editors, most of whom are senior professors at major U.S. or Canadian universities. Contributors to the encyclopedia number more than 6,500, again mostly North American academics. The contributors' list, found at the beginning of Volume 1, includes many well-known scholars and writers, such as Richard Altick, Albert C. Baugh, Ray Allen Billington, Crane Brinton, Carl Carmer, Robert Coles, Theodosius Dobzhansky, Frank Freidel, Walter Goodman, Oscar Handlin, Sidney Hook, Walter Kaufmann, Ernest May, Robert G. McCloskey, Ralph McGill, Harry T. Moore, Dexter Perkins, J.H. Plumb, Allen Walker Read, George Sarton, Arthur M. Schlesinger Jr., Ernest Simmons, and Carl Van Doren.

As this sampling indicates, a relatively high number of the contributors are retired or deceased, but fresh talent is recruited on a regular basis. For example, James Atlas

(of the *New York Times*) and Harry H. Wellington (a Yale University law professor) were among those added to the contributors' list in 1993. All longer articles in the set are signed and routinely include the writer's affiliation or a pertinent publication. The recently revised article "Adoption," for instance, is signed by Lois Ruskai Melina, who is identified as the author of *Making Sense of Adoption*; "Shroud of Turin" is signed by Robert Drews, author of *In Search of the Shroud of Turin*.

The *Americana* consists largely of specific-entry articles, averaging approximately 600 words (or half a page) in length. Many articles, however, are much longer, running to 10 or more pages. The encyclopedia covers practically all important subjects and areas of knowledge. While international in scope, the set's coverage has traditionally centered on U.S. and Canadian people, places, history, and institutions. Bill Katz, the reference authority, elaborates in his *Basic Information Sources* (6th ed., McGraw-Hill, 1992, pp. 240–41):

> As the title implies, the strength of this work is its emphasis on American history, geography, and biography. The *Americana* unquestionably places greater emphasis on these areas than any of the other sets, and it is particularly useful for finding out-of-the-way, little-known material about the United States. However, general coverage of the United States is matched in other major encyclopedias.

In recent years, though, the editors have tended to deemphasize the encyclopedia's coverage of minor American people and places. Specifically, during the past two decades or so many less important historical figures and smaller places in North America have been systematically eliminated from the set, reducing the total number of articles from around 60,000 in 1970 to the present 52,000. Still, the *Americana*, as Katz points out, continues to provide more extensive coverage of North American topics than any other general encyclopedia on the market today.

Due to *Brockhaus's* strong scientific base as well as the predilections of founding editor Lieber and later Frederick Beach, the *Americana* has always been known for first-rate coverage of science and technology. This continues to be true today, as such substantial articles as "Bacteria and Bacteriology," "Brick," "Bridge," "Cell," "Computer," "Evolution," "Genetics," "Genetics, Human," "Heart," "High-Pressure Research," "Human Body," "Lightning," "Magnet and Magnetism," "Mammal," "Nitrogen Compounds," "Nuclear Energy," "Plant, "Plastic," "Plumbing," "Pond," "Set Theory," "Sex," "Star," "Steel," and "Weather" attest.

The social and behavioral sciences also receive strong coverage in the *Americana*. Such articles as "Adoption," "Aggression," "Black Americans," "Business Cycles," "Crime and Criminology," "Homelessness," "Intelligence," "Lobbying," "Persian Gulf War," "Political Action Committee," "Roe v. Wade and Doe v. Bolton," "Savings and Loan Associations," and "Women's Rights Movement" offer thorough encyclopedic treatment of the subject. The arts and humanities are also well-covered, though less extensively than the sciences. Especially valuable are the set's many separate articles on classic works of art, literature, and music, such the statue *Winged Victory*, the novel *Middlemarch*, and the ballet *The Firebird*. There is also an individual article for each book of the Bible.

In some cases, however, the encyclopedia ignores topics that a large, comprehensive general encyclopedia should doubtless cover. By way of example, the omission of any mention of Philip Glass, a prominent living American composer, is inexplicable, as is omission of such major contemporary poets as Philip Larkin, Anne Sexton, and A.R. Ammons. Also missing from the pages of the *Americana* is any mention of such medical topics as carpal tunnel syndrome and chelation therapy. Nor have the editors yet caught up with sexual harassment, although a biography of Clarence Thomas has

been added recently. Obviously, no encyclopedia can be expected to cover every subject under the editorial sun, but these are examples of serious omissions that should be rectified as soon as possible.

Information in the encyclopedia is normally accurate and presented in an unbiased manner. In the words of Francis Lieber in the first edition, the intention of the *Americana* is "not to obtrude opinions but to furnish facts." Each successive editor has honored this commitment to impartiality. In the current printing, the article "Fluoridation," for example, includes a long and balanced discussion of the pros and cons of fluoridating community water supplies under the subheading "Controversy over Fluoridation." Such articles as "Abortion," "Circumcision," "Hypnosis," "Intelligence" (which includes IQ tests), "Scientology," and "Vietnam War"—all controversial or sensitive topics—are equally objective.

As previously noted, the *Americana* is revised continually and on an annual basis. In 1993, a fairly typical year, the editors added 34 new articles, completely revamped another 107, and updated nearly 1,000 others in some manner or other. In addition, 360 new illustrations and maps were added to the set. All of this revision activity involved resetting well over 2,000 pages of text, excluding the index (or somewhat less than 10 percent of the set's 26,740 total pages). It is not surprising, then, that the *Americana* is reasonably current in most instances. Still, there are plenty of times when articles in the encyclopedia are not as up-to-date as they might or should be.

The aforementioned "Shroud of Turin," "Adoption," "Homelessness," "Nuclear Energy," "Heart" (which includes heart diseases and transplants), "Circumcision," and "Intelligence" exemplify articles that are as current as they can be in an annual publication. On the other hand, some articles are quite dated, failing to include significant recent developments. *Examples:* "Galileo," an otherwise excellent article of four and a half pages, fails to note the Roman Catholic Church's recent reversal of its condemnation of the great scientist's alleged heresy, a remarkable admission of error on the part of the church that garnered headlines all over the world. Similarly, "Dead Sea Scrolls," "Apartheid," and the biography of Dr. Charles Drew lack current information. Also, the *Americana* is the only encyclopedia in its class that fails to note the recent adoption of the 27th Amendment to the U.S. Constitution, which prohibits the U.S. Congress from voting itself pay raises in midterm.

A review in *Reference Books Bulletin* (in *Booklist*, September 15, 1993, pp. 178 and 180) of the 1993 printing of the encyclopedia also cites many examples of articles that are not entirely up-to-date:

> Yves Montand's death in November 1991 has not been added to his biography, nor have the deaths in early 1992 of Judith Anderson, Jose Ferrer, Isaac Asimov, and Francis Bacon [the painter] been noted. Ross Perot has no entry and gets only the briefest mention in the general U.S. article. Many entries need to be revised to take out references to the former East and West Germany. There are no 1991 census figures for Canada. *Americana* is riddled with old population figures. Those for Spanish and Belgian cities are from the 1960s.
>
> An article mentioned previously in RBB reviews that still needs updating is *Smoking and Health*. Many country articles need revision to reflect current elections or political unrest. Hurricane Andrew is listed under *Disasters* but not in *Florida*. The riots in Los Angeles after the Rodney King trial are not mentioned.

This review concludes by suggesting the makers of the set "deal with the problem of lack of currency by being more ambitious in the scope of yearly revisions."

Prospective purchasers of the *Americana* should be aware that Grolier publishes and promotes a yearbook entitled *Americana Annual* as a means of keeping the encyclopedia abreast of current developments in all areas of knowledge. The annual is a high quality publication with a number of useful features (including a review of the previous year's events and special reports on timely subjects), but it has no real editorial connection with the encyclopedia and should not be purchased unless the consumer is absolutely convinced it will be used. Too often, encyclopedia annuals are bought but rarely consulted; at the end of 20 years consumers often have little to show for their investment except a collection of expensive dust-catchers.

The editors state in their preface that the *Americana* is intended to "serve as a bridge between the worlds of the specialist and the general reader." Contributors are "reminded of the need to write for the non-specialist reader." Further, they are instructed "not to 'write down' but to present facts and interpretation in an orderly way in a direct style, and to explain technical terms when they are used." In almost all instances the editors and writers achieve these goals. The encyclopedia's writing style is customarily clear and straightforward. Consider, for example, the first two paragraphs of the article "Heart":

> In ancient times the beating heart was regarded as the very soul or spirit of man and the core or center of the body. Certain words pertaining to the spirit, such as "cordial" and "courage" are derived from COR, the Latin word for the heart. St. Valentine's day, which was celebrated as early as the 7th century, has as its emblem the human heart, although it is distorted in shape to resemble that of a diseased heart in which both sides are of equal size. Today, the heart is known as the organ concerned only with pumping the blood through the body, and the soul or spirit of man has been moved to the brain, along with man's thinking, learning, and other higher faculties.
>
> It was obvious even to primitive man that the pulsating heart was a pump distributing to the brain and all other parts of the body important substances, including nourishment from the gastrointestinal tract and liver and a vital spirit from the lungs. However, it was not until the Middle Ages and later that the details of circulation were discovered. First the circulation of the blood through the lungs was worked out by Ibn al-Nafis, Andreas Vesalius, Michael Servetus, and Realdo

Colombo. Next the general body, or systemic, circulation was worked out by Fabricius ab Aquapendente, Andrea Cesalpino, and William Harvey.

As this excerpt clearly shows, the *Americana* is written for adults and older students who possess good reading skills. Further along in the article such technical terms as *aorta, ventricle, pulmonary artery, catecholamines, superior vena cava, sinoatrial node, stroke volume, endocardium, tricuspid valve, papillary muscle,* and *mitral valve* are italicized and defined in context. Also, some longer articles (e.g., "Stock Exchange") include extensive glossaries that furnish dictionary definitions of specialized terms. Nevertheless, the encyclopedia is not normally appropriate for children or younger students. Bill Katz (*Basic Information Sources,* 6th ed., McGraw-Hill, 1992, p. 241) puts it more bluntly: "The set is edited for the adult with a high school education. It is not suitable (despite the zealous efforts of copy writers) for grade school children."

The contents of the encyclopedia are readily accessible in most cases. Cross-references are used sparingly, considering the size of the set. For example, the 12-page article "Heart" contains only one cross-reference ("See also TRANSPLANTS, ORGAN AND TISSUE), even though articles such as "Blood," "Vein," "Anatomy," and "Human Body" offer much related information. Fortunately, the *Americana* does have a large, effective index. Found in Volume 30, the 830-page analytical index consists of more than 353,000 entries. In terms of the ratio of index entries to total words in the encyclopedia (31 million), the *Americana* provides about one index entry for every 90 words of text, or a ratio of 1:90. Among the encyclopedia's chief competitors, COLLIER'S ENCYCLOPEDIA has a much better ratio (1:50), whereas the NEW ENCYCLOPAEDIA BRITANNICA's is about the same (1:90).

Some consumers, especially teachers and librarians, might be interested to know that the *Americana's* index is now available on CD-ROM as part of the *Grolier Master Encyclopedia Index,* which also includes the indexes to the ACADEMIC AMERICAN ENCYCLOPEDIA and the NEW BOOK OF KNOWLEDGE. The disk sells for $149.00 and is available for MS-DOS, Windows, and Macintosh computers.

Bibliographies—lists of recommended books and other sources of additional information on a topic—are appended to all major articles, as well as many shorter ones. The bibliographies tend to be carefully selected titles representing the best or most important works available on a particular subject. But in too many instances, the lists are dated and in need of revision. *Examples:* "Galileo" concludes with a list of 11 titles, all substantial works, but none is more recent than 1988. The same is true of "Dead Sea Scrolls," which includes a bibliography of five studies published between 1978 and 1988; missing from the list are more recent works like Hershel Shanks's indispensable *Understanding the Dead Sea Scrolls,* a 1992 publication.

Illustrations in the *Americana*—85 percent of which are in black-and-white—tend to be informative but uninspiring. Dark, dull photographs predominate. Many years ago, encyclopedia critic Harvey Einbinder criticized the *Americana* and COLLIER'S ENCYCLOPEDIA for the quality of their illustrations in an article entitled "Encyclopedias: Some Foreign and Domestic Developments" in *Wilson Library Bulletin* (December 1980, p. 261):

Revising an encyclopedia is a thankless task. Editors generally have little freedom and authority. They are often forced to utilize continuous revision and are unable to introduce new visual methods of presenting factual information. This handicap is quite noticeable in *Collier's* and the *Americana.* These encyclopedias rely on black-and-white illustrations and rarely use line drawings, diagrams, charts, or colored pictures to supplement their text. As a result, they exude a staid, antiquarian languor, rather than the bustling excitement of a vital repository of contemporary knowledge.

Serious efforts have been underway at Grolier over the past decade or so to improve the *Americana's* illustrations. Regrettably, dramatic progress has not been made. The editors add new visuals each year, many in color, but they tend to be too few and far between to make much of a difference in so large an undertaking. Hence, a review of the 1993 printing of the *Americana in Reference Books Bulletin* (in *Booklist*, September 15, 1993, p. 180) quite fairly comments, "many photographs of places are outdated, and much of the set has a gray look due to the preponderance of black-and-white pictures." Note that rival COLLIER'S ENCYCLOPEDIA has dramatically improved its illustrations in the 1990s.

The set's physical format also leaves something to be desired. The volumes are sturdily bound and will withstand heavy use, but inside the page design is unimaginative and dull, lacking the aesthetic appeal of some of the mid-sized encyclopedias for adults and older students, such as Grolier's own ACADEMIC AMERICAN ENCYCLOPEDIA and the WORLD BOOK ENCYCLOPEDIA. Much of this is due, of course, to the set's general lack of color illustrations. Guide words (or running heads) are provided at the top of each page—except when illustrations interfere, which is often and annoying. The basic typeface (eight-point Times Roman) is legible, but overall the *Americana* will win no awards for its typography.

REPORT CARD: ENCYCLOPEDIA AMERICANA

TOPIC	COVERAGE	ACCURACY	RECENCY	CLARITY
Circumcision	A	A	A	A
Drew, Charles	B	A	B	A
Galileo	B	A	C	A
Glass, Philip	F*	NA	NA	NA
Heart Disease	A	A	A	A
IQ	A	A	A	A
Panda Bears	A	A	A	A
Sexual Harassment	F*	NA	NA	NA
Shroud of Turin	A	A	A	A
Uzbekistan	B	A	B	A

A = Excellent; **B** = Above Average; **C** = Average; **D** = Below Average; **F** = Poor; **NA** = Not Applicable
*No Article

SUMMARY

Encyclopedia Americana, the first general encyclopedia of any consequence published in North America (1829–), is a well-established, ably edited set for adults and older students. It has a number of conspicuous strengths, most notably a clear writing style, accurate and impartial presentation of information,

and strong coverage in the areas of science and technology, the social and behavioral sciences, and U.S. and Canadian biography, geography, and history. In addition, its text is easily accessible, due chiefly to the set's large analytical index. On the debit side, the *Americana* has lackluster illustrations and an uninviting format, but the encyclopedia's greatest limitation is its relatively slow pace of revision, which has resulted in an unacceptable number of articles (and bibliographies) that are not entirely current. The bottom line: A good encyclopedia, but not quite as good as the competition.

OTHER OPINIONS

American Reference Books Annual, 1993, pp. 25–26 (review by Bohdan S. Wynar); *Basic Information Sources* by William A. Katz (vol. 1 of *Introduction to Reference Work*, 6th ed., New York: McGraw-Hill, 1992), pp. 240– 41; *Reference Books Bulletin* (in *Booklist*), September 15, 1993, pp. 178–80; *Reference Sources for Small and Medium-Sized Libraries* (5th ed., Chicago: American Library Assn., 1992), p. 32 (review by Jovian P. Lang).

NEW ENCYCLOPAEDIA BRITANNICA

FACTS

Full Title: *The New Encyclopaedia Britannica in 32 Volumes.* **General Editor:** Robert McHenry. **Publisher:** Encyclopaedia Britannica, Inc. **Former Title:** *Encyclopaedia Britannica* (First to Fourteenth Editions, 1768–1973). **Date Published:** Fifteenth Edition first published as the *New Encyclopaedia Britannica* in 1974; new printing with revisions published annually.

Electronic Versions: BRITANNICA INSTANT RESEARCH SYSTEM (CD-ROM); BRITANNICA ONLINE (ONLINE).

Volumes: 32. **Words:** 44 million. **Pages:** 32,000. **Articles:** 65,100. **Bibliographies:** 1,600. **Illustrations and Maps:** 24,500. **Cross-references:** 17,000. **Index Entries:** 500,000. **Editorial Staff, Advisers, and Contributors:** 5,000. Trim Size: $8\frac{1}{2} \times 10\frac{3}{4}$ in.

Price and Sales Information: $1,194.00 retail; $1,299.00 to schools and libraries. The *New Encyclopaedia Britannica* is sold to individual consumers through authorized sales representatives of the publisher. For additional information about the encyclopedia or to order it, consumers should consult the yellow pages pages of the local telephone directory under "Encyclopedias" for the Encyclopaedia Britannica, Inc. sales representative in their area. If the company is not listed, call toll-free 1-800-858-4895 or write Encyclopaedia Britannica, Inc., Britannica Centre, Customer Service Department, 310 South Michigan Avenue, Chicago, IL 60604.

The *New Encyclopaedia Britannica* is also sold in selected retail stores in North America, such as Sears and Waldenbooks. Interested consumers should contact the company for stores in their areas that sell the encyclopedia.

The *Britannica* is sold to institutions (schools, libraries, etc.) by authorized sales representatives of Encyclopaedia Britannica Educational Corporation, a subsidiary of Encyclopaedia Britannica, Inc. For additional information or to place an order, call toll-free 1-800-621-3900 or write Encyclopaedia Britannica Educational Corporation, 310 South Michigan Avenue, Chicago, IL 60604.

EVALUATION

The *New Encyclopaedia Britannica*—or simply the *Britannica*, as most people call it—is the oldest, largest, best known, and most prestigious general encyclopedia in the English language. This impressive reference work, now in 32 volumes, provides educated adults and serious students with a comprehensive, authoritative compendium of the world's most important knowledge and information. In 1993, the encyclopedia celebrated its 225th year of continuous publication, a remarkable feat of longevity. Need anyone ask why the name *Britannica* is practically synonymous with the word *encyclopedia*?

The *Britannica* first appeared in three alphabetical volumes (A–B; C–L; M–Z) issued in parts (or serially) between 1768 and 1771 in Edinburgh, Scotland. The set, inspired by the success of the influential French *Encyclopédie* (1751–72), was the product of a "Society of Gentlemen" consisting of three enterprising Scots: William Smellie, who served as editor; Andrew Bell, the engraver; and Colin Macfarquhar, the printer. Smellie did the bulk of the writing, drawing liberally on the works of Voltaire, Alexander Pope, Samuel Johnson, Benjamin Franklin, and other sages of the day. Bell illustrated the books with handsome full-page copper-plate engravings, and Macfarquhar printed them in quarto-page sections that were then handsewn and bound, usually by a local cobbler.

The first edition of the *Britannica*—subtitled *A Dictionary of Arts and Sciences*—omitted history and biography, but the second (1778–84) added these areas of knowledge, growing to 10 volumes in the process. The third edition (1788–97) also expanded, this time to 18 volumes; it was the first to use outside contributors as well as the first to be dedicated to the reigning British monarch. This edition also appeared in pirated versions in Dublin and Philadelphia, a sign of the encyclopedia's increasing appeal throughout the English-speaking world. For a carefully researched history of the encyclopedia's first entry into North America, see Robert D. Arner's *Dobson's Encyclopaedia: The Publisher, Text, and Publication of America's First Britannica, 1789–1803* (Univ. of Pennsylvania Press, 1991).

New and larger editions of the *Britannica* were issued regularly during the nineteenth century, including the famous ninth edition (1875–89) in 25 volumes—called the Scholars' Edition because of the great amount of original research that went into its articles. This edition was the first *Britannica* to include a general article about women ("Women, Law Relating to"). In 1901, ownership of the encyclopedia passed to a group of Americans who eventually brought the set, both entrepreneurially and editorially, to the United States, where it has remained ever since.

Interestingly, many casual encyclopedia users in the U.S. and Canada mistakenly believe that the *Britannica* is still edited and produced in Great Britain, a misconception fostered by the editors' continued and, some say, affected use of typical British spellings, such as *centre*, *favour*, and, of course, *encyclopaedia*. The British themselves, though, are well aware that the *Britannica* is no longer part of their dominion and some admit to being unhappy about it. A few years ago, Charles Mosley castigated the encyclopedia in the *Manchester Guardian Weekly* (July 10, 1988), blaming its failings on "the Americans":

> The trouble lies with the crassness of the Americans who have been in sole full-time editorial control . . . . The full horror of what an American editorial monopoly entails is seldom appreciated. The American editors who write short in-house ("micropedia") articles are ignorant and parochial. . . .
>
> In the last few years the Encyclopaedia Britannica has dropped the word

"Encyclopaedia" from its spine. It now reads "Britannica." Yet this is a publication so contemptuous of Britain, the land of its birth, that it cannot be bothered to ascertain correct usage when speaking of the Thames, a publication so insular as to give an entry to Alan Whicker but none to Lords Carrington or Whitelaw. It amounts to more than impertinence.

A decade after passing into American hands, the encyclopedia appeared in a new edition, the much praised eleventh (1910–11). Arguably the most celebrated of all editions of the *Britannica*, the 29–volume eleventh was justly lauded by critics for its impeccable scholarship, elegant style, and substantial literary essays. It was the first edition dedicated to both the king of England and the president of the United States, in this case William Howard Taft; the dual dedication continues to this day, even though the editors winced a bit during the informal Carter years ("Dedicated by permission to President Jimmy Carter and Her Majesty Queen Elizabeth II"). Those keenly interested in the *Britannica*'s history will not want to miss a recently published monograph by Gillian Thomas entitled *A Position to Command Respect: Women and the Eleventh Britannica* (Scarecrow Press, 1992), which studies the 35 female contributors (of a total 1,500) to the eleventh edition.

In the early 1920s, Julius Rosenwald of Sears, Roebuck and Company acquired the encyclopedia and oversaw the production of the twelfth (1922), thirteenth (1926), and fourteenth (1929) editions. In 1936, the editors wisely adopted the practice of continuous revision, which entails issuing updated printings of the set on an annual basis. In 1943, William Benton—advertising millionaire, former U.S. Senator, and then vice president of the University of Chicago—acquired a controlling interest in the *Britannica* from Sears after the university declined it as a gift, because they feared to become directly involved in such a large commercial publishing enterprise. During Benton's ownership, however, the university received royalties (3 percent) based on sales of the encyclopedia in exchange for editorial advice and use of its name, an arrangement that still exists. Benton, who served as the *Britannica*'s publisher for 30 years, died in 1973; his story is told in Sidney Hyman's very readable biography, *The Lives of William Benton* (Univ. of Chicago Press, 1970).

But long before Benton's death, the fourteenth edition had grown stale, despite the editors' annual revisions. Clearly the encyclopedia was living off its reputation and required a complete overhaul to bring it up to speed. Early in the 1960s, a physicist named Harvey Einbinder began publicly documenting the failings of the fourteenth edition, first in the magazine *Columbia University Forum* (Winter 1960) and later in a 390-page book called *The Myth of the Britannica* (Grove Press, 1964). Einbinder's charges hit Britannica headquarters in Chicago like a thunderbolt. Goaded into doing something about their aging encyclopedia, the Senator (as Benton was known to his colleagues) and his brain trust soon were secretly at work on an ambitious new edition, one that they hoped would both silence critics like Einbinder and recapture the encyclopedia's glorious past. Finally, in 1974, a year after Benton's death, the company unveiled an entirely new and in many ways quite radical edition of the *Britannica*.

Produced at a cost of some $32 million, the new fifteenth edition—officially titled the *New Encyclopaedia Britannica* but promoted as *Britannica 3*—appeared in 1974 in 30 volumes. The set was organized into three distinct parts, hence the *Britannica 3* moniker: (1) the *Micropaedia* (or small knowledge), a ten-volume set of approximately 100,000 brief A-to-Z articles of 750 words or less; (2) the *Macropaedia* (large knowledge), a 19-volume A-to-Z library of some 4,200 long scholarly articles reminiscent of those found in the ninth and eleventh editions of the encyclopedia; and (3) the *Propaedia*, a one-volume outline of knowledge and topical guide to the contents of the *Macropaedia*. The *Micropaedia* acted as an index to the *Macropaedia*; there was no index to the *Micropaedia* or separate index to the set.

A firestorm of criticism greeted the new edition and its tripartite (or three-part) arrangement. Many of the *Britannica's* excellent features were obscured because users, including students and librarians, found the set's organization strange, confusing, inefficient, intimidating, overly complicated, or all of these. Not only had the editors of the fifteenth edition abandoned the principle of a separate index, which had been a fixture as far back as the middle of the nineteenth century, they split the set into two different alphabets under two odd-sounding names, *Micropaedia* and *Macropaedia*, thus jeopardizing key ingredients of the encyclopedia's success from the beginning in 1768—simple organization and ease of use. Founding editor Smellie had written that "Utility ought to be the principal intention of every publication. Wherever this intention does not plainly appear, neither the books nor their authors have the smallest claim to the approbation of mankind." It was these words that came to haunt the makers of *Britannica 3*.

The guiding genius behind the fifteenth edition's complex organization was Mortimer J. Adler, perhaps best known for his tireless promotion of the *Great Books of the Western World*, which he edited. A philosopher and teacher, Adler opposed what he has called "alphabetiasis," or the random (and potentially bewildering) fragmentation of knowledge that inevitably results from alphabetical arrangement. Rather, in *Britannica 3*, he imposed a classified system of ordering knowledge (the *Propaedia*) on the big subjects (the *Macropaedia*—the heart of *Britannica 3*), while relegating the indexing function and little subjects to 10 supplementary volumes

(the *Micropaedia*). Not surprisingly, encyclopedia users and critics alike found Adler's reorganization of the *Britannica* unsatisfactory—and said so in loud and unmistakable terms:

- "A single general index to the entire contents of *Britannica 3's* 30 volumes is badly needed," said a review in *Reference Books Bulletin* (in *Booklist*, June 1, 1975, p. 1027).
- "This arrangement has nothing to recommend it except commercial novelty," said Samuel McCracken in his article "The Scandal of 'Britannica 3,'" in *Commentary* (February 1976, p. 63).
- "It is called the *Micropaedia*, for 'little knowledge,' and little knowledge is what it provides. It has proved to be grotesquely insufficient as an index, radically constricting the utility of the *Macropaedia*," said Geoffrey Wolff in his article "Britannica 3, Failures of " in *The Atlantic* (November 1976, p. 107).
- "The conclusion reached by this reviewer is that *Britannica 3* contains much excellent material, but is difficult to use. There are several reasons. The very division of content between *Micropaedia* and *Macropaedia* makes it necessary to consult another volume in the majority of cases; indeed, it was our experience that even simple searches might involve eight or nine volumes. This is not an unhappy experience for the leisurely reader; it can in fact often be a serendipitous one. The reader who wants to 'get it all together' in a short time may feel annoyed and frustrated. . . . By far the greatest source of difficulty in the use of *Britannica 3* is the indexing, and in this encyclopedia the use of the index is absolutely essential," said library science professor Dorothy Ethlyn Cole in a review of the fifthteenth edition in *Wilson Library Bulletin* (June 1974, p. 824).

Finally, after living with *Britannica 3* for more than a decade, the company's brass gave in and tacitly admitted that the public and the critics had been right all along. In 1985, the editors corrected most of the major structural problems that plagued the set. As Philip Goetz, then editor in chief, wrote in his preface to the 1985 printing of the fifteenth edition,

> The changes...are extensive. The entire encyclopaedia has been reset and restructured. The underlying policies of the *Encyclopaedia Britannica* remain unchanged, however. The work continues to be dedicated to intelligibility, to comprehensiveness, to objectivity and neutrality. To these has been added in 1985 a renewed dedication to accessibility, to making all of the riches of this work available to the greatest number of persons. The revision has been characterized by the inclusion of thousands of cross-references, notes, and other aids to the reader as support for the new Index volumes.

Broadly speaking, the 1985 and subsequent printings of the fifteenth edition differ from the 1974–84 printings in these ways: (1) the set has been expanded from 30 to 32 volumes, with approximately one million new words added; (2) the *Micropaedia* has been expanded from 10 to 12 volumes, although the total number of articles has been reduced from about 100,000 to less than 65,000, and the length of the articles, though still short, is no longer limited to 750 words; (3) the *Micropaedia* no longer has an indexing function, although it does furnish some 17,000 cross-references to the *Macropaedia* and the *Britannica World Data Annual* (the set's general yearbook); (4) the *Macropaedia* has been reduced from 19 to 17 volumes, and many of its articles, drastically reduced from 4,207 to 674, have either been consolidated or moved to the *Micropaedia*; (5) a two-volume analytical index of approximately 500,000 entries has been added to the set; (6) the index furnishes access to the entire contents of the encyclopaedia—*Macropaedia, Micropaedia, Propaedia*, and yearbook—whereas previously it was limited to the *Macropaedia*; (7) the *Propaedia* has been simplified and made easier to use;

and (8) the *Britannica Book of the Year*, the set's general yearbook, has been retitled the *Britannica World Data Annual* and now includes current information about countries of the world formerly found in the *Micropaedia*.

Today, the *Britannica* is one of half a dozen world-class encyclopedia produced in North America. Its publisher, the Chicago-based Encyclopaedia Britannica, Inc., is among the largest and most respected publishers of encyclopedias here and abroad. Its product line includes not only the flagship *New Encyclopaedia Britannica* but two multivolume sets for young people, the CHILDREN'S BRITANNICA and YOUNG CHILDREN'S ENCYCLOPEDIA. Britannica also published COMPTON'S ENCYCLOPEDIA until last year, when it was sold to the Tribune Publishing Company. In another major move in 1993, Britannica issued the *New Encyclopaedia Britannica* in a CD-ROM edition called the BRITANNICA INSTANT RESEARCH SYSTEM; and in 1994 the publisher announced that the encyclopedia would become available online via the Internet under the title BRITANNICA ONLINE. In addition to its encyclopedia operation, Britannica owns Merriam-Webster Inc. (the dictionary publisher), Evelyn Wood Reading Dynamics, and several smaller subsidiaries.

Philip (Tom) Goetz, editor in chief of the *Britannica* during 1979–91, was largely responsible for developing and implementing the extensive restructuring of the fifteenth edition that culminated in 1985. A gifted editor, Goetz has worked in various editorial positions at Britannica since 1952 and is now executive vice-chairman of the encyclopedia's board of editors. Robert McHenry is currently the set's general editor, having previously served as managing editor. McHenry is supported by an editorial and administrative staff of about 50, along with a 13-member board of editors (headed by Adler and Goetz), an impressive roster of academic and library advisers, and approximately 5,000 contributors. All of these people are identified in the *Propaedia* volume.

Throughout its illustrious history, the *Britannica* has boasted numerous famous contributors, including Albert Einstein, Sigmund Freud, G.K. Chesterton, Henry Ford, George Bernard Shaw, Sir Walter Scott, Ralph Vaughan Williams, T.E. Lawrence, Lillian Gish, George Jean Nathan, William Hazlitt, Thomas De Quincey, W.E.B. Du Bois, John F. Kennedy, T.H. Huxley, Thomas Babington Macaulay, H.L. Mencken, Leon Trotsky, and Cecil B. DeMille. On the occasion of its 225th birthday, the editors of the *Britannica* put together a collection of reprinted articles from the encyclopedia written by the many notables who have contributed to its pages over the years. Entitled *The Treasury of the Encyclopaedia Britannica*, the 704-page book was published by Viking Penguin in 1992 and sells for $40.00. It is edited by Clifton Fadiman and Robert McHenry, has a preface by Daniel Boorstin, and provides much fascinating reading for anyone who wants to know more about the march of knowledge through the world's oldest continuously published encyclopedia.

The current edition's list of contributors comprises mainly North American and British scholars, often the top people in their field, such as Isaac Asimov, Jacques Barzun, Kenneth E. Boulding, Fawn Brodie, Anthony Burgess, Lawrence Cremin, David Daiches, Michael DeBakey, Theodosius Dobzhansky, Leon Edel, Mircea Eliade, Philip S. Foner, Frank Freidel, Milton Friedman, Arthur Gelb, Sir Lawrence Gowing, Alfred Byrd Graf, Sir Tyrone Guthrie, Eric P. Hamp, Oscar Handlin, Chauncy D. Harris, Robert Heilbroner, Thor Heyerdahl, Gilbert Highet, Robert Lekachman, William Manchester, Martin E. Marty, Arthur Mizener, Howard Nemerov, Allan Nevins, Robert A. Nisbet, Conor Cruise O'Brien, Linus Pauling, Henri M. Peyre, Allen Walker Read, Kenneth

Rexroth, Stanley Sadie, Carl Sagan, Ernest J. Simmons, Lee Strasberg, Allen Tate, Sol Tax, Arnold J. Toynbee, and Alfred North Whitehead.

Many of these people are now retired or dead, but new contributors are added to the *Britannica* each year. For example, Donald H. Reiman (an expert on the poet Shelley), Jane Selverstone (a Harvard University professor of geology), and Nancy Thomson de Grummond (a classics professor at Florida State University) are among dozens of new authorities recruited in recent years. All articles in the *Macropaedia* and some longer ones in the *Micropaedia* are signed with the author's initials, following customary *Britannica* practice. The initials are listed alphabetically at the back of the *Propaedia*; each entry includes the contributor's affiliation and sometimes a major publication, along with the article(s) the person contributed to the encyclopedia.

As in the past, the encyclopedia's coverage is broad, deep, and reasonably well balanced. In a compact but perceptive review in *Reference Sources for Small and Medium-Sized Libraries* (5th ed., American Library Assn., 1992, p. 34), Jovian Lang puts the set's coverage in good perspective: "The sciences, mathematics, scientific biography, biology, medicine, Eastern and African cultures, the fine arts, Chinese history, and biblical literature receive panoramic treatment. Range, depth, and catholicity of coverage are unsurpassed by any other general encyclopedia."

Biographical articles naturally claim a sizable share of the total text, including roughly a third of the *Micropaedia*'s entries. The biographies consistently give not only the pertinent facts but summarize the person's major historical, intellectual, or artistic achievements and themes. Consider for instance the *Micropaedia* article on Philip Glass, which describes one of the composer's major works in these terms:

> Glass's opera *Satyagraha* (1980) was a more authentically "operatic" portrayal of several

incidents from the early life of Mohandas K. Gandhi. In this work, the dronelike repetition of symmetrical sequences of chords attained a haunting and hypnotic power that was well-attuned to the religio-spiritual themes of the libretto, adapted from the Hindu scripture known as the *Bhagavadgita*.

Geographical subjects also usually receive generous coverage. Continents and major countries are exhaustively described in brief, summary articles in the *Micropaedia* followed by long, detailed articles in the *Macropaedia*. Current information appears in the *Britannica World Data Annual*. Conversely, the U.S. states and Canadian provinces are less well covered, grouped by region within the long *Macropaedia* articles "United States of America" and "Canada." States and provinces lack their own maps and generally receive much less attention than in other large multivolume encyclopedias. This is a distinct competitive disadvantage for the *Britannica* in the school and library market, where the quality and quantity of such articles are important to teachers and librarians, to say nothing of students who make extensive use of this sort of material.

The arts and sciences, traditionally emphasized in the *Britannica*, continue to be covered with a thoroughness that only a very large and carefully edited encyclopedia can provide. The social and behavioral sciences are also well covered. In recent times, attention to the harder sciences and technology has steadily increased, reflecting contemporary trends in research and knowledge creation. In fact, scientific and technical topics now account for nearly 40 percent of the set's subject coverage.

Another striking feature of the *Britannica*'s coverage is the conspicuous effort to be as international as possible in all areas. Indeed, it can be stated without fear of contradiction that the fifteenth edition of the *Britannica* accords non-Western cultural, social, and scientific developments more notice than any general English-language encyclopedia currently on the market or, for that matter, ever published. The set's international perspective is exemplified in such articles as "Abortion," "Adoption," "Animals, Cruelty to," "Capital Punishment," "Folk Art," "Garden and Landscape Design," "Homicide," "Homosexual Rights Movement," "Land Reform and Tenure," "Motion Pictures," "Musical Forms and Genres," "Taxation," "Transportation," and "Work and Employment."

On the other hand, the encyclopedia offers little by way of practical, or how-to-do-it, information. For example, *Britannica* users will look in vain for material on how to copyright a book, how to write a business letter, how to compile a research paper, how to address government and religious leaders, how to care for pets, how to remove spots and stains, how to maintain a beautiful lawn, how to raise children, and so on—all subjects most family encyclopedias cover to one degree or another.

Information in the *Britannica* is normally accurate. Minor errors are encountered occasionally, but not often enough in such a large work to cast doubt on the set's overall reliability. One bit of misinformation should be corrected posthaste, however. The article on Dr. Charles Drew in the *Micropaedia* repeats the pernicious and now thoroughly discredited story that the black surgeon and blood bank pioneer bled to death in 1950 because an all-white hospital refused to admit him: "In desperate need of a blood transfusion, he was rushed to the nearest hospital, which turned him away because of his race. He died en route to a hospital for blacks." Not true.

Articles in the encyclopedia on controversial or sensitive topics—abortion, capital punishment, homosexuality, IQ tests, the Vietnam War, etc.—are usually treated in an impartial manner, with all relevant sides of the issue summarized as objectively as humanly possible. *Example:* The *Micropaedia* article "Abortion" explains:

Opponents of abortion, or of abortion for any reason other than to save the life of the mother, argue on religious or humanistic grounds that there is no rational basis for distinguishing the fetus from a newborn infant; each is totally dependent and potentially a member of society, and each possesses a degree of humanity. Proponents of liberalized regulation of abortion hold that, at least during its first three or four months, the fetus exhibits few if any human characteristics; that only a woman herself, rather than the state, has the right to manage her pregnancy in its early stages; and that the alternative to legal, medically supervised abortion is illegal and demonstrably dangerous abortion. The public debate of the issue has demonstrated the enormous difficulties experienced by political institutions in grappling with the complex and ambiguous ethical problems raised by the question of abortion.

As mentioned, the *Britannica*'s editors adopted a policy of continuous annual revision in 1936 and have employed it ever since. Each year an estimated 10 percent or so of the set's more than 30,000 text pages are revised in some manner, ranging from the addition of a brand-new article or complete reworking of an existing one to minor changes in biographical and geographical entries (adding death dates, updating census data, and the like). In the past, the encyclopedia has had a spotty record on revision, the editors tending to pull out all the stops one year and then rest on their oars the next. This stop-go tendency was much in evidence during the troubled 1974–84 years, but since 1985 and the major restructuring, the revision effort has become more consistent.

Today, the encyclopedia is reasonably current. This is particularly true of the *Micropaedia*, which covers topics that are more volatile or prone to change and therefore more closely monitored for revision by the editors. The long essay-type articles in the *Macropaedia*, on the other hand, tend to become dated less quickly than those in the *Micropaedia*, but they also tend to receive less editorial oversight.

Obviously, in an encyclopedia as massive as the *Britannica*, it is not difficult to find articles that are out-of-date or in need of some sort of revision. *Examples:* "Abortion" fails to mention recent U.S. Supreme Court cases that have had a major impact on the subject. "Circumcision" fails to note contemporary arguments against the procedure and the fact that increasingly parents in North America are deciding against circumcision. "Dead Sea Scrolls" contains nothing on current developments regarding the scrolls, either in the area of new discoveries and interpretations or the heated controversy over access. "Galileo" makes no reference to the Roman Catholic Church's recent exoneration of the great Renaissance scientist, an admission of historical error on the part of the church that has received worldwide attention. Many other examples could be cited. Still, considering the magnitude of the set, the editors do an adequate job of keeping the *Britannica* up-to-date.

The publisher of the *Britannica* also offers several yearbooks designed to update the encyclopedia and keep its readers abreast of new knowledge and information. Each of these annual publications is informative and attractive, although only the aforementioned *Britannica World Data Annual* (formerly the *Britannica Book of the Year*) is essential. This 1,000-page book includes important events of the previous year, current statistical information on the countries of the world, and articles and special reports on topics in the news. Its coverage of countries can be accessed via the encyclopedia's two-volume index, an innovative feature. The countries are listed in the index, with references to the *Britannica World Data Annual*. As James Rettig mentions in a review of the 1985 printing in *Wilson Library Bulletin* (October 1985, p. 68), the *Britannica World Data Annual* "is now an integral part of the *Britannica*, tied to it more closely than any other encyclopedia's yearbook." Other Britannica yearbooks are the *Yearbook of Science and the Future* and the *Medical and Health Annual*.

The *Britannica*'s writing style varies, sometimes markedly, from one article to another, especially in the *Macropaedia*, where certain contributors have been given leeway to express themselves subjectively and at some length. The late Anthony Burgess, for example, in the article "Literature, the Art of" turns in a wonderfully readable, quite opinionated essay on the novel that includes such lines as "The inferior novelist tends to be preoccupied with plot" and "Novelists can be elated by good reviews and depressed by bad ones, but it is rare that a novelist's practice is much affected by what he reads about himself in the literary columns." Seldom do present-day encyclopedias include such delicious material.

More typical of the encyclopedia's style is the article "Circulation and Circulatory Systems" in the *Macropaedia*. Written by Dr. Michael DeBakey (the famous heart specialist) and two other medical authorities, the 40-page article treats all pertinent aspects of the circulatory system, including the heart. The article begins this way:

> Within any living organism, the process of circulation involves all of the fluids of the body and permits a continuous integration among various tissues. Important to this process is the intake of metabolic materials, the conveyance of these materials throughout the organism, and the return of harmful by-products to the environment.
>
> Invertebrate animals have a great variety of liquids, cells, and modes of circulation, though many invertebrates have what is called an open system, in which fluid passes more or less freely throughout the tissues or defined areas of tissue. All vertebrates, however, have a closed system—that is, their circulatory system transmits fluid through an intricate network of vessels. This system contains two fluids, blood and lymph, and functions by means of two interacting modes of circulation, the cardiovascular system and the lymphatic system; both the fluid components

and the vessels through which they flow reach their greatest elaboration and specialization in the mammalian systems and, particularly, in the human body.

Generally speaking, articles in the *Britannica* are written in a scholarly though readable manner that normally will be comprehensible to literate adults and interested students at the high school level and beyond. However, some articles, particularly in the physical and mathematical sciences, are written at a level that only specialists and graduate students will readily comprehend. As the excerpt above demonstrates, the encyclopedia does not employ a controlled vocabulary, nor does it write to grade level or use any of the other techniques that enhance or extend readability. Yet some publicists and sales representatives persist in promoting the *Britannica* as suitable for children and young students in the elementary and junior high school grades. Except in the case of truly precocious youngsters, such claims are unfounded and should not be believed.

Access to information in the encyclopedia has been greatly improved since 1985 due to the major restructuring of the set that occurred that year. Most important is the addition of a detailed analytical index to the set. Published in two unnumbered volumes, the index contains more than 2,000 pages and approximately half a million entries. Happily, the index accesses all parts of the encyclopedia—*Macropaedia, Micropaedia, Propaedia,* and *Britannica World Data Annual* (the yearbook). In terms of number of index entries (500,000) to total text words (44 million), the *Britannica*'s index furnishes one entry for roughly every 90 words in the set, or a ratio of 1:90. Among the encyclopedia's chief rivals, COLLIER'S ENCYCLOPEDIA has a much more impressive ratio (1:50) and ENCYCLOPEDIA AMERICANA (1:90) about the same as the *Britannica*'s.

Some consumers, especially librarians and media specialists, will be interested to know that the *Britannica*'s index has recently become available in electronic form on CD-ROM. Called the *Britannica Electronic Index* and sold for $299.00 separately or $99.00 with purchase of the encyclopedia, this index offers much deeper and more sophisticated access to the encyclopedia's contents than the two-volume print index. Not only does the electronic index quickly locate specific topics (people, places, things, titles, concepts, etc.) in the database, it has the capability of retrieving information in ways that can only be accomplished by computerized searching, such as bringing together all references in the set on Russian novelists or capitalism or terms related to the human body. Altogether, the *Britannica Electronic Index* provides some 16 million references to the 44-million-word encyclopedia.

Readers seeking specific topics and facts in the set are also assisted by thousands of cross-references in the *Micropaedia*. Most of these references are to articles in the *Macropaedia*. At the beginning of the *Micropaedia* article "Florida," for instance, is this note: "A brief treatment of Florida follows. For full treatment, *see* MACROPAEDIA: United States of America: *Florida*." Less frequently, cross-references direct the reader from one *Micropaedia* article to another, as in the case of "IQ," which includes a *see* reference to "Intelligence Test." Sometimes, however, the cross-referencing system lets the reader down. A review of the 1993 printing in *Reference Books Bulletin* (in *Booklist*, September 15, 1993, p. 182) offers this example:

> Although there are almost 17,000 cross-references in the *Micropaedia*, internal cross-references are sometimes lacking. The entries *Cranach, Lucas* and *Munch, Edvard*, for example, fail to mention that color reproductions of their work appear in the entry *Painting, The History of Western* in the *Macropaedia*. (This is noted in the index.)

The aforementioned 1985 restructuring of the fifteenth edition of the *Britannica* admirably solved the problem of access to the encyclopedia's contents, but it failed to address a related question concerning the set's organization that still troubles many users: why are there two separate collections of articles, both alphabetically arranged, within the same work? Why do the editors put some articles in the 12-volume *Micropaedia* and others in the 17-volume *Macropaedia*? Won't some users look for information about, say, abortion in the "A" volume of the *Macropaedia* and, not finding it there, assume the subject is not covered in the encyclopedia? It has happened. (The article "Abortion" is, of course, in the "A" volume of the *Micropaedia*.) Editor Goetz provides an answer in his preface to the 1985 printing:

> Every edition of the *Encyclopaedia Britannica* has been characterized by many short articles and some few articles of great length. The Fifteenth Edition is unique in that it separates these two types of article in order to make clearer the different uses they serve— the short article for the seeker of information, of brief, factual data; the longer article for reading and for the more serious study of a major subject.

That is clear enough, but the price of making this rather arcane distinction between short and long articles is an overly complicated organization that ultimately can result in user difficulty and aggravation. Bill Katz, the reference authority, agrees, noting in his *Basic Information Sources* (6th ed., McGraw-Hill, 1992, p. 240) that "The division of the set into two major parts is confusing, and although the format has some benefit for ready-reference work, it is decidedly confusing for laypersons." To be fair, some users of the encyclopedia are quite happy with its present organization. Here, for instance, is what one layperson, Douglas J. Keenan of Thornhill, Ontario (Canada), had to say on the subject in a recent letter to this reviewer:

Ease of access is also quite good. Before purchasing the *Britannica*, I read reviews and found that some reviewers did not like the split between Micropaedia and Macropaedia. It is understandable how the unique organization of the Britannica might make it more difficult to compare with other encyclopedias. As a user, however—rather than a reviewer—the organization proved to deliver exactly what I wanted. It made it easy to look up small facts, or to get a quick overview of a subject, or areas in a subject, while still allowing true depth when that was desired.

Almost every article in the *Macropaedia* and some in the *Micropaedia* conclude with a substantial bibliography, or list of recommended sources for additional information on the subject. The bibliographies are carefully selected and extensively annotated, serving in many instances as small bibliographic essays on the subject. The bibliography accompanying the article "Galileo," for instance, is half a page long and contains authoritative notes on many of the titles listed. It was prepared by the late Giorgio D. de Santillana, author of the *Britannica* article on Galileo and a well-known Galileo scholar. There are two problems with the bibliographies, however. First, they fail to include publishers of the books cited, and second, they are often woefully out-of-date.

Illustrations in the *Britannica* normally add to the substance of the articles they complement, and they are almost always clearly reproduced. *Micropaedia* illustrations, which appear on nearly every page, are typically small, the size of a large postage stamp, and about half are in color. Many more, however, should be in color, not merely for the sake of adding dash to the page but to enhance their informational value. For instance, the article on Washington Allston, said to be "the first important U.S. Romantic painter," informs the reader that "Allston is known for his experiments with dramatic subject matter and his use of light and atmospheric colour," yet the small reproduction

of one of the artist's oil paintings that accompanies the article is in black-and-white. Likewise, the anemone fish is described as "bright orange, with three wide, blue-white bands circling the body," but the illustration is in black-and-white. Numerous similar examples could be cited.

Macropaedia illustrations, usually larger than those in the *Micropaedia*, are mostly in black-and-white, except for 164 color plates. The plates, printed on enameled paper, are excellent. By way of example, see the articles "Birds," "Central Asian Arts," "Coloration," "Decorative Arts and Furnishings," "Exploration," "Insects," "Mimicry," "Religious Symbolism and Iconography," "Rites and Ceremonies," and "Trees." The encyclopedia furnishes adequate map coverage (courtesy of Rand McNally) for the continents and major countries of the world but, as previously mentioned, there are no individual maps in the set for the U.S. states or Canadian provinces, a serious omission.

The *Britannica's* physical format is satisfactory in every respect. The binding is sturdy and attractive, the spine of each volume sporting the encyclopedia's official emblem, a wild Scottish thistle embossed in gold. Inside, befitting the set's image as a serious work of scholarship, the typography is dignified rather than bright and showy. The page layout tends to be formal, sensible, predictable, orderly, and inviting in a refined way. The *Micropaedia* has a three-column layout with narrow margins, whereas the *Macropaedia* is printed in two columns with broad margins. The *Macropaedia's* generous margins include many notes, or sideheads, that assist the reader in locating specific information in the longer articles, e.g., the 25-page article "Nutrition" includes the marginal note "Fluoridation," which points the reader to the paragraph covering that topic. The encyclopedia's 9-point Times Roman type suggests solid authority, the final word.

REPORT CARD: NEW ENCYCLOPAEDIA BRITANNICA

TOPIC	COVERAGE	ACCURACY	RECENCY	CLARITY
Circumcision	B	A	C	A
Drew, Charles	B	D	C	A
Galileo	B	A	C	A
Glass, Philip	A	A	B	A
Heart Disease	A	A	B	B
IQ	A	A	A	A
Panda Bears	A	A	A	A
Sexual Harassment	F*	NA	NA	NA
Shroud of Turin	A	A	A	A
Uzbekistan	A	A	A	A

A = Excellent; B = Above Average; C = Average; D = Below Average; F = Poor; NA = Not Applicable
*No Article

SUMMARY

Now published in 32 volumes comprising 44 million words, the *New Encyclopaedia Britannica* is the oldest, largest, best known, and most formidable general encyclopedia in the English language. Currently in its fifteenth edition, the *Britannica* first appeared in three volumes during 1768–71 in Edinburgh, Scotland, and remained in British hands until the beginning of the twentieth century, when it was sold to a group of Americans. Today the set is published in Chicago by Encyclopaedia Britannica, Inc., one of the preeminent publishers of encyclopedic products in North America and the world.

When the fifteenth edition of the *Britannica* first appeared in 1974, the set—widely known as *Britannica 3* for its tripartite arrangement—was criticized, sometimes harshly, for its overly complex organization and inadequate access to the text, exacerbated by the lack of a comprehensive index. In 1985, a major restructuring, highlighted by the addition of a two-volume analytical index, corrected most, but not all, of the organizational problems.

At the present time, the *Britannica* is one of half a dozen world-class general encyclopedias published in North America. Its conspicuous strengths include broad, deep, and well-balanced coverage of basic knowledge and information presented in articles that are normally authoritative, reliable, objective, reasonably current, and intelligently written for literate adults and serious students at the high school level and beyond. Moreover, access to the set's massive text is now satisfactory, thanks in large measure to the 1985 revision and addition of the aforementioned index.

On the negative side, the *Britannica*'s three-part arrangement (*Micropaedia*, *Macropaedia*, and *Propaedia*) continues to disconcert some users; some articles, mainly in the physical and mathematical sciences, are written at a level well beyond the layperson's grasp; the set's illustrations sometimes lack color where color is clearly required; and there are no individual maps for the U.S. states and Canadian provinces. The bottom line: Great name, great encyclopedia.

OTHER OPINIONS

American Reference Books Annual, 1992, pp. 17–18 (review by Lubomyr R. Wynar); *Basic Information Sources* by William A. Katz (vol. 1 of *Introduction to Reference Work*, 6th ed., New York: McGraw-Hill, 1992), pp. 238–40; *Reference Books Bulletin* (in *Booklist*), September 15, 1993, p. 182 (unsigned review); *Reference Sources for Small and Medium-Sized Libraries* (5th ed., Chicago: American Library Assn., 1992), p. 34 (review by Jovian P. Lang).

COMPARISON CHART
Large Encyclopedias for Adults and Older Students

This chart provides basic statistical information about the three large multivolume general encyclopedias for adults and older students reviewed in *Kister's Best Encyclopedias*. The chart also offers a quick comparative overview of the three titles. How does ENCYCLOPEDIA AMERICANA, for instance, compare with COLLIER'S ENCYCLOPEDIA and the NEW ENCYCLOPAEDIA BRITANNICA in terms of number of words? Articles? Illustrations? Index entries? Price? The chart answers such questions at a glance.

In the case of price information, consumers should understand that prices are subject to change by the publisher or distributor at any time. For the latest price of any encyclopedia, consult *Books in Print* (a standard reference source found in almost all libraries) or, better, call the publisher or distributor direct. Most now have toll-free numbers where the latest information about price and availability can be obtained quickly and efficiently. Telephone numbers are listed in this guide at the beginning of each review under "Price and Sales Information," as well as in the directory of publishers and distributors at the back of the book (see Appendix B, page 460).

The chart's final column assigns a letter grade to each encyclopedia: A = Excellent; B = Above Average; C = Average; D = Below Average; F = Poor. The letter grade represents a final summary of the encyclopedia's detailed evaluation in *Kister's Best Encyclopedias*. Consumers seriously interested in purchasing an encyclopedia are urged to base their selection decisions on the reviews in the book, and not rely solely on the letter grades given in the chart, which are necessarily arbitrary.

TITLE	VOLS.	WORDS	PAGES	ARTICLES	ILLUS & MAPS	CROSS-REFS.	INDEX ENTRIES	LOWEST RETAIL PRICE	RATING
COLLIER'S ENCYCLOPEDIA	24	21 MIL	19,844	25,000	19,000	13,000	450,000	$999.00	A
ENCYCLOPEDIA AMERICANA	30	30.8 MIL	2 6,740	52,000	24,170	40,000	353,000	1,400.00	B
NEW ENCYCLOPAEDIA BRITANNICA	32	44 MIL	32,000	65,100	24,500	17,000	500,000	1,194.00	A

Medium-Sized Encyclopedias for Adults and Older Students

* * * * * * * * *

OVERVIEW

More people want a mid-sized general encyclopedia suitable for adults and older students than any other type of encyclopedia. According to estimates by knowledgeable industry sources, sets in this category account for the largest share of the North American encyclopedia market, both in dollar volume and unit sales. Numbering from 9 to 29 volumes, they tend to be extensive enough to meet the informational needs of most people without being overwhelming or intimidating (as the very large sets can be). Moreover, most encyclopedias in this category are written to appeal to a broad readership, ranging from students at the upper elementary level to educated adults.

In terms of quality, the category is dominated by three titles, namely the WORLD BOOK ENCYCLOPEDIA, COMPTON'S ENCYCLOPEDIA, and the ACADEMIC AMERICAN ENCYCLOPEDIA (which is cloned under a confusing array of other titles, such as the BARNES & NOBLE NEW AMERICAN ENCYCLOPEDIA, the GROLIER ACADEMIC ENCYCLOPEDIA, the GROLIER INTERNATIONAL ENCYCLOPEDIA, the LEXICON UNIVERSAL ENCYCLOPEDIA, and the MACMILLAN FAMILY ENCYCLOPEDIA).

These encyclopedias clearly represent the best of their class. Each possesses many attractive features, including skilled and dedicated editorial staffs, broad and well-balanced coverage, a strong annual revision program, authoritative and reliable articles, a clear writing style, and first-class illustrations. Each has its adherents and the ultimate question of which is best often comes down to personal preference.

How do these three encyclopedias compare?

In terms of sales, WORLD BOOK is the most popular encyclopedia in North America. More sets of WORLD BOOK are sold each year in the U.S. and Canada than any other encyclopedia. Even the formidable NEW ENCYCLOPAEDIA BRITANNICA—possessor of the most esteemed name in English-language encyclopedias—is outsold by WORLD BOOK year in and year out.

First published in 1917, WORLD BOOK soon became a favorite with parents, children, teachers, and librarians—a love affair that continues to this day, and with good reason. Not only does WORLD BOOK pay closer attention to readability than its competitors, it is extremely well-organized for quick and easy retrieval of information. This combination of matchless clarity and superior organization adds up to what some call the WORLD BOOK "knack." A few critics say the encyclopedia is only for young people, but that is wrong; it serves younger and older students and adults equally well. In the judgment of this reviewer, the WORLD BOOK ENCYCLOPEDIA is page-for-page the best encyclopedia currently on the market.

COMPTON'S is also a well-known name among North American encyclopedias, dating back to 1922 when it first appeared as *Compton's Pictured Encyclopedia*. Regrettably, for a period of time during the late 1960s and 1970s, the encyclopedia was not maintained as diligently as it should have been. The set became dated in certain areas, and the illustrations were often too dark and too old. But beginning in the early 1980s and culminating with the 1993 printing, COMPTON'S has been revitalized, and today is entirely competitive with both WORLD BOOK and the ACADEMIC AMERICAN. The fact that COMPTON'S became the first general encyclopedia produced on CD-ROM in a multimedia edition (in 1989) says much about the set's new authority. The COMPTON'S renaissance is due in large part to the talents of its present editor, Dale Good, who is among the best in the business. No one can go wrong today buying and using *Compton's*; it is a first-rate encyclopedia.

Originally published in 1980, the ACADEMIC AMERICAN is the newest—and hence least well-known—of the three top encyclopedias in the mid-sized adult class. It is also the most expensive. The set has outstanding graphics, an excellent index, and an admirable record on continual revision. Although its articles sometimes lack sufficient depth, it provides carefully balanced coverage of basic knowledge and information. The ACADEMIC AMERICAN'S text is clearly more advanced than that found in WORLD BOOK and COMPTON'S, meaning that ordinarily it is not suitable for younger readers. Likewise, the ACADEMIC AMERICAN'S writing style, though lucid enough, tends to be dry and wooden when compared with its competitors. As noted, the encyclopedia is sold around the country and the world under a number of different titles, which can be confusing to consumers; prices can also vary greatly. When all is said and done, the ACADEMIC AMERICAN ENCYCLOPEDIA is not quite as attractive as its chief rivals.

Another good encyclopedia in the mid-sized adult category is FUNK & WAGNALLS NEW ENCYCLOPEDIA, an inexpensive 29-volume set that is merchandised mainly through North American supermarkets on the book-a-week plan. FUNK & WAGNALLS suffers from its supermarket connection and cannot successfully compete with WORLD BOOK, COMPTON'S, and the ACADEMIC AMERICAN, but actually the encyclopedia is an excellent value for the money (well under $200.00). It is a conscientiously prepared set, though it lacks quality illustrations, and the format leaves much to be desired.

Competing with FUNK & WAGNALLS for the supermarket dollar is the smaller but much better illustrated GROLIER ENCYCLOPEDIA OF KNOWLEDGE, a 1991 abridgment of the ACADEMIC AMERICAN. The 20-volume encyclopedia contains about 80 percent of the text of the parent set and is attractively priced at around $120.00, but thus far it has not been revised.

A somewhat similar set in terms of size and coverage is the NEW STANDARD ENCYCLOPEDIA, which has been around since 1930. For many years the set lacked an index and consequently was given short shrift by most critics and consumers, but several years ago it gained credibility with the addition of a full-scale index. NEW STANDARD is a solid, well-maintained encyclopedia, though it is hardly competitive with the likes of WORLD BOOK and COMPTON'S.

Bringing up the rear in the mid-sized adult category are WEBSTER'S FAMILY ENCYCLOPEDIA, a set of 10 paperbound volumes that costs almost nothing but is worth just about the same, and the handsomely produced OXFORD ILLUSTRATED ENCYCLOPEDIA, which is, alas, a cautionary example of how *not* to make an encyclopedia.

ACADEMIC AMERICAN ENCYCLOPEDIA

FACTS

Full Title: *Academic American Encyclopedia.* **Editorial Director:** Lawrence T. Lorimer. **Editor in Chief:** K. Anne Ranson. **Publisher:** Grolier Inc. **Date Published:** First published in 1980; new printing with revisions published annually.

Also published as the BARNES & NOBLE NEW AMERICAN ENCYCLOPEDIA; GLOBAL INTERNATIONAL ENCYCLOPEDIA; GROLIER ACADEMIC ENCYCLOPEDIA; GROLIER INTERNATIONAL ENCYCLOPEDIA; LEXICON UNIVERSAL ENCYCLOPEDIA; and MACMILLAN FAMILY ENCYCLOPEDIA.

Abridged Version: GROLIER ENCYCLOPEDIA OF KNOWLEDGE.

Electronic Versions: ACADEMIC AMERICAN ENCYCLOPEDIA (ONLINE); NEW GROLIER MULTIMEDIA ENCYCLOPEDIA (CD-ROM).

Volumes: 21. **Words:** 9.1 million. **Pages:** 9,864. **Articles:** 28,960. **Bibliographies:** 13,000. **Illustrations and Maps:** 18,000. **Cross-references:** 65,000. **Index Entries:** 201,000. **Editorial Staff, Advisers, and Contributors:** 2,600. **Trim Size:** 8 × 10 in.

Price and Sales Information: $1,150.00 publisher's suggested retail price; $719.00 plus $35.00 shipping and handling to schools and libraries. The *Academic American Encyclopedia* is sold to individual consumers by independent distributors who purchase quantities of the encyclopedia from the publisher, Grolier Inc., which functions as a wholesaler. Distributors set their own prices, which are normally lower than the publisher's suggested retail price of $1,150.00. In most instances, distributors attempt to sell the prospective purchaser a package deal consisting of the encyclopedia and various other reference materials at $1,000.00 or more. For further information about the encyclopedia or to obtain the name of a local distributor, consumers should call 1-203-796-2602 (not a toll-free number) or write Grolier Inc., Sherman Turnpike, Danbury, CT 06816.

The *Academic American* is sold to institutions (schools, libraries, etc.) by authorized sales representatives of Grolier Educational Corporation. For additional information or to place an order, call toll-free 1-800-243-7256 or write Grolier Educational Corporation, Sherman Turnpike, Danbury, CT 06816.

Consumers should also be aware that the *Academic American* is sold through various retail outlets and distributors under a number of different titles. Specifically, it is sold through Barnes & Noble bookstores under the title BARNES & NOBLE NEW AMERICAN ENCYCLOPEDIA; it is sold in discount warehouses and large bookstore chains as the GROLIER INTERNATIONAL ENCYCLOPEDIA and the MACMILLAN FAMILY ENCYCLOPEDIA; it is sold in-home by regional distributors as the GLOBAL INTERNATIONAL ENCYCLOPEDIA, the GROLIER ACADEMIC ENCYCLOPEDIA, and the LEXICON UNIVERSAL ENCYCLOPEDIA; and it is sold in an abridged edition in supermarkets as the GROLIER ENCYCLOPEDIA OF KNOWLEDGE. It is also sold abroad as the GROLIER ACADEMIC ENCYCLOPEDIA, and MACMILLAN FAMILY ENCYCLOPEDIA in countries where "American" in the title might hinder sales.

EVALUATION

Originally published in 1980, the *Academic American Encyclopedia* is the newest major multivolume general English-language encyclopedia on the market, the first such work since the now defunct MERIT STUDENTS ENCYCLOPEDIA appeared in 1967. Whereas its chief rivals—COMPTON'S ENCYCLOPEDIA, FUNK & WAGNALLS NEW ENCYCLOPEDIA, the NEW STANDARD ENCYCLOPEDIA, and the WORLD BOOK ENCYCLOPEDIA—are firmly established, dating back to 1922, 1912, 1930, and 1917 respectively, the *Academic American* has been around for only a decade and a half. Still, during that comparatively short time, the encyclopedia has proved to be a reference work of first importance and a formidable competitor in the marketplace.

The *Academic American* was created from scratch in the late 1970s by the Areté Publishing Company located in Princeton, New Jersey, an American subsidiary of Verenigde Nederlandse Uitgeversbedrijven (VNU), a large publishing conglomerate in the Netherlands. Although financed by Dutch money, the encyclopedia was prepared from the outset with North American readers principally in mind. Areté produced a quality product but the company had no sales organization, the plan being to sell the set exclusively in bookstores and departments stores rather than through presentation in the home, the traditional (and proven) method of merchandising encyclopedias. Most knowledgeable people in the industry predicted the Areté marketing strategy would fail; the company's president, Frank Greenagel, responded, "We're either going to crash and burn, or we're going to blow the hell out of this market" (*New York Times*, May 30, 1980, p. 1-D).

Suffice it to say that Areté and Greenagel did not blow the hell out of the encyclopedia market, and after only a few years, in 1982, VNU gave up on its increas-ingly costly foray into the American reference book business and sold the *Academic American* to Grolier Inc., a leading U.S. encyclopedia publisher. Happily, the set has prospered both financially and editorially under Grolier's ownership. Today the *Academic American* is a mainstay in the publisher's family of general encyclopedias, standing between the larger ENCYCLOPEDIA AMERICANA and the smaller NEW BOOK OF KNOWLEDGE, which is for young people.

Consumers should also be aware that the *Academic American* is marketed by independent distributors under a number of other titles, including the BARNES & NOBLE NEW AMERICAN ENCYCLOPEDIA, the GROLIER INTERNATIONAL ENCYCLOPEDIA, the LEXICON UNIVERSAL ENCYCLOPEDIA, and the MACMILLAN FAMILY ENCYCLOPEDIA. The set is also widely available in electronic form through such popular online computer information services as CompuServe, GEnie, and Prodigy (see page 256); it is also published on CD-ROM for use with personal computers under the title NEW GROLIER MULTIMEDIA ENCYCLOPEDIA.

The *Academic American* is an authoritative encyclopedia designed to serve the informational needs of older students and adults. The 75-member editorial staff brings excellent credentials to the work. Editorial director Lawrence Lorimer is an experienced encyclopedia hand, as is editor in chief K. Anne Ranson, who previously worked on the ENCYCLOPEDIA OF SOCIAL WORK, the *New Columbia Encyclopedia* (predecessor to the COLUMBIA ENCYCLOPEDIA, and Grolier's ENCYCLOPEDIA AMERICANA. The large majority of the more than 2,500 contributors listed at the beginning of Volume 1 are professors at well-known U.S. colleges and universities.

The encyclopedia currently contains about 32,000 entries, of which approximately 29,000 are articles and the rest external cross-references, e.g., "Intelligence Quotient: See

PSYCHOLOGICAL MEASUREMENT." Most articles in the set are of the specific-entry variety. For instance, major battles of the American Civil War—Bull Run, Shiloh, Antietam, Fredericksburg, Vicksburg, Gettysburg, Chattanooga, Chickamauga, etc.—have separate entries rather than being subsumed in the broad-entry article "Civil War, U.S." Likewise, most articles are quite brief, averaging about 350 words (or less than half a page) in length.

The encyclopedia's coverage is admirably broad and well balanced. In their preface, the editors estimate that 36 percent of the text is devoted to the arts and humanities, 35 percent to the sciences and technology, 14 percent to the social and behavioral sciences, 13 percent to geography, and 2 percent to sports and recreation. Within these subjects, biographies account for more than a third of all entries. Prominent twentieth-century figures from all walks of life are especially well covered, as are important mythological characters. The set also includes many articles on individual plays (e.g., *The Glass Menagerie*), novels (*Don Quixote*), poems (*The Waste Land*), treatises (*The Decline of the West*), operas (*Tosca*), and the like—a useful feature for high school and college students.

Unfortunately, although the *Academic American* covers a wide range of topics, its treatment of these topics sometimes lacks sufficient depth, particularly when compared with competing encyclopedias. The *Academic American*'s article on Nicaragua, for example, consists of less than two pages, whereas the WORLD BOOK ENCYCLOPEDIA and COMPTON'S ENCYCLOPEDIA provide two or three times as much coverage. The same is true of articles on the U.S. states, Canadian provinces, North American cities, and other countries and major places of the world. The article "Chelation" concisely describes the process but fails to discuss its application as a controversial medical therapy for arteriosclerosis and other maladies. Dr. Charles Drew, the

African-American physician whose pioneering work with blood plasma helped establish blood banks, is covered in one sentence in the article "Black Americans"; no mention is made of the way Drew died, a topic of considerable interest among students of racism. Many similar examples could be cited.

The editors justify the *Academic American*'s brevity on these grounds: "Students and adults expect an encyclopedia to provide quick access to definitive factual information. Both audiences also want to find a readily intelligible overview of a subject that does not compel the reader to grasp intricate subtleties or wade through drawn-out historical analysis" (preface). This *USA Today* approach to encyclopedia-making has a certain appeal, especially among today's television-bred students. On the other hand, users of encyclopedias frequently want more than bare-bones facts or a terse summary. As an early review of the *Academic American* in *Choice* (March 1981, p. 912) put it, "The AAE's most serious shortcoming is the brevity of its entries. Undergraduates looking for articles that will put their subjects into historical and philosophical perspective will usually find their needs better met by consulting another encyclopedia." James Rettig's review in *Wilson Library Bulletin* (February 1982, p. 460) made much the same point, complaining that many articles "leave the reader wishing the skeleton of facts carried more meat and connecting tissue. They give a teasing, tantalizing taste of their subjects but do not impart enough of its real flavor."

Information in the encyclopedia is normally accurate and presented in an unbiased manner. The many minor errors spotted by critics in the first few editions have since been corrected. Articles dealing with controversial or sensitive issues usually give both sides of the argument. *Example:* The article "Circumcision" notes,

> In modern times circumcision is often performed on newborn males, but physicians disagree on whether or not the procedure is medically advisable (other than in cases of

malformation). On one side, urologists claim that circumcised males have far fewer urinary tract infections and are less at risk for catching sexually transmitted diseases than are uncircumcised males. On the other side, pediatricians say that the medical risks attendant upon the surgery far outweigh the possible future consequences of foregoing the operation."

In a some instances, however, controversy is merely noted but not discussed. For example, in the article "Scientology" the reader learns that the religion "has been the subject of much controversy," but the nature of that controversy is left to the reader's imagination.

As might be anticipated in the case of a relatively new encyclopedia, the *Academic American* tends to be quite contemporary in terms of both content and perspective. Since acquiring the set in 1982, Grolier has put a high priority on keeping it as up-to-date as humanly possible. The 1993 printing, for instance, includes 95 new articles, another 75 articles that have been entirely rewritten, 3,200 more articles that have been revised in some manner, and 362 new or revised illustrations and maps—all involving changes, major and minor, in some 2,500 (or 26 percent) of the encyclopedia's nearly 10,000 pages. Such articles as "Abortion," "Adoption," "Circumcision," "Depression," "Fluoridation," "Germany," "Nuclear Energy," "Nuclear Reactor," "Sexual Harassment," "Shroud of Turin," and "Uzbekistan" are as current as can be expected in an annually revised encyclopedia. (Note that the online version of the encyclopedia—see page 256—is updated quarterly.)

Not all articles in the encyclopedia, however, are as up-to-date as they might be. *Examples:* "Galileo" fails to note that the Roman Catholic Church has recently rescinded the Inquisition's condemnation of the famous astronomer in 1633, which represents a major concession by the modern church. "Nuclear Strategy" continues to discuss the subject in terms of conflict between the U.S. and the Soviets, failing to take into account the end of the Cold War and the demise of the Soviet Union. "Rose" fails to inform the reader that the rose has recently been adopted as the U.S. national flower.

Prospective purchasers of the *Academic American* should also be aware that the publisher offers a yearbook designed to help keep the set abreast of current happenings. The yearbook is a good product that summarizes the events of the previous year, but it has no real editorial connection to the encyclopedia and should not be purchased unless the consumer is convinced it will be used. Too often, such encyclopedia supplements sound good when described by the sales representative but turn out to be little more than dust-catchers.

Over the years, the encyclopedia's writing style and readability have evoked considerable disagreement among users and critics. The aforementioned review in *Choice* (March 1981, p. 914), for instance, states that "the prose style in the AAE is commendable. It is well written, concise, and informative without being condescending or obscure." Jovian Lang, in *Reference Sources for Small and Medium-Sized Libraries* (5th ed., American Library Assn., 1992, p. 30), characterizes the articles as "written in a light, captivating style." But Gary Barber, in *Reference Services Review* (Summer 1982, p. 48), refers to the encyclopedia's "generally undistinguished writing style," which he attributes to "the extreme space constraints imposed on the contributors and AAE's emphasis on straightforward description." And Bill Katz, an astute critic, describes the *Academic American*'s style (in his *Basic Information Sources*, 6th ed., McGraw-Hill, 1992, p. 244) in this way:

> In trying to be all things to all people, the writing style is sometimes too journalistic, too simplistic. But at the same time, thanks to less than firm editorial control, some of the more complicated articles are not that easy to follow. In other words, the presentation is uneven, although generally good enough.

The author of *Kister's Best Encyclopedias* agrees the *Academic American's* writing style leaves something to be desired. In most instances, the style is clear but tends to be dry and stilted—a bit too formal or erudite for easy reading. The first two paragraphs of the article "Heart" typify the encyclopedia's style:

> The human heart is a specialized, four-chambered muscle that maintains BLOOD flow in the CIRCULATORY SYSTEM. Located in the thorax, it lies left of the body's midline, above and in contact with the diaphragm. It is situated immediately behind the breastbone, or sternum, and between the lungs, with its apex tilted to the body cavity's left side. At rest, the heart pumps about 59 cc (2 oz) of blood per beat and 5 l (5 qt) per minute, compared to 120–220 cc (4–7.3 oz) per beat and 20–30 l (21–32 qt) per minute during exercise. The adult human heart is about the size of a fist and weighs about 250–350 gm (9 oz).
>
> Blood supplies food and oxygen to the cells of the body for their life needs and removes the waste products of their chemical processes. It also helps to maintain a consistent body temperature, circulate hormones, and fight infections. Research indicates that the heart itself produces hormonelike chemicals. Brain cells are dependent on a constant oxygen supply, so death ensues shortly if a HEART ATTACK halts circulation to the brain. Such attacks are the number-one cause of death in the United States (see also HEART DISEASES).

Under normal circumstances, the *Academic American* best serves students at the high school and college levels, along with better-educated adults. Much of the text will be beyond the comprehension of most students at the elementary and even junior high school levels, although the editors claim the set "has been created for students at the upper elementary level and in junior high school, high school, or college and for the inquisitive adult" (preface). Interestingly, when the encyclopedia first appeared in 1980 the editors said in their preface that it was "created for students in junior high school, high school, or college and for the inquisitive adult"—the phrase "at the upper elementary level" appeared sometime later, an unsubtle attempt to expand the set's readership at the proverbial stroke of a pen.

Anyone contemplating purchase of the *Academic American* for use by children and younger students should understand that its articles are *not* written to grade level, that the vocabulary is *not* controlled in any discernible manner, and that technical or potentially unfamiliar terms are usually *not* defined in context (see, for example, *thorax, midline, diaphragm, apex,* and *hormones* in the excerpt from "Heart" above)—all writing techniques used to improve comprehension in the better encyclopedias for young people, such as COMPTON'S ENCYCLOPEDIA, NEW BOOK OF KNOWLEDGE, and the WORLD BOOK ENCYCLOPEDIA.

Locating specific facts and topics in the *Academic American* is normally not difficult. A variety of cross-references in the text helps point the user in the right direction. For example, in the excerpt from the article "Heart" above, the words BLOOD, CIRCULATORY SYSTEM, HEART ATTACK, and HEART DISEASES are printed in SMALL CAPITAL LETTERS, indicating that the encyclopedia has articles entitled "Blood," "Circulatory System," "Heart Attack," and "Heart Diseases" where related information can be found. The *Academic American* includes some 65,000 such cross-references.

The set's principal finding device, however, is a large, nearly 600-page analytical index of over 200,000 entries that comprises most of Volume 21. The index, originally prepared by Barbara Preschel, a professional indexer, is outstanding. In terms of the ratio of index entries to total words in the encyclopedic text (9.1 million), the *Academic American* provides one index entry for every 45 text words, or a ratio of 1:45. No other general encyclopedia currently offers such a detailed index; only COLLIER'S ENCYCLOPEDIA comes close, with a ratio of 1:50. Some consumers, especially teachers and librarians, will also be interested to know that the *Academic American's* index is now available on CD-ROM as part of the *Grolier Master Encyclopedia Index,* which also includes the indexes to the other two major Grolier encyclopedias, ENCYCLOPEDIA AMERICANA and the NEW BOOK OF KNOWLEDGE. The disc sells for $149.00 and works on all basic platforms (MS-DOS, Windows, and Macintosh).

Another valuable feature of the encyclopedia is its bibliographies, or lists of materials for further study. Appended to approximately 40 percent of the articles, the bibliographies have been carefully selected to be as useful as possible to students seeking additional information on a topic: "We [the editors] have not attempted, especially in science, to furnish the most definitive work in the field if, in our opinion, that work would be well beyond the comprehension of our intended reader" (preface). In some instances, however, the bibliographies are noticeably dated. *Examples:* The bibliography accompanying the article "Sexual Development" lists six titles, all published in the 1970s; "Sexual Intercourse" lists four titles, three published in the 1970s and one in the 1950s.

The *Academic American*'s illustrations, which make up roughly a third of the total text, add much to the set's informational value. They consist of photographs, diagrams, cutaway drawings, charts, reproductions of paintings and other works of art, and maps, including many useful historical maps. The article "Heart," for instance, has six informative illustrations, including a half-page drawing showing the complete cardiac cycle. Also noteworthy are the captions accompanying all illustrations, which serve as a source of much additional—and valuable—text. *Example:* The article "Motherwell, Robert" is accompanied by a color reproduction of the artist's painting *Summertime in Italy*. The caption reads,

> Summertime in Italy (1960) is representative of Robert Motherwell's bold, architectural compositions, in which abstract geometric forms are executed in slashing brushstrokes. Motherwell, one of the founders and primary exponents of abstract expressionism, is best known for compositions alluding to philosophic ideas.

The encyclopedia's physical format is both carefully constructed and appealing to the eye. Of particular note is the attractive page design, which includes the contemporary "ragged right" (wherein the right-hand margin of each column of type is not justified, or even)—a style that not only looks good but improves reading ease by reducing the amount of hyphenation and maintaining even spacing between words. Overall, the *Academic American* sets a high standard for encyclopedia design.

REPORT CARD: ACADEMIC AMERICAN ENEYCLOPEDIA

TOPIC	COVERAGE	ACCURACY	RECENCY	CLARITY
Circumcision	A	A	A	A
Drew, Charles	F*	NA	NA	NA
Galileo	B	A	C	A
Glass, Philip	A	A	A	A
Heart Disease	B	A	A	B
IQ	B	A	A	A
Panda Bears	A	A	A	A
Sexual Harassment	A	A	A	A
Shroud of Turin	A	A	A	A
Uzbekistan	C	A	A	A

A = Excellent; **B** = Above Average; **C** = Average; **D** = Below Average; **F** = Poor; **NA** = Not Applicable
*No Article

SUMMARY

First published in 1980, the *Academic American Encyclopedia* is the newest multivolume general English-language encyclopedia on the market. During its short existence it has achieved a reputation as a topnotch encyclopedia. Among the set's many strengths are its broad and balanced coverage, up-to-date articles, easy and efficient access to the text, outstanding illustrations, useful bibliographies, and a highly appealing format. On the negative side, the encyclopedia's articles are often quite brief and sometimes lack sufficient depth; also, the writing style tends to be dry and stilted. The editors say the *Academic American* is intended for readers from the upper elementary grades through college and beyond, but in most instances the material is too advanced for elementary and possibly even junior high school students, who will be better served by such competing encyclopedias as COMPTON'S ENCYCLOPEDIA and the WORLD BOOK ENCYCLOPEDIA.

Consumers should also be aware that the *Academic American* is distributed under a number of other titles, including the BARNES & NOBLE NEW AMERICAN ENCYCLOPEDIA, GROLIER ACADEMIC ENCYCLOPEDIA, GROLIER INTERNATIONAL ENCYCLOPEDIA, LEXICON UNIVERSAL ENCYCLOPEDIA, and MACMILLAN FAMILY ENCYCLOPEDIA. There is also an abridged version entitled the GROLIER ENCYCLOPEDIA OF KNOWLEDGE. In addition, the *Academic American* is widely available online via such computerized information services as CompuServe, GEnie, and Prodigy, as well as on CD-ROM as the NEW GROLIER MULTIMEDIA ENCYCLOPEDIA. The bottom line: One of the best midsized encyclopedias available today.

OTHER OPINIONS

American Reference Books Annual, 1993, p. 24 (review by Anna Grace Patterson); *Basic Information Sources* by William A. Katz (vol. 1 of *Introduction to Reference Work*, 6th ed., New York: McGraw-Hill, 1992), pp. 243–45; *Reference Books Bulletin* (in *Booklist*), September 15, 1993, pp. 172–74 (unsigned review); *Reference Sources for Small and Medium-Sized Libraries* (5th ed., Chicago: American Library Assn., 1992), pp. 29–30 (review by Jovian P. Lang).

BARNES & NOBLE NEW AMERICAN ENCYCLOPEDIA

FACTS

Full Title: *Barnes & Noble New American Encyclopedia.* **Editorial Director:** Lawrence T. Lorimer. **Editor in Chief:** K. Anne Ranson. **Publisher:** Grolier Inc. Distributor: Barnes & Noble, Inc. **Date Published:** First published as the *Barnes & Noble New American Encyclopedia* in 1991; new printing with revisions published in 1992.

Also published as the ACADEMIC AMERICAN ENCYCLOPEDIA.
Volumes: 20. **Words:** 9.1 million. **Pages:** 9,864. **Articles:** 28,960. **Bibliographies:** 13,000. **Illustrations and Maps:** 18,000. **Cross-references:** 65,000. **Index Entries:** 201,000. **Editorial Staff, Advisers, and Contributors:** 2,600. **Trim Size:** 8 × 10 in.

Price and Sales Information: $299.00 plus $15.00 shipping and handling. The *Barnes & Noble New American Encyclopedia*—a retitled edition of the 1992 printing of the ACADEMIC AMERICAN ENCYCLOPEDIA—is sold in the main Barnes & Noble Bookstore in New York City and nationally via mail order. Recently, however, a representative of the company indicated that the *Barnes & Noble New American Encyclopedia* will be discontinued as soon as the remaining inventory is exhausted. For further information about the encyclopedia and its status, call toll-free 1-800-242-6657 or write Barnes & Noble, Inc., 120 Fifth Avenue, New York, NY 10011.

CONSUMER NOTE

The 20-volume *Barnes & Noble New American Encyclopedia* has exactly the same contents as the 21-volume ACADEMIC AMERICAN ENCYCLOPEDIA (1992 printing), a major Grolier product. The only difference between the two sets, apart from their distinctive titles and bindings, is that the ACADEMIC AMERICAN has an extra volume (Volume 21), which comprises the set's cumulative, or master, index. *Barnes & Noble*, on the other hand, lacks a cumulative index; rather, its index appears in sections (printed on blue paper) at the end of each of the 20 volumes. For example, Volume 3 covers all articles beginning with the letter "B," followed by all index entries beginning with "B." In addition, *Barnes & Noble* has a cheaper binding than that used for the ACADEMIC AMERICAN, which is designed to withstand heavy use in libraries.

Barnes & Noble, Inc., one of the largest bookstore chains in North America, was founded in 1873 in Wheaton, Illinois. Today the firm's corporate headquarters and flagship store—said to be the largest general interest bookstore in the world—are located in New York City. Its subsidiaries include B. Dalton Bookseller, Scribner's Bookstores, Bookstop, and Doubleday Bookshops. In the case of the ACADEMIC AMERICAN, Barnes & Noble distributes the 1992 printing under its own name and at its own price, which is considerably lower than Grolier's suggested retail price for the encyclopedia. But, as noted, Barnes & Noble has indicated it will no longer distribute the encyclopedia once the present stock has been sold. The company will, however, continue to offer the one-volume BARNES & NOBLE ENCYCLOPEDIA, a retitled edition of the CAMBRIDGE ENCYCLOPEDIA.

For a detailed evaluation of the contents of the *Barnes & Noble New American Encyclopedia*, see the ACADEMIC AMERICAN ENCYCLOPEDIA (page 53).

COMPTON'S ENCYCLOPEDIA

FACTS

Full Title: *Compton's Encyclopedia & Fact-Index.* **Editor:** Dale Good. **Publisher:** Compton's Learning Company, a Tribune Publishing Company. Former Title: *Compton's Pictured Encyclopedia* (1922–67).

Date Published: First published as *Compton's Encyclopedia & Fact-Index* in 1968; new printing with revisions published annually.

Electronic Versions: COMPTON'S CONCISE ENCYCLOPEDIA (CD-ROM); COMPTON'S ENCYCLOPEDIA (ONLINE); COMPTON'S FAMILY EN-

CYCLOPEDIA (CD-ROM); COMPTON'S INTERAC-TIVE ENCYCLOPEDIA (CD-ROM); COMPTON'S MUL-TIMEDIA ENCYCLOPEDIA (CD-ROM).

Volumes: 26. **Words:** 9 million. **Pages:** 10,590. **Articles:** 34,000 (5,250 main articles; 28,750 brief articles in the "Fact-Index"). **Bibliographies:** 450. **Illustrations and Maps:** 22,510. **Cross-references:** 35,500. **Index Entries:** 154,000. **Editorial Staff, Advisers, and Contributors:** 600. **Trim Size:** 7 1/2 ×10 in.

Price and Sales Information: $499.00 retail; $569.00 to schools and libraries. *Compton's Encyclopedia* is sold to individual consumers through authorized sales representatives of the publisher, Compton's Learning Company. For additional information about the set or to order it, call toll-free 1-800-858-4895 or write Compton's Learning Company, 2 Prudential Plaza (Suite 2625), 180 North Stetson Avenue, Chicago, IL 60601-6790.

Compton's is currently sold to educational institutions (schools, libraries, etc.) through Encyclopaedia Britannica Educational Corporation (EBEC). (Part of the agreement between EBEC and the Tribune Co. when *Compton's* was sold to the latter was that the EBEC would continue to sell sets to schools and libraries for two years.) For additional information or to place an order, call toll-free 1-800-544-9862 or write EBEC, Britannica Centre, 310 South Michigan Avenue, Chicago, IL 60604. Educators and librarians receive a substantial discount off the retail price when ordering *Compton's* for their personal use. Call toll-free 1-800-382-FACT for further information or to place an order.

Compton's is also now sold in some independent and university bookstores around the country, including book departments in large department stores. Major national bookstore chains, however, do not carry the encyclopedia. Interested consumers should check directly with the bookstores in their area to determine which, if any, stores sell *Compton's*.

Compton's is also sold via mail order. Consumers receive Volume 1 free and purchase the remaining 25 volumes on a month-by-month basis at a rate of $19.95 per volume plus $1.39 for shipping and handling. Such offers are made through direct mail or telephone solicitation.

EVALUATION

Compton's Encyclopedia first appeared in 1922 in eight volumes as *Compton's Pictured Encyclopedia*, so called because it was the most heavily illustrated encyclopedia of its day. Published by the F. E. Compton Company of Chicago, the set grew to 15 volumes by 1932. In 1961, Encyclopaedia Britannica, Inc., long one of the preeminent names in Anglo-American encyclopedia publishing, acquired *Compton's* and generally upgraded it. In 1969, the encyclopedia was expanded to 24 volumes and retitled simply *Compton's Encyclopedia*, the adjective "Pictured" no longer deemed meaningful since most multivolume encyclopedias of any consequence were now illustrated, some more extensively than *Compton's*. The set attained its present size when two more volumes were added in 1974.

For most of its history, *Compton's* has enjoyed the reputation of a first-class encyclopedia for students of practically all ages as well as for the whole family. It was one of the first encyclopedias to maintain a permanent editorial staff and its editors among the first to recognize the need for continuous revision on an annual basis as a means of staying abreast of new knowledge, which has increased at a dizzying pace since *Compton's* first appeared in the 1920s. It also was one of the first encyclopedias to use color illustrations.

During the 1970s, however, *Compton's* fell on hard times, failing to remain reasonably up-to-date (in both content and design) and therefore increasingly unable to keep pace with its competitors, chiefly the WORLD BOOK ENCYCLOPEDIA, which has long dominated the student and family encyclopedia market in North America. After a period of uncertainty when the publisher considered unloading or even discontinuing the set, a decision was made in the early 1980s to revitalize *Compton's*. This process required a long, hard, expensive effort, but by the end of the decade the encyclopedia had been completely revamped, culminating in the early 1990s in an intellectually and visually impressive encyclopedia that is now once again competitive with the best in its class.

As tangible evidence of the encyclopedia's new vitality, *Compton's* appeared in 1989 in a pathbreaking electronic version on compact disc (CD-ROM). Called COMPTON'S MULTIMEDIA ENCYCLOPEDIA, it was the first reference source on disk to combine text, graphics, sound, and animation with multiple search paths. To validate its pioneering effort, Compton's NewMedia, developer of COMPTON'S MULTIMEDIA ENCYCLOPEDIA, recently obtained a patent from the U.S. Patent Office that recognizes the company as the inventor of multimedia CD-ROM. COMPTON'S INTERACTIVE ENCYCLOPEDIA followed in 1993. The encyclopedia is also available in CD-ROM versions entitled COMPTON'S CONCISE ENCYCLOPEDIA and COMPTON'S FAMILY ENCYCLOPEDIA. It is also available online via America Online, a computerized information service.

In a surprise move, Encyclopaedia Britannica sold its *Compton's* properties (including *Compton's Encyclopedia*, COMPTON'S INTERACTIVE ENCYCLOPEDIA, and COMPTON'S MULTIMEDIA ENCYCLOPEDIA) to the Chicago-based Tribune Company in July 1993 for $57 million. The Tribune Company, a media giant that owns the *Chicago Tribune* plus five other daily papers and a number of radio and television stations, is principally interested in the encyclopedia's potential as an electronic information source.

At present, *Compton's Encyclopedia* is in good editorial hands, literally and figuratively. Dale Good, the current editor, began his career as a music librarian and journal editor at the New York Public Library, then worked for Funk & Wagnalls and Random House on various reference book projects before joining *Compton's* as science and yearbook editor in the early 1980s. He became editor in chief of the encyclopedia in 1986 and is the individual most identified with the resurgence of *Compton's*.

Good is supported by an editorial staff of 80, plus 21 advisers. In addition, *Compton's* lists approximately 500 contributors and editorial consultants, most of whom bring solid credentials to their work, although quite a few are now deceased. All of these people and their affiliations are noted at the front of Volume 1. Of the 34,000 articles in the set, only about 1,100 are signed. These tend to be longer articles that have been added or heavily revised in recent years. *Examples:* "Abortion," "Adoption," "Alcoholism," "Business Cycle," "Genetic Engineering," "Genetics," "Heart," "Mental Illness," "Russia," "Teeth and Gums," and all U.S. state and Canadian province articles.

Compton's aims "to be an innovative, forward-looking reference work that rewards curiosity, inviting the entire family to explore the world in its pages" (preface). It contains about 5,250 main articles in the first 25 volumes. Alphabetically arranged, these articles tend to be substantial treatments of the topic at hand. In addition, there are well over 28,000 very brief articles in Volume 26, called the "Fact Index," which (as its title suggests) serves as both an index to the set and a source of quick reference information. The "Fact Index" is similar to the "Dictionary Index" found in the NEW BOOK OF KNOWLEDGE and the "Reference Index" in CHILDREN'S BRITANNICA.

"Fact-Index" articles treat specific topics not covered in the main body of the encyclopedia. They include people (e.g., the artist Robert Motherwell), smaller places (Moultrie, Georgia), plants and animals (the Mound bird), groups and organizations (Moral Re-Armament), medical concerns (motion sickness), and trendy or ephemeral topics (MTV; the performer Madonna). The "Fact-Index" also provides much eclectic information in tabular form, such as lists of notable bridges, highest mountains, major Academy Awards, and key cabinet and court appointments of each U.S. president. An index to all tables in the "Fact-Index" appears at the front of Volume 26.

The encyclopedia's contents loosely reflect school curricula in the U.S. and Canada. The editors informally monitor curricular trends, although (unlike rival WORLD BOOK ENCYCLOPEDIA) no systematic study of specific schools or subjects taught is undertaken.

Topics not ordinarily associated with the school curriculum—amusement parks, camping, fishing, hunting, games, gardening, pets, etc.—are also covered. Along this line, *Compton's* includes much "how-to" information, although this feature has been de-emphasized in recent years. As noted in a review in *Reference Books Bulletin* (in *Booklist*, May 15, 1992, p. 1709), "Some article revisions reflect a more contemporary outlook and a shift from a 'how-to-do-it' emphasis"; the review goes on to point out by way of example that the newly revised article on gardens and gardening "was very much a 'how-to' in previous editions but is now a survey of the various kinds of gardens."

Coverage of scientific and technical subjects, traditionally one of the encyclopedia's strong suits, continues to be first-rate, exemplified by such long and informative articles as "Animals, Prehistoric," "Arithmetic," "Atomic Particles," "Biochemistry," "Bioengineering," "Birds," "Climate," "Continent," "Flower," "Flowers, Garden,"

"Flowers, Wild," "Genetic Engineering," "Genetics," "Jet Propulsion," "Legume," "Light," "Lightning," "Lizards," "Nuclear Energy," "Oceanography," "Ocean Waves," "Petroleum," "Planets," "Plant," "Plastics," "Star," "Sugar," "Teeth and Gums," "Tools," "Tree," "Wasp," "Watch and Clock," "Zoo," and "Zoology."

Important places—continents, countries, U.S. states, Canadian provinces, major world cities, rivers, lakes, mountains, and the like—also receive generous coverage. *Example:* All U.S. state articles are between 15 and 20 pages in length and include many instructive photographs, several maps (including a detailed political map with gazetteer), short biographies of notable people associated with the state, a historical chronology, a fact summary, and a bibliography; the Canadian provinces receive similar treatment. All of these articles have been redesigned and updated in the 1990s.

Coverage of the humanities, while not as deep as that of the sciences or geography, is adequate and generally well balanced, as substantial articles on such subjects as architecture, calligraphy, drama, folk music, glass and glassware, handicrafts, jazz, mime and pantomime, opera, painting, puppets, quilting, theater, and creative writing attest. Still, some prominent contemporary authors and artists are not covered, such as Roy Campbell, Patrick Henry Bruce, R.B. Kitaj, and Hale Woodruff. Occasionally, too, articles fail to include basic data. For instance, nowhere in the article "Islam" does the reader learn how many adherents are found in the U.S. or Canada.

In the past, coverage of social and behavioral science topics in *Compton's* has been comparatively weak. Happily, during the recent revitalization of the encyclopedia, the editors have made real progress in correcting this deficiency. Particularly noteworthy is the strong effort to improve coverage of persistent social issues, such as abortion, adoption, AIDS, alcoholism, capital punishment, drunk driving, euthanasia and the right to die, homosexuality, missing children, race relations, rape, religious cults, sexual harassment, sexually transmitted diseases, and women's rights—all topics of concern to young people as well as adults. Where controversy exists, the encyclopedia usually provides a fair summary of both sides of the question, as in the articles "Abortion" and "Nuclear Energy."

Compton's is clearly a conscientiously edited encyclopedia. Readers can depend on its information to be accurate and presented in a timely, unbiased manner. Occasionally, small factual errors will be encountered; for instance, the article "Reference Books" says rival WORLD BOOK ENCYCLOPEDIA consists of 24 volumes when actually the number is 22. But such mistakes are few and far between.

Likewise, most articles in Compton's nowadays are admirably up-to-date. As noted earlier, the set had become noticeably stale in the 1970s and early 1980s, but the extensive volume-by-volume revision program launched in 1983 and completed in 1989 brought Compton's back to life, once again rendering it among the best encyclopedias on the North American market. In 1992, the editors redesigned, reillustrated, and reset the entire encyclopedia, outfitting it for the computer age: "A state-of-the-art computerized publishing system [now] makes it possible to update, illustrate, and print Compton's Encyclopedia rapidly, accurately, and economically" (preface). Overall, Encyclopaedia Britannica invested $13.5 million in the set over the past decade. Whether the Tribune Company, the new owner, will continue to maintain the encyclopedia in like fashion remains to be seen.

Editor Good estimates that approximately 18 percent of the encyclopedia's text now receives revision attention annually—that is, nearly 2,000 of the set's more than 10,000 pages have some sort of editorial work done on them each year, ranging from insertion of a new fact or graphic to a completely new or extensively rewritten article. New articles in recent years include "Amino Acids," "Animal Rights," "Artificial Intelligence," "Gangs," "Persian Gulf War," "Unemployment," and biographies of Wayne Gretzky, Magic Johnson, Helmut Kohl, Neil Simon, and Whitney Young, Jr. In addition, many articles have been heavily revised. *Example:* "Communism" has been updated to include substantial material about the collapse of the system in Eastern Europe and the former Soviet Union. And in 1992 the "Fact-Index" was expanded by some 100 pages, with about 2,000 new articles added.

Another way the editors try to keep Compton's current is by publishing Compton's Yearbook, described as "a summary and interpretation of the events of [the year] to supplement Compton's Encyclopedia." Arranged A-to-Z, the yearbook is a quality publication containing much valuable information. But its editorial connection with the encyclopedia itself is tenuous at best, and the yearbook should not be purchased unless the consumer is reasonably sure it will be used. Too often, encyclopedia annuals are bought but rarely consulted; at the end of 20 years consumers often have little to show for their money except a collection of expensive, unused volumes.

Like its chief competitor, the WORLD BOOK ENCYCLOPEDIA, Compton's serves a wide readership, ranging from young people in the upper elementary grades to adults seeking basic knowledge and information. Generally speaking, the encyclopedia is most appropriate for students in grades five through twelve. But unlike WORLD BOOK, Compton's does not employ a controlled vocabulary or check the text against graded word lists to ensure readability at various levels. The editors explain: "By choosing not to limit the vocabulary of its articles to restrictive word lists, Compton's challenges and inspires readers of all ages" (preface). This statement can be accepted on face value as a declaration of noble intentions or viewed as a bit of sophistry; ultimately the user must decide.

Also, as of 1992, the encyclopedia no longer italicizes potentially difficult or unfamiliar terms, a useful feature dropped, according to editor Good, for aesthetic purposes. However, such terms continue to be defined in context. *Examples:* "Abortion" defines such words as *miscarriage* and *sterility* within the context of their use in the article; likewise, terminology associated with the operation itself—*vacuum aspiration*, for instance—is clearly explained in nontechnical language. "Dead Sea Scrolls" defines the word *paleographical* in context as "the study of ancient writing." "Business Cycle" makes such terms as *depression* and *recession* easily comprehensible to ordinary readers. Also, some major articles, such as "Computer" and "Genetics," include glossaries defining basic technical terms.

Articles in *Compton's* are normally written in a clear and informative manner; clarity is obviously valued over stylistic elegance or showiness. Bill Katz sums up the encyclopedia's approach in his *Basic Information Sources* (6th ed., 1992, p. 251): "The writing style is passable, and while far from sparkling, it is clear enough." And Jovian Lang, in *Reference Sources for Small and Medium-Sized Libraries* (5th ed., 1992, p. 31), makes this important point: "The writing is clear and accessible to young readers without being patronizing to older, more advanced users."

The first two paragraphs of the article "Heart" typify the *Compton's* style:

> A muscular, pear-shaped organ slightly larger than a clenched fist, the human heart is the center of the circulatory system. The human heart pumps blood through the body at a rate of more than about 4 quarts (3.8 liters) per minute.
> The heart of an adult weighs between about 8 and 12 ounces (230 and 340 grams) and beats an average of 72 times per minute. During a lifetime of 70 years, it will beat about 2½ billion times and pump a total of 35 million gallons (132 million liters) or more of blood. (See also Blood; Circulatory System.)

Another valuable (though less apparent) feature of *Compton's* is its use of the so-called "pyramid" style of article writing—that is, the most basic facts and simplest concepts are given at the beginning of the article; as the article progresses, the text gradually becomes more detailed and complex. This technique allows people of varying ages and reading levels to use th encyclopedia productively, the idea being that the user will stop reading at the point comprehension ceases or the text becomes too difficult. For example, toward the end "Heart," the article's information, vocabulary, and syntax (or sentence structure) are clearly more advanced than at the beginning:

> Treatment of heart conditions may be possible with prescribed drugs that improve blood flow, reduce blood pressure, prevent blood clots from forming or enlarging, increase the heart's pumping ability, or regulate the heartbeat. Frequently prescribed drugs include anticoagulants that prevent unwanted clotting and vasodilators that widen the blood vessels.

Of all the general encyclopedias on the market today, only *Compton's* and WORLD BOOK successfully employ this subtle but enormously effective stylistic technique.

Compton's has a more complex organization than most encyclopedias. As mentioned earlier, the first 25 volumes comprise some 5,250 substantial alphabetically arranged articles, called "man-text" articles. Most of these articles are the broad-entry variety—that is, they treat specific topics under a broad heading rather than as separate entries. For instance, the planet Uranus is covered in *Compton's* in the article "Planets" rather than having an entry of its own; similarly, dinosaurs are covered in "Animals, Prehistoric." The encyclopedia also contains 28,750 quite brief A-to-Z articles in Volume 26, the aforementioned "Fact-Index."

This means that *Compton's* combines both the broad-entry approach (Volumes 1–25) and the specific-entry approach (Volume 26). It also means that the user must always heed the editors' advice to "Always consult the Fact-Index first" (in "How to Use *Compton's Encyclopedia*" at the beginning of Volume 1). The user who ignores this advice and goes directly to the main A–Z section in Volumes 1–25 may very well miss valuable factual information found in the "Fact Index."

Overall access to information in *Compton's* is quite good, due in part to abundant cross-references in the main articles in Volumes 1–25. For instance, "Abortion" includes cross-references to "Bioethics" and "Birth Control," and "Heart" contains references to "Blood" and "Circulatory System," as seen in the excerpt above. Occasionally, the cross-reference system fails, as in the case of "Roman Catholicism," which lacks a reference to the article "Church and State," where useful information about liberation theology can be found.

But the most important and effective means of accessing material in *Compton's* is through the "Fact Index," which the editors suggest "takes indexing into another dimension of information" (preface). As mentioned, the "Fact-Index" serves as both an index to the set and a source of short articles on specific topics. As an index the "Fact-Index" is excellent, providing easy and detailed access to the encyclopedia's vast contents. Especially helpful is its analytical approach, where index entries for broad topics—"Tree," for example—are broken down into subtopics, such as "bark," "bonsai," "Christmas," "diseases and enemies," "fossils," "fruitgrowing," "lumber," "rubber," and "state trees." The index entry "Abortion" has 14 analytical references, including "adoption," "birth control," and "pregnancy." The entry "Islam" has 94 such references, including "angels and demons," "God," "libraries," and "pilgrimage." This type of close indexing permits the user to retrieve even the smallest or most isolated facts.

However, the index has one important flaw: Articles located in the index itself are usually not indexed or cross-referenced. *Ex-*

ample: A reader seeking information about abstract expressionism will find a brief description of this school of art in the "Fact-Index," along with references to main articles in Volumes 1–25 on painting and six prominent practitioners (De Kooning, Hofmann, Kandinsky, Newman, Pollock, and Rothko). But no reference is given to the "Fact-Index" article on Robert Motherwell, who is described as "one of the founders of abstract expressionism." *Example:* The index entry "Automobile" offers no clue that the "Fact-Index" contains a 23–line article entitled "Electric Automobile"; the user has no way of finding this article except by happenstance.

Users of *Compton's* must remember that the encyclopedia has two alphabets to check, one covering main articles in Volumes 1–25 and the other covering "Fact-Index" articles in Volume 26. This cumbersome organization can be confusing to users, particularly younger ones. It also, as seen above, can cause minor problems in retrieving information from the set. Why, then, do the editors maintain two sets of articles, thus forcing users to consult two different alphabets? The reason, according to editor Good, is strictly economic. When it comes to revision, he says, it is "ten times more economical" to put minor or potentially ephemeral subjects like Robert Motherwell, electric cars, MTV, and Madonna in short articles in one volume (the "Fact-Index") than to have them scattered throughout 25 volumes.

Consumer Note: The "Fact-Index" now appears only in Volume 26, whereas before 1992 portions of the index also appeared at the end of each volume.

The *Compton's* article "Reference Books" advises: "No reference book can be so adequate that it gives all the information every reader may want. As a result . . . reading lists [or bibliographies] are valuable in guiding the reader to that additional information." Regrettably, *Compton's* does not always follow its own advice. In some instances, the encyclopedia does append brief, selected bibliographies to major articles, as in the case of "Women's Rights," which offers a helpful reading list of eight key titles, including Simone de Beauvoir's *The Second Sex* and Betty Friedan's *The Feminine Mystique.* But all too often bibliographies are missing in *Compton's,* even from the most substantial articles. For example, all of these articles lack bibliographies but would be improved by their addition: "Abortion," "Adoption," "Animals, Prehistoric," "Death," "Genetic Engineering," "Genetics," "Great Depression," "Heart," "Hypnosis," "Mental Illness," "Roman Catholicism," and "Suicide." Here is an area the editors need to work on in the future.

Consumer Note: In the past, bibliographies in *Compton's* were customarily divided into materials for younger readers and those for advanced readers. This feature—regrettably—has been dropped in recent editions.

Compton's pioneered the use of illustrations in encyclopedias and was the first to add color in a major way. During the 1970s and early 1980s, however, the set's illustrations grew embarrassingly dated, one reviewer commenting, "Browsing through, one gets a pervasive feeling that many illustrations, though usually pertinent to the article, show hairdos, clothes, and cars that are 15, 20, or more years out of date" (*American Reference Books Annual,* 1982, p. 32).

Fortunately, today this problem has been largely corrected. New color art work, including photographs, charts, graphs, and tables, has replaced most of the outdated illustrations. Approximately 2,000 new four-color photographs along with 1,100 new or revised drawings, again in four-color, were added to the set in 1992 alone; nearly 200 more were added in 1993. Today, about 65 percent of the encyclopedia's 22,500 illustrations and maps are in full color, as opposed to only 35 percent in 1991. In comparison, WORLD BOOK claims 80 percent color and the ACADEMIC AMERICAN ENCYCLOPEDIA 75 percent.

Compton's is an attractive, handsomely turned out encyclopedia. It possesses an inviting two-column page layout and the typefaces are readable and contemporary. The righthand margin of printed text is unjustified—that is, the lines of type are not in alignment. This printing innovation, called "ragged right," was first introduced by the ACADEMIC AMERICAN ENCYCLOPEDIA; it not only appeals to the eye but enhances reading ease by maintaining even spacing between words and reducing the amount of hyphenation. *Compton's* uses high quality coated paper to ensure the best possible reproduction of pictures, graphics, and maps. The washable royal blue binding is stamped with gold lettering and is well sewn to hold up under very heavy use.

As noted, the entire encyclopedia was redesigned and reset in 1992. The *Reference Books Bulletin* review (in *Booklist,* May 15, 1992, p. 1710) sums up the new *Compton's* look this way: "There is no question that *Compton's Encyclopedia* benefits from its new design. The typeface is crisper and cleaner, and new page layouts make illustrations more prominent. Such articles as *Directions,* which used to have an old-fashioned schoolbook appearance, now appear much livelier and more up-to-date, despite the fact that most of the text is unchanged."

SUMMARY

Compton's Encyclopedia is a well-known and highly regarded encyclopedia intended chiefly for older students and adults but also appropriate for younger readers in the upper elementary and junior high school grades. The set's "pyramid" writing style helps make it useful to a wide range of readers. (See page 186 for a review of *Compton's* as an encyclopedia for children and younger students.) The encyclopedia provides strong coverage in the area of science and technology as well as geography, particularly the U.S. states and Canadian provinces. Coverage of the social sciences, traditionally weak, has been much improved in recent years, and controversial subjects are no longer ignored.

As the result of a massive revision program carried out during the 1980s, the set is now quite current, and illustrations—65 percent of which are now in full color—have been enormously improved. Material in *Compton's* is usually easily accessible, although the set's organization (which features articles in two separate alphabets) can be confusing, especially to younger users. Bibliographies, which tend to be too few and far between, need to be expanded.

Thanks to its recent revitalization program, *Compton's* has achieved relative parity with its longtime rival, the WORLD BOOK ENCYCLOPEDIA. It also competes well with the ACADEMIC AMERICAN ENCYCLOPEDIA, which is more suitable for a somewhat older readership, and the NEW BOOK OF KNOWLEDGE, intended specifically for younger readers. Smart consumers will want to test drive all of these excellent encyclopedias before making a final purchase decision. The encyclopedia is also available in several CD-ROM versions, including COMPTON'S MULTIMEDIA ENCYCLOPEDIA and COMPTON'S INTERACTIVE ENCYCLOPEDIA, as well as online via the computerized information service America Online. The bottom line: *Compton's Encyclopedia* has reclaimed its place as one of the best.

OTHER OPINIONS

American Reference Books Annual, 1990, pp. 19–20 (review by Bohdan S. Wynar); *Basic Information Sources* by William A. Katz (vol. 1 of *Introduction to Reference Work*, 6th ed., New York: McGraw-Hill, 1992), pp. 251–53; *Reference Books Bulletin* (in *Booklist*), September 15, 1993, pp. 176–78 (unsigned review); *Reference Sources for Small and Medium-Sized Libraries* (5th ed., Chicago: American Library Association, 1992). p. 31 (review by Jovian P. Lang).

REPORT CARD: COMPTON'S ENCYCLOPEDIA				
TOPIC	COVERAGE	ACCURACY	RECENCY	CLARITY
Circumcision	A	A	A	A
Drew, Charles	B	A	A	A
Galileo	A	A	A	A
Glass, Philip	A	A	A	A
Heart Disease	B	A	A	A
IQ	A	A	A	A
Panda Bears	A	A	A	A
Sexual Harassment	C	A	A	A
Shroud of Turin	A	A	A	A
Uzbekistan	B	A	A	A

A = Excellent; **B** = Above Average; **C** = Average; **D** = Below Average; **F** = Poor; **NA** = Not Applicable

FUNK & WAGNALLS NEW ENCYCLOPEDIA

FACTS

Full Title: *Funk & Wagnalls New Encyclopedia*. **Editorial Director:** Leon L. Bram. **Editor in Chief:** Norma H. Dickey. **Publisher:** Funk & Wagnalls. **Distributor to Schools and Libraries:** World Almanac Education (a Funk & Wagnalls subsidiary). **Former Titles:** *Funk & Wagnalls Standard Encyclopedia of the World's Knowledge* (1912–30); *Funk & Wagnalls New Standard Encyclopedia of Universal Knowledge* (1931–48); *New Funk & Wagnalls Encyclopedia* (1949–53); *Universal Standard Encyclopedia* (1954–58); *Funk & Wagnalls Standard Reference Encyclopedia* (1959–70). **Date Published:** First published as *Funk & Wagnalls New Encyclopedia* in 1971; new printing with revisions published semiannually (twice a year).

Electronic Version: MICROSOFT ENCARTA MULTIMEDIA ENCYCLOPEDIA.

Volumes: 29. **Words:** 9 million. **Pages:** 13,056. **Articles:** 25,000. **Bibliographies:** 1,256. **Illustrations and Maps:** 9,500. **Cross-references:** 88,300. **Index Entries:** 130,000. **Editorial Staff, Advisers, and Contributors:** 1,100. **Trim Size:** 6¼ × 9 in.

Price and Sales Information: $163.81 retail; $189.95 to schools and libraries. *Funk & Wagnalls New Encyclopedia* is sold to individual consumers through supermarkets in the U.S. and Canada. According to the publisher, Funk & Wagnalls, the encyclopedia is unavailable except in those supermarkets currently selling it on a volume-by-volume basis. Consumers who have incomplete sets of the encyclopedia can purchase missing volumes by calling toll-free 1-800-888-8818. Other questions concerning the encyclopedia should be addressed to Funk & Wagnalls, One International Blvd., Suite 444, Mahwah, NJ 07495–0017. The encyclopedia is currently distributed to institutions (schools, libraries, etc.) by World Almanac Education, a subsidiary of Funk & Wagnalls. For additional information or to place an order, call toll-free 1-800-321-1147 or write World Almanac Education, 1277 West 9th Street, Cleveland, OH 44113.

EVALUATION

Funk & Wagnalls is an old and respected name in North American book publishing dating back to the nineteenth century when two enterprising Lutheran ministers, Isaac K. Funk and Adam Willis Wagnalls, established the firm in New York City in 1877. During the early years, Funk & Wagnalls concentrated on books and periodicals for the clergy, but in 1893 the company entered the general reference field with an unabridged dictionary called the *Standard Dictionary of the English Language* (later retitled *Funk & Wagnalls New Standard Dictionary of the English Language*), a hefty tome that spawned a whole family of Funk & Wagnalls dictionaries. Two decades later, in 1912, the first encyclopedia to bear the Funk & Wagnalls name appeared. Entitled *Funk & Wagnalls Standard Encyclopedia of the World's Knowledge*, it consisted of 25 volumes and derived from the *Columbian Cyclopaedia*, a 39–volume set that Funk & Wagnalls had published around the turn of the century.

Funk & Wagnalls Standard Encyclopedia of World's Knowledge continued until 1930, when it was thoroughly revamped and reissued as *Funk & Wagnalls New Standard Encyclopedia of Universal Knowledge* (1931–48), also in 25 volumes. Subsequent major revisions were the *New Funk & Wagnalls Encyclopedia* (1949–53; 36 volumes), the *Universal Standard Encyclopedia* (1954–58; 25 volumes), and *Funk & Wagnalls Standard Reference Encyclopedia* (1959–70; 25 volumes). In 1971, the set underwent its most recent top-to-bottom overhaul, at which time it expanded to 27 volumes and became *Funk & Wagnalls New Encyclopedia*, the sixth edition of the encyclopedia since 1912. In the early 1980s the set added two volumes to reach its present size of 29 volumes.

Since the early 1950s, the encyclopedia has been sold almost entirely on the book-a-week plan through national supermarket chains in the U.S. and Canada, a high-volume, low-markup marketing strategy that has been enormously successful for Funk & Wagnalls. The company estimates that the encyclopedia becomes available to roughly 95 percent of all U.S. households at least once every three years and that, based on unit sales, Funk & Wagnalls is the second largest publisher of general encyclopedias in North America behind World Book, Inc.

Still, the supermarket connection has not done the encyclopedia's reputation much good. There is a strong tendency among some consumers and critics of reference materials to dismiss any publication associated with the supermarket trade as automatically inferior. In the case of *Funk & Wagnalls New Encyclopedia*, however, this prejudice is unwarranted. In recent years, the encyclopedia has earned the approval (if not the affection) of many knowledgeable librarians, teachers, parents, and reviewers as a reputable reference work that competes well in its class, especially when price is a key consideration. Further evidence of the encyclopedia's growing acceptance as a work of stature is seen in the Microsoft Corporation's decision to base its new CD-ROM encyclopedia, MICROSOFT ENCARTA MULTIMEDIA ENCYCLOPEDIA, on *Funk & Wagnalls New Encyclopedia*.

As suggested in the foregoing, *Funk & Wagnalls New Encyclopedia* is an authoritative work. It currently boasts an editorial staff of 93 led by Leon Bram, the set's editorial director. Bram, a senior figure among North American encyclopedists, knows the business inside and out. Likewise, chief editor Norma Dickey brings strong qualifications to the work. The in-house staff is supported by approximately 900 consultants and contributors, most of whom are academics well established in their fields, including such distinguished scholars as Martin Blumenson, John Tyler Bonner, Leon Edel, Rhodes Fairbridge, Stephen Jay Gould, Sanford Kadish, Milton Konvitz, Robert Lekachman, Karl Potter, Benjamin Quarles, John Tebbel, and Lionel Trilling. Consultants and contributors are listed at the end of Volume 28, the latter alphabetically by their initials.

Entries in *Funk & Wagnalls* are, for the most part, quite brief, averaging about 350 words (or half a page) in length, but the set also includes a goodly number of longer survey articles, such as "Ballet," "Economics," "English Literature," "Heart," "Islam," "Islamic Art and Architecture," "Nuclear Energy," "Plant," "Police," "Prints and Printmaking," "Reproductive System," "Russian Revolution," "Ships and Shipbuilding," and "World War II." These extended articles are normally written by an outside authority and signed with the contributor's initials; on the other hand, most of the short articles in the set are staff written and unsigned.

The encyclopedia's coverage is reasonably well balanced, although biographical and geographical topics predominate, accounting for roughly 40 percent of all articles. Major countries and the U.S. states and Canadian provinces receive especially strong coverage. For example, the article "Germany" comprises 24 pages, "Nicaragua" 6 pages, "Florida" 16 pages, and "Manitoba" 10 pages. All such articles include maps (with place-name indexes) and those covering the states and provinces have a double-page summary of basic facts for quick reference. Also well covered are scientific and technical subjects, which account for approximately a quarter of the articles. Coverage of the social and behavioral sciences has recently been enhanced by the addition of two heavily illustrated and complementary features found at the beginning of Volume 1. The first, a 15-page essay entitled "The Course of Human Society," explores the concept of kinship through the ages; the second, "The TimeScope of Human Society," is a 34-page chronology of human history from 200,000 B.C. to the present.

Conversely, the arts and humanities receive short shrift. Most coverage is limited to sweeping survey articles devoted to historical developments at the national or regional level, exemplified by such articles as "German Language," "German Literature," "Latin American Art and Architecture," "Latin American Literature," and "Latin American Music." Unfortunately, newly established authors, artists, and performers tend to be ignored or merely mentioned in an omnibus paragraph. For instance, the encyclopedia fails to furnish basic information about such prominent contemporary writers as Anne Sexton, Margaret Drabble, Maya Angelou, James Wright, Joyce Carol Oates, Nadine Gordimer, Derek Walcott, and Sam Shepard, to name but a few. Coverage of contemporary trends and developments in religion is also disappointing. *Examples:* Smaller, unorthodox but highly visible groups such as Scientology and Hare Krishna are not covered in *Funk & Wagnalls*; L. Ron Hubbard, popular author and founder of Scientology, is ignored; the Shroud of Turin is limited to one unsatisfactory sentence in the article "Turin."

Information in *Funk & Wagnalls* is normally reliable and presented in an impartial manner. Differing points of view on controversial or sensitive subjects are usually identified and discussed. The article "Abortion,"

for instance, includes a section entitled "Resistance and Controversy" that objectively summarizes the basic position of both sides. Likewise, the article "Circumcision" includes information on the current debate over the effectiveness of the procedure:

> The medical case for circumcision is unproved and controversial. Physicians in the 19th century advised the operation for many ailments, including hysteria, venereal disease, hypersexuality, and even hiccups. Modern proponents suggest that diseases result from the buildup of smegma, a substance secreted under the foreskin. Also cited is evidence that circumcised populations (especially Jews) display low rates of penile and cervical cancer. Critics reject the validity of these claims, arguing that such disorders are more likely caused by poor hygiene and by contact with multiple sex partners.

Funk & Wagnalls is a well maintained encyclopedia—meaning that the set is conscientiously revised on a regular basis. In their preface (entitled "Information and the Future") in Volume 1, the editors enunciate their commitment to continuous revision: "Funk & Wagnalls editorial staff, together with its expert consultants and contributors, constantly reviews the currents of change. Updates, additions, and revisions are made at every printing of the encyclopedia. Not only are specific facts within articles, or entire articles, subject to change, but so are major systems." These are not empty words. The set is printed and substantially revised twice each year in the spring and fall. Over the past four years, the editors report that roughly 11,000 of the set's 25,000 articles have undergone some sort of change, a revision rate in excess of 10 percent a year. In addition, nearly 250 new articles and 850 four-color illustrations have been added to the set during that time.

Inevitably, though, there are instances where the encyclopedia is not as up-to-date as it might be. *Examples:* The article "Abortion" fails to cite two recent U.S. Supreme Court cases that have had an important impact on the abortion issue, namely *Rust v. Sullivan* (1991) and *Planned Parenthood of Eastern Pennsylvania v. Casey* (1992). "Dead Sea Scrolls" offers nothing concerning the hot-button issue of access to these ancient documents, nor is there mention of recent research establishing a possible connection between the scrolls and Jesus's putative role as the Messiah. "Heart," current only as of the mid-1980s, fails to cover recent developments in transplantation and artificial hearts. "Turin" notes that "In the cathedral's Chapel of the Holy Shroud is an urn containing a shroud in which, according to tradition, Christ was wrapped for burial," but the article neglects to mention that carbon-14 dating tests conducted several years ago show the shroud to be a fake, having originated around the fourteenth century.

Like most multivolume general encyclopedias on the market today, *Funk & Wagnalls* is supplemented by an annual publication—*Funk & Wagnalls New Encyclopedia Yearbook*—intended to help keep the set reasonably up-to-date. This yearbook contains useful information, but it has no real editorial connection with the encyclopedia and should not be purchased unless the consumer is absolutely convinced it will be used. Too often, encyclopedia annuals are bought but rarely consulted; at the end of 20 years consumers often have little to show for their investment except a collection of expensive dust-catchers. Also available is *Funk & Wagnalls Science Yearbook*.

Funk & Wagnalls is designed primarily for older students and adults seeking nontechnical information or understandable summaries of unfamiliar or complex topics. It is usually written in clear, albeit unexciting prose. In most instances, the encyclopedia will be comprehensible to users reading at the seventh- or eighth-grade level, although scientific articles tend to be written at a somewhat higher level. The first paragraph of the article "Heart" illustrates the point:

HEART, in anatomy, the hollow muscular organ that receives blood from the veins and propels it into and through the arteries. The heart of a human is about the size of a closed fist. It is situated behind the lower part of the breastbone, extending more to the left of the midline than to the right. It is roughly conical in shape, with the base directed upward and to the right and slightly backward; the apex touches the chest wall between the fifth and sixth ribs. The heart is held in place principally by its attachment to the great arteries and veins, and by its confinement in the pericardium, a double-walled sac with one layer enveloping the heart and the other attached to the breastbone, the diaphragm, and the membranes of the thorax.

Note that the encyclopedia does not employ the standard readability techniques such as controlled vocabulary, writing to grade level, and pyramid writing that allow the WORLD BOOK ENCYCLOPEDIA and, to a lesser extent, COMPTON'S ENCYCLOPEDIA to serve a very broad readership. Rarely, too, does *Funk & Wagnalls* define potentially difficult or unfamiliar terms in context. In the excerpt above, for instance, only the word *pericardium* is explained within the text.

The editors of *Funk & Wagnalls* recognize the need to provide easy, effective access to the set's contents: "The various information-finding devices are essential supporting networks to the articles. The index and internal cross-references ensure that all the information in the articles is accessible to the reader and that information need not be repeated in several places, occupying valuable space" (preface). As might be expected, the encyclopedia includes ample *See* and *See also* references within and at the end of articles. All told, the set contains more than 88,000 cross-references. In a sign of the times, the editors apparently are in the process of systematically phasing out use of the abbreviation *q.v.* (Latin for *which see*) to indicate a cross-reference, a once common construction that today probably confuses more readers than it helps.

But the set's principal finding device is a 480-page analytical index of approximately 130,000 entries. Found in the final volume, the index is comprehensive, intelligently constructed, and easy to use. Prepared under the direction of Barbara Preschel, who also supervised the making of the original index for the ACADEMIC AMERICAN ENCYCLOPEDIA, *Funk & Wagnalls'* index furnishes about one entry for every 70 words of encyclopedic text, or a quite favorable ratio of index entries to text words of 1:70. Among *Funk & Wagnalls'* major competitors, only the ACADEMIC AMERICAN ENCYCLOPEDIA (1:45) has a better ratio; the WORLD BOOK ENCYCLOPEDIA (1:70) is on par with *Funk & Wagnalls*. The only negative criticism to be made of the encyclopedia's index is that it fails to include references to illustrations in the text. For instance, the index entry under "Unicorn" leads the reader to page 159 of Volume 26 where there is a short article—sans illustration—describing the unicorn. What the index does not reveal is that a full-page color illustration of a unicorn is included with the article "Tapestry" in Volume 25.

Another distinct strength of the encyclopedia is its extensive and recently revised bibliography, or listing of titles recommended for further reading. Located in Volume 28 following the encyclopedia's "Z" section, the bibliography consists of 260 pages and 1,200 lists containing nearly 9,600 individual titles grouped under hundreds of subjects. Each list is numbered and covers a specific topic. For instance, number 85 is devoted to the Reformation and Counter Reformation and lists 11 titles; number 86 covers the Inquisition and lists four titles. Compiled by Richard S. Halsey (School of Information Science and Policy, State University of New York at Albany) and a dozen other librarians, the bibliography is admirably current and obviously selected with care. All titles are briefly annotated, a valuable feature. Another commendable feature is that articles in the encyclopedia are related to the bibliography by cross-references. The article "Inquisition" in Volume 14, for example,

concludes with this reference: *"For further information on this topic, see the Bibliography in volume 28, section 86."*

Regrettably, the encyclopedia's illustrations are not as impressive as its index or bibliography. Recent revisions have steadily improved the set's lackluster illustrations with the addition of numerous new color photographs and drawings, chiefly in the first six volumes. Still, *Funk & Wagnalls* has a long way to go before its illustrations can honestly be called anything but mediocre. As a recent review in *Reference Books Bulletin* (in *Booklist*, September 15, 1993, p. 180) notes, "The set still has many dark black-and-white pictures." Moreover, some of these pictures lack resolution and some are dated. The addition of color is welcome, but in some instances the color photos are poorly reproduced, having a muddy quality about them. Consumers (and reviewers) must bear in mind, however, that high quality color illustrations cost big dollars to create or license and to reproduce; the reality is that one cannot expect fine illustrations in a 29-volume encyclopedia that sells for under $200.

Aside from the addition of more color, the set's physical format has not changed greatly in recent years. The double-column page layout tends to be unappealing and sometimes confusing, due in part to the lack of spacing between the end of one article and the beginning of another. A decade ago in a review of *Funk & Wagnalls* in *Wilson Library Bulletin* (October 1983, p. 146), James Rettig described the problem this way: "Despite an appealing typeface, one must fault the graphic design on one point. The lack of a line or two of white space between articles makes them appear to run into one another and renders subheadings almost indistinguishable from main headings." *Funk & Wagnalls'* utilitarian binding is adequate, though it cannot match that of any of the set's competitors.

REPORT CARD: FUNK & WAGNALLS NEW ENCYCLOPEDIA

	COVERAGE	ACCURACY	RECENCY	CLARITY
Circumcision	A	A	A	A
Drew, Charles	F*	NA	NA	NA
Galileo	B	B	B	A
Glass, Philip	B	A	A	A
Heart Disease	B	B	B	B
IQ	B	A	A	A
Panda Bears	B	A	A	B
Sexual Harassment	F*	NA	NA	NA
Shroud of Turin	D	B	D	A
Uzbekistan	B	A	A	A

A = Excellent; **B** = Above Average; **C** = Average; **D** = Below Average; **F** = Poor; **NA** = Not Applicable
*No Article

SUMMARY

Funk & Wagnalls New Encyclopedia is an inexpensive, well-maintained family encyclopedia that has risen above the "supermarket" stigma. Specifically, the encyclopedia provides authoritative, reasonably well balanced coverage of the world's basic knowledge and information. In addition, the set's contents are usually up-to-date, its index and cross-references permit easy and effective retrieval of specific facts and topics, and its bibliography furnishes users with carefully chosen lists of books for further study. On the negative side, coverage of the arts and humanities leaves something to be desired, the illustrations are generally undistinguished despite recent efforts to upgrade them, and the set is physically unappealing. The bottom line: Herb Denenberg, a consumer advocate, has called *Funk & Wagnalls New Encyclopedia* "dollar for dollar the best encyclopedia" on the North American market. He's right.

OTHER OPINIONS

Basic Information Sources by William A. Katz (vol. 1 of *Introduction to Reference Work*, 6th ed., New York: McGraw-Hill, 1992), pp. 245–46; *Reference Books Bulletin* (in *Booklist*), September 15, 1993, p. 180 (unsigned review).

GLOBAL INTERNATIONAL ENCYCLOPEDIA

FACTS

Full Title: *Global International Encyclopedia.* **Editorial Director:** Lawrence T. Lorimer. **Editor in Chief:** K. Anne Ranson. **Publisher:** Grolier Inc. **Date Published:** First published as the *Global International Encyclopedia* in 1991; new printing with revisions published annually.

Also published as the ACADEMIC AMERICAN ENCYCLOPEDIA.

Volumes: 21. **Words:** 9.1 million. **Pages:** 9,864. **Articles:** 28,960. **Bibliographies:** 13,000. **Illustrations and Maps:** 18,000. **Cross-references:** 65,000. **Index Entries:** 201,000. **Editorial Staff, Advisers, and Contributors:** 2,600. **Trim Size:** 8 × 10 in.

Price and Sales Information: $1,150.00 publisher's suggested retail price. The *Global International Encyclopedia*—a retitled edition of the ACADEMIC AMERICAN ENCYCLOPEDIA—is sold in-home to individual consumers by independent distributors. Distributors set their own prices, which are normally lower than the publisher's suggested retail price of $1,150.00. In most instances, distributors of the *Global International Encyclopedia* will attempt to sell the prospective purchaser a package deal consisting of the encyclopedia and various other reference materials at $1,000.00 or more. For further information about the encyclopedia or to obtain the name of a local distributor, consumers should call 1-203-796-2602 (not a toll-free number) or write Grolier Inc., Sherman Turnpike, Danbury, CT 06816.

CONSUMER NOTE

Aside from title and binding, the 21-volume *Global International Encyclopedia* is exactly the same work as the 21-volume ACADEMIC AMERICAN ENCYCLOPEDIA, a major Grolier product. Consumers should note that the *Global International* has a cheaper binding than the ACADEMIC AMERICAN, which is designed to withstand heavy use in the library. Prospective purchasers should also be aware that the *Global International* might not be the most recent printing of the encyclopedia. The wise consumer will inquire about the date of the set before committing to purchase.

For a detailed evaluation of the contents of the *Global International Encyclopedia*, see the ACADEMIC AMERICAN ENCYCLOPEDIA (page 53).

GROLIER ACADEMIC ENCYCLOPEDIA

FACTS

Full Title: *Grolier Academic Encyclopedia.* **Editorial Director:** Lawrence T. Lorimer. **Editor in Chief:** K. Anne Ranson. **Publisher:** Grolier Inc. **Date Published:** First published as the *Grolier Academic Encyclopedia* in 1983; new printing with revisions published annually.

Also published as the ACADEMIC AMERICAN ENCYCLOPEDIA.

Volumes: 21. **Words:** 9.1 million. **Pages:** 9,864. **Articles:** 28,960. **Bibliographies:** 13,000. **Illustrations and Maps:** 18,000. **Cross-references:** 65,000. **Index Entries:** 201,000. **Editorial Staff, Advisers, and Contributors:** 2,600. **Trim Size:** 8 × 10 in.

Price and Sales Information: $1,150.00 publisher's suggested retail price. The *Grolier Academic Encyclopedia*—a retitled edition of the ACADEMIC AMERICAN ENCYCLOPEDIA—is sold in North America in-home to individual consumers by independent distributors. In most instances, distributors of the *Grolier Academic Encyclopedia* attempt to sell the prospective purchaser a package deal consisting of the encyclopedia and various other reference materials at $1,000.00 or more. The set is also sold internationally in countries where "American" in the title might hinder sales. For further information about the encyclopedia or to obtain the name of a local distributor, consumers should call 1-203-796-2602 (not a toll-free number) or write Grolier Inc., Sherman Turnpike, Danbury, CT 06816.

CONSUMER NOTE

Aside from title and binding, the 21-volume *Grolier Academic Encyclopedia* is exactly the same work as the 21-volume ACADEMIC AMERICAN ENCYCLOPEDIA, a major Grolier product. A new printing is issued every year. Consumers should note that the *Grolier Academic* has a cheaper binding than the ACADEMIC AMERICAN, which is designed to withstand heavy use in the library.

For more on the contents of the *Grolier Academic Encyclopedia*, see the ACADEMIC AMERICAN ENCYCLOPEDIA (page 53).

GROLIER ENCYCLOPEDIA OF KNOWLEDGE

FACTS

Full Title: *Grolier Encyclopedia of Knowledge*. **Editorial Director:** Lawrence T. Lorimer. **Editor in Chief:** Jeffrey H. Hacker. **Publisher:** Grolier Inc. **Date Published:** 1991; new printing with revisions anticipated in 1994.

Unabridged Version: ACADEMIC AMERICAN ENCYCLOPEDIA.

Volumes: 20. **Words:** 6.5 million. **Pages:** 8,320. **Articles:** 22,000. **Bibliographies:** None. **Illustrations and Maps:** 13,000. **Cross-references:** 40,000. **Index Entries:** 90,000. **Editorial Staff, Advisers, and Contributors:** 2,375. **Trim Size:** 7½ × 9¼ in.

Price and Sales Information: $120.00 (approximate price). The *Grolier Encyclopedia of Knowledge* is sold only in selected supermarkets in North America on a volume-by-volume basis over a period of time. Currently, Volume 1 sells for $0.99, with the remaining 19 volumes priced at $4.99 or $5.99 each. Consumers with questions about the encyclopedia should call the publisher at 1-203-796-2602 (not a toll-free number) or write Grolier Inc., Sherman Turnpike, Danbury, CT 06816.

EVALUATION

Issued in 1991, the 20-volume *Grolier Encyclopedia of Knowledge* is an abridged version of the 21-volume ACADEMIC AMERICAN ENCYCLOPEDIA, an outstanding general encyclopedia for older students and adults that was first published in 1980 and has been revised each year since that time. The abridgment, which is intended exclusively for the supermarket trade, contains about 75 percent of the printed text and 80 percent of the illustrative matter found in the parent encyclopedia. Specifically, the *Grolier Encyclopedia of Knowledge* has 6.5 million words, 8,320 pages, 22,000 articles, and 13,000 illustrations and maps compared with the ACADEMIC AMERICAN's 9.1 million words, 9,864 pages,

28,960 articles, and 18,000 illustrations and maps. In addition, the abridgment has fewer cross-references and a smaller index and physical size than the ACADEMIC AMERICAN.

Remarkably, the *Grolier Encyclopedia of Knowledge* was produced in only 10 months, thanks in large part to the wizardry of contemporary desktop publishing technology. First, the editors reviewed all articles in the ACADEMIC AMERICAN, deciding which ones would be retained without change and which would be condensed or omitted altogether. After completion of this editorial work, the abridged encyclopedic text was converted to electronic files and sent to an outside desktop publishing house, where the design and illustration process was completed very quickly at the rate of about a volume a week over a period of five months. According to a Grolier source, publication of the encyclopedia represents "the biggest desktop publishing project ever, anywhere."

The *Grolier Encyclopedia of Knowledge* retains most of the ACADEMIC AMERICAN's best features. These include broad and carefully balanced coverage, accurate and impartial presentation of material, sound organization and effective access to specific topics and facts, first-rate illustrations, impeccable authority (although articles in the abridgment are not signed), and an especially appealing physical design. Moreover, much of the text cut from the ACADEMIC AMERICAN to make the *Grolier Encyclopedia of Knowledge*— roughly 2.6 million words and 5,000 illustrations—will not be sorely missed by many readers.

Short articles about rather minor people and subjects account for the lion's share of the excised material. *Examples:* All of the following articles found in the ACADEMIC AMERICAN are completely omitted from the *Grolier Encyclopedia of Knowledge*: "Heart of Atlanta Motel, Inc. v. United States" (a 1964 U.S. Supreme Court civil rights case), "Heartbreak House" (a play by George Bernard Shaw), "Hebbel, Christian Friedrich" (a nineteenth-century German writer), "Heda, Willem Claesz" (a seventeenth-century Dutch painter), "Hedayat, Sadeq" (a twentieth-century Iranian writer), "Hedda Gabler" (a play by Henrik Ibsen), "Hedge Sparrow" (a bird), "Heemskerck, Maarten Van" (a sixteenth-century Dutch painter), "Heiberg, Johan Ludvig" (a nineteenth-century Dutch writer), "Heidelberg, University of," "Heidenstam, Verner Von" (a twentieth-century Swedish writer), "Heijermans, Herman" (a twentieth-century Dutch dramatist), "Heilbron, Sir Ian Morris" (a contemporary British chemist), "Heimdall" (a figure in Norse mythology), "Heimskringla" (a Norwegian medieval saga), and "Heine-Geldern, Robert" (a twentieth-century Austro-American archaeologist).

Inevitably, however, some quite useful information found in the ACADEMIC AMERICAN has been dropped from certain articles in the *Grolier Encyclopedia of Knowledge*. The ACADEMIC AMERICAN's article on Galileo, for instance, concludes with a ten-line paragraph summarizing the famous Renaissance scientist's lasting influence; regrettably, this material is not included in the abridgment. In similar fashion, the article "Panda" omits information about recent research concerning the genetic make up and classification of the giant panda, a topic of considerable interest to students of the endangered animal. As a result of these and similar deletions, articles in the *Grolier Encyclopedia of Knowledge* are often overly terse or superficial; the encyclopedia usually provides the requisite facts but too often lacks sufficient depth for readers seeking a thorough summary of a subject. Indeed, in terms of number of words, the *Grolier Encyclopedia of Knowledge* is practically the same size as the single-volume COLUMBIA ENCYCLOPEDIA.

Although published in 1991, the *Grolier Encyclopedia of Knowledge* remains reasonably current, except in those areas subject to frequent or volatile change, such as political events. For instance, the encyclopedia has an article on Sir Henry Clinton, a British general in the American Revolution, but none on Bill Clinton, who was elected president of the U.S. in 1992. Similarly, the set describes Russia, Ukraine, Uzbekistan, etc. as republics of the Soviet Union instead of the independent countries they are today. In other words, the *Grolier Encyclopedia of Knowledge* lacks the high degree of up-to-dateness associated with the ACADEMIC AMERICAN, which is continuously revised on an annual basis. For instance, the 1993 printing of the ACADEMIC AMERICAN added an article on sexual harassment; the 1991 abridgment merely mentions the topic in passing. The editors of the *Grolier Encyclopedia of Knowledge* have indicated they intend to update the set every two or three years, but thus far no new printing has appeared.

Like the ACADEMIC AMERICAN, the *Grolier Encyclopedia of Knowledge* is usually written in a clear manner, but the text tends to be dry and stilted—a bit too formal or erudite for easy reading. The first paragraph of the article "Heart" furnishes a representative sample of the encyclopedia's style:

> The human heart is a specialized, four-chambered muscle that maintains BLOOD flow in the CIRCULATORY SYSTEM. Located in the thorax, it lies left of the body's midline, above and in contact with the diaphragm. It is situated immediately behind the breastbone, or sternum, and between the lungs, with its apex tilted to the left. At rest, the heart pumps about 59 cc (2 oz) of blood per beat and 5 l (5 qt) per minute, compared to 120–220 cc (4–7.3 oz) per beat and 20–30 l (21–32 qt) per minute during exercise. The adult human heart is about the size of a fist and weighs about 250–350 gm (9 oz).

Older students and adults will normally have no serious problems understanding the *Grolier Encyclopedia of Knowledge*, but most students at the elementary and even junior high school levels will find some of the text beyond their comprehension, despite the editors' claim that the set is intended "for every

member of the family—students from the elementary level through college, and the inquisitive adult" (preface). Unlike COMPTON'S ENCYCLOPEDIA and the WORLD BOOK ENCYCLOPEDIA, the ACADEMIC AMERICAN and its abridgment employ none of the techniques—a controlled vocabulary, writing to grade level, pyramid writing, etc.—that help extend or stretch an encyclopedia's readability from the elementary school to adult level.

Locating specific facts and topics in the encyclopedia normally poses few if any problems. The 90,000–entry index is the principal finding device; it comprises more than half of Volume 20. In addition, numerous cross-references help guide the user to related articles.

Approximately 40 percent of all articles in the ACADEMIC AMERICAN include bibliographies, or lists of selected materials for further study. The editors explain: "The goal is to furnish a well-chosen list of standard and recently published works to which readers may turn for further information or additional development of particular points of view" (preface). Unfortunately, in order to save space, the *Grolier Encyclopedia of Knowledge* completely omits these helpful bibliographies.

As noted, the *Grolier Encyclopedia of Knowledge* contains roughly 80 percent of the illustrative matter—photographs, drawings, diagrams, cutaways, art reproductions, graphs, maps, etc.—found in the ACADEMIC AMERICAN. For example, the article "Heart" in the *Grolier Encyclopedia of Knowledge* includes the same illustrations found in the ACADEMIC AMERICAN's "Heart" article except for a drawing of the left ventricle, a cutaway showing cardiac muscle tissue, and a series of diagrams with graphs explaining the interrelationship of the heart, blood pressure, and brain activity. Almost without exception, the illustrations in the abridgment are informative as well as aesthetically pleasing. Certainly, they are well above the quality of illustrations typically found in supermarket encyclopedias, including FUNK & WAGNALLS NEW ENCYCLOPEDIA, the *Grolier Encyclopedia of Knowledge*'s chief competitor. The same can be said of the encyclopedia's overall physical design, which is both practical and appealing to the eye.

SUMMARY

The *Grolier Encyclopedia of Knowledge* is an abridged version of the ACADEMIC AMERICAN ENCYCLOPEDIA aimed directly at the supermarket trade. As such, it competes head-to-head with the larger FUNK & WAGNALLS NEW ENCYCLOPEDIA. The *Grolier Encyclopedia of Knowledge* retains many of the best features of the ACADEMIC AMERICAN, such as impeccable authority, broad and well-balanced coverage, accurate and objective treatment, first-rate illustrations, and an appealing physi-cal design. On the other hand, it suffers from the same weaknesses found in the ACADEMIC AMERICAN, including insufficient depth of coverage and a rather dry, stilted writing style. Furthermore, the *Grolier Encyclopedia of Knowledge* is not revised annually and has dropped the useful bibliographies appended to many articles in the parent set. The bottom line: A very good supermarket encyclopedia.

OTHER OPINIONS

None.

REPORT CARD: GROLIER ENCYCLOPEDIA OF KNOWLEDGE

TOPIC	COVERAGE	ACCURACY	RECENCY	CLARITY
Circumcision	B	A	A	A
Drew, Charles	F*	NA	NA	NA
Galileo	C	A	C	A
Glass, Philip	A	A	A	A
Heart Disease	B	A	A	B
IQ	B	A	A	A
Panda Bears	B	A	A	A
Sexual Harassment	F*	NA	NA	NA
Shroud of Turin	A	A	A	A
Uzbekistan	C	C	D	A

A = Excellent; **B** = Above Average; **C** = Average; **D** = Below Average; **F** = Poor; **NA** = Not Applicable
*No Article

GROLIER INTERNATIONAL ENCYCLOPEDIA

FACTS

Full Title: *Grolier International Encyclopedia.*
Editorial Director: Lawrence T. Lorimer.
Editor in Chief: K. Anne Ranson. **Publisher:** Grolier Inc. **Date Published:** First published as the *Grolier International Encyclopedia* in 1991; new printing with revisions published annually.

Also published as the ACADEMIC AMERICAN ENCYCLOPEDIA.

Volumes: 20. **Words:** 9.1 million. **Pages:** 9,864. **Articles:** 28,960. **Bibliographies:** 13,000. **Illustrations and Maps:** 18,000. **Cross-references:** 65,000. **Index Entries:** 201,000. **Editorial Staff, Advisers, and Contributors:** 2,600. **Trim Size:** 8 × 10 in.

Price and Sales Information: $199.00 in discount stores; $299.00–350.00 in bookstores. The *Grolier International Encyclopedia*—a retitled edition of the ACADEMIC AMERICAN ENCYCLOPEDIA—is sold chiefly in discount warehouse stores such as Sam's Club, Price Club, PACE, and Costco and large North American bookstore chains such as B. Dalton and Bookstop. Barnes & Noble, one of the largest bookstore chains, offers its own edition under the title BARNES & NOBLE NEW AMERICAN ENCYCLOPEDIA. For further information about the encyclopedia or to obtain the name of a local distributor, consumers should call 1-203-796-2602 (not a toll-free number) or write Grolier Inc., Sherman Turnpike, Danbury, CT 06816.

CONSUMER NOTE

The 20-volume *Grolier International Encyclopedia* has exactly the same contents as the 21-volume ACADEMIC AMERICAN ENCYCLOPEDIA, a major Grolier product. The only difference between the two sets, apart from their distinct titles and bindings, is that the ACADEMIC AMERICAN has an extra volume (Volume 21), which comprises the set's cumulative, or master, index. *Grolier International*, on the other hand, lacks a cumulative index; rather, its index appears in sections (printed on colored paper) at the end of each of the 20 volumes. For example, Volume 3 covers all articles beginning with the letter "B," followed by all index entries beginning with "B." In addition, *Grolier International* has a cheaper binding than the ACADEMIC AMERICAN, which is designed to withstand heavy use in the library.

Prospective consumers should also be aware that the *Grolier International* might not be the most recent printing of the encyclopedia. The wise consumer will inquire about the date of the set before committing to purchase.

For a detailed evaluation of the contents of the *Grolier International Encyclopedia*, see the ACADEMIC AMERICAN ENCYCLOPEDIA (page 53).

LEXICON UNIVERSAL ENCYCLOPEDIA

FACTS

Full Title: *Lexicon Universal Encyclopedia.* **Editorial Director:** Lawrence T. Lorimer. **Editor in Chief:** K. Anne Ranson. **Publisher:** Grolier Inc. **Distributor:** Lexicon Publications, Inc. **Date Published:** First published as the *Lexicon Universal Encyclopedia* in 1982; new printing with revisions published annually.

Also published as the ACADEMIC AMERICAN ENCYCLOPEDIA.

Volumes: 21. **Words:** 9.1 million. **Pages:** 9,864. **Articles:** 28,960. **Bibliographies:** 13,000. **Illustrations and Maps:** 18,000. **Cross-references:** 65,000. **Index Entries:** 201,000. **Editorial Staff, Advisers, and Contributors:** 2,600. **Trim Size:** 8 × 10 in.

Price and Sales Information: $1,150.00 publisher's suggested retail price.

The *Lexicon Universal Encyclopedia*—a re-titled edition of the ACADEMIC AMERICAN ENCYCLOPEDIA—is sold in-home to individual consumers by independent distributors. Distributors set their own prices, which are normally lower than the publisher's suggested retail price of $1,150.00. In most instances, distributors of the *Lexicon Universal* will attempt to sell the prospective purchaser a package deal consisting of the encyclopedia and various other reference materials at $1,000.00 or more. For further information about the encyclopedia or to obtain the name of a local distributor, consumers should call 1-203-796-2602 (not a toll-free number) or write Grolier Inc., Sherman Turnpike, Danbury, CT 06816.

CONSUMER NOTE

Aside from title and binding, the 21-volume *Lexicon Universal Encyclopedia* is exactly the same work as the 21-volume ACADEMIC AMERICAN ENCYCLOPEDIA, a major Grolier product. Consumers should note that the *Lexicon Universal* has a cheaper binding than the ACADEMIC AMERICAN, which is designed to withstand heavy use in the library. Prospective purchasers should also be aware that the

Lexicon Universal might not be the most recent printing of the encyclopedia. The wise consumer will inquire about the date of the set before committing to purchase.

For a detailed evaluation of the contents of the *Lexicon Universal Encyclopedia*, see the ACADEMIC AMERICAN ENCYCLOPEDIA (page 53).

MACMILLAN FAMILY ENCYCLOPEDIA

FACTS

Full Title: *The Macmillan Family Encyclopedia.* **Editorial Director:** Lawrence T. Lorimer. **Editor in Chief:** K. Anne Ranson. **Publisher:** Grolier Inc. **Date Published:** First published as the *Macmillan Family Encyclopedia* in 1980; new printing with revisions published annually.

Also published as the ACADEMIC AMERICAN ENCYCLOPEDIA.

Volumes: 20. **Words:** 9.1 million. **Pages:** 9,864. **Articles:** 28,960. **Bibliographies:** 13,000. **Illustrations and Maps:** 18,000. **Cross-references:** 65,000. **Index Entries:** 201,000. **Editorial Staff, Advisers, and Contributors:** 2,600. **Trim Size:** 8 × 10 in.

Price and Sales Information: $199.00 in discount stores; $299.00–350.00 in bookstores. The *Macmillan Family Encyclopedia*—a retitled edition of the ACADEMIC AMERICAN ENCYCLOPEDIA—is sold chiefly in discount warehouse stores such as Sam's Club, Price Club, PACE, and Costco and large North

American bookstore chains such as B. Dalton and Bookstop. Barnes & Noble, one of the largest bookstore chains, offers its own edition under the title BARNES & NOBLE NEW AMERICAN ENCYCLOPEDIA. The *Macmillan Family Encyclopedia* is also sold internationally in countries where "American" in the title might hinder sales. For further information about the encyclopedia or to obtain the name of a local distributor, consumers should call 1-203-796-2602 (not a toll-free number) or write Grolier Inc., Sherman Turnpike, Danbury, CT 06816.

CONSUMER NOTE

The 20-volume *Macmillan Family Encyclopedia* has exactly the same contents as the 21-volume ACADEMIC AMERICAN ENCYCLOPEDIA, a major Grolier product. The only difference between the two sets, apart from their distinct titles and bindings, it that the ACADEMIC AMERICAN has an extra volume (Volume 21), which comprises the set's cumulative, or master, index. *Macmillan Family*, on the other hand, lacks a cumulative index; rather, its index appears in sections (printed on colored paper) at the end of each of the

20 volumes. For example, Volume 3 covers all articles beginning with the letter "B," followed by all index entries beginning with "B." In addition, *Macmillan Family* has a cheaper binding than the ACADEMIC AMERICAN, which is designed to withstand heavy use in libraries.

For a detailed evaluation of the contents of the *Macmillan Family Encyclopedia*, see the ACADEMIC AMERICAN ENCYCLOPEDIA (page 53).

NEW STANDARD ENCYCLOPEDIA

FACTS

Full Title: *New Standard Encyclopedia.* **Editor in Chief:** Douglas W. Downey. **Publisher:** Standard Educational Corporation. **Former Titles:** *Aiton's Encyclopedia* (1910–11); *National Encyclopedia for the Home, School and Library* (1923–26); *Standard Reference Work for the Home, School and Library* (1912–22, 1927–29). **Date Published:** First published as the *New Standard Encyclopedia* in 1930; new printing with revisions published annually.

Volumes: 20. **Words:** 8 million. **Pages:** 10,750. **Articles:** 17,500. **Bibliographies:** 1,000. **Illustrations and Maps:** 13,000. **Cross-references:** 53,600. **Index Entries:** 100,000. **Editorial Staff, Advisers, and Contributors:** 800. **Trim Size:** 6 3/4 × 9 1/4 in.

Price and Sales Information: $900.00 (estimated price). The *New Standard Encyclopedia* is sold to individual consumers by independent distributors who purchase quantities of the encyclopedia from the publisher, Standard Educational Corporation, which functions as a wholesaler. Distributors set their own prices, which currently average in the $800–1,000.00 range; such prices normally include the encyclopedia and various other reference or reading materials. For further information about the encyclopedia or to obtain the name of a local distributor, consumers should call 1-312-346-7440 (not a toll-free number) or write Standard Educational Corporation, 200 West Monroe Street, Chicago, IL 60606.

The *New Standard Encyclopedia* is sold to institutions (schools, libraries, etc.) by authorized sales representatives of Marshall Cavendish Corporation. For additional information or to place an order, call toll-free 1-800-821-9881 or write Marshall Cavendish Corporation, 2415 Jerusalem Avenue, P.O. Box 587, North Bellmore, NY 11710.

EVALUATION

The *New Standard Encyclopedia* aims "to provide as much information of interest to the general reader as is possible within an illustrated set selling for a modest price. Although children as young as nine or ten can understand much of the material, the content is not juvenile and the level of detail is sufficient for basic reference use by persons of any age" (foreword). The encyclopedia currently consists of 20 volumes containing about eight million words and nearly 11,000 pages, making it directly competitive with such formidable sets of similar size and intended readership as the ACADEMIC AMERICAN ENCYCLOPEDIA, COMPTON'S ENCYCLOPEDIA, FUNK & WAGNALLS NEW ENCYCLOPEDIA, and the WORLD BOOK ENCYCLOPEDIA.

The *New Standard* first appeared in 1930 in 10 volumes, deriving from the six-volume *Standard Reference Work for the Home, School and Library* (1912–22, 1927–29), which was also published for a time as the *National Encyclopedia for the Home, School and Library* (1923–26). The sire of all of these titles was *Aiton's Encyclopedia* (1910–11), a five-volume work named after its editor, George Briggs Aiton, a Minnesota educator. Since 1930 when it was acquired by the Standard Education Society (now Standard Educational Corporation) to the present, the *New Standard* has doubled its size, expanding from 10 to 14 volumes in the 1950s, to 17 volumes in the 1983, and finally 20 volumes in 1989, when a full-scale index was added to the set.

Although not as well known as its competitors, the *New Standard* has for many years been recognized as a solid, authoritative mid-sized general encyclopedia for students and the whole family. Moreover, the recent addition of the index has brought the set a degree of critical respect it previously lacked. For instance, the *New Standard* is now being sold in modest quantities to schools and libraries, whereas prior to the index it was unable to compete effectively in the education market.

Douglas W. Downey heads the encyclopedia's editorial staff of 87. Downey, who has held this position for three decades, is an extremely capable editor who has devoted his career to making the *New Standard* the best possible reference work it can be, given the limited economic and human resources available to a relatively small publisher. Most articles in the encyclopedia are written in-house and all are unsigned, but they are rigorously checked for factual accuracy by outside authorities. Downey explains the procedure in his foreword: "Each article published has been reviewed by five or more persons. At least one of these is a recognized authority in the field being covered. This authority, called an *authenticator*, assumes responsibility for accuracy; often several authenticators will review all or part of a given article." More than 700 authenticators, contributors, consultants, and advisers are identified at the beginning of Volume 1. Some of these people are academics but the list also includes many representatives of organizations (e.g., American Heart Association; National Association for the Advancement of Colored People; Laser Institute of America) and corporations (e.g., General Electric Company; Minnesota Mining & Manufacturing Company; Xerox Corporation).

The large majority of articles in the *New Standard* are short, averaging 450 words (or somewhat more than half a page) in length, but some are considerably longer, running to several or more pages. The encyclopedia provides reasonably well-balanced coverage of the major areas of knowledge. Scientific and technical subjects are covered in the most depth, as exemplified by such substantial articles as "Airplane," "Anatomy," "Animal," "Biology," "Bird," "Building Construction," "Computer," "Conservation," "Electronics," "Heart," "Hologram," "Leaves," "Medicine," "Nuclear Energy," "Petroleum," "Plastics," "Space Exploration," "Telephone," "Weather" and "Wood." Prominent historical figures also receive strong coverage, with emphasis on North Americans. Geographical topics emphasize major places in North America as well as the countries and megacities of the world. "Florida," for example, is 14 pages long, "British Columbia" 7 pages, "France" 24 pages, and "Paris" 8 pages.

The encyclopedia also includes a considerable amount of practical information on everyday subjects such as nutrition, consumer protection, first aid, vaccination, fire protection and prevention, plumbing, sewing, canning, veterans' benefits, lawn care, grafting and pruning plants, raising dogs, rules for playing various games, and standard banking services. Along this line, articles often conclude with a list of national organizations and their addresses where additional information on the topic can be obtained. The article "Sex Education," for instance, refers the reader to the American Medical Association, the Council for Sex Information and Education (in California), the National Education Association, and the Sex Information and Education Council of the United States (in New York). Indeed, the *New Standard* probably provides as much or more of this sort of pragmatic information than any other general encyclopedia currently available.

In some instances, though, the encyclopedia's coverage is disappointingly brief or superficial. *Examples:* "Abortion" (half a page long) provides a succinct discussion of U.S. abortion history and law, but information about the operation in other countries is limited to a short paragraph entirely lacking in specifics. The article "Adoption" (only 14 lines—or a fourth of a page—long) is little more than a definition; it totally ignores such profound issues as privacy and the right to know as they pertain to the adoption process. "Heart" (six pages long) includes a summary of diseases of the heart but fails to cover cardiomyopathy and related problems. The popular poet Anne Sexton is limited to one sentence—"Among the most promising Confessional poets were Anne Sexton and Sylvia Plath, both of whose careers were cut short by suicide"—in the article "Literature, American." (Interestingly, Plath has her own entry in the encyclopedia.)

In a review of the *New Standard* in *American Reference Books Annual* (1993, p. 28), D.A. Rothschild makes much the same point: "Some entries are too sparse; for example, the entry on comics has a line about the Comics Code but fails to explain what that entity is and how it has affected comics. Also, the entry on Eugene O'Neill ought to mention the playwright's alcoholism and how it influenced his work." In other instances, the *New Standard* completely ignores important subjects. *Examples:* There is nothing in the encyclopedia on such topics as sexual harassment, circumcision, and chelation therapy, nor on important writers like Charlotte Perkins Gilman, Roy Campbell, and Philip Larkin.

As the Report Card (see below) clearly indicates, the encyclopedia can be relied upon as a trustworthy source of information. Factual accuracy is one of the real strengths of the encyclopedia, obviously the result of editor Downey's authenticator system for fact-checking. Information in the set is also customarily impartial in presentation. Articles on such hot-button issues as abortion, capital punishment, fluoridation, and nuclear energy concisely summarize both sides of the debate as objectively as possible. Occasionally, however, polemical or sensitive questions are glossed over or avoided altogether. For example, putative cultural bias in educational testing is not addressed (in the article "Testing"), and the brief biography of Dr. Charles Drew fails to note the racial controversy surrounding his death.

The *New Standard* is a carefully maintained encyclopedia—meaning that it is conscientiously revised on a regular basis. On average, more than 2,000 (or well over 10 percent) of the set's 17,500 articles are revised in some manner each year, ranging from major rewrites to small changes involving the insertion of a death date or new population figure. In addition, some entirely new articles (87 in 1993) and illustrations (most in color) are added to each annual printing.

Nevertheless, despite the editors' best efforts, the *New Standard* is not always as up-to-date as it could and should be. The article "Dead Sea Scrolls," for example, contains nothing about the present-day contretemps concerning the scrolls' handling and dissemination, nor are recent research findings reported. "Galileo" fails to include information about the Roman Catholic Church's recent acknowledgment that it erred in condemning the great seventeenth-century scientist, an admission that has garnered head-

lines around the world. "Abortion" does not include information about two recent U.S. Supreme Court cases that have had significant impact on the rights of women seeking an abortion. The encyclopedia's foreword states that "Each year up to 40 percent of the pages throughout the encyclopedia are revised, entirely or partially." This assertion might be technically true, but it exaggerates the encyclopedia's normal rate of annual revision, which involves about 2,500 (or one-fourth) of the set's pages and up to 15 percent of its articles each year.

Another method of attempting to keep the *New Standard* current is through publication of an updating supplement entitled *World Progress: The Standard Quarterly Review*. A three-ring booklet that comes with its own binder, *World Progress* is quite different from other encyclopedia updating services in that it appears quarterly. It is written in a lively sytle and covers timely topics in such areas as polictics and government, business and finance, literature, medicine, race relations, sports, and the arts. The final issue each year contains a cumulated index for all four issues. Prospective purhcasers should understand, however, that *World Progress* has no real editorial connection with the encyclopedia itself. Obviously, it should not be purchased unless the consumer is reasonably certain it will be used. Too often such updating supplements are bought but rarely consulted; at the end of 20 years consumers have little to show for their money except a collection of expensive dust-catchers.

The set's writing style is almost always clear, direct, and unpretentious. The goal is clarity rather than fine writing. As explained in the foreword in Volume 1, "Most of the articles are written by members of the encyclopedia's editorial staff . . . . Staff members are qualified in their fields by education and experience and are trained in the techniques of encyclopedia writing." Ordinarily, the text will be comprehensible to users reading at the seventh or eighth grade level and beyond, but it should be noted that the *New Standard* does not employ a controlled vocabulary, nor does it write to grade level or use the pyramid writing approach, all devices used by some encyclopedias (most prominently the WORLD BOOK ENCYCLOPEDIA) to enhance readability.

The first two paragraphs of the article "Heart" typify the *New Standard*'s style:

Heart, the muscular organ that pumps blood through the body. The heart is essential to the life of any animal that depends on blood circulation to supply oxygen and food to the various cells of the body. If the heart stops beating for only a few seconds, permanent damage may be done to the brain. Death usually occurs if the heart stops beating for several minutes. Diseases of the heart and blood vessels lead all others'as a cause of death in most of the world.

Before its function was understood, the heart was thought to be the seat of character and of the emotions, especially love. These ideas about the heart led to such expressions as "softhearted" and "hardhearted," "fainthearted," and "lionhearted." The word "courage" derives from the Latin word for heart (*cor*).

The encyclopedia routinely italicizes and defines in context potentially difficult or unfamiliar terms. In "Heart," for example, more than 40 terms are treated in this manner, including *septum, ventricle, atrial natriuretic factors, superior vena cava, pulmonary veins, aorta, pericardium, cardiac cycle, pacemaker, angina pectoris, myocardial infarction,* and *arrhythmias*. This technique provides a valuable assist to reader comprehension. Another useful feature is pronunciation of all but the most common entry words, e.g., "Apartheid" is pronounced à-pärt'hāt; à-pärt'hĭt.

Finding specific topics and facts in the *New Standard* will normally pose few if any problems for the user. As noted at the outset of this review, the encyclopedia added a much needed index in 1989, a development that has both greatly improved access to the encyclopedia's contents and strengthened its competitive position in the marketplace. James Rettig, in a long and thoughtful review of the set in *Wilson Library Bulletin* (June 1989, p. 125), puts the index situation in good perspective:

For the first time, *New Standard* has a separate index. Heretofore, it has employed a self-indexing system integrated into the A-to-Z sequence of articles. The self-indexing system operated at the article title and subtitle level, but did not analyze articles' contents. While it provided adequate access to the set's contents, the addition of an index significantly increases the set's value as a fact-finding tool.

As Rettig suggests, the index is a good one. Sufficiently detailed, it comprises 446 pages (all of Volume 20) and 100,000 entries, which affords the user a very decent ratio of 1:80 index entries to text words.

In addition to its new index, the *New Standard* includes numerous cross-references in the A-Z listing (e.g., "Intelligence Quotient. See TESTING, subtitle *Intelligence Tests*) and within and at the end of articles. For example, "Heart" contains 16 internal cross-references, all printed in capital letters so they stand out, such as "See also CIRCULATION."

Another useful feature offered by the encyclopedia is inclusion of more than 1,000 bibliographies, or lists of books recommended for further study. Prepared by David King, *New Standard*'s longtime librarian, the bibliographies are appended at the end of articles and are carefully selected and usually up-to-date. A review in *Reference Books Bulletin* (in *Booklist*, September 15, 1993, p. 182) notes, "Bibliographies, which accompany many articles, usually include titles for adults and children. Titles from the 1980s and 1990s predominate. The number of bibliographies updated for this [1993] printing is 233." *Example*: "Heart" concludes with a bibliography of eight titles, all published in the 1980s. Five of the books are suggested for adults, with the other three designated as "For Younger Readers."

Illustrations in the *New Standard* have been steadily upgraded in recent years, but room for improvement still exists. The illustrations, the majority of which are in black-

and-white, usually add to the informational value of the articles they accompany. "Heart," for instance, includes three illustrations, two of which are small and quite dark black-and-white photographs showing a pacemaker and an artificial heart valve; the other is a full-page drawing in color depicting the basic workings of the heart and the circulatory system.

Many new color illustrations have been added to the set during the past decade, including a highly informative acetate overlay that illustrates in considerable detail the many facets of a modern high-rise building (in the article "Building Construction"), but much more of this sort of work needs to be done if the encyclopedia is to be fully competitive with such handsomely turned out sets as the ACADEMIC AMERICAN ENCYCLOPEDIA, COMPTON'S ENCYCLOPEDIA, and the WORLD BOOK ENCYCLOPEDIA. Today, the *New Standard* is comparable with FUNK & WAGNALLS NEW ENCYCLOPEDIA in the area of illustrations, which is not a compliment. On the other hand, the editors of the *New Standard* are aware of the problem and are moving as quickly as time and resources permit to improve the quality of the set's illustrations.

The encyclopedia's physical format is serviceable. The bright red Sturdite binding with black panels and gold lettering is both strong and attractive. The two-column page layout tends to be crowded, and the gutters (or inside margins) narrow. The many small, dark black-and-white illustrations mentioned in the preceding paragraph give the encyclopedia an overall uninviting appearance, but this situation is changing slowly as more color is added to the set. The typefaces used are bold and legible.

REPORT CARD: NEW STANDARD ENCYCLOPEDIA

TOPIC	COVERAGE	ACCURACY	RECENCY	CLARITY
Circumcision	F*	NA	NA	NA
Drew, Charles	C	A	C	A
Galileo	B	A	D	A
Glass, Philip	C	A	B	A
Heart Disease	B	A	B	A
IQ	B	A	B	A
Panda Bears	B	A	B	A
Sexual Harassment	F*	NA	NA	NA
Shroud of Turin	A	A	A	A
Uzbekistan	B	A	A	A

A = Excellent; **B**= Above Average; **C** = Average; **D** = Below Average; **F** = Poor; **NA** = Not Applicable
*No Article

SUMMARY

The *New Standard Encyclopedia*, now published in 20 volumes (up from 17 in 1988), is a well-maintained, carefully edited general reference work for students and the whole family, although it is not as good as its chief competitors, namely the ACADEMIC AMERICAN ENCYCLOPEDIA, COMPTON'S ENCYCLOPEDIA, and WORLD BOOK ENCYCLOPEDIA. The set emphasizes scientific and technical topics, practical information, and North American biography and geography. Conspicuous strengths are accuracy of information, a clear and unpretentious writing style, useful bibliographies, and (since 1989) efficient access to the set's contents via a detailed index and numerous cross-references. On the negative side, the *New Standard*'s articles sometimes lack sufficient depth and timeliness, and the illustrations—often too small and dark—continue to be a liability, although this problem is being addressed.

OTHER OPINIONS

American Reference Book Annual, 1993, pp. 28–29 (review by D.A. Rothschild); *Reference Books Bulletin* (in *Booklist*), September 15, 1993, pp. 182–83 (unsigned review); *Wilson Library Bulletin*, June 1989, pp. 125–26 (review by James Rettig).

OXFORD ILLUSTRATED ENCYCLOPEDIA

FACTS

Full Title: *Oxford Illustrated Encyclopedia: The Physical World* (Volume 1, 1985); *Oxford Illustrated Encyclopedia: The Natural World* (Volume 2, 1985); *Oxford Illustrated Encyclopedia: World History from Earliest Times to 1800* (Volume 3, 1988); *Oxford Illustrated Encyclopedia: World History from 1800 to the Present Day* (Volume 4, 1988); *Oxford Illustrated Encyclopedia of the Arts* (Volume 5, 1990); *Oxford Illustrated Encyclopedia of Invention and Technology* (Volume 6, 1992); *Oxford Illustrated Encyclopedia of Peoples and Cultures* (Volume 7, 1992); *Oxford Illustrated Encyclopedia of the Universe* (Volume 8, 1992); *Oxford Illustrated Encyclopedia: Index and Ready Reference* (Volume 9, 1993). **General Editor:** Harry Judge. **Publisher:** Oxford University Press. **Date Published:** Published volume-by-volume between 1985 and 1993.

Volumes: 9. **Words:** 3 million. **Pages:** 3,300. **Articles:** 20,000. **Bibliographies:** None. **Illustrations and Maps:** 2,500. **Cross-references:** 25,000. **Index Entries:** 36,000. **Editorial Staff, Advisers, and Contributors:** 350. **Trim Size:** 8 1/4 ×10 3/4 in.

Price and Sales Information: $265.00 for the set; individual volumes available for $45.00–$49.95 each. Individual consumers can purchase the *Oxford Illustrated Encyclopedia* in bookstores or, if the set is not in stock, it can be ordered. Similarly, educational institutions (schools, libraries, etc.) can order the encyclopedia or individual volumes through a book wholesaler. To order the set or individual volumes directly from the publisher, call toll-free 1-800-451-7556 or write Oxford University Press, 200 Madison Avenue, New York, NY 10016.

EVALUATION

Published a volume at a time between 1985 and 1993, the handsomely turned out nine-volume *Oxford Illustrated Encyclopedia* is aimed chiefly at older students (high school and up) and educated adults seeking general information on all manner of topics. The set was produced in Great Britain and has a distinct British flavor—elevators, for instance, are covered in the article "Lift" in Volume 6—but for the most part the encyclopedia will be comprehensible to most North American readers. The encyclopedia consists of eight large books, each covering a broad area of knowledge, plus an index volume that provides comprehensive access to the set. Each of the eight subject volumes has its own title (listed at the top of this review). Each volume contains roughly 2,500 brief articles arranged A-to-Z, each can be used independently of the others, and each is edited and written by specialists in the field. For instance, volume 7, the *Oxford Illustrated Encyclopedia of Peoples and Cultures*, is edited by Dr. Richard Hoggart, a prominent British social scientist, and has 80 contributors, most of whom are British academics versed in such fields as sociology, anthropology, economics, government, and the law. However, none of the articles in the encyclopedia is signed. Dr. Harry Judge, identified as Director of the Department of Educational Studies at Oxford University, is the general (or series) editor.

According to Judge's preface in Volume 1, the encyclopedia's volumes "have been carefully arranged in such a way that, taken together, they provide a clear and authoritative map of contemporary knowledge—spanning the sciences and the arts, modern society and its long history, the life of the imagination and the shape of politics, the achievement of men and women and the expanding world of space." An advertisement for the set paints an even grander picture of the encyclopedia's scope, boasting that the set "is nothing less than a complete inventory of human knowledge."

But in reality the *Oxford Illustrated Encyclopedia*'s coverage leaves a great deal to be desired. Even the most casual user will quickly observe that the coverage is troublingly imbalanced, with four (or half) of the subject volumes devoted to science and technology, two to history, and the rest of the world's knowledge relegated to the two remaining volumes. Moreover, the articles, which average just 150 words in length (or seven per page), often provide only the most rudimentary facts. As a result, some important topics receive overly brief or superficial coverage or no coverage at all.

Examples of the encyclopedia's lapses in the area of coverage could fill a book. Here are just a few:

- The only U.S. states covered in the *Oxford Illustrated Encyclopedia* are the original 13 plus Vermont and Florida. Found in volume 3 (devoted to history up to 1800), these articles are only about a dozen lines long and deal solely with the state's early history. The rest of the states—from Alabama to Washington—are completely ignored. A similar pattern obtains for the Canadian provinces, e.g., Quebec is in, British Columbia is out. There are no entries for states or provinces in volume 4, which covers history from 1800 to the present.

- The article "Abortion" fails to mention *Roe v. Wade* or acknowledge the pivotal role of the U.S. Supreme Court in the ongoing debate, saying only that "In the USA, in particular, arguments about the legality and morality of abortion have been brought to the political agenda in recent years by Christian fundamentalists and New Right politicians."

- There are no articles on such medical problems and procedures as carpal tunnel syndrome and chelation therapy, nor is there any information about Dr. Charles Drew in the article "Blood Transfusion"; Drew was a pioneer in blood typing and preservation that helped make transfusions possible.

- There are no articles on such important contemporary writers as Philip Larkin, Roy Campbell, Anne Sexton, Alice Walker, or Toni Morrison.

- The articles "Adoption," "Depression (in economics)," "Depression (in psychiatry)," "Fluoridation," "Heart Disease," "Sexually Transmitted Diseases," and "Transplant Surgery" are so terse as to be of only minimal value to most readers.

Other reviewers have also commented from time to time on the encyclopedia's shallow and erratic coverage. In a review of volume 6 in *Library Journal* (March 1, 1993, p. 70), Joe Accardi notes, "While emerging concepts such as biotechnology and genetic engineering are described, there are no entries for virtual reality or fuzzy logic." M. O'Hara makes the same point even more emphatically in a review of Volume 5 in *Choice* (July–August 1991, p. 1763):

> This title is in reality a hodgepodge of short entries on selected works, authors, artists, architects, choreographers, movements, and national traditions in various fine arts. It is an admirable coffee-table production but lacks any index (there are cross-references) and fails to provide much information not easily available in the most common reference tools . . . . Without a statement of editorial guidelines for inclusion it is difficult to guess the reason behind the omission of an entry for Ernst Haas when Yousef Karsch is included, or why Nadine Gordimer but not Alan Paton is mentioned in the paragraph on South African literature. Where are L. Frank Baum, Robert Penn Warren, Naguib Mahfouz, Isaac Asimov, Elie Wiesel, Charles M. Russell, Michael Graves, Hamada Shoji, and Dave Brubeck? For that matter, where is the entire Harlem Renaissance? Two thumbs down.

Paradoxically, the same information sometimes is repeated in different volumes, as if one editorial hand did not know what the other was doing. The article "Intelligence" in volume 2, for instance, furnishes a brief summary of intelligence and IQ tests and what the scores mean. Very similar information is presented in volume 7 in the articles "Intelligence" and "Intelligence Test." Considering the many important topics the encyclopedia fails to cover, this sort of duplication seems a shameful waste.

The *Oxford Illustrated* is usually accurate, except in instances when the material is out-of-date. Occasionally, however, there are disquieting errors of fact, as in "Panda," which erroneously claims the giant panda "is the biggest and most familiar member of the raccoon family." In actual fact, genetic tests conducted at the National Zoo in Washington, D.C., in the 1980s clearly place the giant panda in the bear family. The encyclopedia is also usually impartial in its presentation of controversial or sensitive information. Such articles as "Abortion," "Capital Punishment," "Homosexuality," and "Intelligence Test" objectively present both sides of the issue. Still, sometimes controversy is ignored, as in "Circumcision," "Contraception," and "Fluoridation."

As mentioned, the encyclopedia has been published over a number of years, beginning in 1985 and concluding with the index in 1993. Obviously, the earlier volumes are becoming dated, in some instances quite noticeably. For example, "Apartheid" and "South Africa" in volume 4 (1988) are woefully out-of-date due to rapidly changing events in that country, whereas "Segregation" in volume 7 (1992) is reasonably current, reporting that the "legislation forming the cornerstones of apartheid [in South Africa] was repealed in 1991." It is not known at this time when or if the set or individual volumes will be revised.

The encyclopedia will normally be comprehensible to older students and adults reading at the tenth grade level and beyond. Technical vocabulary is avoided when possible, but rarely do the writers define potentially difficult or unfamiliar terms in context. Likewise, the editors do not employ a controlled vocabulary nor do they attempt to write to grade level. The writing style has been described by Bill Katz in his *Basic Information Sources* (6th ed. 1992, p. 247) as "extremely easy" and "rather simple." On the other hand, this reviewer finds the style clear but almost always numbing, encyclopediaese at its worst (or best, depending on your perspective).

The first dozen or so lines of the article "Heart" provide a fair sense of the encyclopedia's style:

> Heart is a general term for any muscular organ which pumps blood around the body. In

many invertebrates it is a simple contracting tube which receives blood from one end and then pumps it to the other, creating an open flow along the body.

The vertebrate heart consists of muscular chambers, three in fishes and amphibians, four in others. Blood from the veins, at low pressure after passing through body tissues, is sucked into one of the upper chambers, called an atrium, usually the right in mammals, and then passes into the lower chamber, called the ventricle. In fish and amphibians there is a single ventricle, alternately shared by oxygenated and unoxygenated blood. Other vertebrates have at least a partial separating membrane, dividing the lower chamber into two ventricles.

Unlike most encyclopedias, which organize their information into a single A-to-Z sequence, the *Oxford Illustrated* has eight alphabetical sequences, because each of the subject volumes has its own alphabetical arrangement. This situation, akin organizationally to a thematically arranged encyclopedia, renders the index volume (volume 9) imperative for locating specific topics and facts in an easy and timely manner. Without the index, for instance, the reader has little clue about where to look for information on blood and blood transfusions. As it turns out, "Blood," "Blood Groups," and "Blood Pressure" are found in volume 2 (covering the natural world) and "Blood Gas Analysis" and "Blood Transfusion" in volume 6 (covering inventions and technology). Published in 1993, the index comprises about 36,000 entries in 200 pages; it also includes a so-called "Ready Reference" section consisting of 44 pages of mythical and religious figures and 30 pages of miscellaneous tables.

The set also includes numerous cross-references, both external and internal. They are designated by an asterisk (*). For example, in volume 7 the reader finds "Apartheid *Segregation," which means see the article "Segregation" for information about apartheid. Unfortunately, there are no cross-references from volume to volume. Thus the article "Blood Groups" in volume 2 furnishes two cross-references (*Antibodies and

*Plasma) to articles in that volume, but it does not refer the reader to "Blood Transfusion" in volume 6. Overall, the encyclopedia's cross-reference system is quite limited. It has also been criticized as inconsistent by several reviewers. Here is what the review of volume 5 in *Reference Books Bulletin* (in *Booklist*, April 1, 1991, pp. 1591–92) had to say about the book's cross-references:

> Only one minor flaw mars this otherwise superior work—the cross-references are not as good as they should be. For example, a famous painting by Thomas Eakins illustrates the article *American Art*, but in the entry on Eakins no reference is made to *American Art*. Even when a reference is made to a related topic, it is not always marked by an asterisk. For example, the article on Stephen Sondheim mentions Leonard Bernstein but does not contain an asterisk to let the reader know an article on Bernstein appears in the work. The same is true in the article on Samuel Richardson that mentions Jane Austen without an asterisk by her name.

The best multivolume encyclopedias for adults and older students provide bibliographies, or lists of recommended sources the reader might consult for further information. The *Oxford Illustrated* includes no bibliographies. Should the set be revised, the editors would be wise to consider adding this feature, which can be enormously helpful to students at the secondary school and college levels.

Happily, as its name suggests, the *Oxford Illustrated* includes many illustrations, and they are almost always of very high quality. Indeed, the set's illustrations are hands down its best feature. In both black-and-white and color, the illustrations include sharply reproduced photographs, drawings, diagrams, cartoons, famous paintings, charts, and maps. They tend to be well chosen, well placed, and informative. "Heart," for example, is enhanced by a half-page diagrammatic comparison of the heart of a fish, reptile, and mammal. General editor Judge explains the function of the illustrations in his preface to volume 1:

To be able to see and understand is, for may [sic] topics within the circle of knowledge, at least as important as to be able to read and understand. For the presentation of items which can best be appreciated visually, much research by the staff of the Rainbird Publishing Group has gone into the selection of illustration, and the use of colour is judicious. The intention has been not so much to decorate, although the pictures are handsome, as to supplement and expand the information given in the text.

The encyclopedia's physical format is both attractive and functional. The volumes, which come with colorful dust jackets, are sturdily bound. Either timelines or maps are printed on the endpapers of each volume. The use of quality paper contributes to the excellent reproduction of illustrations in the set. The page design, while not especially different or creative, is aesthetically appealing, as are the various typefaces.

REPORT CARD: OXFORD ILLUSTRATED ENCYCLOPEDIA

TOPIC	COVERAGE	ACCURACY	RECENCY	CLARITY
Circumcision	C	A	C	B
Drew, Charles	F*	NA	NA	NA
Galileo	C	A	C	A
Glass, Philip	B	A	C	A
Heart Disease	C	A	B	B
IQ	B	A	A	A
Panda Bears	B	D	C	A
Sexual Harassment	B	B	B	A
Shroud of Turin	C	B	D	A
Uzbekistan	B	A	B	A

A = Excellent; B = Above Average; C = Average; D = Below Average; F = Poor; NA = Not Applicable
*No Article

SUMMARY

The nine-volume *Oxford Illustrated Encyclopedia* is a British-produced reference work published on a volume-by-volume basis between 1985 and 1993. Intended for older students and adults, it consists of eight subject volumes and an index volume. The encyclopedia's best feature is its illustrations; likewise, its physical format is both attractive and functional. There, however, the plaudits end. The set's negatives include shallow and erratic coverage of basic knowledge, poor organization and an ineffectual system of cross-references, lack of up-to-dateness in the earlier volumes, a clear but soporific writing style, and failure to include bibliographies. The bottom line: An example of how *not* to make an encyclopedia.

OTHER OPINIONS

American Reference Books Annual, 1986, p. 27 (review of volumes 1 and 2 by Phyllis J. Van Orden); *American Reference Books Annual*, 1990, p. 224 (review of volumes 3 and 4 by Phyllis J. Van Orden); *American Reference Books Annual*, 1991, p. 374 (review of volume 5 by Linda Keir Simons); *American Reference Books Annual*, 1993, pp. 612–13 (review of volume 6 by Janice M. Griggs).

Basic Information Sources by William A. Katz (vol. 1 of *Introduction to Reference Work*, 6th ed., New York: McGraw-Hill, 1992), pp. 246–47.

Choice, February 1986, p. 852 (review of volume 1 by N.F. George); *Choice*, February 1986, p. 852 (review of volume 2 by T. Kirk); Choice, July–August 1989, pp. 1822–23 (review of volumes 3 and 4 by R. Fritze); *Choice*, July–August 1991, p. 1763 (review of volume 5 by M. O'Hara); *Choice*, January 1993, p. 774 (review of volume 6 by K.Y. Stabler); Choice, July–August 1993, p. 1753 (review of volume 7 by G.M. Herrmann); *Choice*, October 1993, p. 271 (review of volume 8 by J.O. Christensen).

Library Journal, March 1, 1986, p. 88 (review of volumes 1 and 2 by Joseph Hannibal); *Library Journal*, February 1, 1989, p. 62 (review of volumes 3 and 4 by James Moffet); *Library Journal*, February 15, 1991, p. 188 (review of volume 5 by Mary Molinaro); *Library Journal*, March 1, 1993, p. 70 (review of volume 6 by Joe Accardi).

Reference Books Bulletin (in *Booklist*), June 15, 1986, p. 1520 (unsigned review of volumes 1 and 2); *Reference Books Bulletin* (in *Booklist*), April 1, 1989, p. 1361 (unsigned review of volumes 3 and 4); *Reference Books Bulletin* (in *Booklist*), April 1, 1991, pp. 1591–92 (unsigned review of volume 5); *Reference Books Bulletin* (in *Booklist*), December 1, 1992, p. 690 (unsigned review of volume 6); *Reference Books Bulletin* (in *Booklist*), July 1993, p. 2004 (unsigned review of volume 7); *Reference Books Bulletin* (in *Booklist*), December 1, 1993, p. 716 (unsigned review of volume 8).

WEBSTER'S FAMILY ENCYCLOPEDIA

FACTS

Full Title: *Webster's Family Encyclopedia.* **Variant Title:** *Webster's 10 Volume Family Encyclopedia* (printed on carrying case). **Editors:** Stephen P. Elliott and Alan Isaacs. **Publisher:** Ottenheimer Publishers, Inc. **Distributor:** Arrow Trading Company, Inc. **Former Title:** NEW UNIVERSAL FAMILY ENCYCLOPEDIA. **Date Published:** First published as *Webster's Family Encyclopedia* in 1989; latest edition is Revised Edition published in 1991. **Volumes:** 10 (plus one-volume *Webster's Family Dictionary*); paperbound. **Words:** 1.5 million. **Pages:** 2,834. **Articles:** 25,000. **Bibliographies:** None. **Illustrations and Maps:** 1,200. **Cross-references:** 15,000. **Index Entries:** None. **Editorial Staff, Advisers, and Contributors:** 128. **Trim Size:** 5¼ × 8¼ in.

Price and Sales Information: $19.95. *Webster's Family Encyclopedia* is normally sold through department store catalogs, by mail-order advertisement, or as a premium when buying another product. Individual consumers and educational institutions (schools, libraries, etc.) can order the encyclopedia directly from Arrow Trading Company, Inc., the set's exclusive distributor. For further information or to place an order, call 1-212-255-7688 (not a toll-free number) or write Arrow Trading Company, Inc., 1115 Broadway, New York, NY 10010.

EVALUATION

Published in 10 small paperbound volumes in a cardboard carrying case, *Webster's Family Encyclopedia* originally appeared in North American in 1985 as the now defunct NEW UNIVERSAL FAMILY ENCYCLOPEDIA, a revised and Americanized edition of the *Macmillan Encyclopedia*, a one-volume encyclopedia first published in Great Britain in 1981. The NEW UNIVERSAL FAMILY ENCYCLOPEDIA, also a single-volume work, was a Random House publication, although Ottenheimer Publishers, Inc. held the copyright to everything except the jacket design. The encyclopedia quickly went out of print, but several years later it reappeared as *Webster's Family Encyclopedia*—also called *Webster's 10 Volume Family Encyclopedia* on the carrying case.

Note that *Webster's Family Encyclopedia* actually contains 11 volumes, the extra one being an abridged dictionary entitled *Webster's Family Dictionary*, also issued in paperback. Note also that all volumes in the set prominently display this disclaimer on the title page: "This book is not published by the original publishers of WEBSTER'S DICTIONARY, or by their successors." There is also a 13-volume paperbound edition of the encyclopedia on the market under the same title, known as *Webster's 13 Volume Family Encyclopedia*; it is distributed by the Fingerhut Corporation in St. Cloud, Minnesota as a premium item but has not been seen by this reviewer.

Today the *Webster's Family Encyclopedia* is nominally published by Ottenheimer Publishers and the edition under review here is distributed exclusively by Arrow Trading Company, a company in New York City that deals in premium products. Ottenheimer, located in Baltimore, Maryland, has a reputation for licensing and reprinting older and/or inferior reference materials and then reprinting and distributing them in mass quantities at rock bottom prices. As might be surmised from the foregoing,

the encyclopedia is hardly a work of first importance—but neither is it execrably bad. The editor of the original British edition, Alan Isaacs, is a science writer who has worked on a number of substantial encyclopedia projects; the American editor, Stephen P. Elliott, is also an experienced encyclopedia hand, having served as executive editor of the highly regarded RANDOM HOUSE ENCYCLOPEDIA. The editorial staffs of both the first and revised editions—128 names altogether, including contributors—are listed at the beginning of Volume 1.

Webster's Family Encyclopedia comprises roughly 25,000 entries, 6,000 of which are short biographies of famous people. All articles are quite brief, often little more than dictionary definitions. They average only 60 words in length, or nine articles per page. Quite naturally the coverage, while broad, is very thin and often lacks necessary specifics. For example, the 11-line article "Adoption" defines the term, gives a bit of history, and concludes with a note about the present-day dilemma of "finding adoptive homes for children with special needs," but nowhere does the article deal with the important questions of privacy and the right to know as they pertain to the contemporary adoption process.

The encyclopedia's text is normally accurate, except when it is dated. Occasionally, however, small factual errors are encountered, as in the brief biography of Grandma Moses, which says "she only turned seriously to painting at the age of 67," when in fact she was in her mid-seventies when she began to paint. The encyclopedia also usually presents its material in an impartial manner. "Fluoridation," for instance, notes, "Controversy sometimes arises on the grounds that 'medication' is being forced on people who may not wish to accept it. This measure has been shown to be effective, however, and quite safe in low concentrations." Still, the case of "Circumcision," which fails to mention recent arguments against the procedure, or "Nuclear Energy," which contains nothing about the dangers of nuclear power.

As mentioned, the encyclopedia was first published in 1981 and revised in 1985 when it appeared in North America as the NEW UNIVERSAL FAMILY ENCYCLOPEDIA. Since becoming *Webster's Family Encyclopedia*, the set has been minimally revised twice, most recently in 1991, but essentially it remains much the same as the 1985 version, except for cosmetic updates of major events, such as the reunification of Germany and the breaking apart of the former Soviet Union.

Indeed, many articles in the current edition of the encyclopedia are urgently in need of revision. *Examples:* The article "Abortion" is quite dated, containing nothing regarding important U.S. Supreme Court decisions since 1986. "Apartheid" is woefully out-of-date, and "South Africa" reports, "Despite severe censure from the world community, South Africa has remained dogged in its pursuit of a philosophy of white supremacy." "Dead Sea Scrolls" offers nothing on contemporary findings and controversies surrounding the scrolls. "Galileo" fails to include information about the Roman Catholic Church's recent and remarkable reversal of its stand on Galileo and his once heretical ideas. "Shroud of Turin" fails to note that carbon 14 dating tests conducted in 1988 show the shroud to be a fake.

According to the editors in their preface in volume 1, the encyclopedia aims to serve the general reader as well as students at all levels:

> To make these volumes as useful as possible, all those who contributed to it [sic] were guided by three principles: to write in simple but precise nontechnical language comprehensible to the general reader; to present all material concisely without oversimplification; and to make sure that all articles would be informative and of value to the modern reader, including all levels of students.

For the most part, the encyclopedia can be used by older students at the secondary level and beyond, as well as literate adults. The text is usually too advanced for most elementary school youngsters. Regrettably, the writing style, while customarily clear, tends to be dull and lifeless. The first nine lines of the article "Heart" offers a fair sampling of the encyclopedia's style:

> A four-chambered muscular organ that pumps blood around the body. Two chambers—the left and right atria—dilate to receive oxygen-rich blood from the lungs and oxygen-depleted blood from the rest of the body, respectively (this is called diastole). Contraction of the heart (called systole) starts in the atria, forcing blood into the two ventricles. The left ventricle then contracts to force blood into a large artery—the aorta, which leads from the heart and feeds all the other arteries. The right ventricle pumps blood into the pulmonary artery and to the lungs, where it receives oxygen. Valves between the atria and ventricles and at the arterial exits of the heart prevent the backflow of blood.

Finding material in the encyclopedia is sometimes difficult and frustrating, due to the set's lack of an index and an inadequate network of cross-references. The editors' preface justifies having no index—"The extensive use of cross references makes this encyclopedia virtually self-indexing"—but anyone using the encyclopedia seriously will conclude that the "self-indexing" system leaves much to be desired.

Cross-references to other articles in the set are designated by an asterisk (*) preceding the term; for instance, "Christian Science" says the religion was "founded by Mary Baker *Eddy in 1866," thus alerting the reader that there is an article on Mrs. Eddy in the encyclopedia. Cross-references to illustrations are designated in a similar manner by a raised open square preceding the term. Cross-references tend to be plentiful but too often lacking when needed. For example, the article "Nuclear Energy" fails to furnish cross-references to "Chernobyl" and "Three Mile Island," two of history's worst nuclear power plant accidents. There is no cross-reference from birth control to the article "Contraception." "Heart" lacks a cross-reference to "Transplantation," which covers heart transplants. Conversely, "Adoption" includes a cross-reference to "Minor" ("an unmarried *minor*") but there is no such article in the encyclopedia.

A review in *Reference Books Bulletin* (in *Booklist*, June 15, 1986, p. 1506) of the NEW UNIVERSAL FAMILY ENCYCLOPEDIA, which has almost the same text and exactly the same organization as *Webster's Family Encyclopedia*, also finds fault with the cross-references:

> Cross-referencing is liberal but not exhaustive, and the user must sometimes rely on his or her own knowledge of a subject in order to find the most useful entry, looking under, for example, *Dracula, Count* as well as *Vampire* even though there is no cross-reference from the latter to the former. Cross-referencing is inconsistent at times; for example, *Architecture* contains cross-references to *Cathedral* and *Gothic Revival* but not to entries on other periods and styles, including *Greek Art and Architecture* and *International Style*.

The encyclopedia lacks bibliographies, or lists of recommended sources the reader might consult for additional information—which is especially unfortunate because of the set's superficial coverage of knowledge in all areas. When the editors revise *Webster's Family Encyclopedia* next, they should consider adding bibliographies to selected articles.

Some 1,200 illustrations—mostly photographs, simple diagrams, and line drawings—are found throughout the set. All are in black-and-white and the quality of reproduction is quite poor. In point of fact, some of the photos are so dark and blurry that they have no informational value whatsoever. This criticism is particularly true of photos of exotic animals, such as the panda, okapi, and numbat. On the other hand, some of the diagrams and drawings can be helpful to the reader, such as the half-page illustration with "Heart" showing the heart's central role in the circulatory system of mammals.

The paperbound volumes are simply glued together and will not withstand heavy use. Likewise, the paper used is of very poor quality. Inside, the single-column page design is serviceable but uninviting, the dreary, cheerless, predictable pages lacking any color or imaginative layout. On the plus side, the set comes in an attractive and colorful cardboard carrying case (or tote box), similar to the way the paperbound MODERN CENTURY ILLUSTRATED ENCYCLOPEDIA was boxed some years ago.

REPORT CARD: WEBSTER'S FAMILY ENCYCLOPEDIA

TOPIC	COVERAGE	ACCURACY	RECENCY	CLARITY
Circumcision	D	B	C	A
Drew, Charles	F*	NA	NA	NA
Galileo	C	A	D	A
Glass, Philip	F*	NA	NA	NA
Heart Disease	D	A	C	B
IQ	C	B	C	A
Panda Bears	D	B	C	A
Sexual Harassment	F*	NA	NA	NA
Shroud of Turin	C	B	C	A
Uzbekistan	C	C	D	B

A = Excellent; **B** = Above Average; **B** = Average; **D** = Below Average; **F** = Poor; **NA** = Not Applicable
*No Article

SUMMARY

Webster's Family Encyclopedia—also known as *Webster's 10 Volume Family Encyclopedia*—is essentially an updated reprint of the NEW UNIVERSAL FAMILY ENCYCLOPEDIA, a single-volume work published in 1985 that is no longer in print. Not much good can be said about the encyclopedia. Its coverage, though broad, is very shallow; it is frequently out-of-date; it tends to avoid controversial or sensitive issues; its writing style is dull; it lacks an index and the cross-reference system is unreliable; it has no bibliographies; and its illustrations and physical format are inferior. On the positive side, the articles are clearly written and the price is right. The bottom line: The worst encyclopedia in its class.

OTHER OPINIONS

No other reviews of *Webster's Family Encyclopedia* are currently available. Interested consumers might, however, want to take a look at the long and thoughtful review of the NEW UNIVERSAL FAMILY ENCYCLOPEDIA in *Reference Books Bulletin* (in *Booklist*), June 15, 1986, pp. 1505–08; as explained above, *Webster's Family Encyclopedia* and the NEW UNIVERSAL FAMILY ENCYCLOPEDIA (a now defunct single-volume work published in 1985) contain practically the same text.

WORLD BOOK ENCYCLOPEDIA

FACTS

Full Title: *The World Book Encyclopedia.* **Managing Editor:** Dale W. Jacobs. **Associate Managing Editor:** Gary A. Alt. **Publisher:** World Book, Inc. **Date Published:** First published in 1917; new printing with revisions published annually.

Electronic Version: INFORMATION FINDER (CD-ROM).

Volumes: 22. **Words:** 10 million. **Pages:** 14,000. **Articles:** 17,500. **Bibliographies:** 1,800. **Illustrations and Maps:** 31,300. **Cross-references:** 100,000. **Index Entries:** 150,000. **Editorial Staff, Advisers, and Contributors:** 3,250. **Trim Size:** 7 1/4 × 9 3/4 in.

Price and Sales Information: $679.00 to $849.00 depending on binding; price does not include shipping and handling. The *World Book Encyclopedia* is sold to individual consumers and educational institutions (schools, libraries, etc.) through authorized sales representatives of the publisher. The encyclopedia is not sold in bookstores or similar retail outlets. Individual consumers who own an older set may be eligible to trade it in toward the price of a new printing; trade-ins do not apply to institutional sales. Educators normally receive a discount.

For additional information about the encyclopedia or to order it, consumers should consult the yellow pages of the local telephone directory under "Encyclopedias" for the World Book, Inc. sales representative in their area. If the company is not listed, call toll-free 1-800-621-8202 or write World Book, Inc., 525 West Monroe Street, 20th Floor, Chicago, IL 60661.

EVALUATION

The *World Book Encyclopedia*, long the best-selling encyclopedia in North America, is designed "especially to meet the reference and study needs of students in elementary school, junior high school, and high school. *World Book* also serves as a general family reference tool" (preface). A fixture on the American scene for over 75 years, the encyclopedia first appeared in 1917 in eight volumes that sold for $32.00. An immediate success, the set grew to 10 volumes the following year, 13 volumes in 1929, 19 volumes in 1933, 20 volumes in 1960, and its present 22 volumes in 1972.

Over the years, *World Book* has benefited from enlightened ownership and dedicated editorship. The Hanson-Roach-Fowler Company, the set's first publisher, and later W.F. Quarrie & Company, both of Chicago, published the encyclopedia into the 1940s. During this period, the set established a reputation for high standards under the direction of founding editor Michael Vincent O'Shea, a professor of education at the University of Wisconsin before joining the encyclopedia. In 1945, *World Book* was acquired by Field Enterprises, Inc., a subsidiary of the Marshall Field organization, a giant Chicago corporation. Around this time, John Morris Jones, a Welsh-born educator, became the set's editor. Jones, like O'Shea before him, provided strong and innovative editorial leadership. In 1947, for instance, the entire encyclopedia was revised and restructured, with many new articles and illustrations added to reflect postwar developments and attitudes.

Soon after the death of Jones in 1962, William H. Nault, another educator with impressive credentials and a commitment to quality reference publishing, became *World Book*'s guiding editorial force, a position he held for more than three decades. In 1978, the encyclopedia was acquired by the Scott Fetzer Company of Lakewood, Ohio, a firm that manufactures and sells Kirby vacuum cleaners and related products; today Scott Fetzer and World Book, Inc. are owned by Berkshire Hathaway, Inc., the Omaha-based investment conglomerate headed by billionaire Warren Buffett.

Under William Nault's progressive management, *World Book* has become recognized as one of the best—if not the best—general English-language encyclopedias on the market today. In 1972, Nault and his editorial team added a comprehensive analytical index (volume 22) to the set, which greatly improved access to the encyclopedia's myriad facts. Several years later, they added metric equivalents throughout the set, making *World Book* the first encyclopedia to include both customary (or English) and metric measurements. In 1977, the publisher installed a sophisticated electronic composition system, the most advanced in the encyclopedia industry. The system, which has been upgraded over the years to keep pace with the changing technology, permits editors, writers, and illustrators to work on-screen at computer terminals, thus enhancing both revision and design capabilities. Not long ago an international edition of *World Book* was published for readers outside North America; Chinese and Malaysian editions of the encyclopedia will be published in the near future. These and similar developments have made the name *World Book* synonymous with encyclopedic excellence the world over.

Both Nault and A. Richard Harmet, the set's longtime executive editor, retired in 1993, making way for a new generation of talented editors, headed by Dale Jacobs and Gary Alt. World Book, Inc. also publishes a number of other useful reference products, including INFORMATION FINDER, a CD-ROM version of *World Book*; CHILDCRAFT, an encyclopedic set for preschoolers and beginning readers; and several fine subject encyclopedias, e.g., THE WORLD BOOK ENCYCLOPEDIA OF

PEOPLE AND PLACES and the WORLD BOOK/RUSH-PRESBYTERIAN-ST. LUKE'S MEDICAL CENTER MEDICAL ENCYCLOPEDIA.

World Book maintains a large permanent staff of approximately 75 editors, artists, researchers, indexers, proofreaders, etc., now headed by Jacobs and Alt. In addition, the editors draw upon the expertise of numerous outside authorities who act as advisers, consultants, and contributors. Most of these people are academicians or writers and many are acknowledged leaders in their field, such as Letitia Baldrige (etiquette), Ken Bloom (musical theater), David Broder (U.S. politics), Helen Delpar (Latin America), Roger Ebert (film), Frank Freidel (American History), John Garraty (American biography), Sir Edmund Hillary (mountain climbing), Seymour Lipset (sociology), James McPherson (U.S. Civil War), David Musto (drugs), James S. Reed (ceramics), Leonard Silk (economics), John Tebbel (journalism), and John Noble Wilford (cartography). Everyone involved in the making of the encyclopedia is identified at the front of Volume 1.

At present, the encyclopedia contains approximately 17,500 entries. Most are relatively short, specific-entry articles averaging less than half a page in length, but some are much longer, running to 30 or more pages. For example, the consecutive articles "Healy, James Augustine," "Hearing Aid," "Hearn, Lafcadio," "Hearne, Samuel," "Hearst, Phoebe Apperson," and "Hearst, William Randolph" all comprise less than two pages of text, whereas the next article, "Heart," is more than 15 pages long.

World Book's coverage is fairly apportioned among the major areas of knowledge. Biographical and geographical topics receive especially generous coverage. Considerable attention is accorded continents and countries, the U.S. states and Canadian provinces, and major cities, rivers, lakes, and mountains of the world. Likewise, prominent historical figures such as Galileo, Alexander Hamilton, Lenin, Martin Luther, Mozart, Napoleon, Shakespeare, Daniel Webster, and the U.S. presidents and Canadian prime ministers receive strong coverage. Important contemporary leaders from all walks of life are also well covered in *World Book*. For example, the encyclopedia includes brief biographies of such individuals as Dr. Charles Drew (physician), Philip Glass (composer), Nadine Gordimer (writer), Magic Johnson (basketball player), Kenneth Kaunda (African leader), Danny Kaye (entertainer), Malcolm X (African American leader), Eugenio Montale (poet), Toni Morrison (writer), Robert Motherwell (artist), Ernest Rutherford (scientist), Mike Tyson (boxer), Robert Venturi (architect), and Chen Ning Yang (physicist).

The encyclopedia's coverage of scientific and technical subjects is first-rate, exemplified by such substantial articles as "Air Conditioning," "Animal," "Battery," "Coal," "Cosmic Rays," "Dinosaur," "Flower," "Fluoridation," "Forestry," "Gas," "Insect," "Jet Propulsion," "Lock," "Mammal," "Mineral," "Nuclear Energy," "Ocean," "Petroleum," "Plant," "Satellite, Artificial," "Sound," "Space Exploration," "Tree," "Weather," and "Zoo." Particularly commendable is the encyclopedia's coverage of medical topics. Not only does the set treat all relevant aspects of the human body and major illnesses such as cancer, heart disease, and psychological depression, but it includes many articles on symptoms of disease (e.g., "Backache," "Constipation," "Pus," "Vomiting"), medical procedures and treatments, even experimental or controversial ones ("Chelation Therapy"), and relatively minor or lesser known medical problems ("Carpal Tunnel Syndrome"; "Pelvic Inflammatory Disease"). Pronunciations for potentially unfamiliar terms and names are included. *Example: World Book* informs the reader that *chelation* is pronounced "*kee LAY shuhn.*"

World Book naturally emphasizes topics of interest to North American readers, the set's principal audience. But when appropriate, international developments are covered, as in the article "Abortion," which notes the availability of the drug RU-486 in France and Great Britain. For the most part, the encyclopedia's coverage is determined by an ongoing study of elementary and secondary school curricula in the U.S. and Canada. Called the Nault-Caswell-Brain Curriculum Analysis, the study not only informs *World Book* editors about what subjects are currently being taught at what grade levels, it identifies broad curricular changes and trends. The encyclopedia is also continuously monitored for its effectiveness as a reference source in some 400 selected classrooms in North America. Students doing research fill out cards each time they use the set, indicating what information was sought, what subject headings they searched, and whether they found what they were looking for. This system of structured feedback from readers helps the editors keep *World Book* as current and user-friendly as possible. No other encyclopedia on the market today is so closely in touch with the school curriculum and current informational needs of students.

Do not, however, make the mistake (as some do) of assuming that *World Book* covers only subjects studied in school. In fact, the encyclopedia provides a vast amount of information about non-school or extra-curricular topics of potential interest to both adults and young people, such as air conditioning, automobile manufacture, bicycle safety, boats and boating, canning, camping, cooking, fishing, first aid, fire prevention and safety, furniture, gardening, lawn care, taxes, types of insurance and pensions, Medicare, health maintenance organizations, safety in the home, sewing, skiing, skin diving, tennis, canasta, and all sorts of other sports and games.

Occasionally, *World Book* slips up and fails to cover an important subject. For instance, the article on Charles Drew, the black physician whose research on blood typing and preservation led to the develop-

ment of blood banks, does not include the circumstances of his death, which are a matter of historical controversy and hence should be addressed. (Contrary to popular myth, Dr. Drew did *not* bleed to death outside a segregated whites-only hospital in North Carolina.) In another instance, sexual harassment—a topic of increasing social and legal significance in recent years—is mentioned only in passing in the article on Clarence Thomas in the 1994 printing of the encyclopedia. Barbara Ittner, in a review of the 1992 printing in *American Reference Books Annual* (1993, pp. 30–31), points to other examples:

> There is no listing in either the encyclopedia or the index for virtual reality (or cyberspace, computer simulation, or flight simulation), a scientific topic of great interest to young people. In addition, an important scientific announcement of 1991 has been overlooked—that of fullerenes, sometimes called "Buckminster Fullerenes" or "buckyballs." Quasicrystals, big news in 1985, are also omitted. Fractals appear, but not Benoit Mandelbrot, the individual who brought them into the public eye.

Happily, such lapses are usually rectified in short order. For instance, the 1994 printing does include information about fullerenes, virtual reality, and computer and flight simulation. In all likelihood, an article on sexual harassment will be added to the set in the near future.

Information in *World Book* can be trusted as reliable and impartial. Facts are checked and double-checked by the encyclopedia's research staff. Articles dealing with controversial or sensitive issues almost always present the pros and cons of the subject in an evenhanded manner, as treatment of such polemical topics as abortion, AIDS, birth control, circumcision, electroshock therapy, fluoridation, homosexuality, IQ testing, nuclear power, Scientology, and the Vietnam War attests. Also, in recent years the editors have systematically eliminated sexist language and sexual stereotyping from the encyclopedia's printed text as well as illustrations.

Information in the encyclopedia is normally as current as can be expected in an annually revised reference work. In their preface, the editors state their unequivocal commitment to being as timely as possible and the need for vigorous continuous revision:

> An encyclopedia must be up to date if it is to serve the best interests of its users. A revised edition of *World Book* is published each year. Each edition reflects up-to-date information and the latest changes in educational viewpoints. Every subject area is under continuing surveillance. The annual revision program is never confined to a single area or to certain volumes. Thousands of pages are revised or updated each year.

These are not empty words. For example, in 1993, the publisher spent several million dollars revising and updating the set. More than 2,600 articles were partially revised, another 500 were either entirely new or completely rewritten, and many illustrations and maps were replaced or revamped—all involving changes in roughly half of the encyclopedia's nearly 14,000 pages. This sort of energetic annual revision effort results in an admirably up-to-date encyclopedia. *Examples:* The article "Abortion" discusses the most recent U.S. Supreme Court cases on the subject, including *Planned Parenthood of Eastern Pennsylvania v. Casey* (1992); the article "Depression" (dealing with the psychological disorder) points out the increasing reliance on antidepressant drugs and identifies fluoxetine (or Prozac) as the most commonly prescribed drug; "Galileo" summarizes recent moves by the Roman Catholic Church to rescind the Inquisition's condemnation of the scientist in the seventeenth century; "Germany," recently revised from top to bottom, includes current information on the enormous political, economic, and social changes brought about by the unification of East and West Germany in 1990.

Prospective purchasers of the encyclopedia should be aware that sales representatives will almost surely promote the *World Book Year Book* as an essential means of keeping the encyclopedia up-to-date year after year. The yearbook includes a detailed review of the previous year's events, a number of special reports on newsworthy subjects, a dictionary supplement, and reprints of a dozen or so articles from the latest edition of the encyclopedia. Unlike most encyclopedia yearbooks, the *World Book Year Book* is a good investment. Efforts are made to relate its contents to those of the encyclopedia by means of gummed cross-reference tabs found at the front of the yearbook. The 1993 yearbook, for example, includes a special report on prisons; the tab, which reads "Special Report **Prison**, 1993 Year Book, p. 392," can be affixed to the encyclopedia article "Prison" for future reference. Note that the same entry headings are used in both the encyclopedia and yearbook.

In addition to the *World Book Year Book*, the publisher offers two specialized annual supplements to the encyclopedia, namely *Science Year* and the *World Book Health & Medical Annual* (formerly *Medical Update*). Heavily illustrated and handsomely produced, these annuals are related to the encyclopedia in the same manner as the basic yearbook; both are recommended for libraries and individual consumers where interest warrants.

The encyclopedia's writing style is a key reason why *World Book* continues to outclass its competition year in and year out. Invariably, articles are clearly and interestingly written. But more than that, *World Book* has what many years ago a reviewer in *Choice* (December 1968, p. 1280) called "a knack for clarity on complicated subjects." This "knack"—putting complex ideas and concepts into easily understandable language without sacrificing accuracy of meaning or being condescending to more advanced readers—may seem routine or effortless to the casual encyclopedia user, but in reality it requires much editorial skill and finesse. As one *World Book* editor once put it, "Easy reading is hard writing."

When appropriate, articles are written at the grade level where they are likely to be read or studied. For example, the article "Animal" is written for a younger audience than, say, the article "Nuclear Energy" or "Radiation." All new articles are carefully examined by the encyclopedia's readability consultant, Dr. Joseph O'Rourke of Ohio State University, to ensure that the vocabulary used is geared to the intended grade level. When technical or potentially unfamiliar terms are used in an article, they are italicized and defined or explained in context. In fact, for many years *World Book* has paid stricter attention to vocabulary control and precise levels of readability than any other general encyclopedia on the market.

The first two paragraphs of the article "Heart" typify the encyclopedia's style:

> **Heart** is the wondrous pump that powers the human body. With each heartbeat, it sends life-giving blood throughout the body. Blood carries oxygen and food to all the body cells. The rhythmic beating of the heart begins about seven months before we are born. When the heart stops beating, we die unless a special device circulates and oxygenates our blood.
>
> The heart is a large, hollow, muscular organ divided into two pumps that lie side by side. Veins transport blood from throughout the body to the right-sided pump. That pump sends the blood to the lungs, where it picks up oxygen. The oxygenated blood then flows to the left side of the heart, which pumps it through arteries to the rest of the body. Valves control the flow of blood through the heart. The left-sided pump, which delivers blood throughout the body, is larger and stronger than the right pump.

Another useful writing technique employed by the encyclopedia to make its contents as comprehensible to as many readers as possible is the "pyramid" style—that is, the article begins with the simplest or most elementary material and becomes more detailed or complex as the text progresses. For example, as the reader gets deeper into the article "Heart," its contents and vocabulary become noticeably more advanced:

> The autonomic nervous system controls the heart rate. Special cells send electrical *impulses* (nerve signals) through the heart, causing it to contract and relax rhythmically. The impulse begins in a small bundle of muscle fibers called the *sinoatrial node*, or *S-A node*. The S-A node is often called the *pacemaker* of the heart because it sets the pace of the heartbeat as it sends out rhythmic signals. The S-A node lies in the right atrium near where the superior vena cava enters the heart. The S-A node sends impulses along certain pathways, causing the atria to contract when the electrical signal reaches them. The impulse then arrives at another node, called the *atrioventricular node*, or *A-V node*. The A-V node lies between the atria and ventricles. It delays the nerve signal briefly, allowing the ventricles enough time to fill with blood. As the impulse continues, the ventricles contract.

Like its chief competitor, COMPTON'S ENCYCLOPEDIA, *World Book* is most appropriate for those reading at the seventh grade level and beyond. In addition, much of the text can be comprehended by readers in the upper elementary grades. (See page 206 for a review of *World Book* as an encyclopedia for children and younger students.)

World Book is an intelligently organized encyclopedia and, not surprisingly, locating specific facts and topics in the text normally poses no difficulty for the user. The set's principal finding device is a large, detailed analytical index of more than 150,000 entries. Comprising most of Volume 22 (called *Research Guide/Index*), the index offers one entry for every 70 words of encyclopedic text, an excellent ratio of index entries to total words (1:70), surpassed only by the ACADEMIC AMERICAN ENCYCLOPEDIA (1:45) and COLLIER'S ENCYCLOPEDIA (1:50).

Numerous cross-references throughout the text also help point the reader in the right direction. *Example:* "Heart" (quoted from above) includes *See* references to such related articles as "Blood," "Circulatory System," "Blood Pressure," "Smoking," "Angiography," "Angioplasty," "Electrocardiograph," "Cardiopulmonary Resuscitation,"

"Heart Murmur," and "Tissue Transplant." In addition, nearly 50 *See also* references appear at the end of the article, e.g., "Aorta," "Artery," "Capillary," "DeBakey, Michael," "Harvey, William," "Heart Association, American," "Myocarditis," "Tachycardia," and "Vein."

Approximately 1,600 articles in the encyclopedia conclude with bibliographies, or lists of "Additional Resources," designed to guide readers seeking further information on the subject. The article "Heart," for example, appends a list of nine titles, including Melvin Berger's *The Artificial Heart* (Watts, 1987) and A.C. Greene's *Taking Heart* (Simon & Schuster, 1990). Sometimes the bibliographies are divided into easy reading books (labeled "Level 1") and more advanced titles ("Level 2"). The bibliographies tend to be carefully selected and reasonably current, although in some instances better, more recent titles are available; e.g., the list accompanying "Heart" fails to include the *Yale University School of Medicine Heart Book* (Hearst Books, 1992), an excellent general work on the subject. Some 200 bibliographies are also found in the *Research Guide/ Index* (Volume 22).

Illustrations and maps add significantly to the encyclopedia's informational value. As Bill Katz points out in his *Basic Information Sources* (6th ed., 1992, p. 249), "The most dramatic aspect of the set is the illustration on each and every page. It has more illustrations than any set, adult's or children's, and the 29,000 plates include 24,000 in color. Illustrations take up over one-third of the total space." By way of example, the 15-page article "Heart" contains 20 illustrations (photographs, drawings, cutaways, etc.), all in color except for an X-ray showing a cardiac catheterization, a pen and ink sketch of the heart's anatomy by Leonardo da Vinci, and a William Harvey woodcut of the circulation of blood. Overall, the illustrations and maps found in *World Book* compare favorably with those in the best illustrated encyclopedias available today, including the ACADEMIC AMERICAN ENCYCLOPEDIA, the NEW BOOK OF KNOWLEDGE, and the RANDOM HOUSE ENCYCLOPEDIA.

Available in several bindings, the encyclopedia is both attractive and well made. High quality machine-coated web offset paper is used to obtain the best possible color reproduction. The two-column page layout is inviting to the eye and the various typefaces are legible as well as aesthetically pleasing. Physically, *World Book* is the best-made encyclopedia in its class.

REPORT CARD: WORLD BOOK ENCYCLOPEDIA				
TOPIC	COVERAGE	ACCURACY	RECENCY	CLARITY
Circumcision	A	A	A	A
Drew, Charles	C	A	B	A
Galileo	A	A	A	A
Glass, Philip	A	A	A	A
Heart Disease	A	A	A	A
IQ	A	A	A	A
Panda Bears	A	A	A	A
Sexual Harassment	F*	NA	NA	NA
Shroud of Turin	A	A	A	A
Uzbekistan	A	A	A	A

A = Excellent; **B** = Above Average; **C** = Average; **D** = Below Average; **F** = Poor; **NA** = Not Applicable
*No Article

SUMMARY

The *World Book Encyclopedia*, the best-selling encyclopedia in North America, is a reference work of preeminent quality. The encyclopedia is particularly noteworthy for its close attention to readability, which makes the set useful to a broad range of people, from young students in the upper elementary grades to older students in high school and college as well as adults. *World Book* also deserves high marks for its ease of use, broad and balanced coverage, accurate and up-to-date contents, impartial treatment of controversial or sensitive subjects, and appealing illustrations and layout. First published in eight volumes in 1917, the encyclopedia has been a reference mainstay among U.S. and Canadian readers for more than 75 years. The bottom line: *World Book* is page for page the best general encyclopedia on the market today.

OTHER OPINIONS

American Reference Books Annual, 1993, pp. 29–31 (review by Barbara Ittner); *Basic Information Sources* by William A. Katz (vol. 1 of *Introduction to Reference Work*, 6th ed., New York: McGraw-Hill, 1992), pp. 248–50; *Reference Books Bulletin* (in *Booklist*), September 15, 1993, p. 183 (unsigned review); *Reference Sources for Small and Medium-Sized Libraries* (5th ed., Chicago: American Library Assn., 1992), p. 35 (review by Jovian P. Lang).

COMPARISON CHART

Medium-Sized Encyclopedias for Adults and Older Students

This chart provides basic statistical information about each of the midsized encyclopedias for adults and older students reviewed in *Kister's Best Encyclopedias*. The chart also offers a quick comparative overview of the 14 titles in this category. How do the ACADEMIC AMERICAN ENCYCLOPEDIA, COMPTON'S ENCYCLOPEDIA, and the WORLD BOOK ENCYCLOPEDIA—the three standout sets in the group—compare in terms of numbers of words? Articles? Illustrations? Index entries? Price? What about the FUNK & WAGNALLS NEW ENCYCLOPEDIA, which has more volumes (29) than any of the others, or the OXFORD ILLUSTRATED ENCYCLOPEDIA, which has only nine volumes. The chart answers such questions at a glance.

In the case of price information, consumers should understand that prices are subject to change by the publisher or distributor at any time. For the latest price of any encyclopedia, consult *Books in Print* (a standard reference source found in practically all libraries) or, better, call the publisher or distributor direct. Most now have toll-free numbers where the latest information about price and availability can be obtained quickly and efficiently. Telephone numbers are listed in this guide at the beginning of each review under "Price and Sales Information," as well as in the directory of publishers and distributors at the back of the book (see Appendix B).

The chart's final column assigns a letter grade to each encyclopedia: A = Excellent; B = Above Average; C = Average; D = Below Average; F = Poor. The letter grade represents a final summary of the encyclopedia's detailed evaluation in *Kister's Best Encyclopedias*. Consumers seriously interested in purchasing an encyclopedia are urged to base their selection decisions on the reviews in the book, and not rely solely on the letter grades given in the chart, which are necessarily arbitrary.

Title	Vols.	Words	Pages	Articles	Illus. & Maps	Cross-refs.	Index Entries	Lowest Retail Price	Rating
Academic American Encyclopedia	21	9.1 mil	9,864	28,960	18,000	65,000	201,000	$1,150.00	A
Barnes & Noble New American Encyclopedia[1]	20	9.1 mil	9,864	28,960	18,000	65,000	201,000	299.00	A[1]
Compton's Encyclopedia	26	9 mil	10,590	34,000[2]	22,510	35,500	154,000	499.00	A
Funk & Wagnalls New Encyclopedia	29	9 mil	13,056	25,000	9,500	88,300	130,000	163.81	B
Global International[3] Encyclopedia	21	9.1 mil	9,864	28,960	18,000	65,000	201,000	1,150.00	A[3]
Grolier Academic Encyclopedia[3]	21	9.1 mil	9,864	28,960	18,000	65,000	201,000	1,150.00	A[3]
Grolier Encyclopedia of Knowledge[4]	20	6.5 mil	8,320	22,000	13,000	40,000	90,000	120.00	B
Grolier International Encyclopedia[1]	20	9.1 mil	9,864	28,960	18,000	65,000	201,000	199.00	A[1]
Lexicon Universal Encyclopedia[3]	21	9.1 mil	9,864	28,960	18,000	65,000	201,000	1,150.00	A[3]
Macmillan Family Encyclopedia[3]	21	9.1 mil	9,864	28,960	18,000	65,000	201,000	199.00	A[3]

Title	Vols.	Words	Pages	Articles	Illus. & Maps	Cross-refs.	Index Entries	Lowest Retail Price	Rating
New Standard Encyclopedia	20	8 mil	10,750	17,500	13,000	53,600	100,000	900.00	C
Oxford Illustrated Encyclopedia	9	3 mil	3,300	20,000	2,500	25,000	36,000	265.00	D
Webster's Family Encyclopedia	10	1.5 mil	2,834	25,000	1,200	15,000	None	19.95	D
World Book Encyclopedia	22	10 mil	14,000	17,500	31,300	100,000	150,000	679.00	A

1. Same text as the ACADEMIC AMERICAN ENCYCLOPEDIA but no cumulative index (Vol. 21); portions of the index printed at end of each volume.
2. Encyclopedia has 5,250 main articles; 28,750 brief articles in index.
3. Same text as ACADEMIC AMERICAN ENCYCLOPEDIA.
4. Abridged version of ACADEMIC AMERICAN ENCYCLOPEDIA.

Small Encyclopedias for Adults and Older Students

* * * * * * * * *

OVERVIEW

Someone once said that making a one-volume encyclopedia "is like taking the broth of the universe and condensing it into a bouillon cube." Indeed, the great virtue of single-volume encyclopedias from the consumer's point of view is that they are physically compact and do not take up much room in the home, office, library, etc. Most are desk-size and convenient to handle, although the largest—the COLUMBIA ENCYCLOPEDIA and the RANDOM HOUSE ENCYCLOPEDIA—normally require a stand or flat surface for easy consultation. Accordingly, small-volume encyclopedias are most popular with individuals who live in small homes, town houses, condominiums, and apartments, along with students and office workers who have a limited amount of space for books.

In recent years there has been a flurry of publishing activity in the area of small-volume encyclopedias for adults and older students. Publishers find such encyclopedias attractive ventures for several reasons. First, one- and two-volume encyclopedias are less costly to produce than multivolume sets and hence require a smaller capital investment. Second, they are less costly to maintain, since small encyclopedias are usually not revised on an annual basis as are most multivolume works. Third, small encyclopedias are priced to sell, retailing for no more than $130.00 (and usually much less), whereas a decent multivolume encyclopedia now costs from $500.00 to $1,500.00 or more. And fourth, small encyclopedias are easier for publishers to market than the big sets—that is, one-volume encyclopedias are customarily sold through established retail channels (bookstores, discount stores, etc.) or via direct mail, whereas multivolume encyclopedias are sold chiefly in the home, which requires a sales force and all the expense that goes with it.

Of the 16 small-volume adult encyclopedias currently on the North American market, one—the COLUMBIA ENCYCLOPEDIA—stands out as a work of the highest quality. A physically large book that weighs around 11 pounds and stands a foot high, the COLUMBIA ENCYCLOPEDIA contains approximately 50,000 articles, 3,000 pages, and 6.6 million words. Unlike its major competitors, the encyclopedia originates in North America—"an American encyclopedia written for American readers" (preface). It is thorough, reliable, well-written, and up-to-date, the fifth edition published in 1993. Although relatively expensive ($125.00), the COLUMBIA ENCYCLOPEDIA is enthusiastically recommended as the best single-volume encyclopedia currently available for adults and serious students.

Another fine one-volume encyclopedia is the innovative RANDOM HOUSE ENCYCLOPEDIA, which was designed in Great Britain but has been adapted for North American readers. Like the rival *Columbia Encyclopedia*, it is physically large (12 pounds, 4 inches thick, a foot high), expensive ($129.95), and meticulously edited, but there the similarities between the two encyclopedias end. Whereas the COLUMBIA ENCYCLOPEDIA is a scholarly, alphabetically arranged work with comparatively few illustrations and a totally black-and-white look about it, the RANDOM HOUSE ENCYCLOPEDIA is a popularly written, thematically arranged volume with numerous color illustrations and a bright, visually inviting appearance. It brings knowledge alive, especially for students. On the other hand, because of its organization, the RANDOM HOUSE ENCYCLOPEDIA is less easy to use than the COLUMBIA, and it is not as current, the last edition published in 1990.

Among the smaller, desk-size one-volume encyclopedias for adults and older students, the standout work is the CONCISE COLUMBIA ENCYCLOPEDIA. An updated abridgment of the *New Columbia Encyclopedia* (the fourth edition of the COLUMBIA ENCYCLOPEDIA, published in 1975), the CONCISE COLUMBIA first appeared in 1983 and was revised in 1989. It contains roughly a million words, a thousand pages, and 15,000 authoritative articles. Now in some need of revision, it will most likely be replaced within the next few years by a new concise edition based on the recently published fifth edition (1993) of the COLUMBIA ENCYCLOPEDIA.

Competing directly with the CONCISE COLUMBIA ENCYCLOPEDIA are the AMERICAN SPECTRUM ENCYCLOPEDIA, the CAMBRIDGE ENCYCLOPEDIA (also published as the BARNES & NOBLE ENCYCLOPEDIA), and WEBSTER'S NEW WORLD ENCYCLOPEDIA. Each of these single-volume works has between 1.5 and 2 million words, well over a thousand pages, and between 17,000 and 30,000 short-entry articles. Each originated abroad, each is competently edited, and each is fairly priced—the BARNES & NOBLE ENCYCLOPEDIA is an especially attractive buy at $20.00. Consumers cannot go wrong purchasing and using any of these titles, but none meets the high editorial standards set by the COLUMBIA ENCYCLOPEDIA, the RANDOM HOUSE ENCYCLOPEDIA, and the CONCISE COLUMBIA DNCYCLOPEDIA.

WEBSTER'S NEW WORLD ENCYCLOPEDIA is also published in college and pocket editions, both updated abridgments of the parent work. Likewise, the CAMBRIDGE ENCYCLOPEDIA offers a condensed version in paperback. Consumers looking for a decent one-volume encyclopedia in an inexpensive paperbound edition will find either the WEBSTER'S NEW WORLD ENCYCLOPEDIA: POCKET EDITION ($14.00) or the CAMBRIDGE PAPERBACK ENCYCLOPEDIA ($19.95) a good buy. Two other paperbound single-volume encyclopedias—the NEW AMERICAN DESK ENCYCLOPEDIA and the RUNNING PRESS CYCLOPEDIA—are available, but neither can be recommended.

In a category all its own is the two-volume VOLUME LIBRARY, which first appeared in 1911 and now has the distinction of being the oldest consecutively published small-volume encyclopedia in North America. Never considered a work of first-rate quality, the VOLUME LIBRARY—so named because it divides knowledge into topically arranged chapters or "volumes"—has improved in recent years, due largely to the efforts of editor Gorton Carruth, who has been responsible for the set since the mid-1980s. Still, it has a long way to go before it can be considered a first-choice encyclopedia.

At the bottom of the small-volume heap are BARRON'S NEW STUDENT'S CONCISE ENCYCLOPEDIA, the DICTIONARY OF CULTURAL LITERACY, the KNOWLEDGE ENCYCLOPEDIA, and the aforementioned NEW AMERICAN DESK ENCYCLOPEDIA and the RUNNING PRESS CYCLOPEDIA. Wise consumers will avoid these titles.

AMERICAN SPECTRUM ENCYCLOPEDIA

FACTS

Full Title: *The American Spectrum Encyclopedia: The New Illustrated Home Reference Guide.* **Editor in Chief:** Michael D. Harkavy.

Publisher: American Booksellers Assn. and Spectrum Database Publishing B.V. **Distributor:** Booksellers Order Service. **Date**

Published: 1991.

Volumes: One. **Words:** 1.5 million. **Pages:** 1,312. **Articles:** 17,000. **Bibliographies:** None. **Illustrations and Maps:** 3,850. **Cross-references:** 7,000. **Index Entries:** None. **Editorial Staff, Advisers, and Contributors:** 105. Trim Size: 9¼ × 10¾ in.

Price and Sales Information: $85.00. Individual consumers can purchase the *American Spectrum Encyclopedia* in bookstores or, if the book is not in stock, it can be ordered. Similarly, educational institutions (schools, libraries, etc.) can order it through a book wholesaler. To order the encyclopedia directly from the distributor, call toll-free 1-800-636-0037 or write Booksellers Order Service, 137 West 25th Street, New York, NY 10001.

EVALUATION

The *American Spectrum Encyclopedia* is a physically hefty, handsomely illustrated single-volume encyclopedia intended chiefly for use in the home by adults and older students at the junior high school level and beyond. It competes in a crowded field of small-volume general encyclopedias that includes such formidable titles as the COLUMBIA ENCYCLOPEDIA (which today stands alone as the preeminent one-volume encyclopedia in English), the RANDOM HOUSE ENCYCLOPEDIA, the CAMBRIDGE ENCYCLOPEDIA, the CONCISE COLUMBIA ENCYCLOPEDIA, WEBSTER'S NEW WORLD ENCYCLOPEDIA, and the venerable VOLUME LIBRARY.

Prepared jointly by Uitgeverij Het Spectrum (a top Dutch encyclopedia publisher) and the American Booksellers Association (or ABA, the main trade association for bookstores in the U.S.), the *American Spectrum* is designed specifically for a North American readership. It was published in September 1991 and has not been revised since. Whether there will eventually be an updated edition is questionable, as the encyclopedia—the ABA's first major publishing venture—has apparently not done well in the marketplace. In fact, according to an article by John Mutter entitled "ABA at a Crossroads" in *Publishers Weekly* (March 2, 1992, pp. 9–18), the encyclopedia suffered early return rates by book wholesalers and retailers as high as 90 percent, a disastrous sales performance by any standard.

Be that as it may, the *American Spectrum* appears to be an authoritative encyclopedia, although its articles are unsigned. Certainly the copublishers are reputable. The editor in chief, Michael D. Harkavy, unknown to this critic, is supported by two editorial staffs (U.S. and European), which together number 82 people, as well as a six-member editorial advisory board, which includes Bernard F. Rath, executive director of the ABA, plus two experienced publishers, a librarian, a library school educator, and a psychology professor. There is also an eight-member editorial review board, most of whom are U.S. booksellers. All of these people—not your typical encyclopedia mix but an interesting group—are listed at the front of the volume.

The *American Spectrum* is a specific-entry encyclopedia comprising 17,000 usually very brief articles arranged A-to-Z. Each page contains about a dozen articles, which average roughly 100 words in length. A few articles, such as "Baseball," "Castles," and "Persian Gulf War," are enhanced by one- or two-page spreads featuring captioned illustrations. In a note at the beginning of the book, editor Harkavy explains: "These special spreads provide a highly illustrated overview of the topic and are dedicated to the proposition that sometimes a picture really is worth a thousand words. The selection of topics for additional illustrative treatment has been done on the basis of what is relevant to the U.S. experience on the eve of the 21st century."

The encyclopedia's coverage broadly reflects the U.S. high school curriculum. Again editor Harkavy: "The selection of entries was based on core subjects that form the cornerstone of U.S. high school curricula. This has been accomplished through a consensus of professional educators, teachers, librarians, educational publishing experts, and a team of editorial experts." Biographical and geographical articles account for approximately half the total text. The countries of the world and U.S. states receive especially generous coverage, including attractive information boxes that furnish basic information (population, size, etc.) at a glance. The encyclopedia also appends much useful material, such as a 57-page color world atlas and gazetteer, an illustrated outline of world history, the text of the Declaration of Independence and U.S. Constitution, and lists of U.S. presidents, Supreme Court justices, and national parks.

Although the encyclopedia's reach is broad, its articles tend to lack depth, and there is a disconcerting penchant on the part of the writers to offer vague observations in lieu of hard information. *Examples:* In the article "Abortion," the reader learns, "In 1973, the U.S. Supreme Court ruled in *Roe v. Wade* that abortions in the first or second trimester are legal, but the moral and legal controversy surrounding abortion continues." Exactly how that controversy has played out during the succeeding two decades or more is not discussed. "Christian Science" consists of five lines that tell the reader only that Mary Baker Eddy founded the religion in Boston in 1879 and that it is "based on belief in the power of Christian faith to heal sickness." The 11-line article "Depression" (in economics) offers little more than a dictionary definition of the phenomenon and a passing reference to the Great Depression. "Fluoridation" concludes, "Despite some opposition, many authorities now fluoridate water," but the nature of the opposition is not discussed or even hinted at.

The encyclopedia can usually be trusted as a reliable source of information, although occasionally errors occur. For instance, the article "Panda" erroneously implies the giant panda is a member of the raccoon family. In another instance, the cross-reference from "Eddy, Mary Baker" to "Churches of Christ" is incorrect; the reference should have been to "Christian Science." In addition, the book contains a disquieting number of typographical errors. The encyclopedia is normally impartial in its presentation of information, but frequently controversial or sensitive subject matter is ignored or glossed over. Examples can be found in such articles as "Circumcision," "Dickens, Charles," "Drew, Charles Richard," "Fluoridation," "Hypnosis," "Intelligence Quotient," and "Scientology."

Published in late 1991, the *American Spectrum* is admirably current as of that date. As Sandy Whiteley's review in *Reference Books Bulletin* (in *Booklist*, January 15, 1992, p. 972) points out,

> There are biographies of people of current interest like Steven Jobs, John Major, and Michael Jordan; the article on the Soviet Union says the republics are "clamoring for independence"; and there is a relatively long article with a map for the Persian Gulf War. Entries for places give population; figures for U.S. states and cities are from the 1990 census.

On the other hand, the encyclopedia is now three years old and already events have overtaken it in a number of instances, including the cataclysmic changes in Eastern Europe and the Balkans. For example, all of the entries for the former Soviet republics, such as Uzbekistan, are now in need of revision. In the area of up-to-dateness, the CAMBRIDGE ENCYCLOPEDIA (revised in 1992), the CAMBRIDGE PAPERBACK ENCYCLOPEDIA (published in 1993), the COLUMBIA ENCYCLOPEDIA (last revised in 1993), and WEBSTER'S NEW WORLD ENCYCLOPEDIA: COLLEGE EDITION (published in 1993) are clearly superior to the *American Spectrum*.

As its Report Card (see below) indicates, one of the *American Spectrum's* real strengths is its clarity. The articles are almost always written in a manner that will be readily understandable to readers as young as 13 or 14. In his foreword to the book, Vartan Gregorian (president of Brown University) notes that, "*The American Spectrum Encyclopedia* dispels any commonly held impression that an encyclopedia must not be easy reading and, by definition, must be dull." The article "Heart" (quoted in full here) gives a fair idea of the encyclopedia's style:

> **Heart**, muscular organ whose purpose is to pump blood through the body. The human heart is about the size of the closed fist, shaped like a blunt cone and is located in the chest cavity, slightly left of center. The heart is divided into right and left halves by a muscular partition. Each half is subdivided into two cavities, the upper (atrium) and the lower (ventricle). Blood from the veins of the body flows to the right atrium. From there it goes to the right ventricle, which pumps it to the lungs. From the lungs, the blood, now rich in oxygen, is carried back to the left atrium. It then flows into the left ventricle, from where it is pumped throughout the body. A series of valves between the right and left atria and ventricles and at the entrances to the main blood vessels prevent blood from backing up as it circulates. Diseases of the heart and blood vessels, whiche [sic] cause about half of all deaths in the United States, are called cardiovascular diseases. Three major kinds of heart disease are hypertension, arteriosclerosis, and rheumatic fever. *See also*: Circulatory system.

Finding general information in the *American Spectrum* is usually not difficult because of its specific-entry (as opposed to broad-entry) approach. But locating all material in the book on a specific or related topic can sometimes be a frustrating business. Not only does the encyclopedia lack an index, its cross-reference system does not always guide the reader to pertinent articles. *Examples*: The article "Depression" (in economics) has no cross-reference to the article "Great Depression." Likewise, "Heart" (see above) identifies three major types of heart

disease (hypertension, arteriosclerosis, and rheumatic fever), but fails to indicate that the book contains articles on each of these topics; the article's only cross-reference is "*See also*: Circulatory system." "Christian Science" lacks a cross-reference to "Eddy, Mary Baker" (and, as mentioned, the Mary Baker Eddy article gives an incorrect cross-reference to "Churches of Christ").

Indeed, a case can be made that the *American Spectrum* would be a better encyclopedia if it had a general index. Here is just one of many examples that could be cited to support this conclusion. The reader in search of information on suicide will in all likelihood go directly to that term in the book and, not surprisingly, find the entry "Suicide"; 10 lines long, it is typically a quite superficial treatment of the topic. As there are no cross-references to other articles and no index that might provide access to additional references, the reader will naturally conclude that 10 lines is all the encyclopedia has to offer on suicide. What the reader does not know, or can discover only by serendipity or luck, is that the article "Depression" (in psychology) contains 22 lines devoted entirely to suicide, including several enlightening statistics. Obviously, an index would quickly and efficiently lead the reader to such buried information.

The encyclopedia also lacks bibliographies, or lists of recommended sources that the reader might consult for additional information. This omission is not unexpected; among the small-volume encyclopedias for adults and older students currently available, only the COLUMBIA ENCYCLOPEDIA, the RANDOM HOUSE ENCYCLOPEDIA, and the VOLUME LIBRARY include bibliographies. On the other hand, the lack of bibliographies is yet another competitive disadvantage for the *American Spectrum* in a tough market.

On the bright side, the encyclopedia's illustrations and maps are usually first-rate, adding to the book's value both informationally and aesthetically. The majority (2,100 of 3,850) are in color, and the color reproduction is of very good quality. The article "Heart," for instance, is enhanced by an excellent color drawing of the organ, with the important parts clearly labeled. In her review of the encyclopedia in *Reference Books Bulletin* (in *Booklist*, January 15, 1992, p. 972), Sandy Whiteley offers these observations on the illustrations:

> The 3,800 illustrations are attractive and range from postage-stamp size to more than half a page. They are mostly photographs, but drawings are used when appropriate (e.g., *Archi-*

tecture, Mining, Seismograph). All pictures are captioned but it is not always clear which article is being illustrated.

The *American Spectrum*'s physical format is quite satisfactory. The book, which comes with a colorful jacket, is physically large (9¼ × 10¾ in.), weighs approximately 9 pounds, and is sturdily bound to withstand heavy use. The typography is good-looking and the overall page design bright and attractive. Color reproduction is enhanced by the use of high quality acid-free paper.

SUMMARY

Published in 1991 and not revised since, the *American Spectrum Encyclopedia* is copublished by the Dutch publisher Uitgeverij Het Spectrum and the American Booksellers Association (ABA). It is intended specifically for a North American audience, its coverage loosely reflecting the U.S. high school curriculum. Unfortunately for the ABA, the encyclopedia has been something of a flop saleswise, most likely due to the strong competition among one- and two-volume encyclopedias for adults and older students in the North American market.

The encyclopedia itself is attractively made, offers broad coverage of basic knowl-

edge and information, is very clearly written, and has first-rate illustrations. But it also possesses a number of negatives, including superficial treatment of many topics, a tendency to ignore or gloss over controversial or sensitive subjects, lack of an adequate system of cross-references, no index at all, and no bibliographies. Also, the encyclopedia is not always as accurate as it might be, and increasingly it requires revision, although it is by no means embarrassingly out-of-date. The bottom line: An adequate encyclopedia swamped by the competition.

REPORT CARD: AMERICAN SPECTRUM ENCYCLOPEDIA				
TOPIC	COVERAGE	ACCURACY	RECENCY	CLARITY
Circumcision	C	A	C	A
Drew, Charles	D	A	A	A
Galileo	C	A	B	A
Glass, Philip	B	A	B	A
Heart Disease	C	A	B	A
IQ	C	A	C	A
Panda Bears	D	C	C	A
Sexual Harassment	F*	NA	NA	NA
Shroud of Turin	A	A	A	B
Uzbekistan	C	B	C	A

A = Excellent; **B** = Above Average; **C** = Average; **D** = Below Average; **F** = Poor; **NA** = Not Applicable
*No Article

OTHER OPINIONS

Library Journal, December 1991, p. 130 (review by Kenneth F. Kister); *Reference Books*

Bulletin (in *Booklist*), January 15, 1992, p. 972 (review by Sandy Whiteley)

BARNES & NOBLE ENCYCLOPEDIA

FACTS

Full Title: *The Barnes & Noble Encyclopedia: Based on the Cambridge Encyclopedia.* **Editor:** David Crystal. **Publisher:** Barnes & Noble, Inc. (by arrangement with Cambridge University Press). **Date Published:** 1993 (reprint of the CAMBRIDGE ENCYCLOPEDIA, 1992 revision).

Also published as the CAMBRIDGE ENCYCLOPEDIA.

Volumes: One. **Words:** 1.5 million. **Pages:** 1,488. **Articles:** 30,000. **Bibliographies:** None. **Illustrations and Maps:** 800. **Cross-references:** 75,000. **Index Entries:** None. **Editorial Staff, Advisers, and Contributors:** 120. **Trim Size:** 7½ × 10¼ in.

Price and Sales Information: $19.98 plus tax. The *Barnes & Noble Encyclopedia*—a retitled edition of the CAMBRIDGE ENEYCLOPEDIA (1992 revision)—is sold in Barnes & Noble Bookstores nationwide as well as via mail order through Barnes & Noble in New York City. For further information about the encyclopedia or to order it, call toll-free 1-800-242-6657 or write Barnes & Noble, Inc., 120 Fifth Avenue, New York, NY 10011.

CONSUMER NOTE

The one-volume *Barnes & Noble Encyclopedia* has exactly the same contents as the one-volume CAMBRIDGE ENCYCLOPEDIA (1992 revision). The only difference between the two volumes, apart from their distinctive titles, jackets, and bindings, is their price: the *Barnes & Noble Encyclopedia* currently retails for $19.98 (plus tax), whereas the CAMBRIDGE ENCYCLOPEDIA normally sells for $49.95. This low price makes the *Barnes & Noble Encyclopedia* a very good buy, despite the encyclopedia's many limitations.

Barnes & Noble, Inc., one of the largest bookstore chains in North America, was founded in 1873 in Wheaton, Illinois. Today the firm's corporate headquarters and flagship store—said to be the largest general interest bookstore in the world—are located in New York City. Its subsidiaries include B. Dalton Bookseller, Scribner's Bookstores, Bookstop, and Doubleday Bookshops. In the case of the CAMBRIDGE ENCYCLOPEDIA, Barnes & Noble distributes the 1992 edition under its own name and at its own price, which as noted is considerably lower than the established retail price. In the past, Barnes & Noble has merchandised other encyclopedias in a similar manner, most recently offering Grolier's multivolume ACADEMIC AMERICAN ENCYCLOPEDIA under the title BARNES & NOBLE NEW AMERICAN ENCYCLOPEDIA.

For a detailed evaluation of the contents of the *Barnes & Noble Encyclopedia,* see the CAMBRIDGE ENCYCLOPEDIA (page 118).

BARRON'S NEW STUDENT'S CONCISE ENCYCLOPEDIA

FACTS

Full Title: *Barron's New Student's Concise Encyclopedia.* Project Editor: Carolyn Horne. **Publisher:** Barron's Educational Series, Inc. Former Title: *Barron's Student's Concise Encyclopedia* (1988). **Date Published:** First Edition, 1988; Second Edition, 1993.

Volumes: One. **Words:** 1 million. **Pages:** 1,281. **Articles:** 20,000. **Bibliographies:** None. **Illustrations and Maps:** 500. **Cross-references:** 150. **Index Entries:** 15,000. **Editorial Staff, Advisers, and Contributors:** 67. **Trim Size:** 6¾ × 9¼ in.

Price and Sales Information: $29.95. Individual consumers can purchase *Barron's New Student's Concise Encyclopedia* in bookstores or, if the book is not in stock, it can be ordered. Similarly, educational institutions (schools, libraries, etc.) can order it through a book wholesaler. To order the encyclopedia directly from the publisher, call toll-free 1-800-645-3476 or write Barron's Educational Series, Inc., 250 Wireless Blvd., Hauppauge, NY 11788.

EVALUATION

First published in 1988 as *Barron's Student's Concise Encyclopedia* and updated in a second edition in 1993 under the slightly modified title *Barron's New Student's Concise Encyclopedia*, this desk-size encyclopedia is promoted as an all-purpose reference work for students in high school and college. The book's introduction describes it rather grandly as "a treasury of practical knowledge for students, researchers, writers, or anyone with a need for concise, accurate information drawn from every major field of academic study."

The publisher, Barron's Educational Series, Inc., is best known for its practical books for students, such as study guides to prepare for various national educational tests, books on vocabulary building and improvement, and the occasional general reference publication, which currently includes two encyclopedias, BARRON'S JUNIOR FACT FINDER for younger students, and *Barron's New Student's Concise Encyclopedia* (under review here). The people who write or compile books for Barron's are usually not well-known authorities. This is certainly the case with

Barron's New Student's Concise Encyclopedia. The project editor, editorial staff, writers, and artists—67 unheralded names in all— are listed at the back of book in tiny type just before the index. None of the material in the encyclopedia is signed.

Like several other small-volume encyclopedias for adults and older students (the DICTIONARY OF CULTURAL LITERACY, RANDOM HOUSE ENCYCLOPEDIA, the RUNNING PRESS CYCLOPEDIA, and the VOLUME LIBRARY), *Barron's New Student's Concise Encyclopedia* is arranged topically (as opposed to alphabetically), the contents grouped by subject in 25 sections: "Art," "Biology," "Chemistry," "Computers," "Earth and Space Science," "Economics and Business," "Government," "History—United States," "History— World," "Language Arts," "Law," "Literature," "Living Independently," "Mathematics," "Medical Terms," "Music," "Mythology," "Philosophy," "Physics," "Psychology," "Religion," "Study and Learning Aids," "Technology," "World at a Glance," and "Useful Tables."

As these section headings indicate, scientific and technical subjects receive the lion's share of attention in the encyclopedia, with history, government, and some areas of the humanities also fairly well represented. The book also includes a large amount of useful everyday information, such as toll-free telephone numbers for selected businesses and agencies of the federal government, calorie values for common foods, first aid procedures, how checking accounts work, advice about passports and international travel, and, particularly for students, how to study, take tests, make a speech, use the library, and write a term paper.

The encyclopedia's weakest coverage occurs in the social sciences, where sociology, anthropology, and human cultures around the world are virtually ignored. In addition, *Barron's* contains almost nothing about specific plant and animal life; for instance, the volume completely lacks information about such common animals as dogs, cats, and cows, nor do more exotic creatures like manatees, monkeys, and panda bears fare any better. Likewise, contemporary artists, writers, and musicians are almost completely shut out of the encyclopedia. The Report Card (see below) provides an accurate portrait of the book's erratic coverage.

If the encyclopedia's coverage is severely imbalanced, its treatment of those subjects it does cover is often woefully lacking in substance. Frequently its articles are little more than dictionary-style definitions, as in the case of "Venereal Disease," which comprises two sentences: "A communicable disease transmitted by sexual intercourse or genital contact. Venereal diseases include gonorrhea, syphilis, and granuloma inguinale." And exactly what might "granuloma inguinale" be? The encyclopedia never bothers to explain. Many other articles, including "Abortion," "Adoption," "Capital Punishment," "Circumcision," and "Intelligence Quotient" are equally superficial.

Information found in *Barron's* is normally accurate and presented without discernible bias. In many instances, though, controversial or sensitive subjects are ignored or glossed over. The entry "Capital Punishment," for example, fails to even mention that the death penalty is the subject of much controversy, let alone furnish a summary of the pros and cons of the issue. Similar treatment is given such polemical topics as abortion, tests that measure human intelligence and aptitude, fluoridation of the public water supply, and religious groups like Christian Science and the Seventh-Day Adventist Church. An exception is homosexuality, which *Barron's* treats in a thoughtful, balanced manner.

As noted, *Barron's* was first published in 1988 and later updated in a second edition in 1993. The 1993 edition minimally revised some sections, including "World at a Glance," where basic information about the countries of the world, including the newly formed nations of Eastern Europe, is recorded. In addition, the revised version added some material in the area of health and medicine.

Generally speaking, however, *Barron's* cannot be considered a well-maintained encyclopedia. Some of its articles are plainly out-of-date and some bespeak another era. *Examples:* Sections devoted to the arts generally ignore contemporary trends, creations, and practitioners. The article "The Library: How to Use It" might have been written 25 or 50 years ago, e.g., "The card catalogue is an alphabetical index of all the books in the library"; there is not a single reference in the article to automated catalogs or reference materials in nonprint form, which are now commonplace even in smaller school and public libraries. The article "Galileo" informs the reader that the scientist's work "was condemned by the church in 1616 as dangerous" and that he "was subsequently tried and sentenced to house arrest by the Inquisition," but it fails to mention that in recent times the Roman Catholic Church has reversed itself on the matter of Galileo's heresy.

The encyclopedia's writing style varies markedly from section to section and sometimes from article to article. For example, "Christian Science" is written in nearly impenetrable prose ("One may say, therefore, that Christian Science is a philosophy, a semi-theology, a system of Biblicism, and a psycho-therapy effectively organized, amply financed, and aptly propagated"), whereas "Seventh-Day Adventists" is reasonably clear ("Adventists adhere to a literal interpretation of the Scriptures, and believe the dead are in limbo to be judged at the second coming of Christ"). Another annoying feature of the encyclopedia's style is that technical terms are often used without explanation. In "Galileo," for instance, the reader learns that Galileo's "researches confirmed his belief in the Copernican theory and he openly supported in 1613 this heliocentric theory," but no effort is made to explain or define the terms *Copernican* and *heliocentric*.

The article "Heart" in the medical section is fairly typical of the encyclopedia's style; here is an excerpt:

> The muscular, roughly cone-shaped organ that pumps blood throughout the body. Lying behind the sternum between the lungs, it is about the size of a closed fist, about 12 centimeters (5 inches) long, 8 centimeters (3 inches) wide at its broadest upper part, and about 6 centimeters (2¼ inches) thick and weighs about 275–345 grams (10–12 ounces) in males, 225 to 275 grams (8–10 ounces) in females. Under outer epicardium membranes, the heart wall—myocardium—consists of cardiac muscle; the innermost layer—the endocardium—is continuous with lining of the blood vessels. The heart is divided into left and right sides by a septum; each side has an upper atrium (auricle) and lower ventricle. Through coordinated nerve impulses and muscular contractions, initiated in the sinoatrial node of the right atrium, the heart pumps blood throughout the body.

Readers seeking to locate specific subjects and facts in *Barron's* will find the 15,000-entry index at the back of the book a necessary finding device, due to the book's topical arrangement. The index, however, is not comprehensive nor always reliable. By way of example, the article "Apartheid" contains quite a bit of useful information about the history of South Africa, but the index entry "South Africa" fails to include a reference to "Apartheid." Kathleen Farago, in her review of *Barron's* in *American Reference Books Annual* (1989, p. 16), points out that "the list of toll-free numbers and some other items could not be found in the index." Unfortunately, cross-references are used sparingly and only within sections.

The encyclopedia lacks bibliographies—lists of recommended sources that the reader might consult for additional information. This omission is not unexpected; among the small-volume encyclopedias for adults and older students currently available, only the COLUMBIA ENCYCLOPEDIA, the RANDOM HOUSE ENCYCLOPEDIA, and the VOLUME LIBRARY include bibliographies. On the other hand, the editors of *Barron's* recognize that the encyclopedia is a limited source of information, noting that "it omits far more than it includes" (introduction). Why not, then, provide selected references to sources of further information on major subjects?

The encyclopedia's illustrations are all in black-and-white, except for 32 color plates (mostly historical maps) in the middle of the book. The most effective illustrations are line drawings accompanying articles in "Biology," "Chemistry," and "Physics." On the other hand, the illustrations in "Art" tend to be ineffectual because they lack color; for instance, the article on Henri Matisse speaks of "his use of brilliant and pure colors," but the illustration—a reproduction of *Jazz: Icarus*—is in black-and-white; likewise Marc Chagall's *Green Violinist* is in black-and-white. Numerous similar examples could be cited.

The book's physical format could be improved. The binding is glued, not sewn. Inside, the two-column page layout tends to be unappealing and dull, due in part to the lack of color. On the plus side, the typefaces used are legible and the volume comes with an attractive dust jacket.

REPORT CARD: BARRON'S NEW STUDENT'S CONCISE ENCYCLOPEDIA

TOPIC	COVERAGE	ACCURACY	RECENCY	CLARITY
Circumcision	D	A	C	D
Drew, Charles	F*	NA	NA	NA
Galileo	C	A	C	B
Glass, Philip	F*	NA	NA	NA
Heart Disease	C	A	C	C
IQ	D	A	C	B
Panda Bears	F*	NA	NA	NA
Sexual Harassment	F*	NA	NA	NA
Shroud of Turin	F*	NA	NA	NA
Uzbekistan	C	A	A	B

A = Excellent; **B** = Above Average; **C** = Average; **D** = Below Average; **F** = Poor; **NA** = Not Applicable
*No Article

SUMMARY

Intended chiefly for students at the secondary school and college levels, this single-volume encyclopedia first appeared in 1988 as *Barron's Student's Concise Encyclopedia* and was updated in 1993 under the slightly revised title *Barron's New Student's Concise Encyclopedia*. Arranged topically (as opposed to alphabetically), the book emphasizes scientific and technical subjects as well as practical information of potential interest to students, but overall the coverage is erratic and imbalanced. Other negatives include superficial treatment of many subjects, a tendency to avoid controversial issues, lack of up-to-dateness in certain areas, inconsistent writing styles, an unreliable index, no bibliographies, and dull, uninviting illustrations. The bottom line: Consumers can do much, much better than this mediocre encyclopedia.

OTHER OPINIONS

American Reference Books Annual, 1989, pp. 15–16 (review by Kathleen Farago); *Reference Books Bulletin* (in *Booklist*), February 1, 1994, p. 1023 (unsigned review); *Wilson Library Bulletin*, September 1988, p. 90 (review by James Rettig).

CAMBRIDGE ENCYCLOPEDIA

FACTS

Full Title: *The Cambridge Encyclopedia*. Editor: David Crystal. **Publisher:** Cambridge University Press. **Date Published:** First Edition, 1990; reprinted with revisions in 1992.

Also published as the BARNES & NOBLE ENCYCLOPEDIA.

Abridged Version: CAMBRIDGE PAPERBACK ENCYCLOPEDIA.

Volumes: One. **Words:** 1.5 million. **Pages:** 1,488. **Articles:** 30,000. **Bibliographies:** None. **Illustrations and Maps:** 800.

Cross-references: 75,000. **Index Entries: None. Editorial Staff, Advisers, and Contributors:** 120. Trim Size: 7½ × 10¼ in.

Price and Sales Information: $49.95. Individual consumers can purchase the *Cambridge Encyclopedia* in bookstores or, if the book is not in stock, it can be ordered. Similarly, educational institutions (schools, libraries, etc.) can order it through a book wholesaler. To order the encyclopedia directly from the publisher, call toll-free 1-800-872-7423 or write Cambridge University Press, 40 West 20th Street, New York, NY 10011-4211.

EVALUATION

In the words of editor David Crystal, the single-volume *Cambridge Encyclopedia* aims "to provide a succinct, systematic, and readable guide to the facts, events, issues, beliefs, and achievements which make up the sum of human knowledge" (preface). Essentially, it is a quick-reference desk encyclopedia for adults and older students. British produced, the volume originally appeared in 1990, a collaborative effort between W. & R. Chambers (an old-line publisher of basic reference works based in Edinburgh, Scotland) and Cambridge University Press (one of Great Britain's largest and most prestigious university presses). Cambridge conceived the project and published the book and Chambers handled the editorial and production work.

Thus far the encyclopedia has been revised once, in 1992; further revisions are anticipated every few years or so. In addition, the publisher issued an updated paperbound abridgment in 1993 under the title CAMBRIDGE PAPERBACK ENCYCLOPEDIA, and an even smaller spin-off, the *Cambridge Factfinder*, was published earlier this year; an almanac-like book, it is also a paperbound publication. Consumers should also be aware that the *Cambridge Encyclopedia* (1992 edition) is currently available under the title BARNES & NOBLE ENCYCLOPEDIA. Sold in Barnes & Noble bookstores nationwide at the discount price of $19.98, the BARNES & NOBLE ENCYCLOPEDIA has exactly the same text as the *Cambridge Encyclopedia*.

Editor Crystal brings impressive credentials to the encyclopedia. An Englishman, he is a professor of linguistics (now at the University College of Wales) and author of numerous publications, including the excellent CAMBRIDGE ENCYCLOPEDIA OF LANGUAGE; he is also editor of the CAMBRIDGE PAPERBACK ENCYCLOPEDIA and *Cambridge Factfinder*. In addition to Crystal, the *Cambridge Encyclopedia* lists an editorial staff of 17, plus 103 consultants and contributors, most of whom are affiliated with British universities or other scholarly institutions, such as the British Museum. About a dozen of the contributors are from North America and Australia.

The *Cambridge Encyclopedia* is a short-entry work, its approximately 30,000 A-to-Z articles usually quite brief, averaging only about 50 words in length. It provides comparatively strong coverage of important people, with historical figures like Galileo and Mozart accounting for many entries. Prominent contemporaries from all fields are also well represented, exemplified by Sir Kingsley Amis, James A. Baker, Busby Berkeley, Robert Bolt, Joan Crawford, Elizabeth Dole, Robert Dole, D.J. Enright, Dennis Gabor, Nadine Gordimer, Howard Hawks, Philip Larkin, Roy Lichtenstein, Reginald Mauldling, Marilyn Monroe, John Mortimer, Robert Motherwell, Alan Paton, Ali Akbar Hashemi Rafsanjani, Jonas Salk, Artie Shaw, John van Vleck, and Shirley Williams. Geographical coverage is equally broad. Articles on the U.S. states and Canadian provinces run from 100 to 350 words in length, furnishing a succinct overview of the place; counties in Great Britain are also covered, but not as extensively.

According to J.E. Sheets's review of the encyclopedia in *Choice* (March 1991, p. 1092), some of the biographical and geographical material derives from previously published reference works by Chambers:

> Some of its biographical entries seem to be condensations or paraphrases from *Chambers Biographical Dictionary* (rev. ed.; Edinburgh, 1984) and some of its geographical entries from *Chambers World Gazetteer* (5th ed., 1988). Compare for example the entries for Cornelius Jansen, Jack the Ripper, Java Sea, or Jaipur.

Scientific and technical subjects also receive considerable attention. Coverage of plant and animal life is especially inclusive. In addition, the *Cambridge Encyclopedia* contains numerous specific entries on science topics not found in comparable encyclopedias, such as "Alpha Decay," "Aperture Synthesis," "Background Radiation," "Berry's Phase," "Blueshift," "Cover Crop," "Echolocation," "Globular Cluster," "High Pressure Physics," "Hydrogen Bond," "Integrated Optics," "Luteinizing Hormone," "Nerve Growth Factor," "Occluded Front," "Population Genetics," "Real-time Computing," "Resonant Ionization Spectrometry," "Specific Dynamic Action," "Speckle Interferometry," "Time Dilation," "Vestibular Apparatus," and "Zoosemiotics."

In addition to its A-to-Z articles (which comprise 1,334 pages, or the bulk of the text), the encyclopedia contains a substantial "Ready Reference" section at the back of the book. Printed on yellow paper, the 128-page "Ready Reference" supplement provides much compact information in tabular form on a wide range of subjects, including space exploration, the earth, major religious festivals, the nations of the world, political leaders of various countries, weights and mea-

sures, names and titles, awards, and sports. This appended material can be useful to readers, but it is not without its problems:

> This supplement offers valuable information for those who take the time to study its table of contents or browse through its pages. Unfortunately, the alphabetical portion of the *Encyclopedia* provides inconsistent access to related information in the RR ["Ready Reference"] section. For instance, the entry on Alfred Nobel refers to the RR page listing Nobel Prize winners, but the entry for Joseph Pulitzer does not note the RR page covering Pulitzer Prize winners. (

Quoted from *Reference Books Bulletin* in *Booklist*, November 1, 1990, p. 558).

While the book's coverage tends to be broad and inclusive, its treatment often consists of little more than dictionary-style definitions, devoid of any real encyclopedic depth. This is particularly true of entries covering the social and behavioral sciences. The four-line article "Adoption," for example, provides less information than a good college-level dictionary. The same can be said of "Bankruptcy," "Depression" (in economics), "Euthanasia," "Glasnost," "Homicide," "Libel," "Repression," and "Sexism." Many similar examples could be cited.

As noted at the top of this review, the *Cambridge Encyclopedia* is a British-made encyclopedia. The intention has been to create a single-volume work that can be used profitably by English-speaking people anywhere in the world. Editor Crystal stresses the book's commitment to "internationalism" in his preface, noting that "An encyclopedia for the 1990s must surely reflect international issues, especially in history, politics, and current affairs." In many respects the encyclopedia achieves this ambitious goal. Still, all too often it is unable to transcend its British roots. All too often the *Cambridge Encyclopedia* presents knowledge and information through obviously British editorial eyes, which weakens the book's appeal outside the United Kingdom.

Some articles, for example, deal with rather esoteric bits of British history, such as "Bedchamber Crisis," "Black Rod," "Bloody Assizes," and "Butskellism." In some cases the British emphasis has the potential to mislead, as in "Abortion," which concludes "Unless permitted by the Abortion Acts, induced abortion is a criminal offense." In yet other instances, language can be a barrier, as in "Depression" (in economics), which talks about low "order-books" as a condition of economic depression. Justin Kaplan, in a thoughtful review of the encyclopedia in the *New York Times Book Review* (January 27, 1991, p. 15), offers this perspective on the book's British bias:

> Given the publishing auspices and origins of *The Cambridge Encyclopedia*, it will come as no surprise that its brand of "internationalism" reflects a British point of view. American readers will be grateful for its excellent account of the civil rights movement, as well as for the regard shown for Hank Aaron, Joe DiMaggio and Lou Gehrig (Yogi Berra, Jackie Robinson and Casey Stengel are absent but are in *The Random House Encyclopedia*). But the same readers may find themselves at sea with entries for Walter Lindrum ("Australian billiards player"), Sarah's Bunny (winner of the 1979 Greyhound Derby, run at White City Stadium in London), Sunil Gavaskar ("Indian cricketer, born in Bombay") and Stephen Donoghue ("British jockey, born at Warrington. He won the Derby six times"). "Football hooliganism" of course relates to soccer, a growth sport in this country, but the entry for soccer itself consists only of an inconvenient cross-reference to football.

The *Cambridge Encyclopedia* is usually reliable, although some small but troubling errors have been spotted. *Examples:* The article "Electroconvulsive Therapy" calls ECT a "highly successful treatment" for severe psychiatric disorders, which is not entirely correct; rather, ECT is a quite controversial treatment that some believe can result in brain damage and long-term memory loss. In a captioned illustration with the article "Clock" the word *quartz* is misspelled. In the "Ready Reference" section that lists political

leaders, the U.S. president Benjamin Harrison is given as "Benjamine" Harrison. The running head (or guide word at the top of the page) gives Stephen Donoghue as "Steven" Donoghue. As Justin Kaplan says in his *New York Times Book Review* critique quoted above, "These are small errors, to be sure, but small-scale reliability is something you have a right to demand from a reference book."

The encyclopedia is normally objective in its presentation of information, although occasionally gratuitous opinions intrude, as in "Carpetbaggers," which concludes, "Collectively they [carpetbaggers] have had a bad press, but are now recognized as well-intentioned." In addition, the encyclopedia sometimes avoids controversy and sensitive issues, a tendency seen in such articles as "Christian Science," "Circumcision," "Dead Sea Scrolls," "Intelligence" (which includes IQ tests), "Islam," and "Tchaikovsky, Piotr Ilyich."

In most instances, the encyclopedia is admirably up-to-date. This is particularly so concerning recent political and military developments in such unstable regions as Eastern Europe and the Balkans. Where the book sometimes falls down is not keeping up with nonvolatile subjects. The article "Galileo," for instance, fails to mention the Roman Catholic Church's recent reversal of its longtime condemnation of the great Renaissance scientist, the result of a series of actions initiated by Pope John Paul II in the 1970s that has garnered headlines around the world.

Ordinarily, the encyclopedia—written in what editor Crystal calls "plain English"—will be comprehensible to educated adults and serious students at the secondary school level and beyond. Now and then an article contains an oddly turned or jarring phrase, as in the article on the Russian writer Chekhov ("In 1901 he married the actress Olga Knipper, who remained for many years the admired exponent of female parts in his plays"), but normally the style is straightforward and clear. Sometimes articles on scientific subjects assume a familiarity with specialized terminology. The initial paragraph of the article "Heart" provides a fair sampling of the encyclopedia's writing style:

> A hollow muscular organ, divided into chambers (right and left *atria*, right and left *ventricles*) and enclosed within a fibrous sac (the *pericardium*) found with the thorax. It lies directly under the sternum, being protected by it and the adjacent ribs. It is the first organ to develop in the embryo (in humans by three weeks). In mammals it is separated into right and left halves concerned with pulmonary and systemic circulation respectively. It consists mainly of cardiac muscle (the *myocardium*) enclosed between two sheets of fibrous and elastic tissue, the *epicardium* and the *endocardium*. The myocardium forms a network of sheets and strands which have a characteristic arrangement in different parts of the heart. The heart also possesses a fibrous skeleton which strengthens many of its openings.

Locating specific information in the *Cambridge Encyclopedia* is usually not difficult, given its specific-entry approach, A-to-Z arrangement, and extensive network of some 75,000 cross-references. The book lacks an index, however, which can be a disadvantage. Cross-references, designated by the symbol >>, are especially helpful in guiding the reader to related articles. For instance, "Fluoridation of Water" includes three cross-references, to the articles "Caries," "Fluorine," and "Teeth."

Normally, this system functions well, but occasionally it fails. For example, cross-references from American spelling and usage are not given for such articles as "Aeroplane," "Foetus," "Motor Insurance," and "Tyre." Certainly, few people in the U.S. or Canada would think to look for *airplane* under *aeroplane* or *fetus* under *foetus*. In the case of the Shroud of Turin, readers have no way of knowing that information on the shroud is under "Holy Shroud"; obviously, cross-references from "Shroud" and "Turin" are needed. Also, a detailed index would improve access to the encyclopedia's contents in such instances.

Just as the encyclopedia lacks an index, it lacks bibliographies—lists of recommended sources that interested readers might consult for additional information. This omission is not unexpected; among the small-volume encyclopedias for adults and older students currently available, only the COLUMBIA ENCYCLOPEDIA, the RANDOM HOUSE ENCYCLOPEDIA, and the VOLUME LIBRARY include bibliographies. On the other hand, the lack of bibliographies does nothing to boost the *Cambridge Encyclopedia* in a highly competitive market.

In the area of illustrations, the *Cambridge Encyclopedia* is much like the larger COLUMBIA ENCYCLOPEDIA. Both works rely heavily on printed text and use illustrations very sparingly. In fact, the *Cambridge Encyclopedia* includes only about 800 simple line drawings and maps, most in black-and-white. They are almost always informative, but the absence of color is sometimes a detriment. For instance, recent research suggests that some dinosaurs were brightly colored creatures, but the reader gets no sense of this from the black-and-white drawings that accompany the article "Dinosaur." The book does have 16 four-color plates located between the end of the articles and the "Ready Reference" section. The plates cover a hodgepodge of subjects and quite properly are dismissed as "inconsequential" by James Rettig in his review in *Wilson Library Bulletin* (January 1991, p. 122).

Physically, the encyclopedia, which comes with an attractive jacket, is a reasonably successful production. Its binding is strong and will withstand heavy use. The typefaces used are legible and inviting. Due to the general lack of color and limited graphics, the book's two-column layout tends to be predictable and staid—some might say scholarly. The book is fairly large (7½ × 10¼), but will pose no handling problems for most adults and older students. It weighs about 6½ pounds.

REPORT CARD: CAMBRIDGE ENCYCLOPEDIA				
TOPIC	COVERAGE	ACCURACY	RECENCY	CLARITY
Circumcision	C	A	C	A
Drew, Charles	F*	NA	NA	NA
Galileo	C	A	D	A
Glass, Philip	F*	NA	NA	NA
Heart Disease	B	A	B	B
IQ	D	A	C	A
Panda Bears	C	B	B	A
Sexual Harassment	F*	NA	NA	NA
Shroud of Turin	A	A	A	B
Uzbekistan	C	A	A	A

A = Excellent; **B** = Above Average; **C** = Average; **D** = Below Average; **F** = Poor; **NA** = Not Applicable
*No Article

SUMMARY

The single-volume *Cambridge Encyclopedia* first appeared in 1990 and was revised in 1992. The product of a cooperative effort between W. & R. Chambers and Cambridge University Press (both estimable British publishers), the 30,000-entry encyclopedia best serves as a source of quick-reference information about prominent people and places and specific subjects, such as plants and animals. It provides broad, reasonably current coverage of basic knowledge, but its articles often lack sufficient depth. Other negatives include a pronounced British bias, some small but troubling errors in the text, a tendency to avoid controversial or sensitive issues, occasional failure of the cross-reference system, lack of an index, limited illustrations, absence of color in what illustrations there are, and no bibliographies. Note that the encyclopedia is sold at discount as the BARNES & NOBLE ENCYCLOPEDIA. The bottom line: Definitely *not* the best choice for North Americans seeking a quality one-volume encyclopedia, but a fair bargain at $50.00 or less.

OTHER OPINIONS

Basic Information Sources by William A. Katz (vol. 1 of *Introduction to Reference Work*, 6th ed., New York: McGraw-Hill, 1992), pp. 258–60; *Choice*, March 1991, pp. 1091–92 (review by J.E. Sheets); *Library Journal*, September 1, 1990, pp. 210–12 (review by Brian E. Coutts); *New York Times Book Review*, January 27, 1991, p. 15 (review by Justin Kaplan); *Reference Books Bulletin* (in *Booklist*), November 1, 1990, pp. 558–59 (unsigned review); *Reference Sources for Small and Medium-Sized Libraries* (5th ed., Chicago: American Library Assn., 1992), p. 30 (review by Jovian P. Lang); *Time*, December 10, 1990, p. 98 (review by Stefan Kanfer); *Wilson Library Bulletin*, January 1991, pp. 122–23 (review by James Rettig).

CAMBRIDGE PAPERBACK ENCYCLOPEDIA

FACTS

Full Title: *Cambridge Paperback Encyclopedia.* Editor: David Crystal. **Publisher:** Cambridge University Press. **Date Published:** 1993.

    Unabridged Version: CAMBRIDGE ENCYCLOPEDIA.

Volumes: One. **Words:** 750,000. **Pages:** 970. **Articles:** 19,000. **Bibliographies:** None. **Illustrations and Maps:** 570. **Cross-references:** 26,000. **Index Entries:** None. **Editorial Staff, Advisers, and Contributors:** 14. Trim Size: 6¼ × 9¼ in.

Price and Sales Information: $19.95 paperbound. Individual consumers can purchase the *Cambridge Paperback Encyclopedia* in bookstores or, if the book is not in stock, it can be ordered. Similarly, educational institutions (schools, libraries, etc.) can order it through a book wholesaler. To order the encyclopedia directly from the publisher, call toll-free 1-800-872-7423 or write Cambridge University Press, 40 West 20th Street, New York, NY 10011-4211.

EVALUATION

The 970-page *Cambridge Paperback Encyclopedia*, published in 1993, is a minimally updated paperbound abridgment of the 1,488-page CAMBRIDGE ENCYCLOPEDIA, a hardcover work that first appeared in 1990 and was reissued in a revised printing in 1992. Like its parent volume, the *Cambridge Paperback Encyclopedia* is British-made, is edited by David Crystal, and is an authoritative work for adults and older students that provides broad coverage of the world's basic knowledge and information, especially in the areas of biography, geography, and scientific and technical subjects.

As might be expected, the *Cambridge Paperback Encyclopedia* contains much the same text as the CAMBRIDGE ENCYCLOPEDIA, although numerous articles have been reduced in size and many others have been dropped altogether. "Panda" is an example of a scaled-down article. In the CAMBRIDGE ENCYCLOPEDIA, this article consists of about 100 words, whereas in the abridgment it has been cut down to 68 words. To achieve this reduction, the editors deleted information about the panda's family tree ("related to

raccoons and bears") and its physical characteristics ("front paw with elongated wrist bone which acts like a sixth digit; grasps bamboo shoots between this extra 'thumb' and the first and second true digits"). Hundreds of articles have been edited down in this manner.

The CAMBRIDGE ENCYCLOPEDIA comprises approximately 30,000 entries, whereas the *Cambridge Paperback Encyclopedia* has only about 19,000. Among the thousands of articles excluded from the smaller encyclopedia are "Aperture Synthesis," "Berry's Phase," "Cover Crop," "Dole, Robert," "Donoghue, Stephen," "Football Hooliganism," "Gavaskar, Sunil," "High Pressure Physics," "Luteinizing Hormone," "Motor Insurance," "Motherwell, Robert Burns," "Mourning Dove," "Nerve Growth Factor," "Population Genetics," and "Time Dilation." As this list suggests, editor Crystal's aim has been to omit nothing vital in the abridgment. As always in such work there are anomalies. Why, for instance, are both Robert and Elizabeth Dole included in the CAMBRIDGE ENCYCLOPEDIA, but only Elizabeth makes it into the *Cambridge Paperback Encyclopedia*? Why is a prominent twentieth-century artist like Robert Motherwell dropped while an article on a transitory subject like "Butskellism" is not?

Obviously, the *Cambridge Paperback Encyclopedia* has pretty much the same strengths and weaknesses as the larger work— broad coverage, superficial treatment, a pronounced British bias, occasional errors in the text, a clear writing style, a sometimes faulty system of cross-references, no index, and no bibliographies. (For a detailed evaluation of the CAMBRIDGE ENCYCLOPEDIA, see the review beginning on page 118.) In addition, the paperback's illustrations are all in black-and-white (the parent volume has some color), and its physical format is smaller, including the type size. On the other hand, the paperback version sells for a modest $19.95, whereas the larger hardcover volume normally retails for $49.95.

SUMMARY

New in 1993, the 970-page *Cambridge Paperback Encyclopedia* is a cutdown version of the 1,488-page CAMBRIDGE ENCYCLOPEDIA (1990; revised in 1992). Like its parent work, the abridgment originated in Great Britain and has a strong British flavor; it provides broad coverage but treatment is often superficial; it has a flawed cross-reference system and lacks an index; it includes comparatively few illustrations that, while usually informative, lack color and are uninviting. Still, the encyclopedia is produced by reputable people, provides a goodly amount of quick-reference information, and is competitively priced. The bottom line: While not a distinguished reference work, the *Cambridge Paperback Encyclopedia* is a good buy for the money—though not so good as WEBSTER'S NEW WORLD ENCYCLOPEDIA: POCKET EDITION.

OTHER OPINIONS

None.

REPORT CARD: CAMBRIDGE PAPERBACK ENCYCLOPEDIA

Topic	Coverage	Accuracy	Recency	Clarity
Circumcision	C	A	C	A
Drew, Charles	F*	NA	NA	NA
Galileo	C	A	D	A
Glass, Philip	F*	NA	NA	NA
Heart Disease	B	A	B	B
IQ	D	A	C	A
Panda Bears	C	B	B	A
Sexual Harassment	F*	NA	NA	NA
Shroud of Turin	A	A	A	B
Uzbekistan	D	A	A	A

A = Excellent; **B** = Above Average; **C** = Average; **D** = Below Average; **F** = Poor; **NA** = Not Applicable
*No Article

COLUMBIA ENCYCLOPEDIA

FACTS

Full Title: *The Columbia Encyclopedia.* Editors: Barbara A. Chernow and George A. Vallasi. Project Director: James Raimes. **Publisher:** Columbia University Press. **Distributor:** Houghton Mifflin Company. Former Title: *The New Columbia Encyclopedia* (1975). **Date Published:** First Edition, 1935; Second Edition, 1950; Third Edition, 1963; Fourth Edition, 1975; Fifth Edition, 1993.
Volumes: One. **Words:** 6.6 million. **Pages:** 3,072. **Articles:** 50,000. **Bibliographies:** 8,500. **Illustrations and Maps:** 745. **Cross-references:** 65,000. **Index Entries:**
None. **Editorial Staff, Advisers, and Contributors:** 218. Trim Size: 9¼ × 12 in.
Price and Sales Information: $125.00. Individual consumers can purchase the *Columbia Encyclopedia* in bookstores or, if the book is not in stock, it can be ordered. Similarly, educational institutions (schools, libraries, etc.) can order it through a book wholesaler. To order the encyclopedia directly from the distributor, call 1-800-733-7075 or write Houghton Mifflin Company, 222 Berkeley Street, Boston, MA 02116-3764.

EVALUATION

The *Columbia Encyclopedia* is the largest, most formidable one-volume general encyclopedia currently available in the English language. On the scene now for nearly 60 years, the encyclopedia was first published in 1935 and has been revised on average every 15 years, the second edition appearing in 1950, the third in 1963, the fourth (called the *New Columbia Encyclopedia*) in 1975, and the fifth in 1993. Unlike most of its chief competitors (the RANDOM HOUSE ENCYCLOPEDIA, the CAMBRIDGE ENCYCLOPEDIA, WEBSTER'S NEW WORLD ENCYCLOPEDIA, and the AMERICAN SPECTRUM ENCYCLOPEDIA), which have originated abroad, the *Columbia Encyclopedia* is compiled and published in North America, a product of the Columbia University Press located in New York City. Project editor James Raimes makes the point in his preface to the fifth edition, "This edition is more international than its predecessors, but it remains an American encyclopedia written for American readers."

Over the years, the *Columbia Encyclopedia* has generated a number of spin-off publications. The third edition spawned both an abridged and an illustrated version, namely the *Columbia-Viking Desk Encyclopedia* (one volume; 1968;) and the *Illustrated Columbia Encyclopedia* (22 volumes; 1967); both these titles have long been out of print. In like manner, the fourth edition prompted a single-volume abridgment called the CONCISE COLUMBIA ENCYCLOPEDIA, which is still on the market, as well as an illustrated edition entitled the NEW ILLUSTRATED COLUMBIA ENCYCLOPEDIA (24 volumes; 1978), which is now out of print. Electronic versions of the smaller CONCISE COLUMBIA ENCYCLOPEDIA have also been published recently; see the hand-held COLUMBIA ELECTRONIC ENCYCLOPEDIA and the CONCISE COLUMBIA ENCYCLOPEDIA ON CD-ROM (as part of *Microsoft Bookshelf*). Doubtless the recently published fifth edition of the *Columbia Encyclopedia* will eventually appear in an abridged edition, replacing or updating the CONCISE COLUMBIA ENCYCLOPEDIA. The likelihood of a CD-ROM edition in the near future is also very high.

As the foregoing suggests, the name "Columbia" is widely recognized and respected by those who buy and use encyclopedias in North America. Certainly during its illustrious history, the *Columbia Encyclopedia* has established a firm reputation for thorough and responsible scholarship. From the beginning its editors have drawn heavily on the faculty of Columbia University for contributors and editorial advice—although the university does not officially endorse the encyclopedia (the press is affiliated with the university but operates as a separate, non-profit corporation). Of 114 academic advisers identified at the front of the current edition, 56 (or nearly half) are members of the Columbia University faculty; likewise, all but one of the six-member board of consultants are Columbia professors.

Today, the *Columbia Encyclopedia* is structurally much like the first edition that appeared in 1935. A physically large book (the current edition weighs approximately 11 pounds, stands a foot high, and is three inches thick), it contains thousands of short-entry articles arranged alphabetically that provide basic information about people, places, plants, animals, events, concepts, organizations, etc. The editors have made a determined effort to cover nearly every subject of potential interest to adult readers. "One has to get down to pretty small potatoes to find a topic that is not covered at all," writes Robert M. Adams in his review of the encyclopedia in the *New York Times Book Review* (October 31, 1993, p. 38):

> Teofilo Folengo, for instance, shone briefly in the early 16th century as a leader of the so-called macaronic poets, who wrote a kind of multilingual punning doggerel poetry that ultimately had some influence on Rabelais. Look under "macaroni" or "macaronic" in the Columbia book and you may at best wind up among the pastas, but under "Folengo" you will find a tidy inch or two of print that tells you all you need to know (for starters) about the poet and his harum-scarum career.

Quantitatively, biographies predominate, accounting for roughly 45 percent of all entries. Most cover historical figures ranging from Alexander the Great to Zhou Enlai (with Teofilo Folengo in between), but many diverse contemporary personalities also appear in the pages of the *Columbia Encyclopedia*, including Maya Angelou, Jean Bertrand Aristide, Larry Bird, Johnny Carson, Bill Gates, Magic Johnson, Stephen King, Calvin Klein, Madonna, Michael Milken, Dolly Parton, H. Ross Perot, Janet Reno, Clarence Thomas, and Andrew Lloyd Webber.

Geographical topics account for another 30 percent of the entries. Most localities of any magnitude in the U.S. and Canada receive coverage, as do all countries of the world, including the newly formed nations of Eastern Europe, such as Azerbaijan and Uzbekistan. Simple black-and-white locator maps accompany the country articles. Also covered are the world's major cities, rivers, lakes, mountains, plains, falls, parks, etc., as well as each county in England (metropolitan and nonmetropolitan). Overall, the geographical coverage is quite impressive, exceeding that found in many multivolume encyclopedias.

Scientific and technical subjects also receive strong coverage, continuing a trend established in earlier editions. As might be expected, the new fifth edition has added or updated numerous articles explaining recent developments in key areas of science. By way of example, new articles include "Biological Diversity," "Chaos Theory," "Compact Disc," "Electronics Industry," "Fluxional Molecules," "Genetic Engineering," "Genetic Screening," "Nonlinear Dynamics," "Nuclear Waste," "Quantum Field Theory," "Wind Shear," and "X-Ray Crystallography." The encyclopedia also provides extensive coverage of religious topics, including biblical names. Indeed, in previous editions, every proper name in the King James Version of the Bible had its own entry, with chapter and verse citations given for each. In the current edition, some obscure names have been dropped (e.g., Abban, Agur, Ahasai, Ahi), as have the chapter-verse references, but still the coverage exceeds that of most larger encyclopedias.

Obviously, in such a massive book, inconsistencies in coverage are bound to occur. The subject of adoption, for instance, is accorded roughly the same amount of space as the stink bug; child abuse is covered in 28 lines, whereas children's book illustration receives 148 lines, or more than five times the coverage; carpal tunnel syndrome and chelation therapy are not covered at all; likewise, Charles Drew, the black physician whose research led to the development of blood banks, and Philip Glass, the modern American composer, are inexplicably ignored by the encyclopedia; in the aforementioned *New York Times* review, Robert Adams says he "is shocked to find an encyclopedia entry for Auerbach (Red), the impresario of the Boston Celtics, but none for Auerbach (Erich), the distinguished philologist and comparative linguist." Nevertheless, on balance, the coverage afforded by the *Columbia Encyclopedia* is remarkably broad and equitable.

Reliability has been one of the encyclopedia's distinguishing hallmarks from the outset, and the editors of the new fifth edition have labored painstakingly to continue this tradition. Critics have spotted a few minor errors, but nothing that might tarnish the encyclopedia's well-earned reputation for accuracy. James Rettig, in a review in *Wilson Library Bulletin* (January 1994, p. 84), puts it this way:

> Not even the careful *Columbia* editors can produce 6.6 million words without error. For example, the article on Conway, Arkansas, identifies the University of Central Arkansas by its former name, and the article on Carl Sandburg gives him credit for graduating from Lombard College even though he left without a degree. These very small errors of precise fact stand out because they are such exceptions to the rule of accuracy and reliability.

Information in the encyclopedia is almost always presented in an impartial manner. Likewise, controversial or sensitive issues are treated forthrightly, with the pros and cons carefully summarized. The article

"Euthanasia" is a good example of how the editors and writers deal with a complex, emotionally charged subject:

> Positive euthanasia is illegal in the United States, but physicians may lawfully refuse to prolong life when there is extreme suffering. Dr. Jack Kevorkian, a Michigan physician, has challenged the validity of these laws by assisting patients to die without pain or suffering. Such physician-assisted death is common in the Netherlands, though still officially illegal. Much debate has arisen in the U.S. among physicians, religious leaders, lawyers, and the general public over the question of what constitutes actively causing death and what constitutes merely allowing death to occur naturally. The physician is faced with deciding whether the measures used to keep patients alive are extraordinary in individual situations, e.g., whether a respirator or artificial kidney machine should be withdrawn from a terminally ill patient.

As this excerpt from "Euthanasia" suggests with its reference to Dr. Kevorkian and the current debate over physician-assisted suicide, the new fifth edition of the *Columbia Encyclopedia* is normally up-to-date as of the early 1990s. Project editor Raimes estimates that "about 60% of the fourth edition [1975] of *The Columbia Encyclopedia* was revised for this edition [1993]" (preface). Many new articles have been added to the current edition, while thousands of others have been substantially revised to reflect changing knowledge. New articles include "Alzheimer's Disease," "Bilingual Education," "Bilingualism," "Executive Privilege," "Expert System," "HIV" "Ice Dancing," "Insider Trading," "Iran-Contra Affair," "Iran Hostage Crisis," "Lockerbie," "Money-Market Fund," "Persian Gulf War," "Privacy, Rights of," "Program Trading," "Rustbelt," "Scientology, Church of," and "Sexual Harassment."

Regrettably, some articles have been carried over from the fourth to the fifth edition without sufficient revision. *Examples:* The article "Rose" correctly notes "The rose is the emblem of England and the flower of New York state; the wild rose, of Iowa; the prairie rose, of North Dakota; and the American Beauty, of the District of Columbia," but fails to inform the reader that the rose became the U.S. national flower in 1986. "Turin" refers to "the Cathedral of San Giovanni (late 15th cent.) which has an urn containing a shroud in which, it is said, Jesus was wrapped after the descent from the Cross," but fails to inform the reader that carbon 14 dating tests conducted in 1988 show the shroud to have originated in the fourteenth century. "Circumcision" adequately describes the operation but fails to inform the reader that many people, including some doctors, now regard circumcision as medically unnecessary and even potentially harmful. "Library School," which has exactly the same text as the previous edition, is woefully out-of-date, with statistics current only as of the early 1970s.

The *Columbia Encyclopedia* is intended for adults and students reading at approximately the tenth grade level and beyond. The writing style is admirably clear, concise, and direct. Earlier editions stated that the work is written in "language as intelligible as that of a newspaper." The new fifth edition still adheres to that notion—if the newspaper is the *New York Times* or *Wall Street Journal*. The article "Heart" provides a good example of the encyclopedia's style (the first 22 of 76 lines are quoted):

> **heart,** muscular organ that pumps blood to all parts of the body. The rhythmic beating of the heart is a ceaseless activity, lasting from before birth to the end of life. The human heart is a pear-shaped structure about the size of a fist. It lies obliquely within the chest cavity just left of center, with the apex pointing downward. The heart is constructed of a special kind of MUSCLE called myocardium, and is enclosed in a double-layered, membranous sac known as the pericardium. A wall of muscle divides the heart into two cavities: the left cavity pumps blood throughout the body, while the right cavity pumps blood only through the lungs. Each cavity is in turn divided into two chambers, the upper ones called atria, the lower ones ventricles. Venous blood from the body, containing large amounts of carbon dioxide,

returns to the right atrium. It enters the right ventricle, which contracts, pumping blood through the pulmonary artery to the lungs. Oxygenated blood returns from the lungs to the left atrium and enters the left ventricle, which contracts, forcing the blood into the AORTA, from which it is distributed throughout the body.

Ordinarily, finding specific facts and topics in the encyclopedia can be accomplished without great difficulty, due to the book's A-to-Z arrangement, specific-entry approach, and generous provision of cross-references in the text. As seen in "Heart" above, cross-references appear in SMALL CAPITAL LETTERS (e.g., MUSCLE; AORTA) and direct the reader to other articles in the book that provide additional or related information. Unfortunately, the cross-reference system is not comprehensive nor does it always function effectively. The article "Abortion," for example, contains no cross-reference to the article "Roe vs. Wade," which offers much additional material on the subject. How is the reader to know to look under "Roe vs. Wade"? Are there similar articles in the encyclopedia under other U.S. Supreme Court decisions on abortion? If so, what are their names? What other topics might include information about abortion? In another case, "Depression" fails to direct the reader to "Electroconvulsive Therapy," a controversial treatment for depressive disorders. Many similar examples could be cited.

Erratic cross-referencing would not be a major problem *if* the encyclopedia had an index—but it does not. In fact, the editors in a prefatory section called "How to Use the Columbia Encyclopedia" state emphatically, "Cross-referencing makes an index in *The Columbia Encyclopedia* unnecessary." Anyone who has used the encyclopedia extensively will find this statement dubious at best. For instance, an index would conveniently bring together all references to abortion in the encyclopedia. No longer would the reader have to wonder where else to look for information on the topic. Project editor Raimes boasts in his preface that the encyclopedia "answers more than a million questions, a remarkable figure." Remarkable, yes. But it is equally remarkable that experienced reference book editors really believe that an encyclopedia containing a million facts can attain a high degree of accessibility without a detailed analytical index.

If the encyclopedia's lack of an index is a glaring defect, its bibliographies are a conspicuous strength. An estimated 8,500 articles conclude with bibliographies—or lists of recommended titles for further reading. "Many of the books we cite in our bibliographies were chosen because they themselves contain bibliographies. We envisage an active readership, returning again and again to this Encyclopedia, but being helped by it again and again to read elsewhere" (preface). Normally, the titles selected represent the best books on the subject; moreover, they are usually quite current. *Example:* The article "Dead Sea Scrolls" has a bibliography of eight titles, including *Understanding the Dead Sea Scrolls*, an outstanding anthology compiled by Hershel Shanks and published by Random House in 1992.

Illustrations in the encyclopedia are few and far between, but those that are included add to the informational value of the work. Limited to about 745 black-and-white line drawings, the illustrations mostly depict scientific and technical subjects, such as an abacus, a barometer, the human circulatory system, a female crayfish, a flower at the time of fertilization, the human heart, a warm-air heating system, a fluorescent lamp, DNA, and the ocean floor. Also among the illustrations are simple maps of countries, regions, and historical configurations, e.g., the empire of Alexander the Great. The illustrations in the *Columbia Encyclopedia* stand in total contrast to those found in the rival RANDOM HOUSE ENCYCLOPEDIA, which are colorful, innovative, and profuse.

The encyclopedia's physical format is generally satisfactory. The book—a large one weighing approximately 11 pounds—requires a stand or flat surface for easy consultation. It is thumb-indexed, Smyth sewn, sturdily bound to withstand heavy use, and comes with an attractive jacket. The lightweight acid-free paper is of excellent quality. The type, which tends to be small, is both legible and attractive, but the absence of paragraphing throughout will cause some readers difficulty, especially in cases where articles are more than a column long. Overall, the three-column page layout is dignified but predictable and unexciting.

REPORT CARD: COLUMBIA ENCYCLOPEDIA

TOPIC	COVERAGE	ACCURACY	RECENCY	CLARITY
Circumcision	C	A	C	A
Drew, Charles	F*	NA	NA	NA
Galileo	A	A	A	A
Glass, Philip	F*	NA	NA	NA
Heart Disease	B	A	B	A
IQ	A	A	A	A
Panda Bears	A	A	A	A
Sexual Harassment	A	A	A	A
Shroud of Turin	D	A	D	A
Uzbekistan	A	A	A	A

A = Excellent; **B** = Above Average; **C** = Average; **D** = Below Average; **F** = Poor; **NA** = Not Applicable
*No Article

SUMMARY

One of only a few major single-volume encyclopedias produced in North America, the massive *Columbia Encyclopedia*—6.6 million words, 50,000 articles, 3,072 pages, 11 pounds—is the largest, most authoritative, and best known such work in English. First published in 1935, the encyclopedia is now in its fifth edition (1993). Written for intelligent adults and serious older students, it offers outstanding coverage of basic knowledge and information, with strong emphasis on biographical, geographical, and scientific subjects. Among the encyclopedia's conspicuous strengths are textual reliability, objective and readable presentation of material, excellent bibliographies, and a high level of up-to-dateness as of the early 1990s. Its most discernible weakness is lack of an index, compounded by an erratic system of cross-references. Other negatives include a paucity of illustrations and lack of paragraphing throughout. The bottom line: The best single-volume general encyclopedia currently available in English.

OTHER OPINIONS

Choice, February 1994, p. 912 (review by K.F. Jones); *Library Journal*, September 15, 1993, p. 66 (review by Ken Kister); *New York Times Book Review*, October 31, 1993, pp. 38–39 (review by Robert M. Adams); *Reference Books Bulletin* (in *Booklist*), September 15, 1993, p. 184 (review by Sandy Whiteley); *Wilson Library Bulletin*, January 1994, p. 84 (review by James Rettig).

In addition, useful background information on the encyclopedia can be found in Martin Pedersen's article "Fall Reference Update" (*Publishers Weekly*, August 23, 1993, p. 26).

CONCISE COLUMBIA ENCYCLOPEDIA

FACTS

Full Title: *The Concise Columbia Encyclopedia*. Editors: Barbara A. Chernow and George A. Vallasi. **Publisher:** Columbia University Press. **Date Published:** First Edition, 1983; Second Edition, 1989.

Also published as the *Concise Columbia Encyclopedia in Large Print* (Columbia University Press, 1984; 8 vols.).

British Title: *The Longman Encyclopedia*.

Unabridged Version: *The New Columbia Encyclopedia* (fourth edition, 1975).

Electronic Versions: COLUMBIA ELECTRONIC ENCYCLOPEDIA (Hand-held); CONCISE COLUMBIA ENCYCLOPEDIA (CD-ROM).

Volumes: One. **Words:** 1 million. **Pages:** 954. **Articles:** 15,000. **Bibliographies:** None. **Illustrations and Maps:** 150. **Cross-references:** 50,000. **Index Entries:** None. **Editorial Staff, Advisers, and Contributors:** 131. **Trim Size:** 7¼ × 10¼ in.

Price and Sales Information: $39.95. Individual consumers can purchase the *Concise Columbia Encyclopedia* in bookstores or, if the book is not in stock, it can be ordered. Similarly, educational institutions (schools, libraries, etc.) can order it through a book wholesaler. To order the encyclopedia directly from the publisher, call toll-free 1-800-944-8648 or write Columbia University Press, 562 West 113th Street, New York, NY 10025.

EVALUATION

The one-volume *Concise Columbia Encyclo- pedia*—a desk-sized general reference source aimed specifically at adults and older students in North America—contains more than 15,000 A-to-Z articles and a million words. It first appeared in 1983 and was thoroughly updated in 1989; it has not been revised since. The encyclopedia is a partial abridgment of the much larger 6.6 million-word *New Columbia Encyclopedia* (fourth edition, 1975), which has recently been replaced by the COLUMBIA ENCYCLOPEDIA (fifth edition, 1993), also a single-volume work. A British edition of the *Concise Columbia* is published as the *Longman Encyclopedia* (Longman, 1989).

Two electronic editions of the *Concise Columbia* are also generally available, the most widely known and used being the CD-ROM version that forms part of the popular *Microsoft Bookshelf*, a collection of basic reference sources on disk for use with personal computers; see CONCISE COLUMBIA ENCYCLOPEDIA (CD-ROM) on page 275 for a brief review. The other electronic edition is called the COLUMBIA ELECTRONIC ENCYCLOPEDIA (see page 264), a hand-held, battery-operated product from Franklin Electronic Publishers. In addition, Columbia University Press makes the encyclopedia available online to the Columbia University community via ColumbiaNet, the university library's electronic information network. This arrangement is said to be a unique collaboration between an encyclopedia publisher and a university library system.

The first edition (1983) of the *Concise Columbia* was also published in 1987 in a multivolume large type edition entitled the *Concise Columbia Encyclopedia in Large Print*. Intended for readers with visual problems, the *Concise Columbia Encyclopedia in Large Print* consists of 3,670 pages in eight large volumes (9 × 12 in.) and features 18-point text type, which meets the standards of the National Association for the Visually Handicapped. The large type edition includes all of the articles and most of the illustrations and maps found in the one-volume edition. It remains in print and can be obtained from the publisher (Columbia University Press) at $295.00 for the set.

Since 1935, when the first COLUMBIA ENCYCLOPEDIA made its debut, the name "Columbia" has come to stand for quality small-volume encyclopedias (both general and specialized). The *Concise Columbia* contributes to that tradition admirably. The editors are first-rate reference book professionals. They are supported by a sizable editorial staff, plus more than 50 experienced contributors and 46 subject consultants. Columbia University professors, including some major names (Kenneth Jackson, Robert Stern, Lawrence Cremin, Robert Merton), dominate the consultants' list. It should be noted, though, that the encyclopedia has no official connection with the university—that is, encyclopedias bearing the name "Columbia" are not authorized publications of Columbia University.

In their preface to the second edition entitled "A World of Knowledge at Your Finger Tips," the editors of the *Concise Columbia* state that the volume "places an extraordinary amount of information about the world in useful form at your fingertips. It will answer the sorts of questions we believe you are most likely to ask as you sit at your desk at home, at school, or in the office." As this suggests, the encyclopedia covers all areas of basic knowledge and information. Its coverage is fairly well balanced, although biographical, geographical, and scientific and technical subjects receive the most attention. For example, nearly a third of the book's 15,000 articles deal with people, both living and dead. Countries, states, provinces, and major cities, rivers, lakes, mountains, deserts, and the like are equally well covered. U.S. states usually receive about half a page of text, Canadian provinces a fourth of a page.

Among the 3,000 or so articles devoted to scientific and technical topics are dozens that concisely but authoritatively explain developments in computer science and electronics. Examples are "Artificial Intelligence," "Baud," "Boolean Algebra," "Compact Disc," "Computer," "Computer Graphics," "Computer Program," "Computer Terminal," "Electronic Game," "Electronic Music," "Electronics," "Integrated Circuit," "Logic Circuit," "Microelectronics," "Microprocessor," "Programming Language," "Semiconductor," "Transistor," and "Videotex." Taken together, these and cognate articles provide a reasonably comprehensive summary of the ongoing electronics revolution. Other areas of science and technology receive comparable attention.

The *Concise Columbia* is a specific-entry (as opposed to broad-entry) encyclopedia. Its articles therefore are naturally quite brief, averaging 70–75 words in length (or about 15 per page). But, as the editors point out in their preface, "Our articles always go beyond the mere definitions you would find in a dictionary. We provide context." In many instances, the articles are cut-down or abbreviated versions of those that originally appeared in the now superseded *New Columbia Encyclopedia* (fourth edition, 1975). Quite frequently historical detail found in the larger *New Columbia* has been reduced or eliminated in the *Concise Columbia*, and the bibliographies included in the former have been dropped entirely. A review of the first edition of the *Concise Columbia* in *Reference Books Bulletin* (in *Booklist*, March 1, 1984, p. 952) describes the abridgment process this way:

> Most articles appear to have been condensed or rewritten using material from the older work. Much information provided in the longer *New Columbia Encyclopedia* has had to be sacrificed, and technical topics understandably suffer since explanations are shorter; cultural entries lose some of the details of contextual descriptions.

On the other hand, the *Concise Columbia* updates many of the articles found in the older *New Columbia* and contains much new information, including approximately 1,000 articles covering such contemporary subjects as Alzheimer's disease, health maintenance organizations (HMOs), genetic engineering, AIDS, facsimile machines and transmission, the Chernobyl nuclear disaster, the Alaskan oil spill, the Iran-Contra scandal, and prominent people such as Lech Walesa, Pete Rose, Philip Glass, Nadine Gordimer, Anne Sexton, Kurt Waldheim, Maya Angelou, Toni Morrison, Michael Jackson, George Shultz, and Mikhail Gorbachev.

In keeping with the encyclopedia's efforts to be as concise as possible, a great deal of information is presented in succinct, convenient tabular form. Specifically, there are more than 40 lengthy tables on subjects ranging from African and American Indian languages and Canadian prime ministers to the Olympic Games, rulers of the Roman Empire, theater companies, trigonometric functions, vitamins, and Shakespeare's plays. All tables are listed at the front of the book.

The encyclopedia is normally accurate and impartial in its presentation of information. Moreover, treatment of controversial or sensitive subjects usually includes the pros and cons of the issue. The article "Abortion," for example, informs the reader that, although "attitudes toward abortion have generally become more liberal in the 20th cent.," induced abortion "remains a controversial issue in the U.S., however, and in 1977 Congress barred the use of Medicaid funds for abortion except for therapeutic reasons and in certain other specified instances." Likewise, "Fluoridation" notes that, "While studies have proved fluoridation safe at levels of one part per million, opponents assert that such action constitutes compulsory medication and that those wanting fluoride can use it individually."

Information in the *Concise Columbia* is current as of the late 1980s, which means that the encyclopedia is beginning to show some age spots. Not only are recent headline events—the election of Presidents Clinton in the U.S. and Chamorro in Nicaragua, the breakup of the Soviet Union, the turmoil in what was Yugoslavia, the total defeat of apartheid in South Africa, etc.—missing from the pages of the *Concise Columbia*, so are many other less obvious or dramatic facts, trends, and developments. *Examples:* There is nothing in the encyclopedia on sexual harassment or cardiomyopathy or carpal tunnel syndrome, nor are such important contemporary writers as Philip Larkin and Derek Walcott covered. "Abortion," "Circumcision," "Dead Sea Scrolls," "Galileo," "Islam," "Shock Therapy," and "Uzbekistan" are examples of articles in need of revision. Presumably, a new concise edition based on the recently published COLUMBIA ENCYCLOPEDIA (1993) will eventually be forthcoming. Until that time, however, the present *Concise Columbia* will continue to become more dated with each passing year.

The encyclopedia's writing style is clear, direct, spare, and intelligently constructed. The editors almost always achieve their goal of conveying information "in full sentences as simply and elegantly as possible" (preface). Ordinarily, the text will be comprehensible to educated adults and students at the secondary school and college levels. The article "Heart," reproduced here in its entirety, gives a fair sense of the encyclopedia's style:

> **heart**, muscular organ that pumps blood to all parts of the body. The pear-shaped human heart is about the size of a fist and lies just left of center within the chest cavity. The contractions of heart muscle, or myocardium, are entirely self-stimulated. The heart is divided into two cavities by a wall of muscle; each cavity is divided in turn into two chambers, the upper ones called atria, the lower ones ventricles. Blood from the veins, high in carbon dioxide but low in oxygen, returns to the right atrium. It enters the right ventricle, which contracts, pumping the blood through the pulmonary artery to the LUNGS. Blood rich in oxygen and poor in carbon dioxide returns from the lungs to the left atrium and enters the left ventricle, which contracts, forcing the blood into the aorta, from which it is distributed throughout the body. The blood is prevented from backing up by a series of valves. See CIRCULATORY SYSTEM; see also CORONARY ARTERY DISEASE; TRANSPLANTATION, MEDICAL

Although the *Concise Columbia* lacks an index, finding specific facts and topics in the encyclopedia normally poses few problems, thanks largely to generous use of cross-references within and at the end of articles. Printed in SMALL CAPITAL LETTERS, these *see* and *see also* references direct the reader to related information in the encyclopedia. As the editors note in their preface, "To utilize space efficiently, whenever possible, information included in one article is not repeated in another. Instead, cross-references are used extensively to lead the reader to articles containing additional material relevent [sic] to the entry he or she is consulting." Examples (LUNGS; CIRCULATORY SYSTEM; CORONARY ARTERY DISEASE; TRANSPLANTATION; MEDICAL) can be seen in the article "Heart" reprinted above. Also, many external cross-references are included in the A–Z listing, e.g., "Penis: see REPRODUCTIVE SYSTEM."

A review of the encyclopedia in *Reference Books Bulletin* (in *Booklist*, January 1, 1990, p. 944) accurately describes its cross-reference system as "generally very efficient." Occasionally, however, the system malfunctions. For instance, the encyclopedia has an article entitled "Lie Detector," but fails to provide a cross-reference under the word *polygraph*. Similarly, no cross-reference is given under *deconstruction* to the article "Derrida, Jacques," which contains much useful information on deconstruction. In such instances, a general index would be welcome.

As mentioned, the *Concise Columbia* does not include bibliographies, or lists of recommended sources that the reader might consult for additional information. This omission is not unexpected; among the small-volume encyclopedias for adults and older students currently available, only the larger COLUMBIA ENCYCLOPEDIA, RANDOM HOUSE ENCYCLOPEDIA, and VOLUME LIBRARY offer bibliographies. On the other hand, the lack of bibliographies does the *Concise Columbia* no good in a highly competitive market.

Like its parent (the *New Columbia Encyclopedia*), the *Concise Columbia* is not a heavily illustrated encyclopedia. The relatively few illustrations that are included, however, add significantly to the informational content of the volume. All black-and-white line drawings, the illustrations deal almost exclusively with scientific and technical matters, simply depicting such subjects as the human ear, the human circulatory system, continental drift, vertical faults (in geology), DNA (deoxyribonucleic acid), and the structure of the sun. James Rettig, in a review of the encyclopedia in *Wilson Library*

Bulletin (December 1989, p. 143) takes the interesting position that the *Concise Columbia* does not really need many illustrations: "The absence of illustrations causes no loss, however, for this is the sort of ready reference one consults for verbal rather than visual answers."

In addition to the illustrations, a few simple, black-and-white, staff-drawn political maps of major countries appear throughout the encyclopedia. Also, 16 pages of physical maps by Rand McNally are included in an unpaged section in the center of the book. These maps, all in color, are devoted to the continents of the world and the Pacific and Atlantic Ocean floors.

Physically, the *Concise Columbia* is a well-constructed book, with readable typefaces and a clean (albeit unexciting) layout. Desk-sized (7½ × 10¼ in.), the volume comes with a colorful dust jacket and is reasonably easy to handle, weighing in at about 4½ pounds, or less than half the heft of the *New Columbia Encyclopedia* or its successor, the COLUMBIA ENCYCLOPEDIA.

REPORT CARD: CONCISE COLUMBIA ENCYCLOPEDIA				
TOPIC	COVERAGE	ACCURACY	RECENCY	CLARITY
Circumcision	C	A	C	A
Drew, Charles	F*	NA	NA	NA
Galileo	B	A	D	A
Glass, Philip	B	A	B	A
Heart Disease	B	A	B	A
IQ	F*	NA	NA	NA
Panda Bears	B	A	B	A
Sexual Harassment	F*	NA	NA	NA
Shroud of Turin	F*	NA	NA	NA
Uzbekistan	C	A	C	A

A = Excellent; **B** = Above Average; **C** = Average; **D** = Below Average; **F** = Poor; **NA** = Not Applicable
*No Article

SUMMARY

First published in 1983 and revised in 1989, the *Concise Columbia Encyclopedia* is a desk-sized general encyclopedia based on and abridged from the older and larger *New Columbia Encyclopedia* (1975), which has recently been superseded by the COLUMBIA ENCYCLOPEDIA (1993). It is also published in an eight-volume large type edition (the *Concise Columbia Encyclopedia in Large Print*) and two widely available electronic editions (the COLUMBIA ELECTRONIC ENCYCLOPEDIA and the CONCISE COLUMBIA ENCYCLOPEDIA on CD-ROM as part of *Microsoft Bookshelf*).

The *Concise Columbia* is one of the best small single-volume encyclopedias for adults and older students currently on the North American market. Its strengths include broad and well-balanced coverage, with emphasis on people, places, and scientific and technical subjects; an exceptionally clear writing style; accurate and objective treatment of material, including controversial and sensitive subjects; and an intelligently constructed, usually effective system of cross-references. On the negative side, the encyclopedia, which has not been revised for five years, is beginning to show signs of age; it has few illustrations, none of which are in color except for a 16-page map insert; it lacks bibliographies; and it needs an index to be fully accessible. The bottom line: Still among the best small one-volume encyclopedias, but in need of revision.

OTHER OPINIONS

American Reference Books Annual, 1990, pp. 20–21 (review by Craig W. Beard); *Basic Information Sources* by William A. Katz (vol. 1 of *Introduction to Reference Work*, 6th ed., New York: McGraw-Hill, 1992), pp. 258–60; *Reference Books Bulletin* (in *Booklist*), January 1, 1990, p. 944 (unsigned review); *Reference Sources for Small and Medium-Sized Libraries* (5th ed., Chicago: American Library Assn., 1992), p. 32 (review by Jovian P. Lang); *Wilson Library Bulletin*, December 1989, pp. 142–43 (review by James Rettig).

DICTIONARY OF CULTURAL LITERACY

FACTS

Full Title: *The Dictionary of Cultural Literacy.* Authors: E.D. Hirsch, Jr., Joseph F. Kett, and James Trefil. **Publisher:** Houghton Mifflin Company. **Date Published:** First Edition, 1988; Second Edition, 1993.

Volumes: One. **Words:** 350,000. **Pages:** 619. **Articles:** 5,000. **Bibliographies:** None. **Illustrations and Maps:** 250. **Cross-references:** 20,000. **Index Entries:** 7,500. **Editorial Staff, Advisers, and Contributors:** 30. **Trim Size:** 7½ × 9¼ in.

Price and Sales Information: $24.95. Individual consumers can purchase the *Dictionary of Cultural Literacy* in bookstores or, if the book is not in stock, it can be ordered. Similarly, educational institutions (schools, libraries, etc.) can order it through a book wholesaler. To order the book directly from the publisher, call 1-800-733-7075 or write Houghton Mifflin Company, 222 Berkeley Street, Boston, MA 02116-3764.

EVALUATION

First published in 1988 and substantially revised in 1993, the *Dictionary of Cultural Literacy* contains much general encyclopedic information but is not a typical general encyclopedia. Most encyclopedias aim to cover basic knowledge and information as comprehensively as possible, whereas the *Dictionary* deals only with that body of knowledge "every American needs to know." Here is how the authors explain the purpose of the book:

> Although it is true that no two humans know exactly the same things, they often have a great deal of knowledge in common. . . . The form and content of this common knowledge constitute one of the elements that makes each national culture unique. It is our contention that such a body of information is shared by literate Americans of the late twentieth century, and that this body of knowledge can be identified and defined. This dictionary is a first attempt at that task. It identifies and defines the names, phrases, events, and other items that are familiar to most literate Americans: the information that we call cultural literacy (Introduction).

The idea for the *Dictionary* grew out of an earlier book by E.D. Hirsch called *Cultural Literacy: What Every American Needs to Know* (Houghton Mifflin, 1987). A great success (180,000 copies in hardcover and 200,000 in paperback sold), *Cultural Literacy* postulates that some of today's students in the U.S. are culturally illiterate, that they lack the "shared knowledge" that helped previous generations of Americans succeed in life and the world. The book, which advocates curricular change in the nation's schools, includes a lengthy list of people, places, events, terms, and phrases that Hirsch claims any educated person in this country should be familiar with. The *Dictionary*, published the following year, furnishes encyclopedic summaries of this knowledge core.

Like *Cultural Literacy*, the first edition of the *Dictionary* did enormously well in the marketplace, selling more than 600,000 cop-

ies. In addition, a junior version called the FIRST DICTIONARY OF CULTURAL LITERACY was published in 1989. But not everyone is happy with the notion of cultural literacy or agrees with Hirsch and his colleagues about how to define it. Some critics view Hirsch, an English professor at the University of Virginia at Charlottesville, and his coauthors (also university professors in Virginia) as reactionaries seeking a return to a golden intellectual past that never was. Others see cultural literacy as code words for cultural elitism. Still others question Hirsch's emphasis on factual knowledge as a measure of academic attainment and sophistication. James Rettig, who clearly dislikes the *Dictionary* and what it stands for, frames the issue this way in a review of the second edition in *Wilson Library Bulletin* (December 1993, p. 76):

> One's assessment of this dictionary of diverse facts depends upon one's philosophy of education. If one believes it rests on a foundation of fact that every adult must know to be considered educated, then this is a significant reference book. If, on the other hand, one considers the fact-based approach at best to be uninspired and Gradgrindian and believes that to be educated one must be able to master the theories and mental models that these facts fit into, then this is just a dictionary of diverse facts.

Whether viewed as a vade mecum of everything worth knowing or simply a compilation of "diverse facts," the *Dictionary of Cultural Literacy* does contain much encyclopedic information and as such needs to be judged on how well it performs as a single-volume reference work.

Like several other small-volume adult encyclopedias currently on the market (namely BARRON'S NEW CONCISE STUDENT'S ENCYCLOPEDIA, the RANDOM HOUSE ENCYCLOPEDIA, the RUNNING PRESS CYCLOPEDIA, and the VOLUME LIBRARY), the *Dictionary* is topically (as opposed to alphabetically) arranged. Specifically, it consists of 23 sections, each devoted to a broad subject: "The Bible," "Mythology and Folklore," "Proverbs," "Idioms," "World Literature, Philosophy, and Religion," "Literature in English," "Conventions of Written English," "Fine Arts," "World History to 1550," "World History since 1550," "American History to 1865," "American History since 1865," "World Politics," "American Politics," "World Geography," "American Geography," "Anthropology, Psychology, and Sociology," "Business and Economics," "Physical Sciences and Mathematics," "Earth Sciences," "Life Sciences," "Medicine and Health," and "Technology." A brief essay on the subject introduces each section.

As noted, the Dictionary's coverage is selective rather than comprehensive. In their introduction, Hirsch and his coauthors set forth several criteria, or "tests," designed to determine what should and should not be covered in the book. Only knowledge "likely to be known by a broad majority of literate Americans" is included, while information "so specialized that it is known only by experts" is excluded. Also excluded is very basic and generally known information, "such as the names of colors and animals." Finally, "cultural literacy is not knowledge of cultural events. . . . To become part of cultural literacy, an item must have lasting significance."

As might be expected and the Report Card (see below) documents, the Dictionary's coverage is quite spotty, with nothing on Charles Drew (black physician and blood bank pioneer), Philip Glass (prominent contemporary American composer), panda bears, sexual harassment, and the famous Shroud of Turin. The book also omits any mention of such topics as adoption, carpal tunnel syndrome, psychological depression, fluoridation, and Scientology, as well as important writers and artists like Nadine Gordimer, Philip Larkin, Anne Sexton, and Robert Motherwell. Perhaps all or most of these subjects are outside the announced scope of the Dictionary; sometimes it is difficult to tell. In any event, failure to cover such topics greatly reduces the book's usefulness as a general reference source.

Just as the Dictionary's coverage is erratic, treatment of those topics that are covered is usually so superficial as to be of only minimal reference value to most students and adults. Although encyclopedic in nature, the book—as its title suggests—often attempts little more than dictionary-style definitions. The entry "Homosexuality," for instance, consists of one sentence ("A sexual attraction between persons of the same sex"), with cross-references to "Gay," "Lesbian," and "Heterosexuality." In turn, "Gay" is limited to one line ("Descriptive term for a HOMOSEXUAL"), "Lesbian" to three words ("A HOMOSEXUAL woman"), and "Heterosexuality" to one line ("Sexual attraction between a male and a female").

Much to the embarrassment of the authors, the first edition of the Dictionary contained many factual errors, including several clangers. In the most celebrated instance, Jacksonville was identified as the capital of Florida—this in the section on American geography that begins, "Tests have revealed that many Americans are amazingly ignorant of the geography of their nation." Happily, most of the book's errors have been corrected in the recently published second edition.

The authors are normally impartial in their presentation of information. Likewise, controversial or sensitive subjects usually receive adequate treatment, with the basic issues identified (albeit not fully explored). *Example:* The article "Intelligence Quotient (IQ)" notes, "Psychologists are less confident today than in the past that IQ test scores really measure intelligence. Controversy exists about the effects of race and CLASS on IQ scores. (See NATURE-NURTURE CONTROVERSY)."

In some instances, however, the *Dictionary* fails to inform the reader that a topic is controversial, as in "Shock Therapy," which defines the term as "The treatment of a mentally ill person by passing electric shocks through the BRAIN," but gives no indication that electroshock therapy is and has been a debatable treatment for psychiatric problems.

Thanks to publication of the second edition in 1993, the *Dictionary* is quite current in most areas. The revision effort centered chiefly on new developments in science, medicine, technology, and geography (where such events as the break up of the Soviet Union are described). The authors also added some new information concerning African-American achievements. According to an article in *Publishers Weekly* (August 23, 1993, p. 27), "Houghton Mifflin [the book's publisher] received many letters about the first *Dictionary* and kept a file of reader suggestions and criticisms that the editors used for revisions on the new edition."

The *Dictionary*'s writing style is consistently clear and readable. Its text will be readily comprehensible to literate adults and students reading at the ninth grade level and beyond. The article "Heart," quoted here in its entirety, is typical of the book's style:

The hollow muscular ORGAN that is the center of the CIRCULATORY SYSTEM. The heart pumps BLOOD throughout the intricate system of BLOOD VESSELS in the body.

Access to the *Dictionary*'s contents could hardly be improved. Not only are specific topics and facts easily retrievable through the 7,500-entry index at the back of the book, an extensive network of cross-references effectively guides the reader to related material. For instance, the short article "Heart," reprinted above, includes four cross-references (the words printed in SMALL CAPITAL LETTERS). Whereas the *Dictionary* has an abundance of finding devices, it has no bibliographies, which is strange for a book that claims to have an educational as well as informational mission. In any event, the lack of bibliographies does nothing to enhance the book's reference value.

The illustrations included in the *Dictionary* do enhance the printed text, but they are so few and far between that their impact on the overall work is minimal. All in black-and-white, the 250 illustrations include photographs, drawings, diagrams, reproductions of art work, and maps. Many are portraits of famous people. The physical format is satisfactory. The book, which is well-bound, comes with a dust jacket. Its typography is clean but dull.

REPORT CARD: DICTIONARY OF CULTURAL LITERACY

TOPIC	COVERAGE	ACCURACY	RECENCY	CLARITY
Circumcision	C	A	A	A
Drew, Charles	F*	NA	NA	NA
Galileo	C	A	D	A
Glass, Philip	F*	NA	NA	NA
Heart Disease	D	A	C	A
IQ	B	A	A	A
Panda Bears	F*	NA	NA	NA
Sexual Harassment	F*	NA	NA	NA
Shroud of Turin	F*	NA	NA	NA
Uzbekistan	C	A	A	A

A = Excellent; **B** = Above Average; **C** = Average; **D** = Below Average; **F** = Poor; **NA** = Not Applicable
*No Article

SUMMARY

The single-volume *Dictionary of Cultural Literacy* first appeared in 1988 and was revised in 1993. Selective rather than comprehensive in its approach, the *Dictionary* is a controversial effort by three Virginia professors to identify and summarize that knowledge and information "every American needs to know." The book is encyclopedic in approach, but as a general reference work its coverage has too many gaps to be of much value to most students and adults. Moreover, its treatment of topics that are covered is often extremely superficial, its illustrations are few and far between, and it lacks bibliographies. On the plus side, the *Dictionary* is clearly written, easy to use, and has an interesting (if debatable) premise. The bottom line: Not really suitable as a general reference work.

OTHER OPINIONS

American Reference Books Annual, 1990, p. 128 (review by Robert N. Broadus); *Choice*, April 1989, pp. 1304–05 (review by G.R. Graf); *Reference Books Bulletin* (in *Booklist*), April 1, 1989, pp. 1356–58 (unsigned review); *Wilson Library Bulletin*, December 1993, pp. 76–77 (review by James Rettig).

KNOWLEDGE ENCYCLOPEDIA

FACTS

Full Title: *Knowledge Encyclopedia*. Editor: John Paton. **Publisher:** Arco Publishing Company, Inc. **Date Published:** 1984.
Volumes: One. **Words:** 300,000. **Pages:** 415. **Articles:** 2,500. **Bibliographies:** None. **Illustrations and Maps:** 615. **Cross-references:** 4,000. **Index Entries:** 5,000. **Editorial Staff, Advisers, and Contributors:** 16. **Trim Size:** 7½ × 9¾ in.
Price and Sales Information: $16.95. Individual consumers can purchase the *Knowledge Encyclopedia* in bookstores or, if the book is not in stock, it can be ordered. Similarly, educational institutions (schools, libraries, etc.) can order it through a book wholesaler. Recently, however, a representative of Arco Publishing (the book's publisher) indicated that the *Knowledge Encyclopedia* will probably be discontinued as soon as its remaining inventory is exhausted. To order the encyclopedia directly from the publisher or for further information about its status, call toll-free 1-800-223-2336 or write Arco Publishing Company, Inc., 15 Columbus Circle, New York, NY 10023.

EVALUATION

The single-volume *Knowledge Encyclopedia*, said to be "a work for all members of the family" (preface), first appeared in 1979 in Great Britain, a product of Grisewood & Dempsey, a well-known British publisher of reference books for young people. In 1981, the encyclopedia was updated, and in 1984 Arco Publishing Company of New York issued it for distribution in North America. The editor, John Paton, has a number of encyclopedia credits, including the KINGFISHER CHILDREN'S ENCYCLOPEDIA and the now defunct NEW CAXTON ENCYCLOPEDIA.

As its Report Card (see below) indicates, the encyclopedia furnishes spotty coverage at best. The book emphasizes historical figures, countries of the world, and scientific and technical subjects. Conversely, the arts, humanities, and social sciences receive only cursory attention. The encyclopedia also has a strong British emphasis. For example, the British Parliament is covered, whereas its U.S. and Canadian counterparts are not. Likewise, there is an article on English literature, but none on American or Canadian literature.

Oddly, Australian topics receive extensive coverage in the *Knowledge Encyclopedia. Examples:* The book contains articles on the black swan (a bird native to Australia and the symbol of Western Australia), the echidna (an egg-laying mammal indigenous to Australia), Matthew Flinders (a British explorer credited with naming Australia), Ned Kelly (a famous Australian outlaw), the Murry-Darling (an Australian river system), Newcastle (an Australian port city of some 360,000), and the wattle (a plant whose flower is the Australian national emblem).

While many esoteric topics are covered, the encyclopedia contains absolutely nothing on such general subjects as abortion, adoption, circumcision, economic depression, psychological depression, fluoridation, heart disease, and intelligence tests. Nor are prominent contemporary writers, artists, and musicians such as Philip Larkin, Toni Morrison, Philip Glass, and Robert Motherwell even mentioned.

Just as the *Knowledge Encyclopedia's* coverage is woefully inadequate, its treatment of those topics that are covered is consistently superficial. Articles average about 120 words in length, but many are little more than dictionary definitions, as in the case of "Gene," which devotes all of 60 words to the genetic process. A review in *Reference Books Bulletin* (in *Booklist*, February 15, 1985, p. 844) has this comment on the encyclopedia's shallow treatment: "Students needing a goodly amount of resource material will have to turn to a standard encyclopedia or other nonfiction source; but if they just want to learn a little about a lot of topics, this wide-ranging volume will suit their purposes."

Information in the encyclopedia is usually accurate, although it errs in placing the giant panda in the raccoon family; genetic tests show the animal belongs to the bear family. Likewise, information is objectively presented, although many controversial subjects are avoided. By way of example, the encyclopedia fails to cover such hotly contested issues as abortion, capital punishment, educational tests and testing, fluoridation, religious cults, and sexual harassment. In the area of human sexuality, the book furnishes impartial (albeit very limited) information about sexual intercourse, birth control, homosexuality, and sexually transmitted diseases.

Ordinarily, the encyclopedia—published in 1984—is current only as of the late 1970s or early 1980s. Obviously, it lacks any coverage of such recent events as the unification of East and West Germany, the breakup of the Soviet Union, the turmoil in the former Yugoslavia, the end of apartheid in South Africa, the advent of major political leaders like Presidents Clinton (in the U.S.), Chamorro (Nicaragua), and Yeltsin (Russia), the Challenger disaster, and the AIDS crisis. In its present form, the *Knowledge Encyclopedia* is not viable as a source of reasonably current information. Whether there will eventually be a new edition is not known at this time.

The encyclopedia is aimed chiefly at adults and older students, but it can also be used effectively by students in the upper elementary and junior high school grades who possess good reading skills. Eugenia Schmitz, in a review in *American Reference Books Annual* (1985, p. 15), sums up the encyclopedia's readability range this way: "Simple enough in style for a grade school audience without using controlled vocabulary, and yet interesting to their parents, this is definitely a browsing encyclopedia." The book's writing style tends to be clear and textbookish. The article "Heart," reprinted here in its entirety, is typical:

> **HEART** Hollow muscular organ which pumps BLOOD around the body. All but the simplest animals have some sort of heart. In most cases, this consists of a muscular bag divided into two or more chambers. Mammals, including man, have a four-chambered heart: two upper chambers, or *auricles*, and two lower chambers, or *ventricles*. Pure blood, carrying oxygen, is sent from the left ventricle to the various parts of the body and comes back, carrying CARBON DIOXIDE, to the right auricle. From the right auricle, the blood is driven into the right ventricle, and from there to the LUNGS where it gives up carbon dioxide and collects fresh oxygen. The pure blood is returned to the left auricle then into the left ventricle, ready for another journey round the body. The tubes taking blood away from the heart are called ARTERIES and those bringing it back are called VEINS.

The contents of the *Knowledge Encyclopedia* are easily retrievable in most instances. Cross-references, printed in SMALL CAPITAL LETTERS, appear throughout the text (see "Heart" above for examples), and there is a small but adequate index at the back of the volume. However, articles that use British spelling (e.g., "Tyre") and terminology ("Motor Car") will probably be missed by North American readers due to the lack of cross-references (e.g., "Tire. See Tyre").

Also lacking in the encyclopedia are bibliographies, or lists of recommended sources of additional information. On the other hand, the book does contain many useful illustrations. Colorful, informative, and well reproduced, the illustrations (photographs, drawings, maps, etc.) account for roughly a third of the total text and are clearly the best feature of what is otherwise an undistinguished work. The book's physical format is also good. The binding, which is sewn, will withstand heavy use; inside, the page layout is varied and attractive, helped along by color on most pages and a legible text type.

SUMMARY

The *Knowledge Encyclopedia*, a small British import, was last published in 1984 and urgently requires a thorough revision if it is to remain a viable quick-reference encyclopedia. Intended for "all members of the family" (preface), the current edition not only suffers from lack of up-to-dateness but inadequate coverage and shallow treatment of basic knowledge and information. Only its illustrations and format are satisfactory. The bottom line: Consumers should avoid this encyclopedia.

OTHER OPINIONS

American Reference Books Annual, 1985, p. 15 (review by Eugenia E. Schmitz); *Reference Books Bulletin* (in *Booklist*), February 15, 1985, p. 844 (unsigned review); *Wilson Library Bulletin*, October 1984, p. 147 (review by James Rettig).

REPORT CARD: KNOWLEDGE ENCYCLOPEDIA				
TOPIC	COVERAGE	ACCURACY	RECENCY	CLARITY
Circumcision	F*	NA	NA	NA
Drew, Charles	F*	NA	NA	NA
Galileo	C	A	D	A
Glass, Philip	F*	NA	NA	NA
Heart Disease	F*	NA	NA	NA
IQ	F*	NA	NA	NA
Panda Bears	D	C	C	A
Sexual Harassment	F*	NA	NA	NA
Shroud of Turin	F*	NA	NA	NA
Uzbekistan	F*	NA	NA	NA

A = Excellent; B = Above Average; C = Average; D = Below Average; F = Poor; NA = Not Applicable
*No Article

NEW AMERICAN DESK ENCYCLOPEDIA

FACTS

Full Title: *The New American Desk Encyclopedia.* Editor: Philip D. Morehead. **Publisher:** New American Library, a subsidiary of Penguin USA. Former Titles: *University Desk Encyclopedia* (1977; 1 vol.); *Concord Desk Encyclopedia* (1982; 3 vols.). **Date Published:** First Edition, 1984; Second Edition, 1989; Third Edition, 1993.
    Volumes: One. **Words:** 1.3 million. **Pages:** 1,312. **Articles:** 13,000. **Bibliographies:** None. **Illustrations and Maps:** 200. **Cross-references:** 35,000. **Index Entries:** None. **Editorial Staff, Advisers, and Contributors:** 45. Trim Size: 4¼ × 7 in.

Price and Sales Information: $17.00 paperbound (Meridian Edition). Individual consumers can purchase the *New American Desk Encyclopedia* in bookstores and other retail stores that sell paperbound books; if the book is not in stock, it can be ordered. Similarly, educational institutions (schools, libraries, etc.) can order it through a book wholesaler. To order the encyclopedia directly from the publisher, call toll-free 1-800-526-0275 or write New American Library, c/o Penguin USA, 375 Hudson Street, New York, NY 10014.

EVALUATION

Billed as the "first one-volume encyclopedia to be published in an affordable paperback format" (publisher's advertisement), the *New American Desk Encyclopedia* first appeared in 1984 as an abridged, updated, and retitled version of the *University Desk Encyclopedia.* The *University Desk Encyclopedia,* which has long been out of print, was a mediocre single-volume hardcover work prepared in the Netherlands by the Elsevier Publishing Company and published in North America in 1977 by E.P. Dutton, then an Elsevier subsidiary. Alas, the encyclopedia's only laudable features, its colorful illustrations and fairly attractive format, are absent in the cheaply produced *New American Desk Encyclopedia*. A three-volume version of the *University Desk Encyclopedia* also appeared in 1982 under the title *Concord Desk Encyclopedia*; a boxed paperbound set, it briefly served as a premium for new subscribers to *Time* magazine.

Following its initial publication in 1984, the *New American Desk Encyclopedia* has been minimally revised twice, first in 1989 and again in 1993. The encyclopedia's coverage is fairly well balanced, although biographical, geographical, historical, and scientific topics predominate. Plant and animal life, chemical elements and compounds, natural phenomena, and wars and battles are particularly well covered. Most of the encyclopedia's 13,000 articles are quite brief, averaging roughly 100 words in length (or about 10 articles per page). Not surprisingly, while the coverage tends to be broad, treatment is often shallow, lacking encyclopedic depth and sometimes failing to provide needed explanations. For instance, the article "Fluoridation" informs the reader that "Despite some opposition, many authorities now fluoridate water," but it does not explain who is opposed to fluoridation nor the nature of the opposition. Many similar examples could be cited.

The encyclopedia can also be faulted for occasional factual and typographical errors, as well as questionable interpretations. The article "Galileo," for example, says that the great scientist's "quarrelsome nature led him into an unfortunate controversy with the Church," which seems either a cockeyed reading of history or an unsuccessful attempt at understatement. The article on Dr. Charles Drew, the black physician whose research led to the development of blood banks, credits Drew with founding the American Red Cross blood bank, which is not true. The statement in the article "Pandas" that all pandas are "raccoon-like mammals" might lead readers to assume that the giant panda belongs to the raccoon family, which again is not true.

The encyclopedia normally presents its information in a fair and impartial manner, although most controversial or sensitive issues are ignored or glossed over, as in the case of the previously mentioned article "Fluoridation." As far as up-to-dateness is concerned, the latest (1993) edition of the encyclopedia provides reasonably current information on such headline events as the unification of Germany, the new political configurations in Eastern Europe, and the election of President Clinton in the U.S. On the other hand, less volatile or dramatic developments, such as the Roman Catholic Church's recent acknowledgment of error in the case of Galileo, are usually not reported in the encyclopedia. Hence, despite its 1993 revision date, the *New American Desk Encyclopedia* cannot be considered a well-maintained reference work, its updating more cosmetic than substantive.

The encyclopedia is intended for educated adults and older students at the secondary school level and beyond. Most articles are clearly written, but the style tends to be dry and uneven. Some articles, especially those on scientific subjects, may be too difficult for the average student or layperson. *Example:* The description of Galileo's chief contribution to science will test the comprehension of many readers:

> His most significant contribution to science was his provision of an alternative to the Aristotelian dynamics. The motion of the earth thus became a conceptual possibility and scientists at least had a genuine criterion for choosing between the Copernican and Tychonic hypotheses in ASTRONOMY.

More typical of the encyclopedia's style, however, is this excerpt from the article "Heart," though it too can be difficult going for those with no prior knowledge:

> **HEART,** vital organ in the chest of animals, concerned with pumping the BLOOD, thus maintaining the BLOOD CIRCULATION. The evolution of the vertebrates shows a development from the simple heart found in fish to

the four-chambered heart of mammals. In man, the circulation may be regarded as a figure-eight, with the heart at the cross-over point, but keeping the two systems separate by having two parallel sets of chambers. The pumping in the two sets, right and left, is coordinated, ensuring a balance of flow. Each set consists of an atrium, which receives blood from the LUNGS (left) or body (right), and a ventricle. The atria pump blood into the ventricles, which pump it into the lungs (right) or systemic circulation (left).

Finding information in the *New American Desk Encyclopedia* is usually not difficult, even though the book lacks an index. Its alphabetically arranged articles are of the specific-entry (as opposed to broad-entry) type, which enhances the user's chances of quickly pinpointing a specific topic or fact. In addition, access to specific information in the text is facilitated by an extensive network of 35,000 cross-references. Printed in SMALL CAPITAL LETTERS (as shown in the "Heart" article above), the cross-references normally guide the reader to all pertinent related articles on the subject being studied. Occasionally, though, the cross-reference system fails. For instance, the lengthy article "Mental Illness" includes numerous cross-references (NEUROSIS, SCHIZOPHRENIA, PSYCHOANALYSIS, LOBOTOMY, SHOCK THERAPY, PSYCHOSIS, HYSTERIA, ALCOHOLISM, etc.) but fails to include one to the article "Depression." It is in such instances that an index would be most welcome.

Like most one-volume encyclopedias, the *New American Desk Encyclopedia* lacks bibliographies, or lists of recommended sources for further study. More important is the encyclopedia's lack of illustrations. As mentioned, the hardcover *University Desk Encyclopedia* had quite good color illustrations, but the abridged paperbound *New American Desk Encyclopedia* contains none of these. The only illustrations in the volume are about 200 very small black-and-white location maps, plus a 16-page color atlas of the earth and universe inserted in the center of the book. Likewise, the encyclopedia's physical format is unimpressive. A squat, fat volume (4¼ × 7 in.), the book has a flimsy binding, poor quality paper, an uninviting layout, and type that is excessively small and poorly printed.

SUMMARY

An abridged, updated, and retitled version of the now defunct *University Desk Encyclopedia* (1977), the paperbound *New American Desk Encyclopedia* first appeared in 1984 and has been minimally updated twice, in 1989 and 1993. About the only positive features of the *New American Desk Encyclopedia* are its fairly broad coverage, many cross-references, and inexpensive price. Its substantial negatives include superficial treatment of basic knowledge and information, an unsettling number of factual and interpretative errors, avoidance of controversial or sensitive issues, an uneven and sometimes abstruse writing style, lack of an index, lack of bibliographies, lack of illustrations, and a poor physical format. The bottom line: A bad encyclopedia at any price.

OTHER OPINIONS

None.

REPORT CARD: NEW AMERICAN DESK ENCYCLOPEDIA

TOPIC	COVERAGE	ACCURACY	RECENCY	CLARITY
Circumcision	F*	NA	NA	NA
Drew, Charles	D	C	C	A
Galileo	C	C	D	C
Glass, Philip	F*	NA	NA	NA
Heart Disease	C	A	C	B
IQ	B	A	C	B
Panda Bears	C	C	C	B
Sexual Harassment	F*	NA	NA	NA
Shroud of Turin	F*	NA	NA	NA
Uzbekistan	C	A	A	A

A = Excellent; **B** = Above Average; **C** = Average; **D** = Below Average; **F** = Poor; **NA** = Not Applicable
*No Article

RANDOM HOUSE ENCYCLOPEDIA

FACTS

Full Title: *The Random House Encyclopedia.* Editorial Director: Jess Stein. **Editor in Chief:** James Mitchell. Executive Editor: Stephen P. Elliott. **Publisher:** Random House, Inc. **Date Published:** First Edition, 1977; Second Edition, 1983; Third Edition, 1990.

British Title: *The Joy of Knowledge* (Mitchell Beazley Publishers Ltd., 1977–78; 10 vols.).

Electronic Versions: RANDOM HOUSE ELECTRONIC ENCYCLOPEDIA (Hand-held); RANDOM HOUSE ENCYCLOPEDIA (Floppy Disks).

Volumes: One. **Words:** 3 million. **Pages:** 2,912. **Articles:** 25,880 (880 two-page articles in the "Colorpedia"; 25,000

brief articles in the "Alphapedia"). **Bibliographies:** 93. **Illustrations and Maps:** 13,500. **Cross-references:** 45,000. **Index Entries:** None. **Editorial Staff, Advisers, and Contributors:** 600. Trim Size: 8¼ × 11 in.

Price and Sales Information: $129.95. Individual consumers can purchase the *Random House Encyclopedia* in bookstores or, if the book is not in stock, it can be ordered. Similarly, educational institutions (schools, libraries, etc.) can order it through a book wholesaler. To order the encyclopedia directly from the publisher, call toll-free 1-800-726-0600 or write Random House, Inc., 201 East 50th Street, New York, NY 10022.

EVALUATION

Intended "primarily for teenagers and adults" (preface), the single-volume *Random House Encyclopedia* is a unique amalgam of a traditional A-to-Z encyclopedia and a collection of visually impressive thematic essays for readers raised in the television age. The late

James Mitchell, the encyclopedia's founding editor, explains the idea in his preface to the original edition:

> [T]here are two principal concepts of an encyclopedia. The first is that of a comprehensive fact-book for easy quick-reference use. The second is the complete library—a

collection of treatises on all subjects. In planning *The Random House Encyclopedia*, we examined these two approaches, considering the advantages and disadvantages of each type. The solution we reached—which was to take the two traditions and marry them—was made primarily with the user in mind.

Specifically, the encyclopedia is divided into two major parts, the 1,792-page "Colorpedia" and the 885-page "Alphapedia." In the current edition, the topically arranged "Colorpedia" comprises 880 two-page articles (or spreads) grouped under seven broad headings: "The Universe," "The Earth," "Life on Earth," "Man," "History and Culture," "Man and Science," and "Man and Machines." Within these categories the articles are loosely connected. "Man," for instance, consists of 149 two-page articles beginning with "Primate to Hominid," which is followed by "The First Hominids," "The First Men," "From Ancient to Modern Man," "Spread of Man: 1," "Spread of Man: 2," "Family of Man: Today's Peoples," "Family of Man: How Peoples Differ," and so on to the end of the section, which concludes with "Money and Capital," "Man as an Economic Being," "Industry and Economics," "International Trade and Finance," and "International Cooperation and Development." (In future editions, however, the editors should avoid sexist language in their headings.)

As its name implies, the "Colorpedia" includes many colorful illustrations—approximately 11,000 altogether. The illustrations, which make up about two-thirds of each "Colorpedia" page, are heavily captioned and handsomely reproduced. "For a new generation brought up with television," writes Mitchell in his preface, "words alone are no longer enough, and so in our *Colorpedia* section we have tried to make a new type of compact pictorial encyclopedia for a visually oriented age."

The "Alphapedia," on the other hand, consists of roughly 25,000 alphabetically arranged short-entry articles averaging 100 words in length, or about 30 articles per page. The "Alphapedia" serves chiefly as a source of quick-reference information, but it also provides access to specific topics and facts in the "Colorpedia" via many cross-references. It also includes some illustrations, but they are all small and in black-and-white.

In addition to the "Colorpedia" and "Alphapedia," the *Random House Encyclopedia* contains a chronology of world history called the "Time Chart," a separate bibliography section, and a world atlas. The chronology, which consists of 52 densely packed six-column pages, furnishes a tabular overview of key historical events from 4000–2000 B.C. to the release of Nelson Mandela from prison in South Africa in 1990; it is located between the "Colorpedia" and the "Alphapedia." The bibliography, which follows the "Alphapedia," covers 93 individual topics and comprises a total of 1,500 selected titles. The atlas, found at the very end of the book following the bibliography, features 80 pages of full-color maps by Rand McNally and a 48-page index to nearly 22,000 place-names. A section devoted to flags of the world that appeared in the first two editions has been dropped from the third edition.

Physically an enormous book—it stands 11 inches high, has a thickness of almost 4 inches, and weighs more than 12 pounds—the *Random House Encyclopedia* was first published in 1977 and has been revised twice, in 1983 and 1990. It was conceived in Great Britain by James Mitchell and John Beazley, both now deceased. Experienced and creative makers of contemporary reference products, these two men co-founded Mitchell Beazley Publishers Ltd., which developed and produced the original edition of the encyclopedia at an estimated cost of $10 million. From the beginning, both Mitchell and Beazley realized the potential for adapting the heavily pictorial encyclopedia for markets in other countries and languages. Thus far it has appeared in more than 20 national editions (French, Dutch, Italian, German, Finnish, Norwegian, Russian, etc.), including a 10-volume British version entitled the *Joy of Knowledge* and, of course, the one-volume *Random House Encyclopedia*, which is sold exclusively in North America and competes head-to-head with the COLUMBIA ENCYCLOPEDIA, another massive single-volume work.

The encyclopedia has also recently entered the electronic age. In 1990, SelecTronics Inc. issued the RANDOM HOUSE ELECTRONIC ENCYCLOPEDIA, a lightweight hand-held abridgment of the print encyclopedia that utilizes ROM-chip technology and is battery operated (see page 291 for additional information). At roughly the same time, Microlytics, a division of SelecTronics, brought out the RANDOM HOUSE ENCYCLOPEDIA on floppy disks, a software package based on the print encyclopedia for use with personal computers (see page 293). Also, according to Robert Dahlin's article "Random's Encyclopedia Flourishes into 3rd Edition" (*Publishers Weekly*, July 13, 1990, p. 28), a CD-ROM version of the encyclopedia may be in the offing.

Many prominent people have been involved in the planning, writing, editing, and production of the encyclopedia over the years. In addition to Mitchell and Beazley, the late Jess Stein served as editorial director for the first North American edition. Stein was for many years head of Random House's reference division, which publishes, among other works, an excellent line of dictionaries. The late Stuart Flexner, Stein's successor at Random House and a distinguished lexicographer, was editorial director for the second edition. Providing continuity is Stephen P. Elliott, executive editor for the current edition, who has worked on all three editions. An experienced encyclopedist, Elliott is also one of the principal editors of WEBSTER'S NEW WORLD ENCYCLOPEDIA. Among the approximately 500 contributors to the *Random House En-*

cyclopedia are numerous (mostly British) academics and scholars, including such impressive names as H.J. Eysenck, Patrick Hanks, Alan Isaacs, Kenneth Katzner, Patrick Moore, Geoffrey Parrinder, Martin Seymour-Smith, and Della Summers.

The encyclopedia's coverage is quite broad, but normally not deep. Nor is the coverage particularly well balanced. Scientific and technical subjects receive the lion's share of attention, with the life sciences especially well covered. Coverage in the larger "Colorpedia" tends to be most expansive in those areas that lend themselves to visual treatment, such as the fine arts and the physical, technical, biological, and medical sciences. Conversely, coverage is less extensive in those areas not naturally enhanced by pictorial illustration, such as literature, philosophy, religion, political science, and sociology. For instance, computers, earthquakes, and the human body are subjects best described using a combination of words and pictures, whereas descriptions of, say, capital punishment, poetry, socialism, and Scientology do not especially lend themselves to visual representation.

Hence, the encyclopedia includes no less than seven two-page spreads in the "Colorpedia" on birds and four on amphibians and reptiles, replete with copious and informative drawings showing various species, whereas the important subject of adoption is relegated to a cursory seven-line entry in the "Alphapedia." Stefan Kanfer, in a review of the current edition in *Time* (December 10, 1990, p. 98) is also critical of the encyclopedia's uneven coverage:

> As long as it emphasizes the sweep of history, this encyclopedia has dignity and flair. When it tries to keep up with current events, the book often resembles a hardbound *USA Today*. An untroubled Donald Trump appears, along with Wayne Gretzky, Jimmy Breslin and Oprah Winfrey. Parapsychology and the occult are given two massively illustrated layouts; the Holocaust merits less than half a page. In the section on American writers,

James Baldwin stares out from a large color portrait, while Mark Twain is granted a small black-and-white snapshot, and Henry James is not seen at all, though oddly enough his house is.

In a similar vein, a review in *Reference Books Bulletin* (in *Booklist*, January 1, 1991, p. 946) catalogs some of the encyclopedia's inconsistencies in the area of coverage:

> The editors' choices, particularly in the field of entertainment, are difficult to rationalize. For example, why Cybill Shepherd but not Meryl Streep, Paul Hogan but not Robert Redford? The selection of other topics is also somewhat uneven. For instance, there is an entry for Charles Darnay but not for *A Tale of Two Cities*, and an entry for *Eugénie Grandet* but not for *Les Misérables*. King Hussein of Jordan is included, but not Saddam Hussein of Iraq, and Toni Morrison is covered, but not Alice Walker. Moreover, recent technological innovations such as cellular telephones, camcorders, floppy disks, and high-definition television do not appear in the "Alphapedia," although some of these are treated in relevant articles in the "Colorpedia." Some current health concerns like Lyme disease and bulimia are also not represented. Even AIDS, included in the entry *Autoimmune Disease*, is sparsely treated.

Information in the *Random House Encyclopedia* is normally accurate, although factual and typographical errors occasionally intrude. *Example:* The "Alphapedia" article "Giant Panda" erroneously identifies the animal as a "large bearlike mammal of China, a member of the raccoon family." Actually, genetic studies conducted at the National Zoo in Washington, D.C., a decade ago show conclusively that the giant panda is more closely related to the bear family. *Example:* In the "Colorpedia" article "The American Civil War" the name of Mathew Brady, the famous Civil War photographer, is misspelled as Matthew.

Ordinarily, information in the encyclopedia is presented in an impartial manner. In his preface, editor Mitchell states, "We have done our best to be as balanced as we can; where there is controversy we have tried to present both sides of a case; where there is uncertainty our contributors have been encouraged to say so; where there are questions we have asked them." A good example of the book's effort to be objective is found in the treatment of abortion in the article "Questions of Life and Death" in the "Colorpedia":

> Human characteristics are obvious in a 12-week-old fetus. Its genetic coding has already dictated the color of its eyes and the pattern of its fingerprints, but it is still totally dependent on its mother for oxygen and nourishment. These conflicting factors invite opposing arguments: either that the fetus is simply a part of the mother's body; or that the fetus is a separate human life. Abortion thus becomes, by the first argument justified if the mother wishes it; and by the second, an indefensible act of murder.

The *Random House Encyclopedia* was last revised in 1990, which means it is now noticeably out-of-date in certain areas. For instance, the many monumental political and military events that have occurred around the world since 1990—the fall of Communism, the breakup of the Soviet Union, the chaos in the Balkans, the unification of Germany, the end of apartheid in South Africa, the Persian Gulf War, the election of Presidents Clinton and Chamorro in the U.S. and Nicaragua—are obviously missing from the pages of the encyclopedia. As the Report Card (see below) shows, other less volatile topics are also sometimes not as current as they might be. Examples include articles on the Dead Sea Scrolls, Galileo, and panda bears. J.E. Sheets's review of the current edition in *Choice* (March 1991, p. 1092) provides another good example:

> This reviewer was pleased to see an article in the "Colorpedia" on reference books but was disappointed to find no mention of the widespread use of the CD-ROM format for reference sources. In fact, the entire article is identical to the article in the 1977 edition except for the notation of a 1987 edition of *The Random House Dictionary*.

The encyclopedia's writing style throughout is typically clear, direct, and simple enough to be comprehended by students and adults reading at the junior high school level and beyond. Editor Mitchell notes in his preface to the first edition, "Some younger people should be able to enjoy and to absorb the pages on the animal world, for example, from as young as ten or eleven— but the level has been set primarily for teenagers and adults." "Alphapedia" articles tend to be more formal, or "encyclopedic," than those in the "Colorpedia," which affects a more casual, journalistic style. Here, for example, are the first few sentences of the article "Heart" in the "Alphapedia":

> **Heart,** a chambered muscular organ that contracts rhythmically due to its unique cardiac muscle tissue. Through its contraction it pumps blood throughout the body. In man, the heart is located behind the sternum (breastbone) between the lower parts of the lungs. It lies in a double-walled sac, the pericardium, the outer fibrous layer of which is separated from the inner serous layer by pericardial fluid that serves to protect the heart.

Now compare the "Alphapedia" text on the heart with that found in the "Colorpedia" article "Heart and Blood Circulation." Here is the first paragraph of that article:

> It was the English physician William Harvey (1578–1657) who, in 1628, first deduced that the movement of blood is "constantly in a circle." At the time this was a remarkable observation, since Harvey could not have known of the presence of the base network of capillaries that make up the 60,000mi (96,500km) of human micro-circulation [Key], nor of the oxygen that is exchanged between capillaries and tissues.

(The bracketed word *key* above refers to a basic illustration that accompanies this two-page article.)

Locating specific facts and topics in the *Random House Encyclopedia* is sometimes difficult to accomplish effectively. The "Alphapedia" furnishes some 35,000 cross-references to the "Colorpedia," as well as the "Time Chart" that follows it. For example, the brief article "Heart" in the "Alphapedia" concludes with 15 references to the "Colorpedia" that lead the reader to such two-page spreads as "Heart and Blood Circulation" (quoted from in the preceding paragraph), "The Nervous System," "Breathing and the Lungs," "An Active Old Age," "An Introduction to Illness and Health," "Diseases of Breathing," "Diseases of the Circulation," and "Toward the Chemistry of Life." Cross-references in the "Alphapedia" to the "Colorpedia" are designated by a small open triangle.

In addition, cross-references called "connections" appear at the top left-hand page of each "Colorpedia" article; they are intended to guide the reader to related articles in the "Colorpedia." In the case of "Heart and Blood Circulation," for example, the connections lead to "Diseases of the Circulation," "Breathing and the Lungs," "Muscles and Action," "Keeping Fit," and "Principles of Heredity." There are no cross-references from the "Colorpedia" to the "Alphapedia," but the latter does include approximately 10,000 *see also* references to other articles in the "Alphapedia"; e.g., the "Alphapedia" article "Circumcision" has a *see also* to "Puberty Rites." If all of this sounds complicated, it is.

Over the years, many reviewers (including this one) have criticized the encyclopedia's complicated arrangement and lack of a proper index as deterrents to quick and easy access to material in the volume. The second edition (1983) increased the number of cross-references from 20,000 to 45,000, but that did not stop the criticism. In 1990, when the third edition appeared, Random House's publicity department emphasized the addition of these cross-references: "Responding to the suggestion that the Alphapedia and Colorpedia could be more closely related, the editors of the *sec-*

ond edition [emphasis added] added more than 35,000 index references to the Alphapedia." Some gullible reviewers proclaimed the *third edition* easier to use because it had added 35,000 cross-references—when in fact few if any new cross-references were added in 1990. Even *Library Journal* carried a news item (September 1, 1990, p. 150) that implied the encyclopedia had improved its accessibility, erroneously informing readers in a sub-headline that "New edition revised and expanded to bridge into 1990s; includes 35,000 cross references for ease of use."

In the final analysis, the *Random House Encyclopedia* is best used as a source for browsing through knowledge and making intellectual connections. As a fact-finding source it has considerable limitations and is obviously not as productive to use as an encyclopedia arranged in straight A-to-Z fashion. A review of the current third edition in *Reference Books Bulletin* (in *Booklist*, January 1, 1991, p. 947) puts the situation in good perspective, noting that the encyclopedia's

> arrangement makes it difficult to use effectively and efficiently since the cross-references in the "Alphapedia" to the "Colorpedia" are insufficient to serve as a true index to that section. Locating information on a specific subject can be frustrating and may require skimming the table of contents to the "Colorpedia" in search of relevant articles.

As mentioned, the encyclopedia includes a bibliography section following the "Alphapedia." Consisting of 10 pages of very small type, the bibliographies—or lists of recommended sources of additional information—are grouped under the seven broad "Colorpedia" sections and then divided into more specific topics. For instance, under "The Universe" are lists of books on "General Astronomy," "History of Astronomy," "Telescopes," "The Solar System—General," "Planets, Moons, and Non-Stellar Objects," "The Sun," "Space Exploration," etc. All told, the bibliographies contain some 1,500 citations. Unfortunately, the bibliographies

are often quite dated. *Example:* Of the 17 titles listed for "Space Exploration," 10 were published in the 1970s and three in the 1960s.

The illustrations, which constitute about 40 percent of the total text, contribute enormously to the encyclopedia's informational content, especially in the "Colorpedia," where they account for roughly two-thirds of each two-page spread. Indeed, the *Random House Encyclopedia* is arguably the first encyclopedia in which the illustrations are as vital from an informational standpoint as the written text. Moreover, pictorial matter in the "Colorpedia" is directly related to the printed word by means of bracketed references. For example, in the excerpt from the article "Heart and Blood Circulation" quoted above, the bracketed "Key" refers the reader to a basic illustration in the upper right-hand page showing the human circulatory system; all "Colorpedia" spreads contain such a key illustration, which visually explains the main theme of the article. Later on in "Heart and Blood Circulation" bracketed numbers appear, linking the text with other illustrations accompanying the article.

The "Colorpedia" portion of the encyclopedia is simply stunning in terms of both visual quality and informational content. Also noteworthy is the vast amount of hard factual information conveyed in the picture captions. Likewise, the encyclopedia is very well mapped, including an 80-page color world atlas at the back of the book (maps by Rand McNally) and outstanding historical and thematic maps throughout the "Colorpedia." Overall, the *Random House Encyclopedia* ranks with the best illustrated general encyclopedias on the market today, including the ACADEMIC AMERICAN ENCYCLOPEDIA, the RANDOM HOUSE CHILDREN'S ENCYCLOPEDIA, and the WORLD BOOK ENCYCLOPEDIA.

Still, good as the illustrations are, they have not received a great deal of revision attention since the first edition appeared in

1977, and some are beginning to show signs of rust. James Rettig, an astute critic of reference books, describes the problem at some length in his review of the 1990 edition in *Wilson Library Bulletin* (January 1991, p. 122):

> While the accompanying articles in the Colorpedia have been updated in the small ways characteristic of encyclopedia revision—cramped by the previous edition's layout—the illustrations have not received equal attention. For example, the article on computer hardware illustrates the mouse (here, as in the previous edition, called "a palm-size device") with a clunky antique Lisa rather than a more modern micro; the article on the Soviet Union since World War II continues to show Nixon and Brezhnev toasting and then-VP Bush and Andropov shaking hands instead of Reagan and Gorbachev signing a treaty at the White House—an image more indicative of current superpower relations; and a photo retained from the second edition to illustrate "the latest Ampex" video recorder shows an operator sporting hairstyle and short skirt not seen in combination for two decades!

As far as the book's physical format is concerned, the encyclopedia is both well made and aesthetically appealing, although the basic type, while admirably legible, may be too small for some readers, especially that found in the "Colorpedia" captions. Also, the volume is clumsy to handle, being very heavy (over 12 pounds) and bulky (4 inches thick); normally, it requires a stand or ample tabletop for convenient consultation. The use of recycled paper is commendable.

SUMMARY

Surely one of the most interesting and innovative general encyclopedias currently on the North American scene, the single-volume *Random House Encyclopedia* combines two fundamental types of encyclopedias, the traditional A-to-Z compendium of factual information (here called the "Alphapedia") and the thematically arranged work designed to show interrelationships among various areas of knowledge (the "Colorpedia"). First published in 1977 and revised in 1983 and again in 1990, the encyclopedia has been a huge success around the world, being published in more than 20 foreign adaptations, including the 10-volume *Joy of Knowledge* in Great Britain. Abridged versions are also available in electronic form, namely the RANDOM HOUSE ELECTRONIC ENCYCLOPEDIA, a handheld item, and the RANDOM HOUSE ENCYCLOPEDIA on floppy disks.

Clearly the most exciting part of the encyclopedia is the largest part, the 1,792-page "Colorpedia," which comprises 880 copiously illustrated, topically arranged two-page articles. The 885-page "Alphapedia," the A–Z section, serves chiefly as the encyclopedia's fact-finding component, but it also provides access to specific topics and facts in the "Colorpedia" via numerous cross-references. Proponents of the *Random House Encyclopedia* applaud its thematic approach to knowledge and stunningly good illustrations; detractors find it hard to use, citing its unorthodox arrangement and inadequate system of cross-references. Other minuses include uneven coverage, a growing lack of up-to-dateness, and a physical format that is unwieldy. Other pluses are the encyclopedia's impeccable authority, easy reading style, and objectively presented material. The bottom line: Along with the very different COLUMBIA ENCYCLOPEDIA, the *Random House Encyclopedia*—excellent for browsing but less effective as a fact-finding tool—is the best big one-volume encyclopedia available in the U.S. and Canada today.

REPORT CARD: RANDOM HOUSE ENCYCLOPEDIA

TOPIC	COVERAGE	ACCURACY	RECENCY	CLARITY
Circumcision	C	A	B	A
Drew, Charles	B	A	B	A
Galileo	A	A	D	A
Glass, Philip	F*	NA	NA	NA
Heart Disease	A	A	B	A
IQ	A	A	A	A
Panda Bears	C	C	C	A
Sexual Harassment	F*	NA	NA	NA
Shroud of Turin	F*	NA	NA	NA
Uzbekistan	F*	NA	NA	NA

A = Excellent; **B** = Above Average; **C** = Average; **D** = Below Average; **F** = Poor; **NA** = Not Applicable
*No Article

OTHER OPINIONS

American Reference Books Annual, 1991, pp. 16–17 (review by Anna Grace Patterson); *Basic Information Sources* by William A. Katz (vol. 1 of *Introduction to Reference Work*, 6th ed., New York: McGraw-Hill, 1992), pp. 258–59; *Choice*, March 1991, pp. 1091–92 (review by J.E. Sheets); *Library Journal*, November 15, 1990, p. 67 (review by Kenneth F. Kister); *New York Times Book Review*, January 27, 1991, p. 15 (review by Justin Kaplan); *Reference Books Bulletin* (in *Booklist*), January 1, 1991, pp. 946–47 (un-signed review); *Time*, December 10, 1990, p. 98 (review by Stefan Kanfer); *Wilson Library Bulletin*, January 1991, pp. 122–23 (review by James Rettig).

In addition, useful background information on the encyclopedia can be found in Robert Dahlin's article "Random's Encyclopedia Flourishes into 3rd Edition" (*Publishers Weekly*, July 13, 1990, p. 28) and F. Peter Model's "Eye on Publishing" column (*Wilson Library Bulletin*, October 1990, pp. 77–78).

RUNNING PRESS CYCLOPEDIA

FACTS

Full Title: *Running Press Cyclopedia: The Portable, Visual Encyclopedia*. Compiler and Illustrator: The Diagram Group. **Publisher:** Running Press Book Publishers. **Date Published:** 1993.

British Title: COLLINS GEM ENCYCLOPEDIA.

Volumes: One. **Words:** 100,000. **Pages:** 638. **Articles:** 300. **Bibliographies:** None. **Illustrations and Maps:** 800. **Cross-references:** None. **Index Entries:** 750. **Editorial Staff, Advisers, and Contributors:** None listed. Trim Size: 4¼ × 5¼ in.

Price and Sales Information: $8.95 paperbound. Individual consumers can purchase the *Running Press Cyclopedia* in bookstores and other retail stores that sell paperbound books; if the book is not in stock, it can be ordered. Similarly, educational institutions (schools, libraries, etc.) can order it through a book wholesaler. To order the encyclopedia directly from the publisher, call toll-free 1-800-345-5359 or write Run-

ning Press Book Publishers, 125 South 22nd Street, Philadelphia, PA 19103-4399.

EVALUATION

The peewee-sized *Running Press Cyclopedia*, the smallest one-volume adult encyclopedia currently on the North American market, contains only about 300 articles and 100,000 words; it stands all of 5¼ inches high. Compare these stats with the largest single-volume encyclopedia, the COLUMBIA ENCYCLOPEDIA, which has 50,000 articles, 6.6 million words, and stands a foot high. No wonder the *Running Press Cyclopedia* is advertised as the "Little Know-It All." Published in paperback only, the book originally appeared in Great Britain as the COLLINS GEM ENCYCLOPEDIA.

Described in the preface as "a digest of the basic subjects contained within a single-volume encyclopedia," the compiler estimates that the *Cyclopedia* includes approximately 20,000 individual facts. Much of this information is conveyed visually in the form of charts, drawings, tables, timelines, and the like. The graphics are the work of the Diagram Group, a British company internationally known for its clear and innovative illustrations. The Diagram Group, for example, has compiled several excellent sports encyclopedias over the years, including RULES OF THE GAME.

Like several other small-volume adult encyclopedias currently available (namely BARRON'S NEW CONCISE STUDENT'S ENCYCLOPEDIA, the DICTIONARY OF CULTURAL LITERACY, the RANDOM HOUSE ENCYCLOPEDIA, and the VOLUME LIBRARY), the *Cyclopedia* is organized topically (rather than alphabetically), its contents grouped under six broad headings (or parts), each of which is divided and subdivided into more specific topics (or sections).

Part 1 is "The World"; it is divided into six sections: "The Earth," "Mapping," "The Weather," "The Environment," "World Population," and "Religions." Part 2 is "Countries of the World"; it is divided into two sections: "Population and Wealth" and

"Countries" (which covers the world's nations in tabular form). Part 3 is "History" (which lists major events in world history from the Stone Age to January 1993). Part 4 is "Science"; it is divided into eight sections: "The Universe," "Mathematics," "Physics," "Chemistry," "Biology," "Human Life," "Inventions," and "How Things Work." Part 5 is "The Arts"; it is divided into three sections: "Chronologies" (which cites achievements in music, literature, painting, sculpture, film, etc. from earliest times to Madonna's book *Sex* in 1992), "Visual Arts," and "Performing Arts." Finally, Part 6 is "The United States" (which covers 13 topics, including national symbols, geography, population, climate, agriculture, and the states).

As might be expected in a book so small (and as the Report Card below confirms), the *Cyclopedia*'s coverage is neither comprehensive nor balanced. The emphasis is clearly on geography, history, and science. In fact, Part 4 ("Science") accounts for nearly half the pages of the book. Yet, the social sciences are almost completely ignored. For instance, the book lacks any mention of abortion, adoption, apartheid, depression (either its economic or psychological sense), fluoridation of water supplies, and nuclear disasters such as Three Mile Island and Chernobyl. In addition, biographical coverage of both historical greats and prominent contemporary figures is totally lacking; the only mention of Galileo, for example, is in the "History" timetable, which notes in 1633, "Galileo forced by Inquisition to renounce theories of Copernicus." Many other subjects that readers have a right to expect a general encyclopedia to cover—the Dead Sea Scrolls, heart disease, hypnotism, panda bears, Scientology, etc.—are also missing from the pages of the *Cyclopedia*.

Information in the *Cyclopedia* is normally accurate, objectively presented, and current as of the end of 1992 or beginning of 1993. The writing style, which is clear and straightforward, will be comprehensible to literate adults and students in the junior high school grades and beyond. The following excerpt from the article "The Heart" (in "Human Life" in Part 4) is typical:

> The heart is a muscular pump which drives blood around the body. Its nonstop action supplies oxygen and nutrients to body cells, and removes their waste products. The heart is a fist-sized hollow muscle with a broad top and pointed base. It lies roughly in the middle of the chest. A wall called a septum (**1**) divides the right side (**A**) from the left side (**B**). Each side has an inlet, outlet, and two chambers: atrium and ventricle. Valves (**2**) control the blood flow in and out.

Note that the numbers and letters in parentheses refer to an accompanying diagram of the heart.

Finding specific topics and facts in the text are usually not difficult, due in part to the detailed contents pages at the front of the book (which function as a topical outline) and in part to a 14-page index at the back of the book. The only criticism is that tabular information is not indexed. *Example:* The aforementioned note about Galileo's encounter with the Inquisition in 1633 in the "History" timetable is not accessible via the index.

The *Cyclopedia* has no bibliographies, but it does have excellent illustrations, all in two colors. As mentioned at the outset of this review, the Diagram Group is well-known for its clear, informative, and creative illustrations, and those in this little volume are no exception. In almost every instance, the more than 800 line drawings, tables, charts, cutaways, and timelines add significantly to the book's reference value. The Diagram Group explains its approach in the preface:

> As information can be more clearly presented with the aid of diagrams and charts, much of the *Cyclopedia* has been extensively illustrated with simple line drawings. They readily reveal the pattern of information, whether it relates to the world's distribution of religious faiths, the groups of chemical elements, the orders of classical architecture, or an explanation of how an airplane flies. A second color has also been employed to facilitate access to information. It is used in the text to highlight keywords, dates, and headings, and in diagrams to help clarify the subject.

Note also that the printed text and illustrations are frequently linked by means of parenthetical references, as seen in the "Heart" excerpt above. The *Cyclopedia*'s physical format is satisfactory. Small and squat ($4\frac{1}{4} \times 5\frac{1}{4}$ in.), the paperbound book is lightly sewn and lies perfectly flat when open. Inside, the page layout is both functional and aesthetically appealing. Overall, it is a nicely designed little volume fairly priced at $8.95.

SUMMARY

The single-volume *Running Press Cyclopedia* is the smallest adult encyclopedia on the North American market. A fat little paperback published in 1993, it contains only about 300 articles and 100,000 words. Coverage is lacking for many general subjects and treatment is correspondingly thin, although the book does offer much useful information in visual form, a trademark of the compiler, the Diagram Group. The bottom line: Although this small compendium of facts is worth every penny of its $8.95 price, it is grossly inadequate as a general encyclopedia.

OTHER OPINIONS

None.

REPORT CARD: RUNNING PRESS CYCLOPEDIA

TOPIC	COVERAGE	ACCURACY	RECENCY	CLARITY
Circumcision	F*	NA	NA	NA
Drew, Charles	F*	NA	NA	NA
Galileo	F	A	D	A
Glass, Philip	F*	NA	NA	NA
Heart Disease	F*	NA	NA	NA
IQ	F*	NA	NA	NA
Panda Bears	F*	NA	NA	NA
Sexual Harassment	F*	NA	NA	NA
Shroud of Turin	F*	NA	NA	NA
Uzbekistan	F*	NA	NA	NA

A = Excellent; **B** = Above Average; **C** = Average; **D** = Below Average; **F** = Poor; **NA** = Not Applicable
*No Article

VOLUME LIBRARY

FACTS

Full Title: *The Volume Library: A Modern, Authoritative Reference for Home and School Use.* **Editor in Chief:** Gorton Carruth. **Publisher:** The Southwestern Company. Former Titles: *Cowles Comprehensive Encyclopedia: The Volume Library* (1963–67); *Cowles Volume Library* (1968–69). **Date Published:** Published as the *Volume Library* between 1911 and 1962 and since 1970; new printing with revisions published annually.

Volumes: Two. **Words:** 2.5 million. **Pages:** 2,568. **Articles:** 8,500. **Bibliographies:** 100. **Illustrations and Maps:** 3,000. **Cross-references:** 300. **Index Entries:** 32,000. **Editorial Staff, Advisers, and Contributors:** 112. **Trim Size:** 8¾ × 10¾ in.

Price and Sales Information: $139.95. The *Volume Library* is sold to individual consumers door-to-door chiefly during the summer by college students. It is not normally sold in bookstores or similar retail outlets, although it can be ordered through most bookstores. Educational institutions (schools, libraries, etc.) can order it through a book wholesaler. To order the encyclopedia directly from the publisher, call 1-615-391-2500 (not a toll-free number) or write the Southwestern Company, P.O. Box 305140, Nashville, TN 37230.

EVALUATION

The *Volume Library* is "designed for interested, well-informed people—students and adults who need an authoritative reference book for their home bookshelves, and parents who want to keep abreast of the sub-jects their children are studying in school" (preface). Originally issued in a single volume but expanded to two volumes in 1985, the *Volume Library* has been continuously published for more than 80 years, making it the granddaddy of all small-volume general encyclopedias currently on the North American market.

The *Volume Library* first appeared in 1911 under the imprint of the W.E. Richardson Company of Chicago, the product of a group of educators, mostly professors at the University of Michigan. In the early 1960s, Cowles Communications, Inc. acquired the encyclopedia and revised and retitled it *Cowles Comprehensive Encyclopedia: The Volume Library* (1963–67); later the title was shortened to *Cowles Volume Library* (1968–69). When the encyclopedia's present publisher, the Southwestern Company of Nashville, obtained the rights to the work in 1970, it reverted to its original title.

Despite its longevity, the *Volume Library* has never been considered a first-rate encyclopedia by critics, librarians, and others who are knowledgeable about reference books. Indeed, at one point in the late 1970s it seemed that the *Volume Library* might go the way of its longtime rival, the LINCOLN LIBRARY OF ESSENTIAL INFORMATION, which suffered a painfully drawn out death around that time. However, in the early 1980s, the Hudson Group, Inc., a highly regarded book design and production company located in Pleasantville, New York, took over editorial responsibility for the *Volume Library* by contractual agreement with Southwestern, which remained the publisher. During the decade that the Hudson Group has edited the encyclopedia, the set's quality has improved considerably and all indications are that it is currently doing well as a door-to-door product sold chiefly by college students during the summer months.

Much of the credit for reviving the *Volume Library* belongs to Gorton Carruth, the encyclopedia's chief editor (and key player in the Hudson Group). Carruth, who has produced the standard ENCYCLOPEDIA OF AMERICAN FACTS AND DATES for years, brings substantial experience and strong bona fides to the work. He is supported by a small staff, plus 106 contributors, most of whom are either professors at various U.S. colleges and universities or freelance writers. Contributors' names, degrees, affiliations, and areas of subject responsibility in the encyclopedia are given at the front of both volumes.

Like several other small-volume adult encyclopedias available today, (namely BARRON'S NEW STUDENT'S CONCISE ENCYCLOPEDIA, the DICTIONARY OF CULTURAL LITERACY, the RANDOM HOUSE ENCYCLOPEDIA, and the RUNNING PRESS CYCLOPEDIA, the *Volume Library* is arranged topically (as opposed to alphabetically) in chapters, or "volumes," covering broad subject areas. The latest edition comprises 27 subject volumes: "Animals," "Art," "Asia and Australasia," "Astronomy and Space," "Business and Economics," "Computers," "Chemistry and Physics," "Child and Family," "Earth Sciences," "Europe," "Government and Law," "Health and Life Sciences," "History of the World," "Invention and Technology," "Language," "Literature," "Mathematics," "Middle East and Africa," "People," "Performing Arts," "Plants," "Religion and Philosophy," "Social Sciences," "South and Central America," "Sports and Recreation," "United States and Canada," and "World Environment." A general index (Volume 28) concludes the set.

Each of the 27 subject volumes that make up the *Volume Library* is about 90 pages long and consists primarily of lengthy, broad-entry articles divided into a number of specific topics. *Example:* "Animals" (Volume 1) contains seven long articles: "History of Animals," "Classification of Animals," "Morphology of Animals," "Physiology of Animals," "Behavior of Animals," "Intelligence of Animals," and "Ecology of Animals." Each of these articles is systematically broken down into its logical parts. "Physiology of Animals," for instance, includes such specific topics as "Metabolism," "Digestive Systems," "Respiratory Systems," "Circulatory Systems," "Homeostasis," "Excretory Systems," "Internal Communications," and "External Communications." The "Animals" volume ends with a 30-page "Glossary of Animals," which succinctly covers individual species A-to-Z, from "Aardvark" to "Zebra."

Most of the encyclopedia's subject volumes are organized roughly along the same lines as "Animals." In addition to the broad-entry articles and glossary, the volumes usually contain much information compressed into graphs, charts, and tables, along with numerous illustrations (photographs, drawings, maps, etc.), all in black-and-white except for occasional color plates. At the very end of each volume is a selected bibliography labeled "For Further Reference."

As the volume titles suggest, the *Volume Library* attempts to provide broad and balanced coverage of the world's basic knowledge and information. For the most part, the encyclopedia succeeds quite well—which was definitely *not* the case in the pre-Hudson Group era. Prominent historical figures, major places of the world, and important scientific and technical subjects are especially well covered. North American history and geography receive more than adequate attention in the volume "United States and Canada." The states and provinces, which are regionally grouped, each have a substantial entry, although the small black-and-white maps lack detail and have little reference value.

The encyclopedia also includes an enormous amount of practical information potentially useful to both students and adults. For instance, the "Business and Economics" volume explains how to read stock market reports in the daily newspaper and offers how-to information about starting a small business; "Child and Family" includes "Do's and Don'ts of Pregnancy" and advice concerning personal and family problems, such as alcohol and drug abuse, violence in the home, and stress; "Health and Life Sciences" lists the cholesterol content of common foods and describes how to conduct a breast self-examination; "Language" instructs the reader in how to prepare a resume, write a letter,

conduct research, and improve one's vocabulary; and "World Environment" recommends ways homeowners might save energy.

A supplement to the *Volume Library* (called Book 3) is also available that offers much useful information about taking examinations and how to prepare for such standardized tests as the Scholastic Aptitude Test, the College Board Achievement Tests, and the Graduate Record Examination. This supplement, which also contains many maps and a world atlas, sells for $79.95.

Some subjects in the *Volume Library* are covered in several different volumes. For example, information about intelligence quotients and tests appears in the article "Mental Testing" in the volume "Child and Family," in the article "Intelligence and Creativity" in the volume "Social Sciences," and in the article "Race and Intelligence," also in the "Social Sciences" volume. Usually in such instances new information is given in each article, or the subject is treated from a different perspective. Sometimes, however, the same material is duplicated in different articles, as in the case of psychological depression, which is described in much the same terms in both the "Child and Family" and "Social Sciences" volumes.

While some topics receive an overabundance of attention in the *Volume Library*, many others that merit coverage in any quality general encyclopedia are given short shrift or ignored altogether. As the Report Card (see below) indicates, the *Volume Library* fails to furnish any information on such diverse subjects as circumcision, sexual harassment, the Shroud of Turin, the contemporary composer Philip Glass, and the black physician and blood bank pioneer Charles Drew. Furthermore, the encyclopedia has nothing on adoption, carpal tunnel syndrome, fluoridation, Scientology, and such prominent present-day poets as Philip Larkin, Anne Sexton, Elizabeth Bishop, and Maya Angelou. Toni Morrison, recent recipient of the Nobel Prize for Literature, is mentioned only in passing in a paragraph on promising black writers. Likewise, abortion is mentioned but not fully treated. Such glaring gaps in the *Volume Library*'s coverage need to be addressed before it can be regarded as more than a run-of-the-mill encyclopedia.

Prior to the Hudson Group and Gorton Carruth, the *Volume Library* had a bad record on reliability. A review in *Booklist* (January 1, 1979, p. 771) described the situation in the 1970s this way: "Numerous errors have been found in this encyclopedia. . . .While the error rate seemed lowest in mathematics, biographies, agriculture, and geography, the number of inaccurate statements found elsewhere is beyond an acceptable level." Happily, this problem has been ameliorated during the past 10 or so years; today, the encyclopedia is as accurate as can be expected of a work of more than two million words.

The *Volume Library* normally presents its material in an impartial manner, although as previously noted many contentious or sensitive subjects—abortion, circumcision, fluoridation, Scientology, sexual harassment, etc.—are treated superficially or avoided entirely. A good example of the set's effort to be as objective as possible is found in the article "Race and Intelligence," which summarizes the findings of and reaction to controversial research by the psychologist Arthur Jensen:

> There was a good possibility, he [Jensen] suggested, that blacks might be genetically rather than culturally disadvantaged. Jensen's theories aroused a storm of protest. Some argued that hereditary factors, although they might account for individual differences in IQ, could not be extended to racial groups. Others held that most tests are culturally biased in favor of the white middle class. Still others questioned the value of *any* IQ testing as a measure of intelligence.

Unlike most small-volume encyclopedias, the *Volume Library* is continuously revised with a new printing issued each year. As a result, its text is now reasonably current—another improvement instigated by editor Carruth. For example, the many recent cataclysmic political changes in Eastern Europe are covered, as are major events in South Africa, Nicaragua, and the Middle East. Still, as noted, numerous subjects of potential interest to encyclopedia users—ranging from abortion and adoption to Philip Glass and Toni Morrison—are either inadequately covered or completely missing from the encyclopedia. Likewise, less dramatic or volatile subjects are not always as up-to-date as they might or should be. An example is the article on Galileo in the "People" volume, which notes that the great scientist "was brought to trial before the Inquisition in 1633, where he was forced to renounce the Copernican teachings and put under permanent house arrest," but fails to add that the Roman Catholic Church, at the urging of Pope John Paul II, has recently exonerated Galileo.

Ordinarily, articles in the encyclopedia will be comprehensible to adults and students reading at the ninth or tenth grade level, although the vocabulary is not controlled nor are the articles written to grade level. The writing style tends to be clear, crisp, and readable, as well as fairly consistent from chapter to chapter. The following excerpt describing the heart in the article "Circulatory System" in the "Health and Life Sciences" volume typifies the *Volume Library*'s style:

> The heart is a bundle of muscles, about the size of a fist and weighing less than a pound. On an average, the heart contracts and dilates at a rate of 72 beats a minute, each cardiac cycle lasting about 0.85 second. This adds up to about 100,000 times a day, or nearly 40 million times a year without rest. The only pause a heart takes is the fraction of a second between heartbeats. In the average adult, the heart pumps so steadily and powerfully that, in one minute, it forces 10 pints of blood through more than 1000 complete circuits. This amounts to 5000 to 6000 quarts of blood in a single day.

As explained, the *Volume Library* arranges its contents by subject rather than alphabetically, which means that the index is absolutely essential to finding specific topics and facts in the set. Regrettably, there are few cross-references in the encyclopedia, and these refer only to related material within a particular volume—that is, no cross-references link information from one volume to another. Fortunately, the index, found at the back of the last volume, is a good one, comprising more than 30,000 entries. The index entry "heart," for instance, contains 38 analytical references (e.g., "artificial," "attack," "cardiac arrest," "catheterization," "first surgery on a dog," "pacemaker," "transplant") that direct the reader to a number of pertinent articles throughout the encyclopedia. Overall, information in the *Volume Library* can be retrieved without great difficulty, but still the encyclopedia is not as easy to use, especially for quick reference, as one arranged alphabetically.

Like the competing COLUMBIA ENCYCLOPEDIA and RANDOM HOUSE ENCYCLOPEDIA, the *Volume Library* includes bibliographies that list recommended titles for readers who desire additional information on a subject. The bibliographies—usually a half a page or full page in length—appear at the end of each of the encyclopedia's subject volumes under the heading "For Further Reference." They are usually divided into logical categories; the bibliography at the end of the "Literature" volume, for example, contains six lists under "General," "Ancient," "Eastern," "European," "English," and "American." The bibliographies are carefully selected, although not always up-to-date.

Illustrations in the encyclopedia, which are 95 percent black-and-white, tend to lack visual appeal but they almost always add to the informational value of the set. *Example:* The article "Circulatory System" quoted from above is accompanied by a simple but effective and informatively labeled and captioned drawing showing the workings of the heart. In recent years some color plates have been added throughout the two books. The plates are handsomely reproduced and normally contain useful information, but they are inadequately indexed, which diminishes their reference value. Consumers should also be aware that the aforementioned supplement (or Book 3) to the *Volume Library* contains approximately 500 pages of cartographic material, including black-and-white outline maps helpful for homework assignments and a world history atlas in color. The supplement, which also includes much information about standardized tests, sells for $79.95.

The physical format, which has been improved slowly over the past decade by the present editors, is satisfactory. The two books are strongly bound and conveniently have thumb indexes along the fore-edges showing where each volume (chapter) begins. Inside, each volume is separated by a stiff cover, which is colorfully illustrated. The three-column page layout is uninspiring but functional, and the typefaces are large and readable.

SUMMARY

Continuously published since 1911, the topically arranged *Volume Library* is the granddaddy of small-volume general encyclopedias currently available in North America. Over the past decade, it has been greatly improved due to the experienced editorial hand of Gorton Carruth and his colleagues at the Hudson Group, a highly regarded book design and production company located in Pleasantville, New York. Today, the encyclopedia provides readable

and reasonably broad and balanced coverage of basic knowledge and information, although many glaring omissions can be cited. Other problems include superficial treatment of some subjects, lapses in up-to-dateness, a preponderance of black-and-white illustrations, and insufficient cross-references. The bottom line: Though much improved in recent years, the *Volume Library* still has a long way to go before it can be considered more than a fair-to-middling encyclopedia.

REPORT CARD: VOLUME LIBRARY

TOPIC	COVERAGE	ACCURACY	RECENCY	CLARITY
Circumcision	F*	NA	NA	NA
Drew, Charles	F*	NA	NA	NA
Galileo	B	A	D	A
Glass, Philip	F*	NA	NA	NA
Heart Disease	B	A	B	A
IQ	A	A	A	A
Panda Bears	C	A	A	A
Sexual Harassment	F*	NA	NA	NA
Shroud of Turin	F*	NA	NA	NA
Uzbekistan	C	A	B	A

A = Excellent; **B** = Above Average; **C** = Average; **D** = Below Average; **F** = Poor; **NA** = Not Applicable
*No Article

OTHER OPINIONS

No recent reviews are available.

WEBSTER'S NEW WORLD ENCYCLOPEDIA

FACTS

Full Title: *Webster's New World Encyclopedia*. Editors: Stephen P. Elliott, Martha Goldstein, and Michael Upshall. **Publisher:** Prentice Hall. **Date Published:** 1992.

British Title: *The Hutchinson Encyclopedia*.

Abridged Versions: WEBSTER'S NEW WORLD ENCYCLOPEDIA: COLLEGE EDITION; WEBSTER'S NEW WORLD ENCYCLOPEDIA: POCKET EDITION.

Volumes: One. **Words:** 2 million. **Pages:** 1,230. **Articles:** 25,000. **Bibliographies:** None. **Illustrations and Maps:** 2,500. **Cross-references:** 3,000. **Index Entries:** None. **Editorial Staff, Advisers, and Contributors:** 94. **Trim Size:** 8½ × 10¾ in.

Price and Sales Information: $75.00. Individual consumers can purchase *Webster's New World Encyclopedia* in bookstores or, if the book is not in stock, it can be ordered. Similarly, educational institutions (schools, libraries, etc.) can order it through a book wholesaler. To order the encyclopedia directly from the publisher, call 1-800-223-2348 or write Prentice Hall General Reference, 15 Columbus Circle, New York, NY 10023.

EVALUATION

New in 1992, *Webster's New World Encyclopedia* is a large, attractively produced, alphabetically arranged single-volume general encyclopedia for adults and older students. It has similar specifications to and competes directly with the AMERICAN SPECTRUM ENCY-

CLOPEDIA and the CAMBRIDGE ENCYCLOPEDIA. All three of these encyclopedias feature short entries, contain approximately the same number of articles and pages, and are of recent vintage.

Webster's New World Encyclopedia derives from the British *Hutchinson Encyclopedia*, a one-volume general reference work that has been a staple in homes, libraries, and offices in Great Britain since 1948, when it first appeared as *Hutchinson's Twentieth Century Encyclopedia*. Specifically, *Webster's New World Encyclopedia* is an updated and heavily Americanized version of the most recent edition (ninth) of the *Hutchinson Encyclopedia*, published in 1990. Two abridged editions of *Webster's New World Encyclopedia*—WEBSTER'S NEW WORLD ENCYCLOPEDIA: COLLEGE EDITION (a hardcover publication) and WEBSTER'S NEW WORLD ENCYCLOPEDIA: POCKET EDITION (issued in paperback)—were published in 1993, with another (Concise Edition) said to be forthcoming.

Unlike the competing CAMBRIDGE ENCYCLOPEDIA, which attempts to be "international," *Webster's New World Encyclopedia* has been prepared strictly with a U.S. and Canadian readership in mind. Indeed, few signs of its British origins remain. All of *Hutchinson's* articles were scrutinized and many either completely rewritten or revised in some manner. Moreover, about 1,200 new articles were added, covering subjects of particular interest to North Americans, such as "Aaron, Hank," "Ashe, Arthur," "Brown v. Board of Education" "Civil Rights," "Hudson River School," "Iwo Jima," "O'Keeffe, Georgia," "Palmer, Arnold," "Pony Express," "Roe v. Wade," "Sherman Anti-Trust Act," "Social Security," "Thomas, Clarence," "Underground Railroad," and "Zenger, John Peter."

Conversely, some articles in *Hutchinson*—for example "Admiral's Cup," "Henley-on-Thames," "Master of the Rolls," "National Trust," "Sandhurst," "Stoolball,"

and "Westland Affair"—were dropped from the encyclopedia, deemed too narrowly British for American readers. And, to complete the Americanization process, spelling and usage were systematically changed from British to American English, e.g., *petrol* to *gasoline*, and U.S. measurements were placed before (instead of after) their metric equivalents. In a review in *Choice* (February 1993, p. 947), J.E. Sheets accurately conveys the encyclopedia's American orientation: "Portraits of US presidents are larger than those for British prime ministers, American spellings are used throughout, and such entries as 'robin' or 'constitution' have an American emphasis."

The Americanization project, which required several years to complete, was carried out under the direction of Stephen Elliott, an experienced reference book editor who previously worked on encyclopedias at Grolier and Random House. The encyclopedia's staff of more than 90 editors and writers boasts a number of notable authorities, including John Ayto, Malcolm Bradbury, Peter Fleming, Tom McArthur, David Munro, Ian Ridpath, and Adrian Room. The entire editorial staff is listed at the front of the book.

Webster's New World Encyclopedia provides broad and reasonably well balanced coverage of basic knowledge and information. Prominent people—both historical and contemporary figures—receive a fair amount of attention, as do major places around the world, with countries and the U.S. states and Canadian provinces leading the way. In all, biographical and geographical articles account for roughly 35 percent of the entries. Scientific, technical, and medical subjects are also well covered, as are historical events, such as the Hundred Years' War, the Reichstag fire, and Wounded Knee. Similarly, more than 100 landmark decisions of the U.S. Supreme Court have their own entries.

As mentioned, *Webster's New World Encyclopedia* is a specific-entry work. Articles are naturally quite brief, averaging just under 100 words in length. In some cases, treatment is little more than a dictionary-style definition, as in "Adoption." But in other instances, the encyclopedia manages to pack much information into a relatively small space through economical writing and extensive use of charts, tables, and chronologies. The article "AIDS," for instance, provides outstanding encyclopedic treatment of the topic, a masterpiece of condensation. Still, Mary Jo Walker is not being unfair when she says the encyclopedia's "articles do little more than skim the essentials. For example, someone seeking information on U.S. automobile history will find a cursory sketch that gives coverage to European and Japanese contributions but nary a nod to William C. Durant, founder of General Motors, or Cadillac/Lincoln founder Henry Leland" (*American Reference Books Annual*, 1993, p. 29).

As the Report Card (see below) indicates, the encyclopedia usually can be trusted to have its facts straight, but occasionally it falters. For example, the diagram with "Baseball" erroneously labels home plate "houseplate," an obvious typographical error (the article itself uses the correct term). In his review in *RQ* (Spring 1993, p. 432), Martin Cavanaugh lists a number of other small inaccuracies:

> *Ginger beer* is misalphabetized between *gigabyte* and *Gigli*, when it should be placed between *ginger ale* and *ginkgo*. At the entry for *jerboa*, the *j* is omitted. *Vanzetti* is misspelled *Venzetti* in the photo caption accompanying the entry *Sacco-Vanzetti Case*. In the *football* article, the text incorrectly places the goal posts on the goal lines, while the illustration correctly locates them on the end lines.
>
> Three factual errors were noticed. In the *St. Louis* article, Eliel Saarinen is given credit for designing the Gateway Arch when, in fact, it was his son, Eero. The *Jefferson City* article incorrectly locates that city on the

Mississippi River. In the *Gerald Ford* article, the encyclopedia states that Ford "gave amnesty to those who had resisted the draft for the Vietnam war." This was done by Jimmy Carter on January 21, 1977.

The encyclopedia consistently presents its information without discernible bias. Moreover, when a topic is controversial or sensitive, the text usually informs the reader of the nature of the issue. *Example:* The article "Electroconvulsive Therapy" states, "Although often successful, the treatment can cause distress and loss of concentration and memory, and so there is much controversy about its use and effectiveness." The encyclopedia also deserves generally high marks for up-to-dateness. "Abortion," for instance, discusses the antiprogesterone pill RU 486, and "Turin Shroud" includes the information that recently conducted scientific tests have dated the shroud's origin between 1260 and 1390, meaning that it could not be Christ's burial cloth.

James Moffet points out in his review of *Webster's New World Encyclopedia* in *Library Journal* (August 1992, p. 92) that its articles "are written in plain, explicit prose accessible to a wide audience, with only a small number poorly defined or unclear." In most instances, the encyclopedia can be used profitably by students and adults reading at the ninth grade level or beyond. Potentially difficult or unfamiliar terms are usually defined in context. The article "Heart" is fairly typical of the encyclopedia's style; here is the full text of that article:

> **heart** muscular organ that contracts rhythmically to force blood around the body of an animal with a circulatory system. Annelid worms and some other invertebrates have simple hearts consisting of thickened sections of main blood vessels that pulse regularly. An earthworm has ten such hearts. Vertebrates have one heart. A fish heart has two chambers—the thin-walled atrium (once called the auricle) that expands to receive blood, and the thick-walled ventricle that pumps it out. Amphibians and most reptiles have two atria and one ventricle; birds and mammals have two

atria and two venticles. The beating of the heart is controlled by the autonomic nervous systems and an internal control center or pacemaker, the sinoatrial node.

Locating specific topics and facts in the text ordinarily poses few major difficulties, due largely to the volume's specific-entry approach but also to its use of cross-references. The cross-references, indicated by a small arrow symbol, effectively point the reader to related articles—when they are given. Regrettably, the cross-reference system tends to be inconsistent and cross-references themselves too few and far between. For instance, the article "Depression" (in psychology) furnishes a reference to "Cognitive Therapy" but not to "Electroconvulsive Therapy" and "Antidepressant." The editors state in their brief introduction that "Cross referencing is selective; a cross reference is shown when another entry contains material directly relevant to the subject matter of any entry, and where the reader may not otherwise think of looking." This sounds reasonable, but in actual practice it does not work well, probably because readers do not always think like editors.

What *Webster's New World Encyclopedia* needs, of course, to ensure full access to its contents, but lacks, is a detailed index. One example: The article "Heart" (reprinted in full above) makes no mention of heart disease, nor does the encyclopedia include an article called "Heart Disease" or "Heart Attack" (either of which might include pertinent cross-references to related articles). How then is the reader seeking information about heart disease in this encyclopedia supposed to know where to look? Unfortunately, the only way is to check under such possible terms as *angina, arrhythmia, arteriosclerosis, cardiomyopathy, coronary thrombosis, defibrillator, heart block, pacemaker, pericarditis,* and *rheumatic fever.* This is hardly an efficient or effective way to retrieve information in an encyclopedia.

An index, on the other hand, would bring all material in the book on heart disease together under a single heading.

The encyclopedia also lacks bibliographies, or lists of recommended sources that the reader might consult for additional information. This omission is not unexpected; among the small-volume encyclopedias for adults and older students currently available, only the COLUMBIA ENCYCLOPEDIA, the RANDOM HOUSE ENCYCLOPEDIA, and the VOLUME LIBRARY include bibliographies. On the other hand, the lack of bibliographies is a competitive disadvantage in a tough market.

Happily, the encyclopedia does include illustrations and maps. Numbering about 2,500 in all, they are mostly in color and are nearly always informative and aesthetically pleasing. The "Heart" article, for instance, is enhanced by a clearly rendered, well-captioned color drawing of the organ. The chief complaint about the illustrations is that sometimes they are not placed in good proximity to the article they complement. A review in *Reference Books Bulletin* (in *Booklist,* October 15, 1992, p. 450) explains the problem:

> The encyclopedia is illustrated with more than 2,500 photographs and drawings, many in color. A number of the illustrations help explain technological or biological processes, such as papermaking and acid rain. Also supplementing the text are numerous maps, tables, diagrams, and charts. However, users will miss many of these because they do not appear on the same page as the entry, and the entries provide no reference to illustrations. For example, the World War II chronology is two pages after the article it complements, while the feather diagram appears on the verso of the page with the *Feather* entry.

Physically, *Webster's New World Encyclopedia* is quite satisfactory. The binding is strong and the book, which weighs about six pounds, comes with an attractive blue jacket. Inside, the three-column page layout is both functional and appealing to the eye, with colorful illustrations, maps, and charts often two columns wide. The print, however, is small (albeit legible) and could pose difficulty for readers with any sort of vision problem.

SUMMARY

A heavily Americanized version of the popular British *Hutchinson Encyclopedia*, *Webster's New World Encyclopedia* is intended specifically for North American readers. Published in 1992, it is quite current and has thus far spawned at least two spin-offs, namely WEBSTER'S NEW WORLD ENCYCLOPEDIA: COLLEGE EDITION and WEBSTER'S NEW WORLD ENCYCLOPEDIA: POCKET EDITION. The encyclopedia's coverage is broad and reasonably well balanced, but usually not deep, although it often manages to pack much useful information in a small space, due chiefly to economical writing and judicious use of charts, tables, and chronologies. On the negative side, *Webster's New World Encyclopedia* is not always accurate, its cross-reference system is inadequate, an index is needed, bibliographies are lacking, and its illustrations are sometimes poorly placed. The bottom line: Competes well with all but the largest one-volume encyclopedias.

OTHER OPINIONS

American Reference Books Annual, 1993, p. 29 (review by Mary Jo Walker); *Choice*, February 1993, p. 947 (review by J.E. Sheets); *Library Journal*, August 1992, p. 92 (review by James Moffet); *Reference Books Bulletin* (in *Booklist*), October 15, 1992, pp. 449–50 (unsigned review); *RQ*, Spring 1993, pp. 432–33 (review by Martin A. Cavanaugh); *Wilson Library Bulletin*, November 1992, pp. 96–97 (review by James Rettig).

REPORT CARD: WEBSTER'S NEW WORLD ENCYCLOPEDIA

TOPIC	COVERAGE	ACCURACY	RECENCY	CLARITY
Circumcision	B	A	B	A
Drew, Charles	F*	NA	NA	NA
Galileo	B	A	D	A
Glass, Philip	B	A	A	A
Heart Disease	D	A	B	A
IQ	A	A	A	A
Panda Bears	B	A	B	A
Sexual Harassment	F*	NA	NA	NA
Shroud of Turin	B	A	A	A
Uzbekistan	B	A	B	A

A = Excellent; **B** = Above Average; **C** = Average; **D** = Below Average; **F** = Poor; **NA** = Not Applicable
*No Article

WEBSTER'S NEW WORLD ENCYCLOPEDIA: COLLEGE EDITION

FACTS

Full Title: *Webster's New World Encyclopedia: College Edition.* Editors: Stephen P. Elliott, Martha Goldstein, and Michael Upshall. **Publisher:** Prentice Hall. **Date Published:** 1993.

Unabridged Version: WEBSTER'S NEW WORLD ENCYCLOPEDIA.

Volumes: One. **Words:** 1.7 million. **Pages:** 1,156. **Articles:** 20,000. **Bibliographies:** None. **Illustrations and Maps:** 500. **Cross-references:** 2,600. **Index Entries:** None. **Editorial Staff, Advisers, and Contributors:** 98. Trim Size: 7½ × 9½ in.

Price and Sales Information: $35.00. Individual consumers can purchase *Webster's New World Encyclopedia: College Edition* in bookstores or, if the book is not in stock, it can be ordered. Similarly, educational institutions (schools, libraries, etc.) can order it through a book wholesaler. To order the encyclopedia directly from the publisher, call 1-800-223-2348 or write Prentice Hall General Reference, 15 Columbus Circle, New York, NY 10023.

EVALUATION

Webster's New World Encyclopedia: College Edition (1993) is an updated abridgment of WEBSTER'S NEW WORLD ENCYCLOPEDIA (1992), which in turn is an Americanized version of the ninth edition (1990) of the venerable British *Hutchinson Encyclopedia.* Basically, the two *Webster's,* which aim to provide adults and older students with quick-reference information, are very much alike in terms of coverage, treatment, organization, and reader suitability. (For a detailed evaluation of WEBSTER'S NEW WORLD ENCYCLOPEDIA, see the immediately previous review.) But the two works do differ in a number of ways, some obvious and others not so obvious:

- WEBSTER'S NEW WORLD ENCYCLOPEDIA, the parent (or unabridged) work, is somewhat larger than the abridged *College Edition,* containing approximately 25,000 entries to the *College Edition*'s 20,000 entries. In most instances, the entries omitted from the *College Edition* will not be missed. They tend to deal with relatively

minor people, places, and things, such as "Gers" (a river in France), "Gezira, El" (a plain in the Sudan), "Ghosts" (a play by Ibsen), "Gibbons, Orlando" (a seventeenth-century English composer), "Gibson Desert" (in Australia), "Giessen" (a city in Germany), and "Gilgit" (a region of Kashmir).

- Some articles that appear in both encyclopedias have been edited down or condensed in the *College Edition. Example:* The article "Panda" in WEBSTER'S NEW WORLD ENCYCLOPEDIA notes that the "giant panda is the symbol of the Worldwide Fund for Nature (formerly the World Wildlife Fund)"; this information does not appear in the *College Edition.*

- Articles in WEBSTER'S NEW WORLD ENCYCLOPEDIA are enhanced by some 2,500 informative illustrations and maps, most in color; the *College Edition,* on the other hand, has only about 500 illustrations, all of which are in black-and-white. *Example:* The article "Heart" in the unabridged work offers the reader an informative, clearly labeled color drawing of the organ, whereas the same article in the *College Edition* is unillustrated. The *College Edition's* relatively small number of illustrations and lack of color weaken both its informational content and aesthetic appeal.

- As noted, the *College Edition*, published in 1993, is both an abridged *and* an updated edition of WEBSTER'S NEW WORLD ENCYCLOPEDIA (1992). To the credit of the editors, an impressive amount of revision is evident in the *College Edition*, including many updated articles and much new material. *Examples:* The article "Uzbekistan" has been significantly revised and enlarged to reflect current conditions and Uzbekistan's new status as a country (as opposed to a republic in the former Soviet Union). "Depression" (in psychology) has added a paragraph concerning manic depression, also called bipolar disorder. "Florida" has been updated by the addition of this sentence: "Because of its proximity to Caribbean nations, the state became a haven for refu-

gees from such countries as Cuba and Haiti." New entries not found in WEBSTER'S NEW WORLD ENCYCLOPEDIA but unique to the *College Edition* include "Walcott, Derek," "Gibson, Mel," "GIGO" (the acronym), "Depression" (in weather), "Heart Attack," and "Heart Disease."

- Physically, WEBSTER'S NEW WORLD ENCYCLOPEDIA is considerably larger (8½ ´ 10¾ in.; 6 lbs.) than the desk-sized *College Edition* (7½ × 9½ in.; 4 lbs.). Obviously, most consumers will find the *College Edition* easier and more convenient to handle.

- The *College Edition* sells for a modest $35.00, whereas the larger WEBSTER'S NEW WORLD ENCYCLOPEDIA goes for $75.00. Considering the comparatively small differences between the two titles, the *College Edition* is clearly the better buy. Note also that the recently launched *Webster's New World* encyclopedia family includes an even smaller abridgment, namely WEBSTER'S NEW WORLD ENCYCLOPEDIA: POCKET EDITION, which is published as a trade paperback priced at $14.00 (See review immediately following.)

SUMMARY

The 20,000-entry *Webster's New World Encyclopedia: College Edition* (1993) is an updated abridgment of the 25,000-entry WEBSTER'S NEW WORLD ENCYCLOPEDIA (1992), a single-volume work for adults and older students. Naturally, the two encyclopedias possess much the same text, style, and structure, but the *College Edition* is more current,

physically smaller and hence easier to handle, and considerably less expensive. On the negative side, the *College Edition* lacks the larger encyclopedia's many fine color illustrations. The bottom line: If price is a major consideration, *Webster's New World Encyclopedia: College Edition* is preferable to the larger WEBSTER'S NEW WORLD ENCYCLOPEDIA.

OTHER OPINIONS

Choice, January 1994, p. 764 (review by M.S. Lary); *Wilson Library Bulletin*, No-

vember 1993, p. 106 (review by James Rettig).

REPORT CARD: WEBSTER'S NEW WORLD ENCY: COLLEGE ED.

TOPIC	COVERAGE	ACCURACY	RECENCY	CLARITY
Circumcision	B	A	B	A
Drew, Charles	F*	NA	NA	NA
Galileo	B	A	D	A
Glass, Philip	B	A	A	A
Heart Disease	B	A	B	A
IQ	A	A	A	A
Panda Bears	B	A	B	A
Sexual Harassment	F*	NA	NA	NA
Shroud of Turin	B	A	A	A
Uzbekistan	A	A	A	A

A = Excellent; **B** = Above Average; **C** = Average; **D** = Below Average; **F** = Poor; **NA** = Not Applicable
*No Article

WEBSTER'S NEW WORLD ENCYCLOPEDIA: POCKET EDITION

FACTS

Full Title: *Webster's New World Encyclopedia: Pocket Edition.* Editors: Stephen P. Elliott, Martha Goldstein, and Michael Upshall. **Publisher:** Prentice Hall. **Date Published:** 1993.

Unabridged Edition: WEBSTER'S NEW WORLD ENCYCLOPEDIA.

Volumes: One. **Words:** 925,000. **Pages:** 923. **Articles:** 15,000. **Bibliographies:** None. **Illustrations and Maps:** None. **Cross-references:** 2,000. **Index Entries:** None. **Editorial Staff, Advisers, and Contributors:** 87. **Trim Size:** 5½ × 8½ in.

Price and Sales Information: $14.00 paperbound. Individual consumers can purchase *Webster's New World Encyclopedia: Pocket Edition* in bookstores where it is sold as a trade paperback or, if the book is not in stock, it can be ordered. Similarly, educational institutions (schools, libraries, etc.) can order it through a book wholesaler. To order the encyclopedia directly from the publisher, call 1-800-223-2348 or write Prentice Hall General Reference, 15 Columbus Circle, New York, NY 10023.

EVALUATION

The paperbound *Webster's New World Encyclopedia: Pocket Edition* (1993) is an updated but much reduced edition of WEBSTER'S NEW WORLD ENCYCLOPEDIA (1992), which in turn is an Americanized version of the ninth edition (1990) of the venerable British *Hutchinson Encyclopedia.* The *Pocket Edition* is the smallest member of the recently launched *Webster's New World* encyclopedia family, which also includes a college edition (WEBSTER'S NEW WORLD ENCYCLOPEDIA: COLLEGE EDITION). All of these encyclopedias are single-volume works designed for quick-reference use by adults and older students.

The *Pocket Edition* contains approximately half the number of words and entries found in WEBSTER'S NEW WORLD ENCYCLOPEDIA. Not only are numerous articles in the parent work omitted in the *Pocket Edition,* many others have been condensed, sometimes severely so. *Example:* The article "Galileo" in the *Pocket Edition* consists of about 100 words and deals entirely with Galileo's scientific experiments. By contrast, the same entry in WEBSTER'S NEW WORLD EN-CYCLOPEDIA is nearly three times as long and covers not only Galileo's science but his famous dispute with church officials in Rome and subsequent censure by the Inquisition.

The *Pocket Edition* also completely lacks the 2,500 illustrations and many charts, tables, and chronologies found in WEBSTER'S NEW WORLD ENCYCLOPEDIA. Indeed, the paperback encyclopedia offers nothing but unrelieved black-and-white print, which weakens the volume's aesthetic appeal as well as its informational content. The *Pocket Edi-*

tion is also physically much smaller than the unabridged work. Not surprisingly, it sells for a very affordable $14.00, opposed to $75.00 for the unabridged work and $35.00 for the *College Edition.*

Like WEBSTER'S NEW WORLD ENCYCLOPE-DIA: COLLEGE EDITION, the *Pocket Edition* is sometimes a bit more up-to-date than the parent work—which means it is admirably current. It also occasionally includes articles not found in WEBSTER'S NEW WORLD ENCYCLOPEDIA, such as "Heart Attack" and "Heart Disease."

The *Pocket Edition* naturally possesses many of the same strengths and weaknesses as its parent work in terms of coverage, treatment, organization, and style. For a detailed evaluation of WEBSTER'S NEW WORLD ENCYCLO-PEDIA, see the review beginning on p. 161.

SUMMARY

A trade paperback, *Webster's New World Encyclopedia: Pocket Edition* is a radically cut-down version of WEBSTER'S NEW WORLD ENCYCLOPEDIA. The *Pocket Edition* contains only about half the text of the larger work and none of its many illustrations. On the other hand, the *Pocket Edition* is very cur-

rent, is available in a handy paperbound format, and sells for only $14.00. The bottom line: Along with the CAMBRIDGE PAPER-BACK ENCYCLOPEDIA, this is the best one-volume general encyclopedia in paper covers currently available in North America.

OTHER OPINIONS

None.

REPORT CARD: WEBSTER'S NEW WORLD ENCY: POCKET ED.				
TOPIC	COVERAGE	ACCURACY	RECENCY	CLARITY
Circumcision	D	A	C	A
Drew, Charles	F*	NA	NA	NA
Galileo	D	A	D	A
Glass, Philip	B	A	A	A
Heart Disease	B	A	B	A
IQ	A	A	A	A
Panda Bears	D	A	C	A
Sexual Harassment	F*	NA	NA	NA
Shroud of Turin	B	A	A	A
Uzbekistan	C	A	A	A

A = Excellent; **B** = Above Average; **C** = Average; **D** = Below Average; **F** = Poor; **NA** = Not Applicable
*No Article

COMPARISON CHART

Small Encyclopedias for Adults and Older Students

This chart provides basic statistical information about each of the small one- and two-volume encyclopedias for adults and older students reviewed in *Kister's Best Encyclopedias*. The chart also offers a quick comparative overview of the 16 titles in this category. How does the *Cambridge Encyclopedia*, for instance, compare with similar encyclopedias in terms of number of words? Articles? Illustrations? Index entries? Price? The chart answers such questions at a glance.

In the case of price information, consumers should understand that prices are subject to change by the publisher or distributor at any time. For the latest price of any encyclopedia, consult *Books in Print* (a standard reference source found in nearly all libraries) or, better, call the publisher or distributor directly. Most now have toll-free numbers where the latest information about

price and availability can be obtained quickly and efficiently. Telephone numbers are listed in this guide at the beginning of each review under "Price and Sales Information," as well as in the directory of publishers and distributors at the back of the book (see Appendix B).

The chart's final column assigns a letter grade to each encyclopedia: A = Excellent; B = Above Average; C = Average; D = Below Average; F = Poor. The letter grade represents a final summary of the encyclopedia's detailed evaluation in *Kister's Best Encyclopedias*. Consumers seriously interested in purchasing an encyclopedia are urged to base their selection decisions on the reviews in the book, and not rely solely on the letter grades given in the chart, which are necessarily arbitrary.

Title	Vols.	Words	Pages	Articles	Illus. & Maps	Cross-refs.	Index Entries	Lowest Retail Price	Rating
American Spectrum Encyclopedia	1	1.5 MIL	1,312	17,000	3,850	7,000	None	$85.00	C
Barnes & Noble Encyclopedia[1]	1	1.5 MIL	1,488	30,000	800	75,000	None	19.98	C[1]
Barron's New Student's Concise Encyclopedia	1	1 MIL	1,281	20,000	500	150	15,000	29.95	D
Cambridge Encyclopedia	1	1.5 MIL	1,488	30,000	800	75,000	None	49.95	C
Cambridge Paperback Encyclopedia[2]	1	750,000	970	19,000	570	26,000	None	19.95	C
Columbia Encyclopedia	1	6.6 MIL	3,072	50,000	745	65,000	None	125.00	A
Concise Columbia Encyclopedia	1	1 MIL	954	15,000	150	50,000	None	39.95	B
Dictionary of Cultural Literacy	1	350,000	619	5,000	250	20,000	7,500	24.95	D
Knowledge Encyclopedia	1	300,000	415	2,500	615	4,000	5,000	16.95	F
New American Desk Encyclopedia	1	1.3 MIL	1,312	13,000	200	35,000	None	17.00	D
Random House Encyclopedia	1	3 MIL	2,912	25,880	13,500	45,000	None	129.95	B
Running Press Cyclopedia	1	100,000	638	300	800	None	750	8.95	D

Title	Vols.	Words	Pages	Articles	Illus. & Maps	Cross-refs.	Index Entries	Lowest Retail Price	Rating
Volume Library	2	2.5 mil	2,568	8,500	3,000	300	32,000	139.95	C
Webster's New World Encyclopedia	1	2 mil	1,230	25,000	2,500	3,000	None	75.00	C
Webster's New World Encyclopedia: College Edition[3]	1	1.7 mil	1,156	20,000	500	2,600	None	35.00	C
Webster's New World Encyclopedia: Pocket Edition[3]	1	925,000	923	15,000	None	2,000	None	14.00	C

1. Same text as CAMBRIDGE ENCYCLOPEDIA.
2. Abridged version of CAMBRIDGE ENCYCLOPEDIA.
3. Abridged version of WEBSTER'S NEW WORLD ENCYCLOPEDIA.

Large and Medium-Sized Encyclopedias for Children and Younger Students

* * * * * * * *

OVERVIEW

Consumers interested in a multivolume encyclopedia for children are faced with a wide range of titles that vary greatly in size, price, and quality. The 10-volume GROLIER CHILDREN'S ENCYCLOPEDIA, for instance, contains only 250,000 words in 816 pages, whereas the 26-volume COMPTON'S ENCYCLOPEDIA consists of nine million words in over 10,000 pages. CHARLIE BROWN'S 'CYCLOPEDIA, a supermarket set, sells for approximately $42.00, but the excellent NEW BOOK OF KNOWLEDGE retails for nearly $1,000.00.

Currently, there are 13 multivolume encyclopedias on the North American market suitable for children and younger students. Among those intended exclusively for young people, the standout set is the NEW BOOK OF KNOWLEDGE. Published between 1912 and 1964 as the *Book of Knowledge* and since 1965 as the NEW BOOK OF KNOWLEDGE, the 21-volume encyclopedia offers broad coverage, an engaging style, and first-rate illustrations. But, as noted, it is expensive, and not all consumers are willing to lay out $1,000.00 for a children's encyclopedia, which will be outgrown in a relatively short time.

Less pricey alternatives are the 20-volume CHILDREN'S BRITANNICA ($299.00) and the smaller seven-volume OXFORD CHILDREN'S ENCYCLOPEDIA ($200.00), both quality sets, though not up to new book of knowledge standards. Another possibility is the 22-volume YOUNG STUDENTS LEARNING LIBRARY (also published as the NEW GROLIER STUDENT ENCYCLOPEDIA), but it is an undistinguished set

and seems overpriced at $322.00. Speaking of overpriced, the 10-volume GROLIER CHILDREN'S ENCYCLOPEDIA currently sells for $219.00, which is excessive considering the encyclopedia is also available in a single-volume edition at $29.95 under the title KINGFISHER CHILDREN'S ENCYCLOPEDIA.

Consumers interested in a multivolume set for preschoolers and beginning readers—often called a "pre-cyclopedia"—need look no further than CHILDCRAFT: THE HOW AND WHY LIBRARY, hands-down the best general reference work on the market today for children ages 4–10. Its competitors—CHARLIE BROWN'S 'CYCLOPEDIA and the YOUNG CHILDREN'S ENCYCLOPEDIA (also published as COMPTON'S PRECYCLOPEDIA)—lack CHILDCRAFT's broad and captivating text, superior illustrations, and appealing design. Of course, all of these sets are very quickly outgrown and parents especially must decide if any is worth the investment. On the other hand, all but the smallest public and school libraries should have CHILDCRAFT.

Finally, for those consumers seeking an encyclopedia that will serve the needs of the entire family—children, Mom and Dad, and any other adults who might be around—there are two choices: COMPTON'S ENCYCLOPEDIA and the WORLD BOOK ENCYCLOPEDIA. Both of these encyclopedias have been around for many years, both are exceedingly well edited, both provide balanced coverage of the world's basic knowledge, both offer accurate and up-to-date information, both include informative and aesthetically pleasing illustrations, and, perhaps most important, both present their material in such a way that children and adults can profitably use the encyclopedia. From a purely practical point of view, no family with children can go wrong purchasing either of these two sets. Of the two, WORLD BOOK is clearly the better buy, but COMPTON'S is also a work of considerable merit.

CHARLIE BROWN'S 'CYCLOPEDIA

FACTS

Full Title: *Charlie Brown's 'Cyclopedia.* **Editorial Director:** Pat Fortunato. **Publisher:** Funk & Wagnalls. **Date Published:** First Edition, 1980; Revised Edition, 1990. **Volumes:** 15. **Words:** 225,000. **Pages:** 900. **Articles:** 1,000. **Bibliographies:** None. **Illustrations and Maps:** 1,500. **Cross-references:** None. **Index Entries:** None. **Editorial Staff, Advisers, and Contributors:** 13. **Trim Size:** 8 × 10¾ in.

Price and Sales Information: $42.00. *Charlie Brown's 'Cyclopedia* is sold only in supermarkets in North America. According to the publisher, Funk & Wagnalls, the encyclopedia is unavailable except in those supermarkets currently selling it on a volume-by-volume basis or as a boxed gift set. Questions concerning the encyclopedia should be addressed to Funk & Wagnalls, One International Blvd., Suite 444, Mahwah, NJ 07495-0017.

EVALUATION

Charlie Brown's 'Cyclopedia—a set of 15 thin, abundantly illustrated volumes intended for preschoolers and students in the primary grades—is sold exclusively in North American supermarkets. First published a volume at a time in 1980–81, the encyclopedia grew out of a series of five books entitled *Charlie Brown's Super Book of Questions and Answers, Charlie Brown's Second Super Book of Questions and Answers,* etc., developed by Charles M. Schulz Creative Associates and published by Random House between 1976 and 1981. An immediate hit with children, the *'Cyclopedia* was modestly revised in 1985. In 1990, the set underwent a more extensive revision that expanded it from 720 to 900 pages, each volume being increased from 48 to 60 pages. That edition—the latest—is under review here.

As most consumers will know, the encyclopedia's title refers to a character in Charles Schulz's well-known "Peanuts" comic strip. Captioned cartoons featuring various "Peanuts" figures—Charlie Brown, Snoopy, Lucy, Linus, Sally, Woodstock, et al.—appear throughout the set, adding a light touch to the business of finding and using knowledge and information.

The *'Cyclopedia* is thematically (as opposed to alphabetically) arranged, with each volume devoted to a broad subject or area of knowledge: *Your Amazing Body* (volume 1); *Animals Through the Ages* (volume 2); *Blast Off to Space* (volume 3); *Creatures of Land and Sea* (volume 4); *Cars, Trains, and Other Wheels* (volume 5); *How Machines Work* (volume 6); *A Guide to Planet Earth* (volume 7); *Science Can Be Super* (volume 8); *Our Incredible Universe* (volume 9); *Boats and Things*

That Float (volume 10); *Holidays Around the World* (volume 11); *People and Places* (volume 12); *Electricity and Magnetism* (volume 13); *Clothes from Head to Toe* (volume 14); and *Planes and Things That Fly* (volume 15).

Specific topics are covered in each volume in a question-and-answer format. *Example*: Volume 1 (*Your Amazing Body*) includes articles entitled "What You're Made of," "How You Started," "Your Bones," "Your Teeth," "Your Muscles," "Your Brain and Nervous System in Control," "Eating and Drinking," "Vitamins," "Your Heart," "Your Blood," "When Your Body Aches," and "Drugs and Allergies." These articles consist of quite specific questions followed by brief answers. For instance, "When Your Body Aches" asks and answers such questions as "What happens when you get sick?," "Why can't you get the chicken pox more than once?," "What do 'shots' do for you?," and "What is a fever?"

Like the other encyclopedic sets currently available for preschoolers and beginning readers (CHILDCRAFT, COMPTON'S PRECYCLOPEDIA and the YOUNG CHILDREN'S ENCYCLOPEDIA), the 'Cyclopedia not only furnishes basic information of interest to children but attempts to stimulate the child's innate curiosity about the world and its wonders. The question-and-answer approach employed by the 'Cyclopedia is a particularly effective means of achieving both these goals. For example, volume 14 (*Clothes from Head to Toe*) offers information on such intriguing topics as "Where did people get needles for sewing?," "Did the ancient Greeks wear underwear?," and "When were blue jeans invented?" In addition, colored boxes (or panels) containing interesting facts frequently accompany the Q & A, e.g., "Levi Strauss first went to California to look for gold, but he ended up making much more money from selling pants than from panning gold!"

Unlike its competitors, however, the 'Cyclopedia is very heavily weighted toward science and technology, as the titles of the individual volumes clearly indicate. The subject of space exploration, for instance, receives an entire volume of its own (volume 3, *Blast Off to Space*), whereas famous people, religion, literature, popular music, sports and games, and the countries of the world and other prominent places are either ignored altogether or treated so superficially that little or no practical information can be gleaned. The encyclopedia's lack of balanced coverage is one of its most glaring weaknesses as a general reference source for children.

Prospective purchasers should also note that the 'Cyclopedia—like all the other so-called pre-cyclopedias (CHILDCRAFT, COMPTON'S PRECYCLOPEDIA, and the YOUNG CHILDREN'S ENCYCLOPEDIA)—will be quickly outgrown. After a time, children will find the set too juvenile or "babyish" for them.

Information on topics that the 'Cyclopedia does cover is normally accurate and objective, albeit quite simplistic. For example, the article "Submarines" (in volume 10) notes that "Modern submarines use nuclear energy. It is the most powerful force known. Uranium (you-RAY-nee-um) is the fuel used for nuclear energy. One ounce of it gives out as much energy as is created by burning 100 tons of coal, so nuclear-powered subs can travel long distances without refueling." The set's contents are also reasonably up-to-date, being current as of the late 1980s. For instance, volume 13 contains a rather lengthy article on compact disc players and volume 14 describes the Stealth bomber.

The encyclopedia's writing style, befitting the intended readership, is clear, simple, direct, sometimes informal, and occasionally vivid. Potentially new or difficult terms are often defined in context; some are also pronounced. A good example of the 'Cyclopedia's style is found in the answer to the question "What is a computer?," which introduces the article "The Electronic Age: Computers and Digital Displays":

A computer is a machine that can remember and sometimes even learn. It has special materials in it called semiconductors (seh-mee-kon-DUCK-tours) that help it decide what to do.

Computers can be given instructions on how to do hard things, and then the computer remembers the instructions when it needs them. These instructions are called programs. People who make instructions for computers are called computer programmers. Once a computer is programmed, it can perform millions of instructions in less than a second!

Because it lacks both an index and cross-references, finding specific facts and topics in the 'Cyclopedia is a difficult and unpleasant chore and almost always a hit-and-miss proposition. Only by scanning the contents pages of each volume and extensive browsing in the set—time-consuming operations—can the reader hope to locate all the information on a particular subject. *Example:* Nuclear energy is discussed in the article "Power Plants" in volume 13 and in the aforementioned article "Submarines" in Volume 10, but without an index and cross-references the user has no quick and easy way to zero in on this material. By perusing the contents pages, the reader will eventually find "Power Plants" in volume 13 (*Electricity and Magnetism*), but there is no way

the user can be expected to know that the article "Submarines" contains pertinent information about nuclear energy. Paradoxically, the first edition of the 'Cyclopedia did include a 1,500-entry index in the final volume. Why this necessary finding device was omitted from the latest edition is not explained.

Several types of color illustrations—photographs, diagrams, cutaway drawings, and cartoons—appear throughout the set. The photos, diagrams, and drawings almost always enhance the informational value of the work, and the cartoons add interest and humor. The article "Birds in Flight," for instance, notes in a colored fact panel that "Some birds will fly upside down to attract a mate!" Just below the panel is a cartoon showing Woodstock flying upside down and Snoopy saying, "I think Woodstock is in love again!!" Unfortunately, the color reproduction tends to be garish, a problem exacerbated by the use of cheap paper.

Overall, the set's physical format is satisfactory. The page layout is bright, varied, and appealing to the child's eye, and the binding (covered boards) is strong and will withstand much heavy use by energetic children. And the price—$42.00—is a bargain.

REPORT CARD: CHARLIE BROWN'S 'CYCLOPEDIA

TOPIC	COVERAGE	ACCURACY	RECENCY	CLARITY
Computers	B	A	B	A
Halloween	B	A	C	A
Johnson, Magic	F*	NA	NA	NA
Measles	F*	NA	NA	NA
Nuclear Energy	B	A	C	A
Panda Bears	F*	NA	NA	NA
Rock Music	F*	NA	NA	NA
Rose (Flower)	F*	NA	NA	NA
Russia	F*	NA	NA	NA
Sex Education	C	A	A	A

A = Excellent; **B** = Above Average; **C** = Average; **D** = Below Average; **F** = Poor; **NA** = Not Applicable
*No Article

SUMMARY

Available only in supermarkets, *Charlie Brown's 'Cyclopedia* is a colorful, inexpensive 15-volume set for preschoolers and young students in the primary grades. The *'Cyclopedia*, which is thematically arranged, heavily favors scientific and technical subjects; other areas of knowledge tend to be treated cursorily or not at all. The set's best features are a clear, readable, and interesting writing style and eye-catching (albeit garish) illustrations, including familiar "Peanuts" cartoon characters throughout. On the negative side, the set lacks both cross-references and an index and, as noted, the coverage is badly out of balance. Also, the set will be quickly outgrown. The bottom line: Better encyclopedic sets for preschoolers and beginning readers are available, but none can match the *'Cyclopedia*'s attractive price.

OTHER OPINIONS

None.

CHILDCRAFT

FACTS

Full Title: *Childcraft: The How and Why Library.* **Editor in Chief:** Robert O. Zeleny. **Executive Editor:** Dominic J. Miccolis. **Publisher:** World Book, Inc. **Date Published:** First published in 1934; revised periodically, most recently in 1993.
    Volumes: 15 (plus *Childcraft Dictionary*). **Words:** 750,000. **Pages:** 4,750. **Articles:** 3,000. **Bibliographies:** 255. **Illustrations and Maps:** 4,500. **Cross-references:** None. **Index Entries:** 20,000. **Editorial Staff, Advisers, and Contributors:** 50. **Trim Size:** 7¼ × 9¾ in.

Price and Sales Information: $249.00 plus shipping and handling. *Childcraft* is sold to individual consumers and educational institutions (schools, libraries, etc.) through authorized sales representatives of the publisher. The set is not sold in bookstores or similar retail outlets. For additional information about the set or to order it, consumers should consult the yellow pages of the local telephone directory under "Encyclopedias" for the World Book, Inc. sales representative in their area. If the company is not listed, call toll-free 1-800-621-8202 or write World Book, Inc., 525 West Monroe Street, 20th Floor, Chicago, IL 60661.

EVALUATION

In the words of the editors, *Childcraft* is "a 15-volume resource library designed especially for preschool and primary-grade children and for the older child who needs high-interest, easy-to-read materials. *Childcraft* also serves as a resource for parents, teachers, and librarians" (preface).

The set, which first appeared in 1934–35 in seven volumes, is now 60 years old and still going strong. Along with an annual supplement entitled *Childcraft Annual* (1965–), *Childcraft* is produced by a full-time staff of well-qualified editors, writers, and artists, some of whom also work on the WORLD

BOOK ENCYCLOPEDIA, the publisher's excellent school and family encyclopedia. Outside talent also contributes to the set, including award-winning artists and photographers. Over the years, *Childcraft* has gained widespread recognition as an outstanding source of knowledge and information for children ages 4–10. One significant measure of the set's success is the large number of foreign-language versions it has spawned. These include editions of *Childcraft* in Arabic, Chinese, Finnish, French, Korean, Portuguese, and Spanish, with others—Hebrew, Italian, Thai, and Turkish—in the works.

When it first appeared, *Childcraft* was more a work for adults about children than one for children themselves, but as the set grew and evolved over time, the volumes for children began to outnumber those aimed at parents, teachers, and other adult readers. In 1964, *Childcraft* absorbed the *How and Why Library*, a six-volume reference work published by the L.J. Bullard Company between 1913 and 1959. This move expanded *Childcraft* to its present size of 15 volumes and established its full title as *Childcraft: The How and Why Library*. Moreover, the editors of the watershed 1964 edition chose self-discovery as the set's overriding objective, thus sealing its role as a publication essentially for—and not about—children. J. Morris Jones, then editor of the set, viewed the pages of *Childcraft* as "doors to a child's life and learning," a description as true today as it was 30 years ago.

The set has always been arranged topically (as opposed to alphabetically), with each volume devoted to a broad subject or theme. The current edition consists of 15 numbered volumes: *Once Upon a Time* (volume 1), a collection of nursery rhymes, poems, folk and fairy tales, fables, and stories for reading aloud to preschoolers; *Time to Read* (volume 2), literary works for both young listeners and beginning readers; *Sto-*

ries and Poems (volume 3), a more advanced anthology for young readers age 8 and up; *World and Space* (volume 4); *About Animals* (volume 5); *The Green Kingdom* (volume 6), which deals with the world of plants; *Story of the Sea* (volume 7); *About Us* (volume 8), which explores different human cultures; *Holidays and Birthdays* (volume 9); *Places to Know* (volume 10); *Make and Do* (volume 11), an introduction to practical arts and crafts for young people; *How Things Work* (volume 12); *Mathemagic* (volume 13); *About Me* (volume 14), a first-person examination of the child as a physical and social being; and *Guide to Childcraft* (volume 15), a volume chiefly for parents and teachers that includes extensive material on child development and sensitive issues involving young people (such as drugs, sex, and death), as well as an A-to-Z medical guide and a detailed index to the set.

In 1989, the editors added a general dictionary for children ages 8–11 to *Childcraft*, which, although unnumbered, brings the set's total volumes to 16. Entitled the *Childcraft Dictionary*, it contains approximately 30,000 entries and is, like the numbered 15-volume set, a work of high quality. When *Childcraft* is sold to schools and libraries, however, the dictionary is not included as part of the set, although the *World Book Student Dictionary*, a school (or text) edition of the *Childcraft Dictionary*, can be purchased separately.

As the individual volume titles and the Report Card (see below) plainly indicate, *Childcraft* provides reasonably detailed coverage of many subjects of interest and concern to preschoolers and beginning readers. Much of the set's contents loosely mirror the North American elementary school curriculum, as articles on such topics as comets, fossils, fractions, levers, the White House, the Alamo, animal and plant life, the world's major religions, and weather attest. In addition, the aforementioned supplement, *Childcraft Annual* (published annually since 1965), treats a new topic each year, such as birds, Indians, words, pets, and inventors and inventions.

But users and prospective purchasers of *Childcraft* should understand that the set is not an encyclopedia in the traditional sense, nor does it claim to provide systematic coverage of people, places, events, concepts, etc. Indeed, such areas of knowledge as biography, geography, music, art, and sports are covered only very selectively, if at all. For instance, the set does not even mention such important places as Nicaragua and Tokyo or prominent American leaders as Franklin Roosevelt, Harry Truman, John F. Kennedy, Lyndon Johnson, and Richard Nixon. Readers will also look in vain for such names as Wolfgang Amadeus Mozart and Pablo Picasso.

What *Childcraft* does offer, however, is nearly 5,000 pages of creatively written, attractively presented material designed to stir the curiosity and imagination of children about the world and their place in it. As such, it competes with the other so-called "pre-cyclopedias," namely CHARLIE BROWN'S 'CYCLOPEDIA, COMPTON'S PRECYCLOPEDIA, and the YOUNG CHILDREN'S ENCYCLOPEDIA. All of these sets are appealing to preschoolers and beginning readers, but prospective purchasers should be aware that they are quickly outgrown. After a time, children begin to consider such materials as too juvenile or "babyish" for them.

Childcraft's contents are reliable, unbiased, and reasonably current. By way of example, the article on Halloween in volume 9 describes contemporary customs:

> Some children go out to trick or treat on Halloween. They go from door to door, ring doorbells, and call out, "Trick or treat!" People who answer the doors put treats into the children's bags. In many towns and cities now, children do not go out to trick or treat. It is considered unsafe. Instead, towns, cities, and even neighborhoods have big parties for the children.

In recent years, in an effort to keep the set timely, the editors have strengthened coverage of social and environmental issues. For instance, the article "Putting Atoms to Work" (in volume 12) points out the value of nuclear energy ("power plants that use nuclear energy save a lot of coal, oil, or gas") but also warns of its potential dangers ("Scientists and engineers have to make sure that radioactivity doesn't get out of the power plant and into the air, water, or soil"). In the same vein, a greater emphasis on racial and ethnic diversity is now apparent throughout the set, reflected in the choice of both illustrations and literary selections (stories, poems, folktales, etc.). Some articles, like the one on Halloween cited in the previous paragraph, also convey a more realistic view of contemporary society and its problems.

Hence, earlier criticisms of *Childcraft* as oblivious or insensitive to the real world outside the white, middle-class experience are no longer entirely valid. On the other hand, the set's tone remains positive and cheerful, reassuring the child that the old verities not only exist but predominate. Carol Noll, in a review of the set in *American Reference Books Annual* (1993, p. 25), puts it this way: "As in most such publications for children, the world is seen through rose-colored glasses. Wars are long-ago events commemorated at monuments and on holidays; poverty, unemployment, and divorce do not exist. Of the major problems facing the world, only that of environmental pollution is mentioned in any significant way in the children's volumes."

No one, however, can seriously quarrel with the way *Childcraft* is written. The many literary selections found in the set represent the best expression of such outstanding and diverse writers as Hilaire Belloc, Judy Blume, Lewis Carroll, Beverly Cleary, Emily Dickinson, Eugene Field, Robert Frost, Nikki Giovanni, Kenneth Grahame, Edward Lear, Vachel Lindsay, A.A. Milne, Farley Mowat,

Ogden Nash, Scott O'Dell, Shel Silverstein, Robert Louis Stevenson, Sara Teasdale, and Laura Ingalls Wilder.

Staff-written material in the set is customarily presented in clear, interesting, and vivid prose that will be comprehensible to children in the primary grades and beyond. Potentially new or difficult words are italicized and defined in context. Moreover, most of the subject volumes include glossaries of new words at the back of the book. The glossary in *Story of the Sea* (volume 7), for instance, defines and pronounces such terms as *arthropod, chronometer, crustacean, mammal, mollusk, quadrant,* and *tentacle.* The initial paragraphs of the article on computers entitled "A Machine that Helps You Think" in *How Things Work* (volume 10) furnish a good example of *Childcraft's* writing style:

> If you're an astronaut in a speeding spaceship, you have a problem. The ship is rocketing through space at tremendous speed—thousands of miles an hour. To change direction, you have to figure out where the ship is and how fast it's traveling—and you have only seconds to do it!
>
> You can't think that fast. But a computer can. A computer is a high-speed thinking machine. It can do the figuring for you and tell you where the ship is—*every* second.
>
> Is the computer smarter than you are? Not really. It doesn't "think" the same way you do. A computer has to be told exactly how to think and what to think about. It can't help you fly a spaceship, run a bank, or find a library book unless someone gives it the right information.
>
> People who work with computers write *programs* for them. They figure out exactly what problems a computer needs to solve. Then they give step-by-step instructions for solving the problems. The computer stores the instructions in its *memory*.

Eleven of the 15 numbered *Childcraft* volumes now contain graded bibliographies, up from only four a few years ago. Located at the back of the book, each bibliography annotates (or describes) approximately 25 selected titles where additional information on the subject can be found. The bibliographies are carefully selected and reasonably up-to-date; they will be most useful to parents, teachers, and librarians using *Childcraft* as an educational tool.

Finding specific articles, topics, and facts in the set normally poses no difficulty, thanks to the comprehensive 20,000-entry index at the end of volume 15. Information about computers, for instance, is found in three different volumes and, although the set lacks cross-references in the text, the index quickly and easily steers the reader to each pertinent article. The index not only gives volume and page numbers but indicates if the article contains illustrations.

A conspicuous strength of *Childcraft* is its fine artwork, which includes photographs, diagrams, drawings, and cutaways. The editors do not exaggerate when they say in the preface, "Nearly every graphic technique appears somewhere in *Childcraft*." The illustrations, which are almost all in color, make up roughly half the total text and are nicely varied, informative, and always well reproduced. Happily, the set is printed on high-quality offset paper manufactured specially to obtain the best color reproduction possible.

The set's physical format likewise deserves high praise. The page layout is extraordinarily appealing, designed to capture the young reader's attention immediately and hold it. Particularly effective is the use of white space, which gives the page an inviting, uncluttered look. The binding—washable covered boards—is sturdy and will withstand heavy use by children from toddlers on up.

REPORT CARD: CHILDCRAFT

TOPIC	COVERAGE	ACCURACY	RECENCY	CLARITY
Computers	A	A	A	A
Halloween	A	A	A	A
Johnson, Magic	F*	NA	NA	NA
Measles	A	A	A	A
Nuclear Energy	B	A	B	A
Panda Bears	C	A	B	A
Rock Music	F*	NA	NA	NA
Rose (Flower)	F*	NA	NA	NA
Russia	C	A	A	A
Sex Education	A	A	A	A

A = Excellent; **B** = Above Average; **C** = Average; **D** = Below Average; **F** = Poor; **NA** = Not Applicable
*No Article

SUMMARY

Not strictly an encyclopedia, *Childcraft* is a handsomely turned out, topically arranged 15-volume "resource library" for preschoolers and beginning readers first published in 1934 and frequently revised since that time. The set can also be used profitably by parents, teachers, and librarians as an educational tool. In 1989, a general children's dictionary—the 30,000-entry *Childcraft Dictionary*—was added to the set as an unnumbered volume. *Childcraft* includes informational articles, as well as numerous literary selections, such as stories, poems, nursery rhymes, and folktales. The artwork, which accounts for roughly half the text, is first-rate and the writing style captivating. In recent years, the editors have added racial and ethnic diversity to *Childcraft* (particularly noticeable in the literary selections and illustrations) and broadened the set's reach by touching on some social and environmental issues. Still, the set continues to present a congenial and, in the opinion of some critics, excessively rosy picture of the world. Although quickly outgrown, *Childcraft* is enthusiastically recommended to parents who can afford it; their children will be ever grateful for having *Childcraft* as part of their early education. The set also belongs in public, school, day-care, and kindergarten libraries of any consequence. The bottom line: *Childcraft* is unquestionably the best general reference set for children ages 4–10 currently on the market.

OTHER OPINIONS

American Reference Books Annual, 1993, pp. 24–25 (review by Carol L. Noll); *Basic Information Sources* by William A. Katz (vol. 1 of *Introduction to Reference Work*, 6th ed., New York: McGraw-Hill, 1992), p. 255; *Reference Books Bulletin* (in *Booklist*), June 1, 1990, pp. 1917–18 (unsigned review); *Reference Sources for Small and Medium-Sized Libraries* (5th ed., Chicago: American Library Assn., 1992), p. 30 (review by Jovian P. Lang).

CHILDREN'S BRITANNICA

FACTS

Full Title: *Children's Britannica*. **Editorial Director:** Margaret Sutton. **Editor:** James Somerville. **Publisher:** Encyclopaedia Britannica, Inc. **Date Published:** First published in 1960; latest edition is Fourth Edition published in 1988; new printing with revisions published annually.

Volumes: 20. **Words:** 4 million. **Pages:** 6,830. **Articles:** 10,000 (4,000 main articles; 6,000 brief articles in the "Reference Index"). **Bibliographies:** None. **Illustrations and Maps:** 6,500. **Cross-references:** 2,500. **Index Entries:** 40,000. **Editorial Staff, Advisers, and Contributors:** 900. **Trim Size:** 7¾ × 8½ in.

Price and Sales Information: $299.00 plus shipping and handling. *Children's Britannica* is sold to individual consumers and educational institutions (schools, librar-ies, etc.) through authorized sales representatives of the publisher. The set is not sold in bookstores or similar retail outlets, although it is sometimes sold via mail order. For additional information about the set or to order it, individual consumers should consult the yellow pages of the local telephone directory under "Encyclopedias" for the Encyclopaedia Britannica, Inc. sales representative in their area. If the company is not listed, call toll-free 1-800-858-4995 or write Encyclopaedia Britannica, Inc., Britannica Centre, Customer Service Department, 310 South Michigan Avenue, Chicago, IL 60604. Educational institutions should call toll-free 1-800-544-9862 or write Encyclopaedia Britannica Educational Corporation at the same address.

EVALUATION

A 20-volume general encyclopedia for young people ages 7–14, *Children's Britannica* first appeared in Great Britain in 1960. Major revisions followed in 1969 (Second Edition), 1973 (Third Edition), and, most recently, 1988 (Fourth Edition). The Fourth Edition—the most extensive of the several revisions—is the first to be sold in North America. This edition replaces the publisher's now defunct BRITANNICA JUNIOR ENCYCLOPAEDIA FOR BOYS AND GIRLS, long a staple for elementary school children in the U.S. and Canada that was discontinued in 1984. Indeed, in many respects *Children's Britannica* represents a reincarnation of BRITANNICA JUNIOR, so remarkably similar are the two in size, purpose, content, organization, and style.

According to the editors, the latest edition of *Children's Britannica* was undertaken "to adapt the encyclopedia for young students living in a technological age of the late 20th century and to do so on a broad, international basis" (preface). The key word here is "international," the idea being to create a basic text that, with minimum adaptation, would serve both British-English and American-English markets. Hence the set sold in North America is identical to the one available in Great Britain and throughout the Commonwealth, except for minor alterations in the text such as spelling and usage variants.

Children's Britannica contains 4,000 substantial articles in the first 19 volumes. Arranged alphabetically, these articles are usually of the specific-entry type. For example, measles has its own article in the encyclopedia, whereas in the NEW BOOK OF KNOWLEDGE (*Children's Britannica*'s chief competitor) measles is covered as part of the broad-entry article "Diseases." *Children's Britannica* also includes approximately 6,000 very brief "capsule" articles in volume 20, called the "Reference Index." This A-to-Z volume, which resembles the NEW BOOK OF KNOWLEDGE's "Dictionary Index," COMPTON's ENCYCLOPEDIA's "Fact Index," and the old BRITANNICA JUNIOR's "Ready Reference Index," serves the dual function of index to the set and source of quick reference information on topics that, in the judgment of the editors, do not warrant an entry in the main portion of the encyclopedia. *Example:* Rock music has a six-line entry in the "Reference Index" under "Rock Music," followed by a citation to a lengthy article entitled "Popular Music" in volume 14.

A potential problem with this organization is that children and younger students might miss some useful information in the "Reference Index" if they go directly to the main articles in volumes 1–19. Moreover, they may find the need to consult more than one alphabet for factual information hard to understand. Studies indicate that young people have varying degrees of difficulty with even the simplest indexes and tend to avoid them altogether. Some encyclopedia publishers, however, find it economically advantageous to maintain two sets of articles in the same work, one representing substantial treatment of permanent topics (historical figures, major places, etc.) and the other devoted to short, pithy summaries of less important or ephemeral topics (contemporary celebrities, fads, etc.).

An editorial staff of 37 headed by Margaret Sutton and James Somerville, both experienced encyclopedia editors, is listed at the beginning of Volume 20. All articles in the set are unsigned but hundreds of contributors and verifiers (called "text authorities") are identified at the end of volume 20. The majority are British, although many are from the U.S. and a smattering from other countries. Most are academics or writers who have established themselves as an authority on a particular subject; examples of better-known contributors are John Arlott (the British voice of cricket), Phyllis Bentley (author of books on

the Bronte family), Asa Briggs (prominent British historian), Konrad Lorenz (expert on animal behavior), Eric Partridge (authority on English-language usage and slang), and Roscoe Pound (former head of the Harvard Law School). Suffice it to say that *Children's Britannica* is authoritative.

The encyclopedia adequately covers all basic areas of knowledge, but particularly heavy emphasis is placed on biographical and geographical subjects. For instance, the set has articles on all the countries of the world (including those that made up the former Soviet Union) and major cities of the world, as well as every U.S. state, Canadian province, and county in the British Isles. Major rivers, lakes, mountains, etc. also receive strong attention. Recent scientific developments are also well covered, especially those in the biological and technical sciences, as evidenced by such expansive articles as "Aeronautics," "Bridge," "Building Industry," "Computer," "Genetic Disorders," "Genetic Engineering," "Heart, Human," "Heating and Air Conditioning," "Heredity and Genetics," "Navigation and Pilotage," "Reproduction," "Sex," "Space Exploration," and "Space Flight."

No systematic attempt has been made to relate the encyclopedia's contents to school curricula, either in Great Britain or North America. In their efforts to provide "international" coverage, the editors walk a fine line between catering to the interests and expectations of British and Commonwealth readers on the one hand and American readers on the other. A review in *Reference Books Bulletin* (in *Booklist,* September 15, 1993, p. 174) illuminates this problem:

> Though the editors' intent is to provide an international perspective, a British bias exists, with coverage emphasizing the U.K. and Commonwealth nations. The article *New Zealand,* for instance, is almost as long as *Brazil* and *Mexico* combined. Britons are sometimes covered in more biographical detail. References to association football (i.e., soccer) will not be understood by American children.

James Rettig, in a review in *Wilson Library Bulletin* (November 1988, p. 122), makes much the same criticism:

> The attempt to appeal equally to diverse segments of the international English-language market results in some inconsistencies. For example, the article on air forces includes a section subtitled "The World's Leading Air Forces." It discusses, of course, the United States' and the [former] Soviet Union's air forces. The following subtitled section, "Britain's Royal Air Force," devotes equal space to the RAF. However, the article on universities and colleges offers balanced treatment of the systems on both sides of the Atlantic and briefer discussion of the systems in Australia, New Zealand, and Canada. In attempting to appeal to all of these markets, the *Children's Britannica* takes on multiple identities.

The encyclopedia is conscientiously edited and, as might be expected, its contents are trustworthy and reasonably up-to-date, although occasionally there are lapses. *Example*: The article "Rose" correctly reports that the rose is "the state flower of several states in the United States" but fails to note that it became the national flower by act of the U.S. Congress in 1986.

The encyclopedia can also be relied upon in most instances to present its material as objectively as humanly possible. Happily, unlike its predecessor, the BRITANNICA JUNIOR ENCYCLOPAEDIA, *Children's Britannica* does not normally ignore controversial or sensitive issues, such as drugs and sexuality. For instance, sex among young people is treated in a thoughtful and impartial manner in the article "Sex":

> Standards of what is right and what is wrong also change over time. When effective methods of birth control and abortion became widely available in the early 1960s, young people in many Western societies started to have sexual intercourse at a much earlier age than in any previous generations (as early in some cases as their mid-teens), often with a number of different partners and hoping to avoid the risk of the girl becoming pregnant. Many people have come to accept the idea of living together without being married, a common practice nowadays. But since the dan-

gers of sexually transmitted diseases (see below, under that heading) have become widely recognized, young people everywhere are being pressured once more to form long-term, stable relationships, and not to have sex with several partners.

The encyclopedia is intended chiefly for young students in the upper elementary and junior high school grades, although reading levels vary, sometimes markedly, from article to article. The article "Snake," for instance, will be comprehensible to children reading at the fourth or fifth grade level, whereas the article "Sex" (quoted from in the preceding paragraph) obviously requires more advanced reading skills. This suggests that the articles have been written to grade level, but there is no evidence that the editors tested the articles for readability at various grade levels or used a controlled vocabulary.

Generally speaking, the encyclopedia's writing style tends to be clear but uninspired. The first paragraph of the article "Computer" gives a fair sense of that style:

> A computer is a machine that works according to a program (instructions) to carry out "tasks" on data (information) that has been given, or entered in, to it. The tasks can be calculations with numbers; the compilation of information from data stored within it (such as the payment records of a company's customers); the recognition of shapes contained in pictures or patterns contained in music.

The aforementioned "Reference Index" (volume 20), which is carefully constructed and relatively simple to use, furnishes quick and easy access to the encyclopedia's contents, including illustrations. In the section "How to Use the Index," the editors characterize the index as "a tool for finding a needle in a haystack," an apt metaphor young students will understand. The index contains about 40,000 entries and is analytical—that is, the index not only refers the reader to the main article where the topic is discussed but identifies related articles that treat some aspect of the topic. *Example*: The index entry

"Dinosaur" gives a citation to the main article, in this case "Dinosaur" in Volume 6, followed by subentries citing articles where additional material on dinosaurs can be found: "Extinct Animals," "Fossil," "Geological History," "Mammal," "Prehistoric Life," "Reptile," and "Skeleton." Finding related information in the encyclopedia is also enhanced by numerous cross-references (printed in large capital letters) found within and at the end of articles; e.g., the article on Edmond Halley contains a *see* reference to "COMET."

Children's Britannica unfortunately lacks bibliographies, or lists of recommended sources of information for further study, such as books and educational films. An encyclopedia is often just the first step in finding information about a topic, and most good ones will include suggested titles indicating where to look next. Certainly, the editors of *Children's Britannica* would improve the encyclopedia's usefulness as an information resource for students as well as parents and teachers if, when preparing the next edition, they added some basic bibliographies.

Illustrations, which account for about 30 percent of the set's total text, tend to be, in the words of reviewer James Rettig (*Wilson Library Bulletin*, November 1988, p. 122), "a mixed bag." Some are in color, but black-and-white photographs and diagrams predominate. Some are quite good, such as those accompanying the article "Popular Music"; in other instances, the illustrations are drab, dull, and not terribly informative, as in "Dinosaur" where the prehistoric beasts are depicted in small drawings that lack both color and detail. Like its predecessor, BRITANNICA JUNIOR ENCYCLOPAEDIA, *Children's Britannica* attaches a sizable world atlas near the end of the set. Found in volume 19, the 160-page atlas is prepared by Rand McNally and includes individual maps for the U.S. states and Canadian provinces.

Physically, *Children's Britannica* lacks the aesthetic appeal of its major competitor, the NEW BOOK OF KNOWLEDGE. Bill Katz, a well-known expert on reference materials, puts it this way: "Actually, it [*Children's Britannica*] is not a real challenge to the *New Book of Knowledge*. While basically sound and relatively accurate, it is drab and lacks the flair of the other set" (*Basic Information Sources*, 6th ed., 1992, p. 254). Especially weak is the unimaginative page layout, exacerbated by the many dull illustrations. On the other hand, the typefaces used are quite readable and the binding, which features strong cord stitching inside the spine, is attractive and durable.

REPORT CARD: CHILDREN'S BRITANNICA

TOPIC	COVERAGE	ACCURACY	RECENCY	CLARITY
Computers	B	A	B	A
Halloween	C	A	B	A
Johnson, Magic	F*	NA	NA	NA
Measles	C	A	A	A
Nuclear Energy	B	A	B	A
Panda Bears	C	B	B	A
Rock Music	A	A	A	B
Rose (Flower)	B	A	B	A
Russia	A	A	A	A
Sex Education	B	A	A	A

A = Excellent; **B** = Above Average; **C** = Average; **D** = Below Average; **F** = Poor; **NA** = Not Applicable
*No Article

SUMMARY

Children's Britannica, a British import that strongly resembles the now defunct BRITANNICA JUNIOR ENCYCLOPAEDIA and competes head-to-head with the larger and superior NEW BOOK OF KNOWLEDGE, attempts to provide international coverage of basic knowledge and information for young people ages 7–14 in all English-speaking countries. The effort is not entirely successful. Problems include overemphasis on British topics (people, places, etc.), widely divergent reading levels, lack of vocabulary control, an uninspiring writing style, lack of bibliographies, and too many drab illustrations and a lackluster layout. On the plus side, the encyclopedia is trustworthy, usually up-to-date, impartial in its presentation of information, and well organized for quick and easy access to specific facts and topics, although children and younger students might be confused by the need to consult two alphabets. Also, unlike its predecessor, BRITANNICA JUNIOR, *Children's Britannica* does not shy away from controversial or potentially sensitive subjects, such as drugs and human sexuality. The bottom line: A solid, stolid, stodgy encyclopedia.

OTHER OPINIONS

Basic Information Sources by William A. Katz (vol. 1 of *Introduction to Reference Work*, 6th ed., New York: McGraw-Hall, 1992), pp. 254–55; *Reference Books Bulletin* (in *Booklist*), September 15, 1993, p. 174 (unsigned review); *Reference Sources for Small and Medium-Sized Libraries* (5th ed., Chicago: American Library Assn., 1992), p. 30 (review by Jovian P. Lang); *Wilson Library Bulletin*, November 1988, pp. 121–22 (review by James Rettig).

COMPTON'S ENCYCLOPEDIA

FACTS

Full Title: *Compton's Encyclopedia & Fact-Index*. **Editor:** Dale Good. **Publisher:** Compton's Learning Company, a Tribune Publishing Company. **Former Title**: *Compton's Pictured Encyclopedia* (1922–67). **Date Published:** First published as *Compton's Encyclopedia & Fact-Index* in 1968; new printing with revisions published annually.

Electronic Versions: COMPTON'S CONCISE ENCYCLOPEDIA (CD-ROM); COMPTON'S ENCYCLOPEDIA (ONLINE); COMPTON'S FAMILY ENCYCLOPEDIA (CD-ROM), COMPTON'S INTERACTIVE ENCYCLOPEDIA (CD-ROM); COMPTON'S MULTIMEDIA ENCYCLOPEDIA (CD-ROM).

Volumes: 26. **Words:** 9 million. **Pages:** 10,590. **Articles:** 34,000 (5,250 main articles; 28,750 brief articles in the "Fact Index"). **Bibliographies:** 450. **Illustrations and Maps:** 22,510. **Cross-references:** 35,500. **Index Entries:** 154,000. **Editorial Staff, Advisers, and Contributors:** 600. **Trim Size:** 7½ × 10 in.

Price and Sales Information: $499.00 retail; $569.00 to schools and libraries. *Compton's Encyclopedia* is sold to individual consumers through authorized sales representatives of the publisher, Compton's Learning Company. For additional information about the set or to order it, call toll-free 1-

800-858-4895 or write Compton's Learning Company, 2 Prudential Plaza (Suite 2625), 180 North Stetson Avenue, Chicago, IL 60601-6790.

Compton's is currently sold to educational institutions (schools, libraries, etc.) through Encyclopaedia Britannica Educational Corporation (EBEC). For additional information or to place an order, call toll-free 1-800-544-9862 or write EBEC, Britannica Centre, 310 South Michigan Avenue, Chicago, IL 60604. Educators and librarians receive a substantial discount off the retail price when ordering Compton's for their personal use. Call toll-free 1-800-382-FACT for further information or to place an order.

Compton's is also now sold in some independent and university bookstores around the country, including book departments in large department stores. Major national bookstore chains, however, do not carry the encyclopedia. Interested consumers should check directly with the bookstores in their area to determine which, if any, stores sell Compton's.

Compton's is also sold via mail order. Consumers receive Volume 1 free and purchase the remaining 25 volumes on a month-by-month basis at a rate of $19.95 per volume plus $1.39 for shipping and handling. Such offers are made through direct mail or telephone solicitation.

EVALUATION

The 26-volume *Compton's Encyclopedia* is one of the few general encyclopedia available today that successfully bridges the gap between younger and older readers. Specifically, it is designed to meet the needs of older students and adults seeking quick reference information or a readable overview of an unfamiliar subject, but it can also sometimes be used profitably by children and younger students in the upper elementary grades. A detailed review of *Compton's* appears in the section "Medium-Sized Encyclopedia for Adults and Older Students" in this guide beginning on page 60. The much briefer evaluation here concentrates on the encyclopedia as a source of knowledge and information for young people.

Compton's furnishes adequate coverage of all basic areas of knowledge, including those of interest to children and younger students, as the Report Card shows (see below). Coverage is loosely based on subjects taught in North American elementary and secondary schools, although the editors do not attempt as close or systematic a study of school curricula as rival WORLD BOOK ENCYCLOPEDIA, which also appeals to both younger and older students. *Compton's* places par-

ticular emphasis on scientific and geographic topics, but considerable attention is also devoted to non-academic subjects of interest to young people, such as team sports, swimming, hunting, board games, marbles, hobbies, clothing, dolls, cooking, cosmetics, the circus, magic, movies, popular music, driving an automobile, and sexual development.

Information in *Compton's* can be relied upon as accurate and timely. The set became quite dated in the 1970s and early 1980s, but a massive revision project completed over the past decade has revived the encyclopedia and made it once again competitive with the best titles in its class. In the past, controversial or sensitive subjects were often ignored or treated gingerly, but today the encyclopedia deals with such topics in a direct, mature, and unbiased manner. *Example:* The article "Sexuality" describes sexual fantasies in this way:

> Sexual fantasy or daydreaming is another aspect of human sexuality. This commonly used outlet for sexual feeling can be pleasurable, humorous, and even satisfying. It can also include imagined hostility and behaviors that, if acted upon, would be harmful. Some people feel that portrayals of sex and violence on television and in cinema and music, encour-

age more sex and violence in real life. There are recorded fantasies of sexual experience with every possible object, animal, or person. During fantasy, the person becomes sexually aroused but usually has no intention of acting out the fantasy.

Many younger students will doubtless have difficulty comprehending portions of the encyclopedia's text. Just as it is not curriculum oriented in any hard-and-fast way, *Compton's* is not written to grade level, nor does it employ a controlled vocabulary. Editor Dale Good explains in his preface: "By choosing not to limit the vocabulary of its articles to restrictive word lists, *Compton's* challenges and inspires readers of all ages." As noted in the longer review of the encyclopedia on page 64, this statement can be viewed as either a carefully considered educational position or as a bit of editorial sophistry. In any case, the lack of vocabulary control and precise readability standards in *Compton's* means that students in the elementary and even junior high school grades who possess average reading skills will find much of the encyclopedia's text beyond their capabilities.

On the other hand, *Compton's* does provide some important features designed to aid reader comprehension. Potentially new or difficult terms are often explained in context (although such terms are no longer italicized as they were until quite recently). Some articles—"Computer" and "Genetics" are examples—include glossaries that succinctly define technical vocabulary. Another useful (though less apparent) device to enhance and expand the encyclopedia's readability is its "pyramid" style of article writing—that is, articles begin with the easiest or most elementary facts and become more detailed and complicated as the text progresses. The pyramid technique allows children and younger students to read and comprehend practically any article in the encyclopedia— up to a point. When, or if, the article becomes too complex or dense, readers (no matter what their age) will naturally desist.

The article "Computer" provides a good example of the pyramid style. It begins:

> Generally, any device that can perform numerical calculations—even an adding machine, an abacus, or a slide rule—may be called a computer. Currently, however, the term usually refers to an electronic device that can use a list of instructions, called a program, to perform calculations or to store, manipulate, and retrieve information.

Ten pages later the reader learns:

> The invention of the transistor in 1948 brought about a revolution in computer development. Hot, unreliable vacuum tubes were replaced by small germanium (later silicon) transistors that generated little heat yet functioned perfectly as switches or amplifiers (*see* Transistor).
>
> The breakthrough in computer miniaturization came in 1958, when Jack Kilby, an American engineer, designed the first true integrated circuit. His prototype consisted of a germanium wafer that included transistors, resistors, and capacitors—the major components of electronic circuitry. Using less expensive silicon chips, engineers succeeded in putting more and more electronic components on each chip. The development of large-scale integration (LSI) made it possible to cram hundreds of components on a chip; very-large-scale integration (VLSI) increased that number to hundreds of thousands; and engineers project that ultra-large-scale integration (ULSI) techniques will allow as many as 10 million components to be placed on a microchip the size of a fingernail.

Obviously, most young readers—unless they are Bill Gates wannabes—will find much of the computer article in *Compton's*, which runs to 12 pages, overwhelming. Yet the initial paragraphs will be understandable to students reading at the fourth or fifth grade level.

Compton's contains more than 5,000 main articles in Volumes 1–25. Arranged alphabetically, they are mostly of the broad-entry type. For example, the topic of measles does not have its own entry but is covered in the articles "Disease," "Plagues and Epidemics," and "Vaccines." The encyclopedia also contains almost 29,000 very brief A-to-Z articles in Volume 26. Called the "Fact Index," this volume covers people, places, events, and other subjects not found in Volumes 1–25. Access to specific topics and facts in the encyclopedia is excellent, accomplished chiefly through the "Fact Index," which, as its name implies, functions as both a source of factual information and an index to the set. Younger readers, however, may become confused by the dual purpose of the "Fact Index"; indeed, most children avoid or have trouble with even the simplest indexes. Another source of potential confusion by younger users is the need to consult two alphabets (Volumes 1–25 and Volume 26) for articles.

During the dark days of the 1970s and early 1980s when *Compton's* became noticeably stagnant, the set's illustrations were a particular embarrassment. Dull, drab, and dated, they served as a constant reminder of just how far the set had fallen from its glory days, when excellence in illustrations, or "pictures," was a distinguishing feature of *Compton's*. Happily, today the set's graphics have been greatly improved, a result of the revitalization program carried out in the 1980s and continued into the current decade. Many new informative illustrations, most in color, have been added to *Compton's* in recent years, thus rendering its text more attractive, interesting, and understandable to readers, especially younger ones who might not always understand the words but will appreciate and learn from the pictures.

SUMMARY

Compton's Encyclopedia, like its longtime rival the WORLD BOOK ENCYCLOPEDIA, successfully serves both younger and older students as well as adults. Although *Compton's* (unlike WORLD BOOK) lacks a controlled vocabulary and is not written to grade level, it often defines potentially new or difficult words in context and employs the "pyramid" style of writing, which allows people of almost any age and reading skill to use at least portions of the encyclopedia profitably.

Coverage, which is based loosely on North American school curricula, tends to be well balanced, with scientific and geographic subjects emphasized. Nonschool topics of interest to young people also receive generous attention. Articles are usually up-to-date, thanks to a massive revision effort carried out during the past 10 or so years; likewise, controversial subjects are no longer avoided, but treated in a straightforward, mature, impartial fashion. Illustrations, a particularly rich source of information for children and younger students, have also been much improved in recent years. Access to material in the encyclopedia is excellent, although some children and younger students may be confused by the dual-purpose "Fact Index" and the set's two alphabets. The bottom line: Consumers seeking an encyclopedia for the entire family would do well to look seriously at the current edition of *Compton's*.

OTHER OPINIONS

American Reference Books Annual, 1990, pp. 19–20 (review by Bohdan S. Wynar); *Basic Information Sources* by William A. Katz (vol. 1 of *Introduction to Reference Work*, 6th ed., New York: McGraw-Hill, 1992), pp. 251–53; *Reference Books Bulletin* (in *Booklist*), September 15, 1993, pp. 176–78 (unsigned review); *Reference Sources for Small and Medium-Sized Libraries* (5th ed., Chicago: American Library Assn., 1992), p. 31 (review by Jovian P. Lang).

REPORT CARD: COMPTON'S ENCYCLOPEDIA

TOPIC	COVERAGE	ACCURACY	RECENCY	CLARITY
Computers	A	A	A	C
Halloween	A	A	A	B
Johnson, Magic	A	A	A	A
Measles	C	A	A	B
Nuclear Energy	A	A	A	C
Panda Bears	A	A	A	A
Rock Music	A	A	A	B
Rose (Flower)	A	A	A	B
Russia	A	A	A	A
Sex Education	A	A	A	B

A = Excellent; **B** = Above Average; **C** = Average; **D** = Below Average; **F** = Poor; **NA** = Not applicable

COMPTON'S PRECYCLOPEDIA

FACTS

Full Title: *Compton's Precyclopedia: Based on The Young Children's Encyclopedia.* **Editor in Chief:** Howard L. Goodkind. **Chief Text Editor:** Ryerson Johnson. **Art Director:** Will Gallagher. **Publisher:** Encyclopaedia Britannica, Inc. Former Title: *Compton's Young Children's Precyclopedia* (1971). **Date Published:** First published as *Compton's Precyclopedia* in 1973; revised periodically, most recently in 1988.

Also published as the YOUNG CHILDREN'S ENCYCLOPEDIA.

Volumes: 16 (plus paperbound volume entitled *Teaching Guide and Index to Compton's Precyclopedia*). **Words:** 350,000. **Pages:** 2,944. **Articles:** 650. **Bibliographies:** None. **Illustrations and Maps:** 2,425. **Cross-references:** 500. **Index Entries:** 800. **Editorial Staff, Advisers, and Contributors:** 186. **Trim Size:** 7¾ × 9¼ in.

Price and Sales Information: $289.00 plus shipping and handling. *Compton's Precyclopedia* is currently sold to educational institutions (schools, libraries, etc.) through authorized sales representatives of Encyclopaedia Britannica Educational Corporation (EBEC). It is not sold to individual consumers, although the YOUNG CHILDREN'S ENCYCLOPEDIA (which has the same text) is available. For additional information or to place an order, call toll-free 1-800-544-9862 or write EBEC, Britannica Centre, 310 South Michigan Avenue, Chicago, IL 60604.

CONSUMER NOTE

The 16-volume *Compton's Precyclopedia* originally appeared in 1971 as the *Compton's Young Children's Precyclopedia*, a publication of Encyclopaedia Britannica, Inc. Two years later the set's title was shortened to *Compton's Precyclopedia*. It has been mini- mally revised several times, most recently in 1988. Written for children ages 4–10, the *Precyclopedia* is not a true encyclopedia— that is, it does not attempt comprehensive or systematic coverage of knowledge and information. Rather, it is a beginning reference set designed to introduce "primary school and preschool children to the fun of reading and discovery" (publisher's catalog).

As the set's subtitle indicates, the *Precyclopedia* is "based on" the YOUNG CHILDREN'S ENCYLOPEDIA, a 16-volume work first published in 1970 by Encyclopaedia Britannica as a mail-order and supermarket product for use in the home. Actually, the two titles have exactly the same contents, with two minor differences: (1) the *Precyclopedia*, which is aimed at the school and library market, includes a 24-page "Things to Do" section at the beginning of each volume, whereas YOUNG CHILDREN'S does not; and (2) the *Precyclopedia* comes with a 110-page paperbound supplement entitled *Teaching Guide and Index to Compton's Precyclopedia*, whereas YOUNG CHILDREN'S has no manual (or index).

In July 1993, Encyclopaedia Britannica, Inc. sold its *Compton's* properties—including COMPTON'S ENCYCLOPEDIA, COMPTON'S MULTIMEDIA ENCYCLOPEDIA, and *Compton's Precyclopedia*—to the Chicago-based Tribune Company. Encyclopaedia Britannica, however, continues to own the rights to the YOUNG CHILDREN'S ENCYCLOPE-DIA, which the company now plans to sell in both the home and educational markets. As far as the *Precyclopedia* is concerned, it will continue to be sold by Encyclopaedia Britannica until the inventory of the 1988 edition is exhausted, at which time it will probably disappear from the market; at this point, all indications are that the Tribune Company has no interest in maintaining the title.

For a detailed evaluation of the contents of *Compton's Precyclopedia*, see the YOUNG CHILDREN'S ENCYCLOPEDIA (page 210).

GOLDEN BOOK ENCYCLOPEDIA

FACTS

Full Title: *The Golden Book Encyclopedia.* **Editor in Chief:** Lawrence T. Lorimer. **Publisher:** Western Publishing Company. **Distributors:** Donovan Music and Toy Company (Trade Edition); Children's Press (School and Library Edition). Date Published: First published in 1959; revised periodically, most recently in 1988.

Electronic Version: FIRST CONNECTIONS: THE GOLDEN BOOK ENCYCLOPEDIA (CD-ROM).

Volumes: 20 (plus spiral-bound volume entitled *101 Ways to Use the Golden Book Encyclopedia*). **Words:** 650,000. **Pages:** 1,920. **Articles:** 1,500. **Bibliographies:** One. **Illustrations and Maps:** 2,900. **Cross-references:** 4,000. **Index Entries:** 7,000. Editorial Staff, Advisers, and Contributors: 56. **Trim Size:** 7½ × 10 in.

Price and Sales Information: $85.00 Trade Edition; $59.95 (plus 5 percent shipping and handling) School and Library Edition. *The Golden Book Encyclopedia* is currently sold to individual consumers and educational institutions (schools, libraries, etc.) through two distributors. Donovan Music and Toy Company sells the Trade Edition, intended for use in the home. For additional information or to place an order, call toll-free 1-800-236-7123 or write Donovan, 732 Clinton Street, Waukesha, WI 53186. Children's Press sells the School and Library Edition, intended for use in educational institutions. For additional information or to place an order, call toll-free 1-800-621-1115 or write Children's Press, 5440 North Cumberland Avenue, Chicago, IL 60656-1469.

EVALUATION

The multivolume *Golden Book Encyclopedia* is a heavily illustrated reference work aimed at children ages 7–14 and specifically at students in grades 3–6. The encyclopedia first appeared in 1959 in 16 volumes and was minimally revised in 1961 and again in 1969. It went out of print in 1978 and remained off the market until 1988, when the set received a complete overhaul and was expanded to 20 volumes. The 1988 edition, the most recent available, was prepared by the Macmillan Educational Corporation, then publisher of COLLIER'S ENCYCLOPEDIA and many important subject encyclopedias, in cooperation with Western Publishing Company, the encyclopedia's publisher. Western is best known for its colorfully illustrated children's books, including the Golden Books line.

The *Golden Book Encyclopedia* has never been regarded as a first-class encyclopedia, but the 1988 edition represents a substantial improvement over previous revisions. The editor in chief, Lawrence Lorimer (then of Macmillan and now editorial director at Grolier, Inc.), is an experienced hand at making encyclopedias. Editorial staffers (from both Macmillan and Western), consultants, and contributors—56 names in all—are identified at the beginning of Volume 1. Mostly teachers and writers, the consultants and contributors bring sound credentials to the work; the articles, however, are not signed.

The encyclopedia's volumes are very thin, each containing only 96 pages, for a total of 1,920 pages in the set, which is quite small compared with such competing works as the NEW BOOK OF KNOWLEDGE and CHILDREN'S BRITANNICA. The set's 1,500 articles, which average just over a page in length, cover all areas of knowledge, with emphasis on subjects studied in the upper elementary grades. Although coverage tends to be broad, treatment is often quite perfunctory.

As might be expected, considerable attention is accorded prominent historical figures, such as Jane Addams, Alexander the Great, John James Audubon, Clara Barton, Copernicus, Jefferson Davis, Hernando De Soto, Henry Ford, Homer, Napoleon, Sir Walter Raleigh, Walter Reed, Booker T. Washington, George Washington, and Brigham Young. In the case of U.S. presidents, only the most famous or popular have separate articles; others are very briefly covered in "Presidents of the U.S." For instance, Lyndon Johnson has his own article, Andrew Johnson does not.

Major places—continents, powerful countries, U.S. states, Canadian provinces, large cities around the world—also receive good coverage. On the other hand, smaller, less important countries are covered in regional articles where they receive quite superficial treatment. *Example:* Nicaragua is covered in the article "Central America," which includes a simple map of the region, a chart listing each Central American country and its capital, geographical size, and population, and a sentence or two about each country: "Nicaragua is the largest Central American country. Most of its people live in the Pacific coastal region, where the country's biggest cities and farms are located." This is the sum total of information about Nicaragua in the encyclopedia.

Information in the set is normally reliable and presented in an impartial manner. Unlike earlier editions, the encyclopedia today does not avoid all controversial or sensitive topics. For instance, the articles "Alcohol," "Addiction," "Drugs and Medicines," and "Tobacco" deal with both licit and illicit drugs in a straightforward way; the article "Nuclear Power" contains a fair amount of material on the safety issue, including mention of the accidents at Three Mile Island and Chernobyl. But information concerning human sexuality—a subject of natural interest and concern to students in the elementary grades—remains very much on the "birds and bees" level; nowhere in the *Golden Book Encyclopedia* will the reader encounter such words as *abortion, menstruation,* or *masturbation.*

As noted, the encyclopedia was last revised in 1988. Most articles remain reasonably current, as in the case of "Rock Music," which mentions music videos on cable television and such performers as Michael Jackson and Madonna. Where the set shows its age most clearly is in articles on countries where political reform or revolution has drastically altered the current situation. It is strange, for example, to read "Germany is not one country, but two—West Germany and East Germany" or that "The Soviet Union is the most important and powerful communist country in the world. Its government keeps tight control over the way people work and live." When the encyclopedia will be revised next is not known at this time, but the fact that an electronic version is now available (see FIRST CONNECTIONS) suggests that revisions may become more frequent.

As the Report Card (see next page) indicates, clarity is one of the encyclopedia's strong suits. Articles are normally written in a clear, easy-to-understand manner that relies on a simple sentence structure. There is no evidence that the editors have used a controlled vocabulary or that the articles are written to grade level. On the other hand, potentially unfamiliar or difficult words are italicized and defined in context; for instance, the article "Computer" contains 24 italicized terms, including *mainframe computers, minicomputers, microcomputers, input, output, hardware, processing unit, monitor, disk drives, software, programs,* and *data.* Also, some articles include a brief glossary that defines technical terms. The first two paragraphs of the article "Computer" give a fair idea of the encyclopedia's writing style:

A computer is a machine that can compute—do arithmetic. Computers, however, do much more than arithmetic. They can follow complicated directions. Some of these directions are built into the machine. Others are supplied in other ways. Combining arithmetic with other simple operations lets computers perform many different kinds of tasks.

Computers decide when traffic lights switch from red to green. They help care for patients in hospitals. They keep track of overdue library books. Some people use computers to play games or to make music. Teachers use computers in their classrooms to help them teach and to keep track of students' grades.

Access to the contents of the encyclopedia is quite satisfactory, facilitated by a network of some 4,000 cross-references and a 7,000-entry index found at the end of volume 20. The only problem with the index is that it fails to index the set's many illustrations. *Example:* The index entry "O'Connor, Sandra Day" refers the reader to the article on Ronald Reagan in volume 15, where his appointment of Judge O'Connor to the U.S. Supreme Court is discussed, but there is no entry in the index indicating that there is a captioned photo of the judge in the article "Women's Rights" in volume 20.

In their introduction called "Welcome to the Golden Book Encyclopedia" in volume 1, the editors say, "The information in the *Golden Book Encyclopedia* can give you a head start in learning. It can be a steppingstone to other books and materials about subjects that are exciting to you." After these words one might assume the editors would provide bibliographies recommending additional books and materials for the young reader, but such is not the case. Only the article "Children's Books" contains a bibliography which lists 45 children's classics.

Approximately a third of the encyclopedia's total text is devoted to illustrations, including photographs, diagrams, charts, and maps, most of which are in color. Although often striking and informative, the illustrations are by no means picture perfect.

Color reproduction tends to be brassy and florid, due at least in part to the use of a cheap grade of paper, and some black-and-white photos are too dark or blurry to be effective. A review in *Reference Books Bulletin* (in *Booklist*, November 1, 1989, p. 608) makes a similar criticism: "Many of the pictures are large, taking up as much as half the page. While most of the illustrations are attractive, some of the photographs are in poor focus."

The encyclopedia's physical format is satisfactory. Almost every page has some color and the layout, while not as engaging as that found in such competing sets as the GROLIER CHILDREN'S ENCYCLOPEDIA or the OXFORD CHILDREN'S ENCYCLOPEDIA, will not turn children off or away. The encyclopedia is published in two bindings, the Trade Edition binding intended chiefly for use in the home and the School and Library Edition binding for educational institutions. The latter is a reinforced binding designed to withstand very heavy use.

SUMMARY

First published in 1959 and thoroughly revised in 1988, the *Golden Book Encyclopedia* has never been considered an encyclopedia of first importance. Containing only 1,920 pages in 20 thin volumes, the encyclopedia is too small and superficial to compete effectively with larger, better made sets for young people like the NEW BOOK OF KNOWLEDGE, CHILDREN'S BRITANNICA, COMPTON'S ENCYCLOPEDIA, and the WORLD BOOK ENCYCLOPEDIA.

Also on the negative side, the encyclopedia has become dated in some areas, it lacks bibliographies, and the illustrations are not top quality. Still, the set is reliable, very clearly written, and well organized. A welcome sign for the future of the encyclopedia is its recent appearance in electronic form under the title FIRST CONNECTIONS. The bottom line: Despite its many flaws, the *Golden Book Encyclopedia* is not a bad buy for under $100.00.

OTHER OPINIONS

American Reference Books Annual, 1990, p. 22 (review by Anna Grace Patterson); *Reference Books Bulletin* (in *Booklist*), November 1, 1989, p. 608 (unsigned review).

REPORT CARD: GOLDEN BOOK ENCYCLOPEDIA				
TOPIC	COVERAGE	ACCURACY	RECENCY	CLARITY
Computers	A	A	B	A
Halloween	C	A	C	A
Johnson, Magic	F*	NA	NA	NA
Measles	C	A	B	A
Nuclear Energy	B	A	B	A
Panda Bears	C	A	B	A
Rock Music	A	A	B	A
Rose (Flower)	F*	NA	NA	NA
Russia	C	C	D	A
Sex Education	D	A	D	A

A = Excellent; **B** = Above Average; **C** = Average; **D** = Below Average; **F** = Poor; **NA** = Not Applicable
*No Article

GROLIER CHILDREN'S ENCYCLOPEDIA

FACTS

Full Title: *The Grolier Children's Encyclopedia.* **Editor:** John Paton. **Publisher:** Grolier Educational Corporation. **Former Titles:** *The Doubleday Children's Encyclopedia* (Doubleday, 1990; 4 vols.); FINDING OUT: SILVER BURDETT'S CHILDREN'S ENCYCLOPEDIA (Silver Burdett Company, 1981; 10 vols.). **Date Published:** 1993.

Also published as the KINGFISHER CHILDREN'S ENCYCLOPEDIA (Kingfisher Books, 1992; one vol.).

Volumes: 10. **Words:** 250,000. **Pages:** 816. **Articles:** 1,300. **Bibliographies:** None. **Illustrations and Maps:** 2,000. **Cross-references:** 1,500. **Index Entries:** 6,000. **Editorial Staff, Advisers, and Contributors:** 6. **Trim Size:** 7½ × 10¼ in.

Price and Sales Information: $219.00. The *Grolier Children's Encyclopedia* is sold to educational institutions (schools, libraries, etc.) by authorized representatives of the Grolier Educational Corporation. It is not sold to individual consumers, although the single-volume KINGFISHER CHILDREN'S ENCYCLOPEDIA (which has the same text) is available through bookstores and similar retail outlets. For additional information or to place an order, call toll-free 1-800-243-7256 or write Grolier Educational Corporation, Sherman Turnpike, Danbury, CT 06816.

CONSUMER NOTE

The *Grolier Children's Encyclopedia* has exactly the same text as the KINGFISHER CHILDREN'S ENCYCLOPEDIA, a one-volume work published in 1992 by Kingfisher Books. The major differences between the two encyclopedias, aside from their titles, are (1) the number of volumes, (2) the price, and (3) the intended consumer. Also, the Grolier set has a reinforced library binding, which the Kingfisher book lacks. Still, the *Grolier Children's Encyclopedia* seems wildly overpriced at $219.00 when the one-volume edition sells for a modest $29.95.

For more on the contents of the *Grolier Children's Encyclopedia*, see the KINGFISHER CHILDREN'S ENCYCLOPEDIA, (page 228).

NEW BOOK OF KNOWLEDGE

FACTS

Full Title: *The New Book of Knowledge.* **Editorial Director:** Lawrence T. Lorimer. **Editor in Chief:** Gerry Gabianelli. **Publisher:** Grolier Inc. **Former Title:** *The Book of Knowledge: The Children's Encyclopedia* (1912–65). **Date Published:** First published as the *New Book of Knowledge* in 1966; new printing with revisions published annually.

Volumes: 21 (plus paperbound volume entitled *Home and School Reading and Study Guide*). **Words:** 6.8 million. **Pages:** 10,600. **Articles:** 14,000 (9,000 main articles; 5,000 brief articles in the "Dictionary Index"). **Bibliographies:** 1,000. **Illustrations and Maps:** 25,000. **Cross-references:** 3,700.

Index Entries: 85,000. **Editorial Staff, Advisers, and Contributors:** 1,850. **Trim Size:** 7¾ × 10 in.

Price and Sales Information: $995.00 retail; $679.00 to schools and libraries. The *New Book of Knowledge* is sold to individual consumers and educational institutions (schools, libraries, etc.) through authorized sales representatives of the publisher. The set is not sold in bookstores or similar retail outlets. For additional information about the set or to order it, individual consumers should call 1-203-796-2602 (not a toll-free number) or write Grolier Inc., Sherman Turnpike, Danbury, CT 06816. Educational institutions should call toll-free 1-800-243-7256 or write Grolier Educational Corporation at the same address.

EVALUATION

The alphabetically arranged *New Book of Knowledge* first appeared in 1966, replacing the popular topically arranged *Book of Knowledge* (1912–65), which in turn derived from the British *Children's Encyclopaedia* edited by Arthur Mee, widely regarded as the first modern encyclopedia for children. Intended generally for young people ages 7–14 and particularly for students in grades 3–6, the *New Book of Knowledge* is a product of Grolier Inc., a leading North American publisher of reference materials and one of the largest publishers of encyclopedias in the world. The *New Book of Knowledge* is the smallest of Grolier's three most important general encyclopedias, the others being the medium-sized ACADEMIC AMERICAN ENCYCLOPEDIA and the large ENCYCLOPEDIA AMERICANA.

The *New Book of Knowledge* furnishes extensive and very well balanced coverage of basic knowledge and information. Its contents broadly reflect North American elementary school curricula, as well as extra-curricular and out-of-school interests of young people. The editors' preface clearly sets forth the encyclopedia's scope:

> The *New Book of Knowledge* will be useful to a wide range of readers, starting with preschool children and including students in school up to the age when they are ready for an adult encyclopedia. For the very young child there are carefully selected illustrations that will catch attention and provide early background, as will the various games and activities and the story material composed of recognized classics. Parents will find material to read aloud to preschool children, both for pleasure and as answers to their questions. Students will find a wealth of information and a clarification of concepts that will be useful in their schoolwork. Activities, projects, and experiments are incorporated in order to increase the educational value of subject articles. The content of the encyclopedia was selected by educators who analyzed the curriculum requirements of school systems across the nation and by librarians familiar with the research needs of children. The encyclopedia is designed for the library and the classroom as well as for educational use at home.

The arts and humanities are especially well covered in the *New Book of Knowledge*. Articles on literary topics, for example, frequently include selections from children's literature, such as the *Arabian Nights* stories, the *Cinderella* fairy tale, the poem *Paul Revere's Ride*, and excerpts from the novel *Little Women* by Louisa May Alcott and folktales portraying the exploits of John Henry, Johnny Appleseed, and Pecos Bill. In all, the set contains more than 150 literary selections. Jovian Lang, in a review of the set in *Reference Sources for Small and Medium-Sized Libraries* (5th ed., American Library Assn., 1992, p. 33), makes this related point: "A unique feature is that unlike other, purely curriculum oriented, student encyclopedias, more entertaining articles are written in the first person; for example, Danny Kaye reminisces about his enjoyment of Hans Christian Andersen, and the story 'The Emperor's New Clothes' immediately follows."

In a similar vein, the article "Folk Music" provides samples of the genre, e.g., *Git Along Little Dogies.* Also, survey articles offering a broad perspective on national and regional cultural developments around the world expand the set's humanities coverage, as seen in "African Art," "African Literature," and "African Music."

Scientific and technical subjects also receive impressive coverage. Such articles as "Animals," "Birds," "Biomes," "Body, Human," "Computers," "Diseases," "Genetics," "Heat," "Microscopes," "Nuclear Energy," "Numbers and Number Systems," "Planets," "Plants," "Reproduction," "Tides," and "Underwater Exploration" stand out as models of their kind in a children's encyclopedia. They provide substantial, informative summaries of essential information on complex subjects in a manner that young students can readily understand; all are carefully illustrated to promote comprehension, and some include "wonder" questions (with answers) designed to stimulate the reader's imagination while providing basic factual information. The article "Microscopes," for instance, answers the question "How much magnification can a microscope give?" in three edifying paragraphs.

In addition, the encyclopedia includes numerous practical projects and experiments that will interest and challenge most young readers. *Examples:* "How to Build an Ant Observation Nest" (part of the article "Ants"); "Growing Your Own Crystals" (part of "Crystals"); "Building a Snow House" (part of "Eskimos [Inuit]"); and "An Experiment to Show Osmosis" (part of "Osmosis"). Especially valuable in this connection is the 20-page article "Experiments and Other Science Activities," which explains how to set up and record scientific experiments, advises how to prepare for science fairs, and suggests many ideas for projects in every area of science.

When the *New Book of Knowledge* first appeared, a review in *Choice* (May 1967, p. 276) singled out these various features for special commendation: "A variety of activities, science projects, demonstrations, and questions provide points of departure for exploration, thus serving as a useful supplement to teachers who are seeking ways to arouse children's curiosity and to help them express themselves creatively." This observation is as true today as it was over a quarter of a century ago.

The encyclopedia currently contains about 14,000 entries, of which 9,000 are main articles in Volumes 1–20. Arranged alphabetically, these articles form the informational core of the encyclopedia. Almost all of the articles are signed, either by the author or an authority who has reviewed the material. For instance, the article "Birth Control" was written by Dr. Alan Nourse, who has published books on the subject; the article "Baseball" was reviewed by Peter Ueberroth, former Commissioner of Baseball. All of the more than 1,700 contributors and consultants are listed with their credentials at the end of Volume 20.

The remaining 5,000 entries in the encyclopedia are brief articles found in the "Dictionary Index," portions of which are located at the back of each of first 20 volumes. Printed on blue paper to distinguish it from the main body of the encyclopedia, the "Dictionary Index," which is also arranged alphabetically, serves as both a source of quick reference information and an index to the set, similar to the "Reference Index" found in CHILDREN'S BRITANNICA and the "Fact Index" in COMPTON'S ENCYCLOPEDIA. Articles in the index cover people and other topics deemed not important enough or too ephemeral to be included in the encyclopedia proper. For instance, baseball's Pete Rose is relegated to a brief entry in the index, whereas Babe Ruth has an article in the main section of the encyclopedia. Recently, the editors announced that the

"Dictionary Index" will be phased out over the next few years, but for now users of the *New Book of Knowledge* must be aware of it and how it works.

There can be no doubt that the *New Book of Knowledge* is edited with great care. Its information can be trusted as accurate, unbiased, and reasonably up-to-date. In recent years, the encyclopedia has substantially increased its coverage of controversial or sensitive subjects, bringing a much more realistic (as opposed to sugarcoated) view of the world to its pages. Such issues as nuclear power safety, poverty, birth control, abortion, and AIDS are no longer avoided, but treated in a responsible, impartial manner. The article "Abortion," for example, points out that "there is a major debate in the United States about whether abortion is moral and whether or not it should be legal." Likewise, the article "Ethics" notes:

> One group in the abortion dispute argues that an unborn fetus is not yet a separate person able to survive outside the mother's body. They argue that the woman's right to make her own medical decisions is more important than the fetus's right to live. Those opposed to abortion respond that from the very start, a fetus is a human being with full human rights, including the right not to be killed.

An energetic continuous revision program keeps the *New Book of Knowledge* as current as humanly possible. In recent years, hundreds of new articles have been added to the set and many more have been extensively revised. In 1992, the editors announced that, in addition to its usual annual revisions, the encyclopedia would undergo an ambitious five-year redesign on a volume-by-volume basis, during which time the aforementioned "Dictionary Index" would be completely eliminated. Thus far, over half the volumes have been restructured.

Prospective purchasers of *New Book of Knowledge* should also be aware that the publisher offers a yearbook designed to help keep the set current. Entitled the *New Book*

of Knowledge Annual, it is a quality product that summarizes events of the previous year, but it has no real editorial connection to the encyclopedia and should not be purchased unless the consumer is convinced it will be used. Too often, such encyclopedia supplements turn out to be little more than dust catchers.

The encyclopedia's articles are written in a clear and easily readable style. A controlled vocabulary is employed, and articles are written to grade level. As noted in the editors' preface, "The Dale-Chall readability formula was used to test the reading level of *The New Book of Knowledge*. Professor Jeanne Chall of Harvard University serves as reading consultant to the encyclopedia. Under her direct supervision many original articles were tested with children to make certain the material was comprehensible, informative, and interesting. The comprehension level of articles whose subjects appeal to younger children is lower, whereas other articles, especially those with a technical vocabulary, are at a higher level."

Special efforts are made to capture the reader's attention from the start with interesting first sentences. The initial paragraphs of the 15-page article "Computers" provide a good example of the encyclopedia's writing style.

> One hundred years from now, when historians look back on the second half of the 20th century, they will probably call it The Information Age. Never before have so many people been able to find out so much about so many things in such a short time. Never before have people been able to organize, analyze, and use information so productively. Never before has machinery been able to work so precisely or to perform such complex tasks. One machine more than any other has made these things possible. That machine is the computer.
> Computers help people do amazing things—explore the planets, look inside living bodies and brains without surgery, create imaginary scenes that look real. Computers also help people do everyday tasks better—organize lists, search through library cata-

logs, and print paychecks or bills. You can find computers in offices, factories, schools, libraries, banks, stores, and game arcades. People have computers in their homes, under the hoods of their cars, in their pockets, and on their wrists.

Another effective (though less apparent) writing technique used in the encyclopedia is the "pyramid" approach, wherein articles begin simply and become more detailed and complex as the text progresses. This allows even the youngest readers to get something from almost every article. For example, toward the end of "Computers" the article's content, vocabulary, and syntax (or sentence structure) are clearly more advanced than at the beginning:

> In research laboratories, we find chips and memory devices that can work faster and store more than products now on the market. Those will produce evolutionary changes (improvements of what we now have) in computer systems. But revolutionary changes (new breakthroughs) are also on the way. Scientists are devising new **computer architectures**—new ways of putting electronic circuits together to perform mathematical and logical tasks. Some supercomputers have a few CPUs, but revolutionary future computers, called **neural networks**, will have hundreds or thousands of individual computing units that automatically form many different interconnections.

Note that the technical terms **computer architectures** and **neural networks**—vocabulary unfamiliar to most if not all the encyclopedia's readership—are printed in **bold type** and defined in context. Altogether, the article contains 70 such words and phrases, including **hardware, software, supercomputers, floppy disks, integrated circuits, random-access memory, magnetic tape, computer simulation, artificial intelligence,** and **expert system**. In addition, the article includes a one-page glossary of frequently used computer terms.

The *New Book of Knowledge* is a well-organized encyclopedia. Locating specific facts and subjects in the set is normally not difficult, due in part to the nearly 4,000

cross-references found throughout the text but mostly to the 85,000-entry index that comprises volume 21. The index pinpoints references to all articles where information can be found on a particular topic. For example, the article "Nuclear Energy" is located in volume 13, but the index cites 22 other articles that contain relevant material, including "Energy Supply," "Fermi, Enrico," and "Submarines." Some consumers, especially teachers and librarians, will be interested to know that the index to the *New Book of Knowledge* is now available on CD-ROM as part of the *Grolier Master Encyclopedia Index*, which also includes the indexes to ENCYCLOPEDIA AMERICANA and the ACADEMIC AMERICAN ENCYCLOPEDIA. The disk sells for $149.00 and works on the major platforms (MS-DOS, Windows, and Macintosh).

The index that makes up volume 21 no longer contains the brief articles found in the "Dictionary Index," which is printed on colored paper at the end of Volumes 1–20. As noted, the "Dictionary Index" is currently being phrased out, a move welcomed by all knowledgeable critics for the simple reason that users of the set will no longer be required to look in two different alphabets for information. A review in *Reference Books Bulletin* (in *Booklist*, September 15, 1993, p. 180) flatly states, "Access will be improved by integrating these entries into the main alphabetical sequence of the encyclopedia." Amen.

The *New Book of Knowledge* has 21 numbered volumes, plus an unnumbered paperback volume entitled *Home and School Reading and Study Guide*. Intended for parents, teachers, and librarians, this 98-page booklet provides graded bibliographies on approximately 1,000 subjects keyed to articles in the encyclopedia. For example, 10 recommended titles are listed under the topic "Computers," with indications of whether they are best suited for primary, intermediate, or advanced readers. The bibliographies are carefully chosen and updated on an annual basis. The only criticism of the bibliographies is expressed in a review by Deborah Taylor in *American Reference Books Annual* (1993, p. 27): "One may prefer that bibliographic entries accompany the articles; however, a separate list provides for yearly revisions, helping to maintain currency." The *Home and School Reading and Study Guide* volume also contains detailed suggestions to parents and teachers about how best to use the encyclopedia as an educational tool at various grade levels.

Illustrations in the *New Book of Knowledge* are, in a word, outstanding. They make up approximately a third of the set's total text; over 90 percent are in color. They include handsomely reproduced diagrams, drawings, cutaways, photographs, original artwork, and maps that add immeasurably to the informational content of the encyclopedia. The article "Computers," for example, is enhanced by 17 photographs showing various aspects of the subject, including the components of a personal computer; the article "Dinosaurs" is accompanied by numerous photos and drawings, all in color. New graphics are added to the set each year, over 1,100 in 1993 alone.

Physically, the set is well made and pleasing to the eye. The two-column page layout has enough variety to keep from becoming stale, and the generous use of white space gives the typical page an appealing, uncluttered appearance. Likewise, the typefaces used are legible and attractive. The volumes are constructed to withstand heavy use. Bright and inviting, the *New Book of Knowledge* is an encyclopedia children respond to with enthusiasm.

SUMMARY

The *New Book of Knowledge* is a worthy successor to the longtime favorite *Book of Knowledge* (1912–65). Designed generally for children ages 7–14 and particularly for students in grades 3–6, the encyclopedia provides excellent coverage of both curriculum-related and out-of-school subjects of interest and concern to young people. Conspicuous strengths include accurate, impartial, and up-to-date information, a clear and interesting writing style, first-class illustrations, and much material (including many literary selections and science projects) that promote intellectual growth and curiosity on the part of young readers. Access to the set's contents, which are highly satisfactory, will be further improved when the "Dictionary Index" is finally eliminated, most likely in 1996. The bottom line: An outstanding encyclopedia for young people.

OTHER OPINIONS

American Reference Books Annual, 1993, pp. 26–27 (review by Deborah A. Taylor); *Basic Information Sources* by William A. Katz (vol. 1 of *Introduction to Reference Work*, 6th ed., New York: McGraw-Hill, 1992), pp. 253–54; *Reference Books Bulletin* (in *Booklist*), September 15, 1993, pp. 180–82 (unsigned review; *Reference Sources for Small and Medium-Sized Libraries* (5th ed., Chicago: American Library Assn., 1992), p. 33 (review by Jovian P. Lang).

REPORT CARD: NEW BOOK OF KNOWLEDGE

TOPIC	COVERAGE	ACCURACY	RECENCY	CLARITY
Computers	A	A	A	A
Halloween	A	A	A	A
Johnson, Magic	D	A	D	A
Measles	B	A	A	A
Nuclear Energy	A	A	A	A
Panda Bears	A	A	A	A
Rock Music	A	A	B	A
Rose (Flower)	B	A	B	A
Russia	A	A	A	A
Sex Education	A	A	A	A

A = Excellent; **B** = Above Average; **C** = Average; **D** = Below Average; **F** = Poor; **NA** = Not Applicable

NEW GROLIER STUDENT ENCYCLOPEDIA

FACTS

Full Title: *The New Grolier Student Encyclopedia*. **Editor in Chief:** Terry Borton. **Senior Project Editor:** Rita D'Apice Gould. **Publisher:** Grolier Educational Corporation. **Date Published:** First published in 1988; revised periodically, most recently in 1992.

Also published as the YOUNG STUDENTS LEARNING LIBRARY.

Volumes: 22 (plus *Discovering Maps: A Young Person's World Atlas*). **Words:** 1.5 million. **Pages:** 2,809. **Articles:** 3,000. **Bibliographies:** None. **Illustrations and Maps:** 5,000. **Cross-references:** 10,000. **Index Entries:** 22,000. **Editorial Staff, Advisers, and**

Contributors: 36. **Trim Size:** 8¼ × 10¾ in.

Price and Sales Information: $359.00. The *New Grolier Student Encyclopedia* is sold to educational institutions (schools, libraries, etc.) by authorized representatives of the Grolier Educational Corporation. It is not sold to individual consumers, although they may purchase the YOUNG STUDENTS LEARNING LIBRARY, which has the same text. For additional information or to place an order, call toll-free 1-800-243-7256 or write Grolier Educational Corporation, Sherman Turnpike, Danbury, CT 06816.

CONSUMER NOTE

The *New Grolier Student Encyclopedia* has exactly the same encyclopedic text as the YOUNG STUDENTS LEARNING LIBRARY. The only differences between the two encyclopedias, aside from their titles, are 1) the price, 2) the intended consumer, and 3) the Grolier work does not include a dictionary as part of

the set. Also, the Grolier title has a reinforced library binding, which the YOUNG STUDENTS LEARNING LIBRARY lacks.

For a detailed evaluation of the contents of the *New Grolier Student Encyclopedia*, see the YOUNG STUDENTS LEARNING LIBRARY.

OXFORD CHILDREN'S ENCYCLOPEDIA

FACTS

Full Title: *Oxford Children's Encyclopedia.* **Editor:** Mary Worrall. **Publisher:** Oxford University Press. **Date Published:** 1991.
Volumes: 7. **Words:** 700,000. **Pages:** 1,648. **Articles:** 2,000. **Bibliographies:** None. **Illustrations and Maps:** 3,000. **Cross-references:** 4,000. **Index Entries:** 15,000. **Editorial Staff, Advisers, and Contributors:** 190. **Trim Size:** 8½ × 10¾ in.

Price and Sales Information: $200.00. Individual consumers can purchase the *Oxford Children's Encyclopedia* in bookstores or, if the set is not in stock, it can be ordered. Similarly, educational institutions (schools, libraries, etc.) can order it through a book wholesaler. To order the encyclopedia directly from the publisher, call toll-free 1-800-451-7556 or write Oxford University Press, 200 Madison Avenue, New York, NY 10016.

EVALUATION

The *Oxford Children's Encyclopedia*, in preparation for more than four years, appeared in Great Britain in 1991. A brand-new work intended for children 7–14, the seven-volume set is published by Oxford University Press, a highly respected British publisher of reference materials and scholarly books. Oxford also publishes a general adult encyclopedia entitled the OXFORD ILLUSTRATED ENCYCLOPEDIA, as well as numerous specialized encyclopedic sources, such as the INTERNATIONAL ENCYCLOPEDIA OF COMMUNICATIONS and the OXFORD COMPANION TO POLITICS OF THE WORLD. In 1993, a 58-volume Braille edition of the *Oxford Children's Encyclopedia* appeared in Great Britain under the imprimatur of the National Library for the Blind.

The *Oxford Children's Encyclopedia* contains about 2,000 articles, which average just under a page in length. Volumes 1–5 cover subjects A-to-Z from "Aborigines of Australia" to "Zulus." Volume 6 is devoted exclusively to biography, covering people from "Abraham" to "Zhou Enlai"; the volume also appends four "special features" offering brief biographies of the current British royal family and contemporary film, mu-

sic, and sports stars. Volume 7 is a comprehensive index to the set. The encyclopedia replaces the publisher's old OXFORD JUNIOR ENCYCLOPAEDIA, a much larger, topically arranged set of 13 volumes that has been out of print since the early 1980s.

In 1992, the *Oxford Children's Encyclopedia* became available in the U.S and Canada, but unlike most British-made encyclopedias sold in North America, no attempt was made to "Americanize" the text, even cosmetically. In the *Oxford Children's Encyclopedia*, for instance, *elevators* are *lifts*, *soccer* is *football*, *automobiles* are *motor cars*, *gasoline* is *petrol*, and the metric system rules. As a result, much criticism of the set on this side of the Atlantic has centered on its Britishness and how that affects its value as a reference source for North American youngsters. Marjorie Lewis, in a review in *School Library Journal* (November 1992, p. 140), makes the point:

> There is no entry for Great Britain, but rather United Kingdom, and downright annoying is the fact that some subjects can be found only by browsing ("Motor Cars" are there, but automobiles are not.) Cross-references from Americanisms to Briticisms are rarely given.

A review in *Reference Books Bulletin* (in *Booklist*, June 15, 1992, p. 1886) offers similar criticism:

> The topic selection for a British audience is evident when comparing such articles as the full page on cricket to the half-page coverage of baseball. There are no cross-references from American to British spelling (e.g., from *Tires* to *Tyres*), and the British usage of the word *millions* where we would use *billions* is confusing in the entry *Planets*. (In American English a billion is a thousand million, while in British English it is a million million.)

Justin Kaplan, writing in the *New York Times Book Review* (May 17, 1992, p. 30), also questions the encyclopedia's general lack of accommodation to American readers:

> Oxford is relatively uncompromising in this respect. It gives all its measurements in metric, and some of its vocabulary (for example, "rowlocks" instead of our "oarlocks") and usage ("the River Mississippi"—under "Mark Twain," of course) may puzzle young American readers. They probably also will have trouble putting together experiments that call for "three barley-sugar sweets" and "a round lump of Blu-Tac (about 7 mm across)."

Most understanding of the North American critics concerning the encyclopedia's British orientation is Canadian reviewer Patty Lawlor, who writes in *Quill & Quire* (June 1992, p. 38):

> There is some potentially unfamiliar British vocabulary (e.g., lorries, pitch, noughts and crosses), but it is minimal and should be considered an opportunity to learn something about people in other places.

Most of the encyclopedia's text concerns subjects of universal interest, with a decided emphasis on specific scientific and technical topics, exemplified by such articles as "Animal Behaviour," "Atoms," "Brakes," "Butterflies," "Comets," "Computers," "Dinosaurs," "Evolution of Living Things," "Food," "Geometry," "Hair," "Leaves," "Locks," "Minerals" "Nuclear Power," "Pandas," "Radar," "Reproduction," "Robots," "Rockets," "Sex," "Space Exploration,"

"Wading Birds," and "Waste Disposal." Humanities and social science topics are adequately covered, more often than not in broad-entry articles, e.g., "Ballet," "Battles," "Churches," "Dance," "Factories," "Jewellery," "Languages," "Money," "Music," "Musical Instruments," "Photography," "Renaissance," "Schools," "Sculpture," "Slaves," "Theatres," and "Women's Movement."

Continents and major countries, oceans, rivers, and mountains of the world also receive a fair amount of coverage in the encyclopedia, but smaller places (states, provinces, counties, cities, etc.) are virtually ignored. Hence the reader looking for information about Wisconsin or Alberta will be disappointed. Coverage of people—limited to volume 6—is quite heavy on British and European luminaries, whereas famous Americans (north and south) receive relatively less notice. For instance, the only Johnson who merits an entry is Amy (the British Amelia Earhart); Andrew and Lyndon (along with Jack and Magic) are among the missing Johnsons. Historical and political coverage tends to be similarly skewed, e.g., the article "Parliaments" is two pages in length, "Congress" a quarter of a page.

It should be noted that topics covered in the encyclopedia were determined not only by the editors and subject specialists but the people who actually use the set— children themselves. Among the principal consultants listed at the beginning of volume 1 are the children and staff of six English primary and middle schools. Editor Mary Worrall explains in her introduction:

> As well as experts, children were consulted. We asked them to note down the topics they wanted to read about. There was a lot of interest in science and technology and so there are many detailed articles on these subjects. Children's choices also helped the team to decide which articles should be the longer ones. The final list was a balance between what the experts thought was important and what children wanted to know.

Information found in the *Oxford Children's Encyclopedia* can be relied upon as accurate, impartial, and current as of mid-1991. Controversial or sensitive subjects—poverty, smoking, environmental pollution, nuclear safety, AIDS, human sexuality, even chart-rigging in the music business—are dealt with in a responsible, straightforward fashion and not ignored or sugarcoated, as sometimes occurs in children's encyclopedias. *Example:* The article "Sex" provides clear, factual explanations of human sexual intercourse and major birth control methods. It also includes a paragraph on sexual responsibility:

> Sexual intercourse is also called "making love," because it can give not only a lot of pleasure but a feeling of being very special to the other partner. Ideally, sexual intercourse and caring for the other partner should always go together. Sexual feelings can be very strong indeed, but people should give their partners a choice in whether or not they make love. Many people believe that couples should make love only when they are married and committed to staying together all their lives.

Articles in the *Oxford Children's Encyclopedia* are normally written in a lucid, readable manner. Although the editors have not used a controlled vocabulary, potentially difficult or unfamiliar terms are usually defined within the article itself. In "Sex," for instance, such words as *genitals, uterus, ova, orgasm, ejaculation, fertilization,* and *conception* are defined in context. As noted, occasionally Briticisms will confuse some North American readers, but few will find it more than a minor irritant. The first two paragraphs of the article "Computers" furnishes a good sense of the encyclopedia's writing style:

> You may have used a computer for playing games. Computers are good for zapping aliens. But they can do many other jobs as well. They can do sums more quickly than a calculator and store more information than a roomful of filing cabinets. They can control machines, fly aircraft and help design cars. The jobs they do depend on the instructions they

are given. Today, almost every office and factory uses computers.

> Modern computers are electronic. They work using tiny electric currents. They have thousands of circuits inside them. Most of the circuits are packed together on tiny slices of silicon about the size of your fingernail. Each slice has a casing around it and is called an integrated circuit or chip.

Finding information in the encyclopedia is normally not difficult. Most articles include cross-references to other articles containing related material. "Computers," for example, includes *see also* references to "Calculators," "Electronics," "Information Technology," "Robots," "Transistors," "Valves," "Word Processors," and "Babbage, Charles." But the principal means of pinpointing specific facts and topics in the set is through the 15,000-entry analytical index in volume 7. Here the entry "Computers" leads the user not only to the main article "Computers" and various related articles but many other places in the encyclopedia where computers are discussed, e.g., the article "Detectives," which describes how criminal investigators use computers in their work. At the end of Volume 7 are a number of lists, including countries and their capitals, prime ministers of Great Britain and other Commonwealth countries, U.S. presidents, U.S. states, and Canadian provinces and territories.

The set does not include bibliographies, or lists of materials to guide readers who wish to go beyond what is offered in the encyclopedia. The editors would do well to include such lists in future editions. As editor Worrall notes in her introduction, "The sum total of all human knowledge is, of course, far too great to be included in a set of seven books. Even if we had chosen to produce an encyclopedia of 100 volumes, it would still contain only a tiny part of all known facts."

The encyclopedia is handsomely illustrated with more than 3,000 quality illustrations, almost all of which are in color and were specially commissioned for the work.

They include line drawings, photographs, cutaways, diagrams, charts, and maps. All enhance the set's informational value as well as its aesthetic appeal. The full-page graphic accompanying "Computers," for instance, not only illustrates the components of today's personal computers in a way that aids comprehension but adds a visual quality to the article that captures and holds the reader's attention.

Physically, the *Oxford Children's Encyclopedia* is a carefully constructed reference work. The volumes, which come in a heavy slipcase for easy storage, have wash-able covers and are sewn to withstand heavy use. A high grade of paper has been used to ensure good color reproduction. The two-column page layout is varied, attractive, and uncluttered, featuring excellent use of white space throughout. The only quibble about the layout is best put in a review in *Reference Books Bulletin* (in *Booklist*, June 15, 1992, p. 1886): "Inconsistent column layout may bother some readers; some articles read down a complete column, while others go across the top half of the page in two columns, with another article completing the lower half of the page."

SUMMARY

A product of the prestigious Oxford University Press, the seven-volume *Oxford Children's Encyclopedia* was published in Great Britain from scratch in 1991 after more than four years in the making. Intended for children ages 7–14, the set replaces the publisher's 13-volume OXFORD JUNIOR ENCYCLOPAEDIA, which has been defunct for many years. The persistent criticism of the *Oxford Children's Encyclopedia* in North America centers on its British accent, evident in both the set's language and coverage. In nearly all other respects the set passes muster as a first-class children's encyclopedia. Especially noteworthy are its straightforward approach to controversial or sensitive topics, its clear writing style, and its outstanding illustrations. Although too small to compete head-to-head with the much larger NEW BOOK OF KNOWLEDGE and CHILDREN'S BRITANNICA, the *Oxford Children's Encyclopedia* looks very good indeed when compared with smaller sets in its class. The bottom line: An excellent supplementary encyclopedia for North American school and public libraries.

REPORT CARD: OXFORD CHILDREN'S ENCYCLOPEDIA				
TOPIC	COVERAGE	ACCURACY	RECENCY	CLARITY
Computers	A	A	A	A
Halloween	C	A	B	A
Johnson, Magic	F*	NA	NA	NA
Measles	F*	NA	NA	NA
Nuclear Energy	A	A	A	A
Panda Bears	A	A	A	A
Rock Music	A	A	A	A
Rose (Flower)	F*	NA	NA	NA
Russia	B	B	C	A
Sex Education	A	A	A	A

A = Excellent; **B** = Above Average; **C** = Average; **D** = Below Average; **F** = Poor; **NA** = Not Applicable
*No Article

OTHER OPINIONS

New York Times Book Review, May 17, 1992, p. 30 (review by Justin Kaplan); *Quill & Quire*, June 1992, p. 38 (review by Patty Lawlor); *Reference Books Bulletin* (in *Booklist*), June 15, 1992, pp. 1886–88 (unsigned review); *School Library Journal*, November 1992, p. 140 (review by Marjorie Lewis).

WORLD BOOK ENCYCLOPEDIA

FACTS

Full Title: *The World Book Encyclopedia.* **Managing Editor:** Dale W. Jacobs. **Associate Managing Editor:** Gary A. Alt. **Publisher:** World Book, Inc. **Date Published:** First published in 1917; new printing with revisions published annually.

Electronic Version: INFORMATION FINDER (CD-ROM).

Volumes: 22. **Words:** 10 million. **Pages:** 14,000. **Articles:** 18,000. **Bibliographies:** 1,800. **Illustrations and Maps:** 31,300. **Cross-references:** 100,000. **Index Entries:** 150,000. **Editorial Staff, Advisers, and Contributors:** 3,000. **Trim Size:** 7¼ × 9¾ in.

Price and Sales Information: $679.00 to $849.00 depending on binding; price does not include shipping and handling. The *World Book Encyclopedia* is sold to individual consumers and educational institutions (schools, libraries, etc.) through authorized sales representatives of the publisher. The set is not sold in bookstores or similar retail outlets. For additional information about the encyclopedia or to order it, consumers should consult the yellow pages of the local telephone directory under "Encyclopedias" for the World Book, Inc. sales representative in their area. If the company is not listed, call toll-free 1-800-621-8202 or write World Book, Inc., 525 West Monroe Street, 20th Floor, Chicago, IL 60661.

EVALUATION

Long the best-selling work of its kind in North America, the 22-volume *World Book Encyclopedia* is one of the few general encyclopedias available today that successfully bridges the gap between younger and older readers. Specifically, it is designed "to meet the reference and study needs of students in elementary school, junior high school, and high school. *World Book* also serves as a general family reference tool" (preface). A detailed review of *World Book* appears in the section "Medium-Sized Encyclopedias for Adults and Older Students" in this guide beginning on page 97. The much briefer evaluation here concentrates on the encyclopedia as a reference source for young people.

World Book provides balanced coverage of all basic areas of knowledge, including those of interest to children and younger students, as the Report Card below shows. Currently, the encyclopedia contains approximately 17,500 articles. Most are specific entries averaging less than half a page in length, but others are much longer. For instance, the article on Magic Johnson is a fourth of a page long, whereas "Russia" runs to 32 pages.

For the most part, the encyclopedia's coverage is determined by a continuous study of elementary and secondary school curricula in the U.S. and Canada. Called the Nault-Caswell-Brain Curriculum Analysis, the study not only informs the editors about what subjects are currently being taught at what grade levels, it identifies broad curricular changes and trends. The encyclopedia is also regularly monitored for its effectiveness as a reference source in some 400 selected classrooms in North America. Students doing research fill out cards each time they use the set, indicating what information was sought, what subject headings they searched, and whether they found what they were looking for. The editors receive approximately 100,000 such cards each year, which help them to keep *World Book* as current and user-friendly as possible. In fact, no other encyclopedia on the market today is so closely in touch with the school curriculum and current informational needs of students at all levels.

As might be expected, prominent people and places receive generous coverage in the encyclopedia, as do scientific and technical subjects. Animals and animal life—topics of particular interest to youngsters—are especially well covered. The one-page article "Panda," for instance, furnishes a comprehensive description of these popular and endangered creatures, including an excellent summary of the scientific debate about whether the giant panda belongs to the bear or raccoon family. Major articles append study questions that test the reader's knowledge and comprehension. *Example:* At the end of "Dinosaur" are such questions as "What are some theories that scientists have developed to explain why dinosaurs died out?" "Where are most dinosaur discoveries made today?" and "What kinds of animals besides dinosaurs lived during the Age of Reptiles?"

Although curriculum oriented, the encyclopedia also provides extensive coverage of non-academic subjects of interest to chil-

dren and younger students, such as sports, games, hobbies, bicycles and bicycling, boats and boating, camping, scouting, cooking, clothing, cosmetics, toys, dolls, the circus, magic, movies, television, popular music, childhood diseases, and human sexuality.

Information in *World Book* can be trusted as reliable and up-to-date. The article "Rock Music," for example, concludes with a lengthy section on rock music trends in the 1980s and 1990s, which covers rock videos, the influence of computers and synthesizers on the music, and how the rock culture and society interact. Concerning the latter, the author of the article, music critic Don McLeese, writes,

> Various artists—including the heavy metal band Guns n' Roses and rap groups 2 Live Crew and Public Enemy—sparked controversy in the late 1980's and early 1990's with their rebellious lyrics, aggressive music, and antisocial stance. Concerned parents in such groups as the Parents' Music Resource Center (PMRC) called for record companies to attach warning labels to albums with lyrics that might be objectionable.

Happily for students of all ages, *World Book* provides excellent coverage of controversial or sensitive issues. Such topics as abortion, AIDS, birth control, homosexuality, menstruation, circumcision, boy-girl relationships, and sexual development—all subjects of considerable interest and concern to young people—are treated in an evenhanded, dispassionate manner, with differing points of view noted. *Example:* The article "Circumcision" informs the reader,

> At one time, most United States physicians recommended routine circumcision of newborn males. They felt the operation made the glans easier to clean and thus helped prevent infections of the penis. They also believed circumcision reduced the risk of developing cancer of the penis. Research shows uncircumcised males are more prone to infections of the *urinary tract*, the organs and tubes that produce and eliminate urine. But many physicians argue that proper hygiene can be just as effective in preventing such infections and that routine circumcision is not medically necessary.

Obviously, as the quotes from "Rock Music" and "Circumcision" in the preceding paragraphs suggest, most children and younger students are not likely to comprehend every word in the encyclopedia. On the other hand, *World Book* offers the broadest readability range of any encyclopedia on the market today, including its chief competitor, COMPTON'S ENCYCLOPEDIA.

When appropriate, articles are written at the grade level where they are likely to be read or studied. For example, the article "Dinosaur" is written for a younger reader than, say, the article "Circumcision." All new articles are carefully examined by the encyclopedia's readability consultant, Dr. Joseph O'Rourke of Ohio State University, to ensure that the vocabulary used is geared to the intended grade level. When technical or potentially unfamiliar terms are used in an article, they are italicized and defined or explained in context; see, for example, *urinary tract* in the "Circumcision" excerpt above. In addition, some longer articles— "Computer" and "Space Exploration" are examples—include glossaries that succinctly define technical terms associated with the topic. This sort of close attention to vocabulary control is central to the success of *World Book* and the key reason why it is able to appeal to a readership ranging from students in the elementary grades to college-educated adults.

Articles in the encyclopedia are consistently written in a clear and interesting manner. Indeed, over the years *World Book* has developed a reputation for having a "knack" for putting complex ideas and concepts into easily understandable language without sacrificing accuracy of meaning or being condescending to the more advanced reader. The first paragraph of the article "Computer" gives a good sense of the *World Book* style:

> **Computer** is a machine that performs calculations and processes information with astonishing speed and precision. A computer can handle vast amounts of information and

solve complicated problems. It can take thousands of individual pieces of data and turn them into more usable information—with blinding speed and almost unfailing accuracy. The most powerful computers can perform billions of calculations per second.

Another effective (though less apparent) writing technique used by the editors to make the encyclopedia's contents as comprehensible to as many readers as possible is the so-called "pyramid" approach. The editors explain in their preface: "Many long articles are designed to present simpler concepts and reading levels at the beginning. These articles build toward more sophisticated concepts and reading levels toward the end. The **Leaf** article is an excellent example of this simple-to-more-complex approach." The pyramid style allows children and younger students to read and comprehend practically any article in the encyclopedia—up to a point. When, or if, the article becomes too complex or dense, readers (no matter what their age) will naturally desist.

The encyclopedia is simply and intelligently organized. Not surprisingly, locating specific facts and topics in the text normally poses no difficulty for users, including students at the elementary school level. Numerous cross-references within and at the end of articles help point the reader in the right direction. The article "Computer," for example, includes *see* references throughout the text to such related articles as "Computerized Tomography," "Numeration Systems," "Integrated Circuit," "Semiconductor," and "Transistor." Likewise, numerous *see also* references appear at the end of the article, e.g., "Artificial Intelligence," "Babbage, Charles," "Electronics," "Informational Retrieval," "Microprocessor," and "Turing, Alan M."

In addition, *World Book* possesses an excellent analytical index of some 150,000 entries. Located in volume 22, (called *Research Guide/Index*), the index pinpoints even the smallest facts in the set. For example, the index entry "Computer" not only refers the reader to the 16-page article on the

subject but 60 other articles where computers are mentioned, such as "Bank," "Compact Disc," "Electronic Music," "Map," and
"Robot." Compared with COMPTON'S ENCY-
CLOPEDIA and its "Fact Index" (which functions as both a source of factual information
and an index to set), *World Book* is better
organized and less confusing to use, especially for children and younger students.

Illustrations and maps significantly enhance the encyclopedia's text, making the

articles more attractive, interesting, and informative to readers. This is particularly true
of young readers, who might not always understand the words but will comprehend the
pictures. Specifically, *World Book* includes
over 29,000 illustrations and 2,300 maps, of
which more than 80 percent are in color.
Overall, the artwork compares favorably with
that of any other general encyclopedia available today.

SUMMARY

The *World Book Encyclopedia*, like its longtime rival COMPTON'S ENCYCLOPEDIA, successfully serves both younger and older students
as well as adults. In fact, *World Book*'s readability range—from elementary school students to college-educated adults—is the
broadest of any encyclopedia currently on
the market. The encyclopedia's ability to
appeal to such a broad readership is achieved
by writing articles to grade level, highlight-
ing and defining difficult or potentially unfamiliar terms in context, providing glossaries of technical terms, and employing a
readability specialist to ensure strict vocabulary control. Moreover, the makers of *World
Book* have a "knack" for explaining complex ideas in easy-to-understand language,
and they employ the so-called "pyramid"
writing style, which allows people of almost

any age and reading skill to use at least
portions of the encyclopedia profitably.

The encyclopedia's coverage, which is
based closely on North American school
curricula, emphasizes people, places, and scientific topics, but all important areas of
knowledge are covered in a fair and balanced manner. Nonschool topics of interest
to young people also receive extensive coverage. Articles in *World Book* are consistently accurate, up-to-date, and objective
in presentation. The encyclopedia is intelligently organized and easy to use, an especially important consideration for younger
readers. The illustrations—another area of
particular importance to children and
younger students—are first-rate. The bottom line: *World Book* is the best all-around
encyclopedia for the family with school-age
children.

OTHER OPINIONS

American Reference Books Annual, 1993, pp.
29–31 (review by Barbara Ittner); *Basic Information Sources* by William A. Katz (vol. 1
of *Introduction to Reference Work*, 6th ed.,
New York: McGraw-Hill, 1992), pp. 248–
50; *Reference Books Bulletin* (in *Booklist*),

September 15, 1993, p. 183 (unsigned review); *Reference Sources for Small and Medium-Sized Libraries* (5th ed., Chicago:
American Library Assn., 1992), p. 35 (review by Jovian P. Lang).

REPORT CARD: WORLD BOOK ENCYCLOPEDIA				
TOPIC	COVERAGE	ACCURACY	RECENCY	CLARITY
Computers	A	A	A	A
Halloween	A	A	A	A
Johnson, Magic	A	A	A	A
Measles	A	A	A	A
Nuclear Energy	A	A	A	A
Panda Bears	A	A	A	A
Rock Music	A	A	A	A
Rose (Flower)	A	A	A	A
Russia	A	A	A	A
Sex Education	A	A	A	A

A = Excellent; **B** = Above Average; **C** = Average; **D** = Below Average; **F** = Poor; **NA** = Not Applicable

YOUNG CHILDREN'S ENCYCLOPEDIA

FACTS

Full Title: *The Young Children's Encyclopedia*. **Editor in Chief:** Howard L. Goodkind. **Chief Text Editor:** Ryerson Johnson. **Art Director:** Will Gallagher. **Publisher:** Encyclopaedia Britannica, Inc. Date **Published:** First Edition, 1970; revised periodically, most recently in 1988.

Also published as COMPTON'S PRE-CYCLOPEDIA.

Volumes: 16. **Words:** 325,000. **Pages:** 2,560. **Articles:** 650. **Bibliographies:** None. **Illustrations and Maps:** 2,400. **Cross-references:** 500. **Index Entries:** None. **Editorial Staff, Advisers, and Contributors:** 186. **Trim Size:** 7¾ × 9¼.

Price and Sales Information: $175.00. The *Young Children's Encyclopedia* is sold to individual consumers and educational institu-tions (schools, libraries, etc.) through authorized sales representatives of the publisher. The set is not sold in bookstores or similar retail outlets, although it is sometimes sold via mail order. For additional information about the set or to order it, individual consumers should consult the yellow pages of the local telephone directory under "Encyclopedias" for the Encyclopaedia Britannica, Inc. sales representative in their area. If the company is not listed, call toll-free 1-800-858-4895 or write Encyclopaedia Britannica, Inc., Britannica Centre, Customer Service Department, 310 South Michigan Avenue, Chicago, IL 60604. Educational institutions should call toll-free 1-800-544-9862 or write Encyclopaedia Britannica Educational Corporation at the same address.

EVALUATION

The *Young Children's Encyclopedia*—a 16-volume set intended for children and younger students ages 4–10—was first published in 1970 and has been minimally revised several times over the years, most recently in 1988.

It is also published under the title COMPTON'S PRECYCLOPEDIA. The two sets have exactly the same contents, except that COMPTON'S PRECYCLOPEDIA, which is aimed at the school and library market, offers two features not found in *Young Children's*, namely a 24-page "Things to Do" section at the beginning of each volume and a supplementary paperbound volume containing a teaching guide and index to the set.

Like its chief competitor, CHILDCRAFT, *Young Children's* consists of heavily illustrated stories, folktales, games, riddles, jingles, jokes, and articles on subjects likely to be of interest to young readers. For example, Volume 1 includes a story set in Africa ("Amos Wins the Big Race"); an adventure piece about the Amazon ("Exploring the Amazon River"); chatty biographies of Louisa May Alcott ("Tales of Happy Families") and Susan B. Anthony ("Women: Their Rights and Nothing Less"); two introductory essays on art ("See What I Made" and "Paint Something Different Today"); and three informative descriptions of astronauts at work ("Doing the Job," "A Walk in Space," and "More about Astronauts"). These articles, which are arranged alphabetically by topic, tend to be quite lengthy, averaging just under five pages.

Users and prospective purchasers should understand that *Young Children's* (again like CHILDCRAFT) does not attempt to cover the world's knowledge and information in any comprehensive or systematic manner, and that in the strictest sense it is not an encyclopedia but a browsing set. For instance, there is an article about baseball but none about football, basketball, hockey, or soccer. Information is provided about koala bears but not panda bears. Orchestras, bagpipes, and drums receive coverage but popular music is completely ignored. The same serendipitous approach is taken toward prominent people, places, historical events, plants and animals, and the like.

On the other hand, *Young Children's* does offer some of the appurtenances of a true encyclopedia, such as alphabetical arrangement and cross-references. Considered a "training" encyclopedia by the publisher, the set is designed to introduce preschoolers and beginning readers to the idea of an encyclopedia and how it works, so that they

will be better prepared to cope with larger and more complex encyclopedic works down the road. Prospective purchasers should be aware that *Young Children's* and sets like it—CHARLIE BROWN'S 'CYCLOPEDIA and the aforementioned CHILDCRAFT—will be quickly outgrown. After a relatively short time, children begin to consider such works as too juvenile or "babyish" for them.

Information in *Young Children's* is usually accurate and presented in an impartial manner, although controversial or sensitive subjects are almost always ignored. *Young Children's* presents a cheerful, happy, optimistic view of the world; crime, violence, discrimination, family problems, and other social ills rarely intrude in its brightly colored pages. Articles in *Young Children's* are reasonably current, although timeliness is not as crucial in this type of work as it is in a true encyclopedia. Occasionally, however, the addition of new information would improve an article. The two-page entry on the Panama Canal ("More About Canals"), for instance, lacks any mention of the treaty signed in 1977 that will eventually result in Panamanian control of the canal.

Articles in *Young Children's* are normally written in a clear, interesting, and informal style. Reading levels vary from article to article, but in most instances the text will be comprehensible to beginning readers in the primary grades. Many of the articles are also suitable for reading aloud by parents, teachers, and librarians. The article on computers, entitled "The Machines That Solve Problems," provides a good example of the set's style:

> Until just a few years ago, the machines we call computers were very big and very expensive. Only business and government offices could afford such large and costly machines.
>
> Today, some powerful computers are still very big and very expensive. But other kinds have been made much smaller and so inexpensive that many people have bought them to use right in their own homes.
>
> Computers can find the answers to many kinds of problems that people once had to solve on paper. These machines also have special parts that can remember long lists of

words and numbers, even pictures! Because computers can solve problems and remember facts, they can be very useful.

Access to information in *Young Children's* is facilitated by the set's A-to-Z arrangement, a detailed table of contents in each volume, and cross-references at the end of many articles. The approximately 500 cross-references are especially helpful. For instance, at the end of the article on computers excerpted above is this notation: "*You may learn about what makes the computer work under* Electricity *in Volume 5. Find out how computers help the astronauts under* Space *in Volume 14.*" Still, readers searching for specific topics and facts in *Young Children's* are hampered by the lack of an index to the set. How, for instance, without an index can the reader quickly and easily determine that the article "Inventions" contains extensive information about Orville and Wilbur Wright? Answer: No way. Many similar examples could be cited. The strange part of this is that COMPTON'S PRECYCLOPEDIA (which, as noted, has almost exactly the same text as *Young Children's*) does have an index. Britannica editors should add the index to *Young Children's* at the earliest possible opportunity.

Illustrations, all in color, make up about half the set's total text. Mostly drawings with some cartoons, the illustrations add much to both the instructional and aesthetic appeal of *Young Children's*. The overall appearance of the set is inviting and contemporary, distinguished by a creative page layout and the use of large, readable type faces. Its physical format is satisfactory, except for a few problems: Guide words (or running heads) are not printed at the top of each page, which makes it difficult to locate an article by browsing; some pages lack page numbers, which will confuse or frustrate young readers; and, the most serious complaint, the volumes do not always lie flat when open, thus rendering them physically awkward to use for reference purposes.

Over the years, *Young Children's* has not been reviewed, the publisher preferring to send COMPTON'S PRECYCLOPEDIA out for review, perhaps because it has a stronger and more colorful binding. Most of the notices have been favorable. For example, Jovian Lang, writing about COMPTON'S PRECYCLOPEDIA in *Reference Sources for Small and Medium-Sized Libraries* (5th ed., American Library Assn., 1992, p. 204) says, "The storytelling style and excellent graphics, as well as large type, make it competitive with *Childcraft*." But some critics have expressed reservations, none more forcefully than Bill Katz in his *Basic Information Sources* (6th ed., McGraw-Hill, 1992, pp. 255–56), who writes that the set "offers preschoolers stories, riddles, and television type fare that no self-respecting librarian or parent would give a child. It is virtually worthless as both an encyclopedia and a good reading set."

SUMMARY

A beginning or "training" set designed to introduce preschool and primary school children to the ins and outs of encyclopedias and reference work, the *Young Children's Encyclopedia* is more a collection of stories than a real encyclopedia, although it is arranged alphabetically and does include cross-references. *Young Children's*, which has practically the same text as COMPTON'S PRECYCLOPEDIA, offers an interesting writing style and imaginative illustrations and page layout. On the negative side, the coverage is highly selective, access to specific topics and information in the set suffers due to lack of an index, there are several problems with the physical format, and the set will be quickly outgrown. The bottom line: This colorful "pre-cyclopedia" for children ages 4–10 is no CHILDCRAFT.

REPORT CARD: YOUNG CHILDREN'S ENCYCLOPEDIA

TOPICS	COVERAGE	ACCURACY	RECENCY	CLARITY
Computers	B	A	A	A
Halloween	F*	NA	NA	NA
Johnson, Magic	F*	NA	NA	NA
Measles	F*	NA	NA	NA
Nuclear Energy	D	A	C	B
Panda Bears	F*	NA	NA	NA
Rock Music	F*	NA	NA	NA
Rose (Flower)	D	A	A	A
Russia	C	C	F	B
Sex Education	D	A	A	A

A = Excellent; **B** = Above Average; **C** = Average; **D** = Below Average; **F** = Poor; **NA** = Not Applicable
*No Article

OTHER OPINIONS

As noted, the *Young Children's Encyclopedia* has not been reviewed over the years, the publisher preferring to send out COMPTON'S PRECYCLOPEDIA for review. Interested consumers therefore should consult the following reviews of COMPTON'S PRECYCLOPEDIA, which has the same basic text as *Young Children's: American Reference Books Annual*, 1975, pp. 33–34 (review by Sally Wynkoop); *Basic Information Sources* by William A. Katz (vol. 1 of *Introduction to Reference Work*, 6th ed., New York: McGraw-Hill, 1992), pp. 255–56; *Reference and Subscription Books Review* (in *Booklist*), November 1, 1979, pp. 453–56 (unsigned review); *Reference Sources for Small and Medium-Sized Libraries* (5th ed., Chicago: American Library Assn., 1992), p. 32 (review by Jovian P. Lang).

YOUNG STUDENTS LEARNING LIBRARY

FACTS

Full Title: *Young Students Learning Library.* **Editor in Chief:** Terry Borton. **Senior Project Editor:** Rita D'Apice Gould. **Publisher:** Weekly Reader Books (now Newfield Publications). **Former Title:** *Young Students Encyclopedia* (1972–82). Date Published: First published as *Young Students Learning Library* in 1988; revised periodically, most recently in 1992.

Also published as the NEW GROLIER STUDENT ENCYCLOPEDIA.

Volumes: 22 (plus *Young Students Intermediate Dictionary* and *Young Students World Atlas*). **Words:** 1.5 million. **Pages:** 3,623. **Articles:** 3,000. **Bibliographies:** None. **Illustrations and Maps:** 5,000. **Cross-references:** 10,000. **Index Entries:** 22,000. **Editorial Staff, Advisers, and Contributors:** 36. **Trim Size:** 8¼ × 10¾ in.

Price and Sales Information: $322.20 (or approximately $14.00 per volume). The *Young Students Learning Library* is sold to individual consumers via mail order. Customers receive Volume 1 on approval and the atlas free; Volumes 2 and 3 follow at six-week intervals, again on approval, followed by the remaining volumes in a single delivery. According to promotional literature from the publisher, "This will allow your child to enjoy the complete set while you pay in convenient monthly installments." The encyclopedia is not sold in bookstores or simi-

lar retail outlets. Educational institutions (schools, libraries, etc.) can acquire the encyclopedia under the title NEW GROLIER STUDENT ENCYCLOPEDIA. For additional information about the *Young Students Learning Library* or to order it, call toll-free 1-800-456-8220 or write Newfield Publications (formerly Weekly Reader Books), P.O. Box 16615, Columbus, OH 43216.

EVALUATION

The *Young Students Learning Library*—a multivolume encyclopedia generally designed for children ages 7–14 and specifically for students in grades 3–6—first appeared in 1972 under the title *Young Students Encyclopedia*, a cooperative publishing venture between Xerox Education Publications (which drew on the editorial resources of *My Weekly Reader*, then a Xerox publication) and Funk & Wagnalls, the supermarket reference publisher. This set was revised in 1977 and again in 1982. In 1988, the publisher, now Weekly Reader Books, issued a major revision under the title *Young Students Learning Library*. That work, prepared with editorial assistance from the British reference publisher Grisewood & Dempsey Ltd., was modestly revised in 1991 and 1992, the last time the set has been updated. Note that the encyclopedia is also published in a school and library edition as the NEW GROLIER STUDENT ENCYCLOPEDIA.

Recently, Weekly Reader Books was sold and is now called Newfield Publications. According to a Newfield representative, *Young Students* will be thoroughly revised and slightly expanded (by one volume) sometime in 1994. During its more than 20 years of existence, the encyclopedia has achieved a reputation as an attractive but superficial reference work for young people. It obviously lacks the size and depth to compete head to head with the much larger and editorially superior NEW BOOK OF KNOWLEDGE, CHILDREN'S BRITANNICA, COMPTON'S

ENCYCLOPEDIA, and WORLD BOOK ENCYCLOPEDIA, all of which serve roughly the same readership as *Young Students*. *Young Students* does have the advantage, however, in the area of price, which is considerably lower than the larger sets, with the exception of CHILDREN'S BRITANNICA.

Young Students currently consists of 22 thin numbered volumes, plus two unnumbered volumes: the 800-page *Young Students Intermediate Dictionary* (a work of 34,000 entries) and the 96-page *Young Students World Atlas* (maps by Rand McNally). The latter is offered as a premium when consumers order Volume 1 on approval. The first 22 volumes contain approximately 3,000 A-to-Z articles, which average about a page in length. To a large extent, the encyclopedia's coverage is curriculum oriented: "Subjects represent basic concepts underlying current elementary school curricula as well as children's outside interests" (introduction). As might be expected, all major areas of knowledge are covered, but biographical and geographical subjects predominate, including important historical figures (such as U.S. presidents), the countries of the world, U.S. states and Canadian provinces, and other major places here and abroad. The humanities—art, literature, music, etc.—also receive a surprising amount of attention.

As noted, the articles tend to be brief, sometimes overly so. But they are frequently supplemented by what the editors call "nuggets," or information sidebars. The nuggets, which appear in the outer margins set off by a wide orange bar, convey interesting or curious facts that "will make learning more inviting for readers who like to browse" (introduction). Here is an example of one of three nuggets accompanying the article "Russian History":

> Tsar Peter the Great was a huge man, nearly seven feet tall, with enormous strength and energy. He died at the age of 52 when he caught a chill through diving into icy water to save some soldiers from drowning. It is said that he drove the Russians so hard that when he died a great sigh of relief could be heard all over the country.

Some articles also include hands-on exercises, called "Learn by Doing" activities. Denoted by a small blue square, these educational exercises are intended to make the encyclopedia an interactive learning tool. *Examples:* The article "Poetry" discusses haiku, a popular form of Japanese poetry, and then invites the reader to try to write an original haiku. The article "Air Conditioning" suggests how the reader might construct a primitive air conditioner.

Information in *Young Students* is usually accurate and objective, although occasional errors of fact intrude. For instance, the article "Panda" erroneously states that the giant panda is related to the raccoon family; actually, genetic tests have shown that giant pandas are a subgroup of the bear family. Sometimes, also, controversial or sensitive subjects are glossed over or entirely ignored. Human sexuality is an obvious case in point. Normal, healthy, inquisitive children ages 7–14 naturally have a great interest in and concern about such questions as abortion, birth control, menstruation, masturbation, homosexuality, and circumcision, but they will not find answers in this encyclopedia.

Information in the set is generally current as of 1991, although many significant developments are not covered, as in the case of the Sandinista loss of power in Nica-ragua. Likewise, the article "Popular Music" seems to end in the mid-1980s. Often it is difficult to know if significant facts and events are missing due to lack of diligent revision or due to shallow treatment of the subject.

The encyclopedia's writing style has appropriately been described as "conversational, with facts presented in a clear, noncondescending manner" (*Reference and Subscription Books Reviews* in *Booklist*, July 15, 1980, p. 1690). A controlled vocabulary is employed, and when potentially difficult or unfamiliar terms are used, they appear in italic and are defined or explained in context. For instance, the article "Computer" includes a dozen italicized words, e.g., *transistor, microchip, binary code, hardware, software.* Some articles also include glossaries that briefly define technical terms on the topic. When appropriate, articles are written at the grade level where the topic is most likely to be studied. Moreover, the editors use the so-called "pyramid" style of writing—that is, articles begin with the simplest or most elementary material and then gradually become more detailed and complex as the text progresses. Ordinarily, articles in *Young Students* are most appropriate for students in grades 3–6.

The first few paragraphs of "Computer" are typical of the encyclopedia's style:

> How long would it take you to add together 1+2+3+4+5 and so on up to 1000? Even if you worked quickly, it would take you a long time to get the answer (500,500). Besides you would have to do each of the thousand additions correctly or you would wind up with the wrong answer after all that hard work.
>
> With a home computer, you would need a minute to key in the program or instructions it needs. The computer would then do the additions in about one second. And it would always be right.
>
> To "compute" means to count or to figure. A computer is a machine that solves problems many times faster than a person can. A computer does not think, so a person must give information to the computer, supply instructions on how to solve the problem, and tell in what form the answer is to be given.

The encyclopedia's contents are easily accessible, thanks to a detailed index of 22,000 entries in Volume 22 and to an abundance of cross-references found at the end of most articles. For instance, the article on computers excerpted in the preceding paragraphs concludes with cross-references to five related articles: "Automation"; "Babbage, Charles"; "Binary Code"; "Calculator"; and "Electronics." In addition, the index furnishes 15 citations to articles where information on computers can be found, such as "Computer" (the main article), "Bar Code," and "Robot." As a rule, *Young Students* is well organized and easy to use. Finding specific facts and topics in the set should present no difficulties for most students in the upper elementary grades.

The editors' introduction to the encyclopedia suggests, "Regular use of this set will develop an exciting and rewarding foundation for every child's future," which might be a bit hyperbolic but the sentiment is appreciated. Where the editors are shortsighted, however, is in failing to build on that foundation by providing bibliographies or lists of recommended materials that would help the inquiring child (or parent, teacher, or librarian) go beyond the encyclopedia, which after all is only a beginning place for study and learning. No question, *Young Students* would be an improved encyclopedia if it included carefully prepared bibliographies on selected topics.

Young Students is a heavily illustrated encyclopedia, with roughly 30 percent of the total text given over to photographs, drawings, diagrams, art reproductions, maps, and the like. The illustrations, which now number more than 5,000, are mostly in color and normally add to the informational value of the set, although in some instances the quality of reproduction leaves something to be desired. A more acute problem concerns the placement of illustrations. D.A. Rothschild, in a review in *American Reference Books Annual* (1993, pp. 27–28), explains:

> One of the strengths of this set is the large number of really nice illustrations. . . . One problem, however, is the frequent placement of illustrations or sidebars [nuggets] next to unrelated articles and even on opposite pages. This results from the format, which is two columns of text per page placed near the center of the book, creating a large outside margin for pictures. An extreme example of the confusion this can cause is that a sidebar on Edwin "Buzz" Aldrin appears next to a lengthy chunk of the article on alcoholic beverages and directly under the running head "Alcott, Louisa May." The article on Aldrin barely starts on that page, taking up more space on the next one, where a large photograph of Aldrin will draw readers' attention. They may not even see the sidebar.

The encyclopedia's physical format is generally satisfactory. The page layout is colorful and varied, with wide margins and much white space, although placement of illustrations and nuggets (or information sidebars) are sometimes a problem, as noted above. Though cheaply made, the thin, lightweight volumes are sewn and will hold up well under normal use in the home. The lettering on the spine, however, is much too small to be read comfortably at any distance.

SUMMARY

The *Young Students Learning Library*, formerly the *Young Students Encyclopedia*, provides clear, easily accessible, attractively presented information for children ages 7–14 and specifically for students in grades 3–6. The set's numerous "Learn by Doing" instructional activities found throughout the set are a plus, as are the so-called "nuggets" of information found in the margins of most pages. On the negative side, the encyclopedia's articles often lack depth and are not always as current as they might be. In addition, the editors tend to ignore controversial or sensitive topics, such as human sexuality. The bottom line: A mediocre encyclopedia.

REPORT CARD: YOUNG STUDENTS LEARNING LIBRARY

TOPIC	COVERAGE	ACCURACY	RECENCY	CLARITY
Computers	B	A	A	A
Halloween	C	A	B	A
Johnson, Magic	F*	NA	NA	NA
Measles	C	A	B	A
Nuclear Energy	B	A	B	B
Panda Bears	C	B	B	A
Rock Music	D	A	C	A
Rose (Flower)	B	A	A	A
Russia	C	A	B	A
Sex Education	D	A	C	B

A = Excellent; **B** = Above Average; **C** = Average; **D** = Below Average; **F** = Poor; **NA** = Not Applicable
*No Article

OTHER OPINIONS

American Reference Books Annual, 1993, pp. 27–28 (review by D.A. Rothschild); *Basic Information Sources* by William A. Katz (vol. 1 of *Introduction to Reference Work*, 6th ed., New York: McGraw-Hill, 1992), p. 256; *Reference Books Bulletin* (in *Booklist*), April 15, 1989, pp. 1440–42 (unsigned review).

COMPARISON CHART

Large and Medium-Sized Encyclopedias for Children and Younger Students

This chart provides basic statistical information about each of the large and medium-sized encyclopedias for children and younger students reviewed in *Kister's Best Encyclopedias*. The chart also offers a quick comparative overview of the 13 titles in this category. How does *Children's Britannica*, for instance, compare with similar encyclopedias in terms of number of words? Articles? Illustrations? Index entries? Price? The chart answers such questions at a glance.

In the case of price information, consumers should understand that prices are subject to change by the publisher or distributor at any time. For the latest price of any encyclopedia, consult *Books in Print* (a standard reference source found in practically all libraries and bookstores) or, better, call the publisher or distributor direct. Most now have toll-free numbers where the latest information about price and availability can be obtained quickly and efficiently. Telephone numbers are listed in this guide at the beginning of each review under "Price and Sales Information," as well as in the directory of publishers and distributors at the back of the book (see Appendix B).

The chart's final column assigns a letter grade to each encyclopedia: A = Excellent; B = Above Average; C = Average; D = Below Average; F = Poor. The letter grade represents a final summary of the encyclopedia's detailed evaluation in *Kister's Best Encyclopedias*. Consumers seriously interested in purchasing an encyclopedia are urged to base their selection decisions on the reviews in the book and not rely solely on the letter grades given in the chart, which are necessarily arbitrary.

TITLE	VOLS.	WORDS	PAGES	ARTICLES	ILLUS. & MAPS	CROSS-REFS.	INDEX ENTRIES	LOWEST RETAIL PRICE	RATING
CHARLIE BROWN'S 'CYCLOPEDIA	15	225,000	900	1,000	1,500	NONE	NONE	$42.00	D
CHILDCRAFT	15	750,000	4,750	3,000	4,500	NONE	20,000	249.00	A
CHILDREN'S BRITANNICA	20	4 MIL	6,830	10,000[1]	6,500	2,500	40,000	299.00	B
COMPTON'S ENCYCLOPEDIA	26	9 MIL	10,590	34,000[2]	22,510	35,500	154,000	499.00	B
COMPTON'S PRECYCLOPEDIA[3]	16	350,000	2,944	650	2,425	500	800	289.00	C
GOLDEN BOOK ENCYCLOPEDIA	20	650,000	1,920	1,500	2,900	4,000	7,000	85.00	D
GROLIER CHILDREN'S ENCYCLOPEDIA[4]	10	250,000	816	1,300	2,000	1,500	6,000	219.00	B
NEW BOOK OF KNOWLEDGE	21	6.8 MIL	10,600	14,000[5]	25,000	3,700	85,000	995.00	A
NEW GROLIER STUDENT ENCYCLOPEDIA[6]	22	1.5 MIL	2,809	3,000	5,000	10,000	22,000	359.00	C
OXFORD CHILDREN'S ENCYCLOPEDIA	7	700,000	1,648	2,000	3,000	4,000	15,000	200.00	B
WORLD BOOK ENCYCLOPEDIA	22	10 MIL	14,000	18,000	31,300	100,000	150,000	679.00	A
YOUNG CHILDREN'S ENCYCLOPEDIA[7]	16	325,000	2,560	650	2,400	500	NONE	175.00	C
YOUNG STUDENTS LEARNING LIBRARY[8]	22	1.5 MIL	3,623	3,000	5,000	10,000	22,000	322.20	C

1. Encyclopedia contains 4,000 main articles; 6,000 brief entries in index.
2. Encyclopedia contains 5,250 main articles; 28,750 brief entries in index.
3. Also published as the YOUNG CHILDREN'S ENCYCLOPEDIA.
4. Also published as the KINGFISHER CHILDREN'S ENCYCLOPEDIA in one vol.
5. Encyclopedia contains 9,000 main articles; 5,000 brief entries in index.
6. Also published as the YOUNG STUDENTS LEARNING LIBRARY.
7. Also published as COMPTON'S PRECYCLOPEDIA.
8. Also published as the NEW GROLIER STUDENT ENCYCLOPEDIA.

Small Encyclopedias for Children and Younger Students

* * * * * * * * *

OVERVIEW

There are currently a dozen small, one-volume encyclopedias for children and younger students on the North American market. Most of these encyclopedias originated in Great Britain and later were adapted for U.S. and Canadian readers. Why British publishers should dominate this tiny segment of the American encyclopedia market is something of a mystery. Perhaps the British have a greater appreciation of small children's encyclopedias as early learning tools? Or perhaps, discerning a need and filling it, they have been more enterprising than American publishers? Certainly the record indicates that no major American encyclopedia publisher has ever produced a memorable single-volume encyclopedia for children.

A common problem with almost all small children's encyclopedias is lack of balanced coverage. Most heavily emphasize scientific and technical subjects to the detriment of other areas of knowledge, such as biography, geography, literature, and social studies. Another problem—inevitable in reference works so small—is superficial treatment of those topics that are covered. Still, a good children's encyclopedia of any size should be judged not only on the breadth and depth of its contents, but on how well it engages and stimulates the child's natural intellectual curiosity. Here the encyclopedia's writing style, page layout, quality of illustrations, use of color, and general aesthetic appeal are central to its success or failure as a reference source for young people.

Without question, the two best small encyclopedias available today for children ages 7–14 are the KINGFISHER CHILDREN'S ENCYCLOPEDIA and the RANDOM HOUSE CHILDREN'S ENCYCLOPEDIA. Both are (naturally) of British origin, both are heavily and fetchingly illustrated, and both are authoritative, up-to-date, well-written, and contemporary in design. In addition, both are physically hefty books, each weighing nearly six pounds; KINGFISHER has 816 pages and RANDOM HOUSE 644. (Note that KINGFISHER is also published for schools and libraries in 10 thin volumes under the title GROLIER CHILDREN'S ENCYCLOPEDIA.)

But despite these many similarities, the two encyclopedias differ in significant ways: KINGFISHER is basically a specific-entry encyclopedia, whereas RANDOM HOUSE is of the broad-entry type, which renders KINGFISHER a tad more user-friendly; KINGFISHER has a fairly traditional or structured page layout, whereas the RANDOM HOUSE layout is more creative but also busier; KINGFISHER provides more systematic coverage of U.S. and Canadian topics (people, places, etc.) than its competitor; and, finally, KINGFISHER is more attractively priced ($29.95) than RANDOM HOUSE ($50.00). Both are standout encyclopedias, but the KINGFISHER CHILDREN'S ENCYCLOPEDIA is clearly the first choice.

Other recommended single-volume encyclopedias for children and younger students are BARRON'S JUNIOR FACT FINDER and the USBORNE CHILDREN'S ENCYCLOPEDIA.

Though less impressive than either the KING-FISHER CHILDREN'S ENCYCLOPEDIA or the RANDOM HOUSE CHILDREN'S ENCYCLOPEDIA, these books are quality works, each with particular strengths and limitations as detailed in the reviews that follow.

Finally, the consumer in search of a good single-volume "first" encyclopedia for the preschooler or beginning reader need look no further than Carol Watson's MY FIRST ENCYCLOPEDIA, published by Dorling Kindersley. Simply written and handsomely illustrated, it will appeal to the inquisitive child.

BARRON'S JUNIOR FACT FINDER

FACTS

Full Title: *Barron's Junior Fact Finder: An Illustrated Encyclopedia for Children.* **Author:** Jean-Paul Dupré. **Publisher:** Barron's Educational Series, Inc. **Date Published:** 1989.
Volumes: One. **Words:** 90,000. **Pages:** 304. **Articles:** 134. **Bibliographies:** None. **Illustrations and Maps:** 550. **Cross-references:** None. **Index Entries:** 1,000. **Editorial Staff, Advisers, and Contributors:** 10. **Trim Size:** 6¾ × 10 in.

Price and Sales Information: $19.95. Individual consumers can purchase *Barron's Junior Fact Finder* in bookstores or, if the book is not in stock, it can be ordered. Similarly, schools and libraries can order it through a book wholesaler. To order the encyclopedia directly from the publisher, call toll-free 1-800-645-3476 or write Barron's Educational Series, Inc., 250 Wireless Blvd., Hauppauge, NY 11788.

EVALUATION

Published in North America in 1989, the heavily illustrated *Barron's Junior Fact Finder* is an English-language edition of a small encyclopedia for young people ages 7–14 originally published in France in 1987. It is organized topically (as opposed to alphabetically) in eight chapters representing these areas of knowledge: "History," "Geography," "Language and Its Uses," "Mathematics," "Physical Science," "Natural Science," "English Grammar," and "Arithmetic." Within these chapters are 134 double-page articles (or spreads) covering fairly broad topics. *Example:* The "Natural Science" chapter contains 27 two-page spreads, including "Respiration," "Why Do We Have to Eat," "Good Nutrition," "The Nervous System," and "How Life Begins." These broad articles are naturally subdivided into specific topics, or entries. For instance, "How Life Begins" includes such entries as "Transmission of Life," "Development of an Egg," "The Birth of a Baby," and "From Tadpole to Frog."

Author Dupré's introduction to *Barron's Junior Fact Finder*, addressed to the "young reader," notes that "we have written this book where you will find everything—or almost everything—that you will want to know." This claim, however, is exaggerated. The encyclopedia's contents, while sometimes impressive considering the book's size, are quite selective and fail to cover many subjects of interest to young people. For instance, while mathematics and arithmetic receive considerable attention, astronomy, animal life, sports, holidays, contemporary music, the countries of the world (aside from the U.S. and Canada), and prominent world leaders (including U.S. presidents and Canadian prime ministers) are given short shrift or ignored entirely.

In a review in *American Reference Books Annual* (1990, p. 18), Lois Buttlar comments on this issue, observing that the encyclopedia's "treatment of some subjects seems oversimplified. A discussion of the four great world religions treats both Christianity and Islam in fewer than 100 words each. Likewise, the extent of information explaining numerical bases other than base 10 is very superficial. While earthquakes are mentioned briefly, there are no entries in the index for tornadoes, storms, hurricanes, or weather in general."

Articles in the encyclopedia are almost always written in a clear, accurate, objective, and interesting manner. In some cases, technical terms beyond the grasp of the average elementary school student are used, but such vocabulary is usually italicized and explained in context. The first few paragraphs of the two-page article "Computers" provide a good example of the book's style:

> What is a computer? It is an electronic device that stores instructions (words, numbers, drawings, music) for processing data and then follows these instructions at high speed when requested.
>
> A computer is not intelligent. It processes data only according to the instructions it is given.
>
> The first computers, built around 1950, were very large, took up a great deal of space, and were very expensive. Today, computers are small in size, relatively inexpensive, and a thousand times faster, such as *minicomputers* or *P.C.s* (personal computers).

Finding specific material in *Barron's Junior Fact Finder* is enhanced by both a detailed table of contents and a small,

1,000-entry index at the back of the book. Unfortunately, the index often fails to provide needed entries. *Examples:* Mozart is mentioned—and pictured—in the article "Music and Dance," but the index lacks an entry for the famous composer. Likewise, the average life span of a dog appears in "How Life Begins," but "dog" does not appear in the index. A related problem is the total absence of cross-references in both the text and the index. Not all critics, however, have found the book's poor index and lack of cross-referencing a major drawback: "While indexing is not comprehensive enough for the book to be used for quick reference, by using the table of contents and browsing, students will be able to find the answers to many questions" (*Reference Books Bulletin* in *Booklist*, March 1, 1990, p. 1379).

Colorful, contemporary drawings, found on every page, add substantially to the informational value of the book. As Dupré points out in his introduction, "Each subject is shown on illustrated double pages. Pictures help you to understand and memorize better; diagrams replace long explanations; drawings let you imagine specific scenes." *Examples:* The aforementioned article "Computers" includes a well-captioned drawing showing the major components of today's personal computers. "How Life Begins" is greatly enhanced by realistic artwork depicting human reproduction from conception to birth.

Physically, the encyclopedia possesses an attractive, bright, and varied page layout that will appeal to the child's eye. In addition, the paper is of good quality and the binding strong enough to sustain heavy use by active youngsters. The bright and washable covers are another plus.

REPORT CARD: BARRON'S JUNIOR FACT FINDER				
TOPIC	**COVERAGE**	**ACCURACY**	**RECENCY**	**CLARITY**
Computers	A	A	A	A
Halloween	F*	NA	NA	NA
Johnson, Magic	F*	NA	NA	NA
Measles	F*	NA	NA	NA
Nuclear Energy	B	A	NA	A
Panda Bears	F*	NA	NA	NA
Rock Music	F*	NA	NA	NA
Rose (Flower)	F*	NA	NA	NA
Russia	F*	NA	NA	NA
Sex Education	A	A	A	A

A = Excellent; **B** = Above Average; **C** = Average; **D** = Below Average; **F** = Poor; **NA** = Not Applicable
*No Article

SUMMARY

Barron's Junior Fact Finder, which originated in France in 1987 and was published in English in North America in 1989, is an inexpensive, attractively presented one-volume encyclopedia for children ages 7–14. Topically arranged, its most appealing features are clearly and interestingly written articles enhanced by informative, full-color drawings on every page. On the negative side, the encyclopedia's coverage is quite selective, its treatment of those topics covered sometimes superficial, and its index inadequate. The bottom line: Despite flaws, a good buy for the money.

OTHER OPINIONS

American Reference Books Annual, 1990, pp. 18–19 (review by Lois J. Buttlar); *Reference Books Bulletin* (in *Booklist*), March 1, 1990, p. 1379 (unsigned review).

FACTS PLUS

FACTS

Full Title: *Facts Plus: An Almanac of Essential Information.* **Author:** Susan C. Anthony. **Publisher:** Instructional Resources Company. **Date Published:** First Edition, 1991; Second Edition, 1992.

Volumes: One. **Words:** 100,000. **Pages:** 250. **Articles:** 103. **Bibliographies:** 45. **Illustrations and Maps:** 300. **Cross-references:** None. **Index entries:** 3,500. **Edito-**

rial Staff, Advisers, and Contributors: 15. **Trim Size:** 8¼ × 10¾ in.

Price and Sales Information: $15.95 paperbound, plus $2.50 shipping and handling. Individual consumers can purchase *Facts Plus* in bookstores or, if the book is not in stock, it can be ordered. Similarly, schools and libraries can order it through a book wholesaler. To order the encyclopedia directly from the publisher, call toll-free 1-800-356-9315 or write Instructional Re-sources Company, 1013 East Dimond Blvd. #188, Anchorage, AK 99515.

EVALUATION

Created and written by schoolteacher Susan Anthony, the paperbound *Facts Plus* is a curriculum oriented reference work intended for young North American students in grades 4–8. In the words of Anthony, the book "presents in a concise and understandable format the basic core of information taught in schools and necessary for comprehending books and newspapers intended for the general public. It's arranged to provide a foundation and framework to help learners organize their growing knowledge" (introduction). Although the author calls *Facts Plus* an almanac (presumably because a new edition is scheduled to appear each year), it is encyclopedic in scope and has much in common with other small encyclopedias for children.

The book's contents are arranged topically (as opposed to alphabetically) in 10 chapters, or sections: "Time and Space," "Science and Health," "The Earth and Its People," "The United States," "Maps," "Libraries and Books," "The English Language," "Writing, Music and Art," "Math and Numbers," and "Handbook." Each chapter contains approximately 10 articles covering fairly specific topics. *Example:* "Science and Health" includes articles on the weather, climate, geology, energy, matter, plants and animals, the human body, nutrition and health, and drugs and alcohol. Much of the information in *Facts Plus* is in chart or tabular form. The book concludes with a bibliography of sources and a detailed 18-page index.

As the Report Card below indicates, *Facts Plus* often fails to provide adequate coverage of subjects of concern to young students. On the subject of computers, for instance, the book does not explain what they are and how they operate. The only real mention of computers appears in an article called "The Library," which includes a simple line drawing of a computer worksta-tion accompanied by this caption: "Locating information is easier and faster with computer technology. Modern libraries have the catalog and much other information available on computers." In other instances, the book fails to even mention important subjects, such as childhood diseases, AIDS, and human sexuality. The three-page article "Human Body Systems" purposely excludes the urinary, endocrine, and reproductive systems.

Material in *Facts Plus* is normally accurate, reasonably current, and presented without overt bias; controversial topics, however, are usually ignored, which is a subtle form of bias. The writing style is normally clear in a textbookish fashion, as the two sentences on computers quoted in the previous paragraph show. But occasionally explanatory material can be obscure or confusing or incomplete, as in the case of this description of nuclear energy: "Energy changes from one form to another. For example, *nuclear* energy makes the *light* of the sun, which plants use to make food, stored as *chemical* energy." Few students in the upper elementary or junior high school grades will comprehend this explanation of nuclear energy, particularly when a pie chart on the same page shows nuclear energy as 6 percent of the world's total energy source.

Facts Plus lacks cross-references but specific information is easy to find, thanks to an annotated table of contents and a comprehensive 3,500-entry index at the back of the book. Except for 10 pages of blue-and-white maps, all 300 illustrations in the book are black-and-white drawings. In almost all instances, they contribute substantially to the informational value of the book. Physically, the paperbound book is generally unattractive and the adhesive (or perfect) binding will not hold up to heavy use. On the plus side, it does have large, readable print.

REPORT CARD: FACTS PLUS

TOPIC	COVERAGE	ACCURACY	RECENCY	CLARITY
Computers	D	A	C	B
Halloween	C	B	C	B
Johnson, Magic	D	C	C	A
Measles	F*	NA	NA	NA
Nuclear Energy	F	C	B	D
Panda Bears	F*	NA	NA	NA
Rock Music	F*	NA	NA	NA
Rose (Flower)	F*	NA	NA	NA
Russia	C	A	A	A
Sex Education	F*	NA	NA	NA

A = Excellent; **B** = Above Average; **C** = Average; **D** = Below Average; **F** = Poor; **NA** = Not Applicable
*No Article

SUMMARY

The paperbound *Facts Plus*—subtitled "An Almanac of Essential Information"—was first published in 1991 and revised in 1992; presumably the designation "almanac" means new editions will appear every year. Written by a schoolteacher, the book intends to cover subjects studied in the upper elementary and junior high school grades in North American schools. Unfortunately, coverage of many pertinent topics—computers, childhood diseases, sex education, etc.—tends to be weak or nonexistent. Although usually written in a clear, textbookish style, the book does contain some murky explanations. Its best features are easy access to material and a low price. The bottom line: An eclectic and mostly failed effort to summarize essential information in one volume.

OTHER OPINIONS

Reference Books Bulletin (in *Booklist*), June 1, 1991, p. 1899 (unsigned review); *School Library Journal*, May 1992, pp. 26–27.

FIRST DICTIONARY OF CULTURAL LITERACY

FACTS

Full Title: *A First Dictionary of Cultural Literacy: What Our Children Need to Know.* **Editor:** E.D. Hirsch, Jr. **Publisher:** Houghton Mifflin Company. **Date Published:** 1989 hardcover; 1991 paperbound.

Volumes: One. **Words:** 150,000. **Pages:** 285. **Articles:** 2,000. **Bibliographies:** 80. **Illustrations and Maps:** 400. **Cross-references:** 2,500. **Index entries:** 2,750. **Editorial Staff, Advisers, and Contributors:** 23. **Trim size:** 7½ × 9¼ in.

Price and Sales Information: $14.95 hardcover; $9.95 paperbound. Individual consumers can purchase the *First Dictionary of Cultural Literacy* in bookstores or, if the book is not in stock, it can be ordered. Similarly, schools and libraries can order it through a book wholesaler. To order the encyclopedia directly from the publisher, call 1-800-733-7075 or write Houghton Mifflin Company, 222 Berkeley Street, Boston, MA 02116.-3764

EVALUATION

Dissatisfaction with the U.S. educational system prompted editor Hirsch, an English professor at the University of Virginia at Charlottesville, to compile the *First Dictionary of Cultural Literacy*, an encyclopedic dictionary that "outlines the knowledge that, in the opinion of several hundred teachers and parents across the nation, American children should acquire by the end of the sixth grade" (introduction). Earlier he put together the DICTIONARY OF CULTURAL LITERACY, a similar reference book in one volume intended for older students and adults. To facilitate and promote his work, Hirsch founded the Cultural Literacy Foundation, an organization located in Charlottesville composed of people around the country devoted to improving the U.S. educational system.

Hirsch and his colleagues at the foundation have spent considerable time and energy trying to determine what constitutes the "common core of knowledge" children should know—and hence what should be included in the *First Dictionary of Cultural Literacy*, which functions at least partly as a curriculum guide. Not everyone agrees, however, that their efforts have been entirely successful. James Rettig, writing in *Wilson Library Bulletin* (January 1990, p. 128), finds the book "flawed by its naive Gradgrindian belief that a knowledge of fact and fact alone constitutes cultural literacy." And Kathleen Craver, in a perceptive review in *American Reference Books Annual* (1990, p. 132), points out that the book's contents "reflect a white, male, Western bias and do not evenly represent the diversity of our culture. There are no entries, for example, for James Baldwin, Cinco de Mayo, Carry Nation, or Edith Hamilton."

The *First Dictionary of Cultural Literacy* also fails to include any mention of popular sports (like baseball, football, and basketball), nonreligious holidays (Thanksgiving and Halloween), and domestic animals (dogs and cats), each of which plays a role in the social, intellectual, and cultural development of American children. The most pervasive criticism of the book, however, is its shallow treatment of those topics it does cover. *Examples:* The entire entry "Dinosaur" reads as follows: "Dinosaurs were reptiles that lived millions of years ago and are now extinct. Some types of dinosaurs were small, but others were larger than elephants." The entry "Nicaragua" is equally superficial: "Nicaragua is a Spanish-speaking country in Central America, north of Costa Rica."

Indeed, *superficial* is the one word that has most often been used to describe the contents of Hirsch's book. A review in *Reference Books Bulletin* (in *Booklist*, January 15, 1990, p. 1040) states, "Coverage is broad but superficial," and the aforementioned review by Kathleen Craver finds, "The acquisition of this sort of knowledge is superficial."

Information in the *First Dictionary of Cultural Literacy* is usually reliable (except when out of date, as in the case of entries for Germany, Russia, Yugoslavia, etc.), free from bias (except in the selection of topics covered), and current as of the late 1980s. Almost without exception, the writing style is clear but lifeless; most students in the upper elementary grades will have no problem comprehending the text. The entry "Computer" is typical: "A computer is a device that stores information and follows instructions very rapidly. *See also* FLOPPY DISK; HARDWARE; SOFTWARE."

Finding specific topics and facts in the encyclopedia is normally not difficult, due largely to a comprehensive index at the back of the book and numerous cross-references throughout the text; the cross-references are readily identifiable, printed in small capital letters (see "Computer" in the preceding paragraph for an example). Another useful feature is the section entitled "Guide to Further Reading," which describes approximately 80 reference books children may consult for additional information.

The book also contains approximately 400 black-and-white illustrations, mostly drawings and photographs. While not particularly eye-catching, the illustrations usually enhance the printed text. Physically, the book is reasonably attractive, and both the hardcover and paperbound editions are adequately bound.

SUMMARY

The brainchild of a university professor who is dissatisfied with the U.S. educational system, the *First Dictionary of Cultural Literacy* seeks to identify and concisely explain people, places, events, concepts, and other topics that students should be familiar with by the end of elementary school. The idea of such a book as a curriculum guide or even a sort of national test for passage on to junior high school is both interesting and controversial, but as a source of encyclopedic information, the book is of only marginal value. Many pertinent topics are treated too cursorily or vaguely to be of much use, or they are ignored completely. Moreover, there is evidence of cultural bias in the selection of topics, and the book is no longer trustworthy because of its age. On the plus side, entries are clearly (if dully) written, specific information is easy to retrieve, and the 80-entry "Guide to Further Reading" will be useful to interested students, teachers, and parents. The bottom line: Too superficial to cut the reference mustard.

REPORT CARD: FIRST DICTIONARY OF CULTURAL LITERACY				
TOPIC	COVERAGE	ACCURACY	RECENCY	CLARITY
Computers	D	A	B	A
Halloween	F*	NA	NA	NA
Johnson, Magic	F*	NA	NA	NA
Measles	C	A	A	A
Nuclear Energy	C	A	B	A
Panda Bears	F*	NA	NA	NA
Rock Music	D	A	C	A
Rose (Flower)	F*	NA	NA	NA
Russia	D	F	F	A
Sex Education	D	A	C	A

A = Excellent; **B** = Above Average; **C** = Average; **D** = Below Average; **F** = Poor; **NA** = Not Applicable
*No Article

OTHER OPINIONS

American Reference Books Annual, 1990, pp. 131–32 (review by Kathleen W. Craver); *Reference Books Bulletin* (in *Booklist*), January 15, 1990, pp. 1040–42 (unsigned review); *Wilson Library Bulletin*, January 1990, p. 128 (review by James Rettig).

KINGFISHER CHILDREN'S ENCYCLOPEDIA

FACTS

Full Title: *The Kingfisher Children's Encyclopedia*. **Editor:** John Paton. **Publisher:** Kingfisher Books, an imprint of CKG Publishers, Inc. **Former Titles:** *The Doubleday Children's Encyclopedia* (Doubleday, 1990; 4 vols.); FINDING OUT: SILVER BURDETT'S CHILDREN'S ENCYCLOPEDIA (Silver Burdett Company, 1981; 10 vols.). **Date Published:** First published as the *Kingfisher Children's Encyclopedia* in 1992.

Also published as the GROLIER CHILDREN'S ENCYCLOPEDIA (Grolier Educational Corp., 1993; 10 vols.).

Volumes: One. **Words:** 250,000. **Pages:** 816. **Articles:** 1,300. **Bibliographies:** None. **Illustrations and Maps:** 2,000. **Cross-references:** 1,500. **Index Entries:** 6,000. **Editorial Staff, Advisers, and Contributors:** 6. Trim Size: 7 ½ × 10¼ in.

Price and Sales Information: $29.95. Individual consumers can purchase the *Kingfisher Children's Encyclopedia* in bookstores or, if the book is not in stock, it can be ordered. Similarly, schools and libraries can order it through a book wholesaler. To order the encyclopedia directly from the publisher, call toll-free 1-800-497-1657 or write CKG Publishers, Inc., 95 Madison Avenue, New York, NY 10016.

EVALUATION

First published in Great Britain by Grisewood & Dempsey Ltd. in 1991 in 10 thin volumes, the *Kingfisher Children's Encyclopedia* appeared in North America a year later in a single-volume edition adapted for young readers in the U.S. and Canada. In 1993, it also became available in a 10-volume edition marketed to North American schools and libraries under the title GROLIER CHILDREN'S ENCYCLOPEDIA. The encyclopedia represents an updating of the *Doubleday Children's Encyclopedia* (Doubleday, 1990), published in four volumes and no longer on the market. A much earlier version of the encyclopedia is the now defunct 10-volume FINDING OUT: SILVER BURDETT'S CHILDREN'S ENCYCLOPEDIA. Despite the different titles and varying number of volumes, all of these encyclopedias are essentially—or incestuously—the same work, each containing 816 pages and approximately 250,000 words, 1,300 articles, and 2,000 illustrations.

The one-volume Americanized edition of the *Kingfisher Children's Encyclopedia*, under review here, is published by CKG (Chambers Kingfisher Graham) Publishers, a new publisher that handles Grisewood & Dempsey products in the U.S.; CKG is a subsidiary of the giant French publisher, Groupe de la Cité. The editor is John Paton, an experienced British encyclopedia-maker whose credits include the KNOWLEDGE ENCYCLOPEDIA, the PICTURE ENCYCLOPEDIA FOR CHIL-

DREN, and RAND MCNALLY'S CHILDREN'S ENCY-CLOPEDIA, all one-volume reference works also originally published in Great Britain by Grisewood & Dempsey.

The late Michael Dempsey (of Grisewood & Dempsey) is well known on both sides of the Atlantic as a publisher and editor of encyclopedias for young people, including the HARVER JUNIOR WORLD ENCYCLOPEDIA, which *Kingfisher* resembles in many ways, the TROLL STUDENT ENCYCLOPEDIA, and the GREAT WORLD ENCYCLOPEDIA. Dempsey has also written many children's books on scientific subjects, which perhaps accounts for *Kingfisher*'s noticeable emphasis on the natural and technical sciences.

Kingfisher, which is intended for children ages 7–14, contains approximately 1,300 articles, arranged alphabetically. Unlike its chief competitor, the RANDOM HOUSE CHILDREN'S ENCYCLOPEDIA, *Kingfisher* is basically a specific entry encyclopedia (as opposed to broad entry). For instance, Mozart has his own entry in *Kingfisher*, whereas in the Random House work information about the composer is subsumed in four broad articles, i.e., "Hapsburgs," "Musical Instruments," "Opera and Singing," and "Orchestras."

Kingfisher adequately covers all major areas of knowledge, but clearly scientific topics receive the most attention. For example, the articles "Comet," "Computer," "Dinosaur," "Genetics," "Microscope," "Nuclear Energy," "Ocean," "Reproduction," and "Star" are all a page or more in length—generous coverage for a one-volume children's encyclopedia. Other articles, such as "Aircraft," "Earth," "Insects," "Moon," and "Space Exploration," are double-page spreads. Prominent people (e.g., U.S. presidents), places (e.g., U.S. states and Canadian provinces), and events (e.g., the American Civil War) are also well covered.

Much information in the encyclopedia appears in fact boxes and panels found in the broad margins of each page. *Example:*

The article "Genetics" is accompanied by a fact box that informs the reader, "The chances of a baby being a girl or boy are about the same. But one in 16 families with four children is likely to have four boys, while another such family will have four girls. Much longer strings of boys or girls have been recorded. One French family had nothing but girls—72 of them—in three generations."

The contents of *Kingfisher* are normally accurate and presented in an unbiased manner, although sometimes controversial issues are ignored. The article "Nuclear Energy," for instance, states, "Nuclear energy can be controlled to provide us with power. In a nuclear power plant, control rods are lowered into a reactor to keep the reaction in check," but at no point does the article explain the potential hazards of nuclear power or mention such disasters as Three Mile Island or Chernobyl. The encyclopedia is current as of the early 1990s, as the articles on Russia, Germany, and Nicaragua attest.

The writing style tends to be clear, simple, direct, and interesting to read. Paton and his contributors are especially adept at rendering potentially difficult or confusing ideas and concepts such as heredity, inoculation, and human reproduction comprehensible to young readers. The beginning of the article "Computer" provides a good sense of the encyclopedia's style:

> Computers are playing a bigger and bigger part in all our lives. They can play a game of chess with you, guide a spacecraft, check fingerprints, and draw a map of Australia. They can do all these things, and many more, merely because they can add, subtract, and compare one number with another. Computers are special because they can do millions of calculations in a second.
>
> Although the computer works with numbers, the information it uses does not have to start off as numbers. We can feed almost anything into it, but the first thing the computer does is to turn everything into numbers. But the numbers it uses are not quite the same as ours. We use the numbers 0 to 9. All the

computer needs is 0 and 1. In fact, it can only count up to 1! This is called the BINARY SYSTEM.

The encyclopedia is well organized, and finding specific topics and facts should pose no problem for most students at the elementary or junior high school level. Some 1,500 cross-references throughout the text assist the reader in locating additional information. Most cross-references are found within the articles, designated by small capital letters; see the text of "Computer" in the preceding paragraph for an example. *Kingfisher* also includes two indexes, both found at the back of the book. The first and more useful is an alphabetical index of 4,500 entries that provides quick and easy access to specific information in the 1,300 articles. The other index, which contains 1,500 entries, lists subjects under 17 broad headings, such as "Animals," "Countries and Places," and "Our Earth." The encyclopedia also assigns each entry one of 16 subject symbols designed to help users locate articles on broad topics, such as plants and food, the arts, language and literature, and travel and transportation; for instance, the symbol for travel and transportation is an airplane.

The illustrations, which comprise roughly half the encyclopedia's total text, are almost all in color and most are drawings and photographs. With few exceptions, they add significantly to the informational value of the book, as well as to its aesthetic appeal. Of particular value are the captions accompanying most of the illustrations. By way of example, the article "Computer" includes a photo of a room filled with antiquated computing machines; the caption reads: "The American computer ENIAC was completed in 1946. Early computers such as this filled large rooms, but they were no more powerful than a small modern pocket computer."

Physically, *Kingfisher* has a bright, engaging page layout and large, readable typefaces. The book also has washable covers, is bound to withstand heavy use, and comes with a colorful jacket. A possible drawback concerns the book's weight (nearly six pounds), which could make it difficult for some young people to handle easily.

Considering its size and quality, the encyclopedia is an outstanding bargain at $29.95. This price becomes even more attractive when one learns that the 10-volume school and library edition of *Kingfisher* called the GROLIER STUDENT'S ENCYCLOPEDIA is priced at over $200.00, or that earlier versions of the encyclopedia sold for $69.95 (the *Doubleday Children's Encyclopedia*) and $140.00 (FINDING OUT: SILVER BURDETT'S CHILDREN'S ENCYCLOPEDIA). In addition, *Kingfisher* is considerably less expensive than its rival, the RANDOM HOUSE CHILDREN'S ENCYCLOPEDIA, currently priced at $50.00.

REPORT CARD: KINGFISHER CHILDREN'S ENCYCLOPEDIA				
TOPIC	**COVERAGE**	**ACCURACY**	**RECENCY**	**CLARITY**
Computers	A	A	A	A
Halloween	F*	NA	NA	NA
Johnson, Magic	F*	NA	NA	NA
Measles	C	A	A	A
Nuclear Energy	B	A	B	A
Panda Bears	C	A	C	B
Rock Music	B	A	A	A
Rose (Flower)	F*	NA	NA	NA
Russia	B	A	A	A
Sex Education	A	A	A	A

A = Excellent; **B** = Above Average; **C** = Average; **D** = Below Average; **F** = Poor; **NA** = Not Applicable
*No Article

SUMMARY

Although the *Kingfisher Children's Encyclopedia* originated in Great Britain, the edition sold in North America has been prepared with U.S. and Canadian readers in mind. It is also published on this side of the Atlantic in a 10-volume edition for schools and libraries under the title GROLIER CHILDREN'S ENCYCLOPEDIA. Intended for young readers ages 7–14, the encyclopedia emphasizes scientific subjects, but all major areas of knowledge receive adequate coverage. Material in the book is normally reliable, up-to-date, and presented in an unbiased manner, and the writing style is clear, precise, and interesting. Illustrations, which make up about half the encyclopedia's total text, are uniformly excellent, adding to both the informational and aesthetic value of the book, which is a real bargain at $29.95. The bottom line: Along with the RANDOM HOUSE CHILDREN'S ENCYCLOPEDIA, the *Kingfisher Children's Encyclopedia* is the best single-volume general children's encyclopedia currently on the North American market.

OTHER OPINIONS

Reference Books Bulletin (in *Booklist*), October 15, 1992, pp. 456–57 (unsigned review).

MY FIRST ENCYCLOPEDIA (DORLING KINDERSLEY)

FACTS

Full Title: *My First Encyclopedia*. **Author:** Carol Watson. **Project Editor:** Sheila Hanly. **U.S. Editor:** B. Alison Weir. **Publisher:** Dorling Kindersley. **Distributor:** Houghton Mifflin Company. **Date Published:** 1993.

Volumes: One. **Words:** 15,000. **Pages:** 78. **Articles:** 350. **Bibliographies:** None. **Illustrations and Maps:** 600. **Cross-references:** None. **Index entries:** 750. **Editorial Staff, Advisers, and Contributors:** 21. **Trim Size:** 10 × 13 in.

Price and Sales Information: $16.95. Individual consumers can purchase *My First Encyclopedia* by Carol Watson in bookstores or, if the book is not in stock, it can be ordered. Similarly, schools and libraries can order it through a book wholesaler. To order the encyclopedia directly from the distributor, call toll-free 1-800-225-3362 or write Houghton Mifflin Company, 222 Berkeley Street, Boston, MA 02116-3764.

EVALUATION

Produced by Dorling Kindersley, a British publisher of children's books noted for lavish color illustrations, *My First Encyclopedia* by Carol Watson is, as might be expected, a heavily and colorfully illustrated beginning encyclopedia for children ages 3–8. The book was originally published in Great Britain and in 1993 appeared on this side of the Atlantic in an Americanized edition.

As the Report Card (see below) graphically shows, *My First Encyclopedia* does not attempt a comprehensive survey of basic knowledge and information of potential interest to young children. It contains nothing, for instance, on such subjects as comets, dinosaurs, holidays, and childhood diseases, nor does it cover abstract topics like heredity, nuclear energy, poetry, and religion. Rather, its coverage is highly selective, providing a simple verbal and visual introduction to selected topics, both familiar and esoteric, that preschoolers and beginning readers might encounter or want to know about. Essentially, the book is as much for browsing as it is for reference.

As the introductory "Note to Parents and Teachers" explains, the encyclopedia "is arranged in themes that parallel a child's developing curiosity and interests. Starting with a child's immediate daily experiences, the themes extend to an exploration of the wider world, covering topics such as animals, climatic regions, the people of the world, and even outer space." Altogether the book explores 33 such broad subjects in two-page spreads; each spread covers, on average, 10 specific topics. *Example:* The spread "In the Ocean" contains brief entries on dolphins, sharks, sea horses, octopuses, shrimp, plankton, jellyfish, tropical fish, coral reefs, fishing boats, and scuba divers.

Information found in Dorling Kindersley's *My First Encyclopedia* is naturally quite superficial, but it does serve to introduce language, objects, and concepts to the young child. The encyclopedia's elementary text is accurate, current, and objectively presented. Watson's writing style is simple,

straightforward, and easy for preschoolers or beginning readers to comprehend. The entry "Office Worker" (under "Jobs People Do") typifies the book's style:

> Some people do their jobs in an office. They work at a desk and may use a computer to help them.

Access to specific topics and facts in the encyclopedia is easily accomplished, enhanced by a 750-entry A-to-Z index at the back of the book. Reference books for very young children rarely include an index, but in this case the editors felt one was needed, principally as a training device: "*My First Encyclopedia* is designed to prepare children for more sophisticated information books. A complete alphabetical index is included to simplify the task of locating information on specific topics. You can also encourage children to use the index for cross-referencing."

Large, bright, eye-catching illustrations—all full-color drawings and photographs—make up approximately half the book's total text. In the words of a review in *Publishers Weekly* (May 3, 1993, p. 306), "the full-color, crystal-clear photos steal the show, enabling preschoolers to 'read' the pages on their own and identify familiar objects." The illustrations are also usually informative as complements to the printed text. Happily, children and adults shown in the book represent a multicultural mix; one photo, for example, shows an African American male working as a librarian. Physically, the book is large (10 × 13 in.), handsomely made, and bound in washable laminated covers.

SUMMARY

Dorling Kindersley's *My First Encyclopedia* briefly describes selected topics of potential interest to children ages 3–8. As the Report Card suggests (next page), no effort has been made to deal with knowledge in a comprehensive fashion. Heavily and colorfully illustrated, the book is topically arranged, clearly and simply written, and handsomely produced. It will appeal to both nonreaders and beginning readers. The bottom line: The best of the small "first" encyclopedias currently available.

REPORT CARD: MY FIRST ENCYCLOPEDIA

TOPIC	COVERAGE	ACCURACY	RECENCY	CLARITY
Computers	C	A	A	A
Halloween	F*	NA	NA	NA
Johnson, Magic	F*	NA	NA	NA
Measles	F*	NA	NA	NA
Nuclear Energy	F*	NA	NA	NA
Panda Bears	F*	NA	NA	NA
Rock Music	F*	NA	NA	NA
Rose (Flower)	F*	NA	NA	NA
Russia	F*	NA	NA	NA
Sex Education	F*	NA	NA	NA

A = Excellent; B = Above Average; C = Average; D = Below Average; F = Poor; NA = Not Applicable
*No Article

OTHER OPINIONS

Publishers Weekly, May 3, 1993, p. 306 (unsigned review); *Reference Books Bulletin* (in *Booklist*), July 1993, pp. 2003–04 (unsigned review).

MY FIRST ENCYCLOPEDIA (TROLL)

FACTS

Full Title: *My First Encyclopedia*. **Author and Illustrator:** Alan Snow. **Publisher:** Troll Associates Inc. **Date Published:** 1992.
 Volumes: One. **Words:** 4,000. **Pages:** 30. **Articles:** 90. **Bibliographies:** None. **Illustrations and Maps:** 75. **Cross-references:** None. **Index Entries:** 126. **Editorial Staff, Advisers, and Contributors:** One. **Trim Size:** 10 × 12½ in.

Price and Sales Information: $11.79 hardcover; $4.95 paperbound. Individual consumers can purchase *My First Encyclopedia* by Alan Snow in bookstores or, if the book is not in stock, it can be ordered. Similarly, schools and libraries can order it through a book wholesaler. To order the encyclopedia directly from the publisher, call toll-free 1-800-526-5289 or write Troll Associates Inc., 100 Corporate Drive, Mahwah, NJ 07430.

EVALUATION

Similar in purpose and format to Dorling Kindersley's MY FIRST ENCYCLOPEDIA (see above), Troll's *My First Encyclopedia* by Alan Snow is a simply written, topically arranged, heavily illustrated book for preschoolers and beginning readers. The encyclopedia, which contains only 30 pages (or less than half the size of the Dorling Kindersley book), divides its contents into 11 broad subjects: "Your Body," "People of the World," "Keeping in Touch," "Transport," "Prehistoric World," "Animals Today," "More Animals," "Plants,"

"The Earth," "Space," and "It's the Greatest." Each of these sections (most two pages in length) very briefly covers seven or eight specific topics. *Example:* "Transport" includes entries on cars, trucks, trains, motorcycles, airplanes, helicopters, ships, and speedboats.

As can be seen, the book's focus is almost entirely on scientific and technical subjects. Obviously, many subjects of potential interest to young children are ignored. Treatment of those topics that are covered tends to be quite superficial, with only a few sentences per entry. For instance, "Cars" informs the reader that "Cars are the most popular kind of transport. Most cars have engines that burn gasoline. The gasoline is burned inside the engine. As it burns, it makes the pistons go up and down. The movement of the pistons makes the wheels go around." A review in *Reference Books Bulletin* (in *Booklist*, June 15, 1992, p. 1884) rightly observes, "In a maximum of two pages, with half or more of each page taken up with illustrations, there is little space available for more than a tidbit approach."

What little information there is in the encyclopedia is generally reliable, up-to-date, and presented without apparent bias. Snow's writing style is almost always clear, simple, and to the point. The few words devoted to computers (in "Keeping in Touch") are typical:

Modern technology has given us new machines for communicating with each other. Pictures, sounds, and writing can be sent across the world in just a few seconds. Computers store lots of information. They can send each other messages.

Locating specific topics or facts in Troll's *My First Encyclopedia* is usually not difficult. The 11 sections can be quickly scanned, and there is a small alphabetical index at the back of the book. But the index leaves something to be desired, as Ellen Dibner points out in her review in *School Library Journal* (November 1992, p. 138): "The catchy headings ('Keeping in touch') or the vague ones ('More animals') necessitate using the 126 listings in the index to locate a subject. However, although 'Your body' is a heading, 'body,' or 'human body' are not in the index—only specific parts or systems. Thus, finding the right page for a specific topic is time consuming."

Snow's illustrations, which comprise about half the total text, are all drawings in full color. Bright and bold, they will catch the young reader's eye, but often they lack much informational value. People and animals, for instance, are all depicted as cutesy, cartoon-like characters. Physically, the book is large (10 × 12½ in.), attractively laid out, and the hardcover edition is bound with laminated covers.

REPORT CARD: MY FIRST ENCYCLOPEDIA (TROLL)

Topic	Coverage	Accuracy	Recency	Clarity
Computers	D	A	A	A
Halloween	F*	NA	NA	NA
Johnson, Magic	F*	NA	NA	NA
Measles	F*	NA	NA	NA
Nuclear Energy	F*	NA	NA	NA
Panda Bears	F*	NA	NA	NA
Rock Music	F*	NA	NA	NA
Rose (Flower)	F*	NA	NA	NA
Russia	F*	NA	NA	NA
Sex Education	F*	NA	NA	NA

A = Excellent; **B** = Above Average; **C** = Average; **D** = Below Average; **F** = Poor; **NA** = Not Applicable
*No Article

SUMMARY

Troll's *My First Encyclopedia* is a superficial beginning reference book of only 30 pages written and illustrated by Alan Snow. Topically arranged, its emphasis is almost entirely on science and technology, meaning that many topics of interest to young children are ignored. Troll's *My First Encyclopedia* should not be confused with a book of the same title published by Dorling Kindersley and written by Carol Watson, which is much the superior work (see preceding entry). The bottom line: A mediocre effort.

OTHER OPINIONS

Reference Books Bulletin (in *Booklist*), June 15, 1992, pp. 1884–86 (unsigned review);

School Library Journal, November 1992, p. 138 (review by Ellen Dibner).

RANDOM HOUSE CHILDREN'S ENCYCLOPEDIA

FACTS

Full Title: *The Random House Children's Encyclopedia.* **Senior Editor:** Ann Kramer. **Senior Art Editor:** Miranda Kennedy. U.S. **Editor:** Regina Kahney. **Publisher:** Random House, Inc. **Date Published:** First Edition, 1991; Revised Edition, 1993.

British Title: *The Dorling Kindersley Children's Illustrated Encyclopedia.*

Volumes: One. **Words:** 250,000. **Pages:** 644. **Articles:** 2,500 (425 main entries). **Bibliographies:** None. **Illustrations and Maps:** 3,500. **Cross-references:** 4,000.

Index Entries: 6,000. **Editorial Staff, Advisers, and Contributors:** 88. **Trim Size:** 8½ × 10¾ in.

Price and Sales Information: $50.00. Individual consumers can purchase the *Random House Children's Encyclopedia* in bookstores or, if the book is not in stock, it can be ordered. Similarly, schools and libraries can order it through a book wholesaler. To order the encyclopedia directly from the publisher, call toll-free 1-800-726-0600 or write Random House, Inc., 201 East 50th Street, New York, NY 10022.

EVALUATION

This impressive single-volume encyclopedia for children ages 7–14 first appeared in Great Britain in 1991 as the *Dorling Kindersley Children's Illustrated Encyclopedia.* The publisher, Dorling Kindersley Ltd., is internationally known for high quality children's publications; trademark features include large and colorful close-up photographs and cutaway drawings, a variety of clear and attractive typefaces, and very good paper.

Later in 1991, the encyclopedia appeared in North America under the title *Random House Children's Encyclopedia* in an edition modified for U.S. and Canadian readers. In 1993, the American publisher (Random House) issued a revised edition that updated a number of articles, particularly those dealing with the former Soviet Union and the many political changes that have occurred in Eastern Europe recently. The encyclopedia has also been (or soon will be) published in various national editions in such countries as China, Taiwan, Korea, and Japan. A great success story, the encyclopedia has sold over a million copies around the world since its initial publication in 1991.

The bulk of the *Random House Children's Encyclopedia* consists of approximately 425 main articles, each one or two full pages in length. Arranged alphabetically, these substantial articles are of the broad-entry type—that is, they cover a large subject with smaller, more specific topics treated within. For instance, the article "Festivals and Feasts" includes brief entries on Thanksgiving, Halloween, and the Chinese New Year. The editors estimate that the encyclopedia contains about 2,000 such specific entries, or subentries. As a point of comparison, the other major one-volume encyclopedia for children, the KINGFISHER CHILDREN'S ENCYCLOPEDIA, employs the specific-entry approach, e.g., Thanksgiving has its own main entry.

In addition to its 425 broad articles, the *Random House Children's Encyclopedia* includes a 23-page section called the "Fact Finder" at the back of the book, just before the index. This section furnishes miscellaneous facts on historical, geographical, and scientific topics in tabular or chart form. For instance, lists of U.S. presidents, kings and queens of Great Britain, international organizations, and longest bridges in the world can be found in the "Fact Finder."

The encyclopedia covers all major areas of knowledge adequately, but scientific and technical subjects predominate. Specifically, more than half of the 425 main articles deal with some aspect of the sciences. *Examples:* "Atmosphere," "Atoms and Molecules," "Bears and Pandas," "Beavers," "Bees and Wasps," "Beetles," "Biology," "Birds," "Comets and Meteors," "Computers," "Corals," "Dinosaurs," "Disease," "Doctors," "Electronics," "Engines," "Fossils," "Grasses and Cereals," "Grasshoppers and Crickets," "Heart and Blood," "Heat," "Iron and Steel," "Lasers," "Magnetism," "Microscopes," "Microscopic Life," "Moon," "Planets," "Plastics," "Reproduction," "Seashore Wildlife," "Space Flight," and "Wheels."

About 150 of the 425 articles are devoted to prominent people, places, historical events, and social developments. *Examples:* "Alexander the Great"; "Canada"; "Castles"; "Cities"; "Civil War; American"; "Civil War; English"; "Eskimos"; "India"; "King, Martin Luther"; "Knights and Heraldry"; "Napoleonic Wars"; "Ottoman Empire"; "Reformation"; "Roosevelt, Franklin Delano"; "United Nations"; and "Women's Rights." The remaining main articles—"Architecture," "Ball Games," "Ballet," "Churches and Cathedrals," "Drawing," "Magic," "Opera and Singing," "Popular Music," and "Writers and Poets" are examples—cover the humanities, which obviously receive the least attention.

The encyclopedia provides selective rather than systematic coverage of U.S. and Canadian topics. For example, states and provinces do not have entries, main or sub. Franklin Roosevelt has an entry but Lyndon Johnson is found only in the list of U.S. presidents in the "Fact Finder." Indeed, the only "Johnson" listed in the book's index is Amy Johnson, an early English aviator; among the missing Johnsons are Andrew, Jack, Lyndon, Magic, and Samuel. On the other hand, rival KINGFISHER CHILDREN'S ENCYCLOPEDIA includes an entry for every U.S. president and state and Canadian province.

The *Random House Children's Encyclopedia* is a meticulously edited reference work. Its text is trustworthy, up-to-date, and objectively presented. Racial, ethnic, religious, and gender stereotypes are carefully avoided. *Examples:* The article "Islam" observes that the religion's "popularity has been increased by Islamic fundamentalists—extremely religious people who call for a return to strict, traditional Islamic values"; the article "Doctor" includes a drawing showing a female physician examining a young boy, with the caption "A family physician sometimes visits sick patients in their homes; patients who are well enough visit the physician in his or her office."

The book's writing style is best characterized as clear, straightforward, and clinical. A review of the first edition in *Publishers Weekly* (August 16, 1991, p. 59) notes that, "Wherever necessary, parenthetical explanations of potentially difficult words are included, making the text accessible to children at several reading levels." The initial sentences of the article "Computers" provide a good example of the encyclopedia's style:

> Accurate weather forecasting, safe air travel, reliable medical technology—in today's world we take these things for granted, but they would be impossible without computers. A computer is a special kind of machine. Although it cannot "think" for itself in the same way as a person, a computer works like an electronic brain that can do many tasks and interpret data (information) very quickly.

Locating information in the *Random House Children's Encyclopedia* is usually not difficult, although its broad-entry approach makes it somewhat more complicated to use than its chief competitor, the KINGFISHER CHILDREN'S ENCYCLOPEDIA. Two types of cross-references guide the reader to related material: At the end of each article is a "Find Out More" box, which lists other articles on the subject, and at the top of most pages is a "Running Index" that refers readers to subentries in main articles; e.g., right above the article "Spain and Portugal" are these cross-references: "Spacesuit *see* Astronaut. Spadefoot Toad *see* Conservation and Endangered Species." The encyclopedia also contains a detailed 6,000-entry index, which pinpoints specific topics and facts in the text. As James Rettig points out in *Wilson Library Bulletin* (February 1992, p. 111), "The comprehensive index differentiates among references to main topics, subtopics in other articles, and the Fact Finder." To most effi-

ciently find information, both students and parents would be wise to carefully read the section "How To Use This Book" (just after the contents page) before attempting to use the encyclopedia.

No doubt about it, the illustrations in the *Random House Children's Encyclopedia* are superb, doubtless the best ever seen in a children's encyclopedia. They account for roughly half of the total text of the book and add immeasurably to its value as a source of interesting and reliable information. For instance, the article "Computers" features a cutaway drawing that takes the reader inside a personal computer. As noted at the top of this review, Dorling Kindersley, the encyclopedia's British publisher and holder of its copyright, has a reputation for excellence in the area of color photography and drawings. In point of fact, DK owns its own photo library of nearly half a million images and is fast becoming a potent force in North American publishing for young people. Also interesting is the fact that Bill Gates, head of Microsoft and now an encyclopedia publisher (see MICROSOFT ENCARTA MULTIMEDIA ENCYCLOPEDIA), has recently acquired a sizable interest in DK.

The encyclopedia's physical format is excellent—with a couple of important caveats. The page layout will entice the young (and even old) reader, the illustrations are irresistible as well as informative, the typefaces are readable, and the book is well bound in laminated covers. In some instances, however, the typeface is too small for young eyes; and the book, which weighs almost six pounds, will be too heavy for young hands. In addition, at least one reviewer found the page layout too busy: "While the text is generally clear, locational abilities beyond the reach of many children in the intended audience may be needed in order to work through the crowded pages of graphics and print. Sometimes finding an item mentioned in the index on the appropriate page is tantamount to finding 'Waldo' " (*Reference Books Bulletin*, in *Booklist*, October 15, 1991, p. 468).

REPORT CARD: RANDOM HOUSE CHILDREN'S ENCYCLOPEDIA

TOPIC	COVERAGE	ACCURACY	RECENCY	CLARITY
Computers	A	A	A	A
Halloween	D	A	A	A
Johnson, Magic	F*	NA	NA	NA
Measles	F*	NA	NA	NA
Nuclear Energy	A	A	A	A
Panda Bears	A	A	A	A
Rock Music	A	A	A	A
Rose (Flower)	F*	NA	NA	NA
Russia	A	A	A	A
Sex Education	B	A	A	A

A = Excellent; **B** = Above Average; **C** = Average; **D** = Below Average; **F** = Poor; **NA** = Not Applicable
*No Article

SUMMARY

The *Random House Children's Encyclopedia* is a handsome reference book that will thrill young readers ages 7–14. Especially noteworthy are the book's strong coverage of scientific and technical subjects, its accurate and readable articles, and its absolutely first-rate illustrations. On the negative side, young children might find the book somewhat complicated to use, and North American readers will be frustrated by the lack of systematic coverage of U.S. and Canadian topics. The bottom line: Along with the KINGFISHER CHILDREN'S ENCYCLOPEDIA, the *Random House Children's Encyclopedia* is currently the crème de la crème among single-volume children's encyclopedias.

OTHER OPINIONS

New York Times Book Review, May 17, 1992, p. 30 (review by Justin Kaplan); *Publishers Weekly*, August 16, 1991, p. 59 (unsigned review); *Reference Books Bulletin* (in *Booklist*), October 15, 1991, pp. 467–68 (unsigned review); *Wilson Library Bulletin*, February 1992, p. 111 (review by James Rettig).

RANDOM HOUSE LIBRARY OF KNOWLEDGE: FIRST ENCYCLOPEDIA

FACTS

Full Title: *The Random House Library of Knowledge: First Encyclopedia.* **Authors:** Brian Williams and Brenda Williams. **Publisher:** Random House, Inc. **Date Published:** 1992.

Volumes: One. **Words:** 50,000. **Pages:** 189. **Articles:** 500. **Bibliographies:** None. **Illustrations and Maps:** 300. **Cross-references:** 900. **Index Entries:** 600. **Editorial Staff, Advisers, and Contributors:** 19. **Trim Size:** 9 × 10¾ in.

Price and Sales Information: $18.00. Individual consumers can purchase the *Random House Library of Knowledge: First Encyclopedia* in bookstores or, if the book is not in stock, it can be ordered. Similarly, schools and libraries can order it through a book wholesaler. To order the encyclopedia directly from the publisher, call toll-free 1-800-726-0600 or write Random House, Inc., 201 East 50th Street, New York, NY 10022.

EVALUATION

The *Random House Library of Knowledge: First Encyclopedia* was originally published in Great Britain in 1991 by Kingfisher Books, an imprint of Grisewood & Dempsey Ltd., publisher of numerous reference works for children. The following year Random House published the encyclopedia in North America in an edition adapted for U.S. and Canadian readers ages 7–12. The book's scope and format greatly resemble that of the much larger KINGFISHER CHILDREN'S ENCYCLOPEDIA, also a Grisewood & Dempsey product. For instance, both these single-volume encyclopedias for young people emphasize scientific and technical subjects, both are basically short-entry works, both include much interesting boxed information, and both are loaded with color illustrations—in a few instances the same illustrations.

The *Random House Library of Knowledge: First Encyclopedia* contains roughly 500 articles arranged alphabetically from "Aardvark" to "Zoo" (compared with 1,300 articles in the KINGFISHER CHILDREN'S ENCYCLOPEDIA). Most of the articles tend to be quite brief, although some—"Africa," "Animals," "Earth," "Fish," "Insects," "Moon," "Ships," Solar System," "Space Flight," etc.—are one or two full pages in length. As noted, and confirmed by these examples, the encyclopedia's coverage focuses heavily on science and technology. Some famous people and larger places also receive a fair amount of attention, but smaller countries and places (like Nicaragua, Switzerland, and major cities of the world) are not even mentioned. Many other subjects of interest to young people, such as human sexuality, holidays, sports, and popular music, are also completely neglected.

In a negative review in *School Library Journal* (November 1992, pp. 139–40), Lauren Mayer points out, "Although a one-volume encyclopedia must be selective, here that selectivity manifests itself in uneven coverage of countries, cultures, and people. For example, the French Revolution is given an entry while the American Revolution is not; Winston Churchill and Chaucer are included, but Franklin Delano Roosevelt and Martin Luther King, Jr. are not."

The encyclopedia's contents are reliable—as far as they go. In some instances, the text is vague or overly simple, failing to provide necessary facts or explanations and leaving the young reader confused. *Example:* The article "Panda" notes that, "The giant panda lives in China. It looks like a black and white bear, but it is not a bear. It eats mainly bamboo shoots." If the panda is not a bear, what is it? Many similar examples could be cited. Material in the encyclopedia is reasonably current, although the article "Soviet Union" was prepared just before the breakup of the Soviet Empire and hence is out of date. There is no evidence of bias in the articles.

The writing style has little verve, but is normally clear and direct and in most instances will be comprehensible to youngsters in the upper elementary grades and beyond. The first part of the article "Computer" offers a good example of the book's style:

A computer adds, subtracts, and compares numbers at amazing speed. It can do millions of calculations every second. Computers were invented in the 1940s. Today we use computers at home, school, and work. A computer has a "brain," or central processing unit; an "input" unit, usually linked to a keyboard;

and an "output" unit that produces work. It also has a memory unit where information is stored on magnetic disks.

Normally, readers should have no trouble locating information in the encyclopedia. Most articles conclude with one or more cross-references to a related article, e.g., "Dinosaurs" has cross-references to "Fossil" and "Prehistoric Animals." There is also a 600-entry index at the back of the book that helps readers quickly and easily find specific topics and facts. The only problem with the index is that it does not indicate page numbers for main articles, which can be a problem when there are many numbers involved. *Example:* The index entry "human body" directs the reader to pages 34, 63, 78, 96, 102, 116, 120–1, 136, 162, 173, and 184 in that order; unfortunately, the reader has no idea which of these references is to the main article "Human Body," the obvious starting place for anyone interested in the subject.

The book's 300 illustrations and maps—all full-color drawings and diagrams—are eye-catching and usually add to the informational value of the text. For instance, the two-page article "Prehistorical Animals" consists largely of well-executed pictures of dinosaurs and early amphibians and mammals; succinct captions provide additional information. Lauren Mayer's aforementioned review in *School Library Journal* offers another opinion of the encyclopedia's illustrations: "The illustrations, while colorful and profuse, are of marginal quality and not very informative."

Physically, the *Random House Library of Knowledge: First Encyclopedia* is attractively printed, the page layout will appeal to young readers, and the binding is reasonably sturdy with washable covers.

SUMMARY

As its Report Card shows, the single-volume *Random House Library of Knowledge: First Encyclopedia* furnishes only spotty coverage of basic knowledge and information for children ages 7–12. Although it resembles the KINGFISHER CHILDREN'S ENCYCLOPEDIA in both scope and format, it is a much smaller and less impressive work. The bottom line: Not a first-choice encyclopedia for young people.

REPORT CARD: RANDOM HOUSE LIBRARY OF KNOWLEDGE

TOPIC	COVERAGE	ACCURACY	RECENCY	CLARITY
Computers	C	A	A	A
Halloween	F*	NA	NA	NA
Johnson, Magic	F*	NA	NA	NA
Measles	F*	NA	NA	NA
Nuclear Energy	C	A	A	B
Panda Bears	C	B	B	C
Rock Music	F*	NA	NA	NA
Rose (Flower)	F*	NA	NA	NA
Russia	C	C	C	A
Sex Education	F*	NA	NA	NA

A = Excellent; **B** = Above Average; **C** = Average; **D** = Below Average; **F** = Poor; **NA** = Not Applicable
*No Article

OTHER OPINIONS

Reference Books Bulletin (in *Booklist*), October 15, 1992, pp. 456–57 (unsigned review);

School Library Journal, November 1992, pp. 139–40 (review by Lauren Mayer).

TROLL STUDENT ENCYCLOPEDIA

FACTS

Full Title: *Troll Student Encyclopedia.* **Authors:** Michael Dempsey and Keith Lye. **Publisher:** Troll Associates Inc.. **Date Published:** 1991.
 Volumes: One. **Words:** 100,000. **Pages:** 128. **Articles:** 2,000. **Bibliographies:** None. **Illustrations and Maps:** 200. **Cross-references:** None. **Index Entries:** None. **Editorial Staff, Advisers, and Contributors:** 2. **Trim Size:** 8½ × 10¾ in.

Price and Sales Information: $14.95 hardcover; $9.95 paperbound. Individual consumers can purchase the *Troll Student Encyclopedia* in bookstores or, if the book is not in stock, it can be ordered. Similarly, schools and libraries can order it through a book wholesaler. To order the encyclopedia directly from the publisher, call toll-free 1-800-526-5289 or write Troll Associates Inc., 100 Corporate Drive, Mahwah, NJ 07430.

EVALUATION

The *Troll Student Encyclopedia*—available in both hardcover and paperbound editions—is an inexpensive one-volume reference work for children ages 7–14. Originally published in Great Britain by Grisewood & Dempsey Ltd., the book appeared on this side of the Atlantic in 1991 in an Americanized edition published by Troll Associates, a New Jersey firm known for quality children's educational publications. The lead author, the late Michael Dempsey (of Grisewood & Dempsey), has prepared a number of encyclopedias for young people, including the HARVER JUNIOR WORLD ENCYCLOPEDIA and the GREAT WORLD ENCYCLOPEDIA.

The encyclopedia, which is arranged A-to-Z, contains approximately 2,000 very brief articles, normally only several sentences long. Coverage is necessarily selective. For instance, all U.S. presidents and states and Canadian provinces have entries, as do many historical figures and events, scientific discoveries and phenomena, religions, sports, and holidays. On the other hand, popular music, childhood diseases, and sexual reproduction are among the topics completely ignored.

Topics that are covered in the encyclopedia obviously receive cursory treatment. It is difficult to convey more than a few facts or generalizations about such subjects as comets, computers, dinosaurs, genetics, Islam, nuclear energy, poetry, and space exploration in only three or four sentences. Still, authors Dempsey and Lye more often than not manage to pack much basic information into their short articles. *Example:* The article "Panda, Giant" informs the reader that the animal is a "black and white mammal that lives in the bamboo forests of China. It looks like a bear, but some believe it is related to the raccoon. Now carefully protected, its numbers are decreasing because of the destruction of its habitat (the area in which it lives). The main food of the panda is bamboo shoots."

The encyclopedia is a reliable source of information, except in those cases where the material is no longer current. The articles "Russia" and "Union of Soviet Socialist Republics (USSR)," for example, were prepared before the breakup of the Soviet Union and are now in need of revision. In most instances, however, the book is sufficiently up-to-date, being current as of late 1990. The text is free from overt bias, although unpleasant or controversial topics—human sexuality, nuclear power, the space shuttle Challenger disaster, etc.—tend to be avoided, which is a form of bias.

The *Troll Student Encyclopedia* is written in a clear, textbookish style that will be understandable to most young readers in grades three and up. As seen in the panda article quoted above, potentially unfamiliar or difficult words like *habitat* are defined in context. The article "Computer" offers another good example of the book's style:

> An electronic device that accepts data (information), works on the data as instructed, and gives out the results of its calculation. Computers can work out problems very quickly. They can also store vast amounts of information.

Because of its alphabetical arrangement and specific-entry approach, the encyclopedia is not difficult for children to use, nor will they encounter too many problems locating specific information. Nevertheless, the encyclopedia does lack both cross-references and an index, and there are times when one or the other or both would definitely improve access to the book's contents. *Examples:* Information on heredity is given in the article "Genetics," but if the reader looks only under "heredity"

(where there is no article or cross-reference), it will not be found. Likewise, the reader seeking information on dinosaurs will doubtless find the article "Dinosaurs," but how will that same reader find the article "Tyrannosaurus," which also contains useful information about dinosaurs? Only by knowing terms to look up in the first place or by chance or serendipity.

Unlike most one-volume children's encyclopedias, the *Troll Student Encyclopedia* emphasizes printed text, not pictorial matter. Illustrations—all in color—are included on every page but they are often small and account for a relatively minor portion of the total text. Most of the illustrations are fairly simple drawings, although some photographs of places (e.g., Arlington National Cemetery; Bryce Canyon National Park) are also included. Generally speaking, the illustrations lack distinction. The drawings sometimes have a fuzzy quality about them and the photos often resemble shiny postcards of the place or site. Moreover, some articles lack illustrations that need them—"Computer" and "Nuclear Energy" are examples.

The book's physical format also leaves something to be desired, particularly when compared with most competing encyclopedias. The page layout tends to be monotonous and the binding does not appear strong enough to sustain heavy use. On the plus side, the typefaces are large and readable and the reinforced covers on both the hardcover and paperbound editions are washable.

SUMMARY

A review in *Reference Books Bulletin* (in *Booklist*, September 1, 1991, p. 86) concludes that the *Troll Student Encyclopedia* "will serve children in the lower grades both as a source of information and as a means of learning basic research and library skills." It is true that the authors have crammed much elementary information into the encyclopedia's 2,000 brief entries and that the book is usu-

ally reliable, reasonably current, and written in a clear (albeit dry) manner. On the other hand, the encyclopedia ignores many topics of interest to young people, lacks both cross-references and an index, and has illustrations best characterized as mediocre. The bottom line: Consumers could do better—or worse.

REPORT CARD: TROLL STUDENT ENCYCLOPEDIA

TOPIC	COVERAGE	ACCURACY	RECENCY	CLARITY
Computers	C	B	C	A
Halloween	C	A	B	A
Johnson, Magic	F*	NA	NA	NA
Measles	F*	NA	NA	NA
Nuclear Energy	C	A	B	A
Panda Bears	B	A	A	A
Rock Music	F*	NA	NA	NA
Rose (Flower)	C	B	C	A
Russia	C	C	D	A
Sex Education	F*	NA	NA	NA

A = Excellent; B = Above Average; C = Average; D = Below Average; F = Poor; NA = Not Applicable
*No Article

OTHER OPINIONS

Reference Books Bulletin (in *Booklist*) September 1, 1991, p. 86 (unsigned review).

USBORNE CHILDREN'S ENCYCLOPEDIA

FACTS

Full Title: *The Usborne Children's Encyclopedia.* **Author:** Jane Elliott. **Illustrator:** Colin King. **Editor:** Angela Wilkes. **Publisher:** EDC Publishing, a division of the Educational Development Corporation. **Date Published:** American Edition, 1987.

Volumes: One. **Words:** 35,000. **Pages:** 128. **Articles:** 200. **Bibliographies:** None. **Illustrations and Maps:** 1,000. **Cross-references:** 4. **Index Entries:** 1,300. **Editorial Staff, Advisers, and Contributors:** 7. **Trim Size:** 7¾ × 9¾ in.

Price and Sales Information: $16.95 hardcover; $11.95 paperbound. Individual consumers can purchase the *Usborne Children's Encyclopedia* in bookstores or, if the book is not in stock, it can be ordered. Similarly, schools and libraries can order it through a book wholesaler. To order the encyclopedia directly from the publisher, call toll-free 1-800-331-4418 or write EDC Publishing, P.O. Box 702253, Tulsa, OK 74170.

EVALUATION

The small, colorful *Usborne Children's Encyclopedia* originally appeared in Great Britain in 1986, a product of Usborne Publishing Ltd. The following year, EDC Publishing, a children's book publisher located in Tulsa, Oklahoma, issued an "American Edition," which features a new cover design but no change in the book's contents. The encyclopedia is intended chiefly for children ages 7–12.

When Peter Usborne established Usborne Publishing in 1975, his goal was to create nonfiction books as alluring to young people as such powerful attractions as television, films, popular magazines, and comic books. Over the years, Usborne has been enormously successful, publishing more than 800 titles, including the *Usborne Children's Encyclopedia*, which has become a bestseller among children's books in the United Kingdom. Key to the encyclopedia's appeal is its storytelling approach and many lively illustrations featuring humorous cartoon-like characters, Usborne trademarks.

The book is arranged thematically in six chapters: "Our Planet," "Natural Life," "History," "People," "Science Around Us," and "Appendix", which is devoted entirely to technological developments. Broad subjects are covered in double-page articles or spreads in each chapter. *Example:* "Science Around Us" consists of six double-page spreads entitled "Air and Water," "Light and Color," "Electricity," "Sound," "Transport," and "Medicine." Each spread describes very specific topics in a narrative fashion; under "Medicine," for instance, the reader learns about illness, doctors, medicines, vaccines, hospitals, and blood banks.

The aim of the encyclopedia—to provide "simple explanations of everyday things and key concepts" (back cover)—is best accomplished in the area of science and technology, which accounts for well over half the coverage. As a result, such topics as comets, computers, dinosaurs, energy, flora and fauna, health, and space receive adequate attention, considering the size of the book. On the other hand, as the Report Card on the encyclopedia suggests (see below), many subjects of potential interest or concern to children are ignored altogether. Coverage of U.S. and Canadian topics is especially weak, with nothing on any of the presidents, prime ministers, states, provinces, big cities, North American sports, etc.; an index reference to "football" leads to a brief entry on soccer.

Information found in the *Usborne Children's Encyclopedia* can be relied upon as accurate, reasonably current, and impartial. Occasionally, explanations may be confusing, but this is due more to the effort to compress complex concepts into a few words than error on the writer's part. For instance, in the article "Air and Water" the question of why an iron ship floats is addressed: "An iron ship floats because it pushes aside so much water. The more water something pushes aside, the harder water pushes up against it." Most young readers will find this explanation perplexing.

The large majority of articles in the book, however, are written in an easy, straightforward style that most students in the elementary grades will have no trouble comprehending. These few sentences describing computers are typical:

> Machines now do a lot of the work that people used to do. Computers are programmed to copy human thinking. They can solve some problems faster than a person. Pupils use machines such as computers, tape recorders, calculators and videos to help them learn.

Locating specific topics and facts in the encyclopedia poses no difficulty, thanks to a comprehensive 1,300-entry index at the back of the book. Because the encyclopedia is topically arranged (as opposed to alphabetically) and contains very few cross-references in the text, the index is essential for finding information in the book quickly and easily. There is also a detailed contents page at the front of the book that can help readers zero in on a particular area of knowledge.

As mentioned at the outset, Usborne Publishing is well-known for its lively, whimsical illustrations. In this book, illustrator Colin King provides numerous small cartoon-like drawings that youngsters will usually find both enticing and informative. Physically, the encyclopedia is attractive, nicely printed, and adequately bound with washable covers.

REPORT CARD: USBORNE CHILDREN'S ENCYCLOPEDIA

TOPIC	COVERAGE	ACCURACY	RECENCY	CLARITY
Computers	A	A	A	A
Halloween	F*	NA	NA	NA
Johnson, Magic	F*	NA	NA	NA
Measles	F*	NA	NA	NA
Nuclear Energy	D	A	C	A
Panda Bears	F*	NA	NA	NA
Rock Music	F*	NA	NA	NA
Rose (Flower)	F*	NA	NA	NA
Russia	F*	NA	NA	NA
Sex Education	F*	NA	NA	NA

A = Excellent; B = Above Average; C = Average; D = Below Average; F = Poor; NA = Not Applicable
*No Article

SUMMARY

The *Usborne Children's Encyclopedia*, a small British-made work for young readers ages 7–12, obviously fails to furnish balanced coverage of the world's basic knowledge. On the other hand, its humorous cartoon-like illustrations and storytelling approach—both trademarks of the Usborne style—will appeal to the imagination of many children. Indeed, the encyclopedia is a bestseller in the U.K. The bottom line: Entertaining as well as informative, but too limited in coverage to be a first-rate reference source.

OTHER OPINIONS

None.

WEBSTER'S BEGINNING BOOK OF FACTS

FACTS

Full Title: *Webster's Beginning Book of Facts.* **Authors:** John Dennis, Ryerson Johnson, Bonnie Nims, and Joan Zucker. **Publisher:** Merriam-Webster Inc. **Date Published:** 1978.

Volumes: One. **Words:** 75,000. **Pages:** 384. **Articles:** 88. **Bibliographies:** None. **Illustrations and Maps:** 600. **Cross-references:** None. **Index Entries:** None. **Editorial Staff, Advisers, and Contributors:** 52. **Trim Size:** 7¾ × 9 in.

Price and Sales Information: $12.95. Individual consumers can purchase *Webster's Beginning Book of Facts* in bookstores or, if the book is not in stock, it can be ordered. Similarly, schools and libraries can order it through a book wholesaler. To order the encyclopedia directly from the publisher, call toll-free 1-800-828-1880 or write Merriam-Webster Inc., 47 Federal Street, P.O. Box 281, Springfield, MA 01102.

EVALUATION

Intended for children ages 4–10, *Webster's Beginning Book of Facts* consists of 88 substantial A-to-Z articles derived from the 16-volume YOUNG CHILDREN'S ENCYCLOPEDIA, which is also published as COMPTON'S PRECYCLOPEDIA. The articles, which average about four pages in length, range from "Age" to "Zippers," covering "the kinds of things that young children find endlessly fascinating" (preface). The goal (again from the preface) "is to stimulate and entertain, to amuse and inform, and, while satisfying a child's curiosity, to demonstrate that reading and learning are fun." Like the larger YOUNG CHILDREN'S ENCYCLOPEDIA and COMPTON'S PRECYCLOPEDIA, the book can be used profitably by beginning readers as well as by parents and teachers for reading aloud to preschoolers.

Webster's Beginning Book of Facts appeared in 1978 and has not been revised since. It is published by Merriam-Webster Inc., the highly regarded dictionary firm located in Springfield, Massachusetts. Merriam is also a subsidiary of Encyclopaedia Britannica, Inc., which publishes the YOUNG CHILDREN'S ENCYCLOPEDIA. The book represented Merriam's first foray into children's reference book publishing. An article by Thomas Lask in the *New York Times Book Review* (December 3, 1978, p. 111) furnishes this bit of historical background:

> The decision to enter the juvenile field was a long time aborning, according to William A. Llewellyn, [then] Merriam's president. That was due partly to Merriam's desire to turn out a juvenile in keeping with its image and reputation. "It was tricky picking a book that Merriam ought to do," Mr. Llewellyn said. "We had for many years been looking to do a really beginning dictionary; then we discovered that we couldn't do a beginning dictionary—very young people can't alphabetize. We worked with the Britannica [Merriam's parent company] for about a year to put out a hard factual work that reflected the Merriam-Webster image."

Obviously, as the Report Card emphatically shows (see below), *Webster's Beginning Books of Facts* does not attempt to cover knowledge in any systematic fashion. Rather, coverage is highly selective, with most articles devoted to some aspect of the physical and natural sciences, such as "Astronauts," "Bees," "Bugs," "Cells," "Eagles," "Eggs," "Fossils," "Ice," "Insects," "Life (Strange Forms)," "Mice," "Ocean," "Otters," "Plants (Those That Eat Insects)," "Plants (Why Things Grow)," "Sand," "Seeds," "Shells," "Snakes," "Sun," "Time," "Volcanoes," "Weather (Clouds)," "Weather (Winds)," and "X Ray." Nearly 40 percent of the articles deal with some form of animal life. Missing from the book is such standard encyclopedia fare as entries on prominent people, places, historical events, and human accomplishments in art, music, literature, etc.

Treatment of those topics that are covered in the encyclopedia is accurate, impartial, and, despite the book's age, reasonably current. Likewise, the articles are written in an imaginative, leisurely, easy-to-read narrative that will delight most young children. New or potentially difficult terms are italicized and defined in context. The first part of the four-page article "Ice" typifies the book's style:

> How much ice did you ever see in one place? An ice tray full? A skating rink full? A pond full? A river frozen from bank to bank? That's a lot of ice. But there are places in the world where there is more. Much more.
> You know how high mountains are. There are places where the space between mountains is crammed and jammed and packed full of ice.
> This kind of ice is called a *glacier*.
> Glaciers are the jewels that mountains wear. Sometimes they are as blue as sapphires. When the sun shines on them, glaciers may look like gold. At sunset they may look sparkling ruby red. By starlight they're all diamonds and silver.

Although the articles in *Webster's Beginning Book of Facts* are arranged alphabetically, finding specific information in the 384-page book is often a matter of hit-or-miss, due to the lack of cross-references and an index. *Example:* The reader in search of information about seashells will probably have little difficulty locating the article "Shells," but will the reader also find the material about shells in the article "Money"? Not likely. If *Webster's Beginning Book of Facts* is ever revised, the addition of simple cross-references in the text and an index at the back of the book should be a top priority.

The encyclopedia is heavily illustrated throughout with original artwork in the form of large full-color drawings. The illustrations nicely complement the written narrative, helping to bring the text alive and often providing additional information about the topic. Physically, the book is a handsome production, pleasing to the eye and bound to withstand heavy use by active children.

SUMMARY

As the Report Card below convincingly indicates, *Webster's Beginning Book of Facts* does not attempt to cover knowledge in any systematic way. Rather, it consists of 88 imaginatively written, pleasingly illustrated articles on subjects "that young children find endlessly fascinating" (preface), with a heavy representation from the physical and natural sciences, particularly the animal kingdom. The encyclopedia derives from the multivolume YOUNG CHILDREN'S ENCYCLOPEDIA (also published as COMPTON'S PRECYCLOPEDIA). It will appeal to beginning readers as well as preschoolers (and their parents) as a read-aloud book. The bottom line: Although now more than 15 years old and highly selective, this small book of knowledge continues to have value for young children.

OTHER OPINIONS

None.

REPORT CARD: WEBSTER'S BEGINNING BOOK OF FACTS				
TOPIC	COVERAGE	ACCURACY	RECENCY	CLARITY
Computers	F*	NA	NA	
Halloween	F*	NA	NA	NA
Johnson, Magic	F*	NA	NA	NA
Measles	F*	NA	NA	NA
Nuclear Energy	F*	NA	NA	NA
Panda Bears	F*	NA	NA	NA
Rock Music	F*	NA	NA	NA
Rose (Flower)	F*	NA	NA	NA
Russia	F*	NA	NA	NA
Sex Education	F*	NA	NA	NA

A = Excellent; **B** = Above Average; **C** = Average; **D** = Below Average; **F** = Poor; **NA** = Not Applicable
*No Article

WORLD ALMANAC INFOPEDIA

FACTS

Full Title: *The World Almanac Infopedia: A Visual Encyclopedia for Students.* **Compilers:** Theodore Rowland-Entwistle and Jean Cooke. **Editor:** Rachel Pilcher. **Publisher:** World Almanac, an imprint of Pharos Books. **Distributor:** St. Martin's Press. **Date Published:** 1990.

Volumes: One. **Words:** 100,000. **Pages:** 406. **Articles:** 225. **Bibliographies:** None. **Illustrations and Maps:** 800. **Cross-references:** None. **Index Entries:** 1,500. **Editorial Staff, Advisers, and Contributors:** 5. **Trim Size:** 5 × 8¼ in.

Price and Sales Information: $17.95 hardcover; $8.95 paperbound. Individual consumers can purchase the *World Almanac Infopedia* in bookstores or, if the book is not in stock, it can be ordered. Similarly, schools and libraries can order it through a book wholesaler. To order the encyclopedia directly from the distributor, call toll-free 1-800-288-2131 or write St. Martin's Press, 175 Fifth Avenue, New York, NY 10010.

EVALUATION

Like so many of the single-volume general encyclopedias for children currently on the North America market, the *World Almanac Infopedia* was originally prepared in Great Britain and later adapted for U.S. and Canadian readers. The British publisher, Grisewood & Dempsey Ltd., is well-known for quality children's reference works, including the excellent KINGFISHER CHILDREN'S ENCYCLOPEDIA. Likewise, compilers Theodore Rowland-Entwistle and Jean Cooke, a British husband-and-wife editorial team, are experienced hands at making small encyclopedias for young people; their credits include the JUNIOR ENCYCLOPEDIA OF GENERAL KNOWLEDGE and PURNELL'S PICTORIAL ENCYCLOPEDIA, both now out of print.

The encyclopedia, which is intended for students in the upper elementary grades and beyond, consists of 13 topically arranged chapters: "The Universe," "Planet Earth," "Countries of the World," "History," "Human Body," "Animals," "Plants," "Science and Technology," "Transport," "Communications," "Arts and Entertainment," "Sport," and "Miscellany." In addition, an unpaged

24-page color insert containing a "World Atlas" and "Flags of the World" appears in the middle of "Countries of the World." Fairly substantial articles on specific subjects are found in each chapter. *Example:* "Planet Earth" includes articles on earthquakes and volcanoes, the world's major sources of water, continental drift, the weather, cartography, and time zones.

The *Infopedia*—described as a "mini encyclopedia" on the back cover—packs an enormous amount of factual material into its 408 pages. Much of the information is presented in fact boxes, charts, and glossaries. For example, the aforementioned chapter "Planet Earth" contains these fact boxes: "Earth's Vital Statistics," "Notable Earthquakes," "The Richter Scale," "Longest Rivers," "Largest Lakes," "Highest Mountains," "Famous Waterfalls," "Largest Islands," "Facts about Volcanoes," "Erosion Facts," "Weather Extremes," "Beaufort Scale," "Types of Clouds," and "Facts about Storms." In addition, the chapter includes a two-page chart entitled "Earth's Long History" that shows the planet's geological and biological evolution, as well as three glossaries that define basic terms associated with the weather, maps, and geology.

The publisher boasts that the *Infopedia* "covers all the major subjects a student may encounter" (back cover) and, as noted, the book is packed with facts on a wide variety of topics, particularly in the area of science and technology, which receives the lion's share of attention. Some subjects, however, are less well covered or ignored entirely. For instance, the encyclopedia contains nothing on holidays, the world's religions, or childhood diseases. Other subjects are covered in such a cursory fashion that the information conveyed is of little practical use. *Examples:* The only mention of nuclear energy in the encyclopedia comes in the article "The Sun" (in the chapter "The Universe"), where the reader learns, "Deep inside the Sun the temperature reaches millions of degrees. At such a temperature atoms of its main gas, hydrogen, join together to make the gas helium. This process is called fusion. Scientists are trying to make nuclear power plants here on Earth that will work in the same way." Information in the encyclopedia about poetry is limited to this line in the article "Literature": "Poems and plays are both very ancient forms of literature, but the novel is relatively new."

The encyclopedia is usually accurate, but some material is out-of-date and hence incorrect. For instance, the chapter "Countries of the World" contains much erroneous information about Germany (which is still two nations in the *Infopedia*), Russia (still part of the Soviet Union), and Yugoslavia (still a united "communist country"). A review in *Reference Books Bulletin* (in *Booklist*, December 1, 1990, p. 780) points to similar errors: "Both the map and the flag on the color insert do not reflect that Burma was renamed the Union of Myanmar in 1989. Dominica, Ethiopia, and Kampuchea (Cambodia) approved new flags in 1989, but the old ones are illustrated."

Articles in the *Infopedia* are normally presented in a straightforward, impartial manner. An exception is the two-page article "The Dangers of Drugs" (in the chapter "Human Body"), which passionately condemns drug use; here is an excerpt:

> Nearly all drugs . . . will harm the body in one or more ways, if they are used to excess. For example, sniffing, or "snorting," cocaine will eventually damage the mucus membrane of the nose. Marijuana has been found to harm certain brain cells. And the link between ordinary cigarettes and such diseases as emphysema and lung cancer is now well established.

As the preceding quote shows, the *Infopedia*'s written text is clear and direct; students reading at the fourth or fifth grade level and up will normally have no difficulty comprehending the text. The first part of the three-page section entitled "Computers" furnishes another good example of the book's style:

> The first working electronic computer was built at the University of Pennsylvania in 1945. It was called ENIAC (Electronic Numeral Integrator And Calculator). It weighed 30 tons and occupied a large hall of 1,500 square feet (140 square meters). It contained more than 18,000 valves. Today's personal computers occupy just a small amount of desk space, and have as much power as ENIAC.

Because of the encyclopedia's topical arrangement and because it lacks cross-references in the articles, locating specific facts and information in the *Infopedia* usually requires use of the 1,500-entry index at the back of the book. In most instances, the index is sufficiently detailed to lead the reader to the material being sought. But occasionally the index fails. *Examples:* The index does not include an entry for alcohol or alcoholic beverages or drinking, but the topic is covered extensively in the article "The Dangers of Drugs." Countries of the world have lengthy entries in the chapter "Countries of the World," but inexplicably are not entered in the index.

As the book's subtitle—"*A Visual Encyclopedia for Students*"—implies, the *Infopedia* is heavily illustrated with drawings, photographs, and maps. The illustrations often add to the informational value of the book, but regrettably, except for the atlas and flag insert, they are all reproduced in black-and-white. Even more regrettable is the poor quality of the reproduction of many of the illustrations. The article "Computers," for instance, includes a photo of an ant with a silicon chip, intended to show how small chips are. But the photo is so dark and hazy that the point would be lost if not for the caption.

The encyclopedia's page layout tends to be nicely varied due to the profusion of fact boxes, charts, glossaries, and illustrations, but the lack of color will turn off some young readers. The book's binding and paper quality are adequate, and its compact size is definitely a plus.

SUMMARY

Intended for students in the upper elementary grades and beyond, the British-made *World Almanac Infopedia* attempts to cover all areas of knowledge in 13 topically arranged, fact-filled chapters. Much information is presented economically in fact boxes, charts, and glossaries. Coverage of scientific and technical topics is extensive, albeit uneven; other subject areas tend to be less well covered. Although clearly written, the encyclopedia is dated in places and hence not always as reliable as it might be. Other negatives include lack of cross-references, a less-than-perfect index, and many black-and-white illustrations of poor or mediocre quality. The bottom line: A useful but flawed desk encyclopedia for young students.

OTHER OPINIONS

American Reference Books Annual, 1991, pp. 17–18 (review by Bohdan S. Wynar); *Reference Books Bulletin* (in *Booklist*), December 1, 1990, p. 780 (unsigned review).

REPORT CARD: WORLD ALMANAC INFOPEDIA				
TOPIC	COVERAGE	ACCURACY	RECENCY	CLARITY
Computers	A	A	A	A
Halloween	F*	NA	NA	NA
Johnson, Magic	F*	NA	NA	NA
Measles	F*	NA	NA	NA
Nuclear Energy	F	C	D	F
Panda Bears	D	A	A	A
Rock Music	A	A	A	A
Rose (Flower)	F*	NA	NA	NA
Russia	B	C	F	A
Sex Education	A	A	A	A

A = Excellent; **B** = Above Average; **C** = Average; **D** = Below Average; **F** = Poor; **NA** = Not Applicable
*No Article

COMPARISON CHART

Small Encyclopedias for Children and Younger Adults

This chart provides basic statistical information about each of the single-volume encyclopedia for children and younger students reviewed in *Kister's Best Encyclopedias*. The chart also offers a quick comparative overview of the dozen titles in this category. How does the USBORNE CHILDREN'S ENCYCLOPEDIA, for instance, compare with similar encyclopedias in terms of number of words? Articles? Illustrations? Index entries? Price? The chart answers such questions at a glance.

In the case of price information, consumers should understand that prices are subject to change by the publisher or distributor at any time. For the latest price of any encyclopedia, consult *Books in Print* (a standard reference source found in practically all libraries) or, better, call the publisher or distributor direct. Most now have toll-free numbers where the latest informa-

tion about price and availability can be obtained quickly and efficiently. Telephone numbers are listed in this guide at the beginning of each review under "Price and Sales Information," as well as in the directory of publishers and distributors at the back of the book (see Appendix B).

The chart's final column assigns a letter grade to each encyclopedia: A = Excellent; B = Above Average; C = Average; D = Below Average; F = Poor. The letter grade represents a final summary of the encyclopedia's detailed evaluation in *Kister's Best Encyclopedias*. Consumers seriously interested in purchasing an encyclopedia are urged to base their selection decisions on the reviews in the book, and not rely solely on the letter grades given in the chart, which are necessarily arbitrary.

Title	Vols.	Words	Pages	Articles	Illus. & Maps	Cross-refs.	Index Entries	Lowest Retail Price	Rating
Barron's Junior Fact Finder	1	90,000	304	134	550	None	1,000	$19.95	B
Fact s Plus	1	100,000	250	103	300	None	3,500	15.95	D
First Dictionary of Cultural Literacy	1	150,000	285	2,000	400	2,500	2,750 / 9.95PB	14.95	C
Kingfisher Children's Encyclopedia[1]	1	250,000	816	1,300	2,000	1,500	6,000	29.95	A
My First Encyclopedia (Dorling Kindersley)	1	15,000	78	350	600	None	750	16.95	B
My First Encyclopedia (Troll)	1	4,000	30	90	75	None	126	11.79 / 4.95 PB	D
Random House Children's Encyclopedia	1	250,000	644	2,500[2]	3,500	4,000	6,000	50.00	A
Random House Library of Knowledge: First Ency.	1	50,000	189	500	300	900	600	18.00	C
Troll Student Encyclopedia	1	100,000	128	2,000	200	None	None	14.95 / 9.95 PB	C
Usborne Children's Encyclopedia	1	35,000	128	200	1,000	4	1,300	16.95 / 11.95 P	B
Webster's Beginning Books of Facts	1	75,000	384	88	600	None	None	12.95	C
World Almanac Infopedia	1	100,000	406	225	800	None	1,500	17.95 / 8.95 PB	C

1. Also published as the GROLIER STUDENT'S ENCYCLOPEDIA in 10 vols.
2. Encyclopedia contains 425 main entries and 2,075 subentries.

Electronic Encyclopedias

* * * * * * * * *

OVERVIEW

Not too many years ago the notion of an electronic (or automated) encyclopedia would have struck most people as the stuff of science fiction. How could some machine do the job of those familiar A-to-Z volumes that have so effectively delivered knowledge and information into our homes, schools, libraries, and offices for as long as anyone can remember? A few visionaries, however, knew better. They anticipated a day when the book would no longer be the only or perhaps even the principal medium for conveying encyclopedic knowledge and information.

One of those visionaries was Vannevar Bush, an American scientist and engineer prominent during the World War II era. In July 1945, Bush published a famous article in the *Atlantic Monthly* called "As We May Think" in which he predicted, "Wholly new forms of encyclopedias will appear, ready-made with a mesh of associative trails running through them, ready to be dropped into the memex and there amplified." Memex? With almost eerie accuracy, Bush described today's computer workstation:

> Consider a future device for individual use, which is a sort of mechanized private file and library. It needs a name, and, to coin one at random, "memex" will do. A memex is a device in which an individual stores all his books, records, and communications, and which is mechanized so that it may be consulted with exceeding speed and flexibility. It is an enlarged intimate supplement to his memory.
>
> It consists of a desk, and while it can presumably be operated from a distance, it is primarily the piece of furniture at which he works. On the top are slanting translucent screens, on which material can be projected for convenient reading. There is a keyboard, and sets of buttons and levers. Otherwise it looks like an ordinary desk.

Today, nearly 50 years later, electronic encyclopedia are not only a reality, they threaten to render the print (or hardcover) encyclopedia passé. Increasingly, North Americans are getting their encyclopedic information via popular online information services such as America Online, CompuServe, Delphi, GEnie, and Prodigy. The data is transmitted over telephone lines and accessed at a personal computer, much as Vannevar Bush foresaw. Even the august NEW ENCYCLOPAEDIA BRITANNICA will soon debut on the Internet, the Big Daddy of the computer networks.

In another extraordinary development, encyclopedias have recently become available on CD-ROM, or Compact Disc, Read-Only Memory—"read-only" meaning the user cannot write on the disk or alter its contents in any way. Played through a personal computer, CD-ROMs use optical laser technology to read and retrieve data stored in digital form. One disk is capable of holding (or compressing) an enormous amount of information, including the complete text of a multivolume print encyclopedia. Moreover, most CD-ROM encyclopedias are now enhanced by moving pictures and sound. Called "multimedia" because of their audiovisual features, these encyclopedias normally offer full-motion video, animations, and an assortment of audio (music, speeches, narration, animal sounds). One can only presume that, were he alive today, Vannevar Bush would be amazed by encyclopedias published on disks not much larger than a silver dollar—and that these encyclopedias can talk and move as well! The memex, a radical construct half a century ago, seems quaint by comparison.

Still, exciting as these advances may be, consumers should realize that electronic encyclopedias are in their infancy, not much further along developmentally than the automobile was when Henry Ford began manufacturing the Model T. In point of fact, the online encyclopedia has been around for only a dozen years or so, first introduced in the early 1980s. The earliest CD-ROM encyclopedia—a text-only version of Grolier's *Academic American Encyclopedia*—did not appear until late 1985. And the CD-ROM encyclopedia with multimedia features is an even newer phenomenon, bursting onto the North American scene just a few years ago with the widely publicized launch of *Compton's Multimedia Encyclopedia* in 1989. Today, the leading publishers of encyclopedias in electronic form—Grolier, Compton's NewMedia, Microsoft, Encyclopaedia Britannica, and World Book—are scrambling to keep pace with new technological developments in the areas of data compression and retrieval techniques that promise significant advances in their products during the remainder of this century and surely into the next.

A key question for encyclopedia consumers at this point is, should I go electronic or stick with print? How do the new and still evolving electronic encyclopedias stack up against the tried-and-true print sets? What are the main selling points of the electronic format? The print format?

When compared with their print counterparts, electronic encyclopedias offer these advantages:

- Locating and retrieving information is much faster and more thorough in an electronic encyclopedia. Because of the power of the computer, the entire encyclopedic text, including individual words and word combinations, can be searched completely and systematically at very high speeds. The electronic encyclopedia's database (i.e., its contents) may be programmed for full-text searching using Boolean logic and operators (AND/OR/NOT), proximity searching, hypertext linking, and natural language (or relevance) searching—all sophisticated search options not possible in a print encyclopedia.

- As mentioned, some electronic encyclopedias now include moving pictures and sound. Instead of simply reading about great poets, musicians, and leaders, the encyclopedia user can hear selected portions of their writings, compositions, and speeches, which adds a dimension to knowledge that no print encyclopedia can provide. Likewise, the user's understanding of how, say, a nuclear reactor works or honey bees communicate may be enhanced by a narrated video or animation. Such multimedia features are especially appealing to today's televison-bred children. As data compression technology improves, multimedia will become an essential part of the encyclopedic mix, just as still pictures did earlier.

- Electronic encyclopedias possess the potential for interactivity—that is, users are able to make choices, ask questions, and generally interact with the encyclopedic text, tailoring the search, presentation, and results to their particular informational needs. For instance, the user seeking information about mass transportation may request a map showing all subway systems currently operational around the world. The user might then instruct the encyclopedia to create a country-by-country chart indicating miles of subway track, passengers carried annually, etc. True interactivity, which today is a goal rather than a reality, will eventually permit users to manipulate and coordinate every piece of data in the encyclopedia.

- Electronic encyclopedias have a larger and more flexible storage capacity than print encyclopedias, meaning that no longer must the contents of an encyclopedia be limited to a fixed number of volumes. When new material is added to a print encyclopedia, something of corresponding size must be taken out. In the case of the electronic encyclopedia, there is almost an unlimited capacity for new material.

- Electronic encyclopedias can be revised more easily and frequently than their print counterparts. The ACADEMIC AMERICAN ENCYCLOPEDIA online, for instance, is updated four times a year, whereas practically all print encyclopedias (including the print version of the ACADEMIC AMERICAN) are limited to annual updates.

- Along the same lines, electronic encyclopedias are much less expensive to produce and market than print encyclopedias, which require weeks of costly press time as well as tons of increasingly high-priced materials such as paper, ink, and binding. Another factor in the price equation is the professional encyclopedia sales representative, who has traditionally expected—and received—very generous commissions on hardcover sales. As a result, electronic encyclopedias are now considerably less expensive than print encyclopedias, with the price gap continuing to widen. Philip Elmer-Dewitt put the situation in good perspective recently in an article in *Time* (May 18, 1992, p. 69) entitled "Read a Good PowerBook Lately?":

Ultimately, it may be the economics of publishing, not the aesthetics, that determine what shape literature will take. Fiber-optic wires and data-compression techniques make it possible to deliver books—as well as magazines and newspapers—over telephone or cable-TV lines. In the future, readers may select what they want to read from a menu of titles and have their choices zapped almost instantly to their portable machines. Old-fashioned books will probably never be entirely displaced, but as the cost of digital information continues to fall, and the environmental and production costs of paper keep rising, the pleasure of buying and reading a new hardbound volume may someday be limited to the few who can still afford it.

Most knowledgeable observers agree that the traditional book will be around for a long time. Hardcover encyclopedias are hardly an endangered species. Ink-on-paper, after all, is the established medium for conveying encyclopedic information. Most people are more comfortable with print, individual volumes are easily portable, and browsing in a book beats scanning a computer screen any day. Likewise, "installing" the hardcover set is much easier than dealing with a computer. You buy the print encyclopedia, take it out of the carton, and it's ready to go. There are no messy cords, surge protectors, interminable and costly upgrades, incomprehensible (and sometime ludicrous) terminology, equipment failures, or compatability problems. As Daniel Boorstin, the historian and former Librarian of Congress, has written, "The great power of the printed book is that it requires no technology; it is accessible to anyone who can read." Moreover, the cost of the hardware to run the software—a computer and peripherals required to go online or operate CD-ROMs—must be taken into account.

For those who do opt for an electronic encyclopedia, which ones are the best? Quite obviously, the way to go today is CD-ROM with multimedia features. The consumer gets all of the advantages offered by the electronic format, plus moving pictures and sound, which can add significantly to the encyclopedia's value as an information resource. Among the titles available, the most prominent are COMPTON'S INTERACTIVE ENCYCLOPEDIA, COMPTON'S MULTIMEDIA ENCYCLOPEDIA, MICROSOFT ENCARTA MULTIMEDIA ENCYCLOPEDIA, and the NEW GROLIER MULTIMEDIA ENCYCLOPEDIA (also published as the SOFTWARE TOOLWORKS ILLUSTRATED ENCYCLOPEDIA). Each of these works is a quality production that can be recommended enthusiastically to consumers seeking a state-of-the-art electronic encyclopedia for general family use.

At this time, MICROSOFT ENCARTA stands out as the best of the lot, largely because of its user-friendly interface and excellent multimedia features, which are impressive in terms of both quality and quantity.

FIRST CONNECTIONS: THE GOLDEN BOOK ENCYCLOPEDIA, a multimedia CD-ROM encyclopedia aimed at children and younger students in the elementary grades, obviously lacks the substance of the major titles but teachers and media specialists will find it helpful as a beginning electronic encyclopedia. FIRST CONNECTIONS is currently the only general encyclopedia on CD-ROM for this age group. Another unique multimedia title is the CONCISE COLUMBIA ENCYCLOPEDIA, which is based on the single-volume print encyclopedia of the same name. Bundled (or included) with the *Microsoft Bookshelf* (a basic reference library on CD-ROM), the CONCISE COLUMBIA will appeal to older students and adults, but it is normally useful only for very quick reference.

World Book's INFORMATION FINDER is an impressive CD-ROM encyclopedia but it lacks, at least for now, any multimedia features. However, in 1994 INFORMATION FINDER did add some still pictures and the editors seem to be moving with all deliberate speed toward sound and moving pictures. Another famous name in encyclopedias—Britannica—has also entered the CD-ROM lists, but its BRITANNICA INSTANT RESEARCH SYSTEM (or BIRS) is limited (intentionally) to a quite focused audience, namely professionals working in publishing, journalism, and related areas of the communications industry. BIRS, which is designed as an authoritative and rapid fact-checking tool, emphatically does *not* include multimedia features.

Electronic encyclopedias online are currently limited to the ACADEMIC AMERICAN ENCYCLOPEDIA, COMPTON'S ENCYCLOPEDIA, EVERYMAN'S ENCYCLOPAEDIA, and the KUSSMAUL ENCYCLOPEDIA. Most people who subscribe to an online encyclopedia get the ACADEMIC AMERICAN, not by choice but by default, because the ACADEMIC AMERICAN is the encyclopedia database offered by almost all of the commercial dial-up information services, including CompuServe, Delphi, GEnie, and Prodigy. Among the major services, only America Online carries another title (COMPTON'S). Unfortunately, all online vendors today offer only the encyclopedia's printed text, and not its illustrations, which in the case of both the ACADEMIC AMERICAN and COMPTON'S deprives the user of an important part of the encyclopedia's information base.

The other two online encyclopedias have even worse problems. EVERYMAN'S ENCYCLOPAEDIA, offered by the Dialog Information Services (a major online service for educational and research institutions) is a pathetically inadequate old British encyclopedia. The KUSSMAUL ENCYCLOPEDIA , part of the Delphi service, is of practically no value to users. On the bright side, the 32-volume NEW ENCYCLOPAEDIA BRITANNICA will soon be available, mainly to university libraries, via the Internet under the title BRITANNICA ONLINE.

ACADEMIC AMERICAN ENCYCLOPEDIA (ONLINE)

FACTS

Full Title: *Academic American Encyclopedia.*
Variant Titles: *Grolier Academic American Encyclopedia; Grolier Encyclopedia.* **Publisher:** Grolier Electronic Publishing, Inc. **Vendors:** CompuServe Inc.; Delphi Internet Services Corporation; Dow Jones News/Retrieval Service; GEnie; NVN (National Videotex Network); Prodigy Information Service. **Date Published:** First published online in 1983; updated quarterly.

Print Version: ACADEMIC AMERICAN ENCYCLOPEDIA.

Other Electronic Versions: NEW GROLIER MULTIMEDIA ENCYCLOPEDIA (CD-ROM); SOFTWARE TOOLWORKS ILLUSTRATED ENCYCLOPEDIA (CD-ROM).

Words: 10 million. **File Size:** 33,000 entries. **Still Pictures and Maps:** None. **Video Clips:** None. **Animations:** None. **Audio:** None.

Hardware and Software Requirements: Personal Computer; telephone; modem; and communications software; check with vendor for specifics.

Price and Sales Information: The online version of the ACADEMIC AMERICAN ENCYCLOPEDIA is sold to consumers through a number of commercial online information services. The encyclopedia is just one of many databases offered by each service. Prices vary from service to service, but all charge a monthly membership or subscription fee that covers use of the encyclopedia. For current rates, subscription information, or additional information about the services or encyclopedia, contact these vendors, all of which include the online version of the *Academic American Encyclopedia* as part of their core service:

CompuServe Inc., 5000 Arlington CentreBlvd., Columbus, OH 43220; 800-848-8199 (toll-free).

Delphi Internet Services Corporation, 1030 Massachusetts Avenue, Cambridge, MA 02138; 800-544-4005 or 800-695-4005 (both toll-free).

Dow Jones News/Retrieval Service, P.O. Box 300, Princeton, NJ 08543-0300; 800-522-3567 (toll-free).

GEnie, 401 North Washington Street, Rockville, MD 20850; 800-638-9636 (toll-free).

NVN (National Videotex Network), 5555 San Felipe, Houston, TX 77056; 800-336-9096 (toll-free).

Prodigy Information Service, 445 Hamilton Avenue, White Plains, NY 10601; 800-776-3449 (toll-free).

EVALUATION

The ACADEMIC AMERICAN ENCYCLOPEDIA, a highly regarded 21-volume print encyclopedia intended for adults and older students, was created from scratch in the late 1970s and first published in 1980 by the Aretê Publishing Company, an American subsidiary of VNU, a large Dutch publishing conglomerate. In addition to being the first entirely new general multivolume encyclopedia in English published for many years, the ACADEMIC AMERICAN was also the first English-language encyclopedia of any consequence to be produced in machine-readable form from the outset. In 1982, Grolier, Inc., a major North American encyclopedia publisher, acquired the encyclopedia.

Grolier immediately set about developing the encyclopedia's electronic potential. Grolier Electronic Publishing, Inc., a Grolier subsidiary, was established in 1982 and the following year, in a pioneering effort, the company began marketing the encyclopedia online via Viewtron and Bibliographic Retrieval Services (BRS), both commercial vendors of electronic information. Shortly thereafter the *Academic American* also became available online through such major vendors as Dialog Information Services, Dow Jones News/Retrieval Service, and CompuServe Inc. In the early 1990s, however, Grolier withdrew the encyclopedia from Dialog and BRS, citing lack of adequate compensation.

Currently Grolier licenses the *Academic American* database to such major commerical online information utilities as CompuServe, Delphi, Dow Jones News/Retrieval Service, GEnie, NVN (National Videotex Network), and Prodigy Information Service. The company also sells the online encyclopedia to major educational and research institutions and organizations (large school systems, universities, libraries, etc.) through individual licensing agreements on a flat fee basis.

The *Academic American Encyclopedia* online is based on the 21-volume print set, which contains more than 9 million words, nearly 10,000 pages, and roughly 29,000 articles. See the review beginning on page 53 for a detailed evaluation of the encyclopedia's contents, readability, and treatment of material. Note that the online version is substantially larger than the print set: 10 million versus 9.1 million words; 33,000 versus 29,000 articles. The computer's enormous storage capacity easily accommodates added entries, whereas the print set has a fixed size. In addition, the online version is updated on a quarterly basis, whereas the print set is revised annually. All of which means the two versions—print and electronic—do not and never will have exactly the same text. Both versions, however, include about 13,000 carefully prepared bibliographies designed to assist readers who wish to go beyond the encyclopedia for additional information.

The print set also contains approximately 18,000 illustrations and maps, most of admirably high quality. Regrettably, the *Academic American*'s online version completely lacks pictorial matter at the present time; this is true of the product from any vendor. In this regard, comments in an older review of the online version in *Reference Books Bulletin* (in *Booklist*, April 15, 1984, p. 1168) are pertinent today: "In the online version the Board missed an outstanding feature of the printed books: the excellent illustrations with their lengthy captions which provide information not repeated in the text." In another older review (*RQ*, Winter 1983, p. 222), Toni Risoli makes a similar point and adds a suggestion:

> One omission must be noted. In spite of Grolier's research finding that drawings, photographs, and maps were among those features most desired by their intended audience in an encyclopedia, and notwithstanding the 16,000 illustrations in the printed volumes, there is no way of even identifying the existence of the illustrations in the database [online version]. The illustrations are excellent; in the future, it is highly likely that terminals will have built-in graphics capability; Grolier might, therefore, considering adding both a check tag and a standard description of its illustrations to the database.

Consumers should be aware, however, that the encyclopedia's CD-ROM version—the NEW GROLIER MULTIMEDIA ENCYCLOPEDIA—*does* include pictures (both still and moving) as well as sound. (See page 287 for a review.)

Searching and navigating the *Academic American* online varies somewhat from vendor to vendor, depending on individual interfaces. But basically the encyclopedia is consulted in much the same way as the print set, where the user turns to—or in the case of the online version, types in or clicks on—a specific subject, or keyword, such as "Adoption" or "Galileo." More sophisticated search options, such as full-text searching using Boolean logic and operators, are not currently offered by any of the vendors. It is for this reason that some experienced online searchers lament that the *Academic American* is no longer available on Dialog and BRS, where full-text searching was an option. The NEW GROLIER MULTIMEDIA ENCYCLOPEDIA, however, which is the CD-ROM version, does allow full-text searching.

SUMMARY

The *Academic American Encyclopedia*—a work of high quality for adults and older students—is available in three different versions: print, online, and CD-ROM (as the NEW GROLIER MULTIMEDIA ENCYCLOPEDIA). The online version, reviewed here, is currently available via a number of commercial online information services, including CompuServe and Prodigy. Indeed, it is the best-known and most widely distributed online encyclopedia in North America today. The publisher, Grolier, keeps the encyclopedia admirably current, updating the online version quarterly. The major drawback of the online version is that it lacks the excellent pictorial material found in the print and CD-ROM versions.

If a consumer opts for an electronic encyclopedia, the best choice today in most instances would seem to be one on CD-ROM with multimedia features, such as COMPTON'S MULTIMEDIA ENCYCLOPEDIA, MICROSOFT ENCARTA MULTIMEDIA ENCYCLOPE-

DIA, or the aforementioned NEW GROLIER MULTIMEDIA ENCYCLOPEDIA. On the other hand, if you subscribe to a basic online information service, a general encyclopedia will almost certainly be part of the package—and most likely that encyclopedia will be the *Academic America*. The bottom line: A quality general encyclopedia in any version.

OTHER OPINIONS

No recent reviews are available. For useful background information on the online encyclopedia when it was first introduced, see

Robert T. Grieves' article "Short Circuiting Reference Books" (*Time*, June 13, 1983, p. 76).

BRITANNICA INSTANT RESEARCH SYSTEM (CD-ROM)

FACTS

Full Title: *Britannica Instant Research System.* **Variant Title:** *Britannica Fact-Checking System.* **Publisher:** Encyclopaedia Britannica, Inc. **Date Published:** First published on disk in 1993; updated annually.
Print Version: NEW ENCYCLOPAEDIA BRITANNICA.
Other Electronic Versions: BRITANNICA ONLINE (online).
Words: 44 million. **Articles:** 65,100. **Still Pictures and Maps:** None. **Video Clips:** None. **Animations:** None. **Audio:** None.
Hardware Requirements: Personal Computer with 1.2 gigabyte hard drive; check with publisher for specifics. **Software Requirements:** CD-ROM, 2 discs. **Operating System:** MS-DOS.

Price and Sales Information: The *Britannica Instant Research System* (or *BIRS*), an optical disk version of the NEW ENCYCLOPAEDIA BRITANNICA and its yearbook, is currently licensed to businesses and government organizations at $9,000.00 for one workstation over a three-year period; discounts are available for multiple stations. Schools and libraries may license *BIRS* at $2,995.00 for the first year and $1,990.00 for the following two years (or $995.00 per year). To purchase a *BIRS* license or for additional information about the system, contact Encyclopaedia Britannica, Inc., Britannica Centre, 310 South Michigan Avenue, Chicago, IL 60604; 800-858-4895 (toll-free).

EVALUATION

First published in 1993 and updated annually, the *Britannica Instant Research System* (*BIRS*) is an enormous encyclopedic database published on two CD-ROM discs. The

system comprises the printed text of the 32-volume NEW ENCYCLOPAEDIA BRITANNICA, the largest and best-known encyclopedia in the English language, along with the encyclopedia's current yearbook and *Merriam-Webster's Collegiate Dictionary*. The print encyclopedia contains an estimated 44 million words, 32,000 pages, and 65,100 articles, plus nearly 25,000 illustrations and maps. According to editor Robert McHenry, *BIRS* includes all of the NEW ENCYCLOPAEDIA BRITANNICA'S text—except for illustrations and maps. For a detailed evaluation of the print encyclopedia's contents, readability, and treatment of material, see the review beginning on page 37.

Interested consumers should understand that *BIRS* is not a typical CD-ROM encyclopedia, nor is it intended for home or casual use. Rather, it is designed specifically as a rapid computerized fact-checking system for professionals working in publishing, journalism, and related areas of the communications industry. In a news release from Encyclopaedia Britannica dated August 16, 1993, Karen Barch, a company executive, stressed that *BIRS* is *not* aimed at the home market: "This is a powerful, adult-level research and retrieval tool to be used in the kind of intensive research applications demanded by publishers, news organizations and business and government." *BIRS* is also appropriate for large educational institutions, including university libraries and research institutes.

Central to the system's effectiveness is its rapid searching capability. *BIRS* achieves speed by loading the CD-ROM discs onto the hard drive of the user's computer, instead of relying on a standard CD-ROM drive, which would significantly reduce the system's response time. As Barch points out in Connie Goddard's informative article, "Britannica's Electronic Fact Checker Aims High" (*Publishers Weekly*, November 15, 1993, p. 46), hard drives normally "deliver information in as little as 13 milliseconds, or five to 10 times as fast as the fastest CD-ROM players."

Using *BIRS* is simple. The search system relies on natural language inquiries rather than key words, descriptors, Boolean operators, or the like. Connie Goodard's *Publishers Weekly* article mentioned above explains how *BIRS* works:

> The heart of the Britannica system is its relevance-ranking search and retrieval software. Most electronic reference works carry out their subject searches according to key words and Boolean logic....The BIRS, though, responds to questions in plain English, comparing the words and phrases to produce a context for the search. The system then ranks all the responses it finds according to the likely relevance given the context of the original question.

> "This is an excellent system for answering questions like 'why is the sky blue?' or 'how many hairs are there on a human head?'" Barch says. "These are questions it would be difficult to answer using a print reference index."

BIRS is a result of Encyclopaedia Britannica's recent efforts to find a place for the mammoth NEW ENCYCLOPAEDIA BRITANNICA in the volatile and increasing competitive electronic reference environment. Another such effort is BRITANNICA ONLINE, an online version of the print encyclopedia scheduled to debut on the Internet in the fall of 1994. Some critics, like Gary Samuels of *Forbes* (whose article is cited at the end of this review), believe that Britannica is behind the curve in electronic publishing, especially CD-ROM; others believe the company is asserting a new-found leadership role in the encyclopedia industry. This much is sure: *BIRS* is an impressive, albeit expensive, new product based on an old name.

SUMMARY

The recently published *Britannica Instant Research System (BIRS)*—essentially a CD-ROM version of the 32-volume NEW ENCYCLOPAEDIA BRITANNICA and its yearbook— is designed as a rapid, user-friendly fact-checking service for busy publishers, journalists, and others in the communications business. It is not for children or use in the home. Key elements of *BIRS* are its speed (much, much faster than the typical CD-ROM encyclopedia) and a plain-English search system. A major negative is its steep price. The bottom line: An innovative new product that, along with BRITANNICA ONLINE, brings the oldest, largest, and most distinguished encyclopedia in the English language into the electronic age.

OTHER OPINIONS

None. Useful background information on *BIRS* can be found in Connie Goddard's article "Britannica's Electronic Fact Checker Aims High" (*Publishers Weekly*, November 15, 1993, p. 46). A related article is Gary Samuels' "CD-ROM's First Big Victim" (*Forbes*, February 28, 1994, pp. 42–44), which severely criticizes recent business decisions by Encyclopaedia Britannica management, including the company's alleged failure to fully embrace CD-ROM technology.

BRITANNICA ONLINE

FACTS

Working Title: *Britannica Online*. **Publisher:** Encyclopaedia Britannica, Inc. **Date Published:** In progress, currently being tested; publication online scheduled for September 1994.

    Print Version: NEW ENCYCLOPAEDIA BRITANNICA.

    Other Electronic Versions: BRITANNICA INSTANT RESEARCH SYSTEM (CD-ROM).

    Words: 44 million. **File Size:** 66,000 entries. **Still Pictures and Maps:** 2,000. **Video Clips:** None. **Animations:** None. **Audio:** None.

    Hardware and Software Requirements: Personal Computer; telephone; modem; and communications software; check with publisher for specifics.

    Price and Sales Information: Britannica Online, the online version of the NEW ENCYCLOPAEDIA BRITANNICA, published by Encyclopaedia Britannica, Inc., will soon be available to some consumers via the Internet, the world's largest online information network. People affiliated with large businesses, universities, and research institutions (public and private) can access the Internet through dedicated computers linked by telephone with the network. Corporate and institutional fees are typically $500.00 to $1,500.00 per month.

    Consumers should be aware that, initially, *Brittanica Online* will only be available on the Internet to universities and selected public libraries. The Encyclopaedia Britannica company plans eventually to release the database to a larger commercial audience. For additional information about *Britannica Online*, contact Encyclopaedia Britannica, Inc., Britannica Centre, 310 South Michigan Avenue, Chicago, IL 60604; 800-858-4895 (toll-free).

EVALUATION

At this writing, *Britannica Online*, an online version of the 32-volume NEW ENCYCLOPAEDIA BRITANNICA, has not yet been published, nor has it been seen or used by the author of *Kister's Best Encyclopedias*. In early 1994, the publisher, Encyclopaedia Britannica, Inc., announced that *Britannica Online* (a working title that may or may not become the service's official name) will be launched later in the year, most likely in September. Access will be via the Internet, an immense decentralized network of online databases from around the world linked by computers and high-speed telecommunications lines. The Internet, which has been called a "brain-to-brain" interface, is a main cog in the evolving information superhighway. (See "Price and Sales Information" above about how to gain access to the Internet.)

As noted, *Britannica Online* derives from the 32-volume NEW ENCYCLOPAEDIA BRITANNICA, the largest general print (or hardcover) encyclopedia in the English language. Specifically, the print set contains an estimated 44 million words, 32,000 pages, 65,100 articles, and nearly 25,000 illustrations and maps. See page 37 for a detailed evaluation of the encyclopedia's contents, readability, and treatment of material. The online version will include all of the articles found in the 32-volume set, plus some entries not in the print set. (The computer's expansive storage capacity allows *Britannica* editors to add material to the online version without worrying about space requirements, whereas any addition to the print encyclopedia, which is fixed in size, requires cuts elsewhere.) In the case of the illustrations, however, the online version will be limited, at least at first, to about 2,000. Only those illustrations that are integral to the sense of an article or essential for its comprehension will be included.

Britannica Online is currently being tested by students, faculty, and librarians at the University of California at San Diego. According to one librarian involved in the project, the online version of *Britannica* provides an impressive array of search options not available—or possible—in the print set, such as full-text searching and "hypertext" linking. The latter, akin to cross-referencing in a print encyclopedia, connects related text within the encyclopedia database. Likewise, it allows for linking the encyclopedia's text with relevant material in other databases running on the Internet. *Britannica's* editor, Robert McHenry, gives this example of a hypertext link: At the end of the encyclopedia's article on the Vatican Museum is a "hyperlink" to the description of an exhibit of the museum's treasures in a Library of Congress file; the user clicks on the link and instantaneously brings the Library of Congress material to the *Britannica*.

The speed of the online system is said to be another outstanding feature. Concerning timeliness of information, McHenry hopes to update *Britannica Online* four times a year and, down the road, even more frequently, aiming eventually for "real-time" (or immediate) revision.

Some encyclopedists at rival firms have also expressed initial enthusiasm for *Britannica Online*, based on what they have heard from Britannica representatives and other involved in the project. One experienced editor, for instance, believes that *Britannica Online* potentially represents a major breakthrough for the organization and delivery of encyclopedic information in electronic form, and that it could serve as *the* paradigm for future developments in this exciting area of the knowledge industry. John Markoff, in an article in the *New York Times* (February 8, 1994, p. 1-C) entitled "Britannica's 44 Million Words Are Going

On Line," offers a somewhat more prosaic view: "The development is one of the clearest indications that traditional publishers realize the limitations of offering only hardbound volumes—and are concluding that the opportunities of on-line publishing outweigh the risks."

Interestingly, *Britannica Online* is not the publisher's first foray into the online encyclopedia business. Earlier, in 1981, Mead Data Central distributed an online version of the NEW ENCYCLOPAEDIA BRITANNICA via NEXIS and LEXIS, computer-based information services aimed at researchers in business, government, and the professions. Also interestingly, this pioneering version of *Britannica Online* was deliberately *not* made available to individual consumers or schools and libraries—for fear of jeopardizing sales of the print set and antagonizing the company's professional sales force, which works on commission. In 1985,

however, the encyclopedia was withdrawn from both NEXIS and LEXIS when the publisher (Britannica) and vendor (Mead Data Central) could not agree on who should pay for updating the online file.

It is hardly any wonder, then, that today Britannica is approaching the *Britannica Online* project with very firm ideas about who should call the shots—and reap the profits:

> Encyclopedia Britannica executives said they had decided to become electronic publishers rather than allying themselves with an existing on-line service because of economics. "The main reason we're doing it ourselves is that you just can't make any money licensing your content," said Joseph J. Esposito, president of Encyclopaedia Britannica North America. "If you do believe that content is king, it's rather unfortunate that so many of the content providers have put themselves in a position where they're held hostage to the on-line services." (Quoted from Markoff's *New York Times* article previously cited.)

SUMMARY

Britannica Online, an in-progress online version of the 32-volume NEW ENCYCLOPAEDIA BRITANNICA, the largest and most prestigious general English-language encyclopedia in the world, is currently being tested at the University of California at San Diego. If all goes according to plan, *Britannica Online* will become available initially to universities and some public libraries through the Internet in September of 1994. The bottom line: The project holds great promise—and some perils—for the future of the *Britannica*.

OTHER OPINIONS

None. Informative background information on *Britannica Online* can be found in John Markoff's article "Britannica's 44 Million Words Are Going On Line" (*New York Times*, February 8, 1994, p. 1-C). A related article is Gary Samuels' "CD-ROM's First Big Victim" (*Forbes*, February 28, 1994, pp. 42-44), which severely criticizes recent business decisions by Encyclopaedia Britannica management, especially in the area of electronic product development.

COLUMBIA ELECTRONIC ENCYCLOPEDIA
(HAND-HELD)

FACTS

Full Title: *The Columbia Electronic Encyclopedia.* **Variant Titles:** *Franklin's Concise Columbia Encyclopedia; Franklin's Electronic Concise Columbia Encyclopedia.* **Publisher:** Franklin Electronic Publishers, Inc. **Date Published:** 1991 (based on print version published in 1989).

Print Version: CONCISE COLUMBIA ENCYCLOPEDIA.

Other Electronic Versions: CONCISE COLUMBIA ENCYCLOPEDIA (CD-ROM).

Words: 1 million. **Articles:** 15,000. **Still Pictures and Maps:** None. **Video Clips:** None. **Animations:** None. **Audio:** None.

Hardware and Software Requirements: None.

Price and Sales Information: The *Columbia Electronic Encyclopedia* (model EC-7000) is sold in North America chiefly in department and discount stores as well as retail stores specializing in electronic products. The suggested retail price is $249.95 but the encyclopedia normally sells for well under that figure. It is distributed to the school and library market by Franklin Learning Resources, a division of Franklin Electronic Publishing, Inc., the publisher. The suggested price to educational institutions is $179.95. The *Columbia Electronic Encyclopedia* can also be purchased directly from the publisher. To order the encyclopedia or for additional information, contact Franklin Electronic Publishers, Inc., 122 Burrs Road, Mt. Holly, NJ 08060; 800-543-3511 (toll-free).

EVALUATION

The *Columbia Electronic Encyclopedia*—billed as "the World's First Hand-held Electronic Encyclopedia!" by the publisher when launched in January 1991—is a portable, palm-sized reference work that weighs just 12 ounces. Actually, it is an automated version of the CONCISE COLUMBIA ENCYCLOPEDIA, a high-quality single-volume print encyclopedia for adults and older students that first appeared in 1983 and was thoroughly updated in a second edition in 1989. The CONCISE COLUMBIA, in turn, is an abridgment of the larger *New Columbia Encyclopedia*, published in 1975 and superseded last year by the COLUMBIA ENCYCLOPEDIA, widely regarded as the finest one-volume general encyclopedia available in English.

The CONCISE COLUMBIA contains about a million words, 950 pages, and 15,000 short articles. Like the larger work from which it

derives, the CONCISE COLUMBIA is sparsely illustrated and has no index, but includes many cross-references. See the review beginning on page 131 for a detailed evaluation of the encyclopedia's contents, readability, and treatment of material. The electronic version is published by Franklin Electronic Publishers, a leading North American producer of portable "electronic books," including the Bible and an array of dictionaries. Franklin licenses the CONCISE COLUMBIA'S text from Columbia University Press, the encyclopedia's print publisher.

Physically, the *Columbia Electronic Encyclopedia* (model EC-7000) does not look much like the traditional encyclopedia. About the size of a pocket calculator (5½ × 6 × 1 inches), it has an 8-line high-resolution display screen at the top and a small keyboard, or keypad, for typing at the bottom.

Four AAA batteries must be installed before the encyclopedia can be used. It would be easy to dismiss this encyclopedia as a toy or gimmick. True, it is fun to play with, and it does not look formidable or erudite. But don't be fooled—the *Columbia Electronic Encyclopedia is* a bona fide reference work that contains all 15,000 articles found in the CONCISE COLUMBIA. Moreover, it possesses the potential to be more useful in some respects than its fine print counterpart.

Most impressive is the electronic encyclopedia's search and retrieval system, which is both fast and sophisticated. It allows the user to search all significant words in the database and to narrow the search through word combinations as well as "filters" that delimit by type of article (e.g., biography), geographical location (e.g., countries), subject (e.g., genetics), and time period (e.g., 1960s). For instance, the user can limit a search of "Genetics" to only pertinent articles involving people associated with the subject. Such a search results in a list including such names as Theodosius Dobzhansky, Trofim Denisovich Lysenko, Barbara McClintock, and Gregor Johann Mendel. But, disconcertingly, the search also turns up Gene Tunney, the boxer, doubtless because of his first name. A number of similar indexing bloopers were encountered in the encyclopedia.

Indeed, the *Columbia Electronic Encyclopedia* is far from perfect. The keyboard is awkward to use because of its small size. The display screen is equally frustrating for the same reason. Unlike electronic encyclopedias online or on disk, the hand-held encyclopedia lacks the capability to print out its text. As noted, false references linking topics like "Genetics" and "Tunney, Gene" appear with some frequency. There are no illustrations. Due to the age of the CONCISE COLUMBIA (1989), some material in the *Columbia Electronic* is now dated, severely so in some cases; for instance, important recent political events in Germany, Eastern Europe, the Balkans, and South Africa are not recorded. Finally, the price of the encyclopedia is quite steep, considering that, after all, the work contains only 15,000 relatively brief articles. As Bill Katz, a prominent authority on reference materials, puts it in his *Basic Information Sources* (6th ed., McGraw-Hill, 1992, pp. 258-59), "One may search for key words and names among all the encylopedia entries. The advantage may be there, but does the cost justify it all?"

Interested consumers should note that the *Columbia Electronic Encyclopedia* competes directly with the RANDOM HOUSE ELECTRONIC ENCYCLOPEDIA, another hand-held encyclopedia published at the same time as the *Columbia Electronic*. In fact, the RANDOM HOUSE ELECTRONIC claims the title of "the world's first portable electronic encyclopedia." In any event, the two little electronic encyclopedias are remarkably similar in appearance, design, organization, and size of database.

SUMMARY

Derived from the second edition (1989) of the CONCISE COLUMBIA ENCYCLOPEDIA, a highly regarded single-volume print work for adults and older students, the *Columbia Electronic Encyclopedia* was published in 1991 by Franklin Electronic Publishers, a leading producer of hand-held "electronic books." The electronic encyclopedia, which is about the size of a pocket calculator, might strike some as frivolous. Wrong. It is a genuine—and pricey—reference work that provides much more effective access to its contents than does its print counterpart. But it also has some glaring limitations. The bottom line: Although interesting and innovative, the *Columbia Electronic Encyclopedia* is much too expensive for what it delivers.

OTHER OPINIONS

Basic Information Sources by William A. Katz (vol. 1 of *Introduction to Reference Work*, 6th ed., New York: McGraw-Hill, 1992), pp. 258-59.

COMPTON'S CONCISE ENCYCLOPEDIA (CD-ROM)

FACTS

Full Title: *Compton's Concise Encyclopedia.* **Publisher:** Compton's NewMedia. **Distributor:** Sony Corporation. **Date Published:** 1991.

Print Version: COMPTON'S ENCYCLOPEDIA.

Other Electronic Versions: COMPTON'S ENCYCLOPEDIA (online); COMPTON'S FAMILY ENCYCLOPEDIA (CD-ROM); COMPTON'S INTERACTIVE ENCYCLOPEDIA (CD-ROM); COMPTON'S MULTIMEDIA ENCYCLOPEDIA (CD-ROM).

Words: 9 million. **Articles:** 32,000. **Still Pictures and Maps:** 4,000. **Video Clips:** None. **Animations:** None. **Audio:** None.

Hardware and Software Requirements: None.

Price and Sales Information: *Compton's Concise Encyclopedia* is sold as part of the Sony Corporation's Data Discman, a small portable unit that plays "electronic books" in disk form. Data Discman currently retails for about $450.00, although it can sometimes be purchased in computer and discount stores for less; also, some retail bookstores carry the Discman. For additional information about Data Discman or the encyclopedia, or a list of Sony distributors in your area, contact the Sony Corporation, 655 River Oaks Parkway, San Jose, CA 95134; 800-222-0878 (toll-free).

EVALUATION

Compton's Concise Encyclopedia, a compact disk version of the 26-volume COMPTON'S ENCYCLOPEDIA, is one of three electronic reference works bundled (or included) with the Data Discman (also called the Sony Data Discman), a small hand-held machine introduced by the Sony Corporation in 1991 that plays "electronic books." Not a computer, the battery-operated Discman, which weighs less than two pounds, is designed to access and display information stored on 3-inch compact discs. In many respects, the Discman has much in common with two other hand-held encyclopedias reviewed in this section, namely the COLUMBIA ELECTRONIC ENCYCLOPEDIA and the RANDOM HOUSE ELECTRONIC ENCYCLOPEDIA.

The other titles bundled with the Discman are the *Wellness Encyclopedia* (a Houghton Mifflin publication) and the *World Travel Translator* (a multilingual dictionary published by Passport Books). Sony also has many other "books" (or disks) available for use with the Discman, including the *American Heritage Dictionary*, *Frommer's Guide to America's Most-Travelled Cities*, the *Hoover Handbook*, and an extensive library of literary classics. They sell for $29.95-$69.95 each.

As noted, *Compton's Concise Encyclopedia* is an electronic version of COMPTON'S ENCYCLOPEDIA, a highly regarded 26-volume print (or hardcover) encyclopedia for students and the family. The print set currently contains about 9 million words, 10,500 pages, 34,000 articles (most quite brief), and 22,500 illustrations and maps. See the reviews beginning on page 60 and page 186 for a detailed evaluation of the encyclopedia's contents, readability, and treatment of material. *Compton's Concise Encyclopedia*, as its title suggests, is an abridged or cut-down version of the print set. Missing, for instance, are many of the illustrations that help make COMPTON'S a quality encyclopedia. Specifically, *Compton's Concise* is limited to a few thousand black-and-white drawings.

Using *Compton's Concise Encyclopedia* will pose few if any problems for most people, including computer literate youngsters. Search options include title, subject, keyword, and word combining. For instance, a search of "Oil" AND "Spill" produced 13 hits, or references. But be forewarned, the system is slow; it took about 30 seconds to run the aforementioned search. In a review in *Reference Books Bulletin* (in *Booklist*, January 15, 1992, p. 968), Sandy Whiteley, an experienced critic of reference materials and close observer of trends in the field, nicely describes the Discman, ending with its larger significance:

> The player has a keyboard and five function keys. There are six search capabilities, including subject and keyword. The user interface is consistent across titles, making the product easy to learn to use. The flip-up screen displays only 300 characters at a time, so the fast reader will have to do a lot of scrolling. The player can be plugged into a TV to utilize a larger screen, though the amount of text displayed doesn't change....While Data Discman does not signal the death of the book, it should make all of us think twice as we try to envision the library of the future.

Whether Sony will continue to use *Compton's Concise Encyclopedia* in the Discman in the future is not clear at this point. If it does, the encyclopedia should be updated at regular intervals, preferably at least once a year. Published in 1991 when the Discman first appeared, the encyclopedia today is not yet badly dated, but it will become so if not revised in the near future.

SUMMARY

Compton's Concise Encyclopedia—an optical disk version of COMPTON'S ENCYCLOPEDIA, a 26-volume print set that rates among the best general encyclopedias available today—is one of several reference works bundled with the innovative Data Discman, a handheld device from the Sony Corporation that displays and accesses "electronic books" in disk form. The encyclopedia is easy to use, but it lacks many of the pictures and other graphics that help make the print set such a successful source of information for users of almost any age. In addition, *Compton's Concise Encyclopedia* has not been updated since 1991, when it first appeared as part of the Discman. The bottom line: Certainly *not* the best electronic version of COMPTON'S ENCYCLOPEDIA currently available.

OTHER OPINIONS

Reference Books Bulletin (in *Booklist*), January 15, 1992, p. 968 (review by Sandy Whiteley).

COMPTON'S ENCYCLOPEDIA (ONLINE)

FACTS

Full Title: *Compton's Encyclopedia.* **Publisher:** Compton's NewMedia. **Vendor:** America Online. **Date Published:** First published online in 1992; updated annually.

Print Version: COMPTON'S ENCYCLOPEDIA.

Other Electronic Versions: COMPTON'S CONCISE ENCYCLOPEDIA (CD-ROM); COMPTON'S FAMILY ENCYCLOPEDIA (CD-ROM); COMPTON'S INTERACTIVE ENCYCLOPEDIA (CD-ROM); COMPTON'S MULTIMEDIA ENCYCLOPEDIA (CD-ROM).

Words: 9 million. **File Size:** 34,000 entries. **Still Pictures and Maps:** None. **Video Clips:** None. **Animations:** None. **Audio:** None.

Hardware and Software Requirements: Personal Computer; telephone; modem; mouse; and communications software; check with vendor for specifics.

Price and Sales Information: The online version of *Compton's Encyclopedia* is available to consumers through America Online, a major commercial online information service. The encyclopedia is just one of many databases offered by the service. Currently, America Online charges a flat rate of $9.95 per month, which buys the subscriber five hours of connect-time (or time online); additional time costs $3.50 per hour. For subscription information or more information about the service or the encyclopedia, contact America Online, 8619 Westwood Center Drive (Suite 200), Vienna, VA 22182-2285; 800-827-6364 (toll-free).

EVALUATION

The online version of *Compton's Encyclopedia* is based on the 26-volume COMPTON'S ENCYCLOPEDIA, a general reference work useful for the whole family and particularly students from the upper elementary grades through college. *Compton's* is a high-quality set that has been around since 1922, when it first appeared in eight volumes as *Compton's Pictured Encyclopedia.* The print (or hardcover) version contains approximately 9 million words, 10,000 pages, and 34,000 articles (of which about 5,000 are quite lengthy with the rest very brief), plus more than 22,000 illustrations and maps. Detailed evaluations of the encyclopedia's contents, readability, and treatment of material begin on page 60 and page 186. The online version, which first became available on America Online in 1992, includes the entire text of the print set—except for the illustrations, accompanying captions, and maps. These graphics add much to the informational value of the print encyclopedia, and their omission from the online version obviously reduce its overall effectiveness as a reference source.

Consumers should note, however, that other electronic versions of the encyclopedia—COMPTON'S FAMILY ENCYCLOPEDIA, COMPTON'S INTERACTIVE ENCYCLOPEDIA, and COMPTON'S MULTIMEDIA ENCYCLOPEDIA—do include pictures, maps, and other graphics.

America Online, a popular and fast-growing online information utility that currently boasts more than 600,000 subscribers, employs a Windows-based (or graphical) user interface, which makes navigating the encyclopedia relatively simple once the basics of icons, pull-down menus, and pointing and clicking are mastered. Note that a mouse is required hardware. America Online organizes its database services into eight different categories or sections, such as "Lifestyles and Interests," "Travel and Shopping,"

"Games and Entertainment," and "Learning and Reference." The encyclopedia and other educational resources (e.g., the *National Geographic* magazine) are naturally located in "Learning and Reference," which is opened by clicking on an icon of a light bulb.

Accessing the encyclopedia is equally easy and simple, mainly involving clicking on keywords. As might be expected, search options do not include sophisticated modes such as full-text searching, which involves use of Boolean logic and operators.

SUMMARY

One of the finest general family encyclopedias currently available to North American consumers, *Compton's Encyclopedia* is published in print form, on CD-ROM (as COMPTON'S MULTIMEDIA ENCYCLOPEDIA, COMPTON'S INTERACTIVE ENCYCLOPEDIA, and two other titles), and online. The latter, reviewed here, is prepared by Compton's NewMedia and vended through America Online, a commercial online information service that is growing by the proverbial leaps and bounds. Compared with the print and CD-ROM versions, the online version of *Compton's* suffers from lack of illustrations of any kind.

If a consumer opts for an electronic encyclopedia, the best choice today in most instances would seem to be one on CD-ROM with multimedia capabilities, such as MICROSOFT ENCARTA MULTIMEDIA ENCYCLOPEDIA, the NEW GROLIER MULTIMEDIA ENCYCLOPEDIA, or the aforementioned COMPTON'S MULTIMEDIA ENCYCLOPEDIA. On the other hand, subscribers to America Online can rest assured that they have access to the text (albeit sans illustrations) of a first-rate encyclopedia. The bottom line: Like the ACADEMIC AMERICAN ENCYCLOPEDIA (which is available on practically every online information service except America Online), *Compton's* online returns fair value for the consumer dollar.

OTHER OPINIONS

None.

COMPTON'S FAMILY ENCYCLOPEDIA (CD-ROM)

FACTS

Full Title: *Compton's Family Encyclopedia.* **Publisher:** Compton's NewMedia. **Distributor:** Sony Corporation. **Date Published:** 1991.
    Print Version: COMPTON'S ENCYCLOPEDIA.
    Other Electronic Versions: COMPTON'S CONCISE ENCYCLOPEDIA (CD-ROM); COMPTON'S ENCYCLOPEDIA (online); COMPTON'S INTERACTIVE ENCYCLOPEDIA (CD-ROM); COMPTON'S MULTIMEDIA ENCYCLOPEDIA (CD-ROM).

Words: 9 million. **Articles:** 32,000. **Still Pictures and Maps:** 10,000. **Video Clips:** None. **Animations:** None. **Audio:** 60 minutes.
    Hardware Requirements: Personal Computer (IBM or IBM-compatible); Sony CD-ROM drive; check with distributor for specifics. **Software Requirements:** CD-ROM, 1 disc. **Operating System:** MS-DOS.

Price and Sales Information: *Compton's Family Encyclopedia* is sold as part of the *Sony Laser Library*, a CD-ROM package developed in 1991 by the Sony Corporation that includes a player (or drive), headphones, and six discs (including the encyclopedia). The entire package retails for about $700.00. For additional information about the *Sony Laser Library* or for a list of Sony distributors in your area, contact the Sony Corporation, 655 River Oaks Parkway, San Jose, CA 95134; 800-222-0878 (toll-free).

Consumers should also know that *Compton's Family Encyclopedia* has recently been been phased out by the publisher, Compton's New Media. Although no longer produced, the encyclopedia may be encountered as a discounted item in stores and catalogs that sell computer software. The individual disc originally sold for $395.00 but has recently been marked down to $99.00 or less.

CONSUMER NOTE

Compton's Family Encyclopedia, a CD-ROM version of COMPTON'S ENCYCLOPEDIA, a highly regarded print encyclopedia in 26 volumes, has practically the same contents and design as COMPTON'S MULTIMEDIA ENCYCLOPEDIA, also a CD-ROM product. According to the publisher, Compton's NewMedia, *Compton's Family Encyclopedia* is a "stripped-down" version of COMPTON'S MULTIMEDIA ENCYCLOPEDIA with "slightly lower system requirements." Specifically, when it first appeared in 1989, the much-talked-about COMPTON'S MULTIMEDIA ENCYCLOPEDIA required a computer with a minimum of 640K RAM (random-access memory). Because many homes, schools, and libraries had smaller computers, Compton's NewMedia produced a version of COMPTON'S MULTIMEDIA ENCYCLOPEDIA—called *Compton's Family Encyclopedia*—that would run on computers with less memory than 640K.

Aside from this and their distinctive titles, the major differences between the two encyclopedias are (1) COMPTON'S MULTIMEDIA includes video clips and animations, whereas *Compton's Family* lacks these multimedia features, although it does offer 60 minutes of audio; (2) COMPTON'S MULTIMEDIA has a slightly more sophisticated interface than *Compton's Family*; and (3) COMPTON'S MULTIMEDIA is revised annually, whereas *Compton's Family* has not been updated since it appeared in 1991.

Concerning the last point, note that, although *Compton's Family Encyclopedia* continues to be available as part of the Sony Laser Library and as a discounted item in some stores that sell computer software, the encyclopedia has been discontinued by the publisher, which has no plans to revive it in the future.

For further evaluative information about *Compton's Family Encyclopedia*, see COMPTON'S MULTIMEDIA ENCYCLOPEDIA (page 272). See also Cheryl LaGuardia's informative review of both encyclopedias in *Library Journal* (September 15, 1992, pp. 102–04), which also covers INFORMATION FINDER and the NEW GROLIER MULTIMEDIA ENCYCLOPEDIA.

COMPTON'S INTERACTIVE ENCYCLOPEDIA (CD-ROM)

FACTS

Full Title: *Compton's Interactive Encyclopedia.* Variant Title: *Compton's Interactive Encyclopedia for Windows.* **Publisher:** Compton's NewMedia. **Date Published:** First published on disk in 1993; updated annually.

Print Version: COMPTON'S ENCYCLOPEDIA.

Other Electronic Versions: COMPTON'S CONCISE ENCYCLOPEDIA (CD-ROM); COMPTON'S ENCYCLOPEDIA (online); COMPTON'S FAMILY ENCYCLOPEDIA (CD-ROM); COMPTON'S MULTIMEDIA ENCYCLOPEDIA (CD-ROM).

Words: 9 million. **Articles:** 34,000. **Still Pictures and Maps:** 13,800. **Video Clips:** 30. **Animations:** 32 **Audio:** 50 minutes.

Hardware Requirements: Multimedia Personal Computer; CD-ROM drive; mouse; VGA display; audio board; headphones or speakers; check with publisher for specifics. **Software Requirements:** CD-ROM, 1 disc. **Operating Systems:** Windows; Macintosh.

Price and Sales Information: *Compton's Interactive Encyclopedia* has a suggested retail price of $395.00 for the Windows version and $399.95 for the Macintosh version. The encyclopedia is normally available in stores or through catalogs that sell computer software. It also can be ordered directly from the publisher. For additional information about the encyclopedia or to order it, contact Compton's NewMedia, 2320 Camino Vida Roble, Carlsbad, CA 92009-1504; 800-862-2206 (toll-free).

EVALUATION

First published in 1993, *Compton's Interactive Encyclopedia* is quite similar in content and construction to COMPTON'S MULTIMEDIA ENCYCLOPEDIA, which in 1989 became the first CD-ROM encyclopedia on the market to offer multimedia features, such as full-motion video, narrated animations, and sound in the form of music, speeches, voice-over narration, and the like. Both these CD-ROM encyclopedias are based on COMPTON'S ENCYCLOPEDIA, a highly rated 26-volume print (or hardbound) set for the whole family. The print version currently contains in the neighborhood of 9 million words, 10,500 pages, 34,000 articles (most quite brief), and 22,500 illustrations and maps. See the reviews beginning on page 60 and page 186 for a detailed evaluation of the encyclopedia's contents, readability, and treatment of material.

A unique feature found in *Compton's Interactive Encyclopedia* is called The Virtual Workspace, a tool for managing off-screen windows, similar to the way you might arrange the top of your desk when studying. Rubin Rabinovitz discusses this innovative mode in his review of the encyclopedia in *PC Magazine* (August 1993, p. 554):

> Using The Virtual Workspace, you can open a series of windows on different topics and move them off screen onto a virtual desktop. The Workspace Map, a miniaturized representation of the desktop, shows icons representing the off-screen windows so that you can locate and display them as needed. In case you need to interrupt your work, a group of Virtual Workspace windows can be saved as a file. The Virtual Workspace is a helpful feature, but it will prove somewhat difficult for most children to use.

Like COMPTON'S MULTIMEDIA ENCYCLOPE-DIA before it, *Compton's Interactive Encyclopedia* has been well received in the marketplace, according to the publisher. The critics have likewise praised it. Carol Holzberg, for instance, concludes her review in CD-ROM (September 1993, p. 32) on this upbeat note: "Compton's Interactive Encyclopedia is an all-purpose general reference tool with a spirited collection of sights and sounds to make research more like play."

On the other hand, Cheryl LaGuardia in *Library Journal* (March 15, 1994, p. 109) is not overly impressed with the encyclopedia's user interface:

> CIE's opening search screen brings up an alphabetical listing of articles with a series of buttons running down the screen's righthand side. These buttons are for Idea Search, Ar-ticles, Multimedia, InfoPilot, Topic Tree, Atlas, Timeline, Picture Tour, Dictionary, and Backtrack. Some of these buttons are not sufficiently explicit to covey their uses, and you have to "enter" them just to find out what they do (or you can read the manual if you prefer).
>
> After sampling a couple of the more "usual" devices (Atlas, Picture Tour, etc.), I tried out the InfoPilot, a feature introduced in this new [1994] version of the encyclopedia. Compton's advertises it as a way to discover related articles about your topic. The immediate problem encountered was trying to decode all the boxes that suddenly appeared.... The InfoPilot Screen has that string of search buttons displayed on the right, but the rest of the screen fills with five large boxes and a series of other smaller boxes tucked in among them. After walking through the example in the guide a couple of times, I figured out how to "InfoPilot," but the process was not transparent to me at first (or second, third, or fourth).

SUMMARY

Compton's Interactive Encyclopedia, published in 1993, is an offspring of COMPTON'S MULTIMEDIA ENCYCLOPEDIA, which created a stir—it talked and moved—when it first appeared in 1989. Both these CD-ROM encyclope-dias are based on the multivolume COMPTON'S ENCYCLOPEDIA, a reference mainstay for more than 70 years. The bottom line: One of the best CD-ROM encyclopedias available today.

OTHER OPINIONS

CD-ROM World, September 1993, pp. 30-32 (review by Carol S. Holzberg); *Library Journal*, March 15, 1994, pp. 108–09 (review by Cheryl LaGuardia); *PC Magazine*, August 1993, pp. 554–555 (review by Rubin Rabinovitz); *PC Novice*, October 1993, pp. 64–65 (review by Cindy Krushenisky); *Wilson Library Bulletin*, October 1993, pp. 82–83 (review by Renee Troselius).

COMPTON'S MULTIMEDIA ENCYCLOPEDIA (CD-ROM)

FACTS

Full Title: *Compton's Multimedia Encyclopedia.* **Publisher:** Compton's New Media. **Date Published:** First published on disk in 1989; updated annually.

Print Version COMPTON'S ENCYCLOPEDIA.

Other Electronic Versions: COMPTON'S CONCISE ENCYCLOPEDIA (CD-ROM); COMPTON'S

ENCYCLOPEDIA(online); COMPTON'S FAMILY EN-CYCLOPEDIA, COMPTON'S INTERACTIVE ENCYCLO-PEDIA (CD-ROM).

Words: 9 million. **Articles:** 34,000. **Still Pictures and Maps:** 15,000. **Video Clips:** 30. **Animations:** 45. Audio: 60.

Hardware Requirements: Multimedia Personal Computer; CD-ROM drive; mouse; VGA display; audio board; headphones or speakers; check with publisher for specifics. **Software Requirements:** CD-ROM, 1 disc. **Operating Systems:** MS-DOS; Windows; Macintosh.

Price and Sales Information: *Compton's Multimedia Encyclopedia* has a suggested retail price of $495.00. The encyclopedia is normally available in stores or through catalogs that sell computer software. It can also be ordered directly from the publisher. For additional information about the encyclopedia or to order it, contact Compton's NewMedia, 2320 Camino Vida Roble, Carlsbad, CA 92009-1504; 800-862-2206 (toll-free).

EVALUATION

Compton's Multimedia Encyclopedia—the first encyclopedia of any consequence on CD-ROM to include moving pictures and sound (or multimedia)—received an enormous amount of attention when it was unveiled in September 1989. During the next year or two, the pathbreaking encyclopedia not only won awards from various electronic publishing groups but, more important, it established a strong position in the marketplace, selling especially well to school libraries and media centers where students from the elementary grades to high school were attracted particularly to its multimedia features. In 1992, Grolier countered with its NEW GROLIER MULTIMEDIA ENCYCLOPEDIA and the following year Microsoft entered the field with its formidable MICROSOFT ENCARTA MULTIMEDIA ENCYCLOPEDIA.

As its title suggests, *Compton's Multimedia Encyclopedia* is based on COMPTON'S ENCYCLOPEDIA, a highly regarded 26-volume print (or hardbound) encyclopedia intended for general family use. The print set currently contains roughly 9 million words, 10,500 pages, 34,000 articles (most quite brief), and 22,500 illustrations and maps. See the review beginning on page 60 for a detailed evaluation of the encyclopedia's contents, readability, and treatment of material. In 1993, Compton's introduced a slightly modified and less expensive version

of its multimedia encyclopedia under the title COMPTON'S INTERACTIVE ENCYCLOPEDIA. Thus at the present time, the publisher, Compton's NewMedia, offers two quite similar multimedia encyclopedias on CD-ROM, both based on the print version of COMPTON'S ENCYCLOPEDIA.

Compton's Multimedia Encyclopedia is well organized, offering the user eight different "pathways," or approaches, to finding information in the encyclopedia: "Idea/Picture Search," "Title Finder," "Topic Tree," "U.S. History Timeline," "World Atlas," "Researcher's Assistant," "Science Feature Articles," and "Picture Explorer." Cheryl LaGuardia, in a review in *Library Journal* (September 15, 1992, p. 102)), astutely points out that the encyclopedia's "search philosophy is more of a guided tour through the body of knowledge rather than a search system for random concepts, and this makes sense given the school-age target audience. On the whole, Compton's MultiMedia is an integrated package of information designed to be an effective learning program." In this regard, the publisher has produced three fat paperbound books for teachers to use in conjunction with the encyclopedia: *Lesson Guide for Science Excursions, Lesson Guide for Math Excursions,* and *Lesson Guide for Social Studies Excursions.* These guides include suggested assignments, worksheets, and answer keys.

But LaGuardia goes on to note in her *Library Journal* review, again quite rightly, that competing multimedia encyclopedias tend to be easier to navigate, due to a more user-friendly interface: "Compton's MultiMedia seems like a maze for school-children to find their way through because of the sometimes arcane arrangement of screens and subsets of information." The makers of *Compton's Multimedia Encyclopedia* are working to correct this problem, but they have a way to go to make the encyclopedia as easy to use as the competing NEW GROLIER MULTIMEDIA ENCYCLOPEDIA and MICROSOFT ENCARTA MULTIMEDIA ENCYCLOPEDIA.

The encyclopedia's search options do not include Boolean searching, which would be overly difficult for some younger users, but it does offer a natural language (or plain English) search capability via the "Idea/Picture Search" pathway. This retrieval system, however, can also be confusing to users, especially younger ones. For example, if the user asks "How many drunk drivers are arrested each year in North America?," the encyclopedia will repond with a list of articles that might provide the answer, with the most relevant articles starred, e.g., "Al-coholic Beverages," "Alcoholism," and "Safety." The problem is that many other articles of questionable relevancy are also cited, e.g., "Coffee," "Cyclops," and "Indians, American." A review in *Reference Books Bulletin* (in *Booklist*, June 15, 1990, p. 2018) makes the same point: "The question, 'How do bees make honey?' results in the starred articles *Bee*, *Canada*, and *Honey*. More than 400 additional articles are listed but have little connection with the question."

Compared with rival MICROSOFT ENCARTA, *Compton's Multimedia Encyclopedia* does not contain a great amount of multimedia content, but what the encyclopedia does include is usually of good quality. There are, for instance, a few bird calls, a handful of musical excerpts, and a few lines from speeches by political leaders, such as John F. Kennedy and Martin Luther King, Jr. In addition, 45 full-motion animations cover such topics as how bones are connected and how snakes shed their skin. In the area of still pictures, *Compton's Multimedia Encyclopedia* offers many more than any other electronic encyclopedia currently on the market.

SUMMARY

The first encyclopedia to include sound and moving pictures, pioneering *Compton's Multimedia Encyclopedia* represents an innovative marriage between contemporary digital technology and a fine traditional print encyclopedia, namely the 26-volume COMPTON'S ENCYCLOPEDIA. The multimedia encyclopedia appeals especially to young people, but it also has value as a reference resource for adults and older students. On the negative side, it is not as user-friendly as its chief competitors, MICROSOFT ENCARTA MULTIMEDIA ENCYCLOPEDIA and the NEW GROLIER MULTIMEDIA ENCYCLOPEDIA, and its natural language search option can be confusing, especially to younger users.

OTHER OPINIONS

Basic Information Sources by William A. Katz (vol. 1 of *Introduction to Reference Work*, 6th ed., New York: McGraw-Hill, 1992), pp. 252–53; *Library Journal*, September 15, 1992, pp. 102–04 (review by Cherly LaGuardia); *Newsweek*, March 19, 1990, p. 45 (article by John Schwartz entitled "A Computer Encyclopedia"); *Reference Books*

Bulletin (in *Booklist*), June 15, 1990, pp. 2017–20 (unsigned review); *Reference Sources for Small and Medium-Sized Libraries* (5th ed., Chicago: American Library Assn., 1992), pp. 31–32; *RQ*, Winter 1991, p. 247–48 (review by Mara Sprain); *School Library Journal*, October 1990, p. 60 (unsigned review); *Wilson Library Bulletin*, March 1992, p. 84–86 (review by Charles Anderson).

CONCISE COLUMBIA ENCYCLOPEDIA (CD-ROM)

FACTS

Full Title: *The Concise Columbia Encyclopedia*. **Publisher:** Columbia University Press. **Distributor:** Microsoft Corporation. **Date Published:** First published on disk in 1992 (based on print version published in 1989).

Print Version: CONCISE COLUMBIA ENCYCLOPEDIA.

Other Electronic Versions: COLUMBIA ELECTRONIC ENCYCLOPEDIA (hand-held).

Words: 1 million. **Articles:** 15,000. **Still Pictures and Maps:** 1,400. **Video Clips:** None. **Animations:** 50. **Audio:** 45 minutes.

Hardware Requirements: Multimedia Personal Computer; CD-ROM drive; mouse; VGA display; audio board; headphones or speakers; check with distributor for specifics. **Software Requirements:** CD-ROM, 1 disc. **Operating System:** Windows.

Price and Sales Information: The electronic version of the *Concise Columbia Encyclopedia* is bundled (or included) with *Microsoft Bookshelf*, a collection of reference materials on a single CD-ROM disc produced and distributed by the Microsoft Corporation. *Microsoft Bookshelf* is normally available in stores or through catalogs that sell computer software. The latest edition (1993) carries a suggested retail price of $195.00, but it is often sold for less. The product can also be purchased directly from the Microsoft Corporation, but a company representative advises that "better pricing is usually offered by local software dealers." For additional information about *Microsoft Bookshelf* or the encyclopedia or a list of Microsoft distributors in your area, contact Microsoft Corporation, One Microsoft Way, Redmond, WA 98052-6399; 800-426-9400 (toll-free).

EVALUATION

The CD-ROM edition of the *Concise Columbia Encyclopedia* is not published separately, but rather as part of *Microsoft Bookshelf*, a product of the Microsoft Corporation best described by its subtitle as a "CD-ROM Reference Library." The *Bookshelf*'s current edition (1993) brings together seven popular reference titles: a 65,000-entry edition of the *American Heritage Dictionary* (Houghton Mifflin), *Roget's II Electronic Thesaurus* (Houghton Mifflin), Bartlett's *Familiar Quotations* (Little, Brown), the *Concise Colum-* *bia Dictionary of Quotations* (Columbia University Press), the *Hammond Atlas* (Hammond), the *World Almanac and Books of Facts* (World Almanac Books), and, of course, the *Concise Columbia Encyclopedia* (Columbia University Press). The *Bookshelf*, which first appeared in 1987, has been enormously successful over the years and is now issued annually. It is perhaps most useful to students at the high school and college levels and office workers who require frequent access to basic reference materials.

The CD-ROM version of the *Concise Columbia Encyclopedia* found on the *Bookshelf* is derived from the second edition (1989) of the CONCISE COLUMBIA ENCYCLOPEDIA, a highly regarded one-volume print (or hardcover) encyclopedia for adults and older students. The CONCISE COLUMBIA is actually an updated abridgment of the larger *New Columbia Encyclopedia* (1975), which has recently been revised and published as the COLUMBIA ENCYCLOPEDIA, a work practically everyone agrees is the best single-volume general encyclopedia currently available in English. The print edition of the *Concise Columbia* contains approximately a million words, 950 pages, and 15,000 succinct articles. Like its parent work, the CONCISE COLUMBIA is sparsely illustrated and has no index, although it does include many cross-references. See the review beginning on page 131 for a detailed evaluation of the encyclopedia's contents, readability, and treatment of material.

The *Concise Columbia Encyclopedia* on CD-ROM improves on the print version in several ways. First, access to the encyclopedia's text is greatly enhanced by various search and retrieval options not available in the print volume, such as accessing the database using the Boolean operators AND, OR, NOT, and NEAR—the latter for proximity searching. While this might sound intimidating or too technical for the neophyte, the search options provided in the *Bookshelf* are carefully explained and not overly difficult to master. The good people at Microsoft have accrued a great deal of hard-won experience over the past decade in the business of converting high-quality reference books into high-quality electronic products. The various sources that make up the *Bookshelf*, including the encyclopedia, are good examples, as is Microsoft's excellent MICROSOFT ENCARTA MULTIMEDIA ENCYCLOPEDIA, a much enhanced version of the 29-volume FUNK & WAGNALLS NEW ENCYCLOPEDIA.

The CD-ROM version also outshines the print volume in the area of illustrations and other complements to the text. Specifically, the *Concise Columbia Encyclopedia* in electronic form includes approximately 1,400 still pictures (or "images"), 50 animations in color (half of which are narrated), and a dozen short musical sequences explaining types of serious music (e.g., the fugue). The print version, on the other hand, is almost entirely text-driven, containing only about 150 black-and-white line drawings and simple maps. The CD-ROM encyclopedia's narrated animation of how the heart works and the captioned animation of General Sherman's Southern campaign during the waning days of the Civil War are just two examples of Microsoft's effective application of multimedia in the encyclopedia.

Yet another way the CD-ROM encyclopedia surpasses its print counterpart involves recency of material. As mentioned, the electronic version is based on the second edition of the CONCISE COLUMBIA, published in 1989. But the articles in the encyclopedia in *Microsoft Bookshelf* are current as of the early 1990s. *Example:* The collapse of the former Soviet Union is recorded in the encyclopedia; likewise, the article "Russia" describes Russia as a former republic of the Soviet Union and now an independent country.

Jan Schwenk, in a brief review in *CD-ROM World* (September 1993, p. 40), nicely sums up the general feeling about *Microsoft Bookshelf* and its individual titles, including the encyclopedia:

> There is a very large body of facts and information provided. Enough, in fact, to overwhelm you. However, it is organized and accessible in ways that allow you to seek and select only the info you want. Too much data only exacerbates the information glut; Bookshelf helps you tame it and harness it to your tasks. This is a perfect example of how a computer can really help you do your job cheaper, better, and faster!

SUMMARY

The excellent *Concise Columbia Encyclopedia* on CD-ROM is available only as part of *Microsoft Bookshelf*, a well-known, annually updated CD-ROM library of seven popular reference sources for student and office use. The encyclopedia—based on the second (1989) edition of the single-volume CONCISE COLUMBIA ENCYCLOPEDIA, a work of considerable merit—provides authoritative, up-to-date, easily accessible material enhanced by many still illustrations, plus 50 animations (half of which are narrated) and a dozen musical sequences. The bottom line: A model of how a quality print encyclopedia can be made even better with the addition of electronic enhancements.

OTHER OPINIONS

CD-ROM World, September 1993, p. 34 (review by Carol Holzberg); *CD-ROM World*, September 1993, p. 40 (review by Jan R. Schwenk).

EVERYMAN'S ENCYCLOPAEDIA (ONLINE)

FACTS

Full Title: *Everyman's Encyclopaedia*. British **Publisher:** J.M. Dent & Sons Ltd. British **Vendor:** Learned Information (Europe) Ltd. North American **Vendor:** Dialog Information Services, Inc. **Date Published:** First published online in 1985 (based on print version published in 1978); no updates (closed file).

Print Version: EVERYMAN'S ENCYCLOPAEDIA.

Words: 9 million. File Size: 51,000 entries. **Still Pictures and Maps:** None. **Video Clips:** None. **Animations:** None. **Audio:** None.

Hardware and Software Requirements: Personal Computer; telephone; modem; and communications software; check with vendor for specifics.

Price and Sales Information: The online version of *Everyman's Encyclopaedia* (based on the sixth print edition published in 1978) is available to consumers through Dialog Information Services, Inc., a major commercial online information service intended principally for libraries and research institutions. The encyclopedia is just one of many databases offered by the service. Currently, Dialog charges $0.80 per minute of connect-time (or time online) to use the encyclopedia. For additional information about Dialog or *Everyman's Encyclopaedia* online, contact Dialog Information Services, Inc., 3460 Hillview Avenue, Palo Alto, CA 94304; 800-334-2564 (toll-free).

EVALUATION

The online version of *Everyman's Encyclopaedia* is based directly on the sixth edition of the 12-volume EVERYMAN'S ENCYCLOPAEDIA, an authoritative but outdated British-produced print (or hardcover) encyclopedia for adults and older students. The sixth edition appeared in 1978 but has not been revised since that time and, not surprisingly, is now out of print in both Great Britian and North America. The encyclopedia, which dates back to 1913–14, has long been a British favorite, but its makers today apparently lack the wherewithal, financial and otherwise, to maintain the encyclopedia as a viable source of contemporary information.

The defunct sixth edition contains roughly 9 million words, 8,900 pages, 51,000 articles, and no index. The articles, the large majority of which are quite brief, average about 200 words in length. The print edition also includes some 5,000 informative illustrations (all in black-and-white), plus 600 maps, including a 64-page color atlas in the final volume. For a brief assessment of the encyclopedia's contents, readability, and treatment of material, see page 304 in the "Out-of-Print Encyclopedias" section of this book.

Obviously, *Everyman's Encyclopaedia* is not a household name in North America. In fact, its impact and sales over the years on this side of the Atlantic have been nil. The online version suffers from lack of brand-name recognition, but its substantive shortcomings go much deeper. There is, of course, the crippling problem of the encyclopedia's age. As noted, *Everyman's* has not been revised since 1978—or more than 15 years ago. As far as encyclopedias are concerned today, 15 years is an eternity.

Another problem is the encyclopedia's pronounced bias toward British people, places, events, and institutions, which militates against its usefulness in North America. A.J. Walford, a British authority on reference books, criticized the last (sixth) edition of *Everyman's* on this score in the *Library Association Record* (September 1979, p. 439), pointing out that "the British slant is reflected in such contributions as that on Medi-

cal education: London boroughs and London, Oxford and Cambridge colleges and institutes each have entries. Hull received nearly three pages; Hamburg [Germany] about two-thirds of a page."

Yet another problem is that the online version of *Everyman's* lacks the illustrations found in the print set. Even if Dialog, the American vendor, wanted to include the graphics as part of the database, it could not because of legal restrictions. According to Elizabeth Newlands, a representative of J.M. Dent, *Everyman's* British publisher, "the cost of clearing picture rights for the US was enormous compared with the likely return that we would make in sales, and so we never took the step" (letter from Newlands, dated February 9, 1984, to the author of *Kister's Best Encyclopedias*).

The print encyclopedia was distributed for a time in Canada by Fitzhenry & Whiteside, but today only the online version is available. Like any reputable old encyclopedia, *Everyman's* online has some value as a source of historical information. For a succinct summary of Galileo's scientific achievements and censure by the Inquisition, for instance, it works well. But the reader will not learn that the Roman Catholic Church in recent times has exonerated the famous scientist, acknowledging it was wrong in 1633 to force him to renounce Copernican theory.

On the plus side, the automated version of *Everyman's* provides much greater access to the encyclopedic text than the print set, which included 15,000 cross-references but no general index. Dialog's retrieval system, which includes proximity and full-text searching, renders the database fully accessible to the experienced searcher. But is the database worth searching is the question.

SUMMARY

Although the print set has long been out of print in both Great Britain and North America, *Everyman's Encyclopaedia* continues to be available in an online version via Dialog, a major American vendor of information in electronic form. Unfortunately, the encyclopedia, which is aimed at adults and older students, has not been updated since the last print edition (the sixth, published in 1978), and consequently is dreadfully out-of-date. Moreover, the encyclopedia has a strong British bias and the online version lacks illustrations. *Everyman's* limitations are such that it has little appeal or value to most North Americans other than possibly for historical information. The bottom line: Why Dialog, a major information utility, continues to carry this relic—the only general encyclopedia it offers—is a mystery.

OTHER OPINIONS

Basic Information Sources by William A. Katz (vol. 1 of *Introduction to Reference Work*, 6th ed., New York: McGraw-Hill, 1992), pp. 246-47.

FIRST CONNECTIONS (CD-ROM)

FACTS

Full Title: *First Connections: The Golden Book Encyclopedia.* **Publisher:** Hartley Courseware. **Date Published:** First published on disk in 1993 (based on print version published in 1988).

Print Version: GOLDEN BOOK ENCYCLOPEDIA.

Words: 650,000. **Articles:** 1,500. **Still Pictures and Maps:** 2,900. **Video Clips:** None. **Animations:** 100. **Audio:** 60 minutes.

Hardware Requirements: Personal Computer (Macintosh); CD-ROM drive; mouse; VGA display; audio board; headphones or speakers; check with publisher for specifics. **Software Requirements:** CD-ROM, 1 disc. **Operating System:** Macintosh; MS-DOS version scheduled for July 1994.

Price and Sales Information: *First Connections: The Golden Book Encyclopedia* is currently priced at $149.95. The encyclopedia is normally available in stores or through catalogs that sell computer software. It can also be ordered directly from the publisher. For additional information about the encyclopedia or to order it, contact Hartley Courseware, Inc., 3001 Coolidge (Suite 400), East Lansing, MI 48823; 800-247-1380 (toll-free).

EVALUATION

Published in 1993 by Hartley Courseware (a division of Jostens Learning Corporation), *First Connections: The Golden Book Encyclopedia* is a CD-ROM encyclopedia with multimedia features designed for use with a Macintosh computer. A DOS version is scheduled to appear in July 1994. The encyclopedia—intended chiefly for use in the classroom—is targeted at young students in the elementary grades, but it can be used profitably by most children ages 5–12 in the home or at school. *First Connections*, interestingly, is the only general encyclopedia on CD-ROM currently available aimed specifically at this age group. The others, such as COMPTON'S MULTIMEDIA ENCYCLOPEDIA, MICROSOFT ENCARTA MULTIMEDIA ENCYCLOPEDIA, and the NEW GROLIER MULTIMEDIA ENCYCLOPEDIA, are intended for a somewhat older, more intellectually mature audience.

As its subtitle makes clear, *First Connections* is based on the GOLDEN BOOK ENCYCLOPEDIA, a 20-volume print (or hardcover) ENCYCLOPEDIA FOR YOUNG PEOPLE. The set was first published in 1959 in 16 volumes and last revised in 1988, at which time it expanded to 20 volumes, albeit thin ones. The 1988 edition contains approximately 650,000 words, 1,900 pages, and 1,500 articles, complemented by some 2,900 illustrations and maps. The GOLDEN BOOK ENCYCLOPEDIA has never been considered an encyclopedia of the first order, but neither is it a disreputable work. See the review beginning on page 191 for a detailed evaluation of the encyclopedia's contents, readability, and treatment of material.

First Connections contains practically the same text as the 1988 print set—plus multimedia enhancements produced by Hartley Courseware. The multimedia features are simple but effective, adding to the encyclopedia's value as a source of basic information and knowledge for students at the elementary school level. There are about 100 "movies," or narrated animations; a typical sequence shows a scuba diver exploring under water, while the narrator explains what is happening. There is also a variety of audio in the encyclopedia (music, speeches, sound effects, narrations), totaling about an hour of sound.

Using the CD-ROM encyclopedia should pose few if any real difficulties for today's youngsters, many of whom are more comfortable with electronic equipment and hardware than their parents and teachers. A user-friendly user's guide accompanies *First Connections*. Written at roughly the third grade level, the paperbound guide features Inspector Golden, a cartoonish dog dressed like Sherlock Holmes who appears throughout the encyclopedia as a helpful guide. In the book, the inspector provides a step-by-step introduction to the encyclopedia's contents and organization, with emphasis on accessing the multimedia material. A teacher's guide is also available, with suggestions for using *First Connections* in the classroom.

First Connections has been enthusiastically received to date. Renee Troselius, looking at the encyclopedia strictly through the eyes of a school media specialist, offers this strong endorsement in a review in *Wilson Library Bulletin* (Janaury 1994, p. 126):

> [The encyclopedia] can be used with young learners, older children who have difficulty reading, and English as a second language students. It's a fun-to-explore encyclopedia that should be in the classroom or accessible from the classrom if the library is networked throughout the school. This Mac-based CD makes a wonderful tool for teaching research skills to young learners. Easy to install, the encyclopedia can be navigated without consulting the user guide.

Carol Holzberg, writing in *CD-ROM World* (September 1993, p. 32), is equally impressed:

> Even young children will be able to use the encyclopedia with a minimum of adult supervision. Voice-over narrations (providing directions), plus a very intuitive graphic interface, simplify operation. Four exploration paths enable youngsters to look for articles arranged alphabetically by title, by topic or subtopic, by questions, or by multimedia events (such as maps, pictures, sounds, and speeches)....First Connections is a unique interactive resource with lots of exciting activities.

On the negative side, the CD-ROM encyclopedia, like its print counterpart, is not sufficiently current in some areas. This criticism is especially true in articles on countries where recent political events have radically altered the old order, as in South Africa and Eastern Europe. The publisher is aware of the problem and a Hartley representative has indicated that the encyclopedia might be revised in the near future.

SUMMARY

The only general encyclopedia on CD-ROM produced exclusively for young people, *First Connections: The Golden Book Encyclopedia* is, as its subtitle indicates, based on the GOLDEN BOOK ENCYCLOPEDIA, a 20-volume juvenile encyclopedia first published in 1959 and last revised in 1988. The electronic version is easy to navigate and includes enough multimedia content (about 100 animations and an hour's worth of various sounds) to keep children coming back again and again. The encyclopedia's greatest weakness is lack of recency in some articles. The bottom line: A unique reference source for children.

OTHER OPINIONS

CD-ROM World, September 1993, p. 32 (review by Carol S. Holzberg); *Wilson Library Bulletin*, January 1994, p. 126 (review by Renee Troselius).

INFORMATION FINDER (CD-ROM)

FACTS

Full Title: *Illustrated Information Finder; Information Finder.* **Variant Title:** *Illustrated Information Finder; New Illustrated Information Finder.* **Publisher:** World Book, Inc. **Date Published:** First published on disk in 1989; updated annually.

Print Version: WORLD BOOK ENCYCLOPEDIA.

Words: 10 million. **Articles:** 17,500. **Still Pictures and Maps:** 3,300. **Video Clips:** None. **Animations:** None. **Audio:** None.

Hardware Requirements: Personal Computer; CD-ROM drive; mouse; VGA display; check with publisher for specifics. **Software Requirements:** CD-ROM, 1 disc. **Operating Systems:** MS-DOS (text only); Windows; Macintosh.

Price and Sales Information: The 1994 *Information Finder* is priced at $395.00 for all three versions (DOS, which is text only; Windows; and Macintosh). It is sold to individual consumers and educational institutions (schools, libraries, etc.) through authorized sales representatives of the publisher. Consumers should consult the yellow pages of the local telephone directory under "Encyclopedias" for the World Book, Inc. sales representative in their area. If the company is not listed, contact the publisher for the closest representative to you. *Information Finder* can also be ordered directly from the publisher. For the name of your local World Book representative or for more information about *Information Finder* or to order the encyclopedia, contact World Book, Inc., 525 West Monroe Street, 20th Floor, Chicago, IL 60661; 800-621-8202 (toll-free).

EVALUATION

Information Finder is a CD-ROM version of the WORLD BOOK ENCYCLOPEDIA, an outstanding 22-volume print (or hardcover) encyclopedia for the whole family, from students in the upper elementary grades through college to educated adults. Currently the print set contains approximately 10 million words, 14,000 pages, and 17,500 articles, plus some 31,000 illustrations and maps. The WORLD BOOK—long the bestselling encyclopedia in North America—is especially noted for the clarity and recency of its articles and the informative nature and visual appeal of its many illustrations. See the reviews beginning on page 97 and page 206 for a detailed evaluation of the encyclopedia's contents, readability, and treatment of material.

Information Finder was first issued in 1989, just a few months after the much heralded appearance of COMPTON'S MULTIMEDIA ENCYCLOPEDIA. But *Information Finder* received comparatively little notice, due largely to the fact that it had no pictures, no videos, no animations, no speeches by great leaders or readings by immortal poets, no musical excerpts from Bach or Beethoven, no narrated maps showing how General Sherman marched through the South in 1864, etc. In a word, *Information Finder*, which comprised only the printed text of the WORLD BOOK ENCYCLOPEDIA, was dull compared with the glitzy COMPTON'S MULTIMEDIA ENCYCLOPEDIA, which moved and talked.

It did not take long, however, for those who use CD-ROM encyclopedias extensively—teachers, librarians, media specialists, and the like—to come to appreciate *Information Finder's* strengths, particularly its user-friendly design and powerful search and retrieval capabilities. Cheryl LaGuardia, an experienced CD-ROM reviewer who is head of computer information services at the University of California at Santa Barbara, evaluated the encyclopedia recently in *Library Journal* (September 15, 1992, p. 104):

Information Finder's design struck me as very smart and neat. Here, again, there's a command bar at the top of the screen, but the commands are straightforward. A line tells you to ENTER SEARCH TOPIC, and you can do so in normal language. The system ignores punctuation and spacing in most cases: if you type in "Groundhog Day" the system finds it, although the index lists the topic as "Ground-Hog Day"; if you type "Martin Luther King" it finds it, although he's "King, Martin Luther, Jr." in the index. This kind of flexibility should help in searching the disc.

However, the best aspect of Information Finder is the way it displays articles. When your search is complete, the article appears on a split screen. On the left-hand side is an outline of the entire article including subtopics. On the right-hand side is the actual text of the article. Users are able to run through the information on a topic very quickly, as well as see it in the context of a larger subject. This should serve students well.

Users seeking information about a particular subject can search *Information Finder* by topic, which locates the encyclopedia's main article on the subject as well as related articles, or by keyword, which finds all references to the word in the encyclopedia. A keyword search for material on abortion, for instance, retrieved 112 references (or "hits") in 86 articles; a similar search on asbestos resulted in 140 hits in 43 articles. The keyword searching mode also allows the user to combine words to narrow the search. For instance, a keyword search of "*First* and *Woman* and *Senator*" quickly pulls up the article "Georgia," in which the reader learns that Rebecca L. Felton became the *first* United States *woman senator* in 1922.

Happily, in 1994, the producers of *Information Finder* finally added some pictorial material to the encyclopedia—approximately 3,300 photographs, diagrams, and maps, all derived from the print encyclopedia. On the negative side, this means that only about 12 percent of the excellent illustrations found the current edition of the WORLD BOOK ENCY-

CLOPEDIA are now incorporated in *Information Finder*. Bear in mind, too, that *Information Finder* continues to lack multimedia features (i.e., moving pictures and sound), which continues to place it at a competitive disadvantage vis a vis the NEW GROLIER MULTIMEDIA ENCYCLOPEDIA, MICROSOFT ENCARTA MULTIMEDIA ENCYCLOPEDIA, COMPTON'S INTERACTIVE ENCYCLOPEDIA, and the aforementioned COMPTON'S MULTIMEDIA ENCYCLOPEDIA.

The producers of *Information Finder* naturally put this situation in the best light. Promotional material accompanying the 1994 edition notes,

> Our key strength is still the quality of the text and search system. While our competitors stress "Resources" we stress "Research." The new Illustrated Information Finder incorporates graphics as an enhancement to research.

SUMMARY

First published in 1989, *Information Finder* is a CD-ROM version of the WORLD BOOK ENCYCLOPEDIA, a first-rate print set in 22 volumes. The encyclopedia's pluses include a user-friendly interface and a powerful search and retrieval system. On the debit side, *Information Finder* has lacked illustrations of any kind until 1994, when it added some 3,300 photographs, diagrams, and maps, or about 12 percent of those found in the print set. Moreover, it continues to lack multimedia features (moving pictures and sound). The bottom line: This fine CD-ROM version of the bestselling WORLD BOOK ENCYCLOPEDIA still has a way to go before it achieves its full potential.

OTHER OPINIONS

Basic Information Sources by William A. Katz (vol. 1 of *Introduction to Reference Work*, 6th ed., New York: McGraw-Hill, 1992), pp. 249-50; *CD-ROM Librarian*, June 1990, pp. 26-28 (review by Lois Shumaker); *CD-ROM World*, September 1993, pp. 32-34 (review by Carol S. Holzberg); *Library Journal*, September 15, 1992, pp. 102-04 (review by Cheryl LaGuardia); *Reference Books Bulletin* (in *Booklist*), June 1, 1990, pp. 1918-21 (unsigned review); *RQ*, Winter 1990, pp. 274-76 (review by Carolyn Tynan); *Wilson Library Bulletin*, September 1991, pp. 89-90 (review by Charles Anderson).

KUSSMAUL ENCYCLOPEDIA (ONLINE)

FACTS

Full Title: *The Kussmaul Encyclopedia.* **Publisher:** Delphi Internet Services Corporation. **Date Published:** First published online in 1983; no longer updated (closed file).
Print Version: CADILLAC MODERN ENCYCLOPEDIA.

Words: 3 million. **File Size:** 23,000 entries. **Still Pictures and Maps:** None. **Video Clips:** None. **Animations:** None. **Audio:** None.

Hardware and Software Requirements: Personal Computer; telephone; modem; and communications software; check with publisher for specifics.

Price and Sales Information: The *Kussmaul Encyclopedia*, an online version of the now defunct single-volume CADILLAC MODERN ENCYCLOPEDIA, is available through Delphi Internet Services Corporation. Delphi is a commerical online information service that offers a gateway to the Internet, the world's largest computerized research network. The encyclopedia is just one of many databases accessible through the service. Delphi currently has two subscription plans: the "10/4 Plan," which costs the subscriber $10.00 per month and includes four hours of connect-time (or time online), and the "20/20 Advantage Plan," which costs $20.00 per month and includes 20 hours of connect-time. There is an additional charge for Internet access. For subscription information or additional information about the service or the encyclopedia, contact Delphi Internet Services Corporation, 1030 Massachusetts Avenue, Cambridge, MA 02138; 800-544-4005 (toll-free) or 800-695-4005 (toll-free).

EVALUATION

In the early 1980s, J. Wesley Kussmaul, a bright young entrepreneur from the Boston area, created a pioneering dial-up online information service called Delphi—now Delphi Internet Services Corporation. From the beginning, Kussmaul wanted to offer an encyclopedia as part of his service, and eventually he acquired the electronic publishing rights to the CADILLAC MODERN ENCYCLOPEDIA, a one-volume work for adults and older students published in 1973 and out of print by 1980. Kussmaul converted the encyclopedic text into machine-readable form and, presto, the *Kussmaul Encyclopedia*, named for himself, was born.

The CADILLAC MODERN contained approximately 2.5 million words, nearly 2,000 pages, and 18,000 articles, plus about 1,000 illustrations. It had no index, but included some 50,000 cross-references. For a brief description of the encyclopedia's contents, readability, and treatment of material, see page 301 in the "Out-of-Print Encyclopedias" section of this book. In the early years of Delphi, Kussmaul added some 3,000 entries to the encyclopedia's database. In addition, he cleverly updated the encyclopedia by electronically linking (or cross-referencing) articles to news stories generated by United Press International (UPI), another database then carried by Delphi. For example, the encyclopedia article on the Falkland Islands might provide a reference, or link, to a UPI story on the Falklands War between Great Britain and Argentina.

Regrettably, today the *Kussmaul Encyclopedia* is a closed file, no longer updated in any manner. As Delphi grew—the service is now part of Rupert Murdoch's News Corporation and promotes itself as an open sesame to the Internet—the encyclopedia's prominence diminished, or as Wes Kussmual put it to this author a few years ago, the encyclopedia went "a couple of steps down the menu" in importance to Delphi subscribers. Recently, Delphi added the online version of the ACADEMIC AMERICAN ENCYCLOPEDIA to its service, thus relegating *Kussmaul* to antique status.

Still, it continues to be offered as part of Delphi, although even representatives of the service recommend using the "Grolier" encyclopedia—that is, the ACADEMIC AMERICAN. Anyone who does opt to use *Kussmaul* today will find a quite small and inadequate database that is seriously out-of-date. In addition, it lack any illustrative matter, and the text is searchable by assigned subject headings only.

SUMMARY

Derived from the old (1973) and now defunct CADILLAC MODERN ENCYCLOPEDIA, a one-volume work for adults and older students, the *Kussmaul Encyclopedia* is a small online encyclopedia that generally lacks the depth to satisfy any but the most elementary informational needs. But the greatest drawback to *Kussmaul* is that it has not been updated in a long time and today is woefully out-of-date. The bottom line: The *Kussmaul Encyclopedia* is an interesting pioneering effort in the history of electronic encyclopedias, but even the publisher's representatives recommend against using it.

OTHER OPINIONS

None.

MICROSOFT ENCARTA MULTIMEDIA ENCYCLOPEDIA (CD-ROM)

FACTS

Full Title: *Microsoft Encarta Multimedia Encyclopedia.* **Variant Title:** *Encarta.* **Publisher:** Microsoft Corporation. **Date Published:** First published on disk in 1993; updated annually.

> **Print Version:** FUNK & WAGNALL'S NEW ENCYCLOPEDIA.

> **Words:** 9.5 million. **Articles:** 26,000. **Still Pictures and Maps:** 7,800. **Video Clips:** 45. **Animations:** 100. **Audio:** 8 hours.

> **Hardware Requirements:** Multimedia Personal Computer; CD-ROM drive; mouse; VGA display; audio board; headphones or speakers; check with publisher for specifics. **Software Requirements:** CD-ROM, 1 disc. **Operating Systems:** MS-DOS; Windows; Macintosh.

Price and Sales Information: The 1994 edition of *Microsoft Encarta Multimedia Encyclopedia* is priced at $139.00 for all three versions (DOS; Windows; Macintosh). The encyclopedia is available in stores and through catalogs that sell computer software. It can also be purchased directly from the Microsoft Corporation, but a company representative advises that "better pricing is usually offered by local software dealers." For additional information about *Microsoft Encarta Multimedia Encyclopedia* or a list of Microsoft distributors in your area, contact Microsoft Corporation, One Microsoft Way, Redmond, WA 98052-6399; 800-426-9400 (toll-free).

EVALUATION

Microsoft Encarta Multimedia Encyclopedia— or *Encarta*—is the newest and, in many ways, the best of the CD-ROM encyclopedias on the market today. It offers a user-friendly interface that allows even computer neophytes to navigate the encyclopedia with little or no difficulty. Likewise, it provides a muscular search and retrieval system that invites users to exploit the encyclopedia's database to its fullest. And, in the area of multimedia enhancements, where it truly excels, *Encarta* stands head and shoulders above the competition.

On the other hand, *Encarta*'s printed text derives largely from FUNK & WAGNALLS NEW ENCYCLOPEDIA, a 29-volume print (or hardbound) encyclopedia for the family that is sold chiefly through supermarkets in North America. Competitors ask, holding their noses, how can a "supermarket" encyclopedia be any good, no matter what sort of electronic bells and whistles have be added? Most people who say this—and there are many—have not looked at FUNK & WAGNALLS NEW ENCYCLOPEDIA for a long time, if ever.

They should. True, the encyclopedia does not have much to offer in terms of fine illustrations or aesthetically pleasing page design and layout, but in the case of *Encarta* that criticism is hardly pertinent. As far as the quality of FUNK & WAGNALLS' text is concerned, its articles are normally authoritative, up-to-date, and clearly written. See the review of FUNK & WAGNALLS NEW ENCYCLOPEDIA beginning on page 69 for a detailed evaluation of the encyclopedia's contents, readability, and treatment of material.

Encarta owes its success, at least in large part, to its publisher's strong position in the computer software industry. The Microsoft Corporation is big enough and rich enough and its people talented enough to take on such a project with some reasonable assurance of turning out a first-rate product. How, for instance, have the producers of *Encarta* managed to pack *eight hours* worth of sound into their encyclopedia, when competing works typically offer one hour? Rubin Rabinovitz, reviewing the encyclopedia in *PC Magazine* (August 1993, p. 556), has the answer:

> Compression is the secret, and Microsoft has licensed file-compression algorithms that are far superior to those in rival programs. Its ADPCM (Analog to Digital Pulse Code Modulation) audio-compression technology achieves 30 percent compression for sound clips; other licensed technologies achieve a 12-to-1 compression ratio for graphics files.

Multimedia features in *Encarta* are truly impressive. For instance, the encyclopedia contains more than 1,000 music segments, including nearly 200 national anthems, numerous substantial examples of folk music representing ethnic cultures around the world, and many excerpts from both popular and classic compositions. It also includes about 150 animations and moving sequences, more than 900 interactive maps, and 100 interactive charts, plus 7,800 still pictures. All of this material has been acquired and developed by Microsoft editors.

Not surprisingly, the encyclopedia's reception has been overwhelming positive almost everywhere—except at Compton's, Grolier, and World Book. Merry Mattson is typical. A technology specialist at a high school in Minneapolis, Mattson recently reviewed *Encarta* in *Wilson Library Bulletin* (December 1993, p. 109):

> This is it! This is the multimedia product we have been waiting for. This is the CD-ROM product that will make people go out and buy a CD-ROM player just so they can use *Encarta*. This is the CD-ROM that will make print encyclopedias obsolete. This is the CD-ROM that will set the standard for multimedia reference materials. This is *Microsoft Encarta Multimedia Encyclopedia*. If this sounds like an advertisement for Microsoft, it is because I am very impressed with this product.

And here is what Layne Nordgren, a media specialist at a university in Tacoma, has to say in his review in *CD-ROM Professional* (July 1993, p. 48):

> Encarta encourages exploration and learning, but provides effective tools for refining and focusing searches when needed. The artistic blend of functionality and multimedia content sets very high standards for the competing products from Grolier's and Compton's NewMedia.

Finally, a review of the 1994 edition of *Encarta* in *Choice* (March 1994, p. 1110) states:

Encarta has achieved its objectives by providing an improved presentation of content in a user interface that provides deep, balanced multimedia coverage. Other advantages are enhanced speed and ease of use . . . . Recommended for all academic libraries and for school media centers.

SUMMARY

Microsoft Encarta Multimedia Encyclopedia—usually called simply *Encarta*—is an outstanding new entry in the CD-ROM encyclopedia field. It is produced by the Microsoft Corporation, which knows the business of electronic publishing as well as anyone. This expertise shows up in *Encarta* in many ways, but most significantly in the area of multimedia enhancement, where the encyclopedia simply has it all over the competition—namely, COMPTON'S INTERACTIVE ENCYCLOPEDIA, COMPTON'S MULTIMEDIA ENCYCLOPEDIA, INFORMATION FINDER, and the NEW GROLIER MULTIMEDIA ENCYCLOPEDIA. The bottom line: *Encarta*, overall the best in its class, currently sets the standard for CD-ROM encyclopedias.

OTHER OPINIONS

CD-ROM Professional, July 1993, pp. 46–48 (review by Layne Nordgren); *CD-ROM World*, July 1993, pp. 51–55 (review by Norman Desmarais); *CD-ROM World*, September 1993, pp. 34–36 (review by Carol S. Holzberg); *Choice*, March 1994, p. 1110 (review by M. Green); *Library Journal*, March 15, 1994, pp. 108–09 (revew by Cheryl LaGuardia); *PC Magazine*, August 1993, pp. 555–56 (review by Rubin Rabinovitz); *PC Novice*, October 1993, pp. 63–64 (review by Cindy Krushenisky); *Reference Books Bulletin* (in *Booklist*), August 1993, p. 2084 (review by Charles Anderson); *Wilson Library Bulletin*, December 1993, pp. 109–110 (review by Merry Mattson).

NEW GROLIER MULTIMEDIA ENCYCLOPEDIA (CD-ROM)

FACTS

Full Title: *The New Grolier Multimedia Encyclopedia.* **Variant Title:** *Grolier Multimedia Encyclopedia.* Former Titles: *The Academic American Encyclopedia on CD-ROM* (1985); *The Electronic Encyclopedia* or *The Grolier Electronic Encyclopedia* (1986-87); *The New Grolier Electronic Encyclopedia* (1988-91). **Publisher:** Grolier Electronic Publishing, Inc. **Date Published:** First published on disk in 1985; updated annually.

Print Version: ACADEMIC AMERICAN ENCYCLOPEDIA.

Other Electronic Versions: ACADEMIC AMERICAN ENCYCLOPEDIA (online); SOFTWARE TOOLWORKS ILLUSTRATED ENCYCLOPEDIA (CD-ROM).

Words: 10 million. **Articles:** 33,000. **Still Pictures and Maps:** 3,250. **Video Clips:** 80. **Animations:** 65. **Audio:** 70 minutes.

Hardware Requirements: Multimedia Personal Computer; CD-ROM drive; mouse; VGA display; audio board; headphones or speakers. **Software Requirements:** CD-ROM, 1 disc. **Operating Systems:** MS-DOS; Windows; Macintosh.

Price and Sales Information: The *New Grolier Multimedia Encyclopedia* has a suggested retail price of $395.00, but it is often sold for less. The encyclopedia is nor-mally available in stores and through catalogs that sell computer software. It can also be ordered directly from the publisher. For additional information about the encyclopedia or to order it, contact Grolier Electronic Publishing, Inc., Sherman Turnpike, Danbury, CT 06816; 800-356-5590 (toll-free) or 800-285-4534 (toll-free).

EVALUATION

The ACADEMIC AMERICAN ENCYCLOPEDIA, a highly regarded 21-volume print encyclopedia intended for adults and older students, was created from scratch in the late 1970s and first published in 1980 by the Aretê Publishing Company, an American subsidiary of VNU, a large Dutch publishing conglomerate. In addition to being the first entirely new general encyclopedia in English published for many years, the ACADEMIC AMERICAN was also the first English-language encyclopedia of any consequence to be produced in machine-readable form from the outset. In 1982, Grolier, Inc., a major North American encyclopedia publisher, acquired the encyclopedia.

Grolier immediately set about developing the encyclopedia's electronic potential. Grolier Electronic Publishing, Inc., a Grolier subsidiary, was established in 1982 and the following year, in a pioneering effort, the company began marketing the encyclopedia online via commercial information services. Today, the "Grolier Encyclopedia"—as the *Academic American Encyclopedia* online is often called—dominates these services, available via CompuServe, GEnie, and Prodigy, among others. In October 1985, another milestone in the history of electronic encyclopedias occurred when Grolier introduced the *Academic American* on CD-ROM, said to be the first encyclopedia on disk. Amazing! The entire 21-vol-ume encyclopedia—sans illustrations—compressed on a 4.72-inch optical disc designed to be used with a personal computer! We take CD-ROM and other electronic reference products for granted today, but in 1985 an entire encyclopedia on a tiny disk was big news.

Indeed, it presaged great changes in the publication, use, and merchandising of encyclopedias and other reference materials. In a news release dated July 12, 1985, Frank Farrell, a Grolier executive, announced the new product:

> The hardware needed to scan and display the encyclopedic data are a CD-ROM disk drive, a personal computer and a monitor. Grolier expects that such disk drives will become available for most major personal computers in the near future....The new *AAE* [*Academic American Encyclopedia*] disk provides direct, swift and economical access to a major body of knowledge stored locally—the home, the library, the office. We are also providing dynamic interactive capabilities—easily and comfortably controlled by the user. The new Grolier CD-ROM is the result of three and one-half years of intensive research and development, including experimentation with school groups.

Since its launch in 1985, the Grolier CD-ROM encyclopedia has had several title changes and undergone as many metamorphoses. The initial versions lacked illustrative material of any kind; in 1990, still pictures were added to the encyclopedia, then called the *New Grolier Electronic Encyclopedia*; and most recently, in 1992, the editors added moving pictures and sound (or multimedia), prompting the encyclopedia's current title—the *New Grolier Multimedia Encyclopedia*. Although Compton's (then owned by Encyclopaedia Britannica, Inc.) produced the first multimedia encyclopedia in 1989 (namely COMPTON'S MULTIMEDIA ENCYCLOPEDIA), Grolier has been at the forefront of the development of CD-ROM encyclopedias for more than a decade. It is no wonder, then, that the *New Grolier Multimedia Encyclopedia* is among the best such encyclopedias on the market today, along with COMPTON'S INTERACTIVE ENCYCLOPEDIA, the aforementioned COMPTON'S MULTIMEDIA ENCYCLOPEDIA, and MICROSOFT ENCARTA MULTIMEDIA ENCYCLOPEDIA.

As noted, the *New Grolier Multimedia Encyclopedia* is based on the 21-volume ACADEMIC AMERICAN ENCYCLOPEDIA, a first-rate print (or hardbound) work for adults and older students. Currently, the print set contains more than 9 million words, nearly 10,000 pages, and nearly 29,000 articles. The ACADEMIC AMERICAN is well maintained, boasting a comparatively high rate of annual revision. See the review beginning on page 53 for a detailed evaluation of the encyclopedia's contents, readability, and treatment of material.

Note that the CD-ROM version of the encyclopedia is substantially larger than its print counterpart: 10 million versus 9.1 million words; 33,000 versus 29,000 articles. The computer's enormous storage capacity easily accommodates added entries, whereas the print set has a fixed size. On the other side of the coin, the print set contains some 18,000 high-quality photographs, drawings, cutaways, reproductions of paintings, and maps, most in vivid color. The CD-ROM version, however, includes only a fraction of this material, about 3,000 illustrations and 250 maps. The reason: one picture requires as much digital memory on the CD-ROM

disc as the text of 50 or even a 100 articles, depending on their length. Thus, these two versions of the encyclopedia—print and CD-ROM—do not and never will have exactly the same contents.

The overall quality of the illustrations, maps, and multimedia features found in the *New Grolier Multimedia Encyclopedia* cannot be faulted. The encyclopedia's approximately 80 video clips are especially well selected, including some fine newsreel footage of historical events (the bombing of London during World War II, the Hindenburg disaster, etc.). But in terms of quantity of multimedia, the *New Grolier* has lagged conspicuously behind its Compton's and Microsoft rivals. Grolier is, of course, aware of the problem and is now in the position of playing catch-up. David Arganbright, president of Grolier Electronic Publishing, acknowledged as much in a press release issued June 3, 1993 describing the 1993 edition, in which he says:

> Grolier's focus is still on publishing the best general reference encyclopedia as exemplified by the breadth and depth of the editorial content. However, the marketplace will continue to value multimedia excellence as well as superior editorial content and for that reason the 1993 edition [of the *New Grolier Multimedia Encyclopedia*] will include a rich array of audio-supported features including movies, animations, Multimedia Maps and Knowledge Explorer essays.

The essays Arganbright refers to are innovative "audio-visual" presentations of 4 to 6 minutes on 15 broad topics, including the human body, space exploration, painting and sculpture, music, and Africa. The other new feature, called multimedia maps (or "dynamic" maps), are narrated cartographic animations depicting important historical events, e.g., Magellan's circumnavigation of the globe in the sixteenth century, the U.S. Civil War, and the rise and fall of world communism. Such additions are intended to improve the encyclopedia's competitive position vis-a-vis the COMPTON'S and

Microsoft multimedia encyclopedias; MICROSOFT ENCARTA, new in early 1993, particularly has raised the bar as far as multimedia content is concerned. The *New Grolier Multimedia Encyclopedia*'s new material helps, but the encyclopedia is still somewhat behind the curve in this very visible and increasing market-sensitive area.

The *New Grolier Multimedia Encyclopedia* is well designed and easy to navigate, presenting (metaphorically) nothing like the hazards faced by Magellan on his voyage nearly 500 years ago. Rubin Rabinovitz, a perceptive reviewer of electronic reference products, puts it this way in his review of the *New Grolier* in *PC Magazine* (August 1993, p. 556): "Although a manual is included with the program, you'll probably need it only to get started; a toolbar with icon buttons makes it easy to choose one of the many methods for navigating around the encyclopedia." Layne Nordgren, in a review in *CD-ROM Professional* (May 1993, p. 135), concurs: "Overall I was very impressed with the relatively seamless integration of new media types into the already solid text components of the product. The low cost and reasonable upgrade policy make this encyclopedia an excellent bargain."

The encyclopedia furnishes all of the standard search and retrieval mechanisms that one expects to find in a quality CD-ROM encyclopedia today. For example, its "Word Search" feature—full-text searching employing Boolean logic and operators—renders the encyclopedia's contents accessible in ways no print encyclopedia can hope to emulate. Rubin Rabinovitz (on page 557 of his review cited above) provides this example:

> Still another useful option is to run a Boolean search of the entire encyclopedia. For example, if you want to find out about the Supreme Court during Franklin D. Roosevelt's presidency, you can search for the articles referring to both *Supreme Court* and *Roosevelt*, while excluding all of the articles in which references to the name *Theodore* are in proximity to *Roosevelt*.

Consumers should be aware that articles in the *New Grolier Multimedia Encyclopedia* lack vocabulary control and tend to be written in a somewhat more advanced or "academic" style than those found in the two COMPTON'S multimedia encyclopedias or MICROSOFT ENCARTA. Articles in the latter encyclopedias are normally comprehensible to users reading at the fifth or sixth grade level and up, whereas the *New Grolier*'s text normally requires a somewhat higher reading level.

SUMMARY

The *New Grolier Multimedia Encyclopedia* first appeared in 1985 as the *Academic American Encyclopedia on CD-ROM*, said to be the first encyclopedia published on disc. Today, it is one of the leading CD-ROM encyclopedias on the North American market, along with COMPTON'S INTERACTIVE ENCYCLOPEDIA, COMPTON'S MULTIMEDIA ENCYCLOPEDIA, and MICROSOFT ENCARTA MULTIMEDIA ENCYCLOPEDIA. The *New Grolier Multimedia Encyclopedia* is based on the 21-volume ACADEMIC AMERICAN ENCYCLOPEDIA, an outstanding print set for adults and older students. Consumers should be forewarned that the ACADEMIC AMERICAN, and hence the *New Grolier*, is written at a somewhat higher reading level than its Compton's and Microsoft rivals.

The *New Grolier*'s strongest features are simplicity of design and ease of use, coupled with the full range of search and retrieval options one expects to find in a quality CD-ROM encyclopedia. It includes some well-produced multimedia material (moving pictures and sound), but not so much as its chief rivals. In an effort to catch up to the competition, particularly the multimedia-rich MICROSOFT ENCARTA, the latest edition (1993) of the *New Grolier* has significantly increased its multimedia offerings. The bottom line: An excellent CD-ROM encyclopedia with multimedia features; best for adults and older students.

OTHER OPINIONS

Basic Information Sources by William A. Katz (vol. 1 of *Introduction to Reference Work*, 6th ed., New York: McGraw-Hill, 1992), pp. 245; *CD-ROM Professional*, May 1993, pp. 133-35 (review by Layne Nordgren); *CD-ROM World*, September 1993, p. 36 (review by Carol S. Holzberg); *Library Journal*, September 15, 1992, pp. 102-04 (review by Cheryl LaGuardia); *PC Magazine*, August 1993, pp. 556-57 (review by Rubin Rabinovitz); *PC Novice*, October 1993, p. 63 (review by Cindy Krushenisky).

RANDOM HOUSE ELECTRONIC ENCYCLOPEDIA (HAND-HELD)

FACTS

Full Title: *Random House Electronic Encyclopedia.* **Variant Titles:** *The Pocket Encyclopedia; Random House Pocket Encyclopedia.* **Publisher:** SelecTronics, Inc. **Distributor:** Vitel Electronics, Inc. **Date Published:** 1990 (based on print version published in 1990).

Print Version: RANDOM HOUSE ENCYCLOPEDIA.

Other Electronic Versions: RANDOM HOUSE ENCYCLOPEDIA: ELECTRONIC EDITION (floppy disks).

Words: 1.5 million. **Articles:** 20,000. **Still Pictures and Maps:** None. **Video Clips:** None. **Animations:** None. **Audio:** None.

Hardware and Software Requirements: None.

Price and Sales Information: The *Random House Electronic Encyclopedia* (model RH-3100) is sold in North America chiefly in department and discount stores as well as retail stores specializing in electronic products. The suggested retail price is $400.00 but the encyclopedia, which is currently being closed out, can be had for much less. The *Random House Electronic Encyclopedia* can also be purchased directly from the distributor. For more information about the encyclopedia or to order it, contact Vitel Electronics, Inc., 100 Hollister Road, Teterboro, NJ 07608; 800-443-0594 (toll-free).

EVALUATION

The *Random House Electronic Encyclopedia*, which claims the title of "World's First Portable Electronic Encyclopedia," is a hand-held general encyclopedia that, like the very similar COLUMBIA ELECTRONIC ENCYCLOPEDIA, weighs just 12 ounces. Both encyclopedias derive their computing power from a ROM (Read Only Memory) chip capable of storing and retrieving enormous amounts of data.

Published in late 1990, the *Random House Electronic Encyclopedia* is based on the RANDOM HOUSE ENCYCLOPEDIA, a hefty single-volume print encyclopedia noted especially for its innovative illustrations and complex organization. The print encyclopedia contains approximately 3 million words, 2,900 pages, and 25,880 articles, plus 13,500 graphics, most in color. The book is divided into two basic sections, the 1,800-page "Colorpedia," which consists of 880 topically arranged and heavily illustrated two-page spreads, and the 885-page "Alphapedia," which includes 25,000 alphabetically arranged short-entry articles and acts as an index to the "Colorpedia." See the review beginning on page 146 for a detailed evaluation of the encyclopedia's contents, readability, and treatment of material.

The electronic version of the encyclopedia is published by SelecTronics, Inc., a leading North American producer of electronic reference products, including the Bible and a large line of dictionaries, thesauri, and spell-checkers. SelecTronics licenses the RANDOM HOUSE ENCYCLOPEDIA'S text from Random House, Inc., the encyclopedia's print publisher. As might be expected, the *Random House Electronic Encyclopedia* does not contain anywhere near the amount of material found in the print encyclopedia. Specifically, the print volume's 13,500 illustrations are not included in the electronic version, nor is most of the text of the "Colorpedia" articles. Likewise, the print encyclopedia's extensive picture captions are not included. In reality, the *Random House Electronic Encyclopedia* is a much abridged version of the RANDOM HOUSE ENCYCLOPEDIA, limited largely to the "Alphapedia" portion of the print encyclopedia.

Physically, the *Random House Electronic Encyclopedia* (model RH-3100) looks more like a pocket calculator than an encyclopedia. Palm-sized, it measures $3\frac{1}{4} \times 6\frac{3}{4}$ inches and can be carried in a coat pocket, purse, briefcase, etc. There is a small display screen at the top of the unit and a keypad at the bottom. The little encyclopedia, which is battery-powered, is easy to dismiss as a toy or novelty. But don't be fooled—it is a serious reference work that contains most of the 885-page "Alphapedia" (or reference) section in the RANDOM HOUSE ENCYCLOPEDIA.

Aside from the its size and portability, the electronic encyclopedia's most useful feature is its ability to search for and retrieve information with great speed and thoroughness. The user can access the encyclopedia's text by subject, keyword, or natural language, as well as browse a classified table of contents for pertinent topics. In addition, an extensive network of cross-references helps guide to user to pertinent topics. A news release from SelecTronic dated Janaury 6, 1990 explains:

> A user can enter "father of our country" on the typewriter-style ("QWERTY") keyboard and the unit returns "George Washington." If a user enters "artery block" the unit will return "Thrombosis," "Phlebitis," as well as additional entries that users can view by scrolling. [This reverse dictionary feature utilizes a system developed by the Xerox Corporation called "Word Nerd."] In addition, a user can locate information on a subject or person wherever it appears in an entry. For example, a user can enter "red birds" and locate every type of red bird listed in the text.

Still, the *Random House Electronic Encyclopedia* has a number of drawbacks, including most of those cited in the review of the COLUMBIA ELECTRONIC ENCYCLOPEDIA, its chief competitor in the held-held category. Physically, the encyclopedia is awkward to use and read; it lacks the capability to print out its text; it occasionally makes erroneous intellectual connections during the search and retrieval process; it is outrageously expensive (or was, until being discounted); the text is no longer up-to-date in certain areas; and it lacks illustrations. On this last point, Peter Model sagely observed in his "Eye on Publishing" column in *Wilson Library Bulletin* (October 1990, p. 77) in a piece about tronic version cannot "be regarded as a substitute for the genuine article, which, after all, is a *pictorial* reference work."

Finally, the *Random House Electronic Encyclopedia* is currently being phased out as a product, at least for the time being. According to Vitel Electronics, the distributor, the encyclopedia is now being heavily discounted in various retail outlets, and will be out of print as soon as the stock is exhausted. Furthermore, a SelecTronics representative reports that the company has no plans to produce a new or updated model.

SUMMARY

The *Random House Electronic Encyclopedia*— a small, lightweight, battery-operated encyclopedia that can be carried in a coat pocket or purse—is an electronic abridgment of the RANDOM HOUSE ENCYCLOPEDIA, a well-known one-volume print encyclopedia noted particularly for its eye-catching color illustrations. The electronic version, however, lacks any illustrations, eye-catching or otherwise, and its text is mostly limited to the "Alphapedia" (or reference) portion of the print encyclopedia. Its best feature is its rapid search and retrieval system. But like its rival, the COLUMBIA ELECTRONIC ENCYCLOPEDIA, the encyclopedia has some major problems, including too high a retail price, which is surely one of the reasons it failed in the marketplace and is now being phased out. The bottom line: Although interesting and innovative, the *Random House Electronic Encyclopedia* is too expensive for what it delivers.

OTHER OPINIONS

None.

RANDOM HOUSE ENCYCLOPEDIA: ELECTRONIC EDITION (FLOPPY DISKS)

FACTS

Full Title: *The Random House Encyclopedia: Electronic Edition.* **Publisher:** Microlytics, Inc., a subsidiary of SelecTronics, Inc. **Date Published:** 1990 (based on print version published in 1990).

Print Version: RANDOM HOUSE ENCYCLOPEDIA.

Other Electronic Versions: RANDOM HOUSE ELECTRONIC ENCYCLOPEDIA (hand-held).

Words: 1.5 million. **Articles:** 20,000. **Still Pictures and Maps:** None. **Video Clips:** None. **Animations:** None. **Audio:** None.

Hardware Requirements: Personal Computer (IBM; IBM-compatible; Macintosh); check with publisher for specifics. **Software Requirements:** Floppy disks, 16 disks (5¼ in.) or 8 disks (3½ in.). Operating System: MS-DOS.

Price and Sales Information: The *Random House Encyclopedia: Electronic Edition* currently retails for about $100.00. It is available in most stores and through catalogs that sell computer software or it can be purchased directly from the publisher. For more information about the encyclopedia or to order it, contact Microlytics, Inc., 2 Tobey Village Office Park, Pittsford, NY 14534; 800-828-6293 (toll-free).

EVALUATION

Said to be "the first implementation" of an electronic encyclopedia on disk "which does not require a CD-ROM drive" (publisher's news release, January 10, 1991), the *Random House Encyclopedia: Electronic Edition* is the only general English-language encyclopedia currently available on floppy disks. The disks—16 (5¼ in.) or 8 (3½ in.)—are loaded directly onto the hard drive of the user's computer, and the encyclopedia is immediately ready for use. Why floppy disks instead of CD-ROM? First, no CD-ROM drive is necessary, thus saving the expense of a potentially costly piece of hardware; and second, response time is greatly improved, hard-disk drives being considerably faster than their CD-ROM counterparts. On the flip side, floppy disks eat up a lot of hard-drive space.

Published by Microlytics, Inc., the *Random House Encyclopedia: Electronic Edition* has exactly the same text and electronic configuration as the RANDOM HOUSE ELECTRONIC ENCYCLOPEDIA, a small, 12-ounce, hand-held encyclopedia published by SelecTronics, Inc., the parent company of Microlytics. Indeed, these two seemingly very different encyclopedias—one no larger than a pocket calculator and the other hidden away inside a computer's memory—are actually the same work. Only title, format, and price distinguish one from the other.

Both encyclopedias are based on the third edition (1990) of the RANDOM HOUSE ENCYCLOPEDIA, a huge single-volume print (or hardcover) encyclopedia for adults and older students. This encyclopedia, best known for its outstanding color illustrations and complex organziation, contains approximately 3 million words, 2,900 pages, and 26,900 articles, plus 13,500 graphics. The volume is divided into two basic sections, the 1,800-page "Colorpedia," which consists of 880 topically arranged and heavily illustrated two-page spreads, and the 885-page "Alphapedia," which includes 25,000 alphabetically arranged short-entry articles and acts as an index to the "Colorpedia." See the review beginning on page 146 for a detailed evaluation of the encyclopedias's contents, readability, and treatment of material.

As might be expected, neither of the electronic versions contains anywhere near the amount of material found in the print encyclopedia. Specifically, the print volume's 13,500 illustrations are not included in the *Random House Encyclopedia: Electronic Edition* or the RANDOM HOUSE ELECTRONIC ENCYCLOPEDIA, nor is much of the text of the "Colorpedia." Likewise, the print encyclopedia's extensive picture captions are not included. In reality, the electronic versions are heavy abridgments of the RANDOM HOUSE ENCYCLOPEDIA, limited largely to the "Alphapedia" portion of the encyclopedia.

Doubtless the best feature of both Random House electronic encyclopedias is their ability to search for and retrieve information with great speed and thoroughness. The user can access either encyclopedia by subject, keyword, or natural language, as well as browse a classified table of contents for pertinent topics. A particularly helpful search option is the Reverse Dictionary, which emulates a system created by the Xerox Corporation called "Word Nerd." A lengthy and carefully researched review in *Reference Books Bulletin* (in *Booklist*, July 1991, p. 2064) explains how this search feature works—and sometimes does not work:

> The Reverse Dictionary screen enables the user to search for a term or terms anywhere

within an article or article title. Unless one simply wants to browse, this mode is generally the most effective way of locating information in the *Encyclopedia*. For instance, a search for the term *perestroika* results in no matches in the Outline View mode described above, but produces three matches in the Reverse Dictionary mode. When the user enters a phrase or more than one term, the system assumes the Boolean AND between each word and thus searches for any article that includes all of the terms regardless of their sequence or proximity. As with any free-text keyword search, this can result in inappropriate matches. For example, a search for *world court* generated 35 matches, only a few of which actually had references to the World Court.

Like the RANDOM HOUSE ELECTRONIC EN-CYCLOPEDIA, the *Random House Encyclopedia: Electronic Edition* is far from perfect. As

shown, the Reverse Dictionary search mode often fails to make the right connections. Also, the text, published in 1990, is now dated in places; the Soviet Union, for instance, remains intact in this encyclopedia, and George Bush is still president of the U.S. And the encyclopedia lacks illustrations, one of the glories of the print edition. On this last point, Peter Model gets it right in a column about the RANDOM HOUSE ENCYCLOPE-DIA in *Wilson Library Bulletin* (October 1990, p. 77), when he advises that the electronic versions cannot "be regarded as a substitute for the genuine article, which, after all, is a *pictorial* reference work."

SUMMARY

Said to be the first and certainly today the only general encyclopedia in North America published on floppy disks, the *Random House Encyclopedia: Electronic Edition* is exactly the same work as the RANDOM HOUSE ELECTRONIC ENCYCLOPEDIA; they differ only in title, format, and price. Both these electronic encyclopedias are severe abridgments of the third edition (1990) of the RANDOM HOUSE ENCY-CLOPEDIA, a large one-volume print encyclopedia noted chiefly for its division of knowledge into two sections, the "Colorpedia" and "Alphapedia," and the excellent color illustrations found in the former.

Regrettably, both electronic versions lack any illustrations, colorful or otherwise, and their text is pretty much limited to the "Alphapedia" (or reference) portion of the print encyclopedia. The *Random House Encyclopedia: Electronic Edition*, which operates off the computer's hard drive, currently retails for around $100.00, which seems fair. But it needs to be updated in the near future if it is to remain a viable source of quick-reference information. The bottom line: If you lack and do not plan to invest in a CD-ROM drive, this electronic encyclopedia— the only one available today on floppy disk— is worth serious consideration.

OTHER OPINIONS

Reference Books Bulletin (in *Booklist*), July 1991, pp. 2062-64 (unsigned review).

SOFTWARE TOOLWORKS ILLUSTRATED
ENCYCLOPEDIA (CD-ROM)

FACTS

Full Title: *The Software Toolworks Illustrated Encyclopedia.* **Variant Title:** *Toolworks Illustrated Encyclopedia.* **Publisher:** Grolier Electronic Publishing, Inc. **Distributor:** Software Toolworks, Inc. **Date Published:** First Published on disk as *Software Toolworks Illustrated Encyclopedia* in 1990; updated annually.

Also published as the NEW GROLIER MULTIMEDIA ENCYCLOPEDIA (CD-ROM).

Print Version: ACADEMIC AMERICAN ENCYCLOPEDIA.

Other Electronic Versions: ACADEMIC AMERICAN ENCYCLOPEDIA (online).

Words: 10 million. **Articles:** 33,000. **Still Pictures and Maps:** 3,250. **Video Clips:** 80. **Animations:** 65. **Audio:** 70 minutes.

Hardware Requirements: Multimedia Personal Computer; CD-ROM drive; mouse; VGA display; audio board; headphones or speakers. **Software Requirements:** CD-ROM, 1 disc. **Operating Systems:** MS-DOS; Windows; Macintosh.

Price and Sales Information: The *Software Toolworks Illustrated Encyclopedia* is most frequently sold as part of a software bundle (or program) already installed or built into a personal computer. Such bundles may include a wide variety of software products, such as dictionaries, almanacs, atlases, instructional materials, and games. The price for the package (hardware plus software) will be determined largely by the quality of the hardware, not the software. The encyclopedia is also available separately in some stores and through catalogs that sell computer software. The recommended retail price is currently $395.00. The *Software Toolworks Illustrated Encyclopedia* can also be purchased directly from the distributor. For more information about the encyclopedia or to order it, contact Software Toolworks, Inc., 60 Leveroni Court, Novato, CA 94949; 800-234-3088 (toll-free)

CONSUMER NOTE

Aside from its title, the *Software Toolworks Illustrated Encyclopedia* is exactly the same as the NEW GROLIER MULTIMEDIA ENCYCLOPEDIA, one of the leading CD-ROM encyclopedias currently produced in North America. For a detailed evaluation of the NEW GROLIER MULTIMEDIA ENCYCLOPEDIA, see page 287.

COMPARISON CHART

Electronic Encyclopedias

This chart provides basic statistical information about each of the electronic encyclopedias reviewed in *Kister's Best Encyclopedias*. The chart also offers a quick comparative overview of the 19 titles in this category. How do COMPTON'S MULITIMEDIA ENCYCLOPEDIA, COMPTON'S INTERACTIVE ENCYCLOPEDIA, MICROSOFT ENCARTA MULTIMEDIA ENCYCLOPEDIA, and the NEW GROLIER MULTIMEDIA ENCYCLOPEDIA—the major CD-ROM encyclopedias with multimedia features now on the market—compare in terms of numbers of words? Articles? Still pictures? Video Clips? Animations? Amount of audio? Price? What about the multimedia version of the CONCISE COLUMBIA ENCYCLOPEDIA, which is bundled with *Microsoft Bookshelf*? Or FIRST CONNECTIONS, the recently published multimedia version of the GOLDEN BOOK ENCYCLOPEDIA? How do these works stack up statistically? The chart answers such questions at a glance.

In the case of price information, consumers should understand that prices are subject to change by the publisher, distributor, or vendor at any time. For the latest price of any encyclopedia in the electronic category, call the company that sells it. All have toll-free numbers where the latest information about price and availability can be obtained quickly and efficiently. Telephone numbers are listed in this guide at the beginning of each review under "Price and Sales Information," as well as in the directory of publishers and distributors at the back of the book (see Appendix B).

The chart's final column assigns a letter grade to each encyclopedia: A = Excellent; B = Above Average; C = Average; D = Below Average; F = Poor. The letter grade represents a final summary of the encyclopedia's detailed evaluation in *Kister's Best Encyclopedias*. Consumers seriously interested in purchasing an encyclopedia are urged to base their selection decisions on the reviews in the book, and not rely solely on the letter grades given in the chart, which are necessarily arbitrary.

Electronic Title	Print Version	Format	Words	Articles	Still Picts.	Video Clips	Anima-tions	Audio	Approx. Retail Price	Rating
Academic American Ency.	Academic American Ency.	Online	10 mil	33,000	None	None	None	None	Contact vendor	B
Britannica Instant Research System	New Ency. Britannica	CD-ROM	44 mil	65,100	None	None	None	None	Contact publisher	A
Britannica Online	New Ency. Britannica	Online	44 mil	66,000	2,000	None	None	None	Contact publisher	?[1]
Columbia Electronic Ency.	Concise Columbia	Hand-held	1 mil	15,000	None	None	None	None	$249.95	C
Compton's Concise Ency.	Compton's Ency.	CD-ROM	9 mil	32,000	4,000	None	None	None	450.00[2]	C
Compton's Encyclopedia	Compton's Ency.	Online	9 mil	34,000	None	None	None	None	Contact vendor	B
Compton's Family Ency.	Compton's Ency.	CD-ROM	9 mil	32,000	10,000	None	None	60 min	700.00[3]	B
Compton's Interactive Ency.	Compton's Ency.	CD-ROM	9 mil	34,000	13,800	30	32	50 min	395.00	A
Compton's Multimedia Ency.	Compton's Ency.	CD-ROM	9 mil	34,000	15,000	30	45	60 min	495.00	A
Concise Columbia Ency.	Concise Columbia	CD-ROM	1 mil	15,000	1,400	None	50	45 min	195.00	A
Everyman's Ency.	Everyman's Ency.	Online	9 mil	51,000	None	None	None	None	Contact vendor	F
First Connections	Golden Book Ency.	CD-ROM	650,000	1,500	2,900	None	100	60 min	149.95	B
Information Finder	World Book Ency.	CD-ROM	10 mil	17,000	3,300	None	None	None	395.00	B
Kussmaul Ency.	Cadillac Modern	Online	3 mil	23,000	None	None	None	None	Contact vendor	F
Microsoft Encarta Multimedia Ency.	Funk & Wagnalls	CD-ROM	9.5 mil	26,000	7,800	45	100	8 hours	139.00	A
New Grolier Multimedia Ency.	Academic American	CD-ROM	10 mil	33,000	3,250	80	65	70 min	395.00	A
Random House Electronic Ency.	Random House Ency.	Hand-held	1.5 mil	20,000	None	None	None	None	400.00	D
Random House Ency.	Random House Ency.	Floppy Disk	1.5 mil	20,000	None	None	None	None	100.00	C
Software Toolworks Illus Ency.[4]	Academic American	CD-ROM	10 mil	33,000	3,250	80	65	70 min	395.00	A[4]

1. BRITANNICA ONLINE scheduled to debut on the Internet in September 1994.
2. Sold as part of Sony's Data Discman.
3. Sold as part of the Sony Laser Library.
4. Same text as NEW GROLIER MULTIMEDIA ENCYCLOPEDIA.

Out-of-Print Encyclopedias

* * * * * * * * *

OVERVIEW

Like any commercial product, encyclopedias come and go. Only a relatively few names—*Britannica, Americana, Compton's, World Book, New Book of Knowledge, Columbia, Collier's,* and *Funk & Wagnalls* come quickly to mind—survive in the highly competitive North American marketplace for any real length of time. Those encyclopedias with staying power are inevitably the best known and usually the cream of the crop. Rarely does a mediocre encyclopedia (let alone a poor one) remain on the market for very long; its sins are too public.

Sometimes, however, an encyclopedia starts out well but over time becomes lackluster and eventually loses both its authority and appeal, a casualty of editorial neglect or incompetence or some combination thereof. A case in point is the venerable LINCOLN LIBRARY OF ESSENTIAL INFORMATION. First published in 1924, the LINCOLN LIBRARY was for many years a leading small-volume general encyclopedia for adults and older students, but gradually the editors allowed the encyclopedia to become stale and dated until finally in the mid-1980s it could not in good conscience be sold as a source of current information and was withdrawn from the market. In other instances, an encyclopedia of quality may sink because its publisher suffers a great financial setback or some other cataclysmic problem. An example is the MERIT STUDENTS ENCYCLOPEDIA, a victim of the sudden collapse of the Macmillan publishing empire because of tycoon Robert Maxwell's unexpected (and controversial) death in November 1991.

When, for whatever reason, an encyclopedia is no longer produced by a publisher and its existing stock is exhausted and no new edition or reissue is contemplated, the work is said to be discontinued or out of print. In other words, the encyclopedia is no longer available from the publisher or any distributors or through other normal trade channels, such as book wholesalers or retail bookstores.

This does not necessarily mean that the encyclopedia has totally disappeared from the face of the earth, never to be seen or heard from again. Out-of-print encyclopedias may be encountered in secondhand or remainder bookstores; in discount stores; at estate, garage, or yard sales; in antique or junk shops; at flea markets; or listed for sale in classified advertisements in daily newspapers and weekly shoppers. In addition, one may run across out-of-print encyclopedias at the local public, school, or college library. Just because a reference work is no longer in print does not mean that it has automatically lost all value as a source of information. This is particularly true of established works that have recently fallen on hard times, such as the BRITANNICA JUNIOR ENCYCLOPAEDIA, the NEW CAXTON ENCYCLOPEDIA, and the MERIT STUDENTS ENCYCLOPEDIA.

The possibility also exists that an out-of-print encyclopedia might reappear on the market at any time, either as a reprint of a previous edition or, more likely, in a newly revised edition. Fly-by-night publishers have been known to obtain the rights to a defunct encyclopedia and reissue it, often under a different title, hoping consumers will be conned into thinking it is a new work. Happily, this disreputable practice is less prevalent today than it was a few decades ago, but it still continues and consumers should be ever alert. On the other hand, new editions of once discontinued encyclopedias are a reasonably common occurrence, especially if the title has any sort of name recognition. No one should be surprised, for instance, if the MERIT STUDENTS ENCYCLOPEDIA or the LINCOLN LIBRARY OF ESSENTIAL INFORMATION were to reappear in new editions sometime in the near future.

The encyclopedias described in this section—a total of 73 titles—are all currently out of print. They represent the most significant or visible general English-language encyclopedias discontinued in North America over the past 30 years or so. The roster includes a number of British-made encyclopedias such as CHAMBERS'S ENCYCLOPAEDIA and the NEW CAXTON ENCYCLOPEDIA once, but no longer, distributed in the United States and Canada. For a comprehensive annotated list of older encyclopedias, consult S. Padraig Walsh's *Anglo-American General Encyclopedias: A Historical Bibliography, 1703-1967* (Bowker, 1968).

❊ ❊ ❊

American Educator: A Comprehensive Encyclopedia to Meet the Needs of Home, School, and Library. Lake Bluff, IL: United Educators, Inc., 1919–77. 20 vols. Last priced at $250.00.

The *American Educator* traced its origins back to the six-volume *New Practical Reference Library* (1907–18), which in turn derived from the four-volume *Hill's Practical Reference Library of General Knowledge* (1902–06) and *Hill's Practical Encyclopedia* (1901). Soon after United Educators, Inc. acquired the *American Educator* in 1931, the encyclopedia expanded to 10 volumes. Later, in 1957, the editors added four more volumes, and in 1972, after its last major revision, the set reached its final size of 20 volumes. At this point the *American Educator* contained approximately five million words, 8,000 pages, 13,000 articles, and 12,000 illustrations.

Throughout its history the *American Educator* was never considered a first-class encyclopedia, despite its boast of having more Nobel Prize winners as contributors "than any other encyclopedia in the world." It suffered from a number of obvious weaknesses, such as shallow or incomplete coverage of social science subjects, too many factual inaccuracies, and a lax and inconsistent approach to continuous revision. By the time it went out of print in the late 1970s, the encyclopedia was completely outclassed by the competition, which included the formidable COMPTON'S ENCYCLOPEDIA and WORLD BOOK ENCYCLOPEDIA.

The American Family Encyclopedia: A Concise and Comprehensive Reference Work. New York: Books, Inc., 1963. 8 vols. Last priced at $15.95.

Intended for adults and for students in the middle grades and beyond, this encyclopedia originally appeared between 1938 and 1962 as the one-volume *New American Encyclopedia*, a reference work sold primarily in supermarkets and no relation to the 20-volume NEW AMERICAN ENCYCLOPEDIA described below. In 1963, it was revised and reissued in eight volumes under the title *American Family Encyclopedia*; the set remained on the market until 1973, when it went out of print. At the time, the encyclopedia consisted of roughly one million words, 1,500 pages, 20,000 entries, and 800 illustrations.

A work of conspicuously poor quality, the *American Family Encyclopedia* received negative notices from informed critics. For instance, the Subscription Books Committee of the American Library Association offered this opinion in *Booklist* (January 1, 1966, p. 420): "The Encyclopedia fails to fulfill the aims set forth in the Preface. It is neither up-to-date in coverage nor consistently objective in tone. There is too great an emphasis on lesser figures of the past while neglecting individuals and topics of current interest. The length of an entry is often unrelated to the importance of the subject. The physical format is poor. For these reasons, *The American Family Encyclopedia* is not recommended."

The American Peoples Encyclopedia: A Modern Reference Work. New York: Excelsior Trading Corp. (a subsidiary of Grolier, Inc.), 1948–76. 20 vols. Last priced at $325.50.

Based loosely on material derived from the old *Nelson's Encyclopedia* (1905–40), *The American Peoples Encyclopedia* was first published in 1948 by Spencer Press, a Chicago firm. Until 1958, Sears, Roebuck sold the set exclusively through its retail stores and mail-order catalog division. In 1961, Grolier, a major North American encyclopedia publisher, acquired the rights to *American Peoples* and revitalized it under the direction of Lowell Martin, a well-known librarian and experienced encyclopedia editor. But over the years, Grolier allowed the set to deteriorate and, by the mid-1970s, it had seen better days and was officially discontinued in 1976. Toward the end, *American Peoples* was also published as the *University Society Encyclopedia*, under the imprint of the University Society, Inc. of Midland Park, New Jersey.

Designed for use by adults and older students, the 20-volume *American Peoples* was a substantial encyclopedia comprising roughly 10 million words, 11,000 pages, 35,000 articles, and 13,000 illustrations, most in black-and-white. While never considered a top-notch work, neither was it a disgracefully bad one. Among its strengths were concise, accurate articles on people and places (which accounted for the majority of entries) and reasonably good access to the text. On the negative side, the encyclopedia had a number of readily apparent faults, including dull illustrations, sparse bibliographies, a bland writing style, superficial coverage of many topics, and, during the final years, a general lack of timeliness throughout. Overall, *The American Peoples Encyclopedia* was a competent but undistinguished work. For a lengthy and informative critical review of the 1973 copyright, see *Booklist*, July 15, 1974, pp. 1206–08.

Basic Everyday Encyclopedia. New York: Random House, 1954. 574p. Last priced at $7.95.

This small, well-edited single-volume general encyclopedia for adults contained about 900,000 words and 12,500 quite brief A-to-Z entries in 574 pages. Published only once (in 1954), it proved to be a popular inexpensive volume for a number of years, before growing shopworn and finally going out of print in 1972. It appeared in both hardcover and paperback editions and was edited by Jess Stein, then editor of Random House's reference division.

Britannica Junior Encyclopaedia for Boys and Girls. Chicago: Encyclopaedia Britannica, Inc., 1934–84. 15 vols. Last priced at $279.00.

Despite its name, *Britannica Junior Encyclopaedia* was not an abridged or juvenile version of the old *Encyclopaedia Britannica* (1768–1973) or its successor, the NEW ENCYCLOPAEDIA BRITANNICA. It first appeared in 1931–32 as *Weedon's Modern Encyclopedia*, an eight-volume set published by the S.L. Weedon Company of Cleveland. Encyclopaedia Britannica, Inc., a major North American encyclopedia publisher, quickly obtained the rights to the set and, in 1934, brought out a new edition in 12 volumes under the title *Britannica Junior: An Encyclopaedia for Boys and Girls.* In 1947, the encyclopedia expanded to 15 volumes, its final size. By this time the set contained more than five million words, 8,000 pages, 4,200 lengthy articles, and nearly 12,000 illustrations.

Over the years, *Britannica Junior* achieved a reputation as one of the best multivolume encyclopedias for young people, competing head-to-head with the standout NEW BOOK OF KNOWLEDGE. A conscientiously edited, trustworthy encyclopedia, the set possessed an innovative index and especially good maps, particularly those by Hammond in the world atlas in the final volume. It also had some telling weaknesses, the most obvious being lack of bibliographies, old-fashioned illustrations, avoidance of sensitive subjects (including practically all aspects of human sexuality), and a dull, uninspired writing style.

During the late 1970s and early 1980s, *Britannica Junior* began to have a worn-out air about it, a telltale sign that the editors were failing to maintain the encyclopedia adequately. In 1984, the publisher declared *Britannica Junior* out of print, eventually replacing it with the 20-volume CHILDREN'S BRITANNICA, a set of similar size, style, reading level, and price. For an informative review of the final edition of *Britannica Junior*, see *Reference Books Bulletin* (in *Booklist*), May 15, 1983, pp. 1233–35.

The Cadillac Modern Encyclopedia: The World of Knowledge in One Volume. New York: Cadillac Publishing Company, Inc., 1973. 1,954p. Last priced at $24.95.

Published only once (in 1973) and never revised, the single-volume *Cadillac Modern Encyclopedia* remained in print until 1980. Designed for adults and older students from junior high school through college, it consisted of approximately 2.5 million words, 18,000 succinct articles, and over 1,000 illustrations in nearly 2,000 pages. The encyclopedia—edited by the late Max S. Shapiro, who was also author of the highly successful *Mathematics Made Simple*, published by Doubleday in 1943 and still in print—provided especially strong coverage of the physical and biological sciences. An updated and much modified electronic version of *Cadillac Modern* lives on today as the KUSSMAUL ENCYCLOPEDIA (see page 284).

Chambers's Encyclopaedia. 4th ed. London, England: International Learning Systems Corp., 1973. 15 vols. Last priced at $325.50.

For years the premier British-made general encyclopedia was *Chambers's Encyclopaedia*, which originated in the nineteenth century when the well-known firm of W. & R. Chambers of Edinburgh (Scotland) issued the work in 520 weekly parts between 1859 and 1868. Eventually the parts were cumulated and sold as a 10-volume set. After the *Encyclopaedia Britannica* (now NEW ENCYCLOPAEDIA BRITANNICA) passed into American hands at the turn of the century, *Chambers's* assumed the position of the largest and most distinguished general multivolume encyclopedia published in the United Kingdom. In 1944, the firm of George Newnes Ltd. acquired the rights to the work and, in 1950, issued a heavily revised edition in 15 volumes. Major revisions of the 1950 set appeared in 1955, 1959, and 1966; the 1966 (fourth) edition was reprinted with corrections in 1973, marking the last time the encyclopedia was published.

Today, *Chambers's* is owned by International Learning Systems Corporation Ltd., a subsidiary of the mammoth British Printing Corporation. A fifth edition has been considered, but the cost to do the job right—remember, the set has not been revised for nearly 30 years—is estimated at between $10 million and $20 million, a prohibitive figure under present economic conditions.

The 15-volume *Chambers's Encyclopaedia*, which was distributed for some years in North America by Purnell Educational, contained approximately 14.5 million words, 12,600 pages, 28,000 articles, and 4,500 illustrations, most in black and white. Intended for the "educated layman," the encyclopedia was "primarily a British production and therefore no doubt reflects to some extent the intellectual atmosphere of post-war Britain" (preface). An imposing work, *Chambers's* was best known for its long, accurate, objective articles and authoritative tone; a review in *Choice* (October 1967, p. 793) put it well when it called the encyclopedia "stolid, serious, and scholarly." Limitations included a dull format, unsatisfactory illustrations, an overly learned writing style, skimpy bibliographies, often quite dated material, and—for most North American readers—over-

emphasis on British history, people, places, culture, and achievements.

The Children's Encyclopedia. New York: A.S. Barnes, 1959. 1,147p. Last priced at $8.95.

Edited by Chandler Whipple, this physically large and heavy one-volume encyclopedia for youngsters ages 8–14 covered all basic areas of knowledge in more than 3,000 entries. The text was augmented by over 1,000 drawings, charts, maps, diagrams, and photographs, 90 of which were in full color. Though quantitatively impressive, the *Children's Encyclopedia* failed to make its material consistently interesting and easily accessible to young people. In addition, the volume itself was awkward to handle. It went out of print in the late 1960s.

The Child's World. 4th ed. Chicago: Standard Education Corp., 1974. 8 vols. Last priced at $72.50.

Child's World, first published in 1949 and revised several times subsequently, last appeared in 1974 in eight topically arranged volumes: *Countries and Their Children, How to Live with Your Children, People and Great Deeds, Plant and Animal Ways, Stories of Childhood, The Story World, The World and Its Wonders*, and *The World of the Arts*. Although it contained much encyclopedic information about people, foreign countries, the arts, crafts, and the natural world, the set was not an encyclopedia per se; rather, in the publisher's words, it was designed as "supplementary and enrichment material for the home and classroom library."

Child's World competed (though not very successfully) with the larger and much superior CHILDCRAFT. Sarah Law Kennerly, in a review of the third (1965) edition of *Child's World* in *Library Journal* (September 15, 1966, pp. 4363–65), provides a good perspective on the set's limitations: "Since the publishers insist that *The Child's World* is not a reference tool it is perhaps unfair to judge it by the standards of excellence set by the recommended juvenile encyclopedias. But it is impossible not to notice how much less one's curiosity is stimulated and one's background enriched when reading *The Child's World* than when browsing through the concisely written, clearly expressed, and beautifully illustrated articles in a good children's encyclopedia." In 1977, the publisher reported that the set "has been discontinued and there are no plans to revive it."

Collins Gem Encyclopedia. London, England: William Collins Sons & Company Ltd., 1979. 2 vols. Last priced at $7.90.

The two-volume, British-made *Collins Gem Encyclopedia* was a small pocket-sized work in flexible vinyl covers, each volume measuring 3¼ by 4¾ inches. An abridgment of the larger *Collins Concise Encyclopedia* (1933–76), *Collins Gem* contained roughly half a million words, 1,125 pages, 14,000 very brief entries, and no illustrations. Obviously, the work lacked depth—entries averaged only 32 words in length—but it served as a reliable quick reference source for travelers and others interested only in very basic facts about important people, places, events, concepts, etc. Simon & Schuster, the North American distributor, reported the encyclopedia out of print in the United States and Canada in 1987, but a new edition may reappear at any time.

The Cultural Library. New York: Parents Magazine Educational Press., 1965. 10 vols. Last priced at $149.50.

This multivolume set for young people was on the North American market for more than 50 years until it finally passed from the scene in the late 1960s. First published as *Our Wonder World* (1914–30), it later became the *New Wonder World* (1932–55), and, when acquired by Parents Magazine Educational Press in 1959, it reappeared as the *New Wonder World Encyclopedia.* Several years later the set was again retitled, this time as the *New Wonder World Cultural Library.* Finally, in 1965, it became simply *The Cultural Library.* Intended chiefly for elementary and junior high school students, the encyclopedia was topically arranged with each volume dealing with a broad subject, such as *The Universe, Nature, Agriculture and Industry,* and *The Arts.*

In all, the 10 volumes comprised 2.5 million words, 4,500 pages, and 3,000 illustrations. Although the *Cultural Library* contained much useful information as well as recreational reading material, it was never considered an important reference source for young students, and toward the end it had deteriorated badly. A review by the Subscription Books Committee of the American Library Association in *Booklist* (November 1, 1965, p. 234) tells the story: "Many articles are out-of-date. Inconsistencies and inadequacies in the volume indexes and the master index make them almost useless as guides to the contents of this set, which by its very nature needs a satisfactory device for locating material. Because of inaccuracies, lack of up-to-date material, lack of balance, out-of-date illustrations and unattractive format, the set does not achieve its stated objective as 'one of the most up-to-date and useful reference works for home and school.' The work is not recommended."

Disney's Wonderful World of Knowledge. New York: Danbury Press. (a division of Grolier, Inc.), 1973. 20 vols. Last priced at $229.50.

Originally published in Italian in 16 volumes as *Enciclopedia Disney* in 1970, *Disney's Wonderful World of Knowledge* appeared in North America several years later, a revised and slightly enlarged English-language version of the original. The publisher described the encyclopedia as "a library of human knowledge for children that masterfully combines learning with the magic of vivid color and imagination in 20 beautiful volumes" (advertisement). Its approach to knowledge was quite similar to that found in the smaller CHARLIE BROWN'S 'CYCLOPEDIA.

Aimed mainly at beginning readers and primary school children, *Disney's Wonderful World* contained approximately 750,000 words, 2,500 pages, 1,200 articles, and 4,000 illustrations, all in color. It was topically arranged, with each volume devoted to a particular subject or theme. For instance, volume 1 was *Animals;* volume 2, *Natural Wonders;* volume 3, *Inventions;* volume 4, *Transportation;* volume 5, *Caves to Skyscrapers;* and so on; the final volume comprised an index to the set.

The encyclopedia, which was sold to individual consumers mainly via mail order, never achieved more than second-rate status as a reference work for children. Its colorful illustrations and clever use of Disney characters successfully captured the young reader's attention, but overall the set lacked quality, suffering from imbalanced coverage, inconsistent reading levels, carelessly edited text, an inaccurate index, and, ultimately, out-of-date information. Grolier reported *Disney's Wonderful World* out of print in the early 1980s, but the encyclopedia continues to surface here and there in various distributors' catalogs. In 1993, a Grolier representative confirmed that the set is defunct, but conceded that "the odd set" might still be available.

Dunlop's Illustrated Encyclopedia of Facts. New York: Doubleday, 1969. 864p. Last priced at $8.95.

Compiled by Norris and Ross McWhirter (who also put together the first editions of the *Guinness Book of Records*), this single-volume encyclopedia appeared in North America only once—in 1969. It was published in both hardcover and paperback editions containing some 750,000 words, 2,400 entries, and 400 small black-and-white photographs. The reviews were reasonably favorable, Louis Barron's in *Library Journal* (September 1, 1969, p. 2907) being typical: "Like any one-volume book that claims to contain the 'essential elements' of 'virtually every field of human knowledge' . . . it contains a great deal of simplified nonsense, and many of the illustrations add little but bulk to the book. But so much out-of-the-way information has been brought together here that no library reference desk can afford to be without it." Never revised, the book was reported out of print in the mid-1970s.

Encyclopedia International. Danbury, CT: Lexicon Publications (a subsidiary of Grolier, Inc.), 1963–82. 20 vols. Last priced at $450.00.

For 20 years between 1963 and 1982, *Encyclopedia International*—a serious multivolume general encyclopedia for the whole family and particularly secondary school students—was a mainstay in the Grolier encyclopedia line, positioned between the larger, more advanced ENCYCLOPEDIA AMERICANA and the more elementary NEW BOOK OF KNOWLEDGE. The set contained approximately 9.5 million words, 12,000 pages, 30,000 articles, and 13,000 illustrations, most in black and white. It competed directly with COMPTON'S ENCYCLOPEDIA and WORLD BOOK ENCYCLOPEDIA, both of which had greater name recognition with the encyclopedia-buying public.

Toward the end, the publisher failed to maintain the *International* adequately, allowing it to become badly dated, in some instances embarrassingly so. The encyclopedia's final printing bore a 1982 copyright, and Grolier ceased selling it in 1984 or 1985, after the stock was exhausted. It was eventually replaced in the Grolier encyclopedia hierarchy by the ACADEMIC AMERICAN ENCYCLOPEDIA.

During its period of decline, several independent distributors acquired the rights to peddle older editions of the *International* under different titles, including the *New Age Encyclopedia, Webster's Family Encyclopedia* (published in 20 volumes and unrelated to the 10-volume WEBSTER'S FAMILY ENCYCLOPEDIA that is currently in print), *Webster's New Age Encyclopedia,* and *Webster's New Family Encyclopedia.* Consumers today may still encounter the *International* under these or other titles in shadowy corners of the marketplace. Sometimes, unfortunately, these old editions of the encyclopedia are dressed up to appear new. Caveat emptor.

Encyclopedia of World Knowledge. New York: Encyclopedia of World Knowledge, Inc., 1969. 14 vols. Last priced at $39.75.

This short-lived encyclopedia represented an effort to develop a supermarket edition of the well-known LINCOLN LIBRARY OF ESSENTIAL INFORMATION, which itself is now out of print (see below). Issued in 14 slim volumes and sold on the book-a-week plan, the set reprinted the contents of the two-volume LINCOLN LIBRARY with only slight modifications. It was discontinued in 1972. Why the

Encyclopedia of World Knowledge was phased out so quickly is not known for certain, but most likely the cutthroat nature of the supermarket encyclopedia business played a part in the decision.

The Everyday Reference Library: An Encyclopedia of Useful Information. Chicago: J.G. Ferguson Publishing Co., 1964. 3 vols. Last priced at $29.95.

The Everyday Reference Library first appeared in a single-volume edition in 1951, a revision of *Austin's New Encyclopedia of Usable Information* (1948), which in turn was based on the *Handy Encyclopedia of Useful Information* (1946). In 1964, the publisher expanded the encyclopedia to three volumes containing roughly 1.5 million words, 1,600 pages, 900 entries, and several hundred illustrations. Essentially a compendium of practical "how-to-do-it" information, the set was topically arranged, with volume 1 devoted to information about the home, volume 2 to business, and volume 3 to leisure and recreation.

Although reasonably successful in the marketplace, the *Everyday Reference Library* was a mediocre work at best. Indeed, the Subscription Books Committee of the American Library Association harshly condemned the set: "Because of the need for revision and modernization, the general unevenness and frequent superficiality of subject treatment, and various inaccuracies and omissions, *The Everyday Reference Library* is not recommended for purchase at this time" (*Booklist,* March 15, 1966, p. 671). In 1974, the publisher reported the encyclopedia out of print but added that "a major revision and updating of the set" was being considered; however, no revision (major or minor) has ever appeared.

Everyman's Encyclopaedia (Print Version). 6th ed. London, England: J.M. Dent & Sons Ltd., 1978. 12 vols. Last priced at $401.50 (in Canada).

Everyman's Encyclopaedia—a respected multivolume general encyclopedia of British origin for adults and older students that first appeared in 1913–14 and has been revised periodically over the years—is something of an anomaly at the present time. The most recent edition (the sixth, 1978) has been out of print in both Great Britain and North America for at least several years, but an electronic version of the same edition continues to be available via Dialog Information Services, a computerized database vendor located in California. (For an evaluation of the electronic version of *Everyman's,* see page 278.)

The 12-volume sixth edition of *Everyman's* contained approximately 9 million words, 8,900 pages,

51,000 articles, and 5,000 illustrations, all in black and white. It had—and the electronic version continues to have—a well-deserved reputation as an authoritative, accurate, and unbiased encyclopedia of general knowledge. Another of the set's strengths was its clear, straightforward writing style. Among the encyclopedia's weaknesses were dated material due to infrequent revisions (only five between 1913 and 1978), complete lack of an index, unexciting illustrations, a generally stodgy format, and, from the North American perspective, too heavy an emphasis on British topics.

Over the years, various distributors have sold *Everyman's* in the United States and Canada, although the encyclopedia never made much of an impact on the market in either country, largely due to its strong British slant. The fourth edition (1958) appeared on this side of the Atlantic under the title *Macmillan Everyman's Encyclopedia* and the fifth (1967) as the *International Everyman's Encyclopedia*—an Americanized version in 20 volumes that had roughly one million more words than its British counterpart. Interestingly, the most recent sixth edition of *Everyman's* in print (as opposed to electronic) form could not be distributed in the United States, the reason being, according to the publisher, "that the cost of clearing picture rights for the US was enormous compared with the likely return that we would make in sales, and so we never took that step." Note that the electronic version can be sold in the United States because it contains no illustrations.

J.M. Dent & Sons Ltd., the publisher, reports that it has no plans to produce a new edition of *Everyman's Encyclopaedia*. Presumably bad economic times have put the kibosh on the encyclopedia business in the United Kingdom. Unfortunately, with the demise of *Everyman's*, CHAMBERS'S ENCYCLOPAEDIA (see above), and the NEW CAXTON ENCYCLOPEDIA (see below), there are no major multivolume general encyclopedias being produced in Great Britain today.

Finding Out: Silver Burdett's Children's Encyclopedia. Morristown, NJ: Silver Burdett Company, 1981. 10 vols. Last priced at $140.00.

The 10-volume *Finding Out* was originally published in 1980 in Great Britain by Grisewood & Dempsey Ltd. and adapted for the North American market a year later. Edited by John Paton, a well-known British compiler of reference books for young people, the set contained 250,000 words, 816 pages, 1,300 brief articles, and 2,000 illustrations, almost all in color. It proved to be an accurate, authoritative, clearly written, easily accessible, and physically appealing encyclopedia aimed principally at children in the upper elementary grades. Its greatest drawbacks were overly selective coverage, which very much favored scientific topics, and superficial treatment of some subjects. *Finding Out* went out of print in the United States in 1988, but a revised version with new illustrations continues to be available under the title KINGFISHER CHILDREN'S ENCYCLOPEDIA. In addition, many articles in the now defunct PICTURE ENCYCLOPEDIA FOR CHILDREN (see below) were taken verbatim from *Finding Out*. John Paton edited all of these interrelated encyclopedias.

The Great World Encyclopedia. New York: Two Continents Publishing Group, 1976. 278p. Last priced at $12.95.

An inconsequential single-volume work for older students and adults originally published in Great Britain, the *Great World Encyclopedia* consisted of about 200,000 words, 278 pages, 70 broad articles, and 750 illustrations. The book, edited by Frances M. Clapham, was distributed in North America by Two Continents Publishing Group, which went out of business in the late 1970s; the encyclopedia disappeared from the market around the same time.

Grolier Encyclopedia. New York: Grolier Society, 1944–63. 20 vols. Last priced at $119.50.

Published between 1944 and 1963 in 10- and 20-volume editions, the *Grolier Encyclopedia* derived largely from the old 10-volume *Doubleday Encyclopedia* (1931–41), an American adaptation of the popular British *Harmsworth's Universal Encyclopaedia* (1920–23). In its day, the *Grolier Encyclopedia*—a multivolume work of 5.5 million words, 28,000 concise entries, and about 9,000 illustrations—was a major intermediate-sized general encyclopedia for older students and the family. Over time, however, the set lost its freshness and was unable to compete with better maintained works aimed at the same audience, such as COMPTON'S ENCYCLOPEDIA and WORLD BOOK ENCYCLOPEDIA.

A review by the Subscription Books Committee of the American Library Association in *Booklist* (February 15, 1960, pp. 344–46) documents the set's decline: "The 1958 *Grolier Encyclopedia* has undergone some changes since 1952. However, it does not offer the detail necessary for a basic reference source. Revision, on the whole, is uneven. Current topics are not always covered; nor are recent statistics uniformly available . . . . Although much good illustrative material has been added, too frequently older cuts still in use have deteriorated. *Grolier Encyclopedia* is not recommended."

The publisher discontinued the encyclopedia in 1963, replacing it with ENCYCLOPEDIA INTERNATIONAL (see above), a 20-volume work now also out of print. Eventually, Grolier sold the rights to the *Grolier Encyclopedia* to H.S. Stuttman Company in New York, which merged it with the 15-volume RICHARDS TOPICAL ENCYCLOPEDIA (see below) to create a 30-volume hybrid entitled the UNIFIED ENCYCLOPEDIA (see below).

Grolier Universal Encyclopedia. New York: Grolier, 1965–72. 10 vols. (1965–67); 20 vols. (1968–72). Last priced at $200.00.

Despite the similarity in titles, the *Grolier Universal Encyclopedia* was completely unrelated to the GROLIER ENCYCLOPEDIA (see preceding entry). Rather, the *Grolier Universal* was—at least at the outset—an inexpensive ($99.50) abridgment of the publisher's ENCYCLOPEDIA INTERNATIONAL (see above). It first appeared in 10 volumes in 1965, consisting of roughly five million words, 6,500 pages, 25,000 articles, and 12,000 illustrations.

Although the encyclopedia lacked an index and bibliographies, the condensed set functioned reasonably well as a reliable source of quick-reference information for older students and adults. Later, during the years 1968–72, Grolier reconstructed the same text into 20 thinner volumes, doubled the price (to $200.00), and began selling the *Grolier Universal Encyclopedia* simultaneously under two other titles, namely the *Modern Reference Encyclopedia* and the *New Age Encyclopedia.* (Note that the latter bears no relationship to the NEW AGE ENCYCLOPEDIA described on page 418, a single-volume subject encyclopedia that deals with religion.) In 1972, Grolier abruptly withdrew the *Grolier Universal Encyclopedia* and its clones from the market, relegating them to out-of-print status where they remain to this day.

The Hamlyn Younger Children's Encyclopedia. London, England: Hamlyn Publishing Group Ltd., 1972. 256p. Last priced at $7.95.

A single-volume reference work produced in Great Britain for children ages 7–14, the *Hamlyn Younger Children's Encyclopedia* consisted of 80,000 words, 24 broad topical sections (such as "Our Land and Its People"), and about 800 color drawings. Edited by Kenneth Bailey, the book proved to be inadequate as an encyclopedia for young people, but it possessed potential as a browsing item for the inquiring child. Until it went out of print in 1980, the encyclopedia was distributed in North America by the now defunct A & W Promotional Book Corporation in New York.

Harver Junior World Encyclopedia. Revised ed. Freeport, NY: Harver Educational Services, 1972. 16 vols. Last priced at $70.50.

This multivolume encyclopedia for children at the elementary school level originally appeared in Great Britain in 1960 as the *Junior World Encyclopaedia* under the imprint of Low & Marston Ltd. In 1972, the British publisher Purnell & Sons Ltd. revised, retitled, and adapted the set for the North American market, where it was published by Harver Educational Services. Edited by the late Michael W. Dempsey, a well-known British maker of reference books for youngsters, the 1972 edition contained about one million words, 1,344 total pages, 1,550 articles, and 2,000 illustrations, 90 percent of which were in color. It bore no relationship to the adult HARVER WORLD ENCYCLOPEDIA (see next entry), except that both works had the same publisher and *Harver* in their titles.

Hardly an encyclopedia of first importance, *Harver Junior World* suffered most obviously from superficial and uneven coverage, with strong emphasis on the natural sciences to the detriment of topics in the humanities and social sciences. For instance, subjects of great curiosity to young people, such as human sexuality and drug use, were totally ignored or given short shrift, whereas exotic topics like earwigs, loess, pupa, and show worms received attention. The material was also sometimes unreliable, out-of-date, and poorly arranged for easy access.

Not surprisingly, the encyclopedia had little success in the United States and Canada and was withdrawn from the American market in the late 1970s. In 1980, a representative of the London publisher Macdonald Educational (which acquired the rights to the set) reported that "at present the work is undergoing up-dating and the current edition is going out of print. We do not have any firm dates at present to quote for the new edition." At this point, no new edition of *Harver Junior World Encyclopedia* has ever appeared, either in Great Britain or North America.

Harver World Encyclopedia: Alphabetical Encyclopedia in 20 Volumes. Freeport, New York: Harver Educational Services, 1973–75. 20 vols. Last priced at $375.00.

The 20-volume *Harver World Encyclopedia* consisted of approximately 7.5 million words, 5,850 pages, 20,000 articles, and 16,000 illustrations, well over half in color. Aimed at adults and students at the junior high school level and up, it first appeared in 1973 and again in 1975 in a second edition that added a so-called "Instant Reference Supplement," which upon inspection proved to be nothing more than a very old unabridged English-language dictionary split among the set's 20 volumes. Although intended mainly for a North American audience, the encyclopedia drew most of its editors and writers from Great Britain and its illustrations from the vast picture resources of the Elsevier Company, a highly respected international publisher based in Amsterdam.

Unfortunately, the encyclopedia's overall quality left much to be desired. Weaknesses included overly simplistic and sometimes misleading treatment of complex subjects, too many factual errors, lack of bibliographies, and, perhaps most egregious, lack of an index to the set. Only *Harver World's* illustrations generated much enthusiasm. A review of the first (1973) edition by the Reference and Subscription Books Committee of the American Library Association in *Booklist* (April 1, 1974, p. 831) summed up the response: "The most striking feature of *Harver World Encyclopedia* is its illustrations . . . . Although in many cases photographs and drawings are rather small because of space limitations, they are uniformly clear, easily understood, and sharply reproduced. Color reproduction is particularly outstanding in both photographs and color illustrations."

The North American publisher, Harver Educational Services, folded soon after the second edition of *Harver World* appeared in 1975, after which various independent distributors sold off the remaining stock. The encyclopedia was out of print by 1981 and has apparently never been revised or reissued on either side of the Atlantic.

Home University Encyclopedia: An Illustrated Treasury of Knowledge, with Special Plates and Articles and Departmental Supervision by 462 Leading Editors, Educators and Specialists in the United States and Europe. New York: Books, Inc. (a subsidiary of the Publishers Company), 1941–61. 15 vols. (1st ed.); 12 vols. (2nd ed.). Last priced at $49.50.

Originally published in 1941 and revised only once (in 1961), this intermediate-sized general encyclopedia for the family derived from the old *New York Post World Wide Illustrated Encyclopedia* (1935), which later became the *World Wide Illustrated Encyclopedia* (1937) and was also distributed under the title *University Illustrated Encyclopedia* (1938). The first edition of the *Home University Encyclopedia* comprised 15 volumes, but the second was reorganized into 12 volumes. The 12-volume set contained four million words, 5,000 pages, 40,000 brief entries, and 5,000 illustrations, all in black and white. An inferior work by any standard, the encyclopedia was finally withdrawn from the market in the early 1970s.

The Illustrated Encyclopedia of Learning in 12 Fact-Filled Accurate Volumes Illustrated with More than 6,000 Dramatic Full-Color Pictures. New York: Comet Press., 1969. 12 vols. Last priced at $49.95.

Very similar in size, purpose, scope, style, and format to the 1969 edition of the GOLDEN BOOK ENCYCLOPEDIA, the 12-volume *Illustrated Encyclopedia of Learning* contained 291,000 words, 1,536 pages, 4,500 articles, and over 6,000 drawings, all in color. Edited by Ruth Dimond and intended for elementary school children, the set had little to recommend it. Specifically, it was poorly designed and printed (including the illustrations), provided superficial coverage and treatment of knowledge, and lacked an index as well as cross-references. Moreover, by the time it went out of print in the mid-1980s, the set had become badly dated. An expanded version of the encyclopedia appeared in 1970 under the title LADIES HOME JOURNAL CHILDREN'S ILLUSTRATED ENCYCLOPEDIA FOR LEARNING (see below).

The Illustrated Libraries of Human Knowledge. Columbus, OH: Charles E. Merrill Publishing Company, 1968. 18 vols. Last priced at $137.50.

This topically arranged encyclopedic set for adults and older students was originally produced in Great Britain by the London firm of Aldus Books Ltd. and published in the United States in 1968 by Charles Merrill in a limited edition. It consisted of about one million words, 3,000 pages, and numerous color photographs. In terms of quality, the set lacked bibliographies and adequate indexing, but the text was quite good, being authoritative, informative, interestingly written, and well-illustrated. In 1975, Merrill reported the *Illustrated Libraries of Human Knowledge* out of print in North America, noting that Aldus continued to hold all copyright and distribution rights.

Illustrated World Encyclopedia. Woodbury, NY: Bobley Publishing Corp., 1958–73. 15 & 21 vols. Last priced at $59.95; also published in 1 vol. 1,619p., 1977. Last priced at $19.95.

The *Illustrated World Encyclopedia* derives from a 20-volume set published in 1954 entitled the *Illustrated Encyclopedia of Knowledge*. It was described by Padraig Walsh in his *Anglo-American General Encyclopedias, 1703-1967* (p. 82) as an "extremely poor" work that "was, apparently, designed to be offered as a premium through chain and department stores and food supermarkets, and, in at least one instance, it was offered as an inducement to purchase a television set." Exactly the same encyclopedia with an atlas volume added appeared around the same time under the title *Illustrated Home Library Encyclopedia*.

In 1958, the Bobley Publishing Corporation acquired the rights to the work and changed its title to the *Illustrated World Encyclopedia*. Between 1958 and 1973, Bobley published the encyclopedia in sets of both 15 and 21 volumes, selling them mainly through retail stores and mail-order catalogs at prices considerably lower than the competition, which included such formidable (and much better known) titles as the WORLD BOOK ENCYCLOPEDIA and COMPTON'S ENCYCLOPEDIA. In 1977, the publisher issued a single-volume abridgment of the 21-volume set published in 1973, explaining that "by eliminating all but the best and most important illustrations and by making certain other changes in format, this remarkable one-volume edition was made possible. In fact, for the very first time, virtually the entire encyclopedic content of a well-known, 6,720-page, 21-volume encyclopedia has been re-published in a single 1,600-page volume" (preface).

No matter how many volumes it had, the *Illustrated World Encyclopedia* was always very much a substandard reference work. Deficiencies included uneven coverage, superficial treatment, numerous factual and typographical errors, an inconsistent writing style, frequently out-of-date articles, and illustrations that were often too small, too dark, and of minimal informational value. The only attractive feature of the *Illustrated World* was its bargain-basement price. In 1984, the encyclopedia's editor, Roger Bobley, reported both the single-volume and multivolume editions out of print, although he held out the possibility of a revision sometime in the future.

The Junior Encyclopedia of General Knowledge. London, England: Octopus Books Ltd., 1978. 224p. Last priced at $9.95.

The British-made *Junior Encyclopedia of General Knowledge* was distributed in North America between 1978 and 1985, when it went out of print. A small work of only 224 pages designed for children 8–12 years old, the encyclopedia contained approximately 100,000 words, 100 topically arranged articles of two pages each, and 400 illustrations, all in color. It was edited by the husband-and-wife team of Theodore Rowland-Entwistle and Jean Cooke, who worked together on several other children's encyclopedias, including the WORLD ALMANAC INFOPEDIA and PURNELLS'S PICTORIAL ENCYCLOPEDIA (see below). Overall, the *Junior Encyclopedia* proved to be an attractive and reliable (albeit superficial) reference source for young people.

Junior Pears Encyclopaedia. London, England: Pelham Books Ltd., 1961–. 650p. Last priced at $15.95.

Published every year in Great Britain from 1961 to the present, the well-known and highly respected *Junior Pears Encyclopaedia* has been distributed off and on in North America over the years (most recently by Viking Penguin Inc.), but at present it is no longer available in either the United States or Canada. The same is true of PEARS CYCLOPAEDIA (see below), the adult counterpart to *Junior Pears*. Of course, this situation could change instantly should Pelham Books find a new distributor for its products in North America. Likewise, interested consumers are free to order either or both of the *Pears* books directly from the publisher in England where they are in print (contact Michael Joseph and Pelham Books, 27 Wrights Lane, London W8 5TZ, England) or through a foreign book dealer.

Each annual edition of *Junior Pears*—a single-volume work aimed at children ages 7–14—contains about 280,000 words, 650 pages, 1,500 articles, and 350 illustrations, all black-and-white line drawings. Edited by Edward Blishen since its inception, the encyclopedia is arranged topically, the text grouped by subject under 17 broad headings, such as "The World: Its History; Its Geography; Its Famous People" and "Music and the Arts." According to Blishen's introduction, the basic goal of *Junior Pears* "is to provide information," but he adds, "we've never wanted the book to be merely a bulging collection of facts. We've tried to make it pleasant to read as well as easy to consult." The encyclopedia's contents are accurate, objective, reasonably current, and usually presented in an interesting manner. On the negative side, *Junior Pears* lacks an index and, as a result, access to information is hit-or-miss; but from the North American perspective, the book's major drawback is its heavy British emphasis.

The Ladies' Home Journal Children's Illustrated Encyclopedia for Learning. New York: Ladies Home Journal & Comet Press., 1970. 18 vols. Last priced at $56.00.

Based largely on the 12-volume ILLUSTRATED ENCYCLOPEDIA OF LEARNING (see above), this inferior encyclopedia comprised 18 volumes, 350,000 words, 2,124 pages, 5,000 articles, and more than 6,000 illustrations, all in color. It was heavily advertised in *Ladies' Home Journal* magazine and sold principally by mail order until its demise in 1974. A review in *Booklist* (May 1, 1971, p. 710) correctly dismissed the set, noting that it "has few of the characteristics of a real encyclopedia for children. Material has been selected unevenly; the information given is too brief to be useful to children. The writing is uninteresting, and the illustrations and format are mediocre."

Larousse Illustrated International Encyclopedia and Dictionary. New York: World Publishing, 1972. 1,550p. Last priced at $19.95.

Called by the editor, O.C. Watson, "an American equivalent" of the famous French-language PETIT LAROUSSE ILLUSTRÉ, this practical single-volume reference work for adults and older students combined the functions of dictionary and encyclopedia. It consisted of approximately three million words, 1,500 pages, 15,000 encyclopedic entries, 50,000 dictionary entries, and 3,000 illustrations, many in color. The encyclopedia portion—limited almost exclusively to brief descriptions of people, places, and historical events—proved useful for quick reference. The dictionary entries were also quite concise, providing definitions, pronunciations, parts of speech, etymological information, and excellent illustrative examples (a hallmark of dictionaries bearing the Larousse name). Unfortunately, the *Larousse Illustrated* grew increasingly dated and was finally reported out of print in 1980, with no plans for a new or revised edition.

The Lincoln Library of Essential Information. Columbus, OH: Frontier Press., 1924–85. Vols. varied from 1 to 3. Last priced at $149.50.

In its heyday, the *Lincoln Library of Essential Information* ranked with the COLUMBIA ENCYCLOPEDIA as one of the two best small-volume encyclopedias available in English, but toward the end it was little more than an old-fashioned looking hodgepodge of information, much of it out-of-date. Originally published in 1924, the encyclopedia normally appeared in a new edition every two years until 1985, when it ceased publication. It was first published in one volume but soon split into two volumes. In 1978, it became the *New Lincoln Library Encyclopedia* and expanded to three volumes, but in 1981 the set reverted to its original title and familiar two-volume format.

The final edition of the *Lincoln Library* comprised two volumes, approximately 3.5 million words, 2,500 pages, 25,000 articles, and 1,300 illustrations, most in black and white. Throughout its history, the encyclopedia was arranged topically, the contents grouped by subject in 12 broad sections, or "departments," such as "Geography," "History," "Government," and "Business and Economics." Negative criticisms of the encyclopedia included lack of coverage of controversial issues (e.g., capital punishment, abortion, homosexuality), fragmentation and

repetition of information throughout the various "departments," a stilted and textbookish writing style, dull and uninformative graphics, and out-of-date material in many areas.

Since the *Lincoln Library* went out of print (Frontier Press reportedly sold the last of the 1985 edition in 1988), several publishers have expressed serious interest in acquiring the rights to the work and resuscitating it; after all, the "Lincoln Library" name remains reasonably well-known to the encyclopedia-buying public in North America. But as of this time, none of these publishers appears ready to invest the necessary capital (financial and otherwise) required to bring the encyclopedia up to speed.

Little and Ives Illustrated Ready Reference Encyclopedia. New York: Little and Ives, 1961. 20 vols. Last priced at approximately $25.00.

This inexpensive family encyclopedia was sold in supermarkets on the book-a-week plan until it ceased publication in the mid-1960s. The set consisted of roughly two million words, 3,000 pages, 20,000 articles, and 7,000 color illustrations in 20 slim volumes. It was edited by Franklin Dunham, who also produced two earlier encyclopedias—the *New Pictorial Encyclopedia of the World* (1954) and the *Illustrated Encyclopedia of the Modern World* (1956)—that had practically the same contents as *Little and Ives.* All of these titles lacked the breadth and depth required of a quality encyclopedia, but they enjoyed steady sales and found their way into many homes that otherwise would not have had an encyclopedia. In 1965, the publisher ran into financial difficulties, and the rights to *Little and Ives* were acquired by Grosset & Dunlap of New York, which transformed the set into a single-volume work, sans illustrations, entitled the NEW UNIVERSITY ONE-VOLUME ENCYCLOPEDIA (see below).

The McKay One-Volume International Encyclopedia. New York: McKay, 1970. 1,140p. Last priced at $12.95.

The *McKay One-Volume International Encyclopedia* was a hastily—and unsuccessfully—Americanized version of *Hutchinson's New Twentieth Century Encyclopedia* (1970), a standard British desk encyclopedia first published in 1948. Edited by Edith M. Horsley, it contained over one million words, 1,140 pages, 17,000 concise entries, and 1,500 illustrations, mostly small black-and-white photos and line drawings. Despite minor efforts to revise it for North American readers, the encyclopedia had a distinct British orientation. As the Reference and Subscription Books Review Committee of the American Library Association pointed out (in *Booklist*, June 15, 1972, p. 868), "its British emphasis, use of British spelling and terminology, and lack of adequate coverage of American geography, biography, social, and political events limit its usefulness to the average American home, office, or library, and it cannot be recommended to them." The publisher reported the encyclopedia out of print in 1975.

Merit Students Encyclopedia. New York: Macmillan Educational Company (a division of Macmillan, Inc.), 1967–91. 20 vols. Last priced at $559.00.

A sister set to the larger and more advanced COLLIER'S ENCYCLOPEDIA, *Merit Students Encyclopedia* first appeared in 1967 and abruptly ceased publication in 1991, an apparent casualty of the publisher's sudden financial difficulties due to the untimely death of tycoon Robert Maxwell, whose debt-heavy media empire included Macmillan, Inc. Happily, there is a good possibility the encyclopedia will reappear in the near future, perhaps in a downsized version more closely focused on the elementary and secondary school market. Until such time, *Merit Students* remains out of print, although consumers will encounter it in library reference collections and occasionally on the secondhand book market.

The last printing of the 20-volume set contained approximately nine million words, 12,300 pages, 21,000 articles, and 20,000 illustrations, about a quarter in full color. The encyclopedia had numerous strengths, the most conspicuous being balanced coverage, accurate and objective presentation of information, and an aesthetically pleasing format. The encyclopedia also benefited from an aggressive annual revision program; during the 1980s, for instance, more than half the set's articles were rewritten, revised, or entirely new. Weaknesses included inadequate cross-references, second-rate bibliographies, and some dated illustrations. Overall, *Merit Students Encyclopedia* was a first-class reference source for both students and adults that competed reasonably well with the best sets in its class, namely the WORLD BOOK ENCYCLOPEDIA and COMPTON'S ENCYCLOPEDIA.

Modern Century Illustrated Encyclopedia. New York: Modern Century Illustrated Encyclopedia, Inc. (a division of McGraw-Hill Far Eastern Publishers Ltd.), 1972. 24 vols. Last priced at $19.97 paperbound.

First published in Australia, the *Modern Century Illustrated Encyclopedia* comprised about one million words, 2,300 pages, 2,000 articles, and 3,000 illustrations in 24 small volumes. Intended for children ages 7–14, the set appeared in both hardcover and paperbound editions but was never revised. Over the years, several U.S. distributors were involved,

including Dell Publishing Company and Scholastic Book Services; the encyclopedia eventually disappeared from the North American market in the late 1970s or early 1980s. For a time, it was published in Great Britain by Nile & Mackenzie Ltd. under the title *Encyclopaedia Apollo* in 14 volumes.

Despite its irregular publishing history, the *Modern Century Illustrated Encyclopedia* proved to be a competently produced encyclopedia for young people. It provided balanced, reliable, impartial, and (at the time) reasonably current information on many topics studied in U.S. and Canadian schools. On the negative side, some articles lacked adequate detail, the writing style tended to be dry and uninspiring, the set offered no bibliographies, the illustrations were usually too small to be of much value, and the index was not entirely satisfactory.

My First Encyclopedia A-Z. Morristown, NJ: Silver Burdett Press., 1988. 102p. Last priced at $16.95.

This colorful one-volume encyclopedia by Dorothy Turner covered selected topics of potential interest to children ages 6–10, including astronomy, plant and animal life, major religions, U.S. presidents, kings and queens, musical instruments, and various forms of transportation. Four-color artwork and photographs enhanced the printed text. Altogether, the 102-page book contained about 25,000 words, 200 entries, and 250 illustrations. Reported out of print by the publisher in 1993, *My First Encyclopedia A-Z* might be reprinted or revised and reissued in the near future.

My First Golden Encyclopedia. New York: Golden Press. (a division of Western Publishing Company), 1969. 384p. Last priced at $12.25.

This 384-page encyclopedia for beginning readers was an almost identical reprint of the earlier (and now also defunct) *My First Golden Learning Library,* which appeared in 1965 in 16 very thin volumes of 24 pages each (for a total of 384 pages). Written by Jane Werner Watson and illustrated by William Dugan, both encyclopedias contained about 70,000 words, 650 short articles, and color drawings on every page. Obviously, these simple works lacked value as serious sources of information, but many young children found them intellectually stimulating and instructive. *My First Golden Encyclopedia* was reported out of print in 1978. Note that this encyclopedia bore no relationship to the multivolume GOLDEN BOOK ENCYCLOPEDIA, except for having a similar title and the same publisher

National Encyclopedia. New York: P.F. Collier, 1932–60. 20 vols. Last priced at $199.50.

First published in 1932 as an entirely new work in 11 volumes, the *National Encyclopedia* supplanted *Collier's New Encyclopedia* (1902–29) as the publisher's flagship encyclopedia. The set eventually expanded to 20 volumes comprising seven million words, 7,800 pages, and 33,000 articles. A reasonably good encyclopedia for its time, the *National Encyclopedia* continued under the P.F. Collier imprint until 1950, when the publisher replaced it with COLLIER'S ENCYCLOPEDIA, a larger and vastly superior work that today competes with the NEW ENCYCLOPAEDIA BRITANNICA and ENCYCLOPEDIA AMERICANA.

In time, Educational Enterprises, Inc., a publisher then located in Washington, DC, acquired the rights to the *National Encyclopedia* and, in 1960, issued a minimally revised edition that differed little from the 1950 version. Educational Enterprises continued selling the encyclopedia throughout the 1960s as part of a reference book package deal, periodically promising a substantial revision that never materialized. Exactly when the *National Encyclopedia* finally ceased to be sold is not known, but it was most likely sometime in the early 1970s.

Nelson's Encyclopedia for Young Readers. Nashville, TN: Thomas Nelson Publishers, 1980. 2 vols. Last priced at $34.95.

Nelson's Encyclopedia for Young Readers—a two-volume work for children ages 7–14 edited by Laurence Urdang—contained some 350,000 words, 973 pages, 2,000 articles, and 1,500 illustrations, about half in color. Published in 1980 and never revised, the encyclopedia at first blush appeared to be a colorful, attractive, and readable introduction to basic knowledge, but closer inspection revealed a flawed work suffering from superficial treatment of most topics, disproportionate attention to religious subjects, an ineffective index, and undistinguished illustrations, many of which first appeared in *Black's Children's Encyclopedia*, a British-made work originally published in 1961. *Nelson's Encyclopedia for Young Readers* was reported out of print in 1987.

The New American Encyclopedia: A Treasury of Information on the Sciences, the Arts, Literature, and General Knowledge. Philadelphia: The Publishers Agency, Inc., 1973. 20 vols. Last priced at $133.00.

This encyclopedia had a complex and at times arcane history. Its oldest known ancestor was apparently the *Teacher's and Pupil's Cyclopaedia*, a four-volume set published in 1902; this work became the *New Teacher's and Pupil's Cyclopaedia* when it expanded to five volumes in 1910. Between 1923 and 1927, the encyclopedia also appeared in 10 volumes as the *International Reference Work*. In 1928, its title changed again, this time to the *Progressive Reference Library*, which in turn became the *World Scope Encyclopedia* in 1945. The latter continued in existence until 1963, but during this period it was also issued as the *New World Family Encyclopedia* and the *Standard International Encyclopedia*, both supermarket items.

In 1964, the Publishers Company—later the Publishers Agency—acquired the rights to the *World Scope Encyclopedia*. With practically no revision, *World Scope* was forthwith retitled and sold as the *New American Encyclopedia*, the *World Educator Encyclopedia*, and the *World University Encyclopedia*. A two-volume abridgment also appeared under the old supermarket title *Standard International Encyclopedia*. In 1968, the Publishers Agency decided to create a new and improved edition of the encyclopedia under just one title—the *New American Encyclopedia*.

In an effort to place the *New American Encyclopedia* on a par with such better known and more highly regarded sets as WORLD BOOK ENCYCLOPEDIA and COMPTON'S ENCYCLOPEDIA, the publisher undertook an extensive analysis of seven competing encyclopedias. If at least four of the seven covered a topic, it was automatically included in the new and expanded *New American Encyclopedia*. That set, which appeared in 1973, contained roughly 5.5 million words, 7,500 pages, 27,000 articles, and 9,000 illustrations in 20 volumes.

But despite the publisher's imitative approach and best intentions, the resulting encyclopedia proved to be a palpably inferior work; viewed charitably, it achieved only a minimum level of respectability. Deficiencies included coverage frequently devoid of necessary detail and depth, articles that too often were sadly out-of-date, a choppy and disjointed writing style, numerous errors in the text ranging from glaring typographical mistakes to major factual inaccuracies, and poor access to the set's contents due to a muddled system of cross-references and lack of a general index. In addition, the publisher and/or distributors sometimes used misleading and deceptive advertising to promote the set. As far as is known, the *New American Encyclopedia* is out of print today, but exactly when it ceased publication cannot be pinpointed.

The New Caxton Encyclopedia. 5th ed. London, England: Caxton Publications Ltd., 1979. 20 vols. Last priced at $485.00.

First published as a set (in 18 volumes) in 1966, the British-made *New Caxton Encyclopedia* originally appeared in Great Britain under the title *Purnell's New English Encyclopedia*, a "part-work" issued in 216 weekly supplements, or parts, between 1965 and 1969. The encyclopedia, edited by Bernard Workman, actually grew out of a co-production project involving Caxton Publications and the Istituto Geografico de Agostini, an Italian firm internationally known for its excellent graphics, particularly in the area of cartography. The idea was to produce a richly illustrated general multivolume encyclopedia that could be adapted for various national markets. A second edition of the *New Caxton* appeared in 1969, followed by a third (expanded to 20 volumes) in 1973, and a fourth in 1977. In 1979, the fifth—and thus far the last—edition was published.

The 1979 edition of the *New Caxton* contained approximately six million words, 6,500 pages, 13,000 articles, and 17,000 illustrations, almost all in color and of outstanding quality. Indeed, the illustrations, which included more than 3,000 handsome reproductions of paintings and other works of art, were among the best ever to grace the pages of a general English-language encyclopedia. The publisher used an expensive grade of heavy coated art paper to achieve the highest quality color reproduction possible. Interestingly, the weight of the paper rendered the volumes, which were quite thin, very heavy, each one weighing well over three pounds.

The rest of the encyclopedia was not so impressive, its printed text no match for the illustrations. Specifically, the set's coverage was heavily biased in favor of Western Europe in general and Great Britain in particular; its contents were not always as up-to-date as might have been expected; and access to those contents was unsatisfactory due to a lack of cross-references and a quite poor index. Frances Neel Cheney, in a review of the *New Caxton* in *American Reference Books Annual* (1979, p. 37), put the set in good perspective: "In spite of the many well-chosen illustrations, so well reproduced, the average American library will find the subject matter more fully covered in the standard American encyclopedias."

Over the years, a number of North American distributors sold the *New Caxton Encyclopedia* in the United States and Canada, but today, except perhaps for the odd set or two, it is out of print on this side of the Atlantic. A new (sixth) edition was tentatively scheduled for sometime in the 1980s, but it never came about. Whether Caxton Publications and its parent company, the huge British Printing Corporation (which owns the rights to the set), will eventually invest the resources necessary to bring the encyclopedia up to speed is anyone's guess at this point. What is certain is that the cost of a thoroughgoing revision of an encyclopedia as large as the *New Caxton* becomes more and more formidable with each passing year—which makes such a revision less and less likely.

New Century Book of Facts: A Handbook of Ready Reference. New York: Continental Publishing Company, 1909–64. 1,841p. Last priced at $14.50.

Similar in purpose and design to the LINCOLN LIBRARY OF ESSENTIAL INFORMATION (see above) and the VOLUME LIBRARY, this hefty, single-volume, topically arranged encyclopedia for home and office encompassed about two million words, 1,800 pages, 7,500 discernible entries, and 2,000 illustrations, most in black and white. It began life in 1902 as the *Century Book of Facts*. Seven years later it became the *New Century Book of Facts*, under which title it appeared in periodic new editions until 1964. The publisher scheduled a much needed revision for 1972, but it failed to materialize and soon thereafter the book went out of print. The *New Century Book of Facts* was never considered a first-rate encyclopedia and toward the end it became terribly dated.

The New College Encyclopedia. New York: Galahad Press. (a subsidiary of Ottenheimer Publishers), 1978. 960p. Last priced at $19.95.

Advertised as "brand new" in the September 1, 1978, issue of *Booklist* (p. 71), the one-volume *New College Encyclopedia* no sooner hit the marketplace than it became a remainder item, selling for less than half its original price of $39.95. By 1980 it was out of print. The 960-page book contained about 20,000 brief A-to-Z entries accompanied by 300 full-color graphics of indifferent quality. Published by Galahad Press, an imprint of Ottenheimer Publishers of Baltimore, the encyclopedia most likely derived from the NEW UNIVERSITY ONE-VOLUME ENCYCLOPEDIA (see below), also an Ottenheimer property.

New Golden Encyclopedia. New York: Golden Press. (a division of Western Publishing Company), 1963. 155p. Last priced at $5.00.

Written by Jane Werner Watson, who also produced the similar MY FIRST GOLDEN ENCYCLOPEDIA (see above), this brief and simple encyclopedia for beginning readers consisted of 155 colorfully illustrated pages. It was a revision of Dorothy Agnes Bennett's *Golden Encyclopedia*, published in 1946. The *New Golden Encyclopedia* disappeared from the market in the mid-1970s.

New Human Interest Library. Chicago: Books, Inc. (a subsidiary of the Publishers Company), 1928–68. 7 vols. Last priced at $67.50.

An inferior reference work, this encyclopedia was originally published in 1914 as the *Human Interest Library*. In 1928, the publisher added "New" to the title. Topically arranged by broad subject areas, the seven-volume set comprised about 1.5 million words, 2,800 pages, 10,000 entries, and 3,000 illustrations. The final printing (1968) carried the imprint of the International Book Corporation, a Miami (Florida) distributor. The *New Human Interest Library* was reported out of print in 1972.

The New Illustrated Columbia Encyclopedia. Garden City, NY: Rockville House Publishers, Inc., 1978–80; dist. by Time-Life Books. 24 vols. Last priced at $69.75.

The 24-volume *New Illustrated Columbia Encyclopedia*, published in 1978 and again in 1980 for the supermarket trade and sold via mail order by Time-Life Books, was an expanded version of the one-volume *New Columbia Encyclopedia* (1975), an earlier edition of the erudite COLUMBIA ENCYCLOPEDIA. Aside from their titles and number of volumes, the basic difference between the *New Columbia Encyclopedia* and the *New Illustrated Columbia Encyclopedia* concerned illustrations, the former having only 659, all in black and white, whereas the latter included some 5,000, many in color. Otherwise the text of the two works was practically the same.

The *New Illustrated Columbia Encyclopedia* contained 6.5 million words, 7,522 pages, 50,515 articles, and, as mentioned, 5,000 illustrations. Unfortunately, the illustrations—mostly photographs and art reproductions supplied by the Italian firm of Fratelli Fabbri Editori—were mediocre at best. Some were badly reproduced, being either muddy (if in color) or inordinately dark (if in black and white). Others added little or nothing to the informational content of the encyclopedia, often serving merely as bright or splashy space-fillers. Along these lines, some illustrations tended to be much larger than necessary, as in the case of an Andy Warhol silkscreen of Marilyn Monroe that inexplicably consumed nearly a whole page. In other instances, the illustrations were poorly placed in relation to the articles they complemented.

Augmenting the printed text of a high-quality one-volume encyclopedia with lots of colorful illustrations to create a multivolume set for student and family use sounds like a good idea, but in the case of the *New Illustrated Columbia Encyclopedia* its execution left much to be desired. The articles, written strictly for adults, were much too advanced and demanding for the encyclopedia's intended audience—advertisements described the set as the "right encyclopedia for your children"—and the illustrations added little except bulk. The *New Illustrated Columbia Encyclopedia* was declared out of print in 1985.

New Knowledge Library: Universal Reference Encyclopedia. London, England & Sydney, Australia: Bay Books Pty. Ltd., 1981. 35 vols. Last priced at $299.95.

A set of 35 thin volumes of 96 pages each, the *New Knowledge Library* encompassed approximately two million words, 3,350 pages, 3,000 articles, and 6,000 illustrations, almost all in color. Produced in Australia and distributed in North America by Farwell Promotional Books in Milwaukee, it catered to the reference needs of younger students and children ages 7–14. Although the encyclopedia proved to be reasonably accurate, clearly written, and appealingly illustrated, its coverage had a strong emphasis on topics of particular interest to Australian and New Zealand readers, such as places, people, and plants and animals of the region. In addition, access to the set's contents was hampered due to both a dearth of cross-references and a poorly constructed general index.

Farwell Promotional continued to sell the *New Knowledge Library* through the 1980s, but by 1992 a company representative reported that the set was "no longer available through us. I don't believe it is distributed by anyone in the U.S., and may be out of print in Australia."

The New Talking Cassette Encyclopedia. Mahwah, NJ: Troll Associates, 1984. 100 audiocassette tapes in 10 vols. (or albums). Last priced at $695.00.

As its title suggests, the *New Talking Cassette Encyclopedia* was published in audio rather than print form. It first appeared in 1971 as the *Talking Cassette Encyclopedia* and was reissued in a revised version 13 years later under the title *New Talking Cassette Encyclopedia*. Intended chiefly for classroom use at the kindergarten and elementary school levels, the encyclopedia consisted of 100 audiocassette tapes, each covering a different subject ("Africa," "Agriculture," "Air," "The American Revolution," etc.). Altogether, the set contained approximately 100,000 words, each tape averaging about 1,000 words, or 10 to 12 minutes of listening time. The tapes were arranged alphabetically by title in 10 "volumes," or albums, with access to specific information enhanced somewhat by a small printed index, called the "Cross-Reference Subject Guide."

The *New Talking Cassette Encyclopedia* provided only very selective coverage of the world's knowledge, emphasizing subjects frequently studied in North American elementary schools. By no stretch of the imagination was it considered a full-fledged encyclopedia for children. Rather, it served as an introductory work designed to acquaint young people with the idea of an encyclopedia while at the same time presenting basic factual information in an attention-getting manner. In the early 1990s, Troll Associates reported the encyclopedia out of print, with no immediate plans for reissue or a new edition.

The New Universal Family Encyclopedia. New York: Random House, 1985. 1,079p. Last priced at $34.95.

This one-volume encyclopedia—originally published in Great Britain in 1981 as the *Macmillan Encyclopedia*—appeared in North America in 1985 after being thoroughly "Americanized." It comprised roughly 1.5 million words, 25,000 concise articles, and 1,200 illustrations, all in black and white. Although useful for quick reference in the home, the encyclopedia lacked the scholarly authority and depth of such competing works as the *New Columbia Encyclopedia* (now the COLUMBIA ENCYCLOPEDIA) and the CONCISE COLUMBIA ENCYCLOPEDIA. A review in *Reference Books Bulletin* (in *Booklist*, June 15, 1986, p. 1506) pointed to other problems, noting that the *New Universal Family Encyclopedia*'s "most serious flaws concern recency and illustrative material, supposedly two of the advantages this work has over the *Concise Columbia Encyclopedia*, which is two years older . . . . In many of the photographs, especially those of animals, the subject is blurred or disappears into the background." By 1988, the encyclopedia was out of print.

New Universal Standard Encyclopedia. New York: Funk & Wagnalls, Inc., 1968. 3 vols. Last priced at $48.00.

Published in three excessively large and unwieldy volumes, the *New Universal Standard Encyclopedia* had exactly the same contents as the 25-volume *Funk & Wagnalls Standard Reference Encyclopedia* (1958–71), the immediate predecessor to FUNK & WAGNALLS NEW ENCYCLOPEDIA. The three volumes contained a total of seven million words, 4,060 pages, 30,000 mostly brief articles, and 1,820 illustrations, most in black and white. First sold by Funk & Wagnalls as a special direct-mail edition, the set was later distributed by American Plantations, Inc. of Hialeah, Florida. Eventually, American Plantations sold its remaining inventory of the encyclopedia—some 6,500 sets—to a secondhand bookstore in New York City. As far as is known the *New*

Universal Standard Encyclopedia was never reprinted and has been defunct for many years.

The New University One-Volume Encyclopedia. New York: Grosset & Dunlap, 1968. 830p. Last priced at $9.95.

Derived from the LITTLE AND IVES ILLUSTRATED READY REFERENCE ENCYCLOPEDIA (see above), a set of 20 slim, heavily illustrated volumes published in 1961 and sold in supermarkets, the *New University One-Volume Encyclopedia* contained well over one million words, 20,000 concise entries, and no illustrations. Hardly an outstanding encyclopedia but useful for quick reference in the home, the *New University One-Volume Encyclopedia* appeared only once (in 1968) before being discontinued in the mid-1970s, at which time rights to the book were held by Ottenheimer Publishers of Baltimore. In 1978, Ottenheimer published the NEW COLLEGE ENCYCLOPEDIA (see above); now also defunct, this one-volume encyclopedia had much the same dimensions and contents as the *New University One-Volume Encyclopedia*.

Our Wonderful World: An Encyclopedic Anthology for the Entire Family. New York: Grolier, 1955–72. 18 vols. Last priced at $189.50.

Conceived and edited by Dr. Herbert S. Zim, a noted writer of science books for young people, *Our Wonderful World* first appeared between 1955–57 under the imprint of Spencer Press, a subsidiary of Sears, Roebuck & Company, and for a time it was sold exclusively through the store's retail outlets and mail-order division. In 1961, Grolier, a major U.S. encyclopedia publisher, acquired the set, bringing out a new printing each year until the set's unexpected demise in 1972. Unlike many encyclopedias that have been discontinued over the last few decades, *Our Wonderful World* was genuinely lamented by those who know and appreciate quality reference works.

A fairly sizable set in 18 substantial volumes, the encyclopedia contained approximately 4.5 million words, 8,500 pages, 4,000 basic articles, and 16,000 illustrations, most in black and white. Its contents were topically arranged, organized by 30 broad areas of knowledge, and further subdivided into about 400 thematic units. As the subtitle indicates, the set included much material excerpted from previously published books, articles, pamphlets, and the like. Intended chiefly for young students in the elementary grades through high school, *Our Wonderful World* was an unusual and sometimes fascinating work. A review of the 1963 printing in *Library Journal* (September 15, 1964, p. 3504) put it in good perspective: "This set would not replace any of the good traditional 'ready reference' sets but does make an excellent and worthwhile supplementary set, one which grows on the user as he discovers its many facets."

Oxford Junior Encyclopaedia. London, England & New York: Oxford Univ. Press., 1948–76. 13 vols. Last priced at $189.00.

Widely regarded as one of the best postwar British encyclopedias for young people, the 13-volume *Oxford Junior Encyclopaedia* originally appeared volume-by-volume between 1948 and 1954. In the early 1960s, the publisher issued a second revised edition, and in the 1970s all volumes in the set were modestly updated and reissued in "corrected reprints." Unfortunately, no further revisions have occurred since that time, and the encyclopedia has been unavailable in the United States and Canada since the early 1980s; it has also apparently been phased out in Great Britain. In 1991, the publisher issued the OXFORD CHILDREN'S ENCYCLOPEDIA, a brand-new seven-volume set that effectively replaces *Oxford Junior.*

Despite its fine reputation and impressive authority, *Oxford Junior* never sold well in North America, due largely to its strong British orientation. For instance, information about Santa Claus was found in the article "Father Christmas" and the U.S. Congress was described as a "national parliament." On the plus side, the set proved to be reliable, well-illustrated, and attractively produced. Like OUR WONDERFUL WORLD (see above), *Oxford Junior* was topically arranged, each volume devoted to a broad subject and edited by a specialist. The writing style varied from volume to volume, but in almost all instances the quality of writing remained at a high level—perhaps too high a level for many young people in North America.

Pears Cyclopaedia: A Book of Background Information and Reference for Everyday Use. London, England: Pelham Books Ltd., 1897–. 1,050p. Last priced at $14.95.

The single-volume *Pears Cyclopaedia* has been published continuously on an annual basis in Great Britain since Queen Victoria's Diamond Jubilee in 1897, when it first appeared as *Pears' Shilling Cyclopaedia.* Named for its patron and original publisher, Pears soap, the encyclopedia was an immediate success with the Victorian reading public. Then, as now, it provided an inexpensive desk-sized compendium of both practical and exotic reference information for adults and older students. Also, since 1961, a young people's version of *Pears* has been published under the title JUNIOR PEARS ENCYCLOPAEDIA (see above).

Today, *Pears* continues to be a popular annual in the United Kingdom, a cross between an encyclopedia and an almanac or yearbook. Topically arranged under 18 broad headings, the volume contains about one million words, 1,000 pages, 15,000 articles, and only some 50 illustrations, including a 36-page color world atlas in the middle of the book. Its focus tends to be on current as opposed to retrospective information, with developments in the United Kingdom and the Commonwealth heavily emphasized. From the standpoint of North Americans, *Pears* is altogether too British to be a first-choice reference source, but it is interesting to read and browse through.

Both *Pears* and JUNIOR PEARS have been distributed off and on in North America over the years (most recently by Viking Penguin Inc.), but at present neither is available in the United States or Canada. This situation, however, could change at any time should the publisher, Pelham Books, find a distributor for its products on this side of the Atlantic. Likewise, interested consumers are free to order either or both of the *Pears* books directly from England (contact Michael Joseph and Pelham Books, 27 Wrights Lane, London W8 5TZ, England) or through a foreign book dealer. For a delightful history of *Pears Cyclopaedia,* see Mary-Kay Wilmers' article "Onward and Upward with the Arts: Next to Godliness" in the *New Yorker,* October 8, 1979, pp. 145–63).

Penguin Encyclopedia. New York: Penguin Books, 1966. 647p. Last priced at $2.25 paperbound.

This modestly priced one-volume paperback encyclopedia originally appeared in Great Britain in 1965 and was published in North America a year later. Edited by Sir John Summerscale, it was a work of indifferent quality with strong emphasis on British history and culture. A review in *Choice* (July–August 1966, p. 398) concluded, "The material is clearly presented but this book cites no authorities, does not properly vindicate its claim to contemporaneity, and offers no bibliographies." The encyclopedia went out of print in the early 1970s.

Picture Encyclopedia for Children. 2nd ed. New York: Grosset & Dunlap, 1987. 380p. Last priced at $19.95.

Edited by John Paton, a prolific producer of children's reference sources, the single-volume *Picture Encyclopedia for Children* first appeared in Great Britain in 1982 and then in a revised (second) edition in 1987. It was this revision that Grosset & Dunlap published in North America that same year. Intended for young readers ages 7–12, the encyclopedia contained about 180,000 words, 380 pages, 1,500 brief A-to-Z articles, and 700 illustrations, almost all in color. Much of the text was derived from FINDING OUT: SILVER BURDETT'S CHILDREN'S ENCYCLOPEDIA (see above), also edited by Paton and also now out of print. The *Picture Encyclopedia for Children* presented basic facts in a readable, attractive manner, but its coverage tended to overemphasize scientific and technical topics at the expense of the humanities and social sciences. The encyclopedia—reported out of print in early 1993—may possibly be encountered as a remainder item in discount and secondhand bookstores for the next few years or so.

Pictured Knowledge: The Full-Color Illustrated Encyclopedia for the Family. New York: Little and Ives, 1956–58. 14 vols. Last priced at $13.36.

A profusely illustrated reference set intended chiefly for young people, *Pictured Knowledge* first appeared as early as 1916 in two volumes under the imprint of the old Compton-Johnson Company of Chicago. By 1939 it had grown to 10 volumes. After a lengthy period of being out of print, the encyclopedia reappeared between 1956 and 1958 in 14 volumes, published by Little and Ives, a New York firm. Sold in supermarkets in North America, the topically arranged set contained an estimated three million words, 3,500 pages, 1,600 articles, and 4,000 illustrations, many full-page color photographs.

Unfortunately, the illustrations were generally of inferior quality, the case with most supermarket encyclopedias. In addition, *Pictured Knowledge* lacked a satisfactory index, a problem compounded by the set's topical arrangement. A review by the Subscription Books Committee of the American Library Association published in *Booklist* (December 1, 1959, p. 202) summarized the set's major problems: "Because the material in *Pictured Knowledge* is uneven in quality and range of subject, because the material is poorly arranged and the text is too brief, because many of the illustrations are poorly reproduced, and because the Index is so inadequate, it is not recommended for home, school, or library." *Pictured Knowledge* disappeared from the North American scene in the mid-1960s.

Pocket Encyclopedia. New York: Random House, 1989. 286p. Last priced at $7.95.

Prepared by Jack Adrienne, this small paperbound encyclopedia for children in the elementary grades encompassed approximately 100,000 words, 600 articles, and 650 illustrations in 286 pages. It was published in 1989 and went out of print three years later. A work of acceptable quality, the *Pocket*

Encyclopedia provided clear, basic articles comprehensible to youngsters ages 8–12, but the illustrations were mediocre. As Mary Hartman pointed out in a review in *American Reference Books Annual* (1991, p. 14), "Illustrations are abundant but vary widely in quality. Some of the charts and diagrams are excellent, but the reproductions of black-and-white photographs are dark and dim."

Purnell's First Encyclopedia in Colour. Maidenhead, Berkshire, England: Purnell & Sons Ltd., 1974. 125p. Last priced at $6.95.

Purnell's First Encyclopedia in Colour was a quite small one-volume British-made encyclopedia of little consequence. Edited by the late Michael W. Dempsey, a prolific producer of children's reference books in Great Britain, the book included no introductory matter whatsoever but was clearly intended as a beginning (or first) encyclopedia for preschoolers and youngsters in the primary grades. It contained only about 50,000 words, 300 articles, and 500 illustrations (all in color) in 125 pages. The encyclopedia appeared to be a spin-off of the HARVER JUNIOR WORLD ENCYCLOPEDIA, a multivolume set also edited by Dempsey and now also defunct (see above). The book was distributed in North America by Pergamon Press and its subsidiary, the British Book Centre, until the mid-1980s when it went out of print.

Purnell's Pictorial Encyclopedia. Maidenhead, Berkshire, England: Purnell & Sons Ltd., 1979. 192p. Last priced at $19.95.

Similar in many respects to the JUNIOR ENCYCLOPEDIA OF GENERAL KNOWLEDGE (see above), the one-volume *Purnell's Pictorial Encyclopedia* contained 75,000 words, 192 pages, 88 articles (all two-page spreads), and 550 illustrations, most in black and white. It was produced in Great Britain, edited by Theodore Rowland-Entwistle and Jean Cooke, a husband-and-wife team responsible for a number of children's reference books, including the WORLD ALMANAC INFOPEDIA and the aforementioned JUNIOR ENCYCLOPEDIA OF GENERAL KNOWLEDGE. Intended for students in the upper elementary and junior high school grades, the encyclopedia included some interesting material, written in an admirably clear style, but the coverage was far too selective for the book to be much more than a supplementary source of information. *Purnell's Pictorial Encyclopedia* was distributed in North America by Pergamon Press, which reported the book out of print in 1987.

The Quick Reference Handbook: Basic Knowledge and Modern Technology. Nashville, TN:

Varsity Company (a division of Thomas Nelson, Inc.), 1987. 895p. Last priced at $49.95.

An inferior reference work that competed head-to-head with the VOLUME LIBRARY and the recently discontinued LINCOLN LIBRARY OF ESSENTIAL INFORMATION (see above), this one-volume encyclopedia for adults and older students first appeared as the *Complete Reference Handbook* in 1964; later, it became the *Quick Reference Encyclopedia* (1976), then the *Quick Reference Handbook of Basic Knowledge* (1979), and most recently the *Quick Reference Handbook: Basic Knowledge and Modern Technology* (1987). Although the *Quick Reference Handbook* was reported out of print in 1993, it will almost surely reappear at some point under that title or some similar variation.

The *Quick Reference Handbook* was topically arranged, the contents grouped by subject under 22 sections, or chapters, such as "The English Language," "Authors and Their Works," "American History," "Chemistry," "Western Art," and "The Business World." Overall, the encyclopedia contained roughly 750,000 words, 5,000 individual entries, and 600 illustrations (almost all in black and white) in 895 pages. Regrettably, the book's coverage was highly selective and badly out of balance, with whole areas of knowledge ignored or treated only cursorily. For instance, health and medicine, economics, sociology and anthropology, the performing arts, and computer science were among the subjects neglected in the 1987 edition. In addition, the book's contents were not always accurate nor easily accessible, and its illustrations were of poor quality.

Raintree Children's Encyclopedia. Milwaukee: Raintree Publishers, 1988. 11 vols. Last priced at $180.00 hardcover; $109.45 paperbound.

This attractive, British-made multivolume encyclopedia for young people has been published in Great Britain in three editions (1974, 1980, and 1986) as the *Macmillan Children's Encyclopedia.* The first two editions were not published in the United States or Canada, but the third did appear in North America in 1988 under the title *Raintree Children's Encyclopedia* (which was designated as a fourth edition by the publisher). The encyclopedia consisted of 10 topical volumes—*People, Animals, Plants, The Earth and Beyond, Countries and Customs,* etc.—containing a total of approximately 250,000 words, 1,000 pages, 700 individual entries, and 1,000 colorful illustrations; the final volume comprised an index to the set.

By far, the encyclopedia's best feature was its illustrations, which proved to be attractive, infor-mative, and clearly reproduced. The articles were usually written in a readable and interesting manner, but coverage tended to be spotty and treatment oversimplified. A review in *Reference Books Bulletin* (in *Booklist,* September 1, 1988, p. 55) summed up this criticism: "Children will enjoy reading about familiar topics, and readers introduced to something here might be motivated to learn more about it, though there are no bibliographies. But the child who approaches *Raintree Children's Encyclopedia* with something specific to look up may very well be disappointed. Even if the item is included and can be accessed through the index, the coverage is likely to be superficial."

In 1993, a representative of Raintree Steck-Vaughn Publishers in Austin, Texas (successor to Raintree Publishers of Milwaukee) reported that the *Raintree Children's Encyclopedia* "is out of print and out of stock, and we do not anticipate bringing it back to the market." In all likelihood, a new edition of the *Macmillan Children's Encyclopedia* will be published in due course in Great Britain, but whether it will be distributed in North America (and, if so, under what title) is not known at this time.

Rand McNally Student Encyclopedia in Color. Chicago: Rand McNally, 1972. 544p. Last priced at $7.95.

The *Rand McNally Student Encyclopedia in Color,* a topically arranged single-volume item for students in the upper elementary and junior high school grades, was originally published in Great Britain as the *Hamlyn Children's Encyclopedia in Colour,* a companion to the smaller HAMLYN YOUNGER CHILDREN'S ENCYCLOPEDIA (see above). Kenneth Bailey edited both works. The *Rand McNally Student Encyclopedia* encompassed roughly 250,000 words, 800 individual entries, and 1,000 color illustrations in its 544 pages. The book had limited value as an encyclopedic source of information, largely because of its superficial coverage and inadequate cross-references and index. Rand McNally phased out the encyclopedia in the late 1970s.

Rand McNally's Children's Encyclopedia. Chicago: Rand McNally, 1977. 61p. Last priced at $4.95.

First published in Great Britain in 1976 as *Ward Lock's Children's Encyclopedia,* this small encyclopedia for children ages 7–12 appeared in North America the following year as *Rand McNally's Children's Encyclopedia.* The 61-page book, which was edited by John Paton, a well-known creator of children's reference materials in England, contained only 15,000 words, 27 articles (all two-page spreads), and 300 illustrations, all in color. Its contents, which emphasized scientific and technical subjects, were too limited in scope to be considered truly encyclopedic, and what coverage there was tended to lack detail. In short, this small volume possessed little real reference value, although it served a browsing function. The publisher reported it out of print in 1986.

Richards Topical Encyclopedia. New York: Grolier, Inc., 1939–62. 15 vols. Last priced at $129.50.

As its title makes clear, *Richards Topical Encyclopedia* was arranged topically (or by subject) rather than alphabetically. For instance, volume 13 consisted of biographies of famous philosophers (Descartes, Hume, Kant, etc.) and classical writers (Aeschylus, Cicero, Homer, Horace, Ovid, etc.). The set, intended for young people in the elementary and junior high school grades, first appeared in 1933 in 12 volumes under the title *Richards Cyclopedia,* published by the J.A. Richards Company of New York. Six years later it was revised, enlarged to 15 volumes, and retitled *Richards Topical Encyclopedia.* In the mid-1940s, Grolier, a leading North American encyclopedia publisher, acquired the Richards Company and continued to publish the encyclopedia until 1962, when it was discontinued. At this point the 15-volume set contained about four million words, 8,600 pages, 5,000 individual entries, and 900 illustrations.

In the late 1950s, before *Richards Topical Encyclopedia* went out of print, the H.S. Stuttman Company, by arrangement with Grolier, combined the set with the GROLIER ENCYCLOPEDIA (see above), another multivolume Grolier product on the brink of extinction, to create a rather strange amalgam called the UNIFIED ENCYCLOPEDIA, a 30-volume set published briefly between 1960 and 1964 (see next entry). Also, in 1963, a Spanish-language adaptation of *Richards Topical Encyclopedia* entitled *Nueva Enciclopedia Temática* appeared in Mexico and South America; it, too, is defunct today.

Unified Encyclopedia: A Modern Reference Library of Unified Knowledge for the Parent, Student and Young Reader. New York: Unified Encyclopedia Press. (an imprint of the H.S. Stuttman Company), 1960–64. 30 vols. Last priced at $159.50.

This short-lived and entirely unsuccessful encyclopedia represented a merging of two quite different—and dated—general encyclopedias published by Grolier, a major North American producer of encyclopedias. Specifically, the H.S. Stuttman Company, by arrangement with Grolier, brought together the text of the alphabetically arranged GROLIER ENCYCLOPEDIA (see above), an adult encyclopedia, and the topically arranged RICHARDS TOPICAL ENCYCLOPEDIA (see above), a young people's encyclopedia, to create the *Unified Encyclopedia,* a hybrid work of some six million words, 10,000 pages, 32,500 entries, and 9,000 illustrations in 30 volumes. The encyclopedia first appeared in 1960 and it came as no surprise when the set was withdrawn from the market only a few years later.

The Universal World Reference Encyclopedia. Chicago: Consolidated Book Publishers, 1945–70. 16 vols. Last priced at $199.50.

The *Universal World Reference Encyclopedia* traced its undistinguished origins back to the *Standard American Encyclopedia* (1910–41), a multivolume set that ultimately reached 15 volumes. In 1942, the encyclopedia was revised and reissued as the *International World Reference Encyclopedia* in 10 volumes. Three years later it was reprinted as the *Universal World Reference Encyclopedia,* said to be "20 volumes in 10." In 1958, the editors produced a revised edition in 16 volumes, which encompassed more than four million words, 6,000 pages, 30,000 entries, and 6,500 illustrations, practically all in black and white. The encyclopedia was intended for adults and older students, from junior high school up.

The *Universal World Reference Encyclopedia* was never considered anything more than a second-rate encyclopedia. Bohdan Wynar, in a review of the 1970 (and final) revision in *American Reference Books Annual* (1971, p. 68), found the work, on the whole, "rather disappointing . . . . In most cases the presentation is rather pedestrian, and the quality of illustrations in the text is poor." The Subscription Books Committee of the American Library Association, in its last review of the encyclopedia (in *Booklist,* April 1, 1965, p. 722), likewise found the set wanting: "Because of the lack of authority as evidenced by unsigned articles and the preponderance of contributors who are public relations personnel, the inconsistency and inadequacy in revision and updating, and the uneven and partially out-of-date bibliography, *The Universal World Reference Encyclopedia* is not recommended."

The publisher, Consolidated Book Publishers, had promised a major revision of the *Universal World* in 1970 but produced much less. Soon thereafter, Consolidated scheduled another major revision for 1974, but that date came and went with no revision of any kind. Finally, in 1975, a company representative reported the encyclopedia had been discontinued, with no plans to rejuvenate it.

Wonderland of Knowledge. Lake Bluff, IL: Publishers Productions (a subsidiary of United Educators, Inc.), 1937–73. 12 vols. Last priced at $129.50.

A clearly and simply written 12-volume encyclopedia for children ages 7–14, *Wonderland of Knowledge* contained over three million words, 6,000 pages, some 6,000 alphabetically arranged articles, and 7,500 illustrations, most in color. The set's best features were its easy-to-read text and many bright illustrations. In promotional material the publisher proclaimed *Wonderland* a "unique pictorial encyclopedia" and boasted of "More than 750 new illustrations PLUS more than 150 new living color picture pages (over 5,000 color pictures in all) to captivate the student (and even the comic-book addict) in every curriculum area." As this advertisement suggests, article selection was keyed to North American school curricula.

Although not an outstanding work, *Wonderland of Knowledge* proved to be a quite satisfactory reference source for young people, especially slower students who found the simple writing style and emphasis on pictorial matter appealing. In 1975, the publisher—which also at the time produced the now defunct AMERICAN EDUCATOR (see above)—reported that the set was undergoing a complete overhaul, with an entirely new edition expected in two or three years. For whatever reason, the new edition never appeared and by the end of the decade *Wonderland of Knowledge* had disappeared from the market.

World Wide Encyclopedia. New York: Books, Inc. (a subsidiary of the Publishers Company), 1967. 10 vols. Last priced at $21.95 paperbound.

An inferior, cheaply made work sold in supermarkets and by mail order, the *World Wide Encyclopedia* comprised 10 pocket-sized volumes containing about two million words, 3,200 pages, 20,000 concise entries, and 1,000 illustrations. The encyclopedia, published in both hardcover and paperback editions, was also offered as a premium by various merchandisers. In this and other respects, it resembled WEBSTER'S FAMILY ENCYCLOPEDIA, currently available in an inexpensive 10-volume paperback edition and widely distributed as a premium. The *World Wide Encyclopedia* ceased publication sometime in the mid-1970s.

Young People's Illustrated Encyclopedia. Chicago: Children's Press., 1972. 20 vols. Last priced at $69.95.

This mediocre encyclopedia for elementary school students in grades 3–6 contained roughly 800,000 words, 2,000 pages, 1,600 entries, and 3,500 illustrations, most in color. The set was similar in some ways to the MODERN CENTURY ILLUSTRATED ENCYCLOPEDIA (see above), a 24-volume work now also out of print. McGraw-Hill Far Eastern Press, located in Singapore, prepared both encyclopedias, both encyclopedias employed some of the same editorial staff, and both included some of the same illustrations. But there was little similarity between the text of the two, with the MODERN CENTURY ILLUSTRATED ENCYCLOPEDIA clearly the superior work.

The *Young People's Illustrated Encyclopedia* received less than enthusiastic reviews in North America. Christine Wynar, writing in *American Reference Books Annual* (1973, p. 109), offered a lukewarm endorsement: "While this reference work can never replace a standard encyclopedia such as *World Book*, it can be useful in special situations where additional material on an easy reading level is needed." The Reference and Subscription Books Review Committee of the American Library Association, on the other hand, found little good to say about the encyclopedia: "The producers of *Young People's Illustrated Encyclopedia* fail to meet the curriculum needs of children in grades three to six. It is of extremely limited usefulness. Articles are insufficient in number. They are also inadequate and too brief in coverage. Though profuse, the illustrations are mediocre and often useless for explicating the text or for identification purposes. The finding devices are largely inadequate. Not recommended." (*Booklist*, June 15, 1974, p. 1116).

In 1975, Children's Press, the North American publisher, reported the *Young People's Illustrated Encyclopedia* "temporarily" out of print, but later it was sold via mail order by Parents' Magazine Book Clubs, Inc. in New York. In 1977, a Children's Press representative stated that the encyclopedia was "definitely out of print and will not be reprinted or revised."

Young World: A Child's First Encyclopedia. New York: Random House, 1992. 6 vols. Last priced at $60.00.

Originally published in Great Britain by Kingfisher Books, *Young World* consisted of six thematically arranged volumes of 125 pages each: "All Kinds of Animals," "How Things Are Made," "My Body," "On the Move," "Our Planet Earth," and "Plants." The colorfully illustrated set, which came and went very quickly, was intended for children ages 4–8.

Subject and Foreign Encyclopedias

. . . .

Subject Encyclopedias

✻ ✻ ✻ ✻ ✻ ✻ ✻ ✻

OVERVIEW

In addition to the many general encyclopedias described and evaluated in the pre ceding pages, there are literally thousands of subject encyclopedias available to North American consumers on all manner of topics ranging from pottery to popular music, from metallurgy to gardening, from sex to witchcraft. You name it, and there is probably an encyclopedia about it.

In recent years, publication of subject (or specialized) encyclopedias has far outstripped general encyclopedias in terms of both quantity and quality. This unprecedented outpouring of subject encyclopedias and similar reference works reflects the irresistible human urge toward specialization—hardly a remarkable or unexpected development, considering the incalculable amount of knowledge and information generated since the beginning of recorded history and particularly during the last five hundred years thanks to the advent of the printing press and, now, computer technology.

In the twentieth century, the "information explosion," wherein information and data are said to be doubling approximately every 10 years, has naturally encouraged people to hone in on and master ever smaller, narrower specialties rather than attempt to become proficient in a wide variety of subjects. The day of the so-called "Renaissance man"—a person conversant in all significant areas of knowledge—has long gone.

Today's publishers of reference works closely follow intellectual and societal trends and are well aware of the relentless tendency toward specialization. In response, they are investing heavily in the development of encyclopedias and related sources designed to meet society's demand for specific (as opposed to general) knowledge and information. As one experienced hand recently put it, "What's happening in encyclopedias is not unlike what's happening in other media, with publishers staking out targeted niches." (Quoted from "Tomes Devoted to Suicide, Sex and the South" in the *New York Times*, May 28, 1989, p. 15-F.) In a similar vein, Bill Katz, an authority on reference materials, points out in his *Basic Information Sources* (6th ed., 1992, p. 265), "The reasoning of publishers and producers is that it is no longer possible or profitable to reach out to everyone. The best approach is to prepare a work for a select group, normally a group with both a high interest in the subject and medium-to-high income to purchase the book."

The general encyclopedia obviously remains a very useful and effective reference tool for large numbers of people. Students especially find it helpful because it covers all areas of knowledge, albeit superficially. But for scholars and professional people, an encyclopedia dedicated entirely to their field or area of interest or expertise is often preferable because of its deeper treatment and greater authority. Similarly, in a home where parents and children have a particular bent, say a strong interest in the natural world, the acquisition of a substantial subject encyclopedia might well be a better buy than a general encyclopedia. Or an English major at college might find a subject encyclopedia devoted to world or American literature considerably more useful than a general encyclopedia, which accords Ibsen and Poe only a paragraph or two. Ideally, of course, consumers should have ready access to both general and subject encyclopedias. But when a choice must be made, it is important to know what is available.

This section of *Kister's Best Encyclopedias* provides descriptive and critical information about more than 800 subject encyclopedias, with emphasis on standard works and the best of the newer titles. Most of the encyclopedias reviewed or mentioned are currently in print and can be acquired through retail bookstores, book wholesalers, or directly from the publisher or distributor. (See Appendix B for addresses and telephone numbers of publishers and distributors.)

The encyclopedias in this section are grouped under 30 broad subjects:

- Art (General), Architecture, and Photography
- Astronomy and Space Science
- Biology and Animal Life
- Botany and Horticulture
- Business, Economics, and Statistics
- Chemistry and Chemical Engineering
- Computer and Electronic Sciences
- Decorative Arts and Antiques
- Earth, Energy, and Environmental Sciences
- Education and Libraries
- Engineering and Building Construction
- Film, Radio, Television, and Mass Communications
- Food, Nutrition, and Agriculture
- Geography and Area Studies
- Health, Medicine, and Drugs
- History and Archaeology
- Law and the Judicial System
- Literature, Language, and Publishing
- Military Science and History
- Music
- Physics and Mathematics
- Political Science and Government
- Psychology, Psychiatry, and Parapsychology
- Religion, Philosophy, and Mythology
- Science and Technology (General)
- Sexuality, Human Reproduction, and Child Care
- Social Science, Sociology, and Anthropology
- Sports and Games
- Theater and Dance
- Transportation

❊ ART (GENERAL), ARCHITECTURE, AND PHOTOGRAPHY ❊

American Shelter: An Illustrated Encyclopedia of the American Home. Written by Lester Walker. Overlook Press (dist. by Viking Penguin Inc.), 1981. 320p. $35.00 hardcover; $19.95 paperbound.

Presented in a popular style, this easy-to-use encyclopedia chronologically illustrates the various architectural styles found in North America from 300 A.D. to 1980. Nearly 100 different dwellings are depicted through floor plans, isometric drawings, and explanatory notes. The book, which first ap-

peared in 1981 and in a paperbound edition in 1993, is for those "who want to know, at a glance, the difference between Queen Anne and Second Empire" (*Choice*, March 1982, p. 898).

Artists' and Illustrators' Encyclopedia. Written by John Quick. 2nd ed. McGraw-Hill, 1977. 327p. Out of print (last priced at $32.95).

Intended for working visual artists of all kinds (professional, student, or amateur), Quick's compact, practical encyclopedia "covers materials, tools, techniques, terms, and formulas including those that do not work and those that do" (*Reference Books Bulletin* in *Booklist*, March 15, 1979, pp. 1180–81). Articles are arranged alphabetically from "Abating" to "Yellowing" and vary in length from a line or two to several paragraphs. Although currently out of print, a new (third) edition is expected at any time.

The Britannica Encyclopedia of American Art. Encyclopaedia Britannica Educational Corp., 1973. 669p. Out of print (last priced at $29.95).

This work, now 20 years old and unfortunately out of print, represents the first substantial encyclopedic survey of all important forms of American art, and to date it remains one of the best. The book includes approximately 1,100 entries, most signed by subject specialists, along with 835 illustrations, of which 350 are in full color. A similar but less comprehensive source is the single-volume *Dictionary of American Art* by Matthew Baigell (Harper & Row, 1979), which consists mainly of biographies of American artists but also includes articles on major trends and movements.

Dictionary of Subjects and Symbols in Art. Compiled by James Hall. 2nd ed. Harper & Row, 1979. 349p. $14.00 paperbound.

Alphabetical entries identify and explain the prominent mythological, religious, and literary themes and concepts found in Western art. Entries include figures from Greek and Roman mythology (e.g., Venus), animals associated with people (the lion and St. Jerome), and human phenomena and characteristics (inspiration; ignorance). *Choice* (March 1975, p. 48) described the first edition (1974) as "an impressively erudite yet thoroughly usable dictionary for which students and faculty alike should be grateful." Two comparable sources are Howard Daniel's *Encyclopedia of Themes and Subjects in Painting* (Abrams, 1971) and Gertrude Grace Sill's *Handbook of Symbols in Christian Art* (Macmillan, 1975).

Encyclopedia of American Architecture. Written by Robert T. Packard and Balthazar Korab. 2nd ed. McGraw-Hill, 1994. 630p. $89.50.

First published in 1980 and substantially revised in 1994, the *Encyclopedia of American Architecture* is a valuable introductory reference work for general readers and serious students. The more than 200 nontechnical A-to-Z articles that make up the encyclopedia treat architectural styles, types of buildings, construction materials, and important architects and designers. Black-and-white illustrations accompany most articles and there are some color plates. A review of the first edition in *Booklist* (December 15, 1980, p. 552) put the encyclopedia in good perspective: "Although not a dynamic work, it

is the only one of its kind on American architecture," an observation that holds true for the new edition.

The Encyclopedia of American Comics. Edited by Ron Goulart. Facts on File, 1990. 408p. $39.95 hardcover; $19.95 paperbound.

Although far from a complete record, the *Encyclopedia of American Comics* provides much information about the major comic strips, comic books, and their creators from the end of the nineteenth century to the 1980s. "It has clear reference value and would also be useful as a browsing item" (*Reference Books Bulletin* in *Booklist*, December 15, 1990, p. 881). Those interested in cartoon art will also want to check out the *World Encyclopedia of Comics* (Chelsea House, 1976) and the *World Encyclopedia of Cartoons* (Chelsea House, 1980), both two-volume sets edited by Maurice Horn and furnishing international coverage.

Encyclopedia of Architectural Technology: An Encyclopedic Survey of Changing Forms, Materials, and Concepts. Edited by Pedro Guedes. McGraw-Hill, 1979. 320p. $49.95.

Aimed at both the practitioner and student of architecture, this "handsome volume, with over 500 articles by authorities in the field, approaches architecture not as art, history, or monument but as technological development" (*Wilson Library Bulletin*, October 1979, p. 140). The volume, which contains over 800 illustrations, is international in scope and covers all periods.

Encyclopedia of Architecture: Design, Engineering & Construction. Edited by Joseph A. Wilkes & Robert T. Packard. Wiley, 1988–90. 5 vols. $850.00.

This recently published set is the best all-around architecture encyclopedia currently available. Containing approximately 500 articles complemented by 3,000 illustrations in a total of 4,000 pages, the set offers broad, up-to-date coverage of the field, including major architects, important firms, legal questions, and all significant types of architectural design, buildings, construction materials, and machinery. Sponsored by the prestigious American Institute of Architects and the work of nearly 600 highly qualified contributors, the set possesses impeccable authority. "What has been needed has been a comprehensive first-source encyclopedia on architectural processes and technology to at least get the architectural student or practitioner started in the right direction. This five-volume set seems to fill the bill" (*Choice*, November 1988, p. 458). Complementary sources include Henri Stierlin's two-volume *Encyclopedia of World Architecture* (Facts on File, 1977), which emphasizes floor plans of architectural monuments; the two-volume *International Dictionary of Architects and Architecture* (St. James Press, 1993), which features the work of more than 500 Western architects from ancient Greece to the present; the recently updated *Penguin Dictionary of Architecture* (4th ed., Penguin USA, 1991); and Fletcher Bannister's classic *History of Architecture* (Butterworth, 1987), now in its 19th edition, edited by John Musgrove.

Encyclopedia of Drawing: Materials, Techniques and Style. Written by Clive Ashwin. North Light (dist. by Writer's Digest), 1983. 264p. $22.50.

Intended for "anyone who draws or uses drawings for whatever purpose" (introduction), this well-illustrated encyclopedia covers the history, methods, materials, and vocabulary of drawing. "To those who love drawing and want to learn more about it, *Encyclopedia of Drawing* is a delightful book to consult" (*Reference Books Bulletin* in *Booklist*, September 1, 1984, p. 50). A similar work for painters is Frederick Palmer's *Encyclopedia of Oil Painting: Materials and Techniques* (North Light, 1984).

Encyclopedia of Practical Photography. Edited by John Carroll & William Broecker. Amphoto, 1977–78. 14 vols. Out of print (last priced at $159.95).

It is regrettable that this set is out of print (at least for the present), for it has been called "one of the most ambitious attempts ever made to get all of photography into one set of books" (*New York Times Book Review*, December 3, 1978, p. 84). Produced by the technical and editorial staffs of Eastman Kodak and Amphoto (short for the American Photographic Book Company), the alphabetically arranged encyclopedia furnishes comprehensive coverage of the art and science of photography for amateurs, hobbyists, professionals, teachers, and students—although, naturally, recent advances in photographic technology and techniques are lacking. Numerous color and black-and-white illustrations complement the printed text; there is an extensive index. A review in *Library Journal* (June 1, 1979, p. 1239) praised the set: "As a basic source and instructional guide for amateur photographers, this encyclopedia has no equal." Until a revised edition of the *Encyclopedia of Practical Photography* appears, those interested in photography will be well served by the new (third) edition of the FOCAL ENCYCLOPEDIA OF PHOTOGRAPHY.

The Encyclopedia of Sculpture Techniques. Written by John Mills. Watson-Guptill, 1990. 239p. $32.50.

Mills, a British sculptor, has produced a utilitarian encyclopedia that defines terms prominently associated with the art form, describes tools and techniques, and gives detailed information about such practical matters as formulas for patinas and charts for setting cement. Enhanced by more than 250 practical illustrations, the encyclopedia attempts to treat all types of sculpture, from conventional to experimental. "Mills's book will be of immediate value to budding sculptors at all levels of instruction, to individuals working independently, and to art librarians in need of definitions, formulas, and other technical information" (*American Reference Books Annual*, 1991, p. 417).

The Encyclopedia of Visual Art. Edited by Lawrence Gowing. Encyclopaedia Britannica Educational Corp., 1989. 10 vols. $279.00.

The first five volumes of this readable, handsomely illustrated encyclopedic set survey the history of world art from Paleolithic times to the present. Volumes 6–9 provide biographies of over 1,300 prominent artists; volume 9 also includes a useful glossary of terms. The tenth and final volume offers (1) substantial articles on special topics such as forgery in the art world, how to make the best use of art galleries, and photography as a visual art; (2) a directory of museums and galleries of the world; and (3) an index to the set that also includes thumbnail information on approximately 1,000 artists not covered in volumes 6–9. A comprehensive treatment of world art that comprises nearly a million words and 2,200 illustrations in 2,000 pages, the 10-volume *Encyclopedia of Visual Art* stands between the scholarly 15-volume ENCYCLOPEDIA OF WORLD ART, acknowledged by practically all critics to be the best art encyclopedia available, and the many good single-volume general art encyclopedias available, such as the OXFORD DICTIONARY OF ART. Two older five-volume sets that offer similar coverage are the *McGraw-Hill Dictionary of Art* (McGraw-Hill, 1969) and the *Praeger Encyclopedia of Art* (Praeger, 1971).

Encyclopedia of World Art. Publishers Guild (dist. by Jack Heraty & Associates, Inc.), 1959–68. 15 vols. plus two suppls., 1983; 1987. $1,495.00 (15-vol. set); $99.50 (ea. suppl.).

One of the finest subject encyclopedias ever made, the *Encyclopedia of World Art* was originally published as a joint international effort by the U.S. publisher McGraw-Hill and the Institute for Cultural Collaboration, an Italian agency established in Rome by the G.C. Sansoni Publishing Company of Florence and the Georgio Cini Foundation of Venice. Beautifully and profusely illustrated, it contains approximately 1,000 lengthy, authoritative articles covering the entire spectrum of the visual arts in all periods and countries. Each volume consists of printed text followed by a collection of black-and-white and color plates. In all, more than 16,000 works of art are reproduced in the encyclopedia. Happily, these illustrations are related directly to the text by cross-references and identification numbers and letters; a detailed index in Volume 15 further enhances access to specific information. The two supplements, which are chronologically arranged, update the original set. The *Encyclopedia of World Art* is "one of the greatest sources for expanding knowledge, interest, and understanding in art" (*Library Journal*, February 1, 1969, p. 532).

The Focal Encyclopedia of Photography. Edited by Leslie Stroebel & Richard D. Zakia. 3rd ed. Focal Press, 1993. 914p. $125.00.

Originally published in England in 1956 and revised in 1969 and again in 1993, this standard work is the only substantial photography encyclopedia currently in print. The new edition, which incorporates important recent developments in photographic technology, contains approximately 5,000 entries written by 90 experts from all over the world. Editors Stroebel and Zakia are affiliated with the Rochester Institute of Technology; Focal Press, an imprint of the British publisher Butterworth-Heinemann, has been producing quality professional books on photography for over half a century. While technically oriented, the encyclopedia is equally useful to amateur and professional photographers. "It would be hard to imagine a more complete one-volume work. An essential purchase" (*Choice*, December 1993, p. 584). Another authoritative one-volume encyclopedia on the subject is the *International Center of Photography Encyclopedia of Photography* (Crown, 1984), but unfortunately this fine work has been out of print for a number of years, as has the much esteemed multivolume ENCYCLOPEDIA OF PRACTICAL PHOTOGRAPHY.

Graphic Arts Encyclopedia. Written by George A. Stevenson; revised by William A. Pakan. 3rd ed. Design Press (dist. by TAB Books), 1992. 582p. $57.95.

The alphabetically arranged *Graphic Arts Encyclopedia* provides over 300 articles describing the processes, equipment, techniques, materials, and terms used in copy preparation and reproduction. First published in 1968 and revised in 1979 and most recently in 1992, the encyclopedia covers recent electronic and computer applications along with such standard information as tables showing metrics and their equivalents, paper sizes and weights, and paper cutting requirements. In a review in *American Reference Books Annual* (1993, p. 439), Joan Garner calls the work "a remarkable accomplishment, considering the complexity and extensiveness of the topic. It should prove a valuable source for students and artists out in the field while serving as a quick refresher tool for the professional."

Oxford Dictionary of Art. Edited by Ian Chilvers & Harold Osborne. Oxford Univ. Press, 1988. 576p. $49.95.

Styles, movements, artists, and specialized terms are briefly but authoritatively treated in this handy single-volume general art encyclopedia. All but 300 of the 3,000 entries first appeared in three older Oxford reference works edited by the late Harold Osborne—the *Oxford Companion to Art* (1970), the OXFORD COMPANION TO THE DECORATIVE ARTS (1975), and the *Oxford Companion to Twentieth Century Art* (1982)—but most have been updated and rewritten. Because of space limitations, the *Oxford Dictionary of Art* omits illustrations, bibliographies, and lengthy articles on art in individual countries. "What this dictionary sets out to do it does well; it will become a reference standard" (*American Reference Books Annual*, 1989, p. 363). A paperback spin-off is the somewhat smaller *Concise Oxford Dictionary of Art and Artists* (Oxford Univ. Press, 1990), also edited by Chilvers. Other useful one-volume art encyclopedias include Peter and Linda Murray's *Dictionary of Art and Artists* (3rd ed. Penguin, 1972), David Piper's *Random House Dictionary of Art and Artists* (Random House, 1990), and the *Thames and Hudson Dictionary of Art and Artists* (Thames and Hudson, 1985).

❆ ASTRONOMY AND SPACE SCIENCE ❆

The Astronomy and Astrophysics Encyclopedia. Edited by Stephen P. Maran. Van Nostrand, 1991. 1,002p. $89.95.

By far the most technical astronomy encyclopedia available today, this outstanding work consists of more than 400 authoritative, up-to-date, informatively illustrated articles prepared by leading experts in the field. Its only shortcoming is the index, which lacks sufficient detail. "This volume is now the premier encyclopedia of astronomy, is well worth its price, and should be considered for purchase by every academic and public library" (*Choice*, March 1992, p. 1037); "Aimed at educated laypeople, teachers, science writers, editors, and scientists, the encyclopedia provides the latest theories and data on the heavens, from the Earth's atmosphere to the farthest reaches of the known universe" (*American Reference Books Annual*, 1993, p. 711).

Astronomy from A to Z: A Dictionary of Celestial Objects and Ideas. Written by Charles A. Schweighauser. Sangamon State Univ., 1991. 192p. $14.95 paper.

This inexpensive paperback contains more than 100 brief essays based on previously published newspaper stories. Popularly written and well-illustrated with black-and-white drawings and photographs, the articles cover famous astronomers, constellations and planets, and important concepts in the field. "School and public libraries needing a popular dictionary of astronomy will find *Astronomy from A to Z* a very useful and attractive one. Amateur astronomers will want their own personal copy" (*Reference Books Bulletin* in *Booklist*, June 1, 1991, p. 1894).

The Cambridge Encyclopedia of Space. Edited by Michael Rycroft. Cambridge Univ. Press, 1990. 386p. $79.50.

Handsomely produced and admirably readable, the *Cambridge Encyclopedia of Space* provides the most comprehensive and up-to-date account of space exploration currently available. "This tour de force employs the skills of 100 authors from 13 countries to mold the definitive reference book for the general reader on all aspects of space" (*American Reference Books Annual*, 1992, p. 650). Other useful single-volume encyclopedias covering space are Kenneth Gatland's *Illustrated Encyclopedia of Space Technology* (2nd ed. Crown, 1990) and Bill Yenne's more specialized *Encyclopedia of U.S. Spacecraft* (Exeter Books, 1985), an A-to-Z catalog of all American spacecraft through the mid-1980s.

Encyclopedia of Astronomy and Astrophysics. Edited by Robert A. Meyers. Academic Press, 1989. 807p. $49.95.

This academically oriented (as opposed to popular) one-volume encyclopedia covers the field in a collection of 41 survey articles taken from the 15-volume ENCYCLOPEDIA OF PHYSICAL SCIENCE AND TECHNOLOGY. "The articles are solid expositions of technical topics written by specialists who do not hesitate to use mathematical and chemical equations to express their ideas, although the reader is spared the derivations of these equations" (*College & Research Libraries*, September 1989, p. 572). In many respects, the *Encyclopedia of Astronomy and Astrophysics* is similar to the ASTRONOMY AND ASTROPHYSICS ENCYCLOPEDIA, although it is less expensive, less current, and somewhat less technical.

Encyclopedia of Cosmology: Historical, Philosophical, and Scientific Foundations of Modern Cosmology. Edited by Norriss S. Hetherington. Garland, 1993. 686p. $125.00.

All relevant aspects of cosmology—the study of the origin and organization of the universe—are explored in this valuable new encyclopedia, which consists of signed A-to-Z entries ranging in length from a paragraph or so to 15 or more pages. James Rettig in *Wilson Library Bulletin* (October 1993, p. 86) notes, "With rare exception, the common reader can comprehend these clear explanations of abstruse, abstract concepts without mastery of mathematics." And J.R. Davidson in *Choice* (November 1993, p. 430) recommends the encyclopedia "to readers at all levels to fill the need for a multifaceted overview of the subject."

The Extraterrestrial Encyclopedia: Our Search for Life in Outer Space. Written by Joseph A. Angelo. Rev. ed. Facts on File, 1991. 240p. $40.00.

First published in 1985 and now in a revised edition, the *Extraterrestrial Encyclopedia* furnishes current information on space exploration, particularly as it relates to the search for life beyond the planet Earth. Sometimes quite technical in style and content, the entries cover space projects, missions, and observatories, as well as important people, events, and concepts. Another valuable work on the subject is Jerome Clark's in-progress *UFO Encyclopedia* (Omnigraphics, 1990–), which will eventually comprise three volumes, two of which have been published to date. A couple of older, more limited one-volume sources are Margaret Sachs's *UFO Encyclopedia* (Putnam, 1981) and Ronald Story's *Encyclopedia of UFOs* (Doubleday, 1980).

The International Encyclopedia of Astronomy. Edited by Patrick Moore. Crown, 1987. 464p. $40.00.

This alphabetically arranged encyclopedia of more than 2,500 concise entries provides a reliable, comprehensive, popularly written introduction to the field of astronomy. James Rettig in *Wilson Library Bulletin* (December 1987, p. 94) recommends the work: "Current and readable, this is a good source of basic information on astronomy for high school, public, and college libraries." A number of other helpful single-volume encyclopedias for the layperson interested in astronomy have been published over the years, namely the *Cambridge Encyclopedia of Astronomy* (Crown, 1977), Arnold Weigert and Helmut Zimmerman's *Concise Encyclopedia of Astronomy* (2nd ed. Crane, Russak, 1976), Gilbert Satterthwaite's *Encyclopedia of Astronomy* (St. Martin's Press, 1971), Ian Ridpath's *Illustrated Ency-*

clopedia of Astronomy and Space (Rev. ed. Crowell, 1979), Richard Lewis's Illustrated Encyclopedia of the Universe (Crown, 1983), and David Baker's Larousse Guide to Astronomy (Larousse, 1978).

Isaac Asimov's Library of the Universe. Written by Isaac Asimov; edited by Mark Sachner. Gareth Stevens, 1988. 33 vols. $569.91.

While not a true encyclopedia, this profusely illustrated multivolume set for children in the elementary grades does offer an encyclopedic overview of the universe and modern astronomy. Each 32-page volume treats a specific topic, such as the origin of the universe, comets and meteors, and space satellites; also, each planet is accorded its own volume. Volume 33 is an index to the set. "Clever devices are used, such as drawing an analogy between soap bubbles and the appearance of the universe and comparing raisins in raisin bread to galactic expansion. If the six titles reviewed are any indication of the rest of the set, the whole work is bright, interesting, and informative" (*American Reference Books Annual*, 1991, p. 703).

McGraw-Hill Encyclopedia of Astronomy. Edited by Sybil P. Parker & Jay M. Pasachoff. 2nd ed. McGraw-Hill, 1993. 544p. $75.50.

Most of the more than 250 articles and 400 illustrations that make up this solid one-volume encyclopedia first appeared in the seventh (1992) edition of the MCGRAW-HILL ENCYCLOPEDIA OF SCIENCE AND TECHNOLOGY, an expensive multivolume set. The McGraw-Hill Encyclopedia of Astronomy—a useful source for those who cannot afford or lack access to the parent set—provides a thoroughgoing intro-

duction to all important aspects of the field of astronomy today. The encyclopedia first appeared in 1983.

Moons of the Solar System: An Illustrated Encyclopedia. Written by John Stewart. McFarland, 1991. 244p. $45.00.

Aimed principally at students and interested laypeople, this compact encyclopedia devotes equal attention to "Luna, Earth's Moon" and the 70 other moons that circle the rest of the planets in our solar system. In a review in *American Reference Books Annual* (1993, p. 712), Robert Seal notes that "each entry is a cornucopia of data useful for the researcher or reference librarian."

Patrick Moore's A-Z of Astronomy. Written by Patrick Moore. Rev. ed. Norton, 1987. 240p. $13.50 paper.

Moore is a well-known British science writer who has prepared a number of nontechnical reference works in the field of astronomy, including the excellent INTERNATIONAL ENCYCLOPEDIA OF ASTRONOMY. In this revision of his A-Z of Astronomy (1977), Moore furnishes concise, easily comprehensible definitions and descriptions of astronomical terms, principles, phenomena, and places, as well as biographical information about major astronomers. This inexpensive volume is especially recommended for the personal libraries of amateur astronomers. "One noteworthy and useful feature of this work not found in other astronomy dictionaries, at least in recent years, is its inclusion of historical personages, events, and landmark publications in astronomy" (*American Reference Books Annual*, 1989, p. 642).

❈ BIOLOGY AND ANIMAL LIFE ❈

The Aquarium Encyclopedia. Written by Gunther Sterba; edited by Dick Mills; translated by Susan Simpson. MIT Press, 1983. 605p. $45.00.

Originally published in Germany in 1978, the Aquarium Encyclopedia offers basic information on all aspects of aquarium-keeping and more, including "general and specialist ichthyology, hydrology, fish economy, the biology of freshwater animals and marine biology" (introduction). Library Journal (April 15, 1984, p. 784) cited the encyclopedia as one of its best reference books for 1983: "More than 1,000 clear illustrations, many of them color photographs, will make this appealing for the single-tank hobbyist as well as the professional." Other useful single-volume reference sources for home aquarists—all published by T.F.H. Publications (the publisher's initials stand for Tropic Fish Hobbyists)—are the

Encyclopedia of Marine Invertebrates (1983); Dr. Axelrod's Atlas of Freshwater Aquarium Fishes (6th ed., 1991); and Dr. Burgess's Mini-Atlas of Marine Aquarium Fishes (1991). Another excellent source in one volume is the handsomely turned out Macmillan Book of the Marine Aquarium (Macmillan, 1993) by Nick Dakin.

The Atlas of Cats of the World: Domesticated and Wild. Written by Dennis Kelsey-Wood. T.F.H. Publications, 1989. 384p. $59.95.

No first-rate encyclopedia dealing with cats is currently available, although the Atlas of Cats of the World—a well-written, large-sized, copiously illustrated book—will adequately serve most people's needs for a substantial, up-to-date reference. "Taking an encyclopedic approach, Kelsey-Wood explains the history, domestication, and anatomy of cats of the world" (*Library Journal*, December 1989, p. 108). Judy Gay Matthews, writing in *American Reference Books Annual* (1991, p. 636), also recommends the book: "If only one cat book can be purchased, this is it."

Atlas of Dog Breeds of the World. Written by Bonnie Wilcox & Chris Walkowicz. 3rd ed. T.F.H. Publications, 1991. 912p. $129.95.

Organized alphabetically by breed, this encyclopedic work intends to cover all recognized dog breeds around the world. As such, it offers a broader perspective than the well-known and indispensable *Complete Dog Book*, the American Kennel Club's official encyclopedia (18th ed. Macmillan, 1992). Wilcox and Walkowicz's *Atlas of Dog Breeds* is also better illustrated than the AKC book. In a review of the current edition in *Library Journal* (February 1, 1993, p. 51), Jennifer King praises the *Atlas of Dog Breeds* as "the most comprehensive breed book available to date.... Despite the hefty price, it is far superior to many less expensive works." Another useful single-volume dog encyclopedia is the recently published *Canine Lexicon* (T.F.H., 1993) by Andrew De Prisco and James B. Johnson.

Audubon Society Encyclopedia of North American Birds. Written by John K. Terres. Knopf, 1980; reprinted by Wings Books (dist. by Outlet Book Company), 1991. 1,109p. $39.99.

Students of birds are fortunate to have a number of outstanding encyclopedias available on the subject. Among the best are Terres's *Audubon Society Encyclopedia of North American Birds*, which includes roughly 6,000 alphabetical entries, 625 long articles, and life histories of 847 birds indigenous to North America. "A magnificent one-volume encyclopedia" (*Reference Books Bulletin* in *Booklist*, June 1, 1982, p. 1325). Works of comparable quality treating birds beyond North America include the excellent *Cambridge Encyclopedia of Ornithology* (Cambridge Univ. Press, 1991); Bruce Campbell and Elizabeth Lack's *Dictionary of Birds* (Revised ed. Buteo Books, 1985); Christopher Perrins and Alex Middleton's *Encyclopedia of Birds* (Facts on File, 1985); and Perrins' *Illustrated Encyclopedia of Birds* (Prentice Hall, 1991), which does not quite live up to its subtitle—"*The Definitive Reference to Birds of the World*"—but which is, nevertheless, a valuable work.

Black's Veterinary Dictionary. Edited by Geoffrey P. West. 17th ed. Barnes & Noble Books, 1992. 672p. $67.50.

Black's, first published in Great Britain in 1928 and long established as the premier encyclopedic

dictionary in the field of veterinary medicine, is now in its seventeenth edition. The book's British origin and accent do not diminish its value for North American students and practitioners. "An excellent reference on the anatomy, physiology, diseases, diagnosis and treatment, and first aid of large and small animals" (*American Reference Books Annual*, 1990, p. 628). Competing works are the *Merck Veterinary Manual* (7th ed. Merck, 1991), which has a North American emphasis, and the British-oriented *Concise Veterinary Dictionary* (Oxford Univ. Press, 1988).

The Cambridge Encyclopedia of Life Sciences. Edited by Adrian Friday & David S. Ingram. Cambridge Univ. Press, 1985. 432p. $60.00.

This heavily illustrated, thematically arranged encyclopedia surveys all significant aspects of biology, from microorganisms to complex plant and animal life. For students at the high school and college level, the encyclopedia "is one of the best references on this topic available" (*Library Journal*, December 1985, p. 90). An older but still useful single-volume biology encyclopedia is Peter Gray's *Encyclopedia of the Biological Sciences* (2nd ed. Van Nostrand, 1970; reprinted by Krieger, 1981).

The Complete Encyclopedia of Horses. Written by M.E. Ensminger. A.S. Barnes, 1977. 487p. Out of print (last priced at $29.50).

Ensminger's encyclopedia was once called "the finest horse encyclopedia in print" (*American Reference Books Annual*, 1978, p. 742). Although now out of print, it remains a valuable reference source. Originally published in Great Britain, the encyclopedia treats all important aspects of the horse, including anatomy, diseases, training, breeds, feeds, stabling, racing, riding and hunting terms, and equipment. Complementary sources—all single-volume works currently in print—are Jane Kidd's paperbound *International Encyclopedia of Horse Breeds* (HP Books, 1986), which has also been published in hardcover as the *Illustrated International Encyclopedia of Horse Breeds & Breeding* (Crescent Books, 1989), and James Giffin and Tom Gore's more specialized *Horse Owner's Veterinary Handbook* (Howell Book House, 1989).

Concise Encyclopedia of Biochemistry. Edited by Thomas A. Scott & Mary Brewer. 2nd ed. Walter de Gruyter, 1988. 520p. $89.90.

Originally published in 1983 and revised in 1988, this English-language translation of the German *Brockhaus ABC Biochemie* is the only viable encyclopedia of biochemistry currently available. It contains roughly 4,500 entries, which range from a sentence or two to several columns. Intended for serious students, the material tends to be technical and assumes the reader possesses a familiarity with the vocabulary of biochemistry and biotechnology. The 1988 revision emphasizes recent developments in cell biology and genetic engineering.

The Encyclopedia of Aquatic Life. Edited by Keith Banister & Andrew Campbell. Facts on File, 1985. 349p. $45.00.

Informative, intelligently organized, and beautifully illustrated with some 400 color photos and drawings, this handsome encyclopedia covers fish, aquatic invertebrates, and marine mammals. "The illustrations and their captions convey every bit as much information about the animals' behavior as the text. It is one thing to describe the way ghost crabs burrow into the sand for protection and quite another thing to see a stunning color photograph of a crab so camouflaged" (*Wilson Library Bulletin*, February 1986, p. 62). More specialized are David and Jennifer George's *Marine Life: An Illustrated Encyclopedia of Invertebrates in the Sea* (Wiley, 1979) and Bruce Halstead's *Dangerous Aquatic Animals of the World: A Color Atlas* (Darwin Press, 1992).

Encyclopedia of Bioethics. Edited by Warren T. Reich. Free Press (dist. by Macmillan), 1978. 4 vols. $250.00; reprinted 1982 in 2 vols. $200.00.

Unique among encyclopedias covering the life sciences, the *Encyclopedia of Bioethics* comprises 315 lengthy articles dealing with such ethical and policy questions as abortion, euthanasia, organ transplantation, and psychosurgery. Highly authoritative by virtue of its 285 distinguished contributors, many of whom enjoy international reputations, the encyclopedia is one "of issues and ideas rather than of events" (*Reference Books Bulletin* in *Booklist*, March 15, 1983, p. 988). In 1979 the heavily interdisciplinary encyclopedia received the prestigious Dartmouth Medal, which honors the best reference book of the previous year.

Encyclopedia of Human Biology. Edited by Renato Dulbecco. Academic Press, 1991. 8 vols. $1,950.00.

The recently published *Encyclopedia of Human Biology* stands out as the most extensive, most authoritative, most useful, and most expensive encyclopedia covering the biology of the human species. Edited by Nobel prize winner Renato Dulbecco, the set includes approximately 620 substantial articles prepared by 700 contributors and accompanied by more than 2,000 highly effective illustrations. "The Encyclopedia strives to present a complete overview of the current state of knowledge of contemporary

human biology, organized to serve as a solid base on which subsequent information can be readily integrated," writes Dulbecco in his preface. He continues, "The Encyclopedia is intended for a wide audience, from the general reader with a background in science to undergraduates, graduate students, practicing researchers, and scientists."

The work has received much well deserved praise from critics; this excerpt from a review in *Library Journal* (April 15, 1991, p. 82) is typical: "With its clear organization, comprehensive and thorough coverage, reliable and coherent information, and easy-to-access format, this eight-volume reference on human biology is a unique and valuable addition to the scientific literature." A review in *Choice* (October 1991, p. 256), however, complains that access to information in the set could be improved: "Access . . . is the main difficulty, for three reasons: idiosyncratic cross-referencing, inconsistent phrasing of article titles, and indexing." Notwithstanding, the *Encyclopedia of Human Biology* is one of the finest subject encyclopedias to appear in recent years.

The Encyclopedia of Human Evolution and Prehistory. Edited by Ian Tattersall & others. Garland, 1988. 603p. $95.00.

The first encyclopedia of any magnitude to tackle the complex subject of human and primate evolution, this scholarly work is for advanced students and professionals and not, in the words of James Rettig in *Wilson Library Bulletin* (November 1988, p. 124), for "the casually curious nor beginners. To benefit from its 40 contributors' erudite signed articles, one must have mastery of the vocabulary of paleoanthropology." The 600 articles are extensively illustrated with line drawings and black-and-white photos. Two other recent single-volume encyclopedias also treat the subject, namely the equally authoritative but more readable *Cambridge Encyclopedia of Human Evolution* (Cambridge Univ. Press, 1993), edited by Stephen Jones and others; and Richard Milner's comparatively undemanding *Encyclopedia of Evolution: Humanity's Search for Its Origins* (Facts on File, 1990). An older work is *Grzimek's Encyclopedia of Evolution* (Van Nostrand, 1976), a one-volume complement to the multivolume GRZIMEK'S ANIMAL LIFE ENCYCLOPEDIA; both these works are currently out of print.

The Encyclopedia of Insects. Edited by Christopher O'Toole. Facts on File, 1986. 141p. $24.95.

O'Toole's slim encyclopedia offers a serviceable introduction for nonspecialists to all forms of insect life. In all, 24 groups of insects are covered, with detailed descriptions of their physiology, behavior, distribution, and ecology. "The volume—packed as densely as it is with information—will deservedly find its way onto the bookshelf of the serious naturalist" (*American Reference Books Annual*, 1987, p. 595). A comparable work is the encyclopedic *Audubon Society Book of Insects* (Abrams, 1983).

Encyclopedia of Microbiology. Edited by Joshua Lederberg. Academic Press, 1992. 4 vols. $695.00.

Similar in concept and construction (but not content) to the eight-volume ENCYCLOPEDIA OF HUMAN BIOLOGY, this unique reference set offers a detailed encyclopedic survey of the biology of microscopic organisms. Like the ENCYCLOPEDIA OF HUMAN BIOLOGY, the *Encyclopedia of Microbiology* is published by the Academic Press and edited by a Nobel Laureate. It contains over 200 lengthy articles written for serious students, teachers, and researchers. A particularly valuable feature is inclusion of 1,300 glossary entries, which help readers understand the technical vocabulary of the field. "The scope is broad enough to include viruses, bacteria, protozoa, and the unicellular fungi and algae. . . . There is no comparable work. Highly recommended for libraries that support study, teaching, or research in microbiology" (*Choice*, April 1993, p. 1294).

The Encyclopedia of Reptiles and Amphibians. Edited by Tim Halliday & Kraig Alder. Facts on File, 1986. 143p. $27.95.

Like other titles in the fine Facts on File encyclopedia series in the area of zoology (including the ENCYCLOPEDIA OF AQUATIC LIFE, ENCYCLOPEDIA OF INSECTS, ENCYCLOPEDIA OF SHELLS, *Encyclopedia of Birds*, and *Encyclopedia of Mammals*), this work provides basic, authoritative coverage of the topic—in this case the classes *Amphibia* and *Reptilia*. "This is an excellent compendium; the level of treatment is suitable for public, secondary school, and undergraduate libraries" (*American Reference Books Annual*, 1987, p. 599).

The Encyclopedia of Shells. Edited by Kenneth R. Wye. Facts on File, 1991. 288p. $45.00.

Wye, a well-known authority on conchology, identifies and describes 1,200 shells in this handsomely produced encyclopedia. "It offers detailed photography and succinct entries in an attractive, easy-to-use format" (*Reference Books Bulletin* in *Booklist*, January 15, 1992, p. 972). Interested consumers will also want to check out Tucker Abbott and Peter Dance's *Compendium of Seashells* (4th ed. American Melacologists, 1990), a standard work on shells, and the *Collector's Encyclopedia of Shells* (McGraw-Hill, 1982), which Dance also helped prepare.

The Grolier World Encyclopedia of Endangered Species. Grolier, 1992. 10 vols. $319.00.

Organized by geographical region, this new multivolume encyclopedia furnishes nontechnical information about more than 600 endangered animal species around the world. The set, which draws its data principally from the authoritative "Red List" compiled by the International Union for Conservation of Nature and National Resources, is intended for students and generalists. Approximately 750 full-color photographs enhance the species articles. "A major feature of the work is the more than 700 color photographs ranging in size from a quarter-page to double-page spreads. Every attempt was made to photograph the species in its native habitat. The pictures are clear; the colors, vibrant" (*Reference Books Bulletin* in *Booklist*, September 1, 1993, p. 87). A quite similar encyclopedic set is the recently published 11-volume *Endangered Wildlife of the World* (Marshall Cavendish, 1993). Somewhat more technical and limited to the North American continent is the excellent three-volume *Official World Wildlife Fund Guide to Endangered Species* (Beacham, 1990–92), which describes all species currently under protection of the U.S. Endangered Species Act.

Grzimek's Animal Life Encyclopedia. Edited by Bernhard Grzimek. Van Nostrand, 1972–75. 13 vols. Out of print (last priced at $500.00 hardcover; $250.00 paper).

Long the premier animal encyclopedia, *Grzimek's* was first issued in the late 1960s by the German publisher Kindler Verlag and then translated into English and published in North America a few years later. The work of the late Bernhard Grzimek, a prominent zoologist and former director of the Frankfurt Zoo who died in 1987, the set provides first-rate coverage of the animal kingdom, with four volumes devoted to mammals, three to birds, two to fish and amphibians, and one each to reptiles, insects, mollusks and echinoderms, and lower forms. Because of its readable text and fine illustrations, *Grzimek's* can be used productively by serious students at almost all levels, although its arrangement—topical rather than alphabetical—can frustrate younger readers and inexperienced researchers. Each volume has its own index, but the indexes sometimes require patience and skill to use.

Unfortunately, *Grzimek's* is out of print at the present time, although the mammal volumes have been revised, enlarged, and reissued as a five-volume set entitled GRZIMEK'S ENCYCLOPEDIA OF MAMMALS. The presumption is that the remaining volumes of the original set will eventually be revised in like manner—if a suitable successor to Grzimek can be found to undertake such a monumental project.

Meanwhile, many libraries will have the old (1972–75) edition available, along with the reworked mammal volumes. The ILLUSTRATED ENCYCLOPEDIA OF WILD-LIFE is another useful multivolume animal encyclopedia; while it is in print and is arranged like Grzimek's, it lacks the overall excellence of the latter.

Libraries and individuals in search of a good single-volume animal encyclopedia would do well to look to these works: the *Audubon Society Encyclopedia of Animal Life* (Clarkson N. Potter, 1982) and the *Macmillan Illustrated Animal Encyclopedia* (Macmillan, 1984). Also useful for secondary school students is a four-volume "Encyclopedia of Animals" series issued by Facts on File in 1987; the individual titles, all of which contain 144 pages, are the *Encyclopedia of Animal Behavior*, the *Encyclopedia of Animal Biology*, the *Encyclopedia of Animal Ecology*, and the *Encyclopedia of Animal Evolution*.

Grzimek's Encyclopedia of Mammals. Edited by Bernhard Grzimek. 2nd ed. McGraw-Hill, 1990. 5 vols. $500.00; also available on CD-ROM at $995.00.

A major revision and enlargement of the four volumes on mammals contained in GRZIMEK'S ANI-MAL LIFE ENCYCLOPEDIA and the final legacy of famed German zoologist Bernhard Grzimek (1909–87), this authoritative, superbly illustrated five-volume set is clearly the best mammal encyclopedia currently available and it is likely to remain so for years to come. Outstanding features include the high caliber of contributors, standardized charts for easy comparison of species, 500 distribution maps, and more than 3,500 full-color photographs, many of which are spectacular. "The newer version far surpasses the earlier work in depth and breadth of coverage. . . . Includes many beautiful photographs and excellent maps and diagrams" (Choice, June 1990, p. 1654).

Grzimek's Encyclopedia of Mammals is also published on CD-ROM as part of the *Multimedia Encyclopedia of Mammalian Biology* (McGraw-Hill, 1992). This electronic version, which sells for $995.00 (for a single user), includes the entire text of the print encyclopedia plus sound, graphics, and full-motion video from the archives of the BBC natural history film library; it can be searched by subject, taxonomic group, biogeographic topic, and biological concept. (For a lengthy critical review of the *Multimedia Encyclopedia of Mammalian Biology*, see *Reference Books Bulletin* in *Booklist*, March 1, 1993, p. 1266).

Other recommended mammal encyclopedias in print form are David Macdonald's *Encyclopedia of Mammals* (Facts on File, 1984) in one volume and Ronald Nowak's *Walker's Mammals of the World*

(5th ed. Johns Hopkins Univ. Press, 1991) in two volumes. Also available on CD-ROM is the educationally exciting *Mammals: A Multimedia Encyclopedia*, software produced in 1990 by the National Geographic Society in conjunction with IBM that features full-motion video sequences of animals in action, animal sounds, and a classification game.

The Illustrated Encyclopedia of Wildlife. Grey Castle Press (dist. by Encyclopaedia Britannica Educational Corp.), 1991. 15 vols. $429.00.

This informative, profusely illustrated encyclopedia originally appeared in Great Britain in 1989 in 60 slim volumes containing a total of several thousand pages. Americanized by Grey Castle Press, the 3,053-page set offers expansive treatment of wildlife of the world in a systematic (as opposed to alphabetical) arrangement, similar to the way GRZIMEK'S ANIMAL LIFE ENCYCLOPEDIA is arranged. Especially striking are the 5,400 color illustrations. "As a comprehensive source on international wildlife, this set has wide appeal for both students and adults. . . . Highly recommended for school library media centers, children's departments, and reference departments in public libraries" (*Reference Books Bulletin* in *Booklist*, August 1991, p. 2172). A work of comparable scope, readership, and price is the 25-volume *Marshall Cavendish International Wildlife Encyclopedia* (Marshall Cavendish, 1990), which, unlike the *Illustrated Encyclopedia of Wildlife*, is arranged alphabetically.

The Macmillan Illustrated Encyclopedia of Dinosaurs and Prehistoric Animals: A Visual Who's Who of Prehistoric Life. Written by Dougal Dixon & others. Macmillan, 1988. 312p. $39.95.

Not just another popular dinosaur tome (of which there seems to be a never-ending supply), this scholarly encyclopedia surveys more than 600 prehistoric vertebrate species; the title notwithstanding, only about a fifth of the book deals directly with dinosaurs. "This book is put together by talented artists and renowned vertebrate paleontologists. The more than 60 double-page plates are the most striking feature of the volume" (*Choice*, April 1989, p. 1357). An older but still useful work, the *Encyclopedia of Prehistoric Life* (McGraw-Hill, 1979) provides comparable treatment, although its illustrations are no match for the Macmillan encyclopedia.

The Oxford Companion to Animal Behaviour. Edited by David McFarland. Oxford Univ. Press, 1982; reprinted with corrections, 1987. 657p. $49.95 hardcover; $19.95 paperbound.

"There is only one word to summarize this book—excellent. This 'companion' to animal behavior will undoubtedly become a standard reference volume and remain one for many years" (*Choice*, September 1982, p. 121). The more than 200 articles, each written by a specialist, range in length from a few paragraphs to several pages. The 1987 reprint includes corrections and a revised index. An older (and now out of print) but still valuable work on animal behavior is *Grzimek's Encyclopedia of Ethology* (Van Nostrand, 1977).

World Nature Encyclopedia. Raintree/Steck-Vaughn, 1989. 24 vols. $399.00.

Aimed at youngsters reading at the 5–8 grade levels, the topically arranged *World Nature Encyclopedia* consists of 24 heavily illustrated volumes of 128 pages each, or a total of 3,072 pages of text; each volume covers a particular country or region of the world. The set, first published in Italy in 1985, describes the plant and animal life and climate in each area, as well as the effect humans have on fragile environments and habitats. "A beautiful collection of separate monographs dealing with the natural history of 24 areas of the world, this set has much not found elsewhere" (*Reference Books Bulletin* in *Booklist*, May 15, 1989, p. 1623).

❀ BOTANY AND HORTICULTURE ❀

The American Horticultural Society Encyclopedia of Garden Plants. Edited by Christopher Brickell. Macmillan, 1989. 608p. $49.95.

Although issued under the imprimatur of the American Horticultural Society, this handsome and informative encyclopedia of over 8,000 garden plants was prepared and first published in Great Britain; its contributors are British horticulturists, and editor Brickell is director of the Royal Horticultural Society as well as editor of the new *American Horticultural Society Encyclopedia of Gardening* (Dorling Kindersley, dist. by Houghton Mifflin, 1993). "The *Encyclopedia* is intended for use by both amateur and professional horticulturists. Its beautiful color photographs will be enjoyed by all. While most plants in this book will be familiar to American gardeners, its British origins do pose some limitations on its use in North America. Certain very popular types of plants like roses are represented by European varieties, rather than those normally grown here" (*Reference Books Bulletin* in *Booklist*, March 15, 1990, p. 1496). Reviewing the encyclopedia in *American Reference Books Annual* (1990, p. 625), Lillian Mesner observes, "This book is a magnificent work at a surprisingly modest price. Anyone with interests in garden plants, no matter what aspects, can benefit from the encyclopedia."

Encyclopedia of American Forest and Conservation History. Edited by Richard C. Davis. Macmillan, 1983. 2 vols. $250.00.

Consisting of more than 400 substantial articles from "Afforestation" and "Air Pollution and Forests" to "Wood Preservation" and "World War II and American Forests and Forest Industry," this interdisciplinary work, sponsored by the Forest History Society, aims to be "the standard, authoritative guide and reference to the history of forestry, con-

servation, forest industries, and other forest-related subjects in the United States" (preface). James Rettig in *Wilson Library Bulletin* (April 1984, p. 594) rightly points out that the set's title "gives the mistaken impression that its scope is narrow and its purpose specialized. A perusal of its pages quickly corrects that impression, for it is surprisingly broad and, although written by specialists, was not written for specialists." A more narrowly focused but geographically broader reference dealing with forest products is Aidan Walker's *Encyclopedia of Wood: A Tree-by-Tree Guide to the World's Most Versatile Resource* (Facts on File, 1989).

The Encyclopedia of Flowers. Written by Derek Fell. Smithmark Publishers, 1993. 208p. $19.98.

Fell, who has produced nearly 40 plant and gardening books during his prolific career as a horticultural writer, furnishes expert information on approximately 400 types of flowers, including annuals, perennials, shrubs, and small trees. Each entry describes the flower's leaves, culture, season of bloom, hardiness, and uses, and features a full-color photograph (also by Fell) to facilitate easy identification. An older but equally useful reference is *Simon & Schuster's Guide to Garden Flowers* (Simon & Schuster, 1983) by Guido Moggi and Luciano Giugnolini.

The Encyclopedia of Natural Insect & Disease Control. Edited by Roger B. Yepsen, Jr. Revised ed. Rodale, 1984. 490p. $24.95.

A revision of *Organic Plant Protection* (Rodale, 1976), this well-illustrated encyclopedia "is a guide, arranged in encyclopedic form, to protecting plants from bugs, diseases, and the environment at large. It is addressed to gardeners, small-scale orchardists, and homeowners who wish to avoid using chemical toxins" (introduction). *Westcott's Plant Disease Hand-*

book (5th ed. Van Nostrand, 1990) also devotes considerable attention to pest management and the use of chemicals.

Encyclopedia of Perennials: A Gardener's Guide. Written by Christopher Woods. Facts on File, 1992. 350p. $50.00.

Perennials, the most popular type of garden plant in North America, are listed and described alphabetically by botanical names (followed by common names) in this excellent encyclopedia. From *Acaena* (New Zealand burr) to *Zantedeschia* (calla lily), Wood covers hundreds of species of herbaceous perennials. "Written in clear, nontechnical language, this book is a browser's joy, suitable for both the novice and the sophisticated gardener. Although it is expensive, its layout, binding, paper, and photos are all of the highest quality" (*Library Journal*, May 15, 1992, p. 90). Another useful reference work on the subject is *Rodale's Illustrated Encyclopedia of Perennials* (Rodale, 1993) by Ellen Phillips and Colston Burrell.

Exotica Series 4 International: Pictorial Cyclopedia of Exotic Plants from Tropical and Near-Tropical Regions. Written by Alfred Byrd Graf. 12th ed. Scribner's, 1985. 2 vols. $187.00.

This well-known, authoritative, frequently updated work furnishes concise descriptive information and advice about 8,500 species of exotic plants grown indoors and in greenhouses and, in warmer climates, in outdoor gardens and patios. The volumes consist of 16,300 photos, including some 400 in color, plus explanatory text. Graf, an experienced horticulturist who for many years managed the large greenhouse complex of the Roehrs Company in Rutherford, New Jersey, also produces a companion volume to *Exotica* entitled *Tropica: Color Cyclopedia of Exotic Plants* (3rd revised ed. Scribner's, 1986). And recently he published a valuable new work called *Hortica: A Color Cyclopedia of Garden Flora in All Climates and Indoor Plants* (Macmillan, 1992), which is modeled on the *Exotica* format.

Hortus Third: A Concise Dictionary of Plants Cultivated in the United States and Canada. Compiled by Liberty Hyde Bailey & Ethel Zoe Bailey; revised & expanded by the staff of the Liberty Hyde Bailey Hortorium. 3rd ed. Macmillan, 1976. 1,290p. $135.00.

First published in 1930, revised in 1941 (*Hortus Second*), and now in its third edition, this massive volume provides authoritative information about the uses, propagation, and cultivation of over 20,000 plant species grown in the continental U.S., Canada, Puerto Rico, and Hawaii. Appropriately called the "Bible of nurserymen" (and nurserywomen), *Hortus*

also includes an index to 10,408 common plant names.

The Marshall Cavendish Illustrated Encyclopedia of Plants and Earth Sciences. Edited by David M. Moore. Marshall Cavendish, 1988. 10 vols. $299.95.

A plant dictionary and guide to flowering plants make up the first five volumes of this colorful and profusely illustrated set. Volumes 6–9 are devoted to plant ecology and the earth sciences. The final volume comprises a glossary, bibliography, and alphabetical and thematic indexes. International in scope, the encyclopedia has been prepared by more than 120 specialists in the fields of botany and geology, most associated with British and American universities and museums. James Rettig (*Wilson Library Bulletin*, December 1988, p. 118) advises that the text, "while not scholarly, is demanding. Except for its pictures, this is not a source for use in schools." Carol Noll, reviewing the set for *American Reference Books Annual* (1989, p. 567), enthusiastically recommends the *Marshall Cavendish Illustrated Encyclopedia of Plants and Earth Sciences* as "an outstanding work, with fascinating snippets of information and beautiful illustrations on every page. Despite the multipart arrangement, the central goal of explaining the diversity of plants and their importance to our world is met throughout."

The New Royal Horticultural Society Dictionary of Gardening. Edited by Anthony Huxley & others. Stockton Press, 1992. 4 vols. $795.00.

This expensive British-made multivolume encyclopedia for gardeners—a much needed, much anticipated, thoroughgoing revision of the *Royal Horticultural Society Dictionary of Gardening* (Oxford Univ. Press, 1951; revised ed. 1956)—offers reliable information about the characteristics, culture, and origin of approximately 50,000 plants, including cultivars. In addition to the plant entries, the encyclopedia includes 180 essay-length articles on a variety of pertinent topics, such as bonsai, botanical gardens, conservation, ethnobotany, and garden history and design. The approach is scholarly; as a review in *Reference Books Bulletin* in *Booklist* (September 1, 1992, p. 89) notes, "These volumes will be useful to scientists, growers, botanists, agriculturalists, and gardeners. The set may be too advanced for the casual hobbyist, who may find the scientific approach intimidating." Although international in coverage, the encyclopedia naturally views the gardening world through British eyes—unlike its chief competitor, the 10-volume NEW YORK BOTANICAL GARDEN ILLUSTRATED ENCYCLOPEDIA OF HORTICULTURE, which is the product of an American horticulturist.

The New York Botanical Garden Illustrated Encyclopedia of Horticulture. Written by Thomas H. Everett. Garland, 1981–82. 10 vols. $1,070.00.

Remarkably the work of a single person, the eminent horticulturist Thomas Everett of the New York Botanical Garden, this large, authoritative encyclopedia contains approximately 10,000 photographs and three million words in nearly 4,000 pages covering some 20,000 plant species. Everett, who spent more than 10 years preparing the encyclopedia, says the set's chief purpose is to provide "a comprehensive description and evaluation of horticulture as it is known and practiced in the U.S. and Canada by amateurs and professionals" (preface). The A-to-Z entries follow the nomenclature of HORTUS THIRD, with numerous cross-references from common to scientific names. "This definitive horticultural encyclopedia is indeed an outstanding contribution to horticulture literature. Amateur and professional gardeners will turn to it as an unquestionable authority, and librarians will find invaluable information easily accessible through its extensive cross-references" (*American Reference Books Annual*, 1982, p. 799). Interested consumers should compare the *New York Botanical Garden Illustrated Encyclopedia of Horticulture* with the NEW ROYAL HORTICULTURAL SOCIETY DICTIONARY OF GARDENING, a recently published multivolume work of British origin and emphasis.

The Oxford Encyclopedia of Trees of the World. Edited by Bayard Hora. Oxford Univ. Press, 1981. 288p. $39.95.

"This is an informative and well-illustrated summary of the major genera of trees of the world, and is an excellent general reference source for native and exotic trees of North America" (*American Reference Books Annual*, 1983, p. 631). Articles were prepared by 40 contributors, all specialists with good credentials. A number of other respected single-volume works on trees are available, including *Hillier's Manual of Trees and Shrubs* (5th ed. Van Nostrand, 1983) and Alan Mitchell's *Trees of North America* (Facts on File, 1987).

Popular Encyclopedia of Plants. Edited by Vernon H. Heywood & Stuart R. Chant. Cambridge Univ. Press, 1982. 368p. $42.50.

With emphasis on "the main species of plants used by Man" (introduction), this specialized encyclopedia identifies and concisely describes plants used for food, medicine, building construction, and so on. It contains 2,200 mostly brief articles complemented by over 7,000 full-color illustrations. "The appeal of the book lies in its beautiful, clear color

photographs that appear on every page, set close to the pertinent text and giving scale" (*College & Research Libraries*, January 1983, p. 54).

The RHS Encyclopedia of House Plants Including Greenhouse Plants. Written by Kenneth A. Beckett & the staff of the Royal Horticultural Society. Salem House, 1987. 492p. $34.95.

This good-looking encyclopedia written by an experienced horticulturist begins with chapters on the history of houseplants, how to select and buy them, their cultivation, maintenance, and propagation, and how to deal with pests and disease. The heart of the book—"A to Z of Houseplants"—covers some 4,000 plant species in 800 genera. "Although written mainly for the dedicated gardener who wants to extend his or her collection and knowledge, this beautiful volume will inform and delight the amateur as well" (*Library Journal*, October 1, 1987, p. 86). Another useful albeit less extensive houseplant encyclopedia is the *New Good Housekeeping Encyclopedia of House Plants* (Revised ed. Hearst, 1990), edited by Rob Herwig.

Rodale's All-New Encyclopedia of Organic Gardening: The Indispensable Resource for Every Gardener. Edited by Fern Marshall Bradley & Barbara W. Ellis. Rodale, 1992. 704p. $29.95 hardcover; $17.95 paperbound.

First published in 1959 as the *Encyclopedia of Organic Gardening* and revised in 1978 and again in 1992 (when it was retitled), this highly successful work—more than 700,000 copies of the first two editions have been sold—covers the entire field of horticulture from the organic perspective in 420 A-to-Z entries. The current edition reflects the knowledge and experience of 50 experts on organic gardening. "Composting, xeriscaping, permaculture, environment—all these and 400 or so more [topics] have complete entries. . . . This is an important, complete, well-arranged, and attractive reference tool" (*Library Journal*, March 1, 1992, p. 86).

The Wise Garden Encyclopedia. Edited by E.L.D. Seymour. Revised ed. HarperCollins, 1990. 1,043p. $45.00.

There are three substantial one-volume gardening encyclopedias currently available on the North American market. The *Wise Garden Encyclopedia*, first published in 1970 and completely revised and updated in 1990, presents "in simple, practical, interesting, and helpful form the information that will enable any person to get the most out of gardening" (introduction). The text is liberally sprinkled with small black-and-white line drawings, augmented by a 64-page color insert showing different types of plants.

A work of comparable size, price, and quality is the 1,221-page *Wyman's Gardening Encyclopedia* (2nd ed. Macmillan, 1986), which first appeared in 1971. It has several features that surpass *Wise*, including fuller captions for photographs and drawings and a greater emphasis on plant identification. Also comparable is the *American Horticultural Society Encyclopedia of Gardening* (Dorling Kindersley, dist. by Houghton Mifflin, 1993), the newest of the single-volume gardening encyclopedias. Edited by Christopher Brickell (who also produced the excellent AMERICAN HORTICULTURAL SOCIETY ENCYCLOPEDIA OF GARDEN PLANTS), this handsomely constructed book contains over 3,000 specially commissioned color photographs designed to assist both amateur and professional gardeners; it is comparably priced at $59.95.

Overall, each of these gardening encyclopedias is reasonably comprehensive and up-to-date and can be recommended with enthusiasm. Consumers might also be interested to know that Houghton Mifflin plans at some point to publish a major new edition of *Taylor's Encyclopedia of Gardening*, a highly respected single-volume encyclopedia by Norman Taylor last issued in 1961 (4th ed.); it has been out of print for many years.

❋ BUSINESS, ECONOMICS, AND STATISTICS ❋

Dictionary of United States Economic History. Written by James S. Olson & Susan Wladaver-Morgan. Greenwood, 1992. 667p. $85.00.

A quick reference source, this encyclopedic dictionary comprises 1,300 concise entries covering important people, places, events, laws, government agencies, corporations, court cases, etc. pertaining to American economic history. "This valuable resource should be very useful in academic and large public libraries" (*Library Journal*, October 15, 1992, p. 62). "A valuable ready-reference tool suitable for general readers and college and university libraries" (*Choice*, March 1993, p. 1118). For an older but much more substantial work on the subject, see the three-volume ENCYCLOPEDIA OF AMERICAN ECONOMIC HISTORY.

The Encyclopedia of American Business History and Biography. Series. Edited by William H. Becker. Facts on File/Bruccoli Clark Layman, 1988–. 50 vols. (in progress). $75.00–$85.00 per vol.; series can be purchased from publisher on standing order at 20% discount.

This ambitious, in-progress series is an encyclopedic survey of U.S. business from a historical perspective. Each volume has its own editor; is devoted to a specific industry or business (major industries such as automobiles and railroads are treated in more than one volume); and possesses a standardized format, which includes a lengthy introduction, alphabetically arranged articles on key people and topics written by academic specialists, 150–200 black-and-white illustrations, a select bibliography on the subject, and a detailed index enhanced by numerous cross-references in the text. The first volume in the series, *Railroads in the Age of Regulation, 1900–1980*, edited by Keith Bryant Jr., was published in 1988, followed by Bryant's *Railroads in the*

Nineteenth Century (1988), the *Iron and Steel Industry in the Nineteenth Century* (edited by Paul Paskoff, 1989), and the *Automobile Industry, 1920–1980* (edited by George May, 1989). A review of the latter volume in *Reference Books Bulletin* in *Booklist* (May 1, 1990, p. 1726) sums up the critical reaction thus far: "If all past and future volumes are as interesting, then this encyclopedia will find itself to be well used by students, researchers, and the general reader." To date, more than a dozen of the 50 volumes have appeared.

Encyclopedia of American Economic History: Studies of the Principal Movements and Ideas. Edited by Glenn Porter. Scribner's, 1980. 3 vols. $259.00.

The 72 lengthy and readable articles that make up the *Encyclopedia of American Economic History* present "the views of many specialists on a number of aspects of the collective American economic experience as it is understood in the latter part of the 1970s" (preface). The encyclopedia is more concerned with trends and developments than specific facts and economists. In his review in *American Reference Books Annual* (1981, p. 385), Lubomyr Wynar concludes that the set is "a fundamental reference publication which fills an essential gap in historical and economic reference sources. Highly recommended for public and university libraries." Those who find this encyclopedia helpful will also want to consult Olson's DICTIONARY OF UNITED STATES ECONOMIC HISTORY, a concise, specific-entry encyclopedia that currently serves as a one-volume update to the larger, older *Encyclopedia of American Economic History*.

Encyclopedia of Banking and Finance. Originally prepared by Glenn G. Munn; revised by F.L.

Garcia & Charles J. Woelfel. 9th ed. St. James Press, 1991. 1,097p. $115.00 hardcover; $49.95 paperbound.

First published in 1924, this encyclopedia has become an indispensable one-volume reference for the business community. The latest edition (1991), a heavily revised version of the eighth edition (1983), boasts almost 4,200 entries, including many definitions of banking and financial terms as well as long, detailed articles on such topics as junk bonds, Japanese financial markets, the savings and loan industry, and the Resolution Trust Corporation. Especially informative is the encyclopedia's coverage of federal legislation related to U.S. banking and finance. "Scholars, practitioners, or members of the general public trying to answer a question arising from the many facets of banking and finance should find this [ninth] edition important for both historical and current information" (*Choice*, July/August 1991, p. 1762).

Encyclopedia of Business. Gale Research, 1994 (in progress). 2 vols. $395.00 (tentative).

According to advance word from a Gale representative, the new two-volume *Encyclopedia of Business*—scheduled for publication in late 1994 or early 1995—will provide substantial coverage of all important areas of business, including international developments. It will comprise approximately 750 to 1,000 signed, alphabetically arranged articles dealing with such pertinent topics as acquisitions and mergers, advertising, bankruptcy, business ethics, consumer behavior, database marketing, entrepreneurship, the European Economic Community, government regulation of business, Japanese management techniques, job discrimination, junk bonds, middle management, the Peter Principle, product safety, recession, taxation, Total Quality Management, and venture capital. Access to the text will be enhanced by appropriate indexes. No other encyclopedia currently addresses the whole field of business in such wide-ranging terms. Given Gale's reputation for producing high quality products, the *Encyclopedia of Business* will most likely become an essential first-stop source for business information.

Encyclopedia of Career Change and Work Issues. Edited by Lawrence K. Jones. Oryx Press, 1992. 379p. $67.50.

This timely, authoritative encyclopedia consists of 159 alphabetically arranged articles covering various facets of job-seeking and career development, including interview strategies, labor unions, health benefits, and job retraining. The articles, written by educators and professionals in the field, conclude with helpful bibliographies. "The shortcomings are minor in a very worthwhile and unique work. Although written for the general public and those seeking careers and jobs, the information will also be useful for professionals in the area of careers and jobs" (*Choice*, January 1993, p. 766).

The Encyclopedia of Management. Edited by Carl Heyel. 3rd ed. Van Nostrand, 1982. 1,416p. $57.50.

Heyel's impressive but now somewhat dated encyclopedia covers business management from A to Z, beginning with "Accounting" and ending with "Zero Defects." The more than 350 articles range in length from a few paragraphs to 30 pages. The first edition appeared in 1963, the second in 1973, and the third in 1982; in all likelihood, a fourth revision will be forthcoming in the near future. Meanwhile, the 1982 edition remains a viable reference work. Another title on the subject is the comparatively superficial *Facts on File Encyclopedia of Management Techniques*, a 323-page work prepared by Frank Finch and published by Facts on File in 1985.

Encyclopedia of Statistical Sciences. Edited by Samuel Kotz & Norman L. Johnson. Wiley, 1982–88. 9 vols. plus suppl., 1989. $900.00 (9-vol. set); $65.00 (suppl.).

Intended as an exhaustive encyclopedic treatment of statistical concepts, methods, and applications for those who possess some basic knowledge of mathematics and statistics, this monumental work is far and way the most impressive encyclopedia on the subject currently available. The 5,500-page set consists of more than 2,500 entries by some 750 distinguished contributors. "A decade in the making, *ESS* is a must purchase for college and university libraries, government agencies, and private concerns that need an authoritative reference to the statistical sciences" (*American Reference Books Annual*, 1989, p. 317). A much older work is the two-volume *International Encyclopedia of Statistics*, published by the Free Press in 1978; the set, which offers revised and updated material drawn from the excellent 17-volume INTERNATIONAL ENCYCLOPEDIA OF THE SOCIAL SCIENCES, can still be used profitably by students despite its advanced age.

Encyclopedic Dictionary of Accounting and Finance. Written by Jae K. Shim & Joel G. Siegel. Prentice-Hall, 1989. 504p. $49.95 hardcover; $19.95 paperbound.

More than 500 articles—some just a paragraph and others several pages long—make up this useful quick reference encyclopedia for students and working professionals in accounting, banking, and financial planning. "The work is clearly and authoritatively written, and is excellent for large public libraries, all academic libraries, and anyone with a significant business clientele" (*American Reference Books Annual*, 1990, p. 87). Those seeking a large, comprehensive encyclopedia covering the field of accounting will be disappointed; the most substantial work, Jerome Pescow's three-volume *Encyclopedia of Accounting Systems* (Revised ed. Prentice-Hall, 1976), is now too old to cut the proverbial mustard.

The International Business Dictionary and Reference. Written by Lewis A. Presner. Wiley, 1991. 486p. $45.00.

Presner's *International Business Dictionary and Reference* is more encyclopedic than lexical in approach, although entries normally include definitions of terms with clarifying examples, and various appendixes cover specialized terminology. In all, the encyclopedia succinctly treats 1,500 topics pertaining to international trade, economics, marketing, banking, distribution, law, politics, and the like. It is regrettable that it lacks a comprehensive index. "Despite the difficulty of use created by not having a single alphabetical sequence of terms, either in the main body or in an index, this work cogently and insightfully presents the language of international business" (*Reference Books Bulletin* in *Booklist*, March 1, 1992, p. 1307). A comparable source is William J. Miller's *Encyclopedia of International Commerce* (Cornell Maritime Press, 1985).

Labor Conflict in the United States: An Encyclopedia. Edited by Ronald L. Filippelli. Garland, 1990. 609p. $95.00.

Chosen as one of *Library Journal*'s best reference books for 1990, Filippelli's alphabetically arranged encyclopedia describes 254 disputes involving U.S. workers from 1661 to 1989. The book covers not only major strikes (such as the Pullman Strike of 1894; the N.F.L. Strike of 1987) but lockouts, boycotts, race riots, slave revolts, and radical political agitations. "This is a unique work and will be an indispensable research source for specialists and in subject collections" (*Library Journal*, August 1990, p. 106).

McGraw-Hill Encyclopedia of Economics. Edited by Douglas Greenwald. 2nd ed. McGraw-Hill, 1994. 1,093p. $99.50.

First published in 1982 as simply the *Encyclopedia of Economics* and now thoroughly updated as the *McGraw-Hill Encyclopedia of Economics*, this clearly written single-volume encyclopedia contains more than 300 substantial A-to-Z articles by prominent economists that treat all major aspects of the discipline, including concepts, institutions, and historical periods. "The *Encyclopedia* has been updated by the deletion of some articles (factor cost, Maoism, stagnation thesis), the addition of others (contestable markets, debt and deficits, real business cycles), and the modification of others (e.g., the article on thrift institutions has been recast and retitled 'Thrift Institutions: Problems and Challenges')" (*Wilson Library Bulletin*, January 1994, p. 89). Another useful one-volume encyclopedia covering the entire field of economics is the smaller 876-page *Fortune Encyclopedia of Economics* (Warner, 1993). Edited by David Henderson and attractively priced at $49.95, the *Fortune Encyclopedia* is topically arranged in 14 chapters featuring essays on some 150 economic concepts.

The New Palgrave: A Dictionary of Economics. Edited by John Eatwell & others. Stockton Press, 1987. 4 vols. $750.00.

The premier economics encyclopedia, the *New Palgrave* offers its users a total of 1,916 signed, authoritative, up-to-date articles focusing on economic theory from various points of view, including the analytical, empirical, quantitative, and methodological. In all, the set's four volumes, which weigh a total of 22 pounds, contain 4,194 pages, more than four million words, thousands of cross-references, and a highly detailed subject index. As its title implies, the *New Palgrave* is a revision of an older work, namely Robert Harry Inglis Palgrave's classic *Dictionary of Political Economy*, published in three volumes between 1894 and 1899 and reprinted with corrections as *Palgrave's Dictionary of Political Economy* in 1923–26; Palgrave (1827–1919) was a British banker and financial editor of *The Economist*, the influential British weekly. The new edition boasts a roster of 927 carefully selected contributors, including such well-known names in the field as James Tobin, Milton Friedman, and Kenneth Arrow.

Editor John Eatwell, a lecturer in economics at Trinity College, Cambridge, has been quoted as saying that one of the goals of the set is to challenge Thomas Carlyle's dictum that economics is "the dismal science"; here, as elsewhere, the *New Palgrave* succeeds brilliantly, bringing together an exciting body of contemporary knowledge and making it accessible to serious students and practitioners alike. Be aware, however, that the *New Palgrave*, a work of high scholarship, can be difficult going for the uninitiated or uninspired. Bill Katz puts it this way in his *Basic Information Sources* (6th ed., 1992, p. 269): "Written by experts, most of the material has been carefully edited to be within the grasp of the educated layperson. But not all, and some of the articles require a thorough knowledge of economics jargon as well as a grounding in statistics and mathematics."

The New Palgrave Dictionary of Money and Finance. Edited by Peter Newman & others. Stockton Press, 1992. 3 vols. $595.00.

Unlike the four-volume NEW PALGRAVE: A DICTIONARY OF ECONOMICS, which concentrates on economic theory, this new three-volume encyclopedia deals with the practical world of financial markets and monetary systems. International in scope, the set contains over 1,000 scholarly articles prepared by some 800 experts, most from academe. The text, though consistently well-written, is sometimes beyond the easy comprehension of general readers. The articles, which vary in length from a few paragraphs to essays of 10 or more pages, are arranged alphabetically from "Absolute Priority Rule" to "Zero Coupon Bonds" and cover such broad topics as stock exchanges, bonds, and investment strategies. Valuable bibliographies accompany most articles, and a detailed subject index is found in the final volume. "For those lucky enough to be able to afford the hefty price, it [the *New Palgrave Dictionary of Money and Finance*] is a masterful source of information that will be consulted for years to come. Highly recommended" (*Library Journal*, January 1993, p. 104). A review in *American Reference Books Annual* (1993, p. 105) concurs: "On the whole, this magnificent three-volume compilation is an up-to-date, authoritative reference work in money and finance, with numerous potential users." Consumers should note that the *New Palgrave Dictionary of Money and Finance* duplicates some information found in the companion NEW PALGRAVE: A DICTIONARY OF ECONOMICS, mostly in the area of monetary theory.

The St. James Encyclopedia of Mortgage & Real Estate Finance. Compiled by James Newell & others. St. James Press, 1991. 575p. $55.00.

Also available in a paperback edition entitled simply the *Encyclopedia of Mortgage & Real Estate Finance* from Probus Publishing at $27.50, this handy reference work on the ins and outs of financing real estate contains over 2,000 entries ranging from one line ("Adjudication") to more than 30 pages ("Federal Housing Administration"). The material is clearly presented, sufficiently detailed, and well organized for easy access. "This book will have great utility in public and academic libraries. Because of its exceptionally clear writing and attention to detail, it will be helpful to both the general public and business students" (*Reference Books Bulletin* in *Booklist*, December 1, 1991, p. 723). A comparable source is Jerome Gross's *Webster's New World Illustrated Encyclopedic Dictionary of Real Estate* (3rd ed. Prentice Hall Press, 1987). Much older but more expansive is the 900-page *Arnold Encyclopedia of Real Estate* (Warren, Gorham & Lamont, 1978), which covers the subject from apartments to zoning in some 3,000 concise articles; a yearbook helps keep the encyclopedia reasonably current.

The Thorndike Encyclopedia of Banking and Financial Tables. Edited by David Thorndike. 3rd ed. Warren, Gorham & Lamont, 1987. 1,792p. $125.00.

Primarily for investors and bankers, this well-known and highly regarded encyclopedia furnishes financial and real estate tables for figuring compound interest and annuities, loan payments and amortization, installment loan calculations, bond yields, mortgage rates, etc. Easy-to-understand explanations accompany each table and, when appropriate, examples show how computations were arrived at. Thorndike's encyclopedia first appeared in 1973 and was revised in 1980 and again in 1987; an updating yearbook (or supplement) has been published annually since 1975; it is currently priced at $86.00 per volume.

※ CHEMISTRY AND CHEMICAL ENGINEERING ※

Encyclopedia of Chemical Processing and Design. Edited by John J. McKetta & William A. Cunningham. Marcel Dekker, 1976–. 45 vols. (in progress). $135.00–$165.00 per vol.; series can be purchased from publisher on standing order at $115.00 per vol.

Long, technical articles by recognized authorities in the field make up this large specialized encyclopedia that began in 1976 and is just now nearing completion. The alphabetically arranged set, which will ultimately reach 45 or more volumes, plus a comprehensive index (the lack of which is currently

a source of user frustration), aims to treat all important aspects of the subject, with emphasis on the design of equipment, systems, and controls used in chemical processing.

Its obvious competitor is the much better known KIRK-OTHMER ENCYCLOPEDIA OF CHEMICAL TECHNOLOGY, a multivolume work now being issued in a fourth edition (1991–). In a review of a recently published volume of the *Encyclopedia of Chemical Processing*, Edwin Posey provides this helpful comparative note on the two works: "For similar articles, *Kirk-Othmer* tends to have longer and more useful bibliographic references. The arrangement of the two works differs in that *Kirk-Othmer* tends to get more specific: it has sections on wool and waterproofing, for example, while McKetta and Cunningham have articles such as 'Liquids, Thermal Conductivity Estimation' and 'Lubricating Oils I: Manufacturing Processes.' We would assume that academic libraries supporting strong chemical engineering programs will want to acquire both works simply because different treatments of the same material will be of value" (*American Reference Books Annual*, 1989, p. 589).

Encyclopedia of Polymer Science and Engineering. Edited by Jacqueline I. Kroschwitz & others. 2nd ed. Wiley-Interscience, 1985–90. 17 vols. plus index & suppl. $200.00 per vol.; also available on CD-ROM at $3,500.00.

Successor to the well-received 15-volume first edition published in 1964–71 under the slightly different title of *Encyclopedia of Polymer Science and Technology*, this unique work provides lengthy, signed up-to-date articles on all monomers and polymers. Information includes their properties, analysis and testing, and methods and processes for preparation and manufacture, along with basic theory. The second edition is especially strong on applications in new areas of technology—the biomedical sciences and robotics, for instance—and the latest developments in macromolecular science. Prepared by more than 1,000 specialists, material in the *Encyclopedia of Polymer Science and Engineering* is authoritative, clearly written, and will be comprehensible to serious students and practitioners alike. Students, libraries, and others unable to afford the multivolume set will be pleased to know that a one-volume abridgment of the second edition is available. Entitled the *Concise Encyclopedia of Polymer Science and Engineering* (Wiley-Interscience, 1990), the 1,341-page book is, in the words of *Choice* (February 1991, p. 910), an "intelligently condensed" version of the full encyclopedia; it sells for $135.00.

Kirk-Othmer Encyclopedia of Chemical Technology. Edited by Jacqueline I. Kroschwitz & Mary Howe-Grant. 4th ed. Wiley-Interscience, 1991–. 25 vols. plus index & suppl. (in progress). $275.00 per vol.; $6,696.00 for the set; also available on CD-ROM at $4,500.00 ($1,500.00 annual fee over three years).

Without question the most important encyclopedic work in the field of chemical engineering, the *Kirk-Othmer Encyclopedia of Chemical Technology*— usually cited simply as *Kirk-Othmer* after founding editors Raymond Kirk and Donald Othmer—is cur-

rently undergoing a massive volume-by-volume revision. Begun in 1991 and scheduled for completion in 1998, the new fourth edition will eventually comprise 27 volumes, including an updating supplement and detailed cumulative index to the set. The editors anticipate that 20 percent of the articles will be new, dealing with recent advances in such areas as analytical chemistry, biotechnology, environmental concerns, and computer technology; all other articles will be carefully reviewed and revised as developments require. First published in 1947–60 and revised in 1963–71, 1978–85, and now in the 1990s, *Kirk-Othmer* is the reference of first choice for information on the properties, manufacture, and use of any chemical as well as industrial processes and methods of analysis.

Kirk-Othmer competes directly with two other large sets, the ENCYCLOPEDIA OF CHEMICAL PROCESSING AND DESIGN and ULLMAN'S ENCYCLOPEDIA OF INDUSTRIAL CHEMISTRY. Like the ENCYCLOPEDIA OF POLYMER SCIENCE AND ENGINEERING, *Kirk-Othmer* is currently available on CD-ROM; sold by Dialog on a subscription basis ($1,500.00 annually for three years), the CD-ROM product represents the full text of the 26-volume third edition (1978–85) on disk. The set is also available online via Dialog. Users of *Kirk-Othmer* should also be aware that the publisher offers a one-volume abridged version of the third edition, entitled the *Kirk-Othmer Concise Encyclopedia of Chemical Technology*; the 1,352-page book was published in hardcover in 1985 at $99.95 and in 1989 a paperback edition appeared, priced at an affordable $59.95.

Lange's Handbook of Chemistry. Edited by John A. Dean. 14th ed. McGraw-Hill, 1992. 1,485p. $79.50.

This encyclopedic handbook—a classic desk reference for chemists—first appeared in 1934 under the editorship of Norbert Adolph Lange and has been revised numerous times since, most recently in 1992. The book consists of tables arranged by topic, such as organic chemistry, inorganic chemistry, physical properties, thermodynamic properties, physicochemical relationships, spectroscopy, and practical laboratory information. The current edition has been extensively updated, with much new material added. "Professional chemists, students of chemistry, and others interested in the sciences will find easy access to chemistry and physics data in this one-volume compilation" (*Choice*, December 1992, p. 603). A similar and equally valuable compendium is the *CRC Handbook of Chemistry and Physics*, a single-volume work published annually since 1913 by the Chemical Rubber Company.

McGraw-Hill Encyclopedia of Chemistry. Edited by Sybil P. Parker. 2nd ed. McGraw-Hill, 1993. 1,249p. $95.50.

Over 800 articles on all aspects of chemistry make up this affordable, recently revised one-volume encyclopedia. The articles are drawn from the seventh edition (1992) of the multivolume MCGRAW-HILL ENCYCLOPEDIA OF SCIENCE AND TECHNOLOGY. The *McGraw-Hill Encyclopedia of Chemistry* competes directly with the VAN NOSTRAND REINHOLD ENCYCLOPEDIA OF CHEMISTRY. Both are excellent all-around one-volume encyclopedias for students at the high school level and up, but today the *McGraw-Hill* has a slight edge because of its more recent publication date.

Ullmann's Encyclopedia of Industrial Chemistry. Edited by Wolfgang Gerhartz & others. 5th ed.; 1st English-language ed. VCH, 1985–. 38 vols. (in progress). $180.00 per vol.

Previously published only in German, this first English-language edition of *Ullmann's Encyclopedia of Industrial Chemistry* is currently being issued at the rate of three or four volumes per year, beginning in 1985. The set, which will eventually total 38 volumes, should be completed sometime around 1995 or 1996, if the publisher holds to its announced schedule. Unlike most American-produced encyclopedias (but much in the European tradition), *Ullmann's* is organized both alphabetically and topi-

cally—that is, 28 of the volumes are arranged in A-to-Z fashion while the remaining eight volumes treat basic knowledge by subject. International in scope, the encyclopedia dates back to 1914 and is highly regarded for its technical coverage of industrial processes, products, and chemicals. "Clearly, it stands as one of the preeminent encyclopedias in the field of science and technology and should be acquired by any library that claims to offer comprehensive reference collections in chemistry and technology. The English-language version enhances its desirability" (*American Reference Books Annual,* 1989, p. 646). *Ullmann's* is quite similar in purpose to the KIRK-OTHMER ENCYCLOPEDIA OF CHEMICAL TECHNOLOGY; for an informed analysis of how the two sets compare, see *Choice,* December 1988, pp. 632–33.

Van Nostrand Reinhold Encyclopedia of Chemistry. Edited by Douglas M. Considine. 4th ed. Van Nostrand, 1984. 1,082p. $134.95.

Containing approximately 1,300 A-to-Z articles, all prepared by authorities in the field, this hefty single-volume encyclopedia is a thorough revision of the *Encyclopedia of Chemistry* (3rd ed. Van Nostrand, 1973), edited by Clifford Hampel and Gessner Hawley. Now somewhat dated, the *VNR Encyclopedia of Chemistry* is due for a new edition in the near future. Meanwhile, along with the MCGRAW-HILL ENCYCLOPEDIA OF CHEMISTRY, it remains the best small-volume encyclopedia covering all important aspects of the chemical sciences.

❋ COMPUTER AND ELECTRONIC SCIENCES ❋

Encyclopedia of Artificial Intelligence. Edited by Stuart C. Shapiro. 2nd ed. Wiley, 1992. 2 vols. $275.00.

This outstanding two-volume encyclopedia fully surveys the rapidly changing and expanding field of artificial intelligence (AI) in nearly 200 essay-length articles prepared by leading authorities. The set, first published in 1987 and revised in 1992, also includes 100 or more much shorter entries that briefly describe specific AI systems. Written at a fairly high technical level, the encyclopedia will be "of most use as a starting reference for a technically oriented person, with some background in computer science and AI, who needs or wants to know about some particular aspect of AI" (*American Reference Books Annual,* 1988, p. 683). "This work is a landmark publication representing the history and current knowledge of the science of artificial intelligence" (*Reference Books Bulletin* in *Booklist,* October 15, 1987, p. 378).

Encyclopedia of Computer Science. Edited by Anthony Ralston & Edwin D. Reilly. 3rd ed. Van Nostrand, 1993. 1,664p. $125.00.

An excellent source of both theoretical and practical information about computer science for the nonspecialist, this comprehensive encyclopedia first appeared in 1976, was extensively revised in 1983 (under the expanded title *Encyclopedia of Computer Science and Engineering*), and now has been brought up to speed in a third edition published in 1993. The latest edition contains well over 600 articles, including nearly 175 new ones that cover recent developments in major computing systems, environments, software, etc. This is unquestionably the best single-volume encyclopedia on computer science currently available. "Well-written by academic and industry specialists, the articles are annotated adequately for further research and embedded in an infrastructure that includes a classification, extensive cross-references, appendixes, and a fine index" (*Choice,* May 1993, p. 1438).

The Encyclopedia of Electronic Circuits. Compiled by Rudolf F. Graf. TAB Books, 1985–94. 5 vols. $60.00 hardcover per vol.; $34.95 paperbound per vol.

Graf's huge encyclopedia now contains well over 3,000 schematic drawings of electronic circuits arranged alphabetically by categories. Each volume covers different categories; for instance, volume 1 includes schematics for alarms, fiber optics, light activated circuits, smoke and flame detectors, and timers, while volume 3 covers humidity sensors, integrator circuits, and touch-switch circuits. A cumulative index to the set renders all of this material readily accessible to the user. "This set is extremely popular with engineering students, electronic hobbyists, and others. As it says in the preface, this is truly an invaluable storehouse" (*American Reference Books Annual*, 1992, p. 653). A similar (albeit much older) work is John Douglas-Young's *Illustrated Encyclopedic Dictionary of Electronic Circuits* (Prentice-Hall, 1983).

Encyclopedia of Electronics. Edited by Stan Gibilisco & Neil Sclater. 2nd ed. TAB Books, 1990. 960p. $69.50.

The approximately 3,000 informative, well-illustrated articles that comprise the second edition of the *Encyclopedia of Electronics* range in size from a paragraph to a page or more. The encyclopedia, which is directed mainly at students and laypeople, describes practically all important aspects of electronics and electronics products, including bar codes, cellular telephones, compact disks, and light pens. "Gibilisco and Sclater fill the gap between a language dictionary and a book to be used by a professional in the field. A good source for public, high school, and college libraries, wherever solid introductory material is needed" (*Choice*, December 1990, p. 607).

Encyclopedia of Telecommunications. Edited by Robert A. Meyers. Academic Press, 1988. 575p. $77.00.

This valuable—and unique—encyclopedia contains 28 substantial articles covering the constituent parts of telecommunications. Aimed chiefly at the serious student and interested layperson, the encyclopedia is clearly and authoritatively written. "Entries are written by respected researchers and experts in the field and contain helpful glossaries and bibliographies. Topics include some of the newest developments, such as optical fiber communications, intelligent networks, and videotext, as well as standard topics like antennas, general signal processing, and radio propagation. . . . Highly recommended" (*Choice*, May 1989, p. 1488).

International Encyclopedia of Robotics: Applications and Automation. Edited by Richard C. Dorf. Wiley, 1988. 3 vols. $445.00.

Aimed at the "professional who seeks to understand and use robots and automation" (introduction), the three-volume *International Encyclopedia of Robotics* consists of more than 200 articles by leading theoreticians and engineers, most from the U.S. All significant aspects of robots are covered, including different types, their components, design, application, and social and economic ramifications. The articles tend to be heavily illustrated with pictures and diagrams. In 1990, the publisher issued a condensed version entitled the *Concise International Encyclopedia of Robotics*; a one-volume work of 1,190 pages, the *Concise Encyclopedia* sells for $99.95 and is a boon for students, specialists in the field, and libraries unable to afford the parent set.

Macmillan Encyclopedia of Computers. Edited by Gary G. Bitter. Macmillan, 1992. 2 vols. $150.00.

Although published in two volumes, the *Macmillan Encyclopedia of Computers* contains only about 1,000 pages, making it considerably smaller than the leading one-volume computer encyclopedia, Ralston and Reilly's ENCYCLOPEDIA OF COMPUTER SCIENCE. Nevertheless, the Macmillan work, which is also written for nonspecialists, provides "an excellent introduction to the world of computers, and the brief bibliographies at the ends of entries will lead to more detailed information" (*Reference Books Bulletin* in *Booklist*, September 1, 1992, p. 87). James Rettig in *Wilson Library Bulletin* (June 1992, p. 114) also commends the work: "Overall, the encyclopedia offers a good overview of the computing field and its role in society." But those who must choose between the two titles would do well to pick the ENCYCLOPEDIA OF COMPUTER SCIENCE.

McGraw-Hill Encyclopedia of Electronics and Computers. Edited by Sybil P. Parker. 2nd ed. McGraw-Hill, 1988. 1,047p. $75.00.

The 500-plus articles that make up this useful one-volume work are derived from the sixth edition (1987) of the multivolume MCGRAW-HILL ENCYCLOPEDIA OF SCIENCE AND TECHNOLOGY. By spinning off a one-volume collection of articles from the larger, much more expensive set, the publisher allows students, libraries, and professionals in the field to acquire a valuable encyclopedic source at a reasonable price. The encyclopedia is more technically oriented than the ENCYCLOPEDIA OF COMPUTER SCIENCE and the MACMILLAN ENCYCLOPEDIA OF COMPUTERS, although all three titles can be used profitably by interested students, teachers, and scientists. The

McGraw-Hill work is due for a new edition in the near future.

McGraw-Hill Personal Computer Programming Encyclopedia: Languages and Operating Systems. Edited by William J. Birnes. 2nd ed. McGraw-Hill, 1989. 752p. $99.50.

First published in 1985, Birnes's compendium furnishes detailed information on 28 high-level programming languages (such as BASIC and COBOL), nine software command languages (dBase II, MultiPlan), and 12 operating systems (MS-DOS, AMIGA). The second edition includes new material on neural networks, HyperTalk, and computer-generated music and games. *Choice* (April 1989, p. 1308) highly recommends the encyclopedia: "This reference work is an extremely valuable resource certain to be of interest to students/faculty of computer science, programming professionals, and hobbyists."

The Prentice-Hall Encyclopedia of Information Technology. Written by Robert A. Edmunds. Prentice-Hall, 1987. 590p. $67.50.

Edmunds's encyclopedia, which covers roughly 150 subjects central to the rapidly changing field of information technology, does a good job describing recent developments in communication technology, office automation, computerized systems, software, networks, and storage techniques and devices. The book is written in nontechnical language and provides many examples. "This encyclopedia's topical approach, the nontechnical explanations, and the overall readability of articles make this work a valuable, basic introduction to the subject of information technology" (*American Reference Books Annual*, 1988, p. 247). An earlier work on the subject that complements Edmunds's encyclopedia is Adrian Stokes's *Concise Encyclopedia of Information Technology* (Prentice-Hall, 1983).

❀ DECORATIVE ARTS AND ANTIQUES ❀

The Collectors' Encyclopedia of Antiques. Edited by Phoebe Phillips. Crown, 1973; reprinted by Smith Publications, 1989. 704p. $24.98.

Phillips's well-known encyclopedia—originally published in 1973 under the Crown Publishers imprint but allowed to go out of print in the early 1980s—has recently been reprinted and is now once again available to those in search of an authoritative encyclopedic treatment of the full range of American, British, and European antiques. As noted in *Booklist* (July 1, 1974, p. 1159), the more than 2,000 illustrations add much to the book: "The quality of the colored and black-and-white illustrations is generally on a high level. Integration between the illustrations and the text is provided through the extensive captions which accompany the black-and-white photographs, by means of which much of the detailed information in the encyclopedia is conveyed."

A number of other useful encyclopedias of antiques exist; published in the 1970s, they are all unfortunately out of print at this time: Frances Phipps's *Collector's Complete Dictionary of American Antiques* (Doubleday, 1974); the *Complete Color Encyclopedia of Antiques* (2nd ed. Hawthorn, 1975, edited by L.G.G. Ramsey; Geoffey Wills's *Concise Encyclopedia of Antiques* (Van Nostrand, 1976); George Savage's *Dictionary of 19th Century Antiques and Later Objets d'Art* (Putnam, 1978); James Mackay's *Encyclopedia of Small Antiques* (Harper & Row, 1975); and the *Random House Encyclopedia of Antiques* (Random House, 1973), edited by Ian Cameron and Elizabeth Kingsley-Rowe.

A Complete Dictionary of Furniture. Written by John Gloag; revised & expanded by Clive Edwards. Revised ed. Overlook Press (dist. by Viking), 1991. 828p. $35.00.

First published in 1952 and modestly updated four decades later, Gloag's highly regarded reference comprises some 3,000 entries covering all important aspects of furniture in England since the eleventh century and in North America since the mid-1600s. "This *Dictionary* covers the most extensive time period for both English and North American furniture and furnishings. *A Complete Dictionary of Furniture* is just that, and a very useful reference tool for public and academic libraries" (*Reference Books Bulletin* in *Booklist*, March 15, 1991, p. 1520). Other important encyclopedic sources on furniture are Jonathan Fairbanks and Elizabeth Bidwell Bates's *American Furniture: 1620 to the Present* (Marek, 1981); Charles Boyce's *Dictionary of Furniture* (Facts on File, 1985); and Joseph Aronson's *Encyclopedia of Furniture* (3rd ed. Crown, 1965).

Elements of Style: A Practical Encyclopedia of Interior Architectural Details from 1485 to the Present. Edited by Stephen Calloway. Simon & Schuster, 1991. 544p. $65.00.

This handsomely produced, heavily illustrated encyclopedia offers authoritative material on the principal interior architectural styles found in American and British buildings since the Renaissance. Arranged by period, the book covers everything from Baroque windows to Edwardian bathroom fixtures and more. "Altogether, this is an impressive reference work for architects, interior designers, and historians who need a quick fix on a specific style, feature, or detail" (*Library Journal*, March 15, 1992, p. 76).

The Encyclopedia of Crafts. Edited by Laura Torbet; illustrated by Gary Tong. Scribner's, 1980. 3 vols. Out of print (last priced at $100.00).

Fifty handcrafts ranging from applique and block printing to needlepoint and woodworking are covered in the 12,000 entries that make up this distinctive encyclopedia, now unfortunately out of print. Major articles on each craft emphasize its history, techniques, materials, and equipment. Roughly 2,500 line drawings by Tong enhance the text. "Although the contents may duplicate information found in other titles, the *Encyclopedia* is unique in its inclusiveness and encyclopedic format. It should prove to be a valuable basic tool for professional and amateur alike" (*RQ*, Spring 1981, p. 311).

Encyclopedia of Decorative Arts, 1890–1940. Edited by Philippe Garner. Van Nostrand, 1979. 320p. Out of print (last priced at $35.00).

Beautifully illustrated, this encyclopedia deals with a revolutionary period in the development of the decorative arts: the era of the Bauhaus, of Art Nouveau, Art Deco, and the onset of the international modern movement. Rita Reif, writing in the *New York Times* (December 23, 1979, p. 32), puts the volume in good perspective: "Dozens of books have been written on the Art Nouveau and Art Deco periods covered in this excellent volume. But none has succeeded until now in achieving a larger view of the two styles and their designers. . . . The illustrations and graphics are superb and many will be new even to readers who have studied the many volumes previously produced. It's a feast for the eyes and for the mind—covering furniture, decorative sculpture, jewelry, glass, lighting, tablewares, pottery, posters, rugs and accessories." A comparable work is the *Random House Collector's Encyclopedia: Victoriana to Art Deco* (Random House, 1974), which covers a somewhat larger time period (1851–1939) but is not so well written or illustrated. Both these works are, regrettably, now out of print.

Encyclopedia of Handspinning. Written by Mabel Ross. Interweave Press (dist. by Contemporary Books), 1988. 224p. $21.95.

Ross's attractive, informative, specialized encyclopedia contains brief, alphabetically arranged articles of a few lines to a page in length. "A well-

written, thorough, beautifully produced encyclopedia that covers a wide range of topics related to handspinning, including historical and cross-cultural aspects, spinnable fibers of all kinds, tools, yarn analysis, and spinning techniques. Also included is information on dying [sic], weaving, felting, and commercial yarn processing. . . . There is no other source that brings together so much information on this topic" (*Choice*, September 1988, p. 88).

Encyclopedia of Pottery & Porcelain, 1800–1960. Written by Elisabeth Cameron. Facts on File, 1986. 380p. $35.00.

Cameron expertly furnishes concise information about pottery and porcelain techniques, styles, movements, designers, decorators, factories, marks, and materials in approximately 2,500 A-to-Z entries. International in scope, the encyclopedia's emphasis is on English, American, and European ceramics. Norman Stevens, reviewing the book in *American Reference Books Annual* (1987, p. 366), says, "Within limits this is the best single guide now available in the field of ceramics." Complementing Cameron's encyclopedia is Louise Ade Boger's classic *Dictionary of World Pottery and Porcelain* (Scribner's, 1970), which treats the field from the Bronze Age to modern times. Another well-known work, Frank and Janet Hamer's *Potter's Dictionary of Materials and Techniques* (3rd ed. Univ. of Pennsylvania Press, 1991), serves as a practical encyclopedic guide for potters, both novice and advanced.

The Encyclopedia of Textiles. Written by Judith Jerde. Facts on File, 1992. 260p. $45.00.

Although not as comprehensive as an earlier work prepared by the editors of *American Fabrics and Fashion Magazine* also entitled *Encyclopedia of Textiles* (3rd ed. Prentice-Hall, 1980), Jerde's encyclopedia has the advantage of being much more current. Written for the nonspecialist, Jerde's book emphasizes manufactured rather than handcrafted textiles and includes pertinent information about types of fabrics and fibers, manufacturing processes, finishes, weaves, and dyeing, as well as important names in textile history. "The volume contains 42 full-color and 190 black-and-white photographs. Liberally distributed throughout the text, these illustrations add to the understanding of the technical processes explained and enhance the description of particular types of fabrics" (*Reference Books Bulletin* in *Booklist*, June 1, 1992, p. 1774).

The Encyclopedia of World Costume. Written by Doreen Yarwood. Scribner's, 1978; reprinted by Outlet Book Company, 1988. 471p. $16.99.

This excellent single-volume treatment of costume from the ancient world to the present day includes 650 articles (some quite lengthy) augmented by about 2,000 black-and-while drawings and a detailed index. "Amazingly enough there is an illustration for almost every item discussed in the text, everything from Caucasian folk costumes and children's dress in the 16th century to the history of the ruff and 3,000 years of finger rings" (*Choice*, October 1979, p. 1000). Other serviceable costume encyclopedias include R. Turner Wilcox's *Dictionary of Costume* (Scribner's, 1968); August Racinet's *Historical Encyclopedia of Costume* (Facts on File, 1988), an abridged English-language reissue of Racinet's famous six-volume *Le Costume Historique*, published in France in 1888; and Marion Sichel's multivolume *Costume Reference* (Plays, Inc., 1977–78).

Facts on File Dictionary of Design and Designers. Written by Simon Jervis. Facts on File, 1984. 533p. $35.00.

Jervis (Victoria and Albert Museum) surveys the history of European and American design from 1450 to the present in brief entries describing major styles, movements, exhibitions, associations, publications, and artists. "Excellently organized and very inclusive, this is not only a most useful reference tool to the broad subject of design but opens up many new areas for future design history study" (*American Reference Books Annual*, 1985, p. 316). A more specialized but equally valuable work that nicely complements Jervis's book is John Pile's *Dictionary of 20th-Century Design* (Facts on File, 1990).

Illustrated Dictionary of Jewelry. Written by Harold Newman. Thames & Hudson (dist. by Norton), 1987. 335p. $18.95 paperbound.

International in scope, Newman's encyclopedic *Illustrated Dictionary of Jewelry* comprehensively covers the subject from earliest times to the present in 2,530 brief entries. "A truly unique work. In one handsomely bound volume Newman has combined a wealth of needed information for the jeweler, student, collector, dealer, or interested layperson" (*Choice*, May 1982, p. 1218).

The Oxford Companion to the Decorative Arts. Edited by Harold Osborne. Oxford Univ. Press, 1975. 865p. $22.50 paperbound.

Common and uncommon arts—costume, furniture, jewelry, leatherwork, embroidery, toymaking, landscape gardening, book production, bell-founding, lace-tatting, etc.—are covered by some 75 experts in this handy encyclopedia. A reference mainstay for nearly two decades, the *Oxford Companion to the Decorative Arts* is beginning to show its age; still, it remains an exceptionally useful survey volume. "The *Companion* does not provide definitive treatment of any of its subjects, but it is an excellent starting point for the nonspecialist because of its concise, reliable coverage of a broad range of topics and useful bibliographies" (*Booklist*, June 15, 1976, p. 1486).

The Penguin Dictionary of Decorative Arts. Written by John Fleming & Hugh Honour. Revised ed. Viking, 1990. 935p. $40.00.

Quite similar in purpose, style, size, format, and price to the OXFORD COMPANION TO THE DECORATIVE ARTS, the *Penguin Dictionary of Decorative Arts* is chiefly a guide to the decorative arts of Europe and North America from the Middle Ages onward. The volume, originally published in 1977 and revised in 1990, contains almost 5,000 short entries, of which some 600 are new to the revised edition. Interested consumers cannot go wrong with either of these fine one-volume reference works, although the *Penguin Dictionary of Decorative Arts* is arguably better illustrated and unquestionably more current.

※ EARTH, ENERGY, AND ENVIRONMENTAL SCIENCES ※

Cambridge Encyclopedia of Earth Sciences. Edited by David G. Smith. Cambridge Univ. Press, 1982. 496p. $49.95.

Thematically arranged, this fine survey volume consists of 27 signed, essay-length articles accompanied by approximately 500 informative illustrations. Emphasis is on theoretical aspects of geology, oceanography, paleontology, meteorology, and related earth sciences. "The thorough, well-written coverage of a wide range of topics is suitable for readers at all levels. . . . Recommended for all libraries, and not necessarily only for the reference shelf" (*Choice*, July-August 1982, p. 1534). A larger, more current, and somewhat more technical one-volume encyclopedia on the subject is the MCGRAW-HILL ENCYCLOPEDIA OF THE GEOLOGICAL SCIENCES.

Concise Encyclopedia of Mineral Resources. Edited by Donald D. Carr & Norman Herz. Pergamon Press, 1989. 426p. $170.00; also published by MIT Press at $145.00.

Most but not all of the alphabetically arranged articles that make up this work originally appeared in the eight-volume ENCYCLOPEDIA OF MATERIALS SCIENCE. The articles, written by authorities in the field and normally several pages in length, describe industrial minerals, metals, and fuels within the context of economic geology. Those interested in the subject but who do not want or cannot afford the multivolume encyclopedia (which costs nearly $2,000.00) will find the *Concise Encyclopedia of Mineral Resources* a welcome reference source.

Encyclopedia of Earth Sciences. Edited by Rhodes W. Fairbridge. Van Nostrand, 1966–. 30 or more vols. (in progress). Prices vary from $85.00 to $129.95 per vol.; some vols. out of print.

The *Encyclopedia of Earth Sciences*, an ongoing series of single-volume encyclopedias on specific earth science topics, has been under the general editorship of Rhodes Fairbridge since the beginning when volume 1, the *Encyclopedia of Oceanography*, appeared in 1966. Subsequent volumes include the *Encyclopedia of Atmospheric Sciences and Astrogeology* (1967), the *Encyclopedia of Geomorphology* (1967), the *Encyclopedia of Geochemistry and Environmental Sciences* (1972), the *Encyclopedia of World Regional Geology* (1975), the *Encyclopedia of Sedimentology* (1978), the *Encyclopedia of Paleontology* (1979), the *Encyclopedia of Soil Science* (1979), the *Encyclopedia of Mineralogy* (1981), the *Encyclopedia of Beaches and Coastal Environments* (1982), the *Encyclopedia of Applied Geology* (1984), the *Encyclopedia of Structural Geology and Plate Tectonics* (1987), the *Encyclopedia of Climatology* (1987), the *Encyclopedia of Field and General Geology* (1988), the *Encyclopedia of Geophysics* (1989), the *Encyclopedia of Igneous and Metamorphic Petrology* (1989), and the *Encyclopedia of Solid Earth Geophysics* (1989).

These specialized encyclopedias are written and edited by leading authorities and aimed mainly at professionals and college-level students. A problem, of course, is that some of the volumes are now quite dated and no longer in print. However, the Van Nostrand editor in charge of the series reports that some volumes are currently being revised, e.g., the *Encyclopedia of Geomorphology*, and that a number of new titles are planned or in preparation, e.g., the *Encyclopedia of Quaternary Sciences* and the *Encyclopedia of Hydrology*. In the making for over a quarter of a century and still going strong, the *Encyclopedia of Earth Sciences* is a monumental achievement.

Encyclopedia of Earth System Science. Edited by William A. Nierenberg. Academic Press, 1992. 4 vols. $950.00.

The *Encyclopedia of Earth System Science*—unquestionably the best constructed, best indexed, and most up-to-date encyclopedic source covering all of the earth sciences available in English today—contains approximately 230 alphabetically arranged articles comprising a total of 2,500 pages of text.

Written by internationally known specialists, the articles are enhanced by 1,300 excellent illustrations, 1,600 bibliographies of important books and journal articles, and 1,300 glossary entries that define important technical terms used in the text. "The articles are extremely well written, so that in most cases the educated layperson as well as the researcher is accommodated. By far the most useful aspect of the set is its stress on human environmental involvement with all geologic processes from pure geology to the atmosphere and space" (*Reference Books Bulletin* in *Booklist*, March 15, 1992, p. 1400). No comparable encyclopedia exists.

Encyclopedia of Environmental Control Technology. Edited by Paul N. Cheremisinoff. Gulf Publishing Co., 1989–. 8 vols. (in progress). $155.00 per vol.

Begun in 1989 and scheduled for completion in 1994, the in-progress *Encyclopedia of Environmental Control Technology* deals with all major aspects of environmental and industrial pollution control problems and solutions. The arrangement is thematic (as opposed to alphabetical), with each volume devoted to a broad subject: Volume 1 (1989) covers thermal treatments of hazardous wastes, volume 2 (1989) air pollution, volume 3 (1989) wastewater treatment, volume 4 (1990) hazardous waste containment and treatment, volume 5 (1992) waste minimization and recycling, and volume 6 (1993) pollution reduction and contaminant control. Volumes 7 and 8 are forthcoming. Intended for advanced students and working professionals, the encyclopedia's lengthy articles are written by experts from industry and academia. In a review of volume 1 in *Choice* (June 1989, p. 1701), C.C. Greene says, "The editor's goal in this and future volumes is to provide an overview of state-of-the-art technologies and research activities in the fields of pollution and waste control. . . . Recommended for academic and research libraries supporting civil and environmental engineering programs."

Encyclopedia of Environmental Science and Engineering. Edited by James R. Pfafflin & Edward N. Ziegler. 3rd ed. Gordon and Breach, 1992. 2 vols. $545.00.

First published in two volumes in 1976, then revised and expanded to three volumes in 1983, and now back to two volumes in a third edition issued in 1992, the *Encyclopedia of Environmental Science and Engineering* currently consists of 1,400 pages of reliable information covering all major environmental areas and issues, including such topics as air, water, and soil pollution, public health and safety, fossil fuel production, and hazardous waste management.

The articles, arranged A-to-Z, are written by leading authorities and will ordinarily be comprehensible to serious students, professionals in the field, and interested laypeople who possess at least a rudimentary background in science. Another work that addresses much the same audience is the *McGraw-Hill Encyclopedia of Environmental Sciences* (2nd ed. McGraw-Hill, 1980), although it is now dated and in need of a new edition (which should be forthcoming in the near future).

The Encyclopedia of Environmental Studies. Written by William Ashworth. Facts on File, 1991. 470p. $60.00.

Ashworth's encyclopedia consists of 3,000 concise, alphabetical entries that clearly and accurately cover terms, movements, events, organizations, legislation, regulatory practices, and prominent people associated with environmental science today. Admirably current and written for the layperson with minimal scientific background, the book "is a major contribution to helping the diverse constituency of environmentalism speak the same language. It should be particularly valuable in college library and other general collections" (*American Reference Books Annual*, 1992, p. 719). A complementary work for nonspecialists is Irene Granck and David Brownstone's advocacy oriented *Green Encyclopedia* (Prentice Hall, 1992). In addition, Gale Research has announced a new work tentatively called the *Environmental Encyclopedia*, scheduled for publication sometime in 1994.

The Encyclopedia of Gemstones and Minerals. Written by Martin Holden. Facts on File, 1991. 303p. $45.00.

From actinolite to zircon, Holden's colorfully illustrated encyclopedia describes gems, minerals, and related topics (such as atomic structure and specific gravity) in roughly 250 entries ranging from half a page to three pages in length. "The editorial goal to create a work that would be a primary source of information for student use rather than a technical source for the specialist has been successfully accomplished" (*Reference Books Bulletin* in *Booklist*, March 15, 1992, p. 1402). Interested consumers will also want to look at these excellent works on the subject: Joel Arem's *Color Encyclopedia of Gemstones* (2nd ed. Van Nostrand, 1987), the *Larousse Encyclopedia of Precious Gems* (Van Nostrand, 1992), and the *VNR Color Dictionary of Minerals and Gemstones* (Van Nostrand, 1982) by Michael O'Donoghue.

Encyclopedia of Minerals. Written by Willard L. Roberts & others. 2nd ed. Van Nostrand, 1990. 979p. $99.95.

This definitive encyclopedia provides extensive data on over 3,000 authenticated mineral species, including hundreds of new ones added since the book was first published in 1974. Black-and-white illustrations appear throughout and a center section contains standout color photos of some 300 minerals. "Because of its comprehensive coverage, completeness of entries, and currency of information, this may be the best reference tool in the field of mineral identification" (*American Reference Books Annual*, 1991, p. 716). Another well-known reference source, *Dana's Manual of Mineralogy* (20th ed. Wiley, 1985), includes descriptions of several hundred common minerals, along with essential material on crystallography and physical mineralogy.

The Illustrated Encyclopedia of Fossils. Written by Giovanni Pinna; translated by Jay Hyams. Facts on File, 1990. 240p. $35.00.

Pinna, an Italian paleontologist who has worked for many years at the Museum of Natural History in Milan, traces the evolution of the earth's life forms fossil-by-fossil in this well-illustrated encyclopedia, which "contains a splendid array of color photographs of many types of fossils accompanied by a text describing groups of organisms systematically" (*Library Journal*, March 15, 1991, p. 86). The book is aimed principally at the general reader and student, not the specialist.

International Petroleum Encyclopedia. Edited by Jim West. PennWell Books, 1967– (revised annually). 350p. $115.00.

Published each year since 1967, the single-volume *International Petroleum Encyclopedia* is a prime source for authoritative information about the petroleum and natural gas industries in the U.S. and around the world. It usually has about 350 pages and includes numerous detailed maps, graphs, tables, maps, and informative illustrations; a much needed subject index was added in 1989. "This encyclopedia continues to provide comprehensive coverage of the two industries and has had a long history of serving them well. It is an excellent way of obtaining an overall picture of new developments" (*American Reference Books Annual*, 1993, p. 728).

McGraw-Hill Encyclopedia of the Geological Sciences. Edited by Sybil P. Parker. 2nd ed. McGraw-Hill, 1988. 722p. $85.00.

Authoritative, comprehensive, and easy to use, this encyclopedia offers in-depth coverage of geology, geochemistry, geophysics, and those areas of oceanography and meteorology essential to understanding the materials, processes, composition, and physical characteristics of the earth's solid phase. In toto, the encyclopedia contains 520 articles augmented by 650 illustrations, practically all of which are reprinted from the sixth editon (1987) of the multivolume MCGRAW-HILL ENCYCLOPEDIA OF SCIENCE AND TECHNOLOGY. The encyclopedia is more technically oriented than the competing CAMBRIDGE ENCYCLOPEDIA OF EARTH SCIENCES, although both works can be used profitably by serious students at the high school and college levels as well as by teachers, scientists, and informed laypeople.

The Times Atlas and Encyclopedia of the Sea. Edited by Alastair Couper. HarperCollins, 1989. 272p. $65.00.

Formerly the *Times Atlas of the Oceans* (Van Nostrand, 1983), this retitled and minimally revised edition provides a rich array of information about all relevant aspects of oceanography, including ocean environments, resources, and pollution and the economic importance and military uses of oceans. Especially noteworthy are the outstanding maps, photographs, and graphs throughout the volume. In a review of the original edition in *Library Journal* (November 1, 1983, p. 2074), Jay Kaufman advised that the book "is essential for all libraries serving professional and lay readers interested in the sea. It should facilitate the broader understanding of the oceans that is so crucial to life on earth." A comparable work is the older *Ocean World Encyclopedia* (McGraw-Hill, 1980) by Donald Groves and Lee Hunt; unlike the *Times Atlas and Encyclopedia of the Sea*, the *Ocean World Encyclopedia* is arranged alphabetically, but both are easy to use.

Toxics A to Z: A Guide to Everyday Pollution Hazards. Written by John Harte & others. Univ. of California Press, 1991. 479p. $75.00.

An exhaustive encyclopedia of toxic materials, *Toxics A to Z* describes over 100 potentially hazardous, commonly encountered toxics from acetic acid to zinc. Written in terms comprehensible to the average person, the book thoroughly treats each substance, including its physical and chemical properties, exposure and distribution, potential health and environmental consequences, means of protec-

tion and prevention, and regulatory status. "Popular in presentation and readability, yet technical enough to be a comprehensive guide for those who need a solid introduction to a field that is more important than ever, this volume will be useful for most libraries, either public or academic" (*Choice*, March 1992, p. 1058).

The United States Energy Atlas. Written by David J. Cuff & William J. Young. 2nd ed. Macmillan, 1986. 387p. $85.00.

This encyclopedic survey furnishes definitive information on the location, amount, technology, and uses of practically every known type of energy, from nonrenewable (coal and oil) to renewable (sun and wind) sources. Supporting the text are numerous informative maps, photos, diagrams, and charts. "*The United States Energy Atlas* provides a concise, well-written and well-illustrated overview of energy in the United States today. The authors have succeeded in pulling together widely scattered information into one source. This book is highly recommended for high schools and colleges, as well as for those in the energy industry" (*American Reference Books Annual*, 1987, p. 565).

The Water Encyclopedia: A Compendium of Useful Information on Water Resources. Written by Frits van der Leeden & others. 2nd ed. Lewis Publishers, 1990. 808p. $125.00.

All important aspects of water and related topics—climate, precipitation, hydrology, wastewater, pollution, laws and treaties, etc.—are dealt with in this compilation of some 700 charts, graphs, tables, and maps, reproduced from a variety of reputable sources, both public and private. The encyclopedia, first published in 1970 and extensively revised in 1990, contains no written text, other than a preface and occasional brief notes; it is useful mainly for statistical information. A complementary work is Willard and Ruby Miller's *Water Quality and Availability: A Reference Handbook* (ABC-Clio, 1992), a 430-page encyclopedic reference source that focuses on the water supply in the U.S. and how to preserve it.

❋ EDUCATION AND LIBRARIES ❋

American Educators' Encyclopedia. Written by David E. Kapel & others. Revised ed. Greenwood, 1991. 716p. $95.00.

The best single-volume encyclopedia covering the entire education field available today, the *American Educators' Encyclopedia* provides clear, reliable information on important topics, terminology, and

people in nearly 2,000 concise A-to-Z entries. First published in 1982, the revised edition has added a number of new entries, such as "Acquired Immune Deficiency Syndrome," "Attention Deficit Disorder," "Cooperative Learning," "The Holmes Group," "Master Teacher," and "Zero Rejection." James Rettig in *Wilson Library Bulletin* (April 1992, p. 119) calls the encyclopedia "a reference workhorse for the past decade."

A Critical Dictionary of Educational Concepts: An Appraisal of Selected Ideas and Issues in Educational Theory and Practice. Written by Robin Barrow & Geoffrey Milburn. 2nd ed. Teachers College Press (Teachers College, Columbia Univ.), 1990. 384p. $43.95.

Barrow and Milburn's encyclopedic dictionary explores well over 100 "key concepts" in the education field, e.g., behaviorism, creativity, integrated studies, and research. First published in 1986, the book was revised in 1990. *Choice* (July-August 1987, p. 1672) praised the first edition: "Useful for students of education, this work not only defines terms but also discusses both sides of controversies, and it takes a critical stand on the worth of a particular concept to teaching and learning. . . . The book is a valuable reference book for libraries serving both undergraduate and graduate students."

Encyclopedia of Early Childhood Education. Edited by Leslie R. Williams & Doris Pronin Fromberg. Garland, 1992. 518p. $95.00.

An outstanding specialized encyclopedia, this carefully edited work furnishes roughly 200 signed articles on all pertinent aspects of the education of children from birth to age 8, including theories, movements, curriculum programs, and such practical concerns as day care and AIDS. Articles are arranged topically, grouped within six broad sections. "The contributing authors are among the most outstanding and knowledgeable in their areas. An essay by Maxine Greene on the history of early childhood education is particularly noteworthy, but all of the entries are valuable" (*Choice*, November 1992, p. 518).

The Encyclopedia of Educational Media Communications and Technology. Written by Derick Unwin & Ray McAleese. 2nd ed. Greenwood, 1988. 568p. $135.00.

This useful reference provides both short and long articles "on a broad cross-section of topics of interest to educational technologists. Longer signed articles are written by 70 specialists in the United Kingdom, Australia, Canada, and the United States" (*American Reference Books Annual*, 1990, p. 147). A competing work is the 654-page *International Encyclopedia of Educational Technology* (Pergamon Press, 1989), which consists largely of material reprinted from the multivolume INTERNATIONAL ENCYCLOPEDIA OF EDUCATION.

Encyclopedia of Educational Research. Edited by Marvin C. Alkin. 6th ed. Macmillan, 1992. 4 vols. $330.00.

The *Encyclopedia of Educational Research*, published by Macmillan under the sponsorship of the American Educational Research Association, has long been recognized as one of the premier reference works in the field of education, the first edition appearing in 1940 followed by substantial revisions every 10 years or so thereafter. The recently issued sixth edition—called the Fiftieth Anniversary Edition by the publisher— contains more than 250 admirably current, clearly written articles designed "to summarize research on educational topics of relevance" (introduction). Prepared mainly by professors of education, the articles cover all aspects of the field, including such timely topics as AIDS education, athletics in higher education, the merits of standardized testing, and the schooling of teenage parents. An appendix entitled "Doing Library Research in Education" provides an excellent introduction to education reference sources such as encyclopedias, dictionaries, bibliographies, dissertations, and CD-ROM products. "This edition, like its predecessors, will be useful to college students as well as educational researchers and practitioners and is recommended for undergraduate, graduate, and professional collections" (*Library Journal*, July 1992, p. 74).

Encyclopedia of Higher Education. Edited by Burton R. Clark & Guy Neave. Pergamon Press, 1992. 4 vols. $1,500.00.

New in 1992, the *Encyclopedia of Higher Education* comprises more than 300 substantial articles, including descriptions of 135 national systems of higher education in volume 1, and, in volumes 2 through 4, in-depth treatment of such topics as university administration, finances and funding, research activities and facilities, student recruitment and admissions policies and procedures, and the development of core disciplines. The final volume also contains detailed indexes. The set, which totals roughly two million words in 2,500 pages, draws some material from the publisher's highly regarded 10-volume INTERNATIONAL ENCYCLOPEDIA OF EDUCATION, but most of the text is new, providing an authoritative encyclopedic review of higher education in the 1990s from an international perspective. The *Encyclopedia of Higher Education* effectively replaces the larger but now much dated and out of print 10-volume *International Encyclopedia of Higher Education* (Jossey-Bass, 1977), edited by Asa Knowles. "Arguably, this new effort is one of the most important reference tools in higher education since the Knowles work" (*Choice*, February 1993, p. 938). A smaller, less expansive, and less expensive work is *International Higher Education: An Encyclopedia* (Garland, 1991), a two-volume set edited by Philip Altbach that sells for $150.00 but limits its coverage to 52 countries and regions.

Encyclopedia of Learning and Memory. Edited by Larry R. Squire. Macmillan, 1992. 642p. $105.00.

This excellent specialized compendium contains 189 alphabetically arranged articles prepared by leading authorities in educational psychology and neuroscience. Up-to-date, well-indexed, and scholarly in tone, the encyclopedia emphasizes learning and memory in humans, although some text is devoted to cognitive research involving animals. The book also contains many informative diagrams, photographs, and other illustrations. "Useful to informed lay readers as well as teachers and college students, this volume is recommended for public and undergraduate college libraries" (*Library Journal*, February 15, 1993, p. 160).

Encyclopedia of Library and Information Science. Edited by Allen Kent & others. Marcel Dekker, 1968–83. 35 vols. plus suppls., 1983–. $115.00 per vol.; series can be purchased from publisher on standing order at $99.75 per vol.

Despite many flaws, including alarmingly uneven coverage and lax editing, the massive *Encyclopedia of Library and Information Science* provides useful background information on almost all library topics. The encyclopedia's first volume appeared in 1968, and the basic set was finally completed 15 years later in 1983, having reached a total of 35 volumes, including a two-volume author and subject index. Numerous supplements intended to update old articles and treat new topics have been published since at the rate of more than one a year. At present, the set totals 52 volumes and continues to grow. Bohdan Wynar, writing in *American Reference Books Annual* (1987, p. 228), questions this editorial approach: "The impact of technology on the field of library science in the last 10 years has been felt by all of us. How can this problem be resolved by using supplements? This work has taken more than one and one-half decades to produce. Do we really need to add new articles on John Baskerville or Apollonius Rhodius or Giacomio Casonova? Indeed, they are well written, but there will be no end to these supplements if we continue in this fashion." Wynar wisely advises the editors to put their energies into creating a new edition of this major undertaking.

Encyclopedia of School Administration and Supervision. Edited by Richard A. Gorton & others. Oryx Press, 1988. 352p. $74.50.

Some 250 alphabetically arranged articles from "Academic Learning Time" to "Women in Administration" comprise this useful encyclopedia, which describes contemporary theories, practices, and trends in U.S. elementary and secondary school administration and supervision. The articles are jargon-free and conclude with carefully selected bibliographies. "School board members, supervisors, and administrators will welcome this excellent summary of informwation on leadership improvement in schools" (*Choice*, November 1988, p. 460). An older but still effective reference for school administrators that deals with some of the same issues covered in the *Encyclopedia of School Administration and Supervision* is Richard and Daniel Gatti's *New Encyclopedic Dictionary of School Law* (Parker Publishing, 1983).

Encyclopedia of Special Education: A Reference for the Education of the Handicapped and Other Exceptional Children and Adults. Edited by Cecil R. Reynolds & Lester Mann. Wiley, 1987. 3 vols. $325.00.

This important specialized encyclopedia contains over 2,000 scholarly articles prepared by nearly 400 authorities on all pertinent aspects of special education. Emphasis is on developments in North America, although international perspectives are provided. Topics covered include major court cases and laws, services required to support special education, educational and psychological tests and testing, intervention techniques, and clinical disorders and syndromes. The encyclopedia also includes biographies of prominent practitioners and educators in the field. James Rettig in *Wilson Library Bulletin* (October 1987, p. 82) recommends the set: "This provides excellent exposition of special education topics and meets the needs of its varied audience. A must for academic libraries, it will also be useful in public libraries, especially to parents of students in special education programs." Interested consumers will be pleased to know that in 1990 the publisher issued a one-volume abridged and updated version of the set entitled the *Concise Encyclopedia of Special Education*; this book, which sells for $89.95, claims that "90% of the original articles were condensed and streamlined to give basic facts and reference ideas" (introduction).

The International Encyclopedia of Education. Edited by Torsten Husen & T. Neville Postlethwaite. 2nd ed. Pergamon Press, 1994. 12 vols. $3,795.00.

Winner of the esteemed Dartmouth Medal in 1986 (awarded to the best reference work published the previous year) and highly acclaimed by critics, the 10-volume first edition of the *International Encyclopedia of Education* has been updated and expanded to 12 volumes in 1994. The new edition—unseen by the author of *Kister's Best Encyclopedias*—is said to contain approximately 7,000 pages and expand thematic coverage from 16 to 22 major fields.

The original edition of the encyclopedia is an impressive reference source both quantitatively and qualitatively, encompassing approximately five million words in 6,000 pages of text and nearly 1,500 signed articles by 1,300 respected contributors from over 100 countries. Arranged thematically within 25 broad subject categories, the carefully researched articles treat all relevant facets of education, including administration, continuing education, counseling and guidance, childhood education, economic and funding issues, curricular developments, higher education, special education, and the role of women in education. Another important feature is a survey of the educational systems of 160 countries, which furnishes information similar to that found in Kurian's WORLD EDUCATION ENCYCLOPEDIA. "*The IEE* is an authoritative reference work which represents a significant contribution to the scholarship of pedagogy and is designed to assist a broad range of users" (*American Reference Books Annual*, 1986, p. 118). This fine encyclopedia replaces the once indispensable but now old and out-of-print *Encyclopedia of Education* (Macmillan, 1971), also a 10-volume work.

World Education Encyclopedia. Edited by George Thomas Kurian. Facts on File, 1988. 3 vols. $195.00.

This three-volume set provides basic information and data about the educational systems of 181 nations, as well as commentary on the history and current status of education internationally. Profiles of individual systems are more extensive than those found in the INTERNATIONAL ENCYCLOPEDIA OF EDUCATION, and Kurian covers more countries (181 as

opposed to 160). The *World Education Encyclopedia* "is now likely to be the popular choice for libraries seeking good coverage of comparative education. Its country essays are detailed, well researched, and thoroughly documented. . . . The *Encyclopedia* achieves its goal of presenting a comprehensive overview of the state of world education as the present century approaches its last decade" (*Reference Books Bulletin* in *Booklist*, January 1, 1989, p. 773). Editor Kurian reports that a new edition of the encyclopedia will probably appear within the next year or two.

World Encyclopedia of Library and Information Services. Edited by Robert Wedgeworth. 3rd ed. American Library Assn., 1993. 905p. $200.00.

As its title implies, this encyclopedia surveys the history and present status of librarianship in countries around the world, although developments in U.S. libraries receive the most attention. The encyclopedia, first published in 1980 and revised in 1986 under the title *ALA World Encyclopedia of Library and Information Services*, appeared in a third revision in 1993 as simply the *World Encyclopedia of Library and Information Services*. It now contains approximately 500 signed articles by 430 contributors. In a lengthy critical review of the second edition in *Wilson Library Bulletin* (November 1986, p. 57), Norman Stevens puts the volume in good perspective: "Once again an impressive group of contributors has helped put together a massive array of short articles, arranged in alphabetical order and readily accessed by an outline and a detailed index, on almost all aspects of librarianship throughout the world with an emphasis on the contemporary scene in a historical perspective." The encyclopedia is kept reasonably current by *Libraries and Information Services Today: The Yearly Chronicle* (American Library Assn., 1991–), successor to the *ALA Yearbook of Library and Information Science* (1976–90). A potentially complementary one-volume work (unseen by the author of *Kister's Best Encyclopedias*) is the *Encyclopedia of Library History* (Garland, 1993), edited by Wayne Wiegand and Donald Davis.

※ ENGINEERING AND BUILDING CONSTRUCTION ※

Dictionary of Woodworking Tools c. 1700–1970 and Tools of Allied Trades. Written by R.A. Salaman; revised by Philip Walker. Revised ed. Taunton Press (dist. by Norton), 1990. 546p. $27.95 paperbound.

First published in 1976 and revised in 1990, this encyclopedic dictionary describes all types of hand tools used by carpenters, basket makers, shipbuild-

ers, upholsterers, and the like. Articles run from a few lines to half a dozen or more pages in length; for instance, the entry covering the plane maker is eight pages long. Many informative black-and-white drawings and engravings accompany the readable text. Similar single-volume reference works are Graham Blackburn's *Illustrated Encyclopedia of Woodworking Handtools, Instruments & Devices* (Revised ed. Globe Pequot Press, 1992) and Vic Taylor's *Woodworker's Dictionary* (Storey Communications, 1991). A recently published book that covers both hand and power tools is the 360-page *Reader's Digest Book of Skills & Tools* (Reader's Digest Assn., dist. by Random House, 1993), which is billed as "A Homeowner's Encyclopedia of Tools, Hardware, and Materials."

Encyclopedia of Building Technology. Edited by Henry J. Cowan. Prentice-Hall, 1988. 322p. $75.00.

Cowan, a well-known name in the area of reference works on architecture and building construction, has assembled a handy encyclopedia containing 210 concise articles by leading authorities on various aspects of building technology, such as foundations, scaffolding, curtain walls, balloon frames, and natural ventilation. Written for the nonspecialist, the articles furnish basic information on the topic and conclude with a short bibliography of basic books and articles the reader might profitably consult. Two complementary sources are Hugh Brooks's *Encyclopedia of Building and Construction Terms* (Prentice-Hall, 1983) and the *Concise Encyclopedia of Building & Construction Materials* (MIT Press and Pergamon Press, 1990)—the latter a spinoff of the excellent ENCYCLOPEDIA OF MATERIALS SCIENCE AND ENGINEERING.

Encyclopedia of Fluid Mechanics. Edited by Nicholas P. Cheremisinoff. Gulf Publishing, 1986–93. 10 vols. plus 2 suppls., 1993. $195.00 per vol. (10-vol. set); $139.00 (ea. suppl.); series can be purchased from publisher on standing order at 10% discount.

A large, authoritative, and unique work, the *Encyclopedia of Fluid Mechanics* deals comprehensively with the interdisciplinary field of fluid mechanics and hydraulics. Each of the 10 volumes that makes up the basic set deals with a specific subject: Volume 1, for example, covers flow phenomena and measurement; volume 2, the dynamics of single-fluid flows and mixing; volume 3, gas-liquid flows. Each volume contains over 1,400 pages of text prepared by leading experts from around the world. Supplement 1, published in early 1993, covers applied mathematics in fluid dynamics and includes a detailed index to the 10-volume set; Supplement 2, published in late 1993, treats advances in multiphase flow. Robert Havlik, in a review of the first six volumes in *American Reference Books Annual* (1988, p. 636), rightly concludes, "The work should last for years as the standard reference in the field of fluid dynamics."

Encyclopedia of Materials Science and Engineering. Edited by Michael B. Bever. Pergamon Press, 1986. 8 vols. plus suppl., 1988. $3,050.00 (8-vol. set); $295.00 (suppl.); also published by MIT Press at $2,150.00 (8-vol. set).

Ten years in the making, this distinguished specialized encyclopedia's eight volumes comprise close to 1,600 articles enhanced by more than 3,000 informative illustrations and 1,300 tables packed into 6,100 pages of scholarly text intended for serious students, working engineers, and researchers in the field. The 1,400 contributors represent prominent authorities from over 20 countries. The articles, which are arranged alphabetically, cover 44 broad subject areas within these four categories: "Classes of Materials Based on Their Nature," "Special Classes of Materials Based on Their Applications," "Materials-Related Methods and Phenomena," and "General Subjects." The final volume contains a comprehensive index to the set, plus a 12,500-entry selected bibliography. "This is a beautifully produced encyclopedia on a topic with broad applications in all areas of engineering and physics. Libraries needing materials information, even those already owning *Kirk-Othmer's* [KIRK-OTHMER ENCYCLOPEDIA OF CHEMICAL TECHNOLOGY], which contains substantial materials information, should still consider purchasing this encyclopedia because of its emphasis on metals and metallurgical topics and applications information, and its strong coverage of mechanical, thermal, and electrical properties" (*American Reference Books Annual*, 1987, p. 613).

Consumers should also know that Pergamon Press has recently issued a number of one-volume encyclopedias consisting largely of reprinted articles from the *Encyclopedia of Materials Science and Engineering*. Priced at between $125 and $175 per volume, they include the *Concise Encyclopedia of Composite Materials* (1989), the *Concise Encyclopedia of Wood & Wood-Based Materials* (1989), the *Concise Encyclopedia of Building & Construction Materials* (1990), the *Concise Encyclopedia of Medical & Dental Materials* (1990), and the CONCISE ENCYCLOPEDIA OF MINERAL RESOURCES (1990).

An Encyclopedia of Metallurgy and Materials. Written by C.R. Tottle. Macdonald & Evans, 1984. 380p. Out of print (last priced at $97.50).

Prepared and first published in Great Britain, Tottle's encyclopedia consists of roughly 5,000 concise entries plus 90 pages of tables on the uses and properties of metals, alloys, plastics, and ceramics. "Tottle has produced a comprehensive reference work intended to provide as much information as necessary for an understanding of processes and materials . . . . recommended for acquisition by undergraduate libraries as a useful reference in engineering" (*Choice*, October 1984, p. 254).

How to Clean Everything: An Encyclopedia of What to Use and How to Use It. Written by Alma C. Moore. 3rd ed. Simon & Schuster, 1980. 239p. $6.95 paperbound.

Moore's *How to Clean Everything* is normally one of the most heavily used reference books in public libraries, and at $6.95 it is not beyond the reach of individuals for use in the home. The book describes available cleaning agents and provides precise instructions for cleaning different kinds of materials, finishes, and objects, including blankets, electric irons, jewelry, tiles, wallpaper, playing cards, silk shirts, and shower curtains. This practical encyclopedia concludes with a section on how to remove 150 different kinds of spots and stains. Similar works (all in one volume) are *Heloise from A to Z* (Putnam, 1992), a paperback priced at $10.95; *Don Aslett's Cleaning Encyclopedia* (Dell, 1993), also a paperback priced at $14.95; and *Mary Ellen's Clean House! The All-in-One-Place Encyclopedia of Contemporary Housekeeping* (Crown, 1993), a hardcover book by Mary Ellen Pinkham and Dale Burg that sells for $20.00.

Machinery's Handbook: A Reference Book for the Mechanical Engineer, Designer, Manufacturing Engineer, Draftsman, Toolmaker, and Machinist. Written by Erik Oberg & others; edited by Robert Green. 24th ed. Industrial Press, 1992. 2,543p. $65.00.

First published in 1914 and frequently revised (the previous edition appeared in 1988), this huge one-volume work is encyclopedic in scope, covering practically all facets of the mechanical industries in over 150 sections dealing with materials strength, springs, bearings, lubricants, bolts, etc. Revision in recent editions has emphasized new specifications and standards numbers, along with increasing metrication of the text. La Verne Coan and Suzanne Holler, writing in *Reference Sources for Small and Medium-Sized Libraries* (5th ed. American Library Assn., 1992, pp. 143–44), call the book the "bible of all machinists, metalworkers, designers, and craftspeople . . . . an essential reference wherever machines and mechanical products are involved."

Marks' Standard Handbook for Mechanical Engineers. Edited by Eugene A. Avallone & Theodore Baumeister. 9th ed. McGraw-Hill, 1987. 2,048p. $109.50.

Originally prepared by Lionel S. Marks and published in 1916 as the *Mechanical Engineers' Hand-book*, this truly "standard" work contains a wealth of information for students and working professionals, including much tabular data and encyclopedia-length articles written by specialists in the field. In typical handbook fashion the material is presented in chapters covering such topics as machine elements, fuels and furnaces, power generating pumps and compressors, instrumentation, and environmental control. Fortunately, the volume contains an exhaustive analytical index.

Materials Handbook: An Encyclopedia for Managers, Technical Professionals, Purchasing and Production Managers, Technicians, Supervisors, and Foremen. Written by George S. Brady & Henry R. Clauser. 13th ed. McGraw-Hill, 1991. 1,056p. $74.50.

Widely known in the field as "Brady's," the *Materials Handbook*, first published in 1929 and now in its thirteenth edition, continues to reflect the late George Brady's original aim: "To prepare a one-volume encyclopedia that would intelligently describe the important characteristics of commercially available materials without involvement in details" (introduction). Today the encyclopedia contains approximately 15,000 entries covering both large categories of materials (such as metal alloys, textiles, and plastics) and specific products (cotton, linoleum, tea, walrus hide, etc.). "The *Materials Handbook* is a highly recommended reference book that should be in all core science and technology reference collections in public and academic libraries" (*Reference Books Bulletin* in *Booklist*, December 1, 1991, p. 722).

McGraw-Hill Encyclopedia of Engineering. Edited by Sybil P. Parker. 2nd ed. McGraw-Hill, 1993. 1,264p. $95.50.

Most of the more than 700 articles that make up this source were first published in the seventh (1992) edition of the 15-volume MCGRAW-HILL ENCYCLOPEDIA OF SCIENCE AND TECHNOLOGY. The encyclopedia, which first appeared in 1983, covers all major areas of the engineering sciences (civil, design, electrical, industrial, mechanical, metallurgical, mining, petroleum, nuclear, and production). The articles tend to be technically oriented and will best serve serious students, practitioners, and researchers. Current, authoritative, carefully edited, and reasonably affordable, the *McGraw-Hill Encyclopedia of Engineering* is highly recommended as the only substantial encyclopedia available today that covers the whole field of engineering.

Reader's Digest New Complete Do-It-Yourself Manual. Revised ed. Reader's Digest Assn. (dist. by Random House), 1991. 528p. $30.00.

Previously published in 1973 as the *Reader's Digest Complete Do-It-Yourself Manual*, this readable, easy-to-use book for laypeople provides encyclopedic information on the tools and techniques required to accomplish home improvements, maintenance, and repairs. "Explanations are clear and liberally illustrated, safety is stressed always, and the text is cognizant of environmental issues and energy conservation. A must purchase for libraries" (*Booklist,* November 1, 1991, p. 484). Two older multivolume sets offer similar material: the 26-volume *Complete Handyman Do-It-Yourself Encyclopedia* (Revised ed. H.S. Stuttman, 1983) and the 18-volume *Popular Mechanics Do-It-Yourself Encyclopedia* (Revised ed. Hearst Books, 1978).

Systems and Control Encyclopedia: Theory, Technology, Applications. Edited by Madan G. Singh. Pergamon Press, 1987. 8 vols. $2,300.00.

This outstanding multivolume encyclopedia provides an authoritative summary of what is currently known in the rapidly evolving and highly interdisciplinary field of systems engineering and its various subdisciplines. While all pertinent topics receive adequate attention, artificial intelligence, expert systems, and robotics are accorded especially strong coverage. The articles—prepared by an impressive roster of international authorities—are clearly written, but effective use of the encyclopedia requires a solid engineering and mathematical background. Marilyn Stark, in a lengthy and thoughtful review in *American Reference Books Annual* (1988, pp. 584–85), recommends the set, finding that it "is well edited to maintain consistency and readability of entries, typesetting for complex equations is very good, and illustrations and graphs are excellent. Above all, knowledgeable contributors have summarized areas in systems and control for nonexperts in those areas. For the substantial investment, the quality is high."

FILM, RADIO, TELEVISION, AND MASS COMMUNICATIONS

The American Film Industry: A Historical Dictionary. Written by Anthony Slide. Greenwood, 1986. 431p. $55.00 hardcover; $19.95 paperbound.

Slide's 600-entry encyclopedia furnishes reliable information on significant American film genres and series, studios and production companies, and industry organizations and terminology. It also includes helpful bibliographies at the ends of many articles and indicates sources of archival material. A companion volume is Slide's *International Film Industry: A Historical Dictionary* (Greenwood, 1989). Another complementary, albeit much more specialized, source is Gene Fernett's one-volume *American Film Studios: An Historical Encyclopedia* (McFarland, 1988), which profiles over 60 studios.

Cinemania. Microsoft, 1992– (revised annually). PC software (CD-ROM). $79.95.

This interactive software package offers a wide variety of encyclopedic information about thousands of films made between 1914 and the present, including plot summaries, critical reviews, cast and credit lists, awards, and MPAA ratings. In addition, the user can access biographies (with photos) of some 3,000 important film personalities. Material derives from several established print reference sources, most prominently *Leonard Maltin's TV Movies and Video Guide* (New American Library, 1969–). *Cinemania* is a multimedia CD-ROM product, mean-

ing that it combines sound and graphics with printed text. For instance, users can hear actual dialogue from selected films. Microsoft plans to update *Cinemania* on an annual basis. System requirements include a multimedia PC and MS-DOS version 3.1 or later. (Interested consumers should check with Microsoft for full specifications; call 800-426-9400.)

The Encyclopedia of Animated Cartoons. Written by Jeff Lenburg. Facts on File, 1991. 466p. $40.00.

A much revised and expanded version of Lenburg's earlier *Encyclopedia of Animated Cartoon Series* (Arlington House, 1981), this authoritative source covers the animated cartoon from its inception to the present. "No other work has gleaned and marshaled such a rich and comprehensive, truly encyclopedic, mass of valuable historical and filmographic items for the student of the American animated film" (*Choice,* May 1992, p. 1370).

The Encyclopedia of Television: Series, Pilots, and Specials. Written by Vincent Terrace. Revised ed. New York Zoetrope, 1985–86. 3 vols. $39.95.

The most detailed source on television programs currently available, Terrace's three-volume encyclopedia provides pertinent information about approximately 7,000 series, pilots, and specials produced between 1937 and 1984. Entries in the first two volumes are arranged alphabetically by program and include a plot summary, cast and crew credits, guest stars, network, and date aired. The third volume is an index of actors, producers, writers, and directors. This set expands and updates Terrace's two-volume *Complete Encyclopedia of Television Programs, 1947–1979* (2nd ed. A.S. Barnes, 1979). A complementary source is the single-volume *Complete Directory to Prime Time Network Shows, 1946–Present* (5th ed. Ballantine, 1992).

Encyclopaedia of the Musical Film. Written by Stanley Green. Oxford Univ. Press, 1981. 344p. $15.95 paperbound.

Coverage in this readable encyclopedia includes individual songs, performers, composers, lyricists, directors, and the like from 156 selected American and British musical films ranging from the *Jazz Singer* to *All That Jazz*. Seymour Peck, reviewing the work in the *New York Times Book Review* (November 15, 1981, pp. 13; 38), says "its amusing, informative bits make the book fun to browse through." Peck also notes that Clive Hirschhorn's *Hollywood Musical* (Crown, 1981) covers many more musical films (1,344 in all), although Hirschhorn's work is limited to big studio musicals produced in the U.S.

Halliwell's Film Guide. Written by Leslie Halliwell; updated by John Walker. HarperCollins, 1977– (revised annually). 1,265p. $50.00 hardcover; $20.00 paperbound.

Halliwell's encyclopedic guide to over 14,000 English-language feature films is firmly fixed as a reference standard. Arranged alphabetically by movie title, the concise entries furnish short plot synopses and note such basic facts as running time, date of release, country of origin, production company, and color process along with principal actors and director, producer, and writers. A similar reference work is *Leonard Maltin's TV Movies and Video Guide* (New American Library, 1969–), which is also updated annually. Halliwell, who died in early 1989, also compiled the classic HALLIWELL'S FILMGOER'S COMPANION.

Halliwell's Filmgoer's Companion. Written by Leslie Halliwell; updated by John Walker. 10th ed. HarperCollins, 1993. 1,000p. $60.00 hardcover; $25.00 paperbound.

Like the complementary HALLIWELL'S FILM GUIDE, this one-volume work, which first appeared in 1965, has achieved the status of a reference classic among both film aficionados and librarians; due to Leslie Halliwell's recent death, the current edition was completed by John Walker. International in scope, the *Companion* concentrates on biographies of prominent filmmakers, directors, stars, and writers, as well as key movements, trends, subjects, techniques, and terminology associated with the motion picture arts. The entries, which total well over 10,000, are brief but authoritative. It is regrettable that two similar one-volume works have not been revised since they first appeared: the *Oxford Companion to Film* (Oxford Univ. Press, 1976) and Ephraim Katz's *Film Encyclopedia* (Crowell, 1979); both of these titles are authoritative and remain useful for historical information but urgently need to be updated. The *Encyclopedia of Hollywood* (Facts on File, 1990) by Scott and Barbara Siegel, another single-volume publication, is reasonably current and can be recommended to film buffs, although it is much less extensive than *Halliwell*, *Katz*, or the *Oxford Companion*.

The International Dictionary of Films and Filmmakers. Edited by Nicholas Thomas & James Vinson. 2nd ed. St. James Press (dist. by Gale Research), 1990–93. 5 vols. $495.00.

The first edition (1984–88) of this excellent five-volume encyclopedia comprised carefully crafted, signed essays describing 490 films deemed to be of lasting importance, plus profiles of 1,680 "principal creative figures in the history of film," including actors, directors, writers, and production artists, and a comprehensive title index to the set. The second edition, published between 1990 and 1993, follows the same format and has a like number of volumes but covers more films and people. For instance, volume 1 (*Films*) has added 150 new titles, such as *The Color Purple*, *Hope and Glory*, and Kurosawa's *Ran*; volume 3, devoted to actors and actresses, has added such stars as Whoopi Goldberg, Robin Williams, Gerard Depardieu, and Sigourney Weaver. Moreover, a significant amount of material from the first edition has been revised or updated, including the very useful bibliographies and filmographies, and many black-and-white stills now enhance the text. Intended mainly for students and filmgoers rather than film scholars, the *International Dictionary of Films and Filmmakers* has been well received by critics. James Rettig, in a review of the first volume of the second edition (*Wilson Library Bulletin*, October 1990, p. 127), sounds a typical note: "Already the premier reference book on noteworthy films from around the world, the first volume of the *International Dictionary* isn't just getting bigger; it's also getting better."

International Encyclopedia of Communications. Edited by Erik Barnouw & others. Oxford Univ. Press, 1989. 4 vols. $375.00.

The first and thus far only substantial encyclopedia that comprehensively treats the heavily interdisciplinary field of communications, the four-volume *International Encyclopedia of Communications* is a reliable, up-to-date set consisting of 560 original articles prepared by leading experts from 29 countries. Signed articles ranging in length from 500 to 4,000 words cover such disparate subjects as animal communication and signals, the book, cable television, Walt Disney, fiber optics, historiography, journalism, language, libel, linguistics, the mass media, nonverbal communications, the performing arts, propaganda, speech, and Ludwig Wittgenstein. Sponsored by the prestigious Annenberg School of Communications at the University of Pennsylvania, the encyclopedia—a handsomely made reference work whose text is complemented by some 1,100 informative illustrations—"is a significant scholarly achievement. Its broad and authoritative coverage of the multifaceted aspects of communications provides a synthesis of ideas and concepts that span many disciplines" (*Reference Books Bulletin* in *Booklist*, June 15, 1989, p. 1791).

Les Brown's Encyclopedia of Television. Edited by Les Brown. 3rd ed. Gale Research, 1992. 723p. $39.95 hardcover; $22.95 paperbound (published by Visible Ink Press).

Brown's well-known encyclopedia, first published in 1977, was updated in 1982 and again in 1992. The heavily revised third edition covers all major facets of television, from programs and personalities to the business, legal, regulatory, and technical concerns of the industry. In all, the volume includes nearly 3,000 succinct articles prepared by Brown and other contributors; most are concerned with TV in the U.S., although some coverage of the medium abroad is provided. "*Les Brown's Encyclopedia* is an excellent and easy-to-use resource for information on all aspects of television" (*Reference Books Bulletin* in *Booklist*, September 1, 1992, p. 86). A somewhat similar source is Anthony Slide's TELEVISION INDUSTRY: A HISTORICAL DICTIONARY. Consumers seeking information about specific TV programs will also want to consult Vincent Terrace's ENCYCLOPEDIA OF TELEVISION and the *Complete Directory to Prime Time Network Shows, 1946–Present* (5th ed. Ballantine, 1992).

Magill's Survey of Cinema. Edited by Frank N. Magill. Salem Press, 1980–85. 21 vols. plus annual suppls., 1982–. $1,000.00 (21-vol. set); $50.00 (ea. suppl.).

This impressive collection of essay-length reviews of roughly 3,000 films consists of several distinct parts: English language films are covered in two A-to-Z series, the first in four volumes published in 1980 and the second in six volumes pub-

lished in 1981; silent films comprise three volumes (1982), foreign language films eight volumes (1985), and current films are covered in *Magill's Cinema Annual*, which began in 1982 and serves as a continuing update to the set. Articles on each film include a plot summary, critical notes on directing, acting, screenwriting, cinematography, and the film's place in the history of its genre.

In addition to publication in print form, *Magill's Survey of Cinema* is also available online via Dialog (File 299) at $54.00 per hour. *Magill's Survey* both complements and competes with several other major film encyclopedias, including the single-volume HALLIWELL'S FILM GUIDE, the five-volume INTERNATIONAL DICTIONARY OF FILMS AND FILMMAKERS, and the 12-volume MOTION PICTURE GUIDE. Consumers should also know that a five-volume spin-off of *Magill's Survey of Cinema* has been published in paperback under the title *Magill's American Film Guide*; priced at $135.00, its coverage is limited to 1,000 important American-made films.

Mass Media: A Chronological Encyclopedia of Television, Radio, Motion Pictures, Magazines, Newspapers, and Books in the United States. Compiled by Robert V. Hudson. Garland, 1987. 435p. $70.00.

Hudson's handy volume crams much basic information into its 435 pages. Arranged chronologically in 16 periods covering 1638 to 1985, the encyclopedia traces the origins and development of books, newspapers, magazines, films, and radio and television in the U.S. in brief entries that emphasize key dates, events, and people. A detailed, 75-page index furnishes easy access to specific names and facts. "This is an ambitious book which will respond to a host of inquiries on the mass media and their history" (*American Reference Books Annual*, 1988, p. 365). A complementary work is Richard Hixson's one-volume *Mass Media and the Constitution: An Encyclopedia of Supreme Court Cases* (Garland, 1989), which summarizes major U.S. Supreme Court decisions on press and speech freedom from 1834 to 1986.

The Motion Picture Guide. Edited by Jay Robert Nash & Stanley R. Ross. CineBooks (dist. by R.R. Bowker), 1985–87. 12 vols. plus annual suppls., 1982–. $750.00 (12-vol. set); $119.95 (ea. suppl.).

Jay Robert Nash's description of the *Motion Picture Guide* as "the most important film encyclopedia ever" is hardly an objective judgment, but a good case can be made for its validity. This monumental reference source provides detailed information—

cast and production credits, plot summaries, critical evaluations, MPAA ratings, etc.—on well over 50,000 films made between 1910 and the present time, including virtually all feature films produced in the U.S. and many notable foreign productions; excluded are documentaries, shorts, made-for-TV movies, and X-rated films or those deemed pornographic. The final two volumes consist of indexes to alternative titles, film series, awards, and some 180,000 personal names mentioned in the set.

Anne McGrath, in the column "Eye on Publishing" in *Wilson Library Bulletin* (April 1986, p. 34), notes that "Historians of popular culture will undoubtedly find invaluable the discussions of each movie's genesis and social importance. Were characters modeled on real people? How did a particular story evolve? How does one film made during a certain period compare artistically with its contemporaries?" An updating volume entitled the *Motion Picture Annual* has been published each year since 1982. In addition, the publisher indicates that two complementary works are currently in progress: a 16-volume country-by-country foreign film encyclopedia and a 12-volume biographical encyclopedia on film personalities. Comparable sources are the INTERNATIONAL DICTIONARY OF FILMS AND FILMMAKERS, MAGILL'S SURVEY OF CINEMA, and HALLIWELL'S FILM GUIDE.

The New Video Encyclopedia. Written by Larry Langman & Joseph A. Molinari. Garland, 1990. 312p. $49.95.

A revised version of Langman's *Video Encyclopedia* (Garland, 1983), this useful work focuses on the vocabulary, equipment, production processes, and inventors associated with the television and video industries. It consists of approximately 1,500 brief, alphabetically arranged entries covering such topics as extended resolution format and portable VCRs as well as people like radio and television pioneer David Sarnoff and Vladimir Zworykin, who invented the kinescope picture tube. "Langman and Molinari have created a handy reference tool intended to serve a broad range of video equipment users and consumers. At once both comprehensive and concise, the entries in this encyclopedia should help clarify the jargon and 'video-ese' tossed about by practitioners, authors, and sales personnel" (*Library Journal*, February 1, 1991, p. 72).

The New York Times Encyclopedia of Film, 1896–1979. Edited by Gene Brown. Times Books (dist. by Garland), 1984. 13 vols. $2,000.00.

Not an encyclopedia in the traditional sense, this compilation is a chronologically arranged reprint from microfilm of roughly 5,500 *New York Times* articles on all aspects of film, which have appeared in the *Times* between 1896 and 1979. The articles, however, do not include reviews of films. Reviews have been published separately in a nine-volume set entitled the *New York Times Film Reviews, 1913–1974* (Arno, 1971–75).

The Television Industry: A Historical Dictionary. Written by Anthony Slide. Greenwood, 1991. 374p. $59.50.

Slide, author of the authoritative AMERICAN FILM INDUSTRY: A HISTORICAL DICTIONARY and the *International Film Industry: A Historical Dictionary* (Greenwood, 1989), presents concise information on over 1,000 television production companies, distributors, organizations, genres, technical terms, and industry pioneers; biographical essays on three major network figures—Leonard Goldenson (ABC), William Paley (CBS), and David Sarnoff (NBC)—are appended. As in the case with Slide's film encyclopedias, the emphasis is on the business rather than programming side of the industry. "Although the work is primarily concerned with the American television industry, extensive material on many foreign networks and production companies, especially those in the United Kingdom, is also included. Destined to become an essential reference tool for the study of the television industry, the book is highly recommended for both public and academic libraries" (*American Reference Books Annual*, 1992, p. 370). A similar work is LES BROWN'S ENCYCLOPEDIA OF TELEVISION.

Tune in Yesterday: The Ultimate Encyclopedia of Old Radio, 1925–76. Written by John Dunning. Prentice-Hall, 1976. 703p. Out of print (last priced at $17.95).

Dunning furnishes basic information on hundreds of radio shows that aired between 1925 and 1976, such as "Ma Perkins," "Our Miss Brooks," and "One Man's Family." Entries, which are arranged alphabetically by show, run in length from a few sentences to several pages and include the program's dates, sponsor(s), network, cast, and usually a critical evaluation. "An impressive and important compendium of information on the history, development, and casting of popular radio programming . . .

The book will serve both the casual reader seeking a remembrance of a time when radio was the most popular entertainment medium in the nation and the student of American culture looking for an intelligent and detailed discussion of the dimensions of broadcast creativity" (*Choice*, November 1977, pp. 1204–06). Similar books are Vincent Terrace's *Radio's Golden Years: The Encyclopedia of Radio Programs, 1930–1960* (A.S. Barnes, 1981), a

308-page work that covers more shows (approximately 1,500) but offers less detail than Dunning's *Tune in Yesterday*; and the recently published 806-page *Handbook of Old-Time Radio: A Comprehensive Guide to Golden Age Radio Listening and Collecting* (Scarecrow Press, 1993) by Jon Swartz and Robert Reinehr.

☸ FOOD, NUTRITION, AND AGRICULTURE ☸

The Columbia Encyclopedia of Nutrition. Edited by Myron Winick & others. Putnam, 1988. 349p. $12.95 paperbound.

Written for the layperson, the *Columbia Encyclopedia of Nutrition* contains over 100 articles varying in length from one to many pages on such topics as allergies, breast feeding, caffeine, cancer prevention, cholesterol, diets, exercise, fiber, food balancing, junk food, obesity, salt, and vitamins. The book, sponsored by the Institute of Human Nutrition at Columbia University's College of Physicians and Surgeons, is reliable and reasonably current. "The subject is vital, the text readable and authoritative, the coverage relevant to most readers' interests, and the cost reasonable. *The Columbia Encyclopedia of Nutrition* is recommended for secondary school, public, health science, and academic libraries" (*Reference Books Bulletin* in *Booklist*, September 15, 1988, p. 132). Another excellent single-volume reference source for nonspecialists that nicely complements the *Columbia Encyclopedia* is the *Mount Sinai School of Medicine Complete Book of Nutrition* (St. Martin's Press, 1990). Also useful are John Yudin's *Penguin Encyclopaedia of Nutrition* (Viking, 1985) and the more recent WELLNESS ENCYCLOPEDIA OF FOOD AND NUTRITION.

The Dictionary of American Food and Drink. Written by John F. Mariani. 2nd ed. Hearst, 1994. 475p. $18.00 paperbound.

Mariani's encyclopedic survey of American eating and drinking customs deals with both the familiar (hamburgers, for example) and the exotic (snickerdoodles). *Library Journal* (April 15, 1984, p. 782), in naming the work as one of the best reference books for 1983, called it "A unique compendium on American food and drink in America that is anecdotal and fascinating as well as authoritative. It is especially strong on the history and development of various foods, and the discussions of word derivations are delightful.... Coverage is comprehensive and many entries are actually mini-essays." An updated second edition of Mariani's useful book appeared in 1994 in paper covers.

Encyclopedia of American Agricultural History. Written by Edward L. Schapsmeier & Frederick H. Schapsmeier. Greenwood, 1975. 467p. $55.00.

Intended to "provide information on all areas bearing on agricultural history" (preface) in the United States, this unique encyclopedia comprises some 2,500 concise articles covering pertinent legislation, agencies, publications, people, events, and places. Access to specific information in the book is enhanced by a general index as well as topical indexes that group related subjects.

Encyclopedia of Food Science and Technology. Edited by Y.H. Hui. Wiley, 1992. 4 vols. $595.00.

Aimed principally at food scientists and advanced students in the field, this substantial four-volume encyclopedia furnishes dependable, up-to-date material on the interdisciplinary subject of food science, technology, and engineering. It treats such diverse topics as beekeeping, dairy products, tropical fruits, laws and legislation affecting the food industry, the history of food, and waste management in food processing. In all, the 3,000-page set contains about 400 alphabetically arranged articles prepared by recognized authorities in the field. Coverage of new advances, developments, and applications is especially noteworthy, as evidenced by such articles as "Laboratory Robotics." *Choice* (September 1992, p. 76) recommends the encyclopedia as "an essential title for all industry, research, and academic libraries." A series of three older encyclopedias published by AVI Publishing—the *Encyclopedia of Food Engineering* (2nd ed., 1986), the *Encyclopedia of Food Science* (1978), and the *Encyclopedia of Food Technology* (1974)—offer similar though much less current information. Along with the new ENCYCLOPEDIA OF FOOD SCIENCE, FOOD TECHNOLOGY AND NUTRITION (see next entry), Hui's *Encyclopedia of Food Science and Technology* is a standout encyclopedia in the field.

Encyclopedia of Food Science, Food Technology and Nutrition. Edited by Robert Macrae & others. Academic Press, 1993. 8 vols. $2,100.00.

By far the largest and most expensive encyclopedia covering food and nutrition ever published, this new eight-volume work is published by the Academic Press, known for such high quality multivolume specialized encyclopedias as the ENCY-CLOPEDIA OF PHYSICAL SCIENCE AND TECHNOLOGY and the ENCYCLOPEDIA OF MICROBIOLOGY. The new food encyclopedia continues the publisher's tradition of encyclopedic excellence. It is a work of impressive range and depth, consisting of roughly three million words, 5,000 pages of text, and 500 specially commissioned articles written by the world's leading food scientists and nutritionists. Access to specific topics and facts is assisted by a 50,000-entry subject index in the final volume. The editors are British academicians, but the editorial and advisory boards and contributors come from all over the world. "An important addition to collections on food science and nutrition, aimed at scientists and nonscientists alike" (*Choice*, December 1993, p. 584). A complementary work is Hui's four-volume ENCYCLOPEDIA OF FOOD SCIENCE AND TECHNOLOGY.

Foods and Food Production Encyclopedia. Edited by Douglas M. Considine & Glenn D. Considine. Van Nostrand, 1982. 2,322p. $278.95.

The price might seem high for a one-volume encyclopedia, but purchasers get both quantity and quality for their dollar. This massive volume, appropriate for both specialists and nonspecialists, contains 1.9 million words, 1,201 articles, 1,950 cross-references, 1,006 illustrations, 587 tables, and 7,500 index entries. International in scope, the encyclopedia emphasizes food production from the beginning of the natural growth cycle to the processing of raw-food materials into products for the marketplace. "*Foods and Food Production Encyclopedia* is an excellent reference work that should be of value to library collections from those in high schools to those in large research institutions. Because of its authority, currency, and comprehensive scope, it promises to be of continuing value for some time to come" (*Reference Books Bulletin* in *Booklist*, September 1, 1983, p. 50). A new edition is said to be in the works.

Foods and Nutrition Encyclopedia. Written by Audrey H. Ensminger & others. Pegus Press (dist. by Encyclopaedia Britannica Educational Corp.), 1983. 2 vols. $125.00.

Similar in size and vintage (but not content) to the Considines' FOODS AND FOOD PRODUCTION ENCY-CLOPEDIA, this valuable two-volume encyclopedia offers 2,432 pages of clear, authoritative information on a wide range of topics concerned with the nutrition of food and its relationship to human health. The approximately 2,800 brief articles are accompanied by over 1,600 black-and-white illustrations and 462 tables; a special feature gives the nutritional composition of some 2,500 foods in tabular form. "The language of the entries is purposely kept simple and nontechnical, although technical terms are explained when used" (*American Reference Books Annual*, 1984, p. 722). Consumers should also be aware that a one-volume abridgment of the encyclopedia appeared in 1986 under the title *Food for Health: A Nutrition Encyclopedia*; published by Pegus Press, the volume has added color illustrations and sells for $49.50.

Larousse Gastronomique: All-New American Edition of the World's Greatest Culinary Encyclopedia. Written by Prosper Montagne & Robert J. Courtine; edited by Jenifer Harvey Lang. Revised ed. Crown, 1988. 1,193p. $60.00.

This hefty volume is an updated English-language edition of the famous French food encyclopedia and cookbook first published in 1938. In addition to thousands of recipes, it defines basic cooking terms and offers information on many types of foods and beverages, equipment, preservation, service, etc. Handsomely illustrated with more than 900 full-color photographs and 70 black-and-white drawings, this latest edition of *Larousse Gastronomique*—completely rewritten by Robert Courtine, gastronomy editor of *Le Monde*—has added many entries on wine and much new material on international cuisines. "It is unquestionably the 'world's greatest culinary encyclopedia,' synthesizing the science of nutrition and the art of cooking and providing a monumental historical overview of classical cuisine" (*American Reference Books Annual*, 1989, p. 550). Complementary works are *Cooking A to Z* (Ortho Books, 1988), edited by Jane Horn and Janet Fletcher; Tom Stobart's *Cook's Encyclopedia* (Harper & Row, 1981); and Craig Claiborne's *The New York Times Food Encyclopedia* (Times Books, 1985).

The New Frank Schoonmaker Encyclopedia of Wine. Written by Frank Schoonmaker; revised by Alexis Bespaloff. Revised ed. Morrow, 1988. 624p. $22.95.

Any number of good wine encyclopedias are currently available. Among the best is the *New Frank Schoonmaker Encyclopedia of Wine*, which first appeared in 1964 and quickly achieved "classic" status. *Schoonmaker* covers the important wine producing regions of the world as well as production techniques, major vineyards, regulatory rules and organizations, and key terminology (with helpful pronunciations for foreign terms). New topics in Bespaloff's revision (Frank Schoonmaker died in 1976) include blush wine, vintage port, and the wine industry in England. "This book is designed and produced beautifully and elegantly. Picking a wine may be difficult, even intimidating. Picking a wine dictionary is simple; pick this one" (*Wilson Library Bulletin*, January 1989, p. 125). Other equally useful encyclopedic references on the subject include *Grossman's Guide to Wines, Beers, & Spirits* (7th ed. Scribner's, 1983), *Alexis Lichine's New Encyclopedia of Wine and Spirits* (5th ed. Knopf, 1987), *Hugh Johnson's Modern Encyclopedia of Wine* (3rd ed. Simon & Schuster, 1991), and its companion *Hugh Johnson's World Atlas of Wine* (3rd ed. Simon & Schuster, 1985).

Nutrition and Health Encyclopedia. Written by David F. Tver & Percy Russell. 2nd ed. Van Nostrand, 1989. 639p. $46.95.

First published in 1981, Tver and Russell's encyclopedia offers a cross-disciplinary approach to the study of nutrition, drawing on pertinent information from such fields as physiology, biochemistry, and medicine. The articles, which are usually brief, cover drugs, food additives, human anatomy, malnutrition, toxins, vitamins, and the like. In addition, much valuable tabular data is included among the book's 13 appendixes. "This volume is intended for physicians, scientists, and other health care providers who work with nutritional science. Although the authors claim that their book is also for the public's use, the advanced information presented is usually too complicated for the average reader . . . . a valuable addition to any library serving a clientele concerned with the expanding field of nutritional science" (*American Reference Books Annual*, 1990, pp. 680–81). Consumers seeking a nutrition encyclopedia for nonspecialists should look to the single-volume COLUMBIA ENCYCLOPEDIA OF NUTRITION or two-volume FOODS AND NUTRITION ENCYCLOPEDIA.

The Wellness Encyclopedia of Food and Nutrition: How to Buy, Store, and Prepare Every Variety of Fresh Food. Written by Sheldon Margen & the editors of the University of California at Berkeley *Wellness Letter.* Rebus (dist. by Random House), 1992. 512p. $29.95.

Aimed squarely at the ordinary consumer, this useful reference work furnishes authoritative information on the nutritional value of some 500 familiar whole and fresh foods, such as eggs, fish, meats, poultry, and various fruits, vegetables, and grains. It also includes much practical advice about buying, preparing, and consuming food. James Rettig in *Wilson Library Bulletin* (January 1993, p. 114) likes the encyclopedia: "Everyone eats, and since nearly everyone can eat healthier, the recommended serving of *The Wellness Encyclopedia*—especially for public library reference collections—is one copy." Equally enthusiastic is Barbara Keen in *Library Journal* (February 1, 1993, pp. 74; 76), who writes, "This encyclopedia definitely fills a niche between the highly technical nutrition books and the basic how-to-shop books. Highly recommended."

The World Encyclopedia of Food. Written by L. Patrick Coyle Jr. Facts on File, 1982. 790p. Out of print (last priced at $40.00).

Containing more than 4,000 brief, alphabetically arranged articles totaling half a million words, this readable encyclopedia—now unfortunately out of print—covers practically every food and beverage used anywhere in the world. As *Reference Sources for Small and Medium-Sized Libraries* (5th ed. American Library Assn., 1992, p. 167) notes, the articles "provide information on anything people have eaten, including where it is grown, how it is produced, where it is eaten, its taste, literary and social lore associated with certain foods, and fascinating obscure facts." It is hoped that the publisher will reprint this unique work or commission a new edition.

❋ GEOGRAPHY AND AREA STUDIES ❋

Antarctica: An Encyclopedia. Written by John Stewart. McFarland, 1990. 2 vols. $135.00.

The first (and thus far only) encyclopedia on the subject, Stewart's two-volume work consists of 15,000 readable A-to-Z entries, plus a general chronology, a chronological list of expeditions, and a valuable bibliography. Place-names, such as glaciers and waterways, account for roughly three-fourths of the entries, most of which are quite brief but all give coordinates and, when possible, discoverers. Some entries, however, are essay-length, as in the case of major explorers, expeditions, and disasters. "In sum, this work is comprehensive, handsomely produced, and a valuable addition to collections in larger academic and departmental libraries" (*Library Journal*, January 1991, p. 98).

The Cambridge Encyclopedia of Latin America and the Caribbean. Edited by Simon Collier & others. 2nd ed. Cambridge Univ. Press, 1992. 480p. $55.00.

This handsome, topically arranged encyclopedia treats important facets of the political, social, economic, and cultural life of the countries of Central and South America and the Caribbean. First published in 1985, the encyclopedia was fully revised in 1992, at which time articles were updated and many new maps and color photographs were added. Designed for students at the high school and college levels as well as the general reader, the *Cambridge Encyclopedia of Latin America and the Caribbean* is one of a number of fine regional encyclopedias produced by Cambridge University Press that follow a similar format: the *Cambridge Encyclopedia of Africa* (1981); the *Cambridge Encyclopedia of Australia* (1993); the *Cambridge Encyclopedia of China* (2nd ed. 1991); the *Cambridge Encyclopedia of India, Pakistan, Bangladesh, Sri Lanka, Nepal, Bhutan, and the Maldives* (1989); the *Cambridge Encyclopedia of Japan* (1993); the *Cambridge Encyclopedia of the Middle East and North Africa* (1988); and the recently revised CAMBRIDGE ENCYCLOPEDIA OF RUSSIA AND THE FORMER SOVIET UNION. Each of these titles is authoritatively written, carefully edited, attractively produced, copiously illustrated, and reasonably priced—models of what a good small-volume specialized encyclopedia ought to be.

The Cambridge Encyclopedia of Russia and the Former Soviet Union. Edited by Archie Brown & others. 2nd ed. Cambridge Univ. Press, 1993. 504p. $49.95.

Similar in purpose, concept, arrangement, size, and price to other volumes in the publisher's regional encyclopedia series (see the CAMBRIDGE ENCYCLOPEDIA OF LATIN AMERICA AND THE CARIBBEAN for a description), this work first appeared in 1982 as the *Cambridge Encyclopedia of Russia and the Soviet Union*. The new edition—distinguished by the word *Former* in the title—provides clear, up-to-date information about the post-Soviet world and the many new East European countries that have emerged since the fall of Communism. Another reasonably up-to-date source on the former Soviet states is Andrew Wilson and Nina Bachkatov's *Russia and the Commonwealth A to Z* (HarperPerennial, 1992).

The Canadian Encyclopedia. Edited by James H. Marsh. 2nd ed. Hurtig Publishers (dist. by Gale Research), 1988. 4 vols. $225.00.

The highly acclaimed *Canadian Encyclopedia* is the brainchild of Mel Hurtig, head of Hurtig Publishers located in Edmonton (Alberta) and one of Canada's most outspoken nationalists. He views the encyclopedia as a means of educating Canadians about their country and its people, places, history, land, government, economy, culture, and achievements. First published in three volumes in 1985 and revised and expanded to four volumes in 1988, the encyclopedia now comprises approximately 2,750

pages, 9,500 articles, nearly four million words, and 2,000 illustrations and maps, most in full-color. Significantly, the index has been greatly enlarged and much improved in the revised edition. More than 2,500 leading Canadian authorities have contributed articles to the set, which essentially replaces the older *Encyclopedia Canadiana*, a 10-volume work last published by Grolier in 1975 and now out of print.

In a review of the 1988 edition in *American Reference Books Annual* (1989, p. 52), Shirley Lambert nicely sums up the strengths of the *Canadian Encyclopedia*: "Publication of this encyclopedia was an enormous undertaking; the editors are to be congratulated for their thoroughness and dedication to comprehensiveness. On the whole, the selection of articles reflects a truly Canadian identity, as it was meant to do, and the information presented is both accurate and current." In 1990, Hurtig published the JUNIOR ENCYCLOPEDIA OF CANADA, a companion set for young people in five volumes.

The Concise Encyclopedia of Australia. Edited by John Shaw. 2nd ed. David Bateman Ltd. (dist. by G.K. Hall), 1989. 848p. $54.95.

A revision of the well-received *Collins Australian Encyclopedia* (Collins, 1984), this popularly written encyclopedia offers reliable information about the Australian people and the country's history, political and cultural institutions, flora and fauna, and the like. The 3,000-plus articles are normally brief but some, like "Aborigines" and "Sheep and Wool," run to four or five pages. A review in *Reference Books Bulletin* (in *Booklist*, August 1989, p. 1956) finds the encyclopedia "a highly readable and visually attractive reference work. . . . *The Concise Encyclopedia of Australia* is highly recommended for all types of libraries, high school level and above, not only as a ready-reference source but for more extensive use as well."

Another valuable single-volume reference work on the country is the recently published *Cambridge Encyclopedia of Australia* (Cambridge Univ. Press, 1993), edited by Susan Bambrick. Interested consumers should also be aware of the existence of the larger *Australian Encyclopedia* (5th ed. Australian Geographic Society, 1988), a nine-volume work published in Australia and not currently distributed in North America; for additional information about the set, which sells for around $600 Australian, contact the Australian Geographic Society, P.O. Box 321, Terrey Hills, NSW 2084.

Dictionary of Afro-Latin American Civilization. Written by Benjamin Nuñez with the assistance of the African Bibliographic Center. Greenwood, 1980. 525p. $65.00.

This authoritative reference volume consists chiefly of 4,700 short A-to-Z entries that describe prominent words, phrases, events, and people associated with black culture in Brazil, Jamaica, Haiti, the Anglo-French and Dutch islands, and the Spanish Caribbean. Of interest to specialists and students as well as informed laypeople, the book has received high praise from critics. Two examples: "It is an excellent beginning of what will hopefully be an ongoing study of the cultural impact of the African in Latin America" (*Choice*, April 1980, p. 1076); "The inseparability of black history from the broader history of Latin America makes much of this work useful to researchers on Latin America in general. Highly recommended for libraries with Latin American research collections" (*Library Journal*, September 1, 1980, p. 1722).

Dictionary of Concepts in Physical Geography. Written by Thomas P. Huber & others. Greenwood, 1988. 304p. $59.50.

Eighty-eight concepts essential to the understanding of the multidisciplinary field of physical geography—which includes study of the biosphere, climatology, geology, and remote sensing—are treated in encyclopedic detail in this informative reference source. Each entry provides a concise definition followed by a more expansive discussion that puts the concept in historical perspective and identifies major researchers and theories. A companion volume is Robert Larkin and Gary Peters' *Dictionary of Concepts in Human Geography* (Greenwood, 1983). "The *Dictionary of Concepts in Physical Geography* is a good starting place for obtaining a basic understanding of specific concepts in physical geography and could be used as a beginning for undergraduate research papers as well" (*RQ*, Spring 1989, p. 412). The *Encyclopaedic Dictionary of Physical Geography* (Basil Blackwell, 1985) is a complementary work; it covers many more terms (2,400 as opposed to 88) but in much less detail.

Encyclopaedia Iranica. Edited by Ehsan Yarshater. Routledge & Kegan Paul (dist. by Mazda), 1982–. Estimated 40 vols. (in progress). Price varies from $20.00 to $37.50 per fascicle.

An enormous scholarly undertaking, the in-progress *Encyclopaedia Iranica* intends to cover the 2,500-year-old Persian and Iranian civilization from prehistory to the present in essay-length articles that "provide accurate and up-to-date presentations on topics of archaeological, geographic, ethnographic, historical, artistic, literary, religious, linguistic, philosophical, scientific, and folkloric interest" (introduction). The encyclopedia, begun in 1982 after seven years of painstaking preparation,

will eventually comprise an estimated 40 volumes, although no publication schedule has been issued by editor Yarshater, who is affiliated with the Center for Iranian Studies at Columbia University. At present, the alphabetically arranged set, which is issued in paperbound fascicles (or parts), is up to the letter "C" (volume 5). As Anna DeMiller points out in a progress report in *American Reference Books Annual* (1992, p. 50), "A reader waiting for the entry on Zoroaster will need to be patient." The work—obviously for serious students, teachers, and researchers concerned with Iranian studies and related fields—boasts more than 300 internationally recognized contributors; the first fascicle includes notes on transliteration and a glossary of frequently occurring Persian and Arabic terms.

Encyclopaedia of India. Edited by P.N. Chopra. Rima Publishing House (dist. by South Asia Books), 1992–. 32 vols. (in progress). $1,550.00.

Like ENCYCLOPAEDIA IRANICA, the *Encyclopaedia of India* is an in-progress multivolume set that, once completed, promises to be a reference landmark for years to come. Editor Chopra, an Indian writer and historian who earlier compiled the single-volume *India: An Encyclopaedic Survey* (S. Chand, 1983), plans to devote one volume to each of the 25 states and seven territories that make up India. To date, five of the 32 volumes have appeared, each of which is prepared by a leading Indian scholar and includes material on the history, geography, religion, agriculture, government, education, culture, languages, literature, economy, social mores, and prominent places in the state or territory under scrutiny. "Authoritative and up-to-date (although expensive), this set is highly recommended for all libraries supporting Indian studies" (*Choice*, January 1993, p. 766). Another substantial reference set on Indology is Rajaram N. Saletore's five-volume *Encyclopaedia of Indian Culture* (Sterling Publishers, dist. by Humanities Press, 1981–85)

The Encyclopedia of New England. Edited by Robert O'Brien & Richard D. Brown. Facts on File, 1985. 611p. $29.95.

One of five encyclopedias published in recent years by Facts on File that covers prominent people, places, institutions, and events in distinct regions of the United States, this particular volume contains over 3,000 brief articles devoted to the New England states. The text is enhanced by 90 black-and-white illustrations, a map of each state, several statistical appendixes, and a bibliography. Other titles in the Facts on File series—all similar in size, purpose, construction, and price to the *Encyclopedia of New England*—are the *Encyclopedia of the Central*

West (1989), the *Encyclopedia of the Far West* (1990), the *Encyclopedia of the Midwest* (1988), and the *Encyclopedia of the South* (1985).

Encyclopedia of Southern Culture. Edited by Charles R. Wilson & William Ferris. Univ. of North Carolina Press, 1989. 1,634p. $69.95.

Ten years in the making, the eight-pound *Encyclopedia of Southern Culture* represents the biggest and the best in U.S. regional one-volume encyclopedias. Sponsored by the Center for the Study of Southern Culture at the University of Mississippi at Oxford, it details virtually every aspect of life in the South, from race relations, political ideology, literature, religion, and folklore to hound dogs, snake handlers, mint juleps, chitterlings, Moon Pies, and Paul (Bear) Bryant. Altogether, there are roughly 1,300 entries divided into 24 sections, including such topics as agriculture, the environment, ethnicity, industry, sports, the media, and women. In a lengthy review in the *New York Review of Books* (October 26, 1989, p. 13+), C. Van Woodward lauds the book: "It is an achievement that does credit to both the university and the editors. The editors have secured contributions from some eight hundred specialists, most of them in the South but many from elsewhere. With few exceptions, they appear to take their assignments seriously and give us their best." Two other reference works complementing the *Encyclopedia of Southern Culture* are the aforementioned *Encyclopedia of the South* (Facts on File, 1985) and the ENCYCLOPEDIA OF SOUTHERN HISTORY.

Encyclopedia of the Third World. Edited by George Thomas Kurian. 4th ed. Facts on File, 1991. 3 vols. $225.00.

According to editor Kurian, the Third World accounts for more than half the world's population and two-thirds of its countries. This encyclopedia, a standard reference set first published in 1978 and revised several times, furnishes basic information about each country, such as geographical location and area, weather, population and ethnic composition, languages, religions, colonial history, constitution and government, civil service, foreign policy, health, media, and culture. The encyclopedia is reliable, current, and easy to use and comprehend. "Kurian once again provides the interested student/ scholar with a compendium of vital information necessary to an understanding of these countries" (*American Reference Books Annual*, 1993, p. 63). Kurian also produces two companion works, the two-volume *Encyclopedia of the First World* (Facts on File, 1990) and the single-volume *Encyclopedia of the Second World* (Facts on File, 1991); the latter, which deals with those countries that formed the old Communist bloc, is understandably out of date, despite its relatively recent publication year.

Encyclopedia of Ukraine. Edited by Volodymyr Kubijovyc. Univ. of Toronto Press (dist. by Libraries Unlimited), 1984–93. 5 vols. $700.00.

This alphabetically arranged set—published under the auspices of the Canadian Institute of Ukrainian Studies, the Canadian Foundation for Ukrainian Studies, and the Shevchenko Scientific Society—represents a comprehensive encyclopedic survey of the now independent Ukraine, including the country's history, geography, economy, and cultural heritage. The first two volumes appeared in the 1980s and the final three in late 1993. Critics enthusiastically received the initial volumes; says Bohdan Wynar in *American Reference Books Annual* (1985, p. 46), "This remarkable encyclopedia can safely be recommended to all scholars interested in Eastern Europe as the best work on the subject." A smaller, older but still valuable work is the two-volume *Ukraine: A Concise Encyclopedia* (Univ. of Toronto Press, 1963–70).

Exploring Your World: The Adventure of Geography. Edited by Donald J. Crump. National Geographic Society, 1990. 608p. $31.95.

Intended for young students in the upper elementary and junior high school grades, *Exploring Your World* offers over 330 simply written, well-illustrated articles on various facets of both physical and human geography. The entries, which vary in length from short paragraphs to 10 or more pages, cover both broad topics (such as agriculture, climate, mining, population, and maps and globes) and specific ones (jet streams, fjords, soil). "Well-placed, labeled diagrams and maps as well as captioned photos make this a browser's dream as well as a worthwhile reference source" (*Booklist*, May 1, 1990, p. 1702). A similar but much more extensive source is GEOPEDIA (see next entry).

Geopedia. Encyclopaedia Britannica Educational Corp., 1994. PC software (CD-ROM). $299.00.

New in 1994, *Geopedia* is a multimedia geographical encyclopedia on CD-ROM aimed at students from the upper elementary grades through high school. It consists of more than 1,200 articles covering major places and physical features around the globe. These articles derive from various Britannica reference publications, including the CHILDREN'S BRITANNICA and the yearbook *Britannica World Data Annual*. In addition, *Geopedia* offers approximately 3,000 visuals (maps, charts, graphics, tables, etc.), a world atlas, extensive statistical data on all the countries of the world, and 55 learning activities designed to stimulate young people's interest in geography. The CD-ROM encyclopedia also includes an interactive feature called "Chartmaker," which allows students to create their own charts and graphs. Similar works in print form are *Lands and People* (Revised ed. Grolier, 1993), a familiar six-volume set first published in 1929; and the WORLD BOOK ENCYCLOPEDIA OF PEOPLE AND PLACES, also published in six volumes.

The Great Soviet Encyclopedia. 3rd ed. Macmillan, 1973–83. 32 vols. $2,500.00.

This monumental—and controversial—work is an English-language translation of the third edition of the Russian BOL'SHAIA SOVETSKAIA ENTSIKLOPEDIIA, (see page 449) published in Moscow in 30 volumes between 1969–78. The Russian-language set, usually referred to simply as *BSE*, is the largest and best-known general family and school encyclopedia in the former U.S.S.R. Overall, the set contains more than 100,000 articles in some 21 million words. It puts the Soviet perspective or slant on practically every important subject, from history and politics to the arts and literature; as might be expected, BSE's Marxist-Leninist bias is particularly pronounced in such areas as philosophy, economics, sociology, and political theory. For this reason, the translation project was severely criticized by some. For example, Harvey Einbinder, writing in *Wilson Library Bulletin* (December 1980, p. 260), observed, "Hundreds of thousands of dollars are being spent to translate this work in an apparent belief that American concern with Communist ideology and Soviet military power will ensure substantial library sales, despite the *Encyclopedia*'s biased contents."

Today, such Cold War rhetoric seems quaint, and the encyclopedia is now useful principally for its historical perspective on the vanished Soviet Union. For reasonably current encyclopedic information about Russia and the other East European countries that made up the former Soviet Union, consult the recently published CAMBRIDGE ENCYCLOPEDIA OF RUSSIA AND THE FORMER SOVIET UNION and Andrew Wilson and Nina Bachkatov's *Russia and the Commonwealth A to Z* (HarperPerennial, 1992), both one-volume works.

The Illustrated Encyclopedia of New Zealand. Edited by Gordon McLauchlan. David Bateman Ltd. (dist. by G.K. Hall), 1990. 1,448p. $75.00.

Originally published in Australia and New Zealand in 52 parts, this up-to-date, easy-to-read, handsomely made 1,448-page encyclopedia is actually a much expanded revision of the 656-page *New Zealand Encyclopedia*, published by the Auckland firm of David Bateman Ltd. in 1984 and minimally revised in 1988 under the title *Bateman New Zealand Encyclopedia*. The *Illustrated Encyclopedia of New Zealand* offers extensive information on all aspects of the country, including its history, geography, demographics, politics, climate, literature, and sports. The volume contains nearly 2,500 entries complemented by 2,000 color and 800 black-and-white illustrations, including many maps. "An excellent source of information on New Zealand" (*Library Journal*, October 15, 1990, p. 82).

The Illustrated Encyclopedia of World Geography. Oxford Univ. Press, 1990–93. 11 vols. $45.00 per vol.

Each of the 11 volumes that make up the excellent *Illustrated Encyclopedia of World Geography* covers a broad subject and is edited by a recognized authority in the field. For instance, volume 1 is entitled the *Earth's Natural Forces* (1990) and edited by Kenneth J. Gregory; volume 2 is *World Government* (1990), edited by Peter J. Taylor; volume 3 is *Nature's Last Strongholds* (1991), edited by Robert Burton; volume 4 is *Plant Life* (1991), edited by D.M. Moore. The final volumes, *Planet Management* (edited by Michael Williams) and *World Economy* (edited by Stuart Corbridge) appeared in 1993.

Each volume contains 256 or more pages, is heavily illustrated with color photos and maps, and, unlike most Oxford reference books, is intended for a general (as opposed to academic) audience. In a review of volume 8 (*Resources and Industry*) and volume 9 (*Human Settlement*) in *Library Journal* (May 1, 1993, p. 82), Leonard Grundt calls the set an "outstanding series" and highly recommends it "for libraries serving everyone from junior high school students to general adult readers." In a review of two earlier volumes in *Library Journal* (December 1991, p. 136), Richard Shotwell comments, "These volumes offer a unique worldview of nature, emphasizing aspects that are especially important to understanding each region. The numerous photographs are stunning, and the maps and other illustrations are imaginative and clear."

Ireland: A Cultural Encyclopedia. Edited by Brian de Breffny. Facts on File, 1983. 256p. $35.00.

Forty-five specialists on various aspects of Irish history and culture prepared the approximately 600 articles that make up this fine work. The book is enhanced by some 300 crisp black-and-white and color illustrations. "The expertise of the contributors, an economy of words, and careful work by the general editor have resulted in an encyclopedia that is well balanced, accurate, and informative. The articles, although scholarly in substance, are well suited to users who have only a limited acquaintance with historical or contemporary Irish culture" (*RQ*, Spring 1984, p. 365).

Japan: An Illustrated Encyclopedia. Kodansha America (dist. by Farrar, Straus & Giroux), 1993. 2 vols. $250.00.

Successor to the highly regarded nine-volume *Kodansha Encyclopedia of Japan* (Kodansha, 1983; suppl. 1986), *Japan: An Illustrated Encyclopedia* is an excellent national encyclopedia covering all important facets of Japanese life, with emphasis on the nation's history, customs, arts, places, contemporary society, and prominent people. It contains approximately two million words, 2,000 pages, 12,000 articles, and 4,000 full-color illustrations in two volumes. A noteworthy feature is inclusion of numerous heavily illustrated double-page spreads that illuminate such topics as "A Look into a Contemporary Japanese Home," "How to Make Sushi," "Japanese Management Techniques," and "Echoes of Japan in Western Art." Both Japanese and non-Japanese authorities have contributed to the encyclopedia. Critics have been enthusiastic: "The ponderous style that burdens most reference books is missing here: *Japan* actually invites casual reading" (*Library Journal*, October 1, 1993, p. 89); "Once acquainted with this set, readers will not only use it for reference but will find themselves exploring the many wonderful facets it has to offer. The price of the set is about one-third of the previous edition, making it an affordable resource too" (*Reference Books Bulletin*, in *Booklist*, December 15, 1993, p. 778).

Much of the text derives from the earlier and larger *Kodansha Encyclopedia of Japan*, which comprised well over 3,000 pages as opposed to *Japan's* 2,000. Another important distinction between the two titles is that the earlier work included only about 1,000 black-and-white illustrations whereas *Japan* has four times as many, all in color. Two recommended one-volume encyclopedias on Japan are Dorothy Perkins' *Encyclopedia of Japan: Japanese History and Culture from Abacus to Zori* (Facts on File, 1991) and the *Cambridge Encyclopedia of Japan* (Cambridge Univ. Press, 1993); both of these titles are useful reference works, but neither possesses the range or depth of *Japan: An Illustrated Encyclopedia* or its predecessor, the *Kodansha Encyclopedia of Japan*.

The Junior Encyclopedia of Canada. Edited by James H. Marsh. Hurtig Publishers, 1990. 5 vols. $202.95.

The five-volume *Junior Encyclopedia of Canada* furnishes young Canadians with a comprehensive encyclopedic survey of their country and its history, geography, culture, political system, etc. Although produced by the same editor and publisher who put together the admirable CANADIAN ENCYCLOPEDIA, a four-volume work for adults, the *Junior Encyclopedia* is not a juvenile version of the adult set. Rather, it is an entirely new reference publication.

Three years in the making at a cost of $12.5 million and the first encyclopedia compiled specifically for young people about Canada, the *Junior Encyclopedia of Canada* comprises roughly 4,000 articles written by 130 educators and other experts, along with more than 3,000 quality illustrations, 500 of which are specially commissioned paintings and drawings. Since its publication in 1990, the encyclopedia has been enthusiastically received by English-speaking children, parents, and teachers in Canada. "This work more than fulfills its aim to provide an encyclopedia for young people that gives adequate coverage of Canada and Canadian topics. It is an outstanding achievement" (*American Reference Books Annual*, 1991, p. 14).

Marshall Cavendish Illustrated Encyclopedia: World and Its People. Edited by Emrys Jones. Revised ed. Marshall Cavendish, 1988. 27 vols. $409.95.

This colorful multivolume encyclopedia furnishes sound information on major aspects of physical, political, economic, and human geography. According to the preface, the set "has been designed to provide for a clearly written and comprehensive guide to the geography of the world. It differs from other books on the subject in that it focuses as much attention on major ideas from the physical and cultural environment as on the study of countries and nations." First published in 1978 and revised several times since, the set comprises more than 1,300 articles accompanied by some 1,800 photographs and 250 maps. The final volume includes a 20,000-entry general index and a classified index arranged under 31 areas of study. Lubomyr Wynar, reviewing an earlier edition of the encyclopedia in *American Reference Books Annual* (1982, p. 306) suggests that the set "should be added to reference collections in public and academic libraries. The layperson also will be interested in this well-executed encyclopedic project."

Modern Geography: An Encyclopedic Survey. Edited by Gary S. Dunbar. Garland, 1991. 219p. $50.00.

Approximately 500 succinct, precisely written articles by 95 stellar contributors make up the contents of *Modern Geography*, aptly subtitled "An Encyclopedic Survey." Emphasis is on prominent twentieth-century geographers, both living and dead, but major places, organizations, concepts, and research activity also receive attention. "Readers will enjoy mental cross-referencing success between entry titles and from within articles: a proof of Dunbar's editing acumen. . . . Highest recommendation for all academic libraries" (*Choice*, April 1991, p. 1292).

Reference Handbook on the Deserts of North America. Edited by Gordon L. Bender. Greenwood, 1982. 594p. $95.00.

Written by 23 specialists, this fine encyclopedic survey of the five major deserts of North America describes each desert environment in terms of its geology, ecology, animal and plant life, weather, and desertification activity; also covered is the impact of humans on each desert. The only reference source of its kind, the book "should be on the shelves of all postsecondary academic libraries and is also highly recommended for large public libraries" (*Choice*, November 1982, p. 459).

Rolling Rivers: An Encyclopedia of America's Rivers. Edited by Richard A. Bartlett. McGraw-Hill, 1984. 416p. $34.50.

Arranged geographically, this well-edited, good-looking compendium profiles 117 rivers in the United States, including the Cooper and Yukon in Alaska. The articles—contributed by about 100 authorities, mostly historians—vary in length from three to six pages and provide detailed information about each river. "*Rolling Rivers* is an attractive resource for high school and public libraries, especially for its historical information" (*Reference Books Bulletin* in *Booklist*, April 15, 1985, p. 1173). Two complementary sources, both unfortunately now out of print, are the *Rand McNally Encyclopedia of World Rivers* (Rand McNally, 1980) and the *Standard Encyclopedia of the World's Rivers and Lakes* (Putnam, 1966).

Standard Encyclopedia of the World's Mountains. Edited by Anthony Huxley. Putnam, 1962. 383p. Out of print (last priced at $18.95).

The main portion of this encyclopedia consists of some 300 A-to-Z articles on the world's principal mountain ranges, glaciers, passes, and peaks. The articles, which average about 450 words in length, provide basic geological, ecological, and historical information, including explorations and famous climbs. Over 100 illustrations accompany the text, 16 of which are color plates found throughout the volume; there is also a 1,500-entry gazetteer at the back of the book. Now over 30 years old, the *Standard Encyclopedia of the World's Mountains* is much out-of-date and not surprisingly out of print. Yet it remains a unique and valuable reference source.

Companion volumes (also out of print) are the *Standard Encyclopedia of the World's Oceans and Islands* (Putnam, 1962) and the aforementioned *Standard Encyclopedia of the World's Rivers and Lakes* (Putnam, 1966).

The World Book Encyclopedia of People and Places. World Book, 1992. 6 vols. $149.50.

Prepared by the editors of WORLD BOOK ENCYCLOPEDIA in conjunction with the firms of Mitchell Beazley in England and Bertelsmann Lexikon in Germany, this handsomely produced set covers 215 countries and territories of the world in readable, alphabetically arranged articles aimed at students in the upper elementary and junior high school grades. All material included in the set is original and not derived from the WORLD BOOK ENCYCLOPEDIA or any other source. Mindful that today's television-oriented young people are aware of the real world and its problems, the editors have not attempted to sugarcoat the text.

As James Rettig points out in *Wilson Library Bulletin* (November 1992, p. 97), the articles offer "a frank, albeit concise, assessment of each nation, unflinchingly covering recent political events such as the civil war in Yugoslavia or the racial strife of South Africa. The equally realistic photos show, for example, the bomb-crater-pocked landscape of Vietnam." Rettig recommends the set as one that "will open new worlds around the world to young readers," as does Sandy Whiteley, editor of *Reference Books Bulletin* (in *Booklist*, September 1, 1992, p. 91): "The *World Book Encyclopedia of People and Places* is highly recommended for school and public libraries for its attractive balanced coverage of the world's nations." Competing works are *Lands and People* (Revised ed. Grolier, 1993), a frequently revised six-volume set first published in 1929; the five-volume WORLDMARK ENCYCLOPEDIA OF THE NATIONS; and the GEOPEDIA on CD-ROM.

World Encyclopedia of Cities. Edited by George Thomas Kurian. ABC-Clio, 1993–. 6 vols. $75.00 per vol.

When completed in 1997, this in-progress encyclopedia will comprise an important source of information on hundreds of major cities around the world. The first two volumes, which cover 130 U.S. and six Canadian cities, appeared in 1993. Each city profile includes location and topography, climate, history and historical landmarks, population, demographic composition, government, economy, education, transportation, media, religion, crime, arts and culture, and parks and recreation. The set aims to meet the informational needs of students, teachers, businesspeople, journalists, and specialists in urban planning and policy. Volume 3 (*Europe*) is scheduled for publication in 1994, volume 4 (*Asia and Oceania*) in 1995, volume 5 (*Africa and Latin America*) in 1996, and volume 6 (a gazetteer) in 1997. An older and much less exhaustive work is the four-volume *Cities of the World* (Gale Research, 1982), which drew on the U.S. Department of State *Post Reports* for the bulk of its data.

Worldmark Encyclopedia of the Nations. Edited by Moshe Y. Sachs. 7th ed. Wiley, 1988. 5 vols. $375.00.

Originally published in 1960, the well-known *Worldmark Encyclopedia of the Nations* profiles 176 independent nations and over 80 dependencies around the world, systematically covering 50 standard topics under each country, such as location, size, topography, climate, flora and fauna, environment, population, ethnic groups, languages, religions, history, government, judicial system, economy, income, labor, agriculture, industry, foreign trade, taxation, health, education, libraries and museums, military, and famous persons. Articles on countries appear in volumes 2–5, which are arranged geographically by continent. Volume 1 describes the United Nations and its various agencies.

The *Worldmark Encyclopedia of the Nations*, which is revised about every four years, can be used effectively by students at the junior high school level and up, as well as adults seeking basic information about the countries of the world. As such, the set competes with a number of similar sources, including the six-volume WORLD BOOK ENCYCLOPEDIA OF PEOPLE AND PLACES, *Lands and People* (Revised ed. Grolier, 1993), also a six-volume work, and the GEOPEDIA, a geographical encyclopedia on CD-ROM.

There are also a number of single-volume encyclopedias of countries, such as *Geo-Data: The World Geographical Encyclopedia* (2nd ed. Gale Research, 1989), the *Handbook of the Nations* (9th ed. Gale Research, 1989), the *Statesman's Year-Book: Statistical and Historical Annual of the States of the World* (St. Martin's Press, 1864–, annual), and *World Fact File* (Facts on File, 1990). In addition, two other CD-ROM products now offer country-by-country profiles: *Countries of the World* (Bureau Development, 1991), which contains the full text of 106 U.S. Army Country Series Handbooks plus Hammond maps and other

relevant data on disk; and the *World Factbook* (Quanta Press, 1989, annual), which presents information gathered by the U.S. Central Intelligence Agency on nearly 250 countries from Afghanistan to Zimbabwe (this source is also available in print form from both the U.S. Government Printing Office and Brassey's, a commercial publisher).

Worldmark Encyclopedia of the States. Edited by Moshe Y. Sachs. 2nd ed. Worldmark Press (dist. by Wiley), 1986. 690p. $120.00.

Similar in concept and format (but not content or size) to the WORLDMARK ENCYCLOPEDIA OF NATIONS, this handy volume furnishes reliable information on each of the 50 United States, as well as U.S. dependencies. First published in 1981 and revised in 1986, the book covers 50 topics under each state (location, size, topography, climate, population, etc.), thus facilitating specific comparisons between or among states. It also includes informative maps, charts, and tables. "On balance, this is a quality encyclopedia. The information provided for each state is consistent, and consistently useful" (*American Reference Books Annual*, 1987, p. 47). A valuable complement to the *Worldmark Encyclopedia of the States* is *Facts About the States* (H.W. Wilson, 1989), edited by Joseph Kane and others.

The Young People's Encyclopedia of the United States. Edited by William E. Shapiro. Millbrook, 1992. 10 vols. $239.50.

Among the 1,200 alphabetically arranged articles in this colorfully illustrated 10-volume set for children ages 7–12 are biographies of famous North Americans from all walks of life and two-page spreads profiling the 50 U.S. states and 10 Canadian provinces. Other topics covered include U.S. places, institutions, holidays, plants and animals, historical events, scientific discoveries, ethnic groups and Indian tribes, law and government, folklore and myths, religions, music, architecture, language and literature, sports, and various social issues. The set features much information in easy-to-read boxes, plus nearly 2,000 full-color illustrations and a comprehensive index in the final volume. "It is an attractive and appealing place to begin the study of our nation" (*Reference Books Bulletin* in *Booklist*, October 1, 1992, p. 372).

❊ HEALTH, MEDICINE, AND DRUGS ❊

The American Medical Association Encyclopedia of Medicine. Edited by Charles B. Clayman. Random House, 1989. 1,184p. $44.95.

One of the best popularly written one-volume medical encyclopedias available today, this authori-

tative reference work includes over 5,000 A-to-Z entries covering diseases, symptoms, procedures, treatments, medications, tests, the human anatomy, and other basic medical information. Prepared with the layperson in mind, the encyclopedia's jargon-free text is enhanced by some 2,200 two-color draw-ings and pictures, along with hundreds of tables and diagnostic charts. The volume serves as a compan-ion to the publisher's earlier AMERICAN MEDICAL AS-SOCIATION FAMILY MEDICAL GUIDE, which is designed more with an eye toward self-evaluation of health problems than provision of encyclopedic informa-tion. "A carefully crafted combination of technical and nontechnical language makes the book acces-sible to both laypersons and students while provid-ing succinct descriptions for professionals. . . . Rea-sonably priced and highly recommended for all li-braries" (*Choice*, October 1989, p. 278).

Other useful, reasonably current single-volume medical encyclopedias for the nonspecialist are the *Mosby Medical Encyclopedia* (Revised ed. Penguin USA, 1992), Robert Rothenberg's *New Illustrated Medical Encyclopedia for Home Use* (Revised ed. Galahad, 1986), the *Wellness Encyclopedia* (Houghton Mifflin, 1991), and the WORLD BOOK/ RUSH-PRESBYTERIAN-ST. LUKE'S MEDICAL CENTER MEDI-CAL ENCYCLOPEDIA.

The American Medical Association Family Medi-cal Guide. Edited by Jeffrey R.M. Kunz & Asher J. Finkel. Revised ed. Random House, 1987. 832p. $35.00.

While not strictly an encyclopedia, this con-sumer-friendly medical guide and many others like it furnish encyclopedic information advising those without professional training about how to cope with various health questions such as disease pre-vention and diagnosis, hospitalization, and caring for the sick. The guide, a companion to the excel-lent AMERICAN MEDICAL ASSOCIATION ENCYCLOPEDIA OF MEDICINE, is topically arranged, heavily illustrated, adequately indexed, and written in a manner readily accessible to the layperson. A particularly strong feature is its many symptom flow charts that help users evaluate medical conditions through a series of yes and no questions. First published in 1982 and revised in 1987, the *American Medical Association Family Medical Guide* has been wildly successful, selling well over three and a half million copies, most through direct mail. Similar works of compa-rable size, quality, and price include the *Better Homes and Gardens New Family Medical Guide* (Meredith, 1989), the *Columbia University College of Physicians and Surgeons Complete Home Medical Guide* (Re-vised ed. Crown, 1989), the *Mayo Clinic Family Health Book* (Morrow, 1990), and the *New Good Housekeeping Family Health and Medical Guide* (Hearst Books, 1989).

The Complete Drug Reference. Prepared by the United States Pharmacopeial Convention, Inc.

Consumer Reports Books (dist. by St. Martin's Press), 1991– (revised annually). 1,648p. $39.95.

Previously published as the *United States Pharmacopeia Drug Information for the Consumer*, this outstanding encyclopedia provides reliable, up-to-date information about both prescription and non-prescription drugs available today. It offers more information and is easier to understand and use than the comparable PHYSICIANS' DESK REFERENCE (PDR); for instance, primary access in the *Complete Drug Reference* is alphabetical by generic name whereas in the *PDR* it is by manufacturer. The book includes color photographs of commonly used phar-maceuticals and, in appendixes, chemotherapy regi-mens and advisories for athletes and pregnant and breast-feeding women. "This terrific source of straightforward information on currently marketed prescription and over-the-counter drugs is written in language aimed at the layperson" (*Library Journal*, June 1, 1991, p. 130). In addition to the aforemen-tioned PHYSICIANS' DESK REFERENCE, competing sources include H. Winter Griffith's *Complete Guide to Pre-scription & Non-prescription Drugs* (Putnam, 1992), James Long's *Essential Guide to Prescription Drugs* (Revised ed. HarperCollins, 1990), *Zimmerman's Complete Guide to Nonprescription Drugs* (Gale Re-search, 1993), and the *Pill Book* (Bantam Books, 1990).

Complete Guide to Symptoms, Illness & Surgery. Written by H. Winter Griffith. 2nd ed. Price Stern Sloan, 1989. 1,104p. $15.95 paperbound.

Griffith's affordable encyclopedic guide addresses the questions "What is wrong with me and what can I do?" In clear, nontechnical language, the volume describes nearly 800 symptoms and more than 500 illnesses and 100 surgeries, making it the largest symptomology currently available in North America. In a review of the first edition (1985) in *American Reference Books Annual* (1986, p. 641), Harriette Cluxton enthusiastically endorsed the book: "For all who believe in full participation with their doc-tors in their own medical care, here is a gold mine of authentic information, skillfully presented, with a minimum of medical jargon. Patients' families should find it particularly useful. Not just another 'wellness' text, this is an excellent medical reference book for today's patients." Other recommended symptom encyclopedias for laypeople are Joan Gomez's *Dictio-nary of Symptoms* (Revised ed. Stein & Day, 1985), Sigmund Miller's *Symptoms: The Complete Home Medical Encyclopedia* (Crowell, 1976), and Isadore Rosenfeld's *Symptoms* (Simon & Schuster, 1989). Jack Paar, the entertainer, used Rosenfeld's book to recognize the symptoms of a heart attack: "the book saved my life," said the former talk show host.

The Encyclopedia of Alcoholism. Written by Robert O'Brien & Morris Chafetz. 2nd ed. Facts on File, 1991. 346p. $45.00.

Originally published in 1982, the revised second edition of this informative reference work contains over 600 articles covering major facets of the subject, including 100 new entries on such topics as aspirin and alcohol, drinking and the use of seat belts when driving, outpatient treatment for alcoholism, and the Yale University Center for Alcohol Studies. The book is written in nontechnical language comprehensible to average readers at the high school level and beyond. "Parents, teachers, students, counselors, and others will delve into this carefully crafted encyclopedia for answers to myriad questions relating to the use and abuse of alcohol, its pleasures and its dangers" (*Wilson Library Bulletin*, November 1991, p. 110). A complementary reference is the smaller, 167-page *Alcohol/Drug Abuse Dictionary and Encyclopedia* (Charles C. Thomas, 1988) by John Fay.

The Encyclopedia of Blindness and Vision Impairment. Written by Jill Sardegna & T. Otis Paul. Facts on File, 1991. 329p. $45.00.

A unique work, the *Encyclopedia of Blindness and Vision Impairment* comprises roughly 500 short articles on all aspects of blindness and related eye problems, including diseases, surgery, medications and drugs, guide dogs, public and private organizations, technical terminology, companies that specialize in products for the vision impaired, and legal and economic issues. The goal is to provide practical, jargon-free information of use to both laypeople and professionals in the field. "A clear, concise writing style, a comprehensiveness in coverage, and an easy-to-understand format make this A-to-Z ophthalmologic compendium outstanding" (*Library Journal*, February 1, 1991, p. 74).

The Encyclopedia of Drug Abuse. Written by Glen Evans & others. 2nd ed. Facts on File, 1991. 370p. $45.00.

This authoritative, up-to-date encyclopedia serves as a companion volume to the publisher's ENCYCLOPEDIA OF ALCOHOLISM, now also in its second edition. The *Encyclopedia of Drug Abuse* begins with a lengthy article entitled "History of Drugs and Man" and then presents over 500 concise, alphabetically arranged articles covering specific drugs, laws and organizations pertaining to drug use, medical terminology, and the like. The book "is an excellent resource for secondary school, public, academic, and

health-science libraries. It is a good introduction for those beginning research and a fine ready-reference source for definitions, referrals, and statistics" (*Reference Books Bulletin* in *Booklist*, February 15, 1992, p. 1130).

The Encyclopedia of Genetic Disorders and Birth Defects. Written by James Wynbrandt & Mark D. Ludman. Facts on File, 1991. 426p. $45.00.

The approximately 600 articles that make up this useful, nontechnical subject encyclopedia range in length from a few paragraphs to three or more pages and describe a wide variety of genetic disorders and birth defects from "Aarskog Syndrome" to "Zygodactyly." Articles normally include information about the history of each malady and its discovery, naming, incidence in the population, prognosis, possibility of prenatal detection, and biochemical basis. "*Encyclopedia of Genetic Disorders and Birth Defects* is recommended for large health science collections in both public and academic libraries, community college onwards, especially where pediatrics, child development, or genetics are important" (*Choice*, July–August 1991, p. 1768).

Encyclopedia of Immunology. Edited by Ivan M. Roitt & Peter J. Delves. Academic Press, 1992. 3 vols. $450.00.

Here is another impressive reference set from Academic Press, publisher of such excellent multivolume works in the human and physical sciences as the ENCYCLOPEDIA OF HUMAN BIOLOGY, the ENCYCLOPEDIA OF MICROBIOLOGY, and the ENCYCLOPEDIA OF PHYSICAL SCIENCE AND TECHNOLOGY. The three-volume *Encyclopedia of Immunology* comprehensively treats the broad field of immunology in nearly 600 scholarly articles prepared by leading specialists. The text, which totals 2,032 pages, is enhanced by some 250 illustrations. "The level of writing is advanced, with complex terminology undefined. Undergraduates would find this work difficult, but graduate students and researchers will discover a wealth of information, the core knowledge of the field, very well presented" (*Choice*, December 1992, pp. 600–01).

Encyclopedia of Medical Devices and Instrumentation. Edited by John G. Webster. Wiley, 1988. 4 vols. $625.00.

Editor Webster's goal—description of all medical devices and instrumentation, including various applications of engineering and computer technology to the various specialties and subspecialties of medicine—is not entirely achieved, but this four-volume work represents the most ambitious attempt to date. All told, the encyclopedia presents more than 250 articles on both specific instruments (such as endoscopes and pacemakers) and broad areas (biomedical education). The articles, written by specialists for specialists, are authoritative and reasonably current. "Major strengths of these articles include up-to-date bibliographies, useful illustrations, brief historical overviews of most topics, and thorough cross-indexing in the text" (*American Reference Books Annual*, 1989, p. 610).

Encyclopedia of Medical History. Written by Roderick E. McGrew & Margaret P. McGrew. McGraw-Hill, 1985. 400p. $38.75.

Approximately 100 alphabetically arranged essay-length articles make up this substantial encyclopedic survey of medical history from the earliest times to the present. Written in language comprehensible to students and general readers, the articles treat major medical specialties, maladies, instruments, procedures, treatments, and issues. First the topic is introduced and developments are summarized chronologically. James Rettig in *Wilson Library Bulletin* (November 1985, p. 62) recommends the work: "No one reading about the state of surgery before Dr. Joseph Lister developed antiseptic techniques in the 1860s could possibly pine for the proverbial good old days. The encyclopedia strips away the mystery from medicine. When questions arise in public, high school, and academic libraries about the development of medical practices, this will be just what the doctor, or rather the librarian, orders." For a negative opinion, see Thomas Benedek's review in *American Reference Books Annual* (1986, p. 638).

Those interested in medical history should also check out the new two-volume *Companion Encyclopedia of the History of Medicine* (Routledge, 1994). Edited by W.F. Bynum and Roy Porter, this excellent reference work is much larger (1,400 pages) and much more expensive ($199.95) than the *Encyclopedia of Medical History*, but it provides much more detailed information.

An Encyclopedia of Natural Medicine. Written by Michael T. Murray & Joseph E. Pizzorno. Prima Publishing & Communications (dist. by St. Martin's Press), 1991. 622p. $28.95 hardcover; $18.95 paperbound.

Prepared by two doctors of naturopathy, this useful encyclopedia explains the philosophy and principles of natural medicine and then discusses 62 health problems from cervical dysplasia to varicose veins, with suggested remedies. "This is one of the best books on alternative medicine available. . . . What distinguishes this book is that there is always a clear discussion of the causes of a disease and

extensive references, many from authoritative medical sources" (*Library Journal*, May 1, 1991, p. 72). Other popularly written one-volume encyclopedias emphasizing nontraditional medicine are Kristin Olsen's *Encyclopedia of Alternative Health Care* (Pocket Books, 1990); Carlson Wade's *Home Encyclopedia of Symptoms, Ailments and Their Natural Remedies* (Parker, 1991); Mark Bricklin's *Practical Encyclopedia of Natural Healing* (Revised ed. Rodale, 1983), which has sold almost two million copies over the years; *Rodale's Encyclopedia of Natural Home Remedies* (Rodale, 1982), also compiled by Mark Bricklin, editor of *Prevention* magazine; and the *Visual Encyclopedia of Natural Healing* (Rodale, 1991), subtitled "A Step-by-Step Pictorial Guide to Solving 100 Everyday Health Problems."

Encyclopedia of Neuroscience. Edited by George Adelman. Birkhauser Boston (dist. by Springer-Verlag) 1987. 2 vols. plus suppl., 1989. $165.00 (2-vol. set); $42.50 (suppl.).

This unique encyclopedia—intended chiefly for neuroscientists, researchers, and advanced students—devotes its approximately 700 articles to the rapidly expanding field of neuroscience, which includes neuroanatomy, neurobiology, neurophysiology, neurology, neurosurgery, and every facet of the functioning of the brain. The material is up-to-date and authoritative, the work of over 600 specialists, many from abroad; most articles are accompanied by illustrations and a short bibliography. "This highly recommended source, which includes the most current developments in neuroscience as well as essential background information, is an excellent purchase for academic and special libraries" (*Library Journal*, September 1, 1988, p. 163). Periodic supplements (the first published in 1989) are intended to keep the encyclopedia reasonably current.

Encyclopedia of Pharmaceutical Technology. Edited by James Swarbrick & James C. Boylan. Marcel Dekker, 1988–. 12 vols. (in progress). $180.00 per vol.; series can be purchased from publisher on standing order at $153.00 per vol.

When completed (possibly by the mid-1990s), this large, alphabetically arranged encyclopedia will provide comprehensive coverage of all significant aspects of pharmaceutical technology, including the discovery, development, testing, regulation, manufacturing, commercialization, and post-production considerations of hundreds of licit drugs along with their physicochemical properties and dosage forms. The articles, which customarily run to 20 or more pages in length, are technical in nature and include numerous citations to published literature. In a review of the initial volume, Theodora Andrews puts the set in good perspective: "The editors, who are well-known individuals from academia and industry, felt that the need for such a work was obvious and that it would become a valuable resource for colleagues in pharmaceutical industry, education, and government" (*American Reference Books Annual*, 1989, p. 623).

Gallaudet Encyclopedia of Deaf People and Deafness. Edited by John V. Van Cleve. McGraw-Hill, 1987. 3 vols. $345.00.

Published under the auspices of Gallaudet College, one of the world's foremost educational institutions for the hearing impaired, this first-rate encyclopedia consists of approximately 270 articles on all pertinent aspects of the subject, including "Acoustics," "Audiometry," "Communications Skills," "Educational Legislation," "Gestures," "Hearing Aids," "Hearing Loss," "Legal Rights," "Mouth-Hand Systems," "Otolaryngology," "Psycholinguistics," "Speech Training" and prominent people and organizations associated with the deaf community. When naming the set one of the best reference sources of the 1980s, the editor of *Reference Books Bulletin* (in *Booklist*, December 15, 1989, p. 778) observed, "This unique work, written in a clear and generally accessible manner, will interest scholars and researchers in the field, practitioners who work with the deaf, deaf people themselves, and the general public." A handy single-volume complement to the *Gallaudet Encyclopedia* is Carol Turkington and Allen Sussman's *Encyclopedia of Deafness and Hearing Disorders* (Facts on File, 1992).

Illustrated Encyclopedia of Human Histology. Written by Radivoj V. Krstic. Springer-Verlag, 1984. 450p. $64.00.

This highly specialized technical work treats relevant topics in the interrelated disciplines of human and veterinary histology, histophysiology, cell biology, and embryology. Especially valuable are the halftone illustrations, line drawings, and diagrams that accompany most articles. "With more than 1,500 illustrations, this is an impressive reference volume in histology, and it reflects the enormous progress made in the field during the past three decades that was due to new tools and techniques. Unfortunately, these advances—especially in fine structure elucidation and analysis—are widely scattered throughout the scientific literature and exhibit a disparity of terminology together with a multitude of synonyms. Krstic's work facilitates the orientation of the beginning histology student as well as meeting the needs of the advanced specialist" (*Choice*, May 1985, p. 1306).

Macmillan Health Encyclopedia. Macmillan, 1993. 9 vols. $360.00.

Intended principally for junior and senior high school students, the curriculum-oriented *Macmillan Health Encyclopedia* encompasses more than 1,000 pages of reliable medical information in nine volumes. Each volume treats a broad subject: *Body Systems* (volume 1); *Communicable Diseases* (volume 2); *Noncommunicable Diseases and Disorders* (volume 3); *Nutrition and Fitness* (volume 4); *Emotional and Mental Health* (volume 5); *Sexuality and Reproduction* (volume 6); *Drugs, Alcohol, and Tobacco* (volume 7); *Safety and Environmental Health* (volume 8); and *Health-Care Systems* (volume 9). Individual topics are alphabetically arranged within each volume; for instance, volume 1 begins with "Abdomen" and ends with "Vein." Nearly 500 four-color photographs, 130 anatomical drawings, and 180 charts and diagrams accompany the printed text, which is written in an easy-to-read, nontechnical style. The final volume contains a cumulative index to the set. "*Macmillan Health Encyclopedia*, an excellent reference work created for American students, satisfies the need for health information that is reliable, accurate, and clear. It is also suitable for adults" (*Reference Books Bulletin* in *Booklist*, September 15, 1993, p. 189). The only serious competitor to the *Macmillan Health Encyclopedia* currently available is the 12-volume MARSHALL CAVENDISH ENCYCLOPEDIA OF FAMILY HEALTH (see next entry).

The Marshall Cavendish Encyclopedia of Family Health. Marshall Cavendish, 1991. 12 vols. $459.95.

The *Marshall Cavendish Encyclopedia of Family Health*, a British-produced reference set of 2,808 pages in 12 volumes, is a revision of the *Marshall Cavendish Illustrated Encyclopedia of Family Health*, a 2,692-page work published in 1983 in 24 volumes. Written for laypeople and students at the high school level and beyond, the encyclopedia comprises 900-plus unsigned articles covering major areas of human health, such as anatomy, physiology, reproduction, medicine, and disease. The material is clearly and accurately presented, although some North Americans might be annoyed or frustrated by the use of British terminology and spelling. An appealing feature is the set's many illustrations, most in color. "It is ideal for school libraries and health education collections because it is well illustrated and highly readable. It is also a nice addition for large public libraries with heavy student use" (*Library Journal*, March 15, 1992, p. 78).

The encyclopedia competes directly with the fine new MACMILLAN HEALTH ENCYCLOPEDIA, a nine-volume curriculum-based set. A much less expensive (albeit older and less well-illustrated) popular multivolume medical encyclopedia is *Fishbein's Illustrated Medical and Health Encyclopedia* (H.S. Stuttman, 1983); edited by the late Morris Fishbein, this four-volume set sells for a modest $39.95. Marshall Cavendish also publishes a 14-volume encyclopedia for young people entitled the *Marshall Cavendish Encyclopedia of Health* (1991); containing only 64 pages per volume, it is designed for students in the upper elementary and junior high school grades and sells for $299.95. Although profusely illustrated and reasonably current and reliable, both Marshall Cavendish health encyclopedias seem overpriced, especially when compared with the excellent single-volume titles available (see the review of the AMERICAN MEDICAL ASSOCIATION ENCYCLOPEDIA OF MEDICINE above).

The Merck Manual of Diagnosis and Therapy. Edited by Robert Berkow. 16th ed. Merck, 1992. 2,696p. $26.00 hardcover; also available in 2-vol. paperbound ed. at $12.00 per vol.

A great bargain at under $30.00, this well-known and highly respected volume has been a standard desk reference for physicians since 1899 and, more recently, informed laypeople. Originally sold only to health professionals, the *Merck Manual* over the years achieved fame as an underground medical guide for the general public and, in 1975, Merck finally began selling the manual to laypeople. Still, until recently the publisher refused to promote the book for general use because, according to editor Berkow, "it is written at a level of sophistication likely to confuse or mislead lay readers about the seriousness of symptoms" (*Publishers Weekly*, April 21, 1989, p. 36). Merck, which is revised every four or five years, explains illnesses and diseases, indicates signs and symptoms, and suggests diagnoses and treatments—all in language best suited to those with medical training and experience. The product of more than 270 authorities representing all major medical specialties, the manual is arranged topically, with the first part (or volume) covering general medicine and the second obstetrics, gynecology, pediatrics, and genetics. Remarkably compact, the volume has small print and no illustrations.

The New A to Z of Women's Health: A Concise Encyclopedia. Written by Christine Ammer. Facts on File, 1989. 544p. $29.95.

First published in 1983 as the *A to Z of Women's Health*, this readable, informative reference source contains roughly 1,000 concise articles on various facets of women's health, including such specifics as menstrual problems, breast cancer, toxic shock syndrome, AIDS, cholesterol, infertility, abortion, ex-

ercise, vitamins, and weight control. "It is excellent for women who want to be well informed, responsible health-care consumers. The author provides up-to-date information about women's health in clear, simple language but also is careful to encourage users to seek clinical care and to obtain second opinions" (*Reference Books Bulletin* in *Booklist*, January 15, 1990, p. 1044). Complementary encyclopedic sources on women's health are the *New Our Bodies, Ourselves* (Revised ed. Simon & Schuster, 1992), available in paperback at $20.00, and Denise Foley and Eileen Nechas's *Women's Encyclopedia of Health & Emotional Healing* (Rodale, 1993), subtitled *Top Women Doctors Share Their Unique Self-Help Advice on Your Body, Your Feelings and Your Life*, priced at $27.95.

The Oxford Companion to Medicine. Edited by John Walton & others. Oxford Univ. Press, 1986. 2 vols. $150.00.

This historically oriented encyclopedia of medicine furnishes authoritative information on all important aspects of the subject, ranging from lengthy articles on such medical specialties as neurophysiology and radiology to short entries covering prominent people, schools, hospitals, and medical terms and abbreviations. In all, the two-volume set treats over 10,000 topics in "language sufficiently clear and simple to make them meaningful to the intelligent layman" (introduction). "The *Companion* was compiled with the help of about 150 contributors from Britain and North America. The list of names is very much a who's who of distinguished medical practitioners" (*American Reference Books Annual*, 1987, p. 627).

The Patient's Guide to Medical Tests. Compiled by Cathey Pinckney & Edward R. Pinckney. 3rd ed. Facts on File, 1986. 385p. $27.95 hardcover; $12.95 paperbound.

An updated and expanded version of the *Encyclopedia of Medical Tests* (last published in 1982 by Facts on File), the *Patient's Guide to Medical Tests* work describes more than 1,000 tests and procedures in language readily comprehensible to the average person. In a roundup of recommended medical reference sources, Claudia Perry praises the guide: "The authors are well qualified and clearly present a wealth of detailed information" (*Library Journal*, November 1, 1988, p. 49). Many other similar works are available, including H. Winter Griffith's *Complete Guide to Medical Tests* (Fisher Books, 1988), Philip Shtasel's *Medical Tests and Diagnostic Procedures* (HarperCollins, 1991), and David Sobel and Tom Ferguson's *People's Book of Medical Tests* (Summit Books, 1985). In addition, the Pinckneys have also put together an informative guide to medical tests that can be performed at home called *Do-It-Yourself Medical Testing* (3rd ed. Facts on File, 1989).

Physicians' Desk Reference. Medical Economics, 1947– (revised annually). 1,500p. $49.95; also available on CD-ROM at $595.00.

Popularly known as the *PDR*, this familiar reference source lists and describes some 2,500 prescription drugs, the information derived from official package inserts provided by leading manufacturers. Distributed gratis to more than 500,000 physicians and Veterans Administration hospitals every year, its primary purpose is to advise medical professionals about the proper uses and dosages of pharmaceuticals, along with any contraindications, warnings, side effects, and possible interactions. The *PDR* contains color photographs showing hundreds of tablets and capsules that help the reader identify specific drugs, but the arrangement of material is complex and the text quite technical and often beyond the comprehension of laypeople.

In 1993, the publisher launched an abridged paperback version of the *PDR* intended for those without medical training. Entitled the *PDR Family Guide to Prescription Drugs* and priced at an affordable $24.95, it covers all major prescription drugs and is easier to use and read than the parent volume. Another more simply written and organized source that competes with the *PDR* is the excellent COMPLETE DRUG REFERENCE, which covers both prescription and nonprescription drugs. Consumers should also be aware that the *PDR* is now published on CD-ROM; the disk includes all information in the *PDR* as well as three companion publications, the *Physicians' Desk Reference for Nonprescription Drugs*, the *Physicians' Desk Reference for Ophthalmology*, and the new *PDR Drug Interactions and Side Effects Index*.

Physics in Medicine & Biology Encyclopedia. Edited by T.F. McAinsh. Pergamon Press, 1986. 2 vols. $415.00.

This highly specialized set emphasizes physics-based applications in the areas of medicine and biology, such as nuclear magnetic resonance, Doppler techniques for measuring blood flow, the use of heavy ions and mesons in radiation therapy, digital fluorography, and ultrasonic echocardiography. The more than 240 articles, which presuppose a basic knowledge of physics but not the subject matter itself, have been prepared by leading specialists (most from the United Kingdom) and include detailed bibliographies. The set also furnishes a valuable glossary that defines technical terms used in the encyclopedia. "Because the encyclopedia is aimed essentially at the novice, it will serve as excellent reading for students in either medicine or biology.

In addition, clinicians, medical technologists, and biotechnology researchers will likely find it indispensable" (*American Reference Books Annual*, 1987, p. 620).

Psychedelics Encyclopedia. Written by Peter Stafford. 3rd ed. Ronin Publishing, 1992. 512p. $24.95 paperbound.

Stafford's encyclopedia—first published in 1977—furnishes detailed information about a variety of natural and manufactured mind-altering drugs, such as LSD, PCP, peyote, and marijuana. "This extraordinary volume covers the history of their development and the controversies surrounding them, including the important role played by such figures as Timothy Leary, Richard Nixon, and the CIA in politicizing their use. . . . An excellent reference source for scientific and social research, this book is highly recommended" (*Library Journal*, November 15, 1992, p. 72). Readers interested in Stafford's encyclopedia should also be aware of the *Encyclopedia of Psychoactive Drugs* (Chelsea House, 1985–88). Published in two series of 25 and 32 volumes, this set is designed to give students, teachers, and parents reliable information about both licit and illicit drugs in a readable context. Portions of this set are also available on 10 video tapes under the title *Video Encyclopedia of Psychoactive Drugs* (Schlessinger Video Productions, 1991); the videos, which run 30 minutes each, sell for $39.95 singly or $399.50 for the set.

The World Book/Rush-Presbyterian-St. Luke's Medical Center Medical Encyclopedia: Your Guide to Good Health. World Book, 1991. 1,066p. $39.95.

Prepared by World Book in conjunction with the faculty of Chicago's Rush Medical College, the Rush-Presbyterian-St. Luke's Medical Center (also in Chicago), the American Red Cross, and the National Safety Council, this standout one-volume medical encyclopedia furnishes basic information on all vital aspects of human health in 4,500 concise A-to-Z entries complemented by 1,200 full-color photographs and two-color diagrams. Intended for the family and students at the high school level and beyond, the encyclopedia is handsomely designed and easy to read. It replaces the four-volume *World Book Illustrated Home Medical Encyclopedia* (1984). In his review in *Library Journal* (April 1, 1991, p. 118), James Swanton enthusiastically recommends the work for school and public library collections: "Especially notable and useful are the four appendixes devoted to the diagnosis of symptoms, health maintenance, nutrition and exercise, and growing older." A comparable source is the AMERICAN MEDICAL ASSOCIATION ENCYCLOPEDIA OF MEDICINE.

※ HISTORY AND ARCHAEOLOGY ※

Australians: A Historical Library. Edited by Alan D. Gilbert & others. Cambridge Univ. Press, 1988. 11 vols. $665.00.

Encyclopedic in scope, this unique compendium provides extensive, reliable, heavily illustrated information about the history of Australia. Five volumes cover the country's story from precolonial times to the present; each of the remaining volumes serves a specific reference function: *Events and Places* is a year-by-year chronology and description of important historical places and occurrences; *Historical Statistics* features full-color charts giving data on such topics as population, agriculture, and crime; *A Historical Dictionary* includes succinct biographies of prominent Australians; *A Historical Atlas* offers carefully configured maps depicting the country's growth and development at various points in time; another volume comprises both bibliographies on selected topics and a guide to cultural resources (archives, galleries, libraries, and museums); the final volume is an index to the set. "The editors of this highly readable and visually attractive encyclopedia have worked with over 400 scholars for 10 years to produce the definitive work on the land 'down under' " (*Library Journal*, July 1988, p. 72). Two smaller, single-volume A-to-Z works on Australia are the *Oxford Dictionary of Australian History* (Oxford Univ. Press, 1986), edited by Jan Bassett; and James Docherty's *Historical Dictionary of Australia* (Scarecrow Press, 1993).

The Cambridge Encyclopedia of Archaeology. Edited by Andrew Sherratt. Cambridge Univ. Press, 1980. 495p. Out of print (last priced at $35.00).

Arranged topically rather than alphabetically and intended principally for the nonspecialist, the *Cambridge Encyclopedia of Archaeology* provides an authoritative, interdisciplinary introduction to archaeology as a field of study. The encyclopedia—currently out of print but a strong candidate for reissue or revision in the near future—covers the major archaeological periods, regions, and methods and includes many illustrations that enhance the reader's appreciation and understanding. "The volume is a 'must' purchase for most libraries, and especially those in which the collection in archaeology is not extensive" (*American Reference Books Annual*, 1981, p. 179). A similar source (also now out of print) is the single-volume *Larousse Encyclopedia of Archaeology* (2nd ed. Larousse, 1983), which emphasizes classical archaeology and key excavations of the nineteenth and twentieth centuries.

More specialized are the *Princeton Encyclopedia of Classical Sites* (Princeton Univ. Press, 1976), an imposing work of 1,019 pages edited by Richard Stillwell, which describes 2,800 archaeological sites from the eighth century B.C. to the sixth century A.D., and the *Blackwell Encyclopedia of Industrial Archaeology* (Blackwell, 1993), which deals exclusively with the archaeology of technologically advanced societies.

The Cambridge Historical Encyclopedia of Great Britain and Ireland. Edited by Christopher Haigh. Cambridge Univ. Press, 1985. 392p. $44.50; $18.95 paper.

This handsomely produced encyclopedic survey covers British and Irish history in seven chronological sections, from Roman times to the Common Market era. Informative maps, diagrams, and photographs (in both color and black-and-white) complement the printed text. Approximately 800 brief biographies of famous historical figures are appended. "Readers will find this book useful both as a concise narrative and interpretive history and as a convenient reference work" (*Choice*, February 1986, p. 848).

The Christopher Columbus Encyclopedia. Edited by Silvio Bedini. Simon & Schuster, 1992. 2 vols. $175.00.

Was Columbus a hero or villain? This large (787-page) two-volume encyclopedia, prepared by 150 internationally recognized scholars for the 500th anniversary of Columbus's journey to the "New World," objectively presents both sides of the historical controversy surrounding the famous explorer. Some 350 signed, alphabetically arranged articles furnish information about all significant aspects of Columbian studies, including the man himself, his family and associates, the voyages and discoveries, other early explorers and explorations, the historical period, and the legacy. Excellent bibliographic essays accompany the longer articles, while numerous maps and facsimile documents enhance the text; a detailed index at the end of volume 2 affords easy access to the set's contents. "The encyclopedia deserves to be the centerpiece of every library's suggested reading list or program on Columbus and the Columbian controversy as well as the first bibliographic port of call for everyone exploring the great explorer's life and works" (*Wilson Library Bulletin*, January 1992, p. 126). A useful complement to the *Christopher Columbus Encyclopedia* is Foster Provost's *Columbus Dictionary* (Omnigraphics, 1991), a much less extensive work of 142 pages that treats Columbus and his world in approximately 400 short entries.

Civilization of the Ancient Mediterranean: Greece and Rome. Edited by Michael Grant & Rachel Kitzinger. Scribner's, 1988. 3 vols. $259.00.

The goal of this three-volume set is encyclopedic treatment of the people and achievements of classical Greece and Rome. The work features 95 essay-length articles by 88 qualified contributors arranged in thematic fashion under 14 broad headings, such as "Government and Society" and "Religion." Specific topics covered include agriculture, transportation, building and engineering, social life, sex and reproduction, economic systems, slavery, alphabets and writing, literature, the arts, philosophy, mythology, and wars. A detailed index is found in the final volume. This authoritative work will appeal to scholars as well as interested laypeople and students at the high school level and beyond. A handy one-volume encyclopedic work that covers much of the same ground (albeit not as expansively) is the *Oxford Classical Dictionary* (2nd ed. Oxford Univ. Press, 1970); its 1,176 pages contain substantial signed articles, usually one or two pages in length.

Dictionary of American History. Edited by James T. Adams. Revised ed. Scribner's, 1976. 8 vols. $625.00.

Absolutely essential for practically all North American libraries and often found in the personal libraries of teachers and advanced students of American history, this well-known set is, in the words of reference authority Bill Katz in his *Basic Information Sources* (4th ed. 1982, p. 204), "the standard overview of American history for the layperson and the expert." First published in five volumes in 1940, the revised eight-volume edition contains more than 6,000 entries prepared by some 800 authorities. It treats every major aspect of American history, including political, military, social, cultural, and economic developments. Biographies and historical maps, however, are omitted, as they are extensively covered in two companion works: the multivolume *Dictionary of American Biography* (Scribner's, 1928–) and the *Atlas of American History* (2nd ed. Scribner's, 1984). Interested consumers should also be aware that a comparatively inexpensive one-volume condensation of the *Dictionary of American History* appeared in 1983 under the title *Concise Dictionary of American History*; also published by Scribner's, it currently sells for $65.00.

Dictionary of Scandinavian History. Edited by Byron J. Nordstrom. Greenwood, 1986. 703p. $85.00.

Roughly 400 signed articles contributed by 70 specialists make up this first (and so far only) English-language encyclopedia of Scandinavian history from earliest times to the modern period. Countries covered are Norway, Sweden, Finland, Denmark, and Iceland. "The articles have a uniform, well-edited style, and there is no clumsy diction from non-English-speaking contributors. . . . The biographical and topographical articles (especially on cities and towns) lend much strength to the work" (*American Reference Books Annual*, 1987, p. 205).

Dictionary of the Middle Ages. Edited by Joseph R. Strayer. Scribner's, 1982–89. 13 vols. $990.00.

The definitive encyclopedic work on the Middle Ages, this monumental set contains some 5,000 specially commissioned articles by 1,300 medievalists covering the period 500 to 1500 A.D. Published by Scribner's under the auspices of the American Council of Learned Societies with support from the National Endowment for the Humanities, the encyclopedia is admirably interdisciplinary in approach, dealing with all pertinent areas of life in the Middle Ages (art, literature, language, music, philosophy, religion, government, business, science and technology, etc.). Bill Katz puts the *Dictionary of the Middle Ages* in good perspective in his *Basic Information Sources* (6th ed. 1992, p. 270): "One fascinating point about the coverage is the emphasis on daily life of average people. One moves from the monastery to the farm, not just from the castle to the king. In addition, there are biographical pieces on both famous and minor figures. There are some black-and-white and a few color illustrations, but the strength of the set is the text, not the illustrations. The articles are by 1300 scholars from some 30 countries. It can be read as well as used for a reference work—an almost ideal situation." Two valuable single-volume encyclopedic sources on the Middle Ages are Joseph Dahmus's *Dictionary of Medieval Civilization* (Macmillan, 1984) and the *Middle Ages: A Concise Encyclopaedia* (Thames & Hudson, 1989), edited by H.R. Loyn.

Dictionary of the Russian Revolution. Edited by George Jackson & Robert Devlin. Greenwood, 1989. 704p. $85.00.

The *Dictionary of the Russian Revolution* treats the major occurrences, personalities, parties, movements, and concepts associated with this cataclysmic political, social, and economic event. The articles, which vary in length from several hundred to 4,000 words, are arranged alphabetically and cover the period 1917–21. "The writing throughout the work is clear and interesting. Articles are signed, and most entries cite from three to a half-dozen bibliographic references" (*Reference Books Bulletin* in *Booklist*, October 15, 1989, p. 492). A competing work is the British-made, one-volume *Blackwell Encyclopedia of the Russian Revolution* (Blackwell, 1988), which offers less text (418 versus 704 pages) but includes numerous photographs. Also useful is John Paxton's ENCYCLOPEDIA OF RUSSIAN HISTORY, a single-volume treatment of Russian history from the tenth century through the demise of the Soviet Union.

The Encyclopedia of American Facts and Dates. Edited by Gorton Carruth. 9th ed. HarperCollins, 1993. 1,039p. $40.00.

First published in 1956 and periodically revised (the 7th edition appeared in 1979, the 8th in 1987, and most recently the 9th in 1993), this standard reference source presents the basic facts of American history chronologically—from the Norse explorers to Bill Clinton's election—in four parallel columns covering developments in (1) government, politics, and wars; (2) literature and the arts; (3) science, industry, and economics; and (4) sports and popular entertainment. The book is well organized with easy-to-read type. Comparable (albeit less current) one-volume chronologies are the *Almanac of American History* (Putnam, 1983), edited by Arthur Schlesinger Jr., and *Timetables of American History* (Simon & Schuster, 1981), edited by Laurence Urdang.

Encyclopedia of American History. Edited by Richard B. Morris. 6th ed. HarperCollins, 1982. 1,285p. Out of print (last priced at $29.95).

Acknowledged by just about everyone to be the best all-around one-volume encyclopedia of American history, the sixth edition of this standard work covers events from pre-Columbian times up to 1981, including developments in such areas as space science, technology, and linguistics. The encyclopedia, first published in 1953 and periodically revised over the years, contains approximately 400 biographies of prominent figures in American history among its many brief articles. Richard Morris, the editor and a distinguished historian, died in 1989 and exactly when a new edition of the encyclopedia will be published and who the new editor will be is not known at this time. A more recent work of similar scope and magnitude is the READER'S COMPANION TO AMERICAN HISTORY.

Encyclopedia of American Social History. Edited by Mary Kupiec Cayton & others. Scribner's, 1993. 3 vols. $350.00.

Drawing on the expertise of an impressive group of historians and other social scientists, the new *Encyclopedia of American Social History* consists of 180 original, signed, essay-length articles dealing with important facets of American life and culture, such as immigration, labor, ethnicity, education, the arts, religion, and sports. Specific articles include "Native Peoples Prior to European Arrival," "The American Colonies Through 1700," "Feminist Approaches to Social History," "Oral History," "Commercialization and the Rise of Bourgeois Culture," and "Antebellum African American Culture." A detailed 92-page index renders specific information in the text readily accessible, including many maps, tables, and bibliographies. Although more specialized in coverage than the larger DICTIONARY OF AMERICAN HISTORY (also published by Scribner's), the encyclopedia has the same broad appeal and can be consulted productively by scholars, laypeople, and high school and college students alike. "The lengthy, in-depth articles survey their topics throughout American history, identify changing trends, and analyze their significance" (*Wilson Library Bulletin*, May 1993, p. 116).

The Encyclopedia of Ancient Egypt. Written by Margaret Bunson. Facts on File, 1991. 291p. $40.00.

Although hardly comprehensive in coverage or treatment, this encyclopedia does provide an excellent overview of ancient Egyptian history from the predynastic period to the fall of the New Kingdom. Aimed at secondary school and college students as well as interested laypeople, it contains approximately 1,500 concise A-to-Z articles describing important individuals, places, documents, and objects. Black-and-white illustrations, including maps, appear throughout. "Bunson has addressed a need in the introductory literature of the ancient Near East with this browsing and ready reference tool" (*Choice*, March 1992, p. 1040).

Encyclopedia of Asian History. Edited by Ainslie Embree. Scribner's, 1988. 4 vols. $360.00.

Editor Embree, former chairman of the history department and director of the Southern Asia Institute at Columbia University, has created a topnotch reference work that illuminates the recorded history of Asia from earliest times to the present. The encyclopedia's four volumes comprise about 2,050 pages and nearly 3,000 A-to-Z articles ranging in length from a few lines to 10 pages. Written for the nonspecialist by an impressive roster of contributors, the articles are complemented by 160 photographs and drawings plus 63 original maps. "This first-rate, professionally sound, and invitingly handsome reference work covers most of Asia, including various past and present countries of this region, and comprehensively deals with historical events, the people, places, books, religion, ideas (Marxism, shamanism), music, and phenomena" (*Library Journal*, June 15, 1988, p. 52).

A valuable complement to the *Encyclopedia of Asian History* is David Shavit's 620-page *United States in Asia: A Historical Dictionary* (Greenwood, 1990). Useful single-volume encyclopedias covering the history of individual Asian countries include Hugh O'Neill's *Companion to Chinese History* (Facts on File, 1987), the *Historical Dictionary of Revolutionary China, 1839–1976* (Greenwood, 1992), Parshotam Mehra's *Dictionary of Modern Indian History, 1707–1947* (Oxford Univ. Press, 1985), and Janet Hunter's *Concise Dictionary of Modern Japanese History* (Univ. of California Press, 1984).

The Encyclopedia of Colonial and Revolutionary America. Edited by John M. Faragher. Facts on File, 1989. 448p. $50.00.

Covering American history from the beginning up to circa 1785, this readable encyclopedia consists of 1,500 alphabetically arranged entries from "Abortion" to "Zenger, Peter." Most articles are brief, although some topics such as agriculture, religion, women, and the original 13 colonies receive substantial treatment. "Faragher's single-volume encyclopedia is packed with much information, and it reflects current interest in social as well as economic and political history. . . . This is a superb ready reference tool for all levels. Highly recommended" (*Choice*, July–August 1990, p. 1804). A larger, three-volume work—the *Encyclopedia of the North American Colonies*—appeared in late 1993; published by Scribner's and priced at $320.00, this topically arranged set covers much of the same ground as the *Encyclopedia of Colonial and Revolutionary America* but in much greater detail.

Encyclopedia of Historic Places. Written by Courtlandt Canby. Facts on File, 1984. 2 vols. $175.00.

The *Encyclopedia of Historic Places* provides information about some 10,000 places around the world that are of significant historical interest. James Rettig, reviewing the set in *Wilson Library Bulletin* (June 1984, p. 753), comments: "*Historic Places* has a unique emphasis and should become librarians' first choice as a source for short histories of towns, cities, countries, provinces, states, empires, battle sites, lakes, mountains, rivers, shrines, and archaeological digs."

An Encyclopaedia of Indian Archaeology. Edited by A. Ghosh. Munshiram Manoharlal (dist. by South Asia Books), 1989. 2 vols. $115.00.

The first volume of this definitive survey of archaeological developments in India consists of 20 sections devoted to such pertinent subjects as early Indian cultures, settlements, skeletal remains, pottery, coins, paleobotany, and writing. The second volume, entitled *A Gazetteer of Explored and Excavated Sites in India*, furnishes a 470-page A-to-Z listing of all known archaeological sites in India as of 1979. Together, these volumes "form a superb treatment of Indian archaeology representing high levels of understanding, superb writing, intelligent illustration, and a beautifully executed editorial effort. The simple clarity of the knowledgeable prose makes the work equally accessible to amateurs and professionals" (*Library Journal*, April 15, 1991, p. 82).

Encyclopedia of Russian History: From the Christianization of Kiev to the Breakup of the USSR. Written by John Paxton. ABC-Clio, 1993. 484p. $65.00.

A heavily revised version of Paxton's *Companion to Russian History* (Facts on File, 1983), this handy one-volume A-to-Z encyclopedia contains approximately 2,500 entries covering a thousand years of Russian history. It includes maps, a glossary, and a carefully chosen bibliography. "This first-rate reference monograph will prove an invaluable asset for scholars of Russian literature—no political position is taken or judgment reached—yet it succeeds in its aim to reach as wide a general readership as possible" (*Library Journal*, December 1993, p. 116).

The Encyclopedia of Southern History. Edited by Robert W. Twyman & David C. Roller. Louisiana State Univ. Press, 1979. 1,421p. $95.00.

A model of the best in regional encyclopedia-making, the *Encyclopedia of Southern History* comprises 2,900 articles dealing with the American South on subjects from art to zoology. Prepared by more than 1,100 scholars, mostly U.S. university professors, the encyclopedia emphasizes economic, political, and military developments, although coverage of architecture, art, literature, music, etc. is more than adequate. Potentially controversial topics (such as Reconstruction, miscegenation, and the Ku Klux Klan) are treated without bias. Undoubtedly the best quick-reference source on the region, the *Encyclopedia of Southern History* is, in the words of Raymond Sokolov in the *New York Times Book Review* (May 18, 1980, p. 27), "a valuable, if intimidating compendium of useful information." A much larger and more specialized work is the four-volume

Encyclopedia of the Confederacy published by Simon & Schuster in 1993; edited by Richard N. Current and priced at $355.00, the set features approximately 1,500 signed articles prepared by over 300 scholars.

Encyclopedia of the Holocaust. Edited by Israel Gutman. Macmillan, 1990. 4 vols. $360.00.

All important aspects of the Holocaust—defined by editor Gutman as "the Third Reich's attempt during the period of Nazi power (1933–45) to physically destroy the Jews of Europe" (introduction)—are explored in this outstanding encyclopedia of 950 signed, original articles by leading international authorities. Designed for laypeople, students, and scholars alike, the four-volume set contains articles on significant events that precipitated the Holocaust, the infamous camps, the atrocities and methods of execution, the political situation in Hitler's Germany and beyond, and the many people involved, including Nazi leaders, resistance fighters, prominent Jews of the time, and various world leaders such as Churchill and Pope Pius XII. "This wealth of information about one of the major events in the history of western civilization belongs in all public and academic libraries and large high school libraries" (*Reference Books Bulletin* in *Booklist*, March 1, 1990, p. 1378). A complementary work is the two-volume, German-produced *Encyclopedia of the Third Reich* (Macmillan, 1991), edited by Christian Zentner and Friedemann Bedurftig and translated into English by Amy Hackett.

Encyclopedia of the Renaissance. Edited by Thomas G. Bergin & Jennifer Speake. Facts on File, 1987. 454p. $45.00.

This utilitarian encyclopedia offers authoritative information about the people, events, institutions, ideas, and movements associated with the Renaissance in 2,500 brief, alphabetically arranged articles. The volume, which is especially strong in the areas of literature and art history, includes both black-and-white and color illustrations, a chronology of major political events during the period, and a bibliography divided into nine broad categories. "This A-to-Z encyclopedia is a tapestry of the era's achievements" (*Wilson Library Bulletin*, February 1988, p. 99).

An Encyclopedia of World History: Ancient, Medieval, and Modern, Chronologically Arranged. Edited by William L. Langer. 5th ed. Houghton Mifflin, 1972. 1,505p. $44.00.

Langer's well-known encyclopedia attempts to cover all significant events from prehistoric to modern times in a single volume. First published in 1940

and now in its fifth edition, the work is chronologically arranged in narrative form and emphasizes political, military, and diplomatic history. A new edition should be coming along shortly. Two other recommended—and more recent—one-volume world history encyclopedias are the *Macmillan Concise Dictionary of World History* (Macmillan, 1983), compiled by Bruce Wetterau, and the brand-new *Encyclopedia of World Facts and Dates* (HarperCollins, 1993) by Gorton Carruth, who also produces the standard ENCYCLOPEDIA OF AMERICAN FACTS AND DATES.

The Facts on File Encyclopedia of the 20th Century. Edited by John Drexel. Facts on File, 1991. 1,046p. $79.95.

This hefty single-volume encyclopedia contains over 8,000 brief, unsigned articles devoted to the most important people, places, events, and scientific and artistic achievements of the present century. Most attention is accorded political leaders, but prominent figures from other walks of life (sports, medicine, literature, etc.) are also well represented, as are major wars and military encounters, political conferences and movements, court cases, theories, books, plays, and the like. Two smaller single-volume sources covering the same period are Peter Teed's *Dictionary of Twentieth-Century History* (Oxford Univ. Press, 1992) and David Brownstone and Irene Franck's *Dictionary of 20th Century History* (Prentice Hall, 1990).

Famous First Facts: A Record of First Happenings, Discoveries, and Inventions in the United States. Compiled by Joseph Nathan Kane. 4th ed. H.W. Wilson, 1981. 1,360p. $80.00.

In 1929, Joseph Kane, a meticulous collector of interesting historical facts, approached Halsey W. Wilson, founder and then publisher of the H.W. Wilson Company, with an idea for a reference volume composed of American "firsts." Thus, *Famous First Facts* was born, first published in 1933 and revised and enlarged in 1950, 1964, and, most recently, 1981. The current edition contains over 9,000 historical tidbits from the first ice cream cone to the first television program. Kane also compiles *Facts About the Presidents* (6th ed., 1993) and *Facts About the States* (1989), both H.W. Wilson publications.

The Fitzhenry & Whiteside Book of Canadian Facts and Dates. Compiled by Jay Myers. Fitzhenry & Whiteside, 1986. 354p. $24.95 (in Canada) paperbound.

Intended by Myers as both "a serious reference book and quick fact-finder" and "a narrative history book for personal enjoyment" (preface), this attractively produced paperback chronicles important events in Canadian history beginning with Leif Ericson and ending with Canada's first astronaut in 1984. "*Canadian Facts and Dates* is fairly easy to skim for brief facts, and it certainly deserves hearty welcome as an updating tool for the reference shelf" (*American Reference Books Annual*, 1988, p. 210). Another source of encyclopedic information on Canadian history is the much larger, indispensable CANADIAN ENCYCLOPEDIA, which covers all aspects of the country's life and culture.

Historical Dictionary of European Imperialism. Edited by James S. Olson. Greenwood, 1991. 782p. $99.50.

This handy reference source consists of approximately 800 A-to-Z articles covering major European empires since 1492. "This is a thorough, well-written volume. Absolutely essential for all university, college, and large public libraries" (*Choice*, February 1992, p. 874). The publisher, Greenwood Press, specializes in this sort of single-volume encyclopedic work; comparable volumes include the *Historical Dictionary of Fascist Italy* (1982), the *Historical Dictionary of the Spanish Empire, 1402–1975* (1991), the *Historical Dictionary of the Spanish Civil War, 1936–1939* (1982), the *Historical Dictionary of Modern Spain, 1700–1988* (1990), the *Historical Dictionary of Revolutionary China, 1839–1976* (1992), and the HISTORICAL DICTIONARY OF THE FRENCH REVOLUTION, 1789–1799.

Historical Dictionary of Israel. Written by Bernard Reich. Scarecrow Press, 1992. 351p. $47.50.

Prepared by a recognized authority on the country, this encyclopedic compilation furnishes reliable information on the history of the modern Jewish state, with emphasis on the important people, places, and events. The volume is part of Scarecrow Press's highly regarded Asian Historical Dictionaries series, which includes similar works on Jordan, Vietnam, Indonesia, and several other countries in the region. The publisher also has equivalent series on countries in other parts of the world, such as Africa and South America.

Historical Dictionary of the French Revolution, 1789–1799. Edited by Samuel F. Scott & Barry Rothaus. Greenwood, 1985. 2 vols. $145.00.

Ideal for serious students, teachers, and scholars, this alphabetically arranged encyclopedia describes the people, places, events, organizations, laws, trends, and ideas associated with the French Revolution in 525 alphabetically arranged articles that range in length from a short paragraph to several pages. The two-volume set "is a distinguished contribution. It brings clarity and control to the kaleidoscopic patterns that typify a decade of profound significance" (*American Reference Books Annual*, 1986, p. 191). The *Historical Dictionary of the French Revolution* is part of a series of one- and two-volume works on French history published by Greenwood Press that include the *Historical Dictionary of Napoleonic France, 1799–1815* (1985), the *Historical Dictionary of France from the 1815 Restoration to the Second Empire* (1987), the *Historical Dictionary of the French Second Empire, 1852–1879* (1985), the *Historical Dictionary of the Third French Republic, 1870–1940* (1986), and the *Historical Dictionary of the French Fourth and Fifth Republics, 1946–1991* (1992). Two other sources on the French Revolution should be noted: *A Critical Dictionary of the French Revolution* (Harvard Univ. Press, 1989), edited by François Furet and Mona Ozouf, is a large (1,063-page) single-volume compilation of 90 scholarly articles more concerned with interpretation than presentation of basic facts; and John Paxton's *Companion to the French Revolution* (Facts on File, 1988) is a comparatively small (224-page) volume designed strictly for quick reference.

The Marshall Cavendish Illustrated Encyclopedia of Discovery and Exploration. Marshall Cavendish, 1991. 17 vols. $449.95.

Typical of Marshall Cavendish reference sets, this encyclopedia is generally reliable, competently edited, popularly written, heavily illustrated, adequately indexed, and expensively priced. Originally published by the London firm of Aldus Books Ltd. in the early 1970s and sold at the time in North America by both Grolier and Doubleday under the title *Encyclopedia of Discovery and Exploration*, this set is chronologically arranged and provides a readable survey of "almost every important geographical discovery to take place in the history of mankind" (introduction), from the early efforts of ancient explorers to present-day journeys into space. In a lengthy review in *American Reference Books Annual* (1992, pp. 160–61), Ronald Fritze commends the set, saying it "belongs in every junior high, high school, and public library. Young readers will find it a great source of enjoyable reading and browsing." Two useful one-volume works on the subject are *World Explorers and Discoverers* (Macmillan, 1992), edited by Richard Bohlander, and *The Discoverers: An Encyclopedia of Explorers and Exploration* (McGraw-Hill, 1980), edited by Helen Delpar.

The Oxford Dictionary of Byzantium. Edited by Alexander P. Kazhdan & others. Oxford Univ. Press, 1991. 3 vols. $275.00.

Twelve years in the making, this natural complement to the DICTIONARY OF THE MIDDLE AGES furnishes a unique encyclopedic survey of Byzantine civilization from the fourth through the fifteenth centuries. Comprising some 5,000 articles of varying length prepared by 125 leading authorities, the set offers especially strong coverage of Byzantine agriculture, art, literature, politics, and urban life. The articles are usually well-written and will be comprehensible to interested laypeople as well as serious students at the high school and college levels. "The editor deserves special thanks for the uniformly lucid and readable style, for the clear illustrations, and for the useful maps, though the captions are not very informative" (*Library Journal*, August 1991, p. 88).

The People's Chronology: A Year-by-Year Record of Human Events from Prehistory to the Present. Compiled by James Trager. Revised ed. Holt, 1992. 1,102p. $45.00.

The People's Chronology, first published in 1979 and revised in 1992, is packed with more than 30,000 facts covering all major areas of human endeavor from 3 million B.C. through 1990. An index at the end of the volume provides access to names, places, events, subjects, and the like. Other recommended world chronologies (all single-volume works) are *Asimov's Chronology of the World* (HarperCollins, 1991), the *New York Public Library Book of Chronologies* (Prentice Hall, 1990), and Bernard Grun's *Timetables of History* (3rd ed. Simon & Schuster, 1991).

The Reader's Companion to American History. Edited by Eric Foner & John Garraty. Houghton Mifflin, 1991. 1,226p. $35.00.

Sponsored by the Society of American Historians, this large reference book consists of over 1,000 alphabetically arranged articles contributed by 400 authorities, including some distinguished historians (for instance, Arthur Link writes on Woodrow Wilson). Similar in purpose, size, and scope but not organization and presentation to the older and better known ENCYCLOPEDIA OF AMERICAN HISTORY, the *Reader's Companion* is made up mostly of long, interpretative essays that illuminate important events, periods, and concepts in American history, such as the Civil War, the U.S. Constitution, and the Cold War. All major facets of history—political, military, economic, social, cultural—are covered, which accounts for articles on such topics as baseball, childhood, the feminist movement, abortion, gay rights, domestic work, ecology, fashion, and advertising. Brief biographies of prominent Americans are also found throughout the volume.

"*The Reader's Companion to American History* is informative and readable, an excellent combination of political and social history that can be read and enjoyed by students and the general public" (*Reference Books Bulletin* in *Booklist*, January 1, 1992, p. 852). Other quality one-volume desk encyclopedias on American history are the *Concise Dictionary of American History* (Scribner's, 1983) and the *Scribner Desk Dictionary of American History* (Scribner's, 1984), both abridgments of the eight-volume DICTIONARY OF AMERICAN HISTORY; the now quite dated but still useful *Oxford Companion to American History* (Oxford Univ. Press, 1966), edited by Thomas Herbert Johnson; the recently published *Great American History Fact-Finder* (Houghton Mifflin, 1993) by schoolteachers Ted Yanak and Pam Cornelison; and the aforementioned ENCYCLOPEDIA OF AMERICAN HISTORY.

The Reader's Encyclopedia of the American West. Edited by Howard R. Lamar. HarperCollins, 1977. 1,306p. $30.00.

Employing a broad definition of the region, this encyclopedia covers the people (both real and fictional), places, legends, culture, and events of the American West in some 2,400 signed articles, from "Aberdeen, S.D." to "Zogbaum, Rufus Fairchild" (a Western illustrator). "The book is particularly rich in information on American Indians, their language, and their place in the development of the West. Most articles have bibliographical references. All are well written, with a style and vocabulary appropriate to readers from high school age up" (*Wilson Library Bulletin*, April 1978, p. 652). An older, smaller but complementary work is Denis McLoughlin's *Wild and Woolly: An Encyclopedia of the Old West* (Doubleday, 1975).

The United States in Latin America: A Historical Dictionary. Written by David Shavit. Greenwood, 1992. 471p. $75.00.

To date, Shavit, a professor in the Department of Library and Information Studies at Northern Illinois University, has produced four single-volume encyclopedic works describing the history of U.S. interaction with other parts of the world, all published by Greenwood Press: *The United States in the Middle East: A Historical Dictionary* (1988), *The United States in Africa: A Historical Dictionary* (1989), *The United States in Asia: A Historical Dictionary* (1990), and, most recently, *The United States in Latin America: A Historical Dictionary* (1992). All of these sources are alphabetically arranged and cover prominent people, events, and organizations, although the emphasis in each is on individuals who shaped events. In the Latin American volume, for instance, 217 U.S. diplomats, 73 missionaries, 55 lawyers, and 43 naval officers are among the many biographees. Together, these four reference books form an impressive compendium of historical information about the U.S. and its relations with the developing world.

※ LAW AND THE JUDICIAL SYSTEM ※

The American Law Dictionary. Written by Peter G. Renstrom. ABC-Clio, 1991. 308p. $49.50.

One of more than a dozen encyclopedic dictionaries in the publisher's excellent Clio Dictionaries in Political Science series, this authoritative work provides detailed information about more than 300 legal terms and concepts, such as "docket," "due process of law," "expert witness," "plea bargaining," "sentence," and "summons." Entries, which vary in length from a paragraph or two to more than a page, are arranged A-to-Z within seven topical chapters ("Judicial Organization," "The Criminal Judicial Process," "The Appellate Judicial Process," etc.). Clearly and popularly written, the *American Law Dictionary* is normally easy to use and most helpful as a starting place for laypeople and high school and college students seeking to understand the inner workings of the American legal system. "An excellent index, generous cross-references, and a logical arrangement contribute to the effectiveness of this dictionary as a reliable reference tool" (*Choice*, July-August 1991, p. 1764).

The Constitutional Law Dictionary. Written by Ralph C. Chandler & others. ABC-Clio, 1985–87. 2 vols. plus two suppls. to vol. 1, 1987; 1991. $110.00 (2-vol. set); $50.00 (ea. suppl.).

Like the AMERICAN LAW DICTIONARY, the *Constitutional Law Dictionary* forms part of the Clio Dictionaries in Political Science series, which is designed to assist those without professional training who want an encyclopedic introduction to the essentials of the American political and legal system. The *Constitutional Law Dictionary* comprises two volumes: volume 1 (1985) is entitled *Individual Rights* and volume 2 (1987), *Governmental Powers*; both focus on "concepts of constitutionalism, words and phrases common to American constitutional law, and leading case decisions rendered by the United States Supreme Court" (preface). Supplements are issued periodically to keep the user abreast of new Supreme Court rulings. In a review of volume 1 in *Wilson Library Bulletin* (May 1985, p. 623), James Rettig nicely sums up the whole work: "The clearly written, lengthy two-part entries define a concept or describe the facts of a case and then explain its significance and practical implications. . . . The dictionary is not as basic as the Constitution, but it will be very helpful to people who want to understand that document."

Corpus Juris Secundum: A Complete Restatement of the Entire American Law as Developed by All Reported Cases. West Publishing Co., 1936–. 157 vols. (101 numbered vols., plus annual suppls.) $3,500.00 (estimated price).

Cited as *C.J.S.*, this massive compilation provides an encyclopedic treatment of all legal topics based on reported court cases in the U.S. since 1658. The set is arranged alphabetically by broad topics and kept up-to-date by cumulative annual parts and recompiled volumes. Note that *C.J.S.*— and its equally large and expensive competitor, the multivolume *American Jurisprudence* (2nd ed. Lawyers' Cooperative, 1962–)—are intended for legal professionals experienced in searching the law. Although on occasion these sets can be consulted profitably by laypeople, the magnitude and complexity of the information they contain normally overwhelms or intimidates users who lack training in the law; such individuals will be better served in almost all instances by the GUIDE TO AMERICAN LAW: EVERYONE'S LEGAL ENCYCLOPEDIA, a West Publishing Company set intended specifically for the legal neophyte.

Encyclopedia of the American Constitution. Edited by Leonard W. Levy & others. Macmillan, 1986. 4 vols. plus suppl., 1992. $400.00 (4-vol. set); $90.00 (suppl.).

Published to commemorate the bicentennial of the ratification of the U.S. Constitution in 1787, this magnificent encyclopedia consists of approximately 2,100 signed articles by 260 leading scholars in the fields of law, political science, and history. The articles, which run in length from a paragraph to several pages, cover all significant aspects of the Constitution and constitutional law, including Supreme Court judges and landmark cases, from abortion to zoning. "This richly detailed, skillfully edited, and easy to use reference set belongs in most libraries" (*Library Journal*, December 1986, p. 96). In 1992, a 668-page supplement appeared, updating the encyclopedia's coverage of case law in such areas as civil liberties and environmental regulation and adding pertinent new information—for instance, biographical sketches of Justices Anthony Kennedy and David Souter.

Encyclopedia of the American Judicial System. Edited by Robert J. Janosik. Scribner's, 1987. 3 vols. $259.00.

This first-rate encyclopedia consists of 88 essay-length articles by leading authorities on major components of the American judicial system. Aimed at "the layperson, the university student, and the academic researcher not trained in the ways of the law library" (preface), the articles are arranged thematically under six broad headings: "Legal History," "Substantive Law," "Institutions and Personnel," "Process and Behavior," "Constitutional Law and Issues," and "Methodology." In all, the three-volume set comprises 1,420 pages of readable, highly authoritative information easily accessible via a 57-page index at the end of volume 3. "Most of the essays are analytical as well as expository, reflecting the authors' points of view. Some historical perspective on the topic is usually included, along with a list of relevant cases and an annotated bibliography. This work will be useful to a wide variety of readers and is highly recommended for public and academic libraries" (*Library Journal*, October 15, 1987, p. 75).

Everybody's Guide to the Law: The First Place to Look for the Legal Information You Need Most. Written by Melvin Belli & Allen P. Wilkinson. Revised ed. Harcourt Brace Jovanovich, 1986. 640p. $19.95 hardcover; $11.95 paperbound.

Belli and Wilkinson's book furnishes a quick, readable encyclopedic overview of all important areas of U.S. law, including contracts, real estate, marriage and divorce, wills and estate planning, torts, medical questions, civil rights, and criminal justice. There is also a section on finding the right lawyer, should one be required. Several other one-volume works offer similar information, including Martin J. Ross's *Handbook of Everyday Law* (4th ed. HarperCollins, 1981) and *You and the Law* (3rd ed. Reader's Digest Assn., 1984), but at this time *Everybody's Guide to the Law* is the most current. Such guides best serve those who cannot afford or lack access to the larger, more expansive, and much more expensive GUIDE TO AMERICAN LAW: EVERYONE'S LEGAL ENCYCLOPEDIA.

The Evolving Constitution: How the Supreme Court Has Ruled on Issues from Abortion to Zoning. Written by Jethro K. Lieberman. Random House, 1992. 752p. $26.00.

Lieberman, a law professor and well-known commentator on constitutional matters, presents approximately 1,200 brief, intelligently written articles digesting some 2,370 decisions handed down by the U.S. Supreme Court over the years. Arranged A-to-Z by topic and intended strictly for the general reader, the articles (for example, "Freedom of Religion") deal with both the constitutional history and current legal status of the issues involved. "This excellent reference work details the manner in which the U.S. Supreme Court has interpreted the Constitution for almost 200 years. . . . Highly recommended for public libraries and the general reference collections of academic libraries" (*Library Journal*, December 1992, p. 126). A complementary work is *Historic U.S. Court Cases, 1690–1990: An Encyclopedia* (Garland, 1992). Edited by John W. Johnson and written in jargon-free language by some 80 legal scholars and historians, this 754-page encyclopedia describes approximately 170 landmark decisions issued by various U.S. courts, most from the High Court.

The Family Legal Companion. Written by Thomas Hauser. Revised ed. Allworth Press, 1992. 256p. $16.95 paperbound.

Aimed at readers without legal training, Hauser's encyclopedic guide to family law treats such matters as home ownership, renters' rights and landlords, neighbors, marriage and divorce, children and child custody, and pets. Arranged topically in a question-and-answer format, the book makes no pretense at being comprehensive, but it does have real value as an easy-to-understand quick reference source for the home or library. Similar single-volume works are Lester Wallman and Lawrence Schwarz's *Handbook of Family Law* (Prentice-Hall, 1989) and the *Reader's Digest Family Legal Guide* (Reader's Digest Assn., 1981), edited by Inge Dobelis; the latter is now much in need of revision.

The Guide to American Law: Everyone's Legal Encyclopedia. West Publishing Co., 1983–85. 12 vols. plus suppls., 1987, 1990–92. $1,494.80 (includes suppls.).

Unique among legal encyclopedias, the *Guide to American Law* offers comprehensive coverage of all pertinent aspects of U.S. law in language that can be readily understood by the ordinary person. Alphabetically arranged, the multivolume set contains well over 5,000 articles, which vary in length from short definitional paragraphs to substantial essays of several or more pages. Topics covered include legal principles, concepts, and organizations, landmark judicial decisions, famous legal documents and events, and biographies of prominent figures who have contributed significantly to the development of American law. Supplements help keep the encyclopedia reasonably current. The *Guide to American*

Law, an outstanding reference work that should be found in practically all libraries regardless of type or size, has been widely praised by critics; for instance, Judith Nixon in *Library Journal* (September 15, 1985, p. 73) notes that it "is full enough to satisfy most nonlawyers on any legal subject without being overwhelming," and James Rettig in *Wilson Library Bulletin* (June 1984, p. 755) says, "the text will contribute greatly to ordinary citizens' understanding of the law and its institutions, about which everyone eventually needs intelligible information. Public and academic libraries could be charged with contempt of their clients if they do not buy these volumes."

McCarthy's Desk Encyclopedia of Intellectual Property. Written by J. Thomas McCarthy. BNA Books, 1991. 385p. $57.00 paperbound.

More than 600 concise A-to-Z entries make up this clearly written, authoritative single-volume encyclopedia. It deals with the history, concepts, and important legal cases involving intellectual property, including copyright, patents, trademarks, and trade secrets. At the end of each entry are citations to sources where pertinent additional information can be found. "Drawing on the statutes, regulations, case law, and literature of patent, trademark, and copyright controversies, McCarthy has skillfully created a quick reference resource for students, non-professionals, and experienced attorneys alike" (*American Reference Books Annual*, 1992, p. 206).

The Oxford Companion to Law. Written by David M. Walker. Oxford Univ. Press, 1980. 1,366p. $65.00.

Although now somewhat dated, the *Oxford Companion to Law* remains useful as a reliable source of quick information for laypeople on key legal terms and concepts, definitions of Latin words and phrases used in Anglo-American law, descriptions of types of law and legal processes, prominent figures associated with the law, and the law as historically developed in English-speaking countries and Western Europe. Prepared by a Glasgow University law professor, the volume naturally emphasizes the British legal system, but much of the material is applicable to American and Canadian practice.

The Oxford Companion to the Supreme Court of the United States. Edited by Kermit L. Hall & others. Oxford Univ. Press, 1992. 1,032p. $49.95.

This voluminous A-to-Z encyclopedia describes every significant aspect of the U.S. Supreme Court, from the justices and their work to the ins and outs of constitutional law to the landmark cases, such as *Roe v. Wade* and the *United States v. Nixon*. It contains 1,200 signed entries written by 300 legal scholars in a manner readily comprehensible to the average reader, including interested students at the high school and college levels. Moreover, information in the book is easily retrievable, facilitated by numerous cross-references and case-name and subject indexes. "*The Oxford Companion to the Supreme Court of the United States* belongs in every library, high school and up, and on the shelf of the practitioner and the teacher. It will prove to be the standard reference work on the Supreme Court" (*Reference Books Bulletin* in *Booklist*, December 1, 1992, p. 690). "A vitally important reference tool that should be in every library" (*Choice*, March 1993, p. 1243).

Two recent single-volume works published by Congressional Quarterly Books complement the *Oxford Companion*, namely *Congressional Quarterly's Guide to the U.S. Supreme Court* (2nd ed., 1990) and the *Supreme Court A to Z: A Ready Reference Encyclopedia* (1993). Other useful sources on the High Court are the *Reference Guide to the United States Supreme Court* (Facts on File, 1986), edited by Stephen P. Elliot; and Robert J. Wagman's *The Supreme Court: A Citizen's Guide* (Pharos Books, 1992), both also published in one volume.

The State-by-State Guide to Women's Legal Rights. Compiled by the N.O.W. Legal Defense and Education Fund & Renee Cherow O'Leary. McGraw-Hill, 1987. 523p. $19.95 hardcover; $12.95 paperbound.

A much expanded and heavily revised version of the 224-page *Shana Alexander's State-by-State Guide to Women's Legal Rights* (Wollstonecraft Press, 1975), this handy reference work furnishes nontechnical summaries of the law in all 50 states in such areas of vital concern to women as marriage and divorce, reproductive freedom, adoption, child custody and support, sexual harassment and rape, and discrimination in education and the workplace. State statutes are cited in all instances and court cases when pertinent. The first 100 or so pages of the book are devoted to describing generally how the legal process operates and introducing the law pertaining to women in four major areas: home and family, education, employment, and the community at large. "Written by a communications specialist and a lawyer, this guide is an essential purchase for any library" (*American Reference Books Annual*, 1988, p. 229). A similar but less detailed and up-to-date source is Gayle Niles and Douglas Snider's *Women's Counsel: A Legal Guide for Women* (Arden Press, 1984). Published in paperback at the affordable price of $8.50, this 240-page book lacks the state summaries that make the *State-by-State Guide to Women's Legal Rights* so useful.

❋ LITERATURE, LANGUAGE, AND PUBLISHING ❋

Benét's Reader's Encyclopedia. Originally edited by William Rose Benét. 3rd ed. HarperCollins, 1987. 1,091p. $45.00.

First published in 1948 as the *Reader's Encyclopedia* under the editorship of the late William Rose Benét (who died in 1950), this classic one-volume encyclopedia of world literature has since undergone two revisions, the first in 1965 and then in 1987, when the book was retitled in memory of its founding editor. The latest edition, which has been "expanded, completely revised, and updated," contains over 9,000 entries covering important authors and their works regardless of nationality, genre, or period, as well as literary movements, legends, allusions, terms, and awards. Among the writers added to the new edition are Margaret Drabble, Gabriel García Márquez, Neil Simon, B.F. Skinner, Derek Walcott, and Alice Walker. Regrettably, some useful material found in the earlier editions had to be cut to make way for new entries. "Still one of the great reference books, even if it has lost a little of its air of leisurely pursuit of Benét's 'domain of learning and imagination,' *Benét's Reader's Encyclopedia* is a necessary purchase for all high school, public, and academic libraries" (*Reference Books Bulletin* in *Booklist,* March 1, 1988, p. 1102). A much older work of similar scope is *Cassell's Encyclopedia of World Literature;* published by Morrow in three volumes in 1953 and revised in 1973, this set is dated and understandably no longer in print, although it still offers useful historical information.

Benét's Reader's Encyclopedia of American Literature. Edited by George Perkins & others. HarperCollins, 1991. 1,176p. $45.00.

This excellent new encyclopedia, the work of some 130 scholars, treats the totality of American literature—U.S., Canadian, and Latin American— from the fifteenth century to the present. It succeeds Herzberg's old *Reader's Encyclopedia of American Literature* (Crowell, 1962) and draws some material from the companion BENÉT'S READER'S ENCYCLOPEDIA, which is devoted to all of world literature. The A-to-Z entries cover not only important American writers and their major works but major genres, such as African American literature, Jewish American literature, Native American literature, children's and feminist literature in the Americas, drama as literature, and the American novel. "Added features, such as genealogies of famous literary families, extended essays on all facets of American literature, and biographies on women and ethnic minority writers, make this single-volume work a valuable

asset to any reference shelf" (*Library Journal,* January 1992, p. 104).

Other recommended one-volume encyclopedias of American literature are the *Oxford Companion to American Literature* (5th ed. Oxford Univ. Press, 1983), edited by James D. Hart; the *Concise Oxford Companion to American Literature* (Oxford Univ. Press, 1986), an abridgment of the 1983 *Oxford Companion* also edited by Hart; the *Cambridge Handbook of American Literature* (Cambridge Univ. Press, 1986), edited by Jack Salzman; and the *Harvard Guide to Contemporary American Writing* (Harvard Univ. Press, 1979), edited by Daniel Hoffman.

The Bloomsbury Guide to Women's Literature. Edited by Claire Buck. Prentice Hall, 1992. 1,171p. $40.00 hardcover; $20.00 paperbound.

Approximately 40 authorities have contributed to this outstanding encyclopedic guide, which comprises about 5,000 short entries and 36 essay-length articles on women writers and their literature "from all periods and from the whole world" (introduction). The volume, which focuses on fiction, includes not only celebrated authors like Virginia Woolf, Margaret Drabble, and the Brontë sisters but many less prominent female writers who worked exclusively in such areas as science fiction, romance novels, and children's literature. "*The Bloomsbury Guide to Women's Literature* provides a much needed one-volume reader's companion to women's literature of the world. While it will not substitute for reference works with more in-depth coverage of individual genres or national literatures, it will be a first choice for students of women's writing and for information about the literary endeavors of hundreds, if not thousands, of women excluded by the 'patriarchal tradition' " (*Reference Books Bulletin* in *Booklist,* February 15, 1993, p. 1080). A complementary work is the *Feminist Companion to Literature in English: Women Writers from the Middle Ages to the Present* (Yale Univ. Press, 1990) by Virginia Blain, Patricia Clements, and Isobel Grundy.

Brewer's Dictionary of Phrase and Fable. Edited by Ivor H. Evans. 14th ed. HarperCollins, 1989. 1,220p. $35.00 hardcover; $20.00 paperbound.

Like BENÉT'S READER'S ENCYCLOPEDIA, *Brewer's Dictionary of Phrase and Fable* is a classic reference work. Originally compiled and published in 1870 by Ebenezer Cobham Brewer, a British cleric with a gift for amassing fascinating facts about language, literature, mythology, folklore, and religion, the book has undergone numerous revisions over the years. The current edition (the fourteenth) contains over 15,000 concise entries arranged alphabetically and is the first to include an index. A companion volume is *Brewer's Dictionary of 20th-Century Phrase and Fable* (Houghton Mifflin, 1992).

The Cambridge Encyclopedia of Language. Written by David Crystal. Cambridge Univ. Press, 1987. 472p. $49.50 hardcover; $24.95 paperbound.

A review of this fine encyclopedia in *Reference Books Bulletin* (in *Booklist*, June 15, 1988, p. 1716) astutely points out, "This is that rarity: a work appropriate for both reference and circulating stacks in academic and public libraries and with appeal to the scholar as well as the casual reader." Crystal's readable, topically arranged book covers all major (and some minor) aspects of language, from its structure and acquisition to artificial languages, spelling reform, and word games. A complementary work by Crystal is his recently published *Encyclopedic Dictionary of Language and Languages* (Blackwell, 1993), also a single-volume publication; it provides substantial articles on such topics as language groups, writing systems, punctuation, transformational grammar, neurolinguistics, and phonetics. Two other worthy one-volume encyclopedias on the subject are the *Encyclopaedia of Language* (Routledge, 1990), edited by N.E. Collinge, and Osward Ducrot and Tzvetan Todorov's *Encyclopedic Dictionary of the Sciences of Language* (Johns Hopkins Univ. Press, 1979).

Columbia Dictionary of Modern European Literature. Edited by Jean-Albert Bédé & William Edgerton. 2nd ed. Columbia Univ. Press, 1980. 895p. $163.00.

First published in 1947 and substantially revised in 1980, the *Columbia Dictionary of Modern European Literature* focuses on literary developments in twentieth-century continental Europe. In all, the encyclopedia treats 36 European literatures in more than 1,800 articles prepared by some 500 specialists, including many from abroad. Concise biographical and critical discussions of authors account for the large majority of entries, although lengthy surveys of the various literatures are also included. "The articles are written in a scholarly style and vocabulary, but they will be understandable to high school students and undergraduate students with good reading ability. . . . Large and small libraries will find it an authoritative and useful source" (*Wilson Library Bulletin*, April 1981, p. 619). Among the numerous sources that complement the *Columbia Dictionary of Modern European Literature* are the five-volume ENCYCLOPEDIA OF WORLD LITERATURE IN THE 20TH CENTURY, the recently published *Reader's Encyclopedia of Eastern European Literature* (HarperCollins, 1993),

and several *Oxford Companions* (published by Oxford University Press) devoted to specific national literatures: the *Oxford Companion to French Literature* (1959), the *Oxford Companion to German Literature* (2nd ed., 1986), and the *Oxford Companion to Spanish Literature* (1978).

Compendium of the World's Languages. Compiled by George L. Campbell. Routledge, 1991. 2 vols. $250.00.

Intended chiefly for serious students and linguists, Campbell's two-volume (1,574-page) *Compendium of the World's Languages* describes and analyzes more than 300 individual languages and 41 different language families (e.g., Indo-European). Entries are arranged alphabetically by the common English name of each language and include the language's history, number and location of native speakers, and writing, sound, and grammatical systems. For those languages with a literary tradition, a passage from the *New Testament* is reproduced in the original script. All this information appears in a standardized format, thus facilitating easy comparison between languages. The set "belongs in every serious linguistics reference collection" (*Wilson Library Bulletin*, December 1991, p. 118). A number of similar encyclopedic compilations are available. Among the best are Kenneth Katzner's 376-page *Languages of the World* (Revised ed., Routledge, 1986), which is more popularly written and much less detailed and expensive than Campbell's work; and Bernard Comrie's 1,025-page *World's Major Languages* (Oxford Univ. Press, 1987), which covers only 50 languages but provides greater depth than Campbell.

Cyclopedia of Literary Characters. Edited by Frank N. Magill. Salem Press, 1963. 2 vols. $75.00; also *Cyclopedia of Literary Characters II.* Edited by Frank N. Magill. Salem Press, 1990. 4 vols. $300.00.

Companions to MASTERPLOTS, the publisher's series of plot summaries of important literary works, the *Cyclopedia of Literary Characters* and *Cyclopedia of Literary Characters II* together furnish descriptive information about approximately 28,000 fictional characters found in nearly 3,000 novels, novellas, plays, and epics from around the world, although the emphasis is on Anglo-American literature. Both sets have been well received; these comments about the *Cyclopedia of Literary Characters II* in *Reference Books Bulletin* (in *Booklist*, January 1, 1991, p. 948) are typical: "This set allows users to easily become familiar with personalities from classic fiction or to identify the books in which Jeeves or Billy Pilgrim were characters. Similar works do not contain the depth of character descriptions of this set. In general, the *Cyclopedia of Literary Characters II* does an outstanding job and is recommended for high school, academic, and medium-size and large public libraries."

Comparable works (all in one volume) include the *Dictionary of Fictional Characters* (Revised ed. The Writer, 1992), originally prepared by William Freeman and revised by Martin Seymour-Smith; Laurie Harris's *Characters in 20th-Century Literature* (Gale, 1990) and the companion *Characters in 19th-Century Literature* (Gale, 1992) by Kelly King Howes; Benjamin V. Franklin's *Dictionary of American Literary Characters* (Facts on File, 1989); David Pringle's *Imaginary People: A Who's Who of Modern Fictional Characters* (World Almanac, 1987); and William Amos's *The Originals: An A-Z of Fiction's Real-Life Characters* (Little, Brown, 1985). Note that the two-volume *Cyclopedia of Literary Characters* has also been published under the title *Masterplots Cyclopedia of Literary Characters*.

Dictionary of Concepts in Literary Criticism and Theory. Written by Wendell V. Harris. Greenwood, 1992. 444p. $75.00.

Harris, an English professor at Penn State University, thoroughly explicates 70 important literary concepts—allegory, allusion, classicism, deconstructionism, feminist criticism, imagination, metaphor, modernism, the New Criticism, semiotics, etc.—in encyclopedic articles ranging from three to seven pages in length. "This dictionary is exceptional for its extremely useful bibliographic information and relatively few entries, which are treated in much more depth than in similar dictionaries. . . . An indispensable reference tool for both students and researchers" (*Library Journal*, March 15, 1992, p. 76).

Dictionary of Literary Themes and Motifs. Edited by Jean-Charles Seigneuret. Greenwood, 1988. 2 vols. $225.00.

This excellent encyclopedia contains 143 lengthy A-to-Z articles dealing with such literary subjects as androgyny, the city, evil, marriage, pride, rebellion, responsibility, seduction, stupidity, utopia, and vampirism. Prepared by 98 well-qualified contributors, the articles provide both historical and critical perspectives on each topic through analysis of representative literary works. Volume 2 concludes with a "Cross-Index" of themes and a detailed general index, necessary finding devices in this broad-entry work. "This is a major encyclopedia for comparative literature and, secondarily, the history of ideas . . . . this ambitious new source, unique in English, is important for any four-year college library" (*Library Journal*, September 1, 1988, p. 162).

Dictionary of Oriental Literatures. Edited by Jaroslav Průšek. Basic Books, 1975. 3 vols. Out of print (last priced at $40.00).

A unique encyclopedic overview of Asian literature for the neophyte student and nonspecialist, this set includes roughly 2,000 signed articles that describe the major literary achievements of China, Japan, Korea, India, Pakistan, Bangladesh, Thailand, Indonesia, Egypt, Iran, Turkey, Afghanistan, and numerous other countries, including those of North Africa. Most articles concern literary figures, but important concepts, movements, and terminology are also covered. *Choice* (January 1976, p. 1422) rightly observes that the "dictionary has been long needed, and is not likely to be superseded for many years," which makes its present out-of-print status all the more regrettable. No other broad encyclopedic survey of all Asian literatures is currently available, although some valuable works devoted to specific national literatures do exist. These include the single-volume *Princeton Companion to Classical Japanese Literature* (Princeton Univ. Press, 1985), prepared by Earl Miner, Hiroko Odagiri, and Robert Morrell; and the in-progress *Encyclopaedia of Indian Literature* (Sahitya Akademi, dist. by South Asia Books, 1987–), a highly regarded set edited by Amaresh Datta that will total five volumes when completed.

Dictionary of Twentieth-Century Cuban Literature. Edited by Julio A. Martínez. Greenwood, 1990. 537p. $75.00.

Typical of the many useful encyclopedic dictionaries covering national literatures published by Greenwood Press, the *Dictionary of Twentieth-Century Cuban Literature* includes both brief bio-critical entries on the country's leading contemporary writers and longer survey pieces on literary movements and genres, such as "The Novel of the Cuban Revolution, 1960–1985." All articles (which number about 120) are signed, having been prepared by some 70 specialists, and include bibliographies that cite both English- and Spanish-language works. Similar Greenwood reference publications—all single-volume works edited by respected authorities and priced under $100.00—include the *Dictionary of Albanian Literature* (1986), the *Dictionary of Brazilian Literature* (1988), the *Dictionary of Irish Literature* (1979), the *Dictionary of Italian Literature* (1979), the *Dictionary of Mexican Literature* (1992), the *Dictionary of Modern French Literature* (1986), the *Dictionary of Russian Literature* (1956, reprinted 1971), the *Dictionary of Scandinavian Literature* (1990), and the *Dictionary of Spanish Literature* (1956, reprinted 1972); the latter has been largely replaced by the

Dictionary of the Literature of the Iberian Peninsula, published by Greenwood in 1993 in two volumes.

The Encyclopedia of American Journalism. Written by Donald Paneth. Facts on File, 1983. 548p. Out of print (last priced at $49.95).

Over 1,000 alphabetically arranged articles covering both print and broadcast journalism in the U.S. from the sixteenth century to the early 1980s make up this readable—and unique—encyclopedia. Brief entries predominate but such topics as press freedom, media ownership, and individual components of the media (newspapers, magazines, television, radio, etc.) receive essay-length attention. "The book delivers good histories of newspapers, magazines, journalists, and court cases" (*Wilson Library Bulletin,* November 1983, p. 225). Now somewhat dated and out of print, the *Encyclopedia of American Journalism* is a prime candidate for a new edition in the near future.

The Encyclopedia of Censorship. Written by Jonathon Green. Facts on File, 1990. 388p. $45.00.

Green's encyclopedia comprises about 1,000 A-to-Z articles on important aspects of censorship around the world, including famous (or infamous) works that have been banned over the years, prominent people and organizations involved in the censorship/freedom debate, and major court cases in the U.S. and abroad. In a review in *Choice* (June 1990, p. 1,654), Robert Bravard praises the *Encyclopedia of Censorship* as "a reference work that deftly provides insight into the complexity, the pervasiveness, and the persistence of censorship throughout all known civilization." Complementary sources (all one-volume works) are Leon Hurwitz's *Historical Dictionary of Censorship in the United States* (Greenwood, 1985); *Banned Books, 387 B.C. to 1978 A.D.* (4th ed. Bowker, 1978), originally compiled by Anne Lyon Haight and revised by Chandler Grannis; and the recently published *Intellectual Freedom: A Reference Handbook* (ABC-Clio, 1992) by John B. Harer, a librarian.

Encyclopedia of Literature and Criticism. Edited by Martin Coyle & others. Gale, 1991. 1,299p. $125.00.

Limited to English literature, this hefty volume contains 91 substantial essays devoted to all major aspects of the subject, including poetry, drama, the novel, and criticism. Emphasis is on the American and British literary tradition, but some coverage is also accorded English literature produced in Canada, Australia, India, South Africa, etc. "In addition to comprehensiveness and a narrative format, what distinguishes this work is the fact that the editors encouraged the authors of the essays to be provocative and challenging, rather than to strive for a more definitive, more 'objective' approach. . . . The result is a work that is very much a product of its time, but candidly so, and one that will inform and stimulate the serious student of literature" (*American Reference Books Annual,* 1993, p. 475).

Encyclopedia of Publishing and the Book Arts. Edited by George Thomas Kurian. Holt, 1994 (in progress). 880p. (approx.) Price not set.

Scheduled for publication sometime in 1994 or 1995 and unseen by the author of *Kister's Best Encyclopedias,* this much anticipated reference work is described by editor Kurian as "the first encyclopedia devoted solely to books and book publishing. . . . As a benchmark report on the state of books and book publishing at the end of the bimillennium, the encyclopedia will look at the past, present and future. By distilling and presenting the best ideas on contemporary publishing, the encyclopedia will serve as a usable reference source for publishing professionals" (prospectus). International in scope, the single-volume work will consist of approximately 1,775 A-to-Z entries, of which about 80 will be essay-length articles on such topics as advertising, subsidiary rights, and typography. The text will be enhanced by illustrations (most in black-and-white) and access facilitated by a general index.

Kurian, a well-known and highly respected encyclopedist, brings impeccable credentials to such a project. Moreover, he is supported by an impressive editorial board that includes John F. Baker and Herbert Lottman of *Publishers Weekly* and John Y. Cole of the Center for the Book at the Library of Congress. All indications are that the forthcoming *Encyclopedia of Publishing and the Book Arts* will be a unique and important reference publication. Two complementary one-volume works (both of British origin) are currently available: *Glaister's Glossary of the Book* (2nd ed. Univ. of California Press, 1980), a most useful source compiled by Geoffrey Glaister that treats the vocabulary of the book arts and publishing in encyclopedic fashion; and John Feather's *Dictionary of Book History* (Oxford Univ. Press, 1987), which is also encyclopedic in scope.

Encyclopedia of the British Press, 1440–1991. Written by Dennis Griffiths. St. Martin's, 1993. 694p. $79.95.

This new encyclopedia comprises over 3,000 concise, alphabetically arranged entries covering British newspapers, editors, and journalists from the time of William Caxton, who introduced printing into England in the fifteenth century, to the present.

No other encyclopedic work deals as thoroughly with the history of the British press, although there will doubtless be some overlap with the forthcoming ENCYCLOPEDIA OF PUBLISHING AND THE BOOK ARTS. "Griffiths, a veteran of more than 40 years of the British press (English, Scottish, Irish, and Welsh) has compiled a benchmark work" (*Choice*, May 1993, p. 1440).

Encyclopedia of World Literature in the 20th Century. Edited by Leonard S. Klein. 2nd ed. Continuum Publishing Group, 1981–93. 5 vols. $545.00.

First published in four volumes (1967–75), the indispensable *Encyclopedia of World Literature in the 20th Century* was thoroughly revised and expanded to five volumes in the early 1980s, concluding with a 132-page index volume in 1984. In early 1993, a revised volume 5 appeared; now grown to 726 pages, it includes supplementary text (nearly 50 survey articles plus some 400 articles on authors not previously covered) along with a new index to the set. In all, the encyclopedia now contains well over 2,000 alphabetically arranged articles dealing with all important aspects of world literature in this century, including authors, genres, movements, and national trends. Especially valuable is the set's coverage of Third World literatures. "In summary, the broad scope of the *Encyclopedia of World Literature in the Twentieth Century*, its attention to minor as well as major literatures, its choice of authors, its qualified editor, advisers, and contributors, and its excellent Index recommend it to academic and large public libraries as a source on twentieth-century literature" (*Reference Book Bulletin* in *Booklist*, October 15, 1985, p. 320). A fine one-volume complement to the encyclopedia is Martin Seymour-Smith's *New Guide to Modern World Literature* (HarperCollins, 1985), a revision of *Funk & Wagnalls Guide to Modern World Literature* (Funk & Wagnalls, 1973).

Encyclopedic Dictionary of Semiotics. Edited by Thomas A. Sebeok. Walter de Gruyter, 1986. 3 vols. $440.00.

Sebeok's three-volume encyclopedia is the definitive reference work on semiotics, the study or science of signs and symbols, including both verbal and nonverbal communication. The set contains 426 signed articles by over 200 internationally recognized authorities. The articles, which are arranged A-to-Z, vary in length from a single paragraph to long essays on such topics as semantics and Charles Sanders Peirce (a pioneer in developing semiotics as a field of study). The final volume includes an extensive bibliography. In a review in *American Reference Books Annual* (1988, p. 419), Anna

DeMiller praises the *Encyclopedic Dictionary of Semiotics* as "a significant contribution to the scholarship of semiotics [that] should be the authoritative source in this field for years to come."

Handbook of Latin American Literature. Compiled by David William Foster. 2nd ed. Garland, 1992. 608p. $95.00 hardcover; $18.95 paperbound.

First published in 1987 and revised in 1992, this useful reference work comprises authoritative, readable articles surveying various national Latin American literatures. Arranged alphabetically by country (Argentina, Bolivia, Brazil, etc.), the articles cover principal genres and writers. "Obviously a handbook such as this cannot offer a detailed discussion of each national literature, but the articles are informative, offering perceptive information on the major novelists, essayists, poets, and dramatists of Latin America as well as comments on the dominant features and themes of each country's literary traditions" (*American Reference Books Annual*, 1988, p. 500).

Handbook of Russian Literature. Edited by Victor Terras. Yale Univ. Press, 1985. 558p. $129.00 hardcover; $24.95 paperbound.

Covering 10 centuries of Russian literature, this encyclopedic work is a valuable resource for students, scholars, and interested laypeople. It furnishes reliable information about Russian authors, literary genres and movements, and styles and theories in some 1,000 articles, which run from a paragraph to a dozen pages or more in length. "The *Handbook*'s comprehensive scope and lucid, informative style make it an essential acquisition for academic and appropriate general reference collections" (*Library Journal*, June 1, 1985, p. 116). It effectively replaces William Harkins' *Dictionary of Russian Literature* (Philosophical Library, 1956), long a popular one-volume guide to Russian literature. Complementary works are Wolfgang Kasack's 502-page *Dictionary of Russian Literature Since 1917* (Columbia Univ. Press, 1988) and the in-progress *Modern Encyclopedia of Russian and Soviet Literatures* (Academic International Press, 1977–), an ambitious but uneven set that will eventually comprise 50 volumes.

International Encyclopedia of Linguistics. Edited by William Bright. Oxford Univ. Press, 1991. 4 vols. $395.00.

This fine four-volume encyclopedia—an impeccably edited reference work covering the broad field of language and linguistics—is scholarly in tone and presupposes some specialized knowledge on the part of readers. Consisting of approximately 750 signed articles prepared by leading linguists and language scholars from all over the world, the set emphasizes the interdisciplinary nature of linguistics, treating not only major branches of the field but interrelationships among subdisciplines and linguistic aspects of such fields as education, sociology, psychology, and other behavioral sciences. It also provides strong coverage of both living and extinct languages and language families, thus complementing such sources as David Crystal's CAMBRIDGE ENCYCLOPEDIA OF LANGUAGE and George Campbell's COMPENDIUM OF THE WORLD'S LANGUAGES. "Through the traditional structure of an alphabetically organized encyclopedia, the *International Encyclopedia* explores and explains the Babel of the world's languages and the sometimes equally bewildering specialized concepts and vocabulary of linguistics" (*Wilson Library Bulletin*, March 1992, p. 115).

Another excellent reference source for serious students of linguistics is the recently published *Linguistics Encyclopedia* (Routledge, 1991), a single-volume work edited by Kirsten Malmkjaer and James M. Anderson. Specialists should also be aware that Pergamon Press has this year published a 10-volume set entitled *Encyclopedia of Language and Linguistics* that contains more than 2,000 articles aimed at advanced students and scholars. Edited by R.E. Asher (University of Edinburgh) and J.M.Y. Simpson (University of Glasgow), this huge, authoritative encyclopedia is priced at roughly $3,000.00—well beyond the means of most individuals and libraries.

Masterplots. Edited by Frank N. Magill. Revised ed. Salem Press, 1976. 12 vols. $450.00; also *Masterplots II*. Edited by Frank N. Magill. Salem Press, 1986–90. 30 vols. $2,550.00.

The 12-volume *Masterplots* contains plot summaries and critical assessments of 2,010 of the world's greatest books. *Masterplots II*, inaugurated in 1986, adds thousands of additional titles in seven multivolume series covering American fiction (4 volumes), British and Commonwealth fiction (4 volumes), drama (4 volumes), juvenile and young adult fiction (4 volumes), nonfiction (4 volumes), short stories (6 volumes), and world fiction (4 volumes). While not encyclopedias in the traditional sense, the *Masterplots* volumes summarize much useful information about important literary works. Bill Katz provides a good perspective on *Masterplots* in his *Basic Information Sources* (6th ed., 1992, p. 298): "Students often request plot summaries and other shortcuts to reading. By far the most famous name in this area is Frank N. Magill's *Masterplots*, a condensation of almost every important classic in the English language. Not only are the main characters

well explained, but there is also a critique of the plot's highlights and its good and bad points." Companion volumes are Magill's CYCLOPEDIA OF LITERARY CHARACTERS and CYCLOPEDIA OF LITERARY CHARACTERS II.

McGraw-Hill Encyclopedia of World Drama: An International Reference Work. Edited by Stanley Hochman. 2nd ed. McGraw-Hill, 1984. 5 vols. $380.00

The only multivolume encyclopedia of world drama in English, this outstanding reference set first appeared in 1972 in four volumes and was extensively revised and updated in 1984, at which time it added a fifth volume. Its approximately 1,000 articles, enhanced by numerous black-and-white illustrations, focus on individual playwrights but also cover terms, movements, and styles pertinent to dramatic literature. In response to criticism of the first edition, Hochman's 1984 revision provides greater coverage of the national dramas of Asia, Latin America, Africa, and the Middle East. The revised edition's index is also improved. The encyclopedia is "an invaluable reference work for theater historians, drama critics, teachers, and actors. So comprehensive is its information and so broad is its appeal that even the smallest of public libraries may wish to have it on hand as a guide to dramatic traditions throughout the world" (*American Reference Books Annual*, 1984, p. 458). A useful one-volume complement to the *McGraw-Hill Encyclopedia of World Drama* is the *Crown Guide to the World's Great Plays* (Revised ed. Crown, 1984); first published in 1956, this handy source prepared by Joseph Shipley covers 750 major plays from ancient Greece and Rome to modern times.

The New Encyclopedia of Science Fiction. Edited by James Gunn. Viking-Penguin, 1988. 524p. $24.95.

Gunn's *New Encyclopedia of Science Fiction* consists of over 500 entries covering writers, artists, actors, conventions, and themes associated with the literature of science fiction. Most impressive are 96 essay-length articles, such as "Cyberpunk," "Radio," and "Utopias and Dystopias." "Editor Gunn, himself a respected author, teacher, and scholar, has assembled a distinguished group of contributors . . . to produce an informative and highly entertaining work" (*Choice*, March 1989, p. 1128). Another excellent one-volume work on the subject is John Clute and Peter Nicholls's *Encyclopedia of Science Fiction* (St. Martin's, 1993), which previously appeared as the *Science Fiction Encyclopedia*, published by Doubleday in 1979.

The New Princeton Encyclopedia of Poetry and Poetics. Edited by Alex Preminger & T.V.F. Brogan. 3rd ed. Princeton Univ. Press, 1993. 1,434p. $125.00 hardcover; $29.95 paperbound.

More than 350 leading scholars and poets have contributed to this comprehensive international survey of poetry from the earliest times to the early 1990s. First published in 1965 as the *Princeton Encyclopedia of Poetry and Poetics,* expanded in 1974, and substantially revised and retitled in 1993, the encyclopedia now contains nearly 1,000 entries, including coverage of practically "every significant poetry tradition in the world" (preface). Also covered are the history and techniques of poetry as well as the genre's relationship with other types of literature, but individual poets and works of poetry are not included. A unique encyclopedia, it "has become the standard source for information on the history and criticism of poetry and poetic technique and theory" (*Reference Books Bulletin,* in *Booklist,* December 15, 1993, p. 779). In another review of the current edition (in *Library Journal,* September 1, 1993, p. 174), Peter Dollard concludes the encyclopedia "is an essential purchase for any library supporting the study of poetry; the only problem is that the print is tiny and hard to read."

The Oxford Companion to Canadian Literature. Edited by William Toye. Oxford Univ. Press, 1983. 843p. $49.95.

Similar in purpose, size, format, and price to other *Oxford Companions* treating various national literatures (see, for example, the OXFORD COMPANION TO ENGLISH LITERATURE), this excellent single-volume reference work authoritatively surveys Canadian literature—English and French—in 750 entries. The volume covers individual authors and titles as well as literary periods, genres, and specialized topics, such as Acadian literature, pioneer memoirs, and folklore. "An encyclopedic offering of fact, learning, and perception" (*Choice,* July–August 1984, p. 1591). The *Oxford Companion to Canadian Literature* supersedes the old *Oxford Companion to Canadian History and Literature* (1967), edited by Norah Story. Another one-volume Oxford University Press work complements the *Companion:* Albert and Theresa Moritz's *Oxford Illustrated Literary Guide to Canada* (1987), a popular work for both browsing and reference.

The Oxford Companion to Children's Literature. Written by Humphrey Carpenter & Mari Prichard. Oxford Univ. Press, 1984. 586p. $49.95.

This *Oxford Companion*—a unique and indispensable work for librarians, writers, and students of children's literature, and children themselves—contains approximately 2,000 entries on topics ranging from pop-up books, dime novels, and folktales to prominent authors such as Beatrix Potter, Kenneth Grahame, Lewis Carroll, J.R.R. Tolkien, and Judy Blume. In a full-page review in *School Library Journal* (August 1984, p. 40), Ruth Gordon lauds the book: "It is a most welcome and essential addition to every reference collection of libraries that have anything to do with books for children or with the history of books." Complementary works are Jon C. Stott's less expensive (318-page) *Children's Literature from A to Z: A Guide for Parents and Teachers* (McGraw-Hill, 1984) and Gorton Carruth's 681-page *Young Reader's Companion* (Bowker, 1993), an encyclopedia of more than 2,000 concise entries covering authors, books, and related aspects of children's literature.

The Oxford Companion to Classical Literature. Edited by M.C. Howatson. 2nd ed. Oxford Univ. Press, 1989. 627p. $45.00.

For nearly 40 years, Sir Paul Harvey's first edition of the *Oxford Companion to Classical Literature* served as the preeminent single-volume encyclopedia on the literature of ancient Greece and Rome. A revised edition published in 1989 capably carries on the tradition, covering all important facets of classical literature, including its cultural, political, religious, mythological, and philosophical underpinnings. Edited by M.C. Howatson, a Fellow of St. Anne's College at Oxford University, the revision contains roughly 30 percent more material than the original version, adding articles on such topics as the Achaean Confederacy and the Arian heresy. "This opulent companion offers the general reader help of every kind in the understanding of classical literature" (*Library Journal,* May 1, 1989, p. 74).

The Oxford Companion to English Literature. Edited by Margaret Drabble. 5th ed. Oxford Univ. Press, 1985. 1,156p. $49.95.

First published in 1932, the *Oxford Companion to English Literature* has been a staple in home, public, college, and school library reference collections for over 60 years. The fifth edition, the first produced by well-known novelist Margaret Drabble, contains approximately 9,000 entries, about a third of which were written or substantially revised by Drabble herself. Emphasis is almost exclusively on British authors and their works; other *Oxford Companions* such as the *Oxford Companion to Australian Literature* (1984), the *Oxford Companion to the Literature of Wales* (1986), the *Oxford Companion to American*

Literature (5th ed., 1983), and the OXFORD COMPAN-
ION TO CANADIAN LITERATURE offer similar treatment
of national English literatures outside England. "Edited by novelist Margaret Drabble, the alphabetically arranged volume is notable not only for the
encyclopedic nature of its coverage, but also for the
pithiness of its prose and the ability of its contributors to succinctly place an author or work in its
appropriate literary and sociocultural context"
(*Booklist*, August 1985, p. 1624).

The *Oxford Companion to English Literature*'s major competitor is the excellent *Cambridge Guide to
Literature in English* (2nd ed. Cambridge Univ. Press,
1994). A single-volume work edited by Ian Ousby,
this revision of the *Cambridge Guide to English Literature* (Cambridge Univ. Press, 1983) has a much
broader scope than the *Oxford Companion to English
Literature*, covering English literature wherever it is
found, including Africa, North America, the Caribbean, Australia, New Zealand, and India. Another
recently published competitor is the single-volume
Prentice Hall Guide to English Literature (Prentice
Hall, 1990), edited by Marion Wynne-Davies. Consumers should also be aware that an abridged version of the *Oxford Companion to English Literature*
appeared in 1987 under the title *Concise Oxford
Companion to English Literature*. Edited by Drabble
and Jenny Stringer, this 631-page book is available
from Oxford University Press at $24.95 in hard-
cover and $9.95 in paperback.

*Shakespeare A to Z: The Essential Reference to
His Plays, His Poems, His Life and Times, and
More.* Written by Charles Boyce. Facts on File,
1990. 742p. $45.00 hardcover; $16.00 paperbound (published by Dell).

Originally announced as the *Encyclopedia of
Shakespeare*, Boyce's *Shakespeare A to Z* provides
detailed information in clear, nontechnical language
about all important aspects of the great Elizabethan
writer's life and work, including entries for each play
and significant characters and place-names. "In some
ways this book represents a simple reordering of
what one typically finds in a Shakespeare handbook, but without the long essays about Shakespeare
and his times. It is certainly handy if one wishes to

zero in on one character or play. The book is enriched by many photographs and illustrations of
actors, stage plays, and movie treatments" (*Choice*,
April 1991, p. 1286). Boyce's encyclopedia is more
current but less exhaustive than the much older
Reader's Encyclopedia of Shakespeare (Crowell, 1966),
which is no longer in print.

World Press Encyclopedia. Edited by George Thomas Kurian. Facts on File, 1982. 2 vols. $179.00.

This valuable, albeit now dated, encyclopedia
furnishes an extensive country-by-country survey of
the world's print and broadcast media in lengthy
articles written by some 50 specialists. Each profile
includes standard information about the country's
press, including its history, economic framework,
laws, news agencies, state-press relations, censorship, attitudes toward the foreign press, and education and training of journalists. "This excellent reference tool provides a unique, comprehensive, and
thorough coverage of the state of today's fourth
estate, and is invaluable for students or researchers
in journalism, political history, or current events, as
well as any interested reader concerned with the
flow of information throughout the world" (*American Reference Books Annual*, 1983, p. 519). Editor
Kurian reports that a new edition is under active
consideration and could be published within the
next two or three years.

*Writing A to Z: The Terms, Procedures, and
Facts of the Writing Business Defined, Explained,
and Put Within Reach.* Edited by Kirk Polking &
others. Writer's Digest, 1990. 539p. $24.95
paperbound.

A revision of Polking's popular *Writer's Encyclopedia* (Writer's Digest, 1983), this handy reference
volume consists of roughly 1,200 short, unsigned
entries that offer practical information for writers,
editors, reviewers, and publishers. James Rettig in
Wilson Library Bulletin (January 1991, p. 127) says of
the book, "Anyone who has taken to heart Dr.
Johnson's declaration that 'no man but a blockhead
ever wrote, except for money' will find this a dependable source for answers to the many questions
about copyright, working with editors, etc."

※ MILITARY SCIENCE AND HISTORY ※

Civil War Dictionary. Written by Mark Mayo
Boatner. Revised ed. McKay, 1988. 974p.
$25.00 hardcover; $18.00 paperbound (Random House, 1991).

First published in 1959 and modestly revised in
1988, Boatner's classic encyclopedia of the Ameri-

can Civil War treats the land battles, naval engage-
ments, weapons, issues (political, economic, and
social), and personalities (including all generals on
both sides) of that cataclysmic conflict. The book
also furnishes extensive map coverage of the war.
"With more than 4,000 entries, including 2,000

short biographical sketches of Civil War leaders both civilian and military, this dictionary remains the most comprehensive and consistently accurate reference tool on the American Civil War" (*Choice*, January 1989, p. 775). Comparable one-volume sources are the *Civil War Almanac* (Facts on File, 1982), edited by John Bowman, and the handsomely produced HISTORICAL TIMES ILLUSTRATED ENCYCLOPEDIA OF THE CIVIL WAR.

Dictionary of the Vietnam War. Edited by James S. Olson. Greenwood, 1988. 585p. $65.00 hardcover; $12.95 paperbound (Peter Bedrick Books, 1990).

The *Dictionary of the Vietnam War* contains approximately 900 A-to-Z articles covering the people, events, places, battles, books, and films associated with that war. James Rettig in *Wilson Library Bulletin* (June 1988, p. 140) offers this useful perspective on the book: "Olson's dictionary approaches it [the war] with the scholarly objectivity one would expect from his team of twenty-eight historians, most teachers in universities or high schools. This warts-and-all presentation of the war and its issues includes articles on the anti-war movement, booby traps, the gigantic C-5 Galaxy transport plane, *The Deer Hunter*, Melvin Laird, the 1969 Moratorium Day demonstrations, the Pentagon Papers, punji stakes, Nixon's 'silent majority' speech, tunnel rats, and Watergate." Comparable one-volume works are Harry Summers's *Vietnam War Almanac* (Facts on File, 1985) and the newly published *Encyclopedia of the Vietnam War* (Simon & Schuster, 1994), edited by Stanley Kutler.

The Encyclopedia of American Intelligence and Espionage: From the Revolutionary War to the Present. Written by G.J.A. O'Toole. Facts on File, 1988. 539p. $50.00.

O'Toole, a former CIA officer, provides encyclopedic treatment of U.S. spy activities from the colonial period to contemporary times. The book, which is geared to the general reader, consists of nearly 700 alphabetically arranged articles, most of which deal with prominent people, such as Nathan Hale, William J. ("Wild Bill") Donovan, Allen Dulles, and William Casey. Others cover major organizations (as might be expected the CIA receives the most ink, 18 pages), intelligence operations during nine major wars, and key concepts (e.g., covert action) and events (the attack on Pearl Harbor). O'Toole "has produced a valuable, objective encyclopedia of a little-known but undeniably important aspect of two centuries of military, diplomatic, and political history" (*Wilson Library Bulletin*, October 1988, p. 108).

Similar sources, all one-volume items, are *United States Intelligence: An Encyclopedia* (Garland, 1990) and Wendell Minnick's *Spies and Provocateurs: A Worldwide Encyclopedia of Persons Conducting Espionage and Covert Action, 1946–1991* (McFarland, 1992), both works limited to the period since World War II; Vincent and Nan Buranelli's *Spy/Counterspy: An Encyclopedia of Espionage* (McGraw-Hill, 1982), which covers government snoopery around the world since Elizabethan times; and Richard Deacon's *Spyclopedia: The Comprehensive Handbook of Espionage* (Morrow, 1989), which goes back to 510 B.C. and is also international in scope.

Encyclopedia of Arms Control and Disarmament. Edited by Richard Dean Burns. Scribner's, 1993. 3 vols. $280.00.

Comprehensive, authoritative, and unique, this important new reference work comprises 76 signed, essay-length articles grouped under four broad topics: "National and Regional Dimensions," "Themes and Institutions," "Historical Dimensions to 1945," and "Arms Control Activities Since 1945." A fifth section offers annotated excerpts from 150 historically significant treaties concerned with arms control, with cross-references to pertinent articles. Intended for interested laypeople as well as students, teachers, and researchers, the set covers the history of arms control efforts from antiquity to the present in all regions of the world. Editor Burns, who teaches history at California State University at Los Angeles, is a widely respected expert in the field of arms control; likewise, contributors bring strong credentials to the encyclopedia. "Buttressed with current bibliographies, it is exceedingly useful for the novice or the accomplished scholar. Recommended for academic and most public libraries" (*Library Journal*, July 1993, p. 68).

An Encyclopedia of Battles: Accounts of Over 1,560 Battles from 1479 B.C. to the Present. Compiled by David Eggenberger. Revised ed. Dover, 1985. 533p. $14.95 paper.

An updated and slightly expanded version of Eggenberger's *Dictionary of Battles* (Crowell, 1967), this encyclopedic work provides concise information about all major military encounters in recorded history, beginning with the first battle of Megiddo in 1479 B.C. and concluding with the U.S. invasion of Grenada in 1983. Approximately 100 battle maps supplement the text. The book "is an excellent quick-reference guide for military and nonmilitary historians and is highly recommended for college and public library collections" (*American Reference Books Annual*, 1986, p. 197). Competing single-volume sources are *Brassey's Battles: 3,500 Years of*

Conflict, Campaigns and Wars from A-Z (Brassey's, 1986) by John Laffin; the *Dictionary of Battles: The World's Key Battles from 405 BC to Today* (Holt, 1987), edited by David Chandler; and *Harbottle's Dictionary of Battles* (3rd ed. Van Nostrand, 1979), revised by George Bruce. Another comparable source is the recently published two-volume *Warfare and Armed Conflict* (McFarland, 1992) by Michael Clodfelter. This set, which totals more than 1,400 pages, covers approximately 700 military conflicts (including major riots) from 1618 to the present.

Encyclopedia of Historic Forts: The Military, Pioneer, and Trading Posts of the United States. Written by Robert Roberts. Macmillan, 1987. 894p. $105.00.

Some 3,000 forts found in the U.S. dating back to the sixteenth century are described in this informative work, a 40-year labor of love by the late Robert Roberts, an amateur historian who received posthumous assistance from Alan Aimone, a librarian who specializes in military history. Entries, which are arranged by state and then alphabetically by name of fort, include any earlier names of the installation, construction details, history, and commanders; several hundred captioned photographs, drawings, and plans accompany the text. "Although a number of studies are available on forts in history or historic structures of various US states or regions, this is the first comprehensive effort to treat this subject for the entire country" (*Choice*, March 1988, p. 1070).

Encyclopedia of Terrorism and Political Violence. Written by John Richard Thackrah. Routledge, 1987. 308p. $37.50.

Thackrah, a lecturer at a police college in England, treats important aspects of terrorism and political violence since World War II in some 200 readable A-to-Z entries. Topics include specific events (e.g., the Achille Lauro hijacking), people (Ché Guevara), groups (Basque nationalists), nations (Iran), and concepts (hostage-taking). The encyclopedia "will be of use to researchers studying terrorism and to anyone trying to make some sense of terrorist activities reported in the daily press" (*Reference Books Bulletin* in *Booklist*, March 1, 1988, p. 1119). A somewhat comparable work is Harris Lentz's *Assassinations and Executions: An Encyclopedia of Political Violence, 1865–1986* (McFarland, 1988), a one-volume encyclopedia concerned with "world leaders who have met their end in a violent manner." Two other complementary single-volume references are the *Almanac of Modern Terrorism* (Facts on File, 1991) and *Terrorism: A Reference Handbook* (ABC-Clio, 1992) by Stephen Atkins.

Encyclopedia of the American Revolution. Written by Mark Mayo Boatner. McKay, 1974. 1,290p. $9.98.

Similar in purpose, size, and style to his excellent CIVIL WAR DICTIONARY, Boatner's *Encyclopedia of the American Revolution* covers the period 1763–83—from the Treaty of Paris concluding the French and Indian War to the Treaty of Paris that ended hostilities between the newborn United States of America and Great Britain. The alphabetically arranged articles describe the people, events, and issues of the Revolutionary War. Two other useful, more recently published sources on the subject are the single-volume (845-page) *Blackwell Encyclopedia of the American Revolution* (Blackwell, 1991), edited by Jack Greene and J.R. Pole, and the two-volume (1,800-page) *American Revolution: An Encyclopedia* (Garland, 1993), edited by Richard L. Blanco.

Encyclopedia of the World's Air Forces. Written by Michael J.H. Taylor. Facts on File, 1988. 211p. $35.00.

Taylor, a British expert on military aviation, surveys the air forces of 150 countries, from major powers like the United States and Great Britain to small nations such as Nepal and the Seychelles which have only a few planes. The articles, which range in length from half a page to six pages, are illustrated with color photos of aircraft and include a brief history of each nation's air force and its current status, commitments, budget, and policies. "This handy book belongs in most military collections" (*Library Journal*, April 15, 1989, p. 72). Complementary works (all single volumes) are Bill Gunston's *Illustrated Encyclopedia of Major Military Aircraft of the World* (Crescent Books, dist. by Crown, 1983); the *Rand McNally Encyclopedia of Military Aircraft, 1914–1980* (Rand McNally, 1981), edited by Enzo Angelucci and translated from the Italian by S.M. Harris; Christopher Chant's *World Encyclopedia of Modern Air Weapons* (Patrick Stephens, dist. by Sterling, 1989); and *Jane's All the World's Aircraft* (Jane's Publishing, 1908–), a highly regarded annual that furnishes authoritative information about the current products of the world's aircraft manufacturers.

The Harper Encyclopedia of Military History: From 3500 B.C. to the Present. Written by R. Ernest Dupuy & Trevor N. Dupuy. 4th ed. HarperCollins, 1993. 1,654p. $65.00.

First published in 1970 and revised in 1977 and 1986 as the *Encyclopedia of Military History* and retitled the *Harper Encyclopedia of Military History* in 1993, this standard source surveys all significant aspects of world military history chronologically, describing the major wars, weapons, tactics, leaders, etc. for each period. The new edition is admirably current, including the Persian Gulf War, the collapse of the Soviet Union, and recent upheavals in Eastern Europe and the Balkans. In a review of the latest edition in *Choice* (November 1993, pp. 428–30), P.L. Holmer concludes, ". . . librarians who have learned the value of prior editions will want this improved version." A much larger, more extensive work covering some of the same ground as the *Harper Encyclopedia of Military History* is the new six-volume INTERNATIONAL MILITARY AND DEFENSE ENCYCLOPEDIA.

Historical Dictionary of the Korean War. Edited by James Matray. Greenwood, 1991. 626p. $85.00.

This alphabetically arranged encyclopedia covers all significant aspects of the Korean War, including major personalities (military and civilian), battles, and United Nations actions and documents. "The overall quality of the entries is noteworthy, reflecting well on the editor's efforts at consistency in content and style and balance in treatment of controversy" (*Choice*, February 1992, p. 876). *Library Journal* (April 15, 1992, p. 44) named the *Historical Dictionary of the Korean War* one of its best reference books for 1991: "With a superb bibliography, this is the best reference work published about the war and its consequences." Another useful one-volume work on the war is Harry G. Summers's *Korean War Almanac* (Facts on File, 1990); it includes less information than the *Historical Dictionary* but has superior illustrations and maps.

Historical Times Illustrated Encyclopedia of the Civil War. Edited by Patricia L. Faust & others. HarperCollins, 1986. 849p. $45.00 hardcover; $20.00 paperbound.

Although not as scholarly as Mark Boatner's CIVIL WAR DICTIONARY, the *Historical Times Illustrated Encyclopedia of the Civil War* is an authoritative reference book containing more than 2,000 well-written, reliable articles on the people, places, battles, weapons, and issues involved in the American Civil War. Handsomely produced, it outshines the Boatner work in the area of illustrations and physical format. "In appearance, this volume is reminiscent of the traditional reference volume of the late nineteenth century. In content, it is a splendid reference book of lasting value" (*American Reference Books Annual*, 1988, p. 205).

International Military and Defense Encyclopedia. Edited by Trevor N. Dupuy. Brassey's (dist. by Macmillan), 1993. 6 vols. $1,250.00.

Both Brassey's and Trevor Dupuy—publisher and editor respectively of the new multivolume *International Military and Defense Encyclopedia*—are well-known and highly respected names in the area of military reference. Thus, it comes as no surprise that this encyclopedia is an excellent one, offering authoritative, up-to-date information on practically every important military topic, including combat theory and logistics, air and naval power, manpower and personnel, weapons technology, intelligence, security policy and law, and biographies of prominent military and wartime leaders. Recent military developments in 129 individual countries and regions of the world are also covered. In all, the six-volume, 3,344-page encyclopedia encompasses 786 articles enhanced by more than 400 instructive illustrations, charts, graphs, and photographs. In a review in *Library Journal* (March 15, 1993, p. 70), Raymond Puffer calls the set "a definitive compendium of contemporary military information for the use of today's strategic thinkers and decision makers." Likewise, James Rettig in *Wilson Library Bulletin* (April 1993, p. 122) endorses the set: "This is one of those rare reference works that deserves to be called a classic in its field from the first day of its publication."

Another large and as yet untested work on the subject is the in-progress *International Military Encyclopedia* (Academic International, 1992–). Edited by Norman Tobias, this encyclopedia—projected for 50 or more volumes—is being published volume-by-volume and is available from the publisher by subscription only at $37.00 per volume; for preliminary assessments of the set based on volume 1, see *Wilson Library Bulletin*, February 1993, p. 105; *Choice*, March 1993, pp. 1114–16; and *American Reference Books Annual*, 1993, pp. 293–94.

The Marshall Cavendish Illustrated Encyclopedia of World War I. Edited by Peter Young & Barry Pitt. Marshall Cavendish, 1984. 12 vols. $409.95.

Published in cooperation with the Imperial War Museum in London, this readable, heavily illustrated encyclopedia covers World War I chronologically in some 3,600 pages, beginning with the assassination of Archduke Franz Ferdinand and ending with the election of Warren Harding as U.S. president in 1920. "Many books have been written on World War I, but few if any have covered the subject in as much depth or breadth, or with as many contributing experts and authorities as *The Marshall Cavendish Encyclopedia of World War I*. With its excellent illustrations, its variety of writing styles, and its clear maps and diagrams, this major historical encyclopedia on an important phase of European history is recommended for libraries of all types, as well as for homes where persons are interested in the history of Europe and the world"

(*Reference Books Bulletin* in *Booklist*, June 15, 1985, p. 1440).

The Marshall Cavendish Illustrated Encyclopedia of World War II: An Objective, Chronological and Comprehensive History of the Second World War. Edited by Peter Young. Revised ed. Marshall Cavendish, 1985. 12 vols. $399.95; also available on CD-ROM at $399.95.

First published in 1966 and modestly revised in 1981 and again in 1985, this set—like the companion MARSHALL CAVENDISH ILLUSTRATED ENCYCLOPEDIA OF WORLD WAR I—is a fine survey of one of the world's most devastating wars. Much of the popularly written text is the work of Eddy Bauer, the late Swiss military historian, but the real glory of the encyclopedia is its illustrations. David Eggenberger, in a review in *American Reference Books Annual* (1987, p. 211), comments: "But as good as the text is, the illustration program is better. The editors have capitalized on the most photographed war in history up to that time. Here are a profusion of action photographs from both sides in both black-and-white and color." The CD-ROM version—entitled the *Electronic Encyclopedia of World War II*—appeared in 1993 and features Boolean and proximity searching capabilities.

Many less expensive, single-volume encyclopedic sources on World War II exist, chief among which are the *Dictionary of the Second World War* (Peter Bedrick Books, 1990); *Louis L. Snyder's Historical Guide to World War II* (Greenwood, 1982); the *Encyclopedia of the Second World War* (Presidio Press, 1989) by Bryan Perrett and Ian Hogg; the *Simon and Schuster Encyclopedia of World War II* (Simon & Schuster, 1978); and the recently published *D-Day Encyclopedia* (Simon & Schuster, 1993).

Reference Guide to United States Military History. Edited by Charles R. Shrader. Facts on File, 1991–. 5 vols. (in progress). $50.00 per vol.

The first volume of this in-progress set appeared in 1991 and covers U.S. military history from 1606 to 1815; the second volume, published in 1993, covers 1815 to 1865. Chronologically arranged, these encyclopedic volumes provide narrative history, biographies, and articles on important battles and events, all enhanced by quality maps and illustrations. Eventually, the set will cover the whole of the U.S. military experience. Thus far, reviewers have had nothing but praise for the work; David Lee Poremba in *Library Journal* (April 1, 1993, p. 94) is typical: "In all, this is a comprehensive, easy-to-use reference tool. . . . Strongly recommended."

Warships of the World: An Illustrated Encyclopedia. Written by Gino Galuppini. Times Books (dist. by Outlet Book Company), 1986. 320p. $69.95.

Translated from the Italian, this copiously illustrated encyclopedia covers the history of all types of warships (cruisers, battleships, steamships, submarines, etc.) from earliest times to the twentieth century. A valuable feature is the book's 544 color paintings of various ships. A more detailed but less comprehensive work is the multivolume *Conway's All the World's Fighting Ships* (Naval Institute Press, 1979–85), which provides extensive information about warships from 1860 to the early 1980s in five volumes. Indispensable for current data on warships of the world is the classic annual, *Jane's Fighting Ships* (Jane's Publishing, 1898–).

Weapons: An International Encyclopedia from 5000 BC to 2000 AD. Prepared by the Diagram Group. Revised ed. St. Martin's, 1991. 336p. $27.95 hardcover; $17.95 paperbound.

Originally published in 1981 and updated 10 years later, *Weapons* is (as its subtitle suggests) an encyclopedic history of the instruments of war from the primitive club to the guided missiles and nuclear bombs of the present century. Arrangement is by type and function of weapon, e.g., "Hand-Held Missile-Throwers." A review in *Reference Books Bulletin* (in *Booklist*, July 1991, p. 2071) endorses the book, especially its informative diagrams: "The quality of illustrations is what distinguishes Diagram Group publications, and these are up to the usual standards. More than 2,500 black-and-white drawings are included. . . . Recommended for academic, high school, and public libraries." Another valuable, albeit much less current, single-volume reference on the subject is the *Complete Encyclopedia of Arms and Weapons* (Simon & Schuster, 1979); edited by Leonid Tarussuk and Claude Blair, it is regrettable that this work is now out of print.

※ MUSIC ※

The Definitive Kobbé's Opera Book. Written by Gustave Kobbé; revised & edited by the Earl of Harewood. 1st American ed. Putnam, 1987. 1,404p. $39.95.

Kobbé's has long been a favorite one-volume opera encyclopedia in a crowded field. First published in 1922 and revised and reprinted numerous times since, the first American edition (1987) represents an updating of the ninth edition issued in 1976 under the title *New Kobbé's Complete Opera Book*. The book now contains detailed plots of more than 300 operas as well as lengthy discussions of such composers as Verdi, Wagner, Rossini, Berlioz, and Britten. "We recommend *The Definitive Kobbé's Opera Book* to public, academic, and high school libraries because of its coverage and currency" (*Reference Books Bulletin* in *Booklist*, January 15, 1988, p. 842).

Worthy single-volume competitors to *Kobbé's* include the *Concise Oxford Dictionary of Opera* (2nd ed. Oxford Univ. Press, 1979), written by Harold Rosenthal and John Warrack; the *Encyclopedia of Opera* (Scribner's, 1976), edited by Leslie Orrey; the *Harper Dictionary of Opera and Operetta* (HarperCollins, 1990), edited by James Anderson; the *Metropolitan Opera Encyclopedia: A Comprehensive Guide to the World of Opera* (Simon & Schuster, 1987), edited by David Hamilton; and the *Oxford Dictionary of Opera* (Oxford Univ. Press, 1992), written by John Warrack and Ewan West. In a class (and price) by itself is the recently published NEW GROVE DICTIONARY OF OPERA, a four-volume set that sells for $850.00.

Dictionary of Western Church Music. Written by David Poultney. American Library Assn., 1991. 234p. $40.00.

Poultney, a professor of musicology at Illinois State University, covers approximately 400 topics in this specialized encyclopedia devoted almost exclusively to Christian church music. Articles, which vary in length from a sentence or two to six or seven pages, include prominent composers and musical compositions, genres, and terms. "This lovingly conceived and skillfully executed book will be welcomed by traditional musicians of Roman Catholic, Anglican/Episcopalian, Lutheran, Methodist, and Baptist churches" (*Library Journal*, September 1, 1991, p. 182).

The Encyclopedia of Folk, Country & Western Music. Written by Irwin Stambler & Grelun Landon. 2nd ed. St. Martin's Press, 1983. 902p. Out of print (last priced at $17.95 paper).

Although now dated and no longer in print, this encyclopedia still provides "a breadth of coverage for folk and country recording artists not available elsewhere" (*Library Journal*, January 1, 1983, p. 43). First published in 1969 and greatly enlarged in 1983, the book is especially valuable for biographical information on major performers. It is hoped that a new edition will be forthcoming in the near future. A complementary source that is in print is the much less extensive (208-page) *Harmony Illustrated Ency-*

clopedia of Country Music (Revised ed. Harmony Books, dist. by Crown, 1986).

Encyclopedia of Music in Canada. Edited by Helmut Kallmann & others. 2nd ed. Univ. of Toronto Press, 1992. 1,076p. $95.00.

Initially published in 1981 and revised in 1992, this unique encyclopedia furnishes authoritative information on Canadian composers and their works as well as musical performers (individuals and groups), festivals, schools, organizations, etc. Heavily illustrated and closely indexed, the book covers all major types of music and musicians, from classical and religious to rock and folk. In a review of the first edition in *American Reference Books Annual* (1983, p. 436), John Druesedow called the encyclopedia "the largest and most significant reference work on Canadian music now available." That observation remains true today.

Encyclopedia of Pop, Rock and Soul. Written by Irwin Stambler. Revised ed. St. Martin's Press, 1989. 881p. $35.00 hardcover; $19.95 paperbound.

First published in 1974 and revised in 1989, Stambler's encyclopedia consists of roughly 500 entries focusing on mainstream pop and rock superstar performers and groups. His goal is "to reflect all of the pivotal influences in the evolution of today's popular music spectrum" (introduction). "This book belongs on the reference shelf of every library, and those with more liberal budgets should also consider adding a circulating copy" (*Library Journal*, February 15, 1989, p. 156). Another excellent single-volume reference source on the subject is the *Oxford Companion to Popular Music* (Oxford Univ. Press, 1991) by Peter Gammond; more comprehensive is the much larger four-volume GUINNESS ENCYCLOPEDIA OF POPULAR MUSIC.

Encyclopedia of the Blues. Written by Gérard Herzhaft; translated from the French by Brigitte Debord. Univ. of Arkansas Press, 1992. 513p. $32.00 hardcover; $16.95 paperbound.

Although most entries in the *Encyclopedia of the Blues* are biographical, some coverage is extended to festivals, instruments, and specific subjects, represented by such articles as "Blues Shouters," "Delta Blues," "Female Blues Singers," and "White Blues." The volume, originally published in France as *Encyclopédie du Blues* in 1979, also includes a list of 300 well-known blues songs with a short history of each. A review in *Reference Books Bulletin* (in *Booklist*, January 1, 1993, p. 825) recommends the encyclopedia, noting that "for libraries with an active blues audience, this will be a good addition."

The Great Song Thesaurus. Written by Roger Lax & Frederick Smith. 2nd ed. Oxford Univ. Press, 1989. 774p. $85.00.

More than 11,000 of the best-known songs in the English-speaking world from the sixteenth century through 1987 are briefly described in this well-indexed reference book. First published in 1984 and substantially revised in 1989, the *Great Song Thesaurus* includes popular melodies, folk songs, sea chanteys, college songs, political songs, Christmas carols, and advertising jingles. The second edition has added a new index called "Lyric Key Lines" that furnishes access to songs by memorable lines, as in the case of "Way down upon the Swanee River" from the song *Old Folks at Home.* "'Great' is the operative word here. Originally published five years ago, this thesaurus-almanac-index-encyclopedia smorgasbord of popular American and English song information quickly became a reference mainstay, and the revised second edition is another cornucopia" (*Library Journal*, April 15, 1989, p. 70). A similar source limited to American popular songs is *Lissauer's Encyclopedia of Popular Music in America* (Paragon House, 1991); prepared by Robert Lissauer, this large (1,687-page) volume covers 19,000 songs from 1888 to the present.

The Guinness Encyclopedia of Popular Music. Edited by Colin Larkin. Guinness Publishing (dist. by New England Publishing Associates), 1992. 4 vols. $295.00.

Editor Larkin, a British music journalist, sets out an ambitious agenda for the recently published *Guinness Encyclopedia of Popular Music* in his spirited introduction to the set: "The ultimate intention of this work is once and for all to place popular music shoulder to shoulder with classical and operatic music. . . . Like a bottle of fine claret, popular music now has age on its side." The encyclopedia's four volumes comprise some 14,500 A-to-Z articles (from "Abba" to "Z.Z. Top") in nearly 3,300 pages of text covering all important twentieth-century forms of popular music, including rock, jazz, blues, soul, country, and reggae. The articles, which range from 150 to 3,000 words in length, treat not only individual artists and groups but prominent labels, movements, Broadway shows, festivals, and instruments. Emphasis is naturally on developments in the U.S. and Britain but popular music indigenous to Latin America, Asia, and Africa also receives attention. "It is sure to be a hit with patrons, especially those whose musical taste has been formed by MTV" (*Wilson Library Bulletin*, January 1993, p. 108).

A complementary work is the 21-volume *Marshall Cavendish Illustrated History of Popular Music* (Marshall Cavendish, 1990), an encyclopedic set that furnishes authoritative information about popular music since World War II. Less extensive (and expensive) single-volume complements to the *Guinness Encyclopedia* are the *Oxford Companion to Popular Music* (Oxford Univ. Press, 1991), an outstanding effort by Peter Gammond; the *Penguin Encyclopedia of Popular Music* (Viking, 1989), edited by Donald Clarke; and Stambler's ENCYCLOPEDIA OF POP, ROCK, AND SOUL.

The Heritage Encyclopedia of Band Music: Composers and Their Music. Written by William Rehrig; edited by Paul E. Bierley. Integrity Press, 1991. 2 vols. $110.00.

The goal of this quite specialized encyclopedia is "to document all editions of all music ever published . . . for concert and military bands" (introduction) as well as furnish biographical information about composers of band music. In all, approximately 5,000 compositions and 9,000 composers are covered. J.L. Patterson in *Choice* (April 1992, p. 1212) strongly recommends the set, noting that "this monumental encyclopedia, which took more than a decade to complete, will surely become the standard in the field. It provides band masters with the most complete guide to band music to date."

The International Cyclopedia of Music and Musicians. Edited by Oscar Thompson; revision editor, Bruce Bohle. 11th ed. Dodd, Mead, 1985. 2,609p. Out of print (last priced at $69.95).

Since 1938 when the first edition appeared, the huge *International Cyclopedia of Music and Musicians* has been a music reference mainstay. Now in its eleventh edition (1985), the work is out of print, at least temporarily, but it still represents one of the most substantial and informative all-purpose one-volume music encyclopedias in English, summarizing all important areas of serious music (popular music receives comparatively little attention). Look for a new (twelfth) edition in the near future. A work of comparable size, coverage, and quality is the two-volume (2,048-page) NEW OXFORD COMPANION TO MUSIC.

Music: An Illustrated Encyclopedia. Written by Neil Ardley. Facts on File, 1986. 192p. $18.95.

Intended principally for young people ages 10 and up, this heavily illustrated, clearly presented general music encyclopedia offers basic information on genres, composers and performers, instruments, theory and notation, recording and broadcasting, and key terminology. "Each section of the book contains a chart listing famous works in the form, medium, or genre being discussed, which could be used as a source of suggestions for listening. . . . This is a good book—particularly at the price—and is recommended for public libraries" (*American Reference Books Annual*, 1987, p. 482). A similar work for youngsters is the *Oxford Junior Companion to Music* (2nd ed. Oxford Univ. Press, 1980), edited by Michael Hurd.

The New Grove Dictionary of American Music. Edited by H. Wiley Hitchcock & Stanley Sadie. Grove's Dictionaries of Music, Inc., 1986. 4 vols. $695.00.

This multivolume work—known widely as *Amerigrove*—is the most comprehensive encyclopedia available devoted exclusively to the music of the United States. Covering all types and periods of U.S. music, *Amerigrove* contains approximately 2,500 authoritative articles, of which nearly three-fourths are biographies; the rest treat musical genres, mediums, groups, instruments, publishers, organizations, and various subjects, such as "Advertising," "Criticism," "Jewish-American Music," "Nightclub," "Notation," and "Tuning Systems."

Amerigrove is *not* an abridgment of the 20-volume NEW GROVE DICTIONARY OF MUSIC AND MUSICIANS, although about a third of the articles are revised and updated versions of entries found in the larger work. Reviewers have universally applauded the encyclopedia: Donald Krummel writes in *Choice* (January 1987, p. 725), "Obviously a good deal of imagination and sensitivity has gone into the conception of the set. It clearly deserves high praise." Ross Wood says in *American Reference Books Annual* (1988, p. 510), "*Amerigrove* is an unequivocal triumph, a national dictionary not likely to be equaled or surpassed in our lifetime."

The New Grove Dictionary of Jazz. Edited by Barry Kernfeld. Grove's Dictionaries of Music, Inc., 1988. 2 vols. $350.00.

Although some material in this two-volume set derives from the larger NEW GROVE DICTIONARY OF MUSIC AND MUSICIANS and NEW GROVE DICTIONARY OF AMERICAN MUSIC, an estimated 90 percent of the text is new. Most of the 4,500 entries cover jazz musicians and other people associated with the genre; other entries are devoted to jazz styles, theories, periods, films, festivals, organizations, instruments, record labels, and unique vocabulary. "This massive work deserves highest praise for bringing to jazz music the breadth and rigorous methodology that characterizes Grove projects. Supplementing and updating all extant jazz reference works, this set will prove important for a variety of collections and will not likely be superseded in the near future" (*Library Journal*, February 1, 1989, p. 61). Useful complements to the *New Grove Dictionary of Jazz* are the one-volume *Harmony Illustrated Encyclopedia of Jazz* (Revised ed. Harmony Books, dist. by Crown, 1986) and three classic volumes by Leonard Feather: the *Encyclopedia of Jazz* (1960), the *Encyclopedia of Jazz in the Sixties* (1967), and the *Encyclopedia of Jazz in the Seventies* (1976), all published by Horizon Press; note that the *Encyclopedia of Jazz* was reissued in 1984 in paperback by Da Capo Press.

The New Grove Dictionary of Music and Musicians. Edited by Stanley Sadie. 6th ed. Grove's Dictionaries of Music, Inc., 1980. 20 vols. $2,300.00.

Widely heralded as "the greatest musical dictionary ever published" (by Charles Rosen in the *New York Review of Books*, May 28, 1981, p. 38), "the last word on music" (by R.Z. Sheppard in *Time*, November 17, 1980, p. 110), and "a masterpiece of Britannico-American collaboration with notable contributions from Europe" (by Anthony Burgess in the *Times Literary Supplement*, February 20, 1981, p. 184), the *New Grove* replaces the fifth edition of the old *Grove*, a nine-volume set published in 1955 (the first edition of this justly famous work appeared in four volumes between 1877 and 1890). The *New Grove*'s statistics are impressive: 20 volumes, 22 million words, 18,000 pages, 22,500 articles, 4,500 illustrations, 9,500 cross-references, and 2,400 distinguished contributors, mainly (as Anthony Burgess suggests) from the U.S., U.K., and Western Europe.

One of the great subject encyclopedias of all time, it is comprehensive, authoritative, and essential for all serious music students, teachers, and critics. As Harold Schonberg observed in the *New York Times Book Review* (December 21, 1980, p. 13), "Just about everything one would want to know about matters musical is contained in these 20 volumes." Those who cannot afford or lack access to the *New Grove* should consider the much less expensive, albeit much less extensive, four-volume *Heritage of Music* (Oxford Univ. Press, 1989), a comprehensive encyclopedic set edited by Michael Raeburn and Alan Kendall that currently sells for $195.00. Another useful (but again much smaller) alternative to the *New Grove* is the two-volume NEW OXFORD COMPANION TO MUSIC.

The New Grove Dictionary of Musical Instruments. Edited by Stanley Sadie. Grove's Dictionaries of Music, Inc., 1984. 3 vols. $495.00.

This three-volume set is based on the 20-volume NEW GROVE DICTIONARY OF MUSIC AND MUSICIANS, but it contains much new material, particularly in the areas of non-Western musical instruments and ethnomusicology. Heavily illustrated with over 1,600 black-and-white photographs and drawings (some of which are not entirely clear), the encyclopedia furnishes detailed information on the history, construction, and playing of some 12,000 instruments from practically every culture, past and present. "Encyclopedic in scope and masterful in presentation, *The New Grove Dictionary of Musical Instruments* cannot be considered less than essential for any collection that includes music" (*Choice*, June 1985, p. 1478). A smaller, much less costly encyclopedia on the subject is the single-volume *Oxford Companion to Musical Instruments* (Oxford Univ. Press, 1992) by Anthony Baines; based on the NEW OXFORD COMPANION TO MUSIC, this book sells for a modest $45.00.

The New Grove Dictionary of Opera. Edited by Stanley Sadie. Grove's Dictionaries of Music, Inc., 1992. 4 vols. $850.00.

The latest in the impressive Grove family of multivolume music encyclopedias, the *New Grove Dictionary of Opera* comprises approximately 10,000 articles prepared by 1,300 authorities covering all significant aspects of Western opera, including composers, performers, individual compositions, librettists, companies, theaters, terms, and subjects unique to the genre, including countries and cities famous for opera. The text is enhanced by 1,800 black-and-white illustrations, and volume 4 appends lists of role names and first lines. "Highly recommended as the core opera reference work for all academic and public libraries" (*Library Journal*, February 15, 1993, p. 162); "Superlatives are lacking to describe this wonderful work. A feast for scholars, it can also be an education for opera lovers at any level of sophistication" (*Reference Books Bulletin* in *Booklist*, April 1, 1993, p. 1452). Those who cannot afford this expensive four-volume set should look to the new two-volume *International Dictionary of Opera* (St. James Press, 1993), which is much more affordable at $250.00, or the one-volume DEFINITIVE KOBBÉ'S OPERA BOOK, which currently retails for just $35.00.

The New Oxford Companion to Music. Edited by Denis Arnold. Oxford Univ. Press, 1983. 2 vols. $135.00.

Originally published as the single-volume *Oxford Companion to Music* in 1938 and subsequently revised a number of times, this standard source became the *New Oxford Companion to Music* in 1983, at which time it expanded to two volumes

and increased its text by about 40 percent. The set, which now totals over 2,000 pages, contains approximately 6,600 articles covering more than 2,000 musical terms, 1,300 composers, 1,150 individual works, and 175 instruments. Well over 1,000 illustrations enhance the work, which is aimed largely at the general reader with a serious interest in serious music. "Even though there are entries for Louis Armstrong, Bob Dylan, and reggae, the music of the conservatory and concert hall remains the focus" (*Wilson Library Bulletin*, February 1984, p. 453). A work of comparable size and scope is the 2,609-page INTERNATIONAL CYCLOPEDIA OF MUSIC AND MUSICIANS.

The Norton/Grove Concise Encyclopedia of Music. Edited by Stanley Sadie & Alison Latham. Norton, 1988. 850p. $40.00.

Anyone seeking a good, fairly priced desk-size music encyclopedia that touches all the important bases cannot go wrong with the *Norton/Grove Concise Encyclopedia of Music*, which presents authoritative information on major composers, compositions, performers, instruments, genres, and the like. In all, the book, which is loosely based on the 20-volume NEW GROVE DICTIONARY OF MUSIC AND MUSICIANS, contains 10,000 brief entries and is ideal for interested students who require an affordable, reliable quick-reference source. There are many competing works of similar size, price, and coverage. Among the best are the *HarperCollins Dictionary of Music* (2nd ed. HarperCollins, 1987) by Christine Ammer; the *New Everyman Dictionary of Music* (6th ed. Weidenfeld & Nicolson, 1989) by Eric Blom; the *New Harvard Dictionary of Music* (Revised ed. Harvard Univ. Press, 1986) by Don Michael Randel; and the *Oxford Dictionary of Music* (Oxford Univ. Press, 1985) by Michael Kennedy.

Rock On: The Illustrated Encyclopedia of Rock n' Roll. Written by Norm N. Nite. HarperCollins, 1982–85. 3 vols. $89.90.

Comprising three separately published and titled volumes—*The Solid Gold Years* (1982), *The Years of Change, 1964–1978* (1984), and *The Video Revolution, 1978–1984* (1985)—Norm N. Nite's encyclopedia provides reasonably comprehensive coverage of the rock scene from the seminal 1950s through the mid-1980s, principally through biographies of both groups and individual artists. In his bibliographic essay "Rock and Roll: Dimensions of a Cultural Revolution" in *Choice* (April 1992, p. 1199), Charles Pressler rightly characterizes Nite's work as the "standard encyclopedia of rock and roll events, personalities, songs, and groups." Complementary sources (all single-volume items) are the *Ultimate Encyclopedia of Rock* (HarperCollins, 1993), edited by Michael Heatley; the *Harmony Illustrated Encyclopedia of Rock* (7th ed. Harmony Books, dist. by Crown, 1992), edited by Mike Clifford; the *Encyclopedia of Rock* (Revised ed. Schirmer Books, 1988) by Phil Hardy; and the *Rolling Stone Encyclopedia of Rock & Roll* (Simon & Schuster, 1983), edited by Jon Pareles and Patricia Romanowski.

※ PHYSICS AND MATHEMATICS ※

Encyclopedia of Applied Physics. Edited by George L. Trigg. VCH Publishers, 1991–. 20 vols. (in progress). $295.00 per vol.; $5,950.00 the set.

Scheduled for completion in 1997, this landmark encyclopedia will eventually cover all important aspects of applied physics, including technical and industrial applications and pertinent developments in engineering. The set is sponsored by four major national physics organizations—the American Institute of Physics, the German Physical Society, the Japanese Society of Applied Physics, and the Physical Society of Japan—and will ultimately comprise some 500 alphabetically arranged articles written by prominent scientists and engineers in industry and academia both here and abroad. In a review of volume 1 in *Choice* (March 1992, pp. 1042–44), R.J. Rittenhouse calls the set "an exciting new encyclopedia of physics that promises to be a well-written and illustrated compendium of major fields in physics. . . . The entries have modern subject coverage and, although rigorous, are useful to generalists as well as experts." Likewise, John Trefny in *American Reference Books Annual* (1992, p. 709) likes what he sees in volume 1: "If the exceptional quality of this initial volume is maintained throughout, the result will be of major significance. The scope of the overall project is truly impressive. . . . Most important, the text has a freshness and clarity not commonly found in such works." An older (and now out of print) but still useful multivolume work covering some of the same ground is the *Encyclopaedic Dictionary of Physics* (Pergamon, 1961–75); edited by James Thewlis, this well-known set comprises nine volumes plus five supplements.

Encyclopedia of Lasers and Optical Technology. Edited by Robert A. Meyers. Academic Press, 1991. 764p. $69.95.

This handy one-volume reference work derives from the much larger, more expensive ENCYCLOPEDIA OF PHYSICAL SCIENCE AND TECHNOLOGY, a 15-volume set devoted to all of the physical sciences. The book provides authoritative information on laser and optical technology and will be especially welcome by specialists and physics and engineering libraries unable to afford the parent set.

Encyclopaedia of Mathematics. Edited by M. Hazewinkel. Kluwer Academic, 1988–93. 10 vols. $199.00 per vol.; $1,990.00 for the set.

The 10-volume *Encyclopaedia of Mathematics* is an updated and expanded translation of the *Soviet Mathematical Encyclopaedia*, a five-volume set published in the former Soviet Union between 1977 and 1985. Intended for graduate students, teachers, and working mathematicians, the encyclopedia covers important mathematical concepts, theories, problems, techniques, and terms. The nearly 7,000 articles vary in length from a paragraph or two to a dozen or more pages; longer articles normally include numerous bibliographic citations, AMS (American Mathematical Society) classification numbers, and editorial notes that clarify or augment material translated from the original set. Volume 10, published in 1993, is an index to the set. "Appropriate for special libraries and medium to large university collections, there is little else like this work in the mathematical reference literature" (*American Reference Books Annual*, 1990, p. 740). A complementary work is the ENCYCLOPEDIC DICTIONARY OF MATHEMATICS.

Encyclopedia of Mathematics and Its Applications. Edited by Gian-Carlo Rota. Cambridge Univ. Press, 1976–. 45 vols. to date (in progress). Prices vary from $42.95 to $115.00 per vol.

Each volume in this distinguished encyclopedic series treats a specific mathematical subject and is prepared by a noted international authority. For instance, volume 1 by Luis A. Santalo is entitled *Integral Geometry and Geometric Probability*; volume 2 by George E. Andrews is *The Theory of Partitions*; volume 3 by Robert J. McEliece is *The Theory of Information and Coding: A Mathematical Framework for Communication*. The ultimate goal, according to editor Rota, is "to present the factual body of all mathematics" (introduction) in a manner that can be readily comprehended by the serious nonspecialist. To date, the set, which originates in Great Britain, totals approximately 45 volumes, but new titles continue to be added each year. Interested consumers should be aware that some earlier volumes are currently out of print; most if not all of these volumes will eventually be revised and published in new editions.

Encyclopedia of Modern Physics. Edited by Robert A. Meyers. Academic Press, 1990. 773p. $94.00.

Like the ENCYCLOPEDIA OF LASERS AND OPTICAL TECHNOLOGY, this one-volume encyclopedia derives from the multivolume ENCYCLOPEDIA OF PHYSICAL SCIENCE AND TECHNOLOGY and its yearbooks. The book contains 34 lengthy articles that emphasize topics in the area of applied physics, such as quantum optics and the mechanisms of superconductivity. It will be especially useful to students, practitioners, and libraries that lack access to or cannot afford the multivolume work. "Most entries presuppose a basic knowledge of calculus, chemistry, and physics, though the introductory sections are accessible to the uninitiated. . . . Recommended for large academic or public libraries" (*Choice*, June 1990, p. 1650).

The Encyclopedia of Physics. Edited by Robert M. Besançon. 3rd ed. Van Nostrand, 1985. 1,378p. $149.95 hardcover; $51.95 paperbound.

First published in 1966 and substantially revised in 1974 and again in 1985, Besançon's encyclopedia provides basic information covering the whole field of physics and its major subdisciplines. New developments in such areas as particle physics, gauge theory, quantum chromodynamics, and electroweak theory receive especially strong attention in the latest edition. A noteworthy feature is the writing style, which tends to treat broad, general topics (e.g., solid-state physics) in a fairly rudimentary fashion but becomes more technical and demanding when dealing with advanced subject matter. A review in *American Reference Books Annual* (1987, p. 671) notes that "this is an exceptional work, and will be a welcome tool for the student, librarian, and researcher." Competing single-volume physics encyclopedias are the excellent ENCYCLOPEDIA OF PHYSICS, edited by Rita Lerner and George Trigg, and the equally fine *McGraw-Hill Encyclopedia of Physics* (2nd ed. McGraw-Hill, 1993), edited by Sybil Parker.

Encyclopedia of Physics. Edited by Rita G. Lerner & George L. Trigg. 2nd ed. VCH Publishers, 1991. 1,408p. $175.00.

Similar in size, scope, and quality to Besançon's ENCYCLOPEDIA OF PHYSICS and the recently revised *McGraw-Hill Encyclopedia of Physics* (2nd ed. McGraw-Hill, 1993), Lerner and Trigg's encyclopedia first appeared in 1981 (published by Addison-Wesley) and was extensively revised in 1991. The revised edition contains over 500 clearly written,

signed articles prepared by recognized authorities in the field. It is reliable and reasonably current and can be recommended to serious students and librarians without hesitation. "The editors have produced a new edition that is not only up-to-date in all areas, but visually a much better *Encyclopedia*. VCH, its new publisher, has a reputation for producing excellent reference materials. As with the first edition, the work presents the 'state of physics' as of the time each article was written" (*Reference Books Bulletin* in *Booklist*, August 1991, p. 2171). All three general single-volume physics encyclopedias on the North American market today—Besançon's, the McGraw-Hill work, and Lerner and Trigg's—are first-rate reference sources. But if the consumer must choose one, the latter gets the nod.

Encyclopedic Dictionary of Mathematics. Edited by Kiyosi Ito. 2nd ed. MIT Press, 1987. 4 vols. $350.00.

This outstanding reference set originally appeared in English in two volumes in 1977 and was updated and expanded to four volumes in 1987. Prepared under the auspices of the Mathematical Society of Japan as *Iwanami Sugaku Ziten* and translated into English with the assistance of the American Mathematical Society, the encyclopedia now contains 450 alphabetically arranged articles in 2,148 pages covering all important aspects of the mathematical sciences. The articles, which are not for neophytes, tend to be long, scholarly, and quite technical, affording authoritative coverage of "every significant result of today's mathematics" (foreword). "Every college and university library should have this excellent reference work or its still-useful predecessor" (*Choice*, January 1988, p. 744). Complementing the *Encyclopedic Dictionary of Mathematics* is the 10-volume ENCYCLOPEDIA OF MATHEMATICS and the newly published two-volume *Companion Encyclopedia of the History and Philosophy of the Mathematical Sciences* (Routledge, 1993), edited by Ivor Grattan-Guinness.

Mathematics Illustrated Dictionary: Facts, Figures and People. Written by Jeanne Bendick. Revised ed. Franklin Watts, 1989. 247p. $14.95.

Designed for students in grades 6–12 but also useful for adults who need a basic encyclopedic survey of geometry, algebra, trigonometry, etc., the *Mathematics Illustrated Dictionary* first appeared in 1965 and was updated in 1989. Its roughly 2,000 paragraph-length entries provide reliable, readable encyclopedic information on a wide range of mathematics topics, including fundamental concepts, principles, and terms, as well as brief biographies of prominent mathematicians. "Mathematical principles are generally accompanied by easy-to-understand examples and Bendick makes frequent use of diagrams" (*Reference Books Bulletin* in *Booklist*, March 15, 1990, p. 1500).

The VNR Concise Encyclopedia of Mathematics. Edited by W. Gellert & others. 2nd ed. Van Nostrand, 1989. 776p. $29.95.

The *VNR Concise Encyclopedia of Mathematics*, first published in 1977 and revised in 1989, is an English-language translation of the German *Kleine Enzyklopädie der Mathematik*, a standard one-volume reference aimed principally at high school and college math students as well as interested laypeople.

The book is divided into three parts, the first dealing with elementary mathematics, the second higher mathematics, and the third selected topics in the field, such as number theory, topology, and graph theory. "The treatment of established mathematical subjects is sound. For example, the section on spherical trigonometry could be used by an engineer working with navigation. A nice feature of the arrangement is that formulae appear in yellow, examples in blue, and theorems in red" (*Choice*, October 1990, p. 289). A one-volume work aimed at a similar audience is the *Prentice-Hall Encyclopedia of Mathematics* (Prentice-Hall, 1982).

※ POLITICAL SCIENCE AND GOVERNMENT ※

The American Political Dictionary. Written by Jack C. Plano & Milton Greenberg. 8th ed. Holt, 1989. 608p. $20.00.

A popular reference work with students, teachers, and librarians since it first appeared in 1962, Plano and Greenberg's oft-revised encyclopedic dictionary provides a reliable overview of the U.S. political system. In all, the book contains some 1,200 A-to-Z entries that concisely explain key terms, concepts, agencies, court cases, and laws. A comparable single-volume source is the *HarperCollins Dictionary of American Government and Politics* (HarperCollins, 1992) by Jay Shafritz; this work supersedes the *Dorsey Dictionary of American Government and Politics* (Dorsey Press, 1988), also by Shafritz.

The Blackwell Encyclopaedia of Political Thought. Edited by David Miller. Blackwell, 1987. 570p. $60.00.

This authoritative British-made encyclopedia focuses on important concepts, ideologies, doctrines, theories, and movements central to the Western political experience. Comprising 350 articles that vary in length from a paragraph to several or more pages, the encyclopedia treats subjects (see such articles as "Absolutism," "Alienation," "Anarchism," "Authority," "Church and State," "Civil Disobedience," "Freedom," "Imperialism," "Justice," "Liberalism," "Nationalism," and "Utopianism") as well as prominent political thinkers (e.g., Socrates, Bentham, Locke, Hegel, Hobbes, and Sartre). "This one-volume encyclopedia is an excellent starting point for the user seeking a concise, to-the-point, but not simplistic introduction to political thought" (*American Reference Books Annual*, 1988, p. 276). The *Blackwell Encyclopaedia of Political Institutions* (Blackwell, 1988), a companion volume, emphasizes the machinery (as opposed to theory) of gov-

ernment. Another one-volume work that nicely complements the *Blackwell Encyclopaedia of Political Thought* is the *Dictionary of Modern Political Ideologies* (St. Martin's, 1987); edited by M.A. Riff, it offers 42 lengthy essays discussing various political isms.

The Columbia Dictionary of European Political History Since 1914. Edited by John Stevenson. Columbia Univ. Press, 1992. 437p. $69.50.

Originally published abroad in 1991 as the *Macmillan Dictionary of British and European History Since 1914*, this handy single-volume encyclopedia contains 1,500 compact entries covering major European political leaders, groups, events, and issues from the onset of World War I to the present. "There is extensive cross-referencing between entries, but the lack of an index limits the work's usefulness as a reference tool for librarians with little subject background. Nevertheless, this work is highly recommended for university, college, and large public libraries" (*Choice*, September 1992, p. 74).

Dictionary of American Diplomatic History. Written by John E. Findling. 2nd ed. Greenwood, 1989. 674p. $66.00.

Generally acclaimed as the best one-volume reference work on the history of U.S. foreign policy when first published in 1980, Findling's excellent encyclopedia was updated and expanded in 1989 to include developments during the Reagan and Carter years. The book, which now has more than 1,200 entries, concentrates on individuals and events central to U.S. foreign relations from the beginning of the Republic. "Overall, this is an outstanding compilation and one likely to be frequently consulted by students of American diplomacy" (*Reference Books Bulletin* in *Booklist*, December 15, 1989, p. 854). A complementary work is the three-volume ENCYCLO-PEDIA OF AMERICAN FOREIGN POLICY.

The Dictionary of Contemporary Politics of Central America and the Caribbean. Written by Phil Gunson & Greg Chamberlain. Simon & Schuster, 1991. 397p. $45.00.

Gunson and Chamberlain furnish reliable encyclopedic information about the most important twentieth-century political personalities, parties, organizations, and movements found in the various Central American and Caribbean countries. "This compact political dictionary is a useful source of current information about a turbulent area of the Western Hemisphere. Simple organization and succinct entries make for ease of use, while the 'see also' references help build pathways toward more detailed information" (*Choice*, March 1992, p. 1046); "The editors, all journalists who have specialized in Latin America, have compiled a reference tool almost no library should be without" (*Library Journal*, October 15, 1991, p. 72). Companion volumes covering the political scene in other regions of the world are the *Dictionary of Contemporary Politics of South America* (Macmillan, 1989), also by Gunson and Chamberlain; the *Dictionary of Contemporary Politics of Southern Africa* (Macmillan, 1989) by Gwyneth Williams and Brian Hackland; and the *Dictionary of Contemporary Politics of Southeast Asia* (Routledge, 1993) by Michael Leifer.

A Dictionary of Marxist Thought. Edited by Tom Bottomore & others. 2nd ed. Blackwell, 1992. 672p. $64.95 hardcover; $24.95 paperbound (published by Harvard Univ. Press).

Originally published in 1983, this scholarly work offers up-to-date coverage of both the people and concepts associated with present-day Marxism, a political philosophy and system that has undergone traumatic reversals in recent years but remains a powerful force in many parts of the world. Older sources still valuable for background information on Marxism are Terrell Carver's *A Marx Dictionary* (Barnes & Noble, 1987) and Jozef Wilczynski's *Encyclopedic Dictionary of Marxism, Socialism and Communism* (Walter de Gruyter, 1981), both single-volume works.

Encyclopedia of American Foreign Policy: Studies of the Principal Movements and Ideas. Edited by Alexander DeConde. Scribner's, 1978. 3 vols. $259.00.

A collection of 95 substantial articles that describes and analyzes the fundamental policies, concepts, and issues of U.S. foreign policy (such as Manifest Destiny, the Marshall Plan, the Cold War,

isolationism, and the balance of power), this outstanding set is the work of leading scholars representing a variety of political positions and ideologies. "Written for both scholars and laypersons, this *Encyclopedia* is a unique compilation that admirably complements other types of reference works in the field" (*American Reference Books Annual*, 1981, p. 251). Among these complementary sources are Lester Brune's three-volume *Chronological History of United States Foreign Relations* (Garland, 1985; 1991), John Findling's excellent one-volume DICTIONARY OF AMERICAN DIPLOMATIC HISTORY, and Stephen and Carl Flanders's recently published *Dictionary of American Foreign Affairs* (Macmillan, 1993), also a single-volume work.

Encyclopedia of American Political History: Studies of the Principal Movements and Ideas. Edited by Jack P. Greene. Scribner's, 1984. 3 vols. $259.00.

Similar in purpose, size, and design to the ENCYCLOPEDIA OF AMERICAN FOREIGN POLICY, this set consists of 90 long survey articles covering such broad topics as civil rights, machine politics, suffrage, separation of church and state, populism, egalitarianism, Jacksonian democracy, federalism, the Articles of Confederation, and the New Deal. An extensive index renders specific names and facts easily accessible. A review in *Reference Books Bulletin* (in *Booklist*, August 1985, p. 1644) calls the encyclopedia "an impressive achievement which provides for students of U.S. political history a rare overview of the stuff of politics which many studies have ignored, viz., ideas. It not only informs but also whets one's appetite for further study in a rich field."

Encyclopedia of Government and Politics. Edited by Mary Hawkesworth & Maurice Kogan. Routledge, 1992. 2 vols. $230.00.

Prepared by an impressive roster of academicians from the U.S. and abroad, this scholarly encyclopedia covers contemporary trends in political theory, ideology, institutions, and policies in 84 essay-length articles arranged under 10 broad headings. The set treats government and politics at all levels and, according to the editors, is "post-empiricist" and "post-modernist" in perspective. "This up-to-date and well-executed work provides a sound introduction to all aspects of political study" (*Choice*, March 1993, p. 1110). A perfect complement to the *Encyclopedia of Government and Politics* is the recently published OXFORD COMPANION TO POLITICS OF THE WORLD.

Encyclopedia of Human Rights. Edited by Edward Lawson. Taylor & Francis, 1991. 1,907p. $250.00.

Editor Lawson, who served for 30 years in the United Nation's Division of Human Rights, has brought together an enormous amount of valuable information on the struggle to safeguard and promote human rights since the end of World War II. Arranged alphabetically, entries include important concepts (such as hunger, housing, racial discrimination, and voting rights), major organizations (both governmental and private), essential agreements and documents (e.g., *The Helsinki Accord; The Universal Declaration of Human Rights*), and countries where political and human rights have been a concern to the international community (e.g., Cuba; South Africa). "Lawson's impressive compilation provides comprehensive coverage, great convenience, and historical perspective for information on ongoing international efforts to define, assure, and protect individual rights" (*Wilson Library Bulletin*, November 1991, p. 112).

Encyclopedia of Nationalism. Written by Louis Snyder. Paragon House, 1990. 445p. $35.00.

Unique in its scope and coverage, Snyder's encyclopedia contains over 250 well-written, alphabetically arranged entries dealing with the phenomenon of nationalism in world politics from the nineteenth century to the present. The volume includes concise information about major nationalistic theories, movements, groups, and leaders. "Because this unique work provides many more entries and much more discussion on nationalism than the various dictionaries on American government and politics commonly used in academe, it should be particularly useful to students and professionals in international relations, political theory, and political history" (*Library Journal*, March 1, 1990, p. 90).

Encyclopedia of the American Left. Edited by Mari Jo Buhle & others. Garland, 1990. 928p. $95.00 hardcover; $29.95 paperbound (published by Univ. of Illinois Press).

The first encyclopedia devoted exclusively to the American left, this valuable reference work focuses on the major movements, organizations, concepts, events, and personalities of the radical American left from the post-Civil War period to the end of the 1980s. It consists of approximately 600 articles prepared by 300 highly qualified contributors. "The choice of topics is broad and inclusive. Some articles deal with historic events (e.g., the 1886 Haymarket incident in Chicago), while others deal with broader and sometimes less obvious topics, such as detective fiction and modern dance. . . .

Articles are interesting, well written and suggested readings are current" (*RQ*, Winter 1990, p. 291). Covering the other side of the political coin is the *Dictionary of Conservative and Libertarian Thought* (Routledge, 1991), an informative single-volume work edited by Nigel Ashford and Stephen Davies.

Encyclopedia of the American Legislative System: Studies of the Principal Structures, Processes, and Policies of Congress and State Legislatures Since the Colonial Era. Edited by Joel H. Silbey. Scribner's, 1994. 3 vols. $320.00.

Published in early 1994 and not seen by the author of *Kister's Best Encyclopedias*, this new set is in the same mold as the publisher's ENCYCLOPEDIA OF AMERICAN FOREIGN POLICY and ENCYCLOPEDIA OF AMERICAN POLITICAL HISTORY—three-volume reference works of high quality featuring essay-length articles on broad topics prepared by academic authorities. The *Encyclopedia of the American Legislative System* covers every important facet of lawmaking in the U.S., as these representative articles suggest: "Origins of Congress," "State Legislatures in the Nineteenth Century," "Electoral Realignments," "The Congressional Committee System," "Pressure Groups and Lobbies," "Legislatures and Civil Rights," and "Congress, the Executive, and War Powers." A useful one-volume complement dealing wholly with the U.S. Congress is *Congress A to Z: A Ready Reference Encyclopedia* (2nd ed., Congressional Quarterly, 1993).

Encyclopedia of the American Presidency. Edited by Leonard W. Levy & Louis Fisher. Simon & Schuster, 1993. 4 vols. $355.00.

This brand-new multivolume encyclopedia possesses impressive range and depth. Its roughly 1,000 signed articles cover not only the U.S. presidents from Washington to Clinton, but the major issues and events that have shaped the office over the years. In addition, the set includes articles on the dominant political parties, the cabinet and its responsibilities, presidential elections and transitions, assassinations, and the impeachment process. Editors Levy and Fisher are leading authorities on the American political system and the contributors—400 scholars, journalists, and former presidential advisers—represent the top names in their specialties. "The wealth of information, authoritatively explained and logically and conveniently presented, thoroughly justifies the price" (*Library Journal*, January 1994, p. 104).

Numerous other encyclopedias and fact-finding sources on the U.S. presidents and presidency are available; among the best of these, all single-volume works, are David Whitney's *American Presidents* (7th ed. Prentice Hall Press, 1990); William DeGregorio's *Complete Book of U.S. Presidents* (4th ed. Dembner Books; dist. by Barricade Books, 1993); Joseph Nathan Kane's *Facts About the Presidents* (6th ed. H.W. Wilson, 1993); *The Presidency A to Z: A Ready Reference Encyclopedia* (Congressional Quarterly, 1992), edited by Michael Nelson; Jeffrey Elliot and Sheikh Ali's *Presidential-Congressional Political Dictionary* (ABC-Clio, 1984); and *The Presidents: A Reference History* (Scribner's, 1984), edited by Henry Graff.

The Encyclopedia of the United Nations and International Agreements. Compiled and written by Edmund Jan Osmanczyk. 2nd ed. Taylor & Francis, 1990. 1,220p. $199.00.

Originally published in 1985 and updated in 1990, this A-to-Z compendium furnishes information about the United Nations and its many specialized agencies, intergovernmental and private organizations that cooperate with the U.N., and concepts pertinent to supranational government, diplomacy, and international law. The encyclopedia also includes partial or complete texts of some 3,000 international agreements, conventions, and treaties dating from the late nineteenth century. Access to material is enhanced by detailed subject, personal name, and treaty indexes. A review in *Choice* (March 1991, p. 1102) correctly calls the book "an unparalleled compilation of reference information on the U.N." Regrettably, Edmund Osmanczyk, the person responsible for both editions, died recently, casting doubt on the encyclopedia's future.

The International Relations Dictionary. Written by Jack C. Plano & Roy Olton. 4th ed. ABC-Clio, 1988. 446p. $55.00 hardcover; $24.75 paperbound.

This topically arranged encyclopedic dictionary first appeared in 1969 and has been revised several times since, most recently in 1988. It includes over 700 concise articles in which concepts relevant to international relations and diplomacy (for example, "Apartheid"; "New International Economic Order") are defined and then placed in historical and political context. A review in *Reference Books Bulletin* (in *Booklist*, October 1, 1988, p. 242) concludes, "the latest edition of this standard work will again prove useful in academic and large public libraries, in particular for students of international relations." A competing source is Graham Evans and Jeffrey Newnham's *Dictionary of World Politics: A Reference Guide to Concepts, Ideas and Institutions* (Simon & Schuster, 1990), also a single-volume work.

The Middle East: A Political Dictionary. Written by Lawrence Ziring. 2nd ed. ABC-Clio, 1992. 401p. $56.50 hardcover; $29.95 paperbound.

Ziring's excellent encyclopedic overview of the Middle Eastern political scene was first published in 1984 and substantially revised in 1992. Organized under seven broad topics, it contains approximately 270 lengthy articles covering all significant political aspects of this turbulent region. James Rettig in *Wilson Library Bulletin* (December 1992, p. 110) puts the book in good perspective: "Ziring's dictionary treats the many factions, events, personalities, and conflicts of Middle Eastern politics evenhandedly and is sure, therefore, to offend zealous promoters of any particular view." A similar source covering another politically volatile region of the world is *Latin America: A Political Dictionary* (ABC-Clio, 1992), prepared by Ernest Rossi and Jack Plano.

The Oxford Companion to Politics of the World. Edited by Joel Krieger & others. Oxford Univ. Press, 1993. 1,088p. $49.95.

New in 1993, this large volume contains 650 A-to-Z articles contributed by some 500 internationally known authorities, including such recognizable British and American scholars as Martin Gilbert, Anthony Lake, Martin Lipset, and Garry Wills. Coverage focuses on the current political situation in each country of the world, brief biographical sketches of important national leaders and thinkers, and a wide variety of concepts, events, issues, and organizations pertinent to world politics today (such as AIDS, Chernobyl, class, deindustrialization, democracy, genocide, nationalism, and Tiananmen Square). "One of the strengths of this work is its coverage of the conflicts and issues that are headlines in the news, both today and in the recent past. For instance, in the three pages devoted to Yugoslavia, one can learn the history of the country, the ideology of the competing factions, and the pertinent facts about the current crisis" (*Reference Books Bulletin* in *Booklist*, May 1, 1993, p. 1630). A complementary work is the two-volume ENCYCLOPEDIA OF GOVERNMENT AND POLITICS, which treats world politics in 84 long, analytical articles.

Political Parties and Elections in the United States: An Encyclopedia. Edited by L. Sandy Maisel & Charles Bassett. Garland, 1991. 2 vols. $150.00.

An informative, objective survey of the people, politics, and parties that have formed the U.S. electoral process from colonial times to the present, this two-volume set consists of some 1,200 articles prepared by a team of 250 specialists. The source is especially useful for quick-reference information about little-known or fringe movements, such as the Greenback Party. In a review in *American Reference Books Annual* (1992, pp. 269–70), Carol Wheeler enthusiastically endorses the set: ". . . this new encyclopedia will be a welcome addition to reference collections because of the breadth of its coverage and the analysis and perspective provided by the historians, political scientists, and other scholars who have contributed entries. In addition to being easy to use, it is also fascinating to read." Complementary sources are Peter Renstrom and Chester Rogers's *Electoral Politics Dictionary* (ABC-Clio, 1989); Michael Young's *American Dictionary of Campaigns and Elections* (Hamilton Press, 1987); and Earl Kruschke's *Encyclopedia of Third Parties in the United States* (ABC-Clio, 1991), all one-volume works.

World Encyclopedia of Peace. Edited by Ervin Laszlo & Jong Youl Yoo. Pergamon Press, 1986. 4 vols. $530.00.

Intended for "all men and women who question the dominant logic of doomsday and search for new avenues of peace and understanding among peoples and states" (preface), this unique, sometimes proselytizing encyclopedia deals with crucial issues affecting international relations as well as prominent people who have been involved one way or another in the pursuit of world peace. The first two volumes contain substantial articles—"Aggression," "Conscientious Objection," "Eco-Technology," "Global Families," "Military-Industrial Complex," "Nuclear Winter," "Revolution," and "Terrorism" are examples—written by political scientists and other scholars, mostly from the U.S. and Western Europe. Volume 3 includes the text of 39 treaties concerned with arms control and limiting war among nations,

a chronology of the peace movement from 1815 to 1983, and biographies of all Nobel Peace Prize winners through 1985. The final volume contains subject and name indexes along with a list of contributors, a bibliography, and a directory of organizations devoted to peace. "The worth of this set rests principally with the first two volumes of encyclopedic articles. These provide a valuable overview and analysis of the persons, events, and philosophies involved in the search for peace" (*American Reference Books Annual*, 1988, p. 299). A complementary work is the three-volume ENCYCLOPEDIA OF ARMS CONTROL AND DISARMAMENT.

World Encyclopedia of Political Systems & Parties. Edited by George E. Delury. 2nd ed. Facts on File, 1987. 2 vols. $175.00.

This informative encyclopedia, first published in 1983 and revised four years later, profiles the present-day political scene in more than 175 countries and territories. Area specialists describe the electoral system and major political parties, institutions, and forces in each state, including a summary assessment of the nation's political future. A new edition is said to be in-progress. "This second edition [1987] has been thoroughly updated and considerably improved. More than sixty new contributors have been added, including a number of prominent academics" (*American Reference Books Annual*, 1988, p. 275). Several authoritative sources complement the *World Encyclopedia of Political Systems & Parties*; they are the two-volume POLITICAL PARTIES AND ELECTIONS IN THE UNITED STATES and single-volume *Political Parties of the Americas and the Caribbean: A Reference Guide* (Longman, dist. by Gale, 1992) and *Political Parties of Asia and the Pacific: A Reference Guide* (Longman, dist. by Gale, 1992).

❋ PSYCHOLOGY, PSYCHIATRY, AND PARAPSYCHOLOGY ❋

The Columbia University College of Physicians and Surgeons Complete Home Guide to Mental Health. Edited by Frederic I. Kass & others. Holt, 1992. 640p. $35.00.

Written in reasonably plain, nontechnical language, this encyclopedic guide for laypeople covers the essentials of mental health, including common problems and disorders, assessment techniques, and various treatments. Some 50 experts contributed to the book. "Authoritative yet accessible, the material defines what constitutes various types of mental illness and explains treatment options in a clear, no-nonsense fashion that will help readers determine whether a problem exists and whether it necessitates a visit to a therapist. Introductory chapters

take the terror out of seeking professional counseling by clearly defining the roles of the mental health specialists and summarizing what practitioners do" (*Booklist*, November 15, 1992, p. 569). Comparable reference sources are Frank Bruno's FAMILY MENTAL HEALTH ENCYCLOPEDIA and the recently published ENCYCLOPEDIA OF MENTAL HEALTH.

Dictionary of Concepts in General Psychology. Written by John A. Popplestone & Marion White McPherson. Greenwood, 1988. 380p. $75.00.

Popplestone and McPherson explain 65 broad concepts central to the field of psychology, such as androgyny, behavior, effect, environment, and response. The articles, which average about five pages in length, discuss each concept's origin and historical development as well as current status and specialized applications by particular schools or psychologists. Numerous cross-references and citations to important publications are included. "The dictionary's feature of concept grouping is particularly noteworthy. For example, 'androgyny' is defined in conjunction with masculinity and femininity. . . . Related words are thus perceived more clearly through association" (*Choice*, April 1989, p. 1311). A similar source is Frank Bruno's 275-page *Dictionary of Key Words in Psychology* (Routledge, 1986), which covers many more concepts (260 versus 65) but in much less detail.

The Dictionary of Dreams: 10,000 Dreams Interpreted. Written by Gustavus Hindman Miller. 1901; reprinted by Prentice-Hall, 1985. 636p. $11.00 paperbound.

First published in 1901 as *What's in a Dream?*, this durable reference work has been reprinted a number of times over the years under various titles, including *Ten Thousand Dreams Interpreted* and most recently the *Dictionary of Dreams*. The subjects of dreams—flying, falling, climbing, etc.—are covered A-to-Z. "Interpretations do not take into account the dream theories of psychology and psychoanalysis, and the language may seem old-fashioned, but the publishing history of this title indicates the enduring interest people have in dreams and the ready market for dream books" (*Reference Books Bulletin* in *Booklist*, June 1, 1985, p. 1377). Interested consumers will also want to check out Rosemary Ellen Guiley's new *Encyclopedia of Dreams: Symbols and Interpretations* (Crossroad, 1993), a heavily illustrated book of 260 pages.

A Dictionary of Superstitions. Edited by Iona Opie & Moira Tatem. Oxford Univ. Press, 1989. 494p. $35.00 hardcover; $13.95 paperbound.

Both informative and entertaining, this authoritative reference work describes more than 1,500 strange beliefs and customs, from talking to magpies to bowing to the moon. Emphasis is on superstitions that originated in Great Britain and Ireland, but many will be familiar to North Americans. "The extensive cross-reference system and analytical index are essential to this genre of reference work. In this case, they contribute not just to its usefulness but indeed are part of its fabric, and they are well executed. All libraries will want this book" (*Choice*, March 1990, p. 1110). Two complementary works are Sophie Lasne and Andre Gaultier's *Dictionary of Superstitions* (Prentice-Hall, 1984) and Edwin and

Mona Radford's *Encyclopedia of Superstitions* (Philosophical Library, 1949; reprinted by Greenwood, 1969).

The Encyclopedia of Ghosts and Spirits. Written by Rosemary Ellen Guiley. Facts on File, 1992. 374p. $40.00; $19.95 paperbound.

Guiley—author of a number of reference books on parapsychological subjects, including the *Encyclopedia of Dreams: Symbols and Interpretations* (Crossroad, 1993), *Harper's Encyclopedia of Mystical and Paranormal Experience* (HarperCollins, 1991), and the ENCYCLOPEDIA OF WITCHES AND WITCHCRAFT—tries hard to be objective in this encyclopedia of apparitions and related subjects. The book consists of approximately 400 articles ranging in length from a few sentences to several pages. Topics covered include famous ghosts, mediums, organizations, festivals, etc. "Guiley attempts to present both skeptical and believing viewpoints. If more is presented on the side of believers, this perhaps reflects the fact that the literature itself is more highly weighted in that direction. The entries are generally accurate, concise, and clear" (*Choice*, December 1992, p. 601). Cathy Chauvette, who reviewed Guiley's encyclopedia in *School Library Journal* (June 1993, p. 145), also commends the book: "This is one of those rare miracles—a reference book that is also a terrific read." Competing titles are Daniel Cohen's *Encyclopedia of Ghosts* (Dodd, Mead, 1984; published in paper by Avon in 1992) and Peter Haining's *Dictionary of Ghost Lore* (Prentice-Hall, 1984), both single-volume works.

The Encyclopedia of Mental Health. Written by Ada P. Kahn & Jan Fawcett. Facts on File, 1993. 464p. $45.00.

Similar in concept, coverage, and size to the COLUMBIA UNIVERSITY COLLEGE OF PHYSICIANS AND SURGEONS COMPLETE HOME GUIDE TO MENTAL HEALTH and BRUNO'S FAMILY MENTAL HEALTH ENCYCLOPEDIA, the alphabetically arranged *Encyclopedia of Mental Health* provides nontechnical explanations of basic mental health concepts, disorders, procedures, treatments, and the like. Entries vary in length from a few sentences to a page or two. The book concludes with a list of organizations and a selected bibliography for readers who wish to go beyond the encyclopedia. "In a similar work, *The Columbia University College of Physicians & Surgeons' Complete Home Guide to Mental Health*, concepts are explained not by entry but in chapters based upon broad subject areas. Both approaches are effective, and both books are excellent reference sources required by most library collections" (*Library Journal*, October 1993, p. 89).

Encyclopedia of Occultism & Parapsychology: A Compendium of Information on the Occult Sciences, Magic, Demonology, Superstitions, Spiritism, Mysticism, Metaphysics, Psychical Science, and Parapsychology, with Biographical and Bibliographical Notes and Comprehensive Indexes. Edited by Leslie Shepard. 3rd ed. Gale Research, 1991. 2 vols. $295.00.

Originally published in two volumes in 1978, then expanded to three volumes in 1984, and now back to two volumes as a result of a revision in 1991, this 2,008-page set comprises reworked articles that originally appeared in two older British encyclopedias—Lewis Spence's *Encyclopaedia of Occultism* (1920) and Nandor Fodor's *Encyclopaedia of Psychic Science* (1934)—and much new material added over the years by Shepard. In all, the encyclopedia today contains roughly 6,500 entries treating, as the subtitle suggests, all pertinent aspects of psychical phenomena. "This continues to be an excellent, wideranging source. . . . Highly recommended for its broad, inclusive coverage" (*American Reference Books Annual*, 1992, p. 302).

Other less extensive (and less expensive) reference sources on the subject—all one-volume works—are the *Dictionary of Mysticism and the Esoteric Traditions* (ABC-Clio, 1992) by Nevill Drury (a revision of the author's *Dictionary of Mysticism and the Occult*, published in 1985 by Harper); the *Donning International Encyclopedic Psychic Dictionary* (Donning, 1986) by June Bletzer; the *Encyclopedia of Parapsychology and Psychical Research* (Paragon House, 1991) by Arthur and Joyce Berger; the *Encyclopedia of the Unexplained* (McGraw-Hill, 1974; reprinted by Penguin in 1990 in paper), edited by Richard Cavendish; *Harper's Encyclopedia of Mystical & Paranormal Experience* (HarperCollins, 1991) by Rosemary Ellen Guiley; and Jerome Clark's recently published *Encyclopedia of Strange and Unexplained Physical Phenomena* (Gale Research, 1993).

The Encyclopedia of Phobias, Fears, and Anxieties. Written by Ronald M. Doctor & Ada P. Kahn. Facts on File, 1989. 487p. $40.00.

Doctor and Kahn's encyclopedia offers comprehensive A-to-Z coverage of major phobias and similar psychological apprehensions, including their history, diagnosis, treatment, and nomenclature (both common and medical names are given). "As the only book to bring so much of the literature on phobias together in one place, this volume is recommended for health science collections, college and university reference collections, and public libraries" (*Choice*, March 1990, p. 1110).

Encyclopedia of Psychology. Edited by Raymond J. Corsini & Bonnie D. Ozaki. 2nd ed. Wiley, 1994. 4 vols. $475.00.

Standing between the much larger 12-volume INTERNATIONAL ENCYCLOPEDIA OF PSYCHIATRY, PSYCHOLOGY, PSYCHOANALYSIS, AND NEUROLOGY and the single-volume ENCYCLOPEDIC DICTIONARY OF PSYCHOLOGY, this four-volume set—first published in 1984 and revised in 1994—contains more than 2,100 alphabetically arranged articles prepared by some 500 experts in the field. The articles, which are found in the first three volumes, cover every major area of psychology. They are comprehensive, reliable, admirably current, and written for the "average intelligent layman" (preface). The final volume includes an impressive bibliography and name and subject indexes. James Rettig, in a review of the first edition in *Wilson Library Bulletin* (November 1984, p. 226), warmly endorses the set: "A must purchase for academic libraries, this authoritative, encyclopedic exposition of psychologists, theories, tests, and applications of psychology will also find favor in public libraries."

For those who cannot afford the four-volume set, currently priced at $475.00, the publisher offers a single-volume abridgment of the first edition entitled the *Concise Encyclopedia of Psychology* at $99.95. Edited by Raymond Corsini and published in 1987, this 1,242-page book includes every entry (in condensed form) found in the 1984 edition; presumably a similar condensation of the 1994 edition will eventually appear. Finally, do not confuse either of these two works with the much older and now largely superseded one-volume *Encyclopedia of Psychology* (2nd ed. Continuum, 1979), edited by H.J. Eysenck.

The Encyclopedia of Schizophrenia and the Psychotic Disorders. Written by Richard Noll. Facts on File, 1992. 374p. $45.00.

Noll, a clinical psychologist who specializes in schizophrenia and related maladies, covers all significant aspects of this perplexing disease. Among the 600 or so entries are various theories, therapies, and people associated with schizophrenia historically and medically. The encyclopedia, which is written in nontechnical language, "provides an outstanding overview of this disturbing condition for a wide range of readers. It is an excellent addition to public, academic, and health sciences collections" (*Reference Books Bulletin* in *Booklist*, April 1, 1992, p. 1472). A similar one-volume work covering an equally difficult mental condition is Roberta Roesch's *Encyclopedia of Depression* (Facts on File, 1991).

Encyclopedia of Sleep and Dreaming. Edited by Mary A. Carskadon. Macmillan, 1993. 703p. $105.00.

New in 1993, this excellent single-volume encyclopedia provides multidisciplinary coverage of sleep, dreaming, insomnia, narcolepsy, and related topics. By way of example, its 410 articles include "Aboriginal dreaming," "Amnesia," "Caffeine," "Freud's dream theory," "Hypernychthemeral syndrome," "Metabolic control of REM sleep," "Night sweats," and "Sleeping pills." The articles are up-to-date, clearly written, and authoritative, the work of specialists in the field. "Each entry contains characteristics that make it a beacon for other encyclopedias: clear definitions written and signed by experts, descriptions of current research, references to further reading, and an occasional figure illustrating research results" (*Choice*, September 1993, p. 80). Interested consumers will also want to check out the *Encyclopedia of Sleep and Sleep Disorders* (Facts on File, 1991). Written by Michael Thorpy and Jan Yager, this 298-page book lacks the depth of Carskadon's work but is considerably less expensive ($45.00 versus $105.00).

The Encyclopedia of Suicide. Written by Glen Evans & Norman L. Farberow. Facts on File, 1988. 434p. $45.00.

Intended for students and professionals as well as laypeople, this unique specialized encyclopedia brings together much valuable information about suicide culled from a number of disciplines, including psychology, sociology, literature, and the law. The book consists of more than 500 entries, which run from a few lines to a few pages in length. "While no reference can be truly exhaustive or free from editorial orientations and interests, the encyclopedia makes a good start towards integrating facts, data, and theories about self-destructive behavior" (*American Reference Books Annual*, 1989, p. 613).

The Encyclopedia of Witches and Witchcraft. Written by Rosemary Ellen Guiley. Facts on File, 1989. 421p. $45.00 hardcover; $19.95 paperbound.

This useful encyclopedia describes the beliefs, practices, organizations, and language of witches, both ancient and modern. Especially valuable are the articles on various witch trials in Europe and North America and the biographical sketches of famous witches (Margot Adler, Isaac Bonewits, Janet and Stewart Farrar, Selena Fox, Gerald Gardner, et al). "Although written with a positive bias towards witchcraft and neopaganism and a negative view towards satanism, the comprehensive coverage of

terminology, biography, and history makes this work an important addition to the reference works available on the topic" (*Reference Books Bulletin* in *Booklist*, November 1, 1989, p. 604). An older but still relevant book that nicely complements Guiley's encyclopedia is Rossell Robbins's 576-page *Encyclopedia of Witchcraft and Demonology* (Crown, 1959), which remains in print in an inexpensive paperback edition.

The Encyclopedic Dictionary of Psychology. Edited by Rom Harre & Roger Lamb. MIT Press, 1983. 718p. $95.00.

A superlative single-volume source of basic information about psychology and its major subdisciplines, the *Encyclopedic Dictionary of Psychology* contains approximately 1,300 entries, some of them quite lengthy. The text tends to be scholarly but will be intelligible to most interested laypeople and serious students. The work of more than 250 authorities, the volume has been universally praised by critics; this excerpt from a review in *Library Journal* (February 15, 1984, p. 366) is typical: "The craftsmanship of the editorial effort along with the work's currency and comprehensiveness make this an outstanding reference work for special and general collections."

A complementary work is the *Concise Encyclopedia of Psychology* (Wiley, 1987), the aforementioned one-volume abridgment of the four-volume ENCYCLOPEDIA OF PSYCHOLOGY. Other one-volume psychology encyclopedias are less than satisfactory; for instance, Eysenck's *Encyclopedia of Psychology* (2nd ed. Continuum, 1979) is now quite dated and the *Baker Encyclopedia of Psychology* (Baker Book House, 1985) limits itself to "the Christian perspective" (preface). Finally, do not confuse Harre and Lamb's *Encyclopedic Dictionary of Psychology* with a smaller, much inferior work of the same title edited by Terry F. Pettijohn and published by Dushkin Publishing Company (4th ed., 1991).

The Family Mental Health Encyclopedia. Written by Frank J. Bruno. Wiley, 1989. 422p. $24.95 hardcover; $14.95 paperbound.

Like the COLUMBIA UNIVERSITY COLLEGE OF PHYSICIANS AND SURGEONS COMPLETE GUIDE TO MENTAL HEALTH and Kahn and Fawcett's ENCYCLOPEDIA OF MENTAL HEALTH, this single-volume encyclopedia furnishes clear, reliable, and up-to-date information about mental health for the layperson. Bruno, a psychology professor at San Bernadino Valley College in California, covers roughly 700 topics, including major concepts, theories, illnesses, treatments, and people who have made significant contributions to the mental health field. "Aimed at

The Encyclopaedia of Islam. New edition. E.J. Brill, 1954–. 12 vols. (in progress). $2,300.00 (first 7 vols.).

The projected 12-volume new edition of the *Encyclopaedia of Islam* has been in progress for 40 years. It is obviously an ambitious work of formidable dimensions. The goal is a scholarly synthesis of every important facet of Islamic life, including religious, historical, geopolitical, cultural, ethnographic, and legal developments. Contributors are internationally recognized authorities from the Middle East, Europe, and North America. To date, seven volumes (each about 1,200 pages in length) have been completed; the publisher, E.J. Brill of the Netherlands, hopes to have the remaining five volumes finished within the next 10 years or so. In a review of volumes 2 and 5 in *American Reference Books Annual* (1987, pp. 66–67), Ellen Broidy provides a knowledgeable interim assessment of the project: "*The Encyclopaedia of Islam* is an invaluable resource, well worth the time and effort required to master whatever linguistic difficulties it might present. The articles, even those simply providing brief dictionary-like definitions, are works of scholarship . . . . the *Encyclopaedia of Islam* (new edition) is a landmark publication, a most worthy successor to the earlier *Encyclopaedia of Islam.*"

Interested consumers should also know that the first edition of the encyclopedia, published by Brill between 1913 and 1936, is currently available in a nine-volume paperback reprint edition under the title *E.J. Brill's First Encyclopaedia of Islam, 1913–1936* (E.J. Brill, 1993). This work—correctly promoted by the publisher as "the only complete reference work on Islam now available" (until the New Edition is completed)—contains roughly 5 million words, 5,000 pages, and 9,000 alphabetically arranged articles; it is priced at $485.75.

In addition, two comparatively inexpensive single-volume encyclopedias on Islam are available: the *Shorter Encyclopaedia of Islam* (E.J. Brill, 1953; reprinted 1991), edited by H.A.R Gibb and J.H. Kramers and priced at $63.00, consists mainly of articles on Islamic religion and law derived from the first edition of the *Encyclopaedia of Islam*; and the more recent *Concise Encyclopedia of Islam* (HarperCollins, 1989; $48.00) by Cyril Glasse, which covers various aspects of Islamic religion and customs in approximately 1,200 brief entries. Finally, the two-volume *Muslim Peoples: A World Ethnographic Survey* (2nd ed. Greenwood, 1984; edited by Richard V. Weekes) provides a comprehensive overview of nearly 200 contemporary Islamic ethnic groups around the world, and the single-volume *Islam and Islamic Groups: A Worldwide Reference Guide* (Longman, dist. by Gale Research, 1992; edited by Farzana Shaikh) describes major Islamic political groups.

The Encyclopedia of Native American Religions: An Introduction. Written by Arlene Hirschfelder & Paulette Molin. Facts on File, 1992. 367p. $45.00

This first (and thus far only) encyclopedic treatment of the religious beliefs and ceremonies of Native Americans includes information about key terminology, important sacred sites, specific practices and rituals, landmark court cases, and biographies of religious leaders and Christian missionaries. In all, the encyclopedia has 1,200 concise A-to-Z entries. "This encyclopedia is quite readable and informative. It will be useful in any high school that has a religion curriculum or studies native American culture. Most academic and public libraries should consider it for their collections" (*Reference Books Bulletin* in *Booklist*, May 15, 1992, p. 1716). A complementary work is the excellent 425-page *Dictionary of Native American Mythology* (ABC-Clio, 1992) by Sam Gill and Irene Sullivan.

Encyclopedia of Philosophy. Edited by Paul Edwards. Free Press (dist. by Macmillan), 1967. 8 vols.; reprinted in 1973 in 4 vols. $425.00.

The premier reference work in the field, this outstanding subject encyclopedia treats philosophy (both Eastern and Western) from ancient to modern times. The set consists of nearly 1,500 signed articles prepared by 500 expert contributors from 24 countries. While the text is scholarly, serious students and laypeople will normally find it comprehensible. All major topics and concerns are covered, including the lives and theories of approximately 900 prominent philosophers. Some unexpected articles—"If," "Nothing," and "Popular Arguments for the Existence of God" are examples—add range, depth, and intellectual excitement to the encyclopedia. The final volume contains a detailed name and subject index of some 40,000 entries. Smaller works that furnish encyclopedic information about particular areas of philosophy are the two-volume *Handbook of Metaphysics and Ontology* (Philosophia; dist. by Books International, 1991), edited by Hans Burkhardt and Barry Smith; the *Companion to Epistemology* (Blackwell, 1992), edited by Jonathan Dancy and Ernest Sosa; the *Handbook of World Philosophy: Contemporary Developments since 1945* (Greenwood, 1980), edited by John Burr.

The Encyclopedia of Religion. Edited by Mircea Eliade. Macmillan, 1986. 16 vols. $1,400.00; reprinted in 1993 in 8 vols. $600.00.

One of the most impressive multivolume subject encyclopedias currently available, the *Encyclopedia of Religion* treats the history, beliefs, practices, themes, symbols, and personalities of the world's major and minor religions, both past and present. The set contains approximately 8 million words and 2,750 articles written by 1,400 recognized authorities from many countries. The editor-in-chief—the late Mircea Eliade, a renowned historian of religious ideas who died in 1986 just as the encyclopedia was being issued—and his colleagues have imbued the work with an intellectuality and vision rarely found in modern reference publications. Intended for both the specialist and educated general reader, the set supplants James Hastings's old *Encyclopaedia of Religion and Ethics* (a 13-volume work published by Scribner's between 1907–27) as the standard multivolume encyclopedia in the field. "The advent of the *Encyclopedia of Religion* is truly an exciting event. It will, of course, like Hastings before it, fulfill the typical purposes of a specialized encyclopedia for a generation or more. But, like few other reference works, it will also challenge its readers and broaden their intellectual horizons" (*Wilson Library Bulletin*, September 1987, p. 90). Note that in 1993 the publisher issued the entire set (unrevised) in eight volumes at the attractive price of $600.00.

Encyclopedia of Religion in the South. Edited by Samuel S. Hill. Mercer Univ. Press, 1984. 878p. $45.00.

The longest articles in this useful single-volume encyclopedia are devoted to the religious heritage and institutions of 16 U.S. states—those that made up the old Confederacy plus Kentucky, Maryland, Missouri, Oklahoma, and West Virginia. Briefer articles cover denominations, movements, doctrines, organizations, events, and individuals identified with some aspect of religion in the American South. The volume is "an impressive overview of religion in the southern U.S. from the colonial period to the present" (*Reference Books Bulletin* in *Booklist*, June 15, 1985, pp. 1441–42). The excellent one-volume *Dictionary of Pentecostal and Charismatic Movements* (Zondervan, 1989), edited by Stanley Burgess and others, also contains much information about religious activity in the South.

Encyclopedia of the American Religious Experience: Studies of Traditions and Movements. Edited by Charles H. Lippy & Peter W. Williams. Scribner's, 1988. 3 vols. $259.00.

Aimed mainly at the serious student and layperson (as opposed to the scholar), this three-volume encyclopedia comprises 105 original, topically arranged essays covering the main currents of religious experience in the U.S. (and to some extent Canada) from earliest times to the present day. The essays, which average 12 pages in length, deal with broad topics and themes, such as "Church and State," "The History of Preaching," "Ethnicity and Religion," "The Roman Catholic Heritage," "The Psychology of Religious Experience," and "The Great Awakening." The set boasts a fine index and effective cross-referencing throughout. "An outstanding achievement, this three-volume work will become the standard reference tool in American religion" (*Choice*, May 1988, p. 1380). Complementary sources are the ENCYCLOPEDIA OF AMERICAN RELIGIONS and the DICTIONARY OF CHRISTIANITY IN AMERICA.

Encyclopedia of the Early Church. Edited by Angelo Di Berardino. Oxford Univ. Press, 1992. 2 vols. $175.00.

Translated from the Italian *Dizionàrio Patrìstico e di Antichità Cristiane* published between 1983 and 1988, the scholarly *Encyclopedia of the Early Church* provides detailed information about the first eight centuries of Christianity, including the people, institutions, events, places, ideas, doctrines, issues, and heresies involved in the Church's formative period. Altogether, the two-volume set presents approximately 2,300 entries prepared by an international team of scholars working under the auspices of the prestigious Institutum Patristicum Augustinianum in Rome. The encyclopedia "is attractive in format, solidly bound, comprehensive and rich in content, and highly recommended for libraries" (*American Reference Books Annual*, 1993, p. 591). Less formidable and hence generally more useful for students and nonspecialists is the single-volume *Encyclopedia of Early Christianity* (Garland, 1990), edited by Everett Ferguson. Those seriously interested in the history of the early Christian Church will also want to look into the COPTIC ENCYCLOPEDIA.

The Encyclopedia of Unbelief. Edited by Gordon Stein. Prometheus Books, 1985. 2 vols. $99.95.

From the disarming foreword by Paul Edwards (editor of the ENCYCLOPEDIA OF PHILOSOPHY) to the several appendixes (which include a list of some 500 "Periodicals of Unbelief ?"), this valuable encyclopedia covers intellectual and religious skepticism in all its manifestations, from rationalism to agnosticism to atheism. It consists of more than 200 meaty articles by prominent authorities. Some articles, such as "Existentialism and Unbelief" and "Conjuring and Unbelief in the Supernatural," offer information not found in other standard reference sources. In a thoughtful review in *American Reference Books Annual* (1987, p. 296), Norman Stevens sums up his impressions this way: "This work is not designed as aggressive propaganda but it clearly does advance a particular position. Its articles not only provide historical and other factual information but analyze ideas and, in doing so, present a particular carefully reasoned point of view. This is a challenging work that deserves recognition and use; it may be rejected, without good reason, for its viewpoint." A much less substantial but nevertheless useful work on the subject is the 160-page *Encyclopedia of Heresies and Heretics* (ABC-Clio, 1992) by Chas S. Clifton.

The Facts on File Encyclopedia of World Mythology and Legend. Written by Anthony S. Mercatante. Facts on File, 1988. 807p. $95.00.

Intended to cover "the entire range of world mythology and legend from the ancient Near East to present-day voodoo" (introduction), Mercatante's encyclopedia consists of over 3,200 brief entries enhanced by some 450 black-and-white line drawings. The author not only describes mythic and folkloric figures and the legends associated with them but furnishes references to works of art, music, literature, and film that have drawn on or been influenced by such characters and legends, e.g., George Bernard Shaw's play *Pygmalion*. "Because of the way it gathers such a wealth of information into a single source, *The Facts On File Encyclopedia of World Mythology and Legend* is a useful ready-reference tool for most libraries" (*Reference Books Bulletin* in *Booklist*, January 15, 1989, p. 849).

Numerous other one-volume encyclopedias of mythology are available; among the best are Robert Bell's *Dictionary of Classical Mythology: Symbols, Attributes & Associations* (ABC-Clio, 1982); Pierre Grimal's *Dictionary of Classical Mythology* (Blackwell, 1986); Arthur Cotterell's *Dictionary of World Mythology* (Putnam, 1980; reprinted by Oxford Univ. Press in paper in 1990); and Marjorie Leach's GUIDE TO THE GODS. Also still useful is the old *Funk & Wagnalls Standard Dictionary of Folklore, Mythology, and Legends*, which originally appeared under the Funk & Wagnall imprint in two volumes between 1949 and 1956 and is now available in a single-volume paper reprint edition issued by HarperCollins in 1984.

Guide to the Gods. Written by Marjorie Leach. ABC-Clio, 1992. 995p. $150.00.

Devoted to all types of gods, goddesses, and lesser divinities found in cultures around the world from antiquity to the present, Leach's *Guide to the Gods* identifies and briefly describes more than 20,000 deities, which are grouped by attributes and functions, such as fertility, justice, war, and animals.

"Although there are a number of reference dictionaries and encyclopedias on mythology, this volume uses a unique approach. It is not limited to a specific culture or time period. Greek, Norse, and other Western deities mingle with those of Asia, Africa, Polynesia, and the Americas in a single, accessible source" (*Reference Books Bulletin* in *Booklist*, March 15, 1992, p. 1402). Comparable sources are Manfred Lurker's *Dictionary of Gods and Goddesses, Devils and Demons* (Routledge, 1987); Richard Carlyon's *Guide to the Gods* (Morrow, 1982); Anne Baumgartner's *Ye Gods: A Dictionary of the Gods* (Lyle Stuart, 1984); and Michael Jordan's recently published *Encyclopedia of Gods: Over 2500 Deities of the World* (Facts on File, 1993).

Harper's Bible Dictionary. Edited by Paul J. Achtemeier. HarperCollins, 1985. 1,178p. $39.00.

New in 1985, this excellent encyclopedic Bible dictionary replaces various editions published under the same title since 1952. *Harper's Bible Dictionary* is a nonsectarian work that draws all of its 179 contributors from the Society of Biblical Literature, a highly respected professional association of Bible scholars representing the spectrum of thought within the Judeo-Christian tradition. The volume, which is both authoritative and readable, contains 3,700 concise A-to-Z entries covering all important people, places, events, customs, flora and fauna, words, ideas, and themes found in the Bible; it also provides an outline for each book of the Bible. "Clearly and copiously illustrated with color and black-and-white photographs, maps, and drawings, this splendid volume presents a balanced summary of current biblical scholarship accessible to the general reader, and belongs in every reference collection" (*Library Journal*, January 1986, p. 72).

Many competing one-volume Bible dictionaries exist, with most showing a distinct bias toward a particular denomination or theological position; those closest in quality (if not impartiality) to *Harper's Bible Dictionary* are the *Dictionary of Bible and Religion* (Abingdon, 1986), edited by William Genz; *Eerdmans Bible Dictionary* (Eerdmans, 1987), edited by Allen Meyers; the *Holman Bible Dictionary* (Holman, 1991); the *Mercer Dictionary of the Bible* (Mercer Univ. Press, 1990), edited by Watson Mills and others; the *New Unger's Bible Dictionary* (Revised ed. Moody, 1988); and *Revell's Bible Dictionary* (Revell, 1990), edited by Lawrence Richards. A new entry is the excellent *Oxford Companion to the Bible* (Oxford Univ. Press, 1993); edited by Bruce M. Metzger and Michael D. Coogan, this 900-page dictionary is not as comprehensive as *Harper's Bible*

Dictionary, but it does contain unique material and is nondenominational in approach.

Harper's Encyclopedia of Religious Education. Edited by Iris V. Cully & Kendig Brubaker. HarperCollins, 1990. 717p. $34.95.

Prepared by 270 scholars from the fields of religion, education, history, and psychology, this well-constructed encyclopedia contains over 600 alphabetically arranged, signed articles intended especially for use by religious educators. Emphasis is on Christianity and Judaism but other religions, such as Buddhism and Islam, receive some attention. Articles cover such topics as adolescence, character development, child development, love, maturation, myths, Rosh Hashana, spirituality, and worship, as well as biographies of such thinkers as Erik Erikson and Jean Piaget. "Recommended for public libraries and for academic libraries supporting a curriculum in religious education" (*Choice*, October 1990, p. 283).

The International Standard Bible Encyclopedia. Edited by Geoffrey W. Bromiley & others. Revised ed. Eerdmans, 1979–88. 4 vols. $159.80.

An outstanding work of conservative evangelical Christian scholarship, this four-volume encyclopedia first appeared in 1915 and was revised in 1929 and most recently between 1979 and 1988. The latest edition, which is based on the Revised Standard Version of the Bible, represents a complete rewriting of the encyclopedia, plus the addition of much new illustrative material, including photographs, color plates, and maps. The set—intended principally for Bible scholars, ministers, and interested laypeople—covers all persons and places mentioned in the Bible along with doctrines and practices based on biblical teaching. Important biblical terms are also treated; definitions include Greek or Hebrew origins and other pertinent historical and textual information. "Students, pastors, and researchers engaged in serious study will want to begin with the new *ISBE*; devoted students of the Bible selecting only one research aid of any kind, whether it be a dictionary, concordance, encyclopedia, or commentary, should choose the new *ISBE*" (*American Reference Books Annual*, 1989, p. 527).

Numerous other fine Bible encyclopedias are available, including the excellent new ANCHOR BIBLE DICTIONARY (which represents the latest scholarship), the INTERPRETER'S DICTIONARY OF THE BIBLE, HARPER'S BIBLE DICTIONARY, the five-volume *Zondervan Pictorial Encyclopedia of the Bible* (Zondervan, 1974), the three-volume *Illustrated Bible Dictionary* (Tyndale House, 1980), and the two-volume *Baker Encyclopedia of the Bible* (Baker Book House, 1988).

The Interpreter's Dictionary of the Bible: An Illustrated Encyclopedia Identifying and Explaining All Proper Names and Significant Terms and Subjects in the Holy Scriptures, including the Apocrypha, with Attention to Archaeological Discoveries and Researches into the Life and Faith of Ancient Times. Edited by George Arthur Buttrick. Abingdon, 1962. 4 vols. plus suppl., 1976; set reprinted 1976 in 5 vols. $179.95.

Like the ANCHOR BIBLE DICTIONARY and the INTERNATIONAL STANDARD BIBLE the *Interpreter's Dictionary of the Bible* furnishes an authoritative and comprehensive multivolume survey of the Bible and its text—in this case the King James Version and the Revised Standard Version. The set, which is a cut down version of the *Interpreter's Bible* (a 12-volume work published by Abingdon between 1951 and 1957), first appeared in 1962 in four volumes. A supplementary volume was later added and the original four volumes plus supplement were reprinted as a five-volume set in 1976. Without doubt, the *Interpreter's Dictionary of the Bible* is indispensable for study of the scriptures, but its luster has been reduced somewhat by publication of the aforementioned ANCHOR BIBLE DICTIONARY, which now represents contemporary Bible scholarship much the same way the *Interpreter's Dictionary* did a generation ago.

New Age Encyclopedia: A Guide to the Beliefs, Concepts, Terms, People, and Organizations that Make Up the New Global Movement Toward Spiritual Development, Health and Healing, Higher Consciousness, and Related Subjects. Written by J. Gordon Melton & others. Gale Research, 1990. 586p. $59.50.

This encyclopedia, whose contents are more than adequately described by its lengthy subtitle, is another reference publication in the field of religion featuring the work of Gordon Melton, the foremost chronicler of religious movements in North America. Authoritative, interesting, objective, and well-written, the encyclopedia consists of more than 300 detailed entries plus a master index that makes even the smaller facts readily accessible. James Rettig in *Wilson Library Bulletin* (October 1990, p. 131) recommends the book as "a convenient, unique source of information on movements that one can usually learn about only through alternative press publications rarely collected by libraries. This, then, will be immediately useful to those curious about crystals, fruitarianism, naturopathy, or a host of other New Age phenomena."

New Catholic Encyclopedia: An International Work of Reference on the Teachings, History,

Organization and Activities of the Catholic Church, and on All Institutions, Religions, Philosophies and Scientific and Cultural Developments affecting the Catholic Church from Its Beginning to the Present. Prepared by the Editorial Staff of the Catholic University of America. McGraw-Hill, 1967. 15 vols. plus 3 suppls. (1974, 1979, 1989). Reprinted by New Catholic Encyclopedia, Inc. (dist. by Jack Heraty & Associates, Inc.), 1981. $875.00 plus $45.00 shipping & handling (18 vols.).

Comprising approximately 17,000 articles by 6,200 contributors, accompanied by 7,400 illustrations and 300 maps, the multivolume *New Catholic Encyclopedia* is an excellent specialized encyclopedia, especially for historical information. Particularly noteworthy are the encyclopedia's high degree of scholarship, impartiality, and ecumenical spirit— contributors include many non-Catholics and represent specialists from such diverse fields as theology, philosophy, law, sociology, history, science, education, music, art, and literature. Volume 15 of the basic set furnishes an index of approximately 260,000 entries. Over the years, three single-volume supplements have been issued to help keep the set reasonably current, the most recent appearing in 1989.

The *New Catholic Encyclopedia* replaces the *Catholic Encyclopedia*, a venerable but now much out-of-date work of 18 volumes published by the Gilmary Society between 1907–14. Other smaller but still important reference works dealing with the Catholic faith are the three-volume *Encyclopedic Dictionary of Religion* (Catholic Univ. Press, 1979) and three single-volume titles: *The Catholic Encyclopedia* (Revised ed. Thomas Nelson, 1987), edited by Robert Broderick; the *New Dictionary of Theology* (Michael Glazier, 1987), edited by Joseph Komonchak and others; and the *Encyclopedia of Theology: The Concise Sacramentum Mundi* (Crossroad, 1975), edited by Karl Rahner and others.

The New Encyclopedia of Archaeological Excavations in the Holy Land. Edited by Ephraim Stern. Revised ed. Simon & Schuster, 1993. 4 vols. $355.00.

Originally published in 1975–78 by Prentice-Hall as the *Encyclopedia of Archaeological Excavations in the Holy Land,* this informative four-volume (1,600-page) encyclopedia describes and analyzes all significant archaeological work undertaken since the mid-nineteenth century in Palestine and present-day Israel. Entries are quite detailed and heavily illustrated, mostly with black-and-white photographs. Numerous authorities have contributed to the encyclopedia, which is a useful reference work for biblical archaeologists, religious scholars, serious students, and interested laypeople alike. Complementary sources, both one-volume works, are the *Archaeological Encyclopedia of the Holy Land* (3rd ed. Prentice Hall, 1990), edited by Avraham Negev, and the *New International Dictionary of Biblical Archaeology* (Zondervan, 1983), edited by Edward Blaiklock and R.K. Harrison.

New 20th-Century Encyclopedia of Religious Knowledge. Edited by J.D. Douglas. 2nd ed. Baker Book House, 1991. 896p. $39.95.

This encyclopedia, which views the world through evangelical Protestant eyes, first appeared in 1955 as the *Twentieth-Century Encyclopedia of Religious Knowledge.* That volume was intended as a supplement to the old (and now out-of-print) *New Schaff-Herzog Encyclopedia of Religious Knowledge* (Funk & Wagnalls, 1908–12), a multivolume set derived from a respected German encyclopedia of religion published in the nineteenth century. The *New 20th-Century Encyclopedia of Religious Knowledge* replaces and updates the 1955 edition. The volume contains roughly 2,100 articles covering religious issues, groups, and leaders prominent in this century. Many of the articles are new but some (mostly biographies) are reprinted from the earlier edition. *Reference Books Bulletin* (in *Booklist,* September 15, 1991) calls the encyclopedia "a useful ready-reference source on current and recent developments in religion. It can be recommended especially for public and academic libraries needing a work that emphasizes evangelical viewpoints and interests."

Oxford Dictionary of the Christian Church. Edited by Frank Leslie Cross & Elizabeth A. Livingstone. 2nd ed. Oxford Univ. Press, 1974. 1,518p. $65.00.

Originally published in 1957 and extensively revised in 1974, this valuable one-volume encyclopedia contains about 6,000 entries covering the major terms and names associated with Christianity, such as "Aggiornamento," "Coventry," "Ecumenical Movement," "Humanae Vitae," "Orthodox Church," "Process Theology," "Vatican Council, The Second," and "World Council of Churches." The volume is especially strong on biographies of Christian leaders. The publisher issued an abridged version of the dictionary in 1977 under the title *Concise Oxford Dictionary of the Christian Church;* edited by Elizabeth Livingston, it contains over 5,000 shortened entries in 576 pages and was reissued in a paperback edition in 1989.

The Westminster Dictionary of Christian Ethics. Edited by James F. Childress & John Macquarrie. Revised ed. Westminster, 1986. 704p. $34.95.

A revision of John Macquarrie's *Dictionary of Christian Ethics* (Westminster, 1967), this encyclopedic dictionary furnishes ecumenical treatment of a wide range of controversial religious and moral issues, including abortion, euthanasia, genetics, and scientific experimentation on humans. In addition, ethical concepts, principles, and schools are described and analyzed. In toto, the book contains 620 entries. It "is sufficiently jargon-free to be useful to most laypersons, and should emerge as a standard reference source for years to come" (*American Reference Books Annual*, 1987, pp. 528–29). A competing work is the 472-page *Encyclopedia of Biblical and Christian Ethics* (Revised ed. Thomas Nelson, 1992), edited by R.K. Harrison.

World Christian Encyclopedia: A Comparative Study of Churches and Religions in the Modern World, A.D. 1900–2000. Edited by David B. Barrett. Oxford Univ. Press, 1982. 1,010p. $195.00.

The *World Christian Encyclopedia* is an outstanding collection of information on Christianity and other world religions in 223 countries from 1900 to the present-day—and more. As James Rettig points out in a review in *Wilson Library Bulletin* (June 1982, p. 798), "If this were only a survey of the state of Christianity as professed by more than 1.4 billion believers through 20,800 denominations in over two hundred nations, it would be one of the monumental reference works of recent years. But it is far more than that—atlas, directory, dictionary, statistical abstract, bibliography, and who's who of twentieth-century Christianity." A second edition of the encyclopedia is said to be in progress, tentatively scheduled for completion in 1995; the new edition will expand to three volumes and offer much additional data on ethnic groups, languages, etc. Complementary sources are the DICTIONARY OF CHRISTIANITY IN AMERICA and the OXFORD DICTIONARY OF THE CHRISTIAN CHURCH.

❋ SCIENCE AND TECHNOLOGY (GENERAL) ❋

Album of Science. Edited by I. Bernard Cohen. Scribner's, 1978–1989. 5 vols. $395.00.

Encyclopedic in scope, this impressive pictorial history of science from earliest times to the present encompasses five titled volumes, each written by a distinguished authority: John E. Murdoch's *Antiquity and the Middle Ages* (1984); editor Cohen's *From Leonardo to Lavoisier, 1450–1800* (1980); L. Pearce Williams's *The Nineteenth Century* (1978); Merriley Borell's *Biological Sciences in the Twentieth Century* (1989); and Owen Gingerich's *Physical Sciences in the Twentieth Century* (1989). A review of the last two volumes in *Reference Books Bulletin* (in *Booklist*, January 1, 1990, p. 942) nicely describes the set: "Following the pattern of previous volumes, each chapter opens with a brief outline of major discoveries, principles, and participants in the field, followed by a collection of pictures. Each volume's approximately 400 photographs and drawings show scientists, scientific discoveries, manuscripts, and popular public images. Each picture is accompanied by a descriptive caption, but no other text. The black-and-white photographs are well chosen and will interest students and browsers."

Asimov's Chronology of Science and Discovery. Written by Isaac Asimov. HarperCollins, 1989. 707p. $29.95.

In this useful reference volume, the late Isaac Asimov, a prolific science writer for students and laypeople, summarizes approximately 1,450 notable scientific events and discoveries from 4 million B.C. through 1988, beginning with "Bipedality" and ending with "Greenhouse Effect." The chronologically arranged entries, which run in length from a few sentences to two pages, are readable and factually accurate. Competing one-volume works include *Breakthroughs: A Chronology of Great Achievements in Science and Mathematics, 1200–1930* (G.K. Hall, 1985) by Claire Parkinson; the *Chronology of the History of Science, 1450–1900* (Garland, 1987) by Robert Mortimer Gascoigne; *Milestones in Science and Technology: The Ready Reference Guide to Discoveries, Inventions, and Facts* (2nd ed. Oryx, 1993) by Ellis Mount and Barbara List; and *Timetables of Science: A Chronology of the Most Important People and Events in the History of Science* (Simon & Schuster, 1988) by Alexander Hellemans and Bryan Bunch.

The Cambridge Guide to the Material World. Written by Rodney Cotterill. Cambridge Univ. Press, 1984. 352p. $39.95.

This heavily and colorfully illustrated encyclopedic survey explains physical matter in its many guises, including ceramics, metals, glass, liquid crystals, minerals, water, and the living cell, as well as the atom. "The nonmathematical account provides access for people of many backgrounds to a wonderful picture of the world at the molecular level. This marvelous book should become a reference standard even though the index is too brief and the bibliography does not list page numbers. Highly recommended for all libraries" (*Choice*, July–August 1985, p. 1650).

Dictionary of Science & Creationism. Written by Ronald L. Ecker. Prometheus Books, 1990. 263p. $32.95.

Ecker's encyclopedic dictionary consists of short A-to-Z articles of one to three pages dealing with evolutionary theory and creation science—the latter holds that the Bible's account of the creation of the universe is scientifically valid. Ecker, an avowed anti-creationist, intends "to show the pseudoscientific nature of 'scientific' creationism" (preface), but he frequently refers to the Bible and writings by leading creationists, thus providing the reader with both sides of the issue. Coverage includes key terms used by both scientists (e.g., *fossil record; natural selection*) and creationists (*appearance of age; design argument*). "The dictionary is aimed at a nontechnical audience, and the complexities of evolutionary theory are generally well handled" (*Choice*, July–August 1990, p. 1804). "This *Dictionary* is recommended where a clear, well-documented statement of the pro-evolution position is needed. The *Dictionary* is appropriate for all levels of libraries, from high school through public and academic" (*Reference Books Bulletin* in *Booklist*, May 1, 1990, p. 1736).

Dictionary of the History of Science. Edited by William F. Bynum & others. Princeton Univ. Press, 1981. 494p. $75.00 hardcover; $17.95 paperbound.

Well produced and clearly written, this encyclopedia consists of some 700 alphabetically arranged articles that explore key developments in Western science during the past 500 years. Most articles are brief, but those dealing with major concepts (such as evolution or the Copernican revolution) are essay-length. "In this century, if not earlier, the natural and behavioral sciences have eclipsed the arts as the principal forces shaping our view of the world. This scholarly, high quality dictionary can help students, specialists, and laymen understand how those forces gained strength" (*Wilson Library Bulletin*, March 1982, p. 542). Complementary sources are David Knight's *Companion to the Physical Sciences* (Routledge, 1989) and Paul Durbin's *Dictionary of Concepts in the Philosophy of Science* (Greenwood, 1988), both single-volume works, and the two-volume *History of Science and Technology: A Narrative Chronology* (Facts on File, 1988).

Encyclopedia of Physical Science and Technology. Edited by Robert A. Meyers. 2nd ed. Academic Press, 1992. 18 vols. $2,500.00.

First published in 1987 in 15 volumes and expanded to 18 volumes in 1992, the *Encyclopedia of Physical Science and Technology* is a first-rate multivolume reference work intended for those with a strong science background, including advanced students, researchers, and working scientists. Major areas covered are chemistry, mathematics, physics, computer science and telecommunications, aeronautics, earth and environmental sciences, and nuclear technology. The second edition comprises more than 700 scholarly, peer-reviewed articles (up from 550 in the first edition), which range in length from 15 to 35 or more pages. The text is enhanced by numerous illustrations, tables, and figures throughout. As might be expected, the contributors are recognized authorities in their specialties. Since 1989 the publisher has issued a yearbook to the set that summarizes new advances in the physical sciences and technology. "The yearbook continues the excellence of the encyclopedia both in format and content" (*American Reference Books Annual*, 1990, p. 608). The only reference source comparable in size, scope, and quality to the *Encyclopedia of Physical Science and Technology* is the MCGRAW-HILL ENCYCLOPEDIA OF SCIENCE AND TECHNOLOGY, a 20-volume set aimed at a broader audience.

An Encyclopaedia of the History of Technology. Edited by Ian McNeil. Routledge, 1990. 1,062p. $79.95.

Prepared in Great Britain, this weighty volume sums up the history of technology from the Stone Age to the present in 22 sections, or chapters, covering such topics as architecture, construction materials, energy, transportation, communications, agriculture, and weapons. Approximately 300 drawings and 150 photographs complement the printed text. In a review in *Choice* (November 1990, p. 508), E.R. Webster says "the authors represented in this book are to be congratulated for their readable and reliable surveys of the past and present status of the major areas where mankind has harnessed science for the production of useful products and processes." A comparable (albeit much less extensive) encyclopedia is the 248-page *G.K. Hall Encyclopedia of Modern Technology* (G.K. Hall, 1987), edited by David Blackburn and Geoffrey Holister.

The Encyclopedic Dictionary of Science. Edited by Candida Hunt & Monica Byles. Facts on File, 1988. 256p. $35.00

More a mini-encyclopedia than a true dictionary, this handsomely illustrated volume explains some 7,000 basic concepts in such fields as chemistry, physics, biology, medicine, and the environmental sciences. It is aimed largely at school and college students and laypeople with an interest in and some rudimentary knowledge of scientific principles and vocabulary. Rashelle Karp, in an article on science reference sources for the nonspecialist in *Reference Books Bulletin* (in *Booklist*, February 15, 1992, p. 1122), recommends the book: "Full-page color illustrations for subjects most important for high school-level work (e.g., the ecosystem, digestion, plant evolution, hormones) and longer jargon-free explanations of technical terms will be useful to all." A competing work is the 352-page *Dictionary of Scientific Literacy* (Wiley, 1991) by Richard Brennan.

The Henry Holt Handbook of Current Science & Technology: A Sourcebook of Facts and Analysis Covering the Most Important Events in Science and Technology. Written by Bryan Bunch. Holt, 1992. 689p. $50.00.

The emphasis in Bunch's informative book is on current trends in the fields of astronomy and space science, chemistry, earth and environmental sciences, biology and the life sciences, mathematics, physics, and engineering. Bunch also includes a table of important historical events for each field, as well as predictions concerning future developments. "For its sheer volume and information content, this book may prove to be one of the outstanding science reference books of the year. Scientists, science writers, reference librarians, and anyone interested in current science and technology will find it a valuable addition to their work shelf" (*American Reference Books Annual*, 1993, p. 614). Two complementary sources (both single-volume works) are the *Almanac of Science and Technology: What's New and What's Known* (Harcourt Brace, 1990), edited by Richard Golob and Eric Brus, and *Asimov's New Guide to Science* (Basic Books, 1984) by Isaac Asimov.

The Kingfisher Science Encyclopedia. Edited by Catherine Headlam. CKG Publishers, 1993. 808p. $39.95; also published in 10 vols. in England by Grisewood & Dempsey Ltd. & distributed in North America by Encyclopaedia Britannica Educational Corp. at $299.00 plus $19.00 for shipping & handling.

The Kingfisher Science Encyclopedia—an attractive work for young students in the upper elementary and junior high school grades—contains approximately 1,000 alphabetically arranged entries covering all major areas of science, including astronomy, chemistry, earth science, electronics, life science, mathematics, physics, and technology. Also

among the entries are 200 simple science projects and experiments and biographies of 100 important scientists. More than 2,000 full-color illustrations accompany the 250,000-word text. Originally published in Great Britain in the early 1990s, the encyclopedia is available in a one-volume edition from CKG (Chambers Kingfisher Graham) at $39.95. It is also distributed to schools and libraries by Encyclopaedia Britannica Educational Corporation in 10 thin volumes of about 80 pages each. This set, which contains exactly the same text as the single-volume edition, sells for an expensive $299.00 plus $19.00 shipping and handling. Caveat emptor. Comparable works are the larger multivolume MACMILLAN ENCYCLOPEDIA OF SCIENCE and smaller *Dorling Kindersley Science Encyclopedia* (Dorling Kindersley, dist. by Houghton Mifflin, 1993), an authoritative and colorfully illustrated volume of 448 pages aimed principally at students in the upper elementary grades through high school.

Macmillan Encyclopedia of Science. Macmillan, 1991. 12 vols. $325.00.

The *Macmillan Encyclopedia of Science* is quite similar in purpose, appearance, intended usership, and reference value to the smaller KINGFISHER SCIENCE ENCYCLOPEDIA and larger RAINTREE ILLUSTRATED SCIENCE ENCYCLOPEDIA—all brightly illustrated basic science encyclopedias for young people originating in Great Britain. The *Macmillan Encyclopedia*, which has a total of 1,184 pages (as opposed to 808 for KINGFISHER and 2,160 for RAINTREE), is published in 12 topical volumes of approximately 128 pages each: *Matter and Energy, The Heavens, The Earth, Life on Earth, Plants and Animals, Body and Health, The Environment, Industry, Fuel and Power, Transportation, Communication,* and *Tools and Tomorrow.* The set will appeal mostly to students in junior high school, although motivated children in the elementary grades will find it useful, as will many high school students.

Reference Books Bulletin (in *Booklist*, October 15, 1991, p. 466) correctly calls the encyclopedia "an attractive and appealing reference for school and public libraries serving middle/junior high-age children." Another recently published work with comparable dimensions and features is the 12-volume *Grolier Encyclopedia of Science and Technology* (Grolier, 1993); this set, which contains about 700 alphabetically arranged entries in 1,200 pages, is comparably priced at $319.00.

McGraw-Hill Concise Encyclopedia of Science and Technology. Edited by Sybil P. Parker. 3rd ed. McGraw-Hill, 1994. 2,230p. $115.00.

A condensed version of the 20-volume seventh edition (1992) of the MCGRAW-HILL ENCYCLOPEDIA OF SCIENCE AND TECHNOLOGY, the *McGraw-Hill Concise Encyclopedia of Science and Technology* is a huge volume of over 2,000 pages containing 8,000 authoritative articles augmented by 1,700 photographs and line drawings. Easy to use (but not to handle), the encyclopedia provides an abundance of effective cross-references and a detailed index. It is designed for students at the high school level and beyond, as well as educated laypeople and working scientists.

The volume's chief competitor is VAN NOSTRAND'S SCIENCE ENCYCLOPEDIA, now in its seventh edition (1989) and recently expanded to two volumes. Harold Shane in *Library Journal* (August 1989, p. 124) offers a succinct comparison of the two works: "The *Van Nostrand* is two volumes, 3,180 pages, with 6,773 entries. The *McGraw-Hill* [2nd ed., 1989] is one volume, 2,222 pages, with 7700 entries at about half the price. Each has entries not in the other, but where they overlap, the coverage in the *Van Nostrand* is far more extensive. . . . Both are good references, but for ease of handling, greater depth of coverage, and more rigorous treatment of topics in mathematics and physics, if you must choose only one, take the *Van Nostrand*." Interested consumers should also know that the *McGraw-Hill Concise Encyclopedia* (2nd ed., 1989) is available electronically as part of the *McGraw-Hill Science and Technical Reference Set: Release 2.0* (Revised ed. McGraw-Hill, 1992), a CD-ROM product that also includes the *McGraw-Hill Dictionary of Scientific and Technical Terms*.

McGraw-Hill Encyclopedia of Science and Technology. Edited by Sybil P. Parker. 7th ed. McGraw-Hill, 1992. 20 vols. $1,900.00.

Unquestionably the single most important encyclopedia covering the entire spectrum of science and technology for older students and adults, this well-known and highly regarded set is now in its seventh edition (the first appeared in 1960). It contains well over seven million words, 13,450 pages, and 7,500 articles accompanied by more than 13,000 illustrations—all made readily accessible by two large indexes, one analytical and the other topical. The approximately 3,000 contributors—recognized authorities from around the world—are mainly academicians but many are working scientists in industry and research laboratories. The encyclopedia's main competition comes from the multivolume ENCYCLOPEDIA OF PHYSICAL SCIENCE AND TECHNOLOGY, although it is designed for a somewhat more advanced audience.

Bill Katz, the reference authority, provides a good description of the *McGraw-Hill Encyclopedia of Science and Technology* in his *Basic Information Sources* (6th ed. 1992, pp. 273–74): "There are numerous charts, graphs, and summaries which make even the most detailed articles exceptionally easy to follow. Written with the layperson in mind, the encyclopedia can be read with ease even by the most scientifically naive individual. The writing style is directed to teenagers and adults. The set is ideal for an overview of a given topic, whether it be tube worms or artificial intelligence." The set is updated annually by the *McGraw-Hill Yearbook of Science and Technology*.

Finally, for those who do not want or cannot afford the entire encyclopedia, McGraw-Hill publishes a number of topical volumes based on the 1992 edition: MCGRAW-HILL ENCYCLOPEDIA OF ASTRONOMY, MCGRAW-HILL ENCYCLOPEDIA OF CHEMISTRY, MCGRAW-HILL ENCYCLOPEDIA OF ENGINEERING, *McGraw-Hill Encyclopedia of Environmental Science & Engineering* (1993), and *McGraw-Hill Encyclopedia of Physics* (1993). Each of these titles is published in a single volume and sells for between $75.00 and $95.00.

The New Book of Popular Science. Revised ed. Grolier, 1992. 6 vols. $219.00.

First published in 1924 as the *Book of Popular Science* and retitled the *New Book of Popular Science* in 1978, this standard science encyclopedia for young people in the upper elementary and secondary grades has been revised numerous times during its nearly three quarters of a century of existence, most recently in 1992. The six-volume set continues to be arranged topically: volume 1 covers astronomy, space science, computers, and mathematics; volume 2, earth and environmental sciences; volume 3, physical sciences and biology; volume 4, plant and animal life; volume 5, mammals and human sciences; and volume 6, technology. Currently, the encyclopedia contains about 1.4 million words, over 3,000 pages, and more than 350 articles enhanced by some 3,400 illustrations. The final volume includes a general index to the set; the index is also published separately in paperback form. In a review of the 1992 edition in *American Reference Books Annual* (1993, p. 612), D.A. Rothschild recommends the work: "The changes are substantial enough that libraries with an earlier version, even the previous one, will want to seriously consider its purchase. The set can be recommended with confidence to school, public, and community college libraries." A quite similar work, also topically arranged, is the seven-volume *World Book Encyclopedia of Science* (World Book, 1990).

The Raintree Illustrated Science Encyclopedia. 3rd ed. Raintree/Steck-Vaughn, 1991. 18 vols. $329.00; $299.00 to schools & libraries.

A complete reworking of the *Encyclopedia of Nature and Science* (1974), the British-made *Raintree Illustrated Science Encyclopedia* first appeared in 1979 in 20 volumes and has since been revised twice, first in 1984 and most recently in 1991, when it was reduced to 18 volumes. The encyclopedia, which is intended mainly for students in the elementary and junior high school grades but is also appropriate for high schools students with little interest in or aptitude for science, currently encompasses over 3,000 articles accompanied by 4,000 full-color photographs, charts, diagrams, and tables. "RISE has done a good job updating its material, listening to its library critics, and providing a colorful, appropriately written science reference tool for the 8- to 14-year-old. It will be heavily used in elementary and middle schools and by some reluctant readers of high school age. It is appropriate for home, school, and public library use" (*Reference Books Bulletin* in *Booklist*, June 1, 1992, p. 1778). Comparable works are the smaller MACMILLAN ENCYCLOPEDIA OF SCIENCE and KINGFISHER SCIENCE ENCYCLOPEDIA.

Van Nostrand's Science Encyclopedia. Edited by Douglas M. Considine & Glenn D. Considine. 7th ed. Van Nostrand, 1989. 2 vols. $195.00.

Along with the MCGRAW-HILL CONCISE ENCYCLOPEDIA OF SCIENCE AND TECHNOLOGY, this is the premier small-volume general science encyclopedia for older students and adults. Now in two volumes, *Van Nostrand's Science Encyclopedia* consists of 6,773 alphabetically arranged entries along with more than 3,000 black-and-white illustrations in 3,180 pages. The encyclopedia, which first appeared in 1938, is completely trustworthy, reasonably current, and carefully organized; numerous cross-references and an extensive index (new to the 1989 edition) render the text readily accessible. Harold Shane in *Library Journal* (January 1989, p. 82) calls this work "probably the best scientific encyclopedia available." For a comparative note by Shane, see the MCGRAW-HILL CONCISE ENCYCLOPEDIA OF SCIENCE AND TECHNOLOGY.

The Way Nature Works. Macmillan, 1992. 359p. $35.00.

This handsomely illustrated, thematically arranged encyclopedia for young students furnishes readable articles on significant aspects of the biological and earth sciences, such as plate tectonics, ozone, DNA, reproduction, ecosystems, and environmental pollution. The book, which is divided into nine broad sections, concludes with a detailed index. "*The Way Nature Works* is an excellent addition to the science reference collection for its unique and comprehensive treatment of the natural world and the beauty of its design. For science students in the sixth to ninth grades, it will be popular as a browsing book and useful for the clarity of its explanations. Its low cost makes it affordable for schools and public libraries" (*Reference Books Bulletin* in *Booklist*, February 15, 1993, p. 1085).

❋ SEXUALITY, HUMAN REPRODUCTION, AND CHILD CARE ❋

The A-to-Z of Women's Sexuality: A Concise Encyclopedia. Written by Ada P. Kahn & Linda Hughey Holt. Revised ed. Hunter House, 1992. 362p. $14.95 paperbound.

First published in 1990 in a hardcover edition by Facts on File and reissued in a minimally revised paperback edition in 1992, the *A-to-Z of Women's Sexuality* contains over 2,000 brief entries dealing with both physiological and psychological aspects of female sexuality from "Abdominal Hysterectomy" to "Zygote." The book is readable and authoritative, the work of a medical writer and a physician who specializes in obstetrics and gynecology. In a review of the hardcover edition, *Reference Books Bulletin* (in *Booklist*, September 1, 1990, p. 79) reports that "*The A-to-Z of Women's Sexuality* represents an ambitious attempt to compile a vocabulary of sexuality for a popular audience. The wide-ranging interdisciplinary coverage makes it a good addition for ready reference and the bibliographies will be helpful for those interested in women's studies."

The Columbia University College of Physicians and Surgeons Complete Guide to Early Child Care. Edited by Genell Subak-Sharpe. Crown, 1990. 514p. $32.50.

Encyclopedic in scope, this topically arranged reference work furnishes reliable, up-to-date information on all important facets of child care and development from birth to age five. The book, which is aimed principally at parents, has an easy style and avoids overly technical language. Especially useful are the sections devoted to childhood illnesses, choosing a pediatrician, and the ins and outs of day care. A complementary work is the *Columbia University College of Physicians and Surgeons Complete Guide to Pregnancy* (Crown, 1988).

A *Descriptive Dictionary and Atlas of Sexology.*
Edited by Robert T. Francoeur & others. Greenwood, 1991. 768p. $95.00.

The editors define sexology as "the interdisciplinary science of sex including its anatomical, physiological, psychological, medical, sociological, anthropological, historical, legal, religious, literary, and
artistic aspects." It comes as no surprise, then, that
the approximately 4,500 entries comprising this valuable reference work deal with human sexuality from
all of these perspectives. Emphasis is on terminology
but coverage also includes theoretical concepts, landmark court cases, biographical sketches, important
organizations, and 19 pages of charts and drawings
that make up the elementary "Atlas of Human Sexuality." "In some cases, they [the editors] have gone
beyond a simple definition by giving full encyclopedic discussions with references to further reading,
for example, in the entry *teenage sex.* . . . This
dictionary, while well executed, is clinical in its
approach, making it useful for large public and academic libraries" (*Reference Books Bulletin* in *Booklist*,
December 15, 1991, p. 783). A complementary (albeit much less substantial) reference is the 180-page
Language of Sex: An A-to-Z Guide (Facts on File,
1992) by Michael Carrera.

Encyclopedia of Adolescence. Edited by Richard
M. Lerner & others. Garland, 1991. 2 vols.
$150.00.

This fine two-volume encyclopedia contains 200
essay-length articles offering detailed information
on a wide variety of psychological, biological, and
sociological topics related to human adolescence,
such as "AIDS and Adolescents," "Fathers, Teenage," "Menarche and Body Image," and "Parental
Influence." Intended for advanced students and professionals in the social and medical sciences, the
encyclopedia is scholarly in tone and interdisciplinary in scope. "The critical and often stormy span of
life known as adolescence is superbly covered in
these two hefty volumes that provide up-to-date
research findings, ranging across disciplines from
psychology to medicine to history. . . . Highly recommended" (*Library Journal*, May 15, 1991, p. 77).

The Encyclopedia of Adoption. Written by Christine Adamec & William L. Pierce. Facts on
File, 1991. 382p. $45.00.

The only encyclopedia currently available on
this important subject, the *Encyclopedia of Adoption*
contains approximately 400 alphabetically arranged
articles on such topics as abandonment, adoption
agencies, cocaine babies, grandparents' and unwed
fathers' rights, open adoption, transracial adoption,

and zygote adoption. The articles are authoritative,
up-to-date, and clearly written. "The minor shortcomings of this encyclopedia are outweighed by the
fact that it competently covers an area previously
lacking a comprehensive reference work" (*Library
Journal*, January 1992, p. 104).

The Encyclopedia of Child Abuse. Written by
Robin E. Clark & Judith Freedman Clark. Facts
on File, 1989. 328p. $45.00.

The Clarks' encyclopedia—the only reference
source of its kind currently available—comprises
about 440 entries ranging in length from a sentence
or two to several paragraphs. The entries, which are
normally comprehensible to interested nonspecialists, include medical terms, organizations concerned
with protecting children, types of neglect and abus-
ers, treatment programs, psychological and sociological constructs, and legal principles and cases
concerning child abuse. Among the 15 appendixes
are state-by-state summaries of reporting laws and
child welfare statutes. The encyclopedia "will be
useful to social workers, teachers, parents, concerned
citizens, students, and perhaps even to older victim-
ized children" (*Reference Books Bulletin* in *Booklist*,
October 15, 1989, p. 494).

*Encyclopedia of Childbearing: Critical Perspec-
tives.* Edited by Barbara Katz Rothman. Oryx
Press, 1993. 472p. $74.50.

This unique encyclopedia consists of roughly
250 signed, alphabetically arranged articles by more
than 200 specialists on birth and childbearing representing such diverse fields as anthropology,
demography, ethics, history, law, literature, medicine, midwifery, nursing, philosophy, physical
therapy, political science, psychology, social work,
theology, and women's studies. Topics covered include abortion, adoption, birth centers, birthmothers,
breastfeeding, Cesarean birth, circumcision, infant
mortality, infertility, miscarriage, prenatal care, sex
selection, stillbirth, and teenage childbearing. "A
perfect starting point for undergraduates and general readers, the book is handsomely printed on
permanent paper, with a few black-and-white photographs and drawings. Highly recommended"
(*Choice*, April 1993, p. 1294).

Encyclopedia of Homosexuality. Edited by Wayne
R. Dynes. Garland, 1990. 2 vols. $150.00.

Dynes—author of the widely praised *Homosexuality: A Research Guide* (Garland, 1987)—and his 86
contributors have produced an outstanding two-
volume encyclopedia that offers a wealth of authoritative information about both male and female homosexuality. Useful to specialists as well as inter-

ested students and general readers, the set contains 770 substantial articles covering issues, events, activities, concepts, and people relevant to the gay and lesbian experience in this and other cultures. "Many library collections have insufficient scholarly information on homosexuality; this landmark encyclopedia will go a long way toward strengthening those collections. . . . This work constitutes a masterful summary of current knowledge and informed scholarly opinion about a most controversial topic. High school, college, university, and public libraries should purchase it" (*American Reference Books Annual*, 1991, p. 347).

Human Sexuality: An Encyclopedia. Edited by Vern L. Bullough & others. Garland, 1993. 2 vols. $125.00.

New in November 1993, this two-volume reference work is a prime source of encyclopedic information on the subject of human sexuality for scholars and laypeople alike. The publisher says the new encyclopedia "summarizes the state of knowledge on all aspects of human sexual behavior. Organization is by topical subject matter with cross-references to other articles and a thorough index. Each article is followed by a bibliography of essential primary sources for researching subjects in depth." Garland is also responsible for two other fine sex encyclopedias, namely the ENCYCLOPEDIA OF HOMOSEXUALITY and SEXUALITY AND THE LAW. *Human Sexuality: An Encyclopedia* replaces the once standard but now seriously dated (and out of print) *Encyclopedia of Sexual Behavior* (Revised ed. Aronson, 1973), a large single-volume work of more than 1,000 pages edited by Albert Ellis and Albert Arabanel.

The New Child Health Encyclopedia: The Complete Guide for Parents. Prepared by the Boston Children's Hospital; edited by Frederick H. Lovejoy & David Estridge. Revised ed. Delacorte Press, 1987. 740p. $39.95 hardcover; $19.95 paperbound (published by Dell).

Originally published as the *Child Health Encyclopedia* in 1975, this nontechnical but authoritative encyclopedia draws on the combined experience and knowledge of numerous health professionals associated with the Boston Children's Hospital. Like the comparable COLUMBIA UNIVERSITY COLLEGE OF PHYSICIANS AND SURGEONS COMPLETE GUIDE TO EARLY CHILD CARE, the volume is arranged topically; specifically, it consists of four broad sections—"Keeping Children Healthy," "Finding Health Care for Children," "Emergencies," and "Diseases and Symptoms"—that treat caring for children from head to toe. "It stands out among health guides because it draws on the expertise of over 150 pediatricians and specialists,

and its coverage extends through adolescence" (*Library Journal*, November 15, 1987, p. 72). Other similar works are Penelope Leach's *Child Care Encyclopedia* (Knopf, 1984) and, of course, the classic *Dr. Spock's Baby and Child Care* (Revised ed. Dutton, 1985) by Benjamin Spock and Michael Rothenberg. Also available is the recently published *Lesbian and Gay Parenting Handbook: Creating and Raising Our Families* (HarperCollins, 1993) by April Martin.

The Parent's Desk Reference: The Ultimate Family Encyclopedia from Conception to College. Written by Irene Franck & David Brownstone. Prentice Hall, 1991. 615p. $29.95.

Franck and Brownstone's encyclopedia contains over 2,500 A-to-Z entries covering a wide range of topics pertaining to having and raising children, such as pregnancy, childbirth, nutrition and child care, common childhood diseases and medical problems, genetic disorders in children, psychological and adjustment problems, sexual development and orientation, and educational and legal issues involving young people. Written in a style and language comprehensible to average parents, the book concludes with a "Special Help Section" that offers, among other things, a directory of relevant organizations and a bibliography of books of potential use to parents. "Librarians in school, public, and academic libraries should definitely purchase this encyclopedia for their reference collections. It contains a wealth of information on parenting at an extremely affordable price and will probably serve as a seminal work in this area for several years to come" (*American Reference Books Annual*, 1992, p. 335).

The Practical Encyclopedia of Sex and Health: From Aphrodisiacs and Hormones to Potency, Stress and Yeast Infection. Written by Stefan Bechtel & the editors of *Prevention* & *Men's Health* magazines. Rodale Press, 1993. 352p. $26.95.

This practical, popularly written encyclopedia deals briskly with such common questions about sex as arousal techniques, potency, and sexually transmitted diseases. Typical of Rodale Press publications, the book addresses sex and health from a holistic point of view. Twenty illustrations complement the printed text. "Ever practical and direct, Bechtel draws on research studies (especially the heavily popularized work of such high-profile researchers as Kinsey and Masters and Johnson) to provide basic information about sex and conduct between the sexes" (*Wilson Library Bulletin*, October 1993, p. 96).

Sexuality and the Law: An Encyclopedia of Major Legal Cases. Edited by Arthur S. Leonard. Garland, 1993. 729p. $95.00.

Covering decisions mostly by the U.S. Supreme Court but in some instances by the lower courts (both federal and state), this new encyclopedia summarizes 119 landmark legal decisions involving all aspects of human sexuality, including identity, expression, and discrimination. Specific articles deal with the emerging case law in such areas as sexual bias and orientation, criminal behavior, pornography, domestic relationships, and reproductive rights.

A boon for students at the high school level and up, the book is written in a straightforward, nontechnical style by experts on constitutional law; clear explanations of legal and scientific terms are provided when required. A table of cases and an index follow the articles. "Legal aspects of sexuality are explained with an applicable and pertinent cross section of case law discussion and historical background information. Highly recommended for academic and law libraries" (*Library Journal*, June 1, 1993, p. 106). This volume nicely complements HUMAN SEXUALITY, another fine new encyclopedia from Garland.

❋ SOCIAL SCIENCE, SOCIOLOGY, AND ANTHROPOLOGY ❋

The African American Encyclopedia. Edited by Michael W. Williams. Marshall Cavendish, 1993. 6 vols. $479.95.

New in 1993, this attractive and informative six-volume encyclopedia deals with all significant aspects of black life and culture in the United States from earliest times to the present. It contains nearly 3,000 A-to-Z entries accompanied by 1,500 illustrations in almost 2,000 pages of text prepared by 150 contributors, most of whom are U.S. academics specializing in African American studies. A detailed index to the set is found in the final volume. Up-to-date and objective, the *African American Encyclopedia* is clearly the best general reference source on the subject currently available. A review in *Reference Books Bulletin* (in *Booklist*, July 1993, p. 2,000) concludes that the set "will be extremely useful in public, high school, and college libraries and is highly recommended."

Other important encyclopedic works dealing with the African American experience are the two-volume *Black Women in America: An Historical Encyclopedia* (Carlson Publishing, 1993), edited by Darlene Clark Hine; the 526-page *Chronology of African-American History* (Gale Research, 1991) by Alton Hornsby, Jr.; the 866-page *Dictionary of Afro-American Slavery* (Greenwood, 1988), edited by Randall Miller and John D. Smith; the 198-page *Historical and Cultural Atlas of African Americans* (Macmillan, 1991) by Molefi K. Asante and Mark T. Mattson; the 1,622-page *Negro Almanac: A Reference Work on the African American* (5th ed. Gale Research, 1989), edited by Harry Ploski and James Williams; and the ENCYCLOPEDIA OF AFRICAN-AMERICAN CIVIL RIGHTS. Two older single-volume titles also remain useful for historical information: the *Encyclopedia of Black America* (McGraw-Hill, 1981), edited by W. Augustus Low, and the *Black American Reference Book* (Prentice-Hall, 1976), edited by Mabel M. Smythe.

Dictionary of American Communal and Utopian History. Written by Robert S. Fogarty. Greenwood, 1980. 271p. $45.00.

Fogarty's book focuses on North American communal settlements and their leaders from the eighteenth century to the early years of this century. In all, 140 individuals and 59 communities are described in articles averaging about a page in length. While not definitive, the book "will aid the researcher concerned with America's contribution toward utopian thought and communal organization" (*American Reference Books Annual*, 1981, p. 198). No other such encyclopedic source is available.

Dictionary of Asian American History. Edited by Hyung-Chan Kim. Greenwood, 1986. 627p. $75.00.

The first and thus far only comprehensive encyclopedic work on the subject, the *Dictionary of Asian American History* provides detailed information about the major Asian American ethnic groups, including those of Chinese, Filipino, Japanese, and Korean ancestry. Informative essays on these groups and various topics such as immigration and stereotyping comprise the first 114 pages, but the bulk of the book is devoted to 800 A-to-Z entries covering major events, individuals, organizations, concepts, terms, court cases, immigration laws, and treaties. "This work, the first in its field, will be an essential reference for academic and public libraries" (*Choice*, April 1987, p. 1196). Valuable complementary sources are the *Dictionary of American Immigration History* (Scarecrow Press, 1990), edited by Francesco Cordasco; *Japanese American History: An A-to-Z Reference from 1868 to the Present* (Facts on File, 1993), edited by Brian Niiya; and the indispensable HARVARD ENCYCLOPEDIA OF AMERICAN ETHNIC GROUPS.

Dictionary of Concepts in Cultural Anthropology. Written by Robert H. Winthrop. Greenwood, 1991. 347p. $65.00.

Intended to help guide serious students "through the anthropological labyrinth" (introduction), Winthrop's dictionary furnishes encyclopedic coverage of about 80 concepts central to the field. The seven-page article on evolution, for instance, begins with a succinct definition of the term and then presents detailed information about the history of evolutionary theory and how it has influenced the development and study of cultural anthropology; the article concludes with sources for additional information. "The entries ring with clarity and authority; in place of extended treatment of the fine points within the concepts or an extensive list of terms, the entries offer a basic grounding for the user" (*American Reference Books Annual*, 1993, p. 173). A companion volume is Joan Stevenson's *Dictionary of Concepts in Physical Anthropology* (Greenwood, 1991). Other useful single-volume works on the subject are the *Dictionary of Anthropology* (G.K. Hall, 1986), edited by Charlotte Seymour-Smith, and the now dated (and out of print) *Encyclopedia of Anthropology* (Harper, 1976), edited by David E. Hunter and Phillip Whitten.

Dictionary of Mexican American History. Written by Matt S. Meier & Feliciano Rivera. Greenwood, 1981. 498p. $49.95.

This one-of-a-kind reference work provides concise, reliable coverage of Chicano history from the sixteenth century to the present, including information about important individuals, events, organizations, places, laws, treaties, and terms. Articles range from two or three lines to several pages, but most are about half a page in length. "The index reinforces the cross-referencing for full information retrieval. In Chicano studies collections in academic and public libraries, especially in the Southwest, this will be a standard tool" (*Wilson Library Bulletin*, May 1982, p. 701). The book is similar in purpose and scholarship to the DICTIONARY OF ASIAN AMERICAN HISTORY.

Encyclopedia of Adult Development. Edited by Robert Kastenbaum. Oryx Press, 1993. 592p. $95.00.

Kastenbaum, who has also edited the excellent ENCYCLOPEDIA OF DEATH, brings together an enormous fund of authoritative, up-to-date information on the diverse—and often neglected—subject of adults and adulthood. The encyclopedia's 106 articles deal with such subjects as choosing a mate, divorce, menopause, physical and mental health among adults (including the use and abuse of alcohol and drugs), work, retirement, religion in adult life, and longevity. Written for the nonspecialist but also useful to serious students and practitioners in the social sciences, Kastenbaum's book provides an informed overview of the largest segment of our population. A review by Sandy Whiteley in *Reference Books Bulletin* (in *Booklist*, December 1, 1993, p. 712), concludes, "Academic libraries supporting study in psychology or gerontology will want a copy of the *Encyclopedia of Adult Development*; public libraries should consider purchase too."

Encyclopedia of African-American Civil Rights: From Emancipation to the Present. Edited by Charles D. Lowery & John F. Marszalek. Greenwood, 1992. 658p. $59.95.

Arranged A-to-Z, the 800 succinct articles that make up this outstanding encyclopedia cover practically every major person, event, organization, publication, law, court case, and concept involved in the African American struggle for civil rights from the end of slavery to the beginning of the 1990s. The more than 150 contributors (mostly academics) represent a high level of authority; each article is signed and includes a lengthy and usually impressive bibliography. Anthony Edmonds, in a review in *Library Journal* (May 1, 1992, p. 74), calls the encyclopedia a "monumental compilation of information . . . . a fine work, unique in its focus and comprehensive in its coverage. It will become a standard reference work." A complementary source is the multivolume AFRICAN AMERICAN ENCYCLOPEDIA.

The Encyclopedia of Aging. Edited by George L. Maddox & others. Springer, 1987. 893p. $96.00.

The work of some 220 authorities, this useful single-volume encyclopedia furnishes hundreds of brief, signed articles on a broad range of gerontological topics, including physical, psychological, sociological, and economic problems associated with aging. Aimed largely at serious students, practitioners, and researchers, the articles are clearly written and will normally be comprehensible to the educated layperson. "*The Encyclopedia of Aging* is an excellent reference tool that will meet the needs of a wide variety of audiences served by public and academic libraries" (*American Reference Books Annual*, 1988, p. 323). A competing source is the more recent but much less substantial *Encyclopedia of Aging and the Elderly* (Facts on File, 1992), a 308-page work by F. Hampton Roy and Charles Russell.

The Encyclopedia of American Crime. Written by Carl Sifakis. Revised ed. Smithmark, 1992. 832p. $19.98.

First published in 1982 and modestly updated in 1992 to include infamous killers like Jeffrey Dahmer, the *Encyclopedia of American Crime* consists of more than 1,500 concise articles on prominent U.S. criminals, victims, detectives, judges, lawyers, and criminologists as well as celebrated trials, hoaxes, underworld slang, types of crimes and weapons, and so on. Coverage is from the colonial period to the present day. In a review of the first edition in *Library Journal* (July 1982, p. 1341), Gregor Preston recommends the encyclopedia: "This compendium of alphabetically arranged brief articles on American criminals and crime topics is the most comprehensive popular source available." For a much larger work covering crime and criminals around the world, see Jay Robert Nash's six-volume ENCYCLOPEDIA OF WORLD CRIME.

The Encyclopedia of Crime and Justice. Edited by Sanford H. Kadish. Free Press, 1983. 4 vols. $375.00.

The authoritative *Encyclopedia of Crime and Justice* encompasses 286 alphabetically arranged articles prepared by leading legal scholars, social scientists, historians, and criminal justice professionals. The set focuses on criminal law, the justice system, and the nature, types, and causes of criminal behavior; representative articles are "Abortion," "Actus Reus," "Amnesty and Pardon," "Burden of Proof," "Burglary," "Computer Crime," "Coroner, Role of the," "Discovery," "Exclusionary Rules," "Grand Jury," "Incest," "Mann Act," "Organized Crime," "Prisons," "Psychopathy," "Sentencing," "Speedy Trial," "Terrorism," and "Victimless Crime." The articles are scholarly in tone, clearly written, and useful to a wide audience, including serious students, teachers, practitioners, and interested laypeople.

"This four-volume encyclopedia consists of 286 original articles written and edited by some of the best-known figures in the field of criminal justice. It is a mark of distinction that their work is as close to totally objective as possible in a field that is filled with emotionally laden issues. . . . Among several unique and positive features, most impressive is the excellent index, especially the legal index, which will be useful to students doing research" (*Choice,* March 1984, p. 950). A work of similar magnitude (but not content) is the six-volume ENCYCLOPEDIA OF WORLD CRIME.

Encyclopedia of Death. Edited by Robert Kastenbaum & Beatrice Kastenbaum. Oryx

Press, 1989. 320p. $74.50 hardcover; $15.00 paperbound (published by Avon in 1993).

This unique encyclopedia offers approximately 130 articles on such varied topics as AIDS, brain death, cemeteries, cremation, embalming, euthanasia, funeral customs, grief, hospices, Jonestown, suicide, violent death, and zombies. About half of the articles are contributed by Robert Kastenbaum, a professor of gerontology and also editor of the companion ENCYCLOPEDIA OF ADULT DEVELOPMENT; the rest of the articles are the work of 58 specialists, mostly academics. "As our population ages, we are quickly discovering that we do not know enough about death. This volume forthrightly tackles both the nuts-and-bolts issues and the controversies. . . . An important work, this book is recommended as essential for academic and public libraries" (*RQ,* Fall 1990, pp. 114–15).

Encyclopedia of Human Behavior. Edited by V.S. Ramachandran. Academic Press, 1994. 4 vols. $595.00.

Entirely new in 1994 and admirably contemporary in perspective, this multivolume encyclopedia contains approximately 250 signed, scholarly articles contributed by specialists in such interdisciplinary fields as education, psychology, gerontology, physiology, and anthropology. The set, which is strongly international in scope and emphasis, includes an extensive index and numerous cross-references. This excellent work serves effectively as a complement to the much larger but much older INTERNATIONAL ENCYCLOPEDIA OF THE SOCIAL SCIENCES.

The Encyclopedia of Marriage, Divorce and the Family. Written by Margaret DiCanio. Facts on File, 1989. 607p. $40.00.

DiCanio, a medical sociologist, pulls together contemporary knowledge from numerous fields (medicine, the law, psychology, sociology, etc.) in this 600-entry, multidisciplinary encyclopedia. The focus is on the American family today; topics covered include abortion, alcoholism, amniocentesis, bulimia, childbirth, credit unions, drugs, eating disorders, fast food, gifted children, types of marriage, parenting, sex education, and spouse abuse. The encyclopedia "is a well-researched, readable reference work that provides current information on a large number of important, controversial issues of the day. It is recommended for high schools with family life curricula, as well as public and academic libraries of all sizes" (*Reference Books Bulletin* in *Booklist,* January 1, 1990, p. 948).

The Encyclopedia of Social Work. Edited by Anne Minahan. 18th ed. National Assn. of Social

Workers, 1987. 3 vols. plus suppl., 1990. $85.00 (3-vol. set); $19.95 (suppl.).

Originally published for many years as the *Social Work Year Book* (1929–60), this well-known and highly respected reference publication was retitled the *Encyclopedia of Social Work* in 1965, reflecting its changing purpose and broadening scope. The encyclopedia—currently a wealth of information on a broad array of topics of interest to social workers and others in the behavioral sciences (abortion, foster care, child abuse, poverty, etc.)—is now revised regularly at 10-year intervals: the 17th edition appeared in 1977, the 18th in 1987, and the next revision (the 19th edition) is scheduled for 1997. Occasional supplements are issued to help keep the encyclopedia reasonably current.

Encyclopedia of Sociology. Edited by Edgar F. Borgatta & Marie L. Borgatta. Macmillan, 1992. 4 vols. $340.00.

The *Encyclopedia of Sociology*, a four-volume work comprising roughly 1,800 pages of text, is a comprehensive, authoritative, and up-to-date encyclopedic survey of the field of sociology—the first ever. International in scope, the set contains nearly 400 signed articles by over 300 leading sociologists and researchers, most from North America. The articles—some of which draw on the older INTERNATIONAL ENCYCLOPEDIA OF THE SOCIAL SCIENCES—normally are written in clear, nontechnical language that is readily comprehensible to students and professionals as well as interested laypeople. Typical articles are "Adulthood," "Alienation," "Alternative Life Styles," "Bureaucracy," "Class and Race," "Dependency Theory," "Group Problem Solving," "Hawthorne Effect," "Intermarriage," "Marxist Sociology," "Paradigms and Models," "Role Conflict," and "White Collar Crime."

Upon publication, the set received enthusiastic reviews; for instance, T.N. Smalley writes in *Choice* (July–August 1992, p. 1655) that the encyclopedia "will serve as the premier source of background information and conceptual summaries for the field of sociology for years to come. A must purchase for libraries in all institutions of higher education (including community colleges) and for most public libraries." In 1993, the encyclopedia received the esteemed Dartmouth Medal, which recognizes the single best reference publication of the previous year. No other sociology reference source provides such deep coverage of the field, but for those unable to afford the *Encyclopedia of Sociology* there are several single-volume alternatives that might fill the breach. These are the *Encyclopedic Dictionary of Sociology* (4th ed. Dushkin, 1991), edited by Richard Lachmann; the encyclopedic *HarperCollins Dictionary of Sociology* (HarperCollins, 1991) by David

Jary and Julia Jary; and the *International Encyclopedia of Sociology: A Concise Encyclopedic Reference Work for All Students of the Social Sciences* (Crossroad, 1984), edited by Michael Mann.

Encyclopedia of the Future. Edited by George Thomas Kurian. Macmillan, 1994 (in progress). 2 vols. Price not set.

According to a statement of purpose provided by the editor, Kurian, this in-progress work will be "the first encyclopedia devoted entirely and solely to the future." When completed sometime in 1994 or 1995, it will comprise approximately 300 signed articles by experts from a variety of fields covering such topics as business, health, food and agriculture, the environment, energy, government, war and peace, genetics, sexuality, religion, human rights, crime, and space exploration. If the advisory board—made up of such well-known thinkers as Kenneth Boulding, Ben Bova, Harlan Cleveland, John Deardorff, John Diebold, Amitai Etzioni, Douglas Fraser, Theodore Gordon, Richard Lamm, John Naisbitt, Walter W. Rostow, Glenn Seaborg, Alvin Toffler, Ben Wattenberg, and Murray Weidenbaum—is any indication, the encyclopedia should be one of impressive quality.

Encyclopedia of World Crime: Criminal Justice, Criminology, and Law Enforcement. Written & edited by Jay Robert Nash. CrimeBooks (dist. by Marshall Cavendish), 1990. 6 vols. $600.00.

Jay Robert Nash, author of the classic *Bloodletters and Badmen* (Evans, 1973), among other reference works, is doubtless the best-known encyclopedist of crime in North America if not the world. The six-volume *Encyclopedia of World Crime*, written by Nash with assistance from the research staff of CrimeBooks, Inc. (of which Nash is president), represents his most ambitious effort to date. The first four volumes contain roughly 50,000 A-to-Z entries profiling famous crime figures and prominent judges, lawyers, and law enforcement officials from earliest recorded time to the present. Although international in scope, the encyclopedia emphasizes crime in the United States during the nineteenth and twentieth centuries. Volume 4 concludes with survey articles on such nonbiographical topics as arson, kidnapping, organized crime, prisons, and skyjacking. The writing style tends to be vivid, journalistic, and popular. Volume 5 is a 20,000-entry crime dictionary; note that it has recently been reprinted as a separate work under the title *Dictionary of Crime: Criminal Justice, Criminology and Law Enforcement* (Paragon House, 1992). The final volume comprises detailed name and subject indexes. More than 4,000 black-and-white illustrations enhance the printed text.

This massive encyclopedia—the largest such resource currently available—is equally valuable as a research and browsing tool. As C.H. Handy remarks in *Choice* (December 1990, p. 613), "In addition to providing users with extensive information, it [the encyclopedia] will prove fascinating reading." Nash's popular encyclopedia is comparable in size to the scholarly ENCYCLOPEDIA OF CRIME AND JUSTICE, but the content and style of the two works could not be more different.

Encyclopedia of World Cultures. Edited by David Levinson. G.K. Hall, 1991–. 10 vols. (in progress). Individual vols. $100.00; $1,000.00 (the set).

The ongoing *Encyclopedia of World Cultures* is being produced under the auspices of the Human Relations Area Files (HRAF), a prestigious ethnographic archive founded in the 1940s at Yale University by anthropologist George Peter Murdock to promote cross-cultural study of human society and behavior. Due for completion in 1994 or 1995, the encyclopedia will ultimately profile 1,500 cultural groups from all over the world. The initial volume, subtitled *North America* (1991), describes more than 200 distinct U.S. and Canadian groups, including Native Americans, which account for a majority of the entries; this volume is similar in purpose to the HARVARD ENCYCLOPEDIA OF AMERICAN ETHNIC GROUPS, although that worthy work focuses more heavily on groups of European origin. Other published volumes of the *Encyclopedia of World Cultures* are *Oceania* (volume 2); *South Asia* (volume 3); *Central, Western and Southeast Europe* (volume 4); *Southeast and East Asia* (volume 5); and *Russia and Eurasia-China* (volume 6). A review of volume 3 in *Choice* (December 1992, p. 601) puts the project in good critical perspective: "This South Asia volume and the entire *Encyclopedia of World Cultures* will remain the standard work and an invaluable resource for many years to come." A competing work is the colorful *Illustrated Encyclopedia of Mankind* (Revised ed. Marshall Cavendish, 1989), a 22-volume set edited by Richard Carlisle; suitable for young people, it covers about 500 cultures and is much less scholarly than the *Encyclopedia of World Cultures.*

Handbook of North American Indians. Edited by William C. Sturtevant. Smithsonian Institution (dist. by the U.S. Government Printing Office), 1978–. 20 vols. (in progress). Prices vary from $25.00 to $47.00 per vol.

Encyclopedic in scope, this in-progress work will eventually form a comprehensive study of the history, culture, and anthropology of Native Americans indigenous to Central and North America, including the Eskimo, Aleut, and Inuit peoples. Each volume covers a specific topic or geographical area. For instance, volume 4 deals with the history of Indian-white relations, volume 5 with the Indians of the Arctic, and volumes 9 and 10 with the Indians of the Southwest. The 9 (of 20) volumes published to date are authoritative, clearly written, and extensively illustrated with photographs and high-quality maps.

Complementary reference works are Carl Waldman's one-volume *Encyclopedia of Native American Tribes* (Facts on File, 1988); the initial volume (*North America*) of the ENCYCLOPEDIA OF WORLD CULTURES; and *The American Indian: A Multimedia Encyclopedia* (Facts on File, 1993), a CD-ROM publication comprised of four previously published Facts on File works, including the aforementioned *Encyclopedia of Native American Tribes.* For similar information about Native Americans indigenous to Central and South America, interested consumers should see James S. Olson's *Indians of Central and South America: An Ethnohistorical Dictionary* (Greenwood, 1991), which draws heavily on the old but still valuable seven-volume *Handbook of South American Indians* (U.S. Government Printing Office, 1946–59).

Harvard Encyclopedia of American Ethnic Groups. Edited by Stephan Thernstrom. Harvard Univ. Press, 1980. 1,076p. $95.00.

Over 100 U.S. ethnic groups—from Acadians to Zoroastrians—are described in this outstanding reference work. Prepared by a group of distinguished contributors (with Oscar Handlin as consulting editor), the essay-length articles are erudite yet readable. The encyclopedia also includes 29 thematic essays on such pertinent topics as assimilation, intermarriage, labor, naturalization and citizenship, and ethnic prejudice. When naming the *Harvard Encyclopedia of American Ethnic Groups* as one of the best reference books of the 1980s, Sandy Whiteley of *Reference Books Bulletin* wrote, "This book has proven to be very useful to students of American history and ethnicity and to genealogists" (*Booklist,* December 15, 1989, p. 779). Complementary single-volume sources are the *Dictionary of American Immigration History* (Scarecrow Press, 1990), edited by Francesco Cordasco; *Refugees in the United States: A Reference Handbook* (Greenwood, 1985), edited by David Haines; and volume 1 (*North America*) of the ENCYCLOPEDIA OF WORLD CULTURES.

International Encyclopedia of Population. Edited by John A. Ross. Free Press (dist. by Macmillan), 1982. 2 vols. $250.00.

Consisting of 129 alphabetically arranged articles by 123 specialists from a variety of social science fields, this two-volume encyclopedia provides comprehensive coverage of the main areas of demography, including marriage, mortality, morbidity, and migration, along with such related topics as ecology, family planning, refugees, the status of women, and urbanization. There are also articles on the world's most populous nations and geographical areas. Although now quite dated in places, the *International Encyclopedia of Population* remains a very useful reference source. "Because of its interdisciplinary approach, this encyclopedia will be valuable not only to demographers, but to all social scientists, family planners, public policymakers, librarians, and students, to name a few potential user groups. It should have a long and active shelf life" (*College & Research Libraries*, January 1, 1983, p. 50). A complementary work is the five-volume *Dictionary of Demography* (Greenwood, 1985) by William Petersen and Renee Petersen, which provides detailed information about demographic concepts, terms, and organizations as well as major demographers.

International Encyclopedia of the Social Sciences. Edited by David L. Sills. Free Press (dist. by Macmillan), 1968. 17 vols. plus two suppls., 1979; 1991. 17-vol. set, out of print; reprinted in 8 vols. in 1977. $325.00; $95.00 (ea. suppl.).

A truly monumental reference work, the eight million–word *International Encyclopedia of the Social Sciences* contains 1,716 signed articles covering all important aspects of sociology, anthropology, history, geography, political science, law, psychology, statistics, and various social and behavioral science subfields. The set, which effectively replaces the old *Encyclopedia of the Social Sciences* (1930–35), is noted particularly for the interdisciplinary nature of its text, the high caliber of its contributors, its analytical and comparative (as opposed to historical and descriptive) approach, its excellent bibliographies, and its strong effort to cover the development of the modern social sciences from an international perspective. The articles are scholarly and sometimes require an elementary grounding in the subject, but ordinarily the encyclopedia can be used profitably by college and graduate students, teachers, researchers, and informed laypeople. "The *International Encyclopedia of the Social Sciences* is indeed a reference work of the highest order; Americans may be justly proud of this noble accomplishment" (*Library Journal*, March 15, 1969, p. 1128).

Women's Studies Encyclopedia. Edited by Helen Tierney. Greenwood, 1989–91. 3 vols. $184.90.

The three volumes that make up this excellent encyclopedia are *Views from the Sciences* (volume 1, 1989); *Literature, Arts, and Learning* (volume 2, 1990); and *History, Philosophy, and Religion* (volume 3, 1991). International in scope, but with emphasis on developments in the United States, the set contains readable, signed articles discussing women's contributions in various areas of human endeavor as well as topics of particular concern to women, such as abortion, blues singing, comparable worth, feminism, heroines in literature, the nursing profession, and spouse abuse. Prominent women also receive attention. In a review of the final volume in *Library Journal* (March 15, 1992, p. 80), Susan Parker sums up the critical response to the set: "Crisp editing is responsible for the creation of a rich resource, which this volume represents on its own and as part of a complete work. This work and its companions are highly recommended for most public, high school, and academic libraries." Complementing the *Women's Studies Encyclopedia* are three solid one-volume works: Lisa Tuttle's *Encyclopedia of Feminism* (Facts on File, 1986); the *Handbook of American Women's History* (Garland, 1990), edited by Angela Howard Zophy; and Barbara G. Walker's *Woman's Encyclopedia of Myths and Secrets* (Harper, 1983).

World Encyclopedia of Police Forces and Penal Systems. Written by George Thomas Kurian. Facts on File, 1989. 582p. $95.00.

Kurian's encyclopedia describes the police and prison systems in 183 countries from Afghanistan to Zambia. Each entry summarizes the history, organization, and personnel requirements of the country's law enforcement agencies, as well as crime statistics and data on the corrections system. Kurian "deserves congratulations for attempting such a chore, given the difficulty of obtaining complete and accurate information for countries not as open as the United States. . . . Highly recommended for most public and academic libraries since it is the first of its kind and will not likely be superseded any time soon" (*American Reference Books Annual*, 1990, p. 237). Other recommended encyclopedic works on the subject are John J. Fay's *Police Dictionary and Encyclopedia* (Charles C. Thomas, 1988) and Vergil L. Williams's *Dictionary of American Penology* (2nd ed. Greenwood, 1987)—both one-volume items.

※ SPORTS AND GAMES ※

The Baseball Encyclopedia: The Complete and Official Record of Major League Baseball. Edited by Joseph L. Reichler. 9th ed. Macmillan, 1993. 2,880p. $50.00.

First published in 1969 and now revised and updated every two or three years, the *Baseball Encyclopedia* has achieved the status of reference classic. It provides a comprehensive historical survey of the game from 1876 to the present, including season-by-season statistics for every big league player, no matter how brief or unimposing his career. New to the ninth edition are the official records of the All-American Girls' Professional Baseball League. An inexpensive annual paperback supplement entitled *Baseball Encyclopedia Update* keeps the encyclopedia current during those years in which no new edition is published.

A formidable competitor is the less well known but equally impressive *Total Baseball: The Ultimate Encyclopedia of Baseball* (3rd ed. Warner Books, 1992). Edited by John Thorn and Pete Palmer, this 2,300-page tome first appeared in 1989 and has rapidly gained recognition as a source that offers some useful information and features not found in the *Baseball Encyclopedia*. In addition, *Total Baseball* is published in electronic form on CD-ROM by Creative Multimedia Corp. Other recommended baseball encyclopedias are the *Big League Baseball Electronic Encyclopedia* (Franklin Electronic, 1992), a hand-held unit about the size of a pocket calculator that operates by batteries; and David Neft and Richard Cohen's venerable *Sports Encyclopedia: Baseball* (9th ed. St. Martin's Press, 1989).

Bud Collins' Modern Encyclopedia of Tennis. Edited by Bud Collins & Zander Hollander. 2nd ed. Gale Research, 1993. 604p. $37.95 hardcover; $14.95 paperbound.

The most comprehensive and up-to-date tennis encyclopedia currently available, Collins's encyclopedia covers all important aspects of the game, including its history, tournaments, rules, equipment, and players. The book, which first appeared in 1980, was extensively updated in 1993. It is authoritative, interesting to read, and heavily illustrated. "Not a *Baseball Encyclopedia* in which every player who ever donned a professional baseball uniform is documented, but an encyclopedia of the elites who have played the game, *Bud Collins' Modern Encyclopedia of Tennis* should fill a gap in sports-reference collections" (*Reference Books Bulletin* in *Booklist*, January 1, 1994, p. 847). A similar one-volume work is the

United States Tennis Association Official Encyclopedia of Tennis (3rd ed. HarperCollins, 1981); edited by Bill Shannon, this encyclopedia, while comparable in quality to the Collins book, is obviously in need of a new edition.

The Complete Encyclopedia of Hockey. Edited by Zander Hollander. 4th ed. Gale Research, 1992. 604p. $42.95 hardcover; $22.95 paperbound.

The fourth edition of the *Complete Encyclopedia of Hockey*—the first revision of this standard reference book since 1983—furnishes basic facts about all National Hockey League teams, players, and coaches, plus colorful highlights of each NHL season. Like the BASEBALL ENCYCLOPEDIA, Hollander's encyclopedia includes statistics for every player who has ever appeared in a regular season major league hockey game. For the time being at least, the *Complete Encyclopedia of Hockey* replaces Stan Fischler and Shirley Fischler's *Hockey Encyclopedia* (Macmillan, 1983) as the first source for encyclopedic information about pro hockey.

Dictionary of Concepts in Recreation and Leisure Studies. Written by Stephen L.J. Smith. Greenwood, 1990. 372p. $56.00.

Smith offers encyclopedic treatment of approximately 100 key concepts of interest to students and practitioners in the field of recreation and leisure. Articles include "Activity," "Amateur," "Conservation," "Environment," "Fun," "Game," "National Park," "Park," "Play," "Sport," and "Therapy." "The real value of this book is not as a dictionary in the usual sense, in spite of its title. Rather, it is a primer that will serve both the beginner and the serious student as an introduction to major concepts in the field of recreation and leisure studies. . . . This book is a very worthwhile addition to the literature, since there is currently no other book that adequately addresses its subject" (*Choice*, March 1991, p. 1108).

Encyclopedia of American Wrestling. Written by Mike Chapman. Leisure Press (dist. by Human Kinetics), 1990. 544p. $25.95 paperbound.

Devoted almost exclusively to amateur wrestling in the United States, this encyclopedia includes lists of American champions of major national and international meets as well as biographical, historical, and awards information. A complementary reference source is *Wrestling: Physical Conditioning Encyclopedia* (Athletic Press, 1974), a 416-page volume by John Jesse currently available only in paperback.

The Encyclopedia of Magic and Magicians. Written by T.A. Waters. Facts on File, 1988. 372p. $35.00 hardcover; $19.95 paperbound.

Written by a magician for magicians (both amateur and professional), Waters's encyclopedia comprises more than 2,000 succinct alphabetically arranged entries describing the techniques, props, tricks, routines, and language of the magic business. Also covered are the great illusionists past and present, from Houdini to Doug Henning. The encyclopedia "is a unique reference tool of value to any collection serving amateur magicians or persons interested in the history of magic devices, effects, and illusions or the people who present them" (*Reference Books Bulletin* in *Booklist*, June 15, 1988, p. 1720).

The Encyclopedia of North American Sports History. Written by Ralph Hickok. Facts on File, 1992. 516p. $50.00.

This useful compilation succinctly describes all major and most minor competitive sports played in the United States and Canada, replacing Hickok's earlier *New Encyclopedia of Sports* (McGraw-Hill, 1977), which provides similar information. Among the more than 1,600 alphabetically arranged entries are prominent figures (players, coaches, owners, promoters, et al.), sporting events (such as the Super Bowl), teams, stadiums, organizations, awards, and the sports themselves. The encyclopedia is well-illustrated and has a comprehensive index. "Hickok has developed a reference document that is easy to use and provides quick access for enthusiasts of all ages" (*Library Journal*, January 1992, p. 108).

Encyclopedia of Sporting Firearms. Written by David E. Petzal. Facts on File, 1991. 448p. $50.00.

Petzal's first-class encyclopedia is the basic reference source for information on handguns, rifles, and shotguns as used for sport. Some 2,200 concise entries cover all pertinent aspects of the subject, including types of weapons, terminology, and important manufacturers and individuals in the firearms business, e.g., Colt, Remington, DuPont, and Winchester. "Petzal, the executive editor of *Field & Stream*, has combined his expertise with that of some of the leading contemporary authorities on sporting guns to good effect. For the most part, the individual entries are sensible, and the writing is straightforward and easily understood. . . . This work belongs on the shelves of every gun enthusiast and of any library that serves an audience of sportspersons" (*American Reference Books Annual*, 1992, p. 377).

Encyclopedic Dictionary of Sports Medicine. Written by David F. Tver & Howard F. Hunt. Routledge, Chapman & Hall, 1986. 340p. $35.00.

Arranged alphabetically, this informative reference source describes the full range of injuries and illnesses associated with sports of all kinds. The text tends to be quite technical, but Tver and Hunt do include many helpful illustrations and an extensive glossary of terms. "The intention of the authors of this reference tool is that it will assist doctors and other health professionals working in the area of sports medicine, as well as athletes themselves, in either preventing or detecting sports-related health problems" (*American Reference Books Annual*, 1988, p. 667).

The Football Encyclopedia. Written by David S. Neft & Richard M. Cohen. St. Martin's Press, 1991. 1,008p. $49.95.

Billed as the "complete history of professional NFL football from 1892 to the present," this hefty encyclopedia complements, updates, and largely replaces the authors' earlier *Sports Encyclopedia: Pro Football, the Early Years* (2nd ed. Sports Bookshelf, 1987) and companion *Sports Encyclopedia: Pro Football, the Modern Era, 1960–1990* (8th ed. St. Martin's Press, 1990). Included are statistical tables and scores for every National Football League game played from the league's creation in 1920 through the 1990 season and an alphabetical roster of players from 1960 to 1990. "When it comes to listing pro football records and statistics, this source muscles all others out of the way" (*Wilson Library Bulletin*, December 1991, p. 123). Another useful (albeit now dated) football encyclopedia is Beau Riffenburgh's *Official NFL Encyclopedia* (4th ed. NAL, 1986). Readers interested in college football should check out the recently published *College Football Encyclopedia: The Authoritative Guide to 124 Years of College Football* by Robert Ours (Prima Publishing; dist. by St. Martin's Press, 1993).

Golf Magazine's Encyclopedia of Golf. Edited by George Peper & the Editors of *Golf Magazine.* 2nd ed. HarperCollins, 1993. 518p. $40.00.

First published in 1970 and twice revised (in 1979 and 1993), this comprehensive encyclopedia of golf covers the sport's history, equipment, rules, techniques, terminology, major courses and tournaments, and golfdom's who's who. The current edition includes approximately 175 black-and-white photographs and 200 tables and charts. In a quite positive review, *Reference Books Bulletin* (in *Booklist*, November 15, 1993, p. 644) observes that "This second edition is well worth the wait." A competing work is the 336-page *Random House International Encyclopedia of Golf: The Definitive Guide to the Game* (Random House, 1991) by Malcolm Campbell.

McClane's New Standard Fishing Encyclopedia and International Angling Guide. Edited by A.J. McClane. Revised ed. Holt, 1974. 1,156p. $75.00.

The late A.J. McClane's encyclopedia—an eight-pound tome that has sold almost a million copies since the first edition appeared in 1965—is the most ambitious and best-known reference work on the sport of fishing. From "Aawa" to "Zooplankton," the alphabetical entries cover fishing terms, specific fish (both freshwater and saltwater), fishing localities, biographies of prominent people connected with the sport, etc. Another valuable single-volume reference work on the subject is Joseph Bates's *Fishing: An Encyclopedic Guide to Tackle and Tactics for Fresh and Salt Water* (2nd ed. Dutton, 1985).

The Official Encyclopedia of Bridge. Edited by Harry G. Francis & the Editorial Staff of the American Contract Bridge League. 4th ed. Crown, 1984. 922p. $45.00.

Since its initial publication in 1964, this encyclopedia has been the ultimate authority for the approximately 200,000 members of the American Contract Bridge League. The book admirably meets its stated objective: "to provide an official and authoritative answer to any question a reader might ask about the game of contract bridge and its leading players" (preface). A complementary work is Terence Reese and Albert Dormer's *Bridge Player's Alphabetical Handbook* (Farber & Farber, 1981), a 224-page volume that describes every term used in the game.

The Official NBA Basketball Encyclopedia: The Complete History and Statistics of Professional Basketball. Written by Zander Hollander & Alex Sachare. Random House, 1989. 766p. $29.95.

The *Official NBA Basketball Encyclopedia* supersedes Hollander's earlier *Pro Basketball Encyclopedia* (1977) and NBA's *Official Encyclopedia of Pro Basketball* (1981). As the subtitle suggests, the encyclopedia contains detailed information on the history, teams, players, coaches, records, and rules of professional basketball. Roughly half the book consists of an "All-Time Player Directory" of over 2,600 pro players and their stats. The encyclopedia's "entertaining narrative style, black-and-white photographs, and pleasing format make it attractive for leisure reading as well as reference work" (*Reference Books Bulletin* in *Booklist*, March 1, 1990, p. 1387). A competing volume is David Neft and Richard Cohen's *Sports Encyclopedia: Pro Basketball* (2nd ed.

St. Martin's Press, 1989). Those interested in basketball might also want to check out Jim Savage's *Encyclopedia of the NCAA Basketball Tournament* (Dell, 1990), a single-volume work devoted to college basketball's premier competition.

The Oxford Companion to Chess. Written by David Hooper & Kenneth Whyld. 2nd ed. Oxford Univ. Press, 1992. 483p. $35.00.

Encyclopedic in scope and format and written in a readable style, the *Oxford Companion to Chess* was first published in 1984 and substantially revised in 1992. The current edition contains some 2,600 entries, including definitions of key chess terms, biographies of hundreds of grand masters and other prominent figures in the sport, famous games, and over 600 opening moves (which are cross-referenced to an appendix where they are charted by standard notation). The second (1992) edition "replaces its precursor as the best general reference for the 'royal game'" (*Choice*, April 1993, p. 1296). A similar though much less inclusive work is the 247-page *Chess Encyclopedia* (Facts on File, 1991) by Nathan Divinsky.

Oxford Companion to World Sports and Games. Edited by John Arlott. Oxford Univ. Press, 1975. 1,143p. $35.00.

Although now nearly 20 years old and dated in some respects, this standard encyclopedia remains a valuable reference source for detailed historical information on adult team sports played around the world. The approach is international; for instance, "Football" describes variations in the sport as played in the United States and the United Kingdom. Diagrams of playing fields or courts and summaries of basic rules normally accompany the alphabetically arranged articles. Another useful but also older volume offering similar information is the *Encyclopedia of Sports* (6th ed. A.S. Barnes, 1977), written by Frank Menke and revised by Pete Palmer. Regrettably, this classic work is now out of print. A more current but much less substantial source is RULES OF THE GAME.

Rules of the Game: The Complete Illustrated Encyclopedia of All Major Sports of the World. Compiled by the Diagram Group. Revised ed. St. Martin's Press, 1990. 320p. $24.95.

Rules of the Game, first published in 1974 and revised in 1990, furnishes fundamental information on the history, equipment, and regulations of 150 sports from archery to yacht racing. Some 2,000 clear illustrations comprise much of the text. The book "is a valuable one-volume source for the rules of a wide range of international sports" (*Library*

Journal, November 1, 1990, p. 80). Complementary sources are the older OXFORD COMPANION TO WORLD SPORTS AND GAMES and the *Sports Rules Encyclopedia* (2nd ed. Leisure Press, 1989), edited by Jess R. White; the latter covers only 52 sports, but they are treated in greater depth than in *Rules of the Game*.

Running from A to Z. Written by Cliff Temple. Stanley Paul (dist. by Trafalgar/David & Charles), 1987. 184p. $29.95.

While not a definitive work by any means, *Running from A to Z* does provide encyclopedic information about basic aspects of running, such as training, equipment, major races, and brief biographies of famous runners. No other encyclopedia on the sport is currently available.

Scarne's Encyclopedia of Card Games. Written by John Scarne. HarperCollins, 1983. 448p. Out of print (last priced at $10.10 paperbound).

Scarne, a well-known authority on gambling and odds, covers practically every card game ever devised in this instructional guide and rule book. The encyclopedia also includes sections on techniques for improving card-playing skills and how to detect cheating. The book is currently out of print, but a revision (or reprint) will most likely become available in the near future. A similar work is *Scarne's Encyclopedia of Games* (HarperCollins, 1973). A larger volume (628 pages), it covers major board, dice, tile, guessing, and parlor games, as well as card games; it too is out of print. Also useful is the single-volume *Ainslie's Complete Hoyle* (Simon & Schuster, 1975) by Tom Ainslie, which describes many card, board, and table games.

The World Encyclopedia of Soccer. Edited by Michael LaBlanc & Richard Henshaw. Gale Research, 1993. 504p. $39.95 hardcover; $14.95 paperbound.

This new soccer encyclopedia derives from Richard Henshaw's *Encyclopedia of World Soccer*, published by New Republic Books in 1979. Like its predecessor, the *World Encyclopedia of Soccer* treats the sport comprehensively, offering reliable information about its rules, associations, vocabulary, and prominent players, along with the history of soccer in various countries from Afghanistan to Zambia. There is also a section devoted to the World Cup, which will be played in the United States for the first time in 1994.

The World of Games: Their Origins and History, How to Play Games, and How to Make Them. Written by Jack Botermans & others. Facts on File, 1989. 240p. $29.95.

The *World of Games* limits its coverage to 150 board, dice, card, domino, and activity games that have universal appeal and are played, with variations, all around the world. The entries, which average a page or so in length, give each game's history and rules, as well as instructions for making boards, playing pieces, and the like from easily obtainable materials. Excellent color illustrations accompany the printed text. "The value of this book is in its historical and cross-cultural information (e.g., Native American games) and its handsome illustrations" (*Reference Books Bulletin* in *Booklist*, February 1, 1990, p. 1118).

❈ THEATER AND DANCE ❈

The American Musical Theatre: A Chronicle. Written by Gerald Bordman. 2nd ed. Oxford Univ. Press, 1992. 821p. $49.95.

First published in 1978 and updated in 1992, Bordman's chronological survey covers the musical theater in the United States from colonial times through the 1989–90 season, including every musical ever produced on Broadway. Substantial information—plot summary, list of major characters and who played them, critical commentary, etc.—is provided for each production. In all, Bordman's excellent book describes over 3,000 shows. "Chronicle is too tame a subtitle for this epic book on the American musical. Bordman's aim is to tell the story and make it entertaining. He does it well, and the book is satisfying whether consulted for information or

read for pleasure. Bordman gets his facts straight, and his opinions are trustworthy" (*American Reference Books Annual*, 1993, p. 582).

Other major reference works on the American musical theater are Ken Bloom's two-volume *American Song: The Complete Musical Theatre Companion* (Facts on File, 1985); Richard Lewine and Alfred Simon's single-volume *Songs of the Theater* (H.W. Wilson, 1984); and Thomas S. Hischak's *Stage It with Music: An Encyclopedic Guide to the American Musical Theatre* (Greenwood, 1993), also a single-volume work. Bordman's trilogy—*American Operetta* (Oxford Univ. Press, 1981); *American Musical Comedy* (Oxford Univ. Press, 1982); and *American Musical Revue* (Oxford Univ. Press, 1985)—offers specialized treatment by form of show and effectively supplements his *American Musical Theatre*.

Broadway: An Encyclopedic Guide to the History, People and Places of Times Square. Written by Ken Bloom. Facts on File, 1991. 442p. $50.00.

This readable and informative encyclopedia contains well over 300 A-to-Z entries describing the history of New York's Broadway and Times Square area and its theaters, impresarios, playwrights, composers, actors, producers, directors, restaurants, nightclubs, bars, hotels, publicity stunts, scandals, awards, and much more. Bloom, who has also compiled the aforementioned *American Song: The Complete Musical Theatre Companion* (Facts on File, 1985), enhances the text with some 200 black-and-white photos. "Bloom captures the essence of Broadway and makes the reader nostalgic for days past. Essential for theater collections" (*Library Journal*, November 1, 1990, p. 80).

The Cambridge Guide to American Theatre. Edited by Don B. Wilmeth & Tice L. Miller. Cambridge Univ. Press, 1993. 558p. $49.95.

New in 1993, the *Cambridge Guide to American Theatre* serves as a valuable complement to the older but more extensive and much admired OXFORD COMPANION TO AMERICAN THEATRE. The *Cambridge Guide*, which is encyclopedic in scope, consists of approximately 2,300 succinct A-to-Z entries encompassing all important aspects of the theater in the United States, including well-known plays, famous playhouses, and prominent actors, playwrights, producers, and directors. There are also about 100 topical entries dealing with such diverse subjects as theater architecture, female and male impersonation, magic, costume, Shakespeare on the U.S. stage, dramatic theory, and ethnic contributions to the American theater. "Wonderfully compact, well written, and generously illustrated, this [book] is recommended for most libraries" (*Library Journal*, February 15, 1993, p. 156).

Cambridge Guide to Asian Theatre. Edited by James R. Brandon. Cambridge Univ. Press, 1993. 272p. $49.95.

Similar in concept and construction to the publisher's other theater guides (i.e., the CAMBRIDGE GUIDE TO AMERICAN THEATRE and the CAMBRIDGE GUIDE TO WORLD THEATRE), this new reference work covers the theater arts in 20 Asian countries, including China, India, Pakistan, Korea, Japan, and Vietnam. Facts about major actors, playwrights, and directors appear within the articles on each national theater.

The Cambridge Guide to World Theatre. Edited by Martin Banham. Cambridge Univ. Press, 1989. 1,104p. $49.50 hardcover; $24.95 paperbound.

This fine single-volume encyclopedia is similar in purpose, size, scope, and price to the older and better known OXFORD COMPANION TO THE THEATRE. The newer *Cambridge Guide to World Theatre* furnishes an authoritative overview of the theater in all parts of the world, including countries and regions whose theater traditions are not generally known in the English-speaking world (such as Brazil, India, and the Middle East). In addition to information on national theaters, the book has articles on major theatrical figures as well as pertinent general topics, such as "Animals as Performers," "Cabaret," "Censorship," "Dramatic Theory," "Feminist Theatre," "Gay Theatre," and "Lighting." More than 300 photographs and drawings augment the printed text. "Truly encyclopedic in scope and worldwide in its breadth, this work presents much valuable information in one alphabetical listing about theater—historical, present day, stage, and television—and theater people, etc." (*Choice*, June 1989, p. 1654).

A Companion to the Medieval Theatre. Edited by Ronald W. Vince. Greenwood, 1989. 420p. $75.00.

This carefully researched reference work is intended mainly for students of the theater who are not medieval scholars. The book's alphabetically arranged articles cover major developments in the theater arts between the years 900 and 1500 throughout the world, with individual plays, playwrights, and genres receiving the lion's share of attention. "Procession and spectacle, emblematic costume and decor, place-and-scaffolding staging, the Assumption play, eclogue, farce, mumming, and interlude; the liturgical drama, the Passion play, the saint play, and the morality play; folk drama, courtly entertainment, and tournaments; secular and humanist drama—all are important to the world of medieval theater so thoroughly explored in this invaluable reference companion" (*American Reference Books Annual*, 1990, p. 579).

The Concise Oxford Dictionary of Ballet. Edited by Horst Koegler. 2nd ed. Oxford Univ. Press, 1982. 503p. $17.95 paperbound.

An English-language adaptation of the German *Friedrichs Ballett Lexikon von A-Z* (1972), the *Concise Oxford Dictionary of Ballet* first appeared in 1977 and was thoroughly revised and updated in 1982. It contains more than 5,000 entries covering all important facets of classical dance, including major ballets, dancers, choreographers, composers, theaters, schools and companies, technical terms, and cities around the world known for their appreciation and support of dance as an art form. A complementary work is the recently published INTERNA-TIONAL DICTIONARY OF BALLET. Two other useful titles focus on summarizing the world's best-known ballets: Mary Clarke and Clement Crisp's *Ballet Goer's Guide* (Knopf, 1981) and George Balanchine and Francis Mason's *101 Stories of the Great Ballets* (Doubleday, 1989), both single-volume works.

Dictionary of the Black Theatre: Broadway, Off-Broadway, and Selected Harlem Theatre. Written by Allen Woll. Greenwood, 1983. 359p. $45.00.

This valuable reference source provides concise information about approximately 300 plays, revues, and musicals "by, about, with, for and related to blacks" (preface), as well as the leading people and organizations connected with these productions. "This is a unique, well-executed reference book and a joyous one, celebrating the black theater's past and present and raising hopes for an even greater future" (*American Reference Books Annual*, 1984, p. 464). A complementary work, also in one volume, is Henry T. Sampson's *The Ghost Walks: A Chronological History of Blacks in Show Business, 1865–1910* (Scarecrow Press, 1988).

The Encyclopedia of the New York Stage, 1920–1930 (1985; 2 vols.); *The Encyclopedia of the New York Stage, 1930–1940* (1989; 1,299p.); *The Encyclopedia of the New York Stage, 1940–1950* (1992; 946p.). Edited by Samuel L. Leiter. Greenwood, 1985–92. 4 vols. $175.00 (1920–30); $175.00 (1930–40); $195.00 (1940–50).

Leiter, a drama professor, provides encyclopedic information about well over 5,000 professional theater productions—plays, musicals, revues, and revivals—staged on and off Broadway between 1920 and 1950. The initial publication, which covers the years 1920–30, is in two volumes; the other two, which cover the years 1930–40 and 1940–50, are single-volume works. Entries for each production present such basic information as principal actors, producers, directors, theater, opening date, length of run, production history, plot synopsis, and generous quotations from contemporary reviews. Each title in the series also has a number of useful appendixes, e.g., a subject listing of the plays by type, national origin, and content. In a review of the 1930–40 volume, James Rettig in *Wilson Library Bulletin* (January 1990, p. 126) puts Leiter's work in good perspective: "The thoroughness of coverage and richness of detail on each play exceed most libraries' need for information on a single decade of New York theater seasons; however, libraries with wide-ranging theater history collections will wel-

come the additional depth this gives those collections." Presumably, future volumes covering additional decades (1950–60, etc.) will be forthcoming. A complementary source is the much less extensive and more popularly written *Encyclopedia of the American Theatre, 1900–1975* (Revised ed. A.S. Barnes, 1979), a single-volume work by Edwin Bronner.

Gänzl's Book of the Musical Theatre. Written by Kurt Gänzl & Andrew Lamb. Schirmer, 1989. 1,353p. $75.00.

Modeled after the DEFINITIVE KOBBÉ'S OPERA BOOK, this large encyclopedic work describes more than 300 musical shows (operettas, comic operas, musical comedies, and the like) originating in the United States, Great Britain, France, Spain, Austria, Germany, and Hungary. Entries for each title, which range from four to six pages in length, furnish such essential information as major stage and film productions, a list of characters, and an act-by-act plot summary. "The worldwide proliferation of musical theater makes its documentation in a single volume impossible, but *Gänzl's Book of [the] Musical Theatre* is a most impressive selection from this wealth of material. . . . This is the only source that draws together musicals from more than just America and England. It will become a standard source" (*Library Journal*, April 15, 1989, p. 68). A complementary work is Stanley Green's *Encyclopedia of the Musical Theatre* (Dodd, Mead, 1976; reprinted by Da Capo, 1980), a one-volume encyclopedia that describes musical theater productions in New York and London from the late nineteenth century to 1975.

International Dictionary of Ballet. Edited by Martha Bremser. St. James Press (dist. by Gale Research), 1993. 2 vols. $230.00.

The new *International Dictionary of Ballet* contains more than 700 signed, essay-length profiles of significant ballets, ballet companies, and individual dancers, choreographers, and directors. Approximately 550 drawings and photographs accompany the articles. "It is especially valuable to have illustrations of lesser-known figures of the ballet and of works that may no longer be performed. . . . The *International Dictionary of Ballet* is an excellent compendium of biographical and historical information on the art of ballet and its practitioners" (*Reference Books Bulletin* in *Booklist*, January 15, 1994, p. 959). The set nicely complements and updates the CONCISE OXFORD DICTIONARY OF BALLET.

International Dictionary of Theatre. Edited by Mark Hawkins-Dady. St. James Press (dist. by Gale Research), 1992–. 3 vols. (in progress). $120.00 per vol.; $345.00 the set.

Volume 1 (1992) of this new three-volume reference work on the international theater is devoted to plays; specifically, it summarizes and critiques 620 notable plays representing various nationalities and time periods. Volume 2 (1993) covers prominent playwrights, and volume 3 (scheduled for late 1994) will cover actors, directors, and designers. Altogether the set, when completed, will comprise some 1,600 entries furnishing an authoritative historical survey of theater developments on a worldwide scale. As such, it complements the single-volume OXFORD COMPANION TO THE THEATRE and CAMBRIDGE GUIDE TO WORLD THEATRE.

Kabuki Encyclopedia: An English-Language Adaptation of Kabuki Jiten. Adapted by Samuel L. Leiter. Greenwood, 1979. 572p. $45.00.

An English-language adaptation of a work originally published in Japanese, this alphabetically arranged work presents a comprehensive guide to Kabuki, the traditional Japanese popular drama begun in the seventeenth century and now of much interest to westerners seeking to understand Japanese history and culture. The encyclopedia, which is intended to make "Kabuki accessible to non-Japanese theatre lovers" (introduction), covers virtually every term, name, and subject associated with the genre, including actors, playwrights, plays, theater architecture and management, props, costumes, and music. A review by Richard J. Kelly in *American Reference Books Annual* (1981, p. 478) rightly notes that the *Kabuki Encyclopedia* "should become the first resort for those seeking information on the topic." A companion work is Leiter's *Art of Kabuki: Famous Plays in Performance* (Univ. of California Press, 1979). For an excellent overview of Japanese theater generally, see the new CAMBRIDGE GUIDE TO ASIAN THEATRE.

The Oxford Companion to American Theatre. Written by Gerald Bordman. Oxford Univ. Press, 1984. 734p. $49.95.

An extension of the classic OXFORD COMPANION TO THE THEATRE, this encyclopedic work encompasses some 3,000 A-to-Z entries dealing with the North American theater. Topics covered include individual plays, playwrights, performers, producers, theaters, issues (such as censorship), and allied performing arts (the circus, Wild West shows, vaudeville, etc.). "This most companionable yet of the Oxford 'companions' sets out in concise, accurate, lucid prose the chief figures and works in the history of the American theater from 'Aarons, A.A.' (a 1920s producer) to *Zoo Story*.... Every library from school to university will find this an indispensable and reliable addition to its reference collection" (*Choice*, February 1985, p. 791). In 1987, the publisher issued a 451-page abridgment under the title *Concise Oxford Companion to American Theatre*; it is currently available in both hardcover ($24.95) and paperback ($13.95). A competing work is the recently published CAMBRIDGE GUIDE TO AMERICAN THEATRE.

The Oxford Companion to Canadian Theatre. Edited by Eugene Benson & L.W. Conolly. Oxford Univ. Press, 1989. 662p. $55.00.

The first major reference source to deal with both English and French Canadian theater, this welcome *Oxford Companion* contains 703 signed articles covering major plays, actors, playwrights, theaters, companies, genres, and topics, such as "Acting," "Education and Training," "Feminist Theatre," and "Multicultural Theatre." There are also substantial articles on the growth and development of theater in each of the Canadian provinces and territories. "To those south of the border for whom Canadian theater means little more than Stratford, *The Oxford Companion to Canadian Theatre* offers abundant instruction and delight.... Recommended for libraries supporting programs in Canadian studies, world literature, or drama and theater history" (*Choice*, July–August 1990, p. 1808).

The Oxford Companion to the Theatre. Edited by Phyllis Hartnoll. 4th ed. Oxford Univ. Press, 1983. 934p. $49.95.

Long a standard reference work on theater around the world (the first edition appeared in 1951 and was revised in 1957, 1967, and most recently in 1983), the *Oxford Companion to the Theatre* covers all important aspects of the legitimate theater, including excellent national and regional surveys. "An indispensable reference work for most libraries" (*Choice*, April 1984, p. 1116). Consumers should also be aware of the *Concise Oxford Companion to the Theatre* (Oxford Univ. Press, 1992), a 568-page abridged version of the *Oxford Companion to the Theatre*; edited by Phyllis Hartnoll and Peter Found, the *Concise Oxford* is currently available in hardcover at $35.00. Competing single-volume works are the more recent CAMBRIDGE GUIDE TO WORLD THEATRE; the *Facts on File Dictionary of the Theatre* (Facts on File, 1988), edited by William Packard and others; and the older but still useful *Encyclopedia of World Theater* (Scribner's, 1977), edited by Martin Esslin (also published as the *Illustrated Encyclopaedia of World Theatre* by Thames and Hudson).

Theatre Backstage from A to Z. Written by Warren C. Lounsbury & Norman Boulanger. 3rd revised ed. Univ. of Washington Press, 1989. 213p. $35.00 hardcover; $17.50 paperbound.

Originally published in 1959 as *Backstage from A to Z* and revised and updated several times since, *Theatre Backstage from A to Z* provides encyclopedic information on theater terminology concerning such technical aspects as lighting, sound, scene design, set construction, and props. The heavily illustrated book is aimed chiefly at professionals but will also be useful to serious amateurs. In a review of the third revised edition, *Reference Books Bulletin* (in *Booklist,* February 15, 1990, p. 1190) says, "This new edition includes a wealth of new information. Several hundred new terms have been added, primarily in the areas of computers, lighting, and sound equipment. The detailed entry *Lighting Control* covers the entire

realm of equipment, beginning with the most basic light boards, dimmers, and switchboards and progressing to the most sophisticated state-of-the-art microprocessor remote-control (computer) boards. . . . Highly recommended for most general theater and staging collections."

A companion volume is the same authors' *Theatre Lighting from A to Z* (Univ. of Washington Press, 1992), a 197-page book that greatly expands the lighting entries found in *Theatre Backstage from A to Z.* Another useful nuts-and-bolts reference source for stage people is James Thurston's *The What, Where, When of Theater Props: An Illustrated Chronology from Arrowheads to Video Games* (Betterway Books, 1992), which furnishes encyclopedic treatment of theatrical properties.

❊ TRANSPORTATION ❊

Concise Encyclopedia of Traffic & Transportation Systems. Edited by Markos Papageorgiou. Pergamon Press, 1991. 658p. $410.00.

Prepared by 135 specialists from 16 countries (mostly European), this scholarly encyclopedia deals with major aspects of contemporary transportation engineering, with particular emphasis on the infrastructure and effective use of highway, railroad, air, and maritime systems. The work draws on, updates, and augments material found in the highly regarded SYSTEMS AND CONTROL ENCYCLOPEDIA, published by Pergamon in 1987. Despite its high price, the *Concise Encyclopedia of Traffic & Transportation Systems* has been endorsed by reviewers: Eugene Jackson writes, "The present volume is recommended to those academic and public library collections with major emphasis on traffic-related subjects" (*American Reference Books Annual,* 1993, p. 674), and D.B. Stafford concludes, "Although very expensive, it [the encyclopedia] is recommended for university libraries serving advanced undergraduate and graduate students in systems engineering and traffic and transportation engineering" (*Choice,* March 1992, p. 1111).

Encyclopedia of American Cars, 1946–1959. Written by James H. Moloney & George H. Dammann. Crestline Publishing (dist. by Motorbooks International), 1980. 416p. $29.95.

This interesting and informative encyclopedia provides a detailed history of automobiles manufactured in the United States following World War II through the 1950s, the nostalgic period of tail fins and chromium galore. Heavily illustrated with black-

and-white photos, the book includes a section on experimental and custom-built cars that never made it into production. The prewar years are covered in a companion volume by Moloney and Dammann entitled *Encyclopedia of American Cars, 1930–1942* (Crestline Publishing, 1977); unfortunately, this work is out of print, although Motorbooks (the distributor) indicates it might be reissued in the near future. Two other useful sources of encyclopedic information on American passenger cars are the single-volume *50 Years of American Automobiles, 1939–1989* (Publications International, 1989) and the comprehensive three-volume *Standard Catalog of American Cars* (2nd ed. Krause, 1989), which covers the years 1805–1942 (volume 1), 1946–75 (volume 2), and 1976–86 (volume 3); note that no civilian cars were produced during 1942–45.

Encyclopedia of North American Railroading: 150 Years of Railroading in the United States and Canada. Written by Freeman Hubbard. McGraw-Hill, 1981. 377p. $68.40.

Hubbard's excellent encyclopedia includes A-to-Z articles on important people in the history of North American railroads, individual railroad companies, manufacturers of locomotives and cars, famous trains and train wrecks, railroad unions, railroad slang and business terminology, and the like. "This is a delightful book to browse in and it is potentially useful as an encyclopedic reference source. . . . It would be useful for all libraries from high school to university and would be particularly appropriate in home libraries of railfans or persons with more than a passing interest in railroads" (*Reference Books Bulletin* in *Booklist,* September 1, 1982,

p. 64). Complementary reference sources are the *Historical Guide to North American Railroads* (Kalmbach Publishing, 1985) and the *Train-Watcher's Guide to North American Railroads* (Kalmbach Publishing, 1984), both one-volume works prepared by George H. Drury.

The Illustrated Encyclopedia of General Aviation. Written by Paul Garrison. 2nd ed. TAB Books, 1990. 462p. $34.95 hardcover; $24.95 paperbound.

Although the title suggests Garrison's book is an aviation encyclopedia, it is more accurately an encyclopedic dictionary. The book, which first appeared in 1979 as the *Illustrated Encyclopedia/Dictionary of General Aviation*, contains alphabetically arranged entries describing basic terms and acronyms and abbreviations commonly used in the field, as well as individual airplanes, manufacturers, and related subjects. Garrison also includes directory information concerning aviation associations, agencies, publications, and airshows. Numerous photographs, charts, tables, and other graphics supplement the text. "Garrison is well qualified to compile this dictionary, with more than 24 books published with TAB in the field of aviation. *Illustrated Encyclopedia of General Aviation* is recommended for public and academic libraries" (*Reference Books Bulletin* in *Booklist*, June 15, 1990, p. 2031).

The International Encyclopedia of Aviation. Edited by David Mondey. Revised ed. Crown, 1988. 480p. $24.95.

The best single-volume encyclopedia on the subject currently available, the *International Encyclopedia of Aviation* furnishes a readable, accurate, well-illustrated, and reasonably detailed survey of the history of aviation, including biographies of major figures, definitions of key terminology, and a substantial section on military aviation. British in origin but international in perspective, the encyclopedia first appeared in 1977 and was modestly revised a decade later. Similar (if older and now out-of-print) works are the 218-page *Encyclopedia of Aviation* (Scribner's, 1977) and the 20-volume *Illustrated Encyclopedia of Aviation* (Marshall Cavendish, 1979). Complementary sources are the ILLUSTRATED ENCYCLOPEDIA OF GENERAL AVIATION and the WORLD ENCYCLOPEDIA OF CIVIL AIRCRAFT.

The New Encyclopedia of Motor Cars, 1885 to the Present. Edited by G.N. Georgano. 3rd ed. Dutton, 1982. 688p. Out of print (last priced at $45.00).

Now out of print (at least temporarily) but still enormously useful, Georgano's profusely illustrated encyclopedia describes some 4,300 different models of cars manufactured around the world between 1885 and 1982. Promotional photographs from carmakers accompany many of the models. The book, which also includes brief histories of major auto manufacturers, was first published in 1968 as the *Complete Encyclopedia of Motorcars* and updated twice, in 1973 and 1982. "An incredibly thorough encyclopedia which describes and illustrates the world's output of automobiles" (*Library Journal*, March 1, 1983, p. 450).

The Oxford Companion to Ships and the Sea. Edited by Peter Kemp. Oxford Univ. Press, 1976. 972p. $29.95 paperbound.

This outstanding one-volume encyclopedia consists of 3,700 alphabetically arranged articles on practically every aspect of ships and the sea from earliest recorded history to the present, including famous explorers and their vessels, major sea battles, navigation rules and terms, ship design, sea lore, and writers and artists associated with the sea. Many informative diagrams and photographs enhance the printed text. "The writing is clear and authoritative, the editing experienced and intelligent. . . . This book should prove so informative and entertaining that its binding will not withstand the heavy usage" (*American Reference Books Annual*, 1978, pp. 779–80). Sources complementing the *Oxford Companion* are the 256-page *Encyclopedia of Ships and Seafaring* (Crown, 1980), which is also edited by Peter Kemp, and the small but richly illustrated *Visual Dictionary of Ships and Sailing* (Dorling Kindersley, dist. by Houghton Mifflin, 1991), a 64-page book that appeals to children and adults alike.

Private Pilot's Dictionary and Handbook. Written by Kirk Polking. 2nd ed. Arco, 1986. 245p. $12.95 paperbound.

Based on various U.S. government publications such as the *Airman's Information Manual*, Polking's encyclopedic handbook covers essential terminology, symbols, equipment, operations, procedures, and flight rules for student pilots. Numerous instructional charts, graphs, and other illustrations help make the book a valuable reference for beginning pilots.

Rand McNally Encyclopedia of Transportation. Rand McNally, 1976. 256p. Out of print (last priced at $16.95).

Unfortunately, at this time there is no general transportation encyclopedia on the market for the nonspecialist. The older *Rand McNally Encyclopedia of Transportation* covers all forms of transportation in clear, accurate, popularly written articles suitable for laypeople and students at the high school level and up, but it is quite dated and has long been out of print. A similar work for children and young students is the *Silver Burdett Encyclopedia of Transport* (Silver Burdett, 1983); published in four volumes of 64 pages each, this encyclopedia is also out of print.

World Encyclopedia of Civil Aircraft: From Leonardo da Vinci to the Present. Written by Enzo Angelucci; translated by S.M. Harris. Crown, 1982. 414p. $29.95.

First published in Italy in 1981 under the title *Atlante Enciclopedico degli Aerei Civili del Mondo da Leonardo a oggi*, this excellent encyclopedia covers all types of civil and commercial aircraft from the earliest efforts at flight to space-age vehicles. Angelucci, who has also produced the companion *Rand McNally Encyclopedia of Military Aircraft, 1914–* *1980* (Rand McNally, 1983), furnishes authoritative, detailed information about hundreds of planes. Especially noteworthy are the book's many superbly rendered illustrations. "The rapid development of civilian aviation is graphically depicted. The 165 color plates and some 3000 illustrations spur readers on to new images in flight. The accompanying text, although overshadowed by the illustrations, is lively and informative. . . . Those in fifth grade and up will find it [the encyclopedia] useful for gaining historical perspective of the field" (*School Library Journal*, May 1984, p. 26). Complementary works are the ILLUSTRATED ENCYCLOPEDIA OF GENERAL AVIATION, the INTERNATIONAL ENCYCLOPEDIA OF AVIATION, and the well-known *Jane's All the World's Aircraft* (Jane's Publishing, 1912–), an annual publication currently edited by Mark Lambert and others.

Foreign-Language Encyclopedias

❊ ❊ ❊ ❊ ❊ ❊ ❊ ❊ ❊

OVERVIEW

This section of *Kister's Best Encyclopedias* identifies and briefly describes selected general encyclopedias available in nine major languages other than English: Chinese, Dutch, French, German, Italian, Japanese, Korean, Russian, and Spanish.

Foreign-language encyclopedias are potentially valuable sources of information for English-speaking people in North America, particularly students. While English is very much the predominant language in the United States and Canada (with the obvious exception of the province of Quebec), individuals who are bilingual or multilingual often look to foreign-language encyclopedias for geographical, biographical, cultural, and historical information not ordinarily found in English-language reference works. Bill Katz, a well-known authority on library reference work, elaborates on this point in his *Basic Information Sources* (6th ed., 1992, p. 261):

> Even for users with the most elementary knowledge of the language, several of the foreign works are useful for their fine illustrations and maps. For example, the *Enciclopedia Italiana* [see below under Italian encyclopedias] boasts some of the best illustrations of any encyclopedia, particularly in the area of the fine arts. A foreign encyclopedia is equally useful for point of view: Some American readers may be surprised at the manner in which the Civil War, for example, is treated in the French and the German encyclopedias. Further, the evaluation of American writers and national heroes in these works is sometimes equally revealing about the way Europeans judge the United States. More specifically, the foreign

encyclopedia is helpful for information on less well known figures not found in American or British works, for foreign language bibliographies, for detailed maps of cities and regions, and for other information ranging from plots of lesser-known novels and musicals to identification of place names.

Larger public and academic libraries will almost certainly have at least one encyclopedia in French, Spanish, and German, and possibly other languages as well, depending on the composition and educational requirements of the library's clientele. Likewise, school and public libraries serving communities with large ethnic or nonnative populations will stock encyclopedias in the appropriate language or languages. And individuals proficient in a particular foreign language might want to own an encyclopedia in that language, contingent on their reference needs and the cost involved.

In most instances, the encyclopedias noted in this section of *Kister's Best Encyclopedias* can be acquired through North American book dealers specializing in reference materials published abroad. A leading foreign-language bookseller is the New York firm of French & European Publications, Inc. Established in 1928, the company has been headed for many years by Emanuel Molho, a well-known specialist in the foreign book trade and compiler of *The Dictionary Catalogue* (2nd ed., 1989), a 178-page paperbound price list devoted to dictionaries and encyclopedias in a wide variety of languages. French & European Publications is the largest dealer in French and Spanish books in North America today; in addition, the store stocks materials in many other languages.

Mr. Molho—to whom the author of *Kister's Best Encyclopedias* is grateful for his assistance in preparing this section of the book—offers this general advice to those interested in acquiring foreign-language publications, including encyclopedias and other reference works:

One of the main dilemmas confronting the buyer of foreign-language books is the decision to order through an established importer and pay higher prices, or to deal directly with a foreign publisher or distributor. There are trade-offs in both cases.

Foreign-language book acquisition is not an exercise for the fainthearted. For the most experienced of foreign book importers, it is an exercise fraught with problems and futility; for the uninitiated, it is a virtual impossibility.

The acquisition of foreign-language books begins with a knowledge of what is available abroad, a basic knowledge of foreign languages, and a thorough knowledge of foreign publishers and/or reliable foreign book distributors. It involves corresponding, often in the language of the country from where the books are being bought, translating foreign-language documents and invoices, dealing in international currencies, and clearing customs. It entails long waits for books, errors in fulfillment of orders, exchanging books, returning defective copies, and much frustration from all but a handful of countries. That is why many libraries, bookstores, and individuals opt to deal through a foreign book importer who, within the framework of higher prices than those abroad, performs all of the ancillary acquisition services and often stocks the required books.

In foreign-language encyclopedia and book acquisition, the buyer often has no knowledge of what he or she is ordering. Advice is required on the contents of an encyclopedia,

the number of volumes, date(s) of publication, type of binding, number of illustrations, etc. Unless the customer has access to foreign publishers' catalogs and at least the equivalent of the foreign editions of *Books in Print*, he or she has to rely solely on recommendations from others—such as those provided in this section of *Kister's Best Encyclopedias*. A reliable book importer will be able either to supply the necessary information or, through foreign contacts via telephone or fax, be able to furnish it within a short period of time. The same importer, who often brings in books by air on weekly consolidations, will be able to fill orders within weeks, rather than months, critical for students who require their books before classes start, rather than after they are over, which is often the case when orders are directed abroad.

As a foreign book importer since 1928, French & European Publications is a specialist in every facet of the trade. We suggest that those who have the ability to overcome the myriad of problems of foreign book acquisition buy directly from abroad. For those who have neither the time nor expertise, choose a reliable importer.

For current prices and other pertinent information about foreign-language encyclopedias, write, call, or fax: Mr. Emanuel Molho, French & European Publications, Inc., Rockefeller Center Promenade, 610 Fifth Avenue, New York, NY 10020-2497, 212-581-8810 (telephone) 212-265-1094 (fax).

Two other prominent North American book dealers specializing in foreign-language reference materials are Adler's Foreign Books, 915 Foster Street, Evanston, IL 60201-3199, 708-866-6329 (telephone), 708-866-6287 (fax); and Schoenhof's Foreign Books, 76A Mount Auburn Street, Cambridge, MA 02138, 617-547-8855 (telephone), 617-547-8551 (fax)

❀ CHINESE-LANGUAGE ENCYCLOPEDIAS ❀

The Chinese-Language Concise Encyclopaedia Britannica. Chicago: Encyclopaedia Britannica, Inc. & Taiwan Chung Hwa Book Company Ltd., 1988. 20 vols. $995.00; also available in 10-vol. edition at $395.00.

Two different editions of the *Chinese-Language Concise Encyclopaedia Britannica* are available. The 20-volume set is a Taiwanese translation of the NEW ENCYCLOPAEDIA BRITANNICA rendered in traditional Chinese characters. It comprises roughly 28 million words, 15,300 pages, 85,000 articles, and more than 7,000 illustrations. Approximately 2,600 of the articles are original, written by specialists commissioned to treat particular aspects of Chinese culture and history in greater depth than that found in the English-language version. The 10-volume edition, published in 1984, is largely a translation of the *Micropaedia* portion of the NEW ENCYCLOPAEDIA BRITANNICA in the simplified Chinese characters preferred by the government of the People's Republic of China. It consists of 17 million words, 71,000 articles, and some 5,000 illustrations. The articles are arranged alphabetically according to the Pinyin system of Romanizing titles. Most readers of Chinese in North America will want the traditional-character translation provided in the 20-volume set, although academic libraries serving students from mainland China will find the 10-volume translation also in demand.

※ DUTCH-LANGUAGE ENCYCLOPEDIAS ※

Grote Nederlandse Larousse Encyclopedie. Hasselt: Heideland-Oris, 1972–80. 26 vols. Check with publisher or bookseller for price.

Modeled on the French *Grand Larousse Encyclopédique* (1960–64), this heavily illustrated set is best known for its numerous bibliographies found at the end of each volume. An older set, it may no longer be in print.

Grote Spectrum Encyclopedie. Amsterdam: Het Spectrum, 1974–79. 25 vols. Check with publisher or bookseller for price.

Similar in design and purpose to the English-language ACADEMIC AMERICAN ENCYCLOPEDIA, the *Grote Spectrum Encyclopedie* contains more than 13 million words accompanied with some 24,000 full-color illustrations. Its text is machine-readable, which increases the possibility of more frequent revisions in the future. The publisher's smaller 20-volume *Spectrum Compact Encyclopedie* is based on the *Grote Spectrum*.

Grote Winkler Prins Encyclopedie. 9th ed. Amsterdam: Elsevier, 1985–93. 26 vols. $4,995.00.

The first five editions (1870–1938) of this premier Dutch encyclopedia appeared under the title *Winkler Prins Algemeene Encyclopedie.* The sixth edition (1947–54) shortened the title to *Winkler Prins Encyclopedie* and the seventh edition (1970–78) became the *Grote Winkler Prins Encyclopedie,* the current title. Like its predecessors, the eighth edition was issued volume-by-volume, appearing between 1979 and 1984; the present edition, the ninth, was begun in 1985 and just completed in May 1993. The set, which comprises about 15,000 pages and includes 13,000 illustrations, maintains the same high editorial standards of the earlier editions. A unique feature is an illustrated historical survey of one full century at the beginning of each volume; volume 1, for instance, covers the first century A.D., volume 2 the second century, and so on.

※ FRENCH-LANGUAGE ENCYCLOPEDIAS ※

Dictionnaire Encyclopédique Larousse. Paris: Larousse, 1993 (revised annually). 1,536p. $225.00.

Revised every year, this standard one-volume reference work combines the function of dictionary and encyclopedia, furnishing concise coverage of both the French language and basic factual information on scientific, technical, economic, biographical, and geographical subjects.

Encyclopaedia Universalis. 3rd ed. Paris: Encyclopaedia Universalis France (dist. by Encyclopaedia Britannica in Chicago), 1990. 30 vols. plus 2-vol. suppl. $1,595.00.

Originally published between 1968 and 1974, this highly regarded encyclopedia has since undergone two revisions, first in 1980 and most recently in 1990, when the set was expanded from 20 to 30 volumes. Volumes 1–23, called the *Corpus,* contain more than 10,000 extended articles covering significant areas of knowledge. Volumes 24–26, the *Symposium,* comprise 177 essays on world trends along with recent social, economic, and demographic data on countries. Volumes 27–30, the *Thesaurus-Index,* provide both index references to the *Corpus* and approximately 25,000 capsule articles on quite specific topics. There is also a two-volume supplement that brings together 350 articles dealing with important ideas and concepts. All told, the set offers 33,500 pages of authoritative, reasonably current general information in clear, readable French. A yearbook entitled *Universalia* helps keep *Encyclopaedia Universalis* up-to-date.

Encyclopédie de L'Univers en Couleurs. Paris: Larousse, 1989. 8 vols. $795.00.

Aimed chiefly at secondary school students, this thematically arranged encyclopedia has a strong science orientation, with individual volumes devoted to the natural world, the earth, technology, and the physical sciences. The text is profusely illustrated with some 15,000 photographs, line drawings, diagrams, and the like.

Grand Dictionnaire Encyclopédique Larousse. Paris: Larousse, 1982–89. 10 vols. $1,250.00.

Produced under the editorial supervision of the highly respected Claude Dubois, this multivolume encyclopedia from the house of Larousse adheres to founder Pierre Larousse's philosophy of combining encyclopedic and linguistic entries in one alphabetical sequence. The encyclopedia also features excellent illustrations, as Bill Katz notes in his *Basic Information Sources* (6th ed., 1992, p. 262): "There is a strong emphasis on brilliant illustrations, usually in full color. Each page includes photographs, charts, maps, diagrams and the like. Regardless of one's command of French, everyone will enjoy the illustrations." This set largely supersedes the well-known *Grand Larousse Encyclopédique* (1960–64), also published in 10 volumes.

Grand Larousse Junior. Paris: Larousse, 1992. 10 vols. Check with publisher or bookseller for price.

This colorful, heavily illustrated, handsomely made set for children consists of 10 chronological volumes covering the human experience from prehistory to the present time. Individual volumes, which average 250 pages in length, treat such broad topics as classical civilizations, the Renaissance, the Industrial Revolution, the twentieth century, and the next century.

Grand Larousse Universel en 15 Volumes. Paris: Larousse, 1988. 15 vols. $2,495.00.

A large work containing more than 11,000 pages, 190,000 concise entries (of which about 100,000 deal with French vocabulary), and 25,000 illustrations, the 15-volume *Grand Larousse Universel* provides authoritative information for the French-speaking student. A cut-down version called *Grand Larousse en 5 Volumes* plus an updating supplement entitled *Actua* is available for $995.00.

La Grande Encyclopédie. Paris: Larousse, 1971–90. 20 vols. plus index vol., atlas, and 3 suppls. $2,995.00.

A twentieth-century revision and extension of the great nineteenth-century French encyclopedia of the same title (published in 31 volumes between 1886 and 1902), this lavishly illustrated set contains more than 13,000 pages of text covering approximately 8,000 topics or "articles-dossiers" prepared by internationally respected specialists. All areas of knowledge are treated, but emphasis is on contemporary developments, particularly in the areas of science and technology. Harvey Einbinder, writing in *Wilson Library Bulletin* (December 1980, p. 258), has praised *La Grande Encyclopédie* for its "dazzling profusion of color photographs, drawings, and color plates integrated with a lively, informative text." The 20-volume set is augmented by an index volume, world atlas, and three supplements (1981, 1985, 1990) that help keep the set reasonably current.

Larousse des Jeunes Encyclopédie. Paris: Larousse, 1991. 1,504p. $95.00.

Intended for young students in the elementary grades, the single-volume *Larousse des Jeunes Encyclopédie* is organized A-to-Z around 1,000 essential words and concepts covering major areas of knowledge. The volume, which is clearly written and contains approximately 3,000 color illustrations, represents an ideal reference work for young students in North America learning French as a second language.

Le Petit Larousse Illustré. Paris: Larousse, 1993 (revised annually). 1,784p. $95.00.

Like so many reference books bearing the Larousse imprint, the much esteemed *Petit Larousse* offers the user both lexical and encyclopedic information, the current edition consisting of nearly 60,000 headwords, 25,000 encyclopedic entries, and 3,600 illustrations in almost 1,800 pages of text. This compact work—the best known of all French one-volume reference works—is updated annually. A 1,824-page deluxe edition appears under the title *Petit Larousse en Couleurs*; also published annually, it currently sells for $175.00.

Théma Encyclopédie Larousse. Paris: Larousse, 1990–91. 5 vols. $750.00.

Each of the five volumes comprising this handsomely produced set covers basic knowledge in a broad subject area: Volume 1 is entitled *Human History*; volume 2, *The World Today*; volume 3, *Science and Technology*; volume 4, *Arts and Culture*; and volume 5, *Biology and Medicine*. Intended for secondary school and college students as well as adults, *Théma* is heavily illustrated, with approximately 3,000 photos, 1,000 drawings, and 400 maps.

GERMAN-LANGUAGE ENCYCLOPEDIAS

Brockhaus Enzyklopädie. 19th ed. Wiesbaden: Brockhaus, 1986. 24 vols., plus suppls. $3,995.00.

One of the most famous and successful general encyclopedias in the world, *Brockhaus* is now in its nineteenth edition. The name is as well known in Germany as *Larousse* is in France or *Britannica* is in English-speaking countries. The first edition of *Brockhaus*, the work of innovative German publisher Friedrich Arnold Brockhaus, appeared between 1796 and 1808 under the title *Konversations-Lexikon*. Later, the set became *Brockhaus' Konversations-Lexikon* and, more recently, the sixteenth (1952–63) and eighteenth editions (1977–81) bore the title *Der Grosse Brockhaus*. The set is particularly noted for its short entries, popular approach, and strong emphasis on German historical, geographical, and biographical topics. Numerous smaller works derive from *Brockhaus*, including the six-volume *Der Neue Brockhaus* (7th ed., 1984–85), a two-volume edition entitled *Der Brockhaus* (1984), and the single-volume *Volks-Brockhaus*, which is published annually.

Das Bertelsmann Lexikon: Die Grosse Bertelsmann Lexikothek. Revised ed. Gutersloh: Bertelsmann Lexikon-Verlag, 1984–85. 25 vols. $4,490.00.

This excellent general German-language encyclopedia consists of 10 alphabetically arranged volumes covering basic information in approximately 120,000 concise articles, 14 thematic volumes devoted to lengthy articles on important topics in all areas of knowledge, and an atlas volume. Well illustrated with thousands of full-color photographs, diagrams, maps, etc., the set's authoritative text and modern design made it an instant success in Germany when first published in 1972–76. Interested consumers can acquire the 10 A-to-Z volumes from French & European Publications for $1,495.00, the 14 thematic volumes and atlas for $2,995.00, or the entire set for $4,490.00.

Der Neue Herder. 2nd ed. Freiburg: Herder, 1973–75. 14 vols. $1,195.00.

Along with *Brockhaus*, *Meyer*, and *Bertelsmann*, *Herder* is a major name in encyclopedia publishing in present-day Germany. *Der Neue Herder* (*The New Herder*) derives from the 10-volume *Der Grosse Herder* (5th ed., 1953–56), a medium-sized general encyclopedia noted for its short, reliable articles and excellent illustrations. Of the 14 volumes that comprise the *Neue Herder*, six are arranged alphabetically and eight topically by various scientific subjects.

Meyers Enzyklopädisches Lexikon. 9th ed. Mannheim: Bibliographisches Institut Lexikonverlag, 1973–81. 25 vols. plus suppls. $4,995.00 (suppls. additional).

As indicated above, *Meyer* is a famous name in German encyclopedias. *Meyers Enzyklopädisches Lexikon*, which first appeared between 1840 and 1845, currently contains 250,000 brief entries accompanied by some 26,000 small illustrations, many in full color. Each volume also includes several lengthy essays by special contributors. Note that the incomplete eighth edition (1936–42), entitled *Meyers Neues Lexikon*, embraced Hitler's National Socialism and was heavily tainted by Nazi ideology. As a consequence, the Meyer firm was disbanded after World War II; happily the current edition has returned to the high standards of earlier editions.

❊ ITALIAN-LANGUAGE ENCYCLOPEDIAS ❊

Enciclopedia Einaudi. Torino: G. Einaudi, 1977–84. 16 vols. $2,495.00.

Produced by one of Italy's best known and largest scholarly publishers, this solid middle-sized encyclopedia provides substantial articles on all important aspects of knowledge. The final volume includes an index and many charts and graphs.

Enciclopedia Europea. Milan: Garzanti, 1976–84. 12 vols. $3,500.00.

Garzanti, founded in 1938, is a well-respected Italian reference book publisher. The 12-volume *Europea* is noted for its fine illustrations, authoritative perspective of European developments, and many non-Italian contributors, who include such luminaries as Edward Teller, Arnold Toynbee, and Claude Levi-Strauss. The publisher also issues smaller general encyclopedias, including *Enciclopedia Garzanti* (in five volumes), *Enciclopedia Universale Garzanti* (two volumes), and the single-volume *La Nuova Enciclopedia Universale Garzanti*.

Enciclopedia Italiana di Scienze, Lettere ed Arti. Rome: Istituto della Enciclopedia Italiana, 1929–. 49 vols. (in progress). $17,000.00.

Particularly valuable for its excellent illustrations and color plates, this largest and most famous of all Italian-language general encyclopedias includes long, signed, authoritative articles covering every significant area of knowledge, with particular emphasis on subjects in the arts and humanities. A few articles expound the Fascist point of view (Mussolini himself contributed to the long article "Fascismo" in volume 14), but the overall impartiality of this huge encyclopedia is not seriously compromised. The index (volume 36) contains about 400,000 entries. Ten-year supplements (called appendices) help keep the encyclopedia reasonably up-to-date. At present, the set contains 46 volumes, with three more scheduled for publication by 1995–96. In addition, the publisher has recently produced *Enciclopedia del*

Novecento (1975–89), an eight-volume complement to *Italiana* that concentrates on twentieth-century trends.

Grande Dizionario Enciclopedico UTET. 3rd ed. Torino: Unione Tipografico-Editrice Torinese (UTET), 1966–79. 20 vols. plus suppl. $4,995.00.

This middle-sized adult encyclopedia resembles the ENCICLOPEDIA ITALIANA in format, although it is less detailed, more popularly and concisely written, less impressively illustrated, and less expensive. Volume 20 consists of a 200,000-entry index and an atlas. A supplement entitled *Cronologia Universale* appeared in 1979. A fourth edition is said to be underway.

※ JAPANESE-LANGUAGE ENCYCLOPEDIAS ※

Britannica International Encyclopaedia. Tokyo: TBS-Britannica Company. (dist. by Encyclopaedia Britannica of Chicago), 1975. 29 vols. $2,484.00.

The award-winning *Britannica International Encyclopaedia*, while loosely based on the NEW ENCYCLOPAEDIA BRITANNICA, contains much original material, including articles by prominent Japanese authorities. The set is composed of several distinct parts: the *Main Body* in 20 volumes, which consists of 5,000 lengthy articles and is similar to the *Macropaedia* in the English-language *Britannica*; the *Reference Guide* in six volumes, which provides quick reference entries like the *Micropaedia*; and the *Reader's Guide, Study Guide and Bibliography*, and *General Index*, all single-volume aids to accessing the contents of the *Britannica International Encyclopaedia*. Interested consumers should note that the *Reader's Guide* is available on CD-ROM— but not the encyclopedia itself. The price of the set with the CD-ROM *Reader's Guide* included is $2,863.00.

Daijiten Desuku. Tokyo: Kodansha, 1983. 1,832p. $99.95.

Daijiten Desuku—in English *Encyclopedia of Contemporary Knowledge*—is a serviceable single-volume general encyclopedia in Japanese that features concise

articles accompanied by numerous color illustrations. Kodansha also publishes the excellent English-language JAPAN: AN ILLUSTRATED ENCYCLOPEDIA.

Dai-Nihon Hyakka Jiten. Tokyo: Shôgakukan, 1972–73. 23 vols. Check with publisher or bookseller for price.

Dai-Nihon Hyakka Jiten, or *Encyclopedia Japonica* (as it is known in the West), is a well-edited, handsomely illustrated general encyclopedia for adults. Dated but still very useful for historical information, the set contains numerous short articles on basic subjects, including places and people in North America. For instance, users will find short biographies of such figures as Arthur Miller, Glenn Miller, Henry Miller, and Mitch Miller.

Heibonsha Dai-Hyakka Jiten. Tokyo: Heibonsha, 1984–85. 16 vols. Check with publisher or bookseller for price.

In large measure, this short-entry encyclopedia replaces Heibonsha's well-known *Sekai Dai-Hyakka Jiten*, a 37-volume work first published between 1955 and 1963. The new encyclopedia covers essential knowledge in approximately 7,000 articles. Established more than 80 years ago, Heibonsha is one of Japan's foremost publishers of reference materials.

※ KOREAN-LANGUAGE ENCYCLOPEDIA ※

The Britannica World Encyclopaedia. Seoul: Korea Britannica Corporation (dist. by Encyclopaedia Britannica of Chicago), 1992– (in progress). 27 vols. $1,592.00.

This multivolume encyclopedia is a Korean-language edition of the NEW ENCYCLOPAEDIA BRITANNICA. Published in cooperation with *Dong-A Ilbo*, Korea's national daily newspaper, the *Britannica World*

Encyclopaedia (BWE) began appearing in the fall of 1992 and should be completed by the end 1994, if the publisher holds to its announced schedule. The editors have added material to the original *Britannica* text that is of particular interest to Korean readers and contributed by scholars from that country. According to promotional material issued by the publisher, *BWE* takes into account the current political situation in Korea: "With the aim of providing the most ultimately useful encyclopedia for more than 70 million Koreans throughout the world, the BWE has taken great pains to cover North Korean topics in a realistic manner. In this way the editors have made their own contribution to realizing a unified Korea." How the current political conflicts between the two Koreas will affect the reception and sales of the encyclopedia is difficult to gauge at this point.

❋ RUSSIAN-LANGUAGE ENCYCLOPEDIAS ❋

Bol'shaia Sovetskaia Entsiklopediia. 3rd ed. Moscow: Sovetskaia Entsiklopediia, 1969–78. 30 vols. in 31. Check with publisher or bookseller for price.

The basic general encyclopedia for adults and older students in Russia and Eastern Europe, *Bol'shaia Sovetskaia Entsiklopediia* (or BSE) first appeared in 65 volumes between 1926 and 1947, followed by a 53-volume second edition published between 1949 and 1960, and finally the present 30-volume third edition between 1969 and 1978. Although BSE is reasonably objective in most respects, it naturally exhibits a Marxist-Leninist bias in such areas as philosophy, economics, sociology, and political science. For instance, the American Declaration of Independence is portrayed as the product of a bourgeois revolution. A yearbook, published annually since 1957, helps keep *BSE* abreast of current developments. North Americans should also be aware that an English-language translation of *BSE* is available from Macmillan under the title the GREAT SOVIET ENCYCLOPEDIA (see page 365).

❋ SPANISH-LANGUAGE ENCYCLOPEDIAS ❋

Aula: Enciclopédia del Estudiante. Barcelona: Editorial Planeta, 1988. 10 vols. $350.00.

This encyclopedia for upper elementary and junior high school students treats roughly 1,000 broad topics. Profusely illustrated with color photographs, drawings, and charts, *Aula's* articles are concise, well written, and emphasize Spanish and European history, culture, and achievements.

Diccionario Enciclopédico: Enseñanza General Básica. Chicago: Encyclopaedia Britannica, 1988. 15 vols. $199.00.

Designed for young students in the elementary and intermediate grades, *Diccionario Enciclopédico* contains more than 10,000 very brief entries accompanied with 2,000 color illustrations in 15 volumes consisting of 40 pages each. The set, which provides both encyclopedic and lexical information, was first published in Barcelona by Multilibro. Volume 15 is an index to the set.

Diccionario Enciclopédico Espasa. 9th ed. Madrid: Espasa-Calpe, 1985. 24 vols. $2,495.00.

An encyclopedic dictionary for older students and adults, *Diccionario Enciclopédico Espasa* includes more than 250,000 brief factual articles covering all important areas of knowledge, with emphasis on biographical and geographical topics. The set also furnishes information about words, with definitions in Spanish and equivalencies for most terms in English, French, Italian, and German. The text is complemented by thousands of color illustrations.

Diccionario Enciclopédico Larousse. Barcelona: Editorial Planeta, 1990. 12 vols. $995.00.

Based on the excellent French GRAND DICTIONNAIRE ENCYCLOPÉDIQUE LAROUSSE, this Spanish-language *Larousse* contains well over 100,000 concise entries accompanied by 7,600 photographs, 1,150 drawings, 600 maps, and 100 plates. Authoritative, up-to-date, and reasonably priced, the *Diccionario Enciclopédico Larousse* in 12 volumes represents one of the best buys currently available for public, school, and academic libraries in North America. Prospective purchasers should also know that an eight-volume edition of the set is available at $695.00.

Enciclopedia de los Niños. John Paton, compiler. Madrid: Editorial Everest, 1990. 10 vols. $155.00.

Aimed directly at students in the elementary grades but also useful for older North Americans learning Spanish as a second language, this children's encyclopedia contains approximately 1,200 entries complemented by 2,000 color illustrations. The set originally appeared in English in Great Britain under the Grisewood & Dempsey imprint. A similar set is ENCICLOPEDIA JUVENIL ILUSTRADA.

Enciclopedia de Oro. Mexico City: Novaro, 1984. 16 vols. $225.00.

Like Paton's ENCICLOPEDIA DE LOS NIÑOS and ENCICLOPEDIA JUVENIL ILUSTRADA, *Enciclopedia de Oro* is intended for children in the elementary grades. A Spanish-language translation of the *Little Golden Encyclopedia,* the set is easy to read and has numerous color illustrations.

Enciclopedia General Planeta. Barcelona: Editorial Planeta, 1992. 5 vols. $195.00.

This inexpensive five-volume encyclopedia for adults and older students includes approximately 50,000 brief entries, with emphasis on universally important biographical and geographical topics. The set contains relatively few diagrams and drawings (all in black-and-white) and no photographs. A 64-page color world atlas is found at the end of volume 5.

Enciclopedia Hispánica. Revised ed. Barcelona: Encyclopaedia Britannica, 1992–93. 18 vols. $999.00.

First published in 1990, this outstanding Spanish-language encyclopedia represents a thorough revision and updating of *Enciclopedia Barsa,* a multivolume set that first appeared in the 1950s and was last issued in 1985. Designed principally for students in North American secondary schools and colleges, *Hispánica* "covers the world from a Hispanic perspective—in fact, it's the only truly international encyclopedia in the Spanish language" (1993 publisher's catalog). The set is organized along the lines of the NEW ENCYCLOPAEDIA BRITANNICA, with a two-volume *Micropedia,* 14-volume *Macropedia,* one-volume *Datapedia* (which furnishes maps and information about the countries of the world), and one-volume *Temapedia* (which acts as a thematic guide to the set). Isabel Schon, writing in *Booklist* (July 1992, p. 1965), calls *Hispánica* "Definitely one of the best general encyclopedias in the Spanish language." Given the set's authority and affordable price, it is a first-choice purchase for school and academic libraries in the market for a substantial Spanish-language encyclopedia.

Enciclopédia Ilustrada Cumbre. Mexico City: Promotora Editorial (dist. by Grolier), 1991. 14 vols. $319.00.

Intended for students reading at the seventh grade level and up, this general encyclopedia consists of brief, well-written articles covering all areas of knowledge, with particular emphasis on history, geography, science, and biography. Over 7,000 illustrations, most in black-and-white, augment the printed text.

Enciclopedia Juvenil Ilustrada. Barcelona: Editorial Planeta, 1991. 5 vols. $150.00.

Enciclopedia Juvenil Ilustrada is the Spanish-language edition of the British *Dorling Kindersley Children's Illustrated Encyclopedia,* which is published in North America in one volume as the RANDOM HOUSE CHILDREN'S ENCYCLOPEDIA. This is a good beginning encyclopedia for young students learning Spanish.

Enciclopedia Universal Ilustrada Europeo-Americana. Barcelona: Espasa-Calpe, 1907–33. 70 vols. plus 10-vol. suppl; annual suppls., 1934 to present. $8,995.00.

Known simply as *Espasa* (after the publisher), this monumental work provides comprehensive treatment of the world's most important knowledge in both long and short articles. Physically, the set, which now comprises well over 100 volumes, is the largest ongoing encyclopedia in the world. It eschews periodic revisions (the normal practice) in favor of substantial annual supplements, much like the Italian-language ENCICLOPEDIA ITALIANA. *Espasa,* which currently contains more than one million entries, has long been noted for strong coverage of Spanish and Hispanic American biography and geography. It also serves as a multilingual dictionary translating many terms from Spanish to French, Italian, German, Portuguese, Catalan, Esperanto, and, most important for North Americans, English. Consumers should be aware that the annual supplements, which extend and update *Espasa,* are issued quite late, sometimes five or more years behind schedule. Unfortunately, the encyclopedia's high price will deter many North American libraries and individuals from acquiring the set.

Enciclopedia Universal Sopena. Barcelona: Editorial Ramon Sopena, 1982. 20 vols. $1,995.00.

A combination of Spanish-language encyclopedia and dictionary, *Enciclopedia Universal Sopena* consists of more than 650,000 entries, including 95,000 biographies and 190,000 place-names. Nicely illustrated with both color and black-and-white drawings, photographs, maps, etc., the set is intended mainly for older students and adults but can be used productively by motivated students at the elementary level. Volumes 19 and 20 comprise an extensive thesaurus.

Gran Enciclopedia Larousse. Barcelona: Editorial Planeta, 1992. 24 vols. $2,495.00 plus two atlases at $125.00 ea.

A Spanish-language version of the famous French GRAND LAROUSSE, this large, colorful, handsomely designed encyclopedia contains some 200,000 articles covering all areas of knowledge. A general atlas (*Atlas Geográfico*) and historical atlas (*Atlas Histórico*) complement the set. In addition, a yearbook (*Anuario Planeta*) helps keep the encyclopedia current.

Gran Enciclopedia Rialp: GER. 6th ed. Madrid: Ediciones Rialp, 1989–1991. 25 vols. $3,995.00.

Gran Enciclopedia Rialp—or GER—is an important Spanish-language general encyclopedia prepared by an international editorial team plus some 3,500 contributors from 60 countries. First published in 24 volumes between 1971 and 1976, the set is now in its sixth edition, although much of the original material has not been revised in any significant manner. Intended for adults and older students, GER provides lengthy articles complemented by 20,000 informative illustrations in both color and black-and-white. Reviewing the first edition in *Choice* (May 1977, p. 340), Juan Freudenthal observed that "In the galaxy of Spanish encyclopedias published during this century, GER will undoubtedly rank as one of the major editorial undertakings of its kind, despite its many flaws." Volume 25, added in 1987, is an updating supplement containing recent information about people, places, and political developments.

Imago: Enciclopedia Temática. Madrid: Santillana, 1992. 15 vols. $319.95.

Aimed at junior and senior high school students, *Imago* is a thematically arranged encyclopedia covering general science, mathematics, computers, literature, history, and geography. The well-written text is enhanced by numerous illustrations. Regrettably, the set lacks an index, but as Isabel Schon points out in *Reference Books Bulletin* (in *Booklist*, May 1, 1993, p. 1642), "Despite this serious limitation, many readers will find this encyclopedia useful and informative, especially if they are searching for broad, comprehensive, up-to-date information."

Mis Primeros Conocimientos. Danbury, CT: Grolier, 1989. 10 vols. $169.00.

Originally published in English by Franklin Watts (a Grolier subsidiary) as *My First Knowledge*, this multivolume encyclopedia is intended for young students in the upper elementary and junior high school grades. It contains numerous well-captioned illustrations and emphasizes scientific subjects, such as animals and pets, astronomy, computers, earthquakes and volcanoes, and forms of transportation. In a brief review in *Booklist* (March 1, 1993, p. 1242), Isabel Schon recommends the set: "The excellent Spanish translation (done by Editorial Cumbre in Mexico City) is easy to read and to understand. In addition, numerous full-color illustrations add interest to each topic."

Appendixes

Appendix A

Encyclopedia Resources

* * * * * * * * *

This annotated bibliography directs interested consumers and students to selected books, articles, journals, and other publications about encyclopedias. The bibliography is divided into two parts. The first part, "Evaluating Encyclopedias," covers standard sources that, like *Kister's Best Encyclopedias*, review encyclopedias. The second part, "Making and Using Encyclopedias," identifies published materials concerned with the history, nature, content, production, sale, and use of encyclopedias.

EVALUATING ENCYCLOPEDIAS

American Reference Books Annual. Edited by Bohdan S. Wynar. Littleton, CO: Libraries Unlimited, 1970–. Annual.

American Reference Books Annual—or ARBA— aims to review all English-language reference works published or distributed in North America each year, including general and specialized encyclopedias. Although *ARBA* evaluates close to 1,800 titles each year, it sometimes fails—inexplicably— to review important titles, such as the *American Spectrum Encyclopedia* and the *Oxford Children's Encyclopedia*. In addition, reference sources published in electronic form, including CD-ROM, are almost completely ignored. Reviews of encyclopedias that are covered in *ARBA* are usually informative and occasionally probing.

Choice: Current Reviews for Academic Libraries. Middletown, CT: Assn. of College and Research Libraries, a division of the American Library Assn., 1964–. Monthly.

As its subtitle indicates, *Choice* is a review journal intended for academic librarians, although some public librarians in larger systems also make good use of it. The journal furnishes concise, critical evaluations of both general and reference publications. Subject encyclopedias tend to be well covered, but general encyclopedias are reviewed, if at all, only when first published. While junior-level faculty at North American colleges and universities do most of the reviewing in *Choice*, reference reviews are normally the work of librarians at such institutions.

College and Research Libraries. Chicago: Assn. of College and Research Libraries, a division of the American Library Assn., 1939–. Bimonthly.

Aimed specifically at academic librarians, this journal includes brief evaluative notes on recently published reference sources in its January and July issues. Its encyclopedia reviews are usually limited to selected specialized works.

General Reference Books for Adults: Authoritative Evaluations of Encyclopedias, Atlases, and Dictionaries. Edited by Marion Sader. New York: R.R. Bowker Company, 1988.

Now quite dated, this 614-page book evaluates 215 reference sources, including 15 basic encyclopedias. The unsigned reviews, which average about five pages in length, were prepared for the publisher by Visual Education Corporation, a book packager with no discernible credentials or previous experience in the area of encyclopedia criticism. Oddly, *all* encyclopedias reviewed in *General Reference Books for Adults*—the *Academic American Encyclopedia, Collier's Encyclopedia, Encyclopedia Americana,* the *New Encyclopaedia Britannica,* etc.— are also included in a companion volume entitled *Reference Books for Young Readers* (see below). Even more oddly, the reviews in both publications have practically the same text.

Guide to Reference Books. Edited by Eugene P. Sheehy. 10th ed. Chicago: American Library Assn., 1986; supplement edited by Robert Balay, 1992.

This indispensable guide to reference materials includes annotations (or brief notes) on all types of encyclopedias. The notes are normally descriptive rather than critical, but a brief introduction to general encyclopedias offers practical tips on how to assess such sources. Readers might be interested to know that the *Guide to Reference Books*, which had been prepared at Columbia University's Butler Library from 1902 (the first edition) to 1986 (tenth edition), is now a project of *Choice*, the review magazine (see above). The next edition of the guide—the eleventh—is tentatively scheduled for 1995.

Katz, William A. *Basic Information Sources* (Vol. 1 of *Introduction to Reference Work*). 6th ed. New York: McGraw-Hill, 1992.

Katz, a professor at the School of Information Science and Policy at the State University of New York at Albany, is an internationally known authority on reference sources and services. As in previous editions of this standard reference text, he devotes a long chapter to encyclopedias ("Encyclopedias: General and Subject"), discussing both the genre and the strengths and weaknesses of specific titles. Intended chiefly for library science students, Katz's book, because of its authoritative commentary and readable style, is also a valuable guide for interested consumers.

Library Journal. New York: Cahners Publishing Company, a division of Reed Publishing USA, 1876–. Semimonthly.

The oldest and most popular of the general library periodicals, *Library Journal* devotes a substantial portion of its contents to book reviews prepared by librarians for librarians. The reference reviews, which include new subject encyclopedias, tend to be compact but informative. The magazine also now has a regular column that evaluates CD-ROM products, including encyclopedic works.

Purchasing an Encyclopedia: 12 Points to Consider. Prepared by the Editorial Board of *Reference Books Bulletin*. 4th ed. Chicago: American Library Assn., 1993.

This 48-page paperbound pamphlet reviews nine general encyclopedias and offers advice about selecting an encyclopedia for the home or library. One caveat: libraries that subscribe to *Reference Books Bulletin* (see next entry), from which the nine reviews are taken, can pass up this little booklet, which is priced at $7.95.

Reference Books Bulletin (in *Booklist*). Edited by Sandy Whiteley. Chicago: American Library Assn., 1930–. Semimonthly.

Found at the back of *Booklist* (a general review publication for librarians), *Reference Books Bulletin* publishes approximately 25–30 reviews of new reference titles per issue. The unsigned reviews, which normally range from 1,000 to 1,500 words in length, are prepared by members of the publication's editorial board, a group of U.S. and Canadian librarians who represent a cross-section of the profession. The quality and timeliness of the reviews have improved markedly since Sandy Whiteley took over as editor in 1985. In recent years, the September 15 issue contains an "Annual Encyclopedia Update," a detailed critical survey of the nine or ten major multivolume general encyclopedias on the North American market, with emphasis on their continuous revision programs.

Reference Books for Young Readers: Authoritative Evaluations of Encyclopedias, Atlases, and Dictionaries. Edited by Marion Sader. New York: R.R. Bowker Company, 1988.

The counterpart to *General Reference Books for Adults* (see above), the 615-page *Reference Books for Young Readers* includes over 200 reviews, of which 24 are devoted to encyclopedias. Exactly why such adult encyclopedias as *Collier's Encyclopedia*, *Encyclopedia Americana*, and the *New Encyclopaedia Britannica* are included in a guide for "young readers" is never made clear. In any event, both of these books contain much the same material about encyclopedias. Today, both are quite dated and of limited use to librarians or general consumers.

Reference Sources for Small and Medium-Sized Libraries. Edited by Jovian P. Lang. 5th ed. Chicago: American Library Assn., 1992.

Prepared under the auspices of the Reference and Adult Services Division of the American Library Association, this popular, affordable, up-to-date paperback publication identifies and briefly describes nearly 2,000 basic reference sources, including both general and specialized encyclopedias. The annotations are readable and informative throughout. Editor Lang's section on general encyclopedias (Chapter 3) offers fairly lengthy critical comments on each title. An excellent guide to all types of reference materials.

RQ. Chicago: Reference and Adult Services Division of the American Library Assn., 1960–. Quarterly.

RQ—the journal's official name (it stands for *Reference Quarterly*)—selectively reviews new reference books, including some encyclopedias, in the back of each issue. The signed reviews are normally about 500–800 words in length and are prepared by experienced academic librarians.

School Library Journal. New York: Cahners Publishing Company, a division of Reed Publishing USA, 1954–. Monthly.

All types of materials of potential interest to school and children's librarians, including new encyclopedias, are evaluated in *School Library Journal.* The brief, signed reviews are almost always by working librarians and media specialists.

Wilson Library Bulletin. New York: H.W. Wilson Company, 1914–. Monthly.

Wilson Library Bulletin, one of the leading general library magazines, has a regular column entitled "Current Reference Books" that concisely evaluates 15–20 new titles each issue. Subject encyclopedias receive much attention, but occasionally general encyclopedias are also reviewed. The reviews, prepared by James Rettig, are readable and often furnish comparative references. The magazine has recently added a column covering new reference materials on CD-ROM.

MAKING AND USING ENCYCLOPEDIAS

Anthony, Carolyn. "Selling Encyclopedias Store to Store," *Publishers Weekly,* August 16, 1991, pp. 11–16.

"The continuing explosion of information, the need to find less risky, long-term publishing projects and the growing demand for English-language reference books worldwide," writes Anthony, "have led to increased attention from American publishers to the creation and marketing of reference books." In this article she interviews top editors and marketing people about the current state of the reference book business, with emphasis on subject encyclopedias.

Arner, Robert D. *Dobson's Encyclopaedia: The Publisher, Text, and Publication of America's First Britannica, 1789–1803.* Philadelphia: Univ. of Pennsylvania Press, 1991.

Arner's 295-page account of Philadelphia printer Thomas Dobson (1751–1823) focuses on Dobson's publication of the third edition of the *Encyclopaedia Britannica* in the U.S. soon after the birth of the republic. At that time the *Britannica* was very much a British production, and Arner, an English professor at the University of Cincinnati, shows how the encyclopedia contributed to the intellectual and cultural growth of the new nation.

Bailey, Edgar C. Jr. "Acquisition and Use of General Encyclopedias in Small Academic Libraries," *RQ,* Winter 1985, pp. 218–22.

This readable study, based on a questionnaire survey, "represents an initial attempt to determine precisely which encyclopedias college libraries hold, which are considered most useful, how they are used, and how often new editions are purchased." Interestingly, respondents rated *Encyclopedia Americana* as more useful than the *Academic American Encyclopedia, Collier's Encyclopedia,* the *New Encyclopaedia Britannica,* and the *World Book Encyclopedia.*

Berger, Warren. "What's New in Encyclopedias," *The New York Times,* May 28, 1989, p. 15-F.

Business writer Warren Berger covers various encyclopedia trends—new marketing techniques, the specialized encyclopedia explosion, the advent of CD-ROM—in a full page of *New York Times* text.

Collison, Robert L. *Encyclopedias: Their History Throughout the Ages.* 2nd ed. New York: Hafner Publishing Co., 1966.

Collison's 334-page treatise is described in a lengthy subtitle as "a bibliographical guide, with extensive historical notes, to the general encyclopedias issued throughout the world from 350 B.C. to the present day." The book is esteemed as a history of encyclopedias, but it does not include reviews or much critical information.

"A Consumer's Guide to Encyclopedias," *Consumers' Research,* July 1990, pp. 28–31.

Based on material found in *Purchasing an Encyclopedia: 12 Points to Consider* (see above), a pamphlet prepared by the editorial board of *Reference Books Bulletin,* this article offers helpful suggestions about how to choose an encyclopedia. It also includes a chart giving information about 11 popular multivolume works.

Darnton, Robert. *The Business of Enlightenment: A Publishing History of the Encyclopédie, 1775–1800.* Cambridge, MA: Harvard Univ. Press, 1979.

Darnton, a meticulous historian, details the story of Diderot's celebrated French *Encyclopédie,* incontestably the most influential encyclopedia ever published. "This is intellectual, economic, business, and social history at its best" (*Library Journal,* October 15, 1979, p. 2210). Valuable complements to Darnton's book are the *Encyclopédie and the Age of*

Revolution (see next entry) and P.N. Furbank's *Diderot: A Critical Biography* (Knopf, 1992).

The Encyclopédie and the Age of Revolution. Edited by Clorinda Donato & Robert M. Maniquis. Boston: G.K. Hall, 1992.

This 230-page collection of articles deals generally with encyclopedias and their production in the eighteenth century and specifically with Diderot's famous *Encyclopédie.* Particularly valuable is Frank Kafker's article "The Role of the *Encyclopédie* in the Making of the Modern Encyclopedia."

Hellemans, Alexander. "New Directions for Encyclopedias," *Publishers Weekly,* October 2, 1987, pp. 40–44.

Hellemans, a freelance writer who has contributed articles to several encyclopedias, reviews current developments in the industry, particularly the emergence of encyclopedias in electronic form.

Holzberg, Carol S. "Let Your Fingers Do the Walking: CD-ROM Encyclopedias," *CD-ROM World,* September 1993, pp. 28–37.

"CD-ROM encyclopedias turn research into entertaining journeys of discovery," writes Holzberg, who succinctly reviews nine CD-ROM encyclopedias (both general and specialized) in this popularly written article.

Kister, Kenneth F. "Make Way for Multimedia Encyclopedias," *Family Life,* March–April 1994, p. 62.

A quick look at the newest wave of encyclopedias on disk. They talk and move, but will they replace the traditional bound tomes so many parents grew up with?

Kleinfield, N.R. "The Cheerful Trudge of a World Book Ace," *The New York Times,* March 6, 1988, pp. 1-F+.

While centered on a day in the life of a crack *World Book Encyclopedia* sales representative, Kleinfield's feature article offers a fascinating insight into the business of selling encyclopedias anywhere, anytime, by anyone.

Krushenisky, Cindy. "Lightening Your Load with Multimedia Encyclopedias," *PC Novice,* October 1993, pp. 62–65.

Krushenisky discusses "the new wave" of multimedia encyclopedias on CD-ROM, explaining in nontechnical language how they work and their advantages vis-a-vis traditional print (or hardcover) encyclopedias. She also briefly reviews a number of titles, including the *New Grolier Multimedia Encyclopedia, Microsoft Encarta Multimedia Encyclopedia,* and *Compton's Interactive Encyclopedia.*

Marchionini, Gary. "Information-Seeking Strategies of Novices Using a Full-Text Electronic Encyclopedia," *Journal of the American Society for Information Science,* January 1989, pp. 54–66.

This heavily footnoted article reports on a study of a small group of elementary school children and their first use of a CD-ROM encyclopedia with a full-text search system. Among the author's conclusions: "The results demonstrated that, in general, young novice users could successfully use a full-text, electronic encyclopedia with minimal introductory training." The study is especially valuable for teachers and media specialists, who are actively involved in introducing electronic encyclopedias to young students.

Powers, Alice Leccese. "Volumes of Knowledge," *Creative Ideas For Living,*" January 1988, p. 84.

A brief but intelligently prepared introduction to what parents should look for when buying an encyclopedia.

Rabinovitz, Rubin. "Encyclopedias: The Ideal CD-ROM Reference Library," *PC Magazine,* August 1993, pp. 554–57.

Rabinovitz offers long, informed, thoughtful assessments of three major electronic encyclopedias: *Compton's Interactive Encyclopedia, Microsoft Encarta Multimedia Encyclopedia,* and the *New Grolier Multimedia Encyclopedia.*

Samuels, Gary. "CD-ROM's First Big Victim," *Forbes,* February 28, 1994, pp. 42–44.

Samuels says sales of the *New Encyclopaedia Britannica* are lagging due principally to competition from CD-ROM encyclopedias. Why doesn't Britannica develop its own CD-ROM product for the home and school? Because, suggests Samuels, the company fears "offending its powerful sales force," which is accustomed to healthy commissions on print products.

Walsh, S. Padraig. *Anglo-American Encyclopedias: A Historical Bibliography, 1703–1967.* New York: R.R. Bowker Company, 1968.

The late Padraig Walsh provides extensive notes on 419 general English-language encyclopedias published in North America and Great Britain between 1703 and 1967. This unique work is essential for serious students of the history of encyclopedia publishing.

Wellborn, Stanley N. & Evelyn Bankhead. "Looking for Knowledge, in Volumes," *U.S. News & World Report*, July 27, 1987, pp. 48–49.

This helpful consumer article furnishes solid advice about choosing the best encyclopedia. It also includes thumbnail descriptions of the "top six" general encyclopedias.

Whiteley, Sandy. "Encyclopedias Today: Tradition Meets Innovation," *American Libraries*, May 1992, pp. 402–06.

Whiteley, editor of *Reference Books Bulletin* (see above), discusses six major U.S. encyclopedia publishers, their products, and the growing impact of electronic publishing on the industry. An excellent overview article.

Appendix B

Directory of Encyclopedia Publishers and Distributors

* * * * * * * *

This directory lists North American publishers and distributors of all in-print encyclopedias evaluated in *Kister's Best Encyclopedias*, including general, specialized, and electronic encyclopedias. Entries give the company's name, address, and telephone number (toll-free if available), along with titles published or distributed. In the case of distributors, the publisher is indicated in parentheses following the title. To locate any title listed in the directory, consult the index, which follows.

▓ ▓ ▓

ABC-Clio. 130 Cremona Dr., P.O. Box 1911, Santa Barbara, CA 93116-1911. 800-422-2546 (toll-free).
American Law Dictionary
Constitutional Law Dictionary
Encyclopedia of Russian History
Guide to the Gods
International Relations Dictionary
Middle East: A Political Dictionary
World Encyclopedia of Cities

Abingdon Press (a division of United Methodist Publishing House). P.O. Box 801, 201 Eighth Ave. S., Nashville, TN 37202. 800-251-3320 (toll-free).
Abingdon Dictionary of Living Religions
Interpreter's Dictionary of the Bible

Academic Press, Inc. (a subsidiary of Harcourt Brace & Co.). 525 B St. (Suite 1900), San Diego, CA 92101. 800-321-5068 (toll-free).
Encyclopedia of Astronomy and Astrophysics
Encyclopedia of Earth System Science
Encyclopedia of Food Science, Food Technology and Nutrition
Encyclopedia of Human Behavior
Encyclopedia of Human Biology
Encyclopedia of Immunology
Encyclopedia of Lasers and Optical Technology
Encyclopedia of Microbiology
Encyclopedia of Modern Physics
Encyclopedia of Physical Science and Technology
Encyclopedia of Telecommunications

Adler's Foreign Books. 915 Foster St., Evanston, IL 60201-3199. 708-866-6329.
Foreign-language encyclopedias

Aesculapius Publishers, Inc. 240 E. 76th St. (Apt. 1B), New York, NY 10021. 212-628-1797.
International Encyclopedia of Psychiatry, Psychology, Psychoanalysis, and Neurology (distributed by Macmillan)

Allworth Press. 10 E. 23rd St. (Suite 400), New York, NY 10010. 212-777-8395.
Family Legal Companion

America Online. 8619 Westwood Center Dr. (Suite 200), Vienna, VA 22182-2285. 800-827-6364 (toll-free).
Compton's Encyclopedia (Online)

American Bookseller Association. 137 W. 25th St., New York, NY 10001. 800-637-0037 (toll-free).
American Spectrum Encyclopedia (distributed by the Booksellers Order Service)

American Library Association. 50 E. Huron St., Chicago, IL 60611. 800-545-2433 (toll-free).
Dictionary of Western Church Music
World Encyclopedia of Library and Information Services

American Psychoanalytic Association. 309 E. 49th St., New York, NY 10017. 212-752-0450.
Psychoanalytic Terms and Concepts

Arco Publishing Co., Inc. (a division of Prentice Hall). 15 Columbus Circle, New York, NY 10023. 800-223-2336.
Knowledge Encyclopedia
Private Pilot's Dictionary and Handbook

Arrow Trading Co., Inc. 1115 Broadway, New York, NY 10010. 212-255-7688.
Webster's Family Encyclopedia

Baker Book House. P.O. Box 6287, Grand Rapids, MI 49516-6287. 800-877-2665 (toll-free).
New 20th-Century Encyclopedia of Religious Knowledge

Barnes & Noble Books (a division of Rowman & Littlefield). 4720 Boston Way, Lanham, MD 20706. 301-306-0400.
Black's Veterinary Dictionary

Barnes & Noble, Inc. 120 Fifth Ave., New York, NY 10011. 800-242-6657 (toll-free).
Barnes & Noble Encyclopedia
Barnes & Noble New American Encyclopedia (published by Grolier Inc.)

Barron's Educational Series, Inc. 250 Wireless Blvd., Hauppauge, NY 11788. 800-645-3476 (toll-free).
Barron's Junior Fact Finder
Barron's New Student's Concise Encyclopedia

David Bateman Ltd. *See* **G.K. Hall**

Birkhauser Boston, Inc. (a division of Springer-Verlag). 675 Massachusetts Ave., Cambridge, MA 02139. 800-777-4643 (toll-free).
Encyclopedia of Neuroscience (distributed by Springer-Verlag)

Blackwell Publishers. 238 Main St., Cambridge, MA 02142. 800-488-2665 (toll-free).
Blackwell Dictionary of Judaica
Blackwell Encyclopedia of Political Thought
Dictionary of Marxist Thought

BNA Books. Bureau of National Affairs, 1250 23rd St. N.W. (3rd Floor), Washington, DC 20037. 800-372-1033 (toll-free)
McCarthy's Desk Encyclopedia of Intellectual Property

Booksellers Order Service. 137 W. 25th St., New York, NY 10001. 800-637-0037 (toll-free).
American Spectrum Encyclopedia (published by the American Booksellers Association)

R.R. Bowker Co. (a division of Reed Reference Publishing Co.). 121 Chanlon Rd., New Providence, NJ 07974. 800-521-8110 (toll-free)
Motion Picture Guide (published by CineBooks).

Brassey's (US), Inc. 8000 Westpark Dr. (1st Floor), McLean, VA 22102. 800-257-5755 (toll-free).
International Military and Defense Encyclopedia (distributed by Macmillan)

E.J. Brill USA Inc. P.O. Box 467, 24 Hudson St., Kinderhook, NY 12106. 800-962-4406 (toll-free).
Encyclopaedia of Islam

Britannica. *See* **Encyclopaedia Britannica, Inc.**

Cambridge University Press. 40 W. 20th St., New York, NY 10011-4211. 800-872-7423 (toll-free).
Australians: A Historical Library
Cambridge Encyclopedia
Cambridge Enyclopedia of Archaeology
Cambridge Encyclopedia of Earth Sciences
Cambridge Encyclopedia of Language
Cambridge Encyclopedia of Latin America and the Caribbean
Cambridge Encyclopedia of Life Sciences
Cambridge Encyclopedia of Russia and the Former Soviet Union
Cambridge Encyclopedia of Space
Cambridge Guide to American Theatre
Cambridge Guide to Asian Theatre
Cambridge Guide to the Material World
Cambridge Guide to World Theatre
Cambridge Historical Encyclopedia of Great Britain and Ireland
Cambridge Paperback Encyclopedia
Encyclopedia of Mathematics and Its Applications
Popular Encyclopedia of Plants

Cavendish, Marshall. *See* **Marshall Cavendish Corporation**

Chambers Kingfisher Graham Publishers Inc. *See* **CKG Publishers, Inc.**

Chapman & Hall. *See* **Routledge, Chapman & Hall**

Children's Press. 5440 N. Cumberland Ave., Chicago, IL 60656-1469. 800-621-1115 (toll-free).

> *Golden Book Encyclopedia* (published by Western Publishing Co.)

CineBooks. *See* **R.R. Bowker Co.**

CKG Publishers, Inc. 95 Madison Ave., New York, NY 10016. 800-497-1657 (toll-free).

> *Kingfisher Children's Encyclopedia*
> *Kingfisher Science Encyclopedia*

P.F. Collier, Inc. 866 Third Ave. (17th Floor), New York, NY 10022–6299. 800-257-2755 (toll-free).

> *Collier's Encyclopedia*

Columbia University Press. 562 W. 113th St., New York, NY 10025. 800-944-8648 (toll-free).

> *Columbia Dictionary of European Political History Since 1914*
> *Columbia Dictionary of Modern European Literature*
> *Columbia Encyclopedia* (distributed by Houghton Mifflin Co.)
> *Concise Columbia Encyclopedia*

Compton's Learning Co. (a Tribune Publishing Co.). 2 Prudential Plaza (Suite 2625), 180 N. Stetson Ave., Chicago, IL 60601-6790. 800-858-4895 (toll-free).

> *Compton's Encyclopedia*

Compton's NewMedia (a Tribune Publishing Co.). 2320 Camino Vida Roble, Carlsbad, CA 92009-1504. 800-862-2206 (toll-free).

> *Compton's Concise Encyclopedia* (CD-ROM; distributed by Sony Corporation)
> *Compton's Encyclopedia* (Online; distributed via America Online)
> *Compton's Family Encyclopedia* (CD-ROM; distributed by Sony Corporation)
> *Compton's Interactive Encyclopedia* (CD-ROM)
> *Compton's Multimedia Encyclopedia* (CD-ROM)

CompuServe Inc. 5000 Arlington Centre Blvd., Columbus, OH 43220. 800-848-8199 (toll-free).

> *Academic American Encyclopedia* (Online)

Consumer Reports Books (a division of Consumers Union of the U.S.). 101 Truman Ave., Yonkers, NY 10703. 914-378-2000.

> *Complete Drug Reference* (distributed by St. Martin's Press)

Contemporary Books, Inc. 2 Prudential Plaza (Suite 1200), Chicago, IL 60601. 312-540-4500

> *Encyclopedia of Handspinning* (published by Interweave Press)

Continuum Publishing Group. 370 Lexington Ave., New York, NY 10017. 800-937-5557 (toll-free).

> *Encyclopedia of World Literature in the 20th Century*

Crestline Publishing Co. 1251 N. Jefferson Ave., Sarasota, FL 33577. 813-955-8080.

> *Encyclopedia of American Cars, 1946–1959* (distributed by Motorbooks International)

CrimeBooks, Inc. 1213 Wilmette Ave. (Suite 203), Wilmette, IL 60091-2557. 708-251-8350.

> *Encyclopedia of World Crime* (distributed by Marshall Cavendish)

Crown Publishing Group (an affiliate of Random House, Inc.). 201 E. 50th St., New York, NY 10022. 800-726-0600 (toll-free).

> *Columbia University College of Physicians and Surgeons Complete Guide to Early Child Care*
> *International Encyclopedia of Astronomy*
> *International Encyclopedia of Aviation*
> *Larousse Gastronomique: All-New American Edition of the World's Greatest Culinary Encyclopedia*
> *New Compleat Astrologer: The Practical Encyclopedia of Astrological Science* (published by Harmony Books)
> *Official Encyclopedia of Bridge*
> *World Encyclopedia of Civil Aircraft*

David & Charles. *See* **Trafalgar Square/David & Charles**

Walter de Gruyter, Inc. 200 Saw Mill River Rd., Hawthorne, NY 10532. 914-747-0110.

> *Concise Encyclopedia of Biochemistry*
> *Encyclopedic Dictionary of Semiotics*

Marcel Dekker, Inc. 270 Madison Ave., New York, NY 10016. 800-228-1160 (toll-free).

> *Encyclopedia of Chemical Processing and Design*
> *Encyclopedia of Library and Information Science*
> *Encyclopedia of Pharmaceutical Technology*

Delacorte Press (a division of Bantam Doubleday Dell). 1540 Broadway, New York, NY 10036–4094. 800-221-4676 (toll-free).

> *New Child Health Encyclopedia*

Delphi Internet Services Corporation. 1030 Massachusetts Ave. S., Cambridge, MA 02139-9998. 800-544-4005 (toll-free).
Academic American Encyclopedia (Online)
Kussmaul Encyclopedia (Online)

Design Press. *See* **TAB Books**

Dialog Information Services, Inc. 3460 Hillview Ave., Palo Alto, CA 94304. 800-334-2564 (toll-free).
Everyman's Encyclopaedia (Online)

Donovan Music and Toy Co. 732 Clinton St., Waukesha, WI 53186. 800-236-7123 (toll-free).
Golden Book Encyclopedia (published by Western Publishing Co.)

Dorling Kindersley, Inc. 232 Madison Ave., New York, NY 10016. 212-684-0404.
My First Encyclopedia (distributed by Houghton Mifflin)

Doubleday. Bantam Doubleday Dell Publishing Group Inc., 1540 Broadway, New York, NY 10036. 800-323-9872 (toll-free).
Anchor Bible Dictionary

Dover Publications, Inc. 180 Varick St., New York, NY 10014. 800-223-3130 (toll-free).
Encyclopedia of Battles

Dow Jones News/Retrieval Service. P.O. Box 300, Princeton, NJ 08543-0300. 800-522-3567 (toll-free).
Academic American Encyclopedia (Online)

EDC Publishing (a division of the Educational Development Corporation). P.O. Box 702253, Tulsa, OK 74170. 800-331-4418 (toll-free).
Usborne Children's Encyclopedia

Educational Development Corporation. *See* **EDC Publishing**

Educational Home Systems. 4290 Bells Ferry Rd. (Suite 106–635), Kennesaw, GA 30144. 800-435-2349 (toll-free).
Academic American Encyclopedia (published by Grolier Inc.)
Encyclopedia Americana (published by Grolier Inc.)
Funk & Wagnalls New Encyclopedia (published by Funk & Wagnalls)
New Book of Knowledge (published by Grolier Inc.)

New Grolier Electronic Encyclopedia (published by Grolier Inc.)
New Standard Encyclopedia (published by Standard Educational Corporation)

Wm. B. Eerdmans Publishing Co. 255 Jefferson Ave. S.E., Grand Rapids, MI 49503. 800-253-7521 (toll-free).
Dictionary of Biblical Tradition in English Literature
International Standard Bible Encyclopedia

Encyclopaedia Britannica Educational Corporation (a subsidiary of Encyclopaedia Britannica, Inc.). 310 S. Michigan Ave., Chicago, IL 60604-9839. 800-544-9862 (toll-free).
Britannica International Encyclopaedia (published by TBS-Britannica Co.)
Children's Britannica (published by Encyclopaedia Britannica, Inc.)
Compton's Encyclopedia (published by Compton's Learning Co.)
Compton's Precyclopedia (published by Encyclopaedia Britannica, Inc.)
Diccionairo Enciclopédico (published by Alexander Marketing)
Enciclopedia Hispánica (published by Encyclopaedia Britannica, Inc.)
Encyclopedia of Visual Art
Encyclopaedia Universalis (published by Encyclopaedia Universalis France)
Foods and Nutrition Encyclopedia (published by Pegus Press)
Geopedia (CD-ROM)
Illustrated Encyclopedia of Wildlife (published by Grey Castle Press)
Kingfisher Science Encyclopedia (published by Grisewood & Dempsey Ltd.)
New Encyclopaedia Britannica (published by Encyclopaedia Britannica, Inc.)
Young Children's Encyclopedia (published by Encyclopaedia Britannica, Inc.)

Encyclopaedia Britannica, Inc. Britannica Centre, Customer Service Department, 310 S. Michigan Ave., Chicago, IL 60604. 800-858-4895 (toll-free).
Britannica Instant Research System (CD-ROM)
Britannica Online (Online)
Britannica World Encyclopaedia (published by Korea Britannica Corporation)
Children's Britannica
Chinese-Language Concise Encyclopaedia Britannica
Compton's Precyclopedia
Enciclopedia Hispánica
New Encyclopedia Britannica
Young Children's Encyclopedia

Facts on File, Inc. 460 Park Ave. S., New York, NY 10016. 800-322-8755 (toll-free)
Broadway: An Encyclopedic Guide to the History, People and Places of Times Square
Encyclopedia of Adoption
Encyclopedia of Alcoholism
Encyclopedia of American Business History and Biography
Encyclopedia of American Comics
Encyclopedia of American Intelligence and Espionage
Encyclopedia of Ancient Egypt
Encyclopedia of Animated Cartoons
Encyclopedia of Aquatic Life
Encyclopedia of Blindness and Vision Impairment
Encyclopedia of Censorship
Encyclopedia of Child Abuse
Encyclopedia of Colonial and Revolutionary America
Encyclopedia of Drug Abuse
Encyclopedia of Environmental Studies
Encyclopedia of Gemstones and Minerals
Encyclopedia of Genetic Disorders and Birth Defects
Encyclopedia of Ghosts and Spirits
Encyclopedia of Historical Places
Encyclopedia of Insects
Encyclopedia of Magic and Magicians
Encyclopedia of Marriage, Divorce and the Family
Encyclopedia of Mental Health
Encyclopedia of Native American Religions
Encyclopedia of New England
Encyclopedia of North American Sports History
Encyclopedia of Perennials
Encyclopedia of Phobias, Fears, and Anxieties
Encyclopedia of Pottery & Porcelain, 1800–1960
Encyclopedia of Reptiles and Amphibians
Encyclopedia of Schizophrenia and the Psychotic Disorders
Encyclopedia of Shells
Encyclopedia of Sporting Firearms
Encyclopedia of Suicide
Encyclopedia of Textiles
Encyclopedia of the Renaissance
Encyclopedia of the Third World
Encyclopedia of the World's Air Forces
Encyclopedia of Witches and Witchcraft
Encyclopedic Dictionary of Science
Extraterrestrial Encyclopedia
Facts on File Dictionary of Design and Designers
Facts on File Encyclopedia of the 20th Century
Facts on File Encyclopedia of World Mythology and Legend
Illustrated Encyclopedia of Fossils
Ireland: A Cultural Encyclopedia
Music: An Illustrated Encyclopedia

New A to Z of Women's Health: A Concise Encyclopedia
Patient's Guide to Medical Tests
Reference Guide to United States Military History
Shakespeare A to Z
World Education Encyclopedia
World Encyclopedia of Police Forces and Penal Systems
World Encyclopedia of Political Systems & Parties
World of Games
World Press Encyclopedia

Farrar, Straus & Giroux, Inc. 19 Union Square W., New York, NY 10003. 800-788-6262
Japan: An Illustrated Encyclopedia (published by Kodansha America)

Fitzhenry & Whiteside Ltd. 91 Granton Dr., Richmond Hill, Ontario, Canada L4B 2N5. 416-764-0030.
Fitzhenry & Whiteside Book of Canadian Facts and Dates

Focal Press (an imprint of Butterworth-Heinemann). 80 Montvale Ave., Stoneham, MA 02180. 800-366-2665 (toll-free)
Focal Encyclopedia of Photography

Franklin Electronic Publishers, Inc. 122 Burrs Rd., Mt. Holly, NJ 08060. 800-543-3511
Columbia Electronic Encyclopedia (Hand-held)

Franklin Watts. See **Watts, Franklin**

Free Press (a division of Macmillan Publishing Company, Inc.). 866 Third Ave. (22nd Floor), New York, NY 10022. 800-257-5755 (toll-free)
Encyclopedia of Bioethics (distributed by Macmillan)
Encyclopedia of Crime and Justice (distributed by Macmillan)
Encyclopedia of Philosophy (distributed by Macmillan)
International Encyclopedia of Population (distributed by Macmillan)
International Encyclopedia of the Social Sciences (distributed by Macmillan)

French & European Publications, Inc. Rockefeller Center Promenade, 610 Fifth Ave., New York, NY 10020-2497. 212-581-8810.
Foreign-language encyclopedias

Funk & Wagnalls. One International Blvd. (Suite 444), Mahwah, NJ 07495-0017. 201-529-6900.
Charlie Brown's 'Cyclopedia
Funk & Wagnalls New Encyclopedia

Gale Research Inc. 835 Penobscot Building, Detroit, MI 48226. 800-877-4253 (toll-free)
Bud Collins' Modern Encyclopedia of Tennis
Canadian Encyclopedia (published by Hurtig Publishers)
Complete Encyclopedia of Hockey
Encyclopedia of American Religions
Encyclopedia of Business
Encyclopedia of Literature and Criticism
Encyclopedia of Occultism & Parapsychology
International Dictionary of Ballet (published by St. James Press)
International Dictionary of Films and Filmmakers (published by St. James Press)
International Dictionary of Theatre (published by St. James Press)
Les Brown's Encyclopedia of Television
New Age Encyclopedia
World Encyclopedia of Soccer

Gareth Stevens. *See* **Stevens, Gareth**

Garland Publishing, Inc. 1000A Sherman Ave., Hamden, CT 06514. 800-627-6273 (toll-free).
American Revolution: An Encyclopedia
Encyclopedia of Adolescence
Encyclopedia of Cosmology
Encyclopedia of Early Childhood Education
Encyclopedia of Ethics
Encyclopedia of Homosexuality
Encyclopedia of Human Evolution and Prehistory
Encyclopedia of the American Left
Handbook of Latin American Literature
Human Sexuality: An Encyclopedia
Labor Conflict in the United States: An Encyclopedia
Mass Media: A Chronological Encyclopedia of Television, Radio, Motion Pictures, Magazines, Newspapers, and Books in the United States
Modern Geography: An Encyclopedic Survey
New Video Encyclopedia
New York Botanical Garden Illustrated Encyclopedia of Horticulture
New York Times Encyclopedia of Film, 1896–1979 (published by Times Books)
Political Parties and Elections in the United States: An Encyclopedia
Sexuality and the Law: An Encyclopedia of Major Legal Cases

GEnie. 401 N. Washington St., Rockville, MD 20850. 800-638-9636 (toll-free).
Academic American Encyclopedia (Online)

Gordon and Breach Science Publishers. P.O. Box 786 Cooper Station, New York, NY 10276. 800-545-8398 (toll-free).
Encyclopedia of Environmental Science and Engineering

Government Printing Office. *See* **U.S. Government Printing Office**

Greenwood Publishing Group, Inc. 88 Post Rd. W., P.O. Box 5007, Westport, CT 06881-5007. 800-474-4329 (toll-free).
American Educators' Encyclopedia
American Film Industry: A Historical Dictionary
Companion to the Medieval Theatre
Descriptive Dictionary and Atlas of Sexology
Dictionary of Afro-Latin American Civilization
Dictionary of American Communal and Utopian History
Dictionary of American Diplomatic History
Dictionary of Asian American History
Dictionary of Concepts in Cultural Anthropology
Dictionary of Concepts in General Psychology
Dictionary of Concepts in Literary Criticism and Theory
Dictionary of Concepts in Physical Geography
Dictionary of Concepts in Recreation and Leisure Studies
Dictionary of Literary Themes and Motifs
Dictionary of Mexican American History
Dictionary of Scandinavian History
Dictionary of the Black Theatre
Dictionary of the Russian Revolution
Dictionary of the Vietnam War
Dictionary of Twentieth-Century Cuban Literature
Dictionary of United States Economic History
Encyclopedia of African-American Civil Rights
Encyclopedia of American Agricultural History
Encyclopedia of Educational Media Communications and Technology
Encyclopedia of the New York Stage
Historical Dictionary of European Imperialism
Historical Dictionary of the French Revolution, 1789–1799
Historical Dictionary of the Korean War
Kabuki Encyclopedia
Reference Companion to the History of Abnormal Psychology
Reference Handbook on the Deserts of North America
Television Industry: A Historical Dictionary
United States in Latin America: A Historical Dictionary
Women's Studies Encyclopedia

Grey Castle Press. Pocket Knife Square, Lakeville, CT 06039. 203-435-2518.

Grey Castle Press (continued)
Illustrated Encyclopedia of Wildlife (distributed by Encyclopaedia Britannica Educational Corporation)

Grolier Educational Corporation (a subsidiary of Grolier Inc.) Sherman Turnpike. Danbury, CT 06816. 800-243-7256 (toll-free).
Academic American Encyclopedia (published by Grolier Inc.)
Enciclopédia Ilustrada Cumbre (published by Promotora Editorial)
Encyclopedia Americana (published by Grolier Inc.)
Grolier Children's Encyclopedia
Grolier World Encyclopedia of Endangered Species
Mis Primeros Conocimientos
New Book of Knowledge (published by Grolier Inc.)
New Grolier Student Encyclopedia

Grolier Electronic Publishing, Inc. Sherman Turnpike, Danbury, CT 06816. 800-285-4534 (toll-free).
Academic American Encyclopedia (Online; distributed via CompuServe, Dow Jones News/Retrieval, GEnie, National Videotex, Prodigy)
New Grolier Multimedia Encyclopedia (CD-ROM)

Grolier Inc. Sherman Turnpike, Danbury, CT 06816. 203-796-2602.
Academic American Encyclopedia
Barnes & Noble New American Encyclopedia (distributed by Barnes & Noble)
Encyclopedia Americana
Global International Encyclopedia
Grolier Academic Encyclopedia
Grolier Encyclopedia of Knowledge
Grolier International Encyclopedia
Lexicon Universal Encyclopedia
Macmillan Family Encyclopedia
New Book of Knowledge
New Book of Popular Science

Grove's Dictionaries of Music, Inc. 49 W. 24th St., New York, NY 10010. 800-221-2123 (toll-free).
New Grove Dictionary of American Music
New Grove Dictionary of Jazz
New Grove Dictionary of Music and Musicians
New Grove Dictionary of Musical Instruments
New Grove Dictionary of Opera

Gruyter, Walter de, *See* **de Gruyter, Walter**

Guinness Publishing, *See* **New England Publishing Associates**

Gulf Publishing Company. P.O. Box 2608, Houston, TX 77252-2608. 713-520-4444.
Encyclopedia of Environmental Control Technology
Encyclopedia of Fluid Mechanics

G.K. Hall & Company. 866 Third Ave., New York, NY 10022. 800-257-5755 (toll-free).
Concise Encyclopedia of Australia (published by David Bateman Ltd.)
Encyclopedia of World Cultures
Illustrated Encyclopedia of New Zealand (published by David Bateman Ltd.)

Harcourt Brace Jovanovich, Inc. 1250 Sixth Ave., San Diego, CA 92101. 800-426-6577.
Everybody's Guide to the Law

Harmony Books, *See* **Crown Publishing Group**

HarperCollins Publishers. 10 E. 53rd St., New York, NY 10022. 800-242-7737 (toll-free).
Asimov's Chronology of Science and Discovery
Benet's Reader's Encyclopedia
Benet's Reader's Encyclopedia of American Literature
Brewer's Dictionary of Phrase and Fable
Dictionary of Subjects and Symbols in Art
Encyclopedia of American Facts and Dates
Encyclopedia of American History
Golf Magazine's Encyclopedia of Golf
Halliwell's Film Guide
Halliwell's Filmgoer's Companion
Harper Encyclopedia of Military History
Harper's Bible Dictionary
Harper's Encyclopedia of Religious Education
Historical Times Illustrated Encyclopedia of the Civil War
Reader's Encyclopedia of the American West
Rock On: The Illustrated Encyclopedia of Rock n' Roll
Times Atlas and Encyclopedia of the Sea
Wise Garden Encyclopedia

Hartley Courseware. 3001 Coolidge (Suite 400), E. Lansing, MI 48823. 800-247-1380 (toll-free).
First Connections (CD-ROM)

Harvard University Press. 79 Garden St., Cambridge, MA 02138. 800-448-2242 (toll-free).
Harvard Encyclopedia of American Ethnic Groups

Hearst Books (a division of William Morrow & Company). 1350 Ave. of the Americas, New York, NY 10019. 212-261-6770.
Dictionary of American Food and Drink

Jack Heraty & Associates, Inc. 330 W. Colfax, Palatine, IL 60067. 708-991-0255.
Encyclopedia of World Art (published by the Publishers Guild)
New Catholic Encyclopedia (reprint edition)

Henry Holt and Company, Inc. 115 W. 18th St., New York, NY 10011. 800-628-9658 (toll-free).
American Political Dictionary
Columbia University College of Physicians and Surgeons Complete Home Guide to Mental Health
Encyclopedia of Publishing and the Book Arts
Henry Holt Handbook of Current Science & Technology
McClane's New Standard Fishing Encyclopedia and International Angling Guide
People's Chronology

Houghton Mifflin Company. 222 Berkeley St., Boston, MA 02116-3764. 800-733-7075 (toll-free).
Columbia Encyclopedia (published by Columbia University Press)
Dictionary of Cultural Literacy
Encyclopedia of World History
First Dictionary of Cultural Literacy
My First Encyclopedia (published by Dorling Kindersley, Inc.)
Reader's Companion to American History

Human Kinetics Publishers. P.O. Box 5076, 1607 N. Market St., Champaign, IL 61825-5076. 800-747-4457 (toll-free).
Encyclopedia of American Wrestling (published by Leisure Press)

Hunter House, Inc. P.O. Box 2914, Alameda, CA 94501-0914. 510-865-5282.
A-to-Z of Women's Sexuality: A Concise Encyclopedia

Hurtig Publishers Ltd. 10560 105th St., Edmonton, Alberta, Canada T5H 2W7. 403-426-2359
Canadian Encyclopedia (distributed by Gale Research)
Junior Encyclopedia of Canada

Industrial Press, Inc. 200 Madison Ave., New York, NY 10016. 212-889-6330.
Machinery's Handbook

Instructional Resources Company. 1013 E. Dimond Blvd. #188, Anchorage, AK 99515. 800-356-9315 (toll-free).
Facts Plus

Integrity Press. 61 Massey Dr., Westerville, OH 43081. 614-794-1600.
Heritage Encyclopedia of Band Music

InterVarsity Press P.O. Box 1400, 5206 Main St., Downers Grove, IL 60515. 800-843-7225 (toll-free).
Dictionary of Christianity in America

Interweave Press, Inc. 201 E. Fourth St., Loveland, CO 80537. 800-272-2193 (toll-free).
Encyclopedia of Handspinning (distributed by Contemporary Books)

Kindersley, Dorling. *See* **Dorling Kindersley**

Kingfisher Books (an imprint of CKG Publishers, Inc.). 95 Madison Ave., New York, NY 10016. 800-497-1657 (toll-free).
Kingfisher Children's Encyclopedia

Kluwer Academic Publishers. 101 Philip Dr., Norwell, MA 02061-1677. 617-871-6600.
Encyclopedia of Mathematics

Kodansha America, Inc. 114 Fifth Ave. (18th Floor), New York, NY 10011. 800-788-6262 (toll-free).
Japan: An Illustrated Encyclopedia (distributed by Farrar, Straus & Giroux)

Leisure Press. *See* **Human Kinetics Publishers**

Lewis Publishers (a subsidiary of CRC Press, Inc.). 2000 Corporate Blvd. N.W., Boca Raton, FL 33431. 800-272-7737 (toll-free).
Water Encyclopedia

Libraries Unlimited, Inc. P.O. Box 6633, Englewood, CO 80155-6633. 800-237-6124 (toll-free).
Encyclopedia of Ukraine (published by University of Toronto Press)

Louisiana State University Press. P.O. Box 25053, Baton Rouge, LA 70894-5053. 504-388-6666.
Encyclopedia of Southern History

Macmillan Publishing Company, Inc. 866 Third Ave., New York, NY 10022. 800-257-5755 (toll-free).

Macmillan Publishing Co., Inc. (continued)
American Horticultural Society Encyclopedia of Garden Plants
Baseball Encyclopedia
Coptic Encyclopedia
Encyclopaedia Judaica (published by Keter)
Encyclopedia of American Forest and Conservation History
Encyclopedia of Bioethics (published by the Free Press)
Encyclopedia of Crime and Justice (published by the Free Press)
Encyclopedia of Educational Research
Encyclopedia of Historic Forts
Encyclopedia of Learning and Memory
Encyclopedia of Philosophy (published by the Free Press)
Encyclopedia of Religion
Encyclopedia of Sleep and Dreaming
Encyclopedia of Sociology
Encyclopedia of the American Constitution
Encyclopedia of the Future
Encyclopedia of the Holocaust
Great Soviet Encyclopedia
Hortus Third: A Concise Dictionary of Plants Cultivated in the United States and Canada
International Encyclopedia of Population (published by the Free Press)
International Encyclopedia of Psychiatry, Psychology, Psychoanalysis, and Neurology (published by Aesculapius Publishers)
International Encyclopedia of the Social Sciences (published by the Free Press)
International Military and Defense Encyclopedia (published by Brassey's)
Macmillan Encyclopedia of Computers
Macmillan Encyclopedia of Science
Macmillan Health Encyclopedia
Macmillan Illustrated Encyclopedia of Dinosaurs and Prehistoric Animals
United States Energy Atlas
The Way Nature Works

Marcel Dekker. *See* **Dekker, Marcel**

Marshall Cavendish Corporation. 2415 Jerusalem Ave., P.O. Box 587, North Bellmore, NY 11710. 800-821-9881 (toll-free).
African American Encyclopedia
Encyclopedia of World Crime (published by CrimeBooks)
Marshall Cavendish Encyclopedia of Family Health
Marshall Cavendish Encyclopedia of Personal Relationships
Marshall Cavendish Illustrated Encyclopedia: World and Its People

Marshall Cavendish Illustrated Encyclopedia of Discovery and Exploration
Marshall Cavendish Illustrated Encyclopedia of Plants and Earth Sciences
Marshall Cavendish Illustrated Encyclopedia of World War I
Marshall Cavendish Illustrated Encyclopedia of World War II
New Standard Encyclopedia (published by Standard Educational Corporation)

Mazda Publishers. P.O. Box 2603, 3100 Airway Ave. (Suite 137), Costa Mesa, CA 92626. 714-751-5252.
Encyclopaedia Iranica

McFarland & Company, Inc. Box 611, Jefferson, NC 28640. 919-246-4460
Antarctica: An Encyclopedia
Moons of the Solar System: An Illustrated Encyclopedia

McGraw-Hill, Inc. 1221 Ave. of the Americas, New York, NY 10020. 800-233-1128 (toll-free).
Encyclopedia of American Architecture
Encyclopedia of Architectural Technology
Encyclopedia of Medical History
Encyclopedia of North American Rail Roading
Gallaudet Encyclopedia of Deaf People and Deafness
Grzimek's Encyclopedia of Mammals
Lange's Handbook of Chemistry
Marks' Standard Handbook for Mechanical Engineers
Materials Handbook
McGraw-Hill Concise Encyclopedia of Science and Technology
McGraw-Hill Encyclopedia of Astronomy
McGraw-Hill Encyclopedia of Chemistry
McGraw-Hill Encyclopedia of Economics
McGraw-Hill Encyclopedia of Electronics and Computers
McGraw-Hill Encyclopedia of Engineering
McGraw-Hill Encyclopedia of Science and Technology
McGraw-Hill Encyclopedia of the Geological Sciences
McGraw-Hill Encyclopedia of World Drama
McGraw-Hill Personal Computer Programming Encyclopedia
Rolling Rivers: An Encyclopedia of America's Rivers
State-by-State Guide to Women's Legal Rights

David McKay Company, Inc. (a subsidiary of Random House, Inc.). 201 E. 50th St., New York, NY 10022. 212-751-2600.
Civil War Dictionary
Encyclopedia of the American Revolution

Medical Economics Data. 5 Paragon Dr., Montvale, NJ 07645-1742. 800-442-6657 (toll-free).
Physicians' Desk Reference

Mercer University Press. 1400 Coleman Ave., Macon, GA 31207. 800-637-2378 (toll-free outside Georgia). 800-342-0841 (toll-free in Georgia)
Encyclopedia of Religion in the South

Merck Publishing Group. P.O. Box 2000, Rahway, NJ 07065. 908-594-4600.
Merck Manual of Diagnosis and Therapy

Merriam Webster Inc. 47 Federal St., P.O. Box 281, Springfield, MA 01102. 800-828-1880 (toll-free).
Webster's Beginning Book of Facts

Methuen. *See* **Routledge, Chapman & Hall**

Microlytics, Inc. (a subsidiary of SelecTronics, Inc.). 2 Tobey, Village Office Park, Pittsford, NY 14534. 800-828-6293 (toll-free).
Random House Encyclopedia: Electronic Edition (Floppy Disks)

Microsoft Corporation. One Microsoft Way, Redmond, WA 98052-6399. 800-426-9400 (toll-free).
Concise Columbia Encyclopedia (CD-ROM, published by Columbia University Press); bundled with *Microsoft Bookshelf*
Cinemania (CD-ROM)
Microsoft Encarta Multimedia Encyclopedia (CD-ROM)

Millbrook Press, Inc. 2 Old New Milford Rd., Brookfield, CT 06804. 800-462-4703 (toll-free).
Young People's Encyclopedia of the United States

MIT Press. 55 Hayward St., Cambridge, MA 02142. 800-356-0343 (toll-free).
Aquarium Encyclopedia
Concise Encyclopedia of Mineral Resources
Encyclopedic Dictionary of Mathematics
Encyclopedic Dictionary of Psychology

William Morrow & Company, Inc. 1350 Ave. of the Americas, New York, NY 10019. 800-843-9389 (toll-free).
New Frank Schoonmaker Encyclopedia of Wine

National Association of Social Workers. 750 First St. N.E. (Suite 700), Washington, DC 20002-4241. 800-638-8799 (toll-free).
Encyclopedia of Social Work

National Geographic Society. 1145 17th St. N.W., Washington, DC 20036. 800-368-2728 (toll-free).
Exploring Your World

National Videotex Network. *See* **NVN**

New American Library (a subsidiary of Penguin USA). 375 Hudson St., New York, NY 10014. 800-526-0275 (toll-free).
New American Desk Encyclopedia

New Catholic Encyclopedia, Inc. 330 W. Colfax, Palatine, IL 60067. 708-991-0255.
New Catholic Encyclopedia (reprint edition)

New England Publishing Associates Inc. P.O. Box 5, 59 Parker Hill Rd., Chester, CT 06412. 203-345-4976.
Guinness Encyclopedia of Popular Music (published by Guinness Publishing)

New York Zoetrope. 838 Broadway, New York, NY 10003. 800-242-7546 (toll-free).
Encyclopedia of Television

Newfield Publications. P.O. Box 16615, Columbus, OH 43216. 800-456-8220 (toll-free).
Young Students Learning Library

North Light Books. 1507 Dana Ave., Cincinnati, OH 45207. 800-289-0963 (toll-free).
Encyclopedia of Drawing (distributed by Writer's Digest)

W.W. Norton & Company, Inc. 500 Fifth Ave., New York, NY 10110. 800-223-2584 (toll-free).
Dictionary of Woodworking Tools c. 1700–1970 and Tools of Allied Trades (published by Taunton Press)
Illustrated Dictionary of Jewelry (published by Thames & Hudson)
Norton/Grove Concise Encyclopedia of Music
Patrick Moore's A-Z of Astronomy

NVN (National Videotex Network). 5555 San Felipe (Suite 1200), Houston, TX 77056. 800-336-9096 (toll-free).

Academic American Encyclopedia (Online)

Oryx Press. 4041 N. Central Ave. at Indian School Rd., Phoenix, AZ 85012-3397. 800-279-6799 (toll-free).

Encyclopedia of Adult Development
Encyclopedia of Career Change and Work Issues
Encyclopedia of Childbearing
Encyclopedia of Death
Encyclopedia of School Administration and Supervision

Outlet Book Company, Inc. (a subsidiary of Random House, Inc.). 225 Park Ave. S., New York, NY 10003. 800-726-0600 (toll-free).

Audubon Society Encyclopedia of North American Birds (originally published by Knopf; reprinted by Wings Books)
Encyclopedia of World Costume (reprint edition)

Overlook Press. 149 Wooster St. (4th Floor), New York, NY 10012. 212-477-7162.

American Shelter (distributed by Viking Penguin)
Complete Dictionary of Furniture (distributed by Viking Penguin)

Oxford University Press. 200 Madison Ave., New York, NY 10016. 800-451-7556 (toll-free).

American Musical Theatre: A Chronicle
Concise Oxford Dictionary of Ballet
Dictionary of Superstitions
Encyclopedia of the Early Church
Encyclopaedia of the Musical Film
Great Song Thesaurus
Illustrated Encyclopedia of World Geography
International Encyclopedia of Communications
International Encyclopedia of Linguistics
New Oxford Companion to Music
Oxford Children's Encyclopedia
Oxford Companion to American Theatre
Oxford Companion to Animal Behaviour
Oxford Companion to Canadian Literature
Oxford Companion to Canadian Theatre
Oxford Companion to Chess
Oxford Companion to Children's Literature
Oxford Companion to Classical Literature
Oxford Companion to English Literature
Oxford Companion to Law
Oxford Companion to Medicine
Oxford Companion to Politics of the World
Oxford Companion to Ships and the Sea
Oxford Companion to the Decorative Arts
Oxford Companion to the Mind

Oxford Companion to the Supreme Court of the United States
Oxford Companion to the Theatre
Oxford Companion to World Sports and Games
Oxford Dictionary of Art
Oxford Dictionary of Byzantium
Oxford Dictionary of the Christian Church
Oxford Encyclopedia of Trees of the World
Oxford Illustrated Encyclopedia
World Christian Encyclopedia

Paragon House. 90 Fifth Ave., New York, NY 10011. 800-727-2466 (toll-free).

Encyclopedia of Nationalism

Pegus Press. 648 W. Sierra Ave., P.O. Box 429, Clovis, CA 93612. 209-299-2263.

Foods and Nutrition Encyclopedia (distributed by Encyclopaedia Britannica Educational Corporation)

PennWell Books. 1421 S. Sheridan, Tulsa, OK 74112. 800-752-9764 (toll-free).

International Petroleum Encyclopedia

Pergamon Press Inc. 660 White Plains Rd., Tarrytown, NY 10591-5153. 914-333-2410.

Concise Encyclopedia of Mineral Resources
Concise Encyclopedia of Traffic & Transportation Systems
Encyclopedia of Higher Education
Encyclopedia of Materials Science and Engineering
International Encyclopedia of Education
Physics in Medicine & Biology Encyclopedia
Systems and Control Encyclopedia
World Encyclopedia of Peace

Pharos Books. 200 Park Ave., New York, NY 10166. 800-325-5525 (toll-free).

World Almanac Infopedia (distributed by St. Martin's Press)

Prentice Hall (a subsidiary of Simon & Schuster). 15 Columbus Circle, New York, NY 10023. 800-223-2348 (toll-free).

Bloomsbury Guide to Women's Literature
Dictionary of Dreams (reprint edition)
Encyclopedia of Building Technology
Encyclopedic Dictionary of Accounting and Finance
Parent's Desk Reference: The Ultimate Family Encyclopedia from Conception to College
Prentice-Hall Encyclopedia of Information Technology
Webster's New World Encyclopedia
Webster's New World Encyclopedia: College Edition
Webster's New World Encyclopedia: Pocket Edition

Price Stern Sloan. 11150 Olympic Blvd. (Suite 650), Los Angeles, CA 90064. 800-631-8571 (toll-free).
Complete Guide to Symptoms, Illness & Surgery

Prima Publishing & Communications. 1830 Sierra Gardens (Suite 130), Roseville, CA 95661. 916-786-0426.
Encyclopedia of Natural Medicine (distributed by St. Martin's Press)

Princeton University Press. 41 William St., Princeton, NJ 08540. 800-777-4726 (toll-free).
Dictionary of the History of Science
New Princeton Encyclopedia of Poetry and Poetics

Prodigy Information Service. 445 Hamilton Ave., White Plains, NY 10601. 800-776-3449 (toll-free).
Academic American Encyclopedia (Online)

Prometheus Books. 59 John Glenn Dr., Buffalo, NY 14228-2197. 800-421-0351 (toll-free).
Dictionary of Science & Creationism
Encyclopedia of Unbelief

Publishers Guild. *See* **Jack Heraty & Associates**

Putnam Publishing Group. 200 Madison Ave., New York, NY 10016. 800-631-8571 (toll-free).
Columbia Encyclopedia of Nutrition
Definitive Kobbé's Opera Book

Raintree/Steck-Vaughn Publishers. P.O. Box 26015, Austin, TX 78755. 800-558-7264 (toll-free).
Raintree Illustrated Science Encyclopedia
World Nature Encyclopedia

Random House, Inc. 201 E. 50th St., New York, NY 10022. 800-726-0600 (toll-free).
American Medical Association Encyclopedia of Medicine
American Medical Association Family Medical Guide
Civil War Dictionary
Evolving Constitution: How the Supreme Court Has Ruled on Issues from Abortion to Zoning
Official NBA Basketball Encyclopedia
Random House Children's Encyclopedia
Random House Electronic Encyclopedia (Handheld; distributed by Vitel Electronics)
Random House Encyclopedia
Random House Encyclopedia: Electronic Edition (Floppy Disks; published by Microlytics)

Random House Library of Knowledge: First Encyclopedia
Reader's Digest New Complete Do-It-Yourself Manual (published by Reader's Digest Association)
Warships of the World: An Illustrated Encyclopedia (published by Times Books)
Wellness Encyclopedia of Food and Nutrition (published by Rebus)

Reader's Digest Association, Inc. 260 Madison Ave., New York, NY 10016. 212-850-7007.
Reader's Digest New Complete Do-It-Yourself Manual (distributed by Random House)

Rebus, Inc. 632 Broadway, New York, NY 10012. 212-505-2255.
Wellness Encyclopedia of Food and Nutrition (distributed by Random House)

Reference Book Center. 175 Fifth Ave. (Room 701), New York, NY 10010. 212-677-2160.
Secondhand encyclopedias

Rodale Press, Inc. 33 Minor St., Emmaus, PA 18098-0099. 800-221-7945 (toll-free).
Encyclopedia of Natural Insect & Disease Control
Practical Encyclopedia of Sex and Health
Rodale's All-New Encyclopedia of Organic Gardening

Ronin Publishing, Inc. P.O. Box 1035, Berkeley, CA 94701. 510-540-6278.
Psychedelics Encyclopedia

Routledge, Chapman & Hall, Inc. 29 W. 35th St., New York, NY 10001-2299. 800-634-7064 (toll-free).
Compendium of the World's Languages
Encyclopaedia of the History of Technology
Encyclopedia of Government and Politics
Encyclopedia of Terrorism and Political Violence
Encyclopedic Dictionary of Sports Medicine

Running Press Book Publishers. 125 S. 22nd St., Philadelphia, PA 19103-4399. 800-345-5359 (toll-free).
Running Press Cyclopedia

St. James Press (a subsidiary of Gale Research). 835 Penobscot Building, Detroit, MI 48226. 800-345-0392 (toll-free).
Encyclopedia of Banking and Finance
International Dictionary of Ballet (distributed by Gale Research)
International Dictionary of Films and Filmmakers (distributed by Gale Research)

St. James Press (continued)

International Dictionary of Theatre (distributed by Gale Research)

St. James Encyclopedia of Mortgage & Real Estate Finance

St. Martin's Press. 257 Park Ave. S., New York, NY 10010. 800-221-7945 (toll-free).

Complete Drug Reference (published by Consumer Reports Books)

Encyclopedia of Natural Medicine (published by Prima Publishing & Communications)

Encyclopedia of Pop, Rock and Soul

Encyclopedia of the British Press, 1440–1991

Football Encyclopedia

Rules of the Game: The Complete Illustrated Encyclopedia of All Major Sports of the World

Weapons: An International Encyclopedia from 5000 BC to 2000 AD

World Almanac Infopedia (published by World Almanac Books)

Salem House Publishers. 462 Boston St., Topsfield, MA 01983. 800-624-8947 (toll-free).

RHS Encyclopedia of House Plants Including Greenhouse Plants

Salem Press, Inc. 580 Sylvan Ave., Englewood Cliffs, NJ 07632. 800-221-1592 (toll-free).

Cyclopedia of Literary Characters

Magill's Survey of Cinema

Masterplots

Sangamon State University Press. Springfield, IL 62794-9243. 217-786-6502.

Astronomy from A to Z

Scarecrow Press, Inc. 52 Liberty St., P.O. Box 4167 Metuchen, NJ 08840. 800-537-7107 (toll-free).

Historical Dictionary of Israel

Schirmer Books. 866 Third Ave., New York, NY 10022. 212-702-4283

Gänzl's Book of the Musical Theatre

Schoenhof's Foreign Books. 76A Mount Auburn St., Cambridge, MA 02138. 617-547-8855.

Foreign-language encyclopedias

Charles Scribner's Sons (an imprint of Macmillan Publishing Company). 866 Third Ave., New York, NY 10022. 800-257-5755 (toll-free).

Album of Science

Civilization of the Ancient Mediterranean: Greece and Rome

Dictionary of American History

Dictionary of the History of Ideas

Dictionary of the Middle Ages

Encyclopedia of American Economic History

Encyclopedia of American Foreign Policy

Encyclopedia of American Political History

Encyclopedia of American Social History

Encyclopedia of Arms Control and Disarmament

Encyclopedia of Asian History

Encyclopedia of the American Judicial System

Encyclopedia of the American Legislative System

Encyclopedia of the American Religious Experience

Exotica Series 4 International: Pictorial Cyclopedia of Exotic Plants from Tropical and Near-Tropical Regions

SelecTronics, Inc. 2 Tobey Village Office Park, Pittsford, NY 14534. 800-828-6293 (toll-free).

Random House Electronic Encyclopedia (Handheld; distributed by Vital Electronics)

Simon & Schuster. 1230 Ave. of the Americas, New York, NY 10020. 800-223-2348 (toll-free).

Christopher Columbus Encyclopedia

Dictionary of Contemporary Politics of Central America and the Caribbean

Elements of Style: A Practical Encyclopedia of Interior Architectural Details from 1485 to the Present

Encyclopedia of the American Presidency

How to Clean Everything: An Encyclopedia of What to Use and How to Use It

New Encyclopedia of Archaeological Excavations in the Holy Land

Smithmark Publishers, Inc. 16 E. 32nd St., New York, NY 10016. 800-932-0070 (toll-free).

Encyclopedia of American Crime

Encyclopedia of Flowers

Smithsonian Institution Press. 470 L'Enfant Plaza (Suite 7100), Washington, DC 20560. 202-287-3738.

Handbook of North American Indians (distributed by the U.S. Government Printing Office)

Software Toolworks, Inc. 60 Leveroni Court, Novato, CA 94949. 800-234-3088 (toll-free).

Software Toolworks Illustrated Encyclopedia (CD-ROM)

Sony Corporation of America. 655 River Oaks Parkway, San Jose, CA 95134. 800-222-0878 (toll-free).

Compton's Concise Encyclopedia (CD-ROM; published by Compton's NewMedia); bundled with *Data Discman*

Compton's Family Encyclopedia (CD-ROM; published by Compton's NewMedia); bundled with *Sony Laser Library*
New Grolier Multimedia Encyclopedia (CD-ROM; published by Grolier Electronic Publishing; bundled with *Sony Desktop Library*

South Asia Books. P.O. Box 502, Columbia, MO 65205. 314-474-0116.
Encyclopaedia of India (published by Rima Publishing House)
Encyclopaedia of Indian Archaeology (published by Munshiram Manoharlal)

South Western Company. P.O. Box 305140, Nashville, TN 37230. 615-391-2500.
Volume Library

Springer-Verlag New York, Inc. P.O. Box 2485, Secaucus, NJ 07096-2491. 800-777-4643 (toll-free).
Encyclopedia of Aging
Encyclopedia of Neuroscience (published by Birkhauser Boston)
Illustrated Encyclopedia of Human Histology

Standard Educational Corporation. 200 W. Monroe St., Chicago, IL 60606. 312-346-7440
New Standard Encyclopedia

Steck-Vaughn Publishers. *See* **Raintree/Steck-Vaughn Publishers**

Gareth Stevens, Inc. River Center Building (Suite 201), 1555 N. River Center Dr., Milwaukee, WI 53212. 800-341-3569 (toll-free).
Isaac Asimov's Library of the Universe

Stockton Press. 49 W. 24th St., New York, NY 10010. 800-221-2123 (toll-free).
New Palgrave: A Dictionary of Economics
New Palgrave Dictionary of Money and Finance
New Royal Horticultural Society Dictionary of Gardening

Strand Book Store. 828 Broadway, New York, NY 10003. 212-473-1452.
Secondhand encyclopedias

TAB Books (a division of McGraw-Hill). P.O. Box 40, Blue Ridge Summit, PA 17294-0850. 800-233-1128 (toll-free).
Encyclopedia of Electronic Circuits
Encyclopedia of Electronics
Graphic Arts Encyclopedia (published by Design Press)
Illustrated Encyclopedia of General Aviation

Taunton Press, Inc. 63 S. Main St., P.O. Box 5506. Newtown, CT 06470-5506. 800-243-7252 (toll-free).
Dictionary of Woodworking Tools c. 1700–1970 and Tools of Allied Trades (distributed by W.W. Norton)

Taylor & Francis. 1101 Vermont Ave., NW (Suite 200), Washington, DC 20005-3521. 800-821-8312 (toll-free).
Encyclopedia of Human Rights
Encyclopedia of the United Nations and International Agreements

Teachers College Press. Teachers College, Columbia University, 1234 Amsterdam Ave., New York, NY 10027. 212-678-3929.
Critical Dictionary of Educational Concepts

T.F.H. Publications. 1 T.F.H. Plaza, Union & Third Aves., Neptune City, NJ 07753. 800-631-2188 (toll-free).
Atlas of Cats of the World
Atlas of Dog Breeds of the World

Thames & Hudson Inc. 500 Fifth Ave., New York, NY 10110. 212-354-3763.
Illustrated Dictionary of Jewelry (distributed by Norton)

Times Books. *See* **Outlet Book Company, Inc.**

Trafalgar Square/David & Charles, Inc. P.O. Box 257, Howe Hill Rd., N. Pomfret, VT 05053. 800-423-4525 (toll-free).
Running from A to Z (published by Stanley Paul)

Tribune Publishing Company. *See* **Compton's Learning Company**

Troll Associates Inc. 100 Corporate Dr., Mahwah, NJ 07430. 800-526-5289 (toll-free).
My First Encyclopedia
Troll Student Encyclopedia

U.S. Government Printing Office. Washington, DC 20401. 202-512-2364.
Handbook of North American Indians (published by the Smithsonian Institution)

University of Arkansas Press. 201 Ozark Ave., Fayetteville, AR 72701. 800-525-1823 (toll-free).
Encyclopedia of the Blues

University of California Press. 2120 Berkeley Way, Berkeley, CA 94720. 800-822-6657 (toll-free).
Toxics A to Z

University of Illinois Press. 1325 S. Oak St., Champaign, IL 61820. 800-545-4703 (toll-free).
Encyclopedia of the American Left

University of North Carolina Press. P.O. Box 2288, Chapel Hill, NC 27515-2288. 800-848-6224 (toll-free).
Encyclopedia of Southern Culture

University of Toronto Press. 340 Nagel Dr., Cheektowaga, NY 14225. 716-683-4547.
Encyclopedia of Music in Canada
Encyclopedia of Ukraine (distributed by Libraries Unlimited)

University of Washington Press. P.O. Box 50096, Seattle, WA 98145-5096. 800-441-4115 (toll-free).
Theatre Backstage from A to Z

Van Nostrand Reinhold Company, Inc. 115 Fifth Ave., New York, NY 10003. 800-842-3636 (toll-free).
Astronomy and Astrophysics Encyclopedia
Encyclopedia of Computer Science
Encyclopedia of Earth Sciences
Encyclopedia of Management
Encyclopedia of Minerals
Encyclopedia of Physics
Foods and Food Production Encyclopedia
Nutrition and Health Encyclopedia
Van Nostrand Reinhold Encyclopedia of Chemistry
Van Nostrand's Science Encyclopedia
VNR Concise Encyclopedia of Mathematics

VCH Publishers, Inc. 220 E. 23rd St., New York, NY 10010-4606. 800-367-8249 (toll-free).
Encyclopedia of Applied Physics
Encyclopedia of Physics
Ullmann's Encyclopedia of Industrial Chemistry

Viking Penguin Inc. 375 Hudson St., New York, NY 10014-3657. 800-331-4624 (toll-free).
American Shelter (published by Overlook Press)
Complete Dictionary of Furniture (published by Overlook Press)
New Encyclopedia of Science Fiction
Penguin Dictionary of Decorative Arts

Visible Ink Press (an imprint of Gale Research). 835 Penobscot Building, Detroit, MI 48226. 800-877-4253 (toll-free).
Les Brown's Encyclopedia of Television

Vitel Electronics, Inc. 100 Hollister Rd., Teterboro, NJ 07608. 800-443-0594 (toll-free).
Random House Electronic Encyclopedia (Handheld; published by Selectronics, Inc.)

Walter de Gruyter. *See* **de Gruyter, Walter**

Warren, Gorham & Lamont, Inc. 210 South St., Boston, MA 02111. 800-922-0066 (toll-free).
Thorndike Encyclopedia of Banking and Financial Tables

Watson-Guptill Publications. 1515 Broadway, New York, NY 10036. 800-451-1741 (toll-free).
Encyclopedia of Sculpture Techniques

Franklin Watts. 5450 N. Cumberland Ave., Chicago, IL 60656.
Mathematics Illustrated Dictionary

Weekly Reader Books. *See* **Newfield Publications**

West Publishing Company. 50 Kellogg Blvd., St. Paul, MN 55164-0526. 800-328-9352 (toll-free).
Corpus Juris Secundum
Guide to American Law: Everyone's Legal Encyclopedia

Western Publishing Company. 850 Third Ave., New York, NY 10022. 800-558-5972 (toll-free).
Golden Book Encyclopedia (distributed by the Donovan Music and Toy Company to individual consumers; distributed to schools and libraries by the Children's Press)

Westminster/John Knox Press. 100 Witherspoon St., Louisville, KY 40202-1396. 502-569-5043.
Westminster Dictionary of Christian Ethics

John Wiley & Sons, Inc. 605 Third Ave., New York, NY 10158-0012, 212-850-6000.
Encyclopedia of Architecture
Encyclopedia of Artificial Intelligence
Encyclopedia of Food Science and Technology
Encyclopedia of Medical Devices and Instrumentation
Encyclopedia of Polymer Science and Engineering

Encyclopedia of Psychology
Encyclopedia of Special Encyclopedia
Encyclopedia of Statistical Sciences
Family Mental Health Encyclopedia
International Business Dictionary and Reference
International Encyclopedia of Robotics
Kirk-Othmer Encyclopedia of Chemical Technology
Worldmark Encyclopedia of the Nations
Worldmark Encyclopedia of the States

H.W. Wilson Company. 950 University Ave., Bronx, NY 10452. 800-367-6770 (toll-free).
Famous First Facts

World Almanac Books (a division of Funk & Wagnalls). One International Blvd., Mahwah, NJ 07495-0017. 201-529-6900.
World Almanac Infopedia (distributed by St. Martin's Press)

World Almanac Education (a subsidiary of Funk & Wagnalls). 1277 W. 9th St., Cleveland, OH 44113. 800-321-1147 (toll-free).
Funk & Wagnalls New Encyclopedia (published by Funk & Wagnalls)

World Book, Inc. 525 W. Monroe St. (20th Floor), Chicago, IL 60661. 800-621-8202 (toll-free).
Childcraft
Information Finder (CD-ROM)
World Book Encyclopedia
World Book Encyclopedia of People and Places
World Book/Rush-Presbyterian-St. Luke's Medical Center Medical Encyclopedia

Writer's Digest Books. 1507 Dana Ave., Cincinnati, OH 45207. 800-289-0963 (toll-free).
Encyclopedia of Drawing (published by North Light Books)
Writing A to Z

Yale University Press. 302 Temple St., New Haven, CT 06511. 203-432-0960
Handbook of Russian Literature
Psychoanalytic Terms and Concepts

Zoetrope. *See* **New York Zoetrope**

Index

* * * * * * * *

Encyclopedias reviewed in *Kister's Best Encyclopedias* appear in the index in SMALL CAPITAL LETTERS. Other encyclopedias and publications mentioned in the book, including variant titles, are *italicized* in the index. Following customary practice, the words *encyclopaedia* and *encyclopaedic* are alphabetized in the index

as if they were spelled *encyclopedia* and *encyclopedic*.

Subject (or specialized) encyclopedias are indexed by both title and topic.

For information about encyclopedias as a type of reference work, consult the index entry "Encyclopedias—general information" and its many subheadings.

▓ ▓ ▓

ABINGDON DICTIONARY OF LIVING RELIGIONS, 412
ACADEMIC AMERICAN ENCYCLOPEDIA (Online), 256-59. *See also* 11–12, 284
    chart, 298
    overview, 256
ACADEMIC AMERICAN ENCYCLOPEDIA (Print), 53–59. *See also* 11, 14, 304, 445
    chart, 106
    overview, 51–52
Academic American Encyclopedia on CD-ROM, 287, 290
Academic Press, 12
Accounting, 338-39
Adler's Foreign Books, 444
Adolescence, 425
Adoption, 425
Adult encyclopedias, 23–172
Africa, 362, 404
AFRICAN AMERICAN ENCYCLOPEDIA, 427
African Americans, 414, 427–28, 438
Aging, 428
Agriculture, 359
Ainslie's Complete Hoyle, 436
Air forces, 394
Airman's Information Manual, 441
Airplanes, 394, 441–42
Aiton's Encyclopedia, 82–83

ALA World Encyclopedia of Library and Information Services, 352
ALA Yearbook of Library and Information Science, 352
Albania, 387
ALBUM OF SCIENCE, 420
Alcohol and alcoholism, 370
Alcohol/Drug Abuse Dictionary and Encyclopedia, 370
Alexis Lichine's New Encyclopedia of Wine and Spirits, 361
Almanac of American History, 377
Almanac of Modern Terrorism, 394
Almanac of Science and Technology, 422
America Online, 19, 253, 256, 268
American Booksellers Association, 109–10, 113
American Dictionary of Campaigns and Elections, 407
AMERICAN EDUCATOR, 300
AMERICAN EDUCATORS' ENCYCLOPEDIA, 349–50
AMERICAN FAMILY ENCYCLOPEDIA, 300
AMERICAN FILM INDUSTRY: A HISTORICAL DICTIONARY, 355
American Film Studios: An Historical Encyclopedia, 355
American Furniture, 344
American Heritage Dictionary, 266, 275
American history, 376–78, 381, 403–04

AMERICAN HORTICULTURAL SOCIETY ENCYCLOPEDIA OF GARDEN PLANTS, 334
American Horticultural Society Encyclopedia of Gardening, 334, 337
American Indian: A Multimedia Encyclopedia, 431
American Indians. See Native Americans
American Jurisprudence, 382
AMERICAN LAW DICTIONARY, 382
American literature, 385, 391–92
AMERICAN MEDICAL ASSOCIATION ENCYCLOPEDIA OF MEDICINE, 368–69
AMERICAN MEDICIAL ASSOCIATION FAMILY MEDICAL GUIDE, 369
American Musical Comedy, 436
American Musical Revue, 436
AMERICAN MUSICAL THEATRE, 436
American Operetta, 436
AMERICAN PEOPLES ENCYCLOPEDIA, 301
AMERICAN POLITICAL DICTIONARY, 403
American Presidents, 405
American Reference Books Annual (ARBA), 17, 20, 455
American Revolution, 394
American Revolution, 1775–1783: An Encyclopedia, 394
AMERICAN SHELTER: AN ILLUSTRATED ENCYCLOPEDIA OF THE AMERICAN HOME, 324
American Song: The Complete Musical Theatre Companion, 436–37
AMERICAN SPECTRUM ENCYCLOPEDIA, 109–14
chart, 171
overview, 109
Americana. See ENCYCLOPEDIA AMERICANA
Americana Annual, 34
Amerigrove. See NEW GROVE DICTIONARY OF AMERICAN MUSIC
ANCHOR BIBLE DICTIONARY, 412–13
Ancient history, 376–77
Anglo-American General Encyclopedias: A Historical Bibliography, 1703–1967, 300, 458
Animals and animal life, 329–34
Annotated Dictionary of Modern Religious Movements, 412
Antarctica, 361
ANTARCTICA: AN ENCYCLOPEDIA, 361
Anthropology, 428, 431
Antiques, 344
AQUARIUM ENCYCLOPEDIA, 329
Aquatic life and aquariums, 329, 331–32

ARBA. See American Reference Books Annual
Archaeological Encyclopedia of the Holy Land, 419
Archaeology, 375, 378, 419
Architecture, 324–26, 344–45
Area studies, 361–68
Aretê Publishing Company, 54, 257
Arms and arms control, 393, 407
Arnold Encyclopedia of Real Estate, 340
Art, 324–27
Art of Kabuki, 439
Artificial intelligence, 342
ARTISTS' AND ILLUSTRATORS' ENCYCLOPEDIA, 324–25
Asia, 377–78, 387, 404, 407, 437
Asian Americans, 427
ASIMOV'S CHRONOLOGY OF SCIENCE AND DISCOVERY, 420
Asimov's Chronology of the World, 381
Asimov's New Guide to Science, 422
Assassinations and Executions: An Encyclopedia of Political Violence, 1865–1986, 394
Astrology, 411
Astrology Encyclopedia, 411
Astronomy, 327–29
ASTRONOMY AND ASTROPHYSICS ENCYCLOPEDIA, 327–28
ASTRONOMY FROM A TO Z, 328
Astrophysics, 327–29
Atlante Enciclopedico degli Aerei Civili del Mondo da Leonardo a oggi, 442
Atlas of American History, 376
ATLAS OF CATS OF THE WORLD, 329–30
ATLAS OF DOG BREEDS OF THE WORLD, 330
A-TO-Z OF WOMEN'S SEXUALITY: A CONCISE ENCYCLOPEDIA, 424
Audubon Society Book of Insects, 332
Audubon Society Encyclopedia of Animal Life, 333
AUDUBON SOCIETY ENCYCLOPEDIA OF NORTH AMERICAN BIRDS, 330
AULA: ENCICLOPÉDIA DEL ESTUDIANTE, 449
Austin's New Encyclopedia of Usable Information, 304
Australia, 362, 375, 391
Australian Encyclopedia, 362
AUSTRALIANS: A HISTORICAL LIBRARY, 375
Automobiles, 337, 440–41
Aviation, 441–42
A-Z of Astronomy, 329

Backstage from A to Z, 440
Baker Encyclopedia of Psychology, 410

Baker Encyclopedia of the Bible, 418

Ballet, 437–38

Ballet Goer's Guide, 438

Band music, 398

Bangladesh, 362

Banking, 337-38, 340

Banned Books, 387 B.C. to 1978 A.D., 388

BARNES & NOBLE ENCYCLOPEDIA, 114

    chart, 171

    overview, 109

Barnes & Noble, Inc., 60, 114

BARNES & NOBLE NEW AMERICAN ENCYCLOPEDIA, 59–60

    chart, 106

    overview, 51

Barron's Educational Series, Inc., 115

BARRON'S JUNIOR FACT FINDER, 221–23

    chart, 252

    overview, 220

BARRON'S NEW STUDENT'S CONCISE ENCYCLOPEDIA, 115–18

    chart, 171

    overview, 109

Barron's Student's Concise Encyclopedia, 115, 118

Bartlett's Familiar Quotations, 275

Baseball, 433

BASEBALL ENCYCLOPEDIA, 433

Baseball Encyclopedia Update, 433

BASIC EVERYDAY ENCYCLOPEDIA, 301

Basic Information Sources (Katz), 456

Basketball, 435

Bateman New Zealand Encyclopedia, 365

Battles, 393–94

Behavior and behavioral sciences, 427–32

BENÉT'S READER'S ENCYCLOPEDIA, 385

BENÉT'S READER'S ENCYCLOPEDIA OF AMERICAN LITERATURE, 385

BERTELSMANN LEXIKON: DIE GROSSE BERTELSMANN LEXIKOTHEK, 447

Better Homes and Gardens New Family Medical Guide, 369

Bhutan, 362

Bible, 412–13, 417–18

Big League Baseball Electronic Encyclopedia, 433

Biochemistry, 330–31

Bioethics, 331

Biology, 329–34

Birds, 330

BIRS. See BRITANNICA INSTANT RESEARCH SYSTEM (CD-ROM)

Birth and birth defects, 370

Black American Reference Book, 427

Blacks, 414, 427–28, 438

Black Women in America: An Historical Encyclopedia, 427

Black's Children's Encyclopedia, 311

BLACK'S VETERINARY DICTIONARY, 330

Blackwell Dictionary of Judaica, 414

Blackwell Encyclopedia of Industrial Archaeology, 375

Blackwell Encyclopaedia of Political Institutions, 403

BLACKWELL ENCYCLOPAEDIA OF POLITICAL THOUGHT, 403

Blackwell Encyclopedia of the American Revolution, 394

Blackwell Encyclopedia of the Russian Revolution, 377

Blindness, 370

Bloodletters and Badmen, 430

BLOOMSBURY GUIDE TO WOMEN'S LITERATURE, 385

Blues (music), 397

BOL'SHAIA SOVETSKAIA ENTSIKLOPEDIIA, 449. *See also* 26, 365

Book of Knowledge, 173, 195–96, 200

Book of Popular Science, 423

Booklist, 20, 456

Books and book production, 388

Botany, 334–37

Brady's. See MATERIALS HANDBOOK

Brassey's Battles, 393–94

Brazil, 387

Breakthroughs: A Chronology of Great Achievements in Science and Mathematics, 1200–1930, 420

BREWER'S DICTIONARY OF PHRASE AND FABLE, 385–86

Brewer's Dictionary of 20th-Century Phrase and Fable, 386

Bridge (game), 435

Bridge Player's Alphabetical Handbook, 435

Brill's First Encyclopaedia of Islam, 1913–1936. See E.J. *Brill's First Encyclopedia of Islam, 1913–1936*

Britannica. See NEW ENCYCLOPAEDIA BRITANNICA

Britannica Book of the Year, 41

BRITANNICA ENCYCLOPEDIA OF AMERICAN ART, 325

Britannica Electronic Index, 46

Britannica Fact-Checking System. See BRITANNICA INSTANT RESEARCH SYSTEM

BRITANNICA INSTANT RESEARCH SYSTEM (CD-ROM), 259–61. *See also* 10
  chart, 298
  overview, 256
BRITANNICA INTERNATIONAL ENCYCLOPAEDIA, 448
BRITANNICA JUNIOR ENCYCLOPAEDIA, 301. *See also* 11, 299
BRITANNICA ONLINE (Online), 261-63. *See also* 11
  chart, 298
  overview, 256
Britannica 3. See NEW ENCYCLOPAEDIA BRITANNICA
Britannica World Data Annual, 41, 43–45, 364
BRITANNICA WORLD ENCYCLOPAEDIA, 448–49
BROADWAY: AN ENCYCLOPEDIC GUIDE TO THE HISTORY, 437
Brockhaus, 31, 447
Brockhaus ABC Biochemie, 330
BROCKHAUS ENZYKLOPÄDIE, 447. *See also* 7, 31
Brockhaus' Konversations-Lexikon, 447
BUD COLLINS' MODERN ENCYCLOPEDIA OF TENNIS, 433
Building construction and technology, 352–55
Bush, Vannevar, 253
Business, 337–40
Business of Enlightenment: A Publishing History of the Encyclopédie (Darnton), 7, 457–58
Byzantium, 380-81

CADILLAC MODERN ENCYCLOPEDIA, 301–02
Cadillac Modern Encyclopedia Online. See KUSSMAUL ENCYCLOPEDIA (Online)
CAMBRIDGE ENCYCLOPEDIA, 118–23
  chart, 171
  overview, 109
Cambridge Encyclopedia of Africa, 362
CAMBRIDGE ENCYCLOEDIA OF ARCHAEOLOGY, 375
Cambridge Encyclopedia of Astronomy, 328
Cambridge Encyclopedia of Australia, 362
Cambridge Encyclopedia of China, 362
CAMBRIDGE ENCYCLOPEDIA OF EARTH SCIENCES, 346
Cambridge Encyclopedia of Human Evolution, 331
Cambridge Encyclopedia of India, Pakistan, Bangladesh, Sri Lanka, Nepal, Bhutan, and the Maldives, 362
Cambridge Encyclopedia of Japan, 362, 266
CAMBRIDGE ENCYCLOPEDIA OF LANGUAGE, 386
CAMBRIDGE ENCYCLOPEDIA OF LATIN AMERICA AND THE CARIBBEAN, 361–62
CAMBRIDGE ENCYCLOPEDIA OF LIFE SCIENCES, 330
Cambridge Encyclopedia of Ornithology, 330
CAMBRIDGE ENCYCLOPEDIA OF RUSSIA AND THE FORMER SOVIET UNION, 362

Cambridge Encyclopedia of Russia and the Soviet Union, 362
CAMBRIDGE ENCYCLOPEDIA OF SPACE, 328
Cambridge Encyclopedia of the Middle East and North Africa, 362
Cambridge Factfinder, 119
CAMBRIDGE GUIDE TO AMERICAN THEATRE, 437
CAMBRIDGE GUIDE TO ASIAN THEATRE, 437
Cambridge Guide to English Literature, 392
Cambridge Guide to Literature in English, 392
CAMBRIDGE GUIDE TO THE MATERIAL WORLD, 420–21
CAMBRIDGE GUIDE TO WORLD THEATRE, 437
Cambridge Handbook of American Literature, 385
CAMBRIDGE HISTORICAL ENCYCLOPEDIA OF GREAT BRITAIN AND IRELAND, 375
CAMBRIDGE PAPERBACK ENCYCLOPEDIA, 124–25. *See also* 118-19
  chart, 171
  overview, 109
Cambridge University Press, 11–12, 119
Canada, 362, 366, 379-80, 391, 397, 439
CANADIAN ENCYCLOPEDIA, 362
Canine Lexicon, 330
Card games, 436
Careers, 338
Caribbean, 361–62, 404, 407
Cartoons, 325, 355
Cassell's Encyclopedia of World Literature, 385
Catholic Church, 418–19
Catholic Encyclopedia (Broderick), 419
Catholic Encyclopedia (Gilmary Society), 419
Cats, 329–30
CD-ROM encyclopedias, 253-98. *See also* 8–9, 12–14, 19
Censorship, 388
Century Book of Facts, 312
CHAMBERS'S ENCYCLOPAEDIA, 302. *See also* 300
Characters in 19th-Century Literature, 387
Characters in 20th-Century Literature, 387
CHARLIE BROWN'S 'CYCLOPEDIA, 174–77
  chart, 219
  overview, 173
Charlie Brown's Second Super Book of Questions and Answers, 174
Charlie Brown's Super Book of Questions and Answers, 174
Chemistry and chemical engineering, 340–42
Chess, 435
Chess Encyclopedia, 435
Child abuse, 425

Child care, 424–26
Child Care Encyclopedia, 426
Child Health Encyclopedia, 426
Childbirth, 425
CHILDCRAFT: THE HOW AND WHY LIBRARY, 177–81
    chart, 219
    overview, 173
Childcraft Annual, 177, 179
Childcraft Dictionary, 177–78, 181
CHILDREN'S BRITANNICA, 182–86
    chart, 219
    overview, 173
CHILDREN'S ENCYCLOPEDIA (A.S. Barnes), 302
Children's Encyclopaedia (Arthur Mee), 196
Children's encyclopedias, 173–252
Children's Illustrated Encyclopedia of Learning.
    See LADIES' HOME JOURNAL CHILDREN'S
    ILLUSTRATED ENCYCLOPEDIA OF LEARNING
Children's literature, 391
Children's Literature from A to Z, 391
CHILD'S WORLD, 302
China, 362, 378, 380
CHINESE-LANGUAGE CONCISE ENCYCLOPAEDIA
    BRITANNICA, 444–45
Chinese-language encyclopedias, 444–45
Choice, 455
Christianity, 413, 416, 419–20
CHRISTOPHER COLUMBUS ENCYCLOPEDIA, 375–76
*Chronological History of United States Foreign
    Relations*, 404
Chronology of African-American History, 427
Chronology of the History of Science, 1450–1900,
    420
Church music, 397
CINEMANIA, 355
Cities, 367–68
Cities of the World, 368
Civil War (U.S.), 392–93, 395
Civil War Almanac, 393
CIVIL WAR DICTIONARY, 392–93
CIVILIZATION OF THE ANCIENT MEDITERRANEAN:
    GREECE AND ROME, 376
Cleaning Encyclopedia, 354
*Collector's Complete Dictionary of American
    Antiques*, 344
COLLECTORS' ENCYCLOPEDIA OF ANTIQUES, 344
Collector's Encyclopedia of Shells, 332
College and Research Libraries, 455
College Football Encyclopedia, 434
Collier (P.F.), Inc., 11, 13, 24

COLLIER'S ENCYCLOPEDIA, 24-30. *See also* 11, 14
    chart, 50
    overview, 23–24
Collier's New Encyclopedia, 311
Collier's Year Book, 27–28
Collins Australian Encyclopedia, 362
Collins Concise Encyclopedia, 303
COLLINS GEM ENCYCLOPEDIA, 153–54, 302–03
Color Encyclopedia of Gemstones, 348
COLUMBIA DICTIONARY OF EUROPEAN POLITICAL
    HISTORY SINCE 1914, 403
COLUMBIA DICTIONARY OF MODERN EUROPEAN
    LITERATURE, 386
COLUMBIA ELECTRONIC ENCYCLOPEDIA (Hand-
    held), 264–66
    chart, 298
COLUMBIA ENCYCLOPEDIA, 126–31
    chart, 171
    overview, 108–09
COLUMBIA ENCYCLOPEDIA OF NUTRITION, 359
COLUMBIA UNIVERSITY COLLEGE OF PHYSICIANS AND
    SURGEONS COMPLETE GUIDE TO EARLY CHILD
    CARE, 424
*Columbia University College of Physicians and
    Surgeons Complete Guide to Pregnancy*, 424
COLUMBIA UNIVERSITY COLLEGE OF PHYSICIANS AND
    SURGEONS COMPLETE HOME GUIDE TO MENTAL
    HEALTH, 407
*Columbia University College of Physicians and
    Surgeons Complete Home Medical Guide*, 369
Columbia University Press, 11, 126–27, 132
Columbia-Viking Desk Encyclopedia, 126
Columbian Cyclopaedia, 69
Columbus, Christopher, 375–76
Columbus Dictionary, 375–76
Communes and communal living, 427
*Companion Encyclopedia of the History and
    Philosophy of the Mathematical Sciences*, 402
*Companion Encyclopedia of the History of
    Medicine*, 371
Companion to Chinese History, 378
Companion to Epistemology, 415
Companion to Russian History, 378
Companion to the French Revolution, 380
COMPANION TO THE MEDIEVAL THEATRE, 437
Companion to the Physical Sciences, 421
Compendium of Seashells, 332
COMPENDIUM OF THE WORLD'S LANGUAGES, 386
Complete Book of U.S. Presidents, 406
Complete Color Encyclopedia of Antiques, 344

COMPLETE DICTIONARY OF FURNITURE, 344

Complete Directory to Prime Time Network Shows, 1946-Present, 356–57

Complete Dog Book, 330

COMPLETE DRUG REFERENCE, 369

Complete Encyclopedia of Arms and Weapons, 396

COMPLETE ENCYCLOPEDIA OF HOCKEY, 433

COMPLETE ENCYCLOPEDIA OF HORSES, 330

Complete Encyclopedia of Motorcars, 441

Complete Encyclopedia of Television Programs, 1947–1979, 356

Complete Guide to Medical Tests, 373

Complete Guide to Prescription & Non-prescription Drugs, 369

COMPLETE GUIDE TO SYMPTOMS, ILLNESS & SURGERY, 369–70

Complete Handyman Do-It-Yourself Encyclopedia, 355

Complete Reference Handbook, 317

COMPTON'S CONCISE ENCYCLOPEDIA (CD-ROM), 266–67
  chart, 298

COMPTON'S ENCYCLOPEDIA (Online), 268-69
  chart, 298
  overview, 256

COMPTON'S ENCYCLOPEDIA (Print), 60-68, 186-90
  chart, 106, 219
  overview, 51–52, 173–74

COMPTON'S FAMILY ENCYCLOPEDIA (CD-ROM), 269–70
  chart, 298

COMPTON'S INTERACTIVE ENCYCLOPEDIA (CD-ROM), 271–72
  chart, 298
  overview, 255

Compton's Interactive Encyclopedia for Windows, 271

Compton's Learning Company, 11–12

COMPTON'S MULTIMEDIA ENCYCLOPEDIA (CD-ROM), 272–75. *See also* 11–12
  chart, 298
  overview, 254–55

Compton's Multimedia Publishing Group, 12

Compton's NewMedia, 12

Compton's Pictured Encyclopedia, 51, 60–61, 186, 268

COMPTON'S PRECYCLOPEDIA, 190-91. *See also* 246–47
  chart, 219
  overview, 173

Compton's Yearbook, 64

Compton's Young Children's Precyclopedia, 190

CompuServe, 19, 253, 256–57

Computerized encyclopedias, 253–98. *See also* 8–9, 12–14, 19

Computers and computer science, 342–44

Concise Columbia Dictionary of Quotations, 275

CONCISE COLUMBIA ENCYCLOPEDIA (CD-ROM), 275–77
  chart, 298
  overview, 256

CONCISE COLUMBIA ENCYCLOPEDIA (Print), 131–36
  chart, 171
  overview, 109

Concise Columbia Encyclopedia Hand-held. See COLUMBIA ELECTRONIC ENCYCLOPEDIA (Hand-held)

Concise Columbia Encyclopedia in Large Print, 131–32

Concise Dictionary of American History, 376, 381

Concise Dictionary of Modern Japanese History, 378

Concise Encyclopedia of Antiques, 344

Concise Encyclopedia of Astronomy, 328

CONCISE ENCYCLOPEDIA OF AUSTRALIA, 362

CONCISE ENCYCLOPEDIA OF BIOCHEMISTRY, 330–31

Concise Encyclopedia of Building & Construction Materials, 353

Concise Encyclopedia of Composite Materials, 353

Concise Encyclopedia of Information Technology, 344

Concise Encyclopedia of Islam, 415

Concise Encyclopedia of Medical & Dental Materials, 353

CONCISE ENCYCLOPEDIA OF MINERAL RESOURCES, 346–47. *See also* 353

Concise Encyclopedia of Polymer Science and Engineering, 341

Concise Encyclopedia of Psychology, 409–10

Concise Encyclopedia of Special Education, 351

CONCISE ENCYCLOPEDIA OF TRAFFIC & TRANSPORTATION SYSTEMS, 440

Concise Encyclopedia of Wood & Wood-Based Materials, 353

Concise International Encyclopedia of Robotics, 343

Concise Oxford Companion to American Literature, 385

Concise Oxford Companion to American Theatre, 439

Concise Oxford Companion to English Literature, 392

Concise Oxford Companion to the Theatre, 439
Concise Oxford Dictionary of Art and Artists, 327
CONCISE OXFORD DICTIONARY OF BALLET, 437–38
Concise Oxford Dictionary of Opera, 397
Concise Oxford Dictionary of the Christian
    Church, 419
Concise Veterinary Dictionary, 330
Concord Desk Encyclopedia, 143–44
Congress. See United States Congress
Congress A to Z: A Ready Reference Encyclopedia,
    405
Congressional Quarterly's Guide to the U.S.
    Supreme Court, 384
Constitution. See United States Constitution
CONSTITUTIONAL LAW DICTIONARY, 382
Contemporary Religions: A World Guide, 412
Conway's All the World's Fighting Ships, 396
Cooking A to Z, 360
Cook's Encyclopedia, 360
COPTIC ENCYCLOPEDIA, 413
CORPUS JURIS SECUNDUM, 382
Cosmology, 328
Costume, 345–46
Costume Historique, 346
Costume Reference, 346
Countries, 368
Countries of the World, 368
Country music, 397
Cowles Comprehensive Encyclopedia: The Volume
    Library, 156–57
Cowles Volume Library, 156–57
Crafts, 345
CRC Handbook of Chemistry and Physics, 341
Creationism, 421
Crime, 429-31
CRITICAL DICTIONARY OF EDUCATIONAL CONCEPTS,
    350
Critical Dictionary of the French Revolution, 380
Cronologia Universale, 448
Crown Guide to the World's Great Plays, 390
Cuba, 387
Cults, 414
CULTURAL LIBRARY, 303
Cultural Literacy: What Every American Needs to
    Know (Hirsch), 137
Cyclopaedia (Chambers), 7
CYCLOPEDIA OF LITERARY CHARACTERS, 386–87
CYCLOPEDIA OF LITERARY CHARACTERS II, 386–87

DAIJITEN DESUKU, 448
DAI-NIHON HYAKKA JITEN, 448

Dana's Manual of Mineralogy, 348
Dance, 437–38
Dangerous Aquatic Animals of the World, 331
DAS BERTELSMANN LEXIKON: DIE GROSSE
    BERTELSMANN LEXIKOTHEK, 447
Data Discman, 266–67
D-Day Encyclopedia, 396
De Disciplinis, 6
Deafness, 372
Death, 429
Decorative arts, 344–46
DEFINITIVE KOBBÉ'S OPERA BOOK, 396–97
Delphi Internet Services Corporation, 253,
    256–57, 283–84
Der Brockhaus, 447
Der Grosse Brockhaus, 447
Der Grosse Herder, 447
Der Neue Brockhaus, 447
DER NEUE HERDER, 447
DESCRIPTIVE DICTIONARY AND ATLAS OF SEXOLOGY,
    425
Deserts, 367
Design, 346
Diagram Group, 153–55
Dialog Information Services, 19, 256, 277–79
DICCIONARIO ENCICLOPÉDICO: ENSENANZA GENERAL
    BASICA, 449
DICCIONARIO ENCICLOPÉDICO ESPASA, 449
DICCIONARIO ENCICLIOPÉDICO LAROUSSE, 449
Dictionary Catalogue, 443
Dictionary of Afro-American Slavery, 427
DICTIONARY OF AFRO-LATIN AMERICAN CIVILIZA-
    TION, 362–63
Dictionary of Albanian Literature, 387
Dictionary of American Art, 325
Dictionary of American Biography, 376
DICTIONARY OF AMERICAN COMMUNAL AND
    UTOPIAN HISTORY, 427
DICTIONARY OF AMERICAN DIPLOMATIC HISTORY,
    403–04
DICTIONARY OF AMERICAN FOOD AND DRINK, 359
Dictionary of American Foreign Affiars, 404
DICTIONARY OF AMERICAN HISTORY, 376. See also 4
Dictionary of American Immigration History, 427,
    431
Dictionary of American Literary Characters, 387
Dictionary of American Penology, 432
Dictionary of Anthropology, 428
Dictionary of Art and Artists, 327
DICTIONARY OF ASIAN AMERICAN HISTORY, 427
Dictionary of Battles (Chandler), 394

Dictionary of Battles (Eggenberger), 393
Dictionary of Bible and Religion, 417
DICTIONARY OF BIBLICAL TRADITION IN ENGLISH
  LITERATURE, 413
Dictionary of Birds, 330
Dictionary of Book History, 388
Dictionary of Brazilian Literature, 387
Dictionary of Christian Ethics, 420
DICTIONARY OF CHRISTIANITY IN AMERICA, 413
Dictionary of Classical Mythology (Bell), 417
Dictionary of Classical Mythology (Grimal), 417
Dictionary of Comparative Religion, 412
DICTIONARY OF CONCEPTS IN CULTURAL ANTHRO-
  POLOGY, 428
DICTIONARY OF CONCEPTS IN GENERAL PSYCHOLOGY,
  407–08
Dictionary of Concepts in Human Geography, 363
DICTIONARY OF CONCEPTS IN LITERARY CRITICISM
  AND THEORY, 387
Dictionary of Concepts in Physical Anthropology,
  428
DICTIONARY OF CONCEPTS IN PHYSICAL GEOGRAPHY,
  363
DICTIONARY OF CONCEPTS IN RECREATION AND
  LEISURE STUDIES, 433
*Dictionary of Concepts in the Philosophy of
  Science,* 421
*Dictionary of Conservative and Libertarian
  Thought,* 405
DICTIONARY OF CONTEMPORARY POLITICS OF
  CENTRAL AMERICA AND THE CARIBBEAN, 404
*Dictionary of Contemporary Politics of South
  America,* 404
*Dictionary of Contemporary Politics of Southeast
  Asia,* 404
*Dictionary of Contemporary Politics of Southern
  Africa,* 404
Dictionary of Costume, 346
Dictionary of Crime, 430
DICTIONARY OF CULTURAL LITERARY, 136-40
  chart, 171
  overview, 109
Dictionary of Demography, 432
DICTIONARY OF DREAMS, 408
Dictionary of Fictional Characters, 387
Dictionary of Furniture, 344
Dictionary of Ghost Lore, 408
*Dictionary of Gods and Goddesses, Devils and
  Demons,* 417
Dictionary of Irish Literature, 387
Dictionary of Italian Literature, 387

Dictionary of Key Words in Psychology, 408
DICTIONARY OF LITERARY THEMES AND MOTIFS, 387
DICTIONARY OF MARXIST THOUGHT, 404
Dictionary of Medieval Civilization, 376
DICTIONARY OF MEXICAN AMERICAN HISTORY, 428
Dictionary of Mexican Literature, 387
Dictionary of Modern French Literature, 387
Dictionary of Modern Indian History, 1707–1947,
  378
Dictionary of Modern Political Ideologies, 403
*Dictionary of Mysticism and the Esoteric Tradi-
  tions,* 409
Dictionary of Mysticism and the Occult, 409
Dictionary of Native American Mythology, 415
*Dictionary of 19th Century Antiques and Later
  Objets d'Art,* 344
DICTIONARY OF ORIENTAL LITERATURE, 387
*Dictionary of Pentecostal and Charismatic
  Movements,* 416
Dictionary of Political Economy, 339
Dictionary of Russian Literature, 387, 389
Dictionary of Russian Literature Since 1917, 389
DICTIONARY OF SCANDINAVIAN HISTORY, 376
Dictionary of Scandinavian Literature, 387
DICTIONARY OF SCIENCE & CREATIONISM, 421
Dictionary of Scientific Literacy, 422
Dictionary of Spanish Literature, 387
DICTIONARY OF SUBJECTS AND SYMBOLS IN ART, 325
Dictionary of Superstitions (Lasne and Gaultier),
  408
DICTIONARY OF SUPERSTITIONS (Opie and Tatem),
  408
Dictionary of Symptoms, 369
DICTIONARY OF THE BLACK THEATRE, 438
DICTIONARY OF THE HISTORY OF IDEAS, 413
DICTIONARY OF THE HISTORY OF SCIENCE, 421
*Dictionary of the Literature of the Iberian Penin-
  sula,* 388
DICTIONARY OF THE MIDDLE AGES, 376
Dictionary of the Second World War, 396
DICTIONARY OF THE VIETNAM WAR, 393
DICTIONARY OF THE RUSSIAN REVOLUTION, 376–77
DICTIONARY OF TWENTIETH-CENTURY CUBAN
  LITERATURE, 387–88
Dictionary of 20th-Century Design, 346
Dictionary of 20th Century History (Brownstone
  and Franck), 379
Dictionary of Twentieth-Century History (Teed),
  379
DICTIONARY OF UNITED STATES ECONOMIC HISTORY,
  337

DICTIONARY OF WESTERN CHURCH MUSIC, 397

DICTIONARY OF WOODWORKING TOOLS C. 1700–1970 AND TOOLS OF ALLIED TRADES, 352–53

Dictionary of World Mythology, 417

Dictionary of World Politics, 406

Dictionary of World Pottery and Porcelain, 345

DICTIONNAIRE ENCYCLOPÉDIQUE LAROUSSE, 445

Diderot: A Critical Biography (Furbank), 458

Dinosaurs, 333

Discoverers: an encyclopedia of explorers and exploration, 380

Diseases, 369–70, 372

DISNEY'S WONDERFUL WORLD OF KNOWLEDGE, 303

Divorce, 429

Dizionàrio Patrìstico e di Antichità Cristiane, 416

Dobson's Encyclopaedia: The Publisher, Text, and Publication of America's First Britannica, 1789–1803 (Arner), 38, 457

Dogs, 330

Do-It-Yourself Medical Testing, 374

Dong-A Ilbo, 448

Donning International Encyclopedic Psychic Dictionary, 409

Dorling Kindersley Children's Illustrated Encyclopedia, 235, 450

Dorling Kindersley Ltd., 235, 237

Dorling Kindersley Science Encyclopedia, 422

Dorsey Dictionary of American Government and Politics, 403

Doubleday Children's Encyclopedia, 195, 228

Doubleday Encyclopedia, 305

Dow Jones News/Retrieval Services, 257

Dr. Axelrod's Atlas of Freshwater Aquarium Fishes, 329

Dr. Burgess's Mini-Atlas of Marine Aquarium Fishes, 329

Dr. Spock's Baby and Child Care, 426

Drawing, 326

Dreams, 408

Drugs and drug abuse, 369–72, 374

DUNLOP'S ILLUSTRATED ENCYCLOPEDIA OF FACTS, 303–04

Dutch-language encyclopedias, 445

Earth sciences, 335, 346–49

Economics, 337–40

Education, 349–52

Educational Home Systems, 14

Eerdmans Bible Dictionary, 417

Egypt, 377

E.J. Brill's First Encyclopaedia of Islam, 1913–1936, 415

Elections, 406–07

Electoral Politics Dictionary, 407

Electronic Encyclopedia (Grolier), 287

Electronic Encyclopedia of World War II, 396

Electronic encyclopedias, 253-98. See also 8–9, 12–14, 19

Electronic sciences, 342–44

ELEMENTS OF STYLE: A PRACTICAL ENCYCLOPEDIA OF INTERIOR ARCHITECTURAL DETAILS FROM 1485 TO THE PRESENT, 344–45

Eliade Guide to World Religions, 412

Encarta. See MICROSOFT ENCARTA MULTIMEDIA ENCYCLOPEDIA

Enciclopedia Barsa, 450

ENCICLOPEDIA DE LOS NIÑOS, 449–50

ENCICLOPEDIA DE ORO, 450

Enciclopedia del Novecento, 448

Enciclopedia Disney, 303

ENCICLOPEDIA EINAUDI, 447

ENCICLOPEDIA EUROPEA, 447

Enciclopedia Garzanti, 447

ENCICLOPEDIA GENERAL PLANETA, 450

ENCICLOPEDIA HISPÁNICA, 450

ENCICLOPEDIA ILUSTRADA CUMBRE, 450

ENCICLOPEDIA ITALIANA DI SCIENZE, LETTERE ED ARTI, 447–48. See also 450

ENCICLOPEDIA JUVENIL ILUSTRADA, 450

ENCICLOPEDIA UNIVERSAL ILUSTRADA EUROPEO-AMERICANA, 450

ENCICLOPEDIA UNIVERSAL SOPENA, 450

Enciclopedia Universale Garzanti, 447

Encyclopaedia; seu, Orbis Disciplinarium, tam Sacrarum quam Prophanum Epistemon, 6

ENCYCLOPEDIA AMERICANA, 31–37. See also 7, 11
chart, 50
overview, 23–24

Encyclopaedia Britannica. See NEW ENCYCLOPAEDIA BRITANNICA

Encyclopaedia Britannica Educational Corporation, 11, 13

Encyclopaedia Britannica, Inc., 10–11, 41, 62

Encyclopedia Canadiana, 362

ENCYCLOPEDIA INTERNATIONAL, 304

ENCYCLOPAEDIA IRANICA, 363

Encyclopedia Japonica, 448

ENCYCLOPAEDIA JUDAICA, 414

Encyclopaedia Metropolitana, 6

Encyclopedia of Accounting Systems, 339

ENCYCLOPEDIA OF ADOLESCENCE, 425

ENCYCLOPEDIA OF ADOPTION, 425

ENCYCLOPEDIA OF ADULT DEVELOPMENT, 428

ENCYCLOPEDIA OF AFRICAN-AMERICAN CIVIL RIGHTS, 428

Encyclopedia of African American Religions, 414

ENCYCLOPEDIA OF AGING, 428

Encyclopedia of Aging and the Elderly, 428

ENCYCLOPEDIA OF ALCOHOLISM, 370

Encyclopedia of Alternative Health Care, 371

ENCYCLOPEDIA OF AMERICAN AGRICULTURAL HISTORY, 359

ENCYCLOPEDIA OF AMERICAN ARCHITECTURE, 325

ENCYCLOPEDIA OF AMERICAN BUSINESS HISTORY AND BIOGRAPHY, 337

Encyclopedia of American Cars, 1930–1942, 440

ENCYCLOPEDIA OF AMERICAN CARS, 1946–1959, 440

ENCYCLOPEDIA OF AMERICAN COMICS, 325

ENCYCLOPEDIA OF AMERICAN CRIME, 429

ENCYCLOPEDIA OF AMERICAN ECONOMIC HISTORY, 337

ENCYCLOPEDIA OF AMERICAN FACTS AND DATES, 377

ENCYCLOPEDIA OF AMERICAN FOREIGN POLICY, 404

ENCYCLOPEDIA OF AMERICAN FOREST AND CONSERVATION HISTORY, 334

ENCYCLOPEDIA OF AMERICAN HISTORY, 377

ENCYCLOPEDIA OF AMERICAN INTELLIGENCE AND ESPIONAGE, 393

ENCYCLOPEDIA OF AMERICAN JOURNALISM, 388

ENCYCLOPEDIA OF AMERICAN POLITICAL HISTORY, 404

ENCYCLOPEDIA OF AMERICAN RELIGIONS, 414

Encyclopedia of American Religions: Religious Creeds, 414

ENCYCLOPEDIA OF AMERICAN SOCIAL HISTORY, 377

ENCYCLOPEDIA OF AMERICAN WRESTLING, 433

ENCYCLOPEDIA OF ANCIENT EGYPT, 377

Encyclopedia of Animal Behavior, 333

Encyclopedia of Animal Biology, 333

Encyclopedia of Animal Ecology, 333

Encyclopedia of Animal Evolution, 333

Encyclopedia of Animals, 333

Encyclopedia of Animated Cartoon Series, 355

ENCYCLOPEDIA OF ANIMATED CARTOONS, 355

Encyclopedia of Anthropology, 428

Encyclopedia of Applied Geology, 347

ENCYCLOPEDIA OF APPLIED PHYSICS, 401

ENCYCLOPEDIA OF AQUATIC LIFE, 331

Encyclopedia of Archaeological Excavations in the Holy Land, 419

ENCYCLOPEDIA OF ARCHITECTURAL TECHNOLOGY, 325

ENCYCLOPEDIA OF ARCHITECTURE, 325–26

ENCYCLOPEDIA OF ARMS CONTROL AND DISARMAMENT, 393

ENCYCLOPEDIA OF ARTIFICIAL INTELLIGENCE, 342

ENCYCLOPEDIA OF ASIAN HISTORY, 377–78

Encyclopedia of Associations, 4

Encyclopedia of Astronomy, 328

ENCYCLOPEDIA OF ASTRONOMY AND ASTROPHYSICS, 328

Encyclopedia of Atmospheric Sciences and Astrogeology, 347

Encyclopedia of Aviation, 441

ENCYCLOPEDIA OF BANKING AND FINANCE, 337–38

ENCYCLOPEDIA OF BATTLES, 393–94

Encyclopedia of Beaches and Coastal Environments, 347

Encyclopedia of Biblical and Christian Ethics, 420

ENCYCLOPEDIA OF BIOETHICS, 331

Encyclopedia of Birds, 330, 332

Encyclopedia of Black America, 427

ENCYCLOPEDIA OF BLINDNESS AND VISION IMPAIRMENT, 370

Encyclopedia of Building and Construction Terms, 353

ENCYCLOPEDIA OF BUILDING TECHNOLOGY, 353

ENCYCLOPEDIA OF BUSINESS, 338

ENCYCLOPEDIA OF CAREER CHANGE AND WORK ISSUES, 338

ENCYCLOPEDIA OF CENSORSHIP, 388

ENCYCLOPEDIA OF CHEMICAL PROCESSING AND DESIGN, 340–41

Encyclopedia of Chemical Technology. See KIRK-OTHMER ENCYCLOPEDIA OF CHEMICAL TECHNOLOGY

Encyclopedia of Chemistry, 342

ENCYCLOPEDIA OF CHILD ABUSE, 425

ENCYCLOPEDIA OF CHILDBEARING, 425

Encyclopedia of Climatology, 347

ENCYCLOPEDIA OF COLONIAL AND REVOLUTIONARY AMERICA, 378

ENCYCLOPEDIA OF COMPUTER SCIENCE, 342

Encyclopedia of Computer Science and Engineering, 342

Encyclopedia of Contemporary Knowledge, 448

ENCYCLOPEDIA OF COSMOLOGY, 328

ENCYCLOPEDIA OF CRAFTS, 345

ENCYCLOPEDIA OF CRIME AND JUSTICE, 429

Encyclopedia of Deafness and Hearing Disorders, 372

ENCYCLOPEDIA OF DEATH, 429

ENCYCLOPEDIA OF DECORATIVE ARTS, 1890–1940, 345

Encyclopedia of Depression, 409

Encyclopedia of Discovery and Exploration, 380

ENCYCLOPEDIA OF DRAWING, 326

Encyclopedia of Dreams, 408

ENCYCLOPEDIA OF DRUG ABUSE, 370

ENCYCLOPEDIA OF EARLY CHILDHOOD EDUCATION, 350
Encyclopedia of Early Christianity, 416
ENCYCLOPEDIA OF EARTH SCIENCES, 347
ENCYCLOPEDIA OF EARTH SYSTEM SCIENCE, 347
Encyclopedia of Economics, 339
Encyclopedia of Education, 352
ENCYCLOPEDIA OF EDUCATIONAL MEDIA COMMUNI-
CATIONS AND TECHNOLOGY, 350
ENCYCLOPEDIA OF EDUCATIONAL RESEARCH, 350
ENCYCLOPEDIA OF ELECTRONIC CIRCUITS, 343
ENCYCLOPEDIA OF ELECTRONICS, 343
ENCYCLOPEDIA OF ENVIRONMENTAL CONTROL
TECHNOLOGY, 347
ENCYCLOPEDIA OF ENVIRONMENTAL SCIENCE AND
ENGINEERING, 347-48
ENCYCLOPEDIA OF ENVIRONMENTAL STUDIES, 348
ENCYCLOPEDIA OF ETHICS, 414
Encyclopedia of Evolution, 331
Encyclopedia of Feminism, 432
Encyclopedia of Field and General Geology, 347
ENCYCLOPEDIA OF FLOWERS, 334
ENCYCLOPEDIA OF FLUID MECHANICS, 353
ENCYCLOPEDIA OF FOLK, COUNTRY & WESTERN
MUSIC, 397
Encyclopedia of Food Engineering, 359
Encyclopedia of Food Science, 359
ENCYCLOPEDIA OF FOOD SCIENCE AND TECHNOLOGY, 359
ENCYCLOPEDIA OF FOOD SCIENCE, FOOD TECHNOLOGY
AND NUTRITION, 359–60
Encyclopedia of Food Technology, 359
Encyclopedia of Furniture, 344
ENCYCLOPEDIA OF GEMSTONES AND MINERALS, 348
ENCYCLOPEDIA OF GENETIC DISORDERS AND BIRTH
DEFECTS, 370
*Encyclopedia of Geochemistry and Environmental
Sciences*, 347
Encyclopedia of Geomorphology, 347
Encyclopedia of Geophysics, 347
Encyclopedia of Ghosts, 408
ENCYCLOPEDIA OF GHOSTS AND SPIRITS, 408
Encyclopedia of Gods, 417
ENCYCLOPEDIA OF GOVERNMENT AND POLITICS, 404
ENCYCLOPEDIA OF HANDSPINNING, 345
Encyclopedia of Heresies and Heretics, 417
ENCYCLOPEDIA OF HIGHER EDUCATION, 350–51
ENCYCLOPEDIA OF HISTORIC FORTS, 394
ENCYCLOPEDIA OF HISTORICAL PLACES, 378
Encyclopedia of Hollywood, 356
ENCYCLOPEDIA OF HOMOSEXUALITY, 425–26
ENCYCLOPEDIA OF HUMAN BEHAVIOR, 429
ENCYCLOPEDIA OF HUMAN BIOLOGY, 331

ENCYCLOPEDIA OF HUMAN EVOLUTION AND
PREHISTORY, 331
ENCYCLOPEDIA OF HUMAN RIGHTS, 405
Encyclopedia of Hydrology, 347
*Encyclopedia of Igneous and Metamorphic
Petrology*, 347
ENCYCLOPEDIA OF IMMUNOLOGY, 370
ENCYCLOPAEDIA OF INDIA, 363
ENCYCLOPAEDIA OF INDIAN ARCHAEOLOGY, 378
Encyclopaedia of Indian Culture, 363
Encyclopaedia of Indian Literature, 387
ENCYCLOPEDIA OF INSECTS, 331-32
Encyclopedia of International Commerce, 339
Encyclopaedia of Islam (First Edition), 415
ENCYCLOPAEDIA OF ISLAM (New Edition), 415
Encyclopedia of Japan, 366
Encyclopedia of Jazz, 399
Encyclopedia of Jazz in the Seventies, 399
Encyclopedia of Jazz in the Sixties, 399
Encyclopedia of Jewish History, 414
Encyclopedia of Jewish Symbols, 414
Encyclopedia of Judaism, 414
Encyclopaedia of Language, 386
Encyclopedia of Language and Linguistics, 390
ENCYCLOPEDIA OF LASERS AND OPTICAL TECHNOL-
OGY, 401
ENCYCLOPEDIA OF LEARNING AND MEMORY, 351
ENCYCLOPEDIA OF LIBRARY AND INFORMATION
SCIENCE, 351
Encyclopedia of Library History, 352
ENCYCLOPEDIA OF LITERATURE AND CRITICISM, 388
ENCYCLOPEDIA OF MAGIC AND MAGICIANS, 434
Encyclopedia of Mammals, 332–33
ENCYCLOPEDIA OF MANAGEMENT, 338
Encyclopedia of Marine Invertebrates, 329
ENCYCLOPEDIA OF MARRIAGE, DIVORCE AND THE
FAMILY, 429
ENCYCLOPEDIA OF MATERIALS SCIENCE AND
ENGINEERING, 353
ENCYCLOPAEDIA OF MATHEMATICS, 401
ENCYCLOPEDIA OF MATHEMATICS AND ITS APPLICA-
TIONS, 401–02
ENCYCLOPEDIA OF MEDICAL DEVICES AND INSTRU-
MENTATION, 370–71
ENCYCLOPEDIA OF MEDICAL HISTORY, 371
Encyclopedia of Medical Tests, 373
ENCYCLOPEDIA OF MENTAL HEALTH, 408
ENCYCLOPEDIA OF METALLURGY AND MATERIALS,
353–54
ENCYCLOPEDIA OF MICROBIOLOGY, 332
Encyclopedia of Mineralogy, 347

ENCYCLOPEDIA OF MINERALS, 348

Encyclopedia of Military History, 394

ENCYCLOPEDIA OF MODERN PHYSICS, 402

Encyclopedia of Mortgage & Real Estate, 340

ENCYCLOPEDIA OF MUSIC IN CANADA, 397

ENCYCLOPEDIA OF NATIONALISM, 405

ENCYCLOPEDIA OF NATIVE AMERICAN RELIGIONS, 415

Encyclopedia of Native American Tribes, 431

ENCYCLOPEDIA OF NATURAL INSECT & DISEASE CONTROL, 334–35

ENCYCLOPEDIA OF NATURAL MEDICINE, 371

Encyclopedia of Nature and Science, 424

ENCYCLOPEDIA OF NEUROSCIENCE, 371

ENCYCLOPEDIA OF NEW ENGLAND, 363–64

ENCYCLOPEDIA OF NORTH AMERICAN RAILROADING, 440–41

ENCYCLOPEDIA OF NORTH AMERICAN SPORTS HISTORY, 434

Encyclopedia of Occultism, 409

ENCYCLOPEDIA OF OCCULTISM & PARAPSYCHOLOGY, 409

Encyclopedia of Oceanography, 347

Encyclopedia of Oil Painting, 326

Encyclopedia of Opera, 397

Encyclopedia of Organic Gardening, 336

Encyclopedia of Paleontology, 347

Encyclopedia of Parapsychology and Psychical Research, 409

ENCYCLOPEDIA OF PERENNIALS, 335

ENCYCLOPEDIA OF PHARMACEUTICAL TECHNOLOGY, 371–72

ENCYCLOPEDIA OF PHILOSOPHY, 415

ENCYCLOPEDIA OF PHOBIAS, FEARS, AND ANXIETIES, 409

ENCYCLOPEDIA OF PHYSICAL SCIENCE AND TECHNOLOGY, 421

ENCYCLOPEDIA OF PHYSICS (Besancon), 402

ENCYCLOPEDIA OF PHYSICS (Lerner and Trigg), 402

ENCYCLOPEDIA OF POLYMER SCIENCE AND ENGINEERING, 341

Encyclopedia of Polymer Science and Technology, 341

ENCYCLOPEDIA OF POP, ROCK AND SOUL, 397

ENCYCLOPEDIA OF POTTERY & PORCELAIN, 1800–1960, 345

ENCYCLOPEDIA OF PRACTICAL PHOTOGRAPHY, 326

Encyclopedia of Prehistoric Life, 333

Encyclopedia of Psychic Science, 409

Encyclopedia of Psychoactive Drugs, 374

Encyclopedia of Psychoanalysis, 412

ENCYCLOPEDIA OF PSYCHOLOGY (Corsini and Ozaki), 409

Encyclopedia of Psychology (Eysenck), 409–10

ENCYCLOPEDIA OF PUBLISHING AND THE BOOK ARTS, 388

Encyclopedia of Quaternary Sciences, 347

ENCYCLOPEDIA OF RELIGION, 415–16. *See also* 14

Encyclopedia of Religion and Ethics, 416

ENCYCLOPEDIA OF RELIGION IN THE SOUTH, 416

Encyclopedia of Religions in the United States, 414

ENCYCLOPEDIA OF REPTILES AND AMPHIBIANS, 332

Encyclopedia of Rock, 401

ENCYCLOPEDIA OF RUSSIAN HISTORY, 378

ENCYCLOPEDIA OF SCHIZOPHRENIA AND THE PSYCHOTIC DISORDERS, 409

ENCYCLOPEDIA OF SCHOOL ADMINISTRATION AND SUPERVISION, 351

Encyclopedia of Science Fiction, 390

ENCYCLOPEDIA OF SCULPTURE TECHNIQUES, 326

Encyclopedia of Sedimentology, 347

Encyclopedia of Sexual Behavior, 426

Encyclopedia of Shakespeare. See SHAKESPEARE A TO Z

ENCYCLOPEDIA OF SHELLS, 332

Encyclopedia of Ships and Seafaring, 441

ENCYCLOPEDIA OF SLEEP AND DREAMING, 410

Encyclopedia of Sleep and Sleep Disorders, 410

Encyclopedia of Small Antiques, 344

ENCYCLOPEDIA OF SOCIAL WORK, 429–30

ENCYCLOPEDIA OF SOCIOLOGY, 430

Encyclopedia of Soil Science, 347

Encyclopedia of Solid Earth Geophysics, 347

ENCYCLOPEDIA OF SOUTHERN CULTURE, 364

ENCYCLOPEDIA OF SOUTHERN HISTORY, 378–79

ENCYCLOPEDIA OF SPECIAL EDUCATION, 351

ENCYCLOPEDIA OF SPORTING FIREARMS, 434

Encyclopedia of Sports, 435

ENCYCLOPEDIA OF STATISTICAL SCIENCES, 338

Encyclopedia of Strange and Unexplained Physical Phenomena, 409

Encyclopedia of Structural Geology and Plate Tectonics, 347

ENCYCLOPEDIA OF SUICIDE, 410

Encyclopedia of Superstitions, 408

ENCYCLOPEDIA OF TELECOMMUNICATIONS, 343

ENCYCLOPEDIA OF TELEVISION, 355–56

ENCYCLOPEDIA OF TERRORISM AND POLITICAL VIOLENCE, 394

Encyclopedia of Textiles (American Fabrics and Fashion Magazine), 345

ENCYCLOPEDIA OF TEXTILES (Jerde), 345

ENCYCLOPEDIA OF THE AMERICAN CONSTITUTION, 382–83

ENCYCLOPEDIA OF THE AMERICAN JUDICIAL SYSTEM, 383

ENCYCLOPEDIA OF THE AMERICAN LEFT, 405

ENCYCLOPEDIA OF THE AMERICAN LEGISLATIVE SYSTEM, 405

ENCYCLOPEDIA OF THE AMERICAN PRESIDENCY, 405–06

ENCYCLOPEDIA OF THE AMERICAN RELIGIOUS EXPERIENCE, 416

ENCYCLOPEDIA OF THE AMERICAN REVOLUTION, 394

Encyclopedia of the American Theatre, 1900–1975, 438

Encyclopedia of the Biological Sciences, 330

ENCYCLOPEDIA OF THE BLUES, 397

ENCYCLOPEDIA OF THE BRITISH PRESS, 1440–1991, 388–89

Encyclopedia of the Central West, 363–64

Encyclopedia of the Confederacy, 379

ENCYCLOPEDIA OF THE EARLY CHURCH, 416

Encyclopedia of the Far West, 364

Encyclopedia of the First World, 364

ENCYCLOPEDIA OF THE FUTURE, 430

ENCYCLOPAEDIA OF THE HISTORY OF TECHNOLOGY, 421

ENCYCLOPEDIA OF THE HOLOCAUST, 379

Encyclopedia of the Jewish Religion, 414

Encyclopedia of the Midwest, 364

ENCYCLOPAEDIA OF THE MUSICAL FILM, 356

Encyclopedia of the Musical Theatre, 438

Encyclopedia of the NCAA Basketball Tournament, 435

ENCYCLOPEDIA OF THE NEW YORK STAGE, 1920–1930, 438

ENCYCLOPEDIA OF THE NEW YORK STAGE, 1930–1940, 438

ENCYCLOPEDIA OF THE NEW YORK STAGE, 1940–1950, 438

Encyclopedia of the North American Colonies, 378

ENCYCLOPEDIA OF THE RENAISSANCE, 379

Encyclopedia of the Second World, 364

Encyclopedia of the Second World War, 396

Encyclopedia of the Social Sciences, 432

Encyclopedia of the South, 364

Encyclopedia of the Third Reich, 379

ENCYCLOPEDIA OF THE THIRD WORLD, 364

Encyclopedia of the Unexplained, 409

ENCYCLOPEDIA OF THE UNITED NATIONS AND INTERNATIONAL AGREEMENTS, 406

Encyclopedia of the United States Congress,

Encyclopedia of the Vietnam War, 393

ENCYCLOPEDIA OF THE WORLD'S AIR FORCES, 394

Encyclopedia of Themes and Subjects in Painting, 325

Encyclopedia of Theology, 419

Encyclopedia of Third Parties in the United States, 407

Encyclopedia of UFOs, 328

ENCYCLOPEDIA OF UKRAINE, 364

ENCYCLOPEDIA OF UNBELIEF, 416–17

Encyclopedia of U.S. Spacecraft, 328

ENCYCLOPEDIA OF VISUAL ART, 326

Encyclopedia of Witchcraft and Demonology, 410

ENCYCLOPEDIA OF WITCHES AND WITCHCRAFT, 410

Encyclopedia of Wood, 334

Encyclopedia of World Architecture, 326

ENCYCLOPEDIA OF WORLD ART, 326–27

ENCYCLOPEDIA OF WORLD COSTUME, 345–46

ENCYCLOPEDIA OF WORLD CRIME, 430–31

ENCYCLOPEDIA OF WORLD CULTURES, 431

Encyclopedia of World Facts and Dates, 379

Encyclopedia of World Faiths, 412

ENCYCLOPEDIA OF WORLD HISTORY, 379

ENCYCLOPEDIA OF WORLD KNOWLEDGE, 304

ENCYCLOPEDIA OF WORLD LITERATURE IN THE 20TH CENTURY, 389

Encyclopedia of World Regional Geology, 347

Encyclopedia of World Soccer, 436

Encyclopedia of World Theater, 439

Encyclopedia publishers and distributors, 460–75

ENCYCLOPAEDIA UNIVERSALIS, 445

Encyclopedias—general information, 3–20

  accessibility, 5, 18, 254

  accuracy, 17–18

  adult encyclopedias, 23–172

  arrangement, 5

  bias, 5–6, 18

  bibliographies, 18

  CD-ROM encyclopedias, 253–98. *See also* 8-9, 12–14, 19

  charts, 50, 105–07, 170–72, 218–19, 251-52, 297-98

  children's encyclopedias, 173–252

  choosing an encyclopedia, 15–20

  comparison charts, 50, 105–07, 170–72, 218–19, 251-52, 297–98

  computerized encyclopedias, 253-98. *See also* 8–9, 12–14, 19

  continuous revision, 18

  coverage, 17

  definition, 3–4

  electronic encyclopedias, 253–98. *See also* 8–9, 12–14, 19

  evaluating an encyclopedia, 15–20

  foreign-language encyclopedias, 9, 443–51

  history, 5–8

  illustrations, 5, 19, 254

  indexes, 5, 18

  large-print encyclopedias, 131–32

Encyclopedias—general information (*Continued*)
  multimedia encyclopedias, 253–98. *See also* 19
  one- and two-volume encyclopedias, 11,
    108–72, 220–52
  online encyclopedias, 253–98. *See also* 8–9,
    12–14, 19
  organization, 5
  out-of-print encyclopedias, 299–319
  physical format, 19, 255
  pictures, 5, 19, 254
  prices, 12, 19–20
  publishers and distributors, 10–12, 17, 254,
    460–75
  purpose, 3–8
  reader suitability, 17
  reviews and reviewers, 20, 455–57
  revision, 5, 18, 255
  sales methods and practices, 12–14
  sales statistics, 10
  secondhand encyclopedias, 14–15
  special features, 19
  specialized encyclopedias, 9, 12, 323–442
  subject encyclopedias, 9, 12, 323–442
  supermarket encyclopedias, 52, 70, 79, 286
  teachers' attitudes toward, 9–10
  types, 8–9
  up-to-dateness, 5, 18, 255
  used encyclopedias, 14–15
  writing style, 17
  yearbooks, 18
Encyclopedias: Their History Throughout the Ages
  (Collison), 457
ENCYCLOPEDIC DICTIONARY OF ACCOUNTING AND
  FINANCE, 338–39
Encyclopedic Dictionary of Judaica, 414
Encyclopedic Dictionary of Language and lan-
  guages, 386
Encyclopedic Dictionary of Marxism, Socialism and
  Communism, 404
ENCYCLOPEDIC DICTIONARY OF MATHEMATICS, 402
Encyclopedic Dictionary of Physical Geography, 363
Encyclopaedic Dictionary of Physics, 401
ENCYCLOPEDIC DICTIONARY OF PSYCHOLOGY (Harre
  and Lamb), 410
Encyclopedic Dictionary of Psychology
  (Pettijohn), 410
Encyclopedic Dictionary of Religion, 419
ENCYCLOPEDIC DICTIONARY OF SCIENCE, 421–22
ENCYCLOPEDIC DICTIONARY OF SEMIOTICS, 389
Encyclopedic Dictionary of Sociology, 430
ENCYCLOPEDIC DICTIONARY OF SPORTS MEDICINE, 434

Encyclopedic Dictionary of the Sciences of
  Language, 386
Encyclopedic Handbook of Cults in America, 414
Encyclopédie, 3, 7–8, 38, 457–58
Encyclopédie and the Age of Revolution, 7, 458
ENCYCLOPÉDIE DE L'UNIVERS EN COULEURS, 446
Encyclopédie du Blues, 397
Endangered species, 332
Endangered Wildlife of the World, 332
Energy, 348–49
Engineering and engineering sciences, 352–55
English literature, 391–92
Environment and environmental sciences, 347–49
Environmental Encyclopedia, 348
Espasa. See ENCICLOPEDIA UNIVERSAL ILUSTRADA
  EUROPEO-AMERICANA
Espionage, 393
Essential Guide to Prescription Drugs, 369
Ethics, 414, 420
Ethnic groups, 431
Europe, 380, 386, 403
Europea. See ENCICLOPEDIA EUROPEA
Evelyn Wood Reading Dynamics, 41
EVERYBODY'S GUIDE TO THE LAW, 383
EVERYDAY REFERENCE LIBRARY, 304
EVERYMAN'S ENCYCLOPAEDIA (Online), 277–79
  chart, 298
  overview, 256
EVERYMAN'S ENCYCLOPAEDIA (Print), 304–05
Evolution, 331
EVOLVING CONSTITUTION: HOW THE SUPREME COURT
  HAS RULED ON ISSUES FROM ABORITION TO
  ZONING, 383
EXOTICA SERIES 4 INTERNATIONAL: PICTORIAL
  CYCLOPEDIA OF EXOTIC PLANTS FROM TROPICAL
  AND NEAR-TROPICAL REGIONS, 335
EXPLORING YOUR WORLD: THE ADVENTURE OF
  GEOGRAPHY, 364
EXTRATERRESTIAL ENCYCLOPEDIA, 328
Eyes, 370

Facts About the Presidents, 379, 406
Facts About the States, 368, 379
Facts on File, 12
FACTS ON FILE DICTIONARY OF DESIGN AND DESIGN-
  ERS, 346
Facts on File Dictionary of the Theatre, 439
Facts on File Encyclopedia of Management
  Techniques, 338
FACTS ON FILE ENCYCLOPEDIA OF THE 20TH
  CENTURY, 379

FACTS ON FILE ENCYCLOPEDIA OF WORLD MYTHOLOGY AND LEGEND, 417

FACTS PLUS, 223-25
chart, 252

Familiar Quotations, 275

Family, 383, 429

FAMILY LEGAL COMPANION, 383

FAMILY MENTAL HEALTH ENCYCLOPEDIA, 410–11

FAMOUS FIRST FACTS, 379

Federal Trade Commission. *See* United States Federal Trade Commission

Feminist Companion to Literature in English, 385

50 Years of American Automobiles, 1939–1989, 440

Film, 355–58

Film Encyclopedia, 356

FINDING OUT: SILVER BURDETT'S CHILDREN'S ENCYCLOPEDIA, 305

Firearms, 396, 434

FIRST CONNECTIONS: THE GOLDEN BOOK ENCYCLOPEDIA (CD-ROM), 279–81
chart, 298
overview, 256

FIRST DICTIONARY OF CULTURAL LITERACY, 225–28
chart, 252

Fish and fishing, 329, 331, 435

Fishing: An Encyclopedic Guide to Tackle and Tactics for Fresh and Salt Water, 435

Fishbein's Illustrated Medical and Health Encyclopedia, 373

FITZHENRY & WHITESIDE BOOK OF CANADIAN FACTS AND DATES, 379–80

Flowers, 334–35

Fluid mechanics, 353

FOCAL ENCYCLOPEDIA OF PHOTOGRAPHY, 327

Folk music, 397

Food, 359–61

Food for Health: A Nutrition Encyclopedia, 360

FOODS AND FOOD PRODUCTION ENCYCLOPEDIA, 360

FOODS AND NUTRITION ENCYCLOPEDIA, 360

Football, 434

FOOTBALL ENCYCLOPEDIA, 434

Foreign-language encyclopedias, 9, 443–51

Forests, 334

Forts, 394

Fortune Encyclopedia of Economics, 339

Fossils, 348

France, 380, 386-87

Franklin Electronic Publishers, Inc., 12

Franklin's Concise Columbia Encyclopedia. See COLUMBIA ELECTRONIC ENCYCLOPEDIA (Hand-held)

Franklin's Electronic Concise Columbia Encyclopedia. See COLUMBIA ELECTRONIC ENCYCLOPEDIA (Hand-held)

French & European Publications, Inc., 443–44

French-language encyclopedias, 445–46

Friedrichs Ballett Lexikon von A-Z, 437

From Archetype to Zeitgeist: Powerful Ideas for Powerful Thinking, 413

Frommer's Guide to America's Most-Travelled Cities, 266

Funk & Wagnalls, 11, 69–70

Funk & Wagnalls Guide to Modern World Literature, 389

FUNK & WAGNALLS NEW ENCYCLOPEDIA, 69–74
chart, 106
overview, 52

Funk & Wagnalls New Encyclopedia on CD-ROM. See MICROSOFT ENCARTA MULTIMEDIA ENCYCLOPEDIA (CD-ROM)

Funk & Wagnalls New Encyclopedia Yearbook, 72

Funk & Wagnalls New Standard Dictionary of the English Language, 69

Funk & Wagnalls New Standard Encyclopedia of Universal Knowledge, 69

Funk & Wagnalls Science Yearbook, 72

Funk & Wagnalls Standard Dictionary of Folklore, Mythology, and Legends, 417

Funk & Wagnalls Standard Encyclopedia of the World's Knowledge, 69

Funk & Wagnalls Standard Reference Encyclopedia, 69–70. 314

Furniture, 344

Future, 430

Gale Encyclopedia of Business. See ENCYCLOPEDIA OF BUSINESS

Gale Research, 12

GALLAUDET ENCYCLOPEDIA OF DEAF PEOPLE AND DEAFNESS, 372

Games, 433–36

GÄNZL'S BOOK OF THE MUSICAL THEATRE, 438

Gardens and gardening, 334–37

Gemstones, 348

General Reference Books for Adults, 455

Genetics and genetic disorders, 370

GEnie, 19, 253, 256–57

Geo-Data: The World Geographical Encyclopedia, 368

Geography, 361–68

Geology and geological sciences, 346–49

GEOPEDIA, 364–65

GER. See GRAN ENCICLOPEDIA RIALP: GER
German-language encyclopedias, 447
Germany, 386
Ghost Walks: A Chronological History of Blacks in Show Business, 1865–1910, 438
Ghosts, 408
G.K. Hall Encyclopedia of Modern Technology, 421
Glaister's Glossary of the Book, 388
GLOBAL INTERNATIONAL ENCYCLOPEDIA, 74–75
  chart, 106
Glossary of Psychoanalytic Terms and Concepts, 412
GOLDEN BOOK ENCYCLOPEDIA, 191–94
  chart, 219
Golden Book Encyclopedia on CD-ROM. See FIRST CONNECTIONS: THE GOLDEN BOOK ENCYCLOPEDIA (CD-ROM)
Golden Encyclopedia, 312
Golf, 434–35
GOLF MAGAZINE'S ENCYCLOPEDIA OF GOLF, 434–35
Government, 403–07
GRAN ENCICLOPEDIA LAROUSSE, 451
GRAN ENCICLOPEDIA RIALP: GER, 451
GRAND DICTIONNAIRE ENCYCLOPÉDIQUE LAROUSSE, 446. *See also* 449
Grand Larousse en 5 Volumes, 446
Grand Larousse Encyclopédique, 445–46. *See also* 450
GRAND LAROUSSE JUNIOR, 446
GRAND LAROUSSE UNIVERSEL EN 15 VOLUMES, 446
GRANDE DIZIONARIO ENCICLOPEDICO UTET, 448
GRANDE ENCYCLOPÉDIE, 446
GRAPHIC ARTS ENCYCLOPEDIA, 327
Great American History Fact-Finder, 381
Great Books of the Western World, 40
Great Britain, 375, 388–89
GREAT SONG THESAURUS, 398
GREAT SOVIET ENCYCLOPEDIA, 365. *See also* 26, 449
GREAT WORLD ENCYCLOPEDIA, 305
Greater Mirror, 6
Greece, 376
Green Encyclopedia, 348
Greenwood Publishing Group, 12
GROLIER ACADEMIC ENCYCLOPEDIA, 75–76
  chart, 106
  overview, 51
Grolier Academic American Encyclopedia. See ACADEMIC AMERICAN ENCYCLOPEDIA (Print); ACADEMIC AMERICAN ENCYCLOPEDIA (Online)

GROLIER CHILDREN'S ENCYCLOPEDIA, 195
  chart, 219
  overview, 173
Grolier Educational Corporation, 11
Grolier Electronic Encyclopedia, 287
Grolier Electronic Publishing, 12, 288
Grolier Encyclopedia. See ACADEMIC AMERICAN ENCYCLOPEDIA (Print); ACADEMIC AMERICAN ENCYCLOPEDIA (Online)
GROLIER ENCYCLOPEDIA (1944–63), 305–06
GROLIER ENCYCLOPEDIA OF KNOWLEDGE, 76–79
  chart, 106
  overview, 52
Grolier Encyclopedia of Science and Technology, 422
Grolier, Inc., 10–11, 13, 32, 54
GROLIER INTERNATIONAL ENCYCLOPEDIA, 80
  chart, 106
  overview, 51
Grolier Master Encyclopedia Index, 35, 57–58, 199
GROLIER UNIVERSAL ENCYCLOPEDIA, 306
GROLIER WORLD ENCYCLOPEDIA OF ENDANGERED SPECIES, 332
Grosse Brockhaus, 447
Grosse Herder, 447
Grossman's Guide to Wines, Beers, & Spirits,
GROTE NEDERLANDSE LAROUSSE ENCYCLOPEDIE, 445
GROTE SPECTRUM ENCYCLOPEDIE, 445
GROTE WINKLER PRINS ENCYCLOPEDIE, 445
Grove's Dictionaries of Music, 12
GRZIMEK'S ANIMAL LIFE ENCYCLOPEDIA, 332–33
Grzimek's Encyclopedia of Ethology, 334
Grzimek's Encyclopedia of Evolution, 331
GRZIMEK'S ENCYCLOPEDIA OF MAMMALS, 333
GUIDE TO AMERICAN LAW: EVERYONE'S LEGAL ENCYCLOPEDIA, 383–84
Guide to Reference Books, 9, 455
Guide to the Gods (Carlyon), 417
GUIDE TO THE GODS (Leach), 417
Guinness Book of Records, 303
GUINNESS ENCYCLOPEDIA OF POPULAR MUSIC, 398
Guns, 396, 434

HALLIWELL'S FILM GUIDE, 356
HALLIWELL'S FILMGOER'S COMPANION, 356
Hamlyn Children's Encyclopedia in Colour, 317
HAMLYN YOUNGER CHILDREN'S ENCYCLOPEDIA, 306
Hammond Atlas, 275
Handbook of American Women's History, 432
Handbook of Demoninations in the United States, 414
Handbook of Everyday Law, 383

Handbook of Family Law, 383

HANDBOOK OF LATIN AMERICAN LITERATURE, 389

Handbook of Living Religions, 412

Handbook of Metaphysics and Ontology, 415

HANDBOOK OF NORTH AMERICAN INDIANS, 431

Handbook of Old-Time Radio, 359

HANDBOOK OF RUSSIAN LITERATURE, 389

Handbook of South American Indians, 431

Handbook of Symbols in Christian Art, 325

Handbook of the Nations, 368

Handbook of World Philosophy, 415

Handy Encyclopedia of Useful Information, 304

Harbottle's Dictionary of Battles, 394

Harmony Illustrated Encyclopedia of Country Music, 397

Harmony Illustrated Encyclopedia of Jazz, 399

Harmony Illustrated Encyclopedia of Rock, 401

Harmsworth's Universal Encyclopaedia, 305

Harper Dictionary of Modern Thought, 413

Harper Dictionary of Opera and Operetta, 397

HARPER ENCYCLOPEDIA OF MILITARY HISTORY, 394–95

HarperCollins, 12

HarperCollins Dictionary of American Government and Politics, 403

HarperCollins Dictionary of Music, 400

HarperCollins Dictionary of Sociology, 430

HARPER'S BIBLE DICTIONARY, 417

Harper's Encyclopedia of Mystical and Paranormal Experience, 408–09

HARPER'S ENCYCLOPEDIA OF RELIGIOUS EDUCATION, 418

Hartley Courseware, 12

HARVARD ENCYCLOPEDIA OF AMERICAN ETHNIC GROUPS, 431

Harvard Guide to Contemporary American Writing, 385

HARVER JUNIOR WORLD ENCYCLOPEDIA, 306

HARVER WORLD ENCYCLOPEDIA, 306–07

Hazardous wastes, 349

Health, 368–74

Health and Medical Horizons, 28

Hearing and hearing disorders, 372

HEIBONSHA DAI-HYAKKA JITEN, 448

Heloise from A to Z, 354

HENRY HOLT HANDBOOK OF CURRENT SCIENCE & TECHNOLOGY, 422

HERITAGE ENCYCLOPEDIA OF BAND MUSIC, 398

Heritage of Music, 399

Higher education, 350–52

Hillier's Manual of Trees and Shrubs, 336

Hill's Practical Encyclopedia, 300

Hill's Practical Reference Library of General Knowledge, 300

Hispánica. See ENCICLOPEDIA HISPÁNICA

Histology, 372

Historia Naturalis, 5

Historic U.S. Court Cases, 1690–1990: An Encyclopedia, 383

Historical and Cultural Atlas of African Americans, 427

Historical Dictionary of Australia, 375

Historical Dictionary of Censorship in the United States, 388

HISTORICAL DICTIONARY OF EUROPEAN IMPERIALISM, 380

Historical Dictionary of Fascist Italy, 380

Historical Dictionary of France from the 1815 Restoration to the Second Empire, 380

HISTORICAL DICTIONARY OF ISRAEL, 380

Historical Dictionary of Modern Spain, 1700–1988, 380

Historical Dictionary of Napoleonic France, 1799–1815, 380

Historical Dictionary of Revolutionary China, 1839–1976, 378, 380

HISTORICAL DICTIONARY OF THE FRENCH REVOLUTION, 1789–1799, 380

Historical Dictionary of the French Fourth and Fifth Republics, 1946–1991, 380

Historical Dictionary of the French Second Empire, 1852–1879, 380

HISTORICAL DICTIONARY OF THE KOREAN WAR, 395

Historical Dictionary of the Spanish Civil War, 1936–1939, 380

Historical Dictionary of the Spanish Empire, 1402–1975, 380

Historical Dictionary of the Third French Republic, 1870–1940, 380

Historical Encyclopedia of Costume, 346

Historical Guide to North American Railroads, 441

Historical Guide to World War II. See Louis L. Snyder's Historical Guide to World War II

HISTORICAL TIMES ILLUSTRATED ENCYCLOPEDIA OF THE CIVIL WAR, 395

History, 375–82

History of Architecture, 326

History of Science and Technology, 421

Hockey, 433

Hockey Encyclopedia, 433

Hollywood Musical, 356

Holman Bible Dictionary, 417

Holocaust, 379

Holy Land, 419

Home Encyclopedia of Symptoms, Ailments and Their Natural Remedies, 371

HOME UNIVERSITY ENCYCLOPEDIA, 307

Homosexuality, 425–26

Homosexuality: A Research Guide, 425

Hoover Handbook, 266

Horse Owner's Veterinary Handbook, 330

Horses, 330

Hortica: A Color Cyclopedia of Garden Flora in All Climates and Indoor Plants, 335

Horticulture, 334–37

Hortus Second, 335

HORTUS THIRD: A CONCISE DICTIONARY OF PLANTS CULTIVATED IN THE UNITED STATES AND CANADA, 335

How and Why Library, 178

HOW TO CLEAR EVERYTHING: AN ENCYCLOPEDIA OF WHAT TO USE AND HOW TO USE IT, 354

Hudson Group, 157, 160

Hugh Johnson's Modern Encyclopedia of Wine, 361

Hugh Johnson's World Atlas of Wine, 361

Human behavior, 427–32

Human reproduction, 424–27

HUMAN SEXUALITY: AN ENCYCLOPEDIA, 426

Hutchinson Encyclopedia, 161–62, 165–66, 168

Hutchinson's New Twentieth Century Encyclopedia, 309

Hutchinson's Twentieth Century Encyclopedia, 162

Illustrated Bible Dictionary, 418

Illustrated Columbia Encyclopedia, 126

ILLUSTRATED DICTIONARY OF JEWELRY, 346

Illustrated Encyclopedia/Dictionary of General Aviation, 441

Illustrated Encyclopedia of Astronomy and Space, 328–29

Illustrated Encyclopedia of Aviation, 441

Illustrated Encyclopedia of Birds, 330

ILLUSTRATED ENCYCLOPEDIA OF FOSSILS, 348

ILLUSTRATED ENCYCLOPEDIA OF GENERAL AVIATION, 441

ILLUSTRATED ENCYCLOPEDIA OF HUMAN HISTOLOGY, 372

Illustrated Encyclopedia of Knowledge, 307

ILLUSTRATED ENCYCLOPEDIA OF LEARNING, 307

Illustrated Encyclopedia of Major Military Aircraft of the World, 394

Illustrated Encyclopedia of Mankind, 431

ILLUSTRATED ENCYCLOPEDIA OF NEW ZEALAND, 365

Illustrated Encyclopedia of Space Technology, 328

Illustrated Encyclopedia of the Modern World, 309

Illustrated Encyclopedia of the Universe, 329

ILLUSTRATED ENCYCLOPEDIA OF WILDLIFE, 333

Illustrated Encyclopedia of Woodworking Handtools, Instruments & Devices, 352–53

ILLUSTRATED ENCYCLOPEDIA OF WORLD GEOGRAPHY, 365

Illustrated Encyclopaedia of World Theatre, 439

Illustrated Encyclopedic Dictionary of Electronic Circuits, 343

Illustrated Home Library Encyclopedia, 308

Illustrated Information Finder. See INFORMATION FINDER (CD-ROM)

Illustrated International Encyclopedia of Horse Breeds & Breeding, 330

ILLUSTRATED LIBRARIES OF HUMAN KNOWLEDGE, 307

ILLUSTRATED WORLD ENCYCLOPEDIA, 307–08

Imaginary People: A Who's Who of Modern Fictional Characters, 387

IMAGO: ENCICLOPEDIA TEMÁTICA, 451

Immunology, 370

India, 362–63, 378, 387

India: An Encyclopaedic Survey, 363

Indians (American). *See* Native Americans

Indians of Central and South America: An Ethnohistorical Dictionary, 431

INFORMATION FINDER, 281–83
    chart, 298
    overview, 256

Information science and technology, 344, 351

Infopedia. See WORLD ALMANAC INFOPEDIA

Insects, 331–32, 334–35

Intellectual Freedom: A Reference Handbook, 388

Intellectual property, 384

INTERNATIONAL BUSINESS DICTIONARY AND REFERENCE, 339

International Center of Photography Encyclopedia of Photography, 327

INTERNATIONAL CYCLOPEDIA OF MUSIC AND MUSICIANS, 398

International Dictionary of Architects and Architecture, 326

INTERNATIONAL DICTIONARY OF BALLET, 438

INTERNATIONAL DICTIONARY OF FILMS AND FILMMAKERS, 356

International Dictionary of Opera, 400

International Dictionary of Religion, 412

INTERNATIONAL DICTIONARY OF THEATRE, 438–39

INTERNATIONAL ENCYCLOPEDIA OF ASTRONOMY, 328–29

INTERNATIONAL ENCYCLOPEDIA OF AVIATION, 441

INTERNATIONAL ENCYCLOPEDIA OF COMMUNICA-TIONS, 356–57

INTERNATIONAL ENCYCLOPEDIA OF EDUCATION, 351–52

International Encyclopedia of Educational Technology, 350

International Encyclopedia of Higher Education, 350

International Encyclopedia of Horse Breeds, 330

INTERNATIONAL ENCYCLOPEDIA OF LINGUISTICS, 389–90

INTERNATIONAL ENCYCLOPEDIA OF POPULATION, 431–32

INTERNATIONAL ENCYCLOPEDIA OF PSYCHIATRY, PSYCHOLOGY, PSYCHOANALYSIS, AND NEUROL-OGY, 411

INTERNATIONAL ENCYCLOPEDIA OF ROBOTICS, 343

International Encyclopedia of Sociology, 430

International Encyclopedia of Statistics, 338

INTERNATIONAL ENCYCLOPEDIA OF THE SOCIAL SCIENCES, 432

International Everyman's Encyclopaedia, 305

International Film Industry: A Historical Dictio-nary, 355, 358

International Higher Education: An Encyclopedia, 351

INTERNATIONAL MILITARY AND DEFENSE ENCYCLOPE-DIA, 395

International Military Encyclopedia, 395

INTERNATIONAL PETROLEUM ENCYCLOPEDIA, 348

International Reference Work, 311

International relations, 403–04, 406

INTERNATIONAL RELATIONS DICTIONARY, 406

INTERNATIONAL STANDARD BIBLE ENCYCLOPEDIA, 418

International World Reference Encyclopedia, 318

Internet, 19, 253, 256, 261–62, 284

INTERPRETER'S DICTIONARY OF THE BIBLE, 418

Introduction to Reference Work (Katz), 456

Iran, 363

Ireland, 365-66, 375, 387

IRELAND: A CULTURAL ENCYCLOPEDIA, 365–66

ISAAC ASIMOV'S LIBRARY OF THE UNIVERSE, 329

Islam, 415

Islam and Islamic Groups: A Worldwide Reference Guide, 415

Israel, 380

Italiana. See ENCICLOPEDIA ITALIANA DI SCIENZE, LETTERE ED ARTI

Italian-language encyclopedias, 447–48

Italy, 380, 387

Jane's All the World's Aircraft, 394, 442

Jane's Fighting Ships, 396

Japan, 362, 366, 378, 387, 439

JAPAN: AN ILLUSTRATED ENCYCLOPEDIA, 366

Japanese American History: An A-to-Z Reference from 1868 to the Present, 427

Japanese Americans, 427

Japanese-language encyclopedias, 448

Jazz, 399

Jewelry, 346

Jewish-American History and Culture: An Encyclopedia, 414

Jewish Encyclopedia, 414

Jewish Time Line Encyclopedia, 414

Jews and Judaism, 414

Journalism, 388

Joy of Knowledge, 146, 148, 152

Judaism, 414

Judicial system, 382–84

JUNIOR ENCYCLOPEDIA OF CANADA, 366

JUNIOR ENCYCLOPEDIA OF GENERAL KNOWLEDGE, 308

JUNIOR PEARS ENCYCLOPAEDIA, 308

Junior World Encyclopedia, 306

KABUKI ENCYCLOPEDIA, 439

KINGFISHER CHILDREN'S ENCYCLOPEDIA, 228–31
 chart, 252
 overview, 220-21

KINGFISHER SCIENCE ENCYCLOPEDIA, 422

Kirk-Othmer Concise Encyclopedia of Chemical Technology, 341

KIRK-OTHMER ENCYCLOPEDIA OF CHEMICAL TECH-NOLOGY, 341

Kleine Enzyklopädie der Mathematik, 403

KNOWLEDGE ENCYCLOPEDIA, 140–43
 chart, 171
 overview, 109

Kobbé's. See DEFINITIVE KOBBÉ'S OPERA BOOK

Kodansha Encyclopedia of Japan, 366

Konversations-Lexikon, 7, 31, 447

Korean-language encyclopedias, 448–49

Korean War, 395

Korean War Almanac, 395

KUSSMAUL ENCYCLOPEDIA (Online), 283–85
 chart, 298
 overview, 256

LA GRANDE ENCYCLOPÉDIE, 446

La Nuova Enciclopedia Universale Garzanti, 447

Labor, 339

LABOR CONFLICT IN THE UNITED STATES: AN ENCYCLOPEDIA, 339

LADIES' HOME JOURNAL CHILDREN'S ILLUSTRATED ENCYCLOPEDIA OF LEARNING, 308–09
Lands and People, 367–68
LANGE'S HANDBOOK OF CHEMISTRY, 341
Language, 386, 389–90
Language of Psychoanalysis, 412
Language of Sex: An A-to-Z Guide, 425
Languages of the World, 386
Large-print encyclopedias, 131–32
LAROUSSE DES JEUNES ENCYCLOPÉDIE, 446
Larousse Encyclopedia of Archaeology, 375
Larousse Encyclopedia of Astrology, 411
Larousse Encyclopedia of Precious Gems, 348
LAROUSSE GASTRONOMIQUE: ALL-NEW AMERICAN EDITION OF THE WORLD'S GREATEST CULINARY ENCYCLOPEDIA, 360
Larousse Guide to Astronomy, 329
LAROUSSE ILLUSTRATED INTERNATIONAL ENCYCLOPE-DIA AND DICTIONARY, 309
Lasers, 401
Latin America, 361–63, 381–82, 389, 404, 406
Latin America: A Political Dictionary, 406
Law, 382–84, 427
Law enforcement, 432
Le Costume Historique, 346
LE PETIT LAROUSSE ILLUSTRÉ, 446
Leonard Maltin's TV Movies and Video Guide, 355–56
LES BROWN'S ENCYCLOPEDIA OF TELEVISION, 357
Lesbian and Gay Parenting Handbook, 426
Lexicon Technicum, 7
LEXICON UNIVERSAL ENCYCLOPEDIA, 81
    chart, 106
    overview, 51
Libraries, 351–52
Libraries and Information Services Today: The Yearly Chronicle, 352
Library Journal, 456
Life sciences, 329–34
LINCOLN LIBRARY OF ESSENTIAL INFORMATION, 309
Linguistics, 386, 389–90
Linguistics Encyclopedia, 390
Lissauer's Encyclopedia of Popular Music in America, 398
Literature, 385–92
LITTLE AND IVES ILLUSTRATED READY REFERENCE ENCYCLOPEDIA, 309
Little Golden Encyclopedia, 450
Lives of William Benton (Hyman), 39
Longman Encyclopedia, 131–32

Louis L. Snyder's Historical Guide to World War II, 396

MACHINERY'S HANDBOOK, 354
Machines and machinery, 354
Macmillan Book of the Marine Aquarium, 329
Macmillan Children's Encyclopedia, 317
Macmillan Concise Dictionary of World History, 379
Macmillan Dictionary of British and European History, 403
Macmillan Encyclopedia, 94, 314
MACMILLAN ENCYCLOPEDIA OF COMPUTERS, 343
MACMILLAN ENCYCLOPEDIA OF SCIENCE, 422
Macmillan Everyman's Encyclopedia, 305
MACMILLAN FAMILY ENCYCLOPEDIA, 81–82
    chart, 106
    overview, 51
MACMILLAN HEALTH ENCYCLOPEDIA, 372
Macmillan Illustrated Animal Encyclopedia, 333
MACMILLAN ILLUSTRATED ENCYCLOPEDIA OF DINOSAURS AND PREHISTORIC ANIMALS, 333
Macmillan, Inc., 12
Macropaedia. See NEW ENCYCLOPAEDIA BRITANNICA
Magic and magicians, 434
Magill's American Film Guide, 357
Magill's Cinema Annual, 357
MAGILL'S SURVEY OF CINEMA, 357
Maldives, 362
Mammals, 333
Mammals: A Multimedia Encyclopedia, 333
Management, 338
Marine life, 329–31
Marine Life: An Illustrated Encyclopedia of Invertebrates in the Sea, 331
MARKS' STANDARD HANDBOOK FOR MECHANICAL ENGINEERS, 354
Marriage, 429
Marshall Cavendish, 12
MARSHALL CAVENDISH ENCYCLOPEDIA OF FAMILY HEALTH, 372–73
Marshall Cavendish Encyclopedia of Health, 373
MARSHALL CAVENDISH ENCYCLOPEDIA OF PERSONAL RELATIONSHIPS: HUMAN BEHAVIOR, 411
Marshall Cavendish Encyclopedia of World War I, 395
MARSHALL CAVENDISH ILLUSTRATED ENCYCLOPEDIA: WORLD AND ITS PEOPLE, 366
MARSHALL CAVENDISH ILLUSTRATED ENCYCLOPEDIA OF DISCOVERY AND EXPLORATION, 380

Marshall Cavendish Illustrated Encyclopedia of Family Health, 372

MARSHALL CAVENDISH ILLUSTRATED ENCYCLOPEDIA OF PLANTS AND EARTH SCIENCES, 335

MARSHALL CAVENDISH ILLUSTRATED ENCYCLOPEDIA OF WORLD WAR I, 395–96

MARSHALL CAVENDISH ILLUSTRATED ENCYCLOPEDIA OF WORLD WAR II, 396

Marshall Cavendish Illustrated History of Popular Music, 398

Marshall Cavendish International Wildlife Encyclopedia, 333

Marx Dictionary, 404

Mary Ellen's Clean House! The All-in-One-Place Encyclopedia of Contemporary Housekeeping, 354

Mass communications, 355–59

MASS MEDIA: A CHRONOLOGICAL ENCYCLOPEDIA OF TELEVISION, RADIO, MOTION PICTURES, MAGAZINES, NEWSPAPERS, AND BOOKS IN THE UNITED STATES, 357

Mass Media and the Constitution: An Encyclopedia of Supreme Court Cases, 357

MASTERPLOTS, 390

Masterplots Cyclopedia of Literary Characters. See CYCLOPEDIA OF LITERARY CHARACTERS

Masterplots II, 390

Materials and materials science, 353–54

MATERIALS HANDBOOK, 354

Mathematics, 401–03

MATHEMATICS ILLUSTRATED DICTIONARY, 402–03

Mayo Clinic Family Health Book, 369

MCCARTHY'S DESK ENCYCLOPEDIA OF INTELLECTUAL PROPERTY, 384

MCCLANE'S NEW STANDARD FISHING ENCYCLOPEDIA AND INTERNATIONAL ANGLING GUIDE, 435

McGraw-Hill, 12

MCGRAW-HILL CONCISE ENCYCLOPEDIA OF SCIENCE AND TECHNOLOGY, 422–23

McGraw-Hill Dictionary of Art, 326

McGraw-Hill Dictionary of Scientific and Technical Terms, 423

MCGRAW-HILL ENCYCLOPEDIA OF ASTRONOMY, 329

MCGRAW-HILL ENCYCLOPEDIA OF CHEMISTRY, 342

MCGRAW-HILL ENCYCLOPEDIA OF ECONOMICS, 339

MCGRAW-HILL ENCYCLOPEDIA OF ELECTRONICS AND COMPUTERS, 343–44

MCGRAW-HILL ENCYCLOPEDIA OF ENGINEERING, 354

McGraw-Hill Encyclopedia of Environmental Science & Engineering, 423

McGraw-Hill Encyclopedia of Environmental Sciences, 348

McGraw-Hill Encyclopedia of Physics, 402–423

MCGRAW-HILL ENCYCLOPEDIA OF SCIENCE AND TECHNOLOGY, 423. *See also* 14–15

MCGRAW-HILL ENCYCLOPEDIA OF THE GEOLOGICAL SCIENCES, 348–49

MCGRAW-HILL ENCYCLOPEDIA OF WORLD DRAMA, 390

MCGRAW-HILL PERSONAL COMPUTER PROGRAMMING ENCYCLOPEDIA, 344

McGraw-Hill Science and Technical Reference Set, 423

McGraw-Hill Yearbook of Science and Technology, 423

MCKAY ONE-VOLUME INTERNATIONAL ENCYCLOPEDIA, 309–10

Mechanical engineering, 354

Mechanical Engineers' Handbook, 354

Medical and Health Annual, 45

Medical tests, 373–74

Medical Tests and Diagnositic Procedures, 373

Medical Update, 101

Medicine, 368–74, 434

Mental health, 407–08, 410–11

Mercer Dictionary of the Bible, 417

MERCK MANUAL OF DIAGNOSIS AND THERAPY, 373

Merck Veterinary Manual, 330

MERIT STUDENTS ENCYCLOPEDIA, 310. *See also* 28, 299–300

Merriam-Webster Inc., 41, 246

Metals and metallurgy, 353–54

Metropolitan Opera Encyclopedia, 397

Mexico, 387

Mexican Americans, 428

MEYERS ENZYKLOPÄDISCHES LEXIKON, 447

Meyers Neues Lexikon, 447

Microbiology, 332

Microlytics, 12

Micropaedia. See NEW ENCYCLOPAEDIA BRITANNICA

Microsoft Bookshelf, 256, 275–77

Microsoft Corporation, 12, 237, 275–76, 285–86

MICROSOFT ENCARTA MULTIMEDIA ENCYCLOPEDIA (CD-ROM), 285–87. *See also* 3, 12, 70

chart, 298

overview, 255–56

Middle Ages, 376, 437

Middle Ages: A Concise Encyclopedia, 376

Middle East, 362, 406

MIDDLE EAST: A POLITICAL DICTIONARY, 406

Midwest (U.S.), 364

Milestones in Science and Technology, 420

Military science and history, 392–96

Minerals and mineralogy, 346–48

MIS PRIMEROS CONOCIMIENTOS, 451

MODERN CENTURY ILLUSTRATED ENCYCLOPEDIA, 310

Modern Encyclopedia of Russian and Soviet Literatures, 389

MODERN GEOGRAPHY: AN ENCYCLOPEDIC SURVEY, 366–67

Modern Reference Encyclopedia, 306

Molho, Emanuel, 443–44

MOONS OF THE SOLAR SYSTEM: AN ILLUSTRATED ENCYCLOPEDIA, 329

Mosby Medical Encyclopedia, 369

Motion Picture Annual, 358

MOTION PICTURE GUIDE, 357–58

Motion pictures, 355–58

Mount Sinai School of Medicine Complete Book of Nutrition, 359

Moutains, 367

Multimedia Encyclopedia of Mammalian Biology, 333

Multimedia encyclopedias, 19, 253–98

Music, 356, 396–401

MUSIC: AN ILLUSTRATED ENCYCLOPEDIA, 398–99

Musical instruments, 399–400

Musical theater, 436, 438

Muslim Peoples: A World Ethnographic Survey, 415

Muslims, 415

MY FIRST ENCYCLOPEDIA (Dorling Kindersley), 231–33
  chart, 252
  overview, 221

MY FIRST ENCYCLOPEDIA (Troll), 233–35
  chart, 252

MY FIRST ENCYCLOPEDIA A-Z, 310

MY FIRST GOLDEN ENCYCLOPEDIA, 310

My First Golden Learning Encyclopedia, 310

My First Knowledge, 451

My Weekly Reader, 214

Myth of the Britannica (Einbinder), 39

Mythology, 417

NATIONAL ENCYCLOPEDIA, 311

National Encyclopedia for the Home, School and Library,

Nations, 368

Native Americans, 415, 431

Natural medicine, 371

NBA's Official Encyclopedia of Pro Basketball, 435

Negro Almanac, 427

Nelson's Encyclopedia, 301

NELSON'S ENCYCLOPEDIA FOR YOUNG READERS, 311

Nepal, 362

Neue Brockhaus, 447

NEUE HERDER, 447

Neuroscience, 371

NEW A TO Z OF WOMEN'S HEALTH: A CONCISE ENCYCLOPEDIA, 373

NEW AGE ENCYCLOPEDIA (Gale), 418

New Age Encyclopedia (Grolier), 304, 306

New Age movement, 418

NEW AMERICAN DESK ENCYCLOPEDIA, 143–46
  chart, 171

New American Encyclopedia (Books, Inc.), 300

NEW AMERICAN ENCYCLOPEDIA (Publishers Agency), 311

NEW BOOK OF KNOWLEDGE, 195–201
  chart, 219
  overview, 173

New Book of Knowledge Annual, 198

NEW BOOK OF POPULAR SCIENCE, 423

NEW CATHOLIC ENCYCLOPEDIA, 418–19

NEW CAXTON ENCYCLOPEDIA, 311–12. See also 299–300

NEW CENTRY BOOK OF FACTS, 312

NEW CHILD HEALTH ENCYCLOPEDIA, 426

NEW COLLEGE ENCYCLOPEDIA, 312

New Columbia Encyclopedia, 126, 131–33, 135–36, 313

NEW COMPLEAT ASTROLOGER: THE PRACTICAL ENCYCLOPEDIA OF ASTROLOGICAL SCIENCE, 411

New Dictionary of Theology, 419

NEW ENCYCLOPAEDIA BRITANNICA, 37–49. See also 7–8, 10, 14, 444–45, 448, 450, 457
  chart, 50
  overview, 23–24

New Encyclopaedia Britannica on CD-ROM. See BRITANNICA INSTANT RESEARCH SYSTEM (CD-ROM)

New Encyclopaedia Britannica Online. See BRITANNICA ONLINE (Online)

NEW ENCYCLOPEDIA OF ARCHAEOLOGICAL EXCAVA-TIONS IN THE HOLY LAND, 419

NEW ENCYCLOPEDIA OF MOTOR CARS, 1885 TO THE PRESENT, 441

NEW ENCYCLOPEDIA OF SCIENCE FICTION, 390

New Encyclopedia of Sports, 434

New Encyclopedic Dictionary of School Law, 351

New England (U.S.), 363–64

New Everyman Dictionary of Music, 400

NEW FRANK SCHOONMAKER ENCYCLOPEDIA OF WINE, 360–61

New Funk & Wagnalls Encyclopedia, 69–70
NEW GOLDEN ENCYCLOPEDIA, 312
New Good Housekeeping Encyclopedia of House Plants, 336
New Good Housekeeping Family Health and Medical Guide, 369
New Grolier Electronic Encyclopedia, 287, 289
NEW GROLIER MULTIMEDIA ENCYCLOPEDIA (CD-ROM), 287–91
  chart, 298
  overview, 255
NEW GROLIER STUDENT ENCYCLOPEDIA, 201
  chart, 219
  overview, 173
NEW GROVE DICTIONARY OF AMERICAN MUSIC, 399
NEW GROVE DICTIONARY OF JAZZ, 399
NEW GROVE DICTIONARY OF MUSIC AND MUSICIANS, 399
NEW GROVE DICTIONARY OF MUSICAL INSTRUMENTS, 399-400
NEW GROVE DICTIONARY OF OPERA, 400
New Guide to Modern World Literature, 389
New Harvard Dictionary of Music, 400
NEW HUMAN INTEREST LIBRARY, 313
NEW ILLUSTRATED COLUMBIA ENCYCLOPEDIA, 313
New Illustrated Information Finder. See INFORMATION FINDER   (CD-ROM)
New Illustrated Medical Encyclopedia for Home Use, 369
New International Dictionary of Biblical Archaeology, 419
NEW KNOWLEDGE LIBRARY, 313
New Kobbé's Complete Opera Book, 397
New Lincoln Library Encyclopedia, 309
New Our Bodies, Ourselves, 373
NEW OXFORD COMPANION TO MUSIC, 400
NEW PALGRAVE: A DICTIONARY OF ECONOMICS, 339–40
NEW PALGRAVE DICTIONARY OF MONEY AND FINANCE, 340
New Pictorial Encyclopedia of the World, 309
New Practical Reference Library, 300
NEW PRINCETON ENCYCLOPEDIA OF POETRY AND POETICS, 391
NEW ROYAL HORTICULTURAL SOCIETY DICTIONARY OF GARDENING, 335
New Schaff-Herzog Encyclopedia of Religious Knowledge, 419
NEW STANDARD ENCYCLOPEDIA, 82–88
  chart, 107
  overview, 52

New Standard Jewish Encyclopedia, 414
NEW TALKING CASSETTE ENCYCLOPEDIA, 313–14
New Teacher's and Pupil's Cyclopaedia, 311
NEW 20TH-CENTURY ENCYCLOPEDIA OF RELIGIOUS KNOWLEDGE, 419
New Unger's Bible Dictionary, 417
NEW UNIVERSAL FAMILY ENCYCLOPEDIA, 314. *See also* 93-97
NEW UNIVERSAL STANDARD ENCYCLOPEDIA, 314
NEW UNIVERSITY ONE-VOLUME ENCYCLOPEDIA, 314
NEW VIDEO ENCYCLOPEDIA, 358
New Wonder World, 303
New Wonder World Cultural Library, 303
New Wonder World Encyclopedia, 303
NEW YORK BOTANICAL GARDEN ILLUSTRATED ENCYCLOPEDIA OF HORTICULTURE, 336
New York Post World Wide Illustrated Encyclopedia, 307
New York Public Library Book of Chronologies, 381
NEW YORK TIMES ENCYCLOPEDIA OF FILM, 1896–1979, 358
New York Times Film Reviews, 1913–1974, 358
New York Times Food Encyclopedia, 360
New Zealand, 365
New Zealand Encyclopedia, 365
NORTON/GROVE CONCISE ENCYCLOPEDIA OF MUSIC, 400
Nueva Enciclopedia Temática, 318
Nuova Enciclopedia Universale Garzanti, 447
Nutrition, 359–61
NUTRITION AND HEALTH ENCYCLOPEDIA, 361
NVN (National Videotex Network), 257

Occult, 408-10
Ocean World Encyclopedia, 349
Oceans and oceanography, 349
OFFICIAL ENCYCLOPEDIA OF BRIDGE, 435
OFFICIAL NBA BASKETBALL ENCYCLOPEDIA, 435
Official NFL Encyclopedia, 434
Official World Wildlife Fund Guide to Endangered Species, 332
On the Disciplines, 6
One- and two-volume encyclopedias, 11, 108–72, 220-52
101 Stories of the Great Ballets, 438
Online encyclopedias, 253-98. *See also* 8–9, 12–14, 19
Opera, 396–97, 400
Organic Plant Protection, 334

Originals: An A-Z of Fiction's Read-Life Charac-ters, 387
Ottenheimer Publishers, 94
Our Bodies, Ourselves. See New Our Bodies, Ourselves
Our Wonder World, 303
OUR WONDERFUL WORLD, 314–15
Out-of-print encyclopedias, 299–319
OXFORD CHILDREN'S ENCYCLOPEDIA, 202-06
   chart, 219
Oxford Classical Dictionary, 376
Oxford Companion to American History, 381
Oxford Companion to American Literature, 385, 391–92
OXFORD COMPANION TO AMERICAN THEATRE, 439
OXFORD COMPANION TO ANIMAL BEHAVIOUR, 333–34
Oxford Companion to Art, 327
Oxford Companion to Australian Literature, 391
Oxford Companion to Canadian History and Literature, 391
OXFORD COMPANION TO CANADIAN LITERATURE, 391
OXFORD COMPANION TO CANADIAN THEATRE, 439
OXFORD COMPANION TO CHESS, 435
OXFORD COMPANION TO CHILDREN'S LITERATURE, 391
OXFORD COMPANION TO CLASSICAL LITERATURE, 391
OXFORD COMPANION TO ENGLISH LITERATURE, 391
Oxford Companion to Film, 356
Oxford Companion to French Literature, 386
Oxford Companion to German Literature, 386
OXFORD COMPANION TO LAW, 384
OXFORD COMPANION TO MEDICINE, 373
Oxford Companion to Music, 400
Oxford Companion to Musical Instruments, 400
OXFORD COMPANION TO POLITICS OF THE WORLD, 406
Oxford Companion to Popular Music, 397–98
OXFORD COMPANION TO SHIPS AND THE SEA, 441
Oxford Companion to Spanish Literature, 386
Oxford Companion to the Bible, 417
OXFORD COMPANION TO THE DECORATIVE ARTS, 346
Oxford Companion to the Literature of Wales, 391
OXFORD COMPANION TO THE MIND, 411
OXFORD COMPANION TO THE SUPREME COURT OF THE UNITED STATES, 384
OXFORD COMPANION TO THE THEATRE, 439
Oxford Companion to Twentieth Century Art, 327
OXFORD COMPANION TO WORLD SPORTS AND GAMES, 435
OXFORD DICTIONARY OF ART, 327
Oxford Dictionary of Australian History, 375
OXFORD DICTIONARY OF BYZANTIUM, 380–81
Oxford Dictionary of Music, 400

Oxford Dictionary of Opera, 397
OXFORD DICTIONARY OF THE CHRISTIAN CHURCH, 419
OXFORD ENCYCLOPEDIA OF TREES OF THE WORLD, 336
OXFORD ILLUSTRATRATED ENCYCLOPEDIA, 88–93
   chart, 107
   overview, 52
OXFORD ILLUSTRATED ENCYCLOPEDIA OF INVENTION AND TECHNOLOGY, 88
OXFORD ILLUSTRATED ENCYCLOPEDIA OF PEOPLES AND CULTURES, 88–89
OXFORD ILLUSTRATED ENCYCLOPEDIA OF THE ARTS, 88
OXFORD ILLUSTRATED ENCYCLOPEDIA OF THE UNIVERSE, 88
Oxford Illustrated Literary Guide to Canada, 391
Oxford Junior Companion to Music, 399
OXFORD JUNIOR ENCYCLOPAEDIA, 315
Oxford University Press, 12

Pakistan, 362
Palgrave's Dictionary of Political Economy, 339
Parapsychology, 408–10
PARENT'S DESK REFERENCE: THE ULTIMATE FAMILY ENCYCLOPEDIA FROM CONCEPTION TO COLLEGE, 426
PATIENT'S GUIDE TO MEDICAL TESTS, 373–74
PATRICK MOORE'S A-Z OF ASTRONOMY, 329
PDR. See PHYSICIANS' DESK REFERENCE
PDR Drug Interactions and Side Effects Index, 374
PDR Family Guide to Prescription Drugs, 374
Peace, 393, 407
PEARS CYCLOPAEDIA, 315
Pears' Shilling Cyclopaedia, 315
Penguin Dictionary of Architecture, 326
PENGUIN DICTIONARY OF DECORATIVE ARTS, 346
PENGUIN ENCYCLOPEDIA, 315
Penguin Encyclopaedia of Nutrition, 359
Penguin Encyclopedia of Popular Music, 398
People's Book of Medical Tests, 373
PEOPLE'S CHRONOLOGY, 381
Pergamon Press, 12
Petit Larousse en Couleurs, 446
PETIT LAROUSSE ILLUSTRÉ, 446. *See also* 309
Petroleum, 348
Pharmacology and pharmaceuticals, 371–72, 374
Philosophy, 413, 415
Photography, 326–27
PHYSICIANS' DESK REFERENCE, 374
Physicians' Desk Reference for Nonprescription Drugs, 374
Physicians' Desk Reference for Ophtalmology, 374
Physics, 401-02

PHYSICS IN MEDICINE & BIOLOGY ENCYCLOPEDIA, 374
PICTURE ENCYCLOPEDIA FOR CHILDREN, 315–16
PICTURED KNOWLEDGE, 316
Pill Book, 369
Planeta Internacional, 24
Plants and plant life, 334–37
Plays, 390, 437-39
POCKET ENCYCLOPEDIA (Random House), 316
Pocket Encyclopedia (SelecTronics). *See* RANDOM HOUSE ELECTRONIC ENCYCLOPEDIA (Hand-held)
Poetry, 391
Police, 432
Police Dictionary and Encyclopedia, 432
Political parties, 406–07
POLITICAL PARTIES AND ELECTIONS IN THE UNITED STATES: AN ENCYCLOPEDIA, 406–07
Political Parties of Asia and the Pacific: A Reference Guide, 407
Political Parties of the Americas and the Caribbean: A Reference Guide, 407
Political science, 403–07
Pollution, 349
Polymer science, 341
POPULAR ENCYCLOPEDIA OF PLANTS, 336
Popular Mechanics Do-It-Yourself Encyclopedia, 355
Popular music, 397–98
Population, 431-32
Porcelain, 345
Position to Command Respect: Women and the Eleventh Britannica (Thomas), 39
Post Reports (U.S. Department of State), 368
Potter's Dictionary of Materials and Techniques, 345
Pottery, 345
Practical Encyclopedia of Natural Healing, 371
PRACTICAL ENCYCLOPEDIA OF SEX AND HEALTH, 426
Praeger Encyclopedia of Art, 326
Prehistory and prehistoric life, 331, 333
Prentice Hall, 11–12
PRENTICE-HALL ENCYCLOPEDIA OF INFORMATION TECHNOLOGY, 344
Prentice-Hall Encyclopedia of Mathematics, 403
Prentice Hall Guide to English Literature, 392
Presidency A to Z: A Ready Reference Encyclopedia, 406
Presidential-Congressional Political Dictionary, 406
Presidents: A Reference History, 406
Presidents and presidency (U.S.), 405–06
Press, 392
Princeton Companion to Classical Japanese Literature, 387

Princeton Encyclopedia of Classical Sites, 375
Princeton Encyclopedia of Poetry and Poetics, 391
PRIVATE PILOT'S DICTIONARY AND HANDBOOK, 441
Pro Basketball Encyclopedia, 435
Prodigy Information Service, 19, 253, 256–57
Profiles in Belief: The Religious Bodies of the United States and Canada, 414
Progressive Reference Library, 311
Propaedia. See NEW ENCYCLOPAEDIA BRITANNICA
PSYCHEDELICS ENCYCLOPEDIA, 374
Psychiatry, 411
Psychoanalysis, 411–12
PSYCHOANALYTIC TERMS AND CONCEPTS, 411–12
Psychology, 407–12
Publishing, 388-89
Purchasing an Encyclopedia, 456
PURNELL'S FIRST ENCYCLOPEDIA IN COLOUR, 316
Purnell's New English Encyclopedia, 312
PURNELL'S PICTORIAL ENCYCLOPEDIA, 316

Quick Reference Encyclopedia, 317
QUICK REFERENCE HANDBOOK, 316–17
Quick Reference Handbook of Basic Knowledge, 317

Radio, 358-59
Radio's Golden Years: The Encyclopedia of Radio Programs, 1930–1960, 358–59
Railroads, 337, 440–41
RAINTREE CHILDREN'S ENCYCLOPEDIA, 317
RAINTREE ILLUSTRATED SCIENCE ENCYCLOPEDIA, 424
Rand McNally Encyclopedia of Military Aircraft, 1914–1980, 394, 442
RAND MCNALLY ENCYCLOPEDIA OF TRANSPORTA-TION, 441–42
Rand McNally Encyclopedia of World Rivers, 367
RAND MCNALLY STUDENT ENCYCLOPEDIA IN COLOR, 317
RAND MCNALLY'S CHILDREN'S ENCYCLOPEDIA, 317–18
RANDOM HOUSE CHILDREN'S ENCYCLOPEDIA, 235-38.
  See also 450
  chart, 252
  overview, 220-21
Random House Collector's Encyclopedia, 345
Random House Dictionary of Art and Artists, 327
RANDOM HOUSE ELECTRONIC ENCYCLOPEDIA (Hand-held), 291–93
  chart, 298
RANDOM HOUSE ENCYCLOPEDIA (Print), 146–53.
  See also 3
  chart, 171
  overview, 108–09

RANDOM HOUSE ENCYCLOPEDIA: ELECTRONIC EDITION (Floppy disks), 293–95
   chart, 298
Random House Encyclopedia of Antiques, 344
Random House, Inc., 11
Random House International Encyclopedia of Golf, 435
RANDOM HOUSE LIBRARY OF KNOWLEDGE: FIRST ENCYCLOPEDIA, 238–41
   chart, 252
Random House Pocket Encyclopedia. See RANDOM HOUSE ELECTRONIC ENCYCLOPEDIA (hand-held)
READER'S COMPANION TO AMERICAN HISTORY, 381
Reader's Digest Book of Skills & Tools, 353
Reader's Digest Family Legal Guide, 383
READER'S DIGEST NEW COMPLETE DO-IT-YOURSELF MANUAL, 355
Reader's Encyclopedia, 385
Reader's Encyclopedia of American Literature, 385
Reader's Encyclopedia of Eastern European Literature, 386
Reader's Encyclopedia of Shakespeare, 392
READER'S ENCYCLOPEDIA OF THE AMERICAN WEST, 381
Real estate, 340
Recreation, 433
Reference Book Center, 15
Reference Books Bulletin (in Booklist), 17, 20, 456
Reference Books for Young Readers, 456
REFERENCE COMPANION TO THE HISTORY OF ABNORMAL PSYCHOLOGY, 412
Reference Guide to the United States Supreme Court, 384
REFERENCE GUIDE TO UNITED STATES MILITARY HISTORY, 396
REFERENCE HANDBOOK ON THE DESERTS OF NORTH AMERICA, 367
Reference Sources for Small and Medium-sized Libraries, 456
Refugees in the United States: A Reference Handbook, 431
Religion, 412-20
Religions of the World, 412
Renaissance, 379
Reptiles, 332
Revell's Bible Dictionary, 417
Revolutionary War (American), 394
RHS ENCYCLOPEDIA OF HOUSE PLANTS INCLUDING GREENHOUSE PLANTS, 336
RICHARDS TOPICAL ENCYCLOPEDIA, 318
Rivers, 367

Robots and robotics, 343
Rock music, 400–01
ROCK ON: THE ILLUSTRATED ENCYCLOPEDIA OF ROCK N' ROLL, 400
RODALE'S ALL-NEW ENCYCLOPEDIA OF ORGANIC GARDENING, 336
Rodale's Encyclopedia of Natural Home Remedies, 371
Rodale's Illustrated Encyclopedia of Perennials, 335
Roget's II Electronic Thesaurus, 275
ROLLING RIVERS: AN ENCYCLOPEDIA OF AMERICA'S RIVERS, 367
Rolling Stone Encyclopedia of Rock & Roll, 401
Rome, 376
Royal Horticultural Society Dictionary of Gardening, 335
RQ (Reference Quarterly), 456
RULES OF THE GAME: THE COMPLETE ILLUSTRATED ENCYCLOPEDIA OF ALL MAJOR SPORTS OF THE WORLD, 435–36
Running, 436
RUNNING FROM A TO Z, 436
RUNNING PRESS CYCLOPEDIA, 153-56. *See also* 8
   chart, 171
   overview, 109
Russia, 362, 376–77, 387, 389
Russia and the Commonwealth A to Z, 362, 365
Russian-language encyclopedias, 449

Scandinavia, 376, 387
SCARNE'S ENCYCLOPEDIA OF CARD GAMES, 436
Scarne's Encyclopedia of Games, 436
Schizophrenia, 409
Schoenhof's Foreign Books, 444
School Library Journal, 457
Science, 420–24
Science fiction, 390
Science Fiction Encyclopedia, 390
Science Year, 101
Scientific American, 31
Scribner Desk Dictionary of American History, 381
Scribner's (Charles) Sons, 12
Sculpture, 326
Secondhand encyclopedias, 14–15, 299
Sekai Dai-Hyakka Jiten, 448
Semiotics, 389
Sex and sexuality, 424–27
SEXUALITY AND THE LAW: AN ENCYCLOPEDIA OF MAJOR LEGAL CASES, 427
SHAKESPEARE A TO Z, 392
Shakespeare, William 392

Shana Alexander's State-by-State Guide to Women's Legal Rights, 384

Shells, 332

Ships, 396, 441

Shorter Encyclopaedia of Islam, 415

Silver Burdett Encyclopedia of Transport, 442

Simon and Schuster Encyclopedia of World War II, 396

Simon & Schuster's Guide to Garden Flowers, 334

Sleep, 410

Soccer, 436

Social sciences, 427–32

Social work, 429–30

Social Work Year Book, 430

sociology, 430

SOFTWARE TOOLWORKS ILLUSTRATED ENCYCLOPEDIA (CD-ROM), 296
  chart, 298
  overview, 255

Songs, 398, 436–37

Songs of the Theater, 436

Sony Laser Library, 270

South (U.S.), 364, 378–79, 416

South America, 361–63, 381–82, 404, 406

Southwestern Company, 11

Soviet Mathematical Encyclopedia, 401

Soviet Union, 362, 365, 376–77

Space science, 327–29

Spain, 380, 386-88

Spanish-language encyclopedias, 449–51

Special education, 351

Specialized encyclopedias, 9, 12, 323–442

Spectrum Compact Encyclopedie, 445

Speculum Majus, 6

Spies and Provocateurs: A Worldwide Encyclopedia of Persons Conducting Espionage and Covert Action, 1946–1991, 393

Spies and spying, 393

Sports, 433–36

Sports Encyclopedia: Baseball, 433

Sports Encyclopedia: Pro Basketball, 435

Sports Encyclopedia: Pro Football, the Early Years, 434

Sports Encyclopedia: Pro Football, the Modern Era, 1960–1990, 434

Sports Rules Encyclopedia, 436

Spyclopedia: The Comprehensive Handbook of Espionage, 393

Spy/Counterspy: An Encyclopedia of Espionage, 393

Sri Lanka, 362

ST. JAMES ENCYCLOPEDIA OF MORTGAGE & REAL ESTATE FINANCE, 340

St. Martin's Press, 12

Stage It with Music: An Encyclopedic Guide to the American Musical Theatre, 436

Standard American Encyclopedia, 318

Standard Catalog of American Cars, 440

Standard Dictionary of the English Language, 69

Standard Educational Corporation, 11, 83

Standard Encyclopedia. See NEW STANDARD ENCYCLOPEDIA,

STANDARD ENCYCLOPEDIA OF THE WORLD'S MOUNTAINS, 367

Standard Encyclopedia of the World's Oceans and Islands, 367

Standard Encyclopedia of the World's Rivers and Lakes, 367

Standard International Encyclopedia, 311

Standard Reference Work for the Home, School and Library, 82–83

STATE-BY-STATE GUIDE TO WOMEN'S LEGAL RIGHTS, 384

States (U.S.), 368

Statesman's Year-Book, 368

Statistics, 338

Strand Book Store, 15

Subject encyclopedias, 9, 12, 323–442

Suicide, 410

Supermarket encyclopedias, 52, 70, 79, 286

Supernatural, 408–10

Superstitions, 408–09

Supreme Court. See United States Supreme Court

Supreme Court: A Citizen's Guide, 384

Supreme Court A to Z, 384

Symptoms, 369

Symptoms: The Complete Home Medical Encyclopedia, 369

Symptoms of illness and disease, 369–71

SYSTEMS AND CONTROL ENCYCLOPEDIA, 355

Systems engineering, 355

Talking Cassette Encyclopedia, 313

Taylor's Encyclopedia of Gardening, 337

Teacher's and Pupil's Cyclopaedia, 311

Technology, 420–24

Television, 355–58

TELEVISION INDUSTRY: A HISTORICAL DICTIONARY, 358

Ten Thousand Dreams Interpreted, 408

Tennis, 433

Terrorism, 394

Terrorism: A Reference Handbook, 394

Textiles, 345

Thames and Hudson Dictionary of Art and Artists, 327

Theater, 390, 436–40

THEATRE BACKSTAGE FROM A TO Z, 439–40

Theatre Lighting from A to Z, 440

THÉMA ENCYCLOPÉDIE LAROUSSE, 446

Third world, 364

THORNDIKE ENCYCLOPEDIA OF BANKING AND FINANCIAL TABLES, 340

TIMES ATLAS AND ENCYCLOPEDIA OF THE SEA, 349

Times Atlas of the Oceans, 349

Timetables of American History, 377

Timetables of History, 381

Timetables of Jewish History, 414

Timetables of Science, 420

Tools, 352–53

Toolworks Illustrated Encyclopedia. See SOFTWARE TOOLWORKS ILLUSTRATED ENCYCLOPEDIA

Total Baseball: The Ultimate Encyclopedia of Baseball, 433

TOXICS A TO Z, 349

Train-Watcher's Guide to North American Railroads, 441

Transportation, 440–42

Treasury of the Encyclopaedia Britannica, 42

Trees, 334, 336

Trees of North America, 336

Tribune Company, 62

TROLL STUDENT ENCYCLOPEDIA, 241–43
chart, 252

Tropica: Color Cyclopedia of Exotic Plants, 335

TUNE IN YESTERDAY: THE ULTIMATE ENCYCLOPEDIA OF OLD RADIO, 1925–76, 358–59

Twentieth-Century Encyclopedia of Religious Knowledge, 419

UFO Encyclopedia (Clark), 328

UFO Encyclopedia (Sachs), 328

UFOs. See Unidentified Flying Objects (UFOs)

Ukraine, 364

Ukraine: A Concise Encyclopedia, 364

ULLMANN'S ENCYCLOPEDIA OF INDUSTRIAL CHEMISTRY, 342

Ultimate Encyclopedia of Rock, 400

Unidentified flying objects (UFOs), 328

UNIFIED ENCYCLOPEDIA, 318

United Nations, 406

United States Congress, 405

United States Constitution, 357, 382–83

UNITED STATES ENERGY ATLAS, 349

United States Federal Trade Commission, 13

United States in Africa: A Historical Dictionary, 381

United States in Asia: A Historical Dictionary, 378, 381

UNITED STATES IN LATIN AMERICA: A HISTORICAL DICTIONARY, 381–82

United States in the Middle East: A Historical Dictionary, 381

United States Intelligence: An Encyclopedia, 393

United States Pharmacopeia Drug Information for the Consumer, 369

United States Tennis Association Official Encyclopedia of Tennis, 433

United States Supreme Court, 383–84, 427

Universal Jewish Encyclopedia, 414

Universal Standard Encyclopedia, 69–70

UNIVERSAL WORLD REFERENCE ENCYCLOPEDIA, 318

Universalia, 445

University Desk Encyclopedia, 143–45

University Illustrated Encyclopedia, 307

University Society Encyclopedia, 301

USBORNE CHILDREN'S ENCYCLOPEDIA, 243–45
chart, 252
overview, 220

Used encyclopedias, 14–15

Van Nostrand Reinhold, 12

Van Nostrand Reinhold Color Dictionary of Minerals and Gemstones. See VNR Color Dictionary of Minerals and Gemstones

Van Nostrand Reinhold Concise Encyclopedia of Mathematics. See VNR CONCISE ENCYCLOPEDIA OF MATHEMATICS

VAN NOSTRAND REINHOLD ENCYCLOPEDIA OF CHEMISTRY, 342

VAN NOSTRAND'S SCIENCE ENCYCLOPEDIA, 424

Veterinary medicine, 330

Video, 358

Video Encyclopedia, 358

Video Encyclopedia of Psychoactive Drugs, 374

Vietnam War, 393

Vietnam War Almanac, 393

Vision and vision problems, 370

Visual Dictionary of Ships and Sailing, 441

Visual Encyclopedia of Natural Healing, 371

VNR Color Dictionary of Minerals and Gemstones, 348

VNR CONCISE ENCYCLOPEDIA OF MATHEMATICS, 403

VNR Encyclopedia of Chemistry. See VAN
NOSTRAND REINHOLD ENCYCLOPEDIA OF
CHEMISTRY
Volks-Brockhaus, 447
VOLUME LIBRARY, 156–61
chart, 172
overview, 109

Wales, 391
Walker's Mammals of the World, 333
Ward Lock's Children's Encyclopedia, 317
Warfare and Armed Conflict, 394
WARSHIPS OF THE WORLD: AN ILLUSTRATED
ENCYCLOPEDIA, 396
Water, 349
WATER ENCYCLOPEDIA, 349
*Water Quality and Availability: A Reference
Handbook,* 349
WAY NATURE WORKS, 424
Weapons, 396
WEAPONS: AN INTERNATIONAL ENCYCLOPEDIA FROM
5000 BC TO 2000 AD, 396
Weaving, 345
WEBSTER'S BEGINNING BOOK OF FACTS, 245–47
chart, 252
WEBSTER'S FAMILY ENCYCLOPEDIA (Ottenheimer),
93–97
chart, 107
overview, 52
Webster's Family Encyclopedia (Webster Publish-
ing Company), 304
Webster's New Age Encyclopedia, 304
Webster's New Family Encyclopedia, 304
WEBSTER'S NEW WORLD ENCYCLOPEDIA, 161–65
chart, 172
overview, 109
WEBSTER'S NEW WORLD ENCYCLOPEDIA: COLLEGE
EDITION, 166–68
chart, 172
overview, 109
WEBSTER'S NEW WORLD ENCYCLOPEDIA: POCKET
EDITION, 168–69
chart, 172
overview, 109
*Webster's New World Illustrated Encyclopedic
Dictionary of Real Estate,* 340
Webster's 10 Volume Family Encyclopedia, 93–94.
97
Webster's 13 Volume Family Encyclopedia, 94
Weedon's Modern Encyclopedia, 301
Wellness Encyclopedia, 266, 369

WELLNESS ENCYCLOPEDIA OF FOOD AND NUTRITION,
361
West (U.S.), 364, 381
Westcott's Plant Disease Handbook, 334–35
WESTMINSTER DICTIONARY OF CHRISTIAN ETHICS,
420
*What, Where, When of Theater Props: An
Illustrated Chronology from Arrowheads to
Video Games,* 440
What's in a Dream?, 408
*Wild and Woolly: An Encyclopedia of the Old
West,* 381
Wiley (John) & Sons, 12
Wilson Library Bulletin, 457
Wine, 360–61
Winkler Prins Algemeene Encyclopedie, 445
WISE GARDEN ENCYCLOPEDIA, 336–37
Witches and witchcraft, 410
Woman's Encyclopedia of Myths and Secrets, 432
Women, 373, 384–85, 424, 432
Women's Counsel: A Legal Guide, 384
*Women's Encyclopedia of Health & Emotional
Healing,* 373
WOMEN'S STUDIES ENCYCLOPEDIA, 432
WONDERLAND OF KNOWLEDGE, 319
Wood and woodworking, 334. 353
Woodworker's Dictionary, 353
World Almanac and Book of Facts, 275
WORLD ALMANAC INFOPEDIA, 248–50
chart, 252
WORLD BOOK ENCYCLOPEDIA, 97–104, 206–10
chart, 107, 219
overview, 51–52, 173–74
WORLD BOOK ENCYCLOPEDIA OF PEOPLE AND PLACES,
367
World Book Encyclopedia of Science, 423
World Book Encyclopedia on CD-ROM. See
INFORMATION FINDER (CD-ROM)
World Book Health & Medical Annual, 101
*World Book Illustrated Home Medical Encyclope-
dia,* 374
World Book, Inc., 10–11, 98
WORLD BOOK/RUSH-PRESBYTERIAN-ST. LUKE'S
MEDICAL CENTER MEDICAL ENCYCLOPEDIA, 374
World Book Student Dictionary, 178
World Book Year Book, 101
WORLD CHRISTIAN ENCYCLOPEDIA, 420
WORLD EDUCATION ENCYCLOPEDIA, 352
World Educator Encyclopedia, 311
World Encyclopedia of Cartoons, 325
WORLD ENCYCLOPEDIA OF CITIES, 367–68

WORLD ENCYCLOPEDIA OF CIVIL AIRCRAFT, 442
World Encyclopedia of Comics, 325
WORLD ENCYCLOPEDIA OF FOOD, 361
WORLD ENCYCLOPEDIA OF LIBRARY AND INFORMA-
    TION SCIENCE, 352
World Encyclopedia of Modern Air Weapons, 394
WORLD ENCYCLOPEDIA OF PEACE, 407
WORLD ENCYCLOPEDIA OF POLICE FORCES AND PENAL
    SYSTEMS, 432
WORLD ENCYCLOPEDIA OF POLITICAL SYSTEMS &
    PARTIES, 407
WORLD ENCYCLOPEDIA OF SOCCER, 436
World Explorers and Discoverers, 380
World Fact File, 368
World Factbook, 368
WORLD NATURE ENCYCLOPEDIA, 334
WORLD OF GAMES: THEIR ORIGINS AND HISTORY, 436
WORLD PRESS ENCYCLOPEDIA, 392
World Progress: The Standard Quarterly Review, 85
*World Religions from Ancient History to the
    Present*, 412
World Scope Encyclopedia, 311
World Travel Translator, 266
World University Encyclopedia, 311
WORLD WIDE ENCYCLOPEDIA, 319
World Wide Illustrated Encyclopedia, 307
World War I, 395–96
World War II, 396
WORLDMARK ENCYCLOPEDIA OF THE NATIONS, 368
WORLDMARK ENCYCLOPEDIA OF THE STATES, 368
World's Major Languages, 386

Wrestling, 433
Wrestling: Physical Conditioning Encyclopedia, 433
Writer's Encyclopedia, 392
Writing, 392
WRITING A TO Z, 392
Wyman's Gardening Encyclopedia, 337

Ye Gods: A Dictionary of the Gods, 417
Yearbook of Science and the Future, 45
You and the Law, 383
YOUNG CHILDREN'S ENCYCLOPEDIA, 210–13. *See
    also* 246–47
    chart, 219
    overview, 173
YOUNG PEOPLE'S ENCYCLOPEDIA OF THE UNITED
    STATES, 368
YOUNG PEOPLE'S ILLUSTRATED ENCYCLOPEDIA, 319
Young Reader's Companion, 391
Young Reader's Encyclopedia of Jewish History, 414
Young Students Encyclopedia, 213–14, 216
Young Students Intermediate Dictionary, 213–14
YOUNG STUDENTS LEARNING LIBRARY, 213–17
    chart, 219
    overview, 173
Young Students World Atlas, 213–14
YOUNG WORLD, 319

*Zimmerman's Complete Guide to Nonprescription
    Drugs*, 369
Zondervan Pictorial Encyclopedia of the Bible, 418